the Vampire Bund

BOOKS 1-3

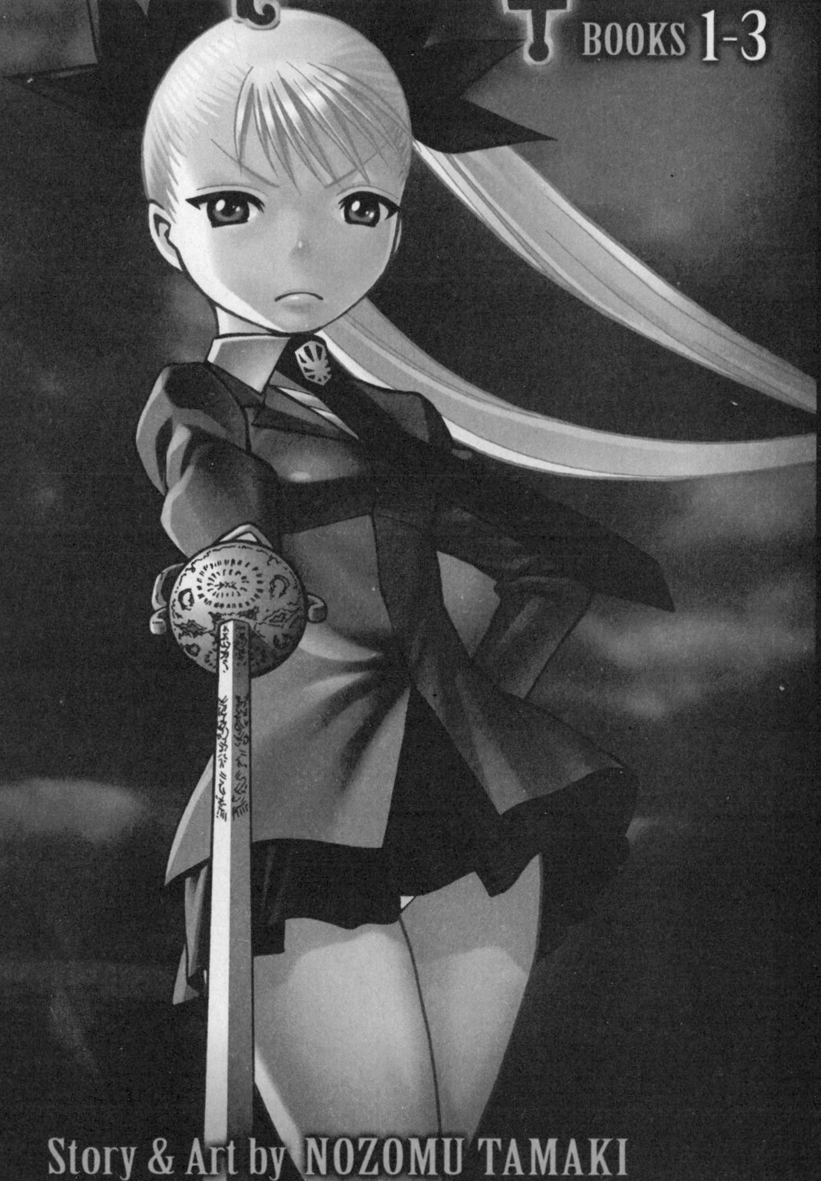

Story & Art by NOZOMU TAMAKI

Nozomu Tamaki Presents Dance In The Vampire Bund 1

DANCE IN THE VAMPIRE BUND
1
NOZOMU TAMAKI

Sein Reich komme!

Nichts ist wirklicher als diese Illusion.

Sie hat die Dome erbaut,

sie hat die Dome zertrümmert,

Jahrtausende haben gesungen,

gelitten,

gemordet für dieses Reich,

das niemals kommt

—und dennoch macht es die ganze menschliche Geschichte!

Let His kingdom come!
Nothing is more real than this illusion.
It has smashed the cathedrals.

Millennia have sung, suffered, and murdered one another
For this illusive kingdom that never comes.
—And so it is responsible for the whole of human history.

Frisch "Nun singen sie wieder"

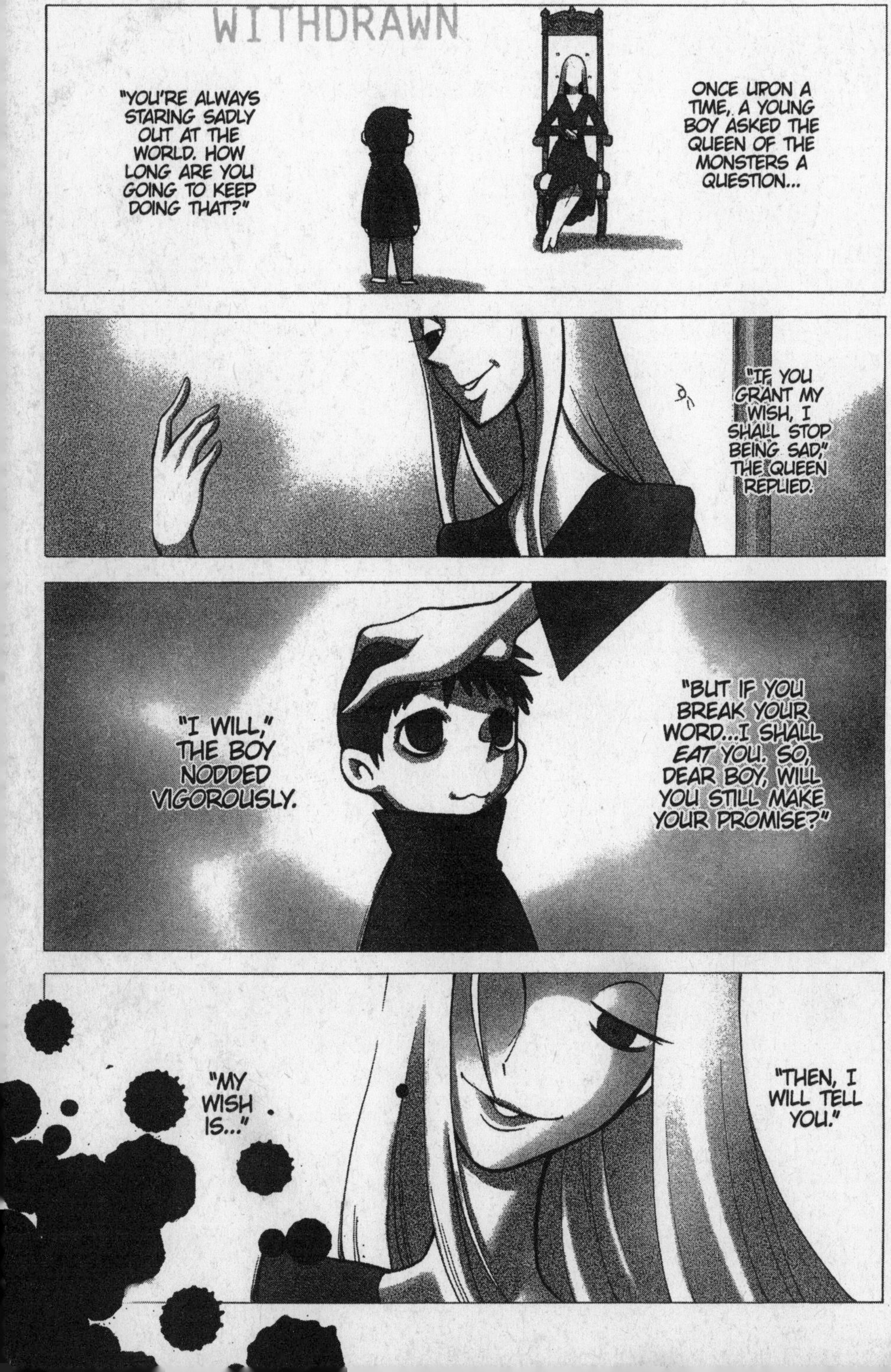
ONCE UPON A TIME, A YOUNG BOY ASKED THE QUEEN OF THE MONSTERS A QUESTION...
"YOU'RE ALWAYS STARING SADLY OUT AT THE WORLD. HOW LONG ARE YOU GOING TO KEEP DOING THAT?"
"IF YOU GRANT MY WISH, I SHALL STOP BEING SAD," THE QUEEN REPLIED.
"BUT IF YOU BREAK YOUR WORD...I SHALL *EAT* YOU. SO, DEAR BOY, WILL YOU STILL MAKE YOUR PROMISE?"
"I WILL," THE BOY NODDED VIGOROUSLY.
"THEN, I WILL TELL YOU."
"MY WISH IS..."

Chapter 1: The Covenant

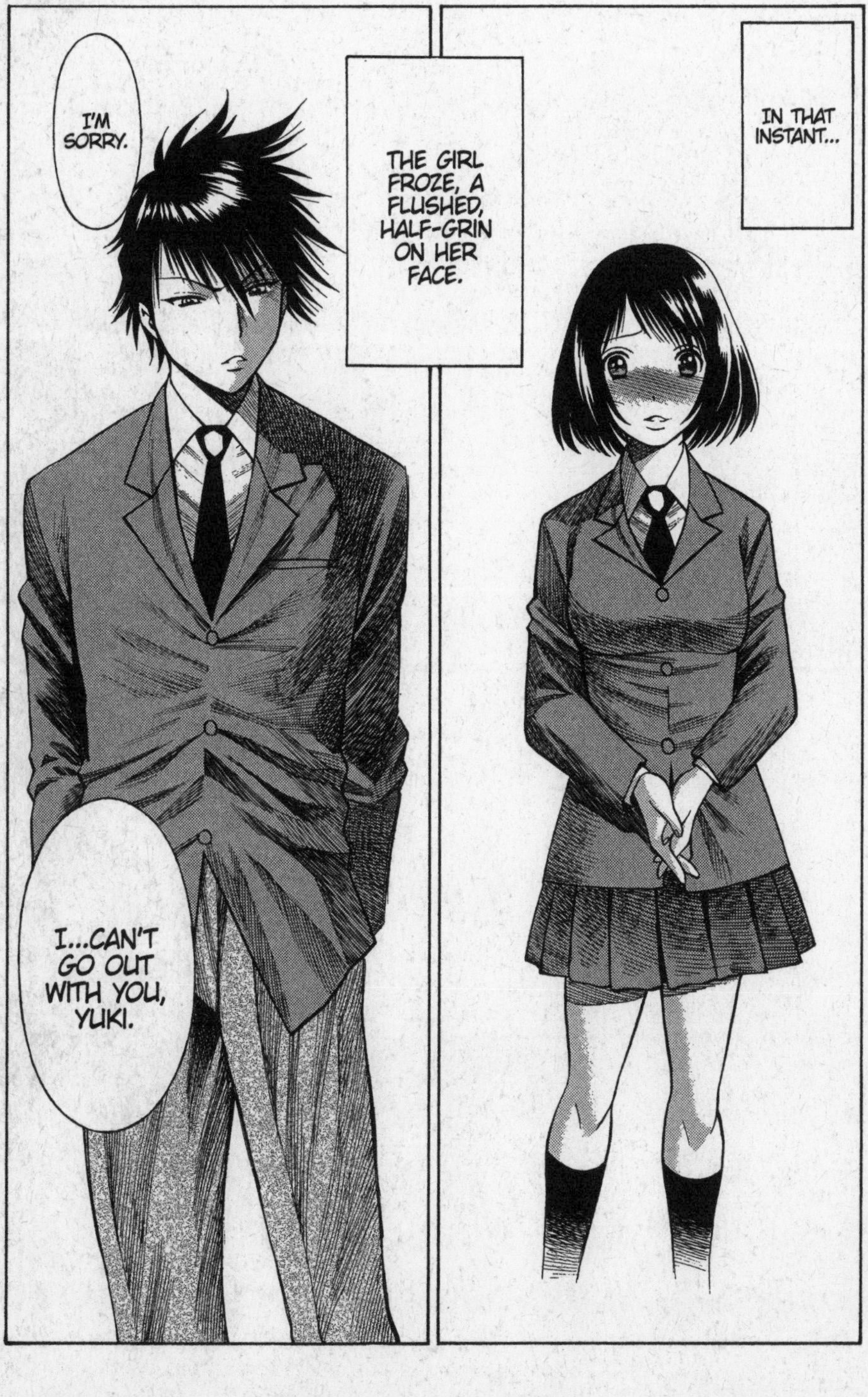
IN THAT INSTANT...
THE GIRL FROZE, A FLUSHED, HALF-GRIN ON HER FACE.
I'M SORRY.
I...CAN'T GO OUT WITH YOU, YUKI.

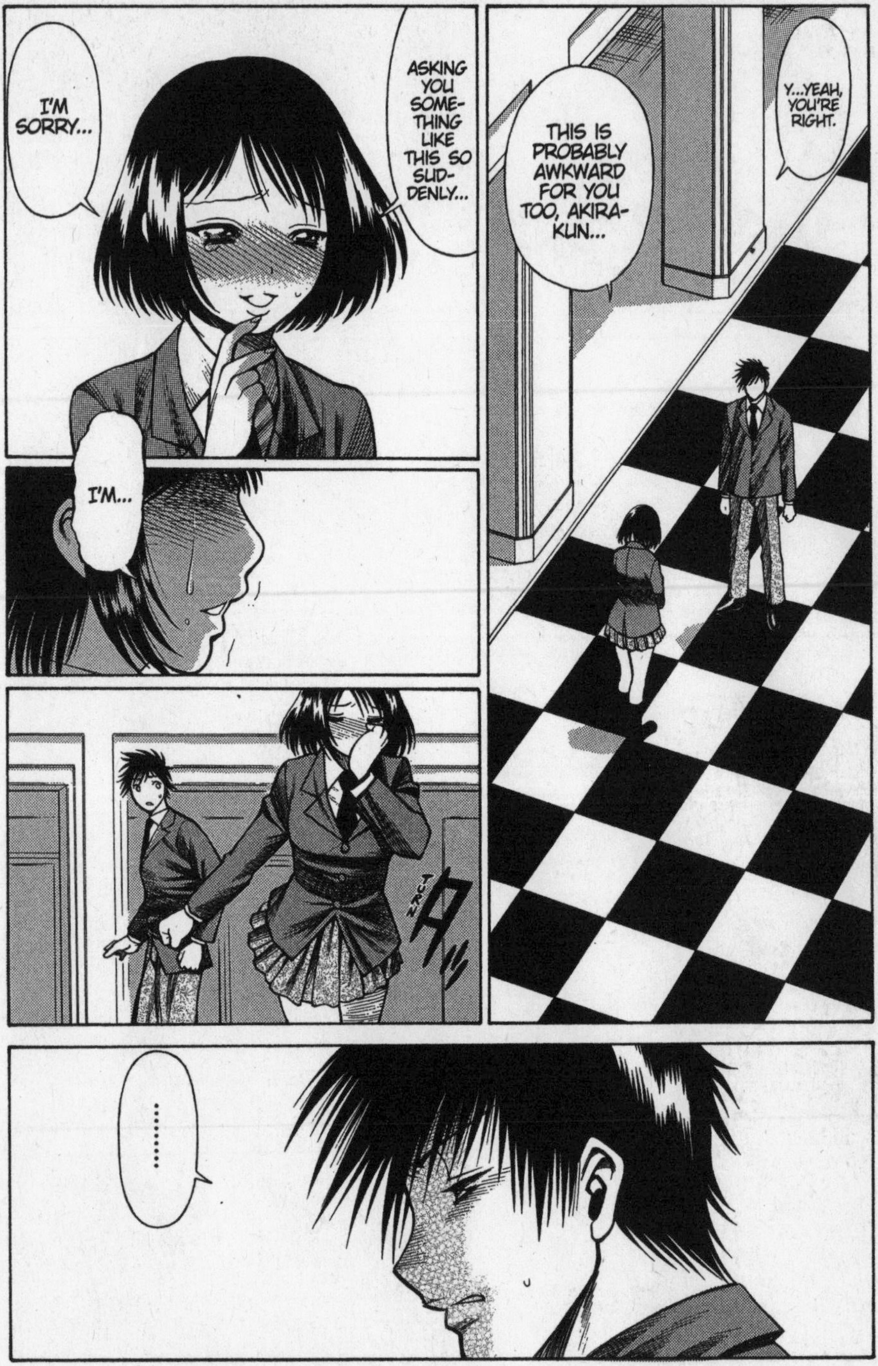
Y...YEAH, YOU'RE RIGHT.
THIS IS PROBABLY AWKWARD FOR YOU TOO, AKIRA-KUN...
ASKING YOU SOMETHING LIKE THIS SO SUDDENLY...
I'M SORRY...
I'M...
TURN
....

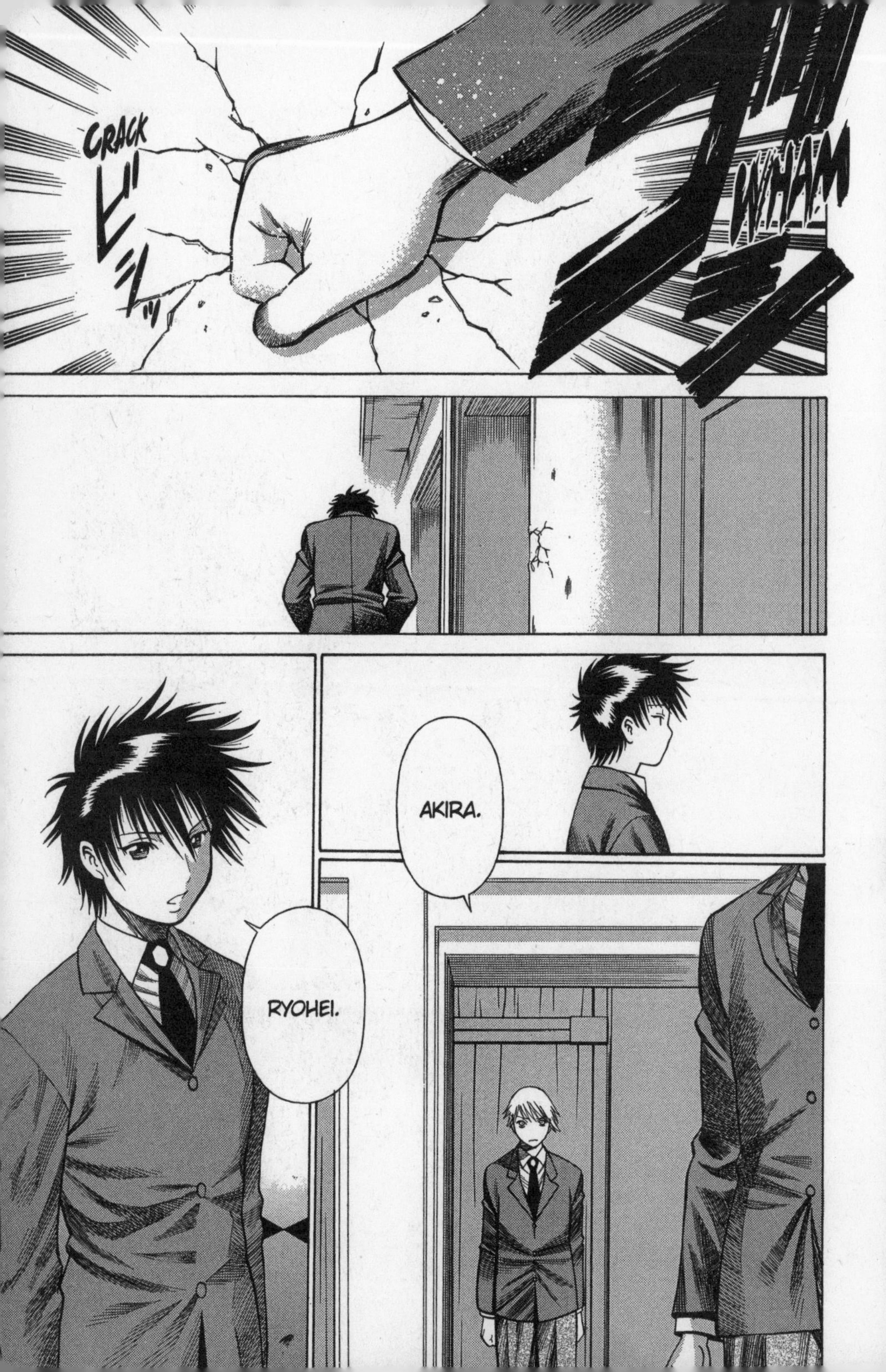
WHAM
CRACK
AKIRA.
RYOHEI.

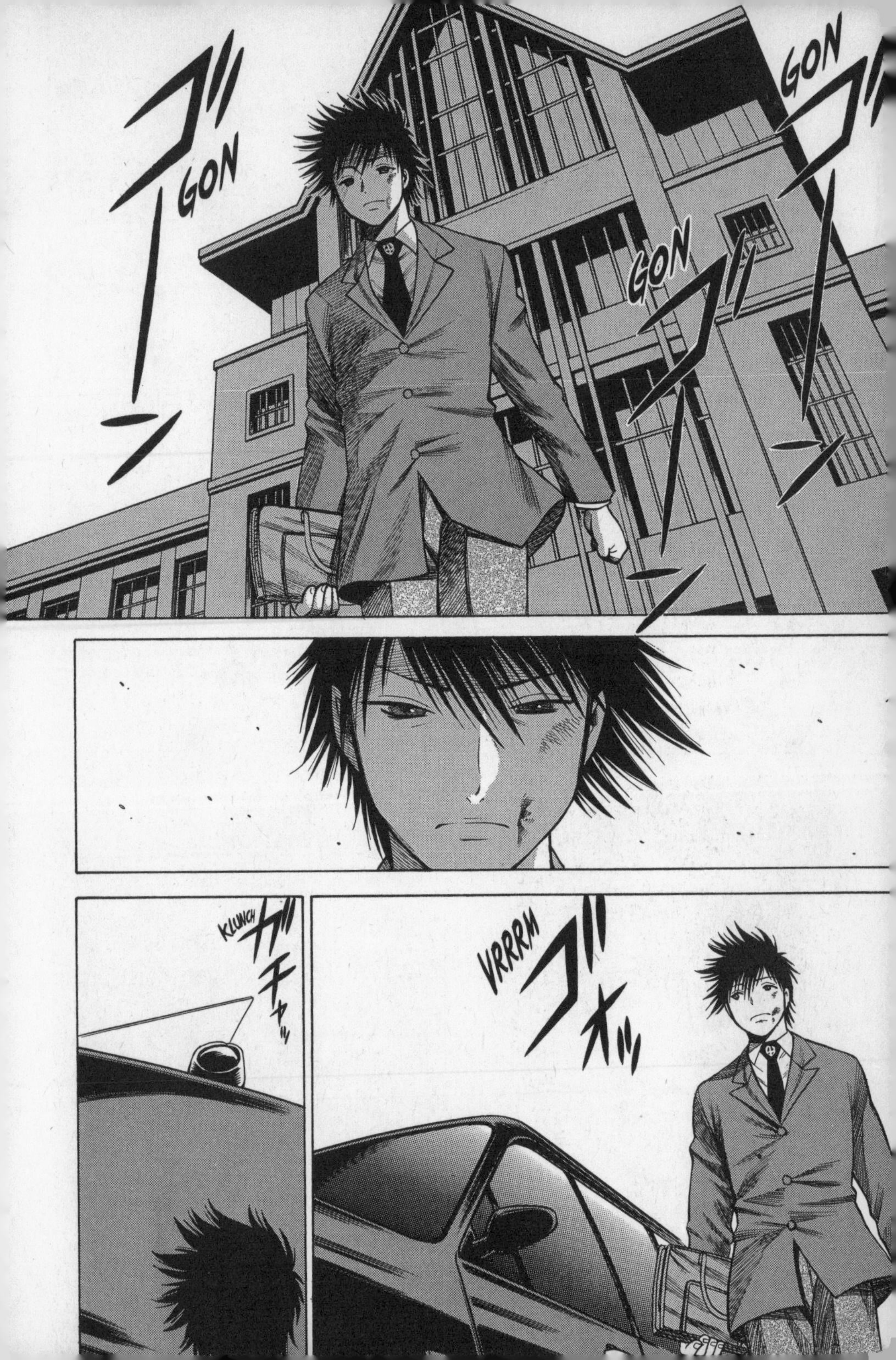
GON
GON
GON
VRRRM
KLUNCH

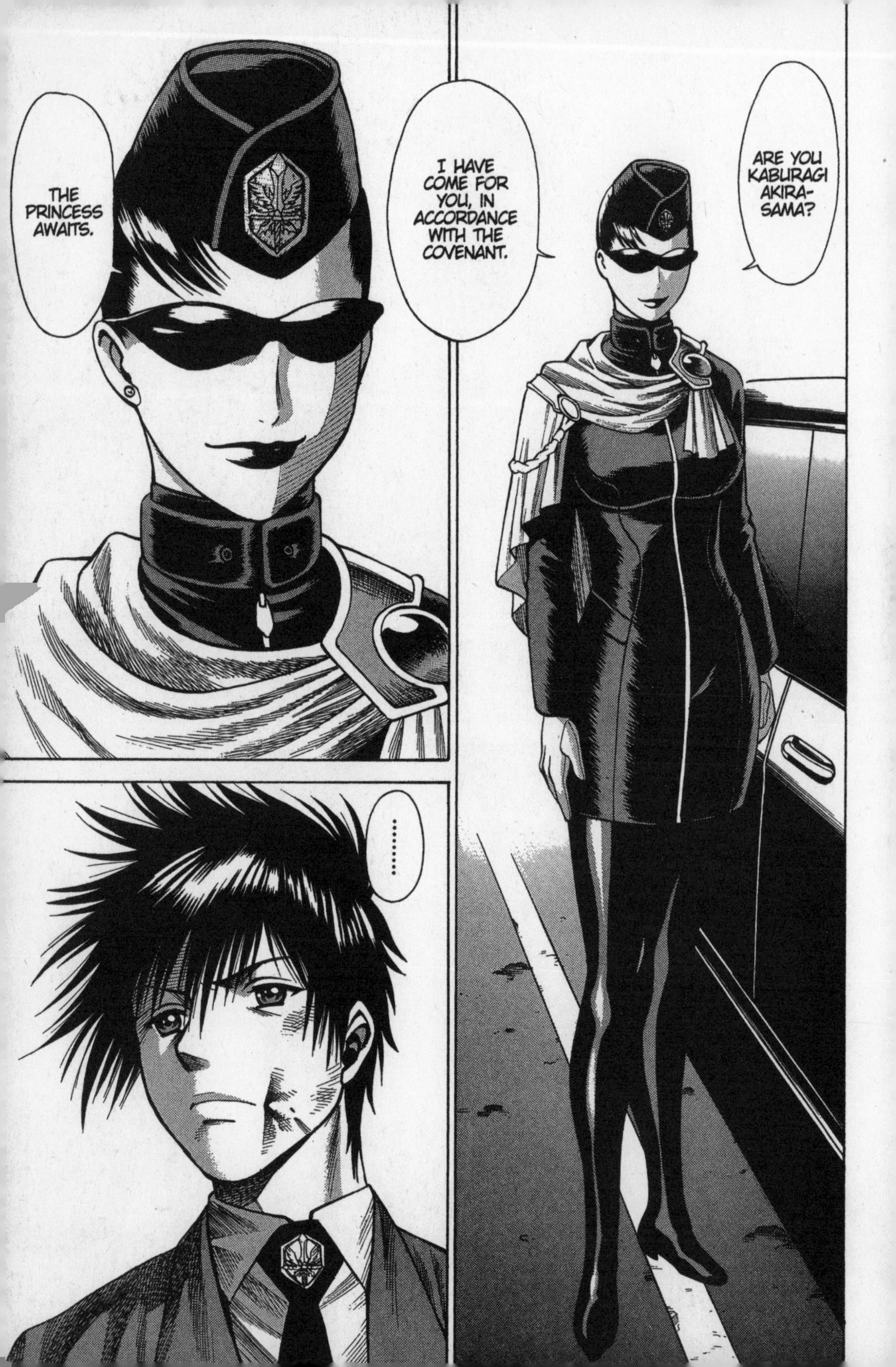
ARE YOU KABURAGI AKIRA-SAMA?
I HAVE COME FOR YOU, IN ACCORDANCE WITH THE COVENANT.
THE PRINCESS AWAITS.
....

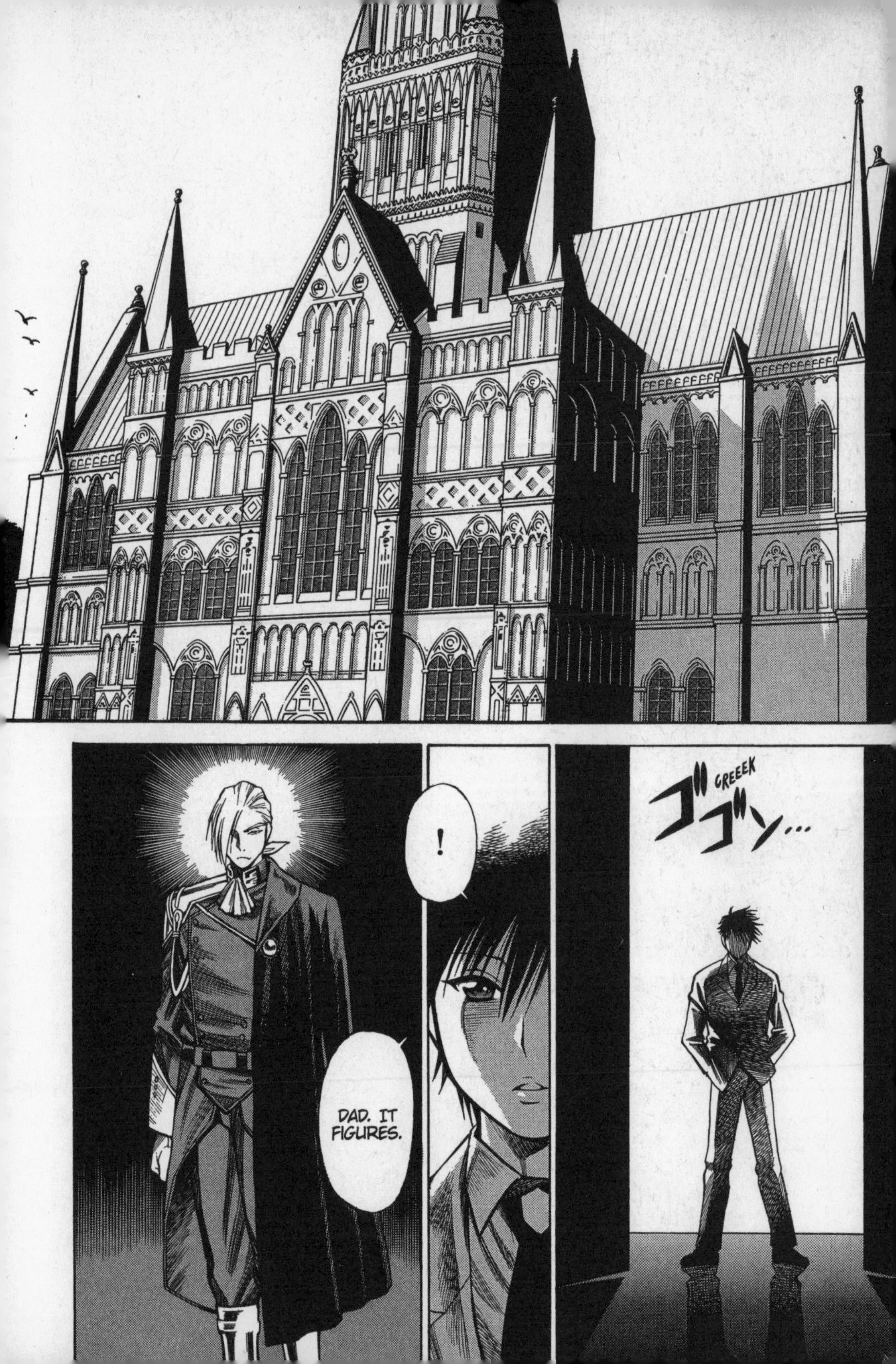

ゴゴン…
CREEEK
!
DAD. IT FIGURES.

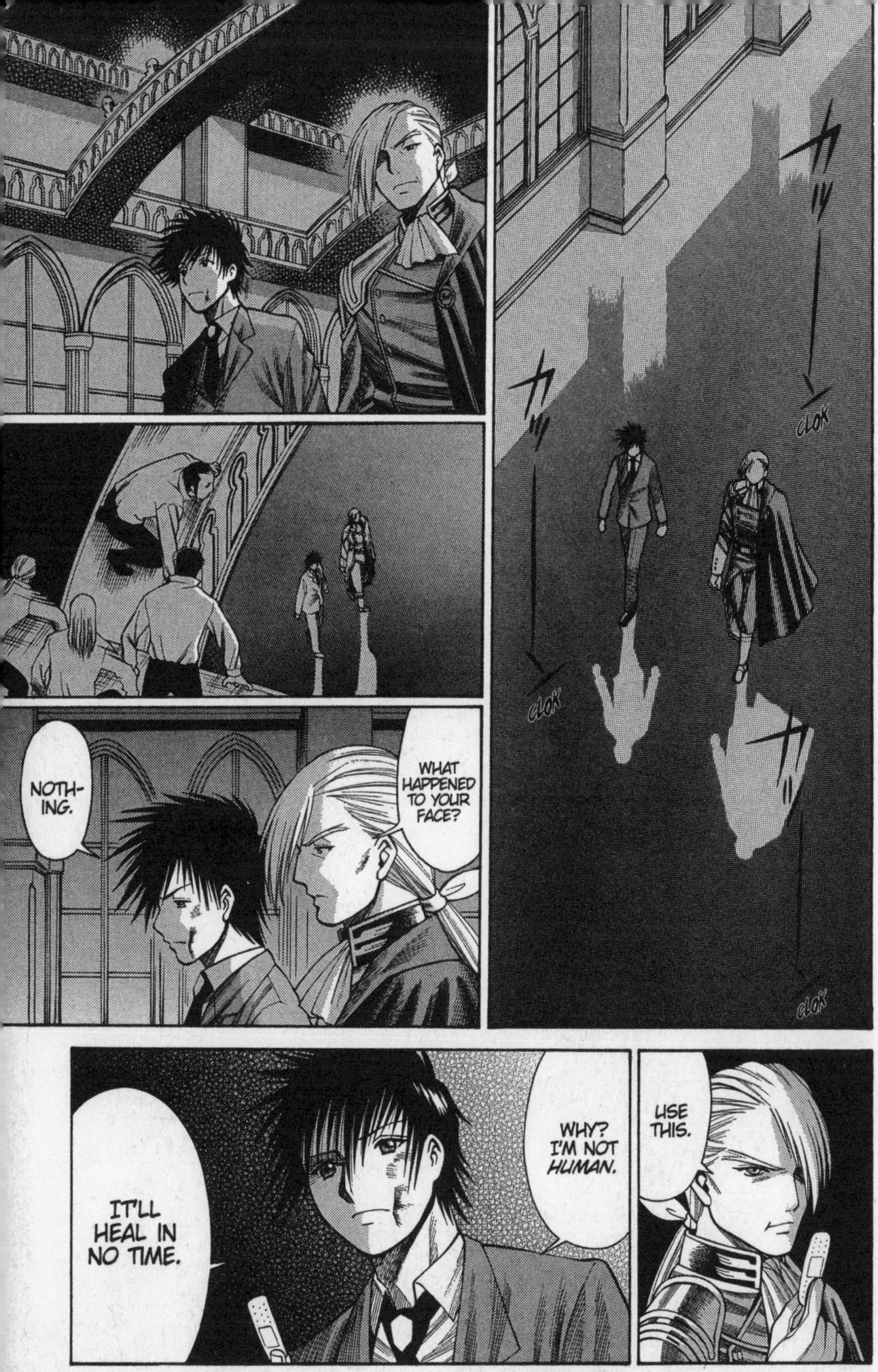
CLOK
CLOK
CLOK
WHAT HAPPENED TO YOUR FACE?
NOTH-ING.
USE THIS.
WHY? I'M NOT *HUMAN.*
IT'LL HEAL IN NO TIME.

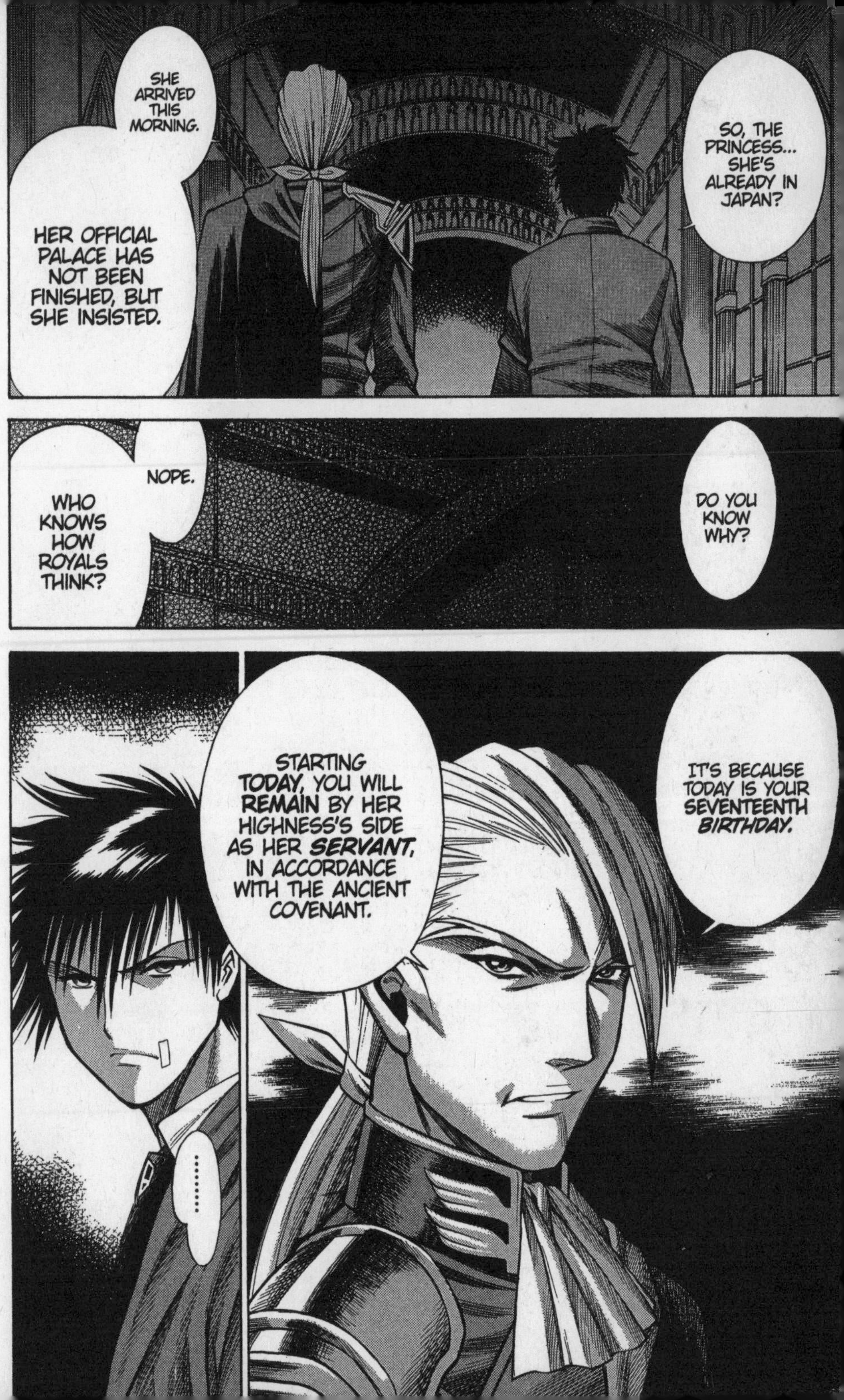
SO, THE PRINCESS... SHE'S ALREADY IN JAPAN?
SHE ARRIVED THIS MORNING.
HER OFFICIAL PALACE HAS NOT BEEN FINISHED, BUT SHE INSISTED.
DO YOU KNOW WHY?
NOPE.
WHO KNOWS HOW ROYALS THINK?
IT'S BECAUSE TODAY IS YOUR SEVENTEENTH *BIRTHDAY.*
STARTING **TODAY,** YOU WILL **REMAIN** BY HER HIGHNESS'S SIDE AS HER ***SERVANT,*** IN ACCORDANCE WITH THE ANCIENT COVENANT.
......

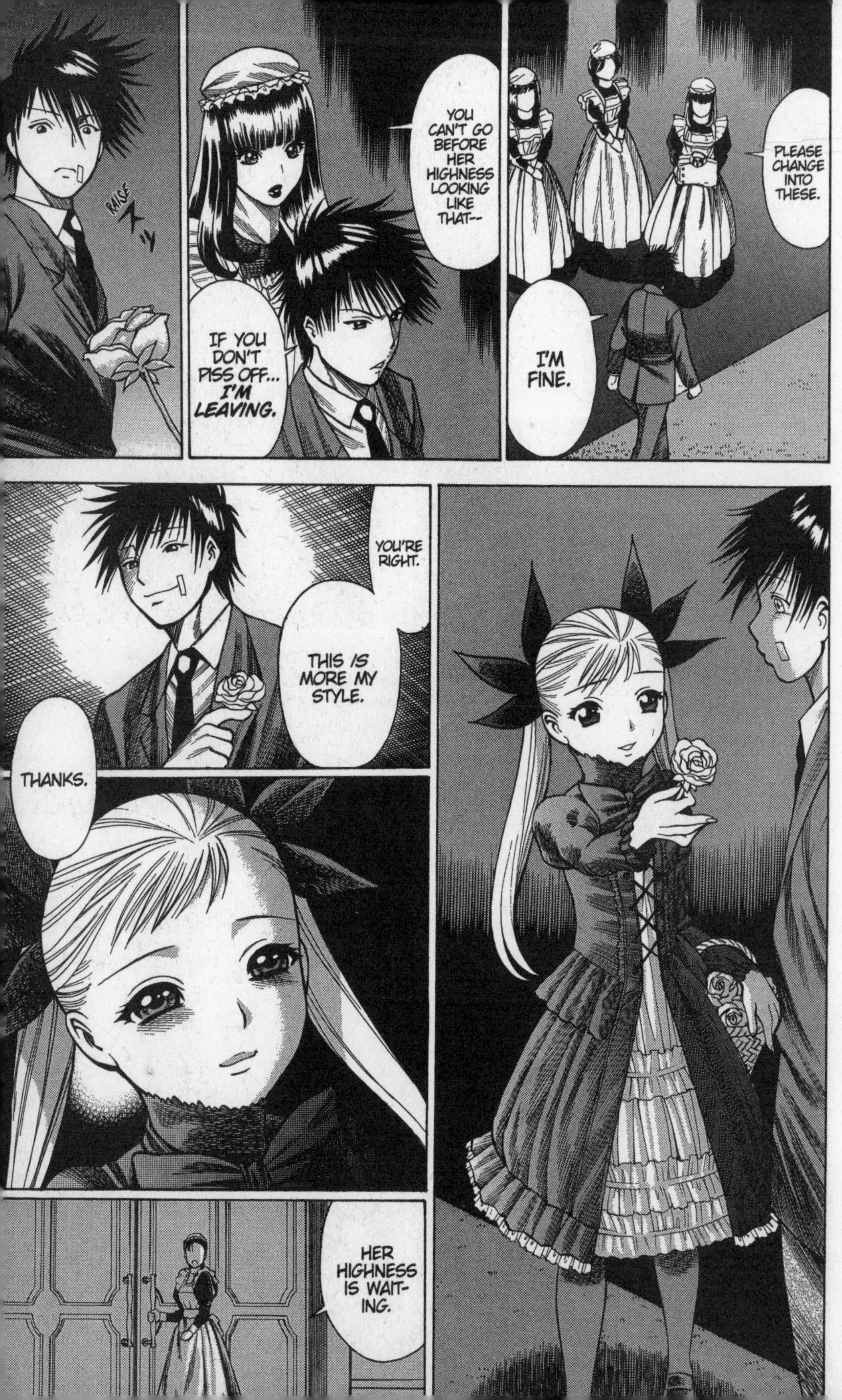

PLEASE CHANGE INTO THESE.
I'M FINE.
YOU CAN'T GO BEFORE HER HIGHNESS LOOKING LIKE THAT--
IF YOU DON'T PISS OFF... *I'M LEAVING.*
RAISE
YOU'RE RIGHT.
THIS IS MORE MY STYLE.
THANKS.
HER HIGHNESS IS WAIT-ING.

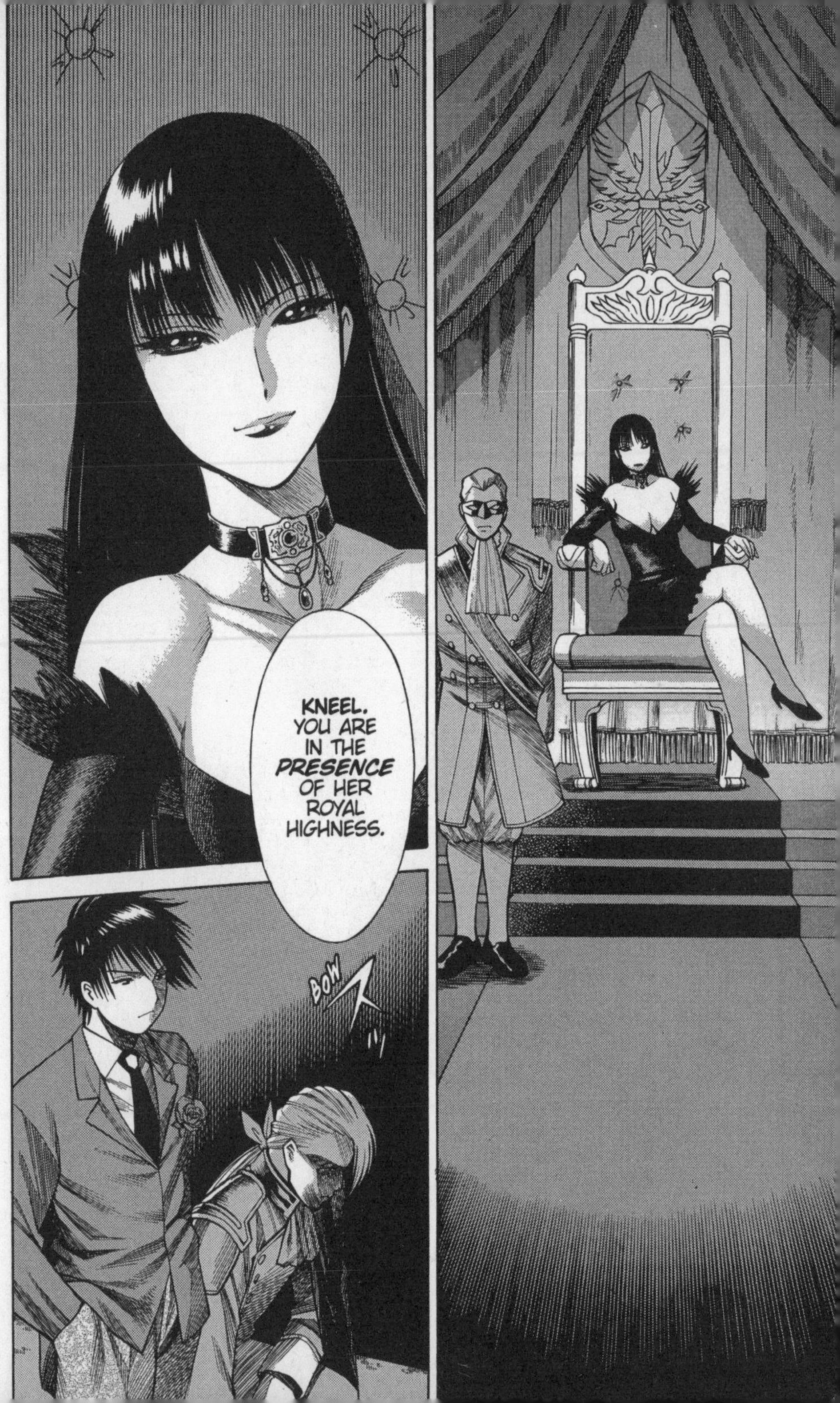
KNEEL. YOU ARE IN THE PRESENCE OF HER ROYAL HIGHNESS.
BOW

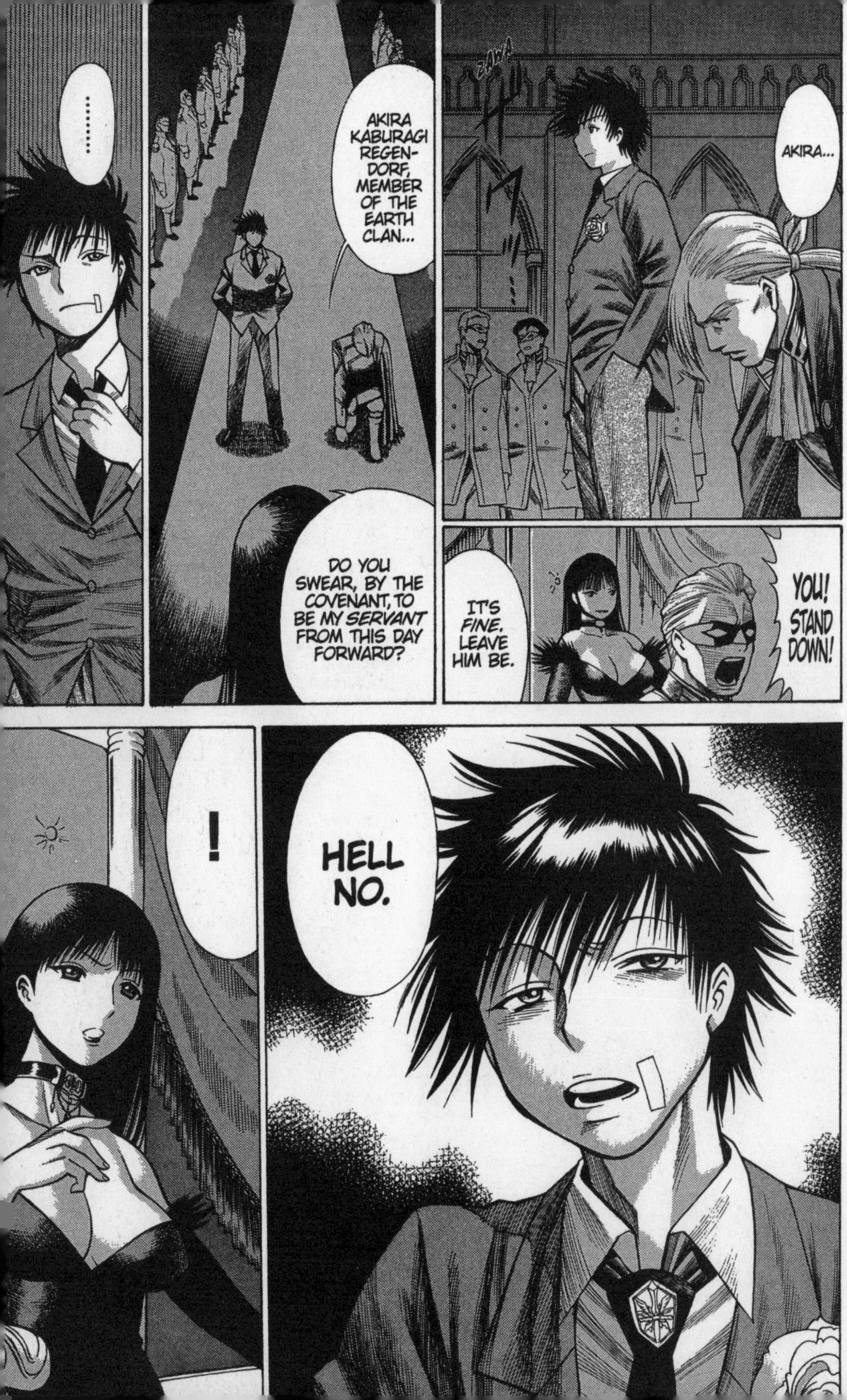
ZAWA
AKIRA...
YOU! STAND DOWN!
IT'S FINE. LEAVE HIM BE.
AKIRA KABURAGI REGENDORF, MEMBER OF THE EARTH CLAN...
DO YOU SWEAR, BY THE COVENANT, TO BE MY SERVANT FROM THIS DAY FORWARD?
......
HELL NO.
!

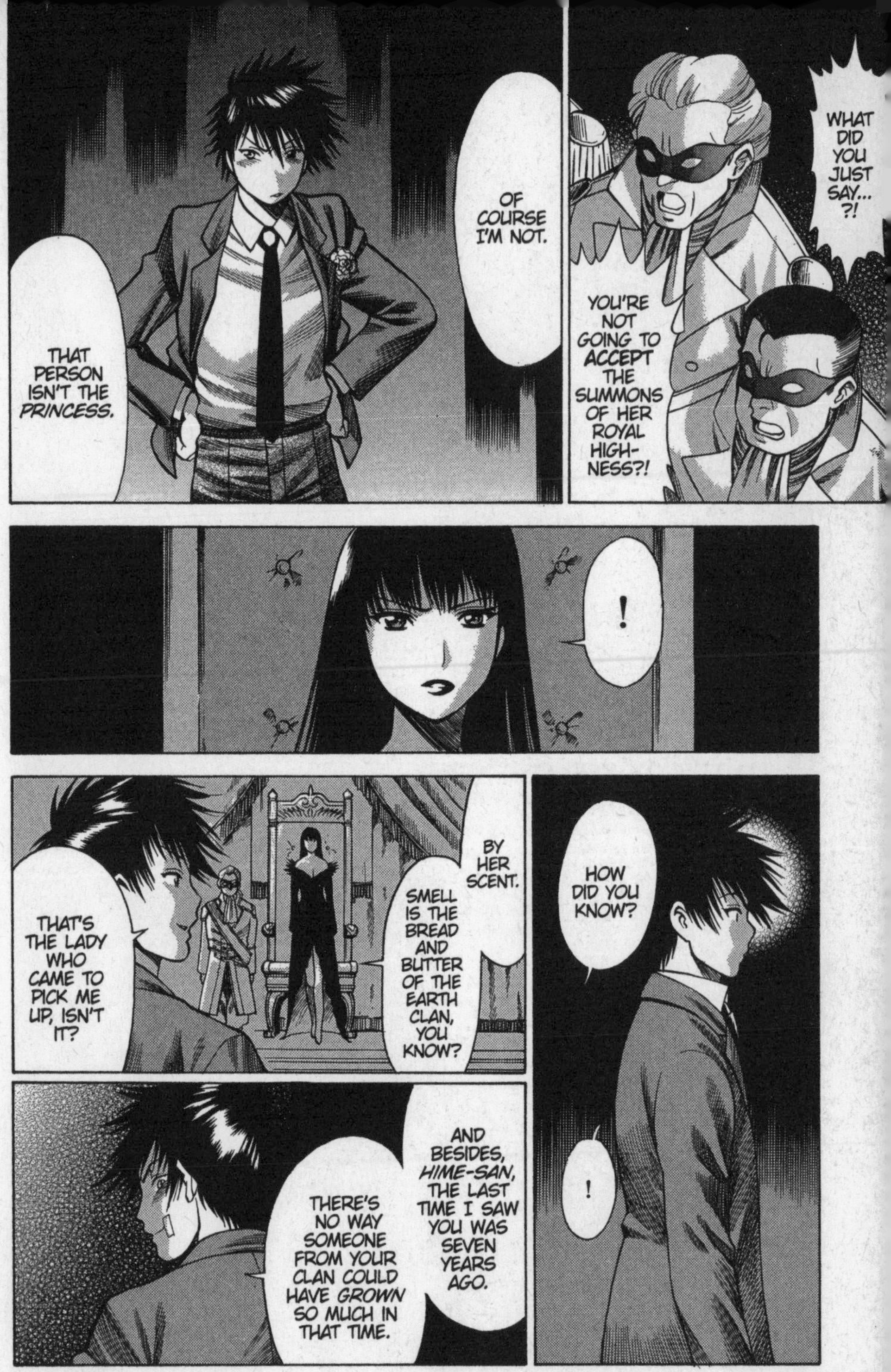
WHAT DID YOU JUST SAY...?!
YOU'RE NOT GOING TO ACCEPT THE SUMMONS OF HER ROYAL HIGHNESS?!
OF COURSE I'M NOT.
THAT PERSON ISN'T THE *PRINCESS.*
!
HOW DID YOU KNOW?
!
BY HER SCENT.
SMELL IS THE BREAD AND BUTTER OF THE EARTH CLAN, YOU KNOW?
THAT'S THE LADY WHO CAME TO PICK ME UP, ISN'T IT?
AND BESIDES, *HIME-SAN,* THE LAST TIME I SAW YOU WAS SEVEN YEARS AGO.
THERE'S NO WAY SOMEONE FROM YOUR CLAN COULD HAVE *GROWN* SO MUCH IN THAT TIME.

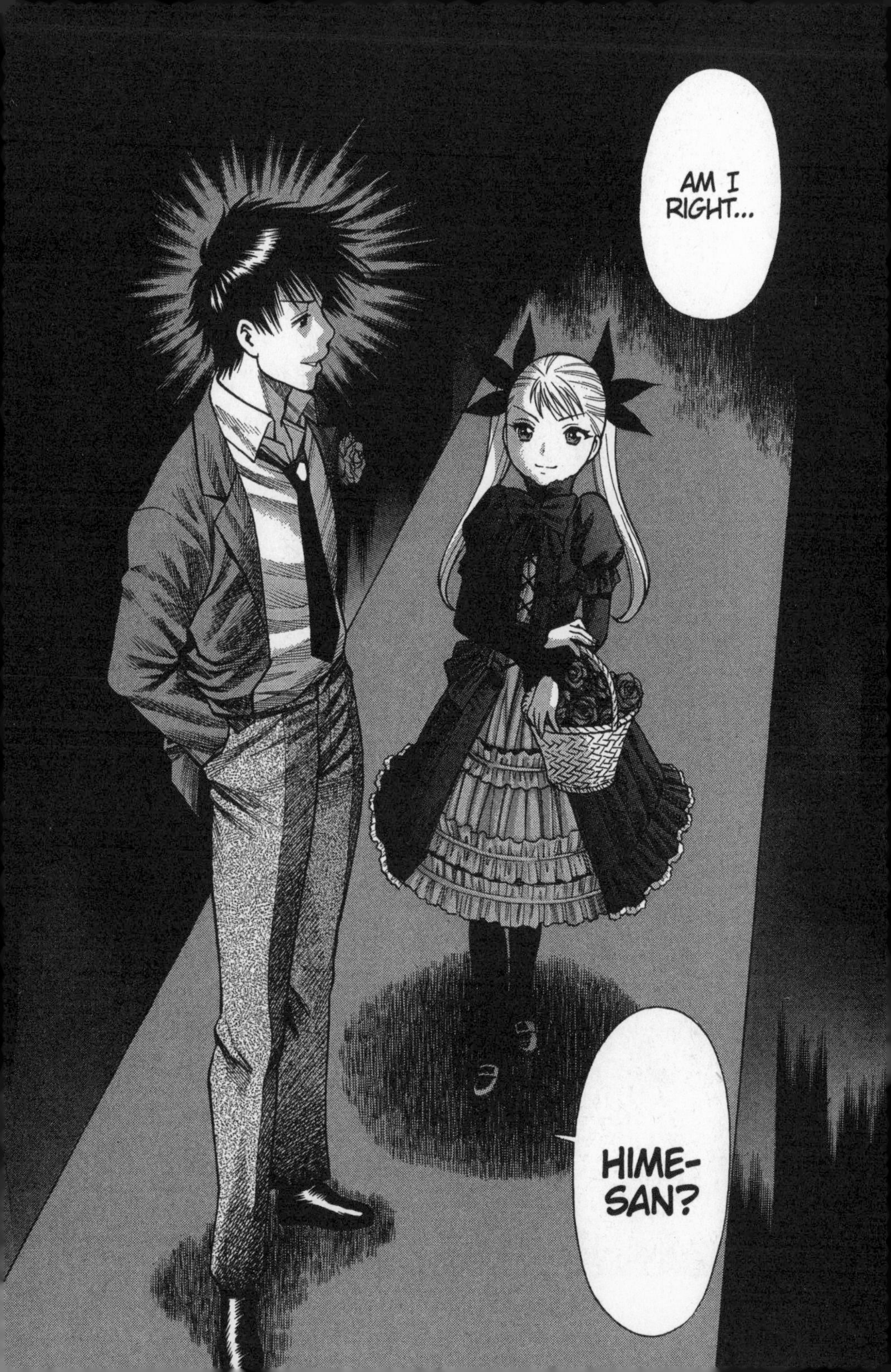
AM I RIGHT...
HIME-SAN?

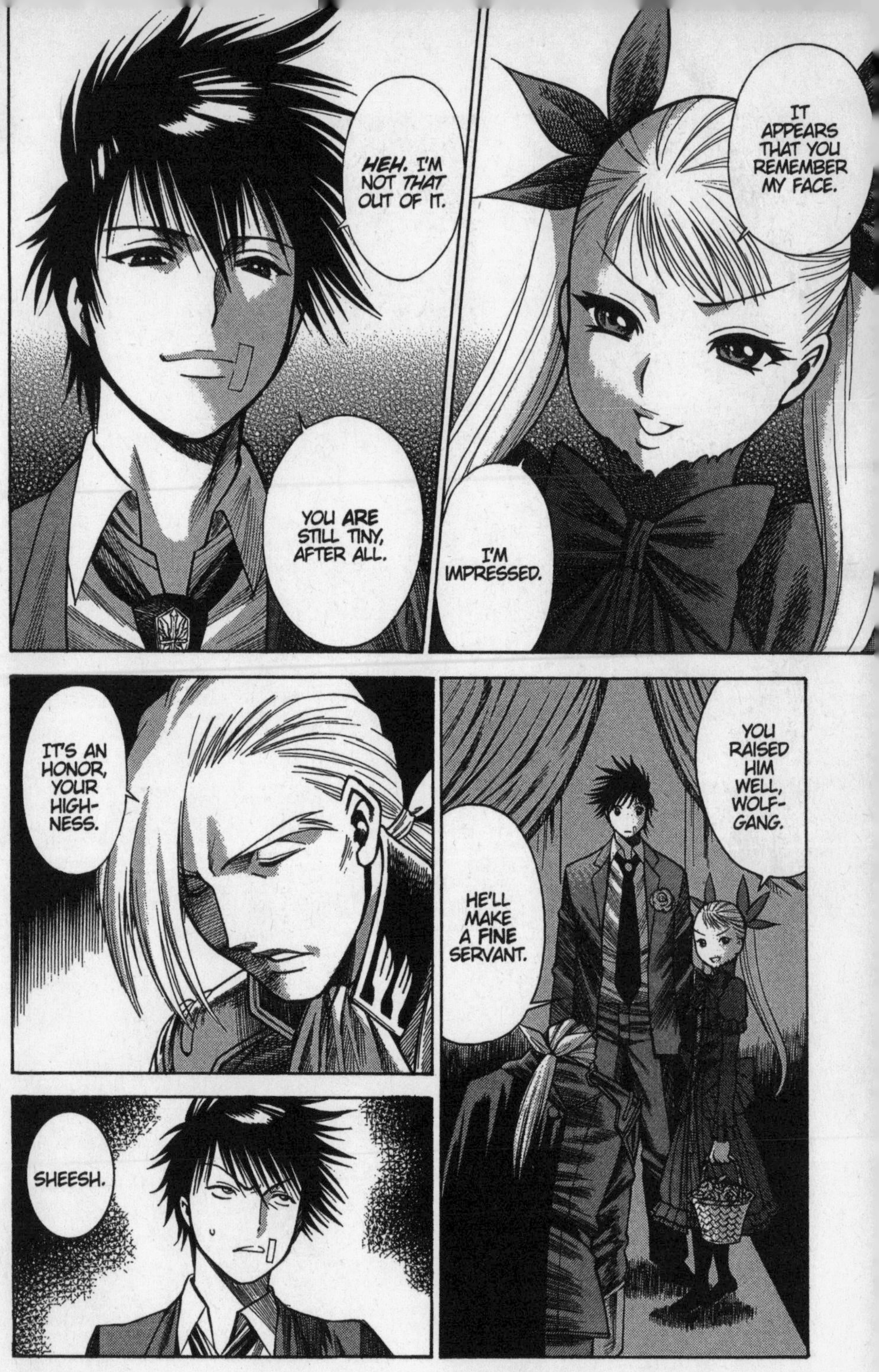
IT APPEARS THAT YOU REMEMBER MY FACE.
I'M IMPRESSED.
HEH. I'M NOT THAT OUT OF IT.
YOU ARE STILL TINY, AFTER ALL.
YOU RAISED HIM WELL, WOLF-GANG.
HE'LL MAKE A FINE SERVANT.
IT'S AN HONOR, YOUR HIGH-NESS.
SHEESH.

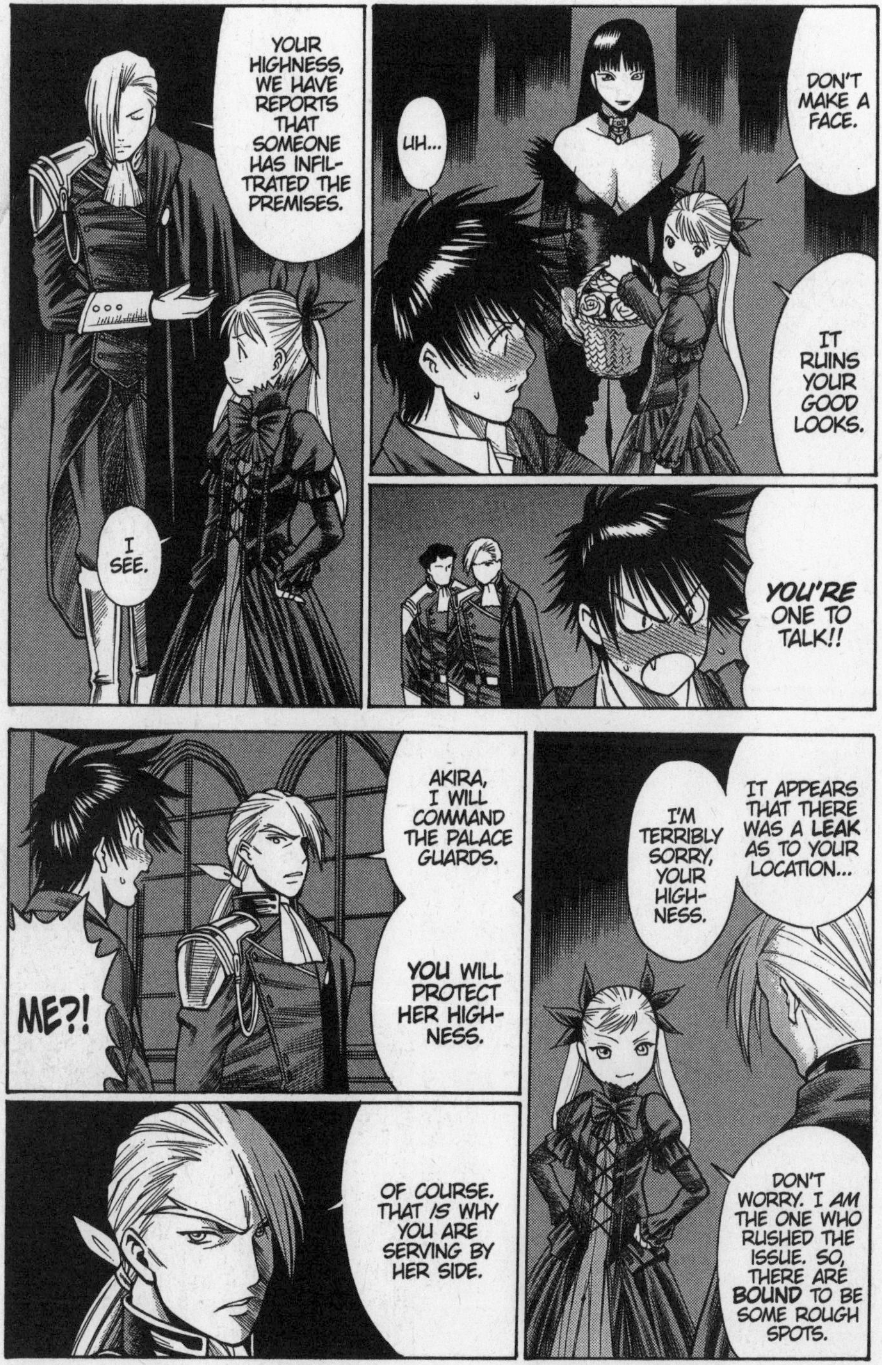
DON'T MAKE A FACE.
UH...
IT RUINS YOUR GOOD LOOKS.
YOU'RE ONE TO TALK!!
YOUR HIGHNESS, WE HAVE REPORTS THAT SOMEONE HAS INFILTRATED THE PREMISES.
I SEE.
IT APPEARS THAT THERE WAS A LEAK AS TO YOUR LOCATION...
I'M TERRIBLY SORRY, YOUR HIGHNESS.
DON'T WORRY. I AM THE ONE WHO RUSHED THE ISSUE. SO, THERE ARE BOUND TO BE SOME ROUGH SPOTS.
AKIRA, I WILL COMMAND THE PALACE GUARDS.
YOU WILL PROTECT HER HIGHNESS.
ME?!
OF COURSE. THAT IS WHY YOU ARE SERVING BY HER SIDE.

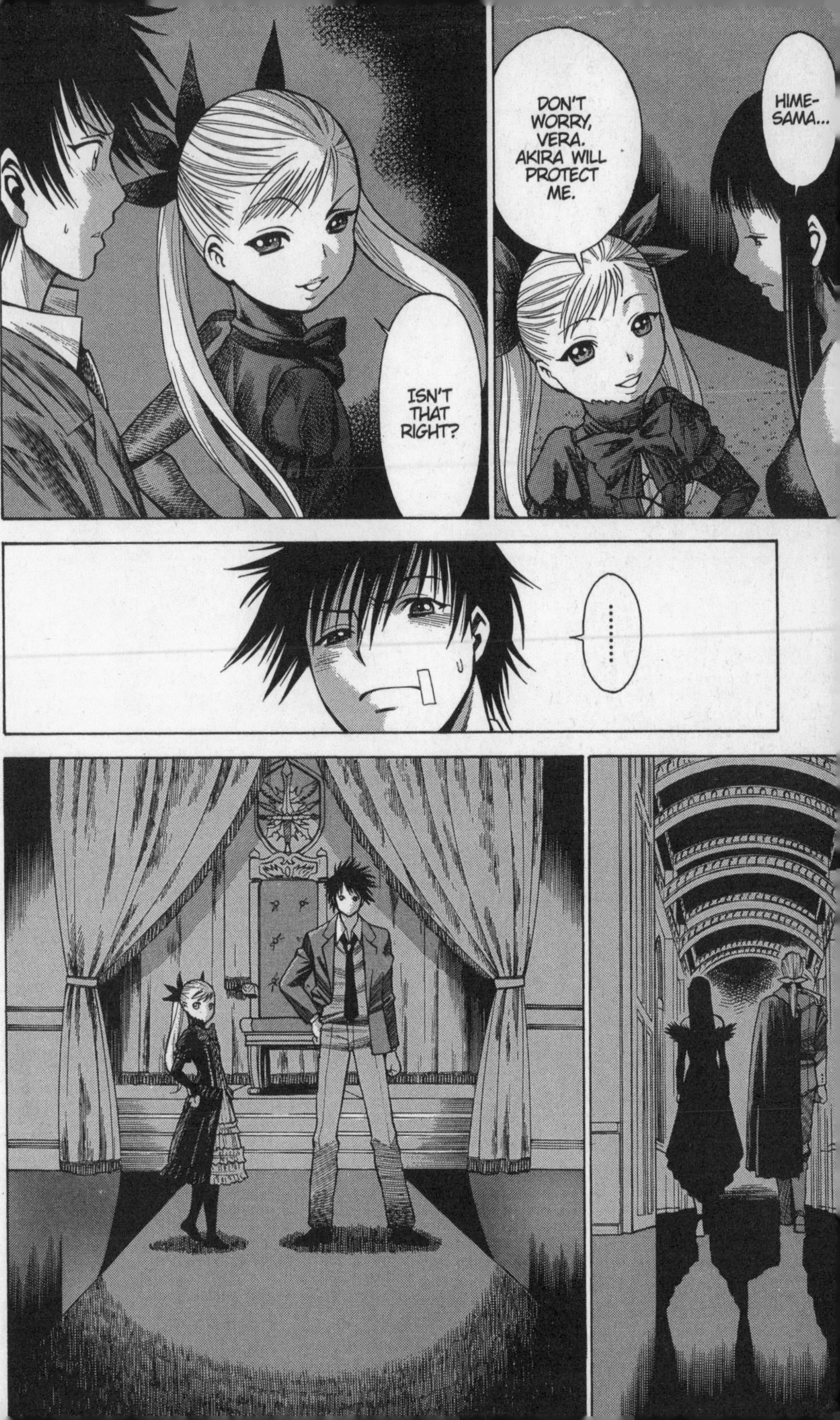
HIME-SAMA...
DON'T WORRY, VERA. AKIRA WILL PROTECT ME.
ISN'T THAT RIGHT?
......

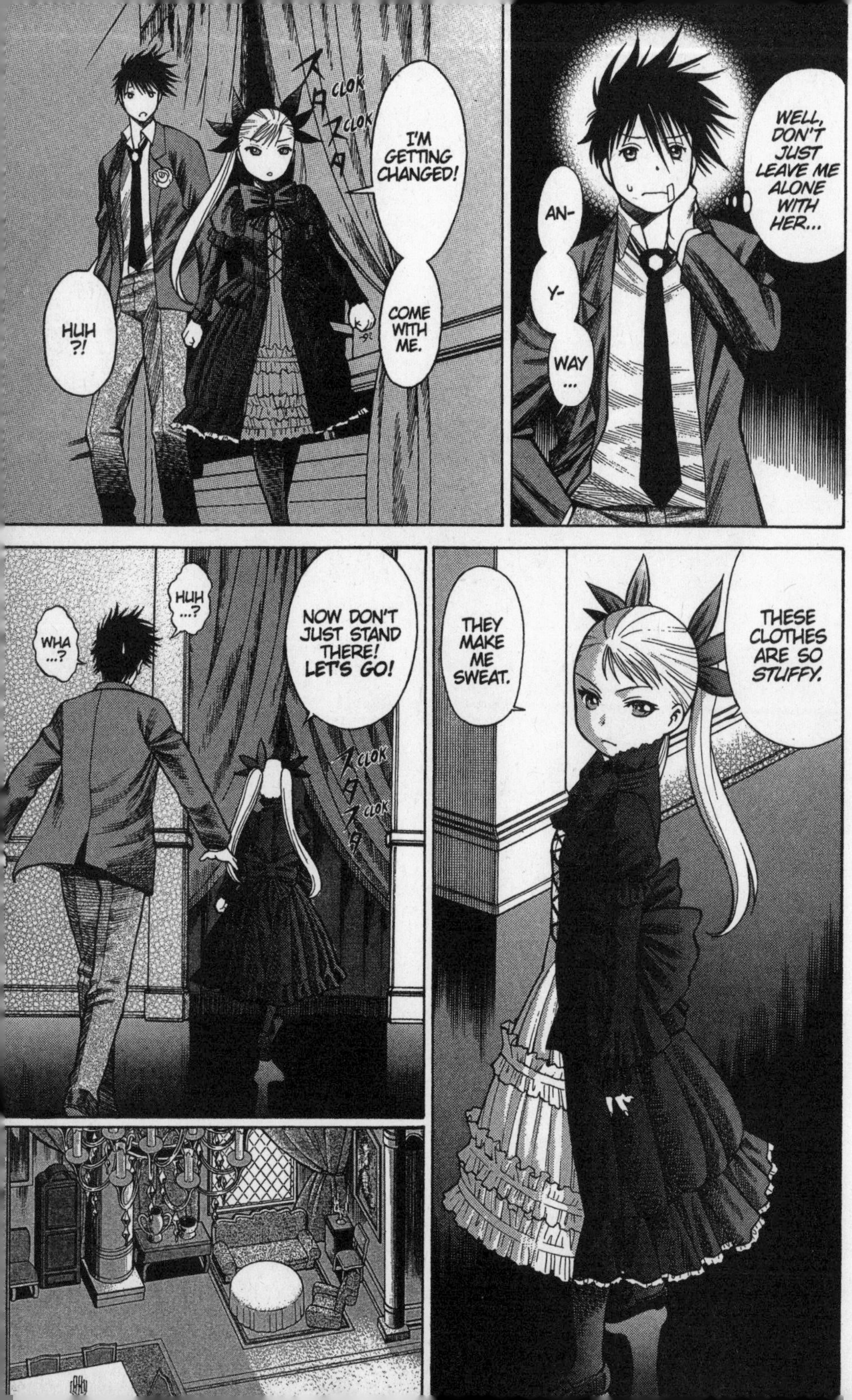
WELL, DON'T JUST LEAVE ME ALONE WITH HER...
AN- Y- WAY ...
CLOK CLOK
I'M GETTING CHANGED!
COME WITH ME.
HUH ?!
THESE CLOTHES ARE SO STUFFY.
THEY MAKE ME SWEAT.
NOW DON'T JUST STAND THERE! LET'S GO!
HUH ...?
WHA ...?
CLOK CLOK

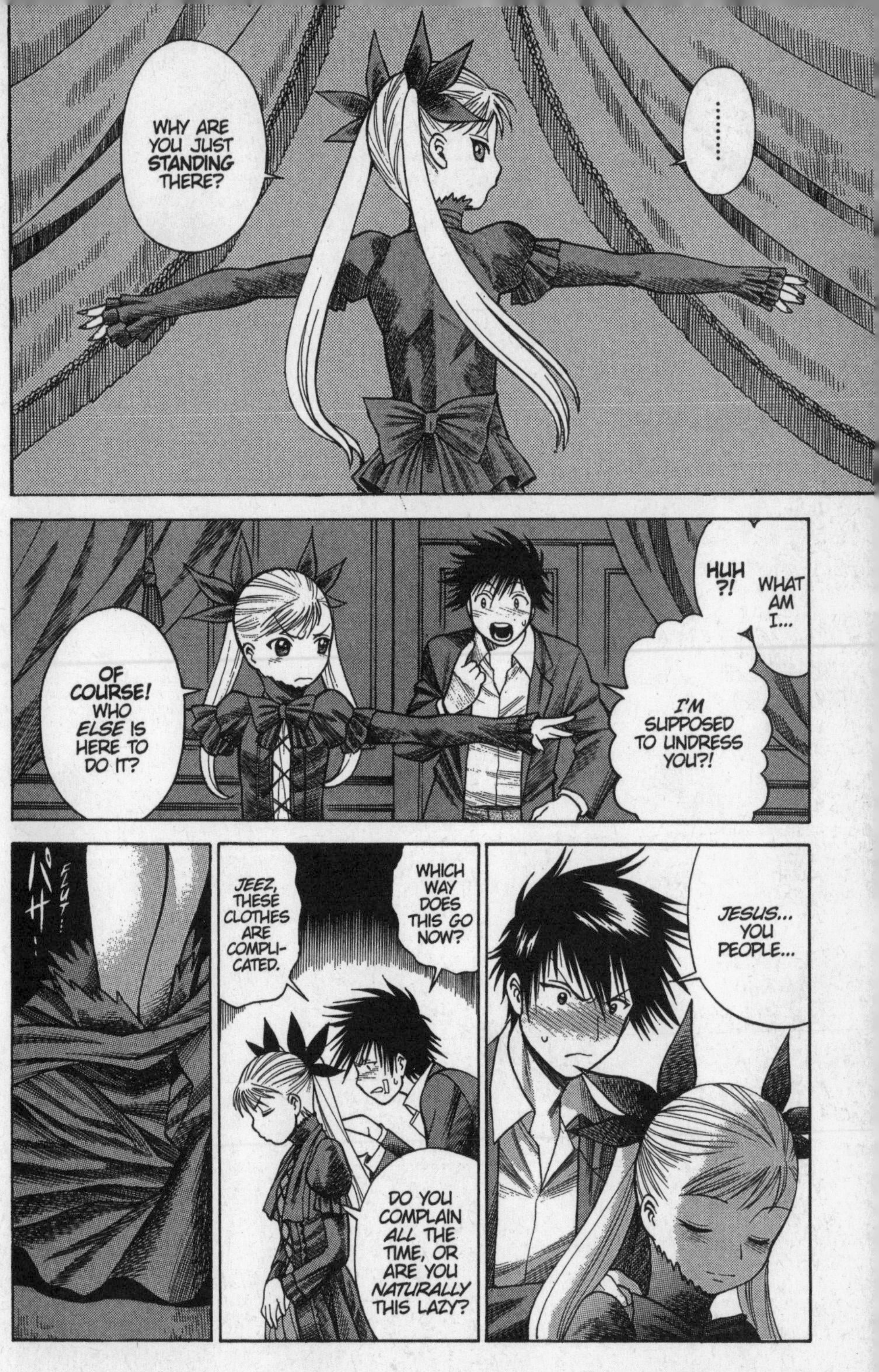
......
WHY ARE YOU JUST STANDING THERE?
HUH?! WHAT AM I...
I'M SUPPOSED TO UNDRESS YOU?!
OF COURSE! WHO *ELSE* IS HERE TO DO IT?
JESUS... YOU PEOPLE...
WHICH WAY DOES THIS GO NOW?
JEEZ, THESE CLOTHES ARE COMPLICATED.
DO YOU COMPLAIN *ALL* THE TIME, OR ARE YOU *NATURALLY* THIS LAZY?
パサ… FLUT...

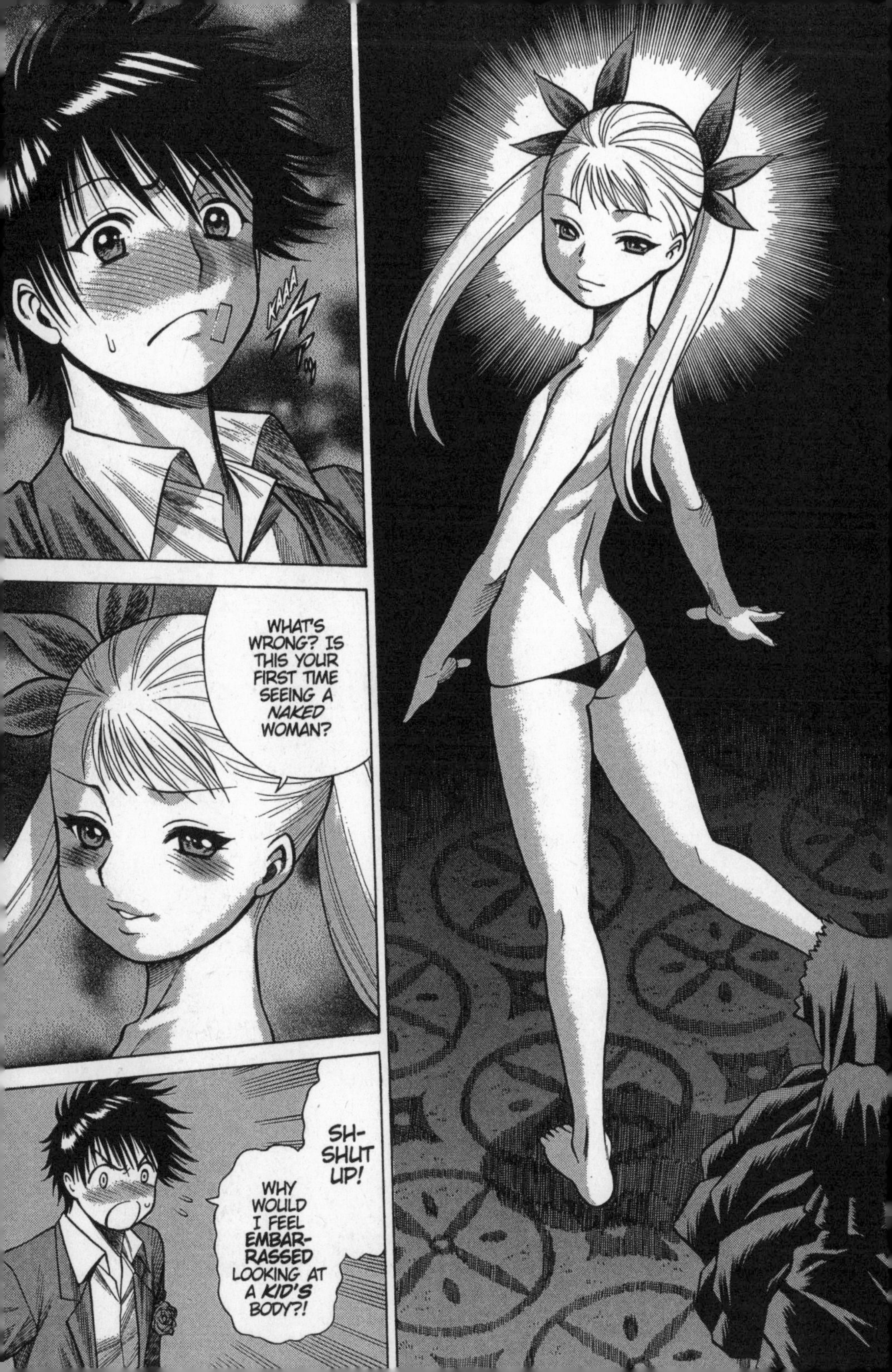
KAAAA
WHAT'S WRONG? IS THIS YOUR FIRST TIME SEEING A *NAKED* WOMAN?
SH-SHUT UP!
WHY WOULD I FEEL EMBARRASSED LOOKING AT A *KID'S* BODY?!

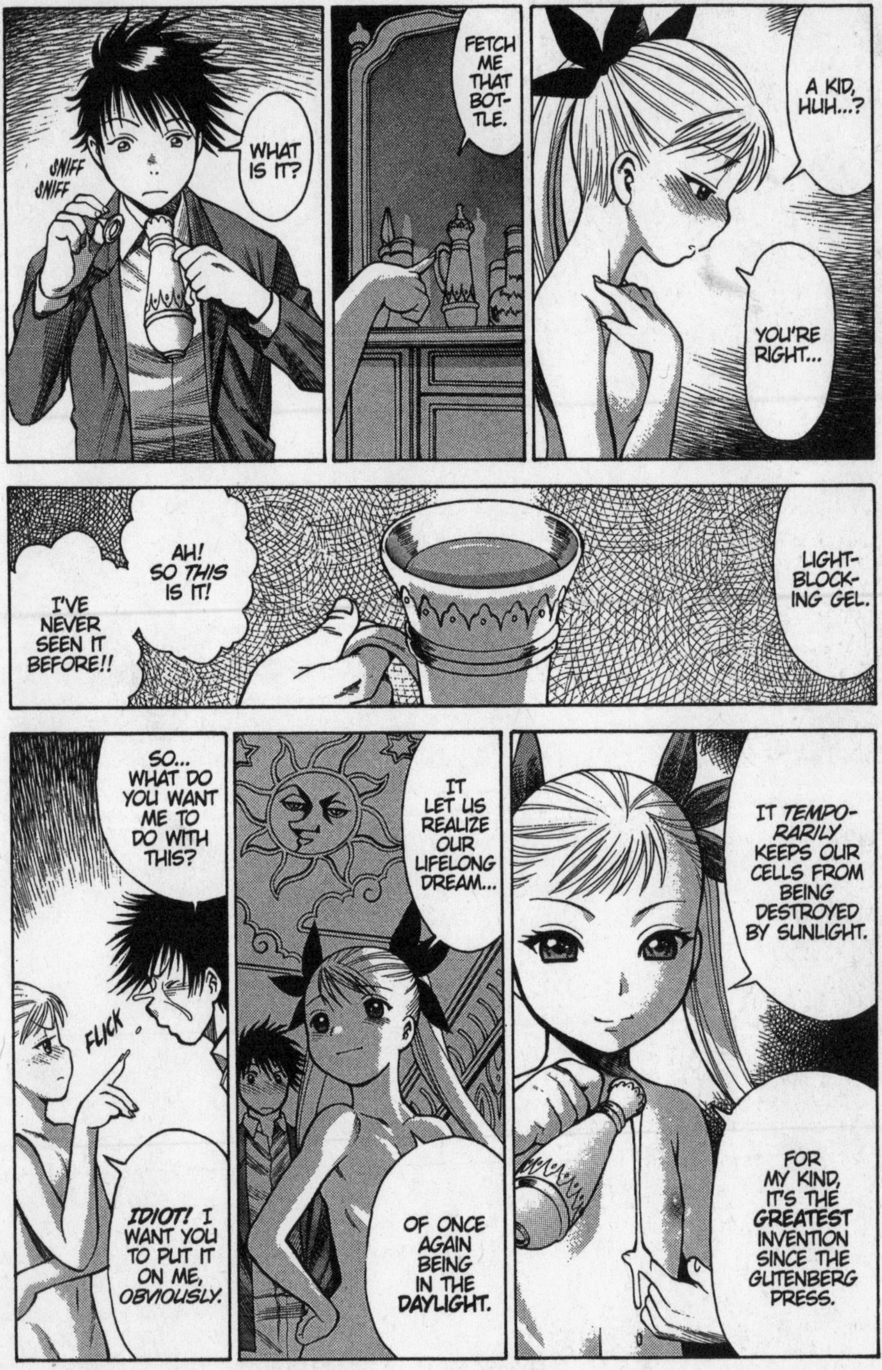
A KID, HUH...?
YOU'RE RIGHT...
FETCH ME THAT BOTTLE.
WHAT IS IT?
SNIFF SNIFF
LIGHT-BLOCKING GEL.
AH! SO *THIS* IS IT!
I'VE NEVER SEEN IT BEFORE!!
IT *TEMPORARILY* KEEPS OUR CELLS FROM BEING DESTROYED BY SUNLIGHT.
FOR MY KIND, IT'S THE **GREATEST** INVENTION SINCE THE GUTENBERG PRESS.
IT LET US REALIZE OUR LIFELONG DREAM...
OF ONCE AGAIN BEING IN THE **DAYLIGHT**.
SO... WHAT DO YOU WANT ME TO DO WITH THIS?
FLICK
IDIOT! I WANT YOU TO PUT IT ON ME, *OBVIOUSLY*.

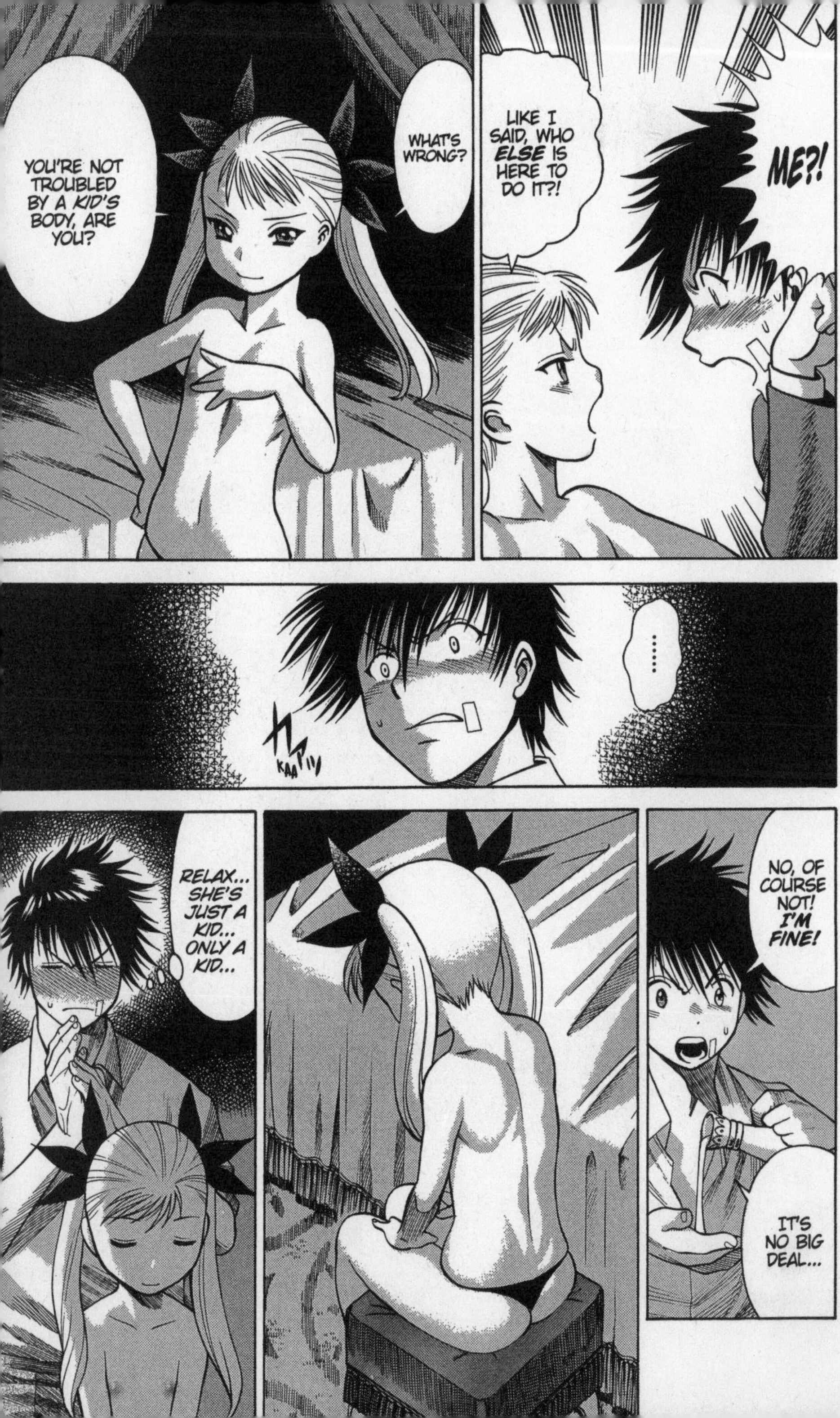
ME?!
LIKE I SAID, WHO ELSE IS HERE TO DO IT?!
WHAT'S WRONG?
YOU'RE NOT TROUBLED BY A KID'S BODY, ARE YOU?
......
KAA
NO, OF COURSE NOT! I'M FINE!
IT'S NO BIG DEAL...
RELAX... SHE'S JUST A KID... ONLY A KID...

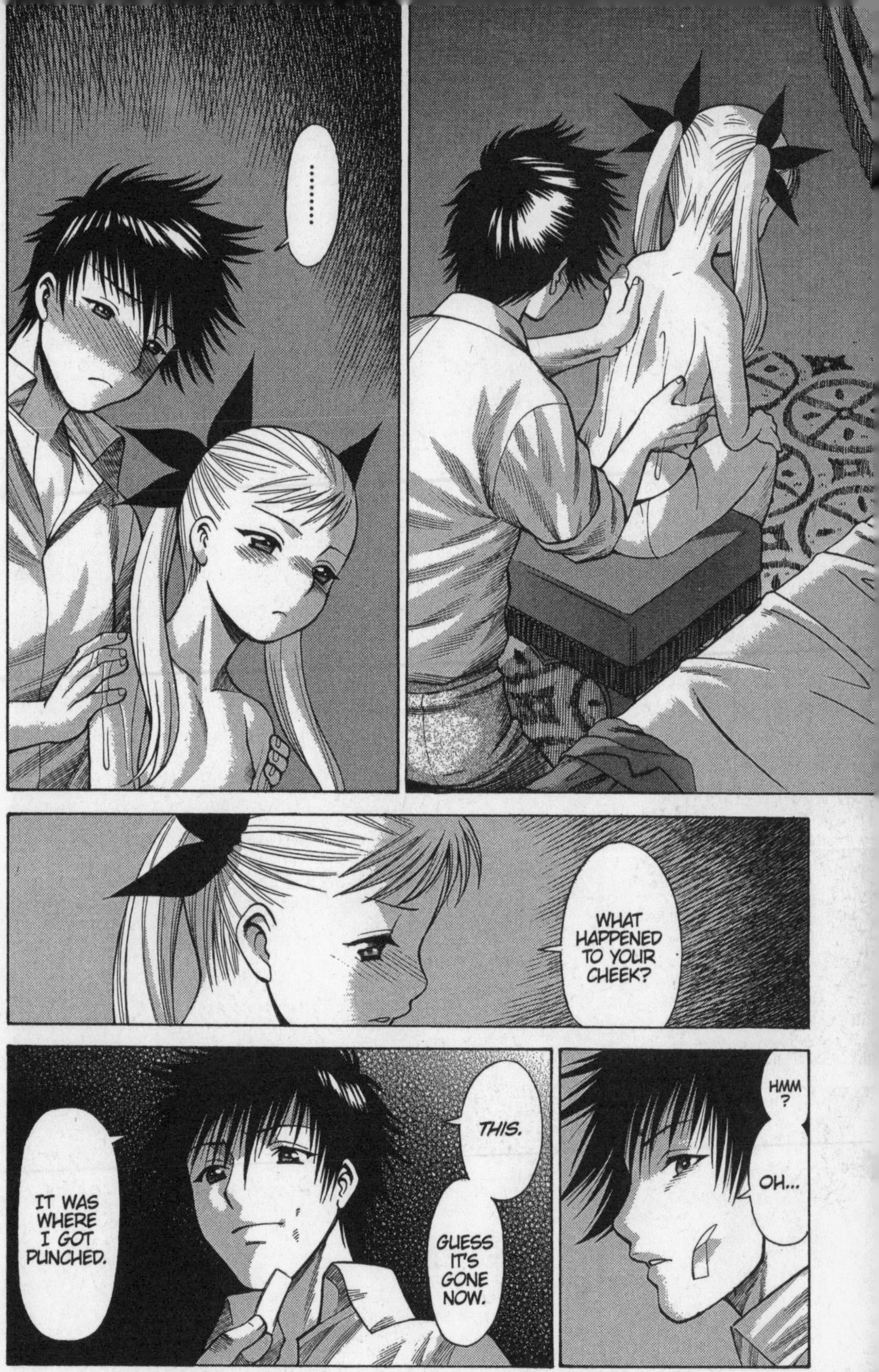
……
WHAT HAPPENED TO YOUR CHEEK?
HMM?
OH...
THIS.
GUESS IT'S GONE NOW.
IT WAS WHERE I GOT PUNCHED.

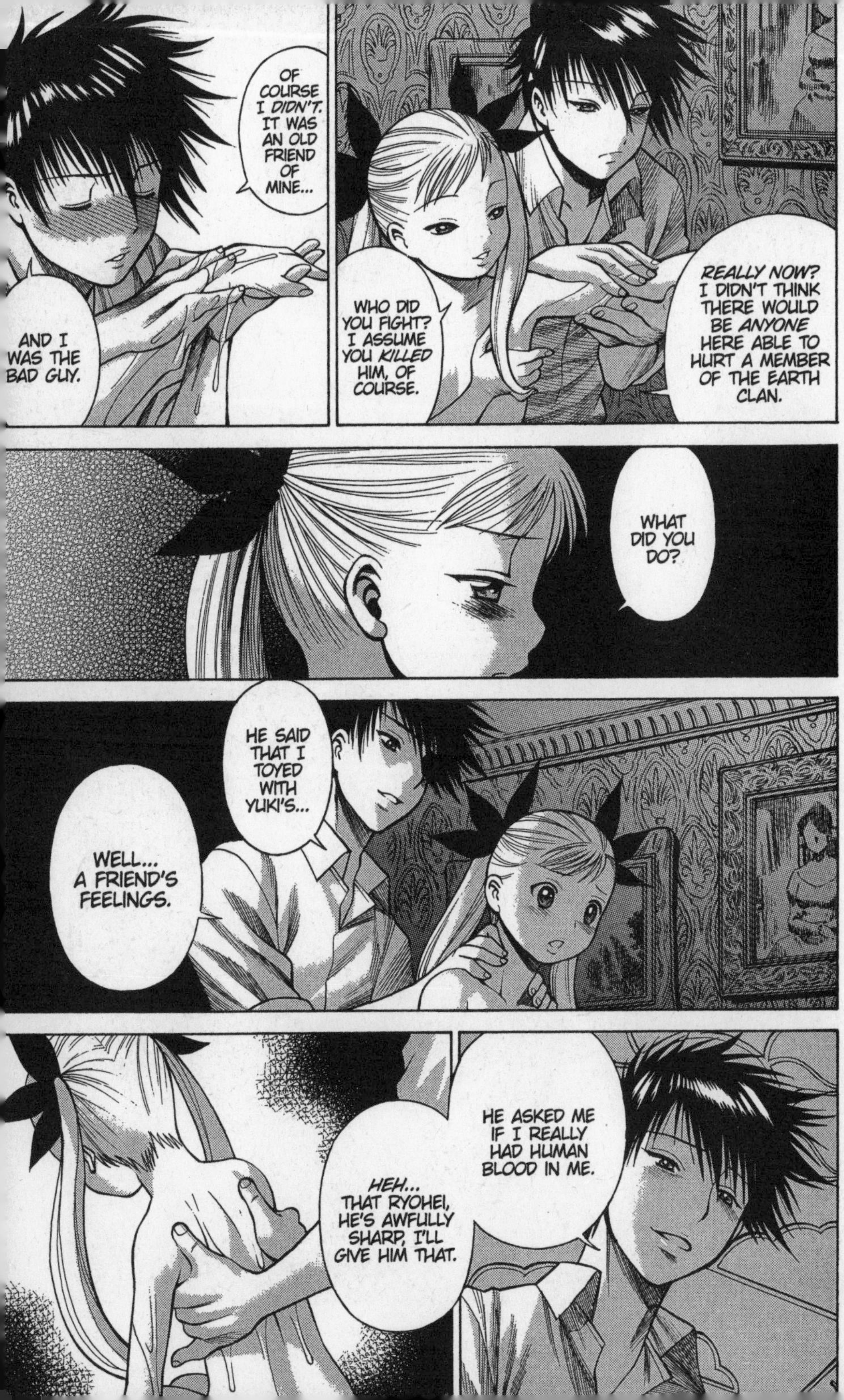
REALLY NOW? I DIDN'T THINK THERE WOULD BE ANYONE HERE ABLE TO HURT A MEMBER OF THE EARTH CLAN.
WHO DID YOU FIGHT? I ASSUME YOU KILLED HIM, OF COURSE.
OF COURSE I DIDN'T. IT WAS AN OLD FRIEND OF MINE...
AND I WAS THE BAD GUY.
WHAT DID YOU DO?
HE SAID THAT I TOYED WITH YUKI'S...
WELL... A FRIEND'S FEELINGS.
HE ASKED ME IF I REALLY HAD HUMAN BLOOD IN ME.
HEH... THAT RYOHEI, HE'S AWFULLY SHARP, I'LL GIVE HIM THAT.

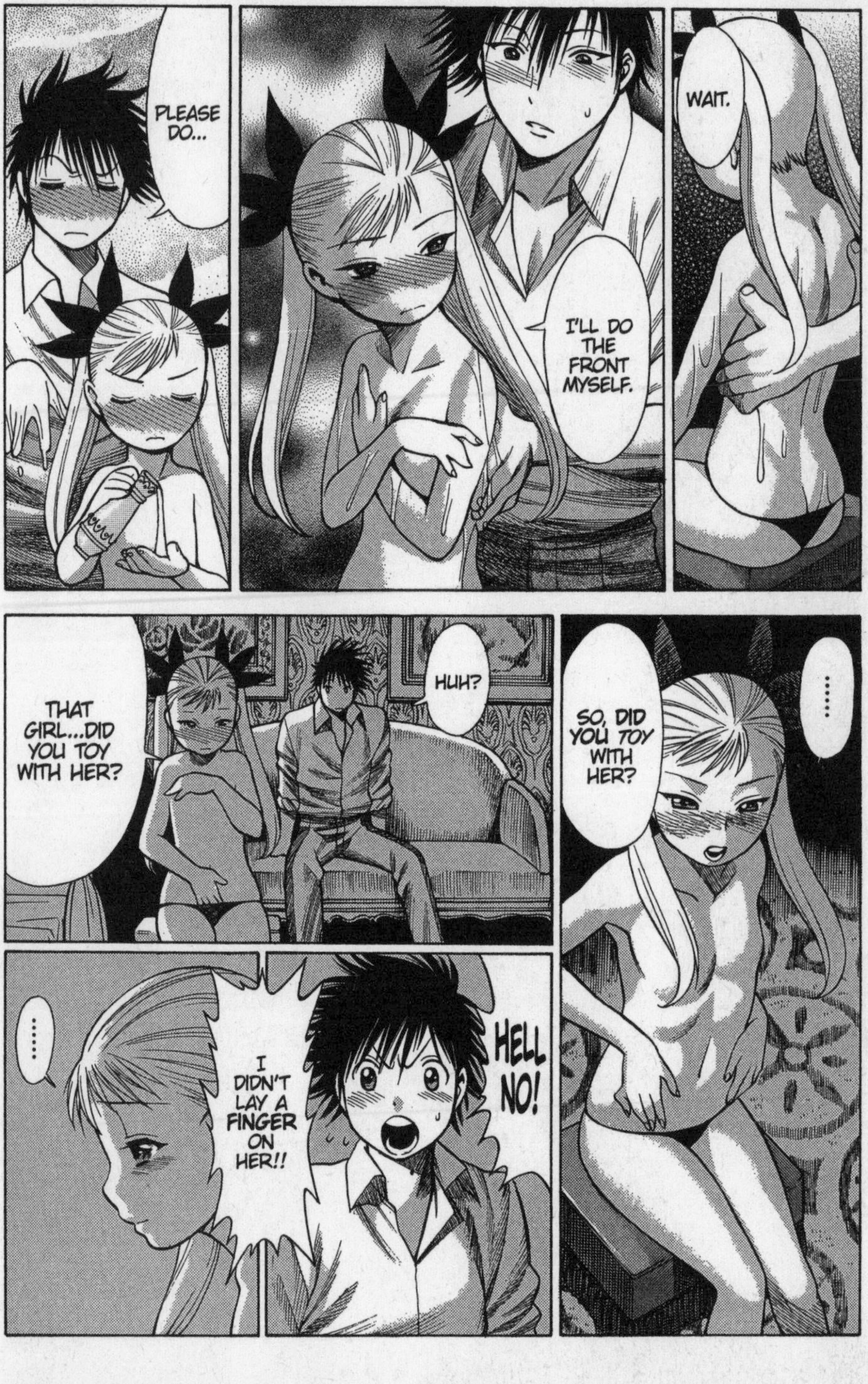
WAIT.
I'LL DO THE FRONT MYSELF.
PLEASE DO...
......
SO, DID YOU *TOY* WITH HER?
HUH?
THAT GIRL...DID YOU TOY WITH HER?
HELL NO!
I DIDN'T LAY A FINGER ON HER!!
......

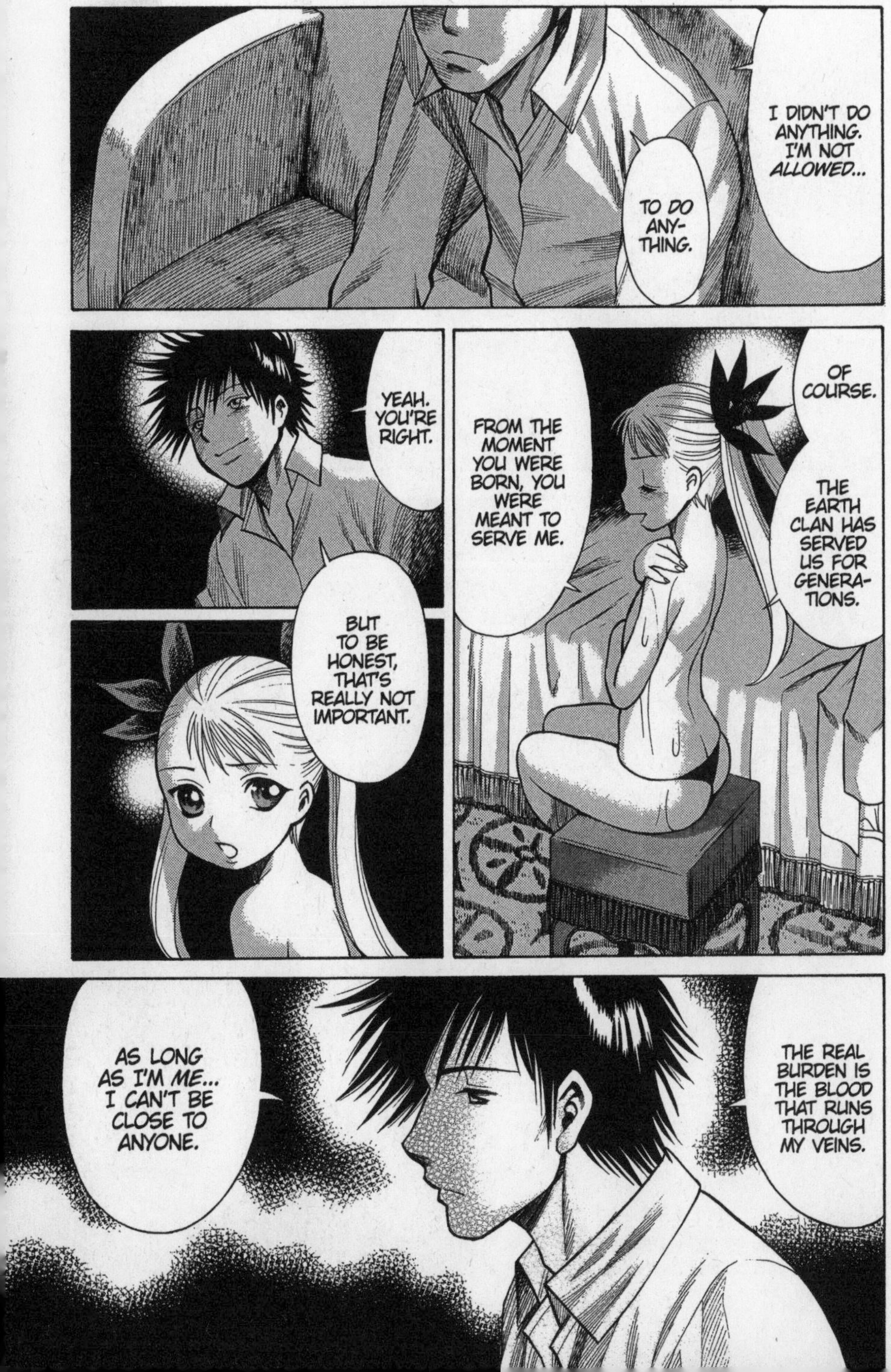
I DIDN'T DO ANYTHING. I'M NOT *ALLOWED*...
TO DO ANY-THING.
OF COURSE.
THE EARTH CLAN HAS SERVED US FOR GENERA-TIONS.
FROM THE MOMENT YOU WERE BORN, YOU WERE MEANT TO SERVE ME.
YEAH. YOU'RE RIGHT.
BUT TO BE HONEST, THAT'S REALLY NOT IMPORTANT.
THE REAL BURDEN IS THE BLOOD THAT RUNS THROUGH MY VEINS.
AS LONG AS I'M *ME*... I CAN'T BE CLOSE TO ANYONE.

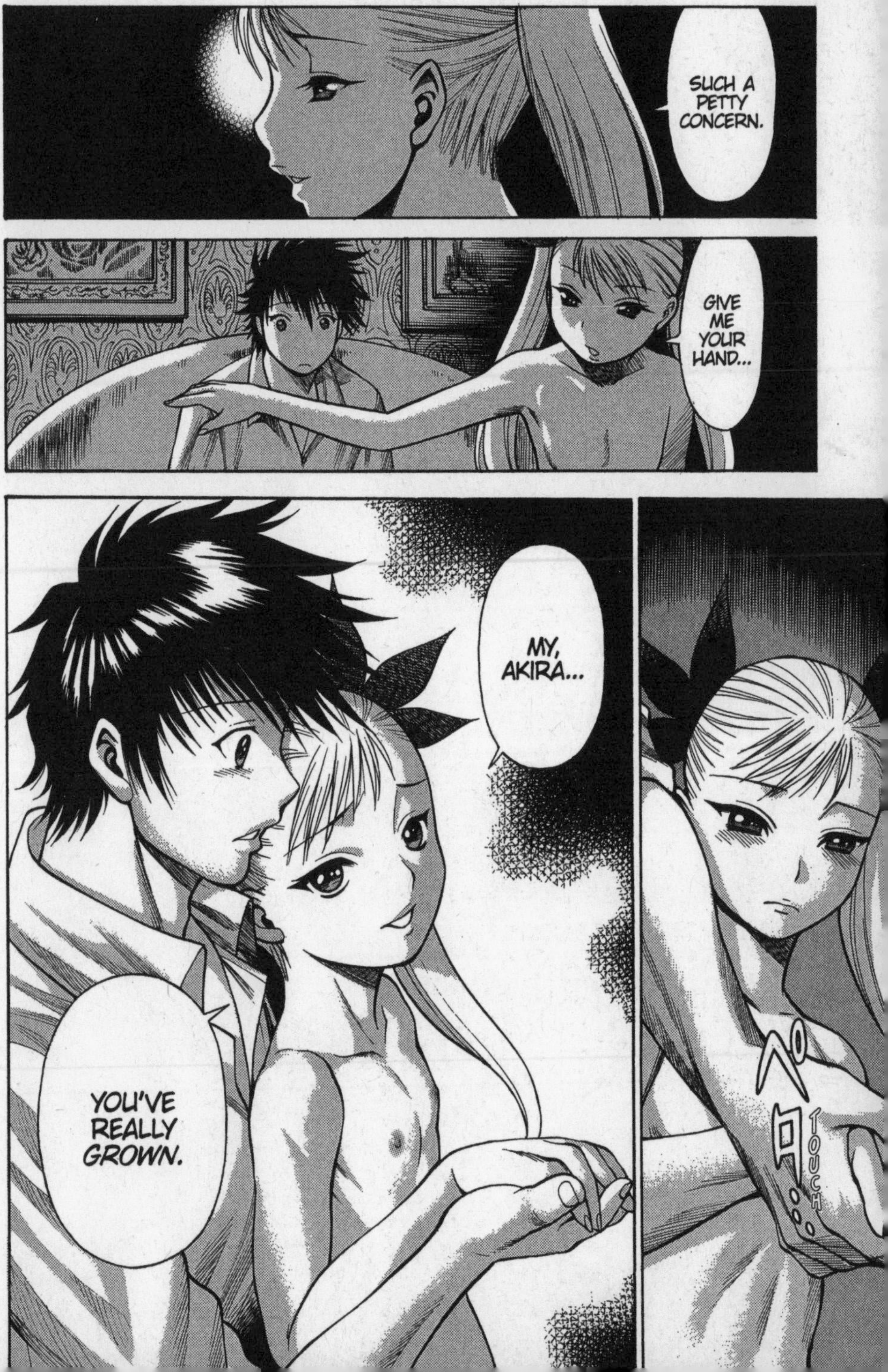
SUCH A PETTY CONCERN.
GIVE ME YOUR HAND...
ペロ
TOUCH
MY, AKIRA...
YOU'VE REALLY GROWN.

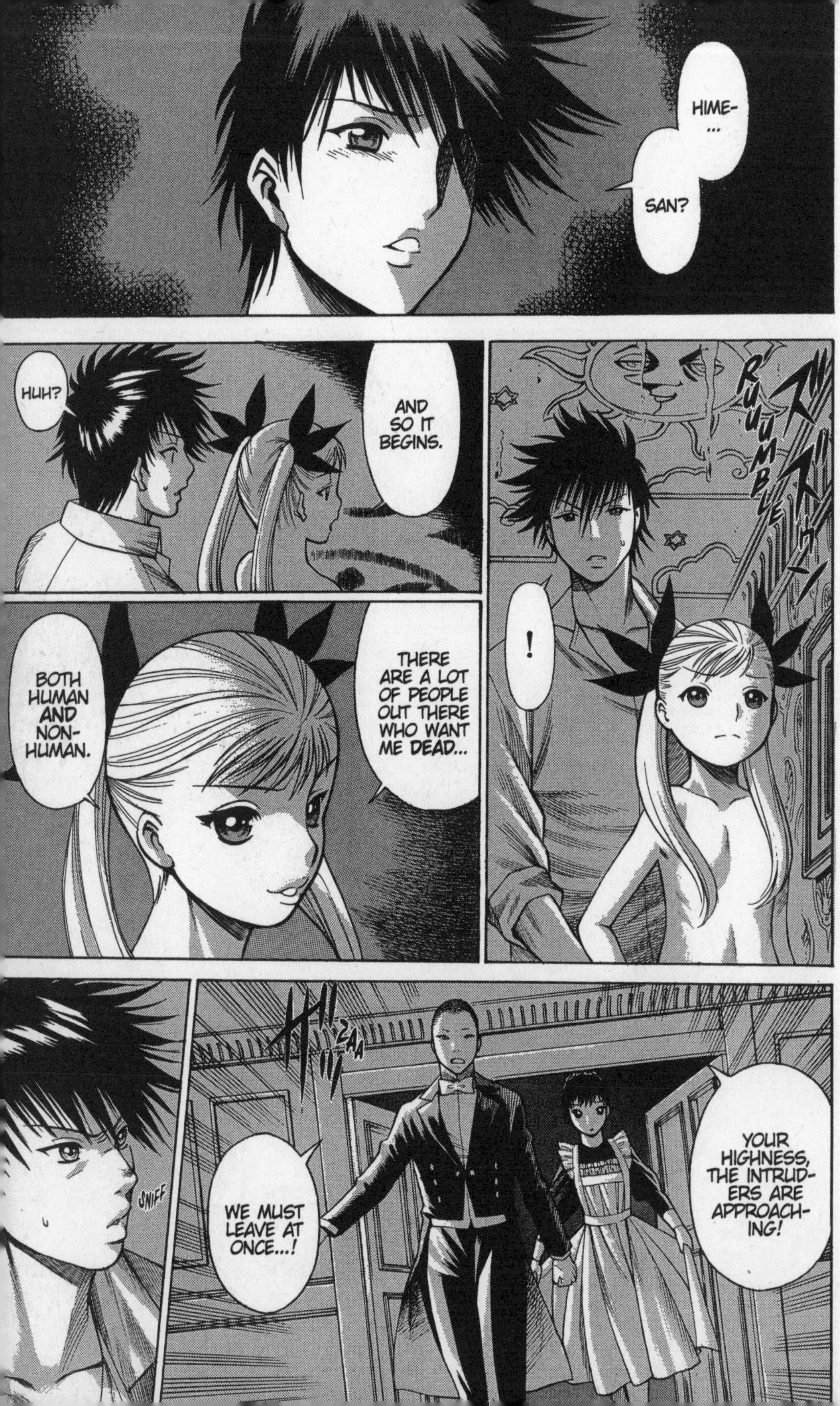
HIME-...
SAN?
RUUMBLE
!
AND SO IT BEGINS.
HUH?
THERE ARE A LOT OF PEOPLE OUT THERE WHO WANT ME DEAD...
BOTH HUMAN AND NON-HUMAN.
ZAA
YOUR HIGHNESS, THE INTRUDERS ARE APPROACHING!
WE MUST LEAVE AT ONCE...!
SNIFF

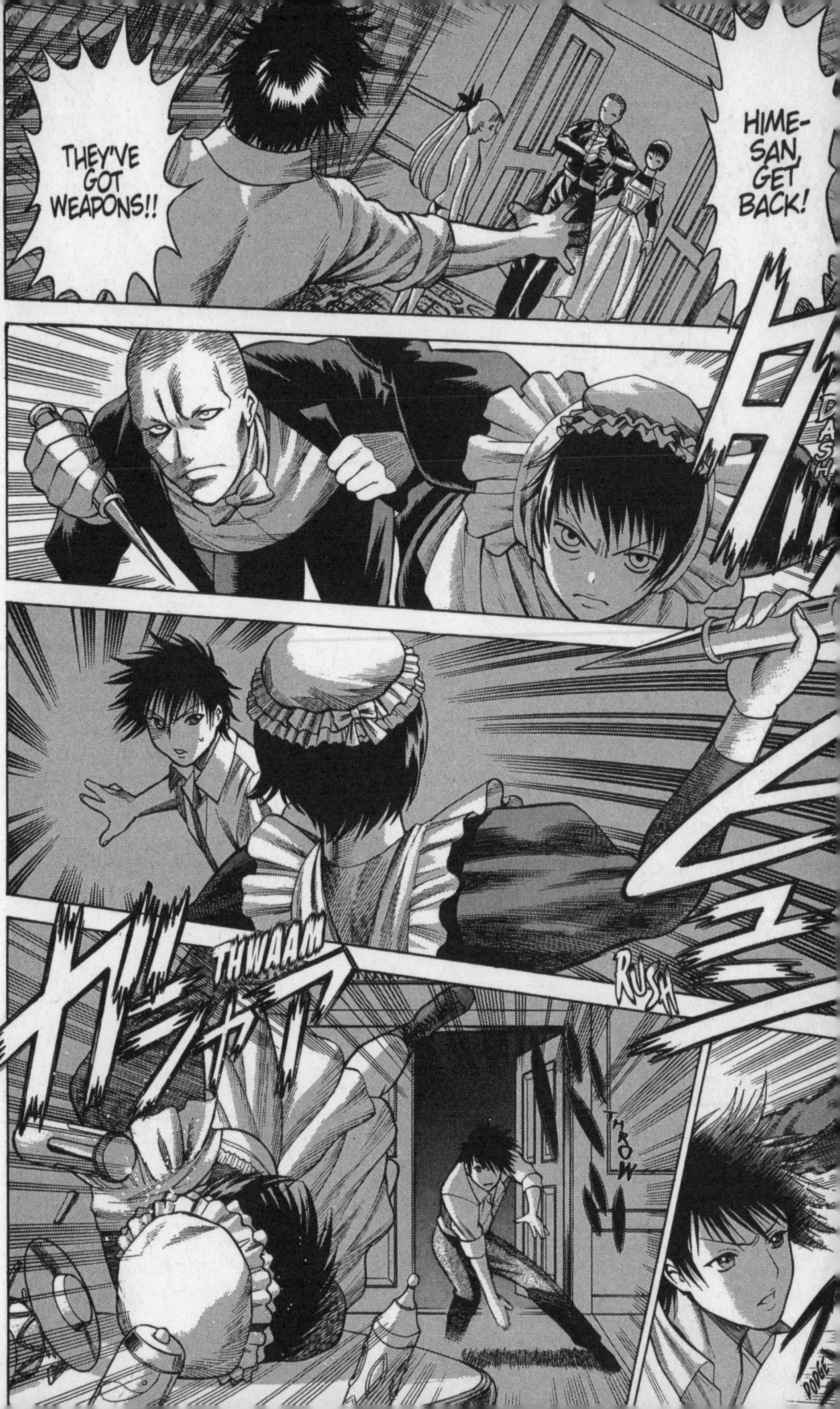
HIME-SAN, GET BACK!
THEY'VE GOT WEAPONS!!
DASH
RUSH
THWAAM
THROW
DODGE

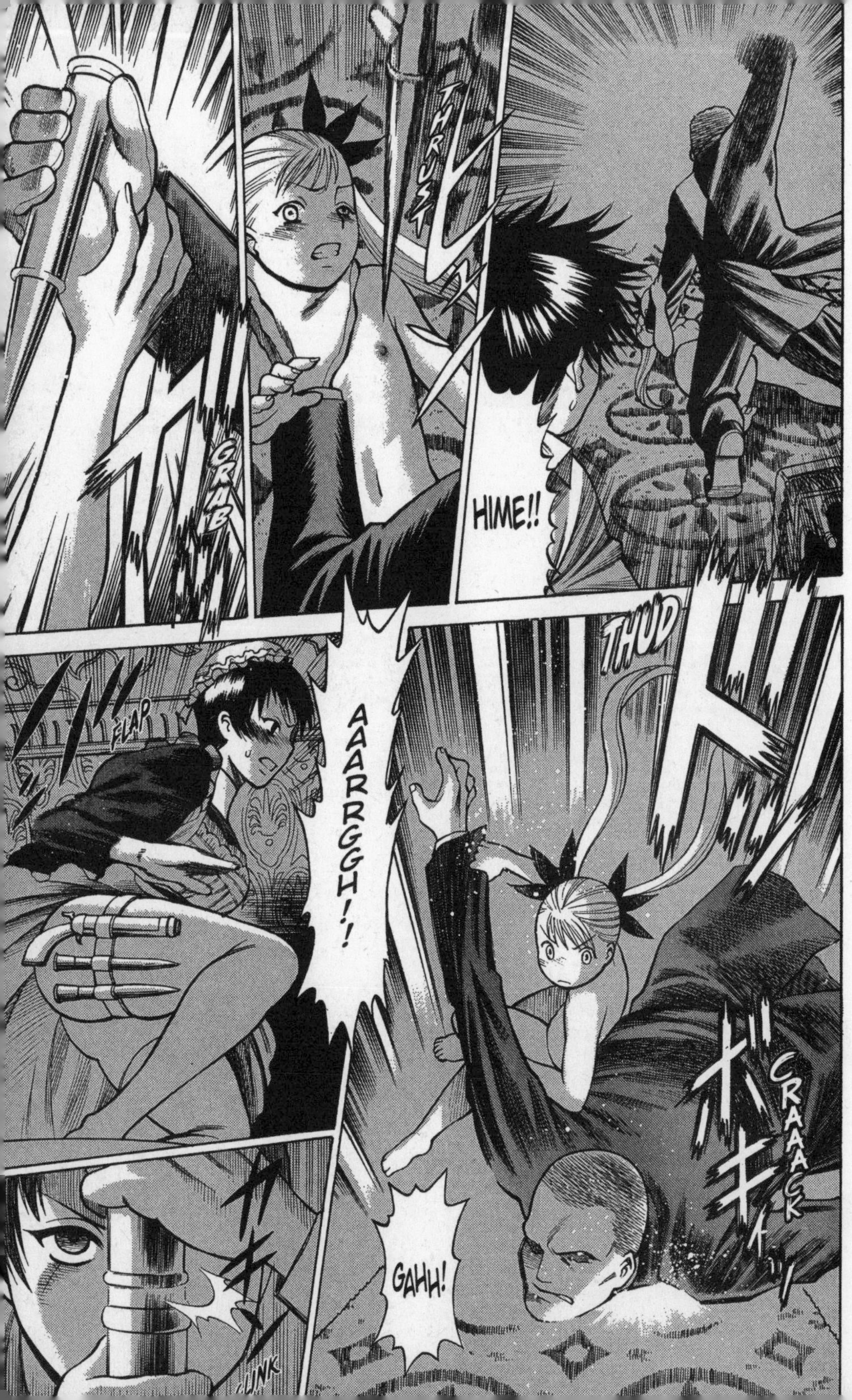
HIME!!
THRUST
GRAB
THUD
CRAAACK
GAHH!
AAARRGGH!!
FLAP
CLINK

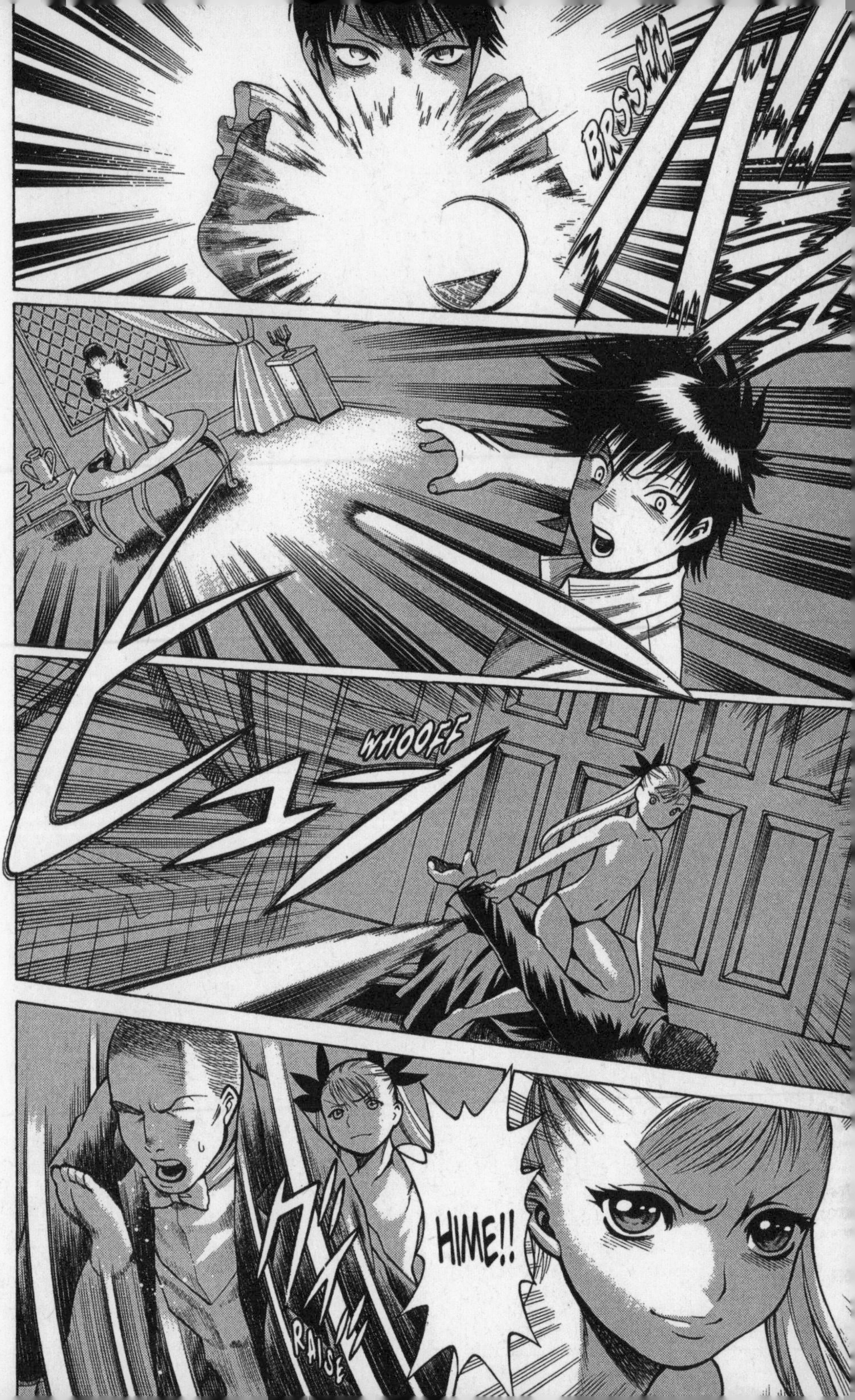
BRSSHH
WHOOFF
HIME!!
RAISE

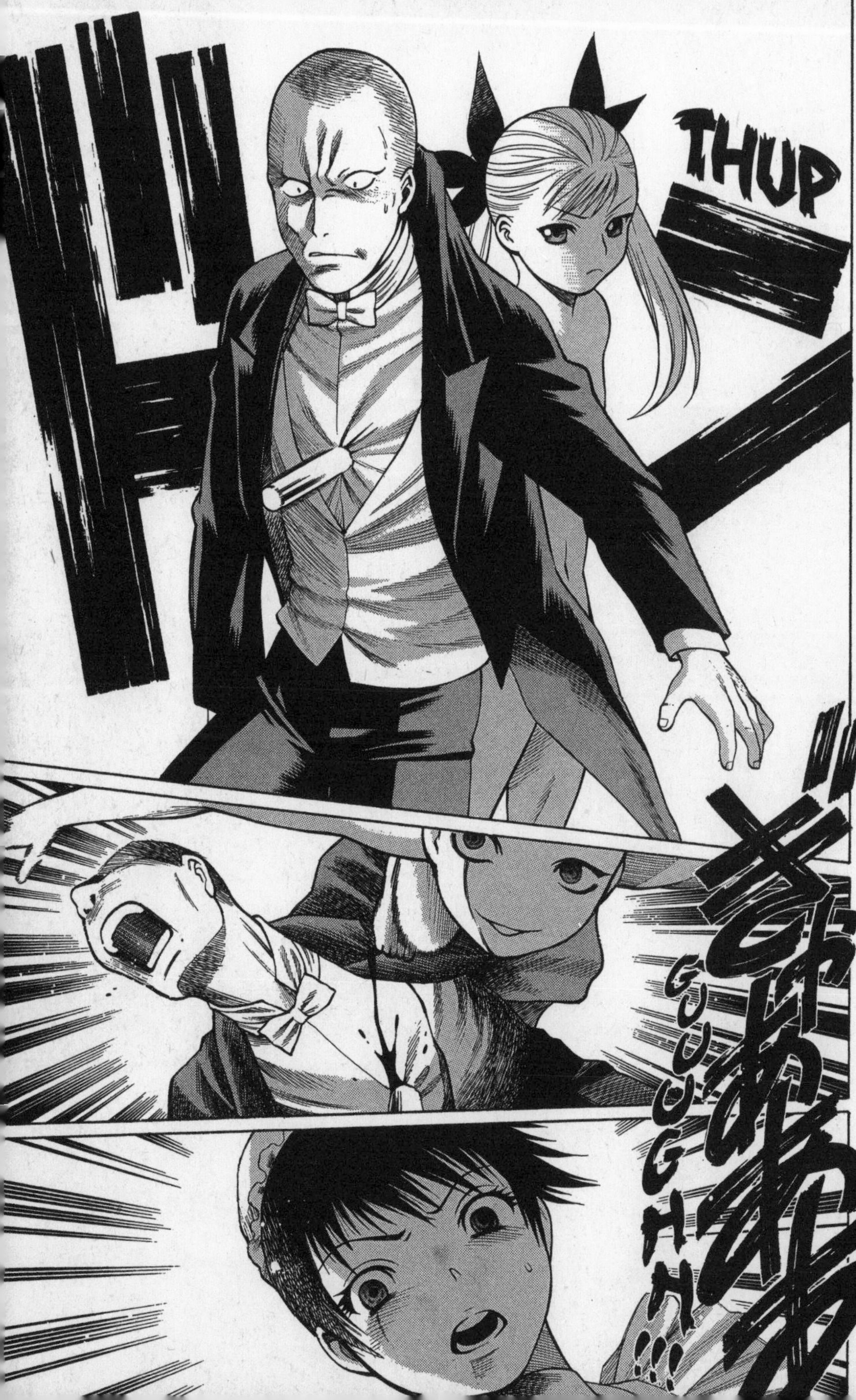
THUP
GUUUGHH!!!

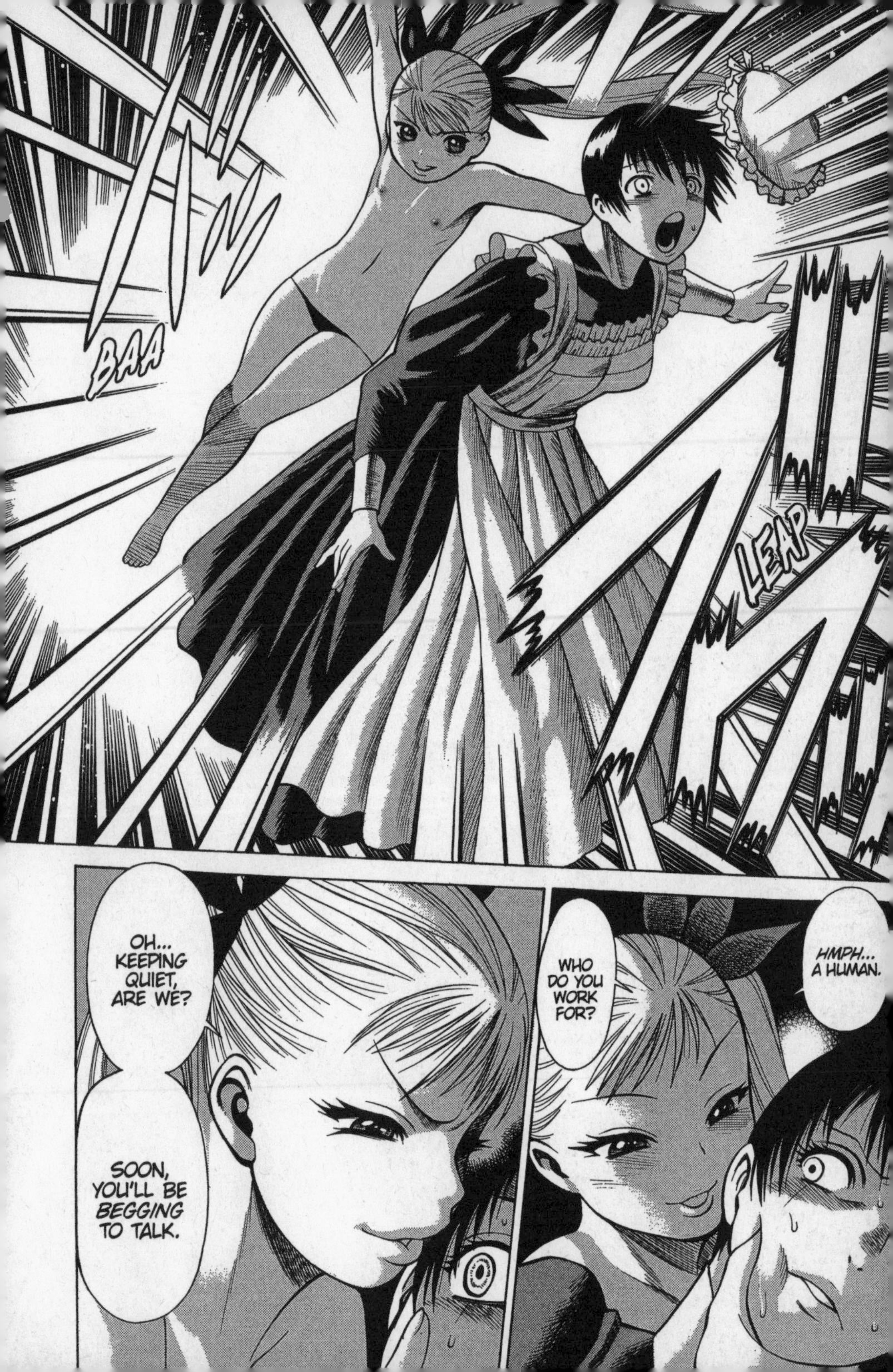
LEAP
BAA
HMPH... A HUMAN.
WHO DO YOU WORK FOR?
OH... KEEPING QUIET, ARE WE?
SOON, YOU'LL BE BEGGING TO TALK.

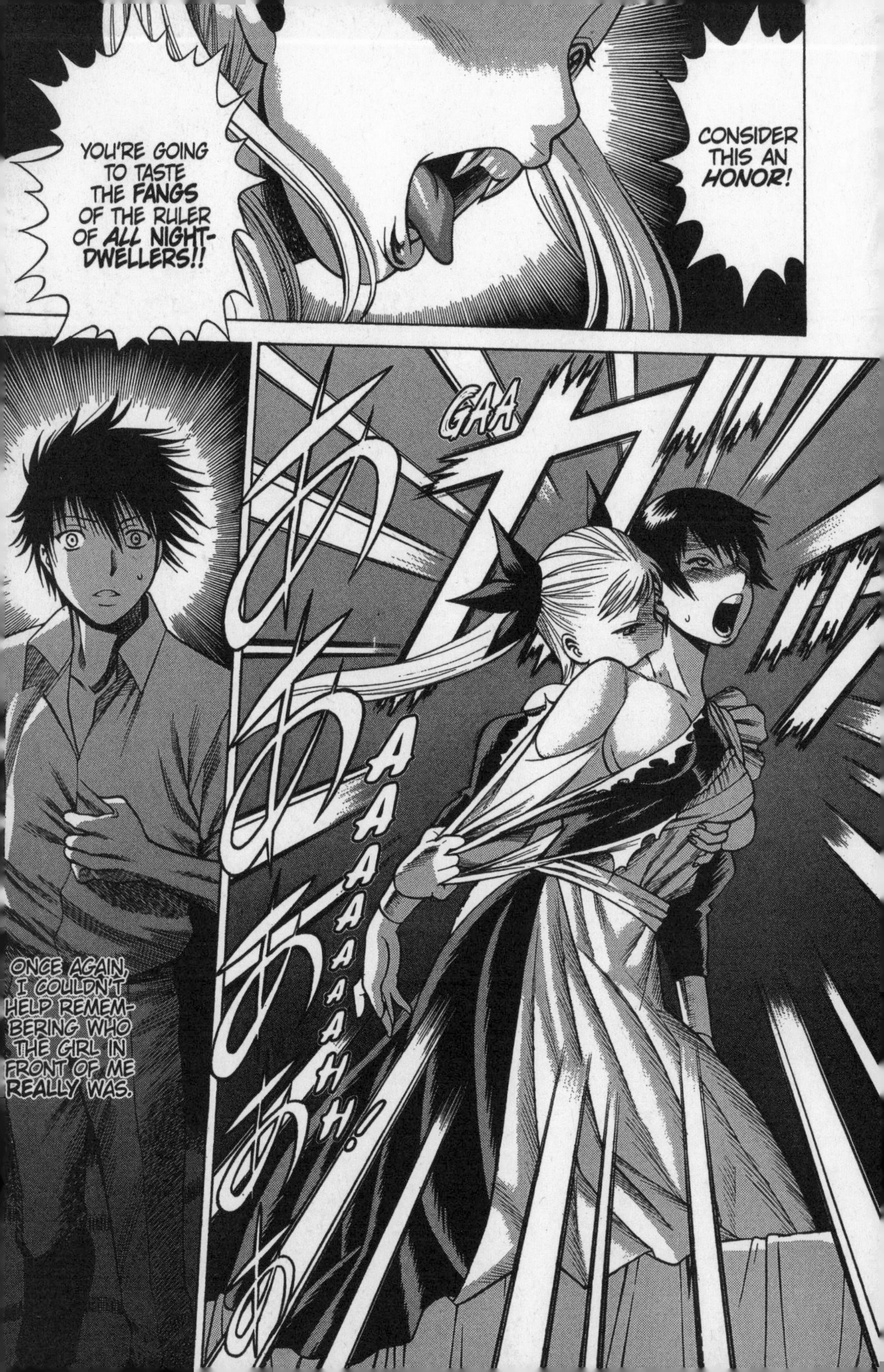
CONSIDER THIS AN *HONOR!*
YOU'RE GOING TO TASTE THE **FANGS** OF THE RULER OF ***ALL*** **NIGHT-DWELLERS!!**
GAA
AAAAAAAHH!
ONCE AGAIN, I COULDN'T HELP REMEMBERING WHO THE GIRL IN FRONT OF ME **REALLY** WAS.

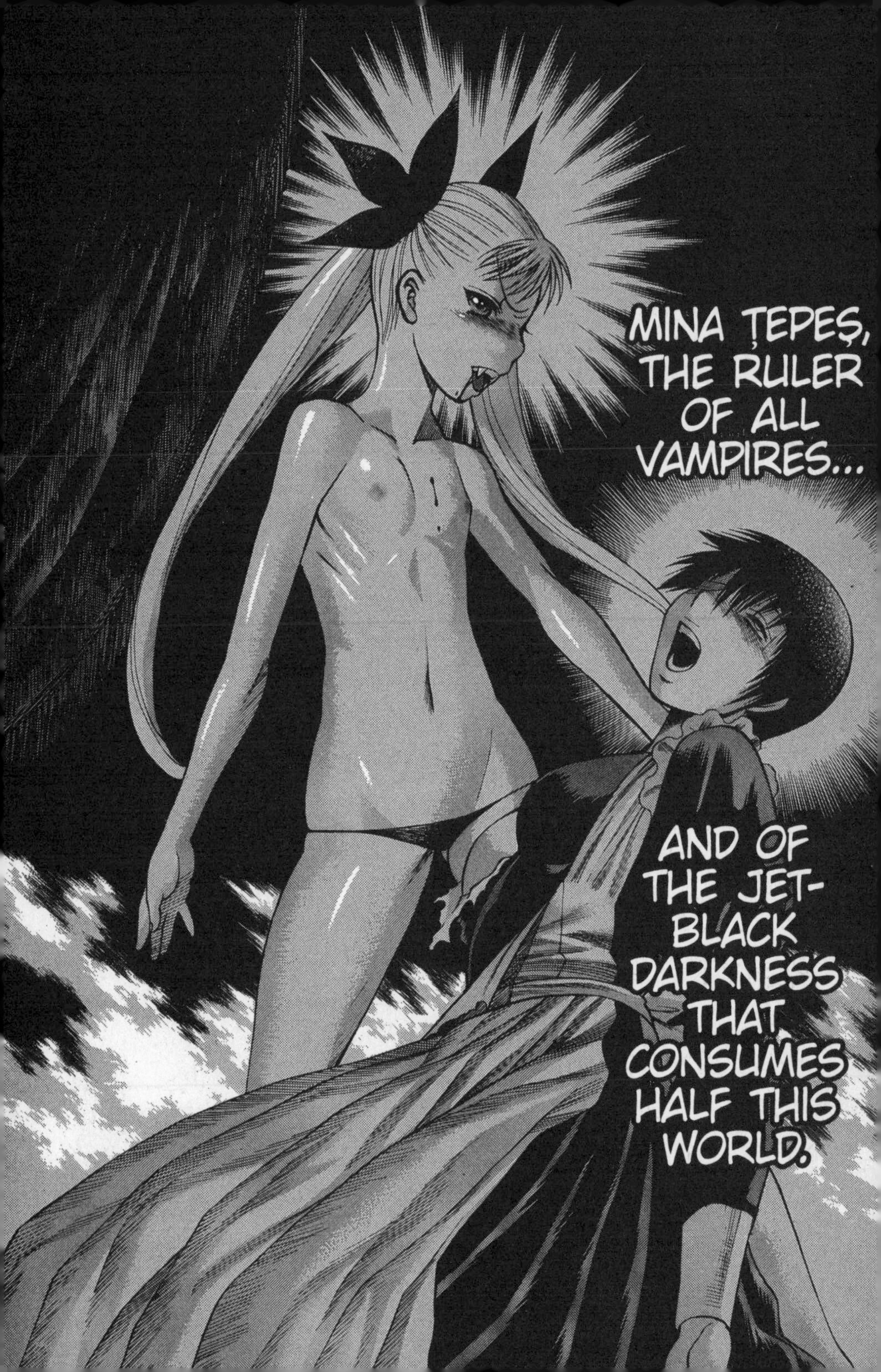
MINA ȚEPEȘ, THE RULER OF ALL VAMPIRES...
AND OF THE JET-BLACK DARKNESS THAT CONSUMES HALF THIS WORLD.

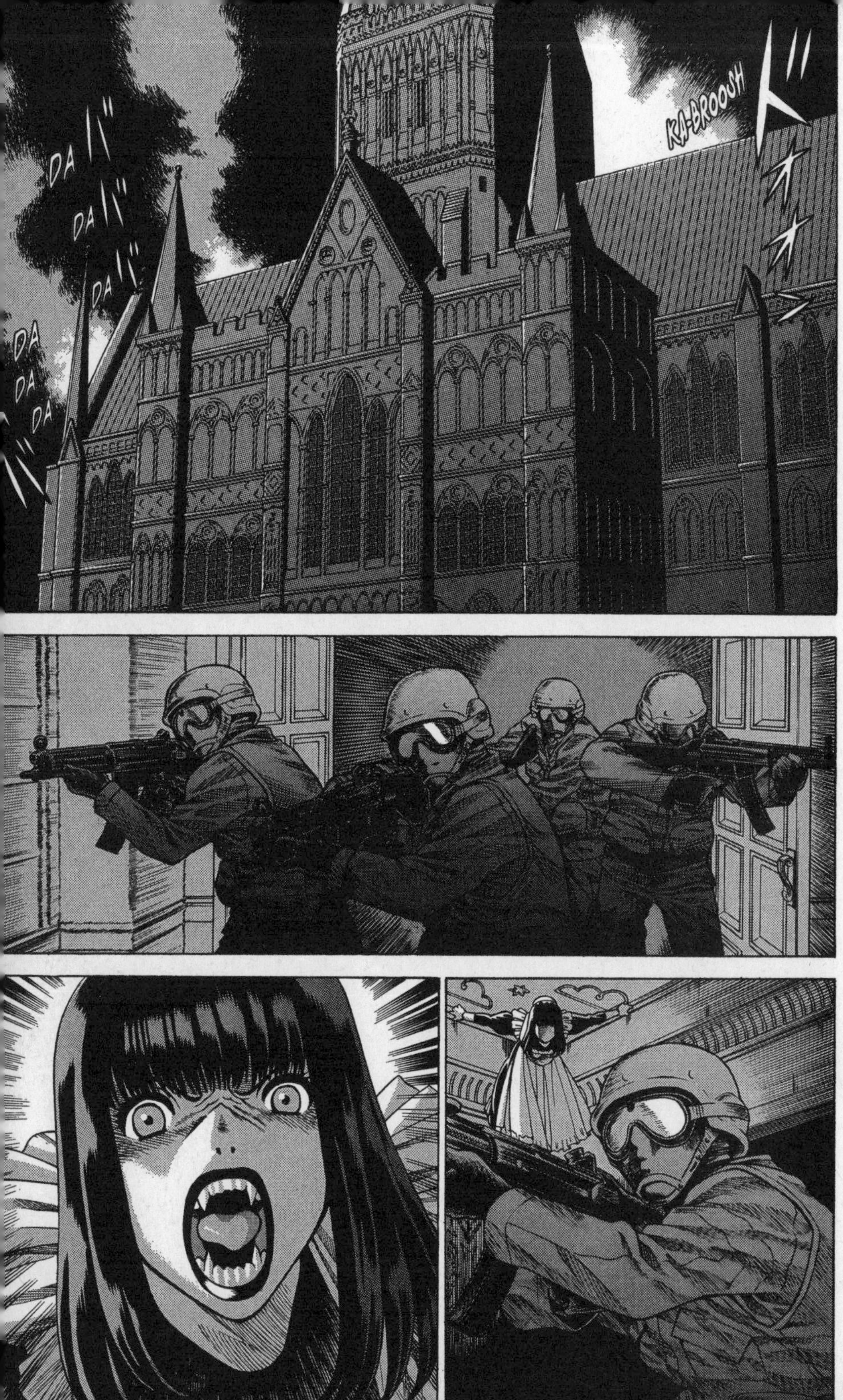

KA-BROOSH
ドォォォン
DA
DA
DA
バババ
DA
DA
DA

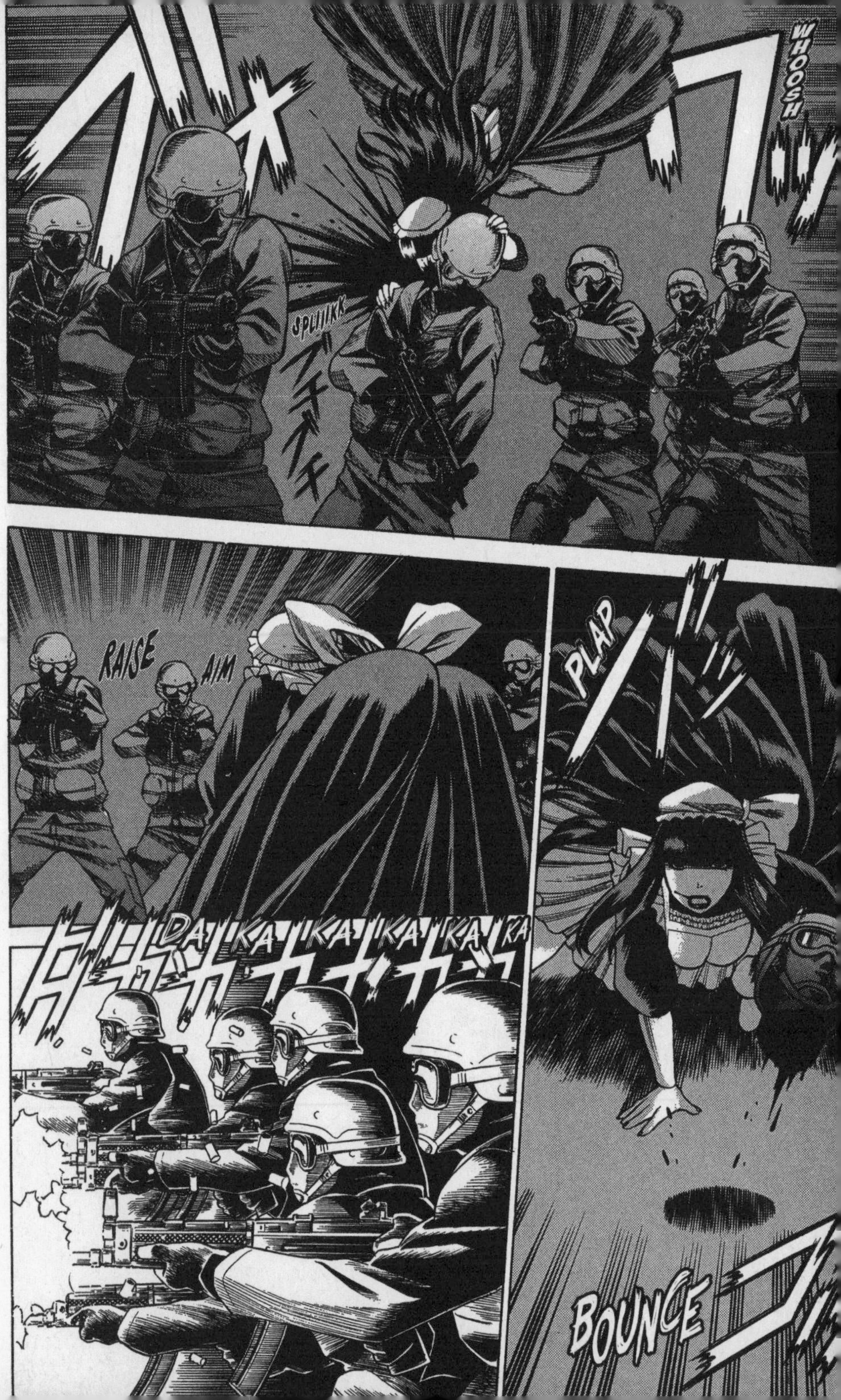
WHOOSH
SPLIIIKK
PLAP
BOUNCE
RAISE
AIM
DA KA KA KA KA KA KA

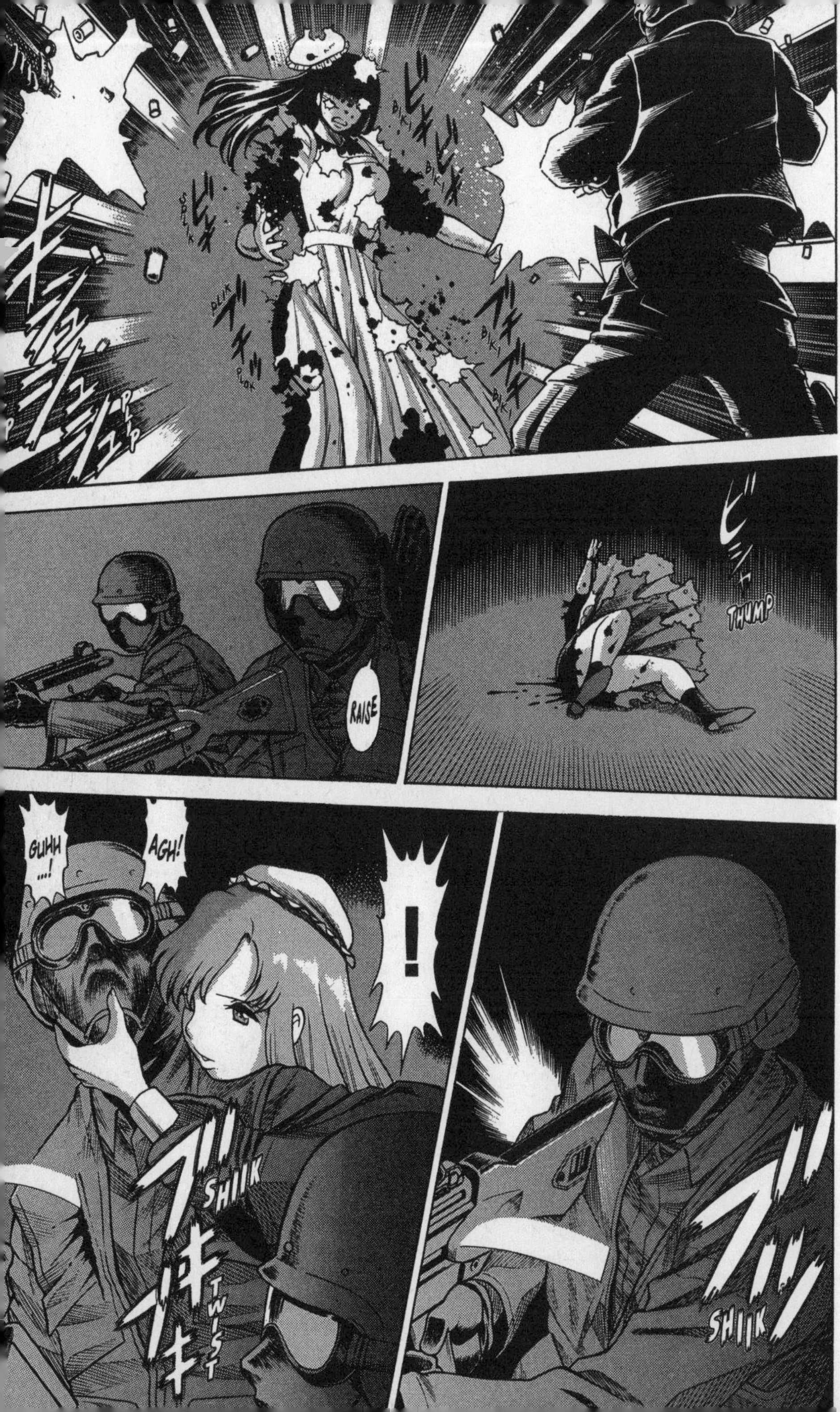
BIKI
SPLIK
PLIK
PLOK
PLIP
THUMP
RAISE
SHIIK
!
AGH!
GUHH ...!
SHIIK
TWIST

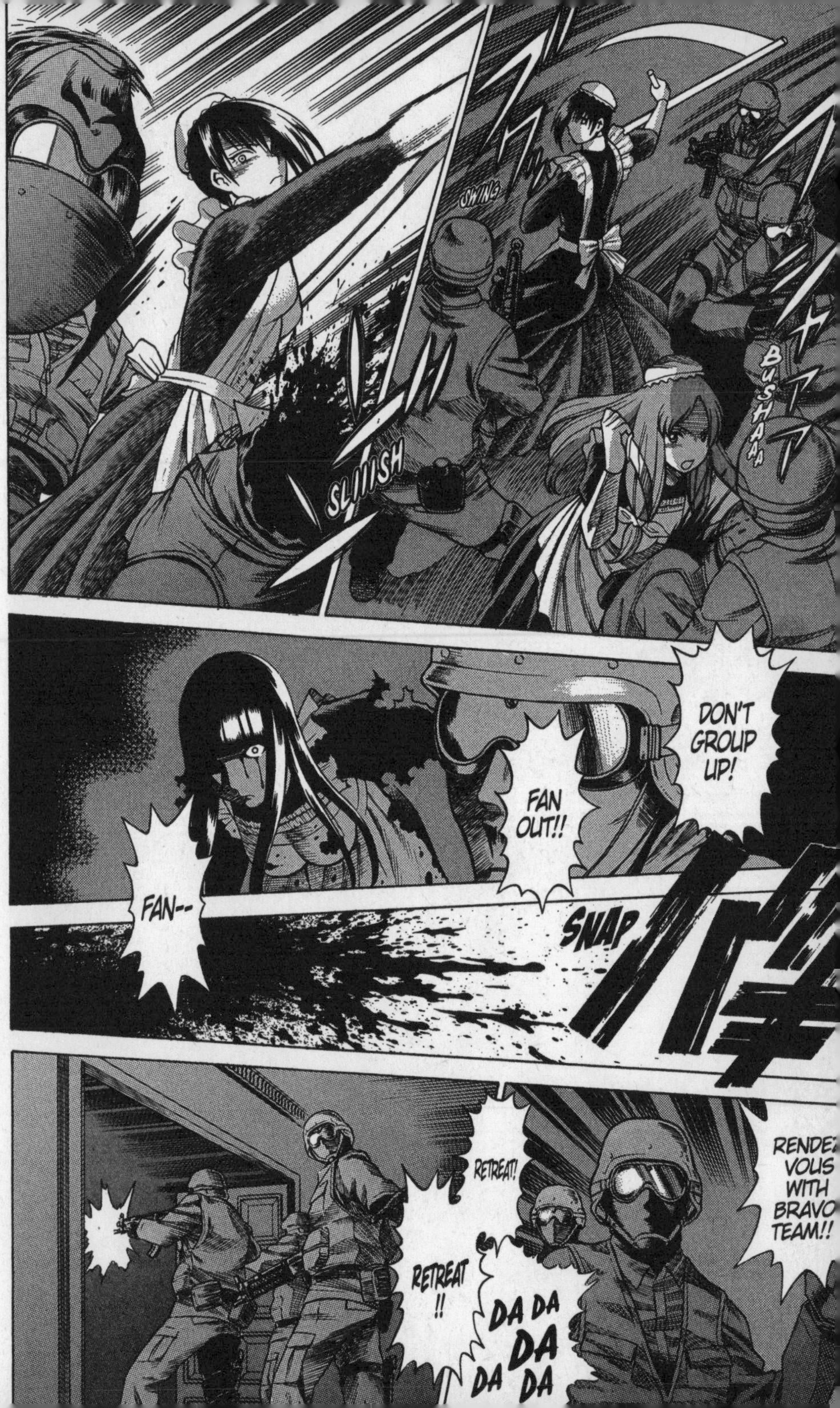

BUSHAAA
SWING
SLIIISH
DON'T GROUP UP!
FAN OUT!!
SNAP
FAN--
RENDEZ VOUS WITH BRAVO TEAM!!
RETREAT!
RETREAT!!
DA DA DA DA DA DA

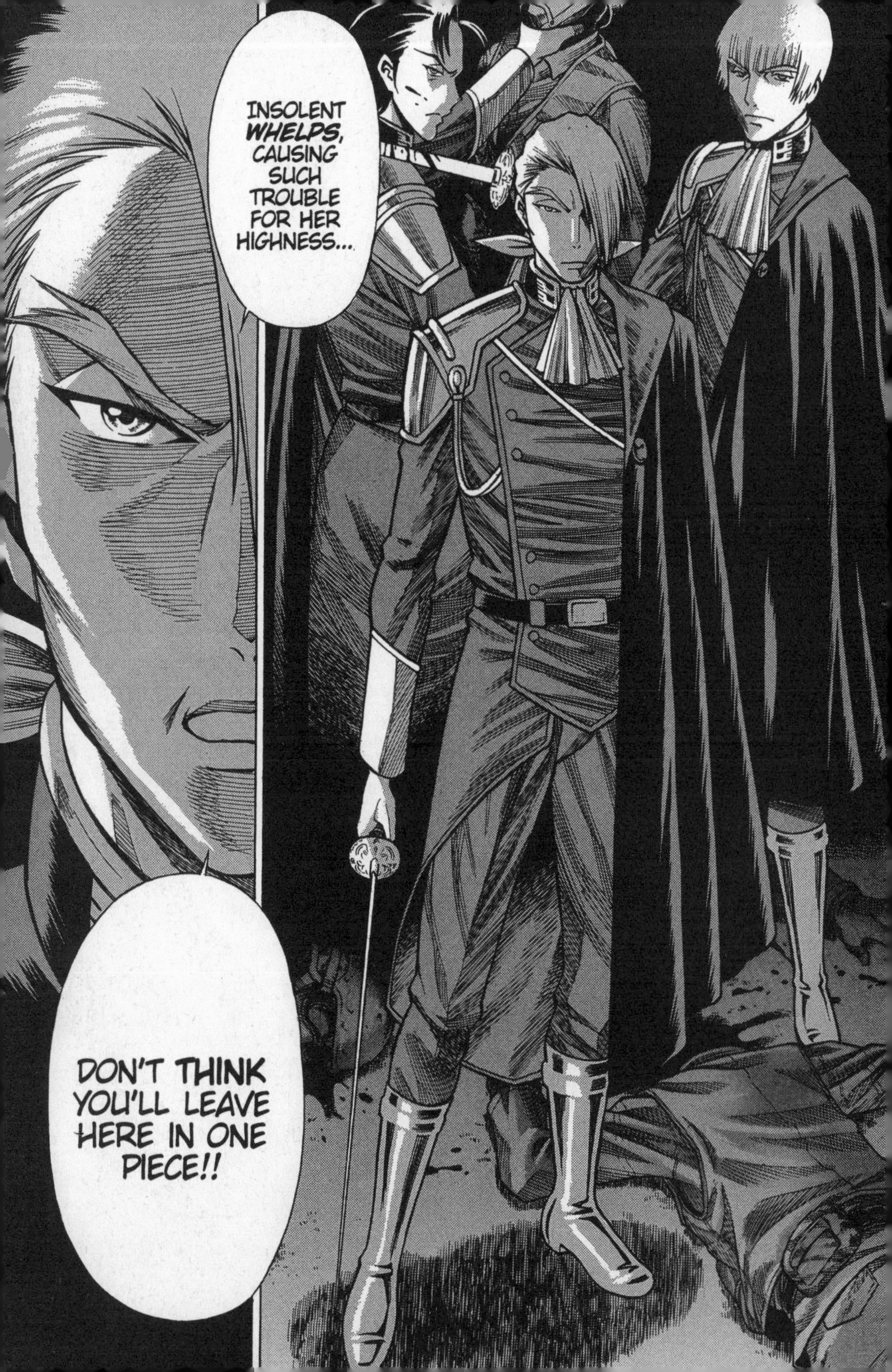
INSOLENT WHELPS, CAUSING SUCH TROUBLE FOR HER HIGHNESS...
DON'T THINK YOU'LL LEAVE HERE IN ONE PIECE!!

Chapter 2: Choice

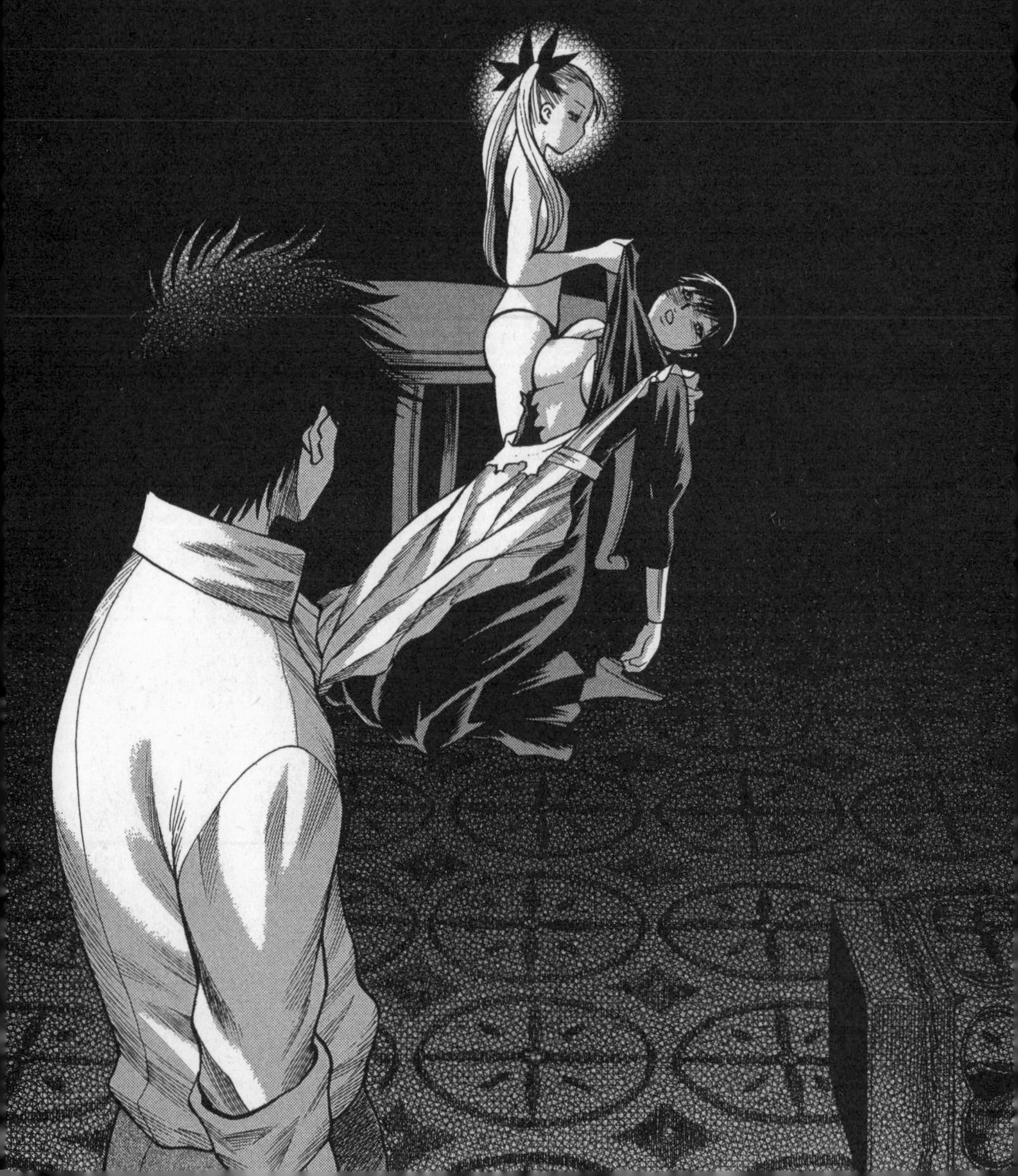

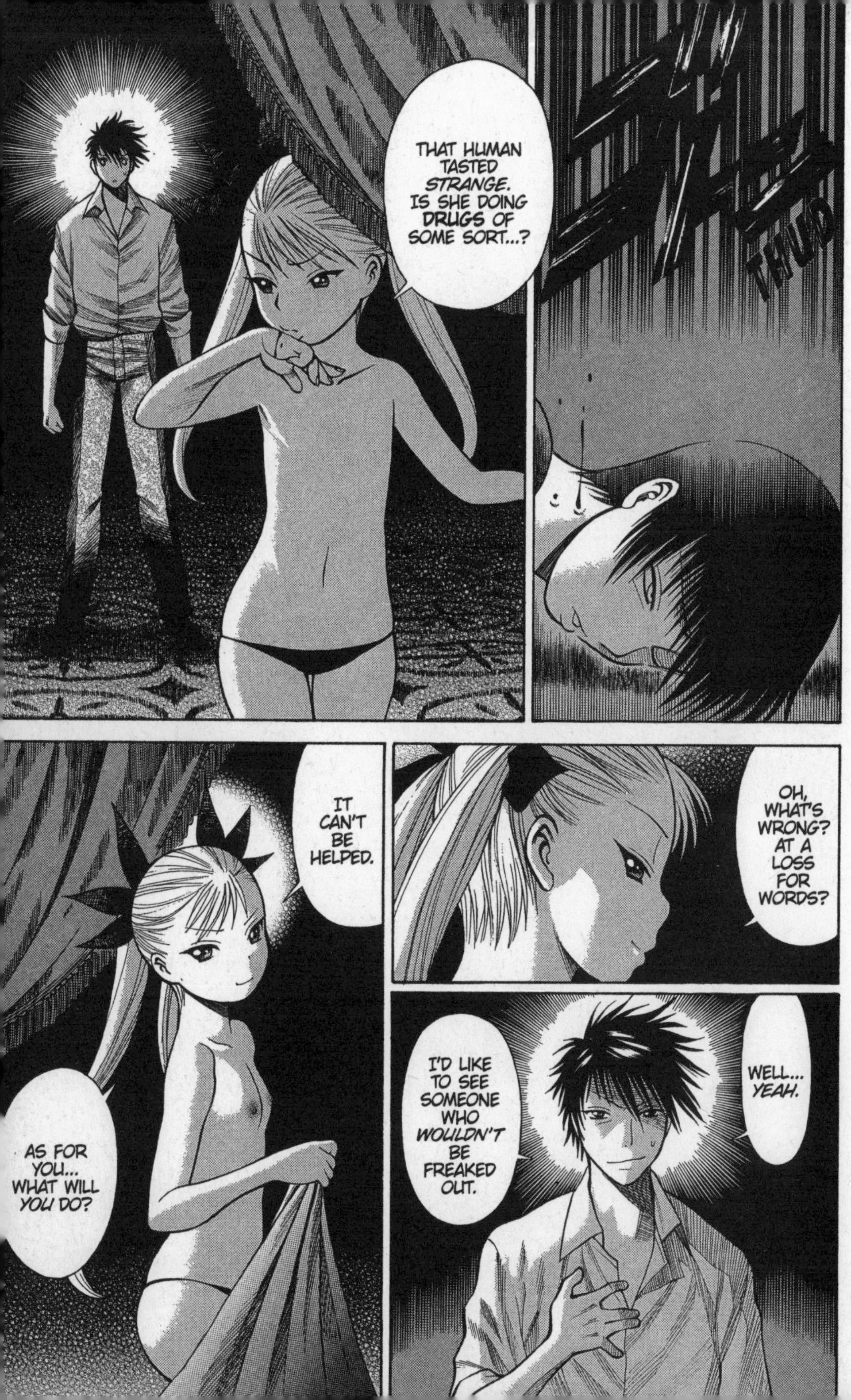
THUD
THAT HUMAN TASTED STRANGE. IS SHE DOING DRUGS OF SOME SORT...?
OH, WHAT'S WRONG? AT A LOSS FOR WORDS?
WELL... YEAH.
I'D LIKE TO SEE SOMEONE WHO WOULDN'T BE FREAKED OUT.
IT CAN'T BE HELPED.
AS FOR YOU... WHAT WILL YOU DO?

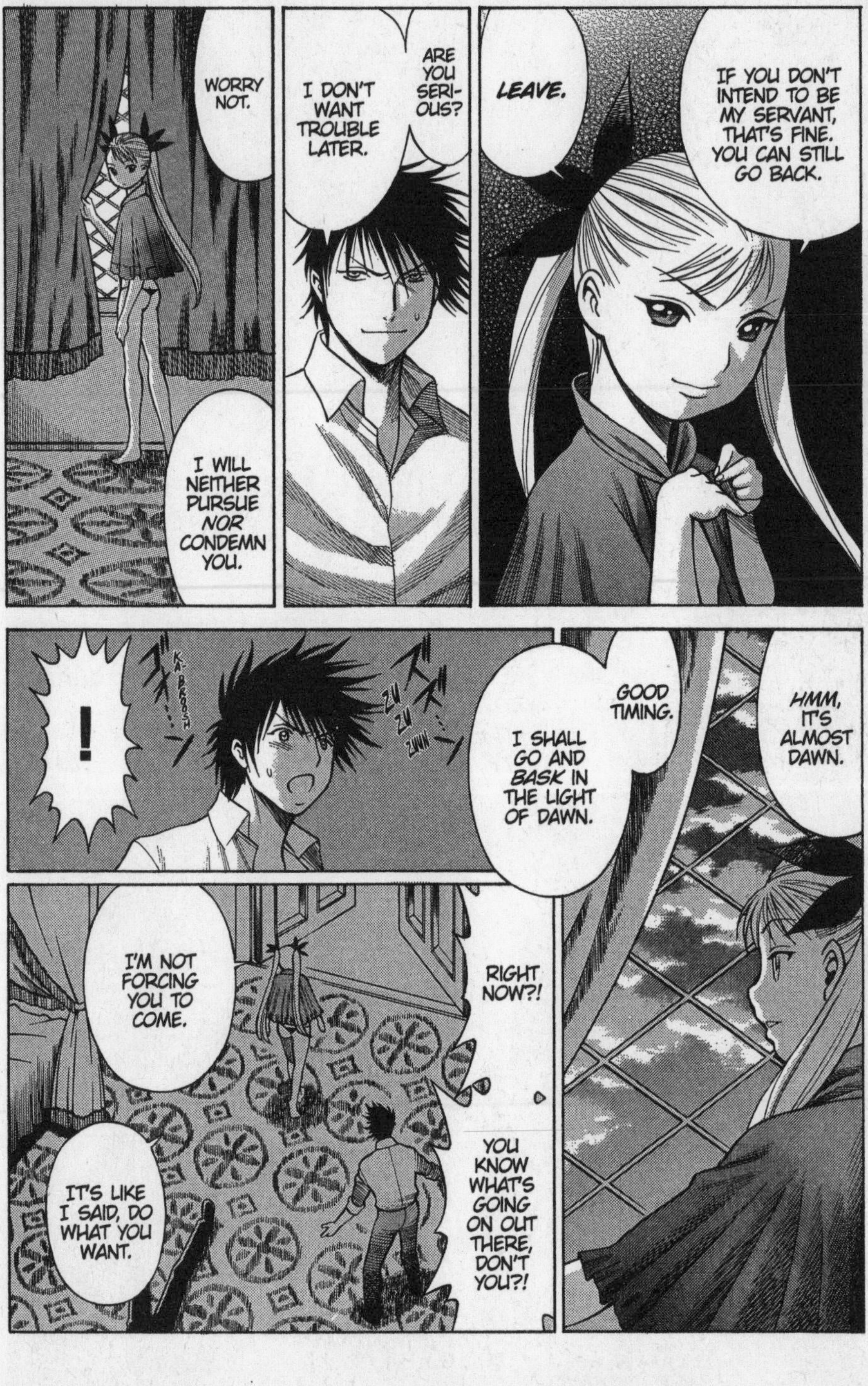
IF YOU DON'T INTEND TO BE MY SERVANT, THAT'S FINE. YOU CAN STILL GO BACK.
LEAVE.
ARE YOU SERI-OUS?
I DON'T WANT TROUBLE LATER.
WORRY NOT.
I WILL NEITHER PURSUE *NOR* CONDEMN YOU.
HMM, IT'S ALMOST DAWN.
GOOD TIMING.
I SHALL GO AND *BASK* IN THE LIGHT OF DAWN.
!
KA-BROOSH
ZU ZU ZUUN
RIGHT NOW?!
YOU KNOW WHAT'S GOING ON OUT THERE, DON'T YOU?!
I'M NOT FORCING YOU TO COME.
IT'S LIKE I SAID, DO WHAT YOU WANT.

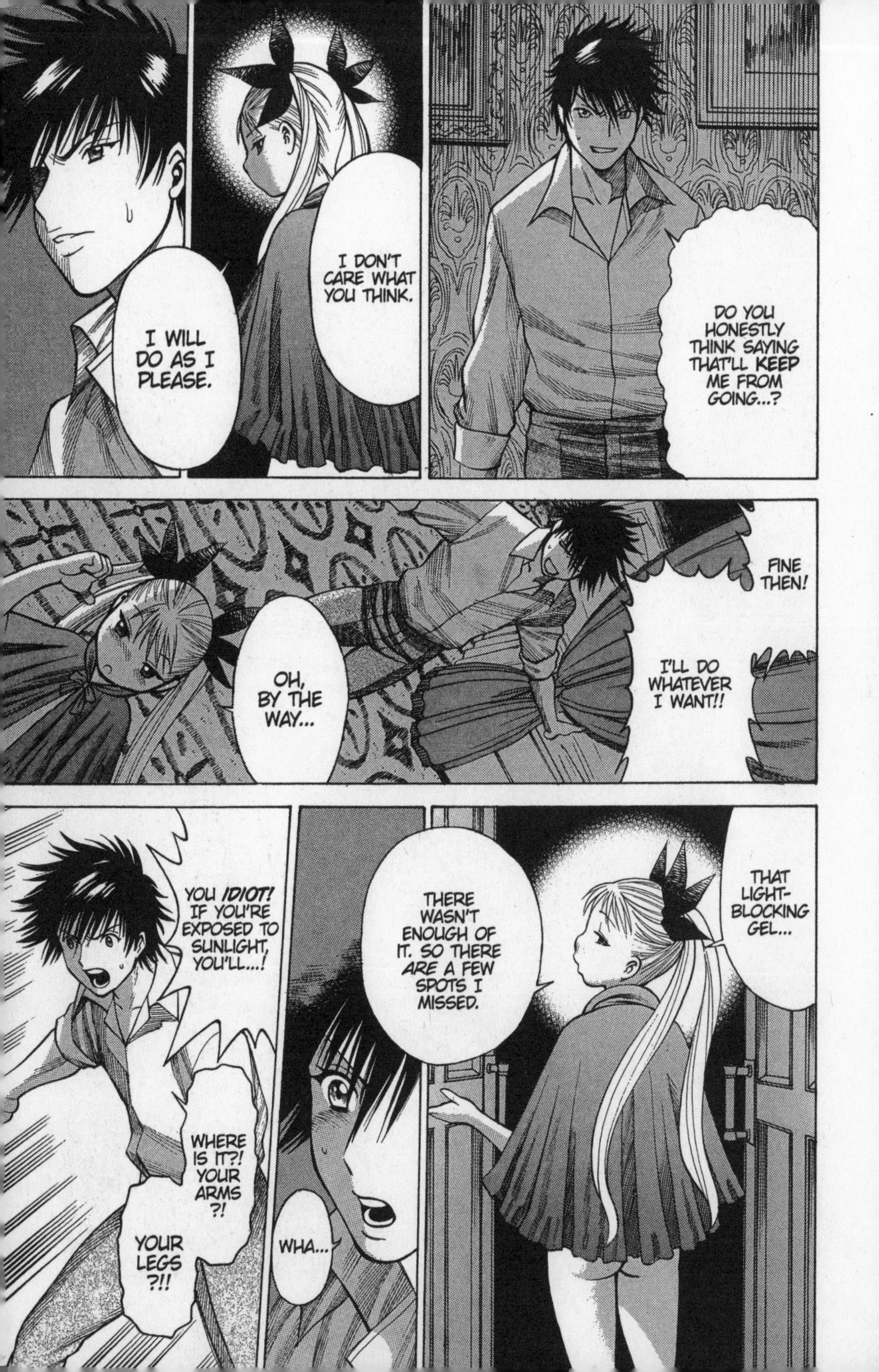
DO YOU HONESTLY THINK SAYING THAT'LL KEEP ME FROM GOING...?
I DON'T CARE WHAT YOU THINK.
I WILL DO AS I PLEASE.
FINE THEN!
I'LL DO WHATEVER I WANT!!
OH, BY THE WAY...
THAT LIGHT-BLOCKING GEL...
THERE WASN'T ENOUGH OF IT. SO THERE *ARE* A FEW SPOTS I MISSED.
WHA...
YOU *IDIOT!* IF YOU'RE EXPOSED TO SUNLIGHT, YOU'LL...!
WHERE IS IT?! YOUR ARMS?!
YOUR LEGS?!!

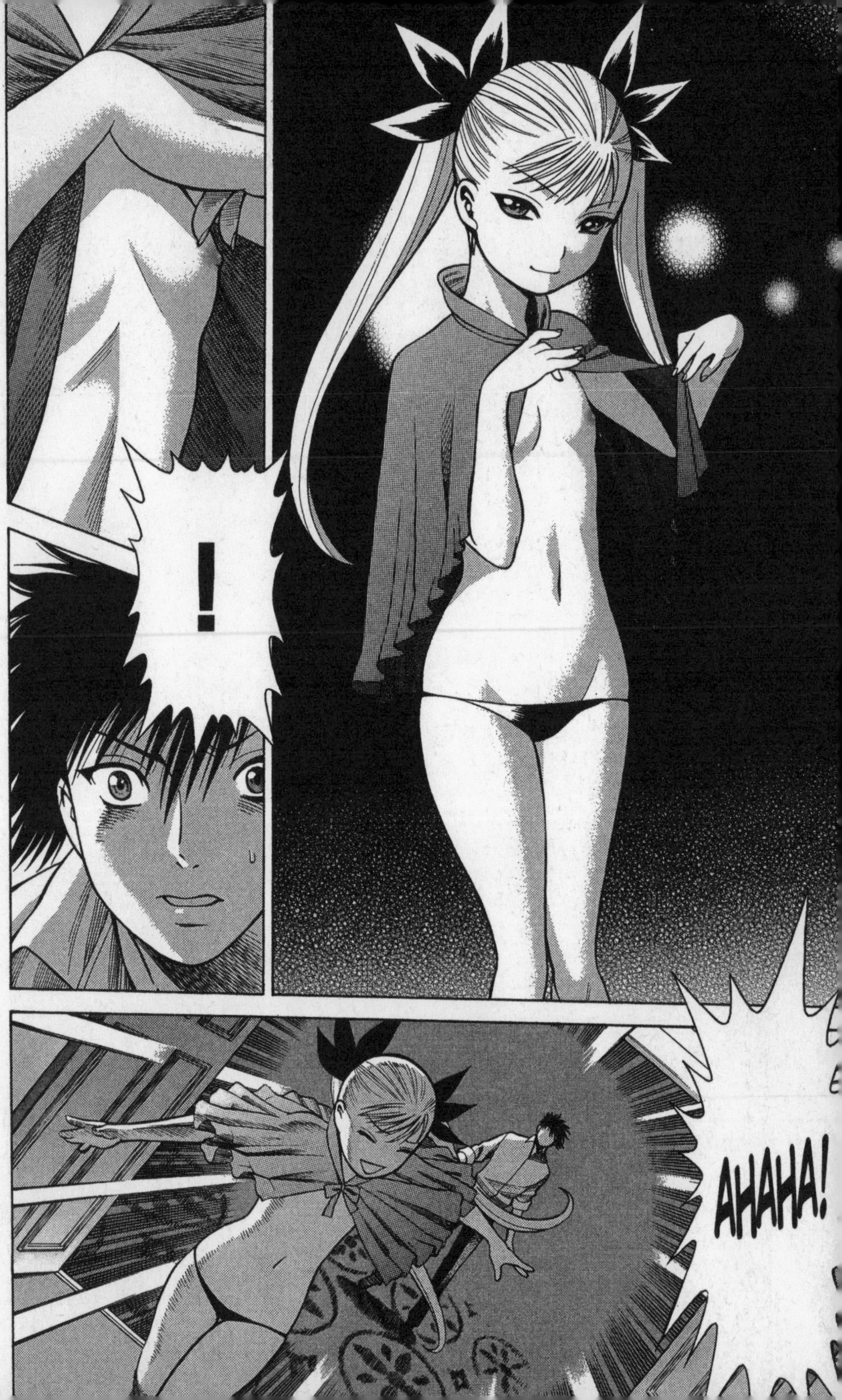
!
AHAHA!

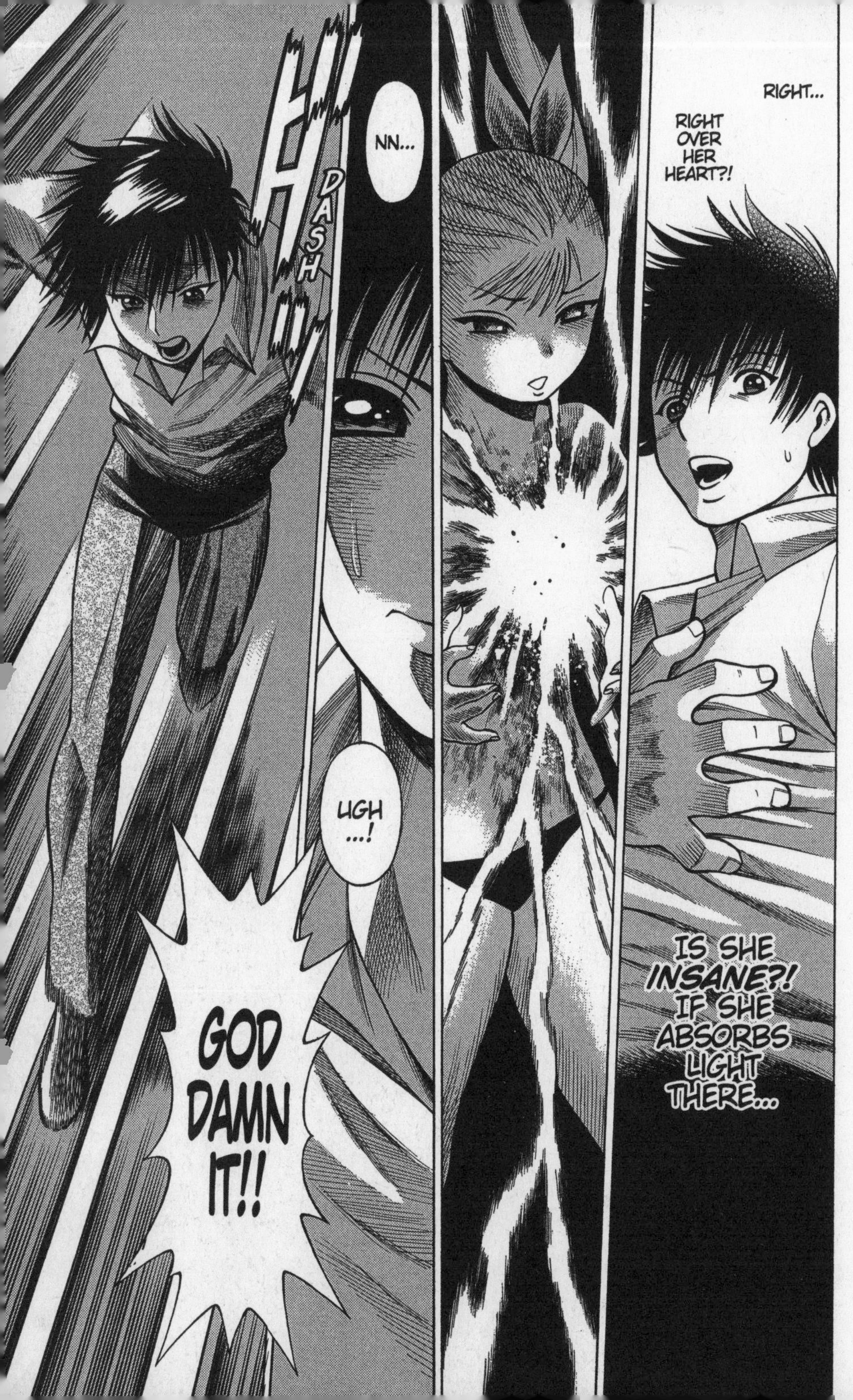
RIGHT...
RIGHT OVER HER HEART?!
IS SHE INSANE?! IF SHE ABSORBS LIGHT THERE...
NN...
UGH ...!
DASH
GOD DAMN IT!!

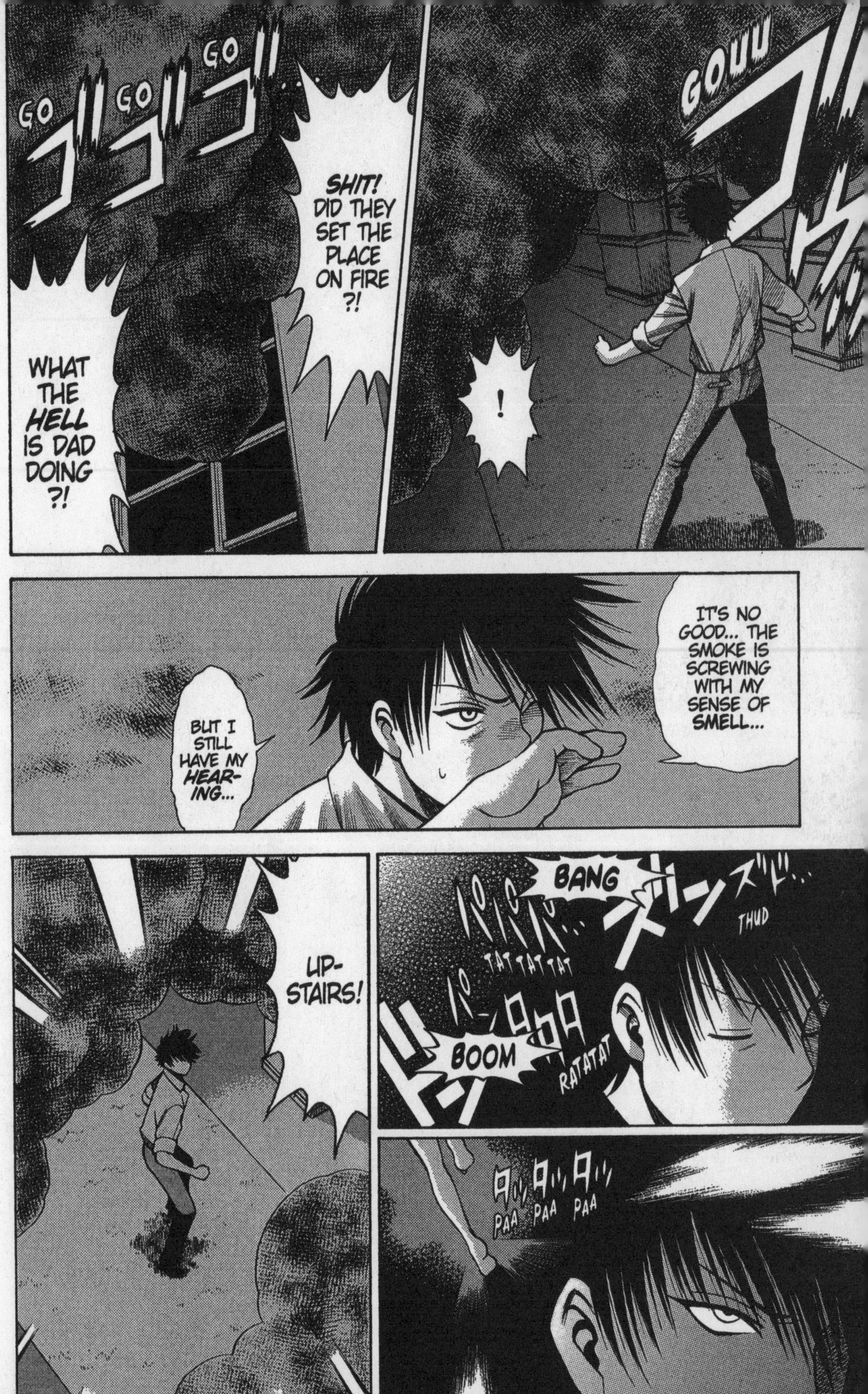
GOUU
!
GO GO GO
SHIT! DID THEY SET THE PLACE ON FIRE ?!
WHAT THE HELL IS DAD DOING ?!
IT'S NO GOOD... THE SMOKE IS SCREWING WITH MY SENSE OF SMELL...
BUT I STILL HAVE MY HEARING...
BANG
THUD
TAT TAT TAT
BOOM
RATATAT
PAA PAA PAA
UP-STAIRS!

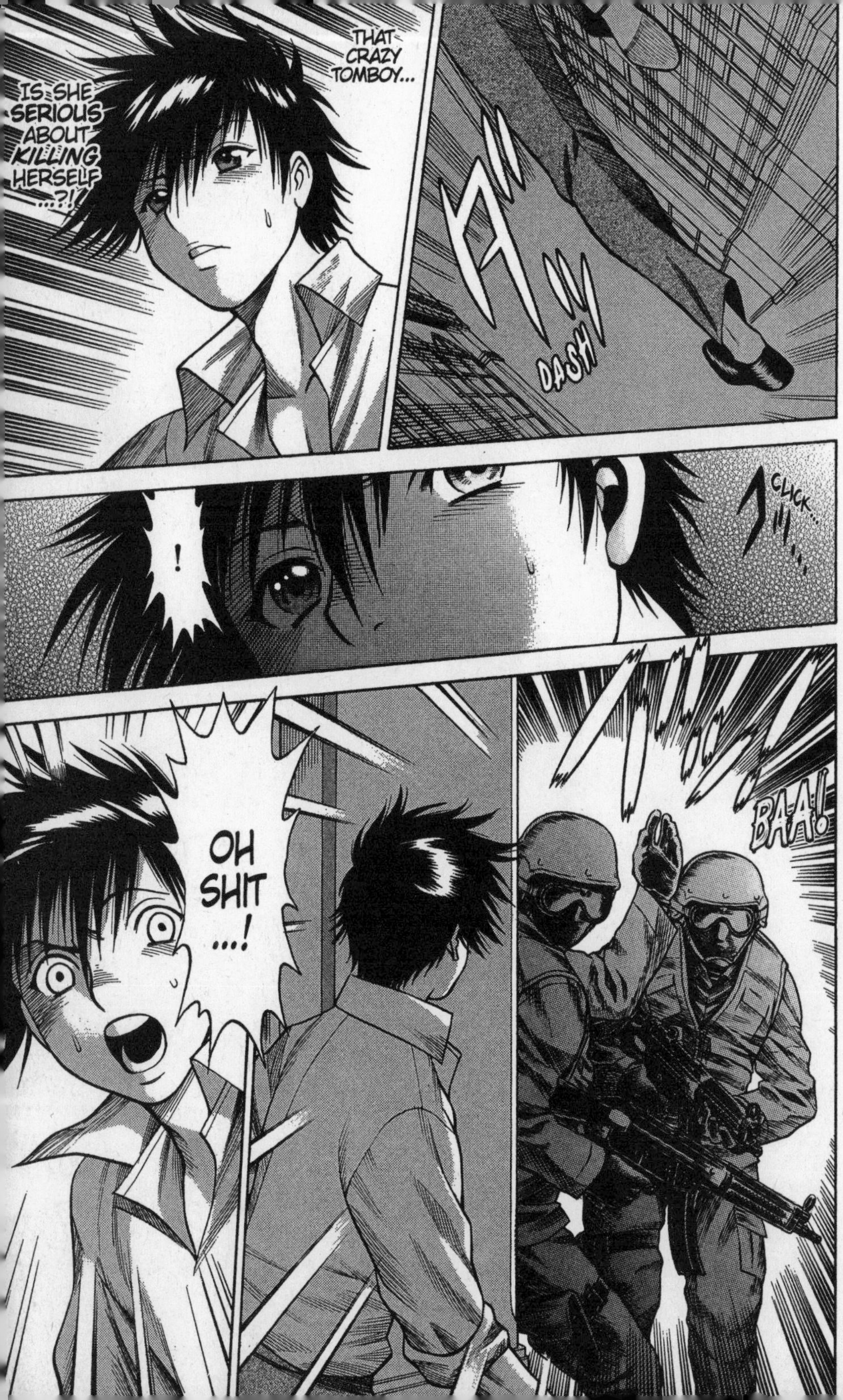
DASH
THAT CRAZY TOMBOY...
IS SHE SERIOUS ABOUT KILLING HERSELF ...?!
CLICK...
!
BAA!
OH SHIT ...!

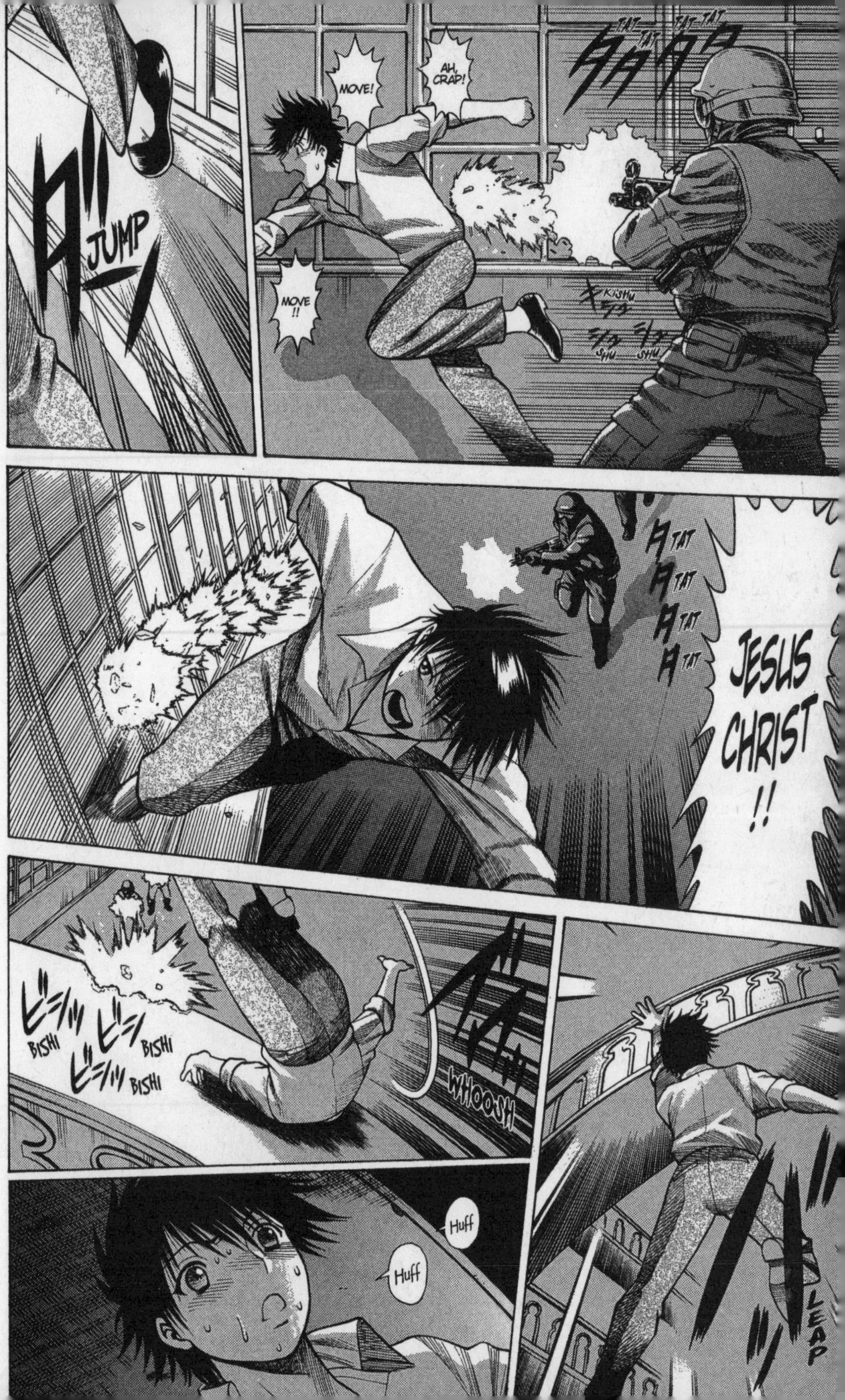
TAT TAT TAT TAT
AH, CRAP!
MOVE!
KISHU
SHU
SHU
MOVE!!
JUMP
TAT
TAT
TAT
TAT
JESUS CHRIST!!
LEAP
WHOOSH
BISHI
BISHI
BISHI
Huff
Huff

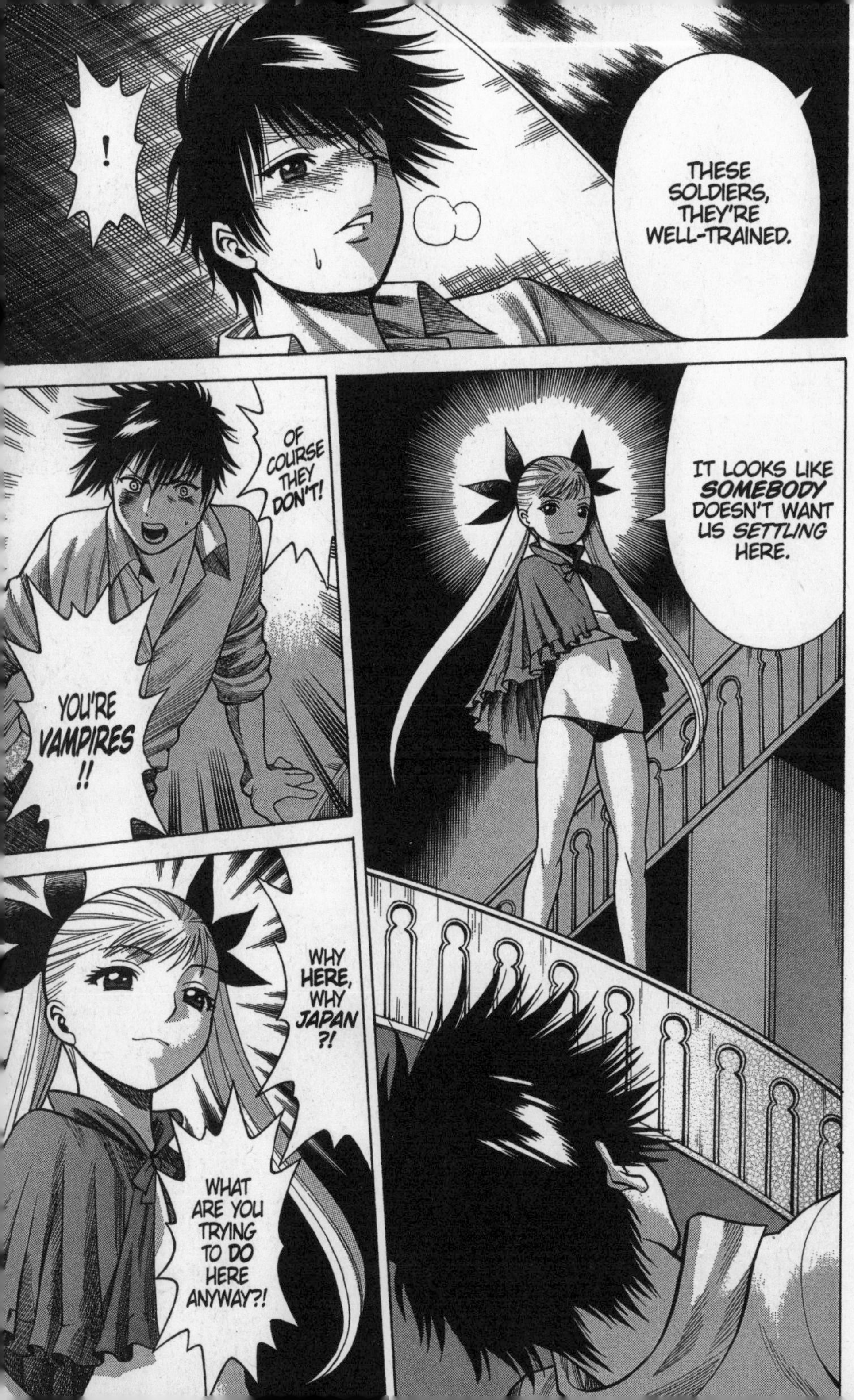
THESE SOLDIERS, THEY'RE WELL-TRAINED.
!
IT LOOKS LIKE SOMEBODY DOESN'T WANT US SETTLING HERE.
OF COURSE THEY DON'T!
YOU'RE VAMPIRES !!
WHY HERE, WHY JAPAN ?!
WHAT ARE YOU TRYING TO DO HERE ANYWAY?!

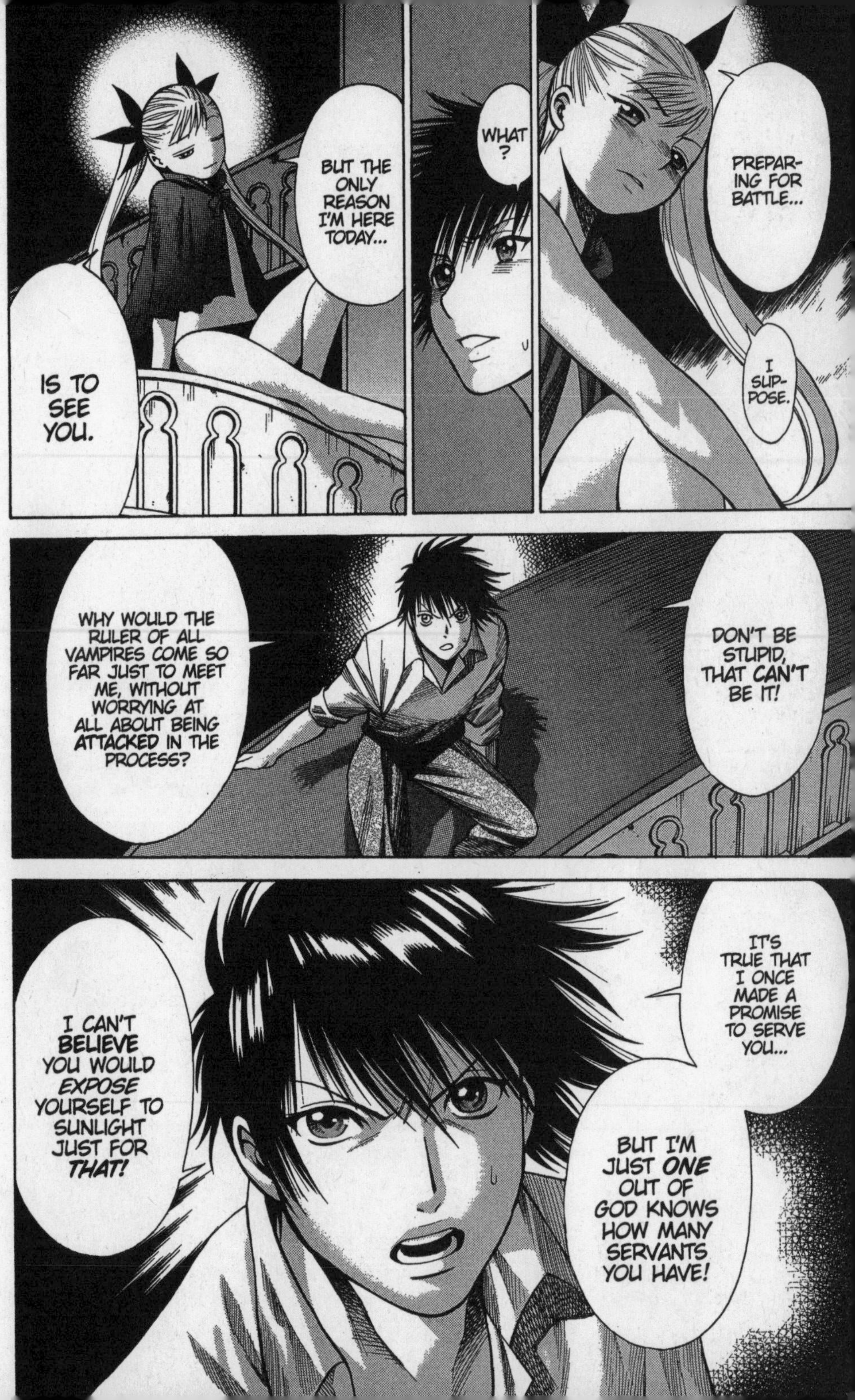
PREPARING FOR BATTLE...
I SUPPOSE.
WHAT?
BUT THE ONLY REASON I'M HERE TODAY...
IS TO SEE YOU.
DON'T BE STUPID, THAT CAN'T BE IT!
WHY WOULD THE RULER OF ALL VAMPIRES COME SO FAR JUST TO MEET ME, WITHOUT WORRYING AT ALL ABOUT BEING ATTACKED IN THE PROCESS?
IT'S TRUE THAT I ONCE MADE A PROMISE TO SERVE YOU...
BUT I'M JUST ONE OUT OF GOD KNOWS HOW MANY SERVANTS YOU HAVE!
I CAN'T BELIEVE YOU WOULD EXPOSE YOURSELF TO SUNLIGHT JUST FOR THAT!

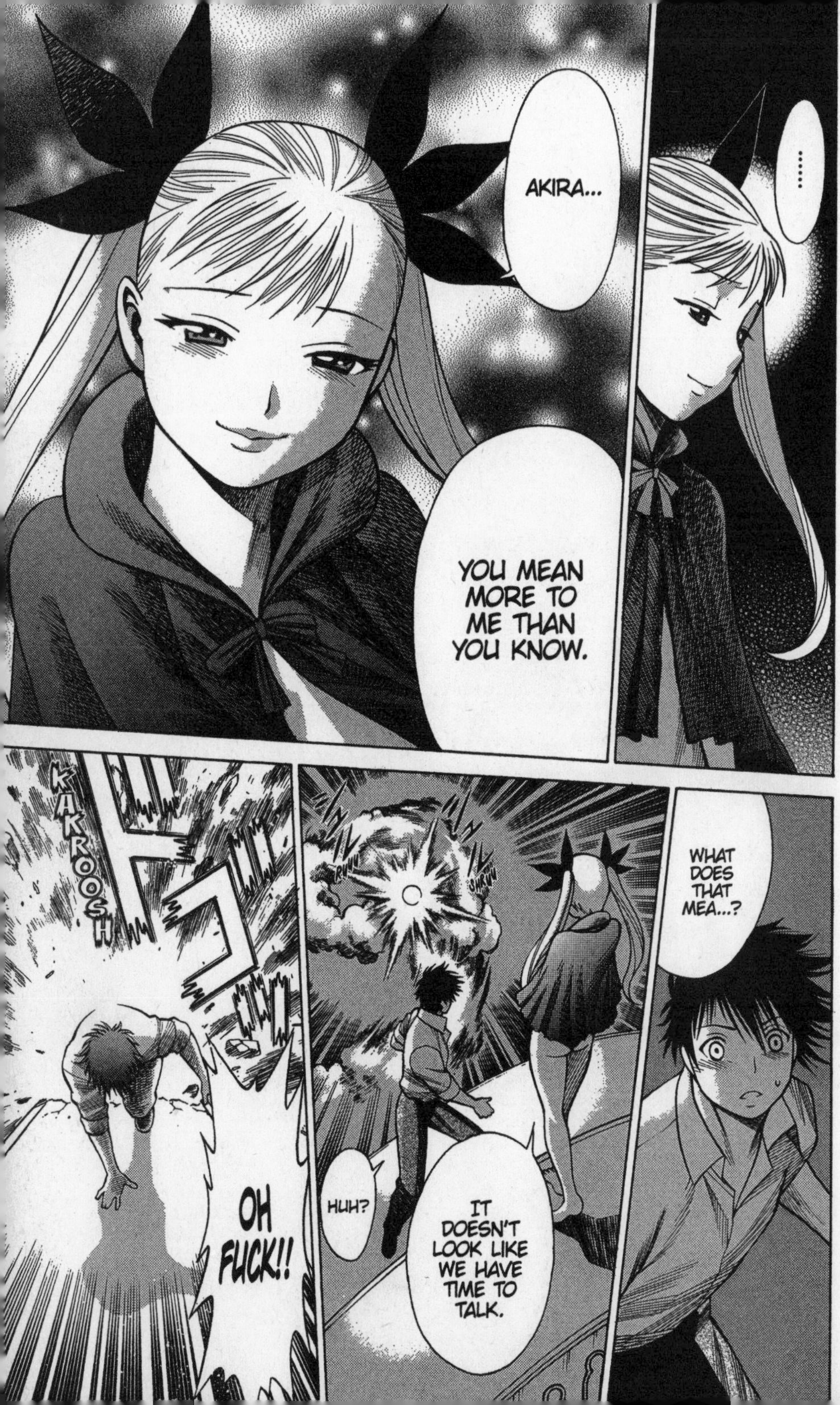
......
AKIRA...
YOU MEAN MORE TO ME THAN YOU KNOW.
WHAT DOES THAT MEA...?
IT DOESN'T LOOK LIKE WE HAVE TIME TO TALK.
HUH?
KAKROOSH
OH FUCK!!

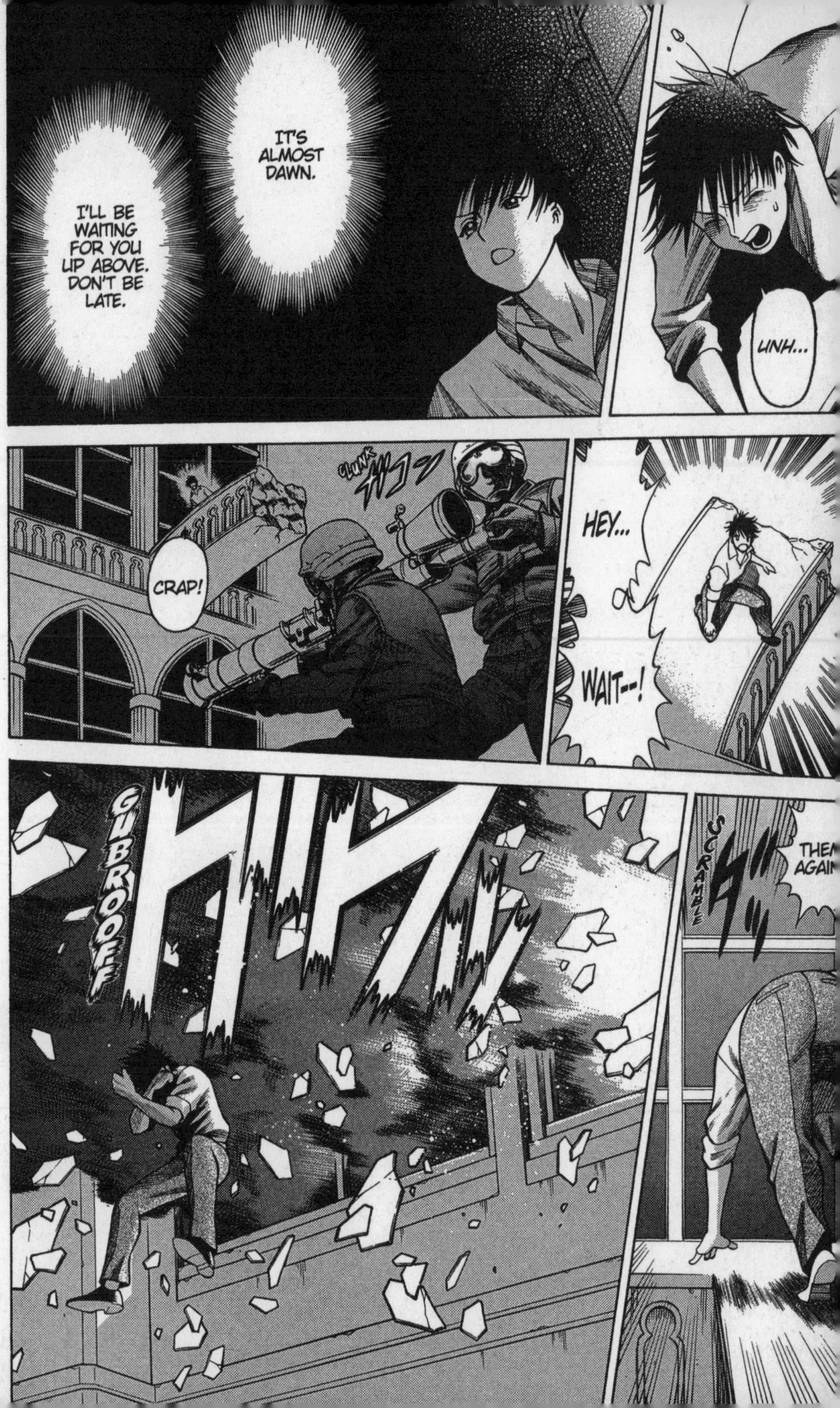
UNH...
IT'S ALMOST DAWN.
I'LL BE WAITING FOR YOU UP ABOVE. DON'T BE LATE.
HEY...
WAIT--!
CLUNK
CRAP!
SCRAMBLE
THEM AGAI
GUBROOOFF

GUESS SHE MEANT UP THERE.

ALL RIGHT, BETTER GET MOVING...

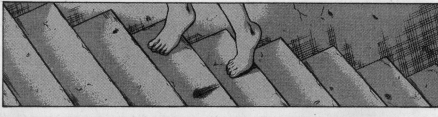

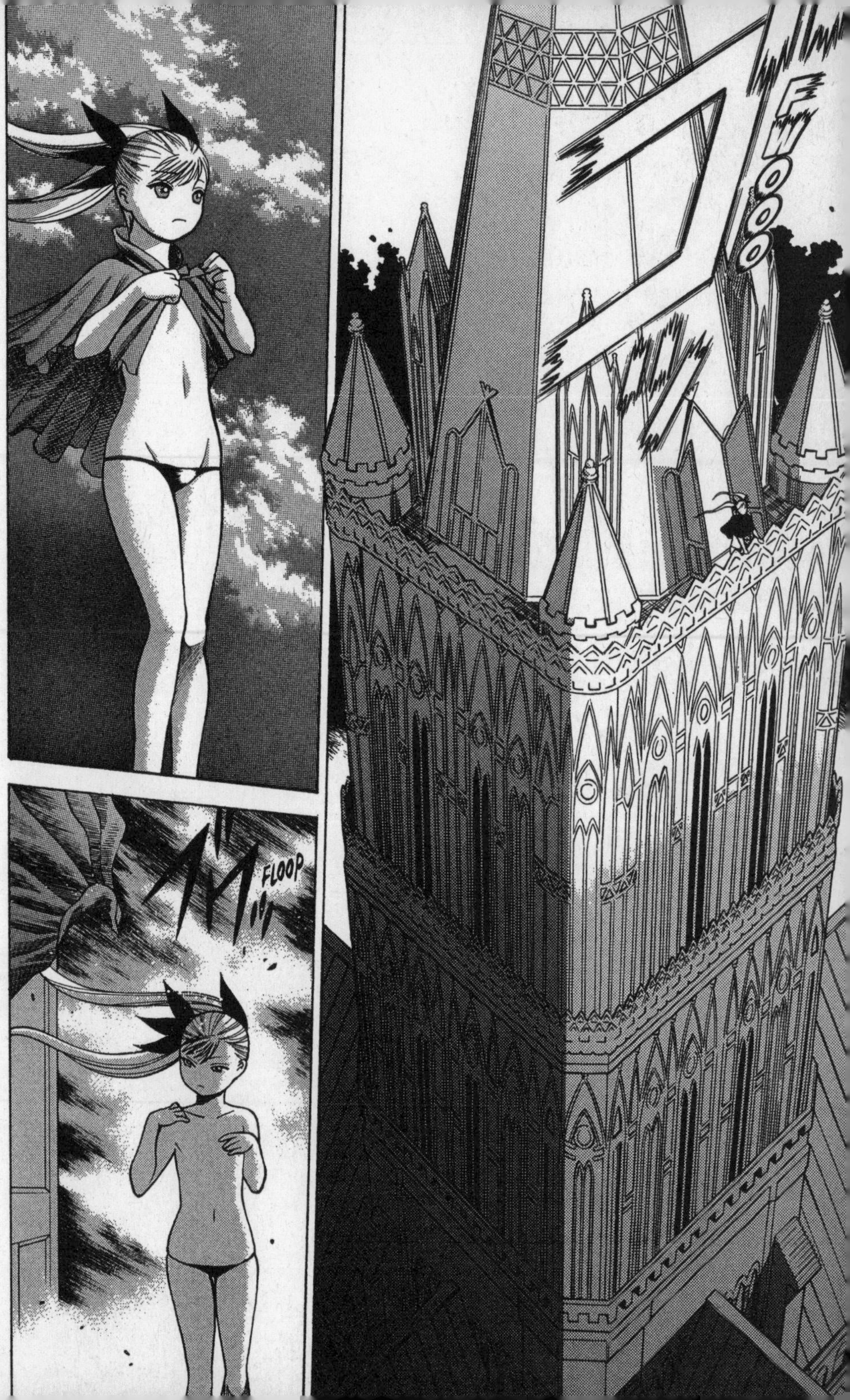
FWOOO
FLOOP

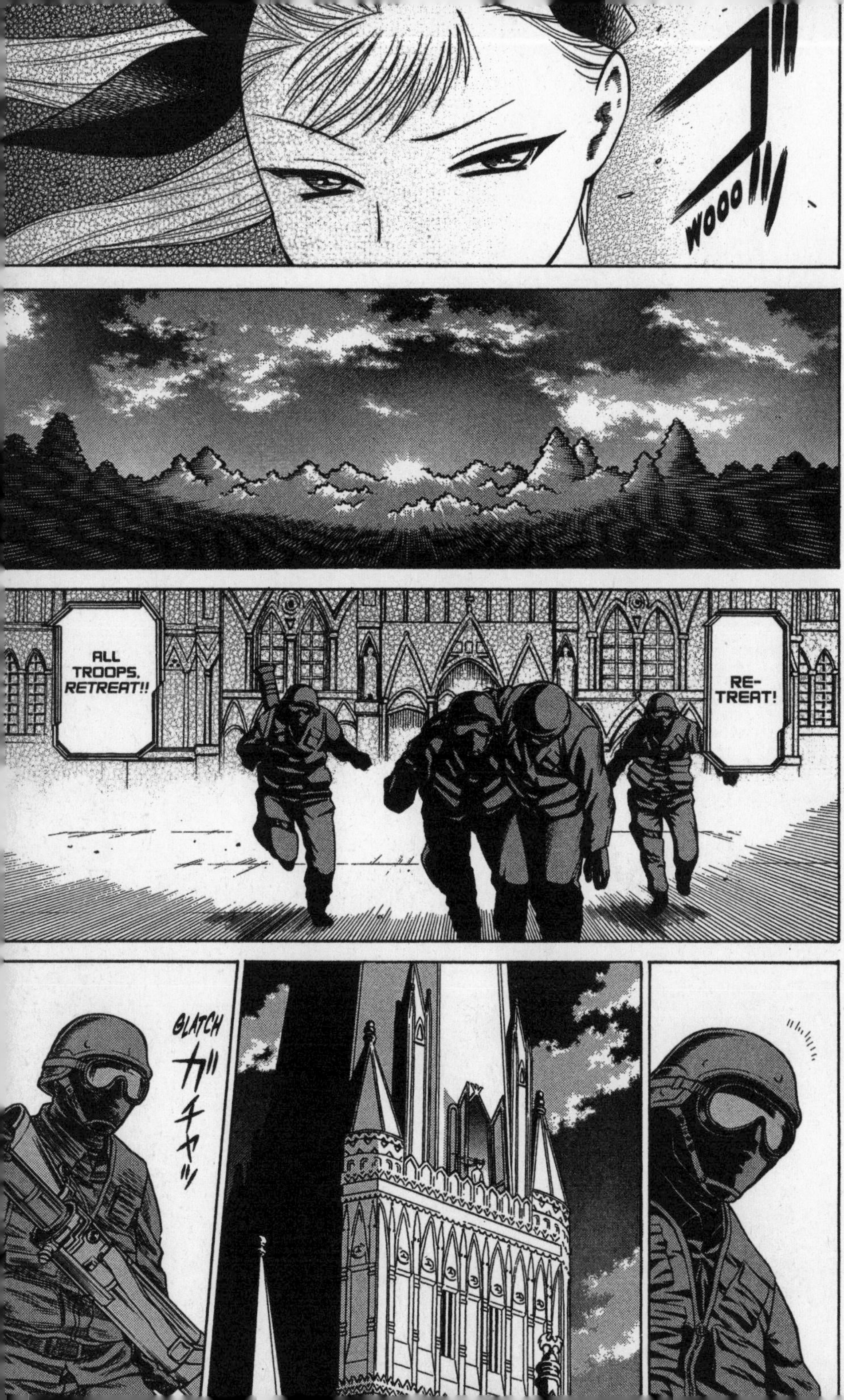
WOOO
RE-TREAT!
ALL TROOPS, RETREAT!!
CLATCH
ガチャッ

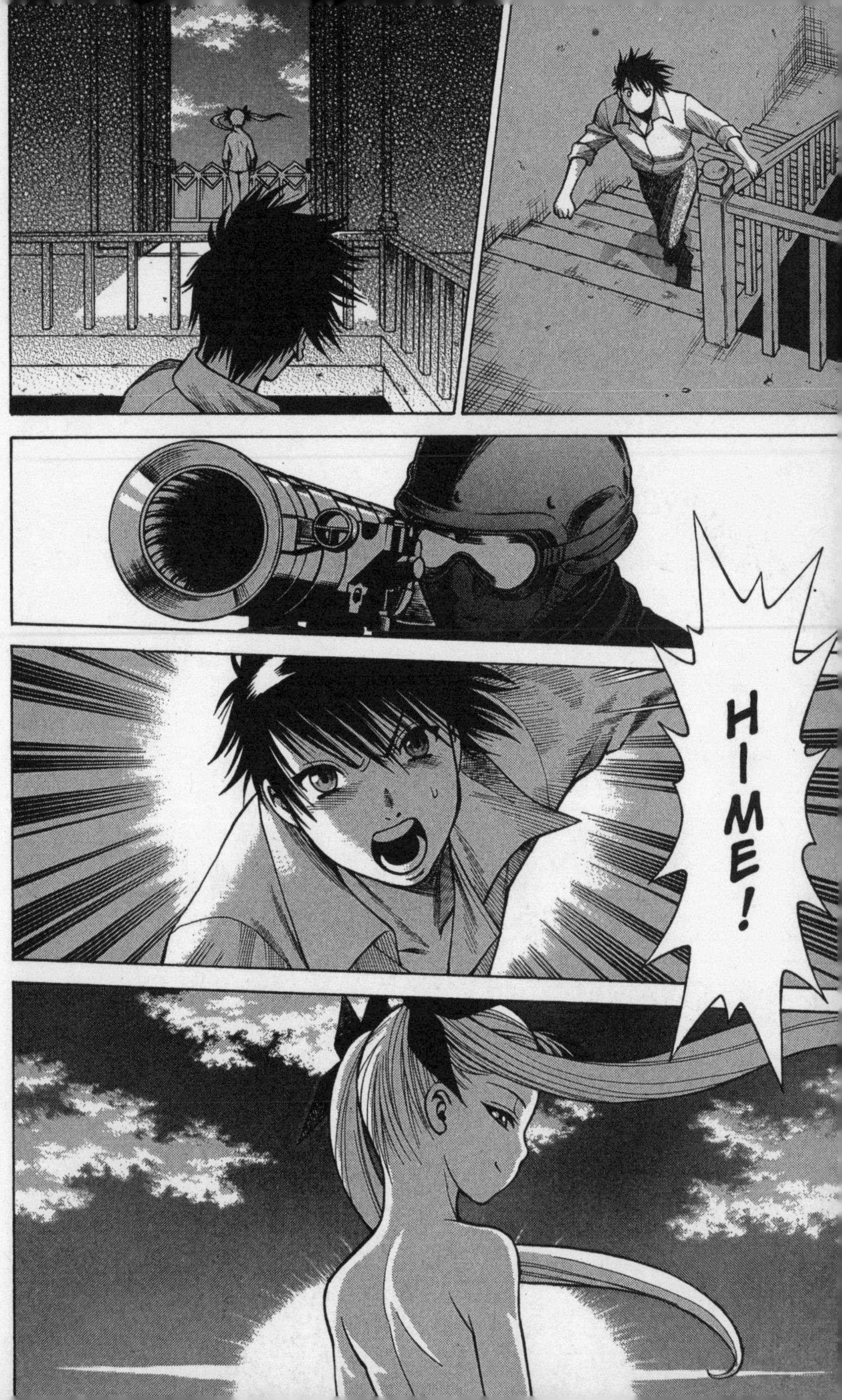
HIME!

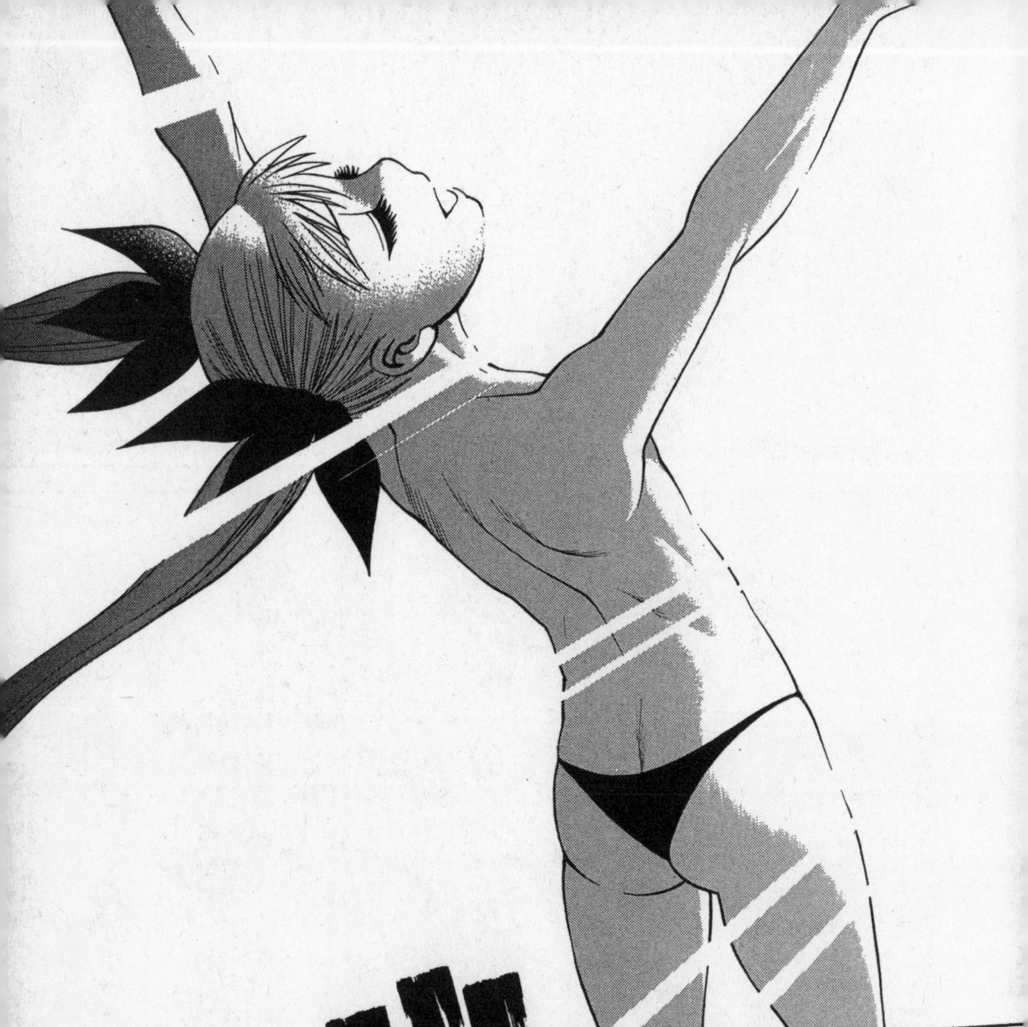
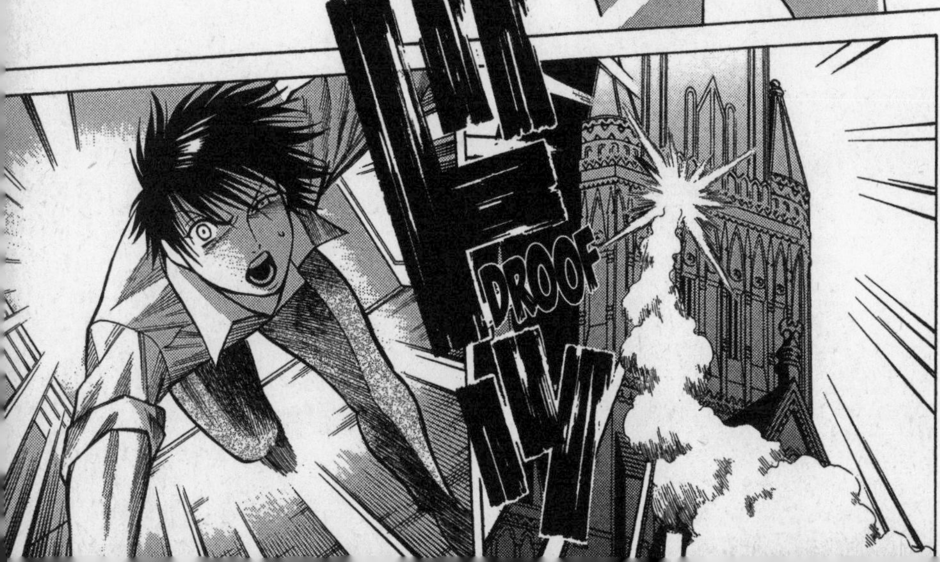
DROOF

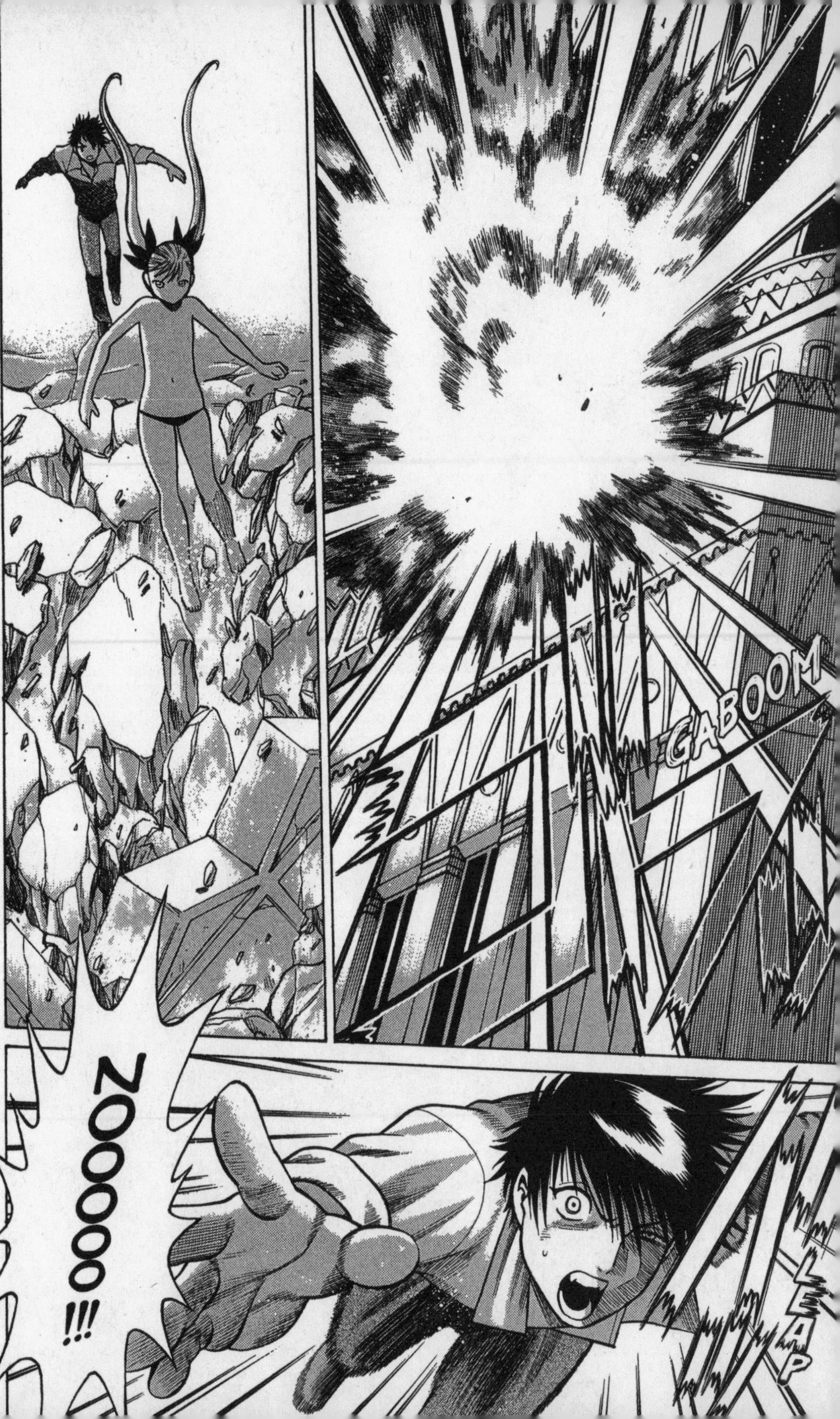
GABOOM
LEAP
ZOOOOOO!!!

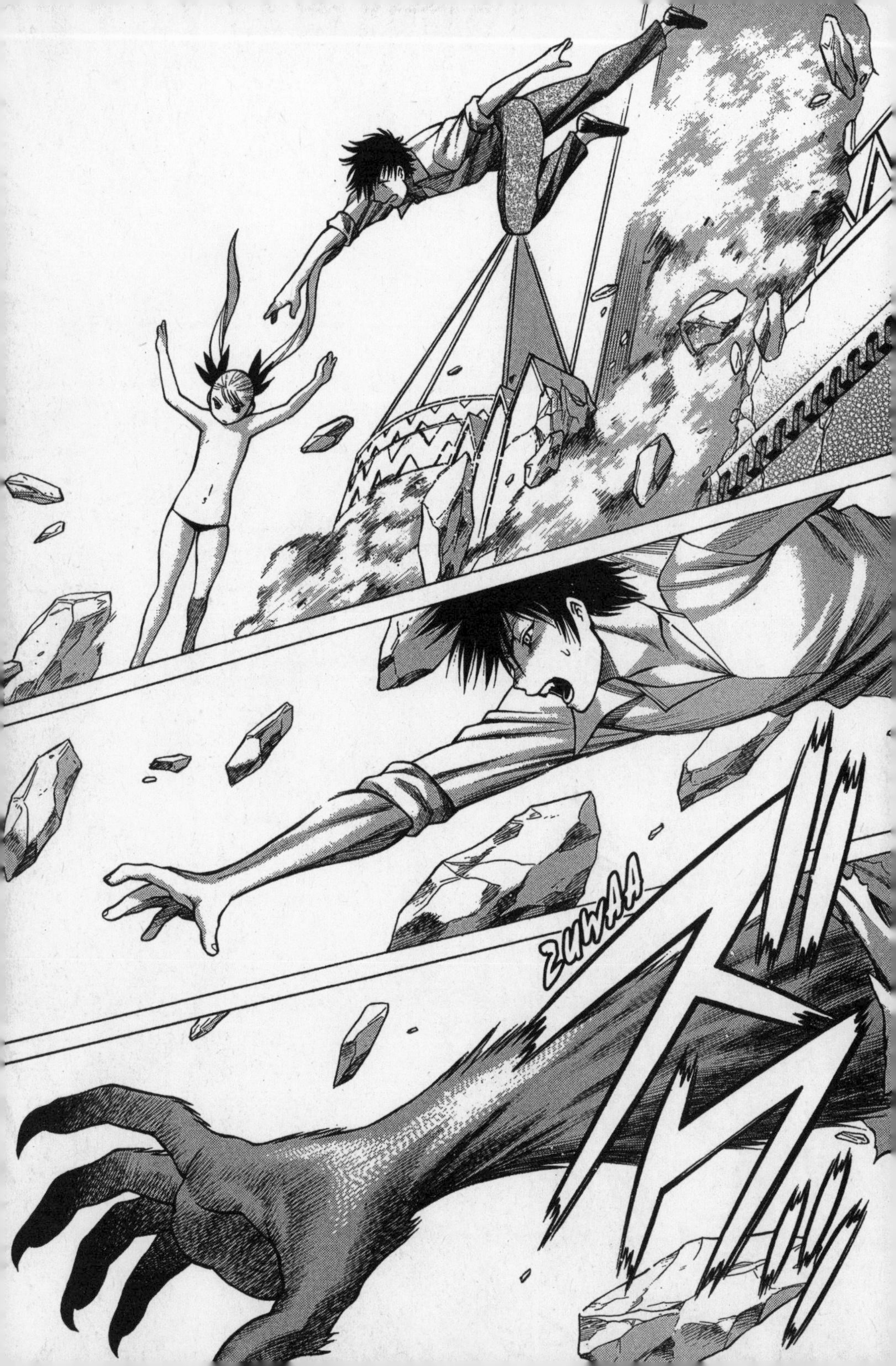
ZUWAA

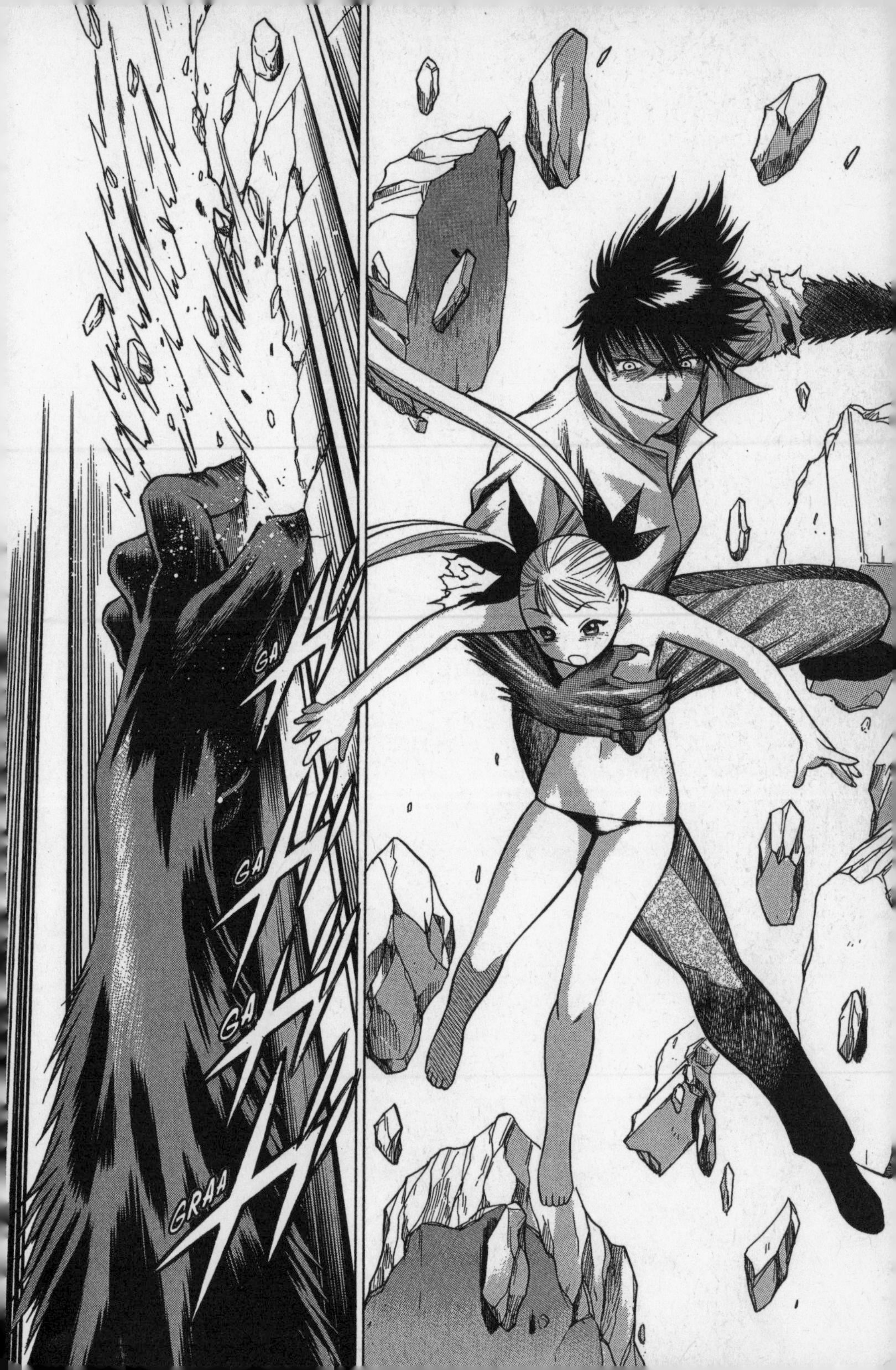
GA
GA
GA
GRAA

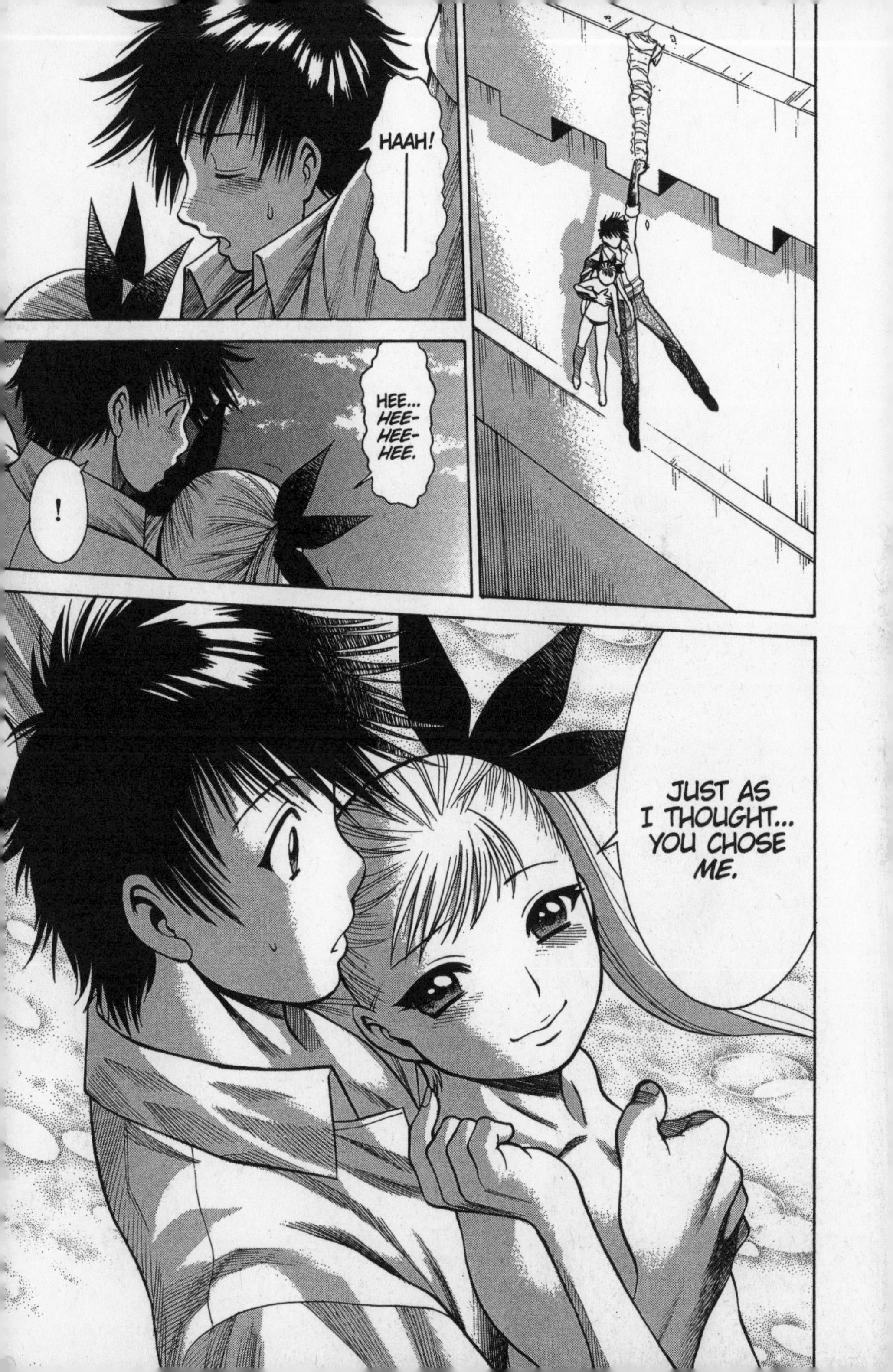
HAAH!
HEE... HEE-HEE-HEE.
!
JUST AS I THOUGHT... YOU CHOSE ME.

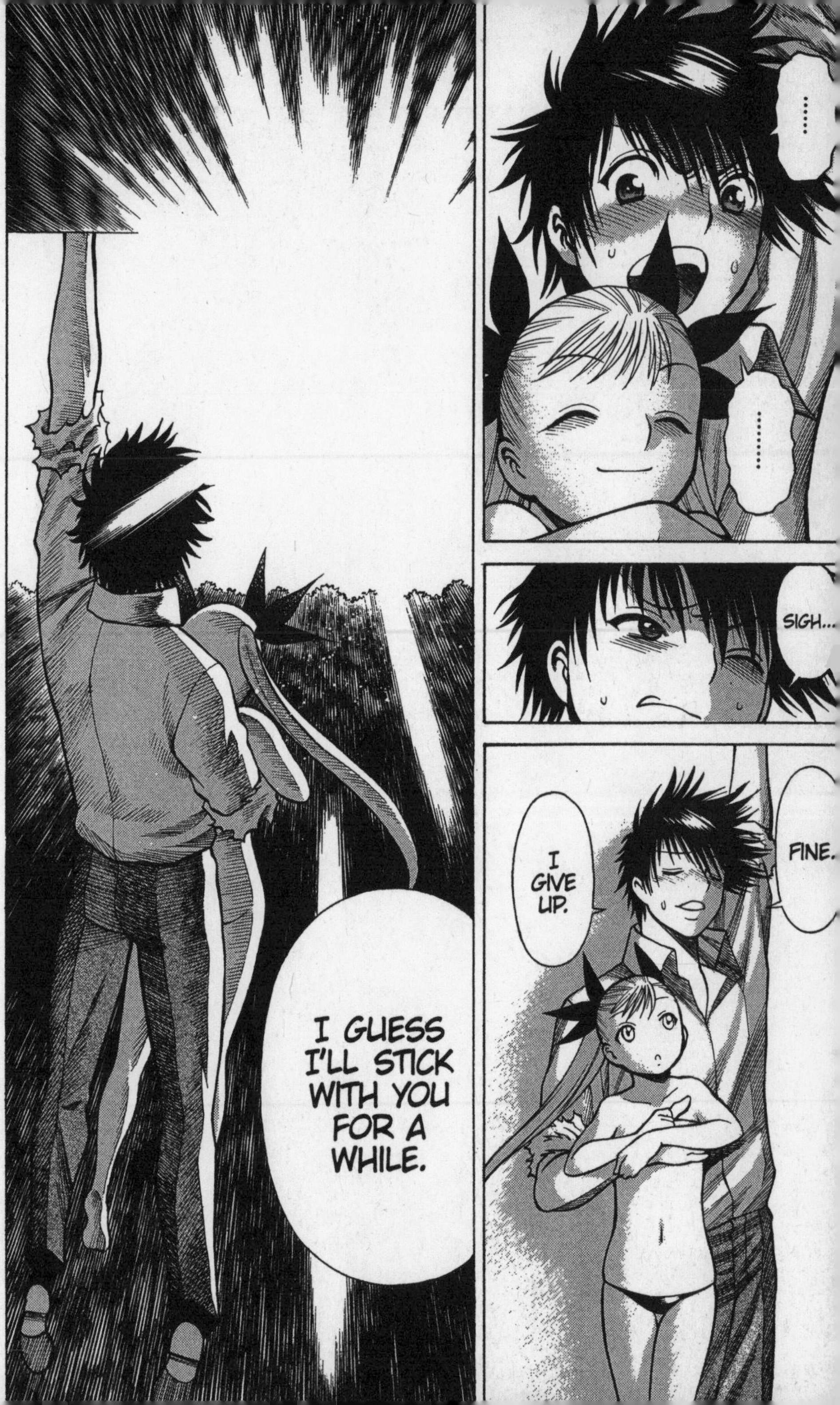
……
……
SIGH…
FINE.
I GIVE UP.
I GUESS I'LL STICK WITH YOU FOR A WHILE.

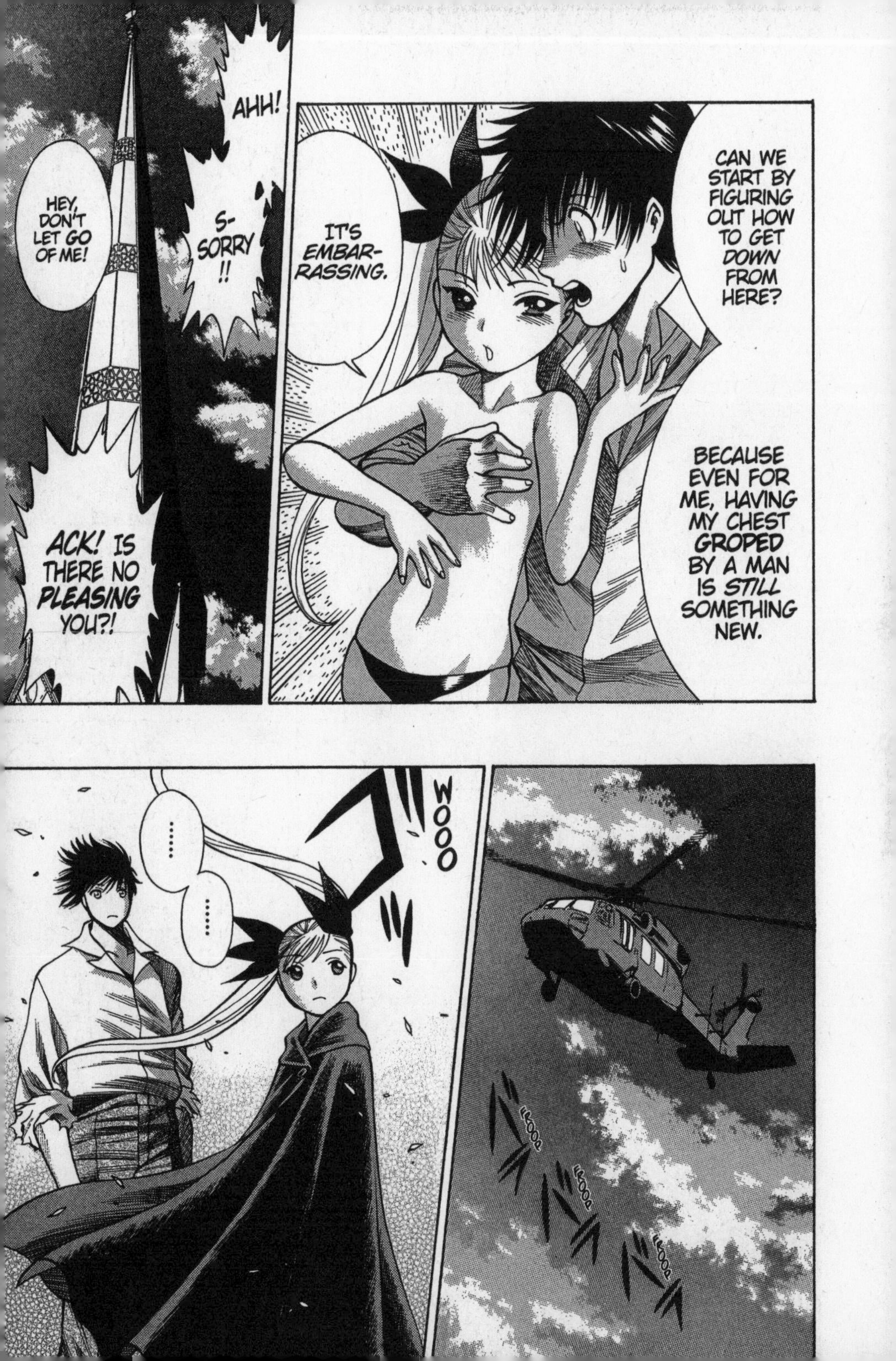
CAN WE START BY FIGURING OUT HOW TO GET DOWN FROM HERE?
BECAUSE EVEN FOR ME, HAVING MY CHEST GROPED BY A MAN IS STILL SOMETHING NEW.
IT'S EMBARRASSING.
AHH!
S-SORRY!!
HEY, DON'T LET GO OF ME!
ACK! IS THERE NO PLEASING YOU?!
WOOO
......
......

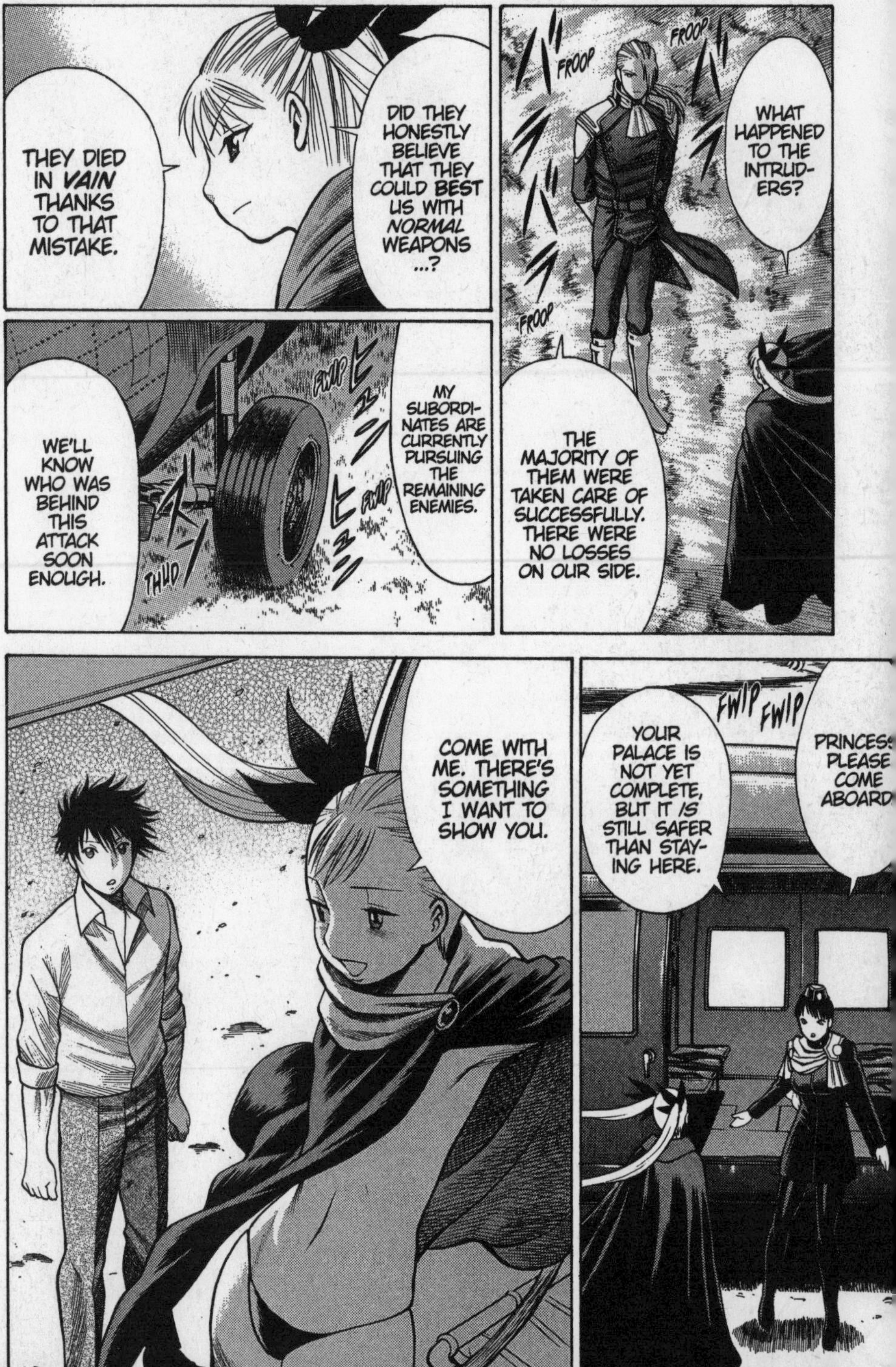
FROOP
FROOP
WHAT HAPPENED TO THE INTRUD-ERS?
FROOP
THE MAJORITY OF THEM WERE TAKEN CARE OF SUCCESSFULLY. THERE WERE NO LOSSES ON OUR SIDE.
DID THEY HONESTLY BELIEVE THAT THEY COULD BEST US WITH NORMAL WEAPONS ...?
THEY DIED IN VAIN THANKS TO THAT MISTAKE.
MY SUBORDI-NATES ARE CURRENTLY PURSUING THE REMAINING ENEMIES.
FWIP
FWIP
THUD
WE'LL KNOW WHO WAS BEHIND THIS ATTACK SOON ENOUGH.
PRINCESS PLEASE COME ABOARD
FWIP FWIP
YOUR PALACE IS NOT YET COMPLETE, BUT IT IS STILL SAFER THAN STAY-ING HERE.
COME WITH ME. THERE'S SOMETHING I WANT TO SHOW YOU.

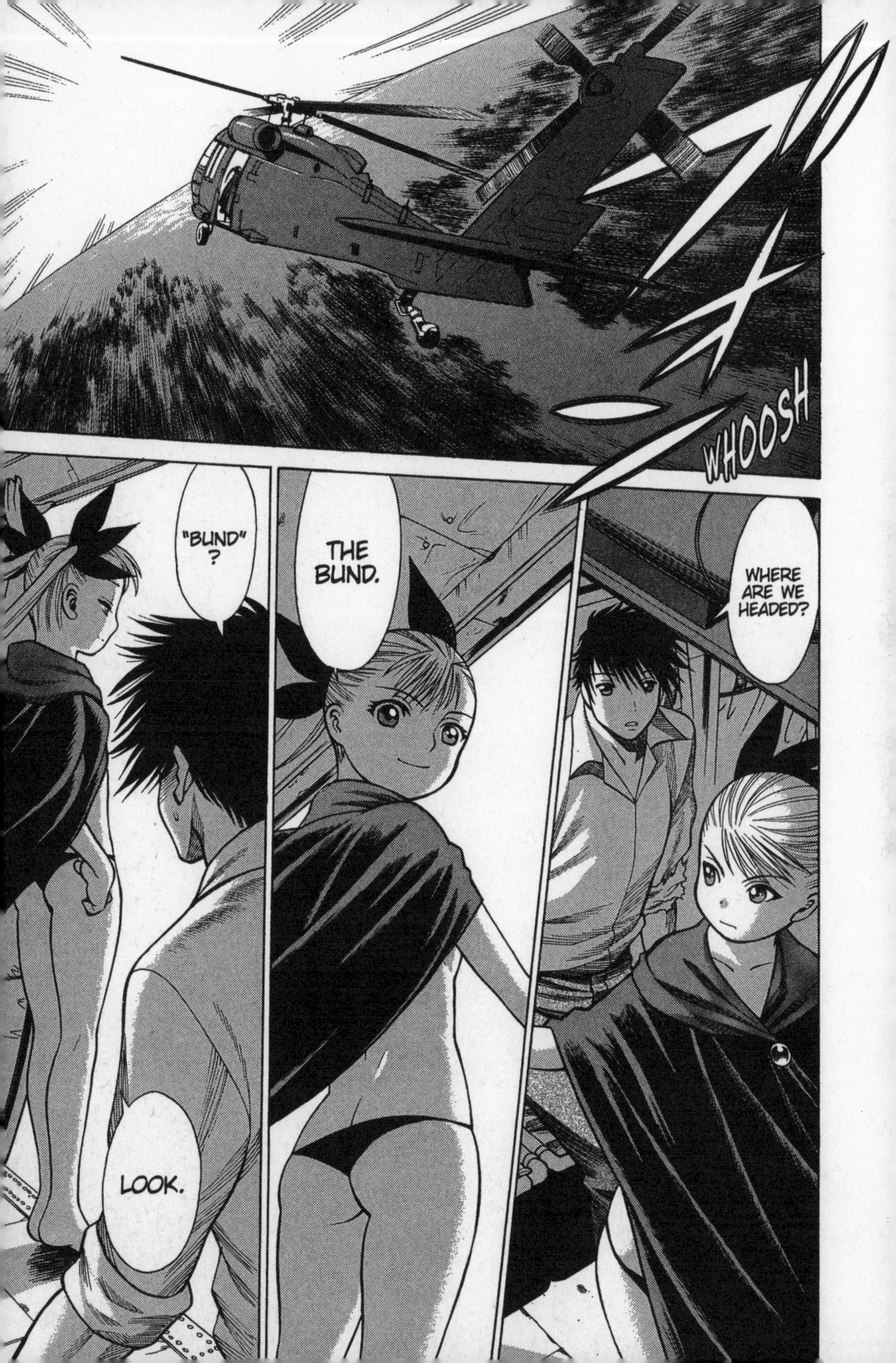
WHOOSH
WHERE ARE WE HEADED?
THE BUND.
"BUND"?
LOOK.

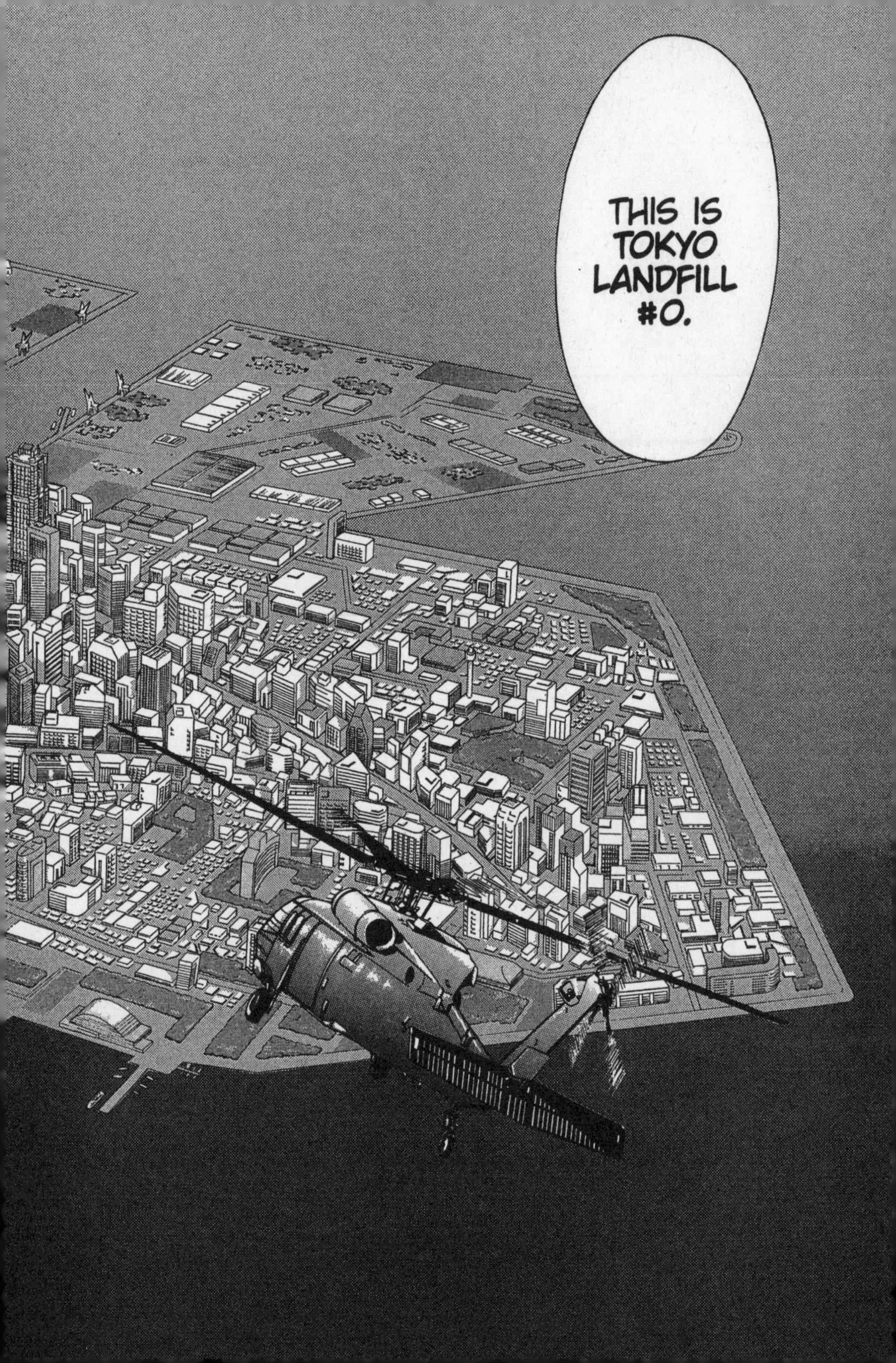
THIS IS TOKYO LANDFILL #0.

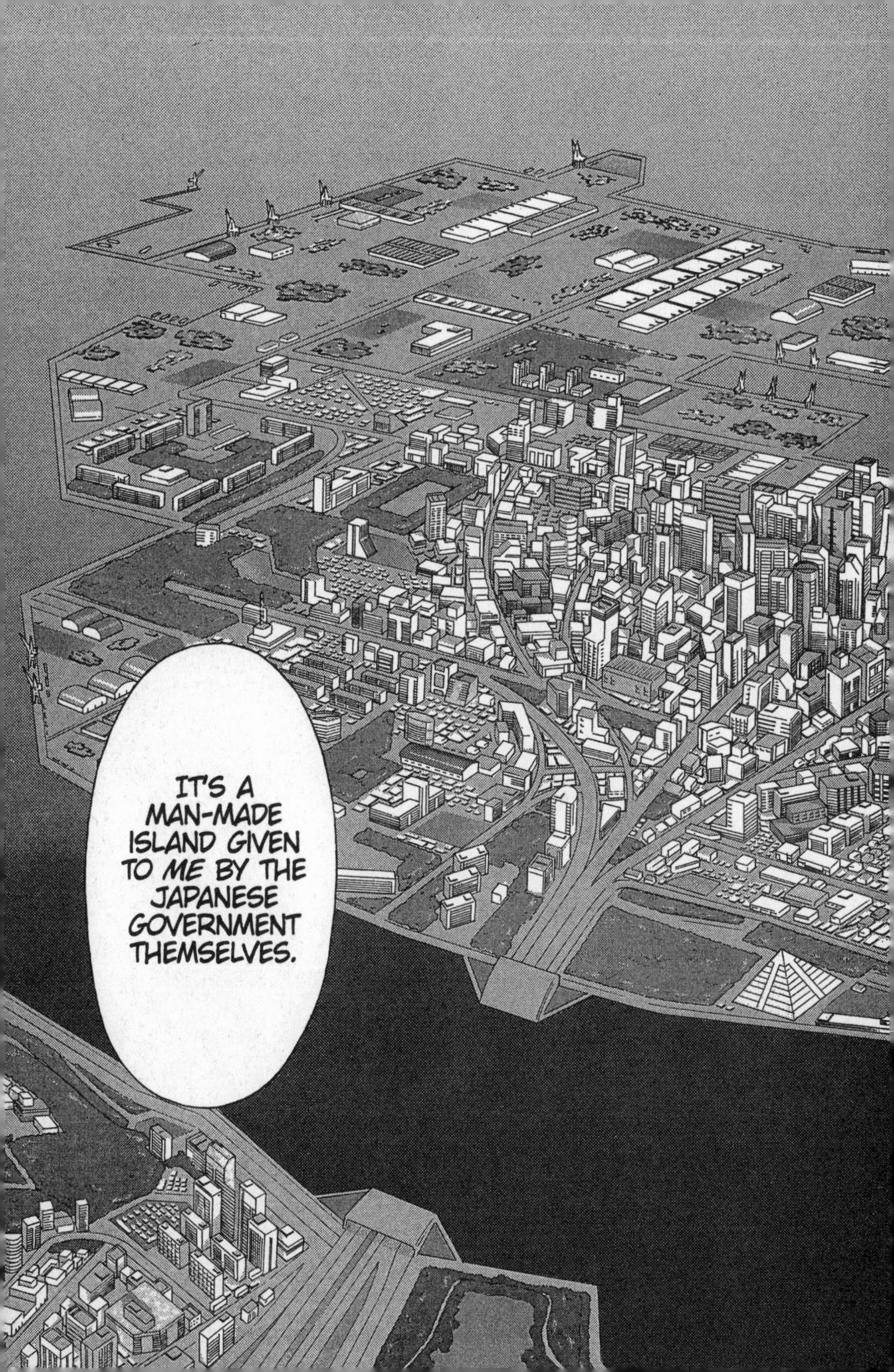
IT'S A MAN-MADE ISLAND GIVEN TO *ME* BY THE JAPANESE GOVERNMENT THEMSELVES.

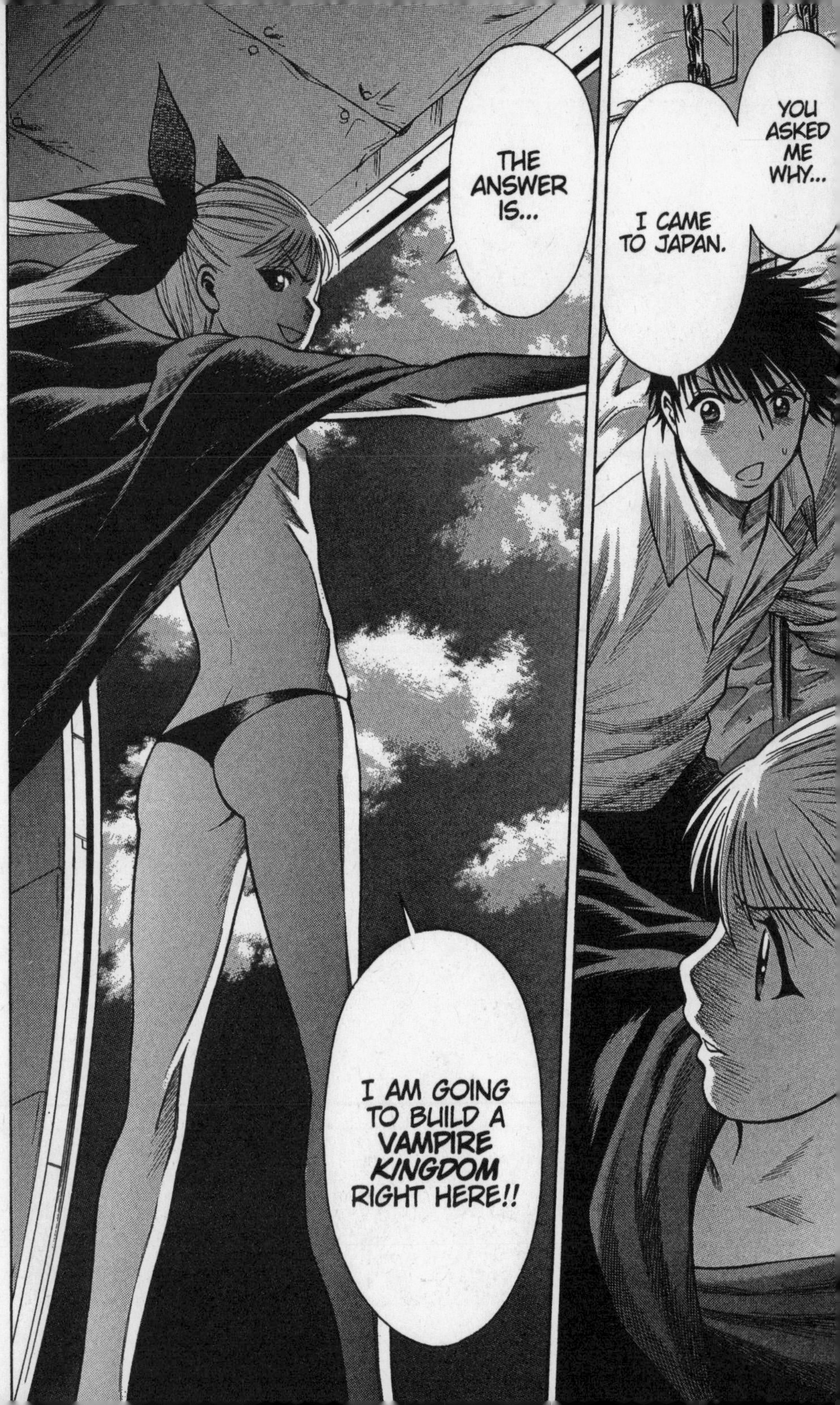
YOU ASKED ME WHY...
I CAME TO JAPAN.
THE ANSWER IS...
I AM GOING TO BUILD A VAMPIRE *KINGDOM* RIGHT HERE!!

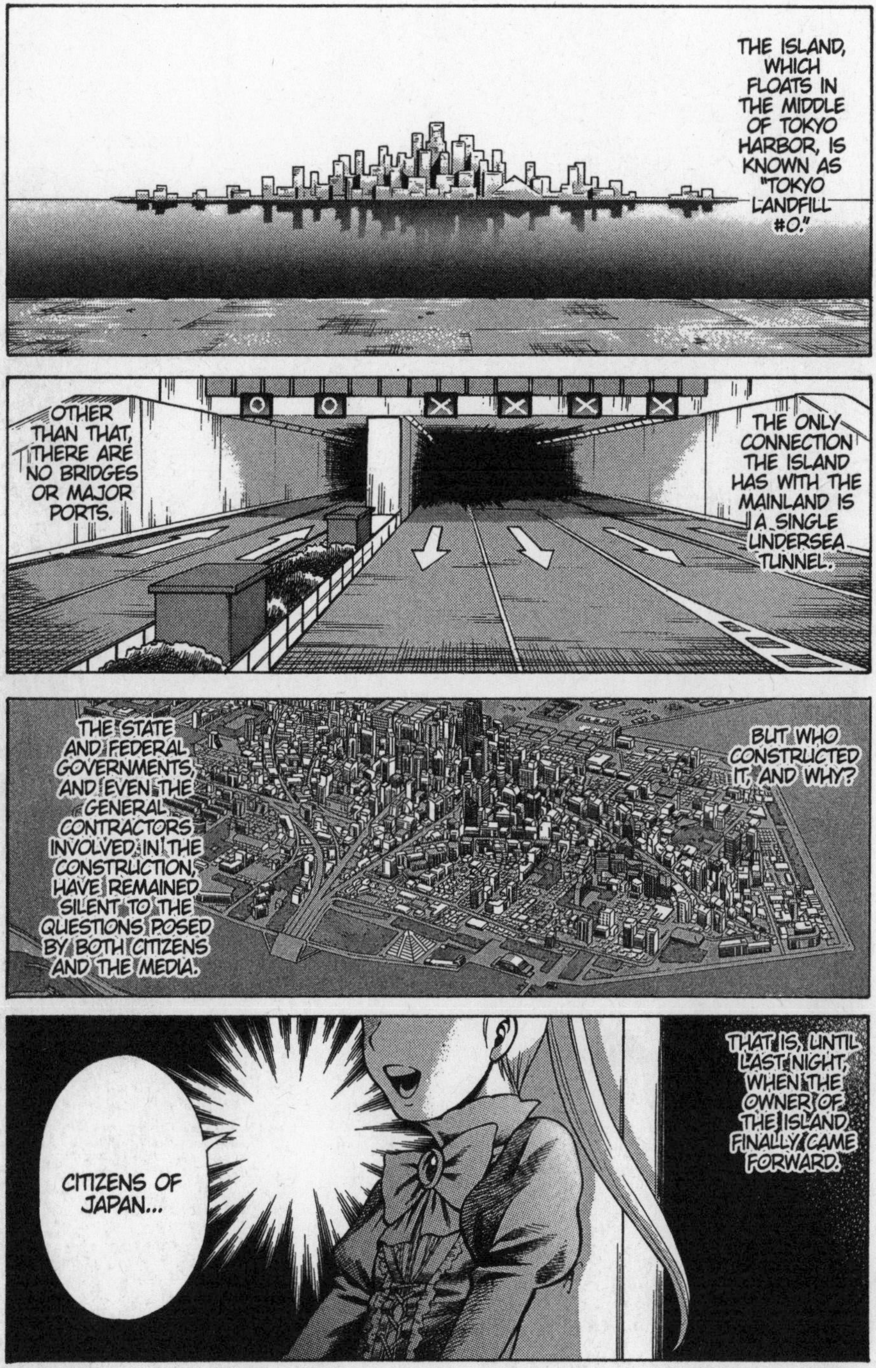
THE ISLAND, WHICH FLOATS IN THE MIDDLE OF TOKYO HARBOR, IS KNOWN AS "TOKYO LANDFILL #0."
THE ONLY CONNECTION THE ISLAND HAS WITH THE MAINLAND IS A SINGLE UNDERSEA TUNNEL.
OTHER THAN THAT, THERE ARE NO BRIDGES OR MAJOR PORTS.
BUT WHO CONSTRUCTED IT, AND WHY?
THE STATE AND FEDERAL GOVERNMENTS, AND EVEN THE GENERAL CONTRACTORS INVOLVED IN THE CONSTRUCTION, HAVE REMAINED SILENT TO THE QUESTIONS POSED BY BOTH CITIZENS AND THE MEDIA.
THAT IS, UNTIL LAST NIGHT, WHEN THE OWNER OF THE ISLAND FINALLY CAME FORWARD.
CITIZENS OF JAPAN...

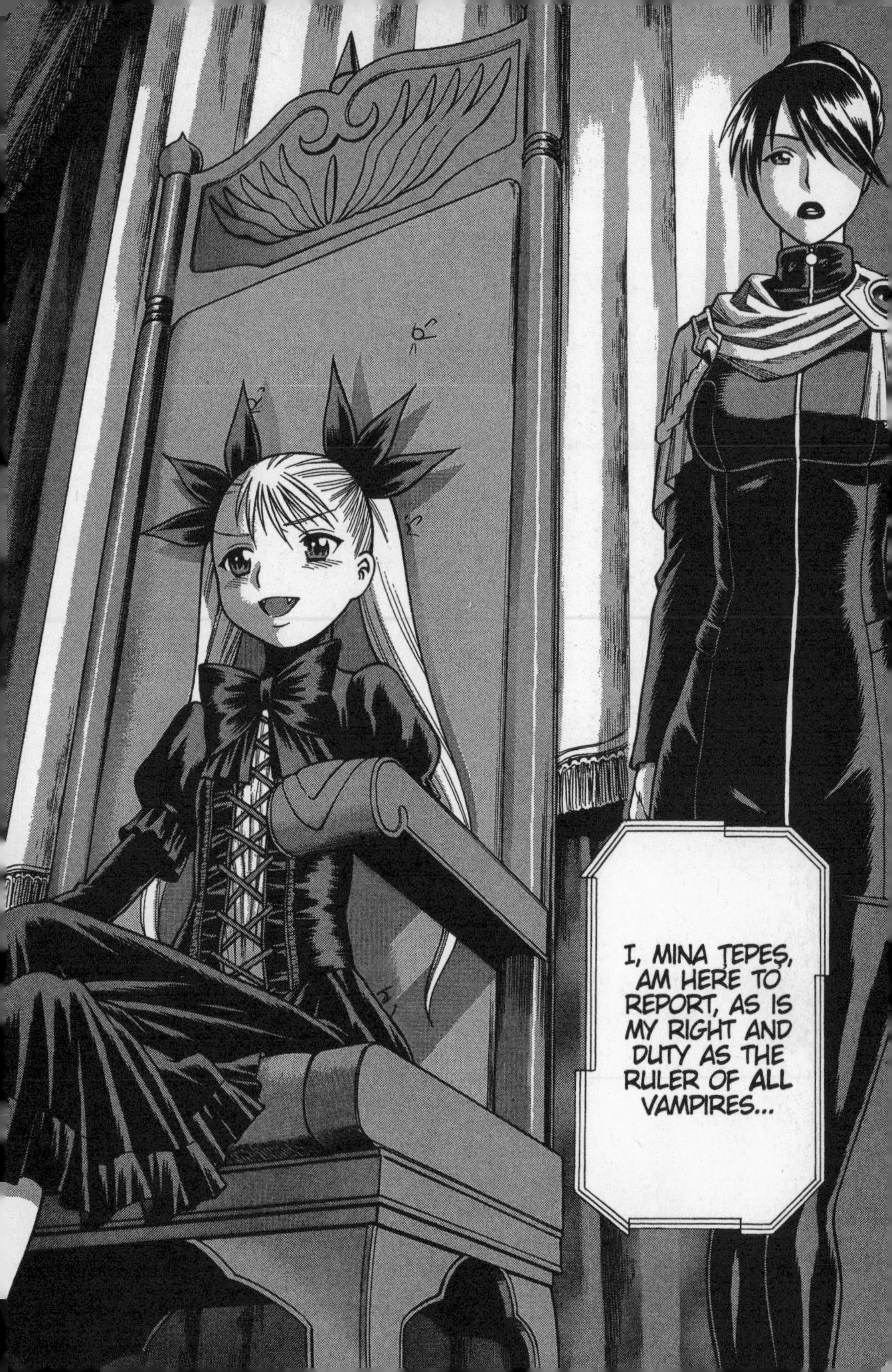
I, MINA ȚEPEȘ, AM HERE TO REPORT, AS IS MY RIGHT AND DUTY AS THE RULER OF ALL VAMPIRES...

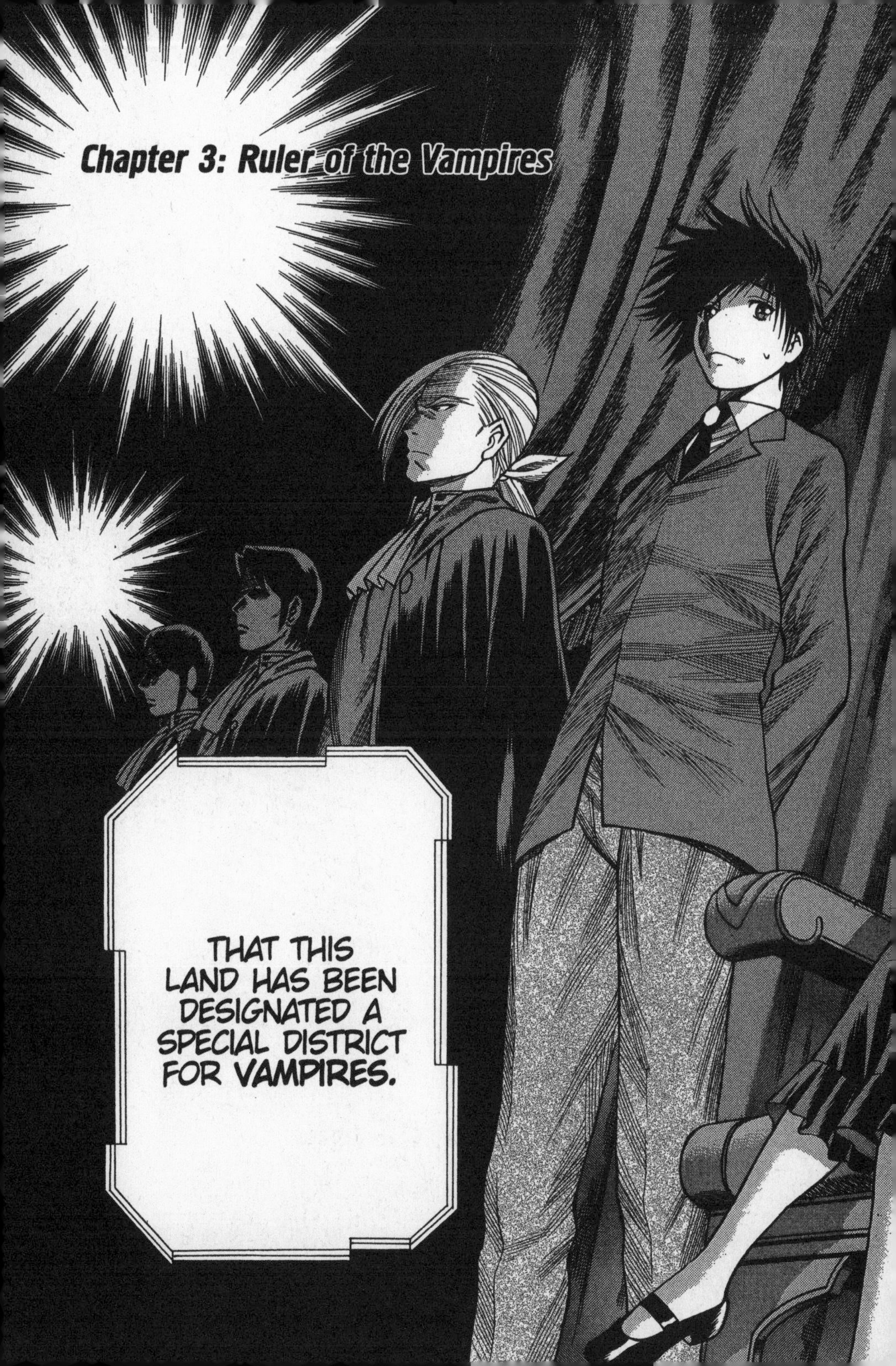
Chapter 3: Ruler of the Vampires
THAT THIS LAND HAS BEEN DESIGNATED A SPECIAL DISTRICT FOR VAMPIRES.

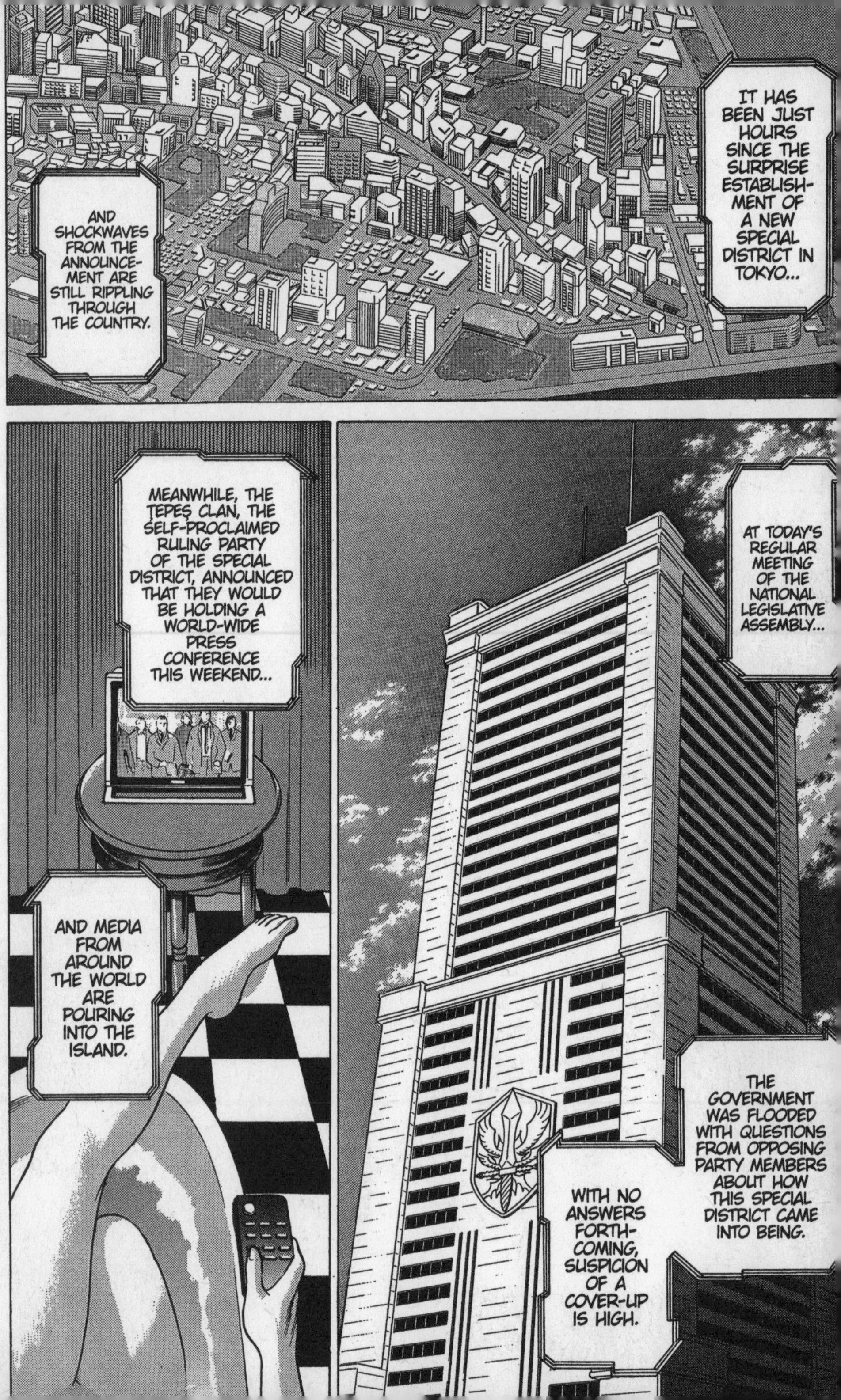
IT HAS BEEN JUST HOURS SINCE THE SURPRISE ESTABLISHMENT OF A NEW SPECIAL DISTRICT IN TOKYO...
AND SHOCKWAVES FROM THE ANNOUNCEMENT ARE STILL RIPPLING THROUGH THE COUNTRY.
AT TODAY'S REGULAR MEETING OF THE NATIONAL LEGISLATIVE ASSEMBLY...
THE GOVERNMENT WAS FLOODED WITH QUESTIONS FROM OPPOSING PARTY MEMBERS ABOUT HOW THIS SPECIAL DISTRICT CAME INTO BEING.
WITH NO ANSWERS FORTHCOMING, SUSPICION OF A COVER-UP IS HIGH.
MEANWHILE, THE TEPES CLAN, THE SELF-PROCLAIMED RULING PARTY OF THE SPECIAL DISTRICT, ANNOUNCED THAT THEY WOULD BE HOLDING A WORLD-WIDE PRESS CONFERENCE THIS WEEKEND...
AND MEDIA FROM AROUND THE WORLD ARE POURING INTO THE ISLAND.

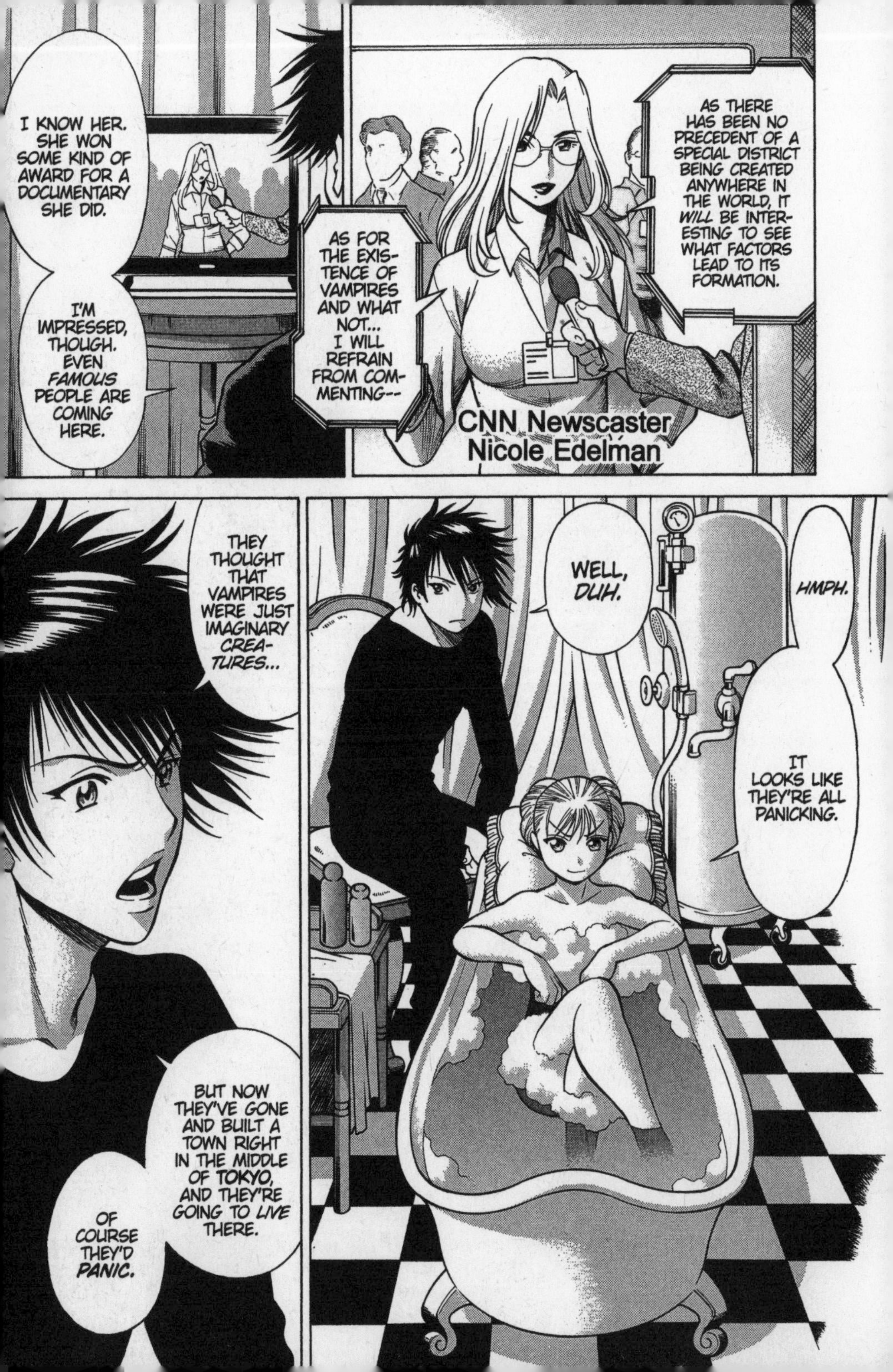
AS THERE HAS BEEN NO PRECEDENT OF A SPECIAL DISTRICT BEING CREATED ANYWHERE IN THE WORLD, IT *WILL* BE INTERESTING TO SEE WHAT FACTORS LEAD TO ITS FORMATION.
AS FOR THE EXISTENCE OF VAMPIRES AND WHAT NOT... I WILL REFRAIN FROM COMMENTING--
CNN Newscaster Nicole Edelman
I KNOW HER. SHE WON SOME KIND OF AWARD FOR A DOCUMENTARY SHE DID.
I'M IMPRESSED, THOUGH. EVEN *FAMOUS* PEOPLE ARE COMING HERE.
HMPH.
IT LOOKS LIKE THEY'RE ALL PANICKING.
WELL, *DUH.*
THEY THOUGHT THAT VAMPIRES WERE JUST IMAGINARY *CREATURES...*
BUT NOW THEY'VE GONE AND BUILT A TOWN RIGHT IN THE MIDDLE OF TOKYO, AND THEY'RE GOING TO *LIVE* THERE.
OF COURSE THEY'D *PANIC.*

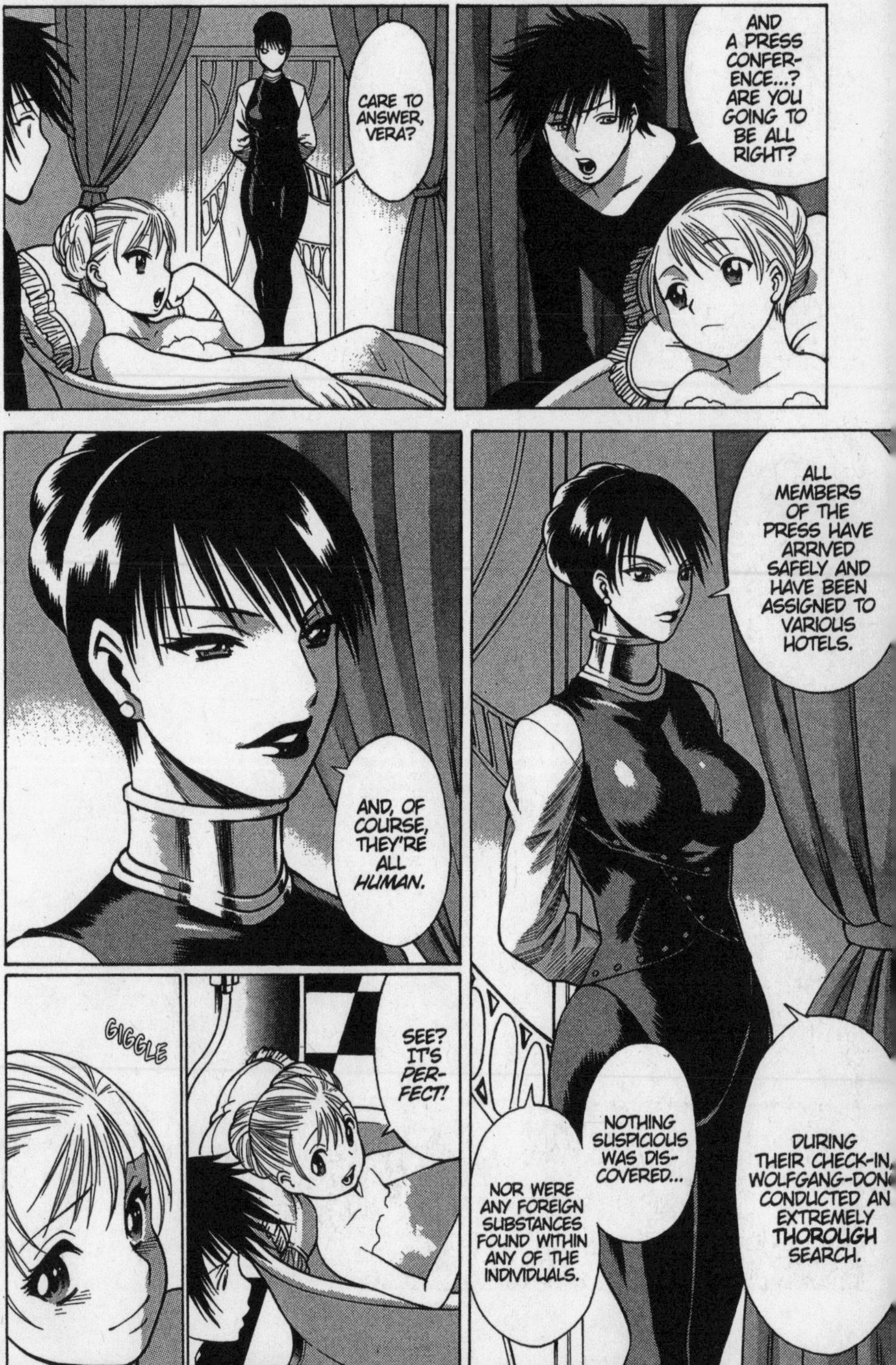
AND A PRESS CONFERENCE...? ARE YOU GOING TO BE ALL RIGHT?
CARE TO ANSWER, VERA?
ALL MEMBERS OF THE PRESS HAVE ARRIVED SAFELY AND HAVE BEEN ASSIGNED TO VARIOUS HOTELS.
DURING THEIR CHECK-IN, WOLFGANG-DON CONDUCTED AN EXTREMELY *THOROUGH* SEARCH.
NOTHING SUSPICIOUS WAS DISCOVERED...
NOR WERE ANY FOREIGN SUBSTANCES FOUND WITHIN ANY OF THE INDIVIDUALS.
AND, OF COURSE, THEY'RE ALL *HUMAN*.
SEE? IT'S PERFECT!
GIGGLE

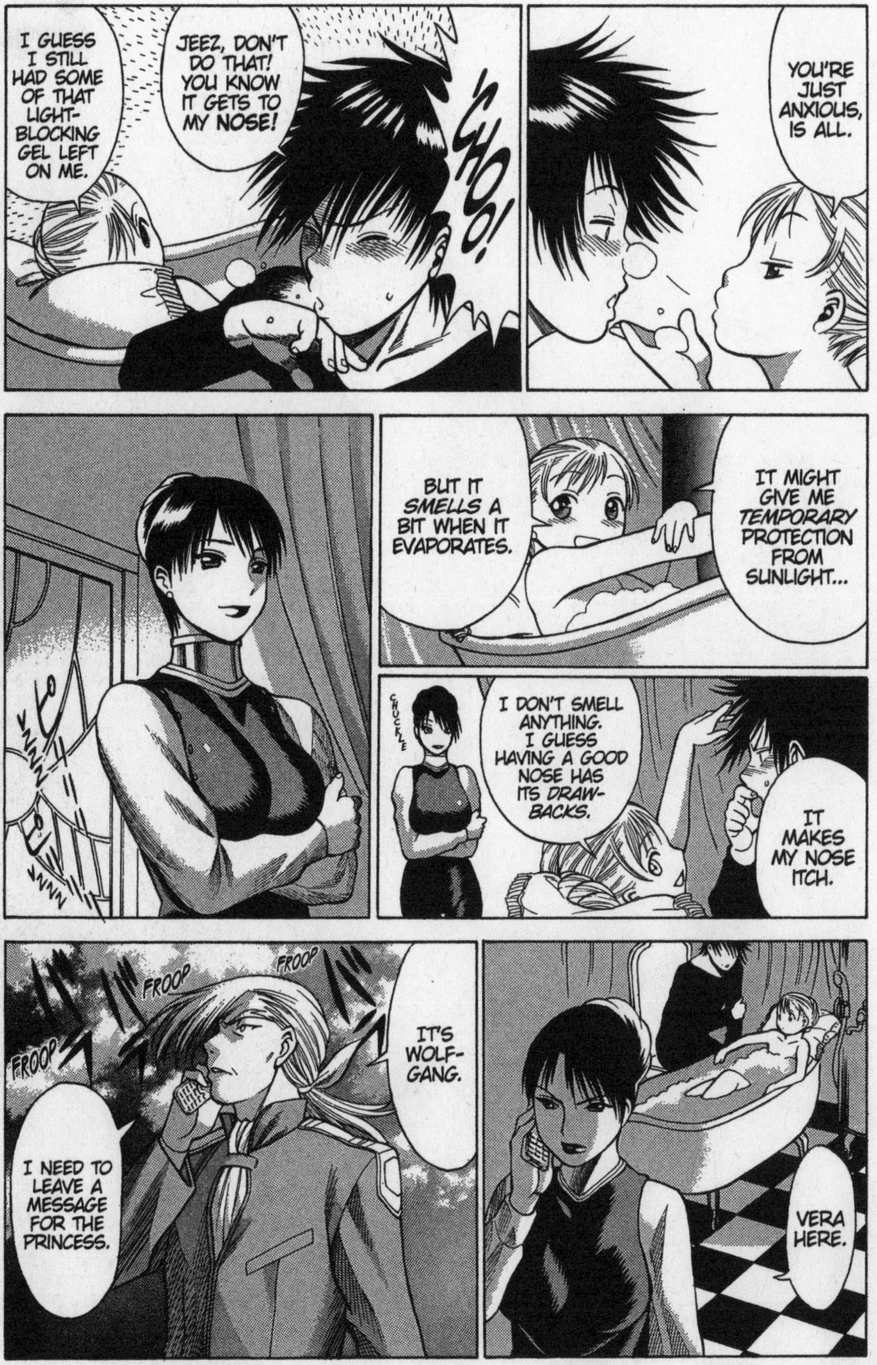
YOU'RE JUST ANXIOUS, IS ALL.
'CHOO!
JEEZ, DON'T DO THAT! YOU KNOW IT GETS TO MY NOSE!
I GUESS I STILL HAD SOME OF THAT LIGHT-BLOCKING GEL LEFT ON ME.
IT MIGHT GIVE ME *TEMPORARY* PROTECTION FROM SUNLIGHT...
BUT IT *SMELLS* A BIT WHEN IT EVAPORATES.
IT MAKES MY NOSE ITCH.
I DON'T SMELL ANYTHING. I GUESS HAVING A GOOD NOSE HAS ITS *DRAW-BACKS.*
CHUCKLE
VNNNN
VNNN
VERA HERE.
FROOP
FROOP
FROOP
IT'S WOLF-GANG.
I NEED TO LEAVE A MESSAGE FOR THE PRINCESS.

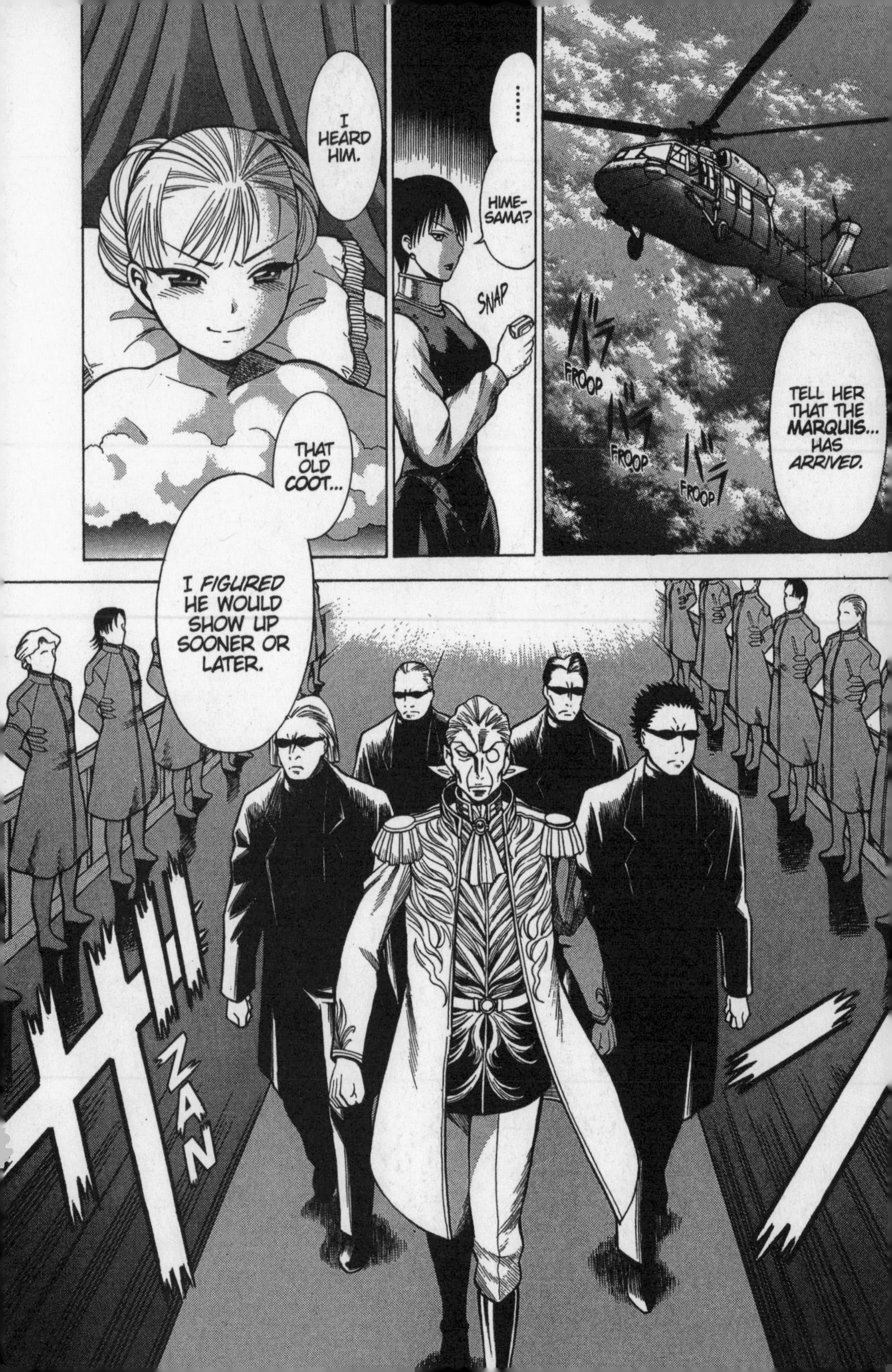
FROOP
FROOP
FROOP
TELL HER THAT THE MARQUIS... HAS ARRIVED.
......
HIME-SAMA?
SNAP
I HEARD HIM.
THAT OLD COOT...
I FIGURED HE WOULD SHOW UP SOONER OR LATER.
ZAN

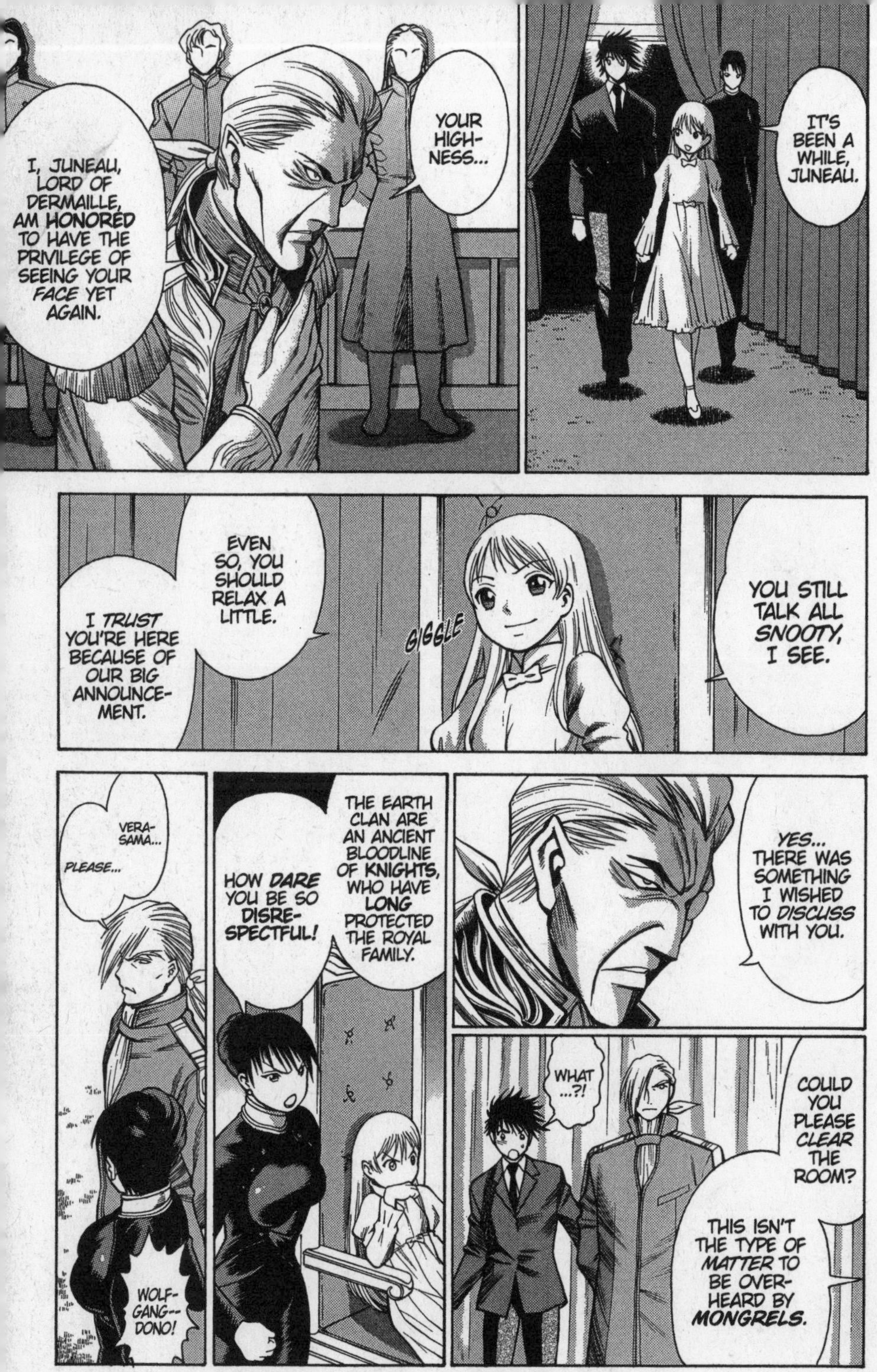
IT'S BEEN A WHILE, JUNEAU.
YOUR HIGHNESS...
I, JUNEAU, LORD OF DERMAILLE, AM HONORED TO HAVE THE PRIVILEGE OF SEEING YOUR FACE YET AGAIN.
YOU STILL TALK ALL SNOOTY, I SEE.
GIGGLE
EVEN SO, YOU SHOULD RELAX A LITTLE.
I TRUST YOU'RE HERE BECAUSE OF OUR BIG ANNOUNCEMENT.
YES... THERE WAS SOMETHING I WISHED TO DISCUSS WITH YOU.
COULD YOU PLEASE CLEAR THE ROOM?
THIS ISN'T THE TYPE OF MATTER TO BE OVERHEARD BY MONGRELS.
WHAT ...?!
THE EARTH CLAN ARE AN ANCIENT BLOODLINE OF KNIGHTS, WHO HAVE LONG PROTECTED THE ROYAL FAMILY.
HOW DARE YOU BE SO DISRESPECTFUL!
VERA-SAMA... PLEASE...
WOLFGANG--DONO!

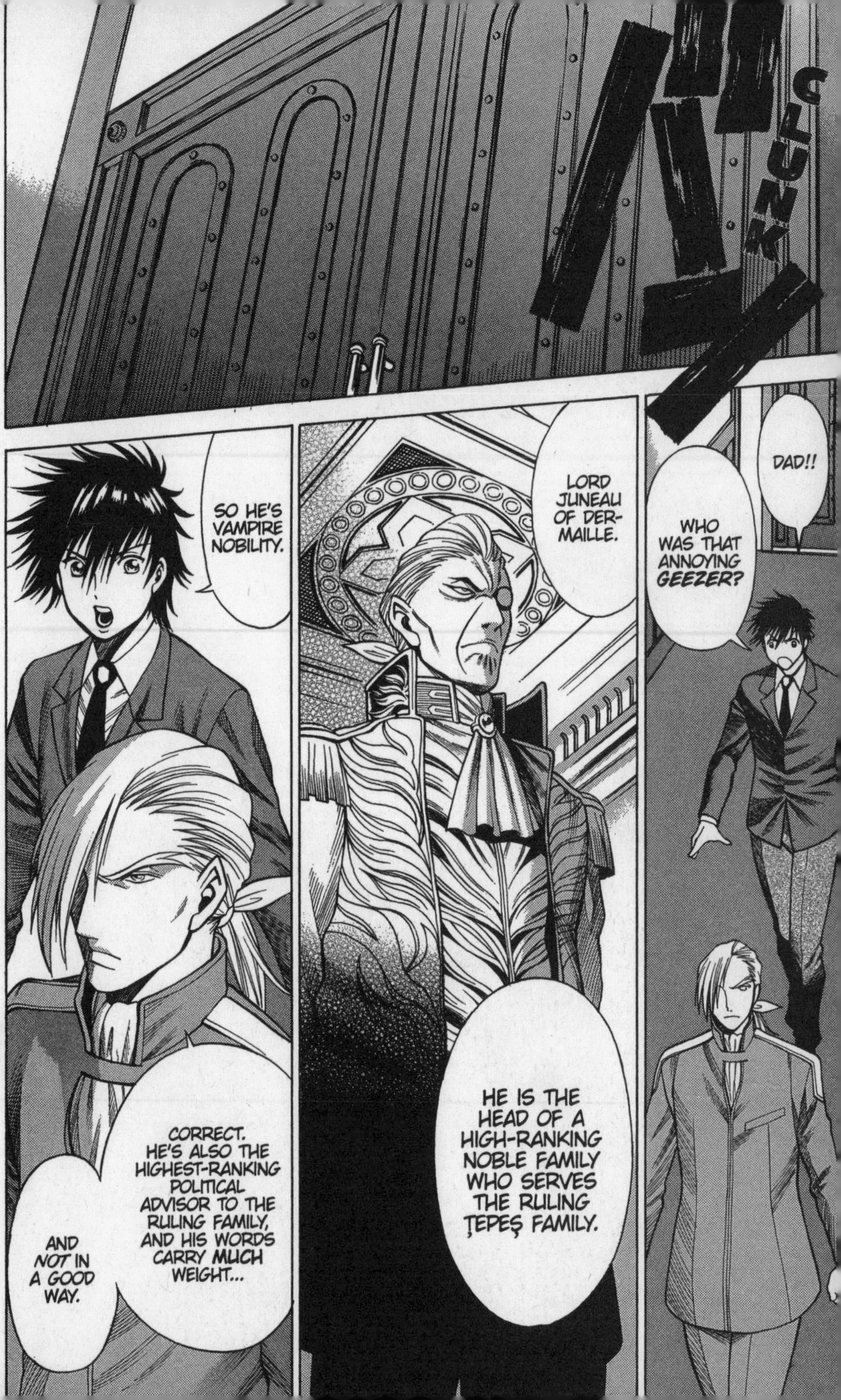
CLUNK
DAD!!
WHO WAS THAT ANNOYING GEEZER?
LORD JUNEAU OF DER-MAILLE.
HE IS THE HEAD OF A HIGH-RANKING NOBLE FAMILY WHO SERVES THE RULING ȚEPEȘ FAMILY.
SO HE'S VAMPIRE NOBILITY.
CORRECT. HE'S ALSO THE HIGHEST-RANKING POLITICAL ADVISOR TO THE RULING FAMILY, AND HIS WORDS CARRY MUCH WEIGHT...
AND NOT IN A GOOD WAY.

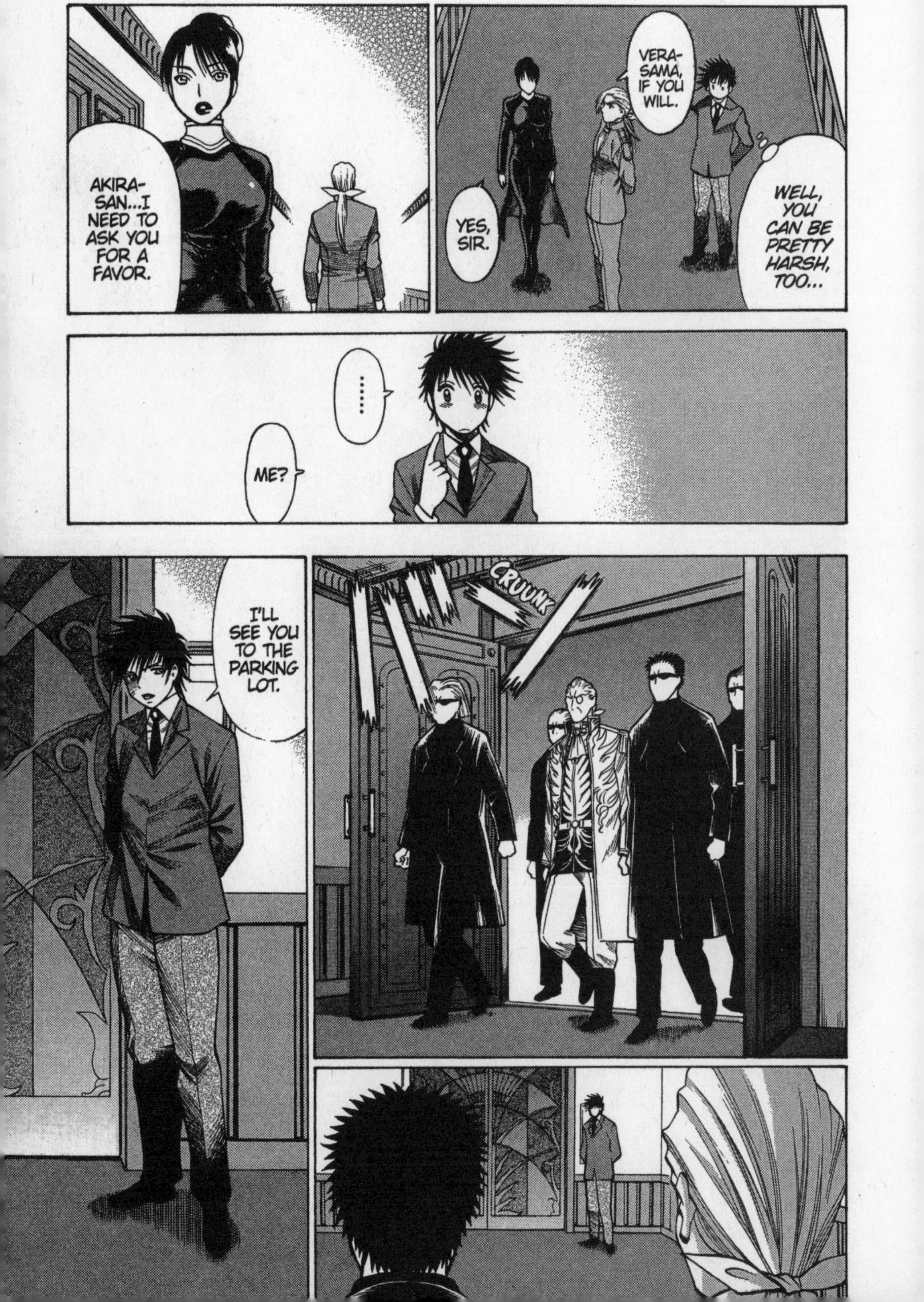
VERA-SAMA, IF YOU WILL.
WELL, YOU CAN BE PRETTY HARSH, TOO...
YES, SIR.
AKIRA-SAN...I NEED TO ASK YOU FOR A FAVOR.
......
ME?
CRUUNK
I'LL SEE YOU TO THE PARKING LOT.

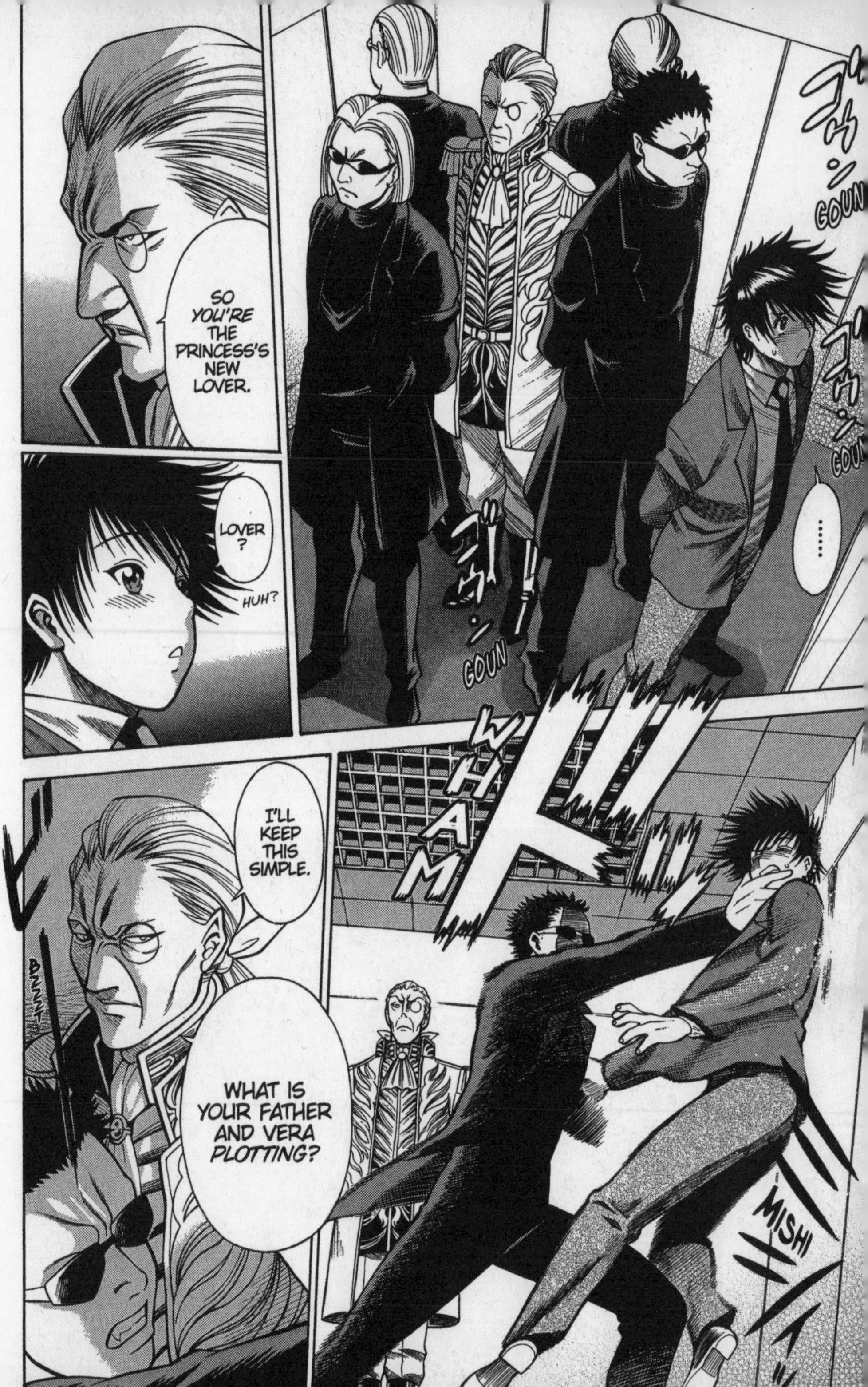
GOUN
GOUN
......
GOUN
SO YOU'RE THE PRINCESS'S NEW LOVER.
LOVER?
HUH?
WHAM
MISHI
I'LL KEEP THIS SIMPLE.
BZZZT
WHAT IS YOUR FATHER AND VERA PLOTTING?

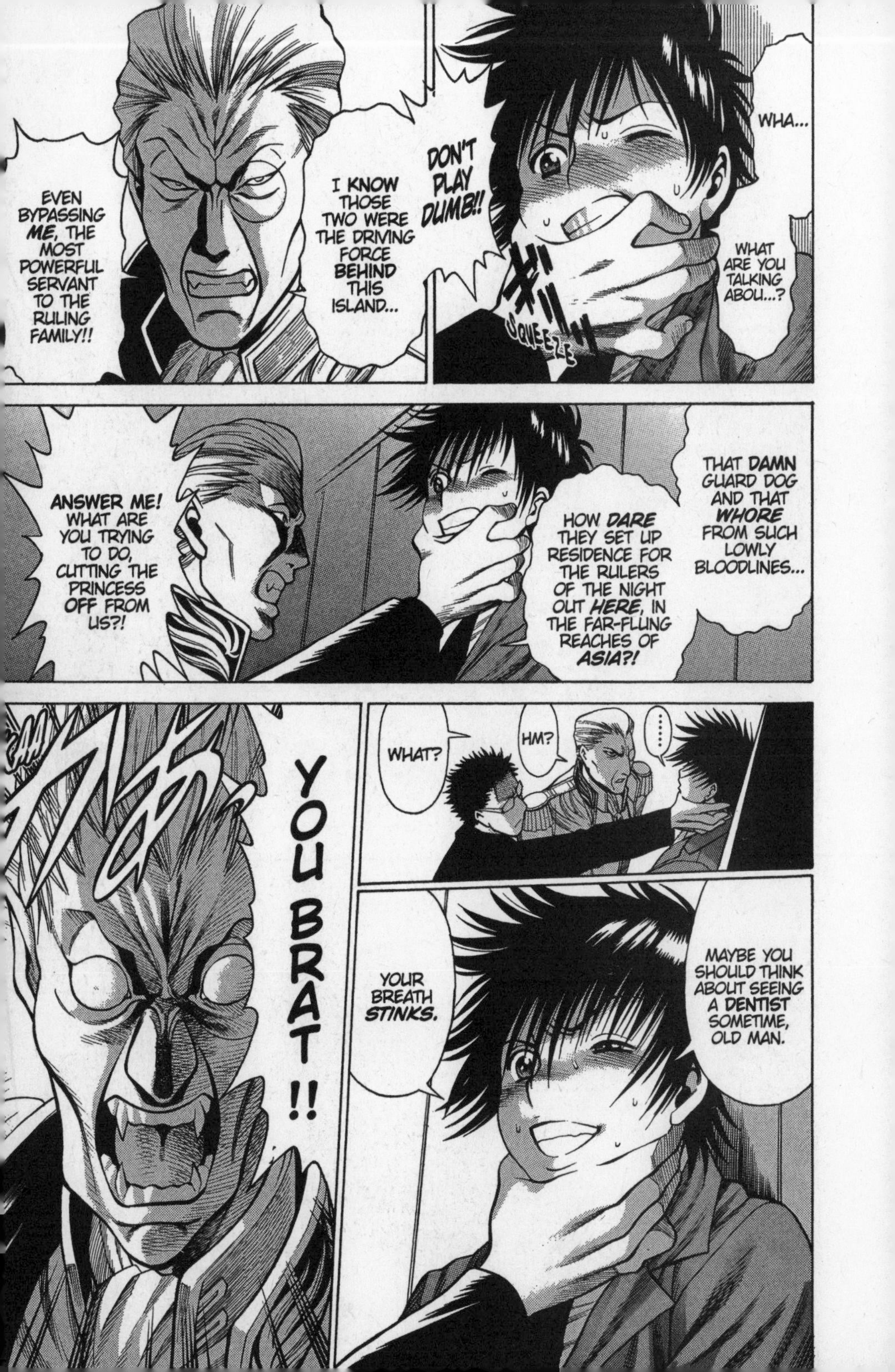
WHA...
WHAT ARE YOU TALKING ABOU...?
DON'T PLAY DUMB!!
SQUEEZE
I KNOW THOSE TWO WERE THE DRIVING FORCE BEHIND THIS ISLAND...
EVEN BYPASSING ME, THE MOST POWERFUL SERVANT TO THE RULING FAMILY!!
THAT DAMN GUARD DOG AND THAT WHORE FROM SUCH LOWLY BLOODLINES...
HOW DARE THEY SET UP RESIDENCE FOR THE RULERS OF THE NIGHT OUT HERE, IN THE FAR-FLUNG REACHES OF ASIA?!
ANSWER ME! WHAT ARE YOU TRYING TO DO, CUTTING THE PRINCESS OFF FROM US?!
......
HM?
WHAT?
MAYBE YOU SHOULD THINK ABOUT SEEING A DENTIST SOMETIME, OLD MAN.
YOUR BREATH STINKS.
YOU BRAT!!

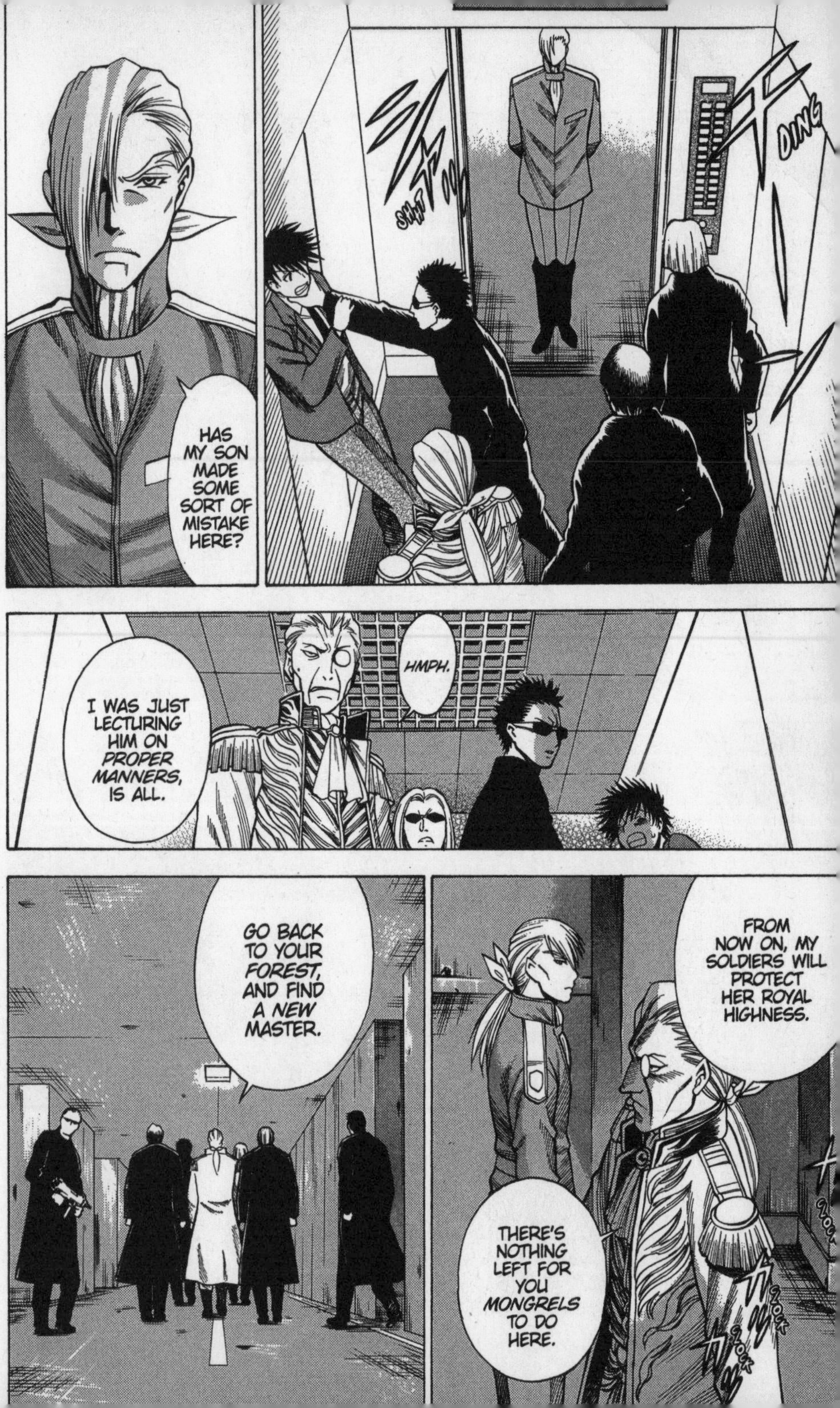
DING
HAS MY SON MADE SOME SORT OF MISTAKE HERE?
HMPH.
I WAS JUST LECTURING HIM ON PROPER MANNERS, IS ALL.
FROM NOW ON, MY SOLDIERS WILL PROTECT HER ROYAL HIGHNESS.
THERE'S NOTHING LEFT FOR YOU MONGRELS TO DO HERE.
GO BACK TO YOUR FOREST, AND FIND A NEW MASTER.

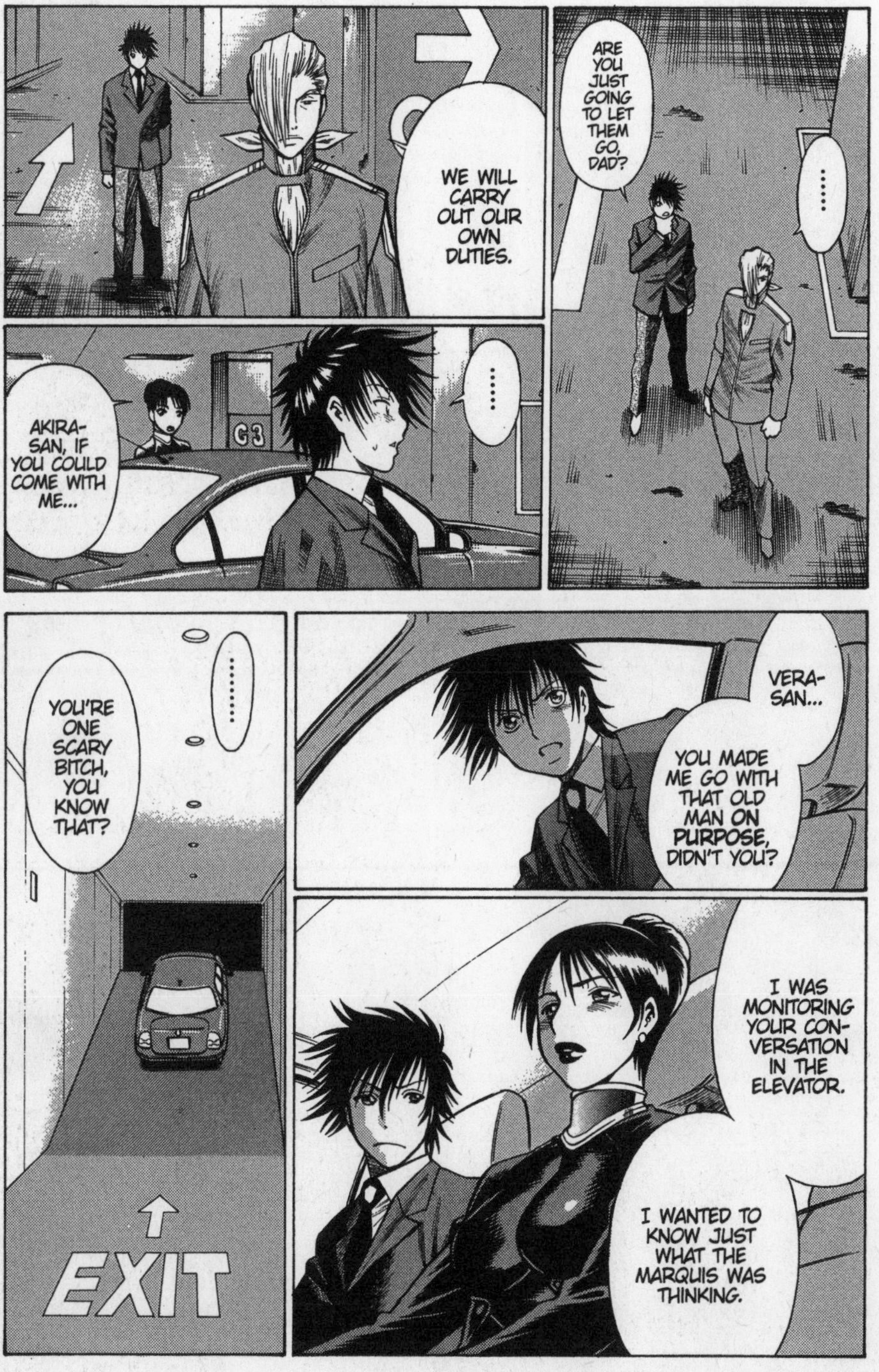
ARE YOU JUST GOING TO LET THEM GO, DAD?
......
WE WILL CARRY OUT OUR OWN DUTIES.
......
AKIRA-SAN, IF YOU COULD COME WITH ME...
VERA-SAN...
YOU MADE ME GO WITH THAT OLD MAN ON PURPOSE, DIDN'T YOU?
I WAS MONITORING YOUR CON-VERSATION IN THE ELEVATOR.
I WANTED TO KNOW JUST WHAT THE MARQUIS WAS THINKING.
......
YOU'RE ONE SCARY BITCH, YOU KNOW THAT?
EXIT

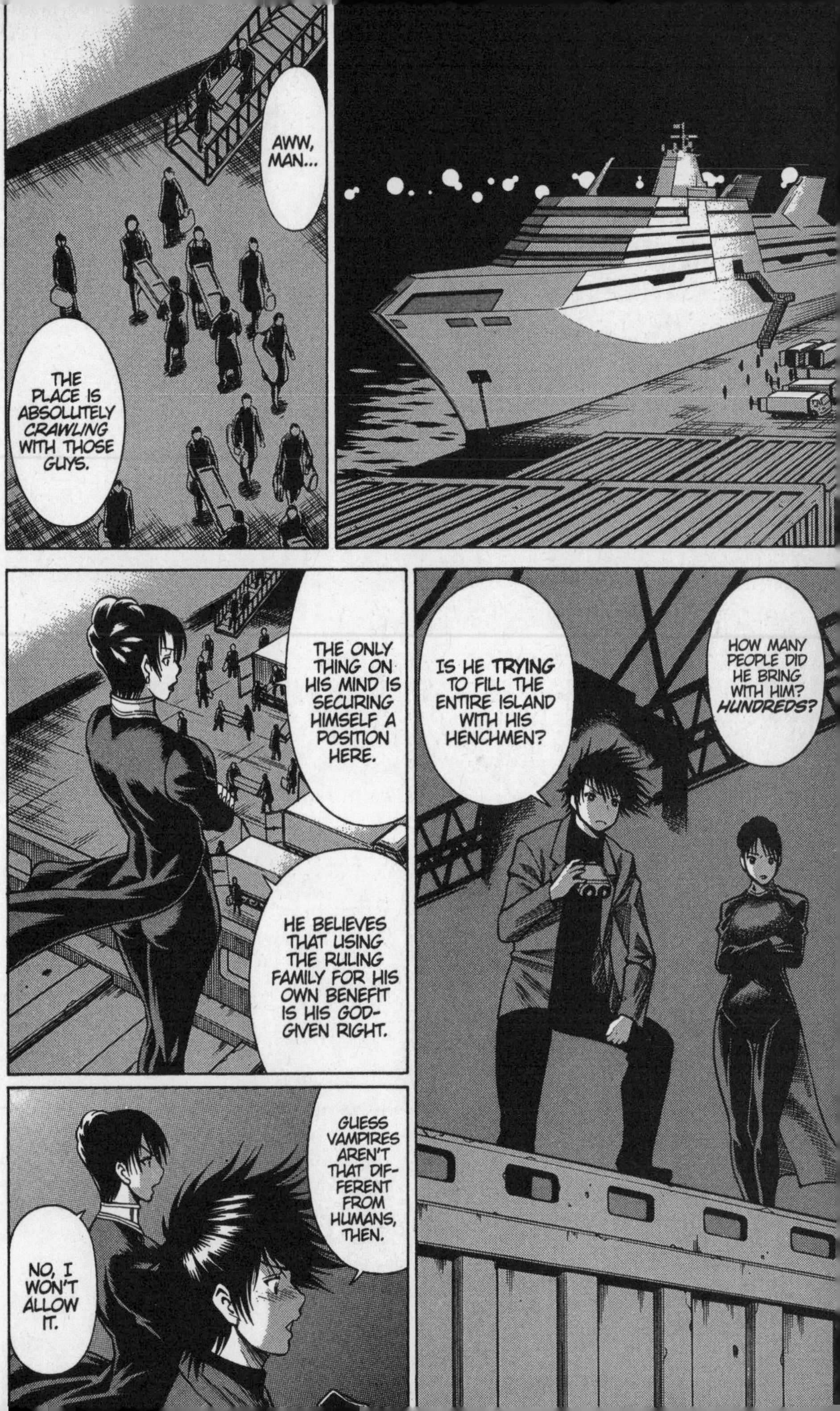
AWW, MAN...
THE PLACE IS ABSOLUTELY *CRAWLING* WITH THOSE GUYS.
HOW MANY PEOPLE DID HE BRING WITH HIM? *HUNDREDS?*
IS HE **TRYING** TO FILL THE ENTIRE ISLAND WITH HIS HENCHMEN?
THE ONLY THING ON HIS MIND IS SECURING HIMSELF A POSITION HERE.
HE BELIEVES THAT USING THE RULING FAMILY FOR HIS OWN BENEFIT IS HIS GOD-GIVEN RIGHT.
GUESS VAMPIRES AREN'T THAT DIF-FERENT FROM HUMANS, THEN.
NO, I WON'T ALLOW IT.

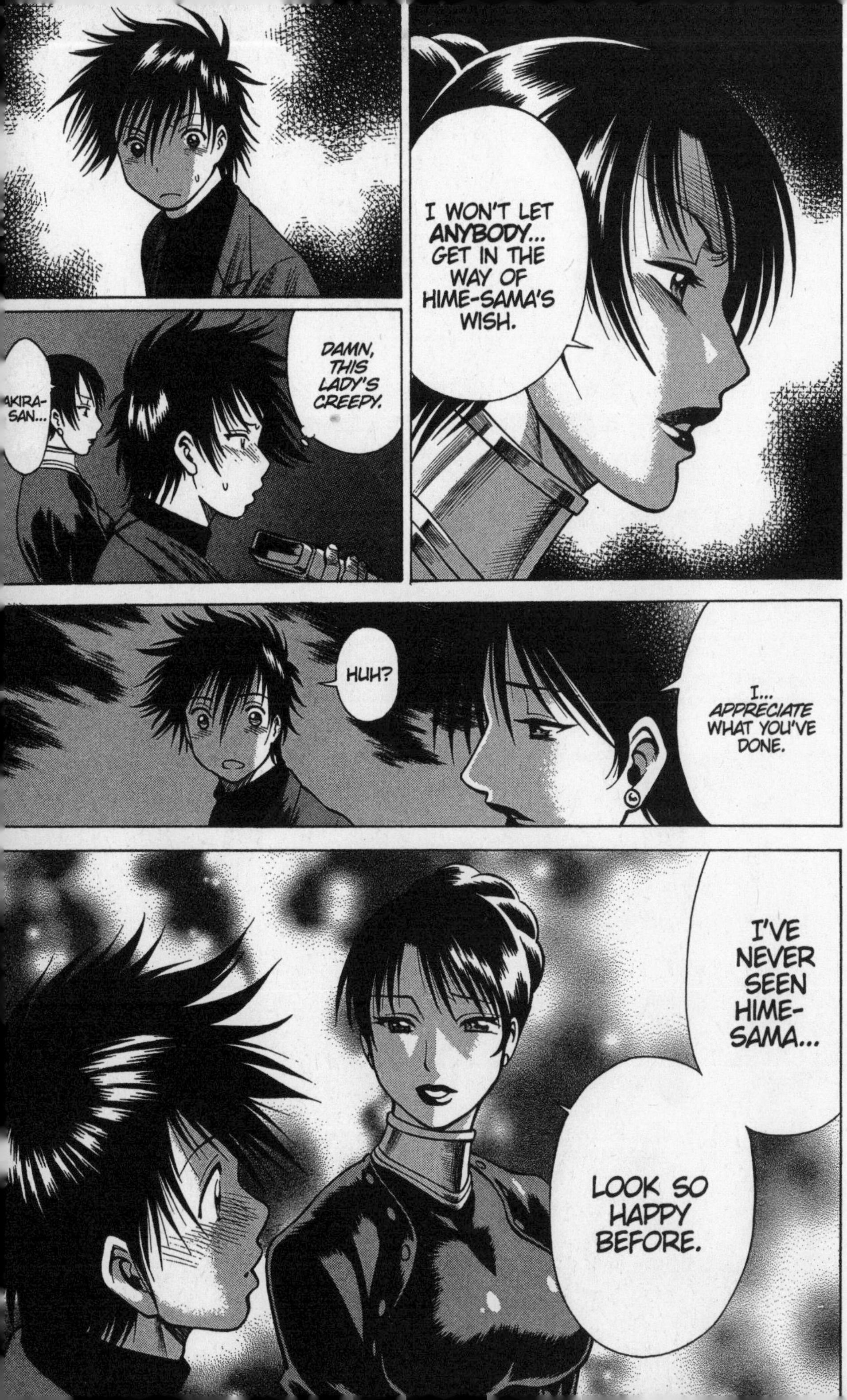
I WON'T LET ANYBODY... GET IN THE WAY OF HIME-SAMA'S WISH.
DAMN, THIS LADY'S CREEPY.
AKIRA-SAN...
I... APPRECIATE WHAT YOU'VE DONE.
HUH?
I'VE NEVER SEEN HIME-SAMA...
LOOK SO HAPPY BEFORE.

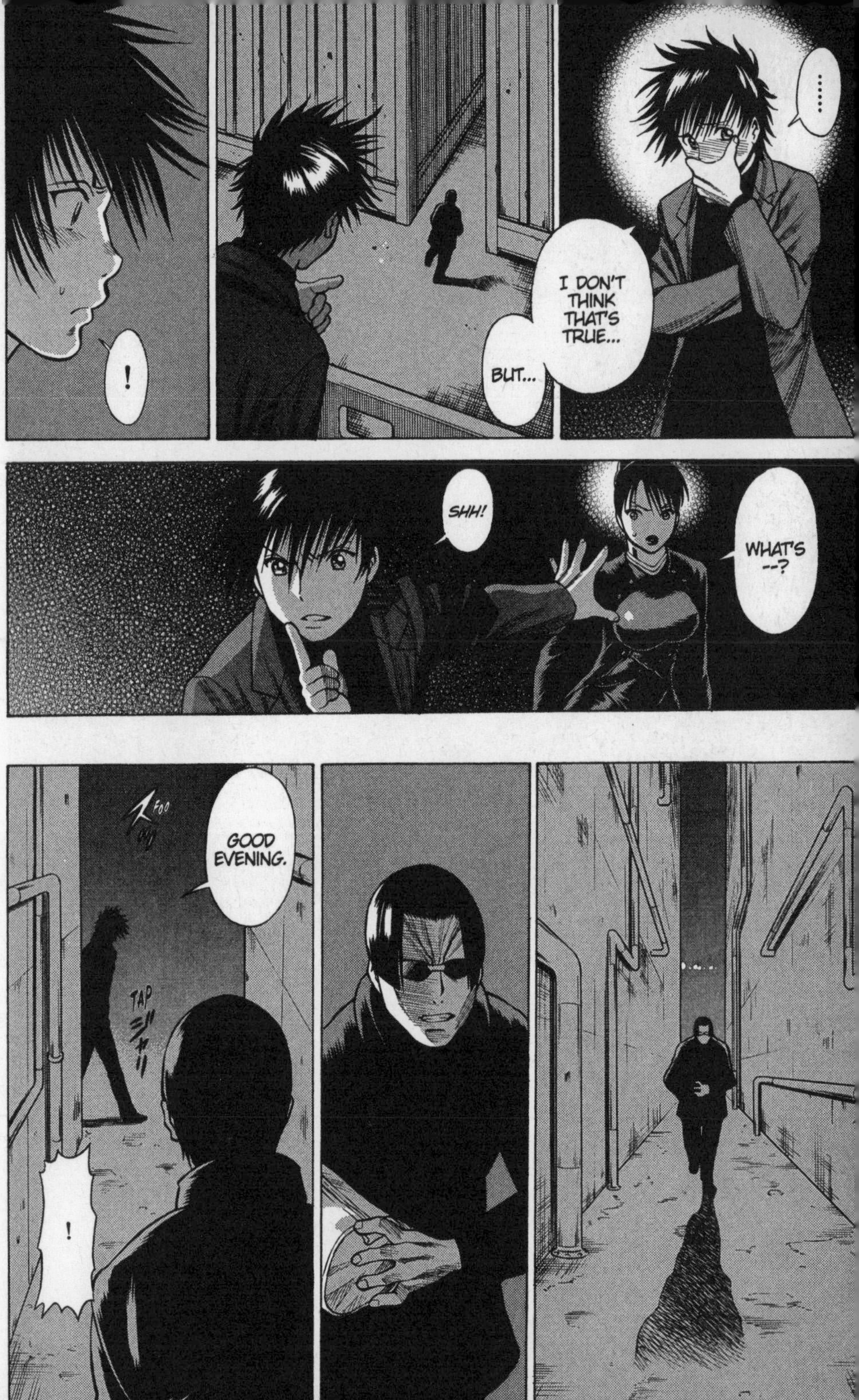
......
I DON'T THINK THAT'S TRUE...
BUT...
!
WHAT'S --?
SHH!
GOOD EVENING.
FOO
TAP
!

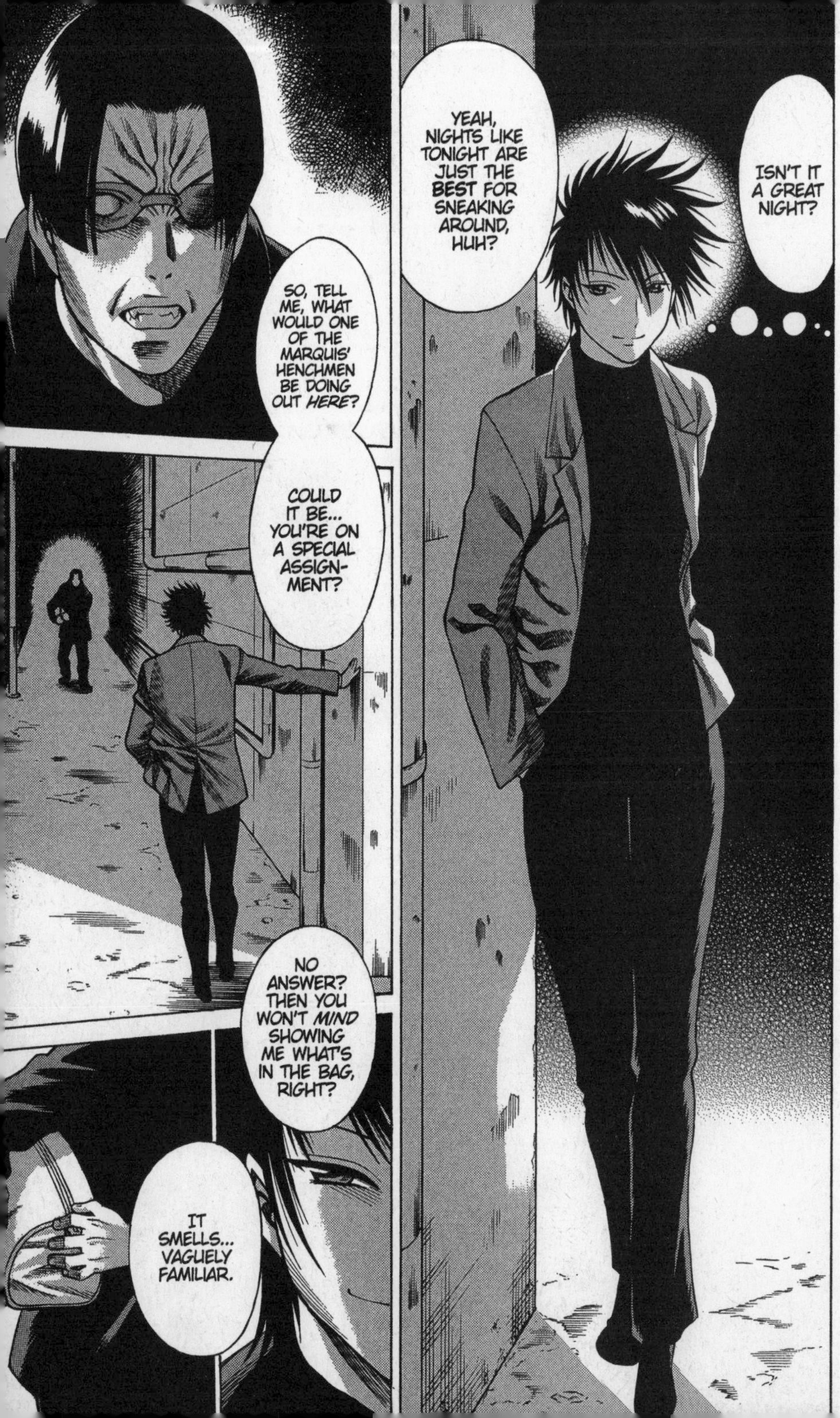
ISN'T IT A GREAT NIGHT?
YEAH, NIGHTS LIKE TONIGHT ARE JUST THE BEST FOR SNEAKING AROUND, HUH?
SO, TELL ME, WHAT WOULD ONE OF THE MARQUIS' HENCHMEN BE DOING OUT *HERE*?
COULD IT BE... YOU'RE ON A SPECIAL ASSIGNMENT?
NO ANSWER? THEN YOU WON'T *MIND* SHOWING ME WHAT'S IN THE BAG, RIGHT?
IT SMELLS... VAGUELY FAMILIAR.

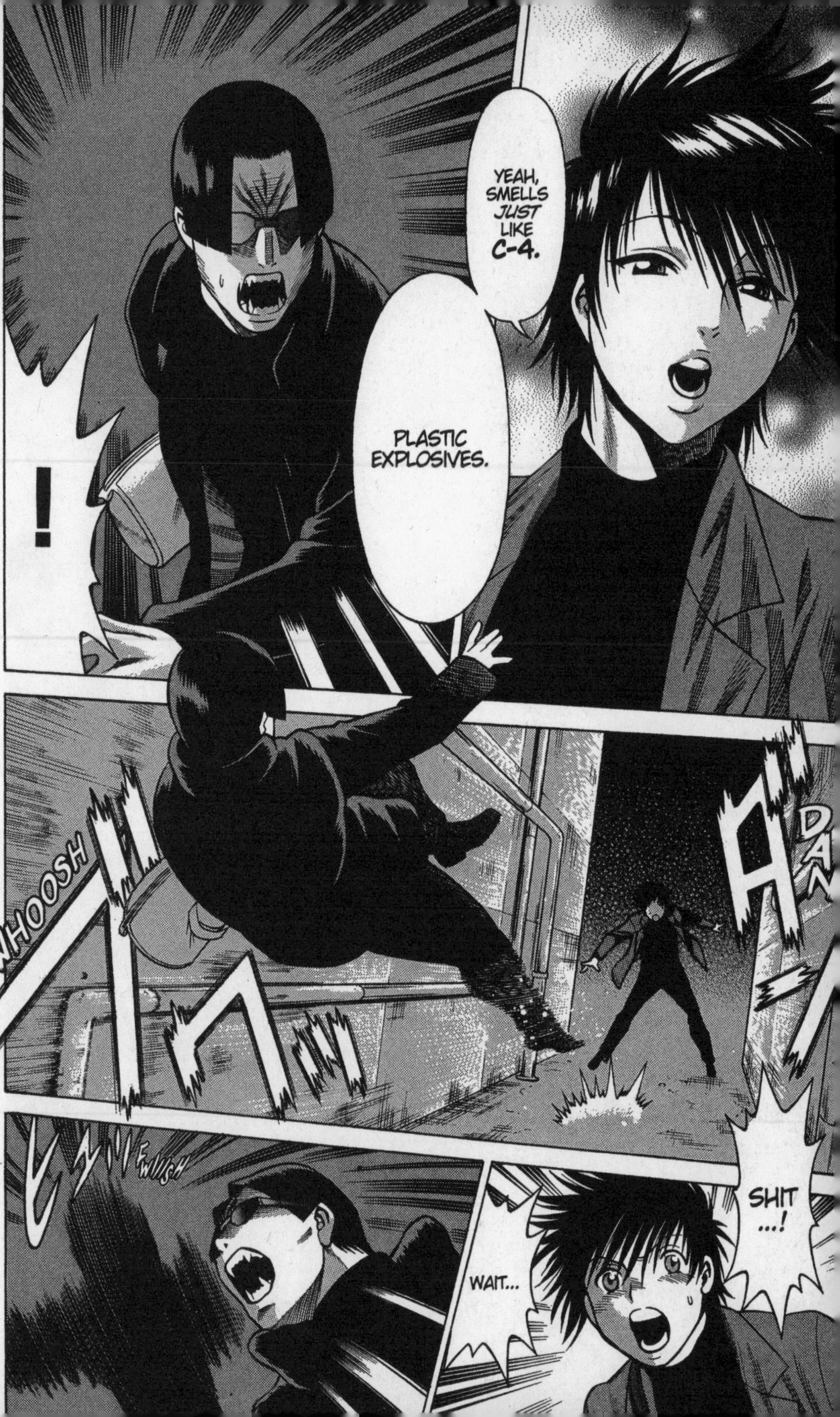
YEAH, SMELLS JUST LIKE C-4.
PLASTIC EXPLOSIVES.
!
DAN
WHOOSH
SHIT ...!
WAIT...
FWISH

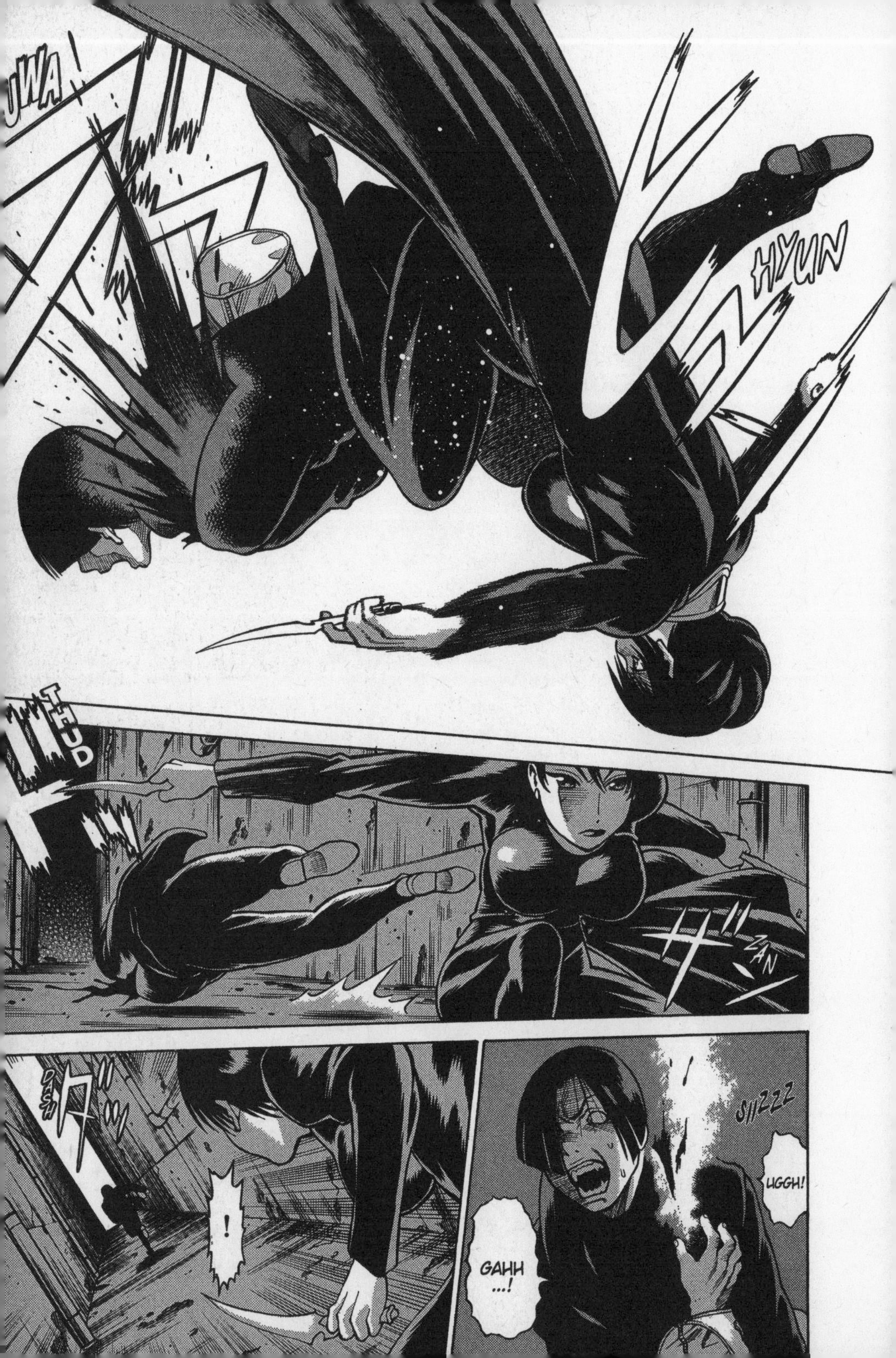
HYUN
UWA!
ZAN
THUD
SIIZZZ
UGGH!
GAHH ...!
DASH
!

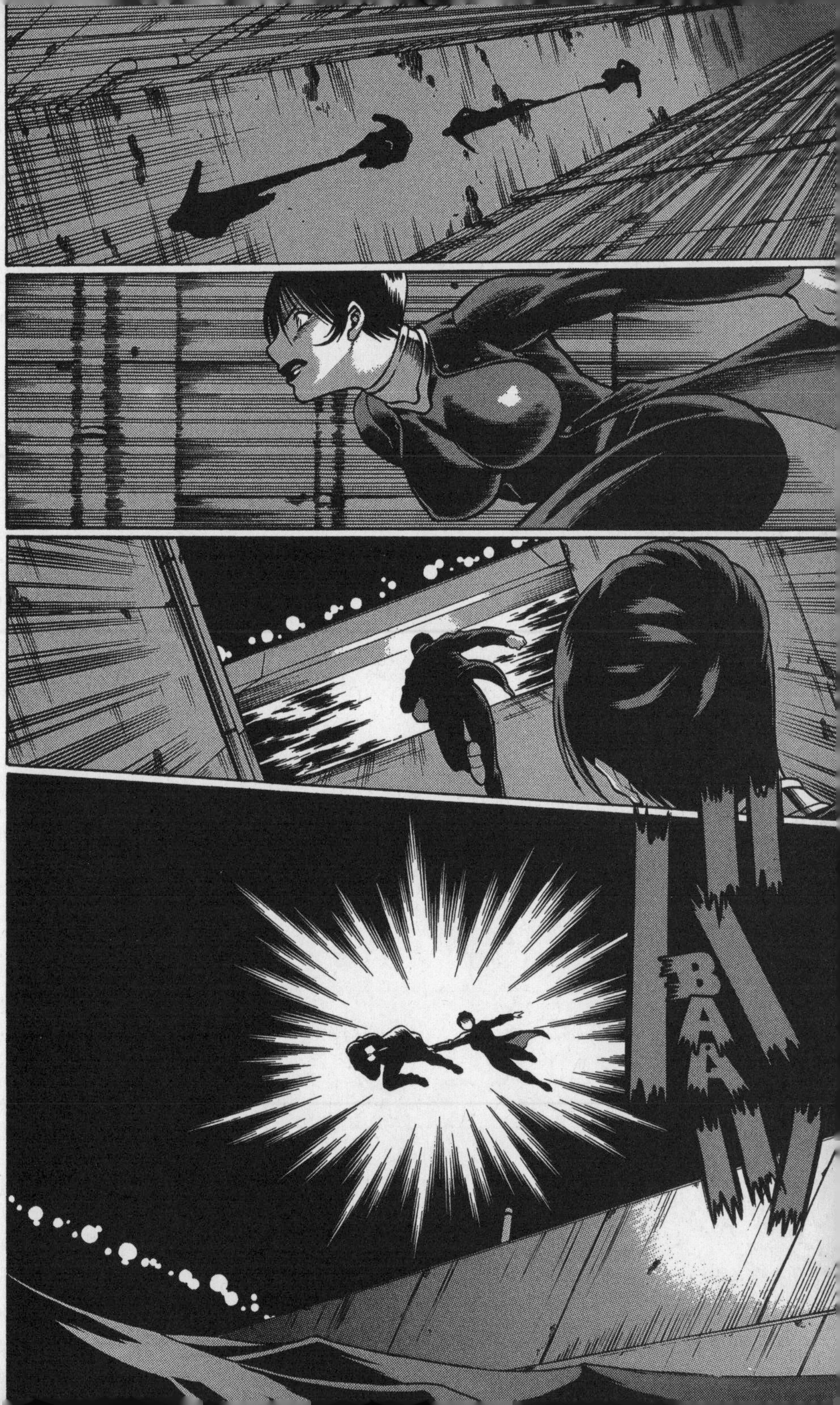
BAA

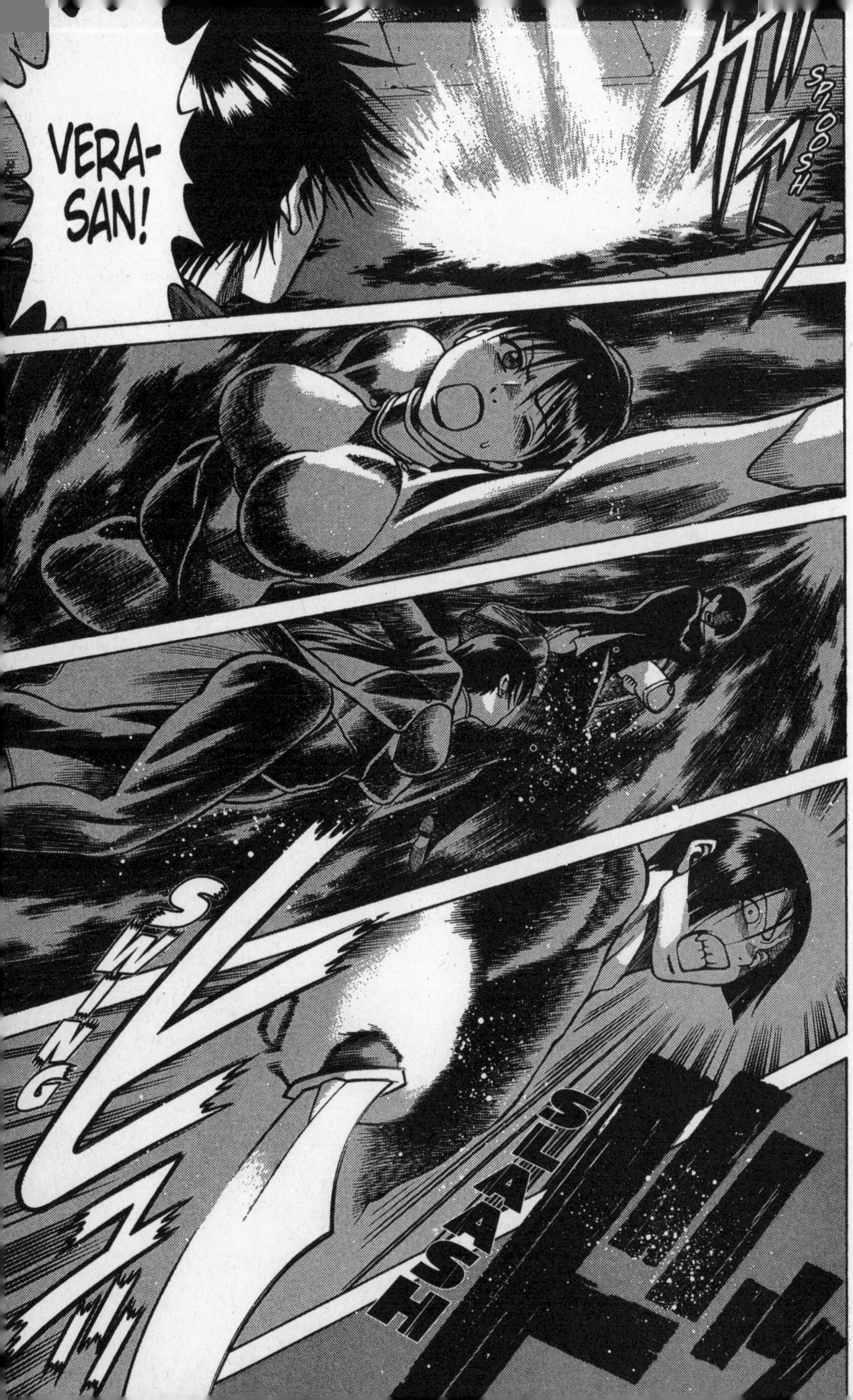
SPLOOSH
VERA-SAN!
SWING
SHAAASH

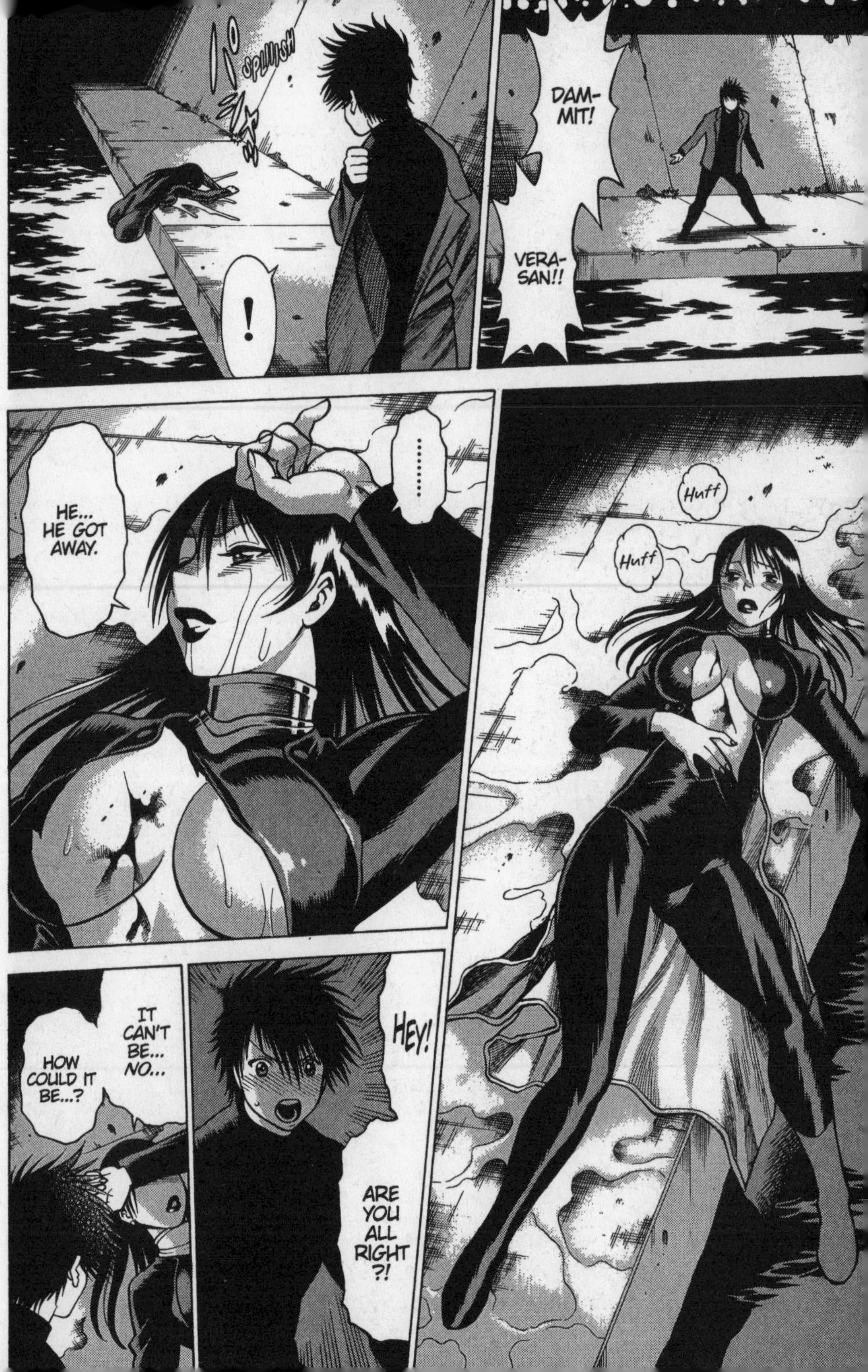
DAM-
MIT!
VERA-
SAN!!
SPLIIISH
!
Huff
Huff
......
HE...
HE GOT
AWAY.
HEY!
ARE
YOU
ALL
RIGHT
?!
IT
CAN'T
BE...
NO...
HOW
COULD IT
BE...?

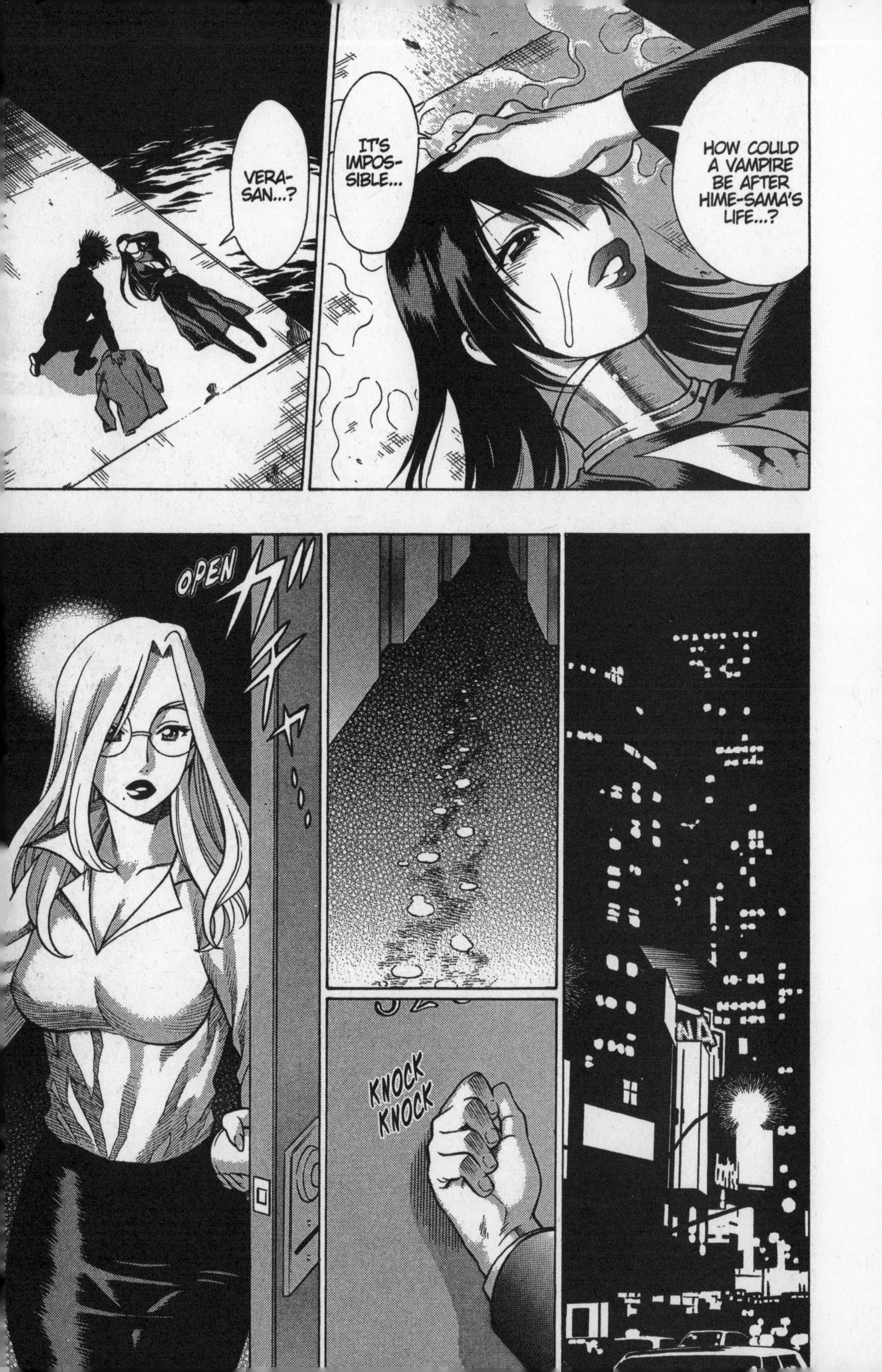
HOW COULD A VAMPIRE BE AFTER HIME-SAMA'S LIFE...?
IT'S IMPOSSIBLE...
VERA-SAN...?
KNOCK KNOCK
OPEN

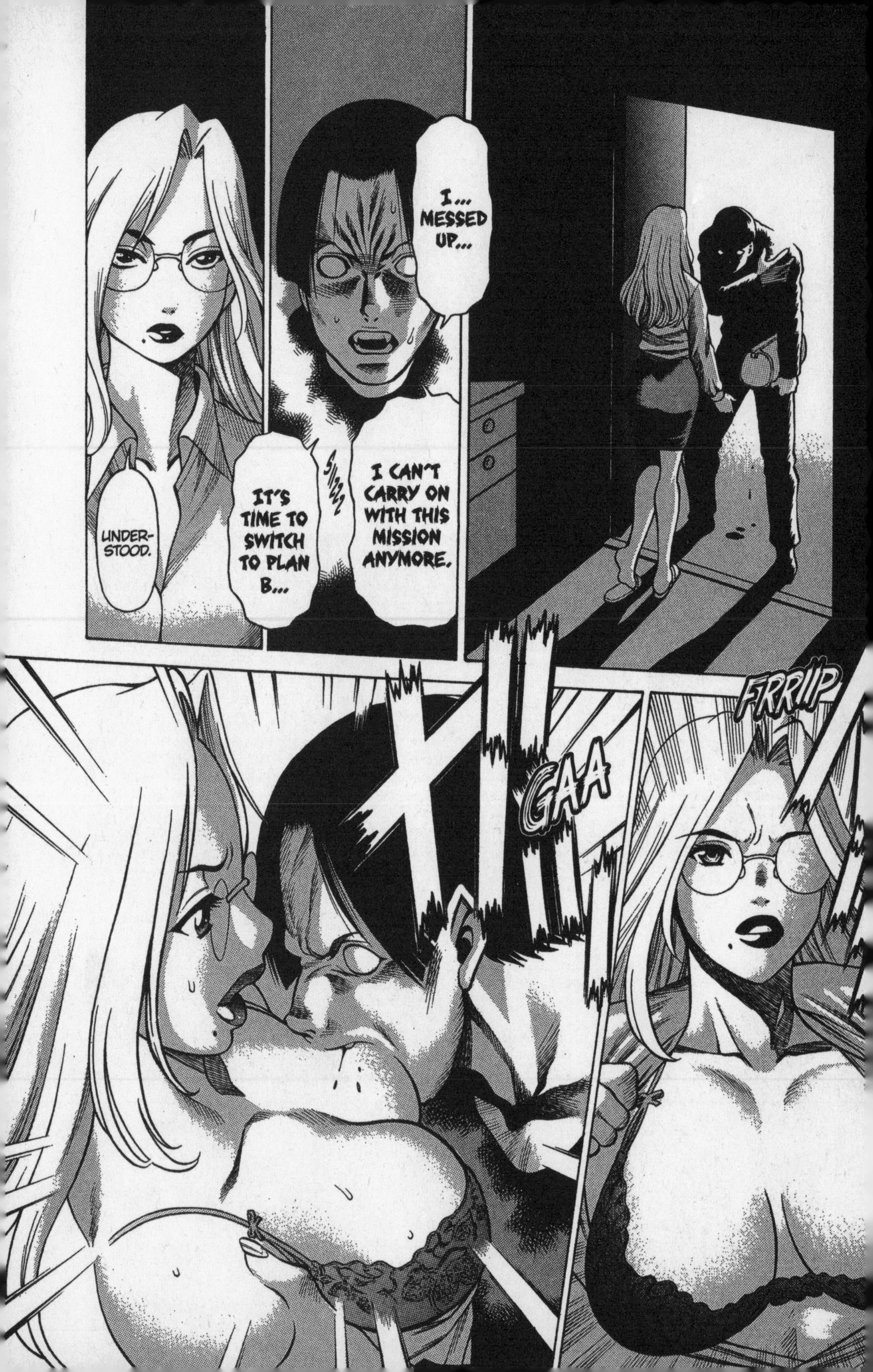

I... MESSED UP...
I CAN'T CARRY ON WITH THIS MISSION ANYMORE.
IT'S TIME TO SWITCH TO PLAN B...
UNDER-STOOD.
FRRIIP
GAA

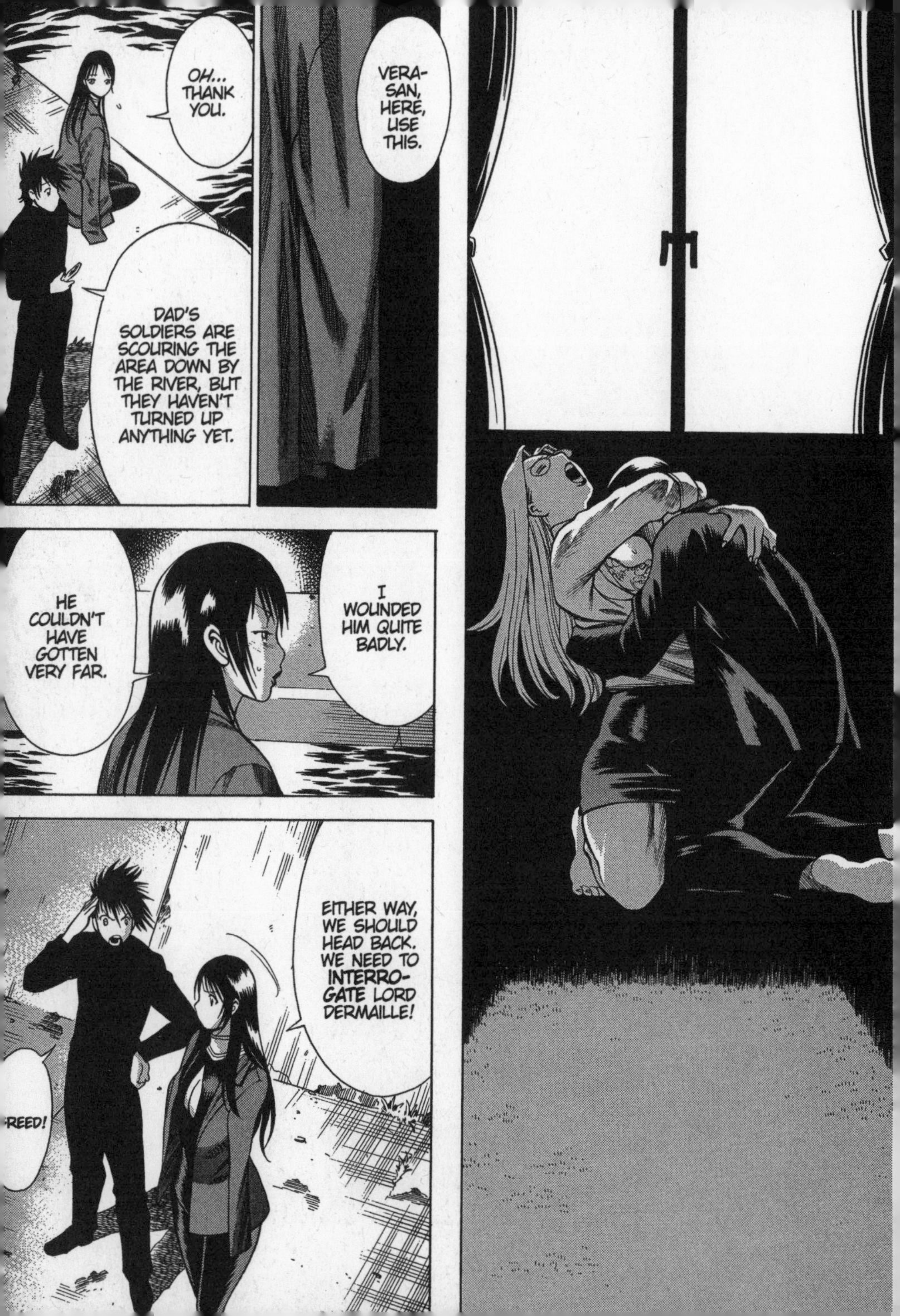
VERA-SAN, HERE, USE THIS.
OH... THANK YOU.
DAD'S SOLDIERS ARE SCOURING THE AREA DOWN BY THE RIVER, BUT THEY HAVEN'T TURNED UP ANYTHING YET.
I WOUNDED HIM QUITE BADLY.
HE COULDN'T HAVE GOTTEN VERY FAR.
EITHER WAY, WE SHOULD HEAD BACK. WE NEED TO INTERRO-GATE LORD DERMAILLE!
FREED!

※ Special Air Service – The British Army's principle special forces unit.

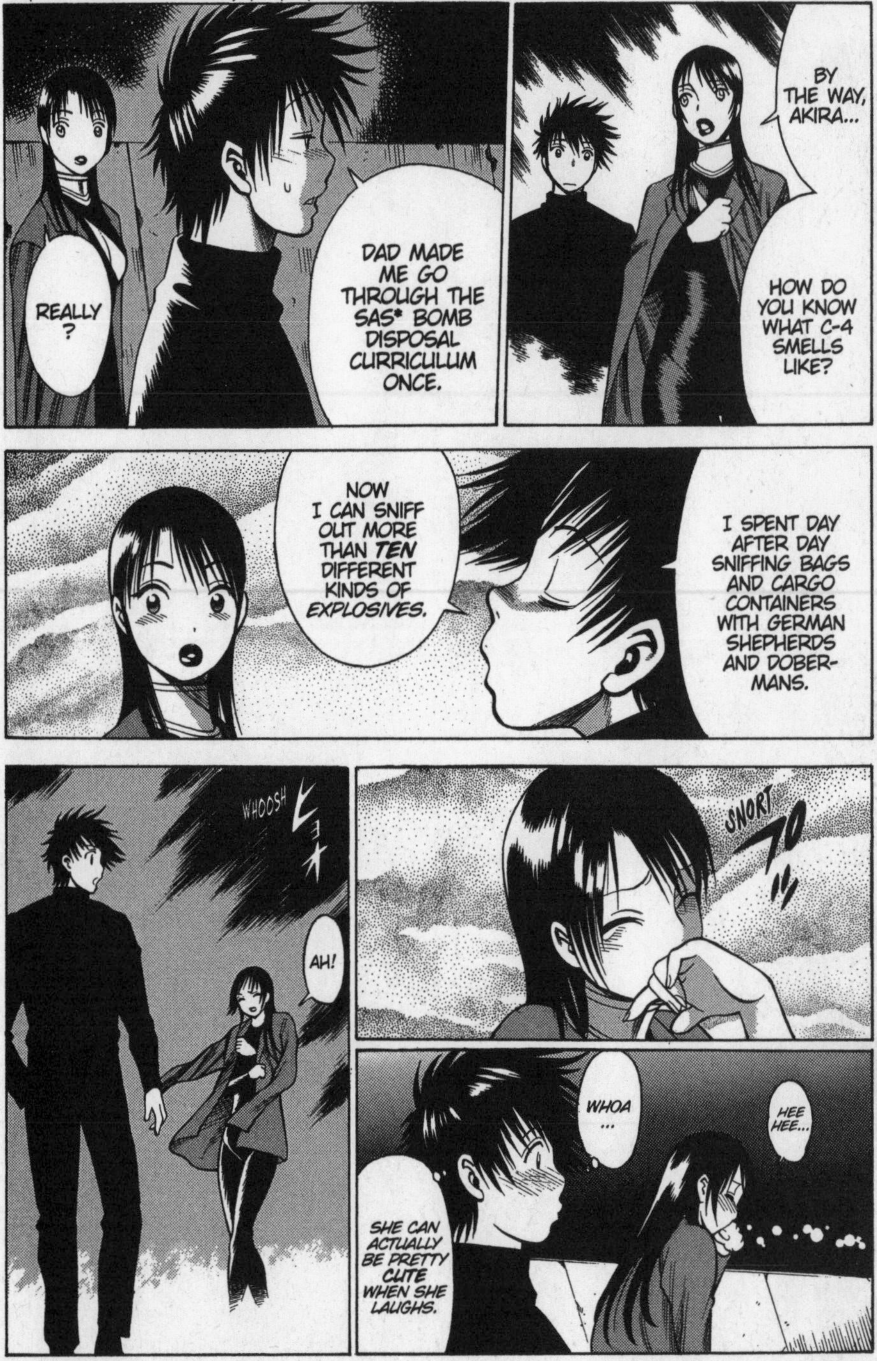
BY THE WAY, AKIRA...
HOW DO YOU KNOW WHAT C-4 SMELLS LIKE?
DAD MADE ME GO THROUGH THE SAS* BOMB DISPOSAL CURRICULUM ONCE.
REALLY ?
I SPENT DAY AFTER DAY SNIFFING BAGS AND CARGO CONTAINERS WITH GERMAN SHEPHERDS AND DOBER-MANS.
NOW I CAN SNIFF OUT MORE THAN TEN DIFFERENT KINDS OF EXPLOSIVES.
SNORT
HEE HEE...
WHOA ...
SHE CAN ACTUALLY BE PRETTY CUTE WHEN SHE LAUGHS.
WHOOSH
AH!

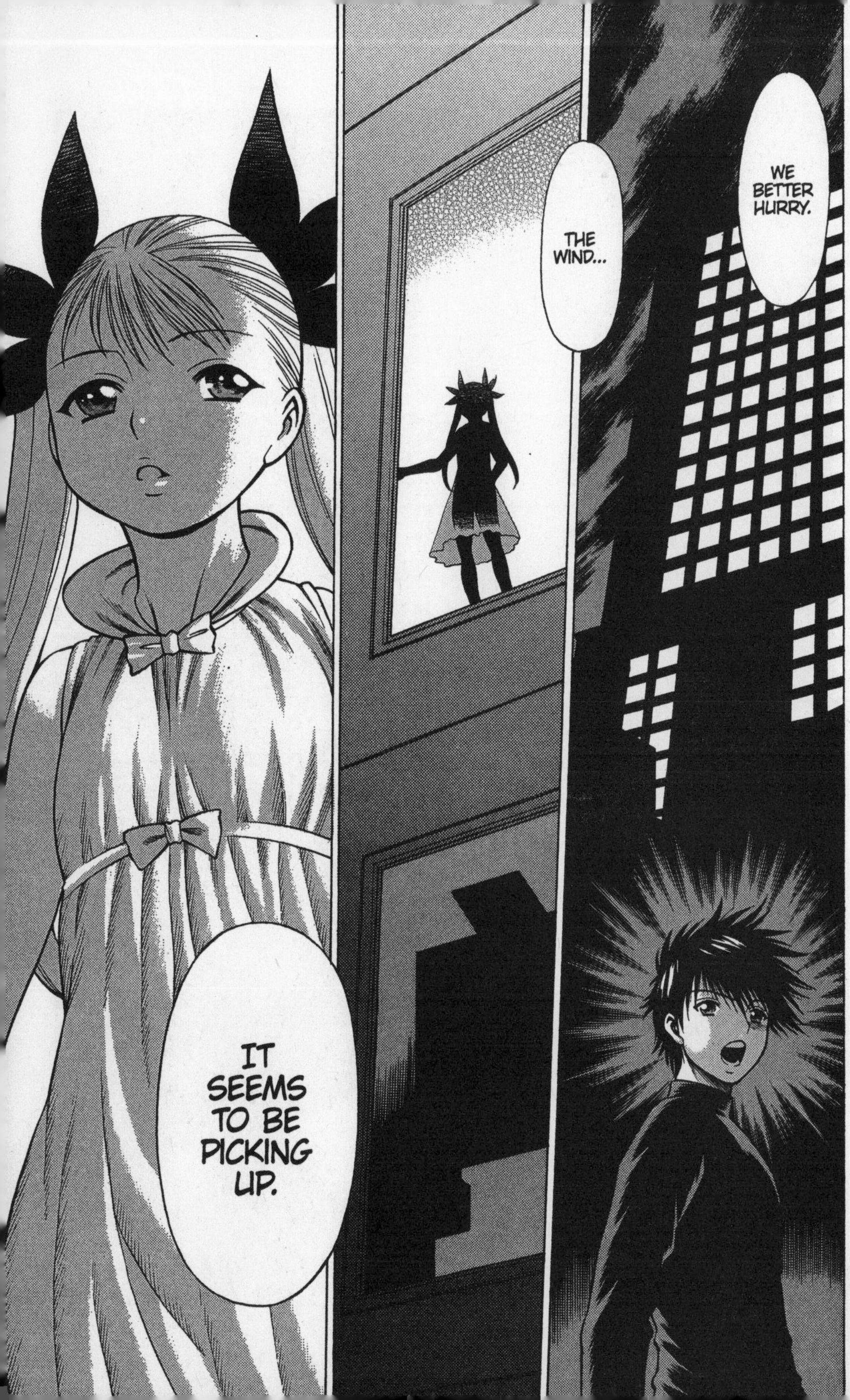
WE BETTER HURRY.
THE WIND...
IT SEEMS TO BE PICKING UP.

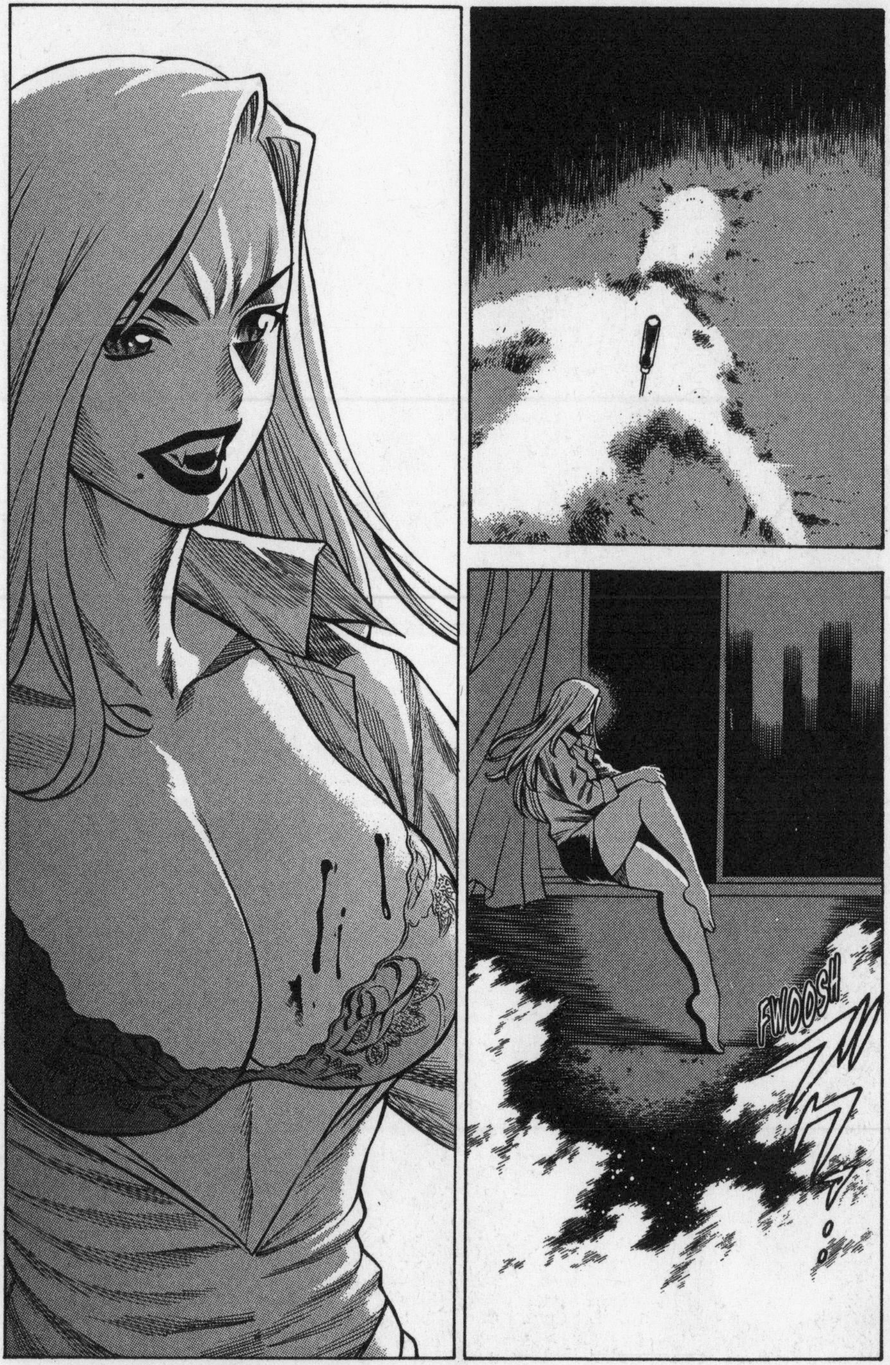
FWOOSH

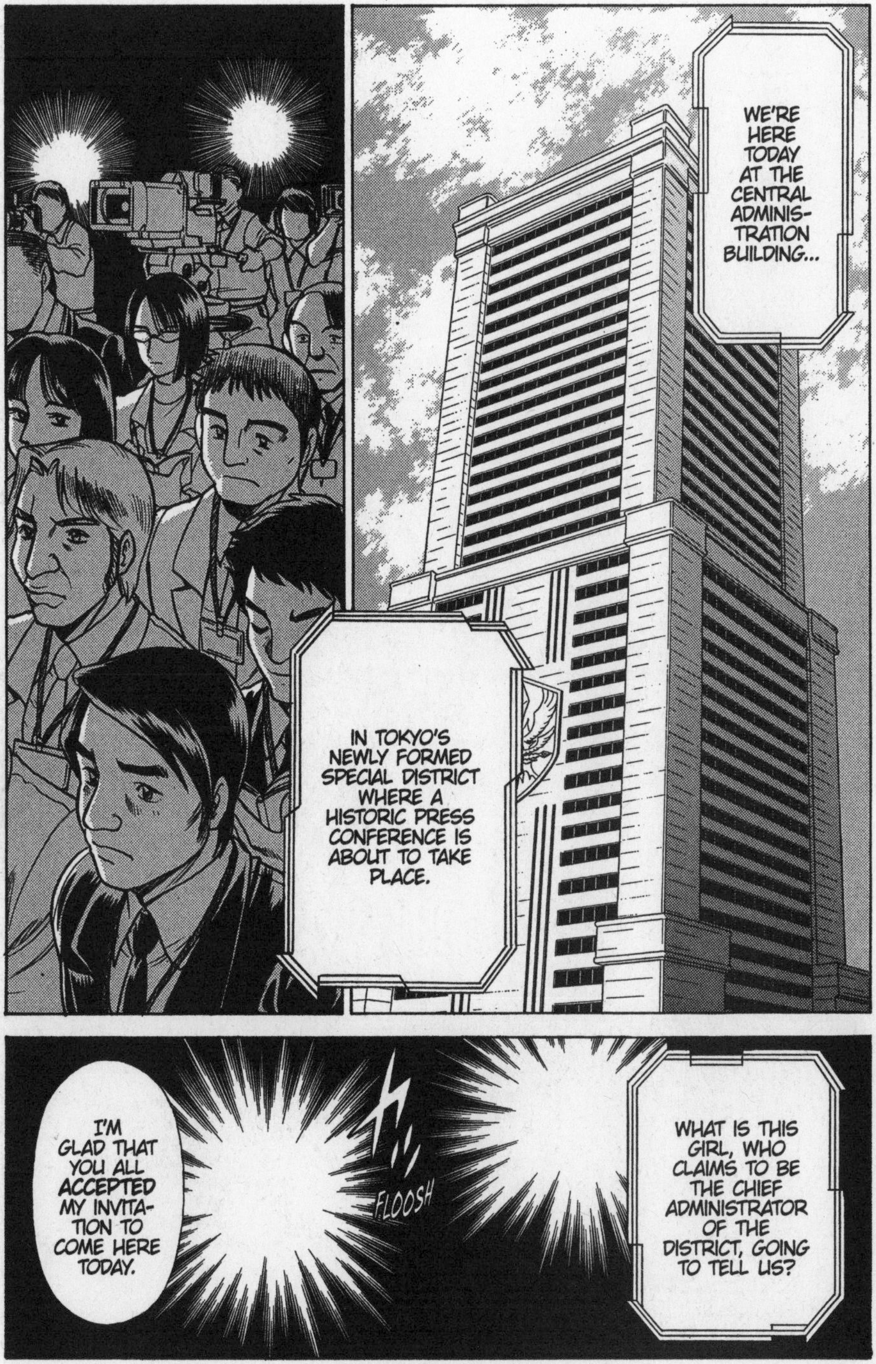
WE'RE HERE TODAY AT THE CENTRAL ADMINIS-TRATION BUILDING...
IN TOKYO'S NEWLY FORMED SPECIAL DISTRICT WHERE A HISTORIC PRESS CONFERENCE IS ABOUT TO TAKE PLACE.
WHAT IS THIS GIRL, WHO CLAIMS TO BE THE CHIEF ADMINISTRATOR OF THE DISTRICT, GOING TO TELL US?
FLOOSH
I'M GLAD THAT YOU ALL ACCEPTED MY INVITA-TION TO COME HERE TODAY.

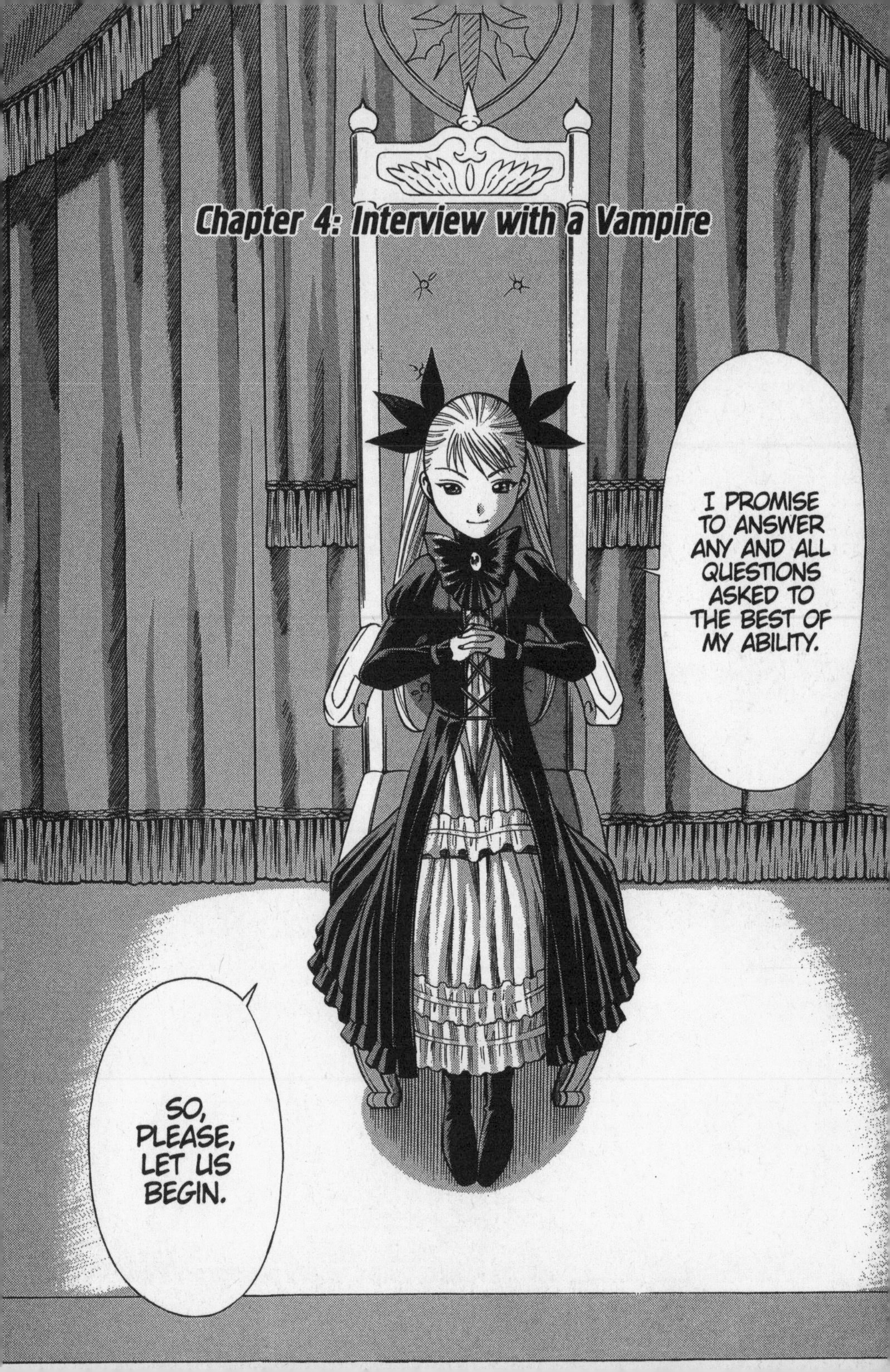
Chapter 4: Interview with a Vampire
I PROMISE TO ANSWER ANY AND ALL QUESTIONS ASKED TO THE BEST OF MY ABILITY.
SO, PLEASE, LET US BEGIN.

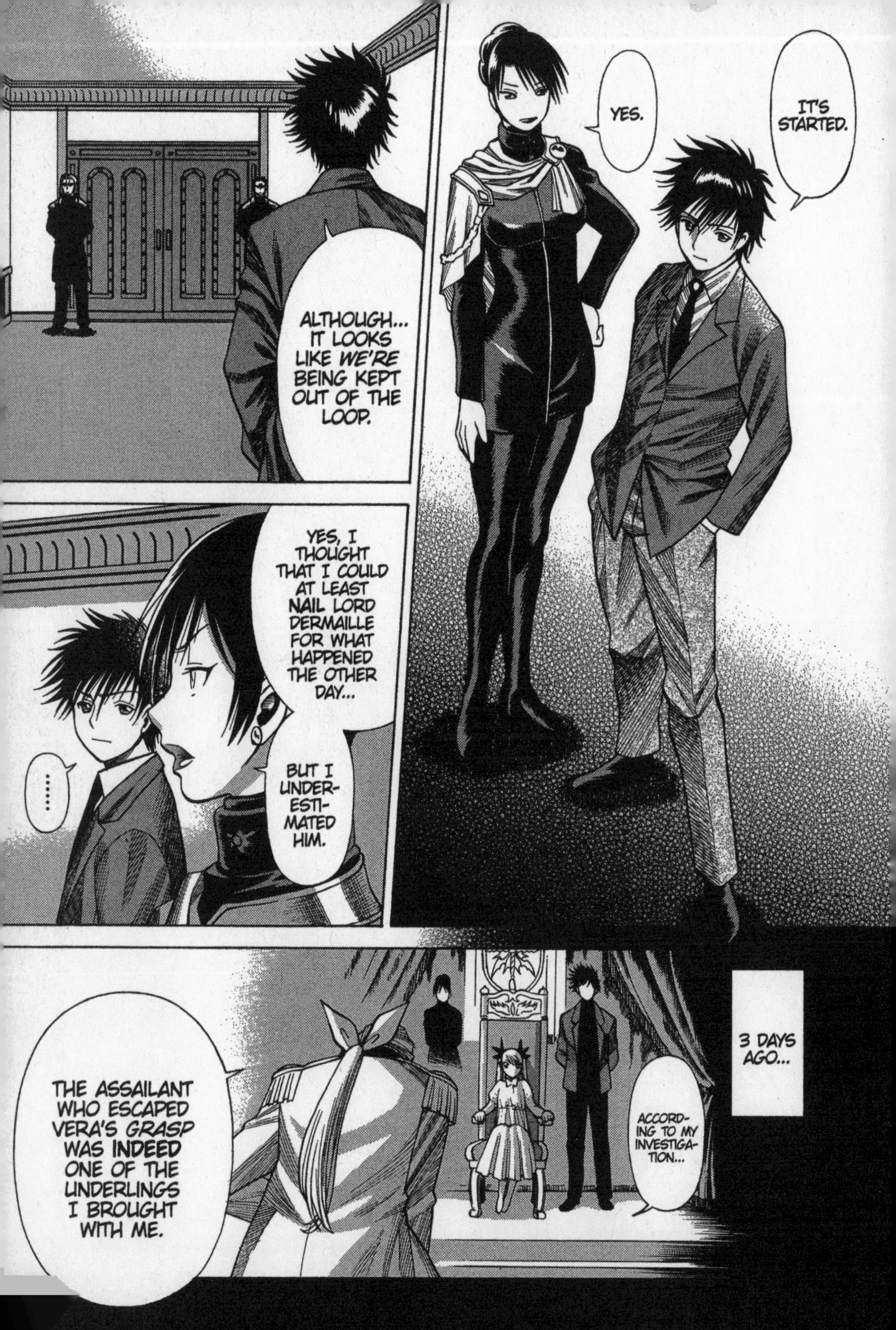
IT'S STARTED.
YES.
ALTHOUGH... IT LOOKS LIKE WE'RE BEING KEPT OUT OF THE LOOP.
YES, I THOUGHT THAT I COULD AT LEAST NAIL LORD DERMAILLE FOR WHAT HAPPENED THE OTHER DAY...
BUT I UNDER-ESTI-MATED HIM.
......
3 DAYS AGO...
ACCORD-ING TO MY INVESTIGA-TION...
THE ASSAILANT WHO ESCAPED VERA'S GRASP WAS INDEED ONE OF THE UNDERLINGS I BROUGHT WITH ME.

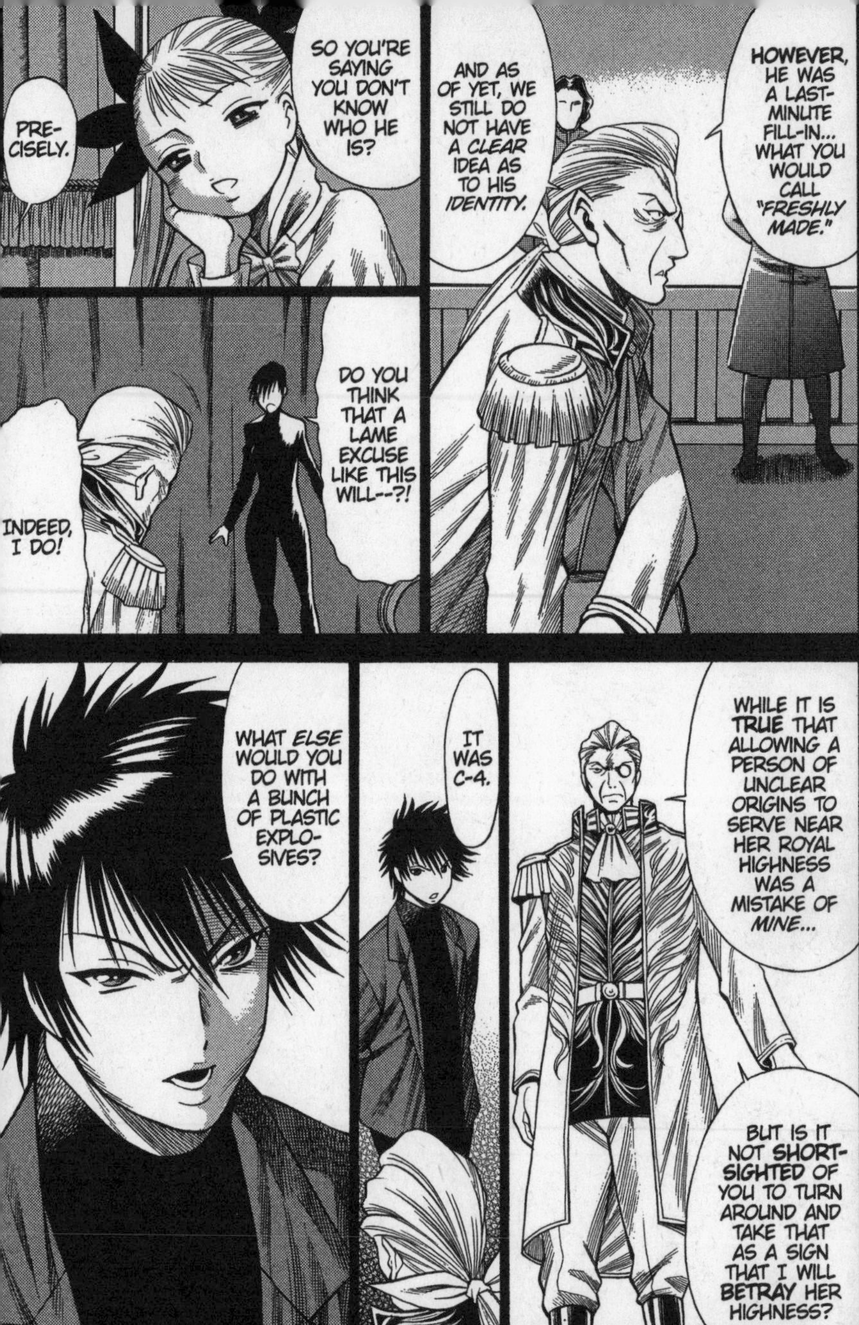
HOWEVER, HE WAS A LAST-MINUTE FILL-IN... WHAT YOU WOULD CALL "FRESHLY MADE."
AND AS OF YET, WE STILL DO NOT HAVE A CLEAR IDEA AS TO HIS IDENTITY.
SO YOU'RE SAYING YOU DON'T KNOW WHO HE IS?
PRE-CISELY.
DO YOU THINK THAT A LAME EXCUSE LIKE THIS WILL--?!
INDEED, I DO!
WHILE IT IS TRUE THAT ALLOWING A PERSON OF UNCLEAR ORIGINS TO SERVE NEAR HER ROYAL HIGHNESS WAS A MISTAKE OF MINE...
BUT IS IT NOT SHORT-SIGHTED OF YOU TO TURN AROUND AND TAKE THAT AS A SIGN THAT I WILL BETRAY HER HIGHNESS?
IT WAS C-4.
WHAT ELSE WOULD YOU DO WITH A BUNCH OF PLASTIC EXPLOSIVES?

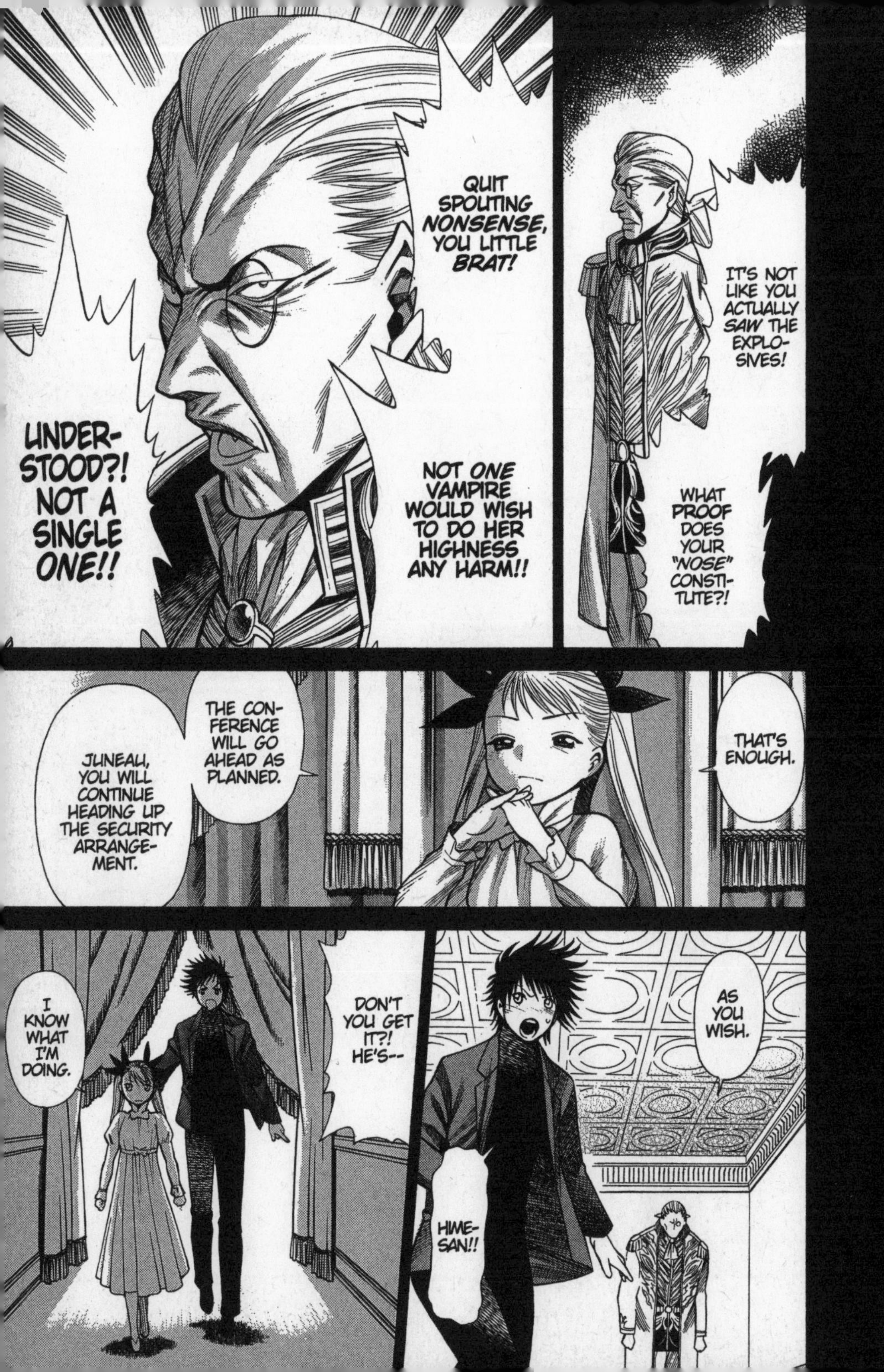
IT'S NOT LIKE YOU ACTUALLY SAW THE EXPLOSIVES!
WHAT PROOF DOES YOUR "NOSE" CONSTITUTE?!
QUIT SPOUTING NONSENSE, YOU LITTLE BRAT!
NOT ONE VAMPIRE WOULD WISH TO DO HER HIGHNESS ANY HARM!!
UNDERSTOOD?! NOT A SINGLE ONE!!
THAT'S ENOUGH.
THE CONFERENCE WILL GO AHEAD AS PLANNED.
JUNEAU, YOU WILL CONTINUE HEADING UP THE SECURITY ARRANGEMENT.
AS YOU WISH.
HIME-SAN!!
DON'T YOU GET IT?! HE'S--
I KNOW WHAT I'M DOING.

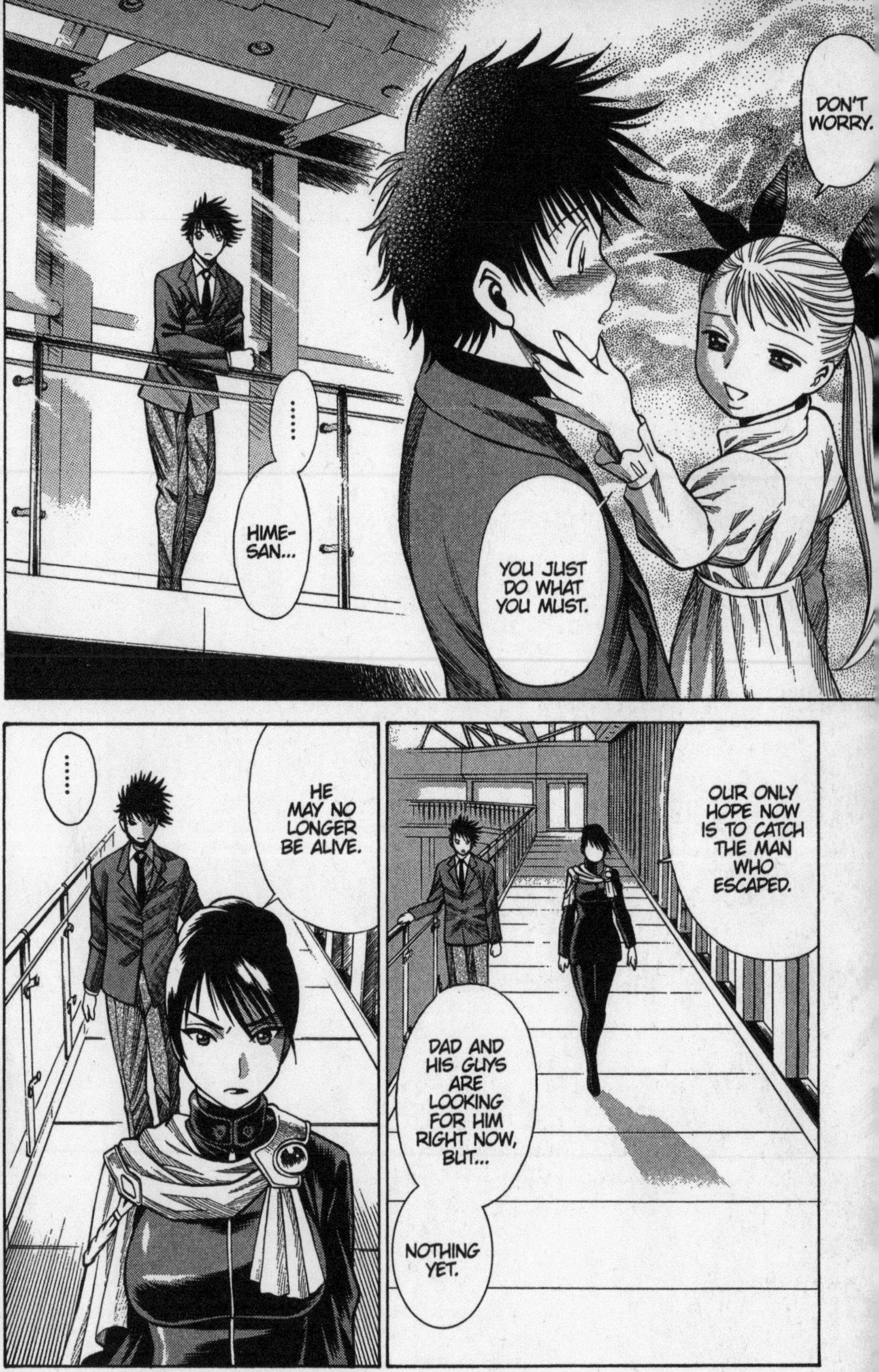
DON'T WORRY.
YOU JUST DO WHAT YOU MUST.
……
HIME-SAN...
OUR ONLY HOPE NOW IS TO CATCH THE MAN WHO ESCAPED.
DAD AND HIS GUYS ARE LOOKING FOR HIM RIGHT NOW, BUT...
NOTHING YET.
HE MAY NO LONGER BE ALIVE.
……

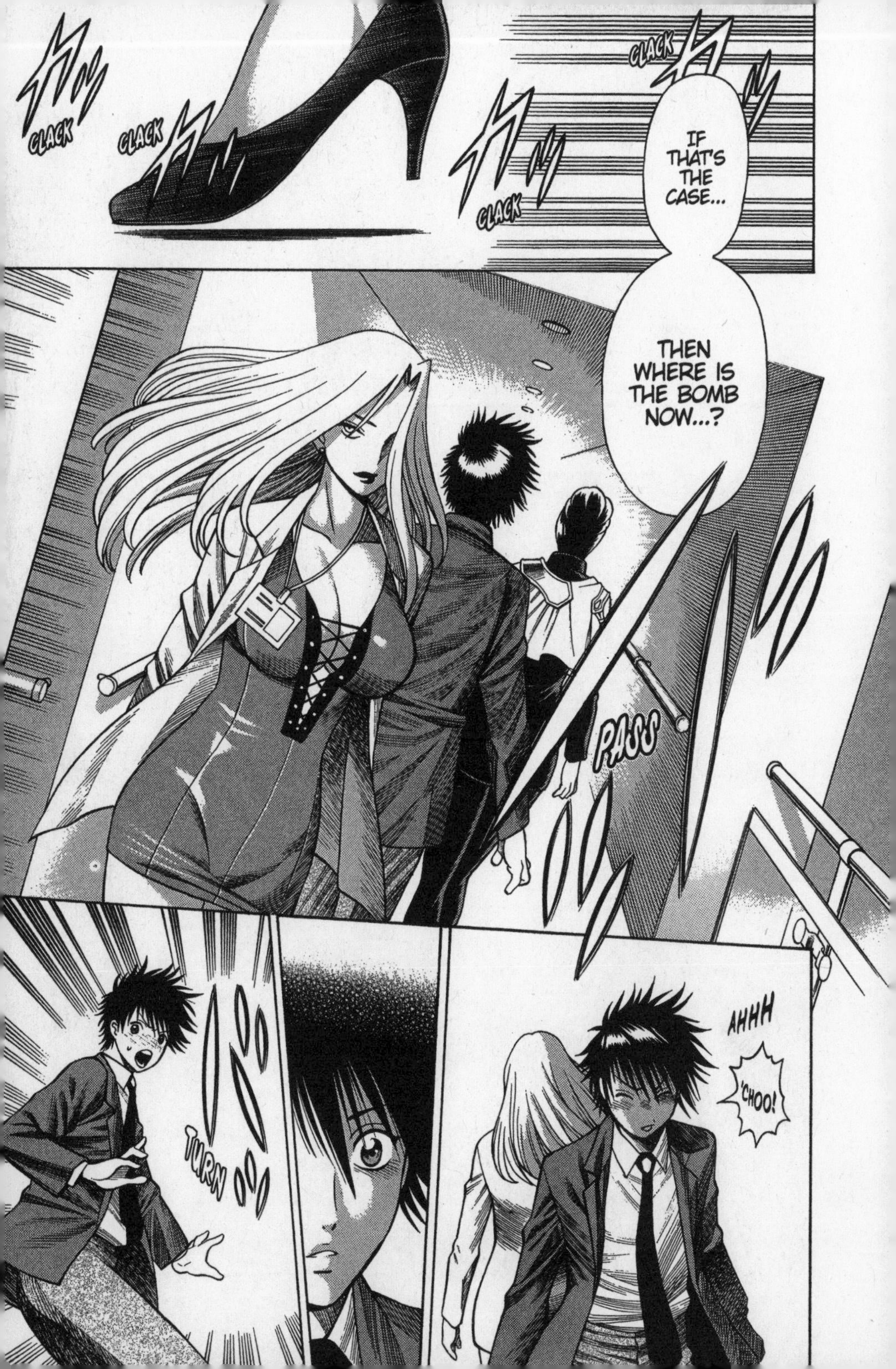
CLACK
IF THAT'S THE CASE...
CLACK
CLACK
CLACK
THEN WHERE IS THE BOMB NOW...?
PASS
AHHH
'CHOO!
TURN

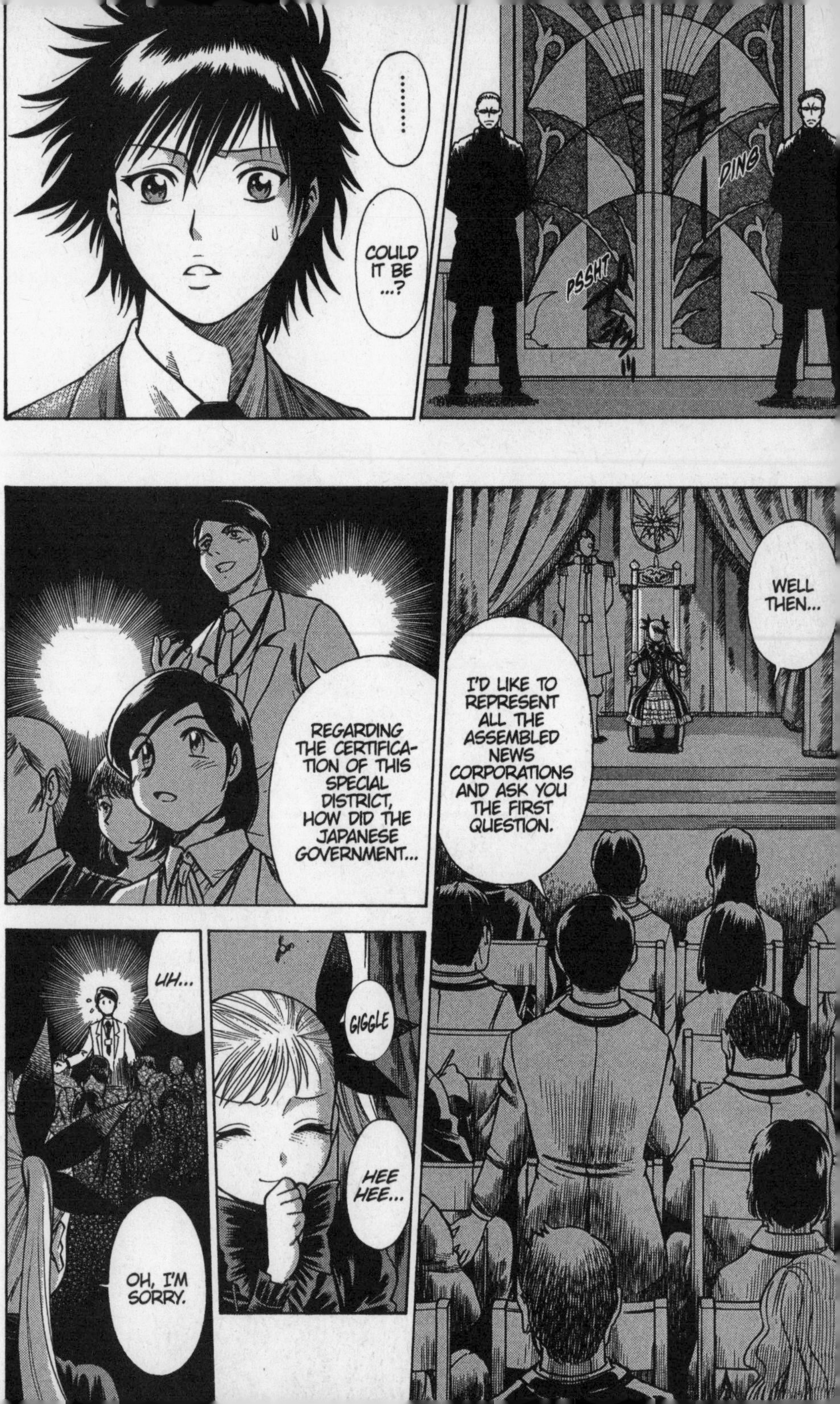
DING
PSSHT
......
COULD IT BE ...?
WELL THEN...
I'D LIKE TO REPRESENT ALL THE ASSEMBLED NEWS CORPORATIONS AND ASK YOU THE FIRST QUESTION.
REGARDING THE CERTIFICATION OF THIS SPECIAL DISTRICT, HOW DID THE JAPANESE GOVERNMENT...
GIGGLE
HEE HEE...
UH...
OH, I'M SORRY.

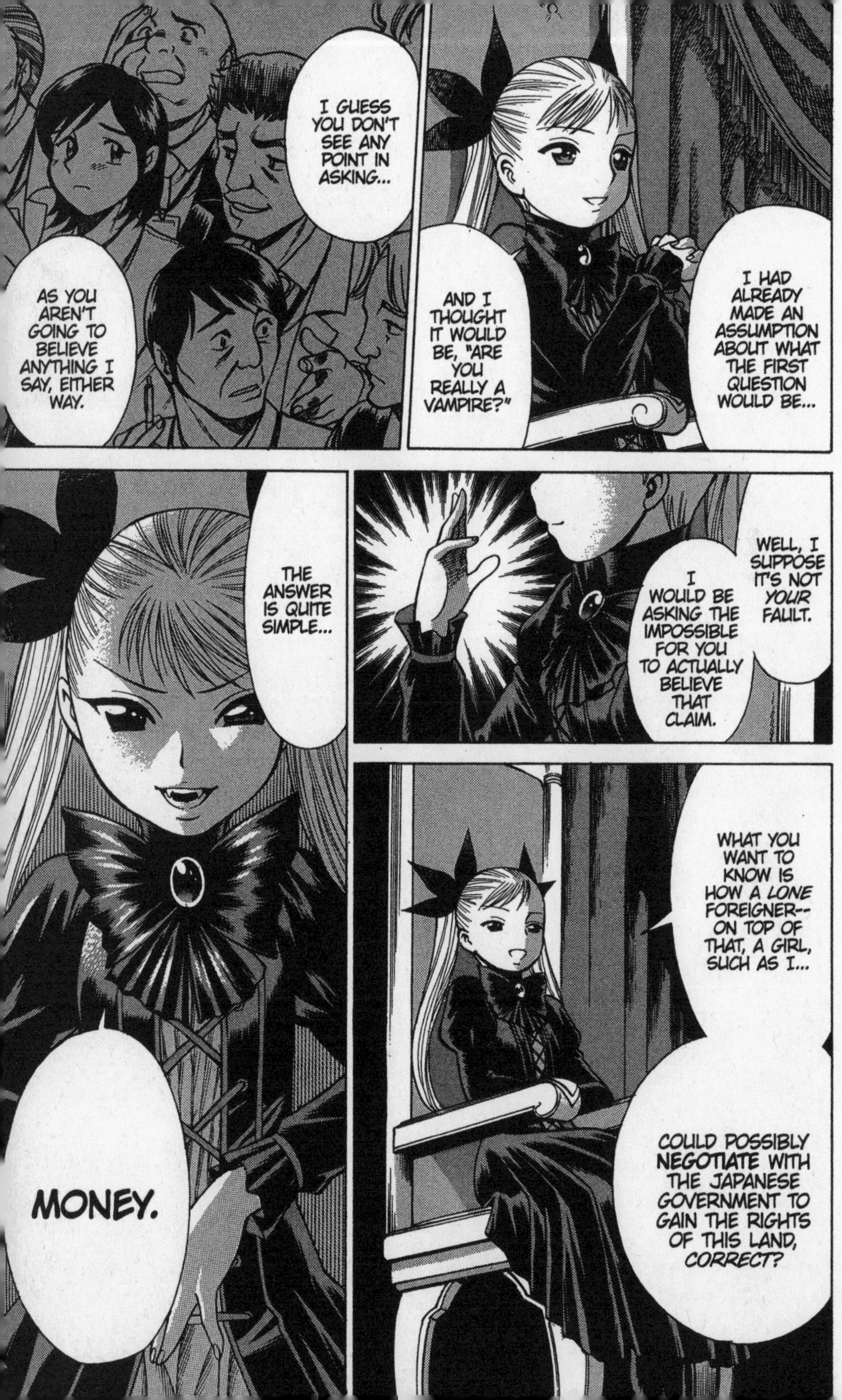
I HAD ALREADY MADE AN ASSUMPTION ABOUT WHAT THE FIRST QUESTION WOULD BE...
AND I THOUGHT IT WOULD BE, "ARE YOU REALLY A VAMPIRE?"
I GUESS YOU DON'T SEE ANY POINT IN ASKING...
AS YOU AREN'T GOING TO BELIEVE ANYTHING I SAY, EITHER WAY.
WELL, I SUPPOSE IT'S NOT *YOUR* FAULT.
I WOULD BE ASKING THE IMPOSSIBLE FOR YOU TO ACTUALLY BELIEVE THAT CLAIM.
WHAT YOU WANT TO KNOW IS HOW A *LONE* FOREIGNER-- ON TOP OF THAT, A GIRL, SUCH AS I...
COULD POSSIBLY **NEGOTIATE** WITH THE JAPANESE GOVERNMENT TO GAIN THE RIGHTS OF THIS LAND, *CORRECT?*
THE ANSWER IS QUITE SIMPLE...
MONEY.

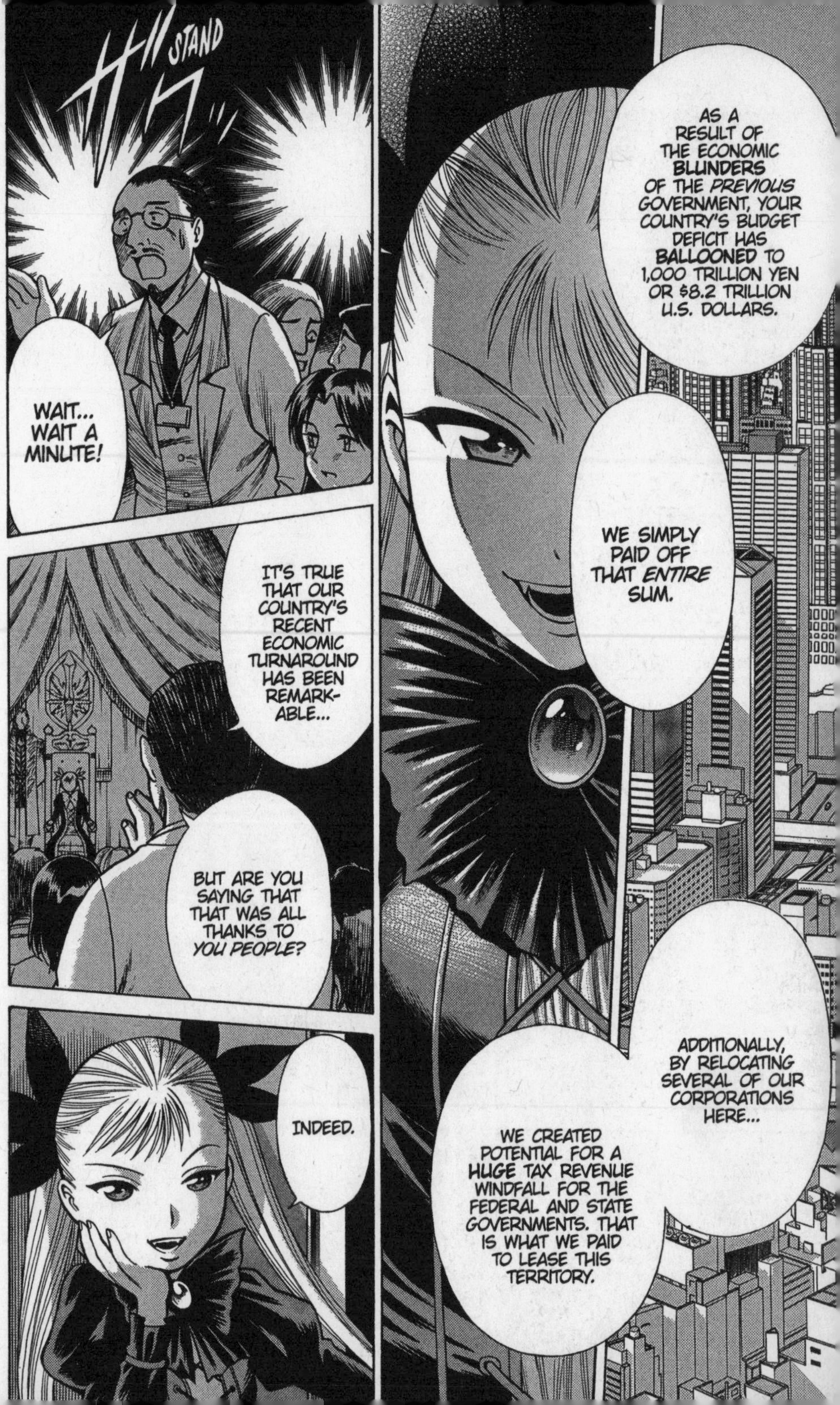
AS A RESULT OF THE ECONOMIC BLUNDERS OF THE PREVIOUS GOVERNMENT, YOUR COUNTRY'S BUDGET DEFICIT HAS BALLOONED TO 1,000 TRILLION YEN OR $8.2 TRILLION U.S. DOLLARS.
WE SIMPLY PAID OFF THAT ENTIRE SUM.
ADDITIONALLY, BY RELOCATING SEVERAL OF OUR CORPORATIONS HERE...
WE CREATED POTENTIAL FOR A HUGE TAX REVENUE WINDFALL FOR THE FEDERAL AND STATE GOVERNMENTS. THAT IS WHAT WE PAID TO LEASE THIS TERRITORY.
STAND
WAIT... WAIT A MINUTE!
IT'S TRUE THAT OUR COUNTRY'S RECENT ECONOMIC TURNAROUND HAS BEEN REMARK-ABLE...
BUT ARE YOU SAYING THAT THAT WAS ALL THANKS TO YOU PEOPLE?
INDEED.

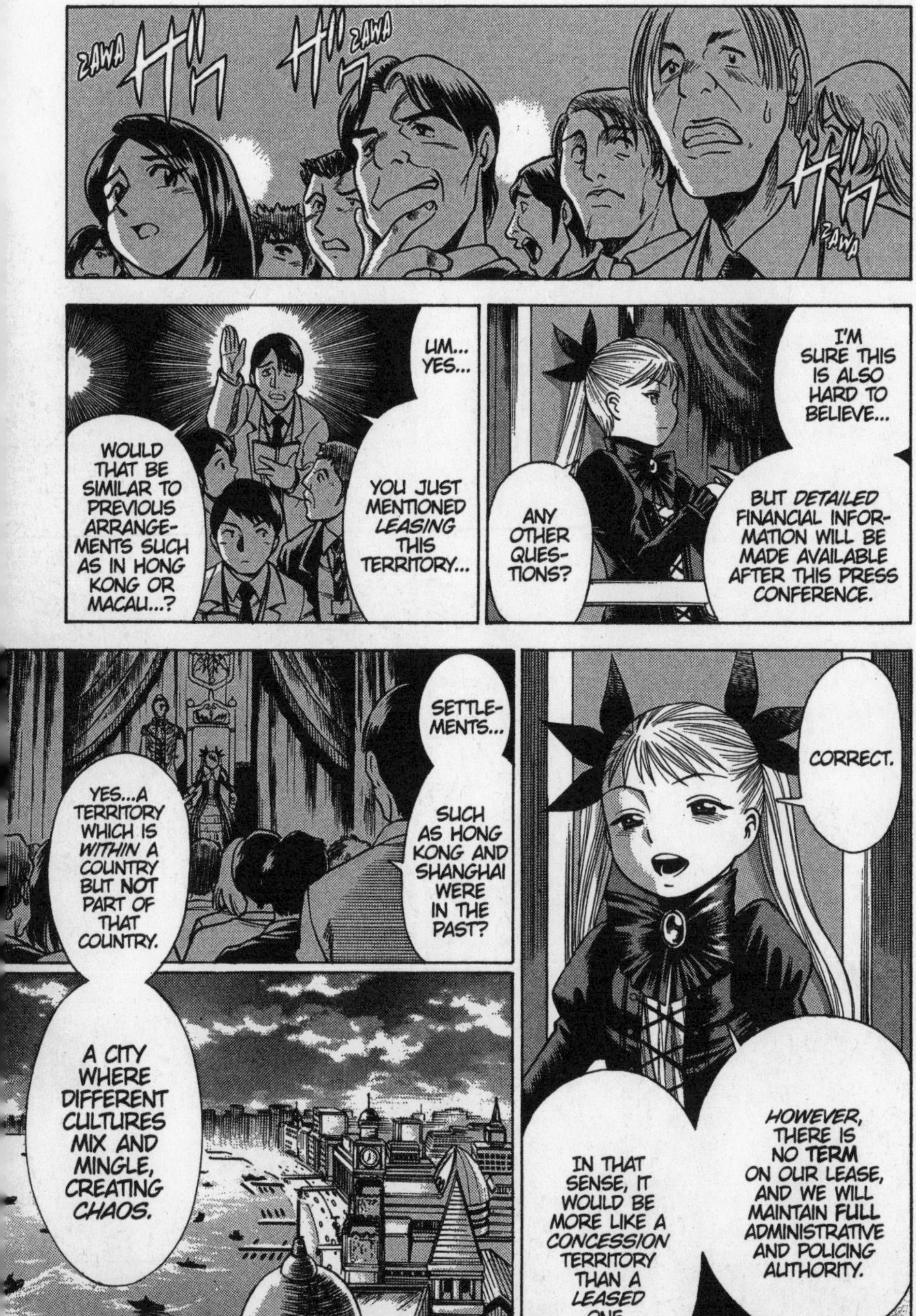
ZAWA
ZAWA
ZAWA
I'M SURE THIS IS ALSO HARD TO BELIEVE...
BUT *DETAILED* FINANCIAL INFORMATION WILL BE MADE AVAILABLE AFTER THIS PRESS CONFERENCE.
ANY OTHER QUESTIONS?
UM... YES...
YOU JUST MENTIONED *LEASING* THIS TERRITORY...
WOULD THAT BE SIMILAR TO PREVIOUS ARRANGEMENTS SUCH AS IN HONG KONG OR MACAU...?
CORRECT.
HOWEVER, THERE IS NO TERM ON OUR LEASE, AND WE WILL MAINTAIN FULL ADMINISTRATIVE AND POLICING AUTHORITY.
IN THAT SENSE, IT WOULD BE MORE LIKE A *CONCESSION* TERRITORY THAN A *LEASED* ONE.
SETTLEMENTS...
SUCH AS HONG KONG AND SHANGHAI WERE IN THE PAST?
YES...A TERRITORY WHICH IS *WITHIN* A COUNTRY BUT NOT PART OF THAT COUNTRY.
A CITY WHERE DIFFERENT CULTURES MIX AND MINGLE, CREATING *CHAOS*.

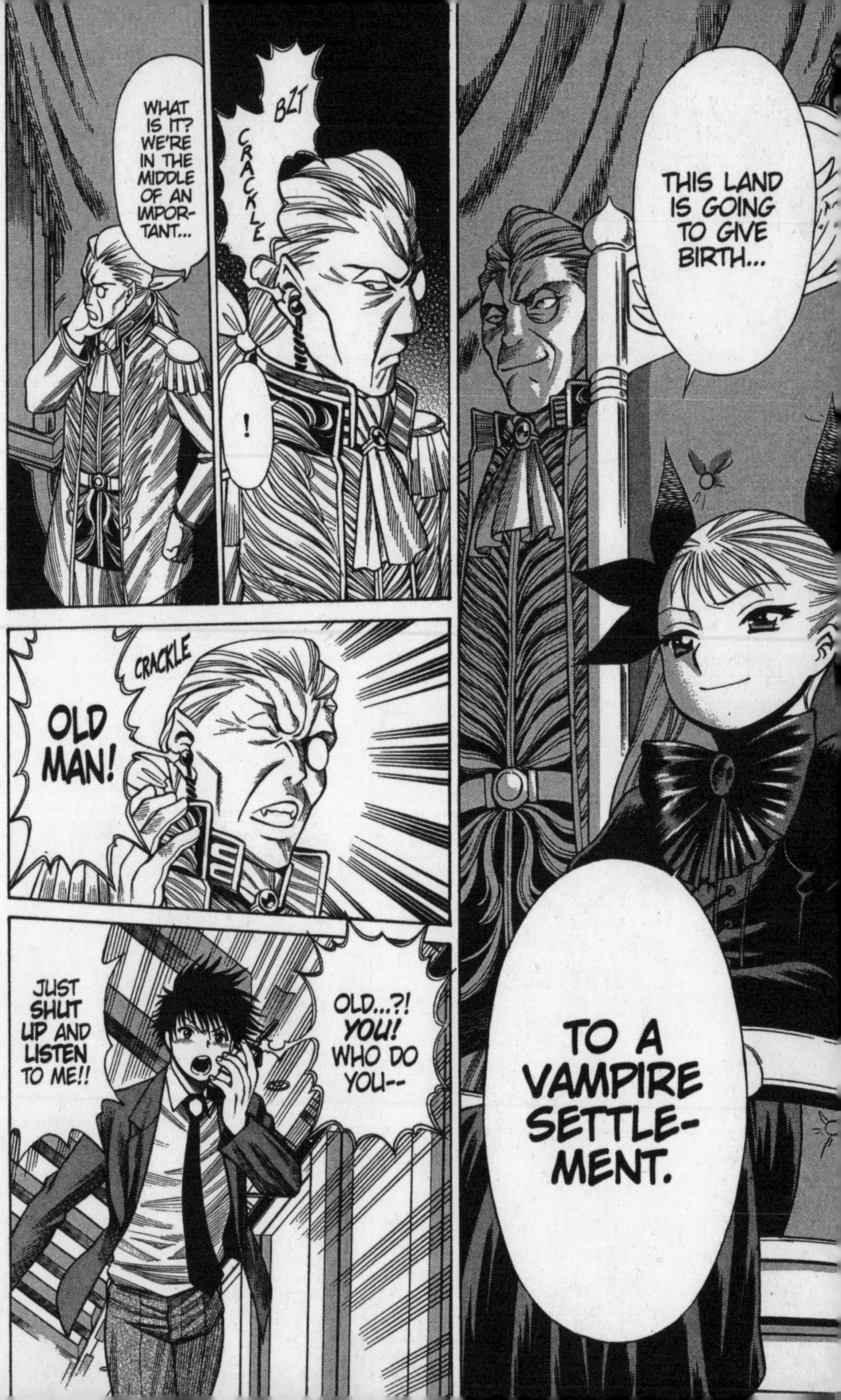
THIS LAND IS GOING TO GIVE BIRTH...
TO A VAMPIRE SETTLE-MENT.
BZT
CRACKLE
!
WHAT IS IT? WE'RE IN THE MIDDLE OF AN IMPOR-TANT...
CRACKLE
OLD MAN!
OLD...?! YOU! WHO DO YOU--
JUST SHUT UP AND LISTEN TO ME!!

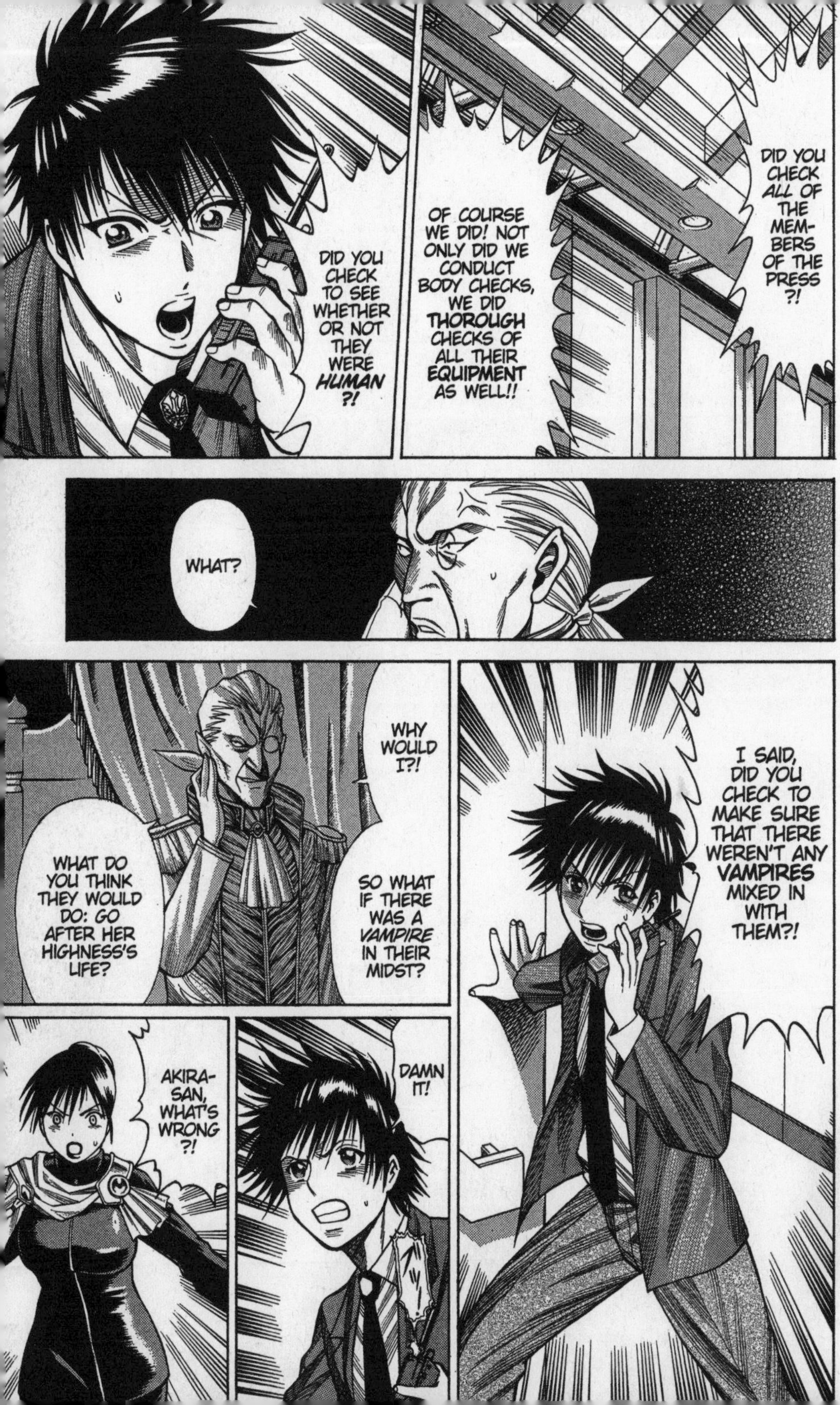
DID YOU CHECK ALL OF THE MEMBERS OF THE PRESS?!
OF COURSE WE DID! NOT ONLY DID WE CONDUCT BODY CHECKS, WE DID THOROUGH CHECKS OF ALL THEIR EQUIPMENT AS WELL!!
DID YOU CHECK TO SEE WHETHER OR NOT THEY WERE HUMAN?!
WHAT?
I SAID, DID YOU CHECK TO MAKE SURE THAT THERE WEREN'T ANY VAMPIRES MIXED IN WITH THEM?!
WHY WOULD I?!
SO WHAT IF THERE WAS A VAMPIRE IN THEIR MIDST?
WHAT DO YOU THINK THEY WOULD DO: GO AFTER HER HIGHNESS'S LIFE?
DAMN IT!
AKIRA-SAN, WHAT'S WRONG?!

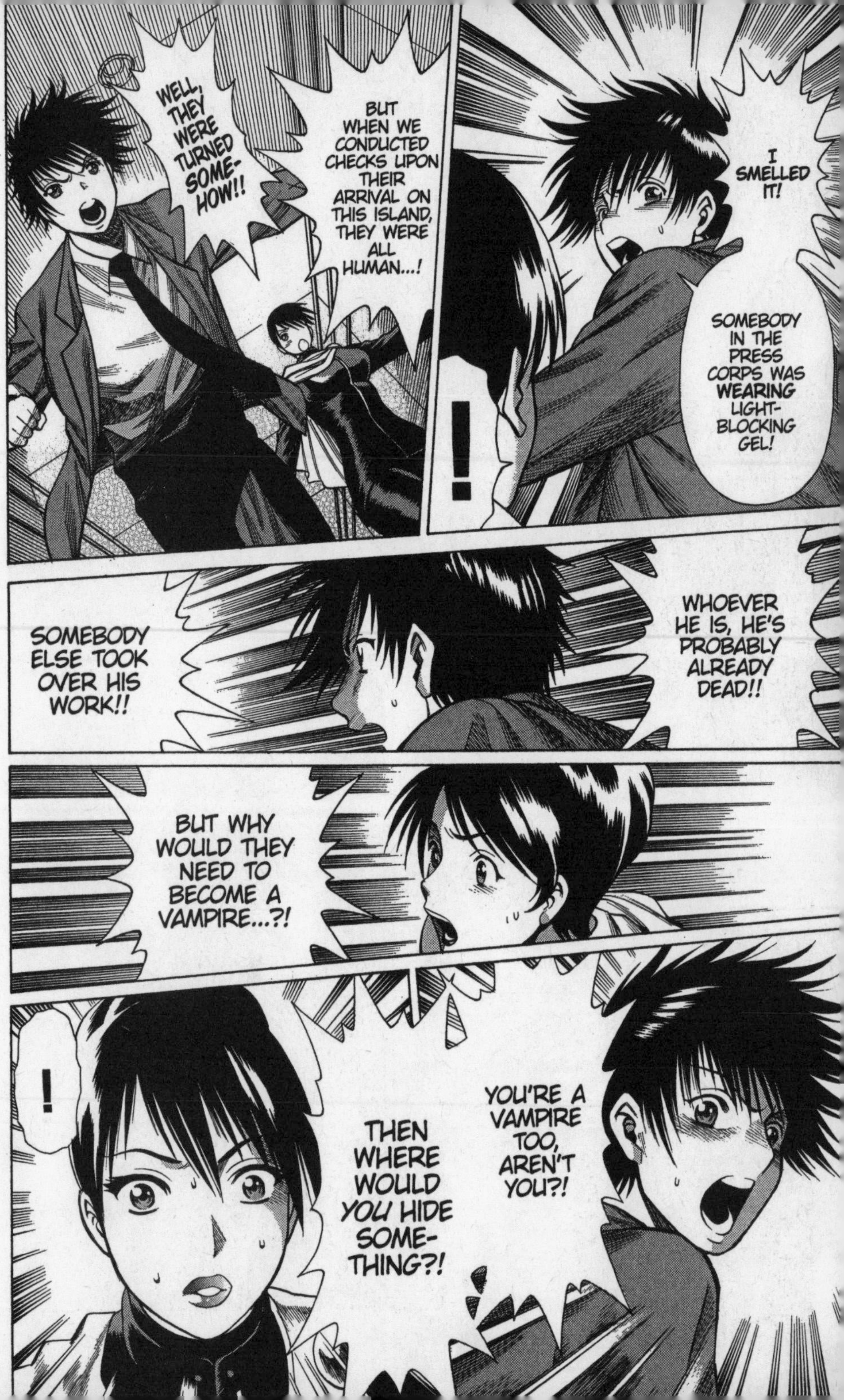
I SMELLED IT!
SOMEBODY IN THE PRESS CORPS WAS WEARING LIGHT-BLOCKING GEL!
!
BUT WHEN WE CONDUCTED CHECKS UPON THEIR ARRIVAL ON THIS ISLAND, THEY WERE ALL HUMAN...!
WELL, THEY WERE TURNED SOME-HOW!!
WHOEVER HE IS, HE'S PROBABLY ALREADY DEAD!!
SOMEBODY ELSE TOOK OVER HIS WORK!!
BUT WHY WOULD THEY NEED TO BECOME A VAMPIRE...?!
YOU'RE A VAMPIRE TOO, AREN'T YOU?!
THEN WHERE WOULD *YOU* HIDE SOME-THING?!
!

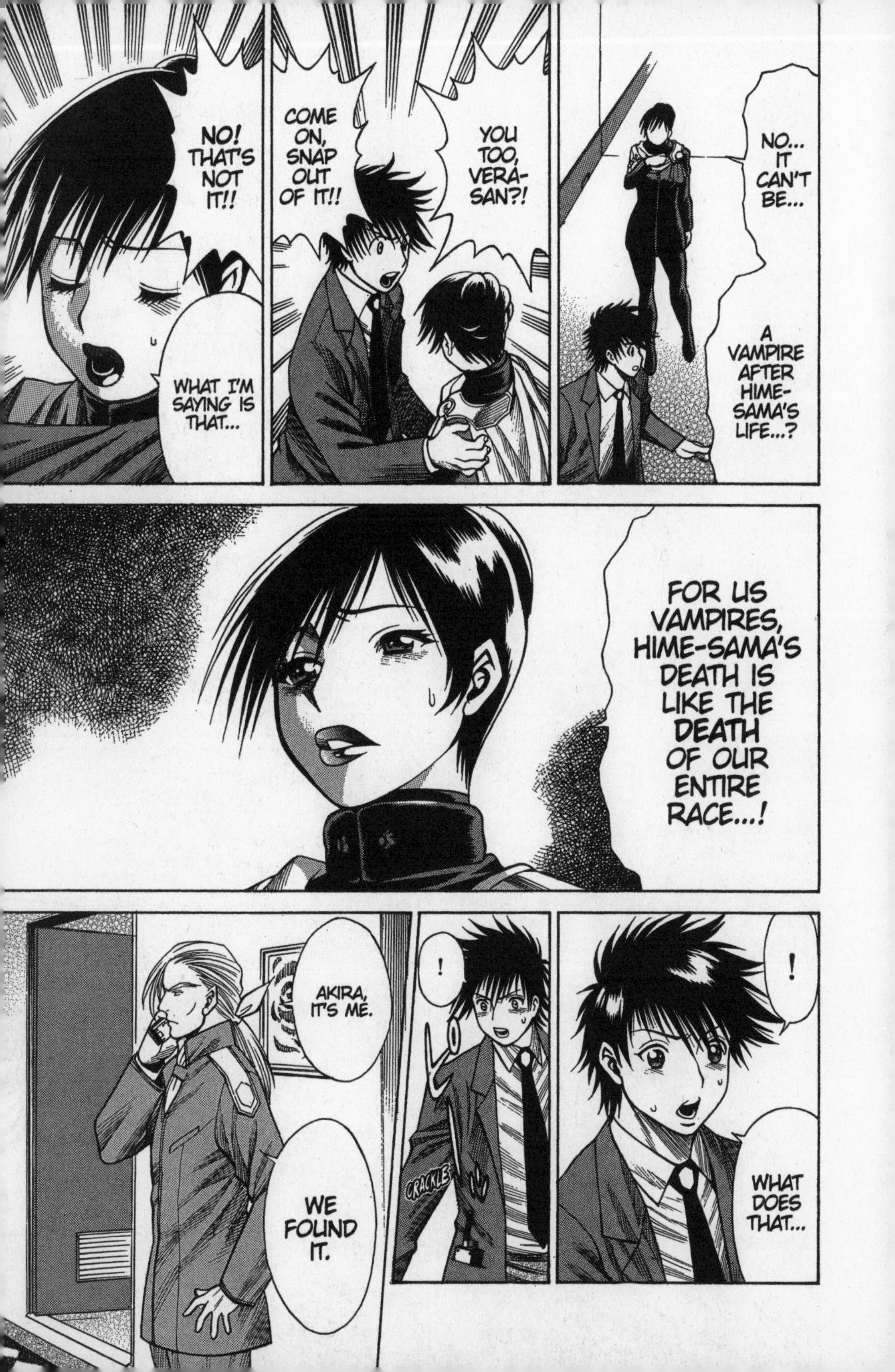
NO... IT CAN'T BE...
A VAMPIRE AFTER HIME-SAMA'S LIFE...?
YOU TOO, VERA-SAN?!
COME ON, SNAP OUT OF IT!!
NO! THAT'S NOT IT!!
WHAT I'M SAYING IS THAT...
FOR US VAMPIRES, HIME-SAMA'S DEATH IS LIKE THE DEATH OF OUR ENTIRE RACE...!
!
WHAT DOES THAT...
!
CRACKLE
AKIRA, IT'S ME.
WE FOUND IT.

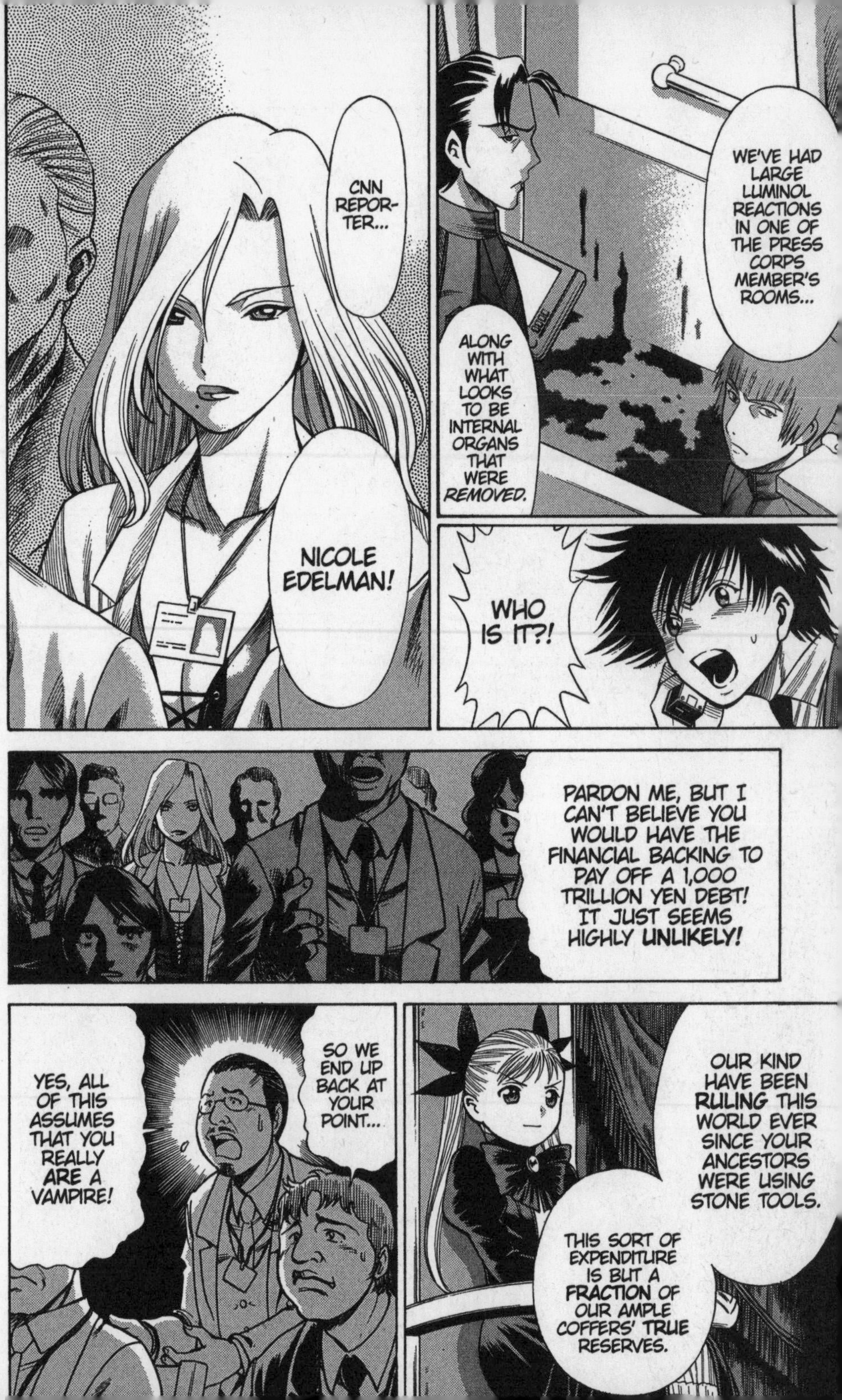
WE'VE HAD LARGE LUMINOL REACTIONS IN ONE OF THE PRESS CORPS MEMBER'S ROOMS...
ALONG WITH WHAT LOOKS TO BE INTERNAL ORGANS THAT WERE *REMOVED.*
WHO IS IT?!
CNN REPORTER...
NICOLE EDELMAN!
PARDON ME, BUT I CAN'T BELIEVE YOU WOULD HAVE THE FINANCIAL BACKING TO PAY OFF A 1,000 TRILLION YEN DEBT! IT JUST SEEMS HIGHLY **UNLIKELY!**
OUR KIND HAVE BEEN **RULING** THIS WORLD EVER SINCE YOUR ANCESTORS WERE USING STONE TOOLS.
THIS SORT OF EXPENDITURE IS BUT A **FRACTION** OF OUR AMPLE COFFERS' TRUE RESERVES.
SO WE END UP BACK AT YOUR POINT...
YES, ALL OF THIS ASSUMES THAT YOU REALLY **ARE** A VAMPIRE!

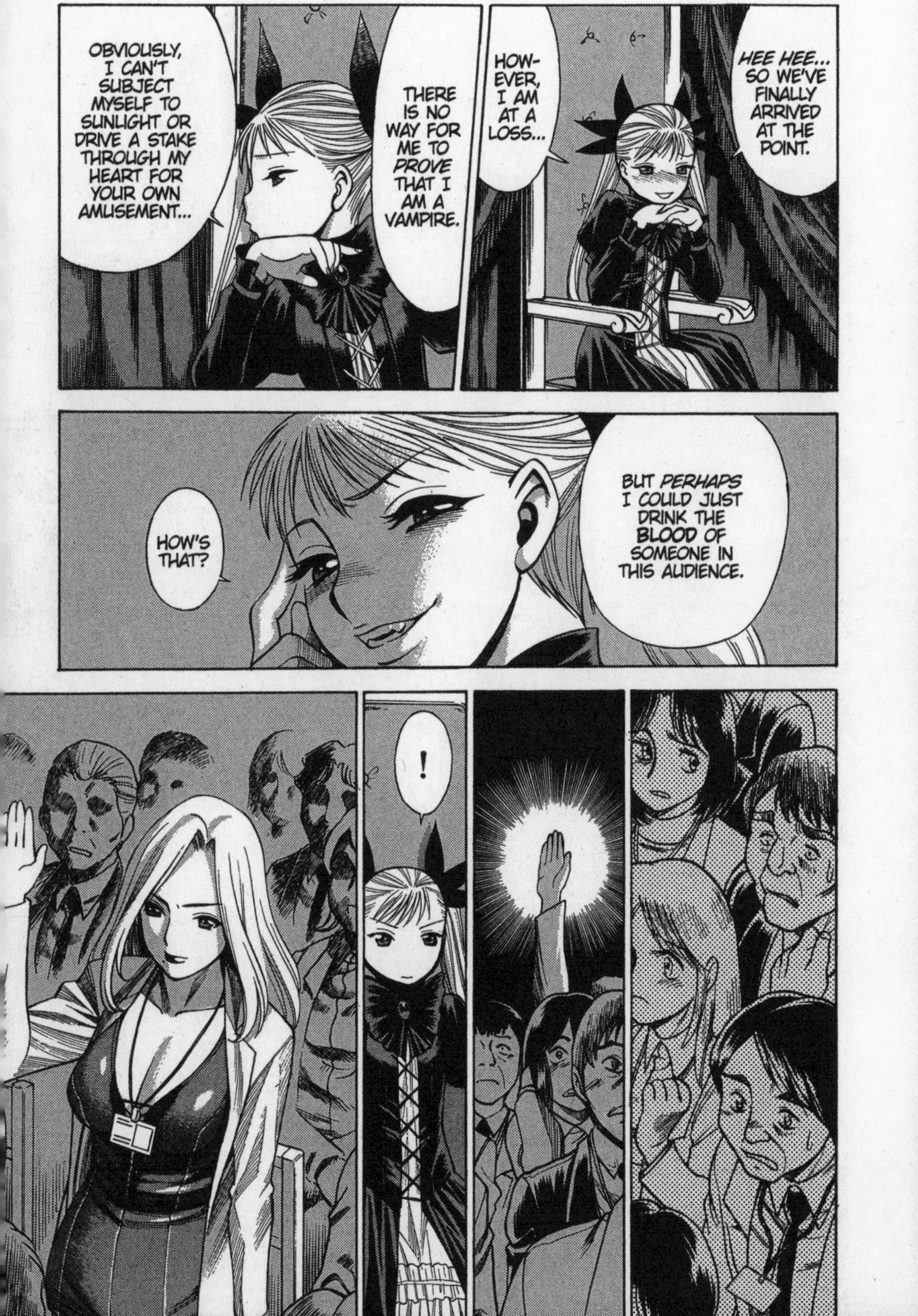
HEE HEE... SO WE'VE FINALLY ARRIVED AT THE POINT.
HOW-EVER, I AM AT A LOSS...
THERE IS NO WAY FOR ME TO *PROVE* THAT I AM A VAMPIRE.
OBVIOUSLY, I CAN'T SUBJECT MYSELF TO SUNLIGHT OR DRIVE A STAKE THROUGH MY HEART FOR YOUR OWN AMUSEMENT...
BUT *PERHAPS* I COULD JUST DRINK THE **BLOOD** OF SOMEONE IN THIS AUDIENCE.
HOW'S THAT?
!

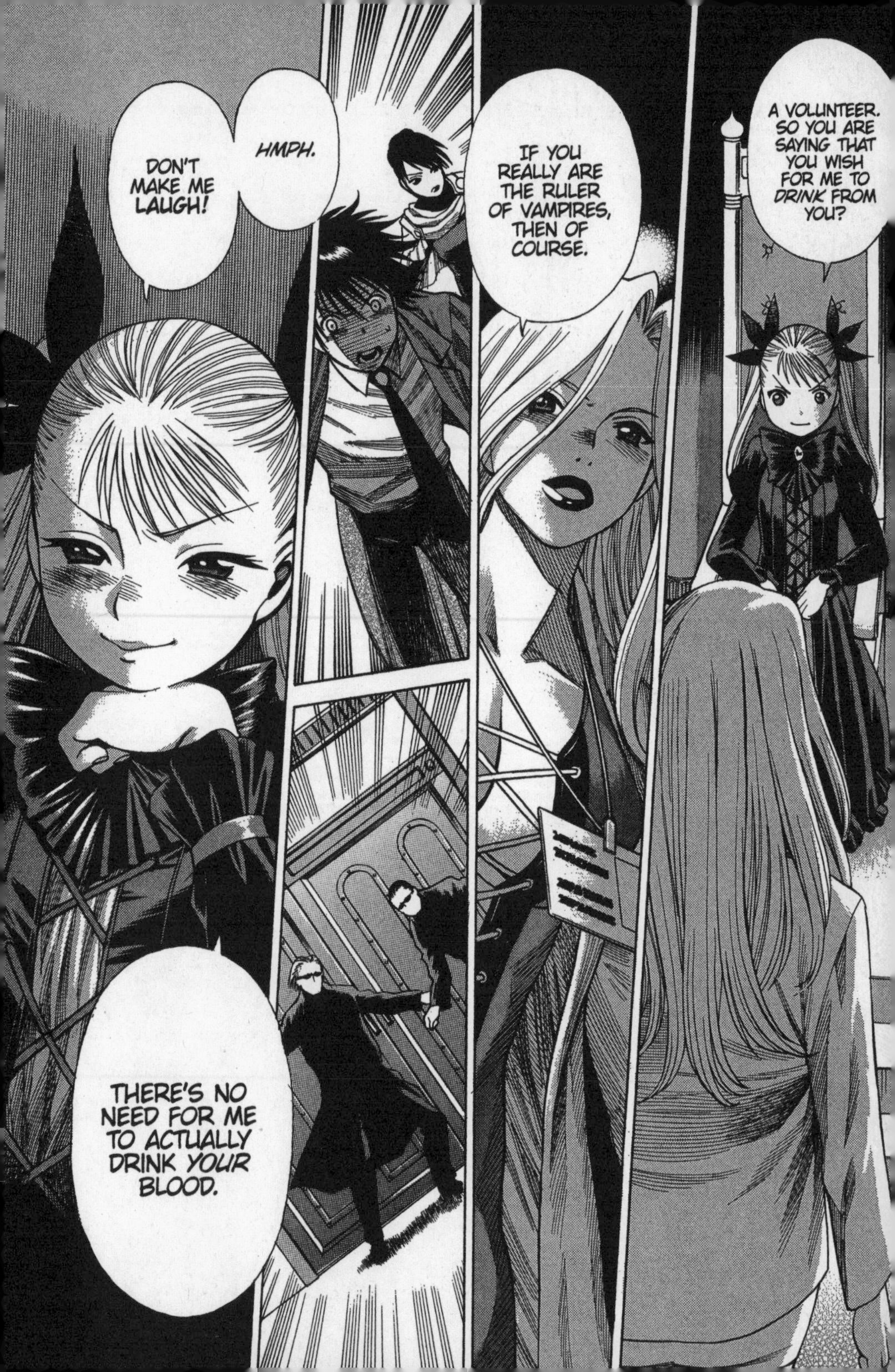
A VOLUNTEER. SO YOU ARE SAYING THAT YOU WISH FOR ME TO *DRINK* FROM YOU?
IF YOU REALLY ARE THE RULER OF VAMPIRES, THEN OF COURSE.
HMPH.
DON'T MAKE ME LAUGH!
THERE'S NO NEED FOR ME TO ACTUALLY DRINK *YOUR* BLOOD.

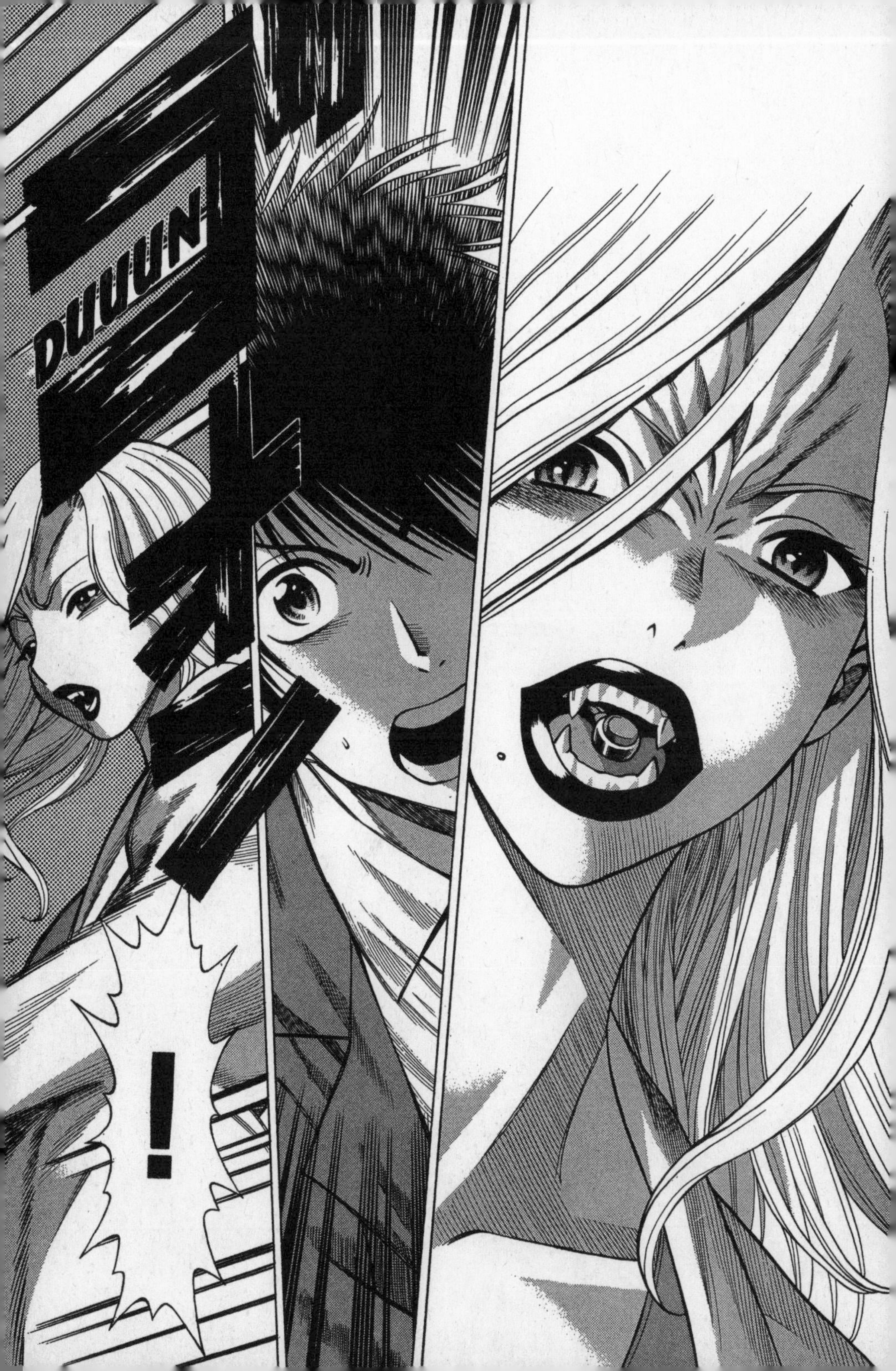
DUUUN
!

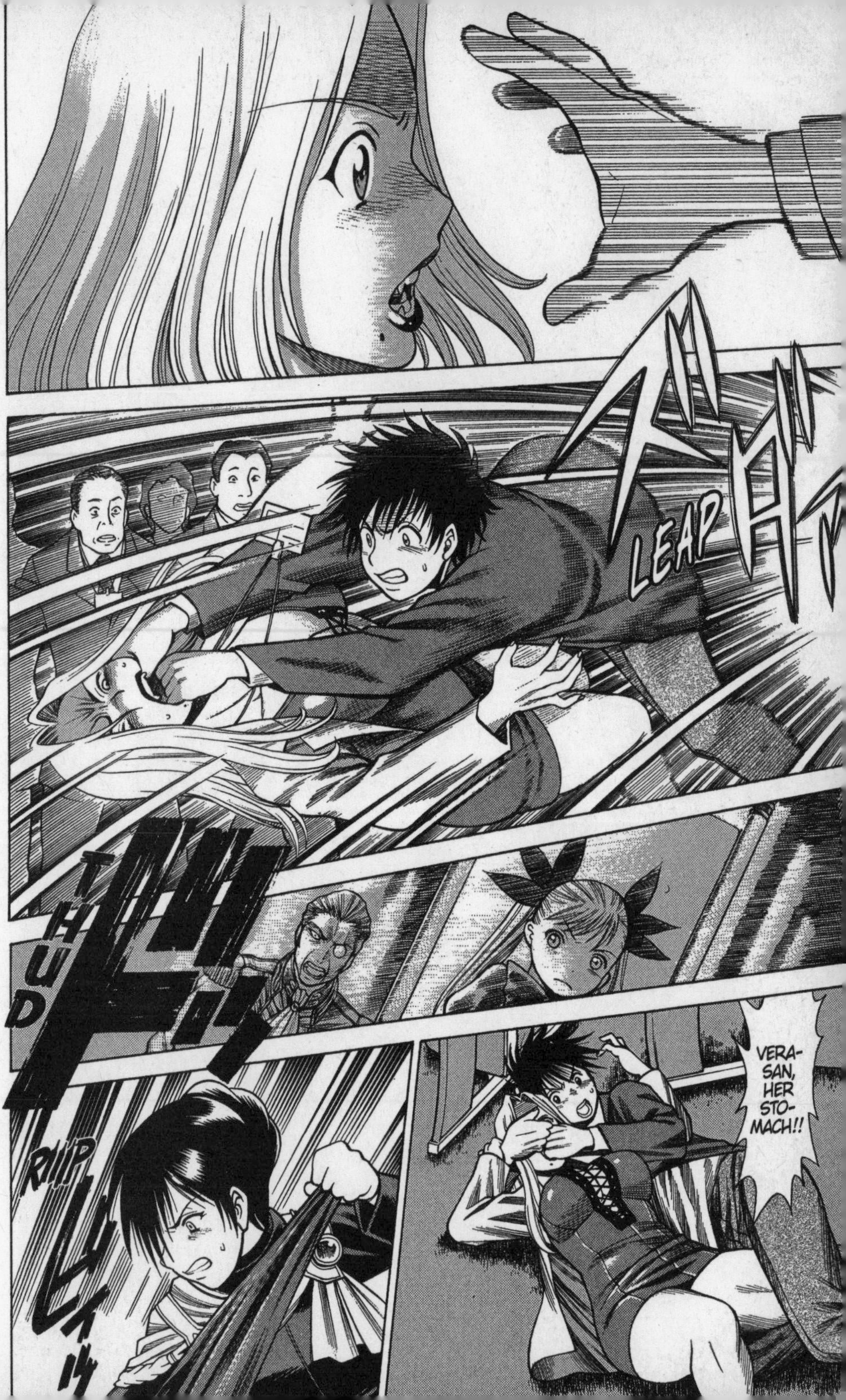
LEAP
THUD
VERA-SAN, HER STO-MACH!!
RIIP

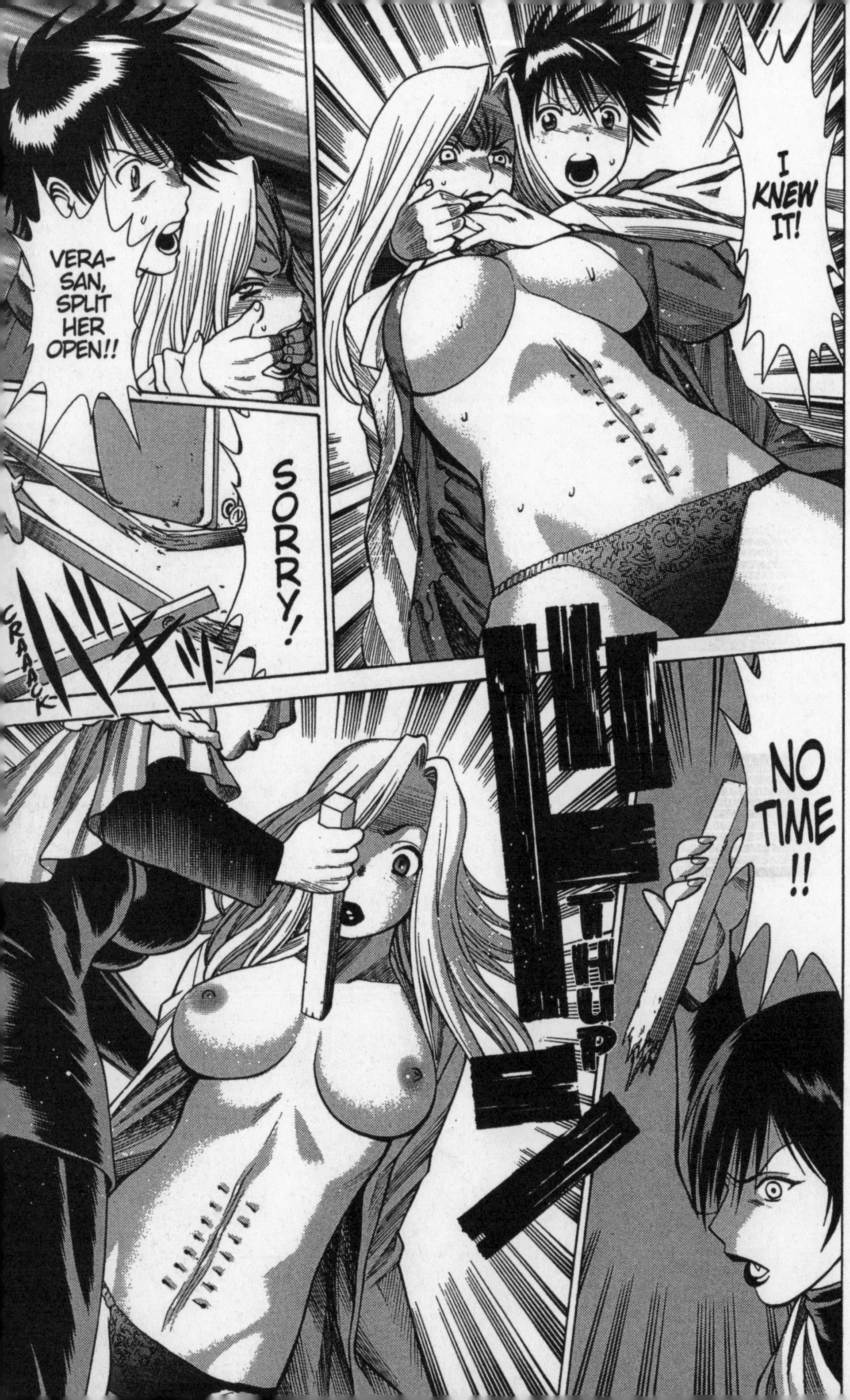
I KNEW IT!
VERA-SAN, SPLIT HER OPEN!!
SORRY!
CRAAACK
NO TIME!!
THUP

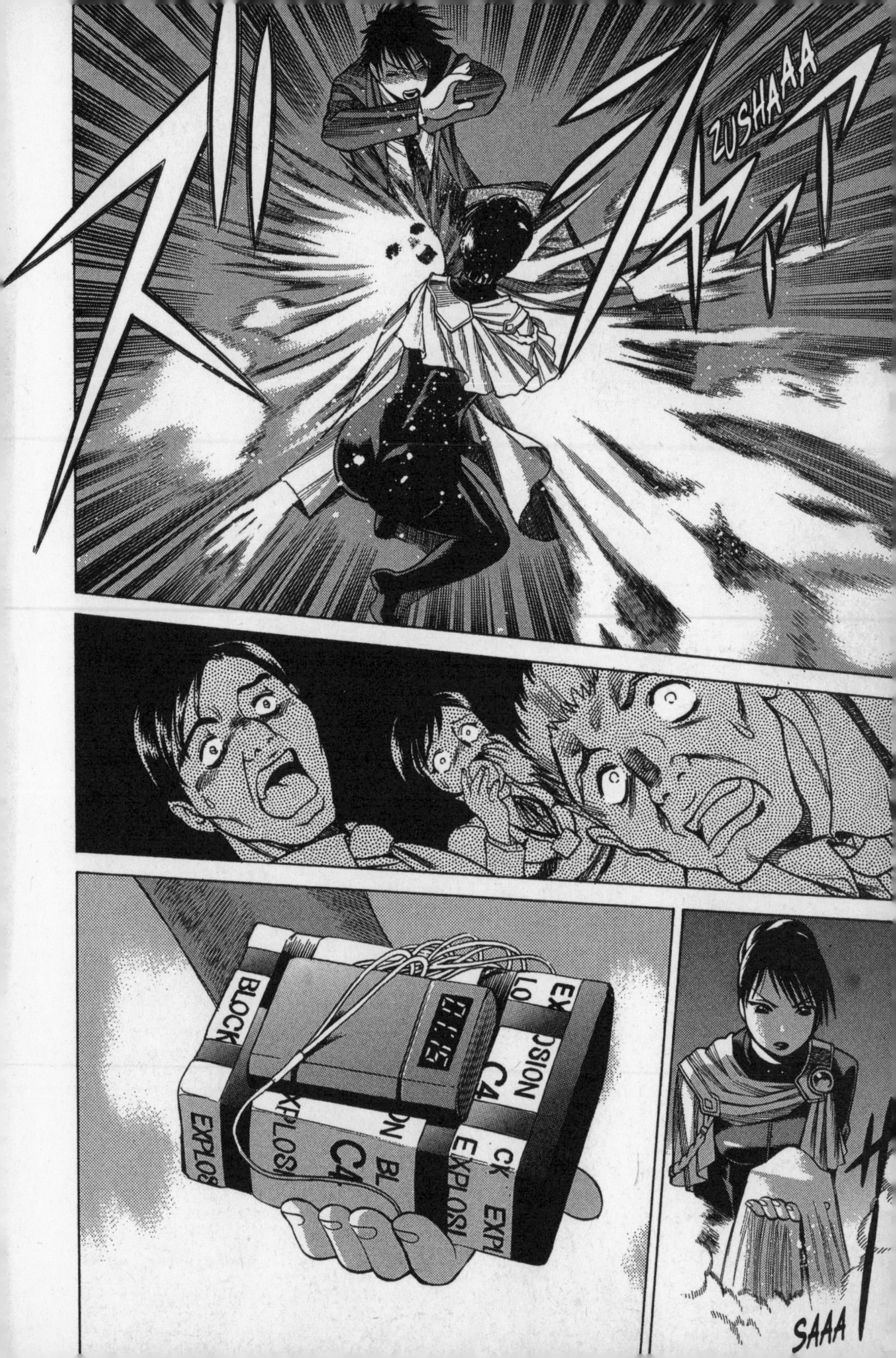
ZUSHAAA
SAAA
EX
LO
OSION
C4
BLOCK
EXPLOSI
ON
BL
C4
CK
EXPLOSI
EXPL
EXPLOS

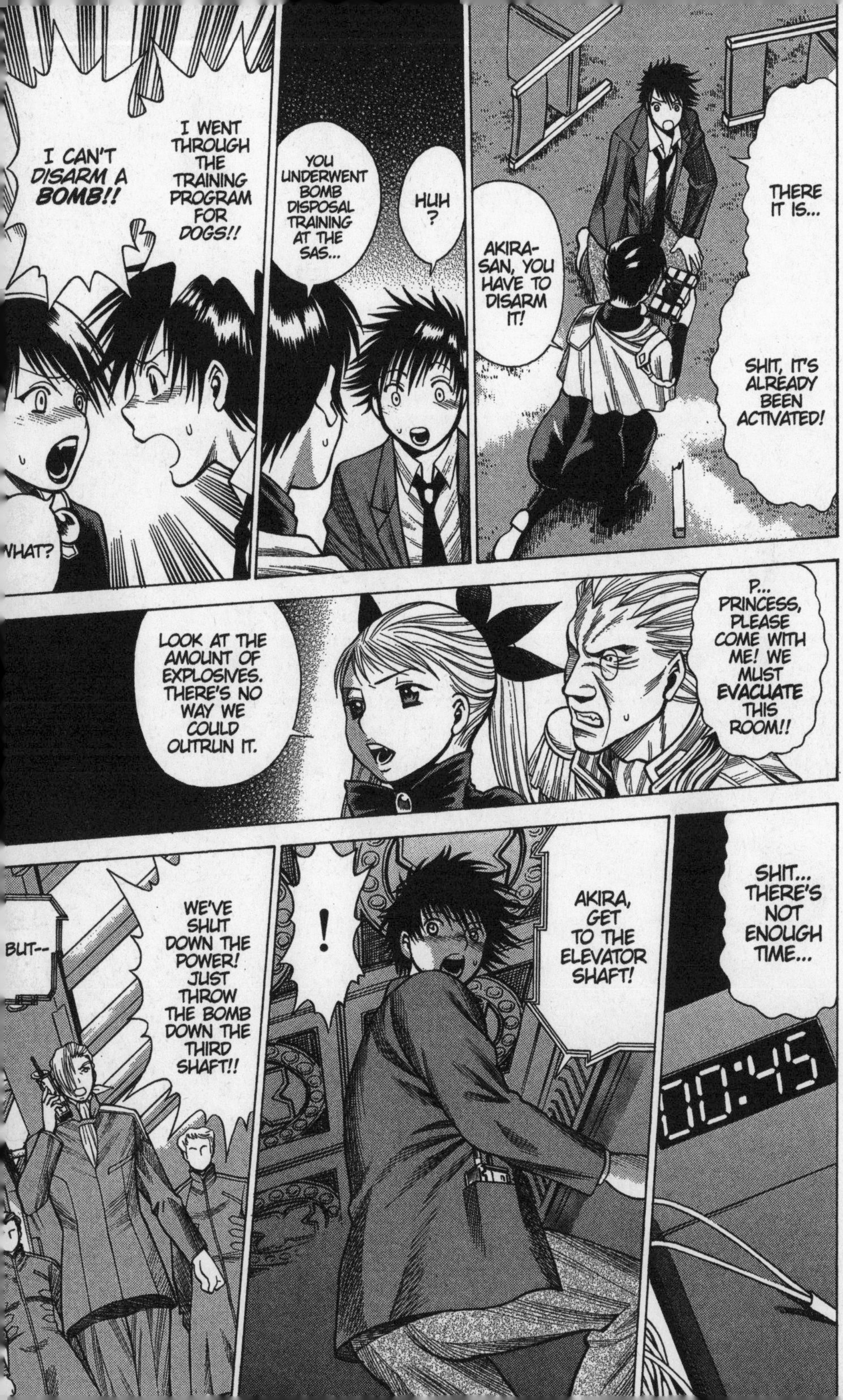
THERE IT IS...
SHIT, IT'S ALREADY BEEN ACTIVATED!
AKIRA-SAN, YOU HAVE TO DISARM IT!
HUH?
YOU UNDERWENT BOMB DISPOSAL TRAINING AT THE SAS...
I WENT THROUGH THE TRAINING PROGRAM FOR DOGS!!
I CAN'T DISARM A BOMB!!
WHAT?
P... PRINCESS, PLEASE COME WITH ME! WE MUST EVACUATE THIS ROOM!!
LOOK AT THE AMOUNT OF EXPLOSIVES. THERE'S NO WAY WE COULD OUTRUN IT.
SHIT... THERE'S NOT ENOUGH TIME...
00:45
AKIRA, GET TO THE ELEVATOR SHAFT!
!
WE'VE SHUT DOWN THE POWER! JUST THROW THE BOMB DOWN THE THIRD SHAFT!!
BUT--

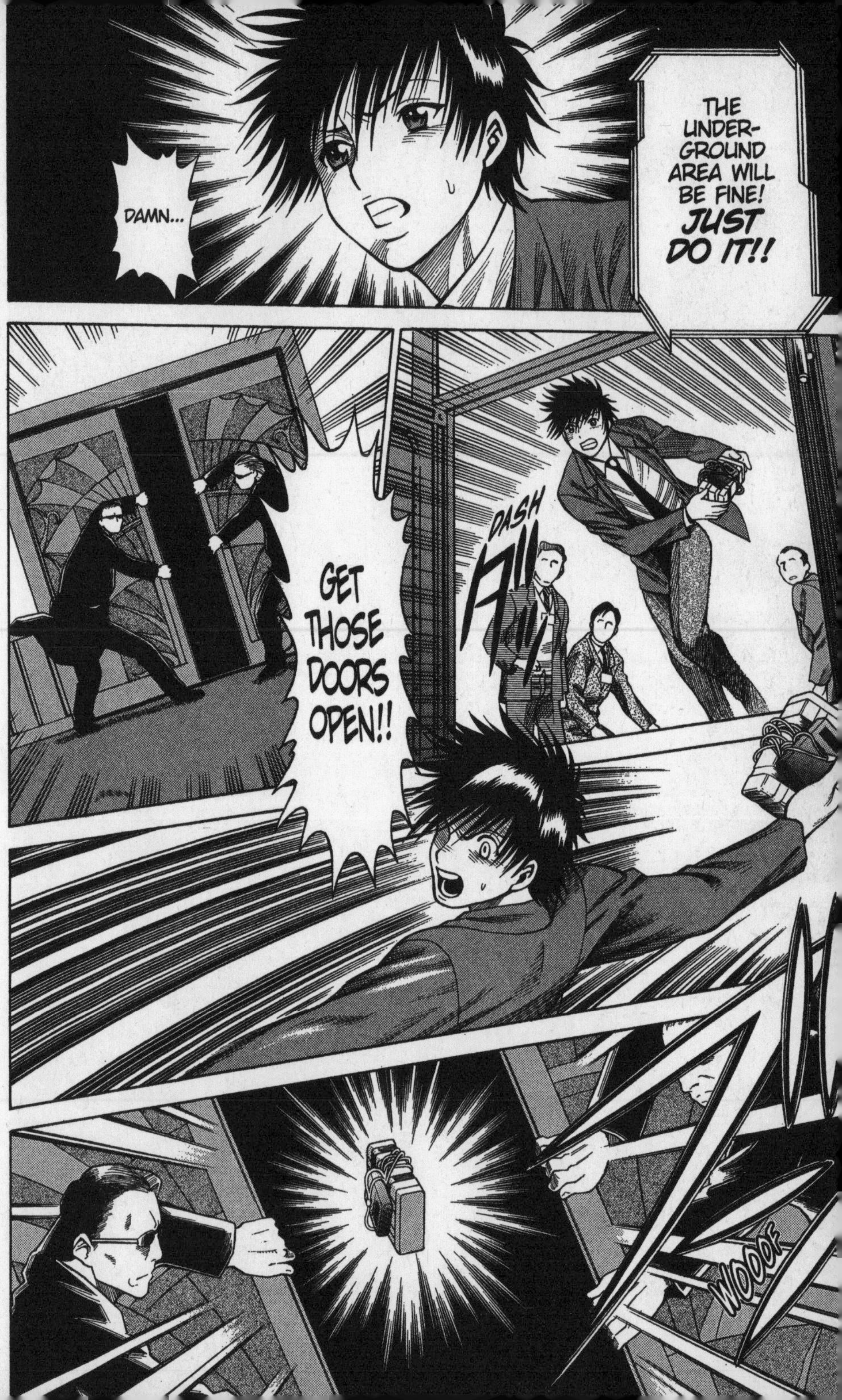
THE UNDER-GROUND AREA WILL BE FINE! JUST DO IT!!
DAMN...
DASH
GET THOSE DOORS OPEN!!
WOOOF

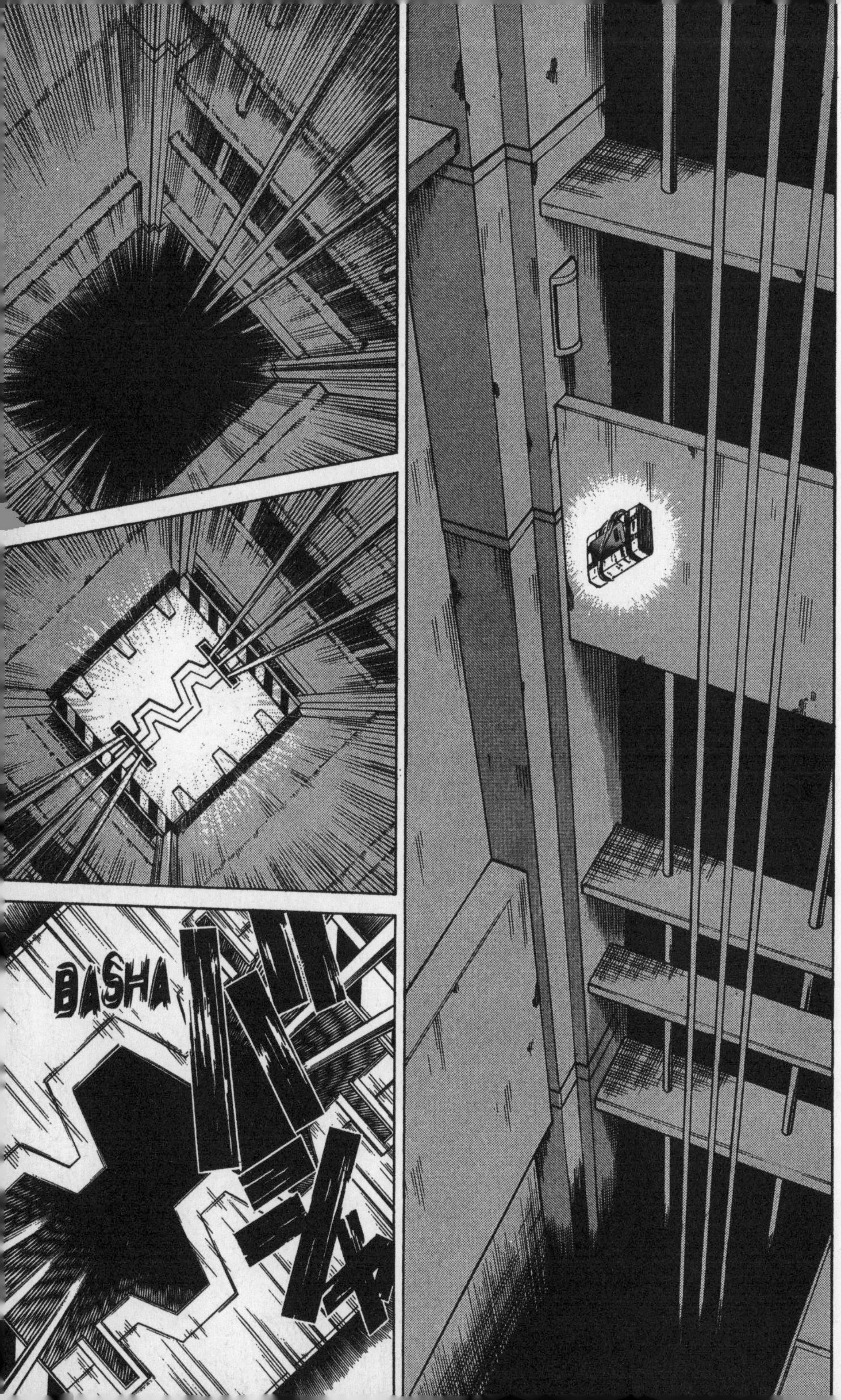
BASHA

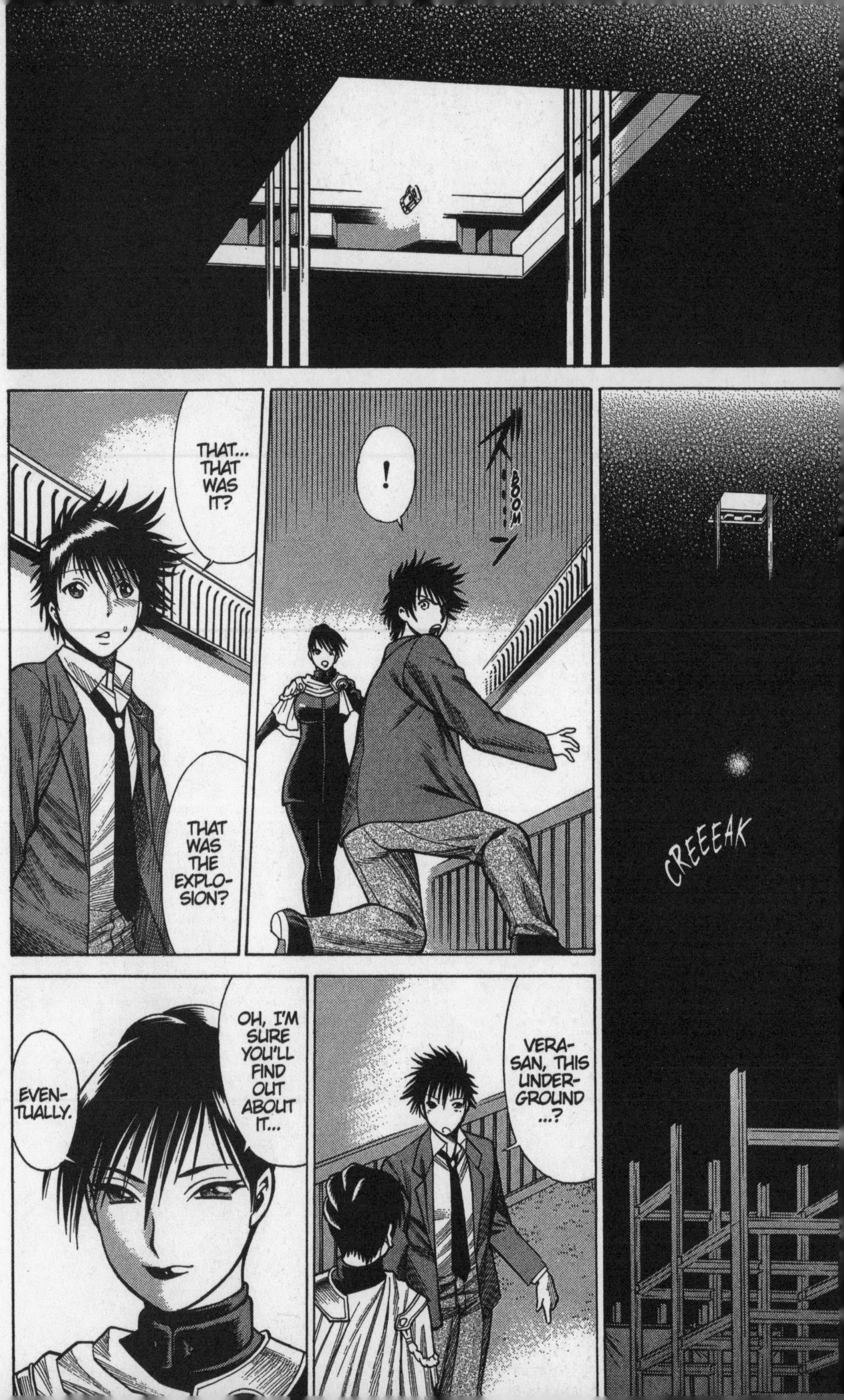
CREEEAK
!
BOOM
THAT... THAT WAS IT?
THAT WAS THE EXPLOSION?
VERA-SAN, THIS UNDERGROUND ...?
OH, I'M SURE YOU'LL FIND OUT ABOUT IT...
EVEN-TUALLY.

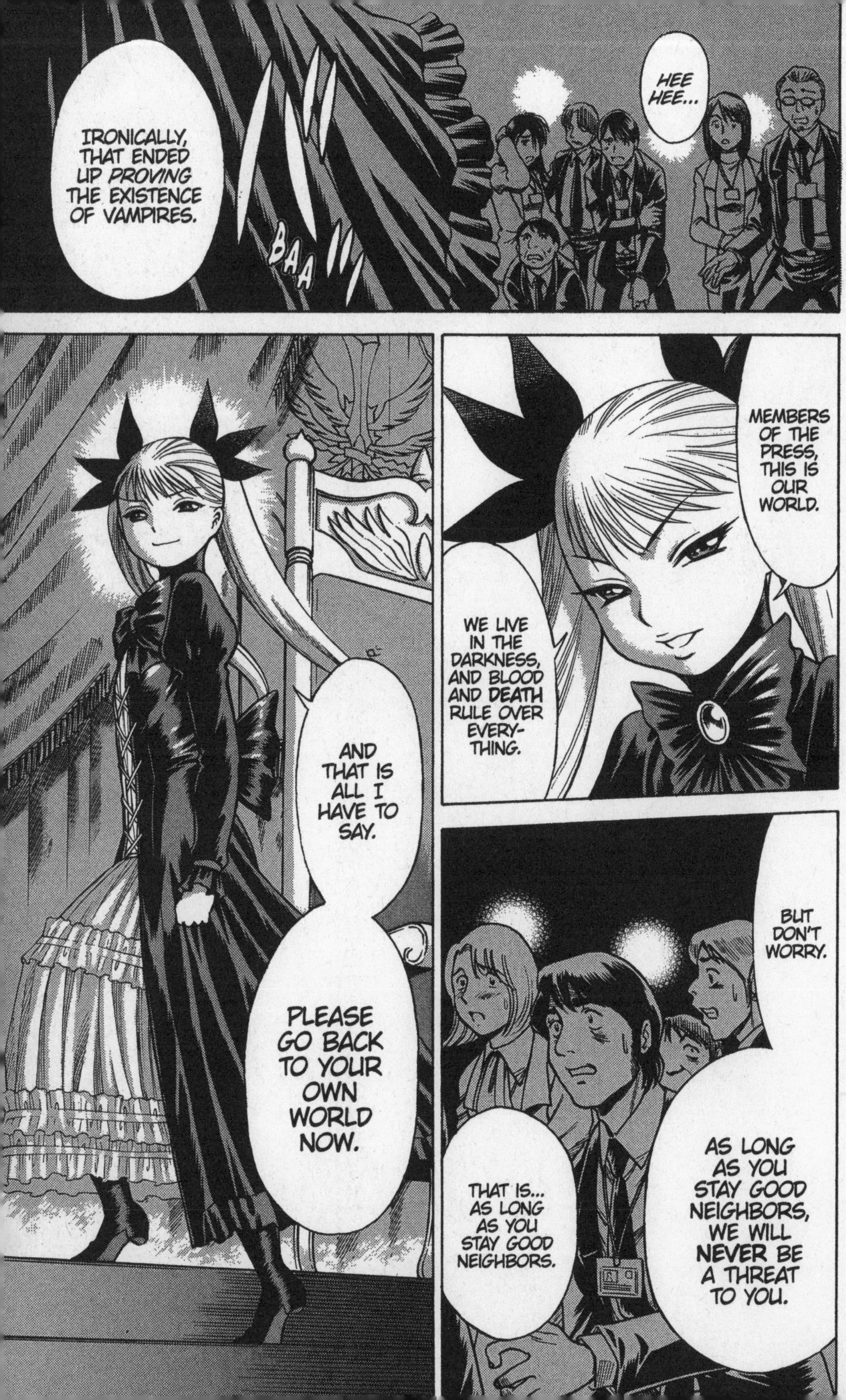
HEE HEE...
IRONICALLY, THAT ENDED UP *PROVING* THE EXISTENCE OF VAMPIRES.
BAA
MEMBERS OF THE PRESS, THIS IS OUR WORLD.
WE LIVE IN THE DARKNESS, AND BLOOD AND DEATH RULE OVER EVERY-THING.
BUT DON'T WORRY.
AS LONG AS YOU STAY GOOD NEIGHBORS, WE WILL **NEVER** BE A THREAT TO YOU.
THAT IS... AS LONG AS YOU STAY GOOD NEIGHBORS.
AND THAT IS ALL I HAVE TO SAY.
PLEASE GO BACK TO YOUR OWN WORLD NOW.

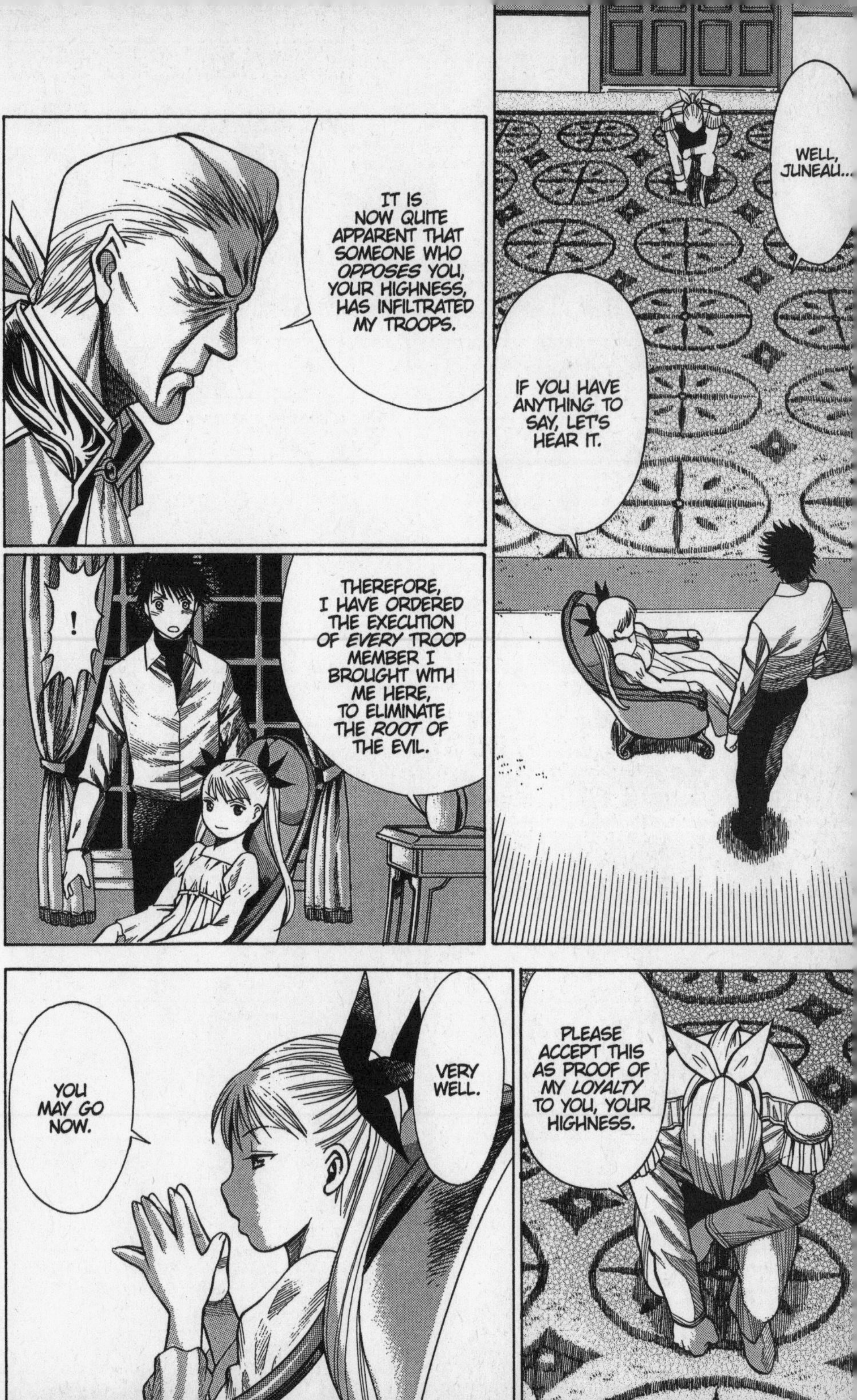
WELL, JUNEAU...
IF YOU HAVE ANYTHING TO SAY, LET'S HEAR IT.
IT IS NOW QUITE APPARENT THAT SOMEONE WHO *OPPOSES* YOU, YOUR HIGHNESS, HAS INFILTRATED MY TROOPS.
THEREFORE, I HAVE ORDERED THE EXECUTION OF *EVERY* TROOP MEMBER I BROUGHT WITH ME HERE, TO ELIMINATE THE *ROOT* OF THE EVIL.
!
PLEASE ACCEPT THIS AS PROOF OF MY *LOYALTY* TO YOU, YOUR HIGHNESS.
VERY WELL.
YOU MAY GO NOW.

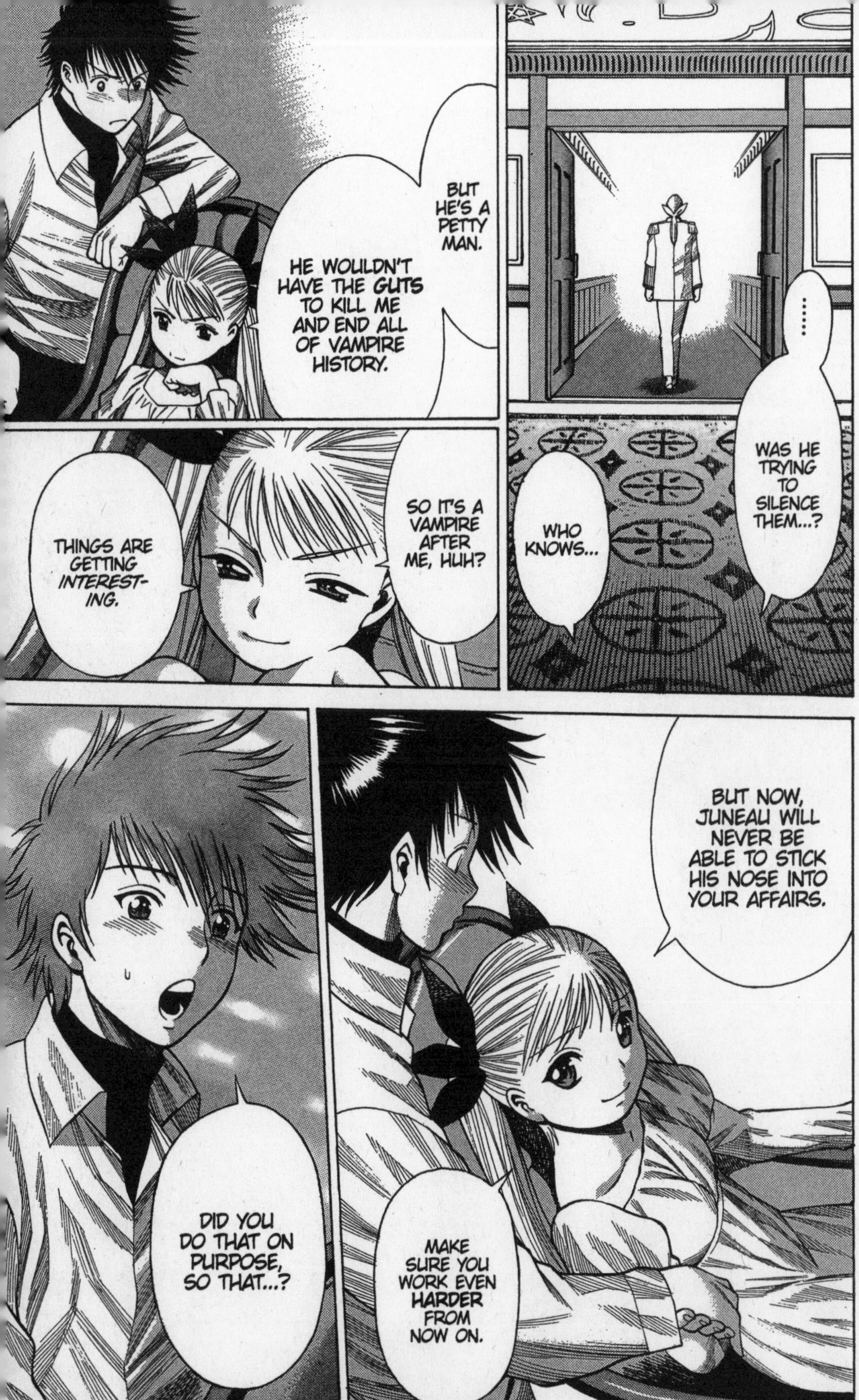
......
BUT HE'S A PETTY MAN.
HE WOULDN'T HAVE THE GUTS TO KILL ME AND END ALL OF VAMPIRE HISTORY.
WAS HE TRYING TO SILENCE THEM...?
WHO KNOWS...
SO IT'S A VAMPIRE AFTER ME, HUH?
THINGS ARE GETTING INTEREST-ING.
BUT NOW, JUNEAU WILL NEVER BE ABLE TO STICK HIS NOSE INTO YOUR AFFAIRS.
MAKE SURE YOU WORK EVEN HARDER FROM NOW ON.
DID YOU DO THAT ON PURPOSE, SO THAT...?

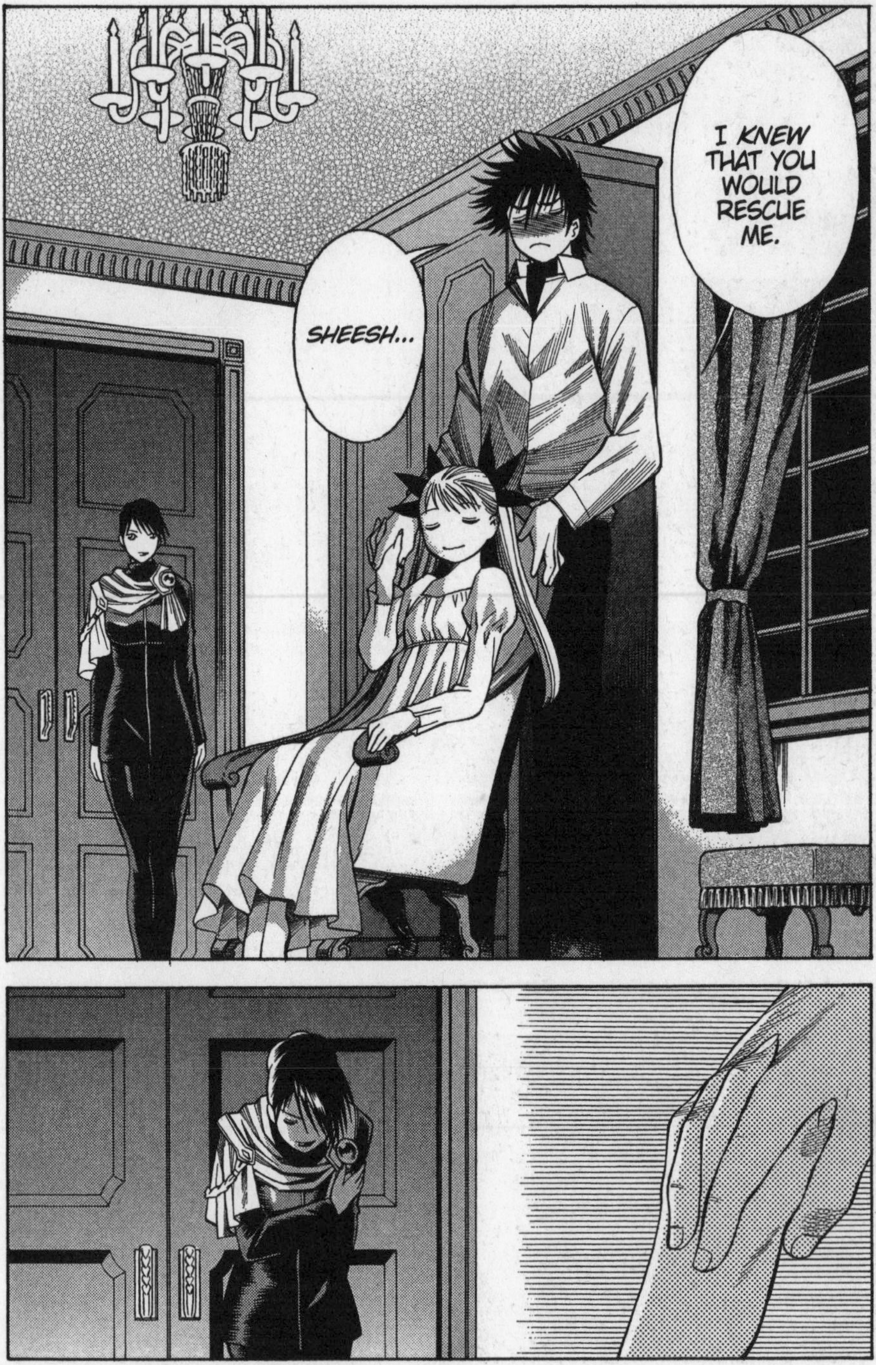
I KNEW THAT YOU WOULD RESCUE ME.
SHEESH...

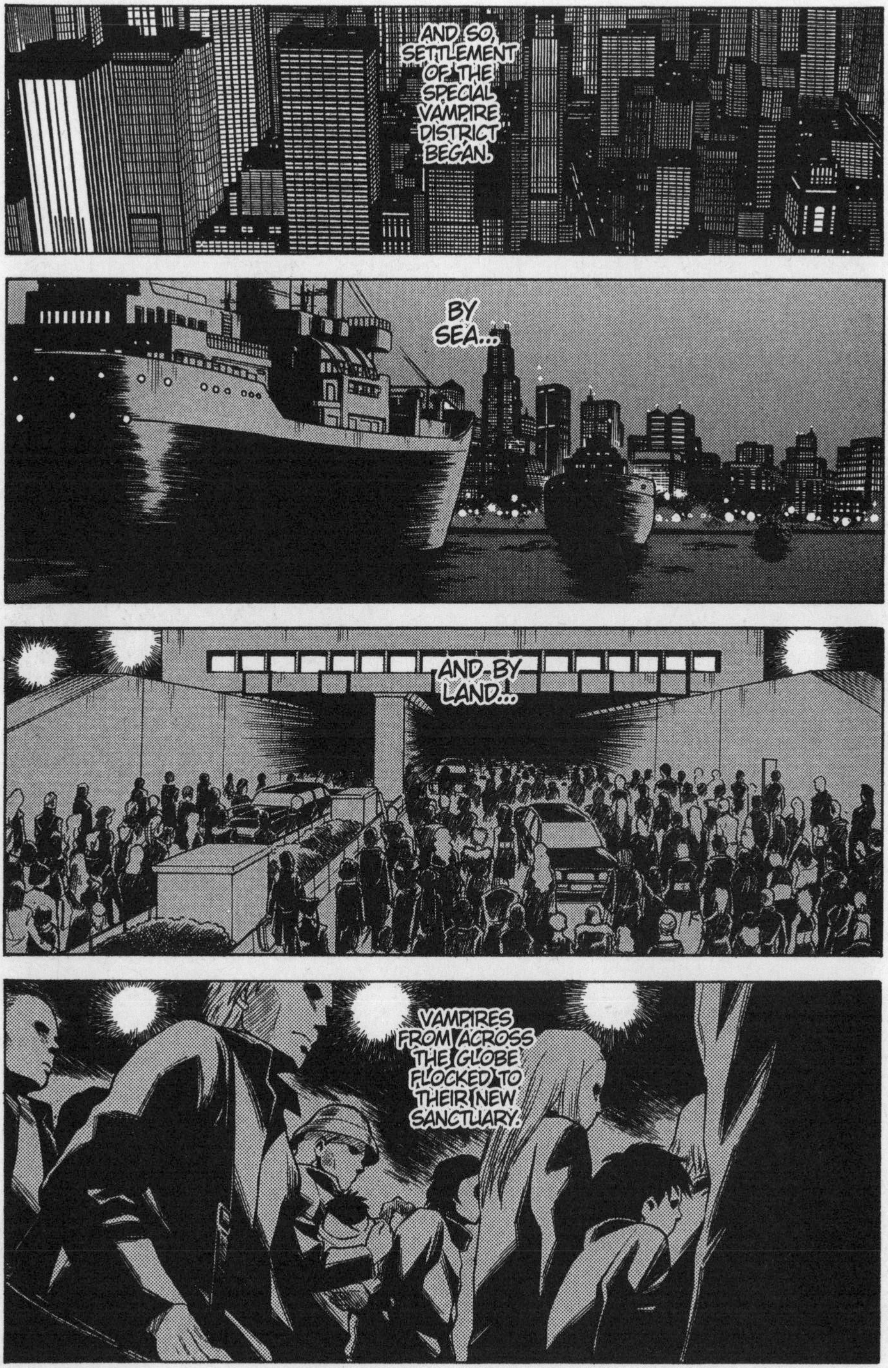
AND SO, SETTLEMENT OF THE SPECIAL VAMPIRE DISTRICT BEGAN.
BY SEA...
AND BY LAND...
VAMPIRES FROM ACROSS THE GLOBE FLOCKED TO THEIR NEW SANCTUARY.

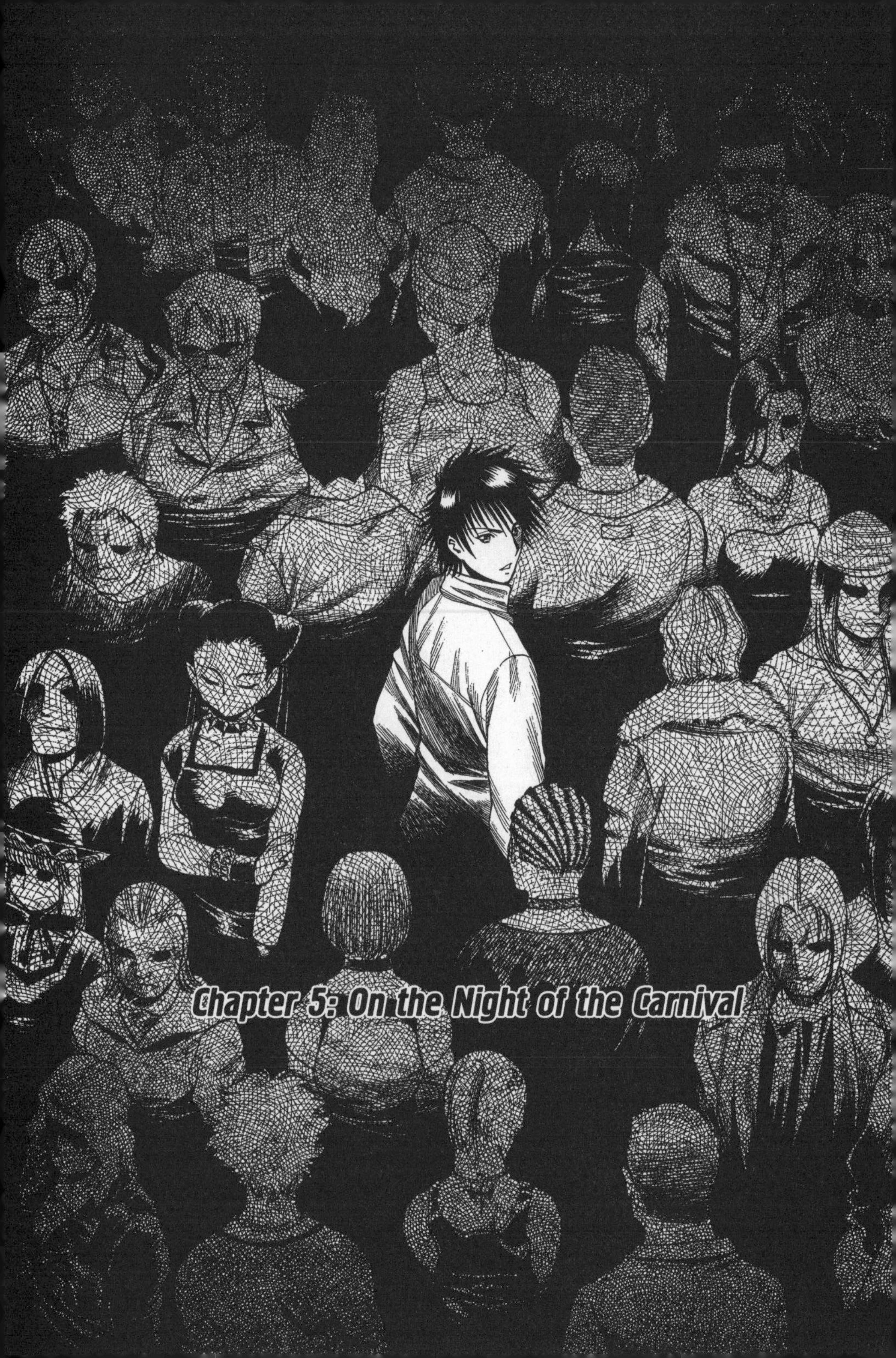
Chapter 5: On the Night of the Carnival

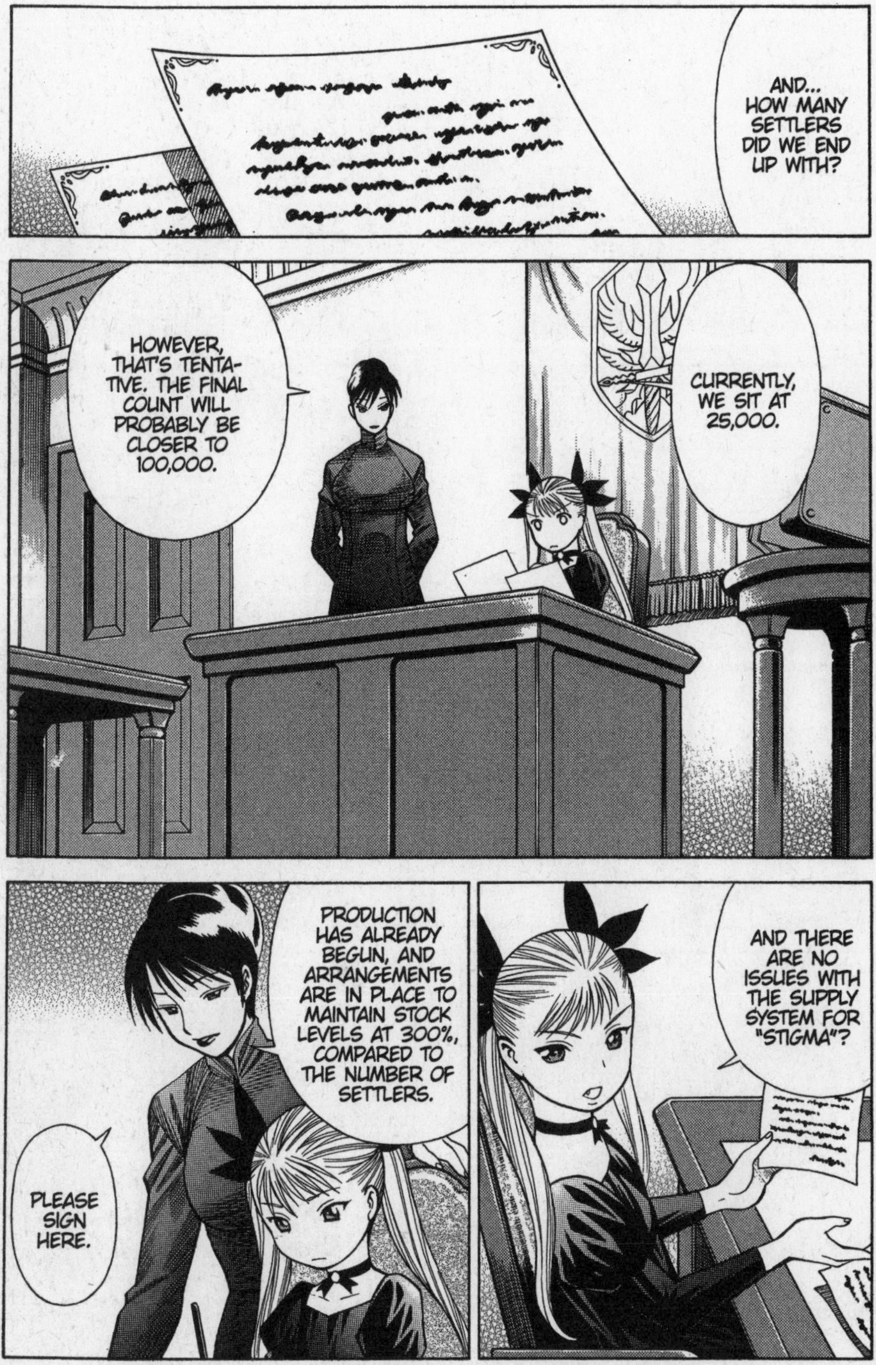
AND... HOW MANY SETTLERS DID WE END UP WITH?
CURRENTLY, WE SIT AT 25,000.
HOWEVER, THAT'S TENTA-TIVE. THE FINAL COUNT WILL PROBABLY BE CLOSER TO 100,000.
AND THERE ARE NO ISSUES WITH THE SUPPLY SYSTEM FOR "STIGMA"?
PRODUCTION HAS ALREADY BEGUN, AND ARRANGEMENTS ARE IN PLACE TO MAINTAIN STOCK LEVELS AT 300%, COMPARED TO THE NUMBER OF SETTLERS.
PLEASE SIGN HERE.

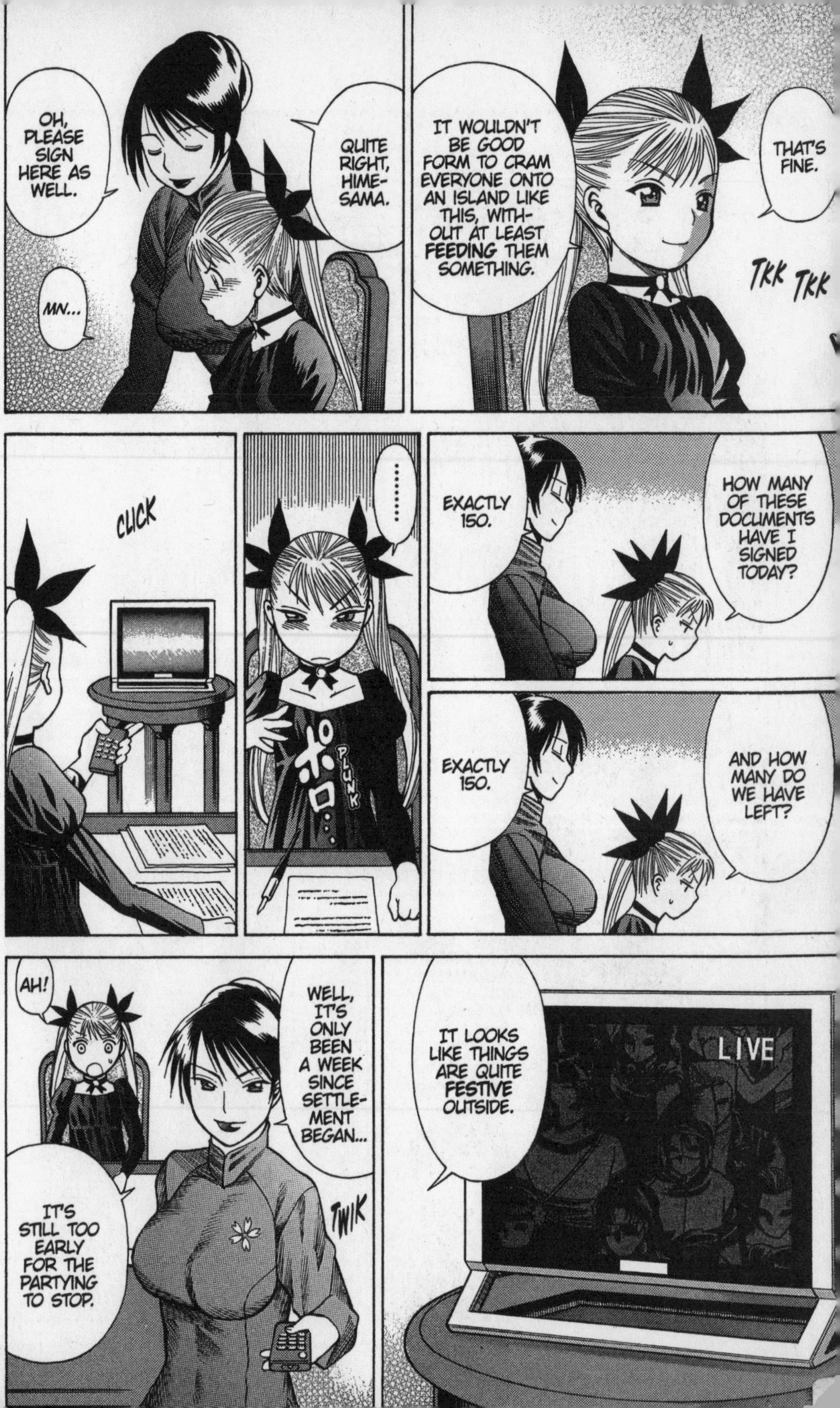

THAT'S FINE.
IT WOULDN'T BE GOOD FORM TO CRAM EVERYONE ONTO AN ISLAND LIKE THIS, WITH-OUT AT LEAST FEEDING THEM SOMETHING.
TKK TKK
QUITE RIGHT, HIME-SAMA.
OH, PLEASE SIGN HERE AS WELL.
MN...
HOW MANY OF THESE DOCUMENTS HAVE I SIGNED TODAY?
EXACTLY 150.
AND HOW MANY DO WE HAVE LEFT?
EXACTLY 150.
....
PLUNK
CLICK
IT LOOKS LIKE THINGS ARE QUITE FESTIVE OUTSIDE.
LIVE
WELL, IT'S ONLY BEEN A WEEK SINCE SETTLE-MENT BEGAN...
AH!
TWIK
IT'S STILL TOO EARLY FOR THE PARTYING TO STOP.

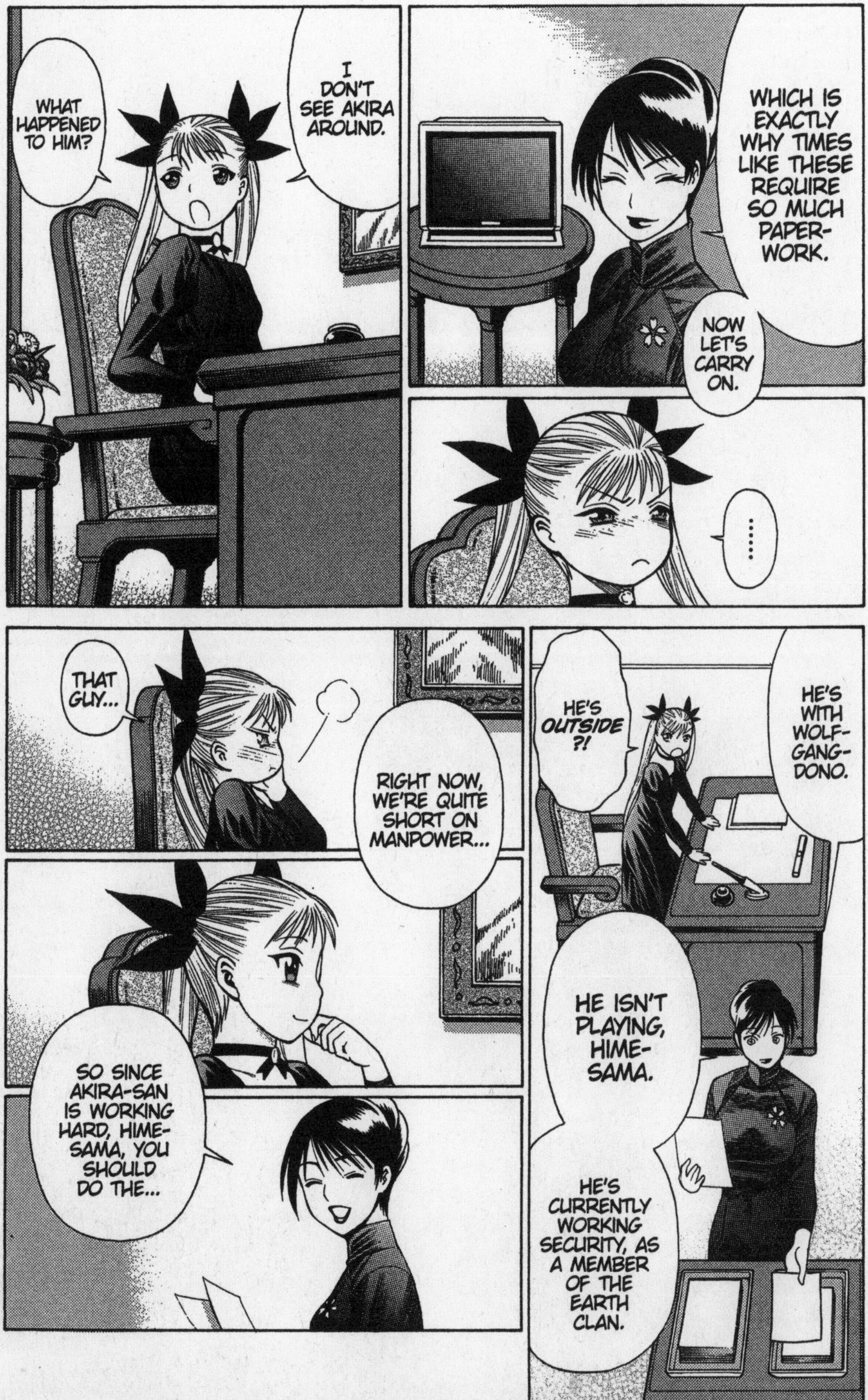
WHICH IS EXACTLY WHY TIMES LIKE THESE REQUIRE SO MUCH PAPER-WORK.
NOW LET'S CARRY ON.
......
I DON'T SEE AKIRA AROUND.
WHAT HAPPENED TO HIM?
HE'S WITH WOLF-GANG-DONO.
HE'S *OUTSIDE* ?!
HE ISN'T PLAYING, HIME-SAMA.
HE'S CURRENTLY WORKING SECURITY, AS A MEMBER OF THE EARTH CLAN.
THAT GUY...
RIGHT NOW, WE'RE QUITE SHORT ON MANPOWER...
SO SINCE AKIRA-SAN IS WORKING HARD, HIME-SAMA, YOU SHOULD DO THE...

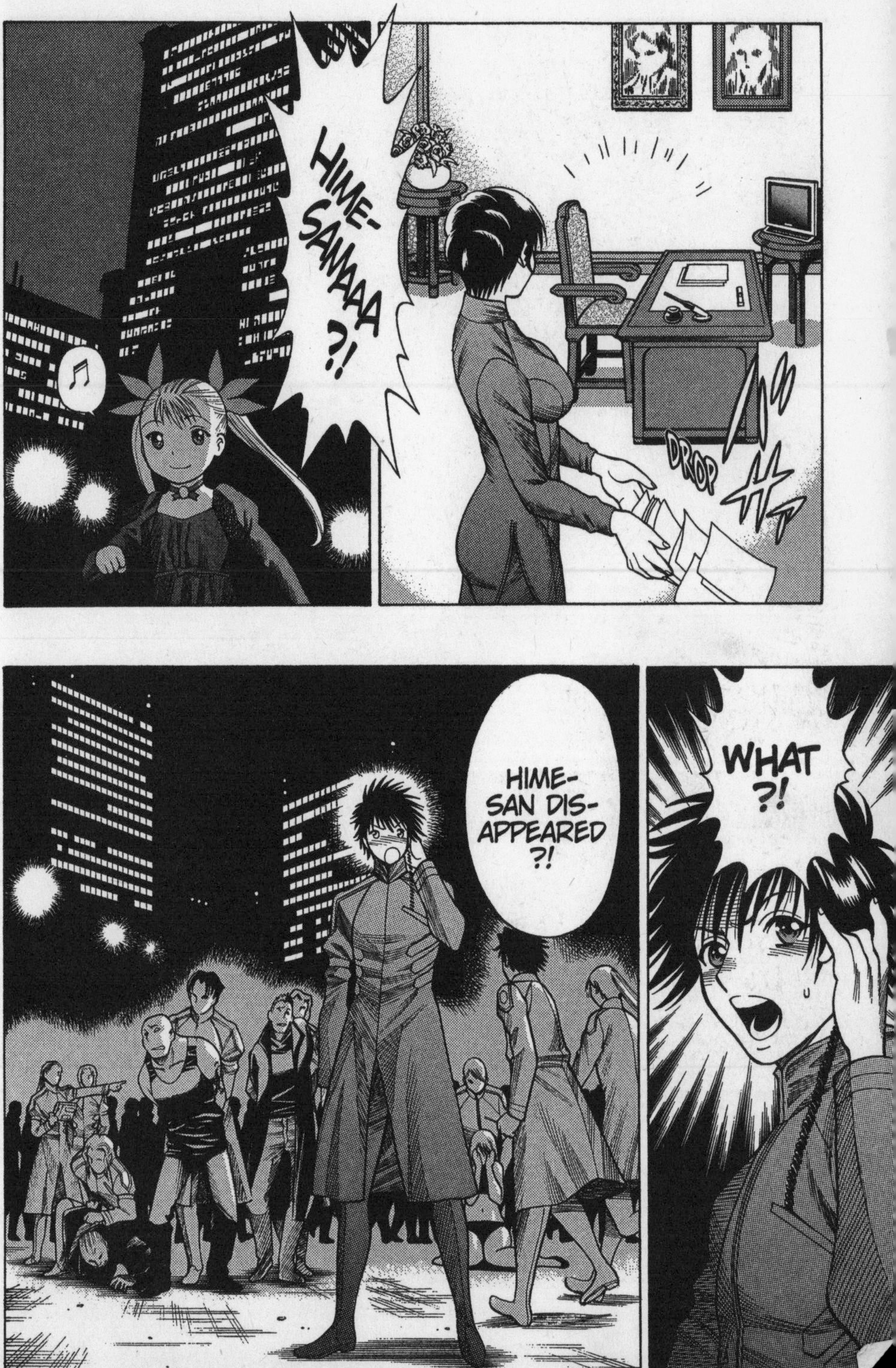
DROP
HIME-SAMAAAA?!
♪
WHAT?!
HIME-SAN DIS-APPEARED?!

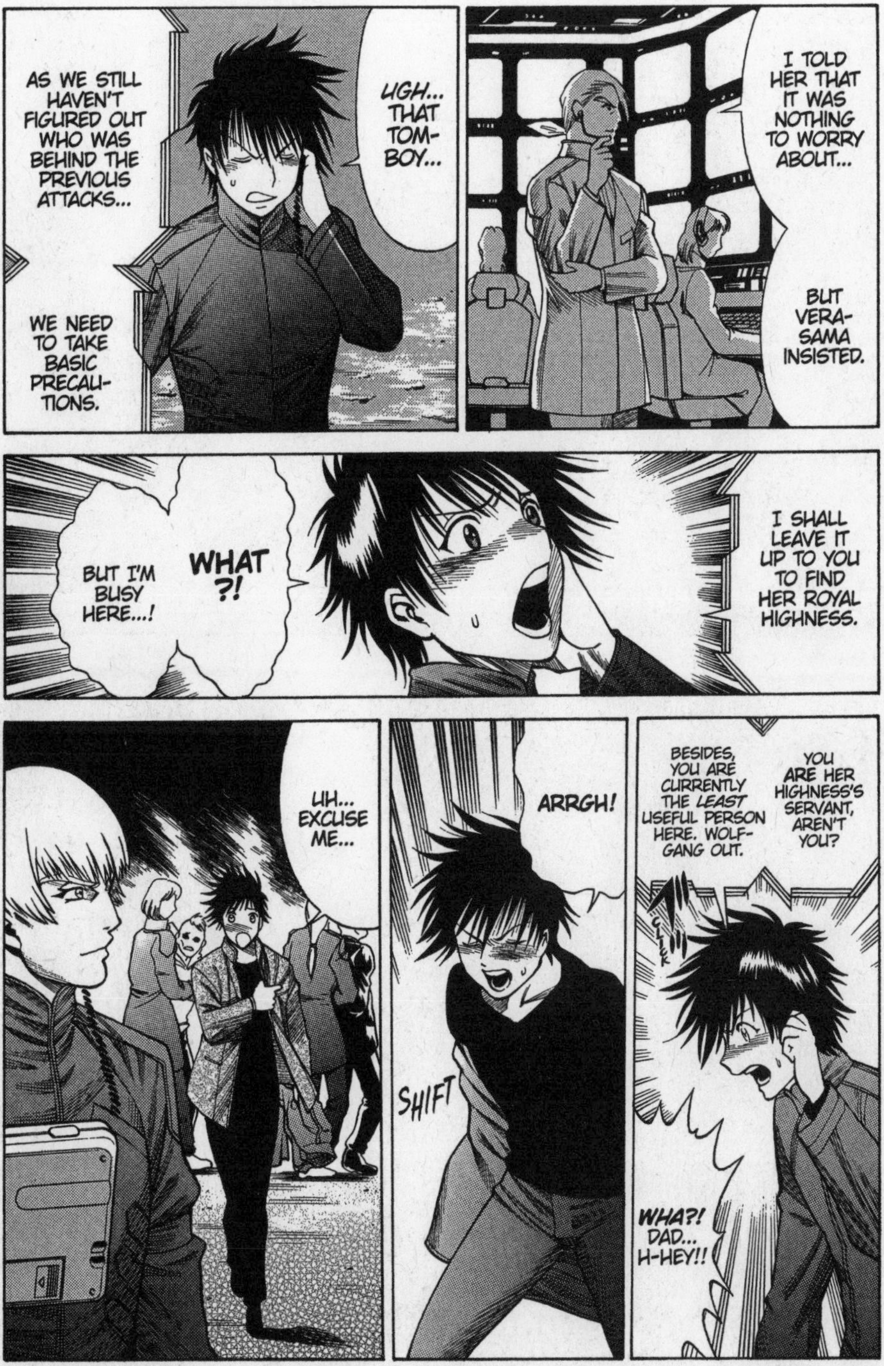
I TOLD HER THAT IT WAS NOTHING TO WORRY ABOUT...
BUT VERA-SAMA INSISTED.
UGH... THAT TOM-BOY...
AS WE STILL HAVEN'T FIGURED OUT WHO WAS BEHIND THE PREVIOUS ATTACKS...
WE NEED TO TAKE BASIC PRECAU-TIONS.
I SHALL LEAVE IT UP TO YOU TO FIND HER ROYAL HIGHNESS.
WHAT?!
BUT I'M BUSY HERE...!
YOU ARE HER HIGHNESS'S SERVANT, AREN'T YOU?
BESIDES, YOU ARE CURRENTLY THE LEAST USEFUL PERSON HERE. WOLF-GANG OUT.
CLICK
WHA?! DAD... H-HEY!!
ARRGH!
SHIFT
UH... EXCUSE ME...

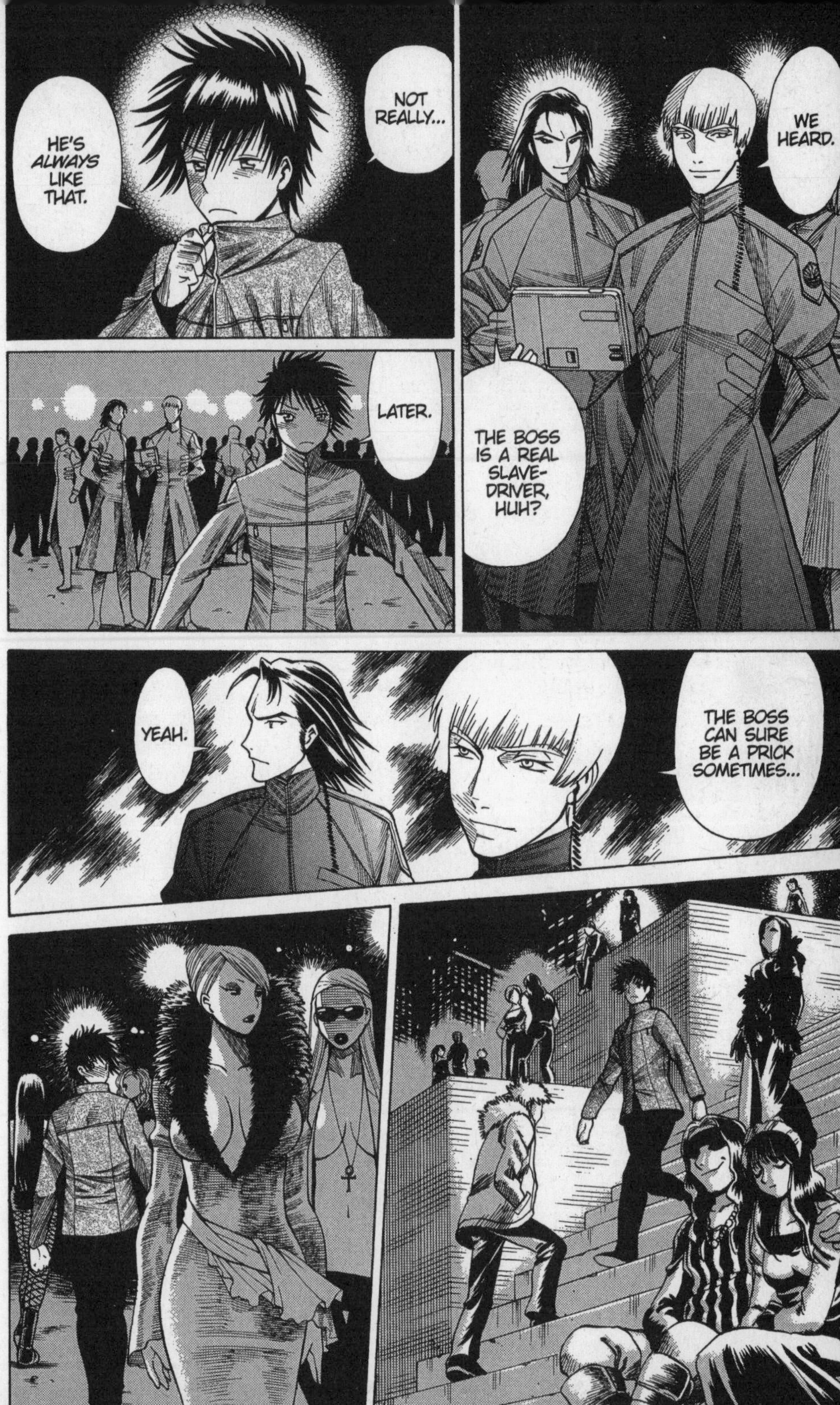
WE HEARD.
THE BOSS IS A REAL SLAVE-DRIVER, HUH?
NOT REALLY...
HE'S *ALWAYS* LIKE THAT.
LATER.
THE BOSS CAN SURE BE A PRICK SOMETIMES...
YEAH.

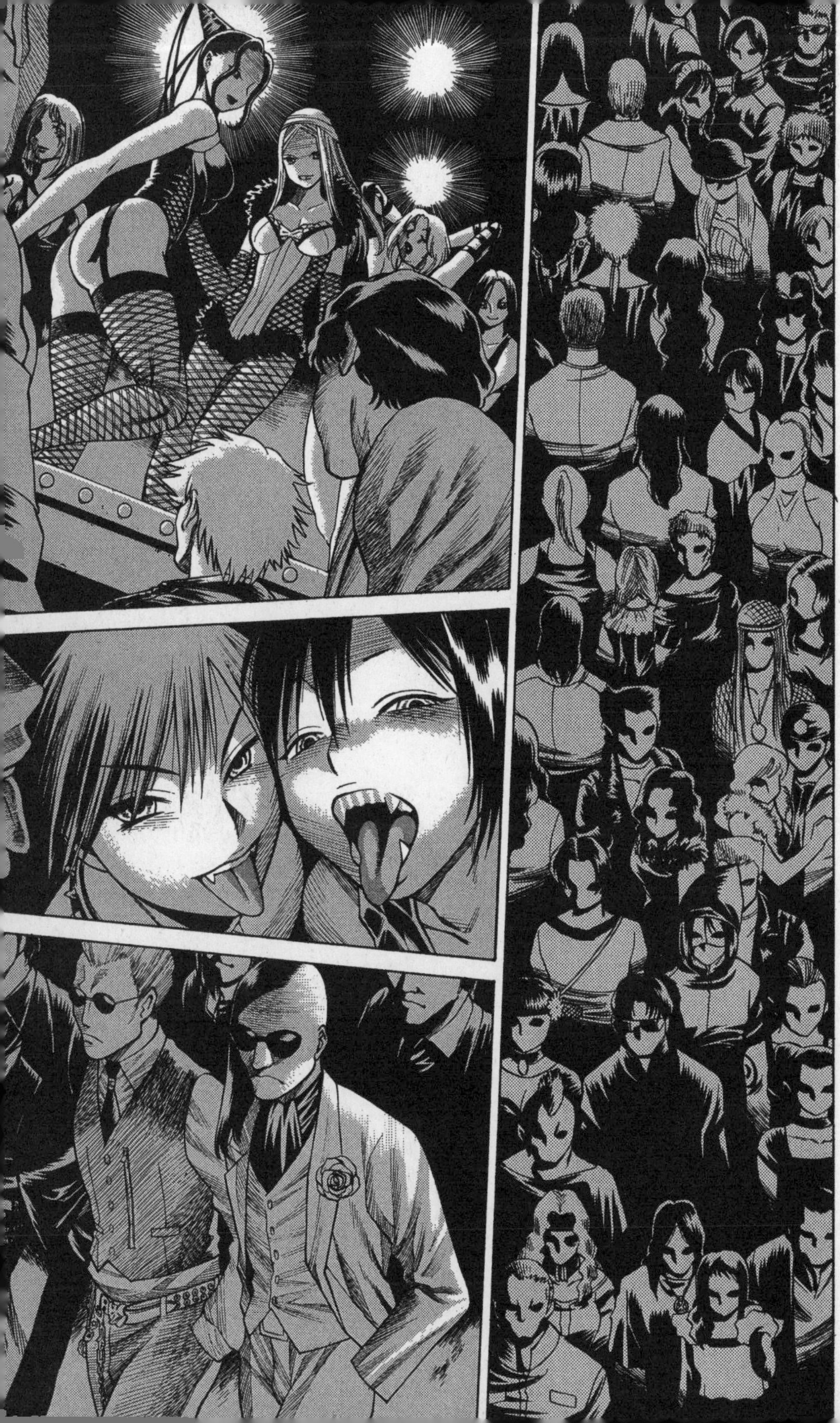

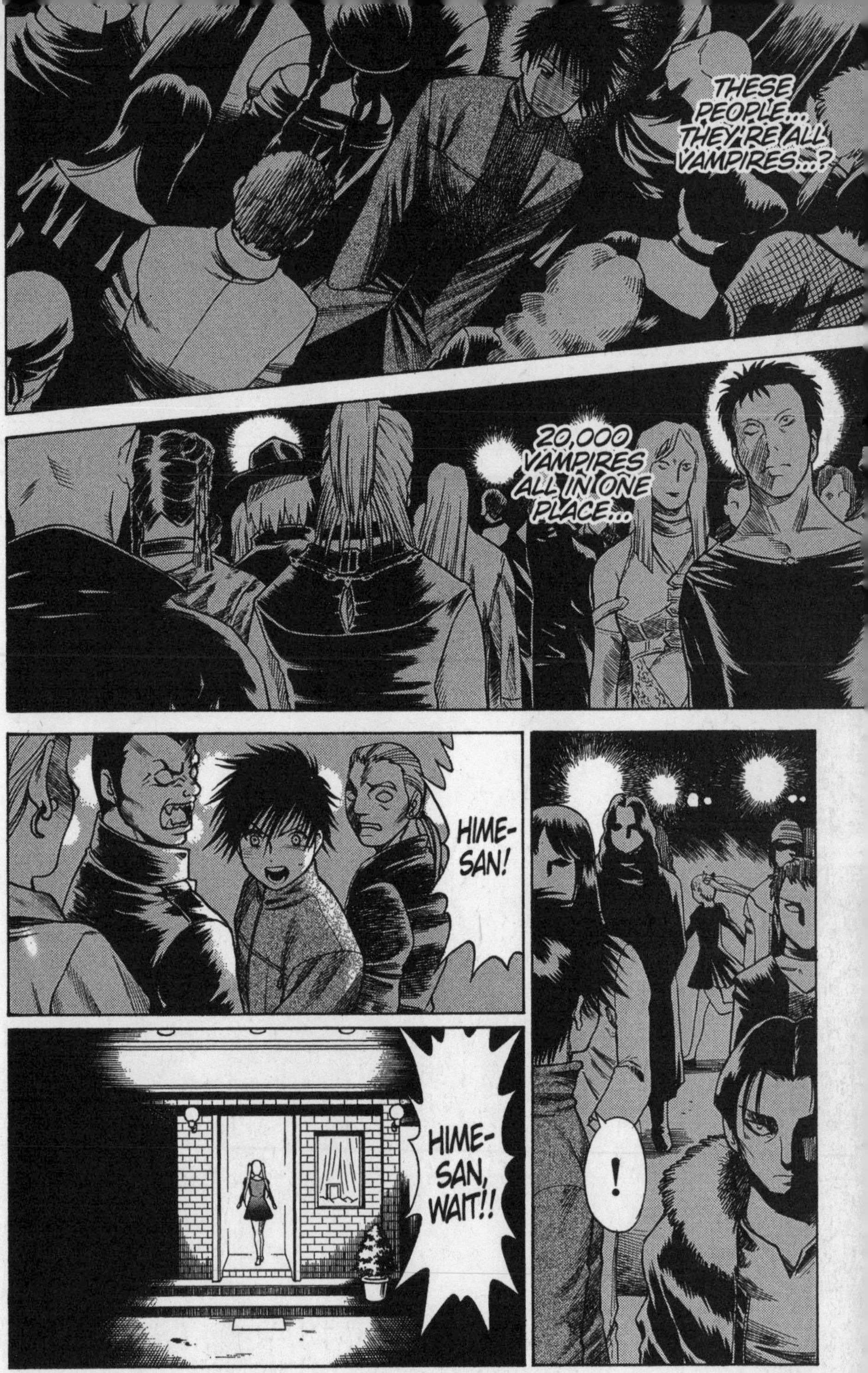
THESE PEOPLE... THEY'RE ALL VAMPIRES...?
20,000 VAMPIRES ALL IN ONE PLACE...
!
HIME-SAN!
HIME-SAN, WAIT!!

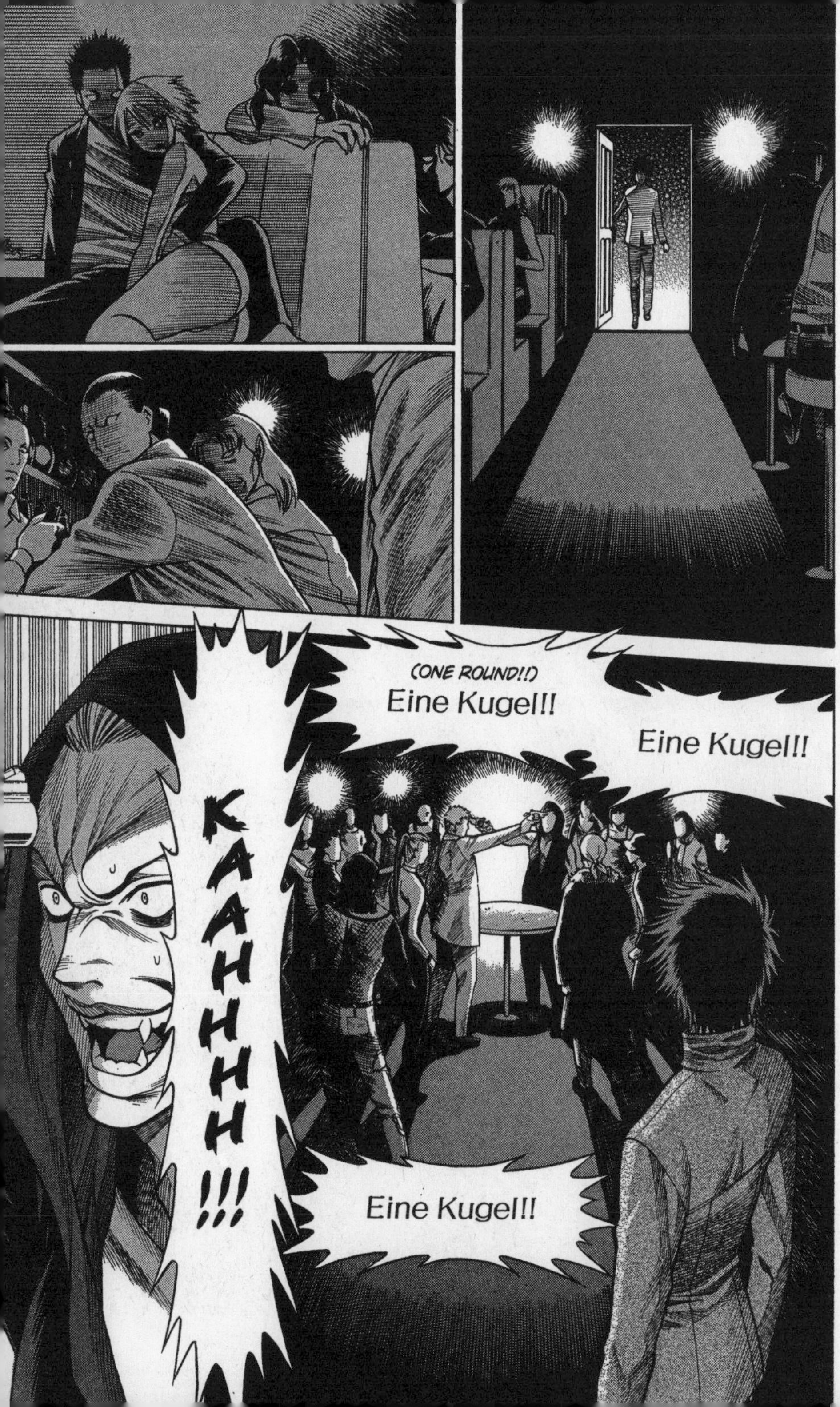
(ONE ROUND!!)
Eine Kugel!!
Eine Kugel!!
KAAHHHH!!!
Eine Kugel!!

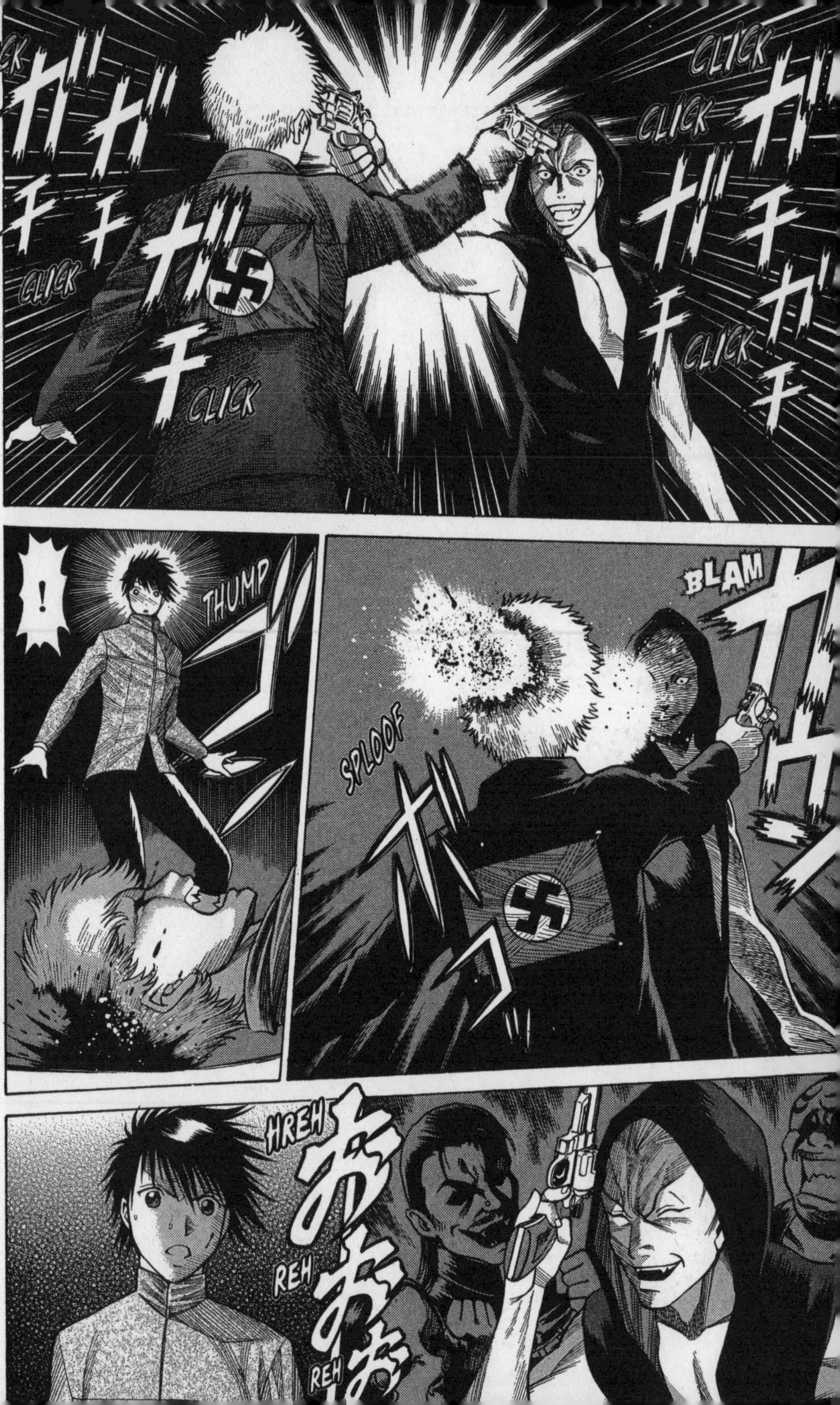
CLICK
CLICK
CLICK
CLICK
CLICK
CLICK
BLAM
SPLOOF
!
THUMP
HREH
REH
REH

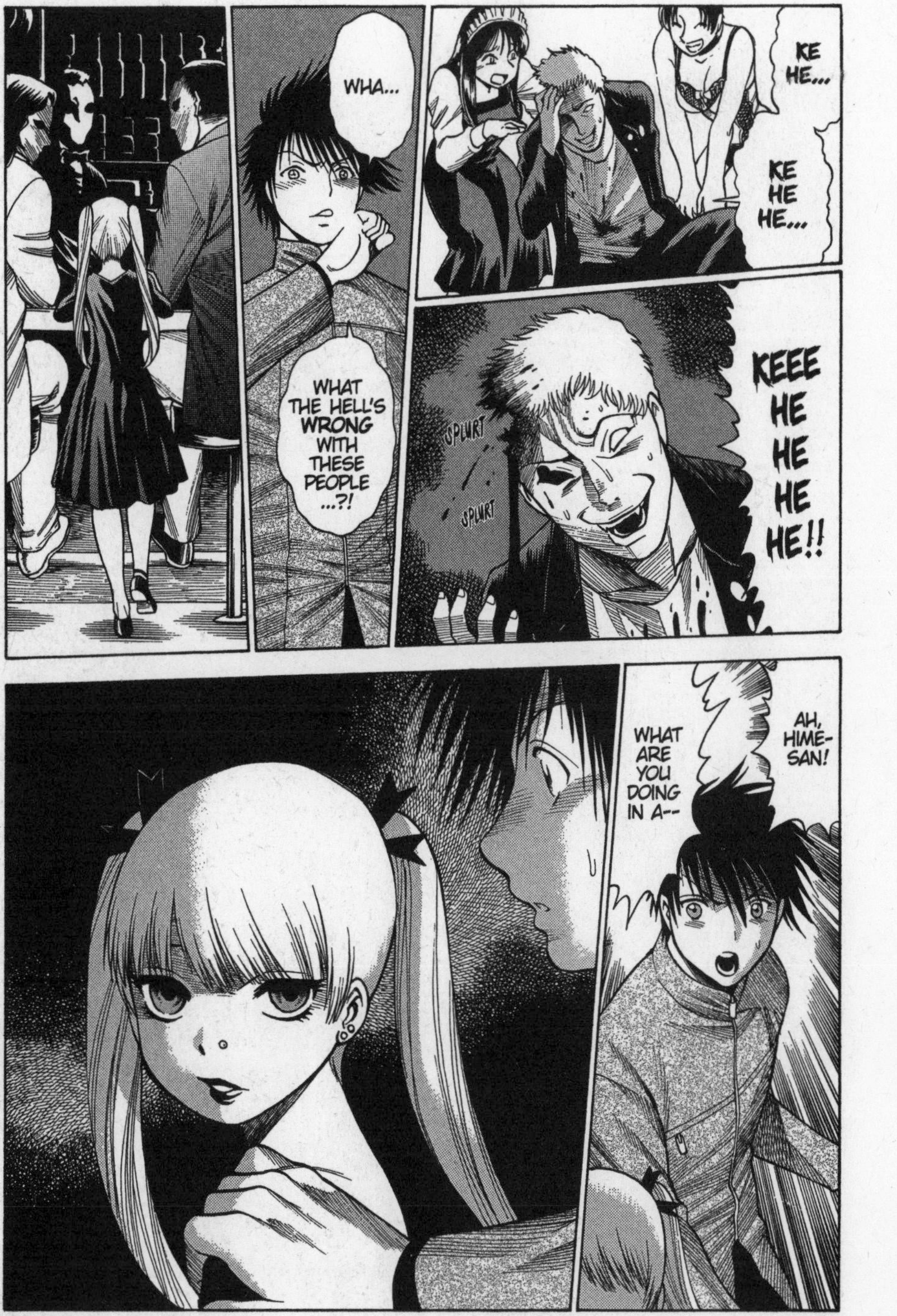
KE HE...
KE HE HE...
SPLURT
SPLURT
KEEE HE HE HE HE!!
WHA...
WHAT THE HELL'S WRONG WITH THESE PEOPLE ...?!
AH, HIME-SAN!
WHAT ARE YOU DOING IN A--

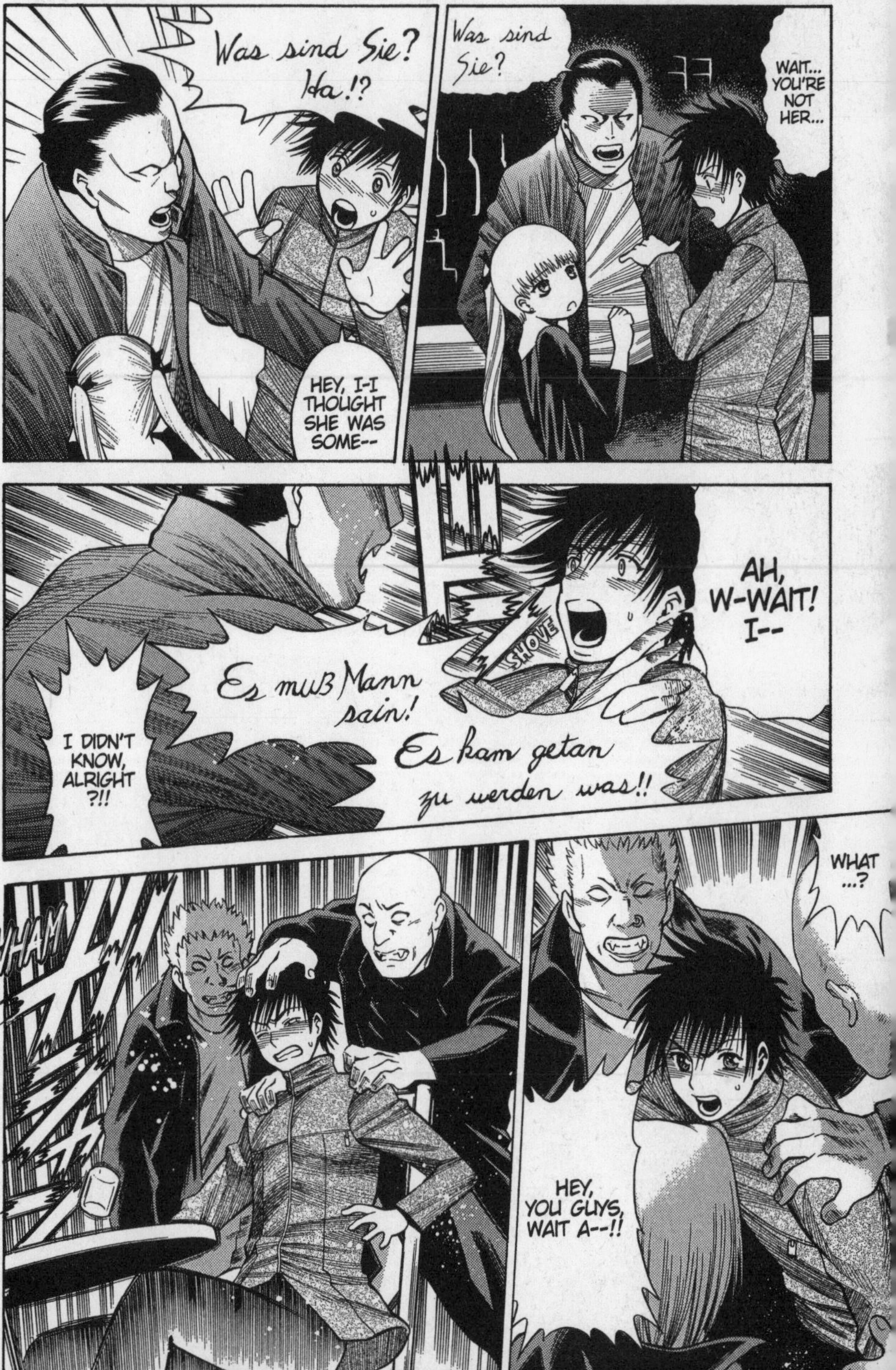
Was sind Sie?
WAIT... YOU'RE NOT HER...
Was sind Sie? Ha!?
HEY, I-I THOUGHT SHE WAS SOME--
AH, W-WAIT! I--
SHOVE
Es muß Mann sain!
Es kam getan zu werden was!!
I DIDN'T KNOW, ALRIGHT?!!
WHAT ...?
HEY, YOU GUYS, WAIT A--!!
WHAM

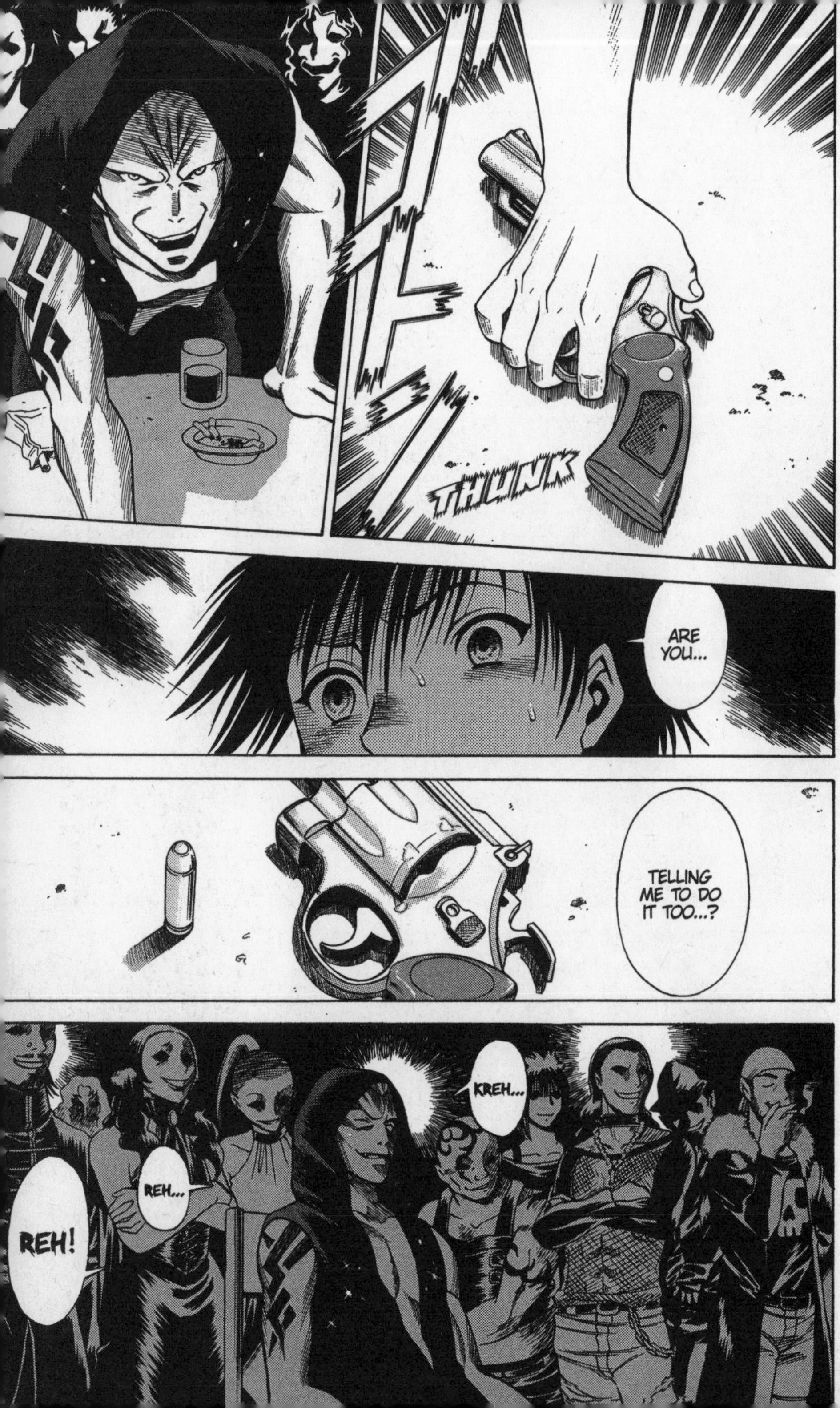
THUNK
ARE YOU...
TELLING ME TO DO IT TOO...?
KREH...
REH...
REH!

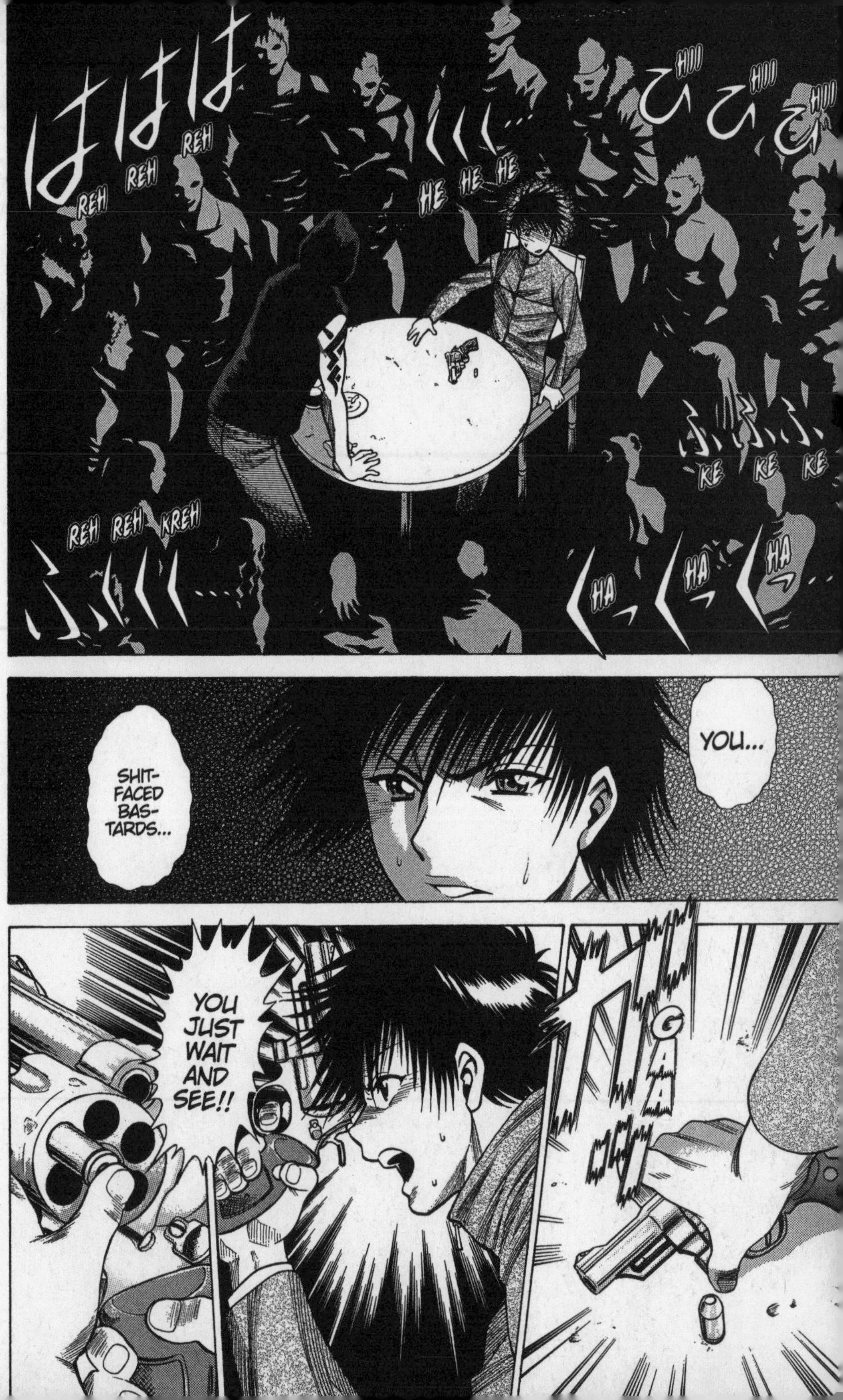
HII HII HII
HE HE HE
REH REH REH
KE KE KE
HA HA HA
REH REH KREH
YOU...
SHIT-FACED BAS-TARDS...
YOU JUST WAIT AND SEE!!

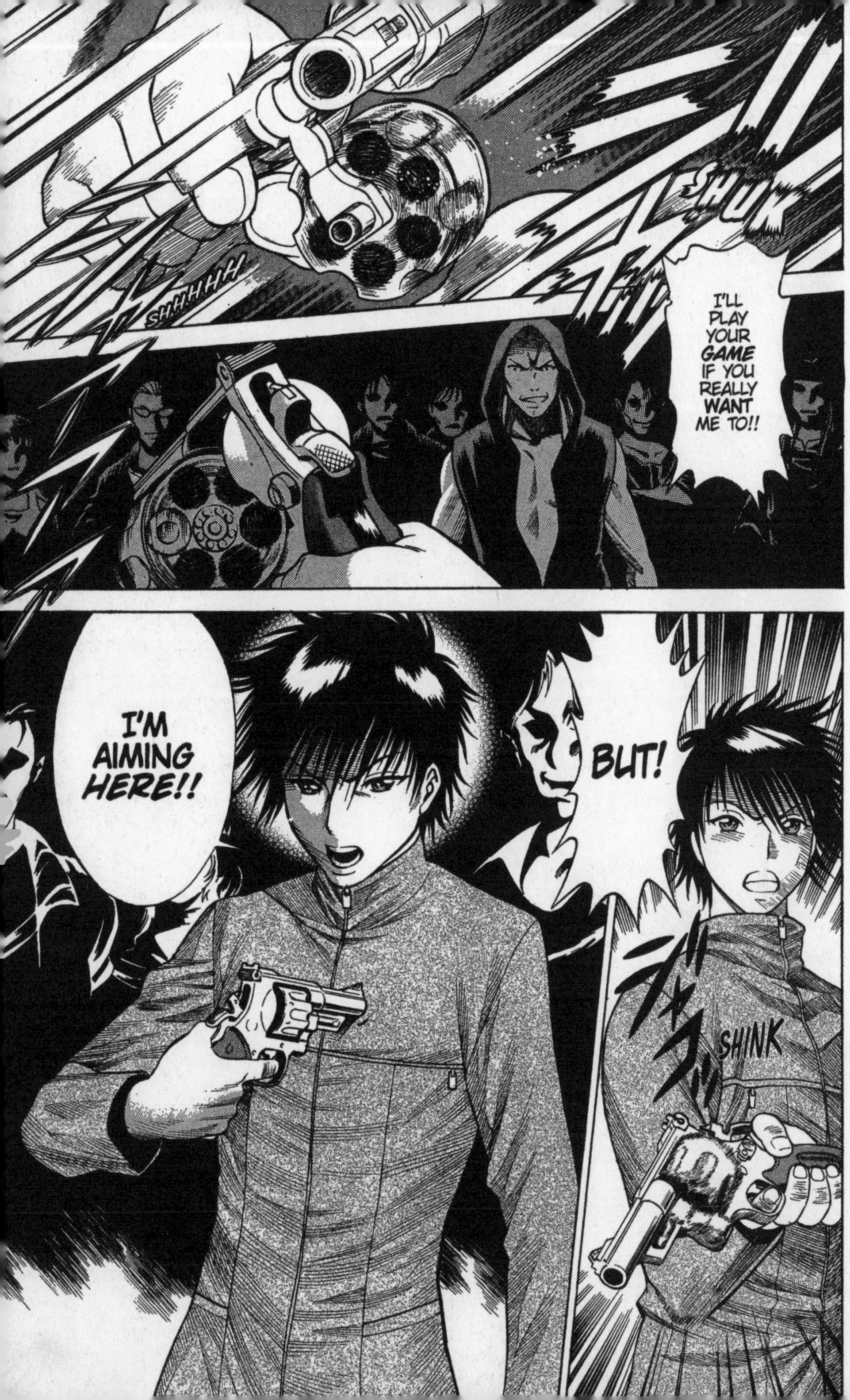
CHUK
SHHHHHH
I'LL PLAY YOUR GAME IF YOU REALLY WANT ME TO!!
BUT!
I'M AIMING HERE!!
SHINK

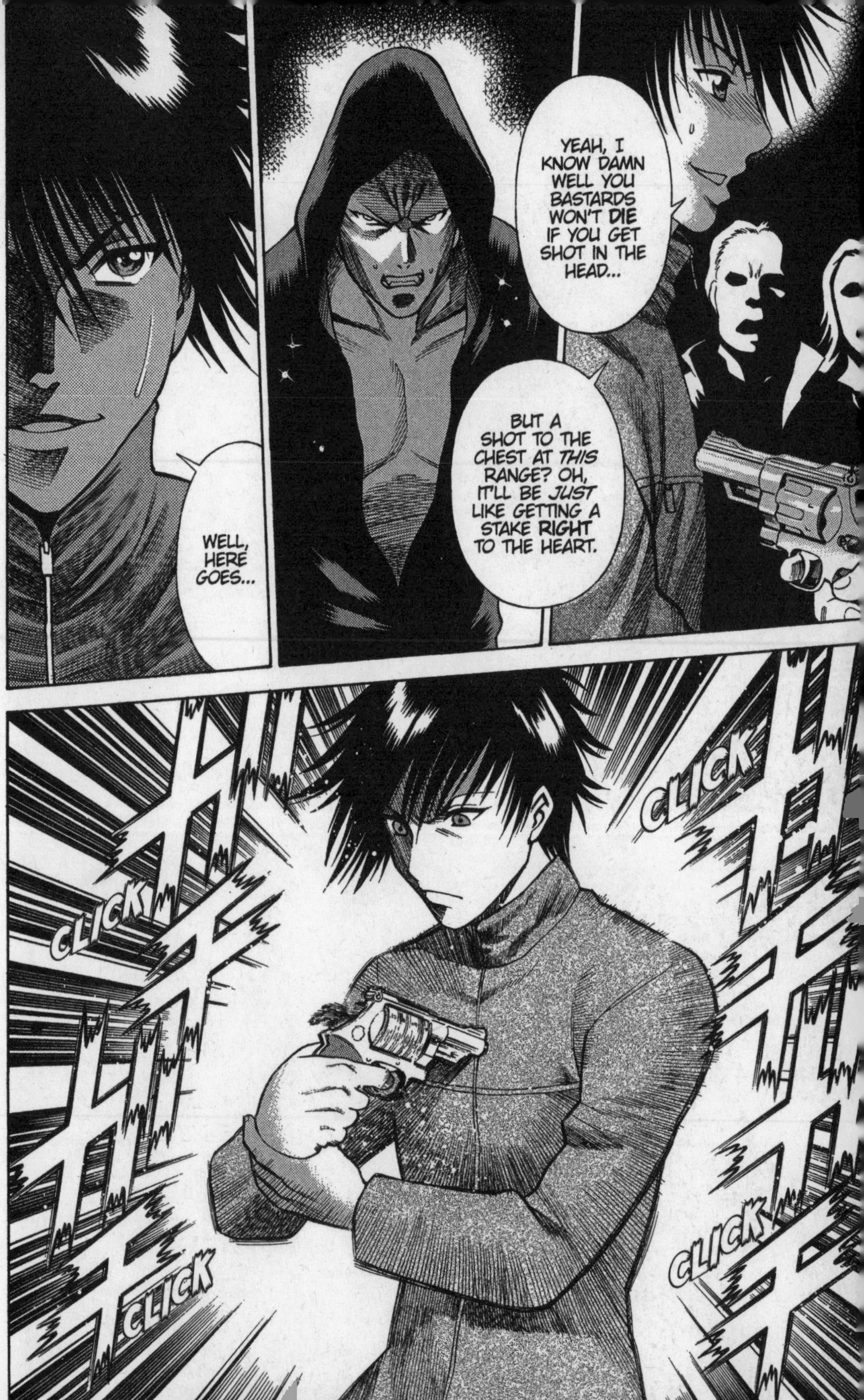
YEAH, I KNOW DAMN WELL YOU BASTARDS WON'T DIE IF YOU GET SHOT IN THE HEAD...
BUT A SHOT TO THE CHEST AT THIS RANGE? OH, IT'LL BE JUST LIKE GETTING A STAKE RIGHT TO THE HEART.
WELL, HERE GOES...
CLICK
CLICK
CLICK
CLICK

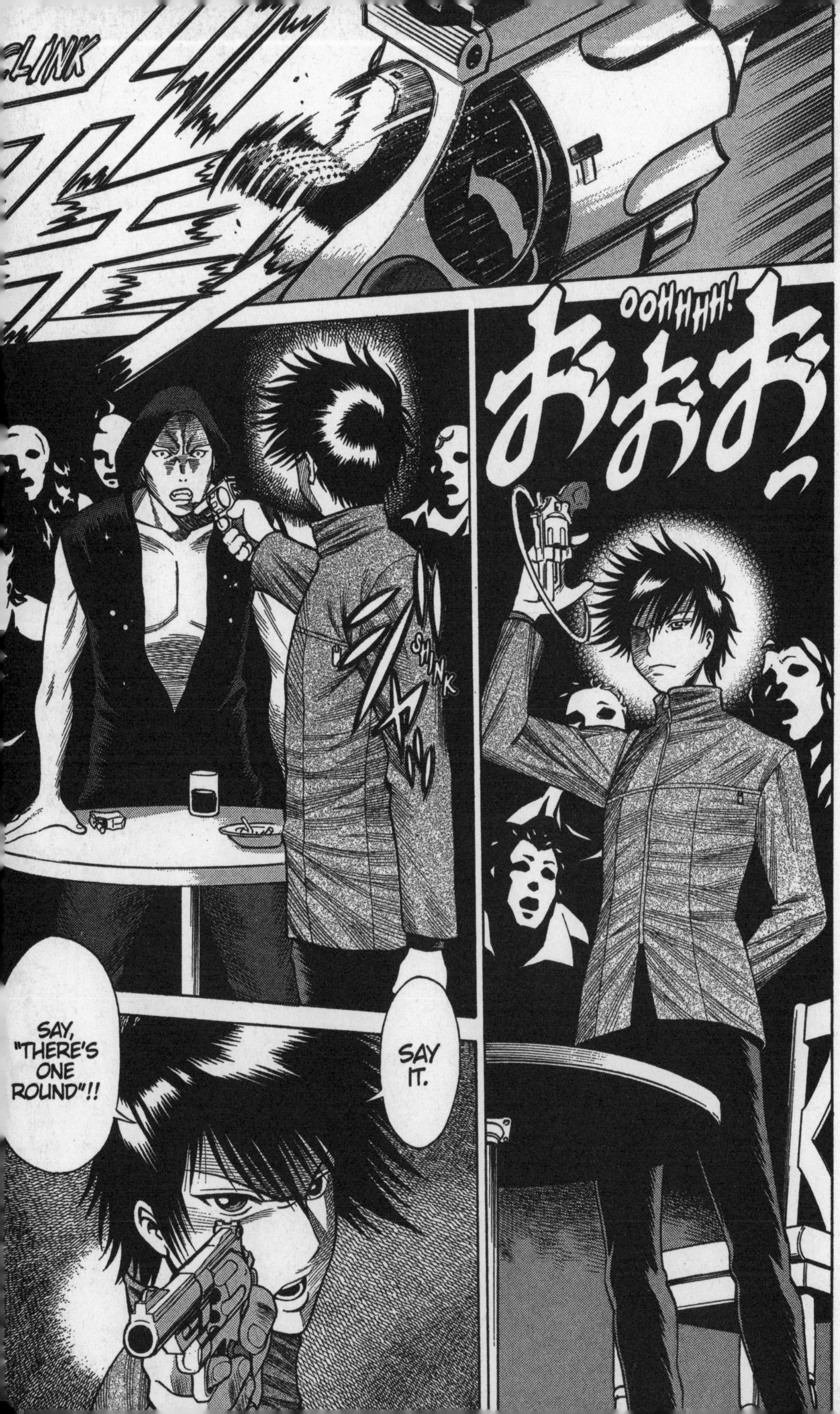
LINK
OOHHHH!
おおおっ
SHINK
SAY IT.
SAY, "THERE'S ONE ROUND"!!

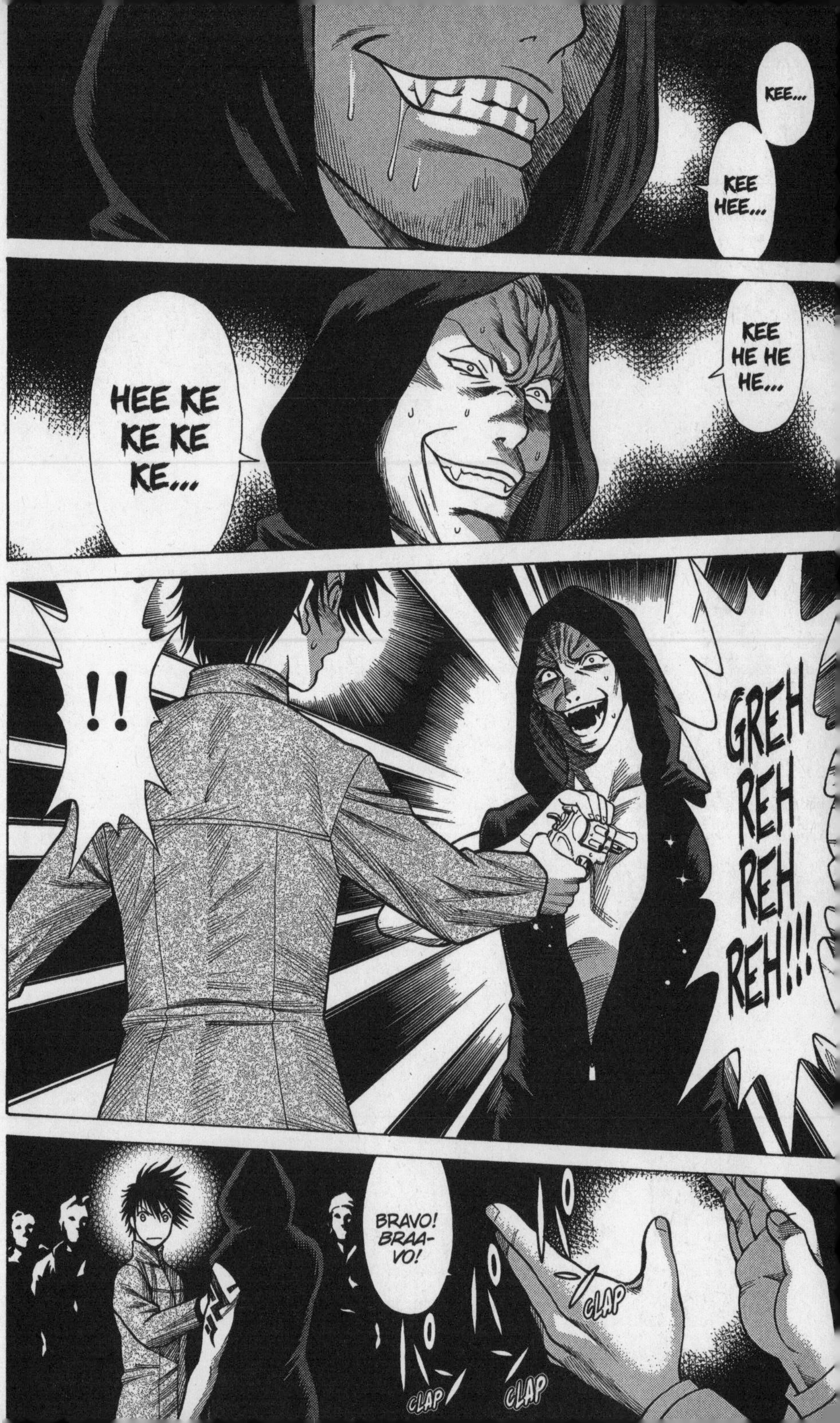
KEE...
KEE HEE...
KEE HE HE HE...
HEE KE KE KE KE...
GREH REH REH REH REH!!!
!!
CLAP
BRAVO! BRAA-VO!
CLAP
CLAP

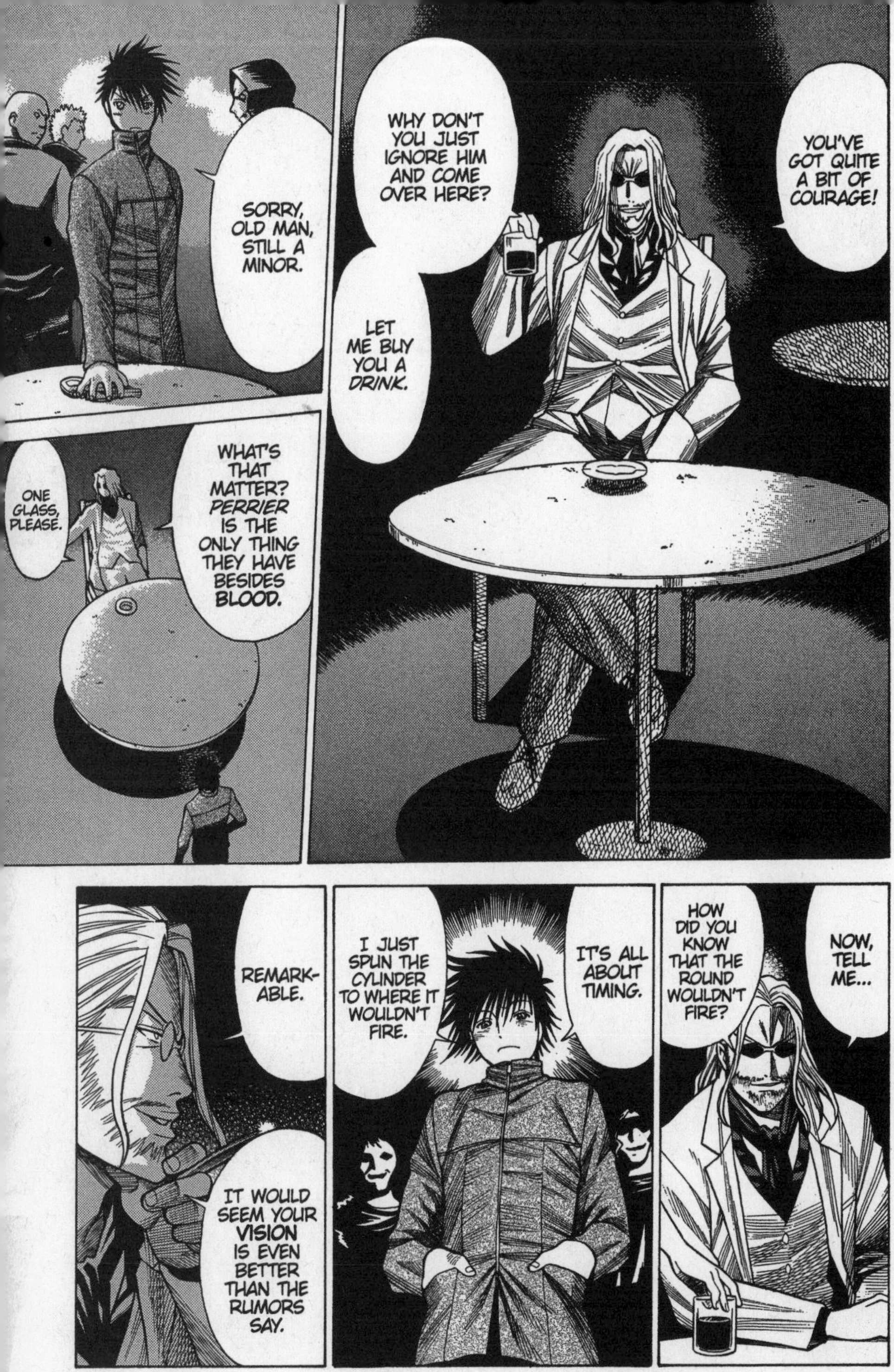
YOU'VE GOT QUITE A BIT OF COURAGE!
WHY DON'T YOU JUST IGNORE HIM AND COME OVER HERE?
LET ME BUY YOU A *DRINK.*
SORRY, OLD MAN, STILL A MINOR.
WHAT'S THAT MATTER? *PERRIER* IS THE ONLY THING THEY HAVE BESIDES **BLOOD.**
ONE GLASS, PLEASE.
NOW, TELL ME...
HOW DID YOU KNOW THAT THE ROUND WOULDN'T FIRE?
IT'S ALL ABOUT TIMING.
I JUST SPUN THE CYLINDER TO WHERE IT WOULDN'T FIRE.
REMARK-ABLE.
IT WOULD SEEM YOUR **VISION** IS EVEN BETTER THAN THE RUMORS SAY.

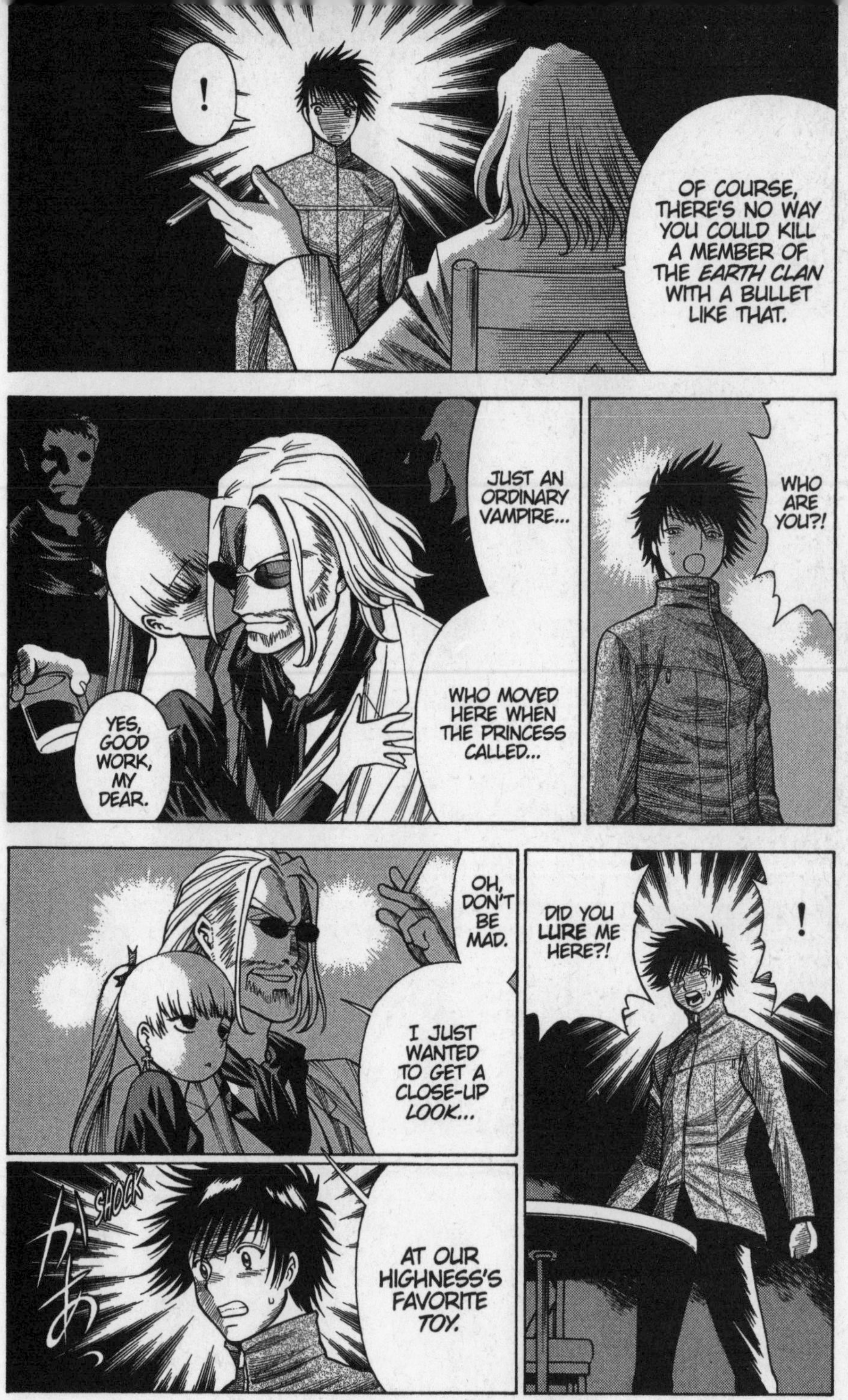
OF COURSE, THERE'S NO WAY YOU COULD KILL A MEMBER OF THE *EARTH CLAN* WITH A BULLET LIKE THAT.
!
WHO ARE YOU?!
JUST AN ORDINARY VAMPIRE...
WHO MOVED HERE WHEN THE PRINCESS CALLED...
YES, GOOD WORK, MY DEAR.
!
DID YOU LURE ME HERE?!
OH, DON'T BE MAD.
I JUST WANTED TO GET A CLOSE-UP *LOOK*...
AT OUR HIGHNESS'S FAVORITE *TOY*.
SHOCK

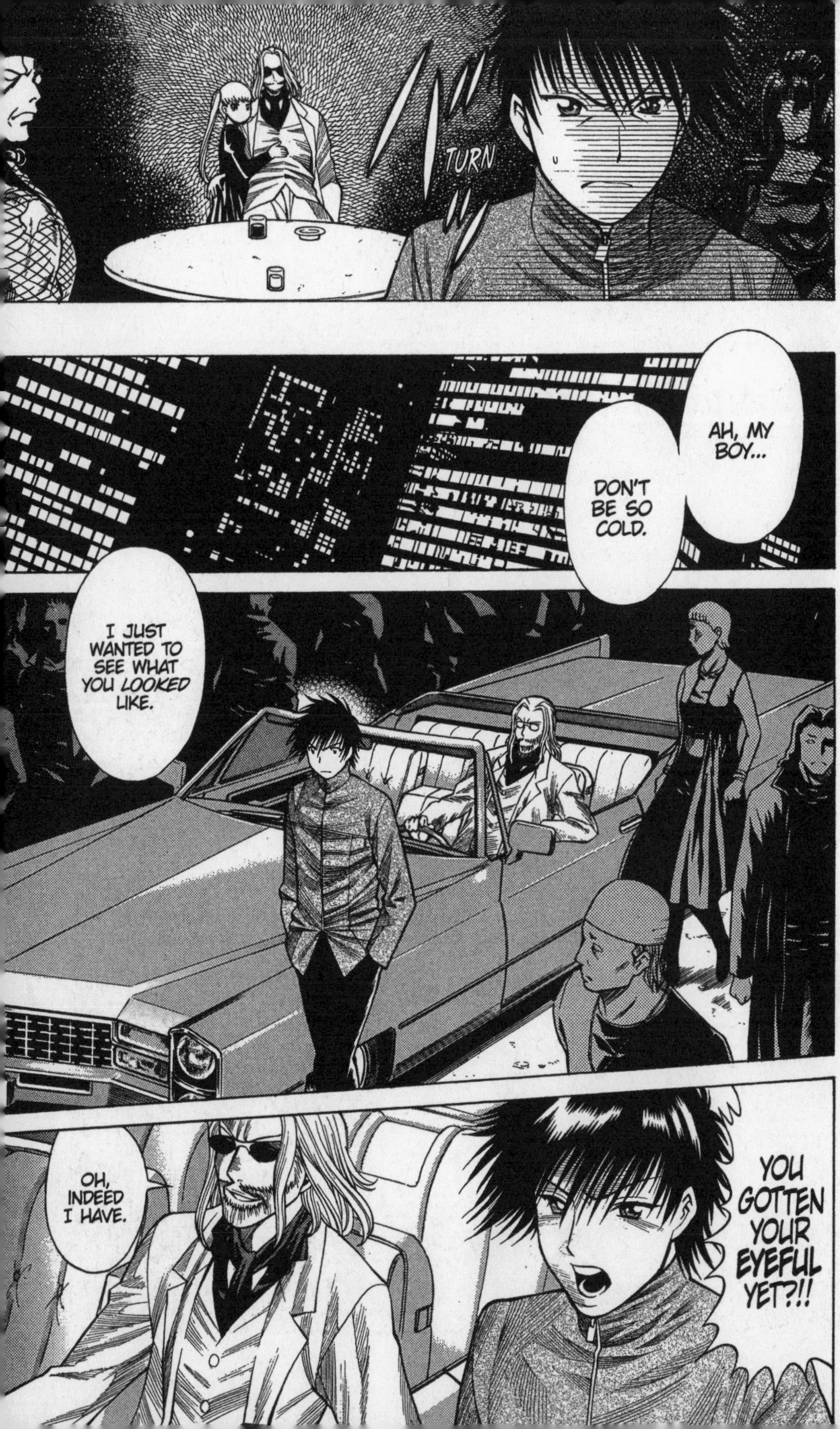
TURN
AH, MY BOY...
DON'T BE SO COLD.
I JUST WANTED TO SEE WHAT YOU LOOKED LIKE.
YOU GOTTEN YOUR EYEFUL YET?!!
OH, INDEED I HAVE.

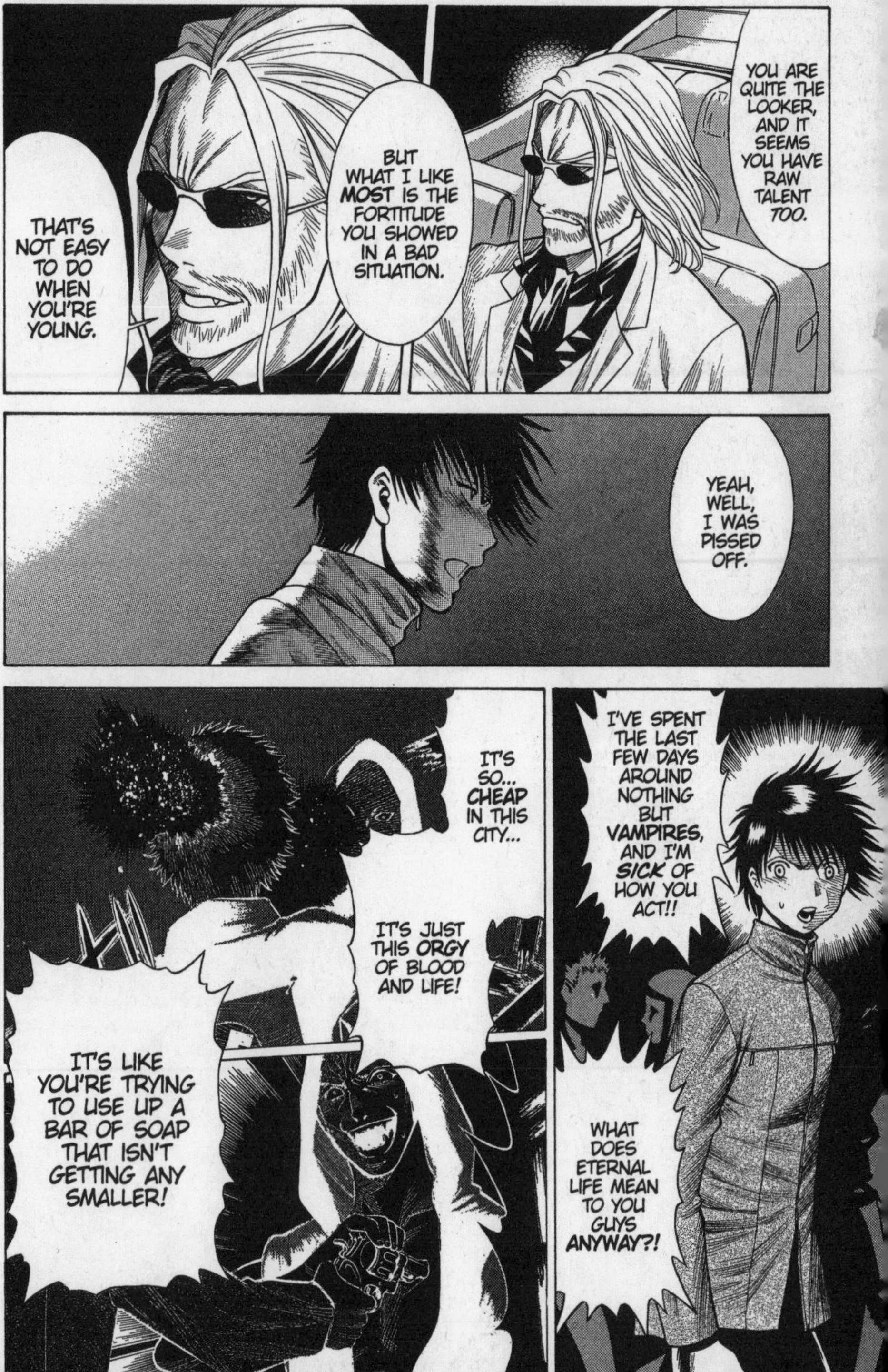
YOU ARE QUITE THE LOOKER, AND IT SEEMS YOU HAVE RAW TALENT *TOO.*
BUT WHAT I LIKE **MOST** IS THE FORTITUDE YOU SHOWED IN A BAD SITUATION.
THAT'S NOT EASY TO DO WHEN YOU'RE YOUNG.
YEAH, WELL, I WAS PISSED OFF.
I'VE SPENT THE LAST FEW DAYS AROUND NOTHING BUT **VAMPIRES,** AND I'M ***SICK*** OF HOW YOU ACT!!
WHAT DOES ETERNAL LIFE MEAN TO YOU GUYS **ANYWAY?!**
IT'S SO... **CHEAP** IN THIS CITY...
IT'S JUST THIS **ORGY** OF BLOOD AND LIFE!
IT'S LIKE YOU'RE TRYING TO USE UP A BAR OF SOAP THAT ISN'T GETTING ANY SMALLER!

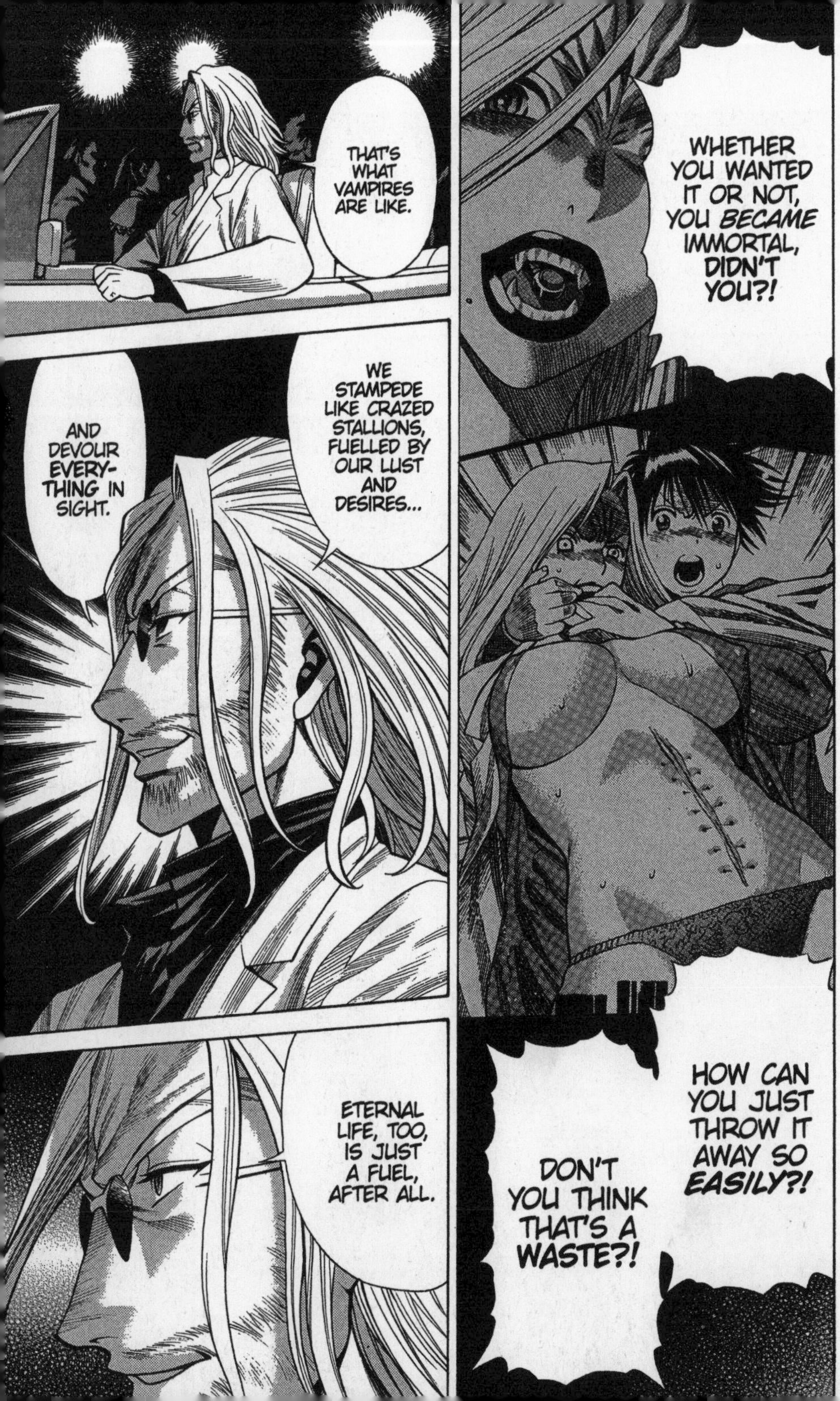
WHETHER YOU WANTED IT OR NOT, YOU *BECAME* IMMORTAL, DIDN'T YOU?!
HOW CAN YOU JUST THROW IT AWAY SO *EASILY?!*
DON'T YOU THINK THAT'S A WASTE?!
THAT'S WHAT VAMPIRES ARE LIKE.
WE STAMPEDE LIKE CRAZED STALLIONS, FUELLED BY OUR LUST AND DESIRES...
AND DEVOUR EVERY-THING IN SIGHT.
ETERNAL LIFE, TOO, IS JUST A FUEL, AFTER ALL.

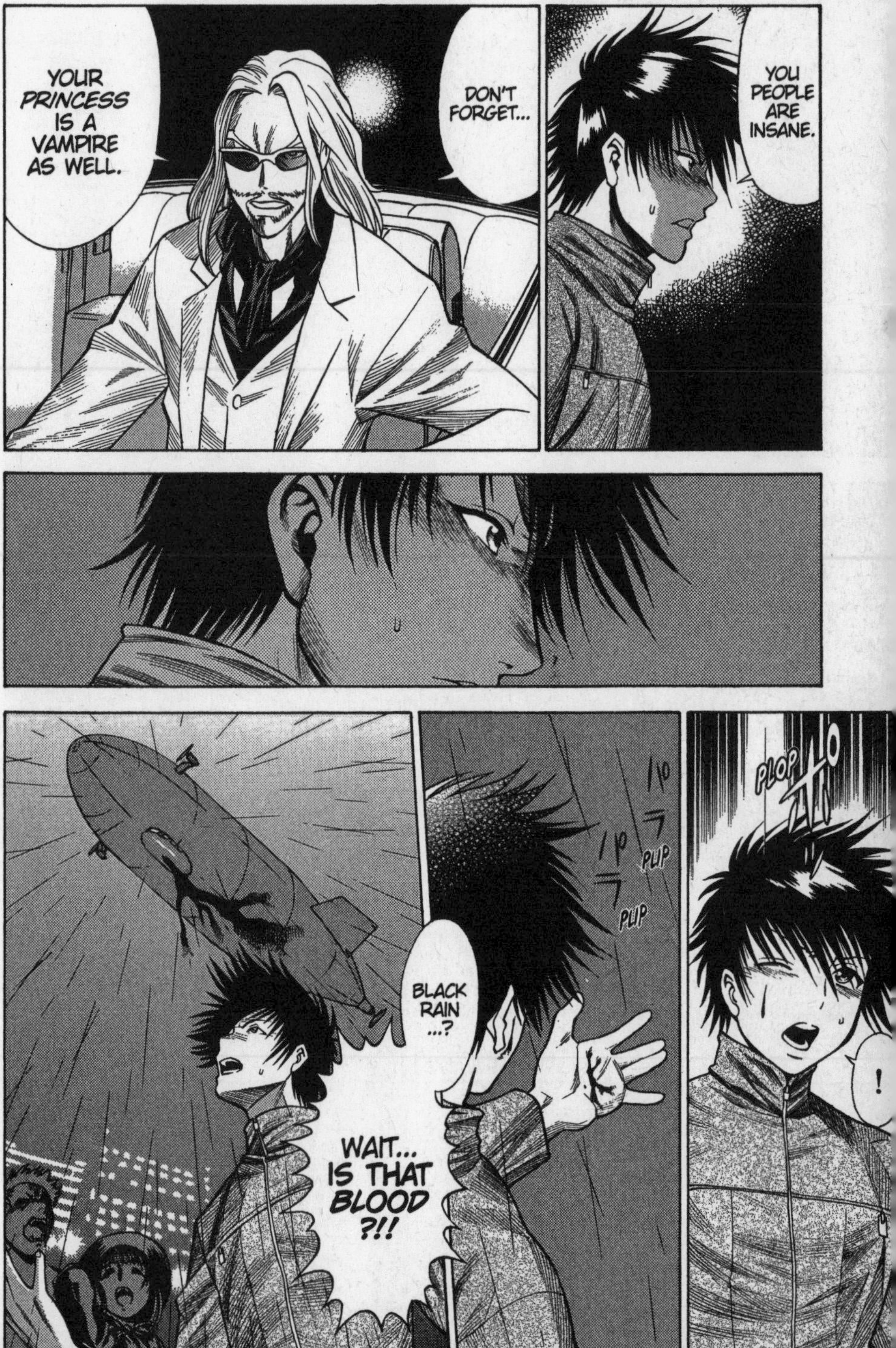
YOU PEOPLE ARE INSANE.
DON'T FORGET...
YOUR PRINCESS IS A VAMPIRE AS WELL.
PLOP
!
PLIP
PLIP
BLACK RAIN ...?
WAIT... IS THAT BLOOD ?!!

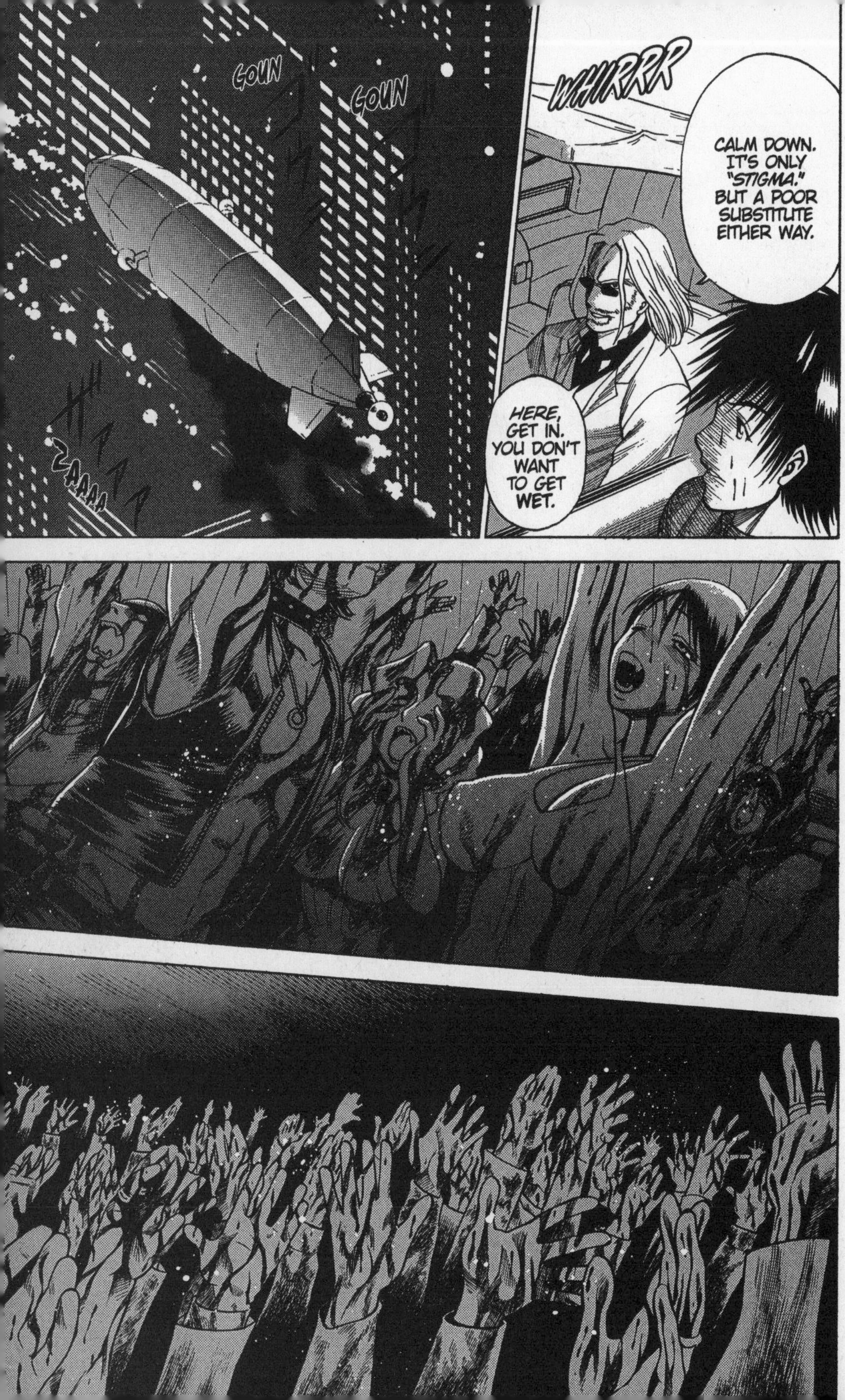
CALM DOWN. IT'S ONLY "STIGMA." BUT A POOR SUBSTITUTE EITHER WAY.
WHIRRR
HERE, GET IN. YOU DON'T WANT TO GET WET.
GOUN
GOUN
ZAAAA

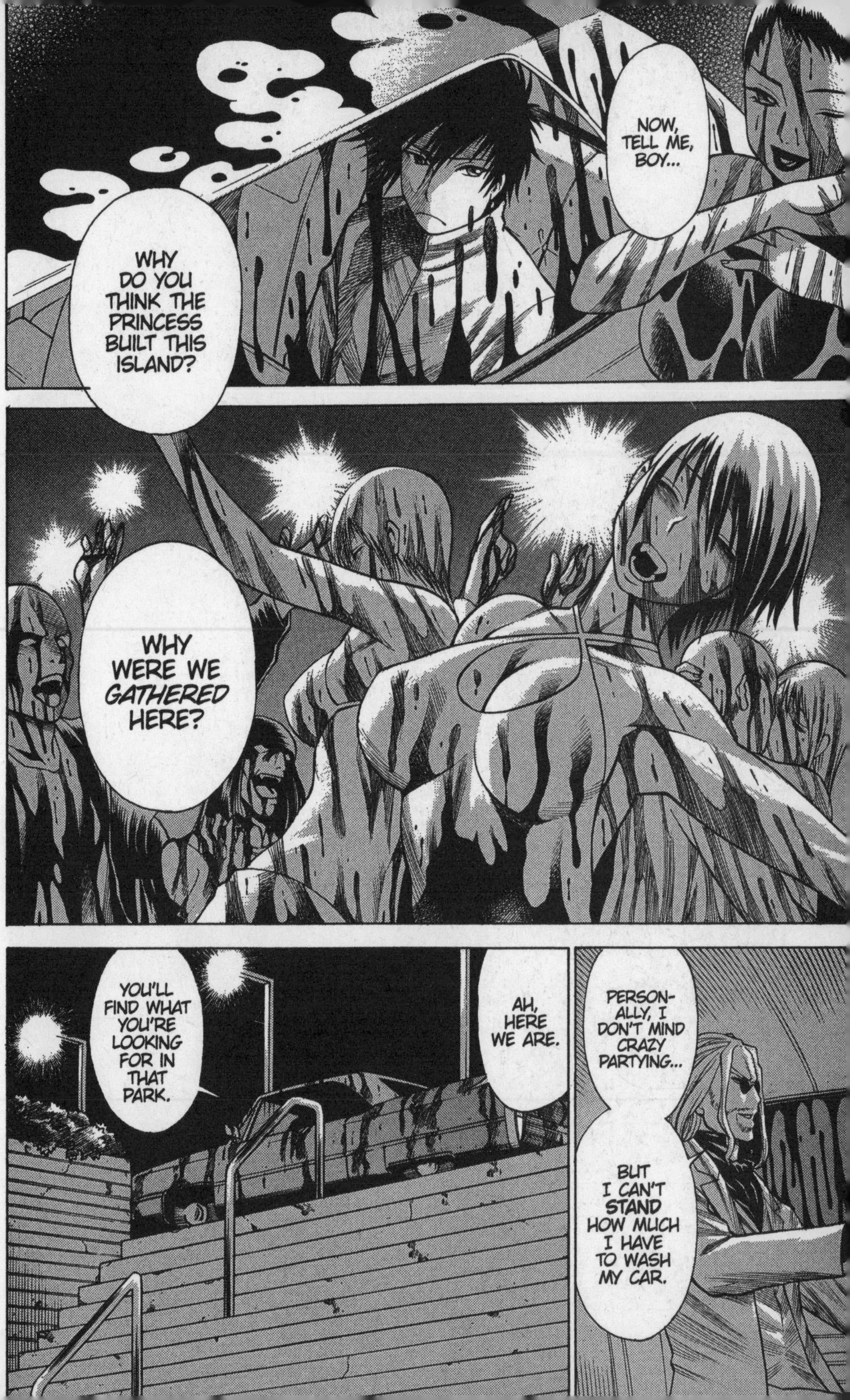
NOW, TELL ME, BOY...
WHY DO YOU THINK THE PRINCESS BUILT THIS ISLAND?
WHY WERE WE GATHERED HERE?
PERSON-ALLY, I DON'T MIND CRAZY PARTYING...
BUT I CAN'T STAND HOW MUCH I HAVE TO WASH MY CAR.
AH, HERE WE ARE.
YOU'LL FIND WHAT YOU'RE LOOKING FOR IN THAT PARK.

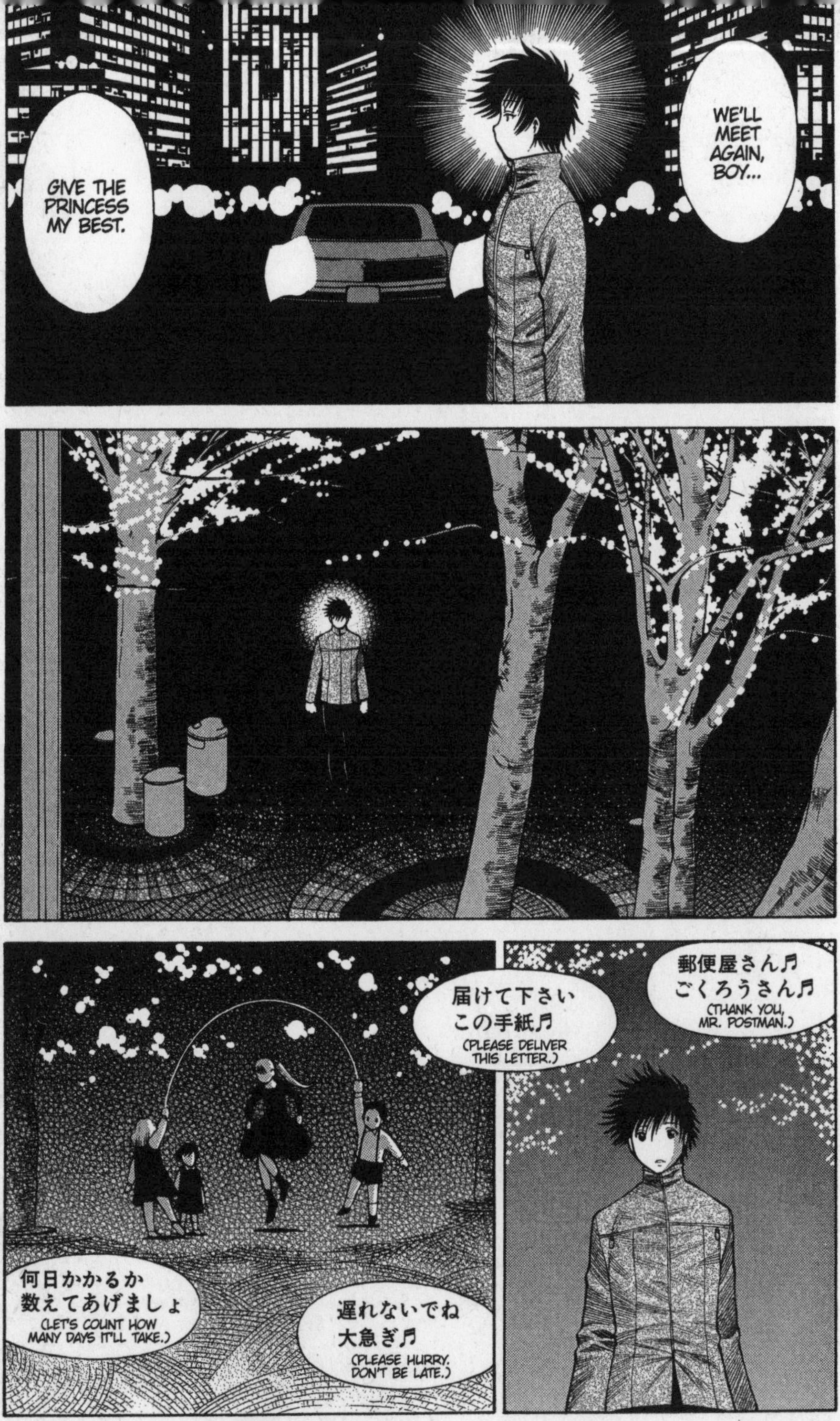
WE'LL MEET AGAIN, BOY...
GIVE THE PRINCESS MY BEST.
郵便屋さん♬ ごくろうさん♬
(THANK YOU, MR. POSTMAN.)
届けて下さい この手紙♬
(PLEASE DELIVER THIS LETTER.)
遅れないでね 大急ぎ♬
(PLEASE HURRY. DON'T BE LATE.)
何日かかるか 数えてあげましょ
(LET'S COUNT HOW MANY DAYS IT'LL TAKE.)

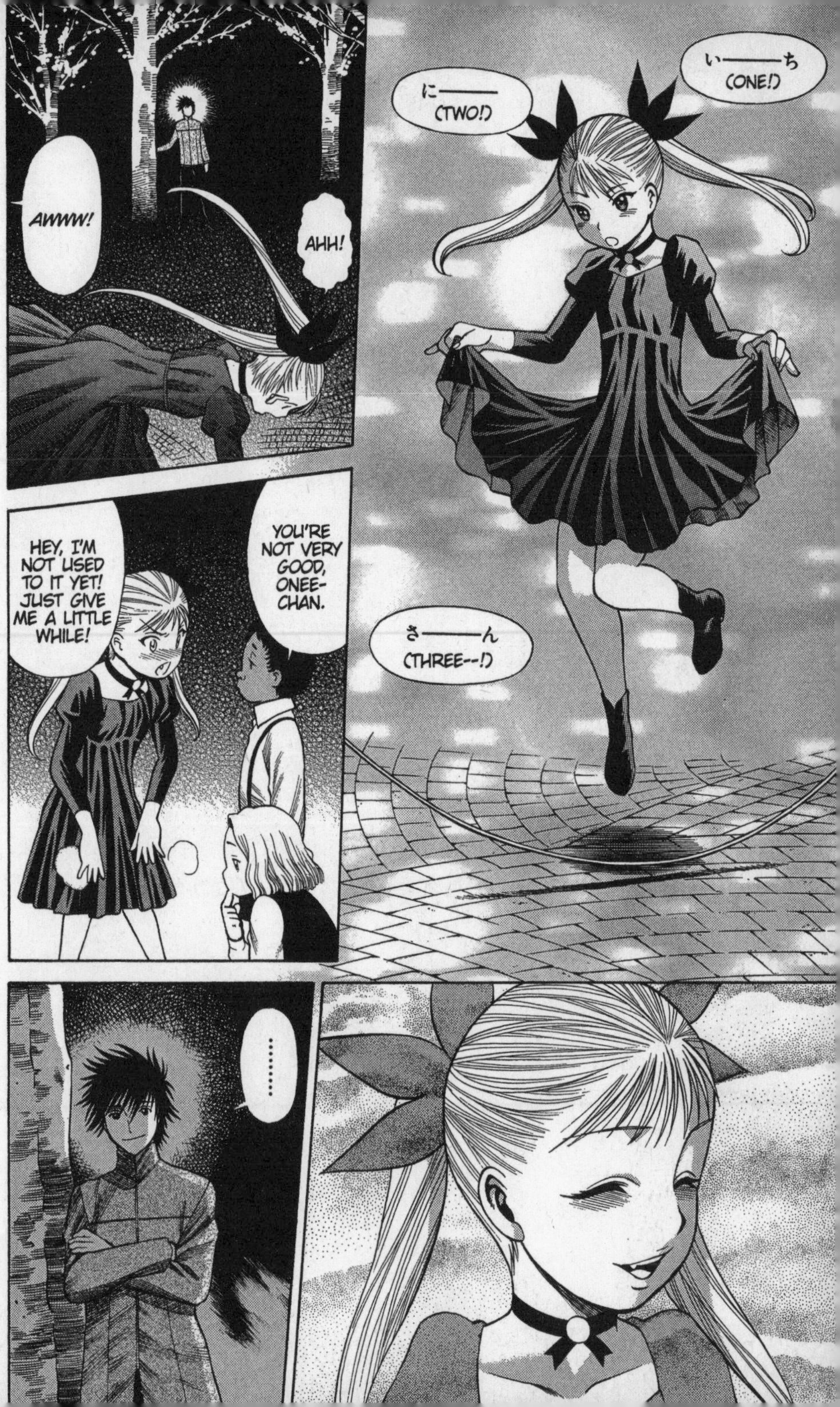

いーーーち (ONE!)
にーーー (TWO!)
さーーーん (THREE--!)
AHH!
AWWW!
YOU'RE NOT VERY GOOD, ONEE-CHAN.
HEY, I'M NOT USED TO IT YET! JUST GIVE ME A LITTLE WHILE!
....

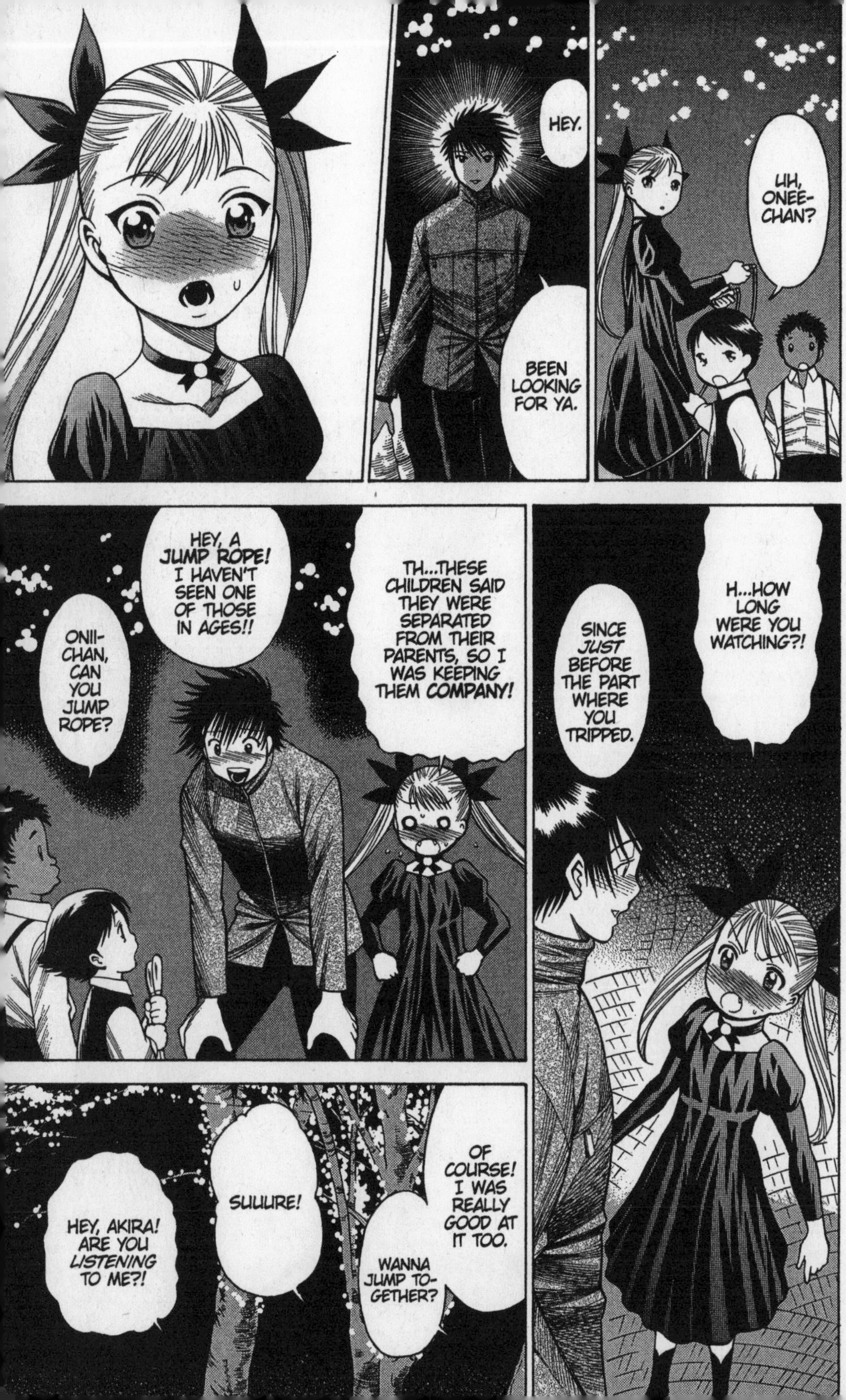
UH, ONEE-CHAN?
HEY.
BEEN LOOKING FOR YA.
H...HOW LONG WERE YOU WATCHING?!
SINCE JUST BEFORE THE PART WHERE YOU TRIPPED.
TH...THESE CHILDREN SAID THEY WERE SEPARATED FROM THEIR PARENTS, SO I WAS KEEPING THEM COMPANY!
HEY, A JUMP ROPE! I HAVEN'T SEEN ONE OF THOSE IN AGES!!
ONII-CHAN, CAN YOU JUMP ROPE?
OF COURSE! I WAS REALLY GOOD AT IT TOO.
WANNA JUMP TO-GETHER?
SUUURE!
HEY, AKIRA! ARE YOU LISTENING TO ME?!

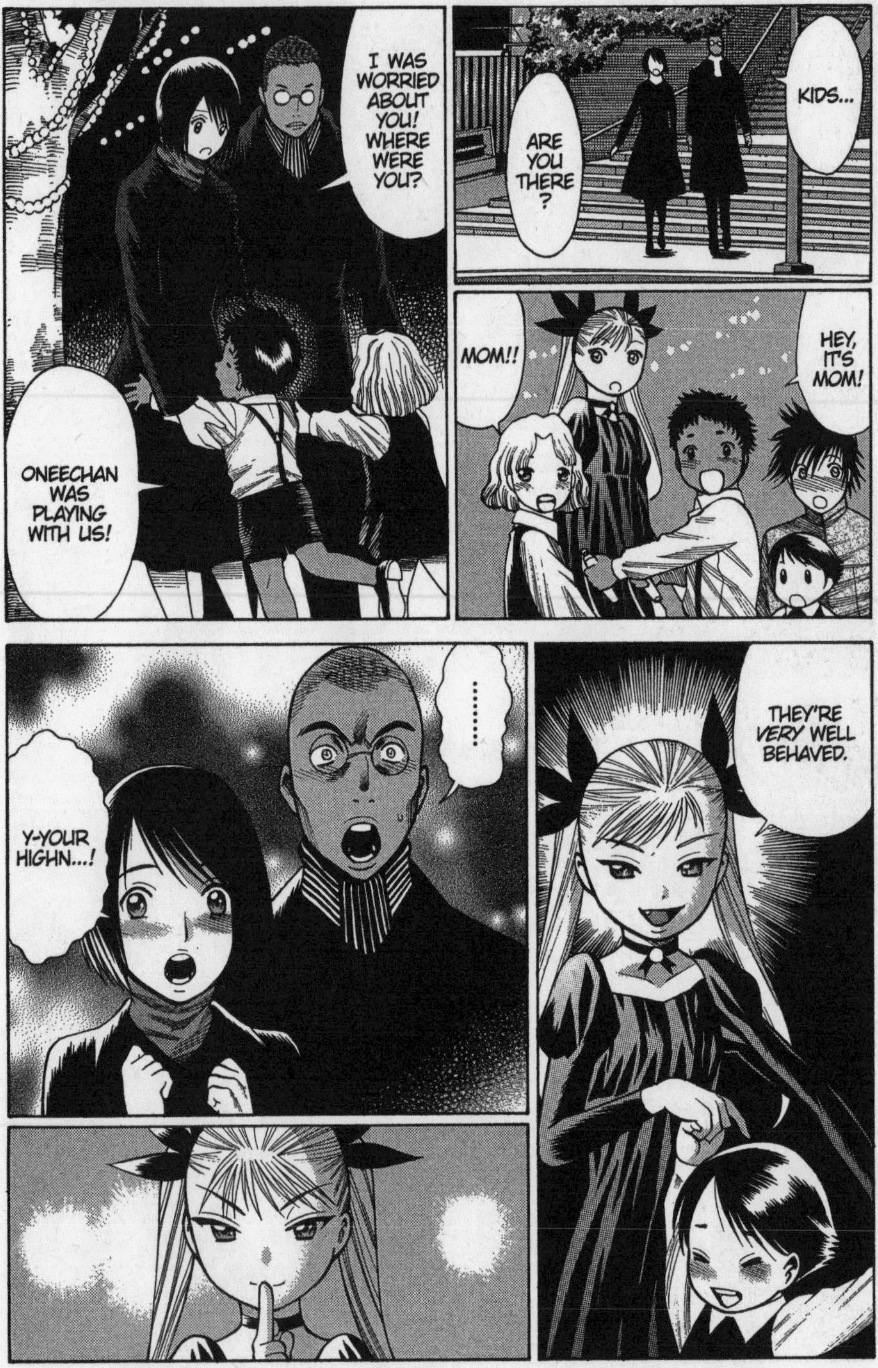
KIDS...
ARE YOU THERE?
HEY, IT'S MOM!
MOM!!
I WAS WORRIED ABOUT YOU! WHERE WERE YOU?
ONEECHAN WAS PLAYING WITH US!
THEY'RE *VERY* WELL BEHAVED.
......
Y-YOUR HIGHN...!

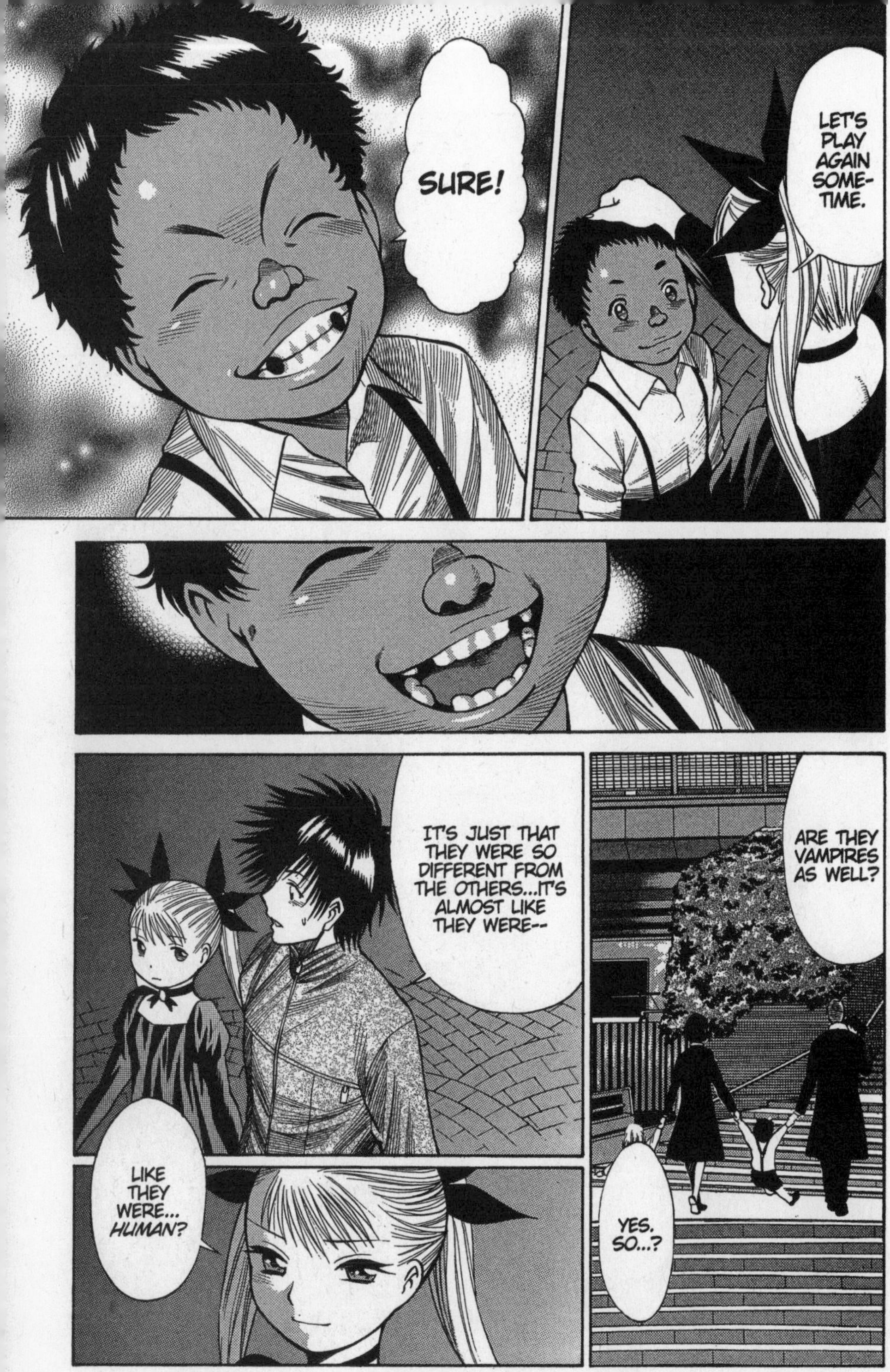
LET'S PLAY AGAIN SOME-TIME.
SURE!
ARE THEY VAMPIRES AS WELL?
YES. SO...?
IT'S JUST THAT THEY WERE SO DIFFERENT FROM THE OTHERS...IT'S ALMOST LIKE THEY WERE--
LIKE THEY WERE... *HUMAN?*

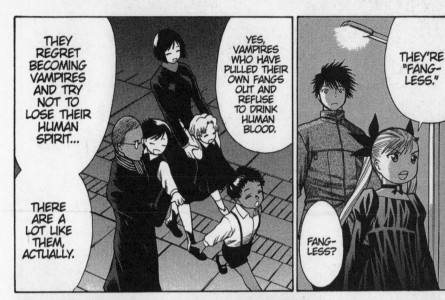

THEY'RE "FANG-LESS."
FANG-LESS?
YES, VAMPIRES WHO HAVE PULLED THEIR OWN FANGS OUT AND REFUSE TO DRINK HUMAN BLOOD.
THEY REGRET BECOMING VAMPIRES AND TRY NOT TO LOSE THEIR HUMAN SPIRIT...
THERE ARE A LOT LIKE THEM, ACTUALLY.
AND IT'S BECAUSE OF THIS, THEY WERE PERSECUTED NOT ONLY BY HUMANS BUT OTHER VAMPIRES AS WELL.
THEY WERE FORCED TO LEAD A LIFE OF EXILE.
BUT THAT'S OVER NOW.
NOW, WE HAVE THE BUND.
AS LONG AS IT'S HERE, THEIR PEACE WILL *NEVER* BE DISTURBED AGAIN.
....

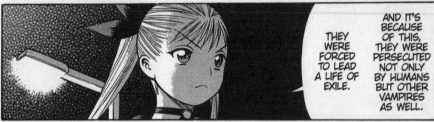

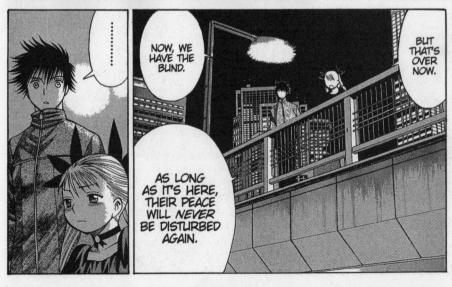

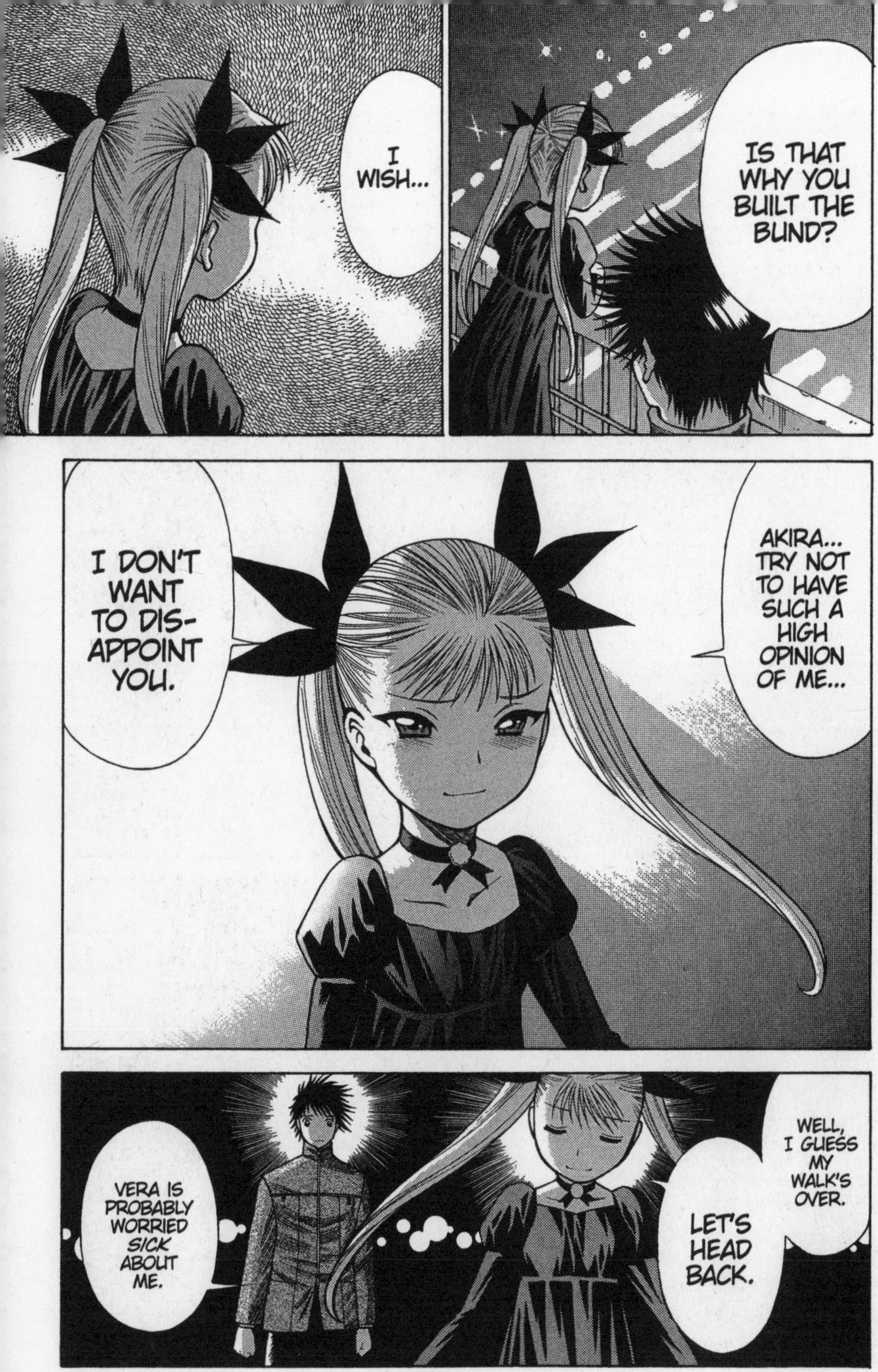
IS THAT WHY YOU BUILT THE BUND?
I WISH...
AKIRA... TRY NOT TO HAVE SUCH A HIGH OPINION OF ME...
I DON'T WANT TO DIS-APPOINT YOU.
WELL, I GUESS MY WALK'S OVER.
LET'S HEAD BACK.
VERA IS PROBABLY WORRIED SICK ABOUT ME.

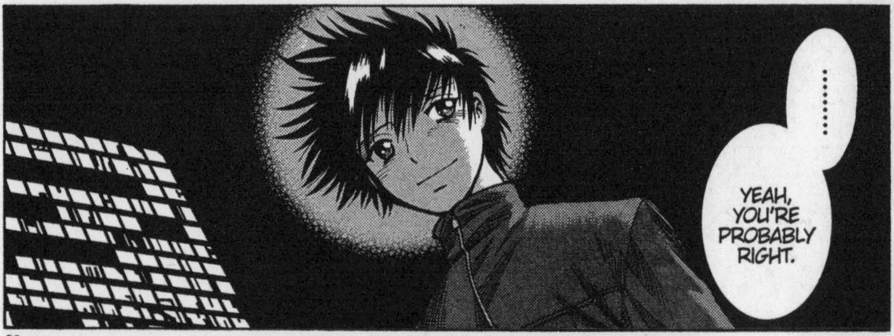
......
YEAH, YOU'RE PROBABLY RIGHT.

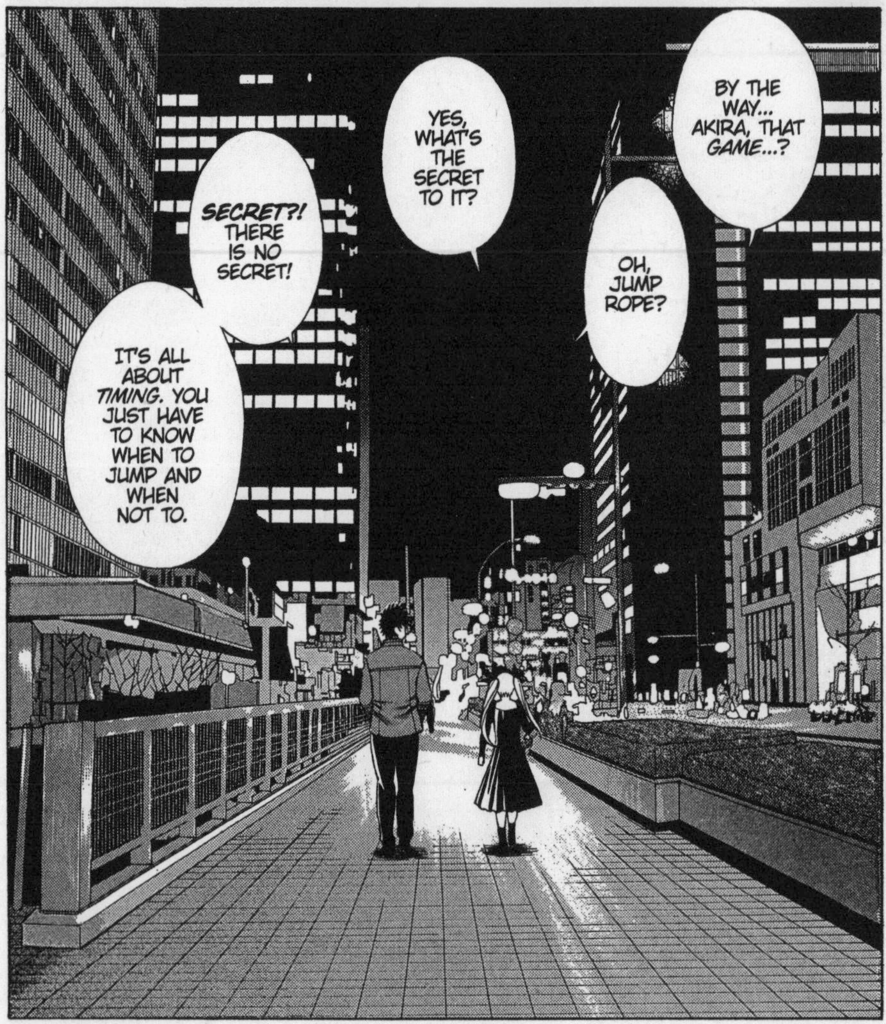
BY THE WAY... AKIRA, THAT *GAME*...?
OH, JUMP ROPE?
YES, WHAT'S THE SECRET TO IT?
SECRET?! THERE IS NO SECRET!
IT'S ALL ABOUT *TIMING*. YOU JUST HAVE TO KNOW WHEN TO JUMP AND WHEN NOT TO.

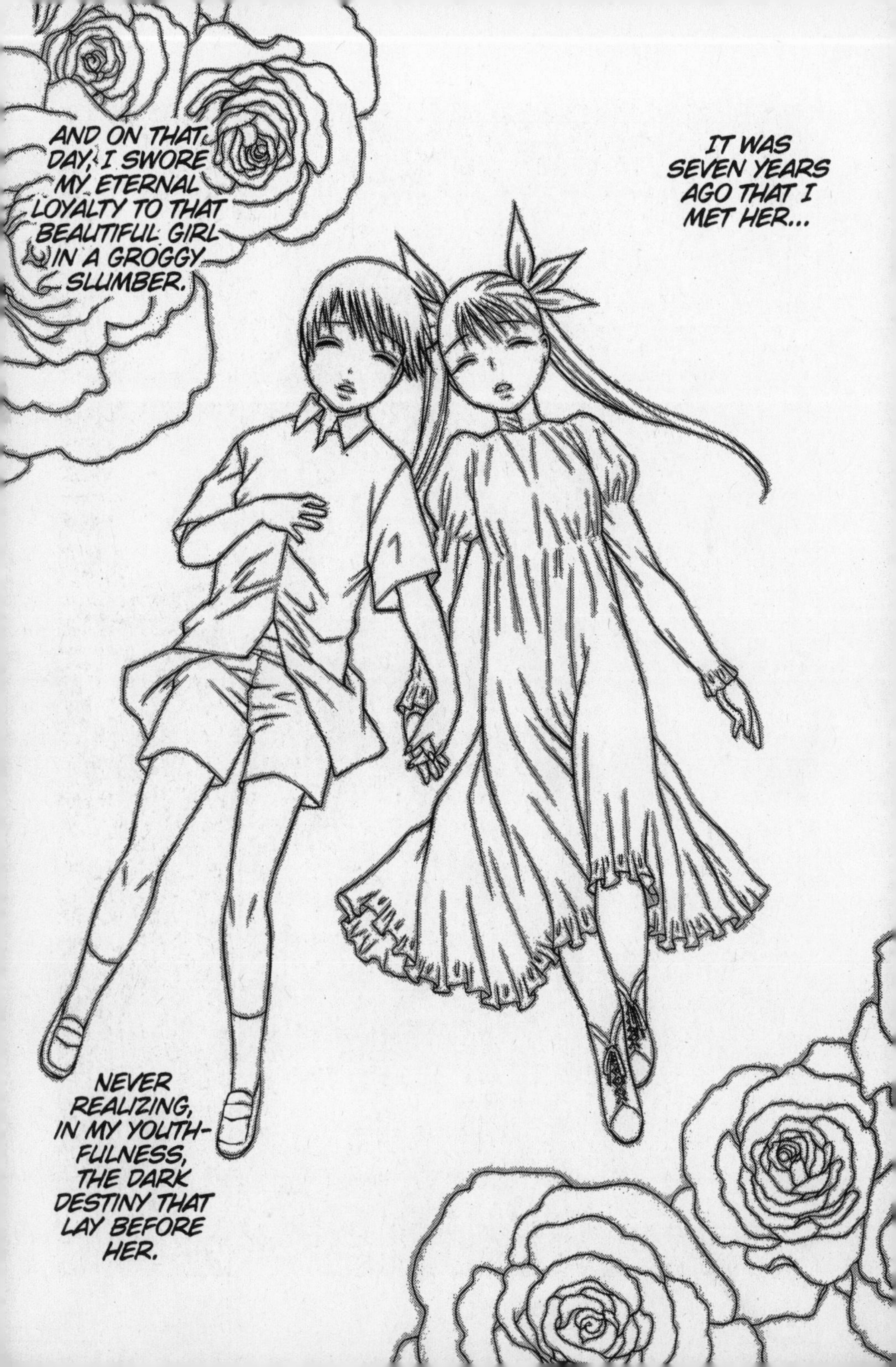
IT WAS SEVEN YEARS AGO THAT I MET HER...
AND ON THAT DAY, I SWORE MY ETERNAL LOYALTY TO THAT BEAUTIFUL GIRL IN A GROGGY SLUMBER.
NEVER REALIZING, IN MY YOUTH-FULNESS, THE DARK DESTINY THAT LAY BEFORE HER.

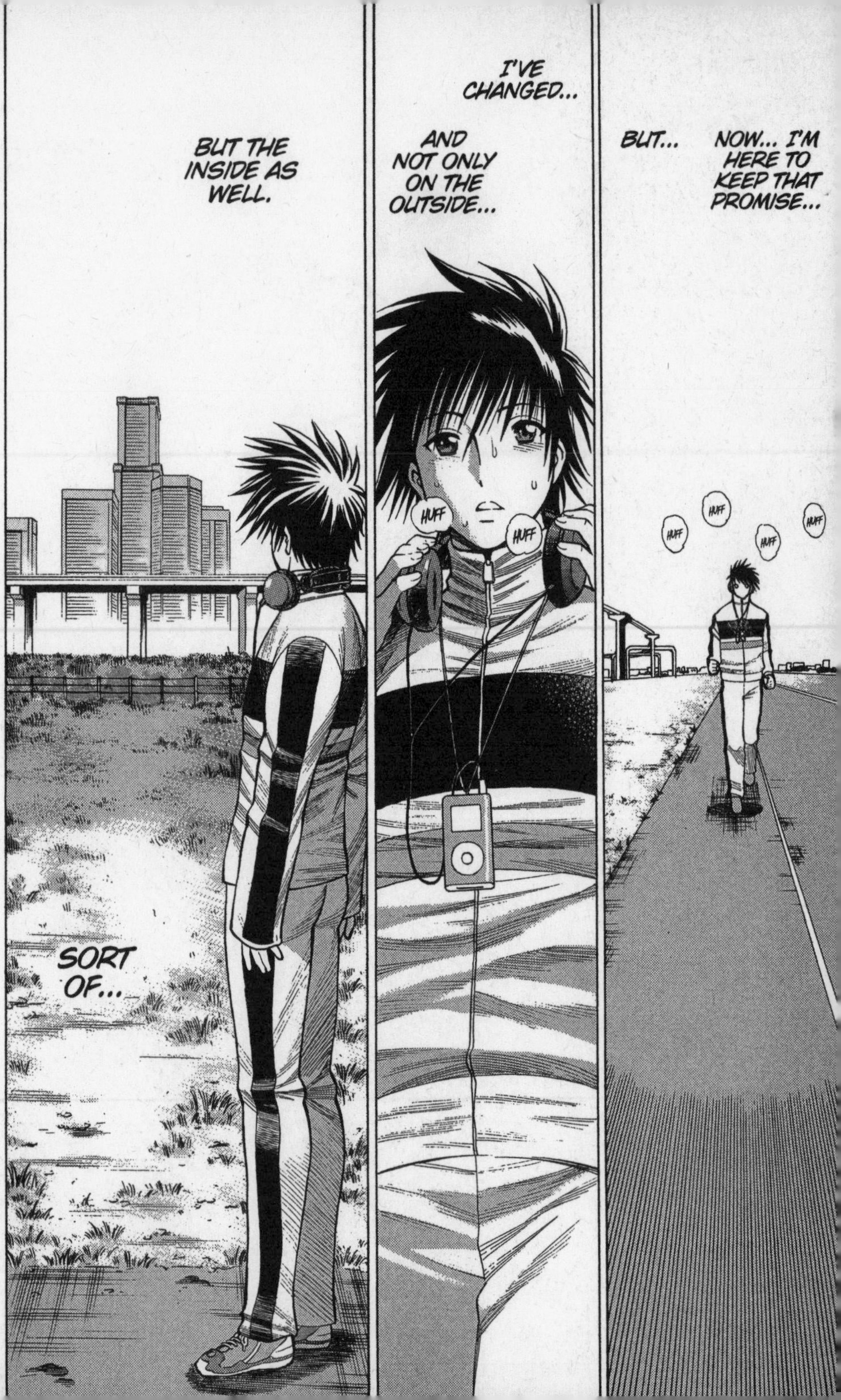
NOW... I'M HERE TO KEEP THAT PROMISE...
BUT...
HUFF
HUFF
HUFF
HUFF
I'VE CHANGED...
AND NOT ONLY ON THE OUTSIDE...
HUFF
HUFF
BUT THE INSIDE AS WELL.
SORT OF...

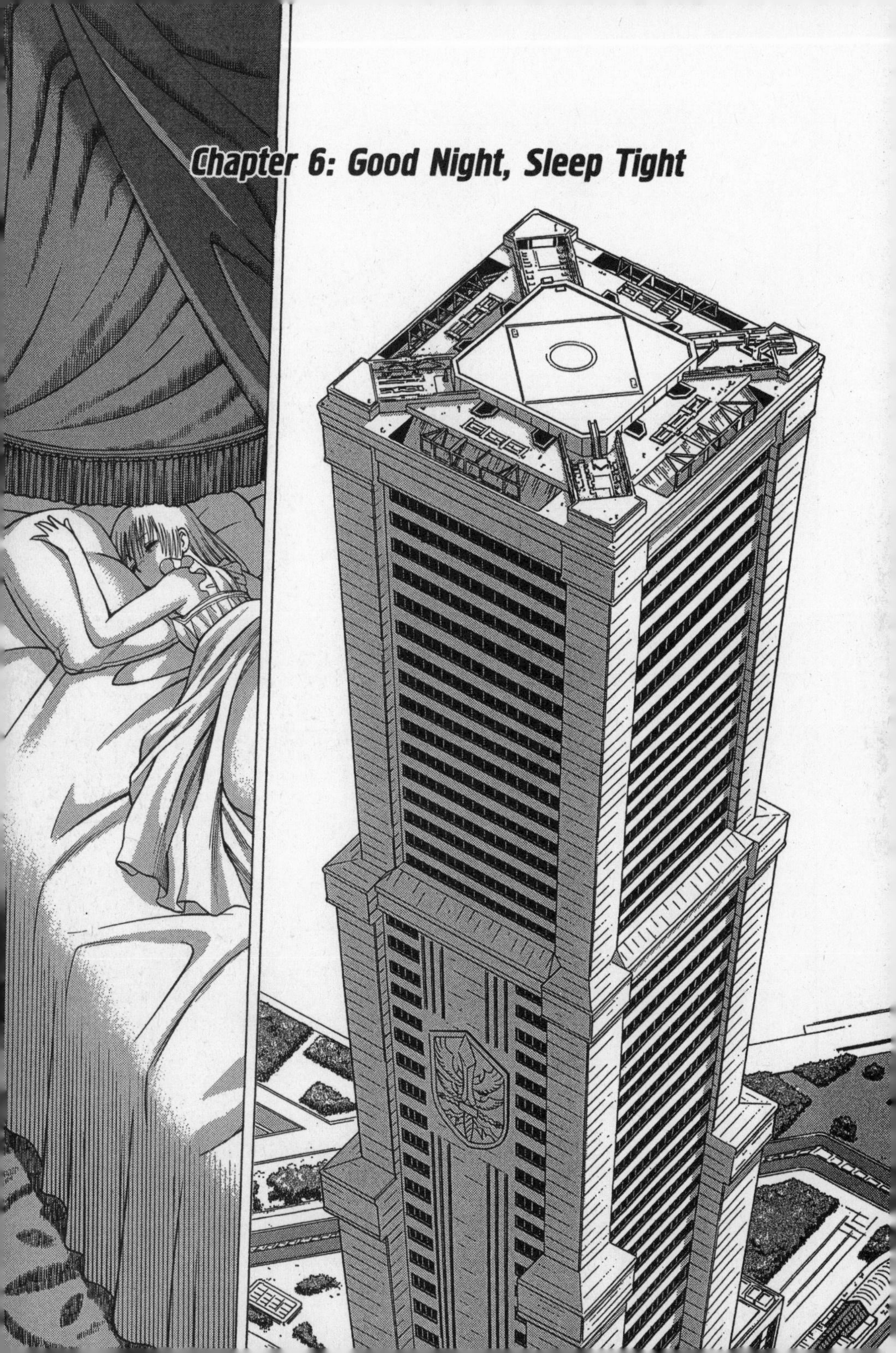
Chapter 6: Good Night, Sleep Tight

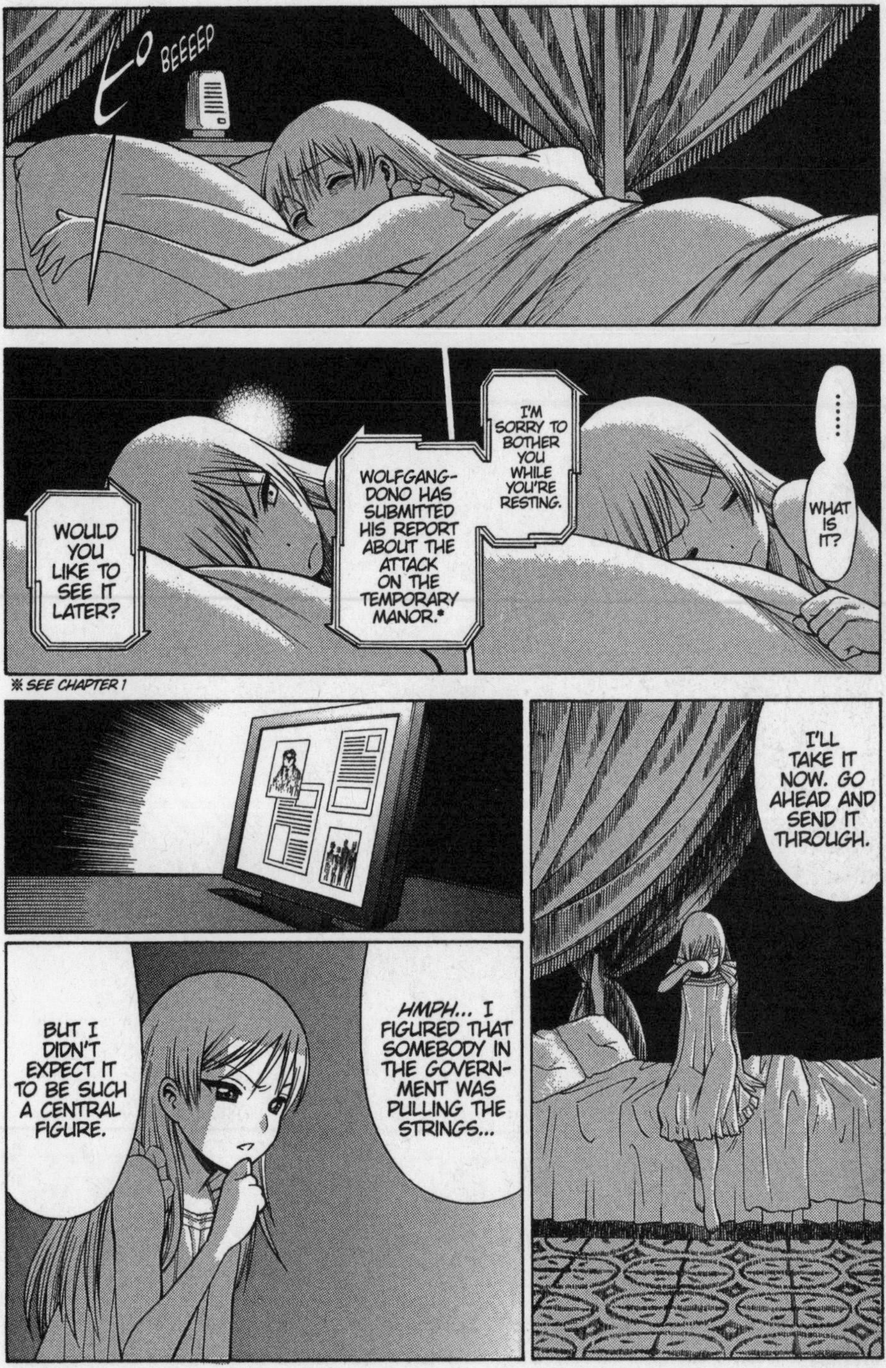
BEEEEP
......
WHAT IS IT?
I'M SORRY TO BOTHER YOU WHILE YOU'RE RESTING.
WOLFGANG-DONO HAS SUBMITTED HIS REPORT ABOUT THE ATTACK ON THE TEMPORARY MANOR.*
WOULD YOU LIKE TO SEE IT LATER?
I'LL TAKE IT NOW. GO AHEAD AND SEND IT THROUGH.
HMPH... I FIGURED THAT SOMEBODY IN THE GOVERNMENT WAS PULLING THE STRINGS...
BUT I DIDN'T EXPECT IT TO BE SUCH A CENTRAL FIGURE.

※ SEE CHAPTER 1

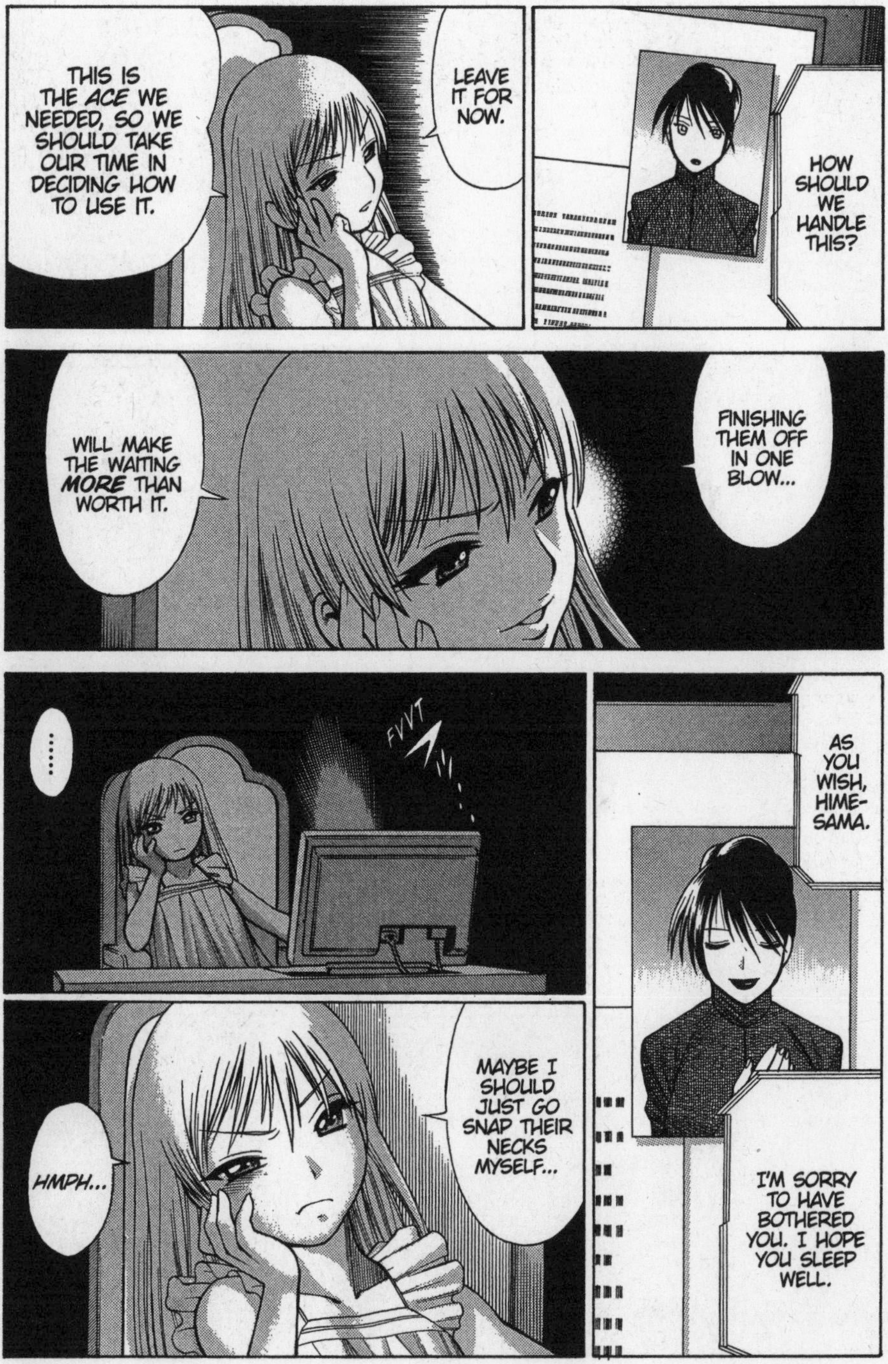
HOW SHOULD WE HANDLE THIS?
LEAVE IT FOR NOW.
THIS IS THE ACE WE NEEDED, SO WE SHOULD TAKE OUR TIME IN DECIDING HOW TO USE IT.
FINISHING THEM OFF IN ONE BLOW...
WILL MAKE THE WAITING MORE THAN WORTH IT.
AS YOU WISH, HIME-SAMA.
I'M SORRY TO HAVE BOTHERED YOU. I HOPE YOU SLEEP WELL.
......
FVVT
MAYBE I SHOULD JUST GO SNAP THEIR NECKS MYSELF...
HMPH...

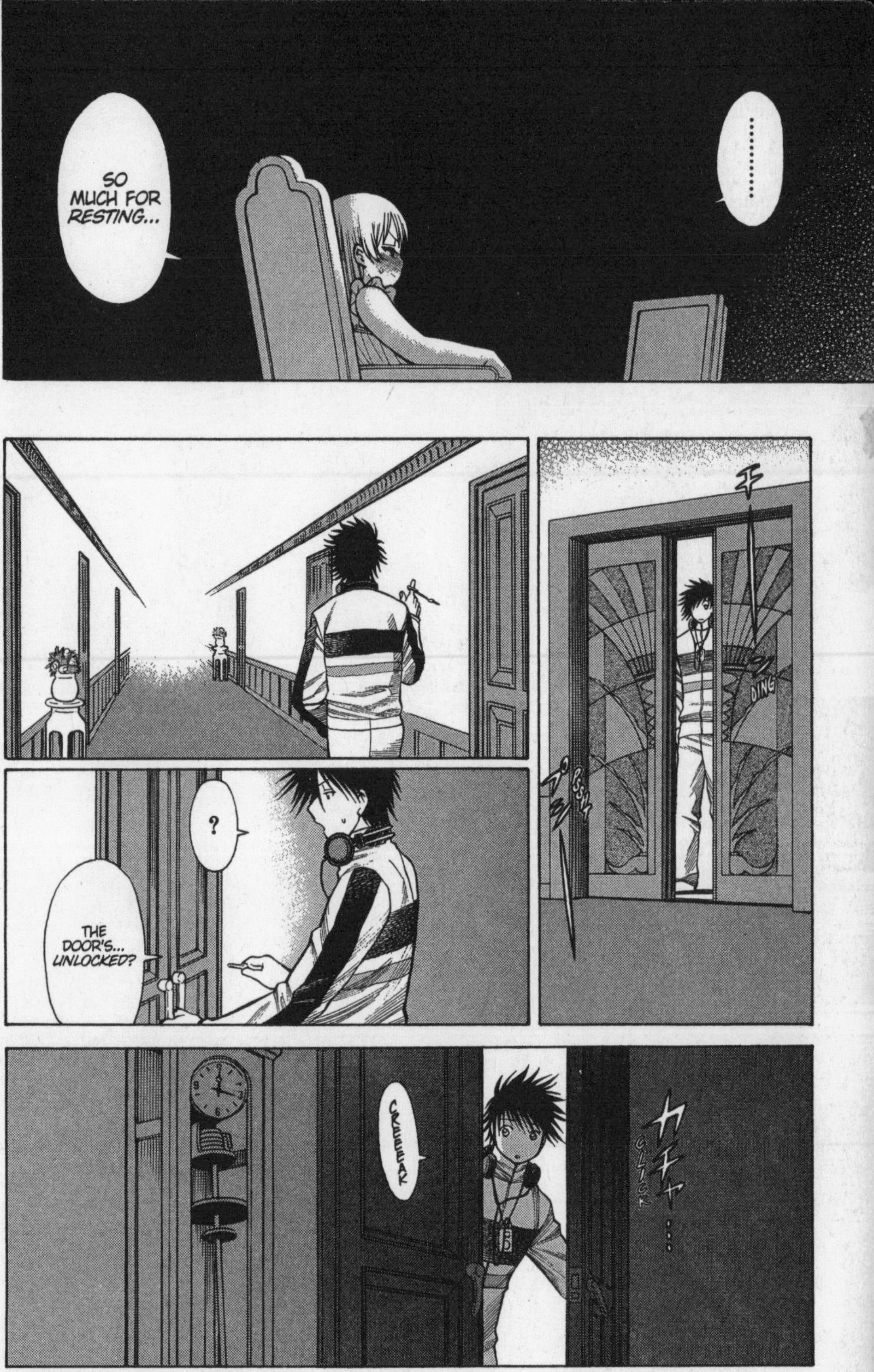
......
SO MUCH FOR RESTING...
DING
PSSH
?
THE DOOR'S... UNLOCKED?
カチャ...
CLICK
CREEEAK

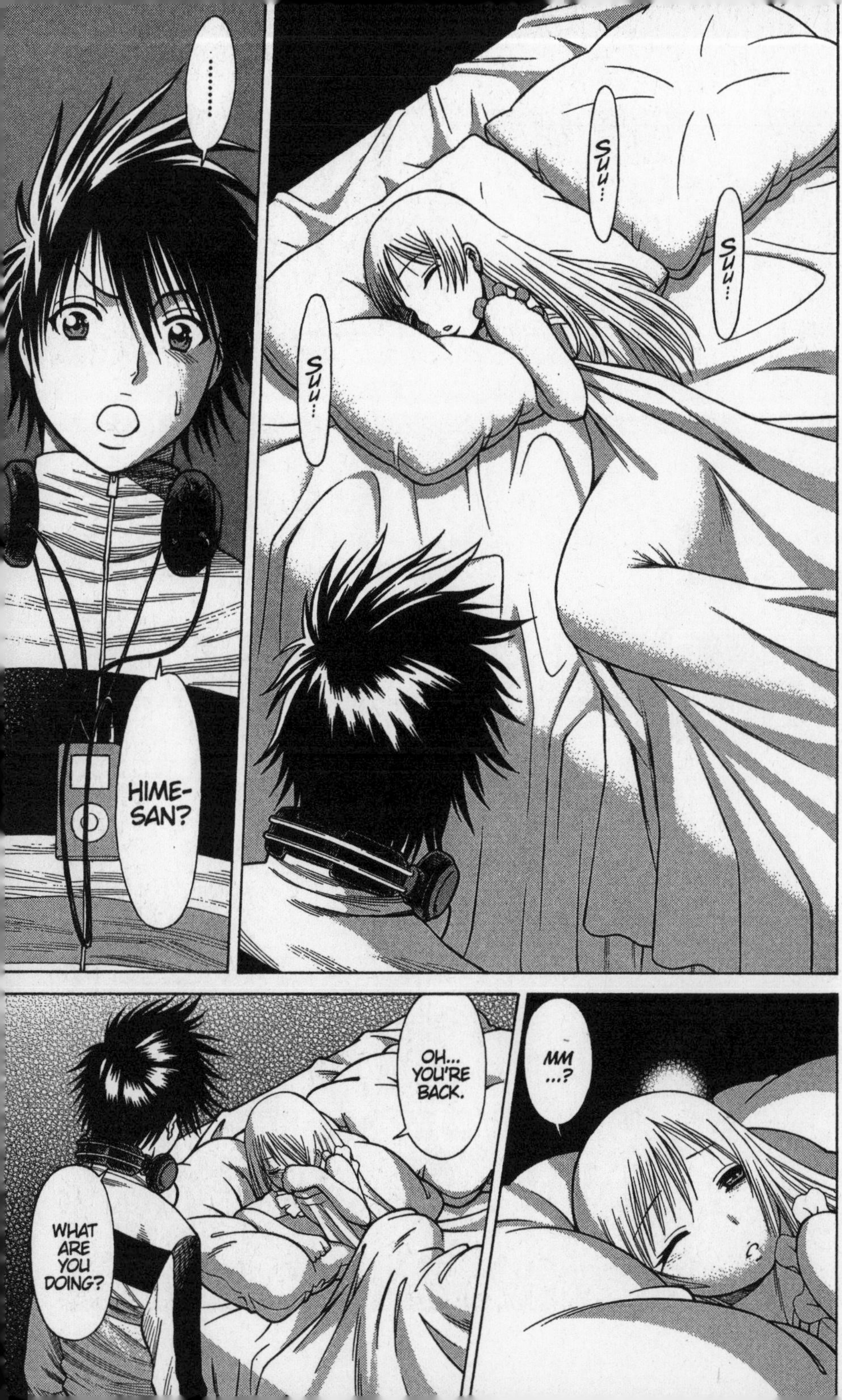
Suu...
Suu...
Suu...
......
HIME-SAN?
MM ...?
OH... YOU'RE BACK.
WHAT ARE YOU DOING?

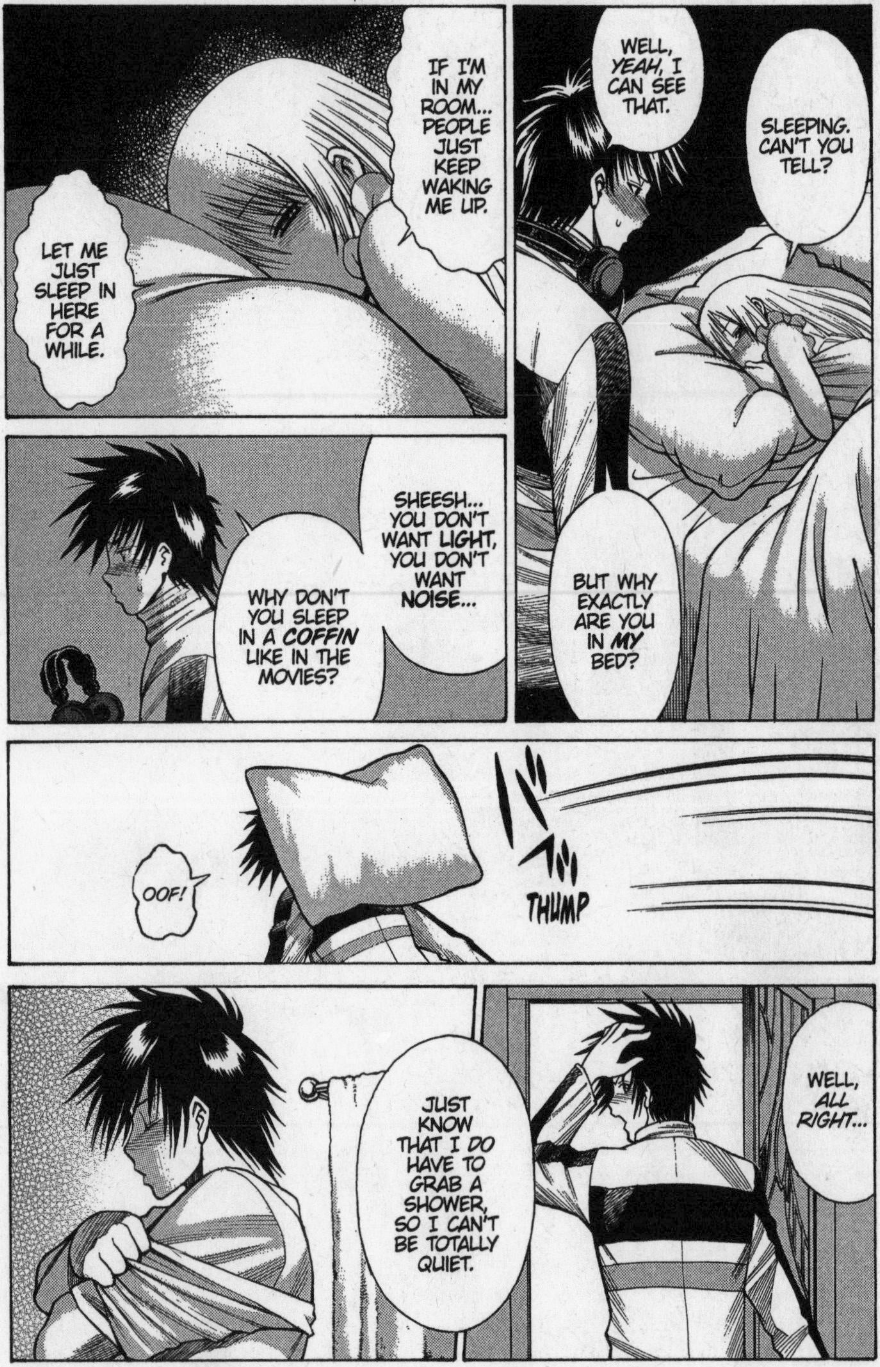
SLEEPING. CAN'T YOU TELL?
WELL, *YEAH,* I CAN SEE THAT.
BUT WHY EXACTLY ARE YOU IN *MY* BED?
IF I'M IN MY ROOM... PEOPLE JUST KEEP WAKING ME UP.
LET ME JUST SLEEP IN HERE FOR A WHILE.
SHEESH... YOU DON'T WANT **LIGHT,** YOU DON'T WANT **NOISE...**
WHY DON'T YOU SLEEP IN A ***COFFIN*** LIKE IN THE MOVIES?
THUMP
OOF!
WELL, *ALL RIGHT...*
JUST KNOW THAT I *DO* HAVE TO GRAB A SHOWER, SO I CAN'T BE TOTALLY QUIET.

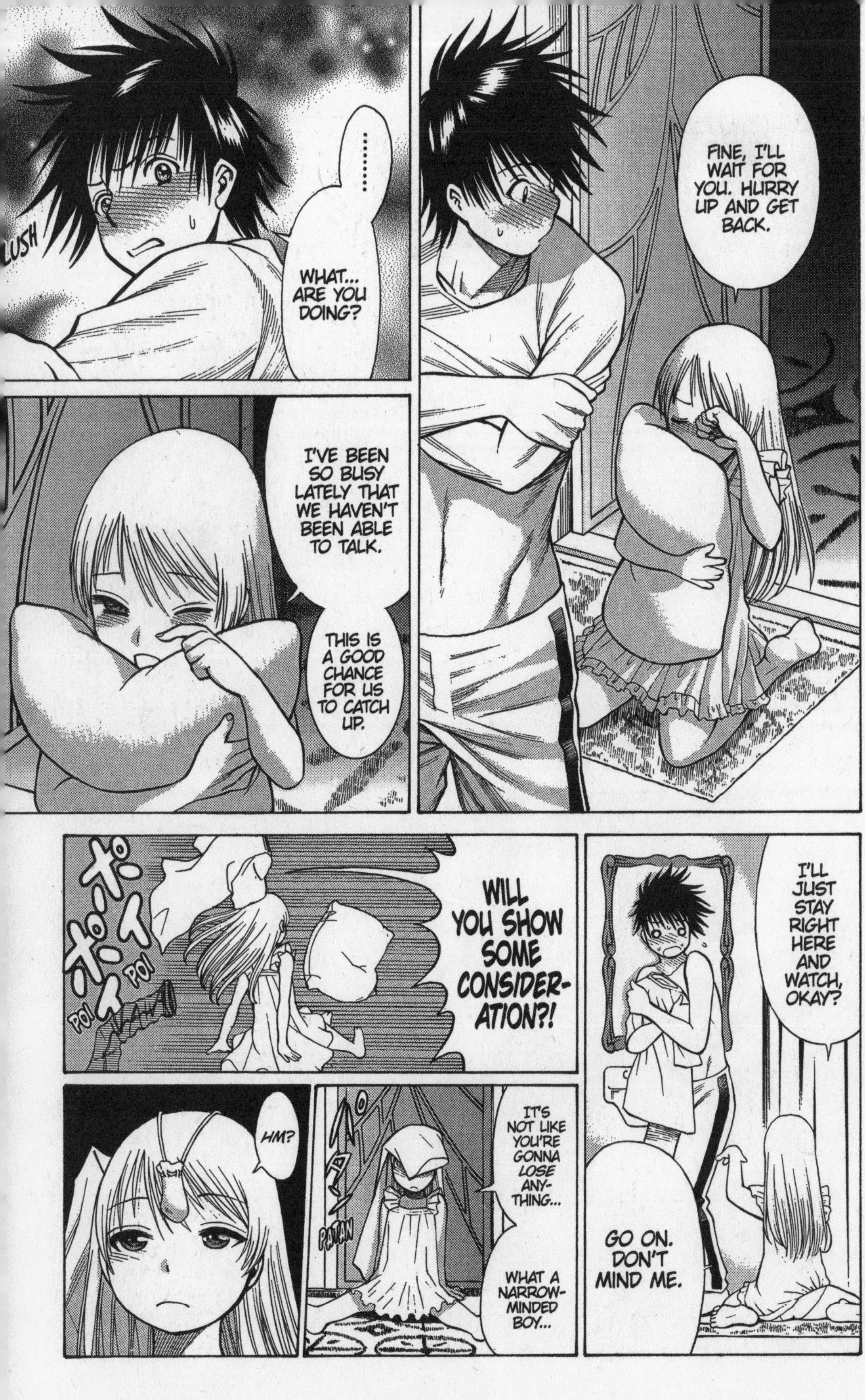
FINE, I'LL WAIT FOR YOU. HURRY UP AND GET BACK.
......
LUSH
WHAT... ARE YOU DOING?
I'VE BEEN SO BUSY LATELY THAT WE HAVEN'T BEEN ABLE TO TALK.
THIS IS A GOOD CHANCE FOR US TO CATCH UP.
I'LL JUST STAY RIGHT HERE AND WATCH, OKAY?
GO ON. DON'T MIND ME.
WILL YOU SHOW SOME CONSIDER-ATION?!
POI
POI
IT'S NOT LIKE YOU'RE GONNA LOSE ANY-THING...
WHAT A NARROW-MINDED BOY...
PATAN
HM?

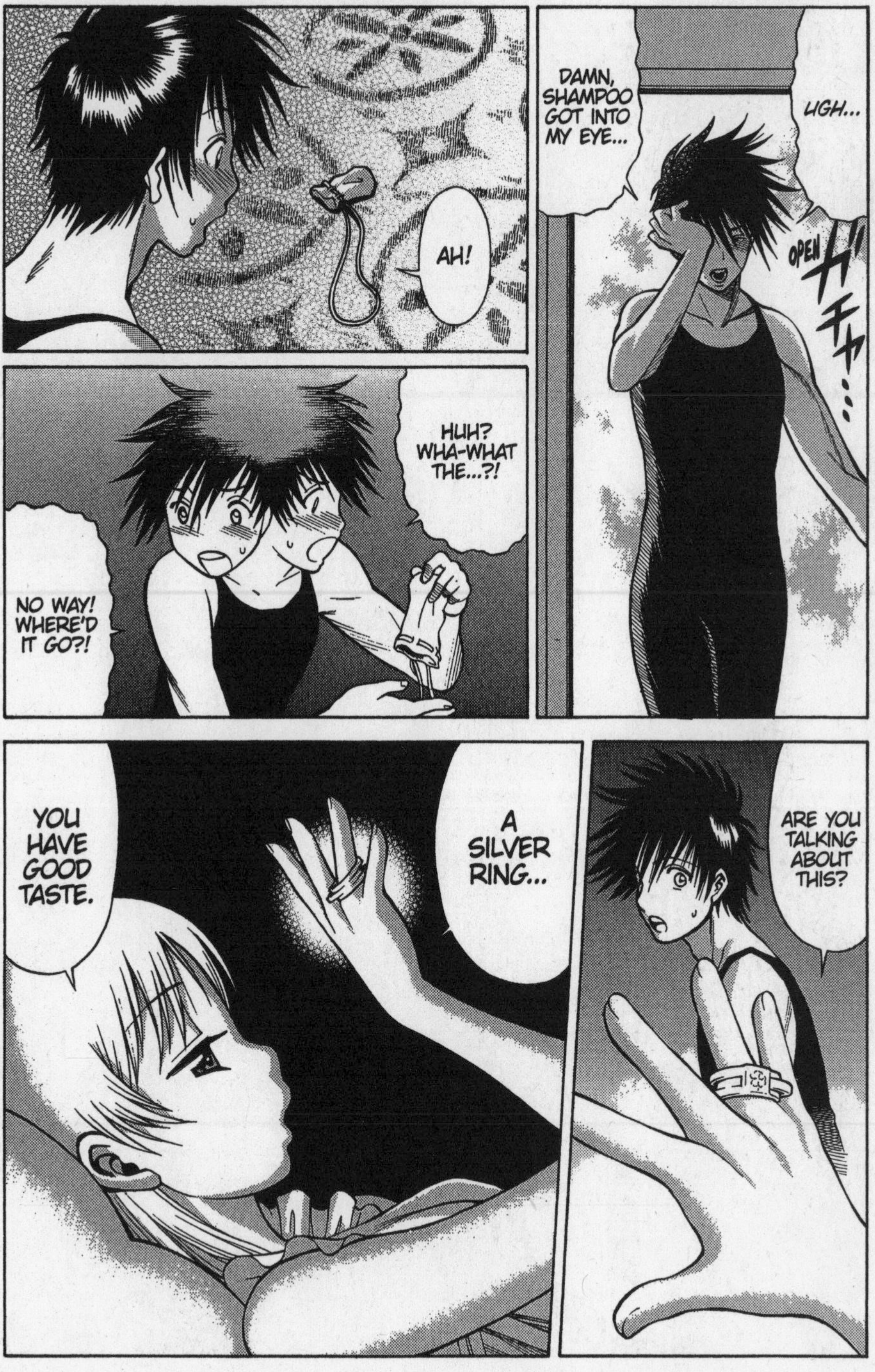
UGH...
DAMN, SHAMPOO GOT INTO MY EYE...
OPEN ガチャ...
AH!
HUH? WHA-WHAT THE...?!
NO WAY! WHERE'D IT GO?!
ARE YOU TALKING ABOUT THIS?
A SILVER RING...
YOU HAVE GOOD TASTE.

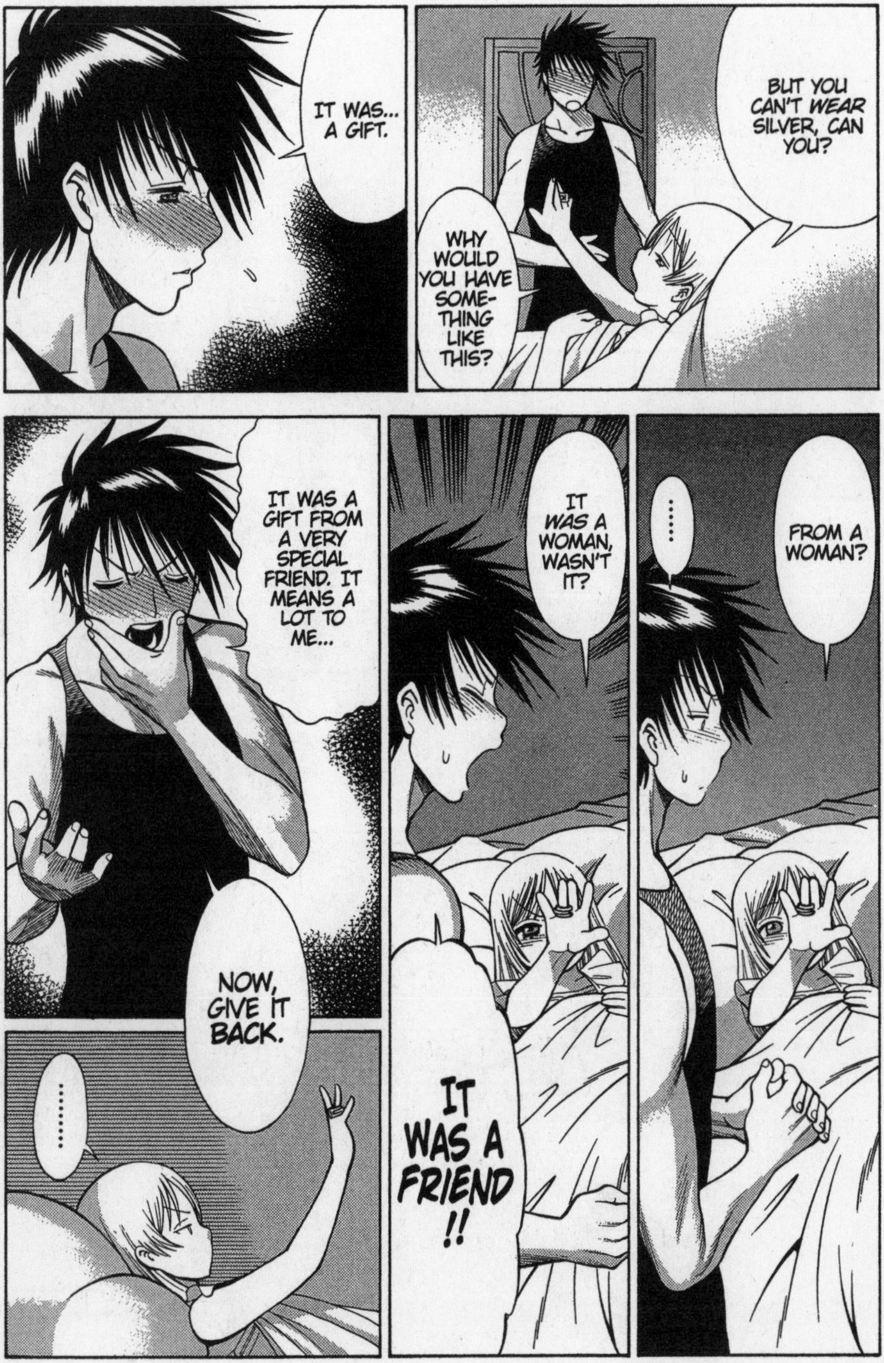
BUT YOU CAN'T *WEAR* SILVER, CAN YOU?
WHY WOULD YOU HAVE SOME-THING LIKE THIS?
IT WAS... A GIFT.
FROM A WOMAN?
......
IT *WAS* A WOMAN, WASN'T IT?
IT WAS A FRIEND!!
IT WAS A GIFT FROM A VERY SPECIAL FRIEND. IT MEANS A LOT TO ME...
NOW, GIVE IT BACK.
......

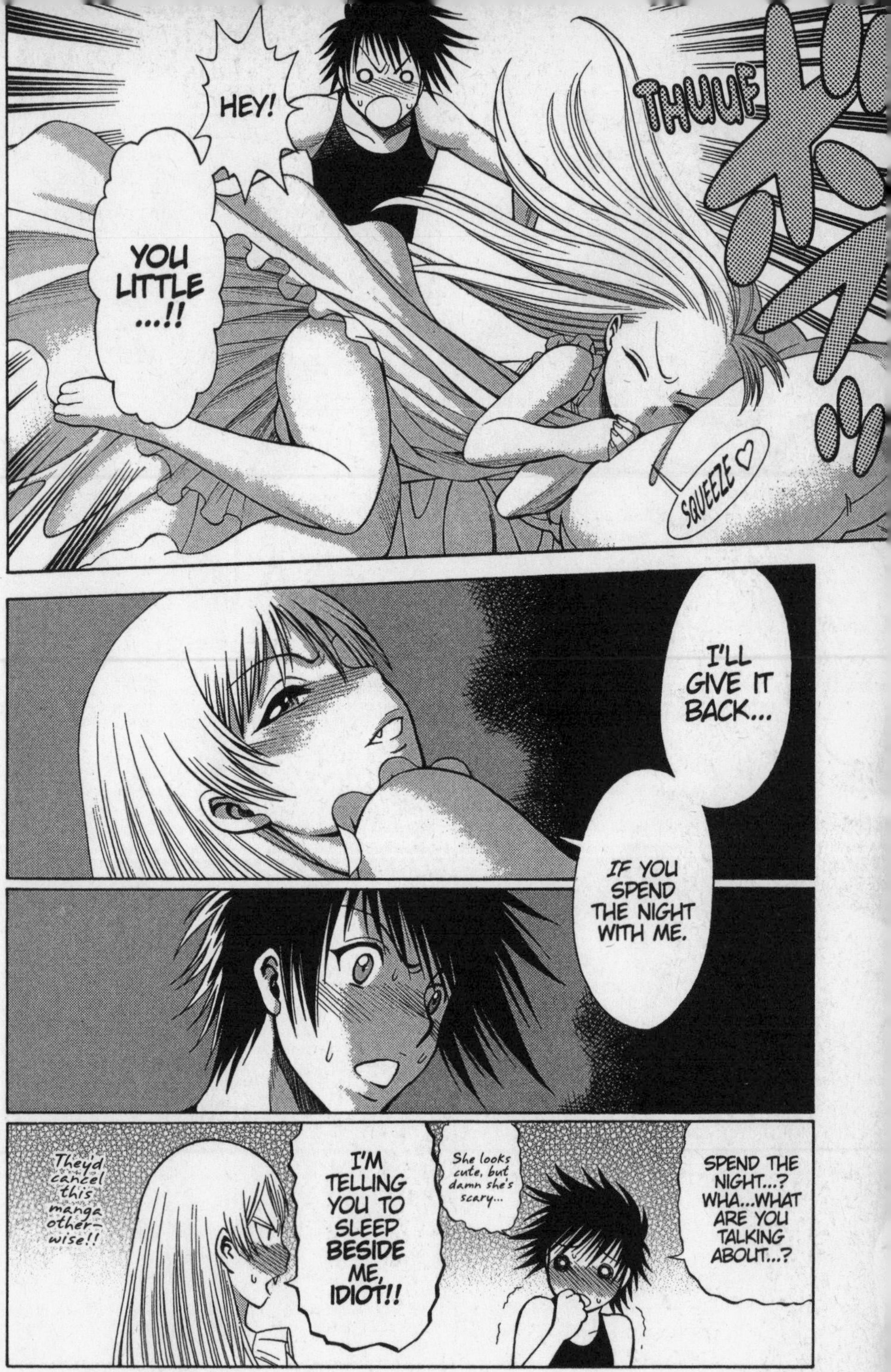
THUUF
HEY!
YOU LITTLE ...!!
SQUEEZE ♡
I'LL GIVE IT BACK...
IF YOU SPEND THE NIGHT WITH ME.
SPEND THE NIGHT...? WHA...WHAT ARE YOU TALKING ABOUT...?
She looks cute, but damn she's scary...
I'M TELLING YOU TO SLEEP BESIDE ME, IDIOT!!
They'd cancel this manga other-wise!!

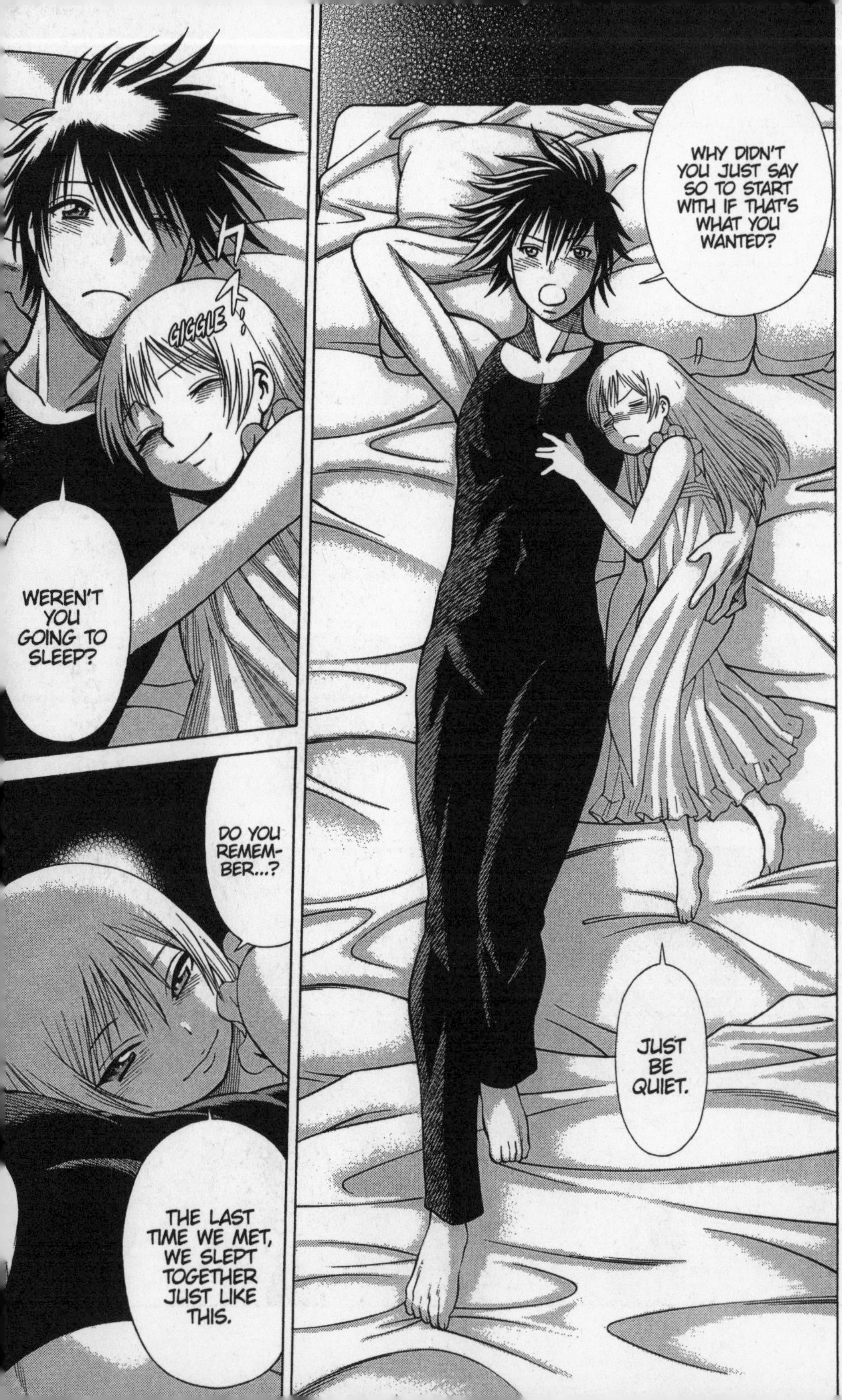
WHY DIDN'T YOU JUST SAY SO TO START WITH IF THAT'S WHAT YOU WANTED?
JUST BE QUIET.
GIGGLE
WEREN'T YOU GOING TO SLEEP?
DO YOU REMEM-BER...?
THE LAST TIME WE MET, WE SLEPT TOGETHER JUST LIKE THIS.

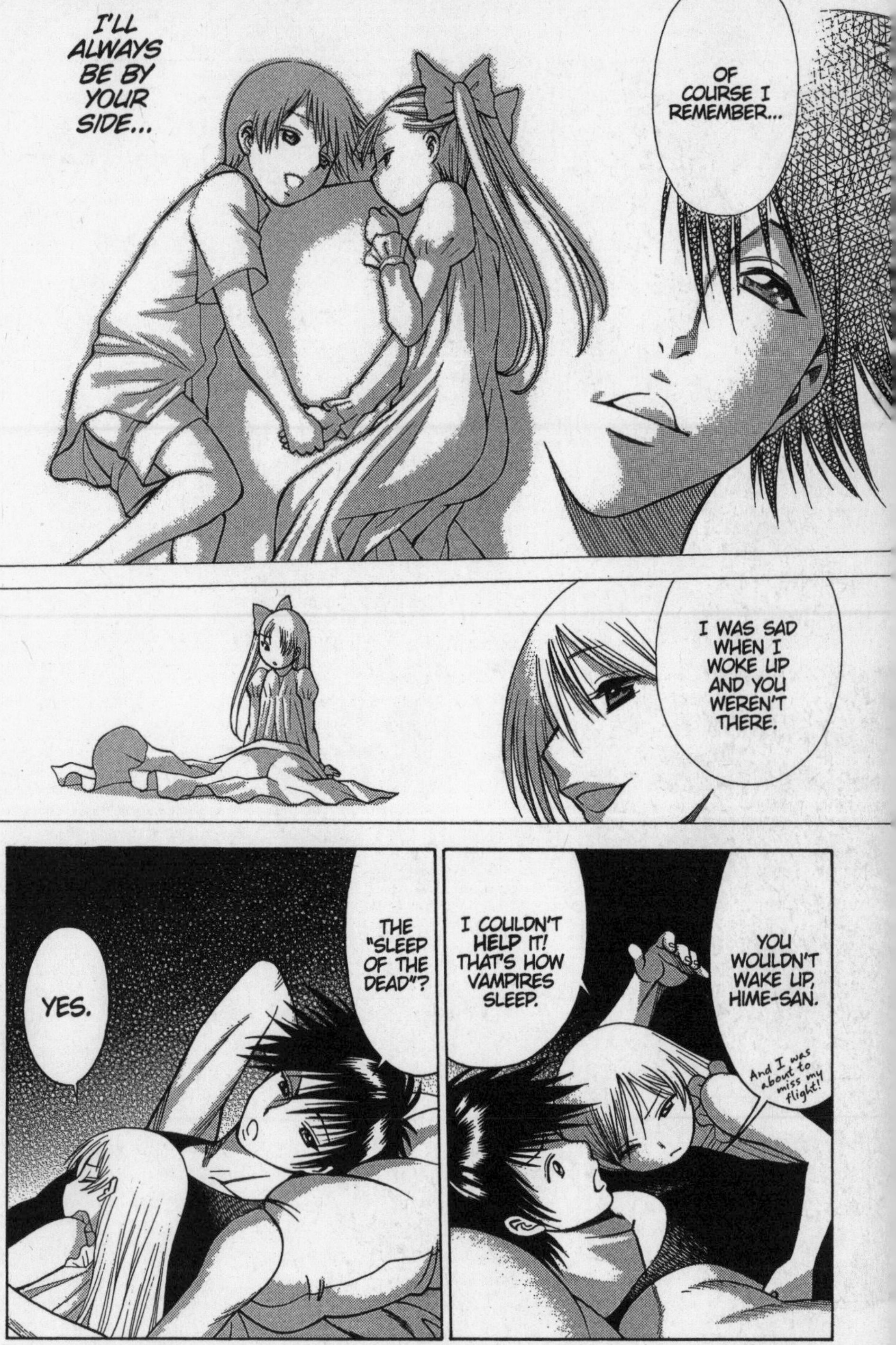
OF COURSE I REMEMBER...
I'LL ALWAYS BE BY YOUR SIDE...
I WAS SAD WHEN I WOKE UP AND YOU WEREN'T THERE.
YOU WOULDN'T WAKE UP, HIME-SAN.
And I was about to miss my flight!
I COULDN'T HELP IT! THAT'S HOW VAMPIRES SLEEP.
THE "SLEEP OF THE DEAD"?
YES.

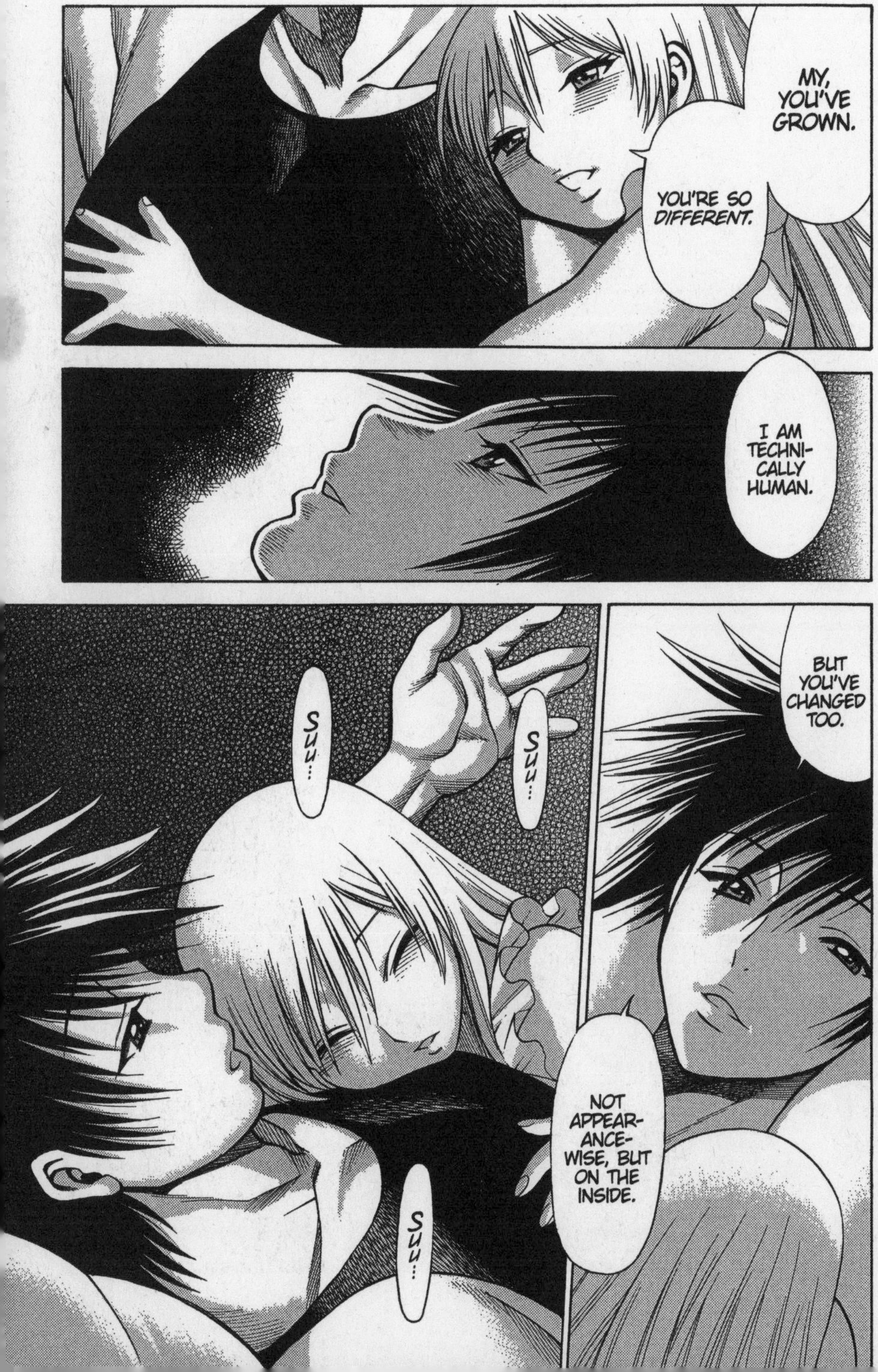
MY, YOU'VE GROWN.
YOU'RE SO DIFFERENT.
I AM TECHNICALLY HUMAN.
BUT YOU'VE CHANGED TOO.
NOT APPEARANCE-WISE, BUT ON THE INSIDE.
Suu...
Suu...
Suu...

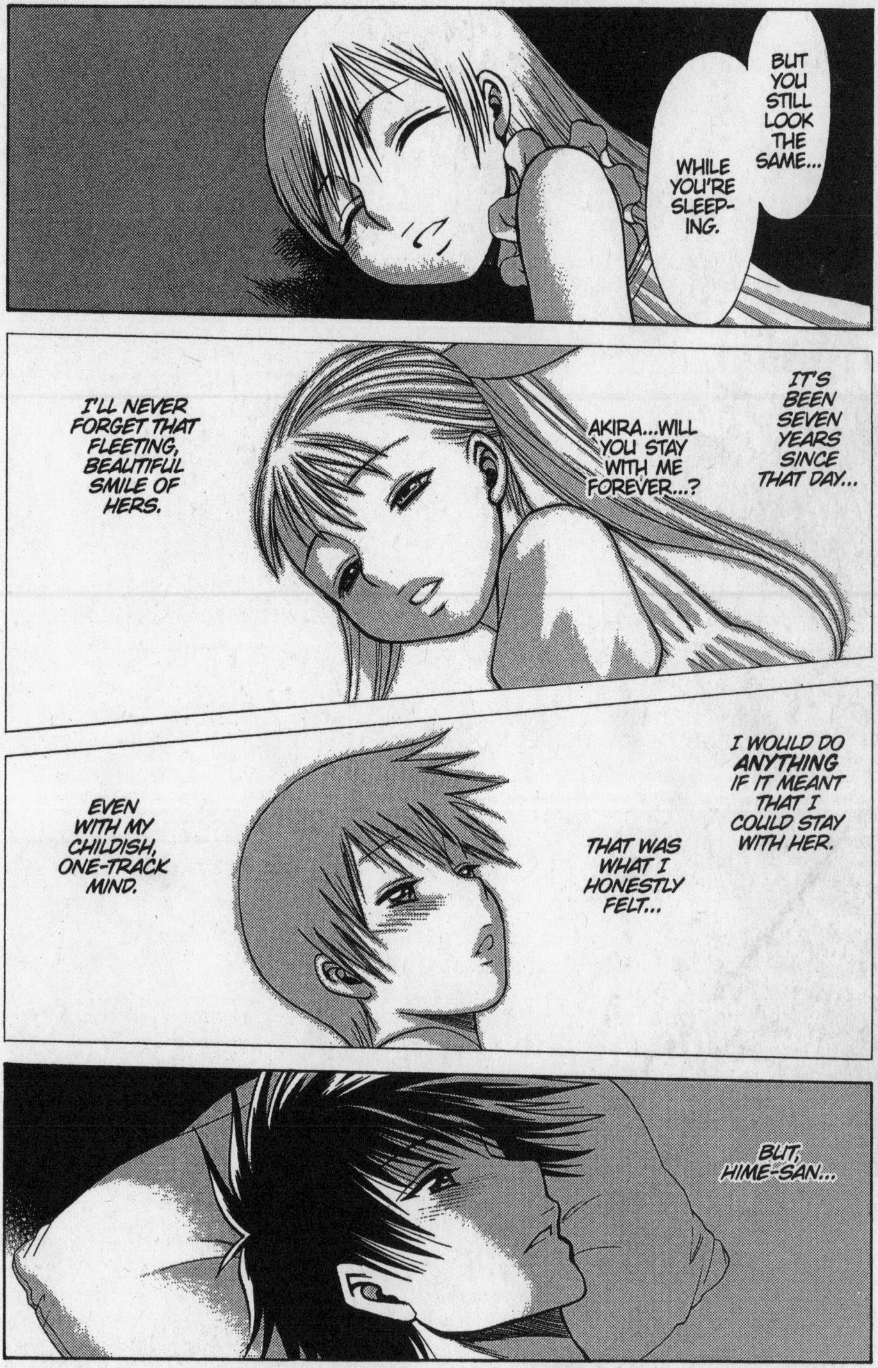
BUT YOU STILL LOOK THE SAME...
WHILE YOU'RE SLEEP-ING.
IT'S BEEN SEVEN YEARS SINCE THAT DAY...
AKIRA...WILL YOU STAY WITH ME FOREVER...?
I'LL NEVER FORGET THAT FLEETING, BEAUTIFUL SMILE OF HERS.
I WOULD DO **ANYTHING** IF IT MEANT THAT I COULD STAY WITH HER.
THAT WAS WHAT I HONESTLY FELT...
EVEN WITH MY CHILDISH, ONE-TRACK MIND.
BUT, HIME-SAN...

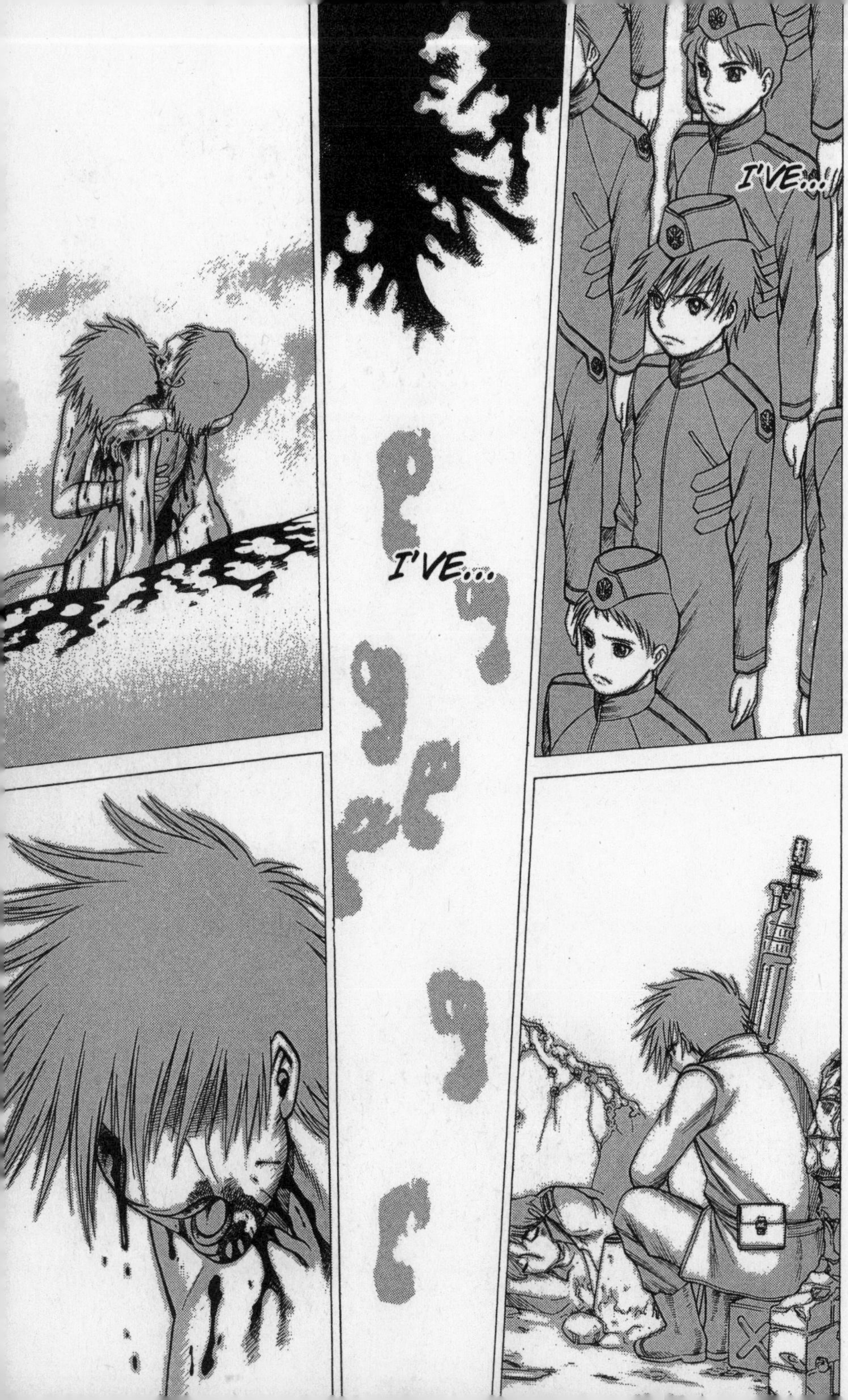
I'VE...
I'VE...

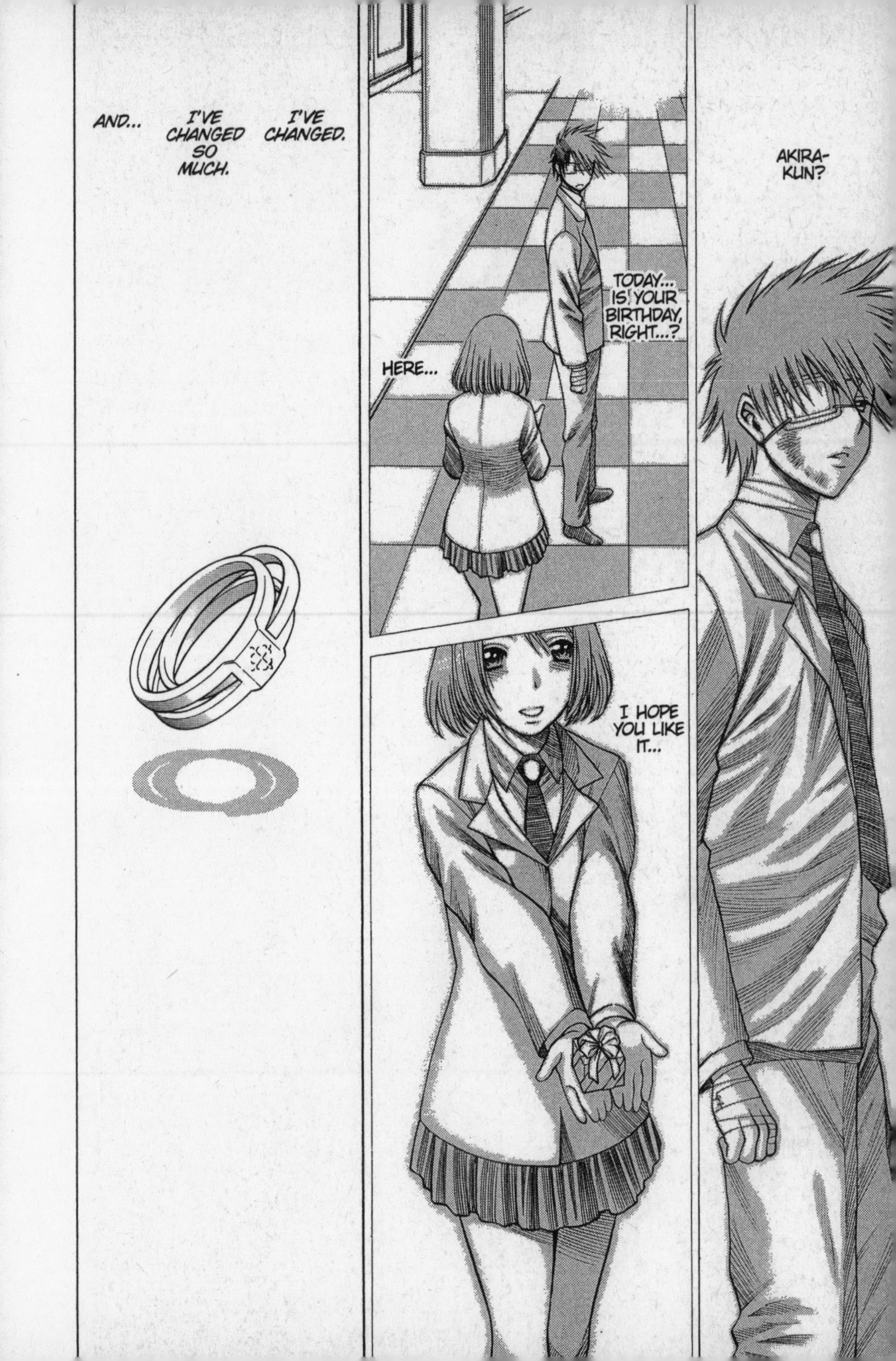
AKIRA-KUN?
TODAY... IS YOUR BIRTHDAY, RIGHT...?
HERE...
I HOPE YOU LIKE IT...
I'VE CHANGED.
I'VE CHANGED SO MUCH.
AND...

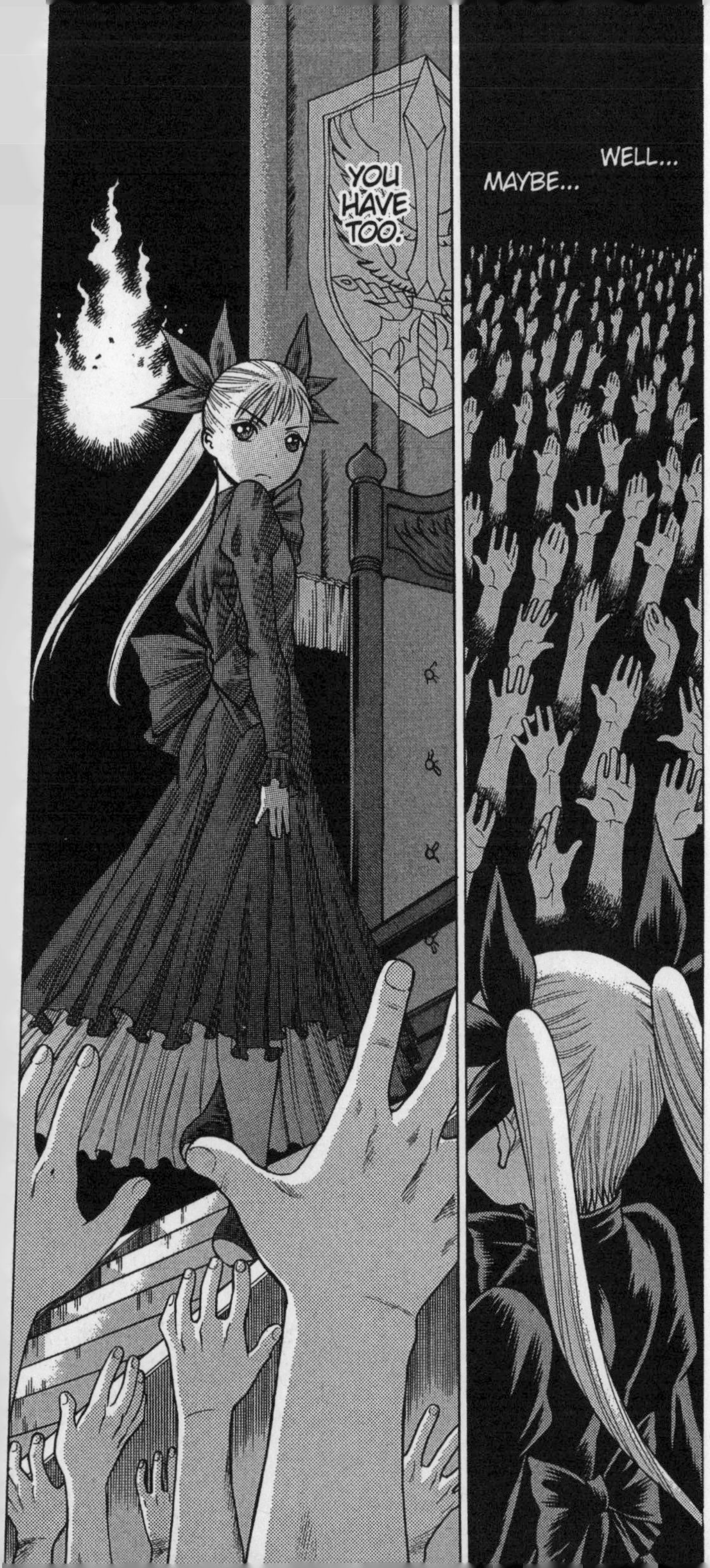
WELL...
MAYBE...
YOU HAVE TOO.

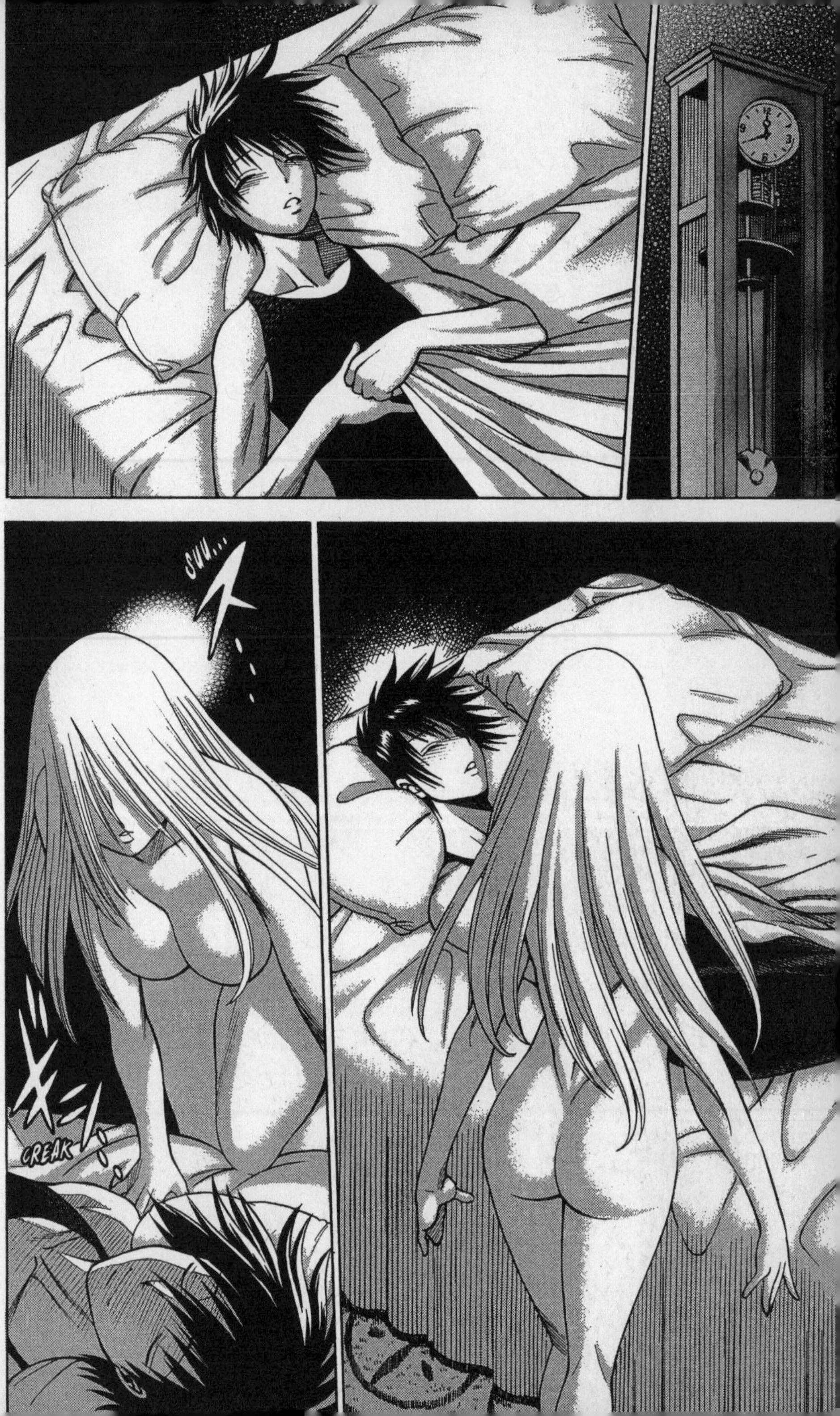
SUU...
CREAK

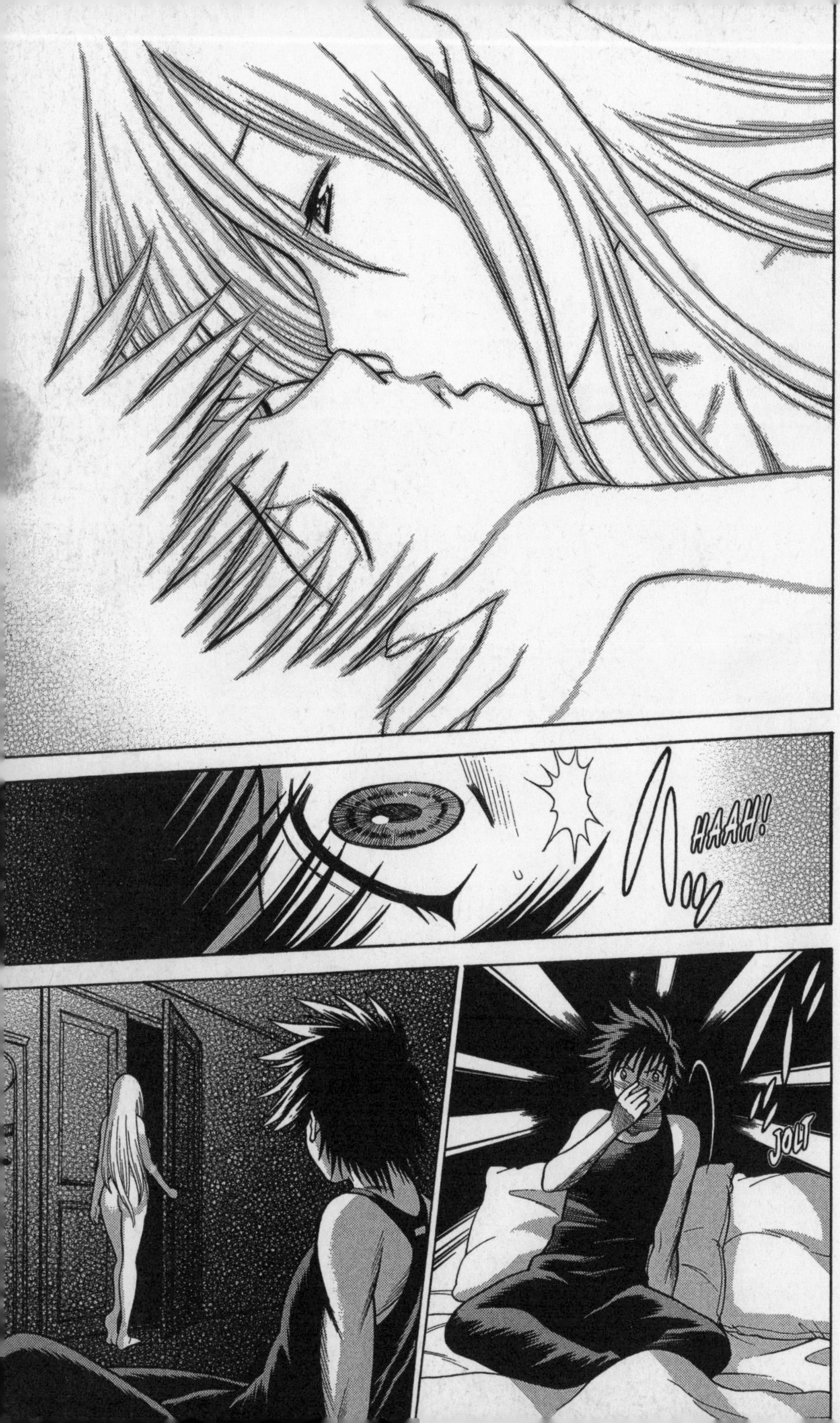
HAAH!
JOLT

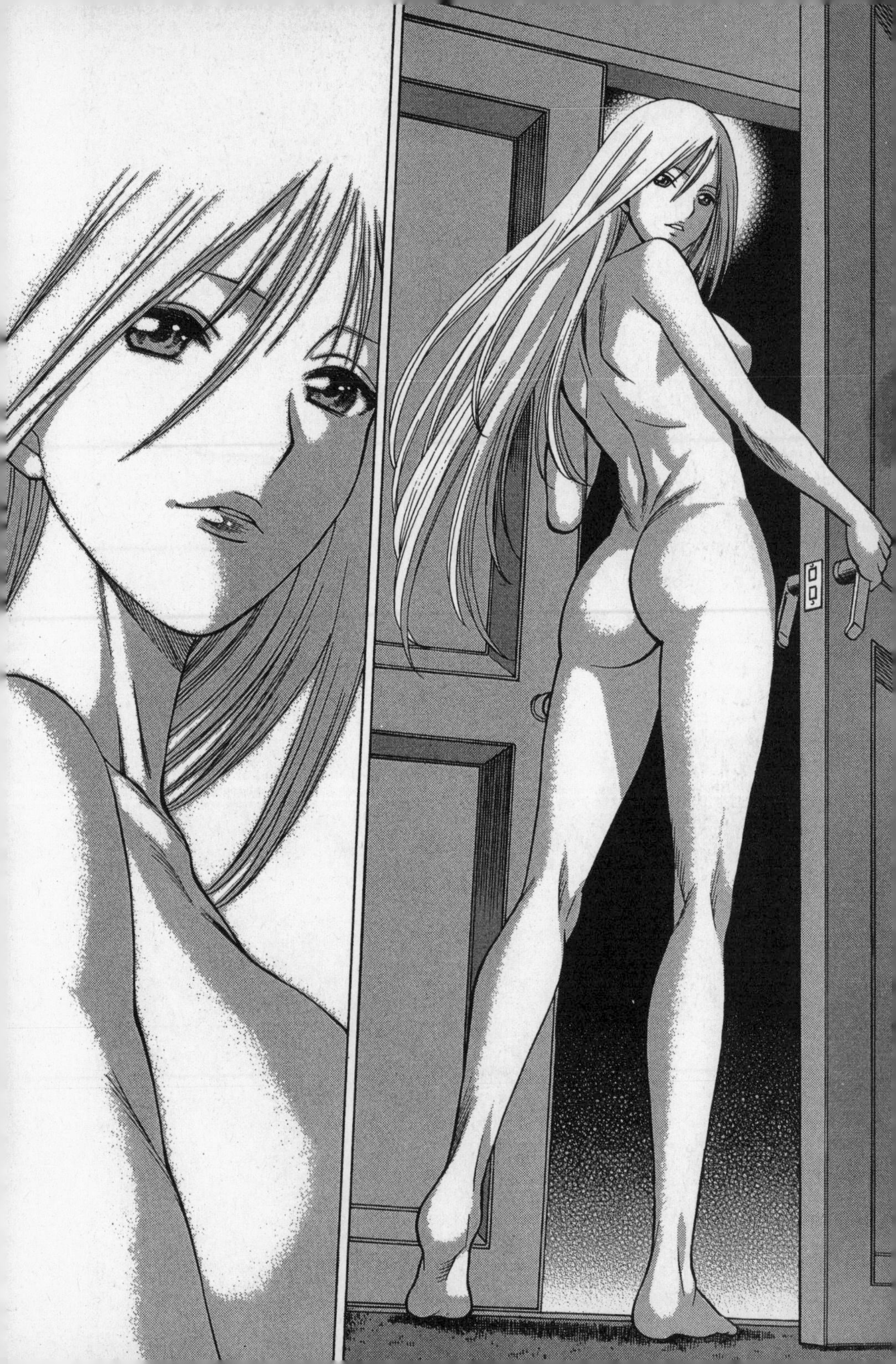

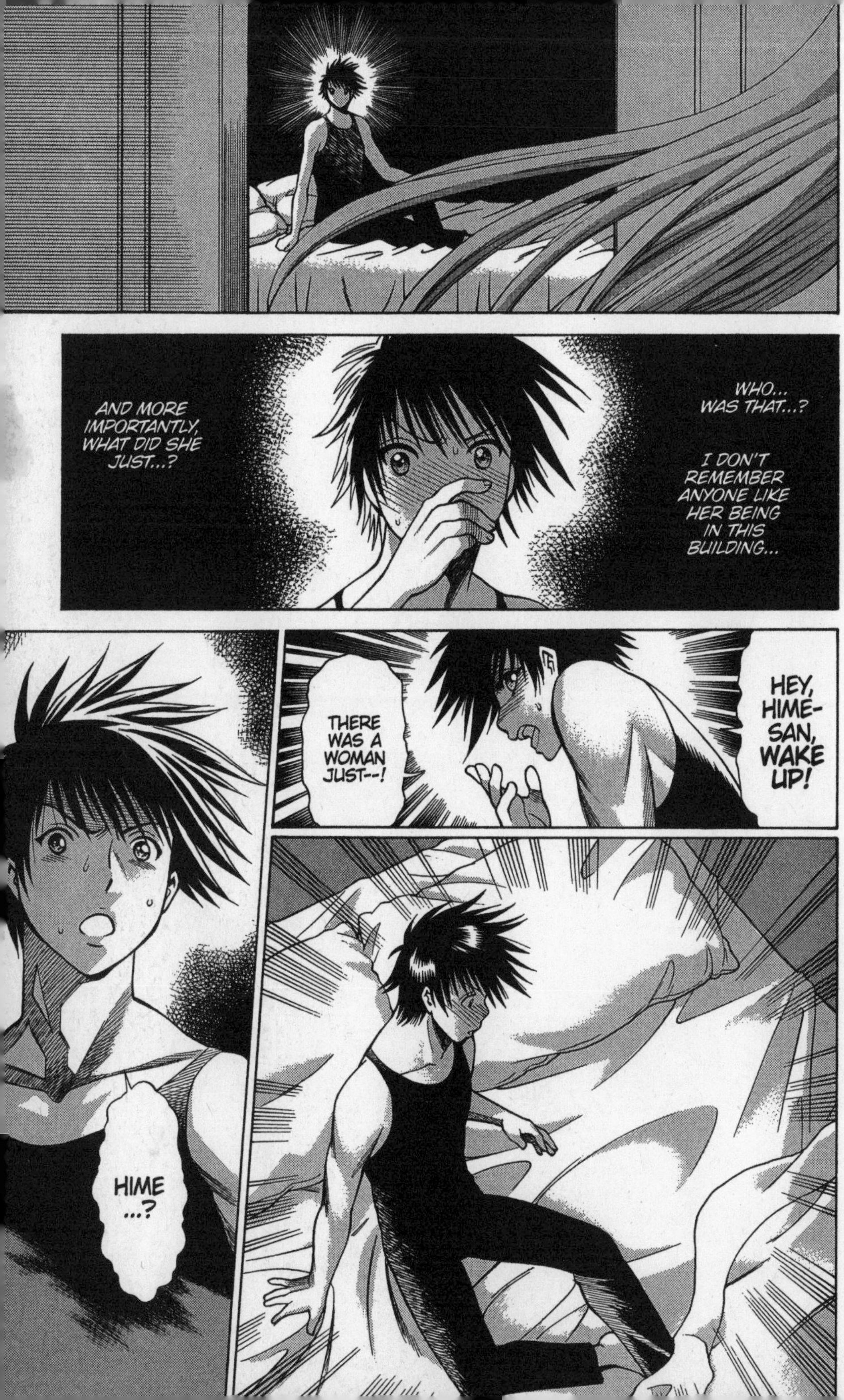
WHO... WAS THAT...?
I DON'T REMEMBER ANYONE LIKE HER BEING IN THIS BUILDING...
AND MORE IMPORTANTLY, WHAT DID SHE JUST...?
HEY, HIME-SAN, WAKE UP!
THERE WAS A WOMAN JUST--!
HIME ...?

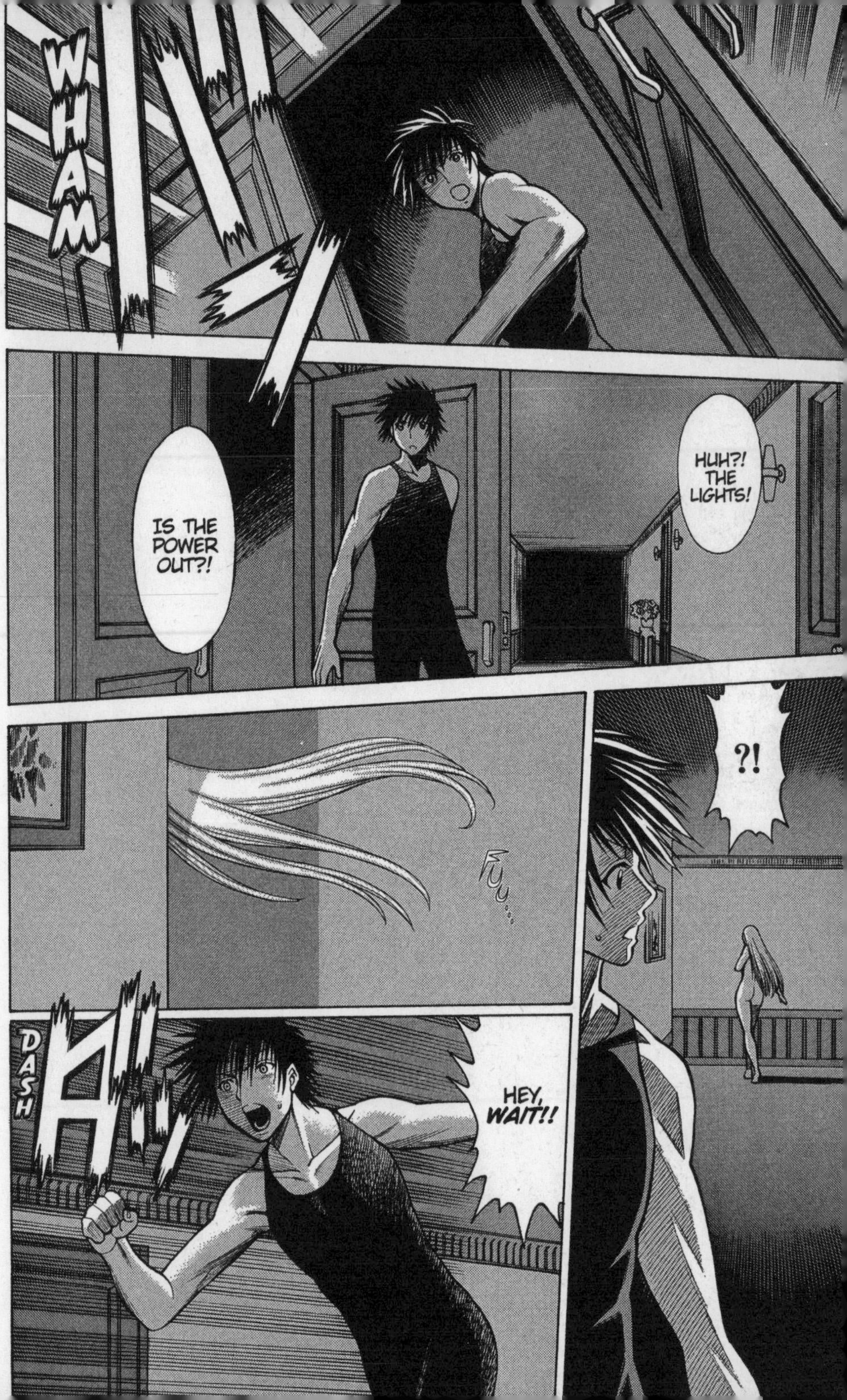
WHAM
HUH?! THE LIGHTS!
IS THE POWER OUT?!
?!
FUU...
DASH
HEY, WAIT!!

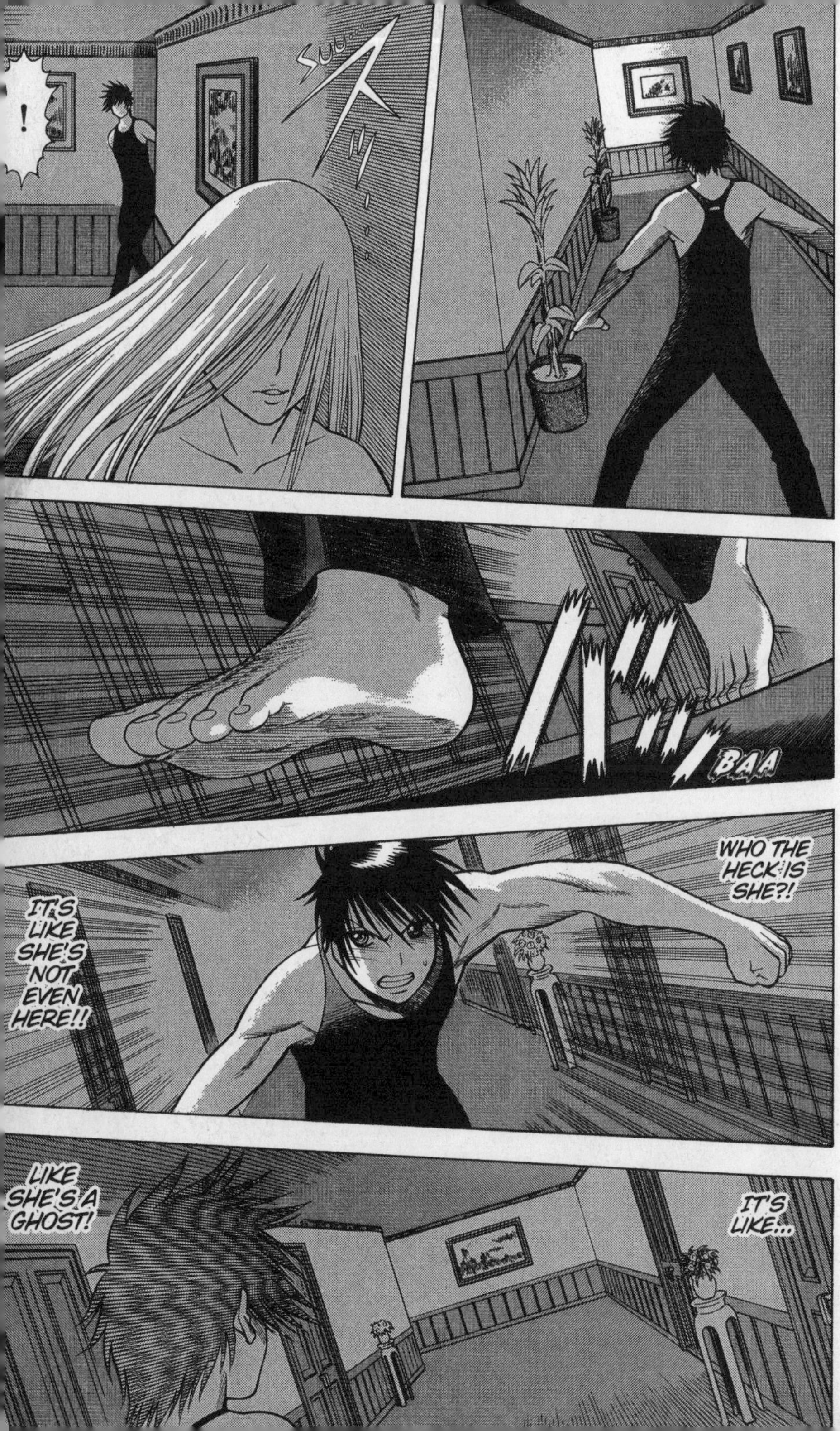
SUU...
!
BAA
WHO THE HECK IS SHE?!
IT'S LIKE SHE'S NOT EVEN HERE!!
IT'S LIKE...
LIKE SHE'S A GHOST!

CREAK...

BAA

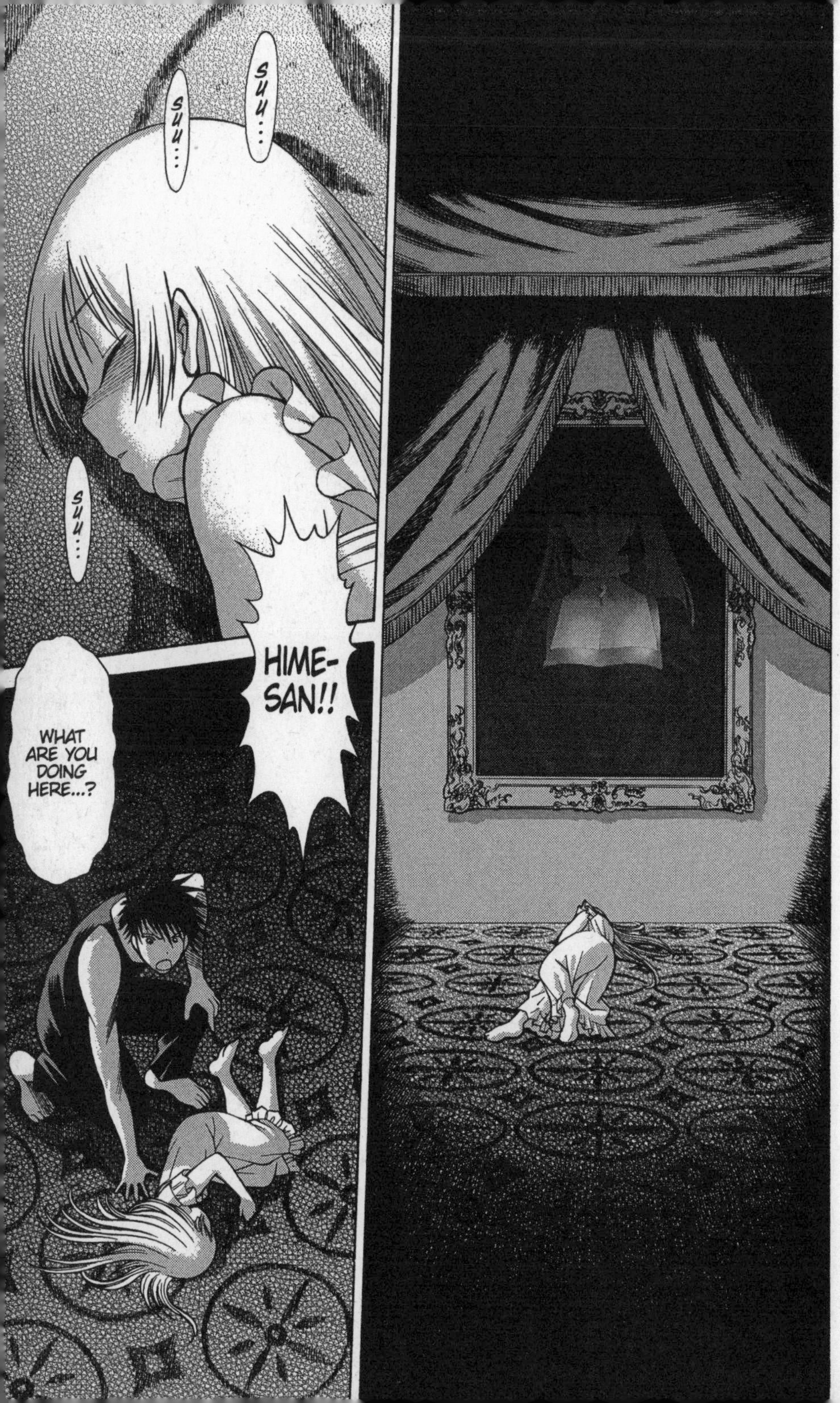
SUU....
SUU....
SUU....
HIME-SAN!!
WHAT ARE YOU DOING HERE...?

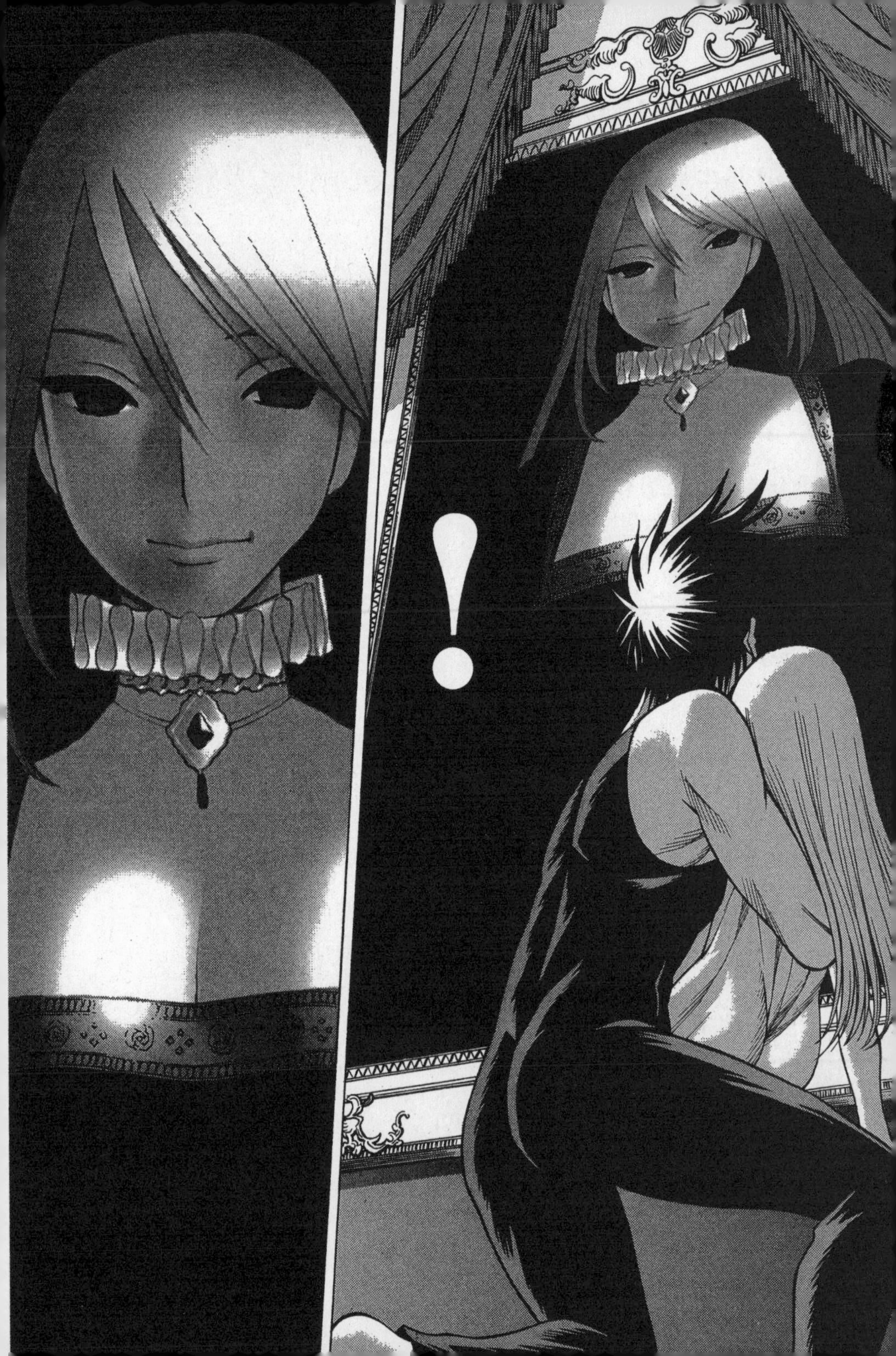
!

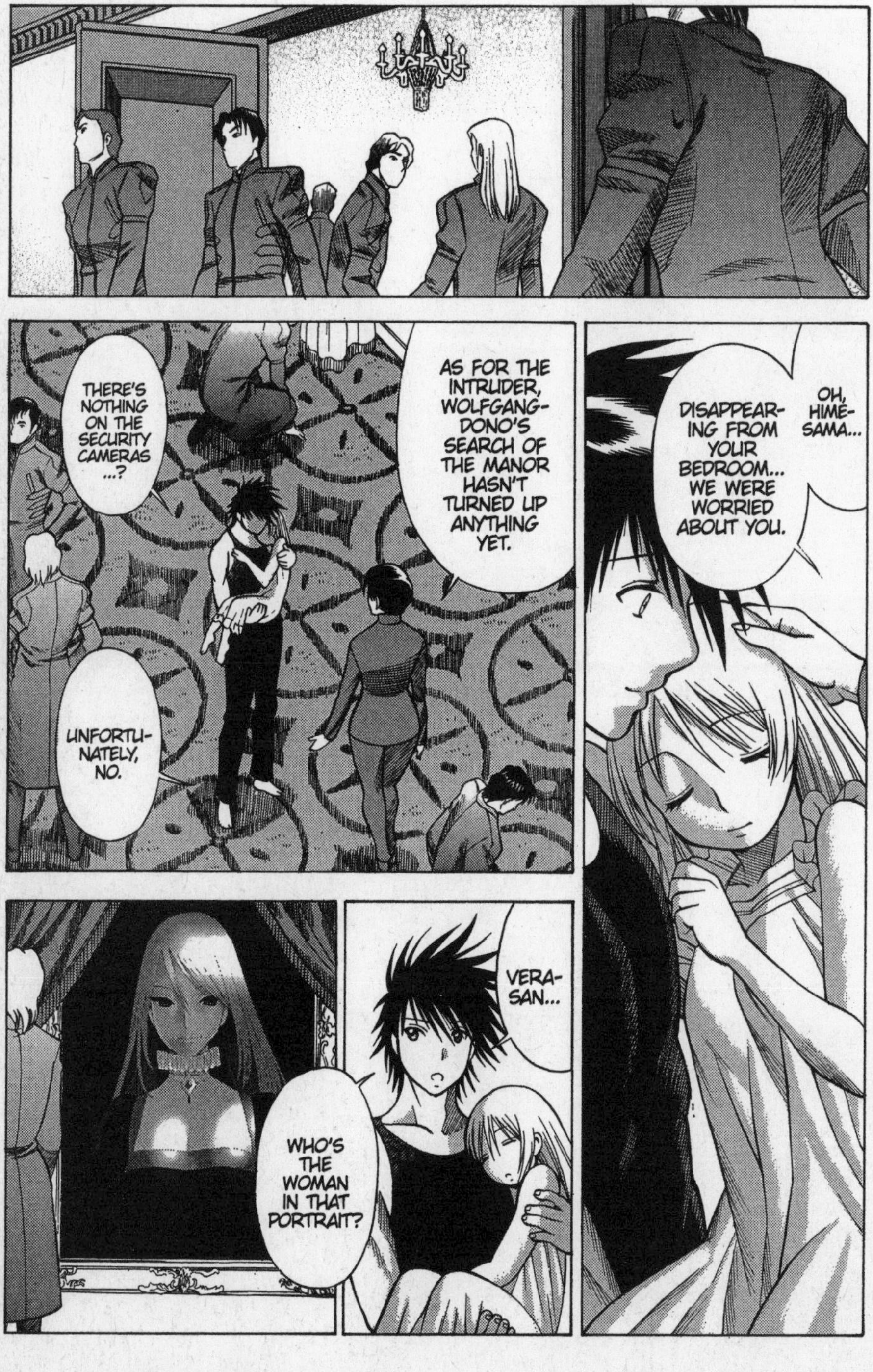
OH, HIME-SAMA...
DISAPPEARING FROM YOUR BEDROOM... WE WERE WORRIED ABOUT YOU.
AS FOR THE INTRUDER, WOLFGANG-DONO'S SEARCH OF THE MANOR HASN'T TURNED UP ANYTHING YET.
THERE'S NOTHING ON THE SECURITY CAMERAS ...?
UNFORTUNATELY, NO.
VERA-SAN...
WHO'S THE WOMAN IN THAT PORTRAIT?

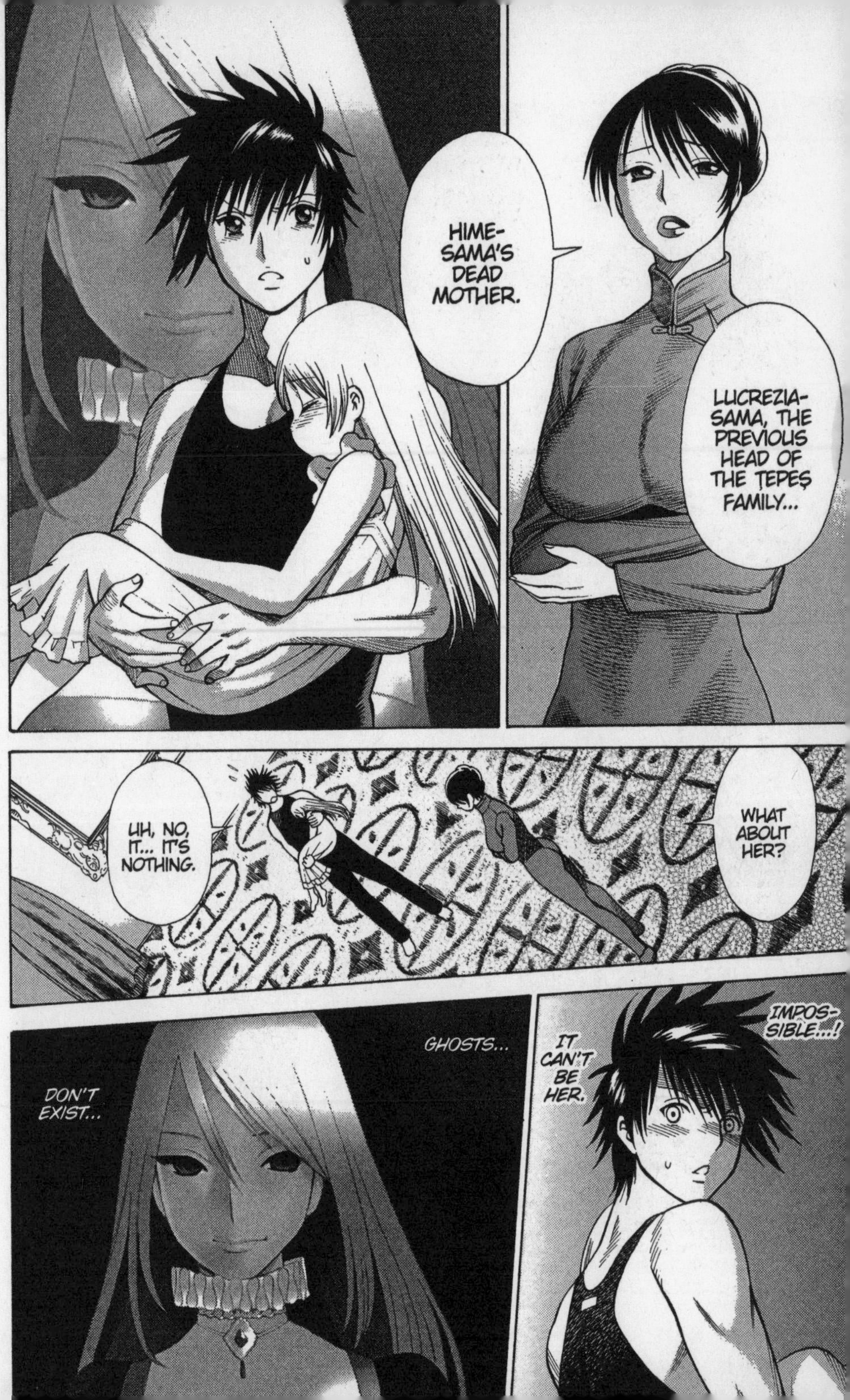
LUCREZIA-SAMA, THE PREVIOUS HEAD OF THE ȚEPEȘ FAMILY...
HIME-SAMA'S DEAD MOTHER.
WHAT ABOUT HER?
UH, NO, IT... IT'S NOTHING.
IMPOSSIBLE...!
IT CAN'T BE HER.
GHOSTS...
DON'T EXIST...

......
AKIRA...
I'M RIGHT HERE.
SQUEEZE
I THOUGHT YOU'D LEFT ME BEHIND AGAIN.
SILLY, I WOULD NEVER DO THAT.
YOU WERE THE ONE WHO LEFT ME BEHIND TODAY.

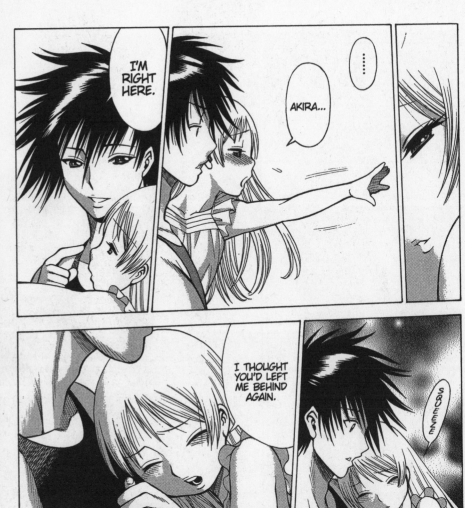

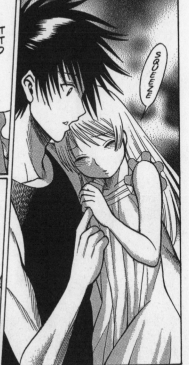

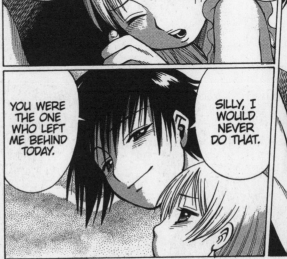

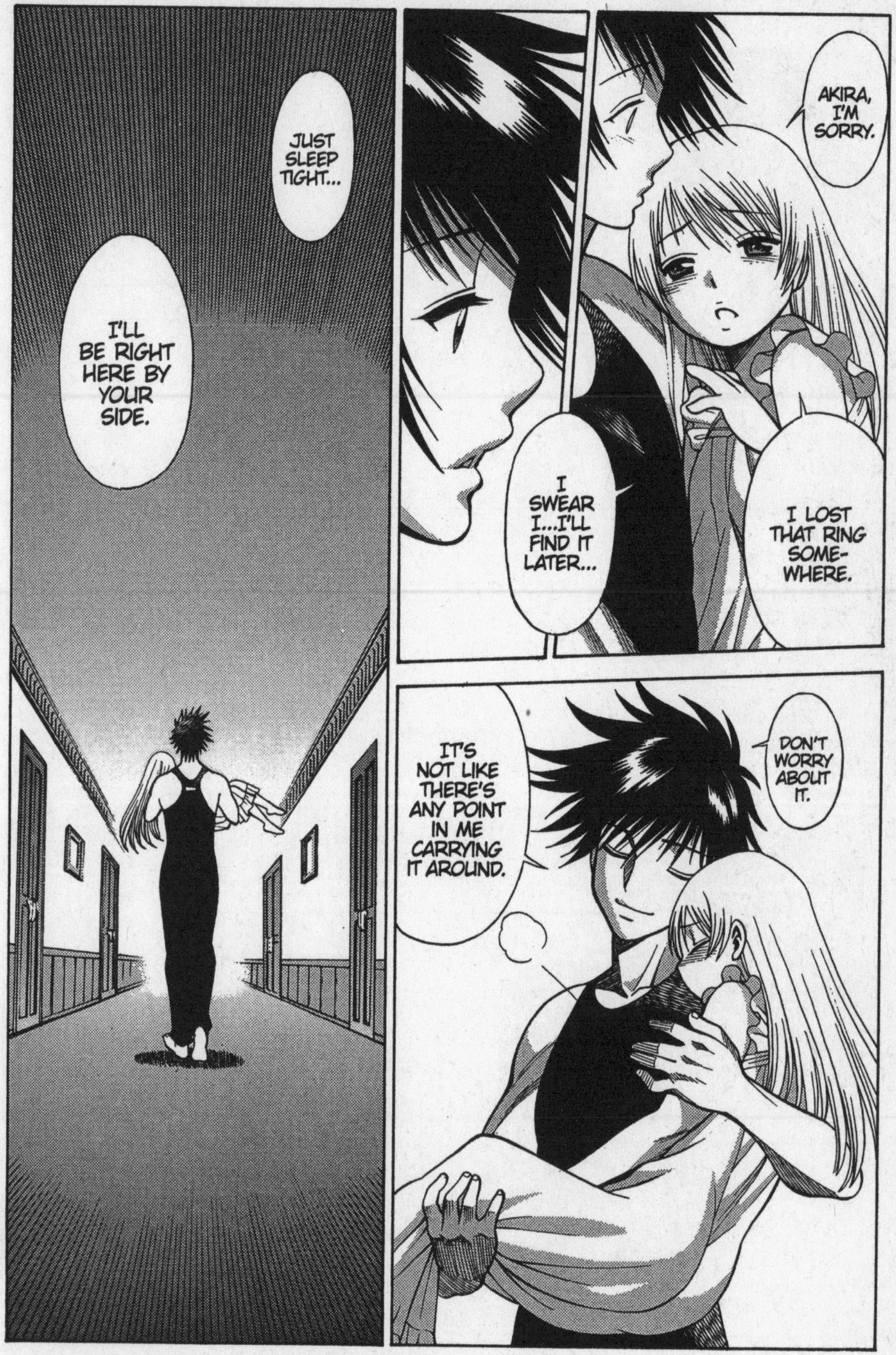
AKIRA, I'M SORRY.
I LOST THAT RING SOME-WHERE.
I SWEAR I...I'LL FIND IT LATER...
DON'T WORRY ABOUT IT.
IT'S NOT LIKE THERE'S ANY POINT IN ME CARRYING IT AROUND.
JUST SLEEP TIGHT...
I'LL BE RIGHT HERE BY YOUR SIDE.

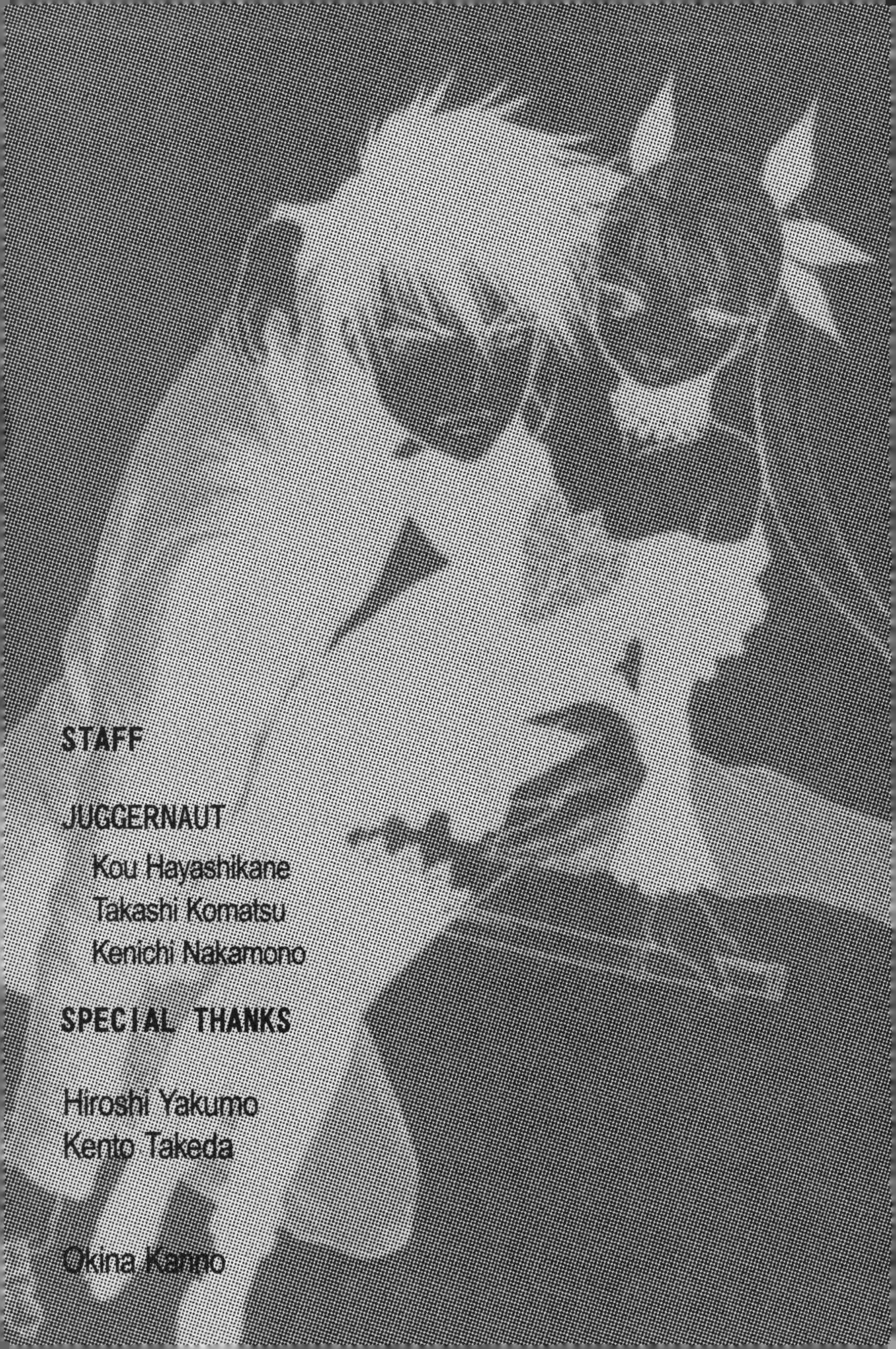

STAFF

JUGGERNAUT

Kou Hayashikane
Takashi Komatsu
Kenichi Nakamono

SPECIAL THANKS

Hiroshi Yakumo
Kento Takeda

Okina Kanno

Dance with the Vampire Maid

Book-only, freshly-penned 4-koma strips

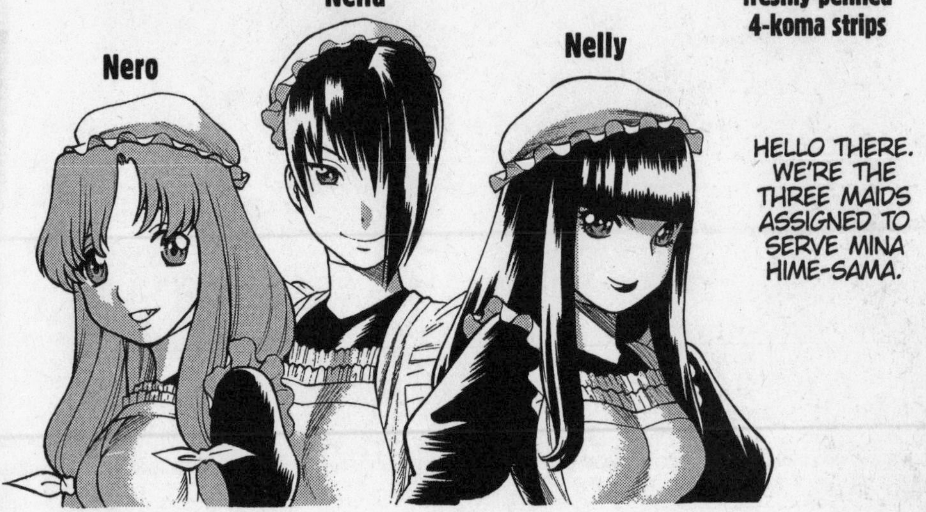

HELLO THERE. WE'RE THE THREE MAIDS ASSIGNED TO SERVE MINA HIME-SAMA.
Nelly
Nella
Nero

EARLIER TODAY, ONE OF HIME-SAMA'S NEW SERVANTS ARRIVED...
I DON'T LIKE THAT BOY.
DID YOU HEAR WHAT HE SAID?
IF YOU DON'T PISS OFF... I'M LEAVING.
THAT RUDE BASTARD!
SHOCK
HEEE HE HE
I'M GOING TO TORMENT HIM UNTIL HE LEAVES!
HEY LOOK, IT'S THAT GUY.
ペコ
BOW
......
I'LL BE WORKING HERE, STARTING TODAY.
I HOPE YOU CAN GIVE ME INSTRUCTIONS AND GUIDANCE.
IT TURNS OUT, AKIRA-KUN WAS AN UNEXPECTEDLY POLITE BOY...

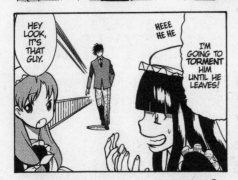

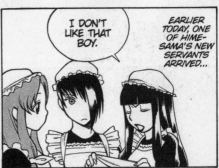

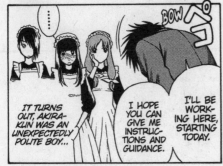

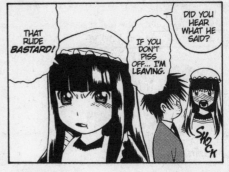

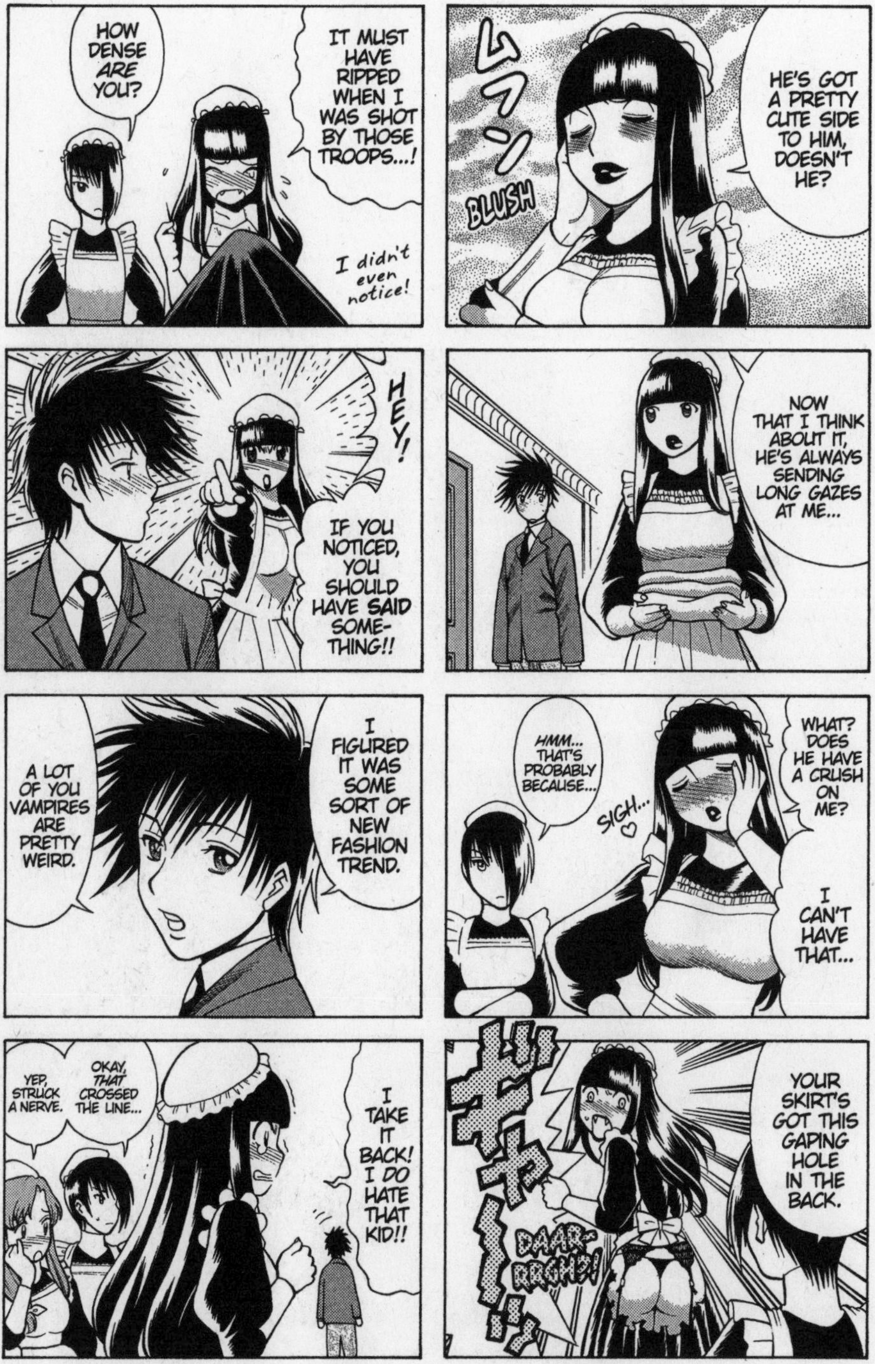

HE'S GOT A PRETTY CUTE SIDE TO HIM, DOESN'T HE?
BLUSH
IT MUST HAVE RIPPED WHEN I WAS SHOT BY THOSE TROOPS...!
HOW DENSE *ARE* YOU?
I didn't even notice!
NOW THAT I THINK ABOUT IT, HE'S ALWAYS SENDING LONG GAZES AT ME...
HEY!
IF YOU NOTICED, YOU SHOULD HAVE **SAID** SOMETHING!!
WHAT? DOES HE HAVE A CRUSH ON ME?
HMM... THAT'S PROBABLY BECAUSE...
SIGH...♡
I CAN'T HAVE THAT...
I FIGURED IT WAS SOME SORT OF NEW FASHION TREND.
A LOT OF YOU VAMPIRES ARE PRETTY WEIRD.
YOUR SKIRT'S GOT THIS GAPING HOLE IN THE BACK.
DAAR-RRGH!!
I TAKE IT BACK! I *DO* HATE THAT KID!!
OKAY, *THAT* CROSSED THE LINE...
YEP, STRUCK A NERVE.

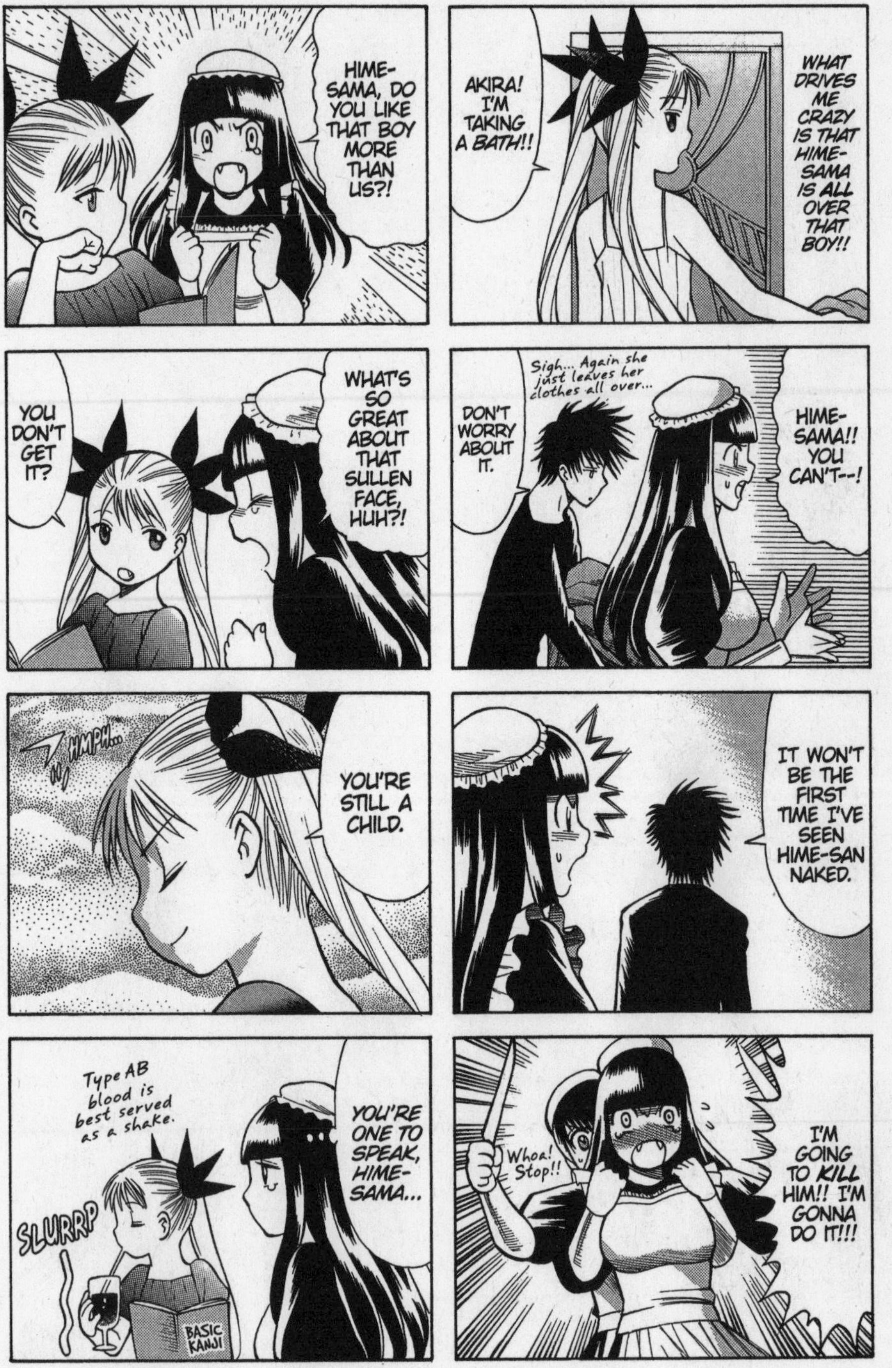
WHAT DRIVES ME CRAZY IS THAT HIME-SAMA IS ALL OVER THAT BOY!!
AKIRA! I'M TAKING A BATH!!
HIME-SAMA!! YOU CAN'T--!
Sigh... Again she just leaves her clothes all over...
DON'T WORRY ABOUT IT.
IT WON'T BE THE FIRST TIME I'VE SEEN HIME-SAN NAKED.
I'M GOING TO KILL HIM!! I'M GONNA DO IT!!!
Whoa! Stop!!
HIME-SAMA, DO YOU LIKE THAT BOY MORE THAN US?!
WHAT'S SO GREAT ABOUT THAT SULLEN FACE, HUH?!
YOU DON'T GET IT?
YOU'RE STILL A CHILD.
HMPH...
YOU'RE ONE TO SPEAK, HIME-SAMA...
Type AB blood is best served as a shake.
SLURRP
BASIC KANJI

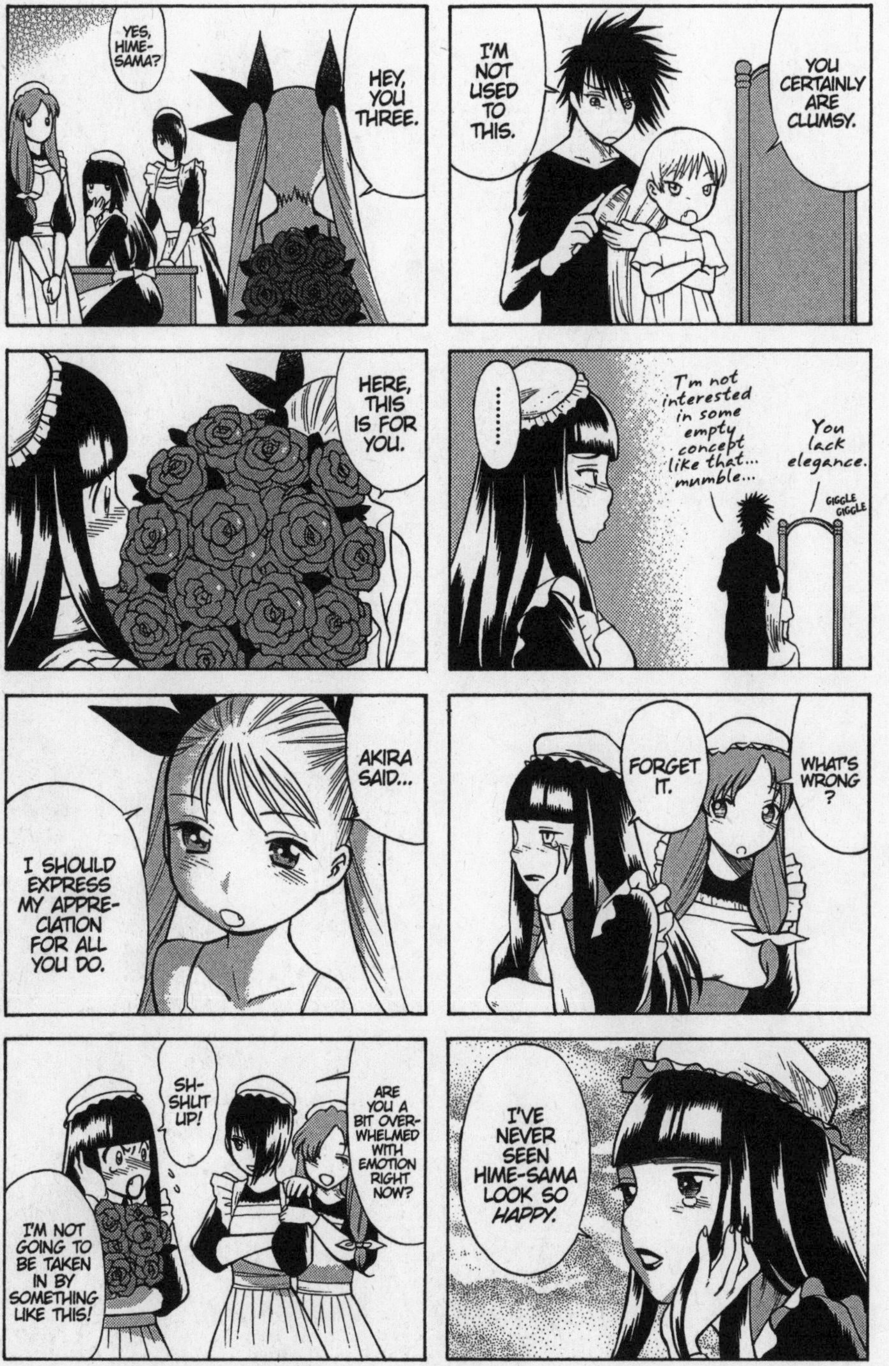
YOU CERTAINLY ARE CLUMSY.
I'M NOT USED TO THIS.
HEY, YOU THREE.
YES, HIME-SAMA?
You lack elegance.
GIGGLE GIGGLE
I'm not interested in some empty concept like that... mumble...
....
HERE, THIS IS FOR YOU.
WHAT'S WRONG?
FORGET IT.
AKIRA SAID...
I SHOULD EXPRESS MY APPRECIATION FOR ALL YOU DO.
I'VE NEVER SEEN HIME-SAMA LOOK SO *HAPPY.*
ARE YOU A BIT OVERWHELMED WITH EMOTION RIGHT NOW?
SH-SHUT UP!
I'M NOT GOING TO BE TAKEN IN BY SOMETHING LIKE THIS!

Tamaki Nozomu Presents Dance In The Vampire Bund 2

DANCE IN THE VAMPIRE BUND
2
NOZOMU TAMAKI

Homme, si, le cœur plein de joie ou d'amertume,

Tu passais vers midi dans les champs radieux,

Fuis! la Nature est vide et le Soleil consume:

Rien n'est vivant ici, rien n'est triste ou joyeux.

Viens! Le Soleil te parle en paroles sublimes;

Dans sa flamme implacable absorbe-toi sans fin;

Et retourne à pas lents vers les cités infimes,

Le cœur trempé sept fois dans le Néant divin.

Humans, if you choose to allow your hearts to
shake with joy and sink with sadness,
And go down the bright mid-day trail, then flee, for
nature is inane, and the sun will burn your flesh.
For all living things, there is neither joy nor sadness.

Cometh! The sun shall beckon you with noble words.
Sink into those fires of hell for eternity, and then with
heavy feet plod back to your humble town.
Wallowing seven times in the nihilism that is God.

Leconte de Lisle, Poèmes antiques

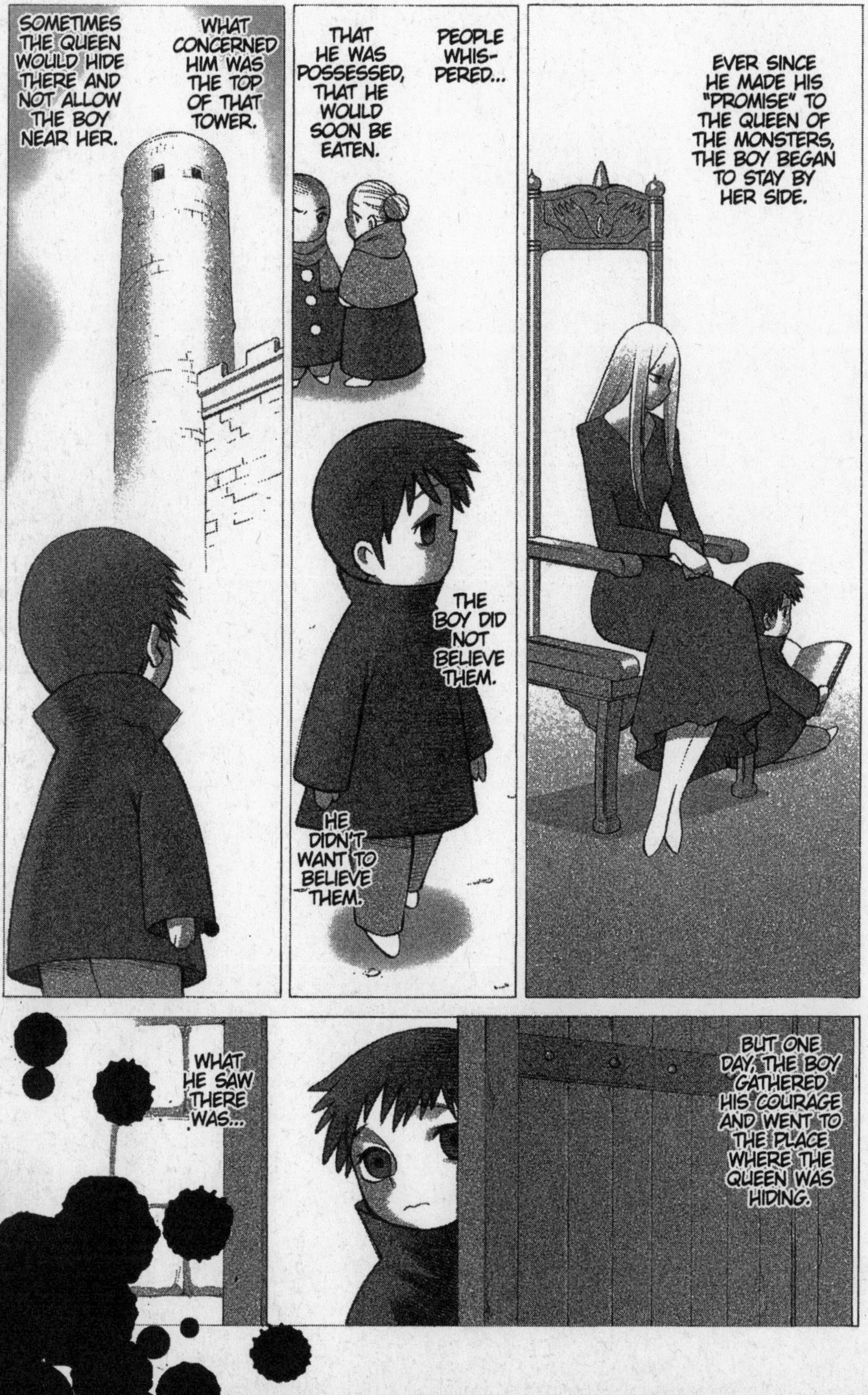
EVER SINCE HE MADE HIS "PROMISE" TO THE QUEEN OF THE MONSTERS, THE BOY BEGAN TO STAY BY HER SIDE.
PEOPLE WHISPERED...
THAT HE WAS POSSESSED, THAT HE WOULD SOON BE EATEN.
THE BOY DID NOT BELIEVE THEM.
HE DIDN'T WANT TO BELIEVE THEM.
WHAT CONCERNED HIM WAS THE TOP OF THAT TOWER.
SOMETIMES THE QUEEN WOULD HIDE THERE AND NOT ALLOW THE BOY NEAR HER.
BUT ONE DAY, THE BOY GATHERED HIS COURAGE AND WENT TO THE PLACE WHERE THE QUEEN WAS HIDING.
WHAT HE SAW THERE WAS...

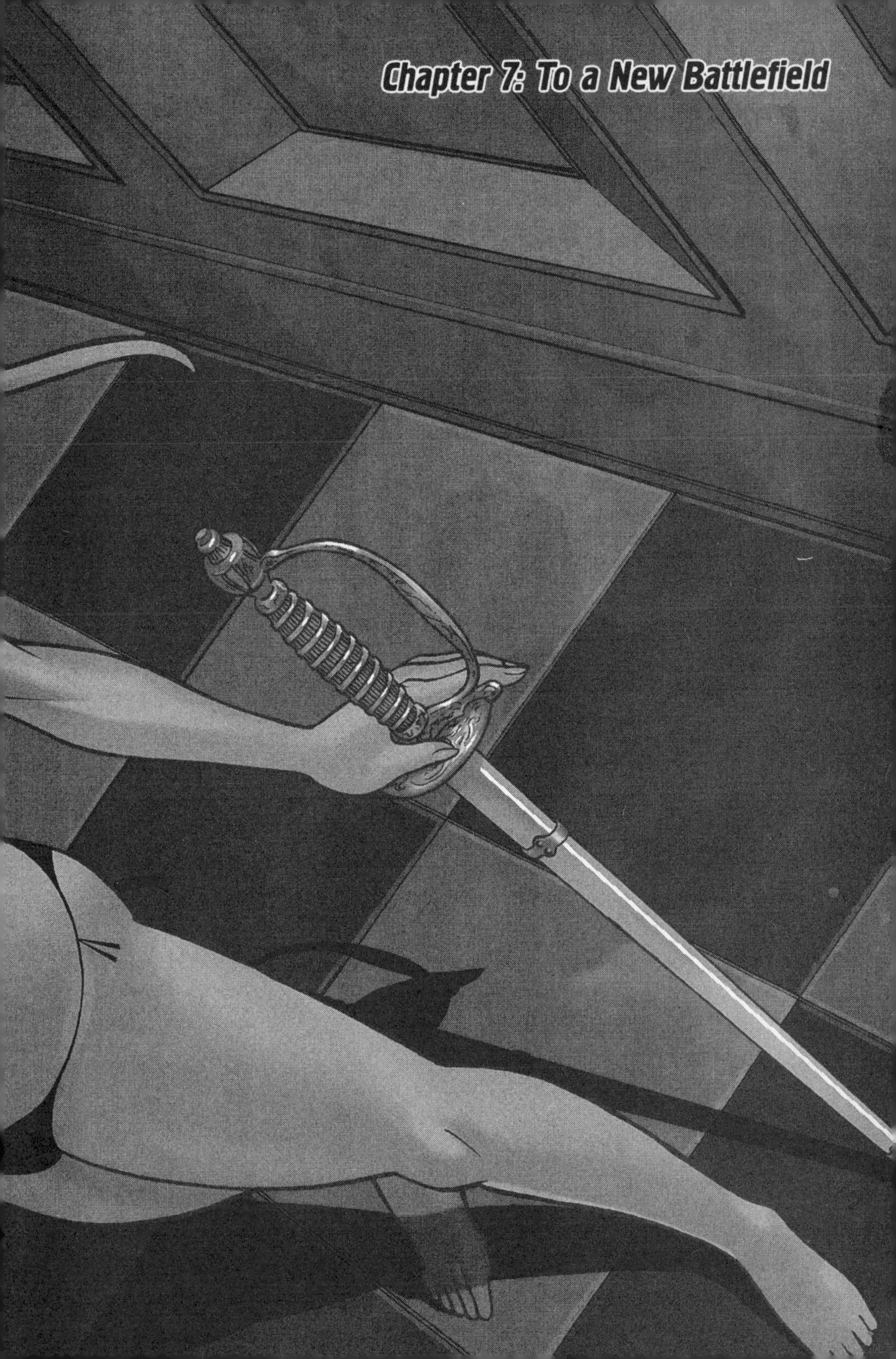
Chapter 7: To a New Battlefield

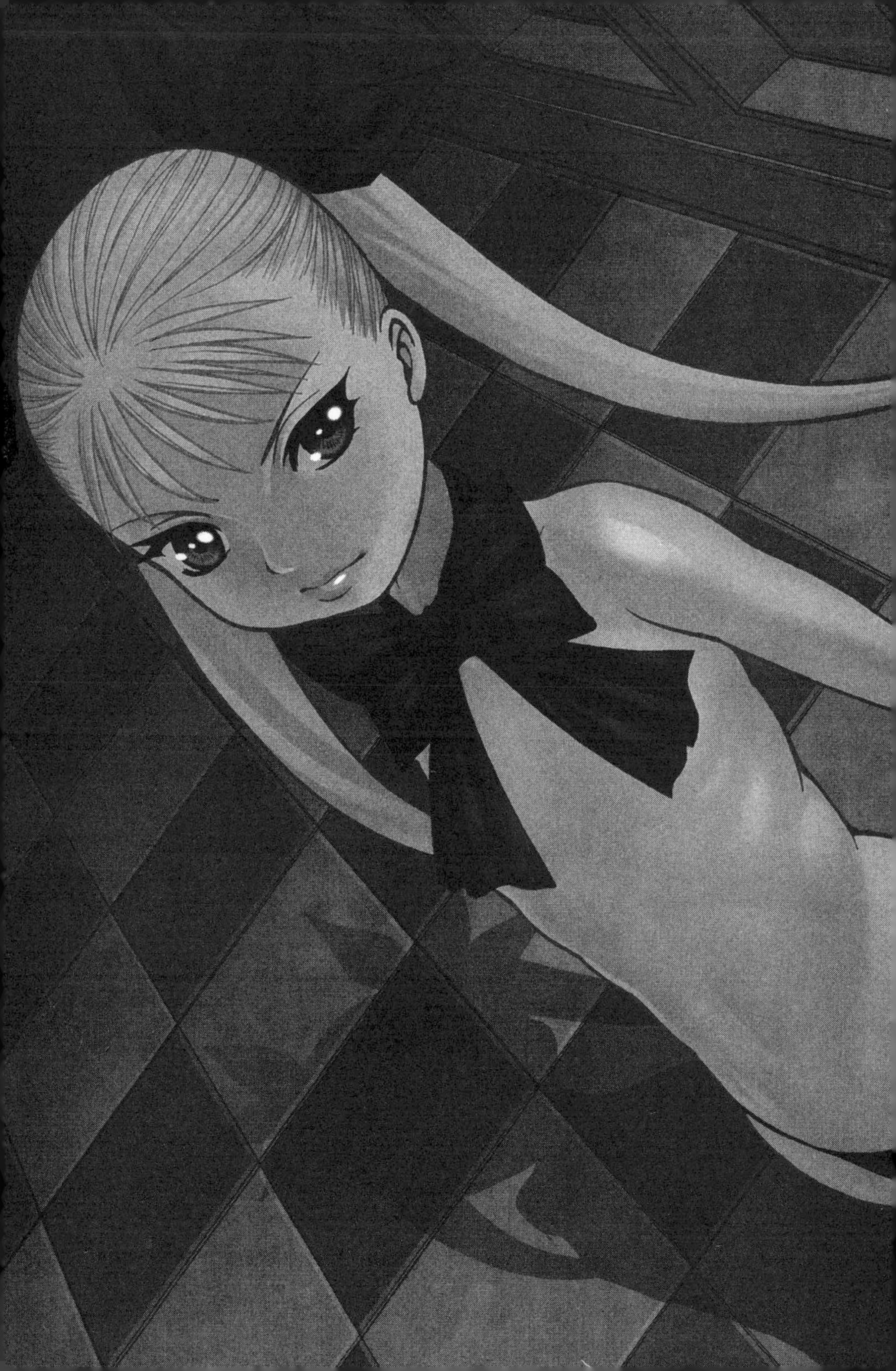

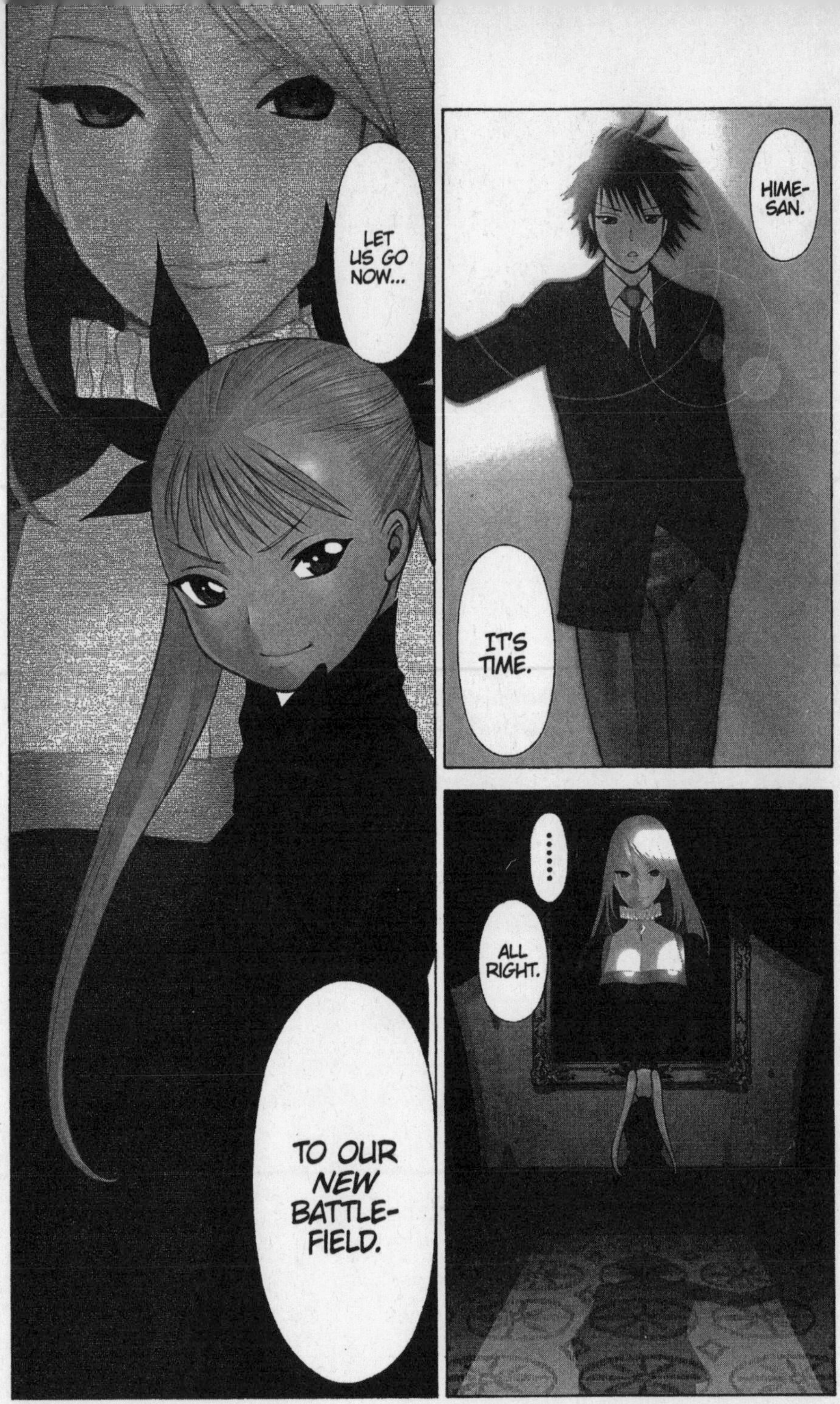
HIME-SAN.
IT'S TIME.
......
ALL RIGHT.
LET US GO NOW...
TO OUR NEW BATTLE-FIELD.

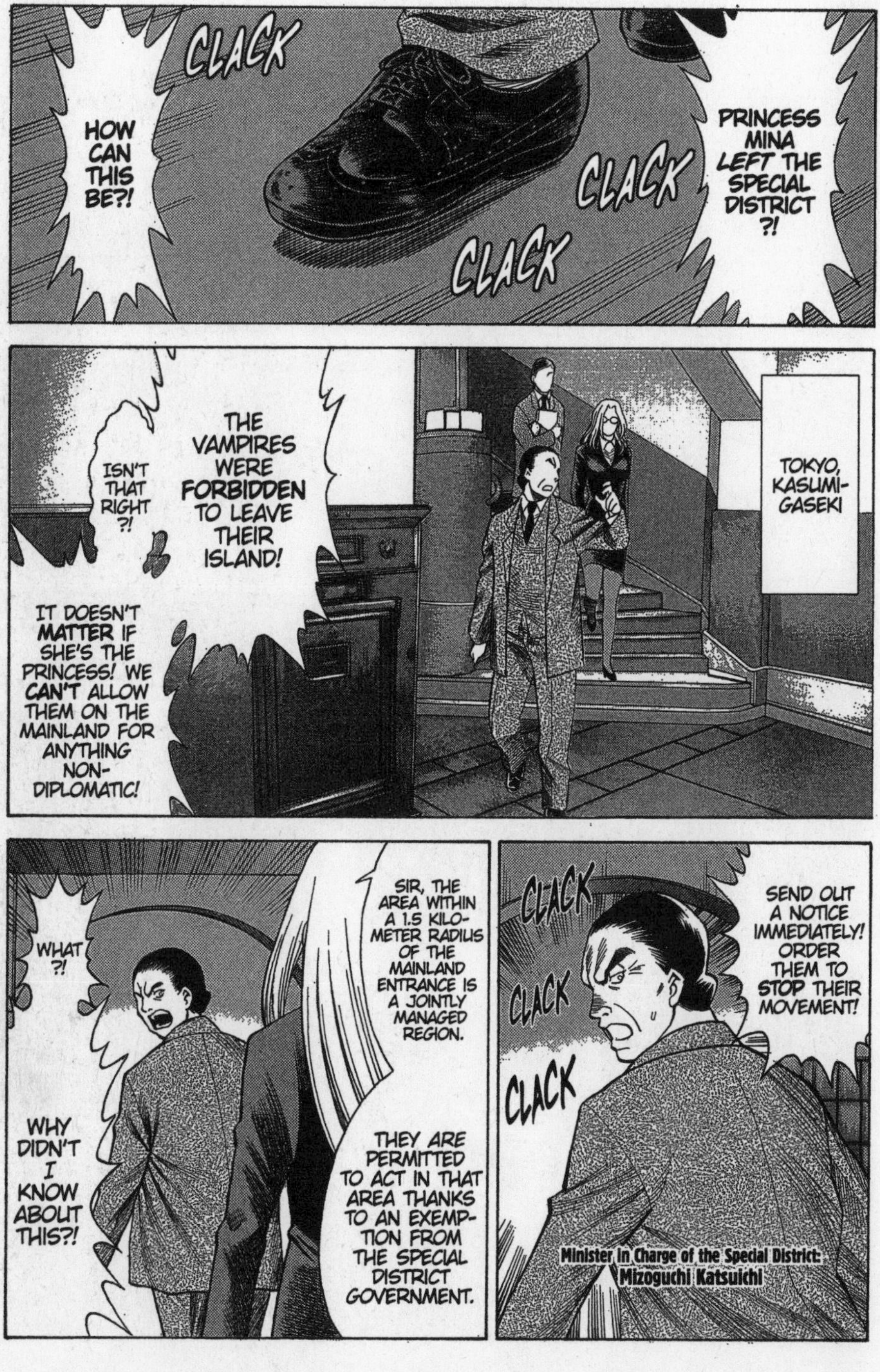

PRINCESS MINA LEFT THE SPECIAL DISTRICT?!
CLACK
CLACK
CLACK
HOW CAN THIS BE?!
TOKYO, KASUMIGASEKI
THE VAMPIRES WERE FORBIDDEN TO LEAVE THEIR ISLAND!
ISN'T THAT RIGHT?!
IT DOESN'T MATTER IF SHE'S THE PRINCESS! WE CAN'T ALLOW THEM ON THE MAINLAND FOR ANYTHING NON-DIPLOMATIC!
SEND OUT A NOTICE IMMEDIATELY! ORDER THEM TO STOP THEIR MOVEMENT!
CLACK
CLACK
CLACK
Minister in Charge of the Special District: Mizoguchi Katsuichi
SIR, THE AREA WITHIN A 1.5 KILOMETER RADIUS OF THE MAINLAND ENTRANCE IS A JOINTLY MANAGED REGION.
WHAT?!
THEY ARE PERMITTED TO ACT IN THAT AREA THANKS TO AN EXEMPTION FROM THE SPECIAL DISTRICT GOVERNMENT.
WHY DIDN'T I KNOW ABOUT THIS?!

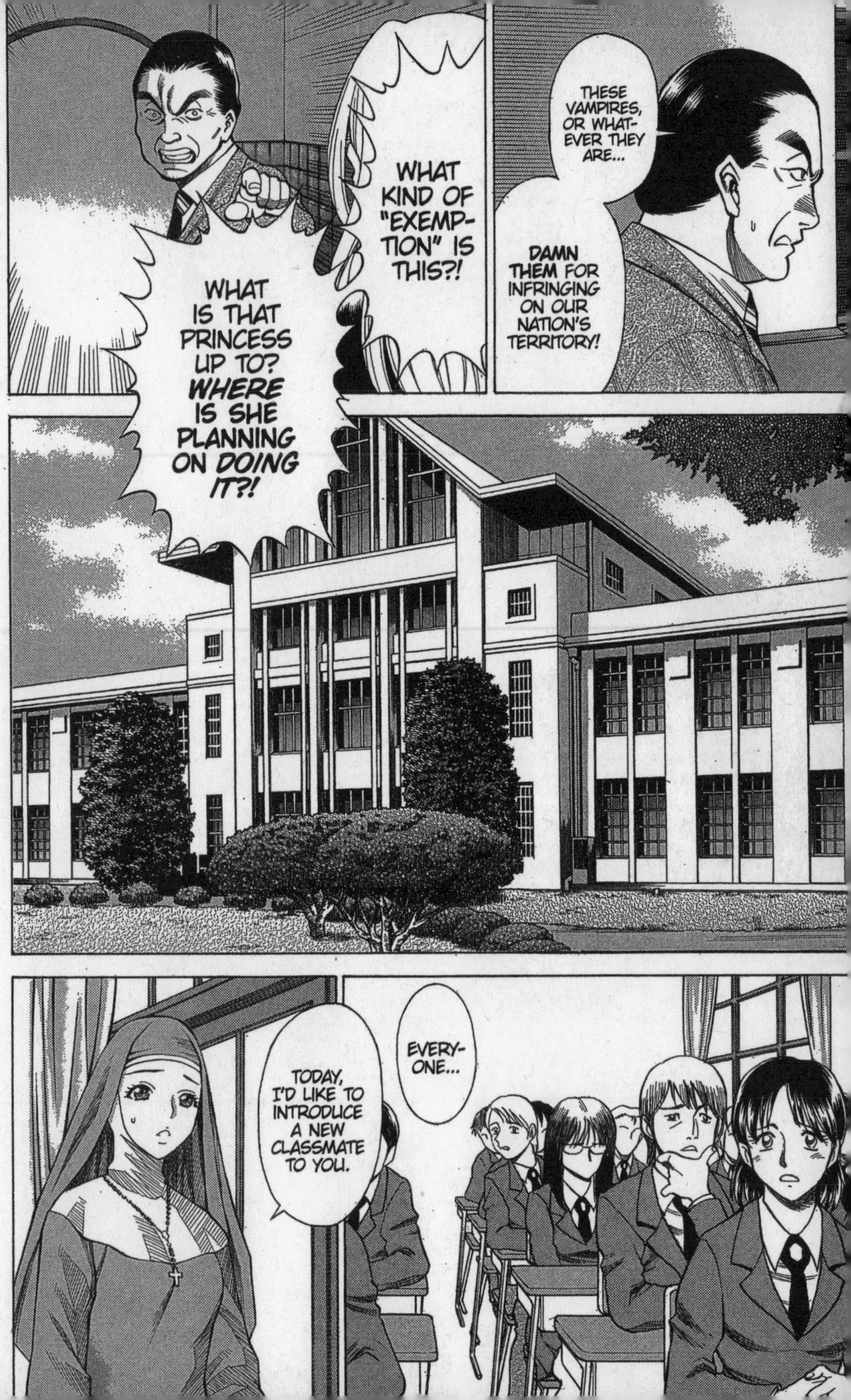
THESE VAMPIRES, OR WHAT-EVER THEY ARE...
DAMN THEM FOR INFRINGING ON OUR NATION'S TERRITORY!
WHAT KIND OF "EXEMP-TION" IS THIS?!
WHAT IS THAT PRINCESS UP TO? *WHERE* IS SHE PLANNING ON *DOING IT*?!
EVERY-ONE...
TODAY, I'D LIKE TO INTRODUCE A NEW CLASSMATE TO YOU.

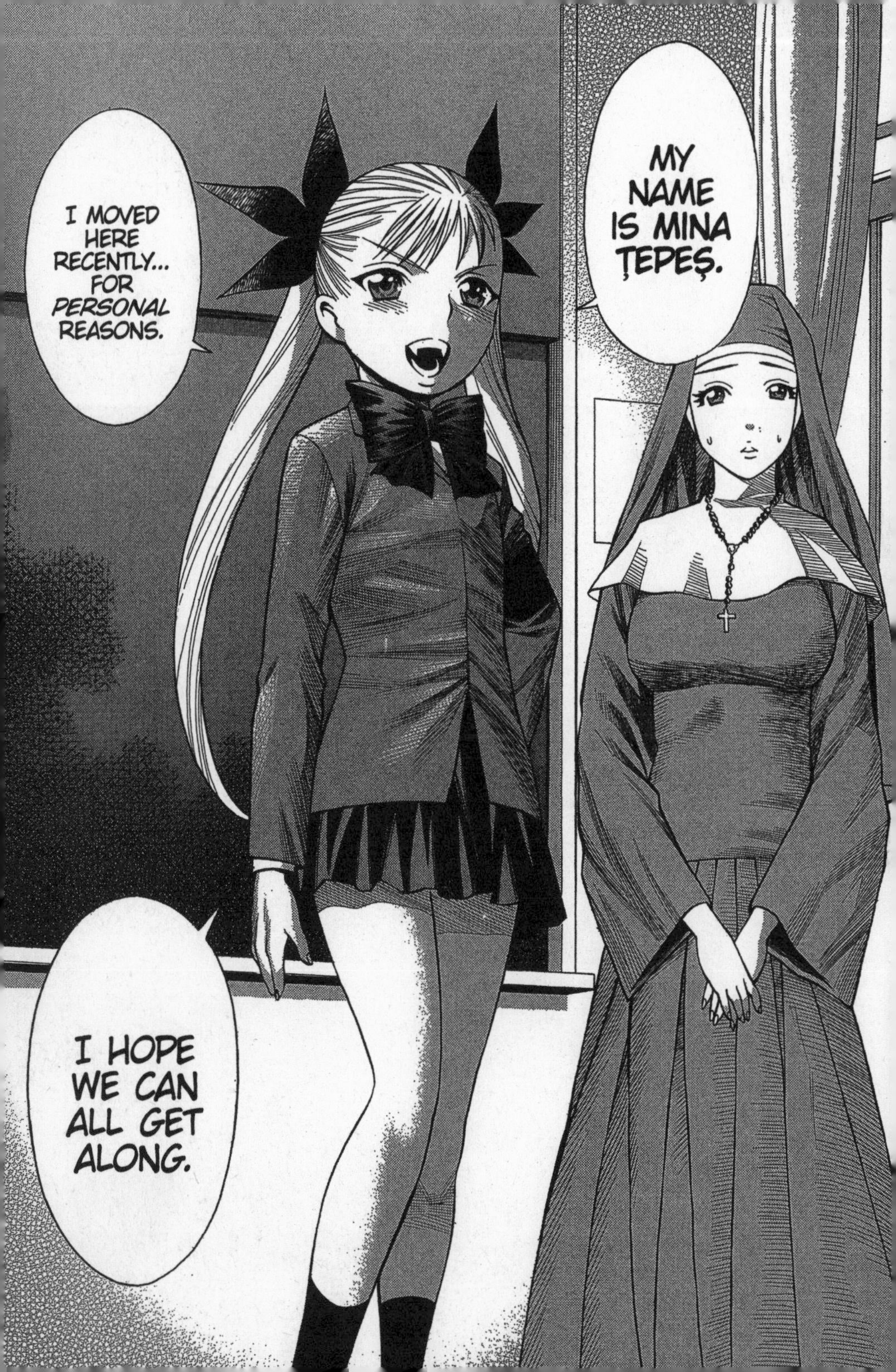
MY NAME IS MINA ȚEPEȘ.
I MOVED HERE RECENTLY... FOR *PERSONAL* REASONS.
I HOPE WE CAN ALL GET ALONG.

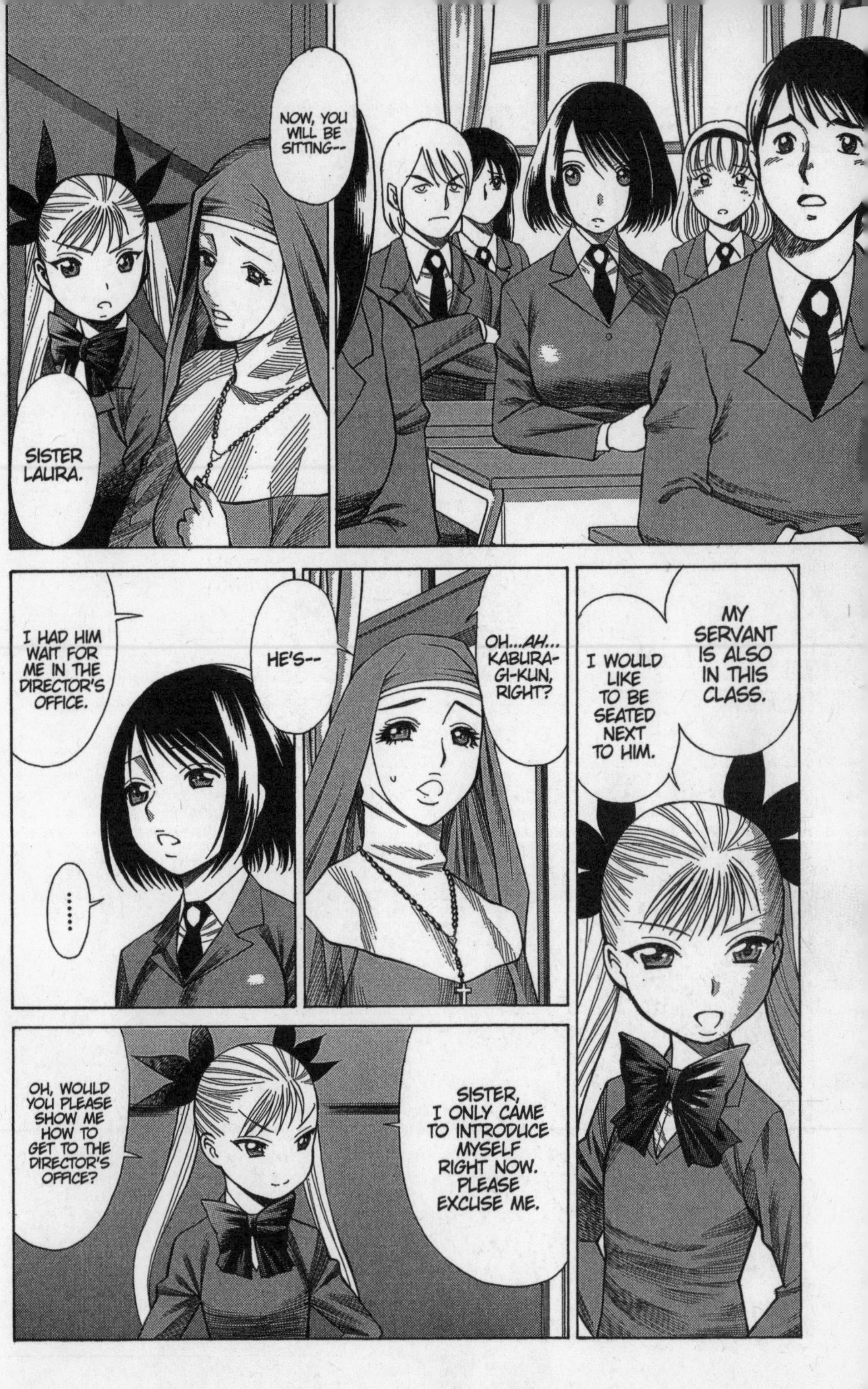
NOW, YOU WILL BE SITTING--
SISTER LAURA.
MY SERVANT IS ALSO IN THIS CLASS.
I WOULD LIKE TO BE SEATED NEXT TO HIM.
OH...*AH*... KABURAGI-KUN, RIGHT?
HE'S--
I HAD HIM WAIT FOR ME IN THE DIRECTOR'S OFFICE.
......
SISTER, I ONLY CAME TO INTRODUCE MYSELF RIGHT NOW. PLEASE EXCUSE ME.
OH, WOULD YOU PLEASE SHOW ME HOW TO GET TO THE DIRECTOR'S OFFICE?

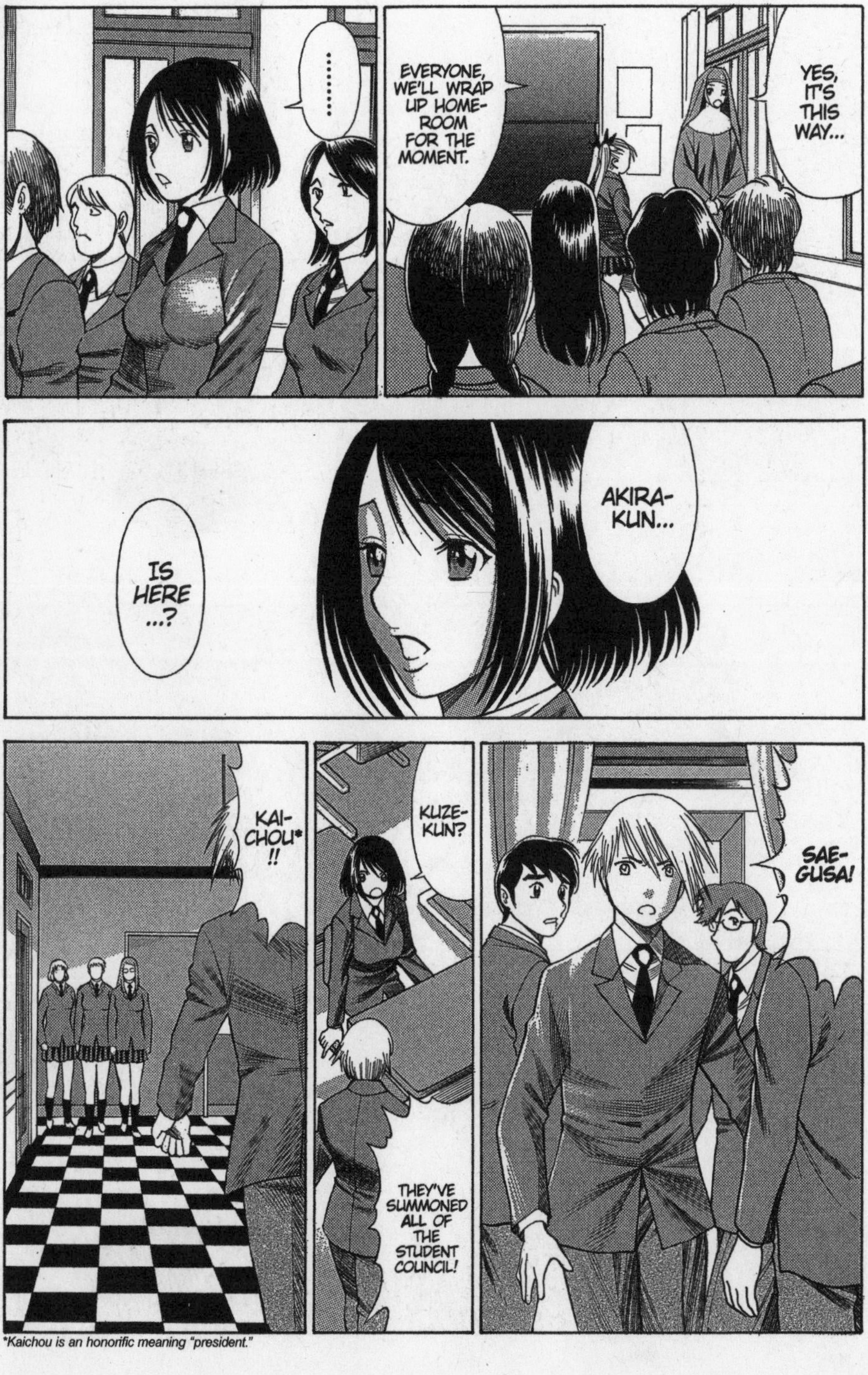
YES, IT'S THIS WAY...
EVERYONE, WE'LL WRAP UP HOME-ROOM FOR THE MOMENT.
......
AKIRA-KUN...
IS HERE ...?
SAE-GUSA!
KUZE-KUN?
THEY'VE SUMMONED ALL OF THE STUDENT COUNCIL!
KAI-CHOU* !!

*Kaichou is an honorific meaning "president."

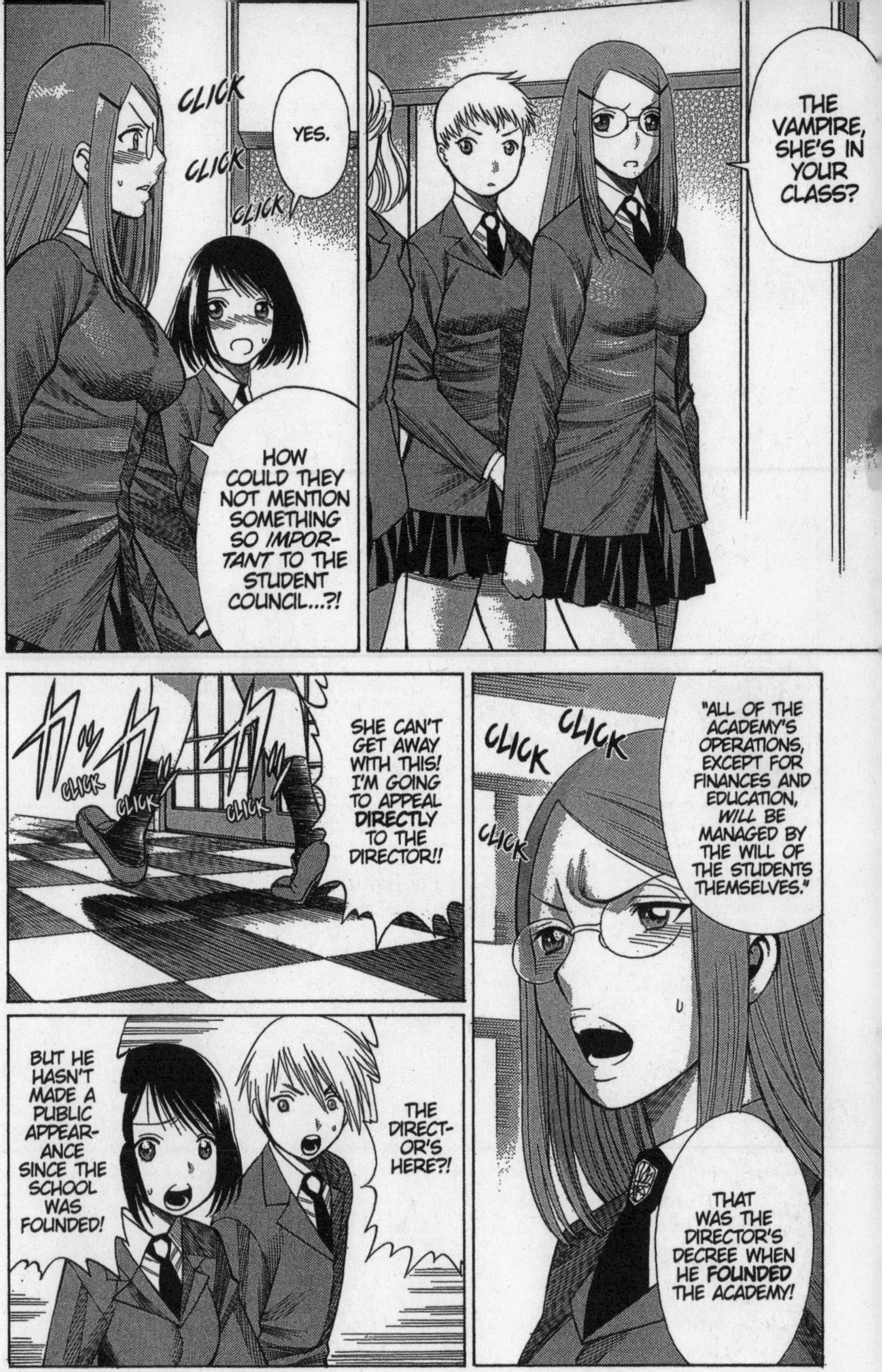
THE VAMPIRE, SHE'S IN YOUR CLASS?
YES.
CLICK
CLICK
CLICK
HOW COULD THEY NOT MENTION SOMETHING SO *IMPORTANT* TO THE STUDENT COUNCIL...?!
CLICK
CLICK
CLICK
"ALL OF THE ACADEMY'S OPERATIONS, EXCEPT FOR FINANCES AND EDUCATION, *WILL* BE MANAGED BY THE WILL OF THE STUDENTS THEMSELVES."
THAT WAS THE DIRECTOR'S DECREE WHEN HE **FOUNDED** THE ACADEMY!
SHE CAN'T GET AWAY WITH THIS! I'M GOING TO APPEAL **DIRECTLY** TO THE DIRECTOR!!
カッ
CLICK
カッ
CLICK
カッ
CLICK
THE DIRECTOR'S HERE?!
BUT HE HASN'T MADE A PUBLIC APPEARANCE SINCE THE SCHOOL WAS FOUNDED!

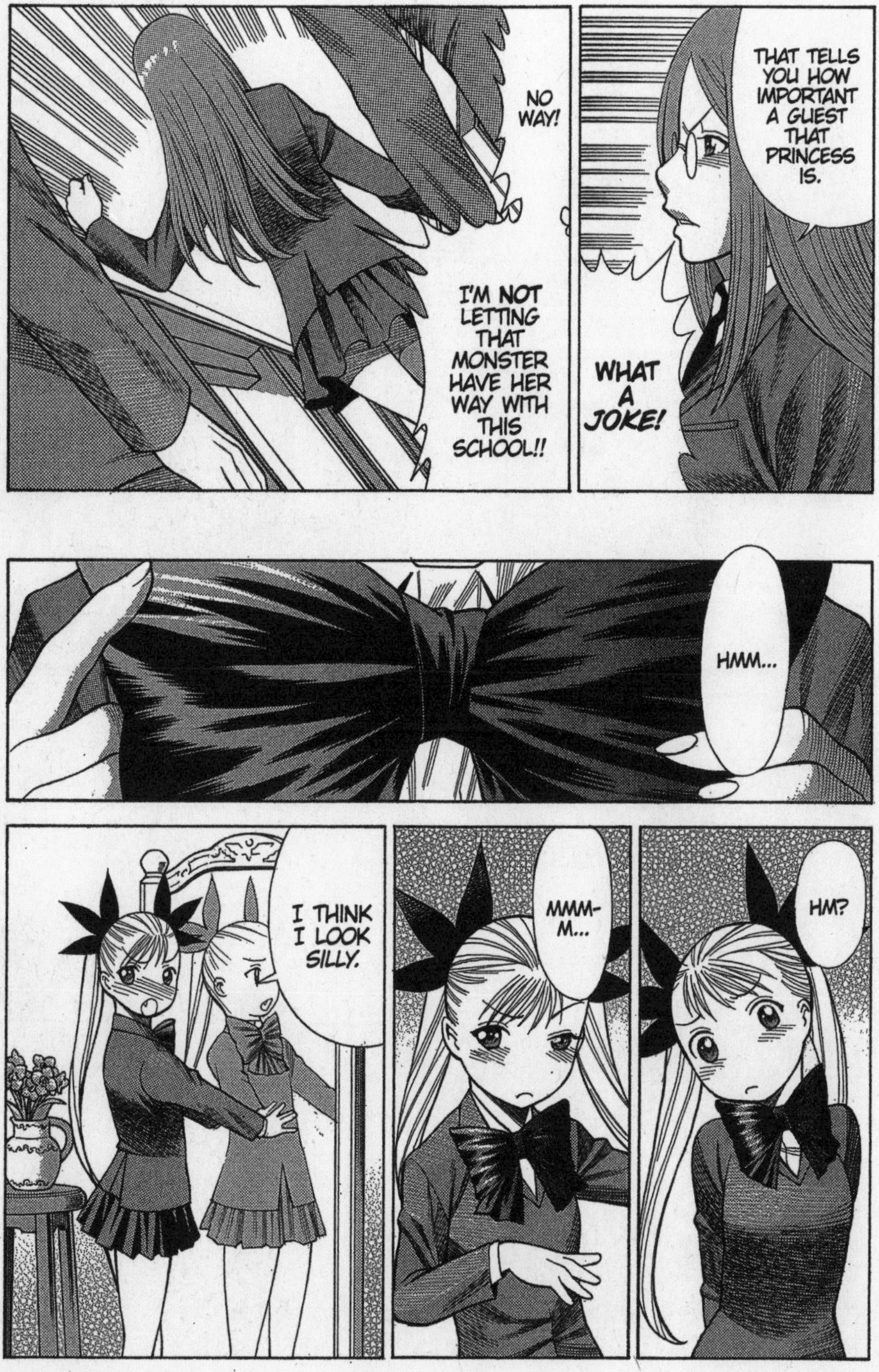
THAT TELLS YOU HOW IMPORTANT A GUEST THAT PRINCESS IS.
WHAT A JOKE!
NO WAY!
I'M NOT LETTING THAT MONSTER HAVE HER WAY WITH THIS SCHOOL!!
HMM...
HM?
MMMM-M...
I THINK I LOOK SILLY.

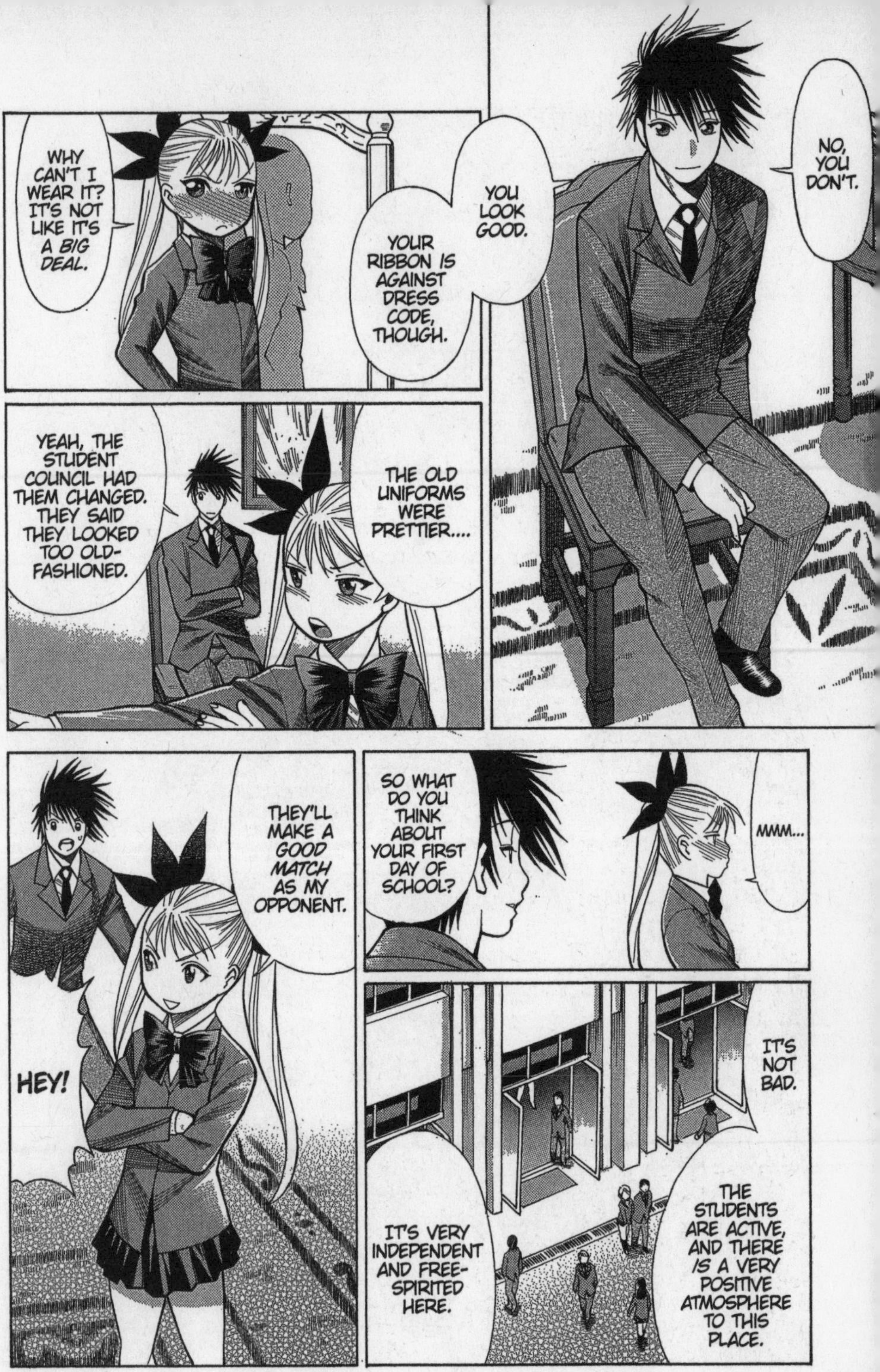

NO, YOU DON'T.
YOU LOOK GOOD.
YOUR RIBBON IS AGAINST DRESS CODE, THOUGH.
WHY CAN'T I WEAR IT? IT'S NOT LIKE IT'S A *BIG* DEAL.
THE OLD UNIFORMS WERE PRETTIER....
YEAH, THE STUDENT COUNCIL HAD THEM CHANGED. THEY SAID THEY LOOKED TOO OLD-FASHIONED.
SO WHAT DO YOU THINK ABOUT YOUR FIRST DAY OF SCHOOL?
MMM...
IT'S NOT BAD.
THE STUDENTS ARE ACTIVE, AND THERE *IS* A VERY POSITIVE ATMOSPHERE TO THIS PLACE.
IT'S VERY INDEPENDENT AND FREE-SPIRITED HERE.
THEY'LL MAKE A GOOD *MATCH* AS MY OPPONENT.
HEY!

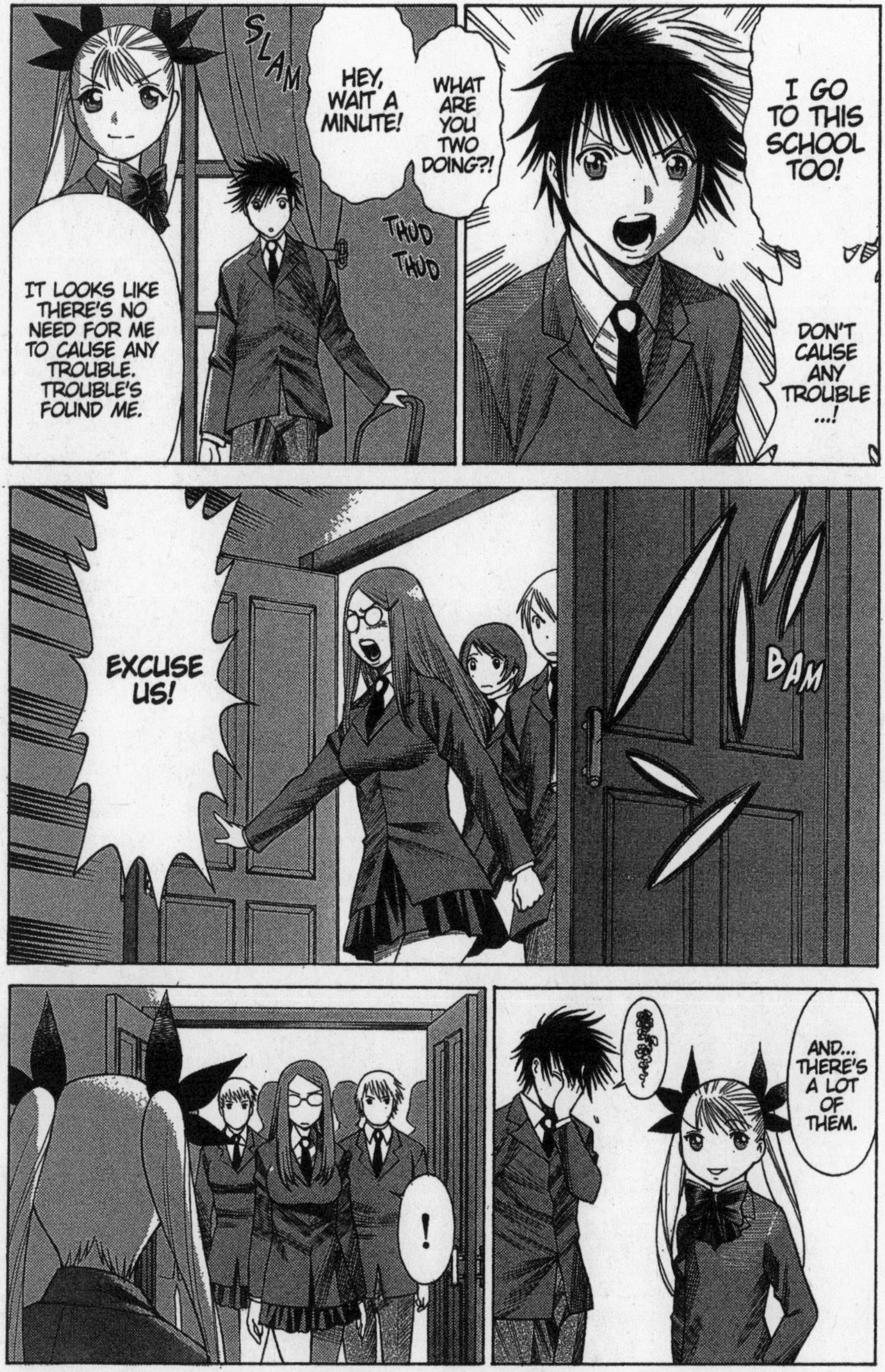
I GO TO THIS SCHOOL TOO!
DON'T CAUSE ANY TROUBLE ...!
SLAM
HEY, WAIT A MINUTE!
WHAT ARE YOU TWO DOING?!
THUD THUD
IT LOOKS LIKE THERE'S NO NEED FOR ME TO CAUSE ANY TROUBLE. TROUBLE'S FOUND ME.
BAM
EXCUSE US!
AND... THERE'S A LOT OF THEM.
!

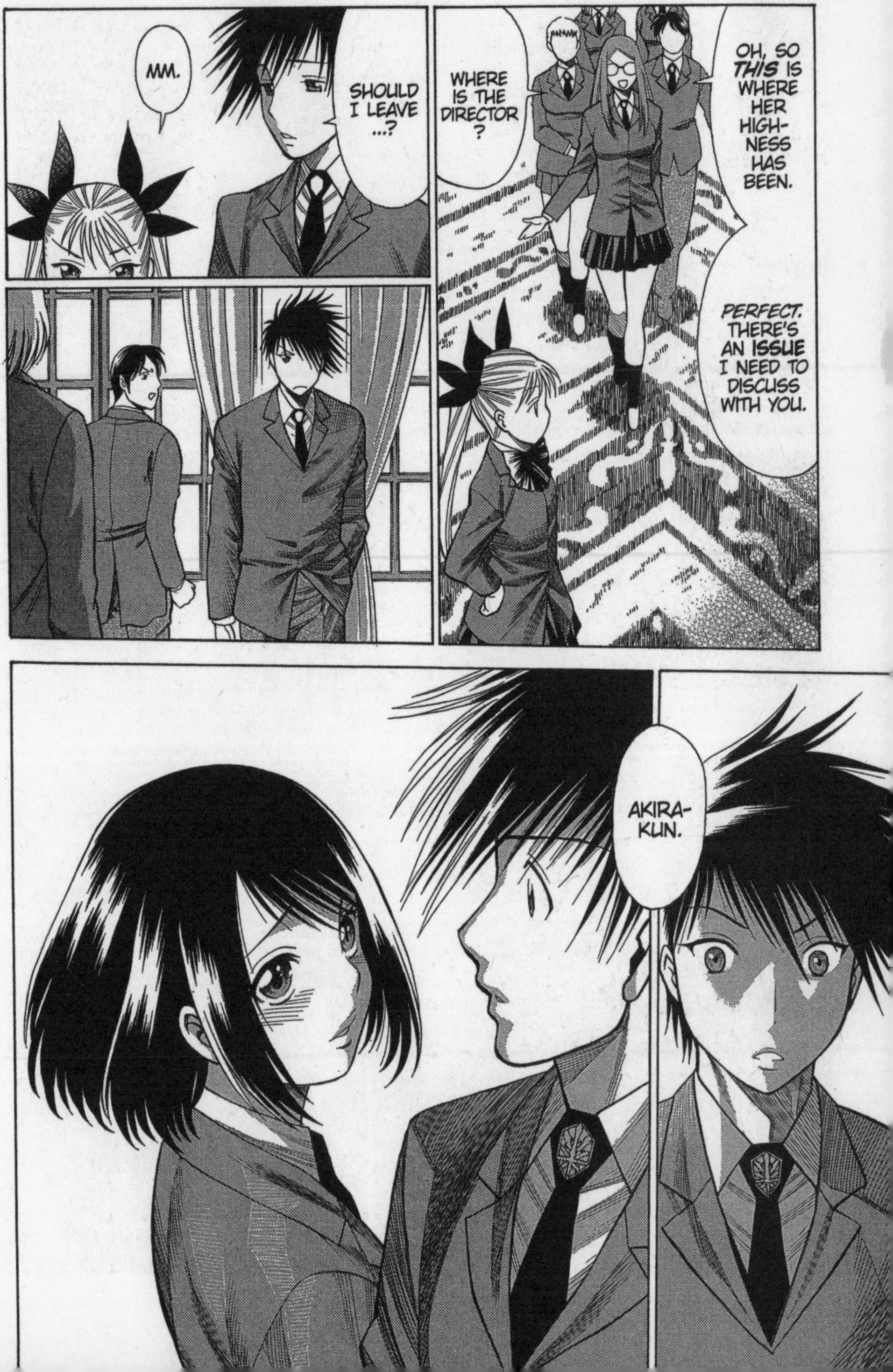
OH, SO THIS IS WHERE HER HIGHNESS HAS BEEN.
WHERE IS THE DIRECTOR?
PERFECT. THERE'S AN ISSUE I NEED TO DISCUSS WITH YOU.
SHOULD I LEAVE ...?
MM.
AKIRA-KUN.

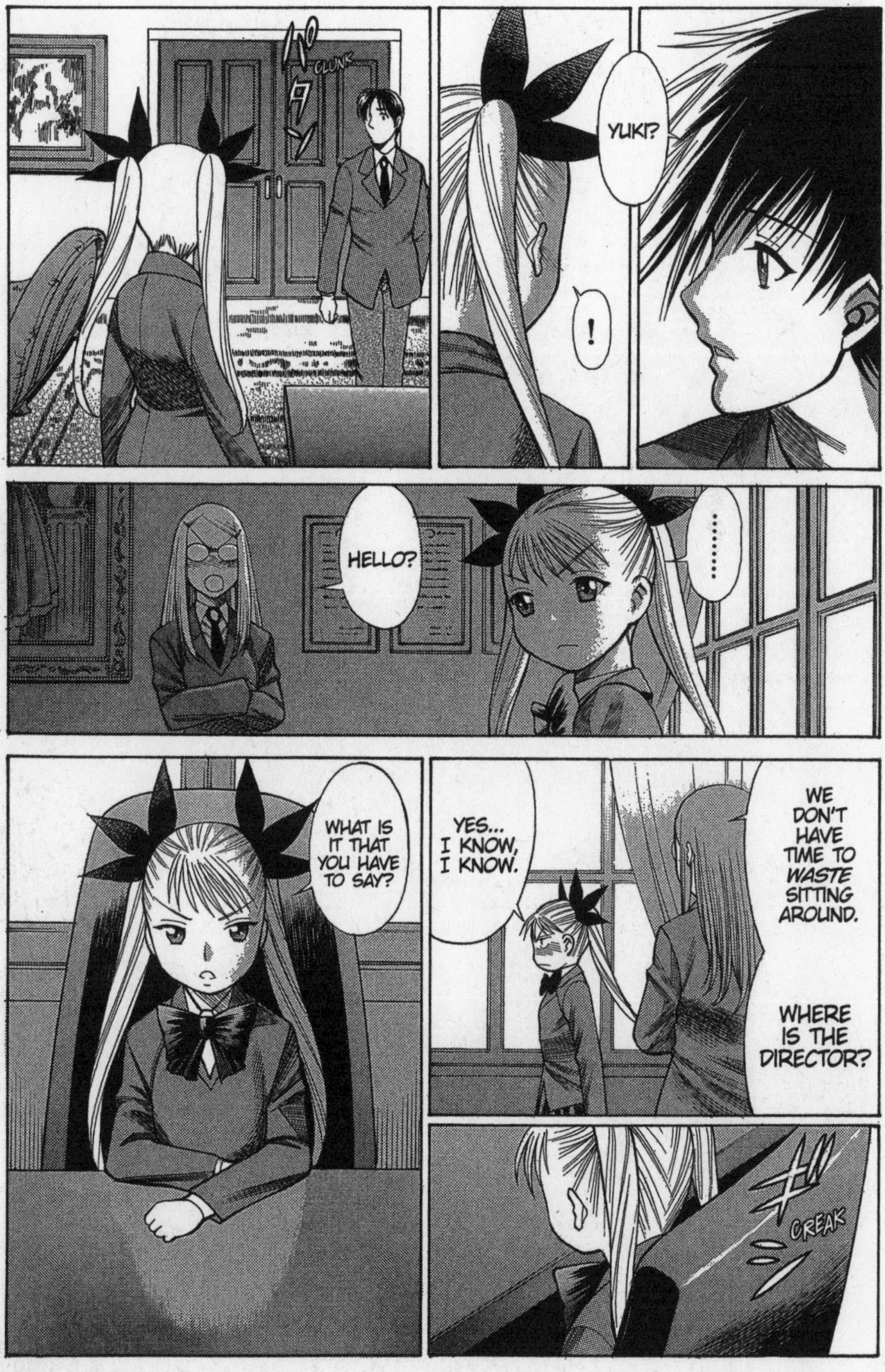
YUKI?
!
パタン
CLUNK
......
HELLO?
WE DON'T HAVE TIME TO *WASTE* SITTING AROUND.
WHERE IS THE DIRECTOR?
YES... I KNOW, I KNOW.
CREAK
WHAT IS IT THAT YOU HAVE TO SAY?

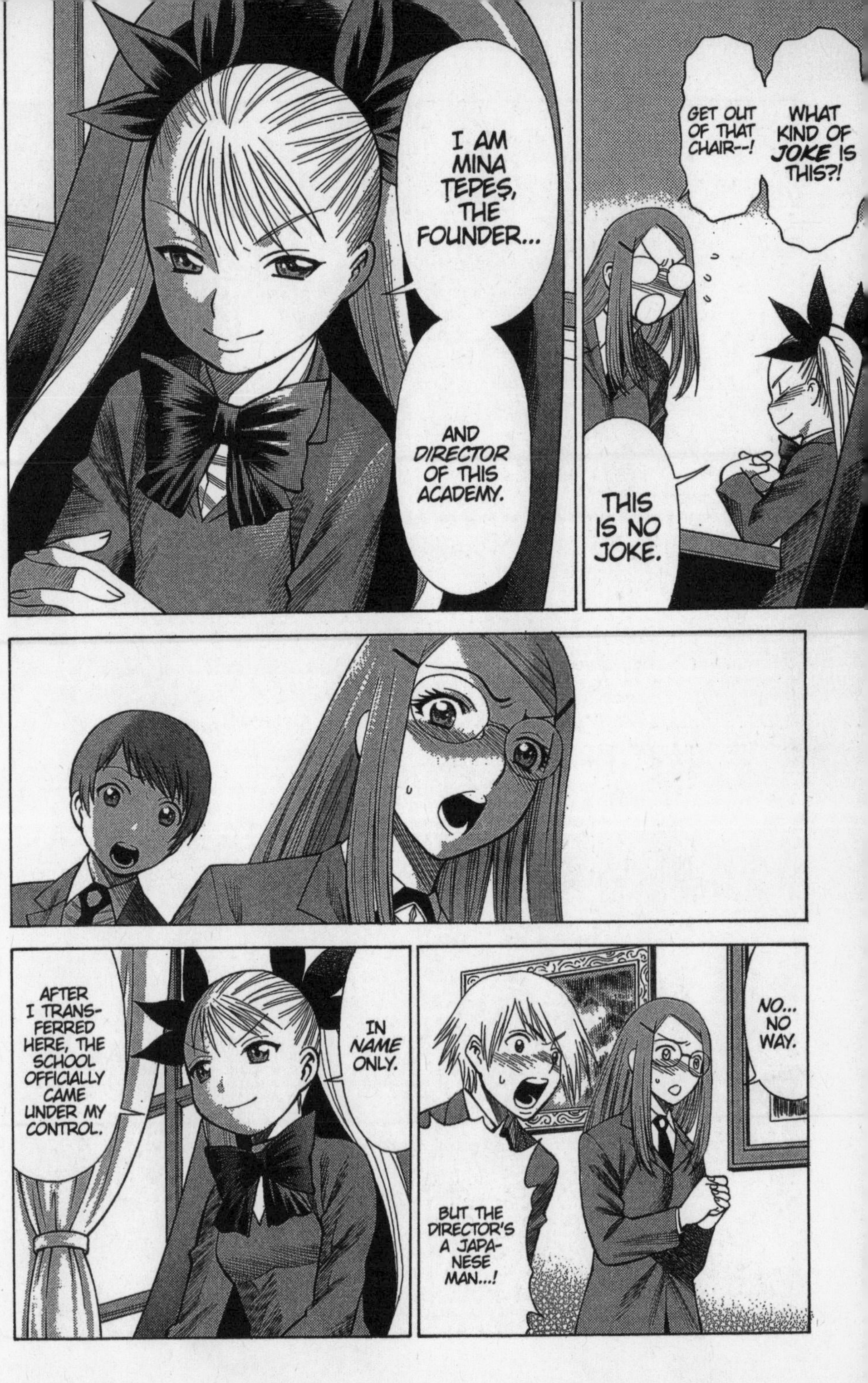
WHAT KIND OF JOKE IS THIS?!
GET OUT OF THAT CHAIR--!
THIS IS NO JOKE.
I AM MINA TEPEŞ, THE FOUNDER...
AND DIRECTOR OF THIS ACADEMY.
NO... NO WAY.
BUT THE DIRECTOR'S A JAPA-NESE MAN...!
IN NAME ONLY.
AFTER I TRANS-FERRED HERE, THE SCHOOL OFFICIALLY CAME UNDER MY CONTROL.

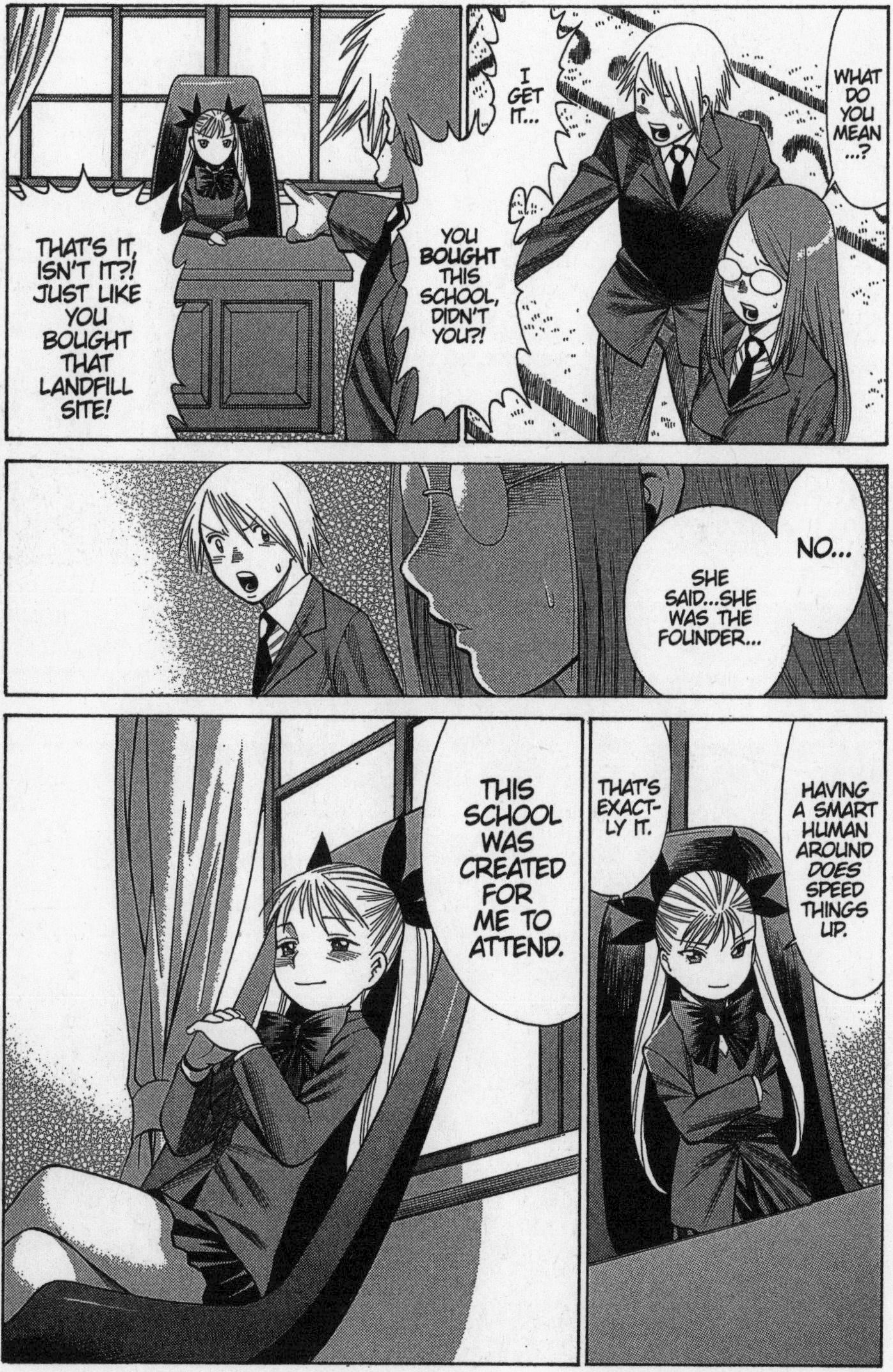
WHAT DO YOU MEAN ...?
I GET IT...
YOU BOUGHT THIS SCHOOL, DIDN'T YOU?!
THAT'S IT, ISN'T IT?! JUST LIKE YOU BOUGHT THAT LANDFILL SITE!
NO...
SHE SAID...SHE WAS THE FOUNDER...
HAVING A SMART HUMAN AROUND *DOES* SPEED THINGS UP.
THAT'S EXACT-LY IT.
THIS SCHOOL WAS CREATED FOR ME TO ATTEND.

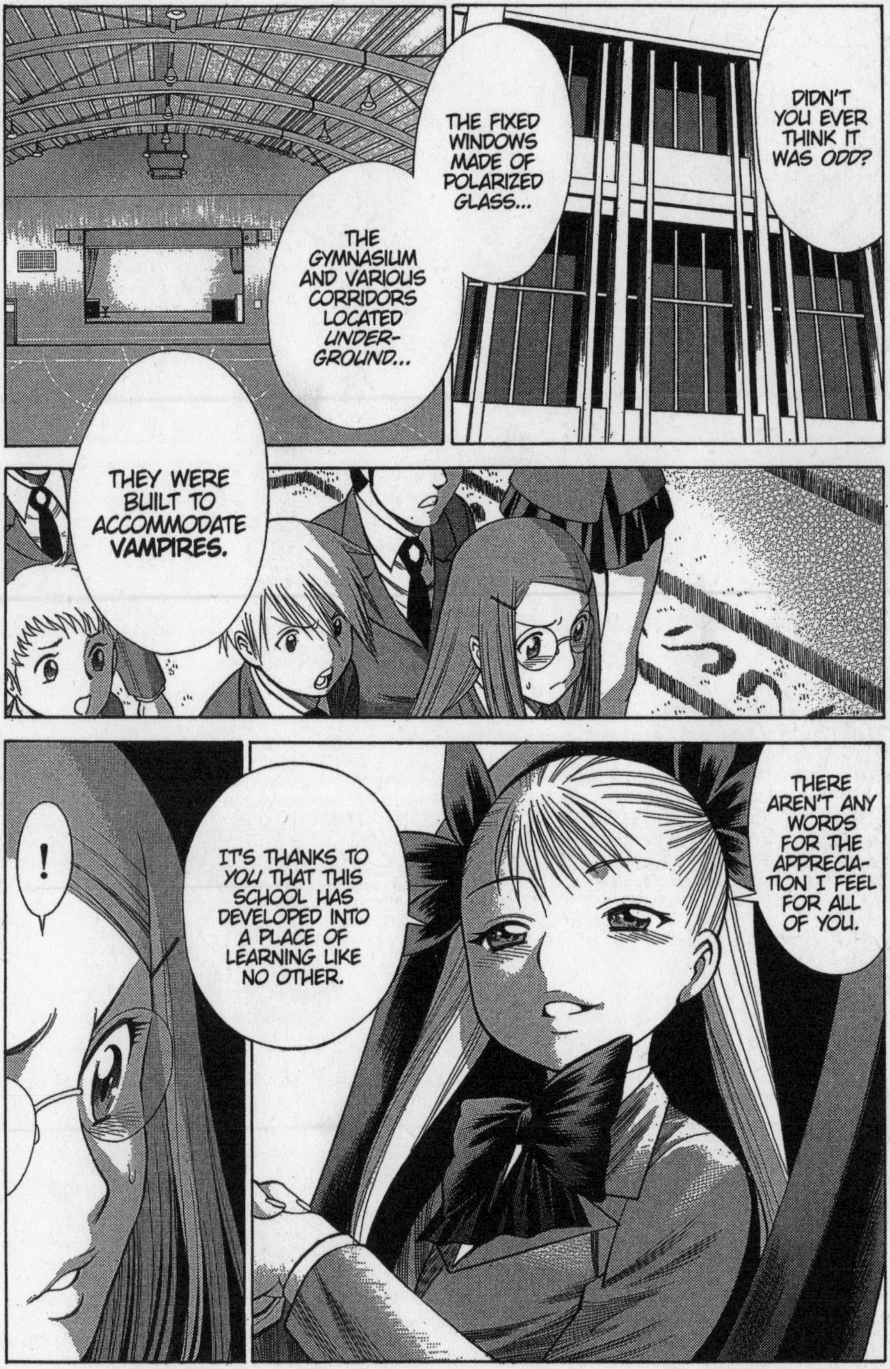
DIDN'T YOU EVER THINK IT WAS ODD?
THE FIXED WINDOWS MADE OF POLARIZED GLASS...
THE GYMNASIUM AND VARIOUS CORRIDORS LOCATED UNDER-GROUND...
THEY WERE BUILT TO ACCOMMODATE VAMPIRES.
THERE AREN'T ANY WORDS FOR THE APPRECIA-TION I FEEL FOR ALL OF YOU.
IT'S THANKS TO YOU THAT THIS SCHOOL HAS DEVELOPED INTO A PLACE OF LEARNING LIKE NO OTHER.
!

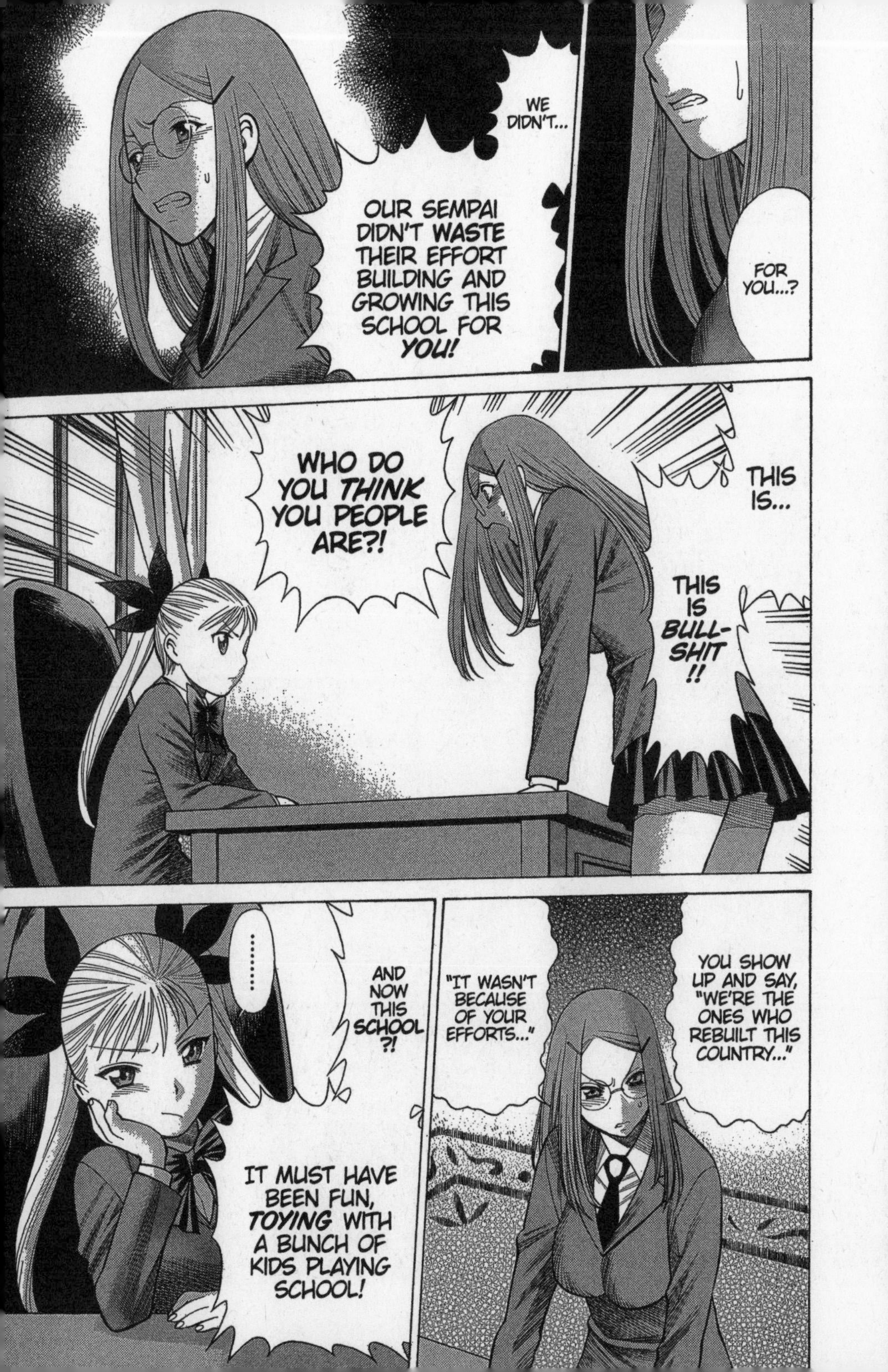
FOR YOU...?
WE DIDN'T...
OUR SEMPAI DIDN'T WASTE THEIR EFFORT BUILDING AND GROWING THIS SCHOOL FOR YOU!
THIS IS...
THIS IS BULL-SHIT!!
WHO DO YOU THINK YOU PEOPLE ARE?!
YOU SHOW UP AND SAY, "WE'RE THE ONES WHO REBUILT THIS COUNTRY..."
"IT WASN'T BECAUSE OF YOUR EFFORTS..."
AND NOW THIS SCHOOL?!
....
IT MUST HAVE BEEN FUN, TOYING WITH A BUNCH OF KIDS PLAYING SCHOOL!

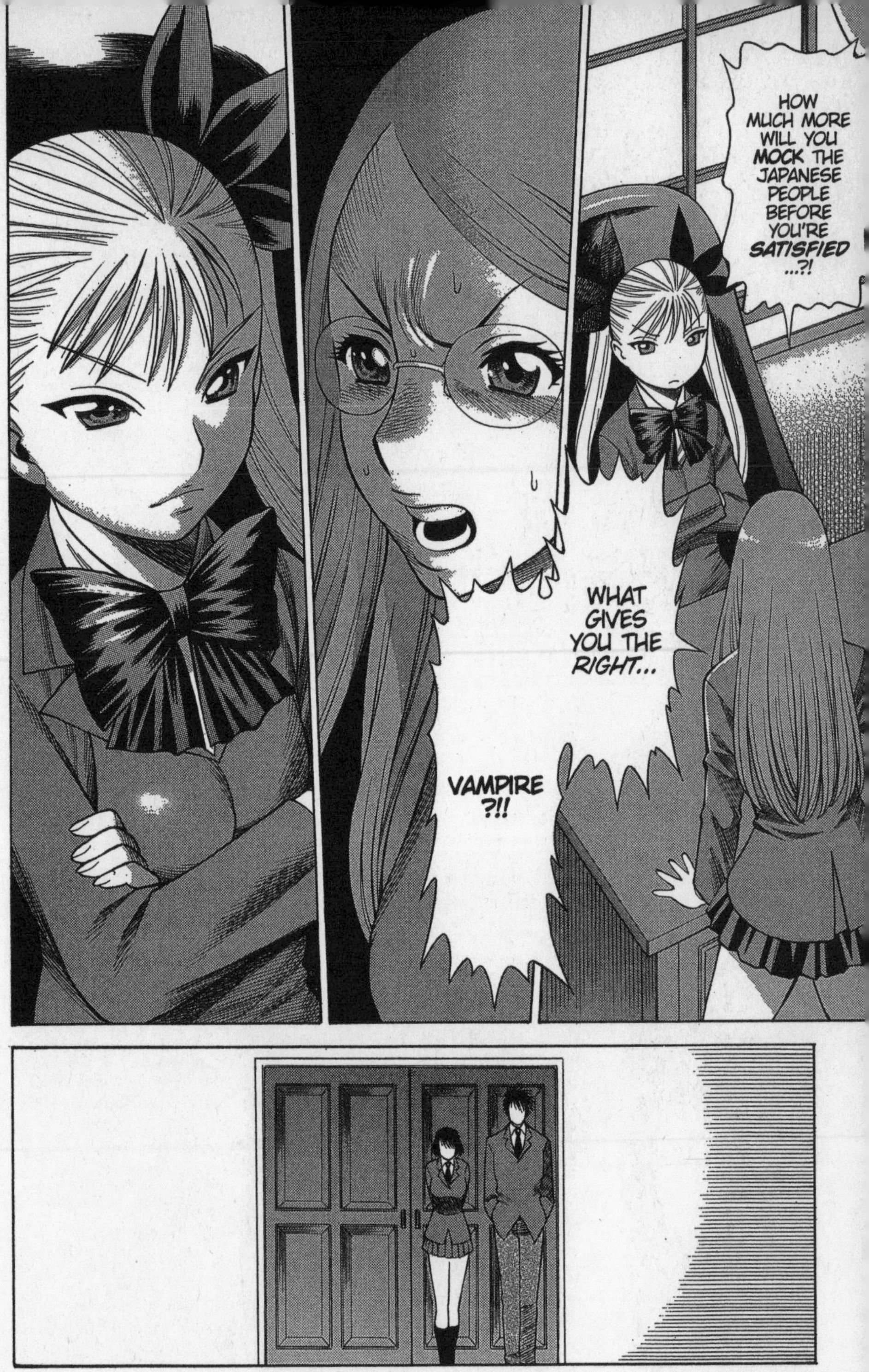
HOW MUCH MORE WILL YOU MOCK THE JAPANESE PEOPLE BEFORE YOU'RE SATISFIED ...?!
WHAT GIVES YOU THE RIGHT...
VAMPIRE ?!!

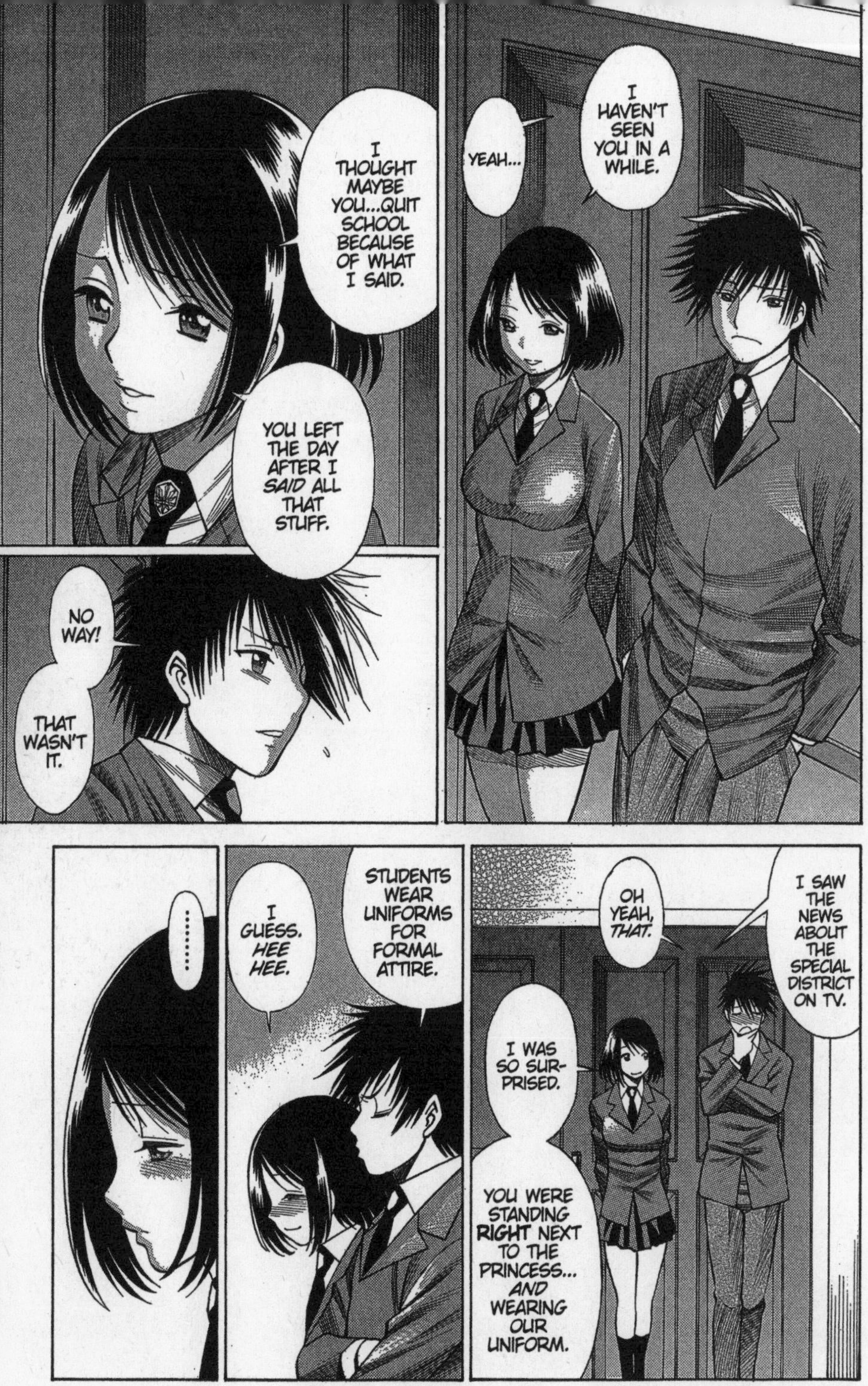
I HAVEN'T SEEN YOU IN A WHILE.
YEAH...
I THOUGHT MAYBE YOU...QUIT SCHOOL BECAUSE OF WHAT I SAID.
YOU LEFT THE DAY AFTER I *SAID* ALL THAT STUFF.
NO WAY!
THAT WASN'T IT.
I SAW THE NEWS ABOUT THE SPECIAL DISTRICT ON TV.
OH YEAH, *THAT.*
I WAS SO SURPRISED.
YOU WERE STANDING **RIGHT** NEXT TO THE PRINCESS... *AND* WEARING OUR UNIFORM.
STUDENTS WEAR UNIFORMS FOR FORMAL ATTIRE.
I GUESS. *HEE HEE.*
....

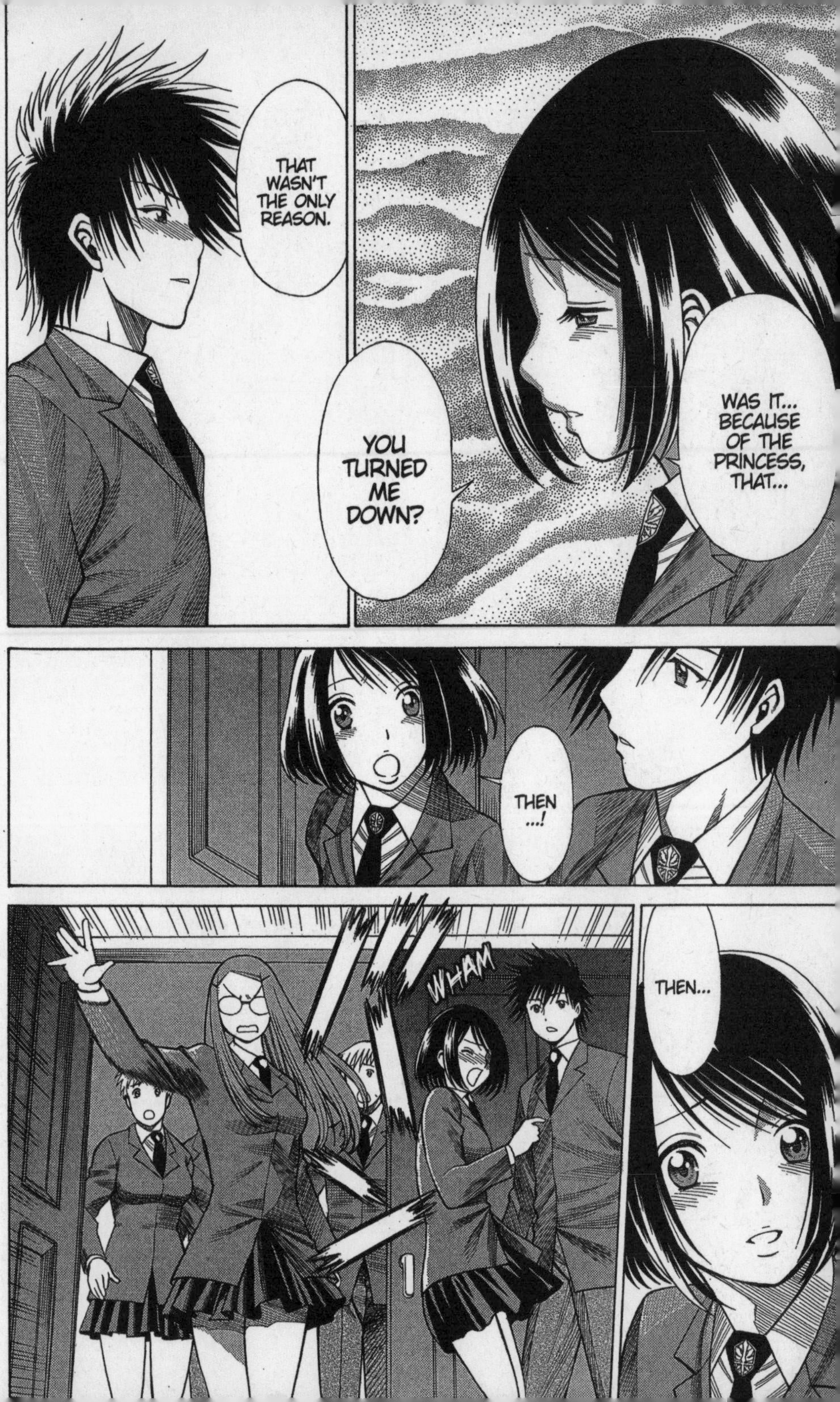
WAS IT... BECAUSE OF THE PRINCESS, THAT...
YOU TURNED ME DOWN?
THAT WASN'T THE ONLY REASON.
THEN ...!
THEN...
WHAM

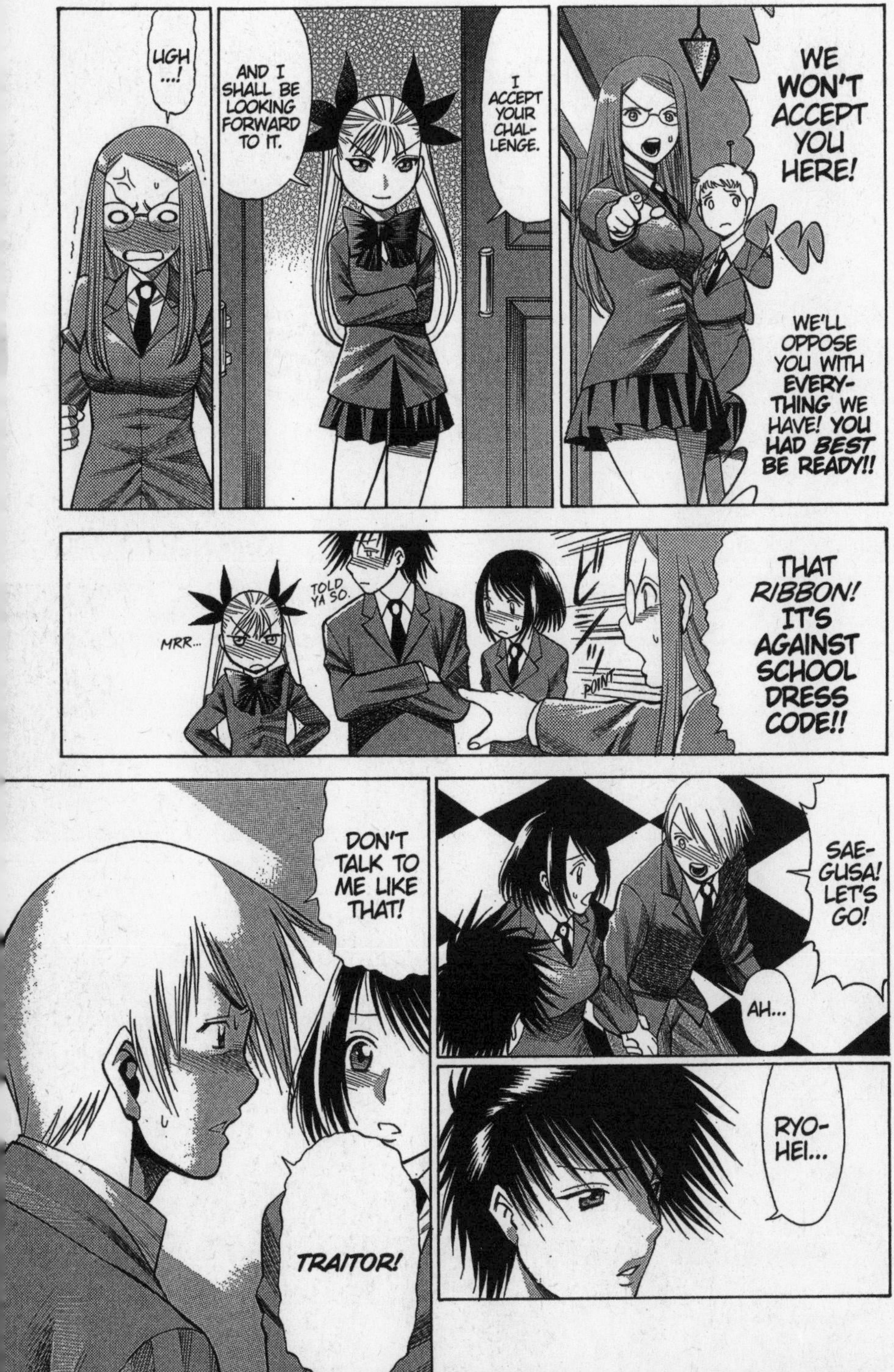
WE WON'T ACCEPT YOU HERE!
WE'LL OPPOSE YOU WITH EVERY-THING WE HAVE! YOU HAD *BEST* BE READY!!
I ACCEPT YOUR CHAL-LENGE.
AND I SHALL BE LOOKING FORWARD TO IT.
UGH ...!
THAT *RIBBON!* IT'S AGAINST SCHOOL DRESS CODE!!
POINT
TOLD YA SO.
MRR...
SAE-GUSA! LET'S GO!
AH...
RYO-HEI...
DON'T TALK TO ME LIKE THAT!
TRAITOR!

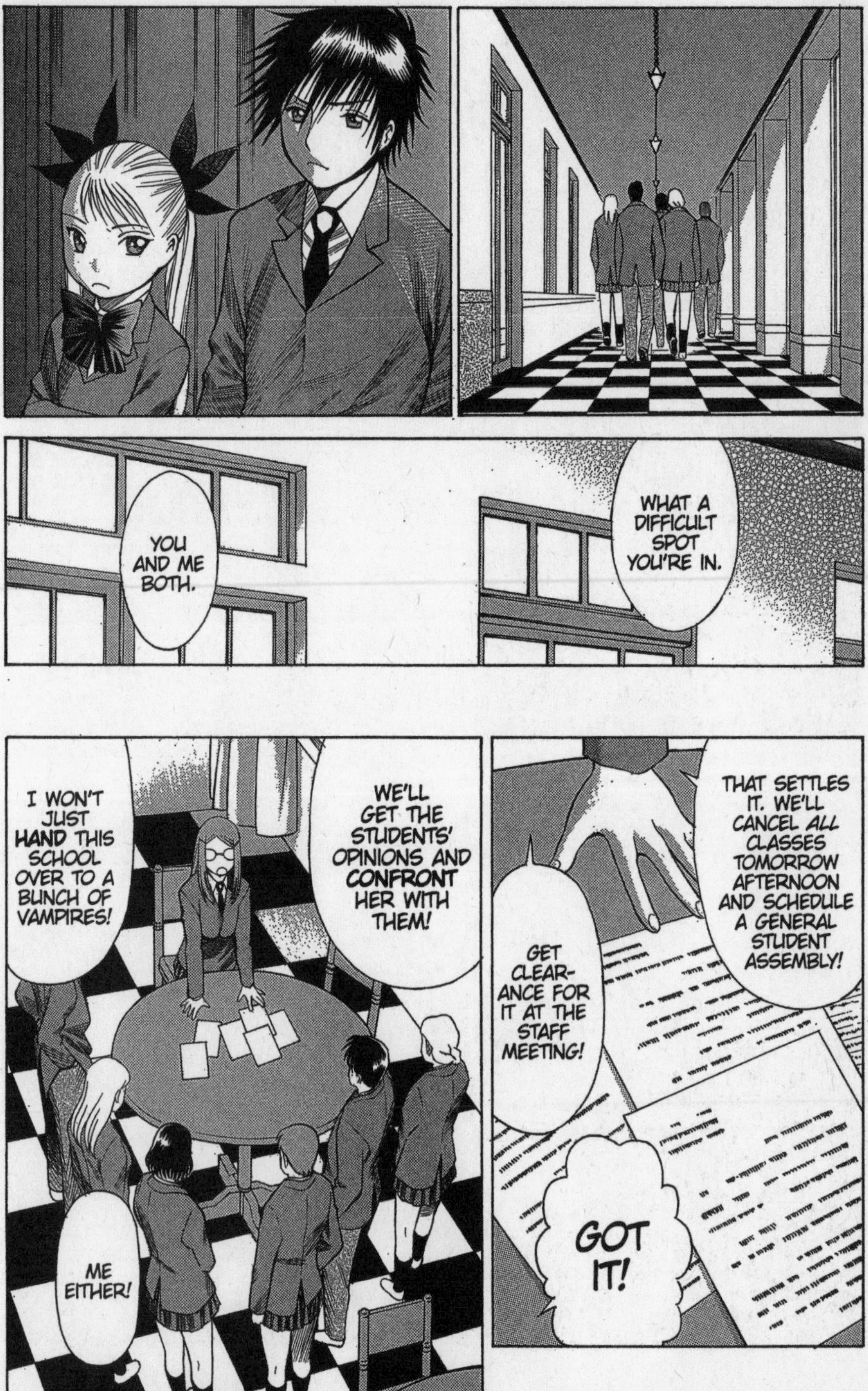
WHAT A DIFFICULT SPOT YOU'RE IN.
YOU AND ME BOTH.
THAT SETTLES IT. WE'LL CANCEL ALL CLASSES TOMORROW AFTERNOON AND SCHEDULE A GENERAL STUDENT ASSEMBLY!
GET CLEAR-ANCE FOR IT AT THE STAFF MEETING!
GOT IT!
WE'LL GET THE STUDENTS' OPINIONS AND CONFRONT HER WITH THEM!
I WON'T JUST HAND THIS SCHOOL OVER TO A BUNCH OF VAMPIRES!
ME EITHER!

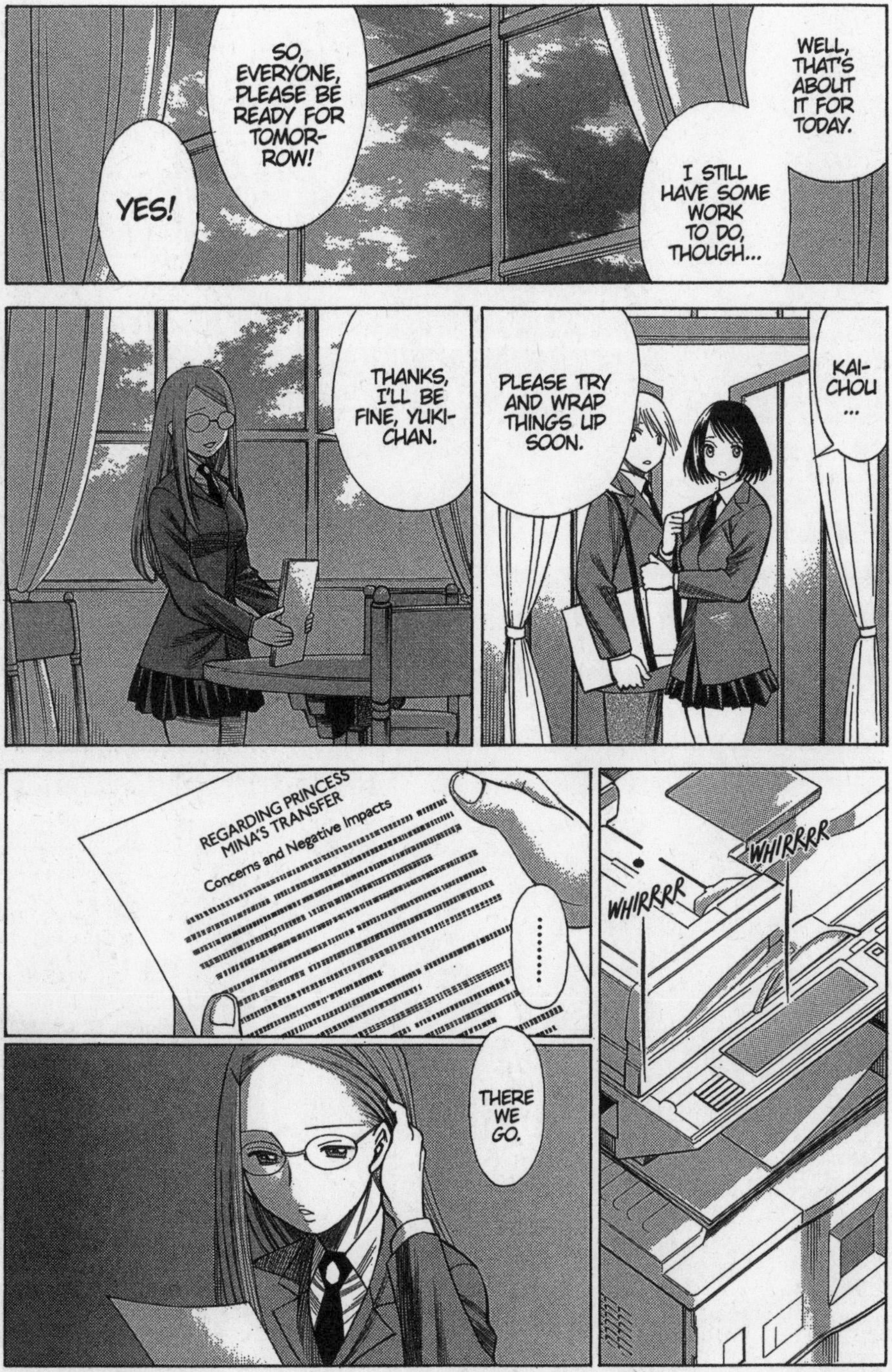
WELL, THAT'S ABOUT IT FOR TODAY.
I STILL HAVE SOME WORK TO DO, THOUGH...
SO, EVERYONE, PLEASE BE READY FOR TOMOR-ROW!
YES!
KAI-CHOU ...
PLEASE TRY AND WRAP THINGS UP SOON.
THANKS, I'LL BE FINE, YUKI-CHAN.
WHIRRRR
WHIRRRR
REGARDING PRINCESS MINA'S TRANSFER
Concerns and Negative Impacts
....
THERE WE GO.

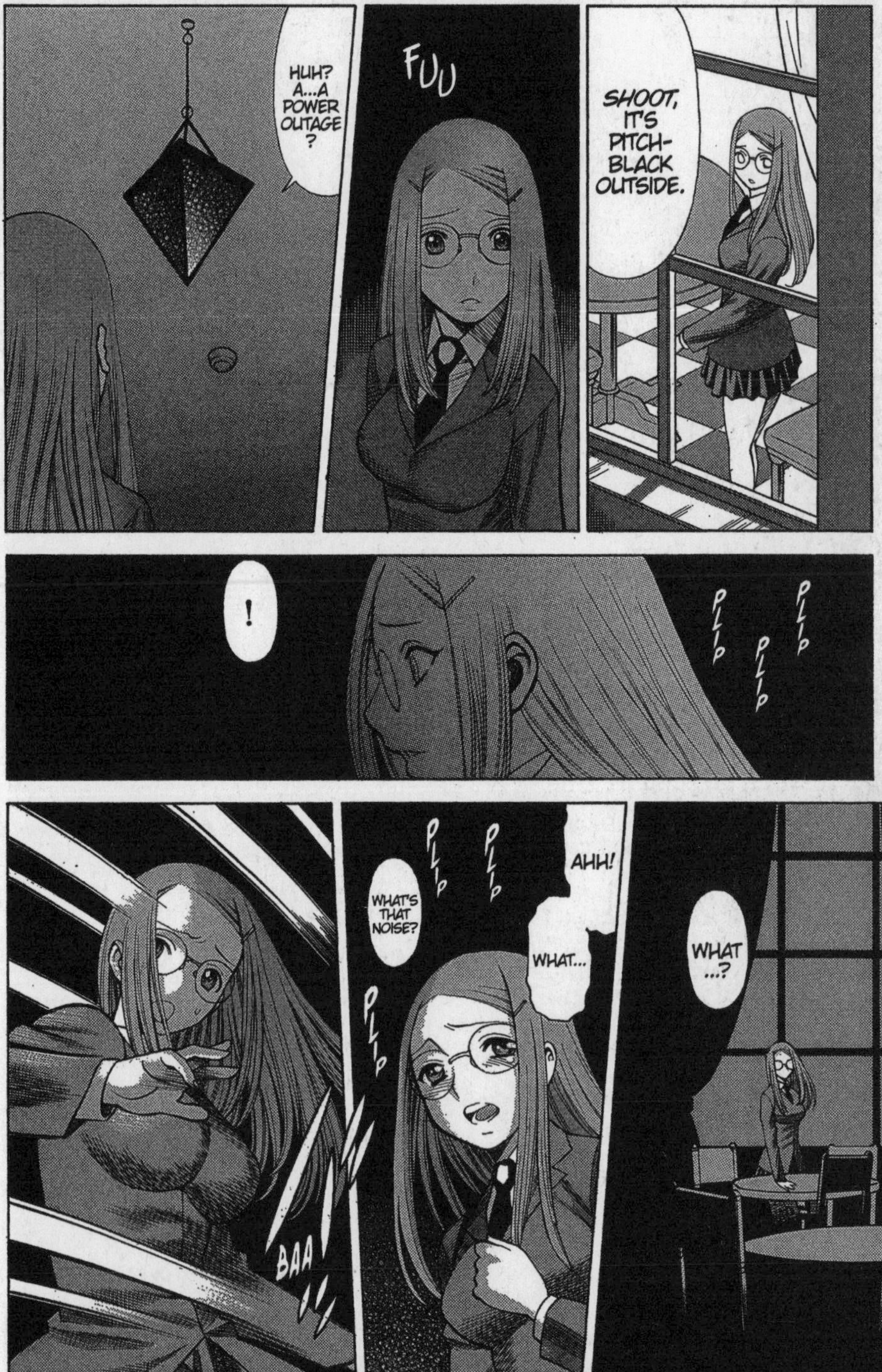
SHOOT, IT'S PITCH-BLACK OUTSIDE.
FUU
HUH? A...A POWER OUTAGE?
PLIP
PLIP
PLIP
!
WHAT...?
AHH!
PLIP
PLIP
WHAT...
WHAT'S THAT NOISE?
PLIP
BAA

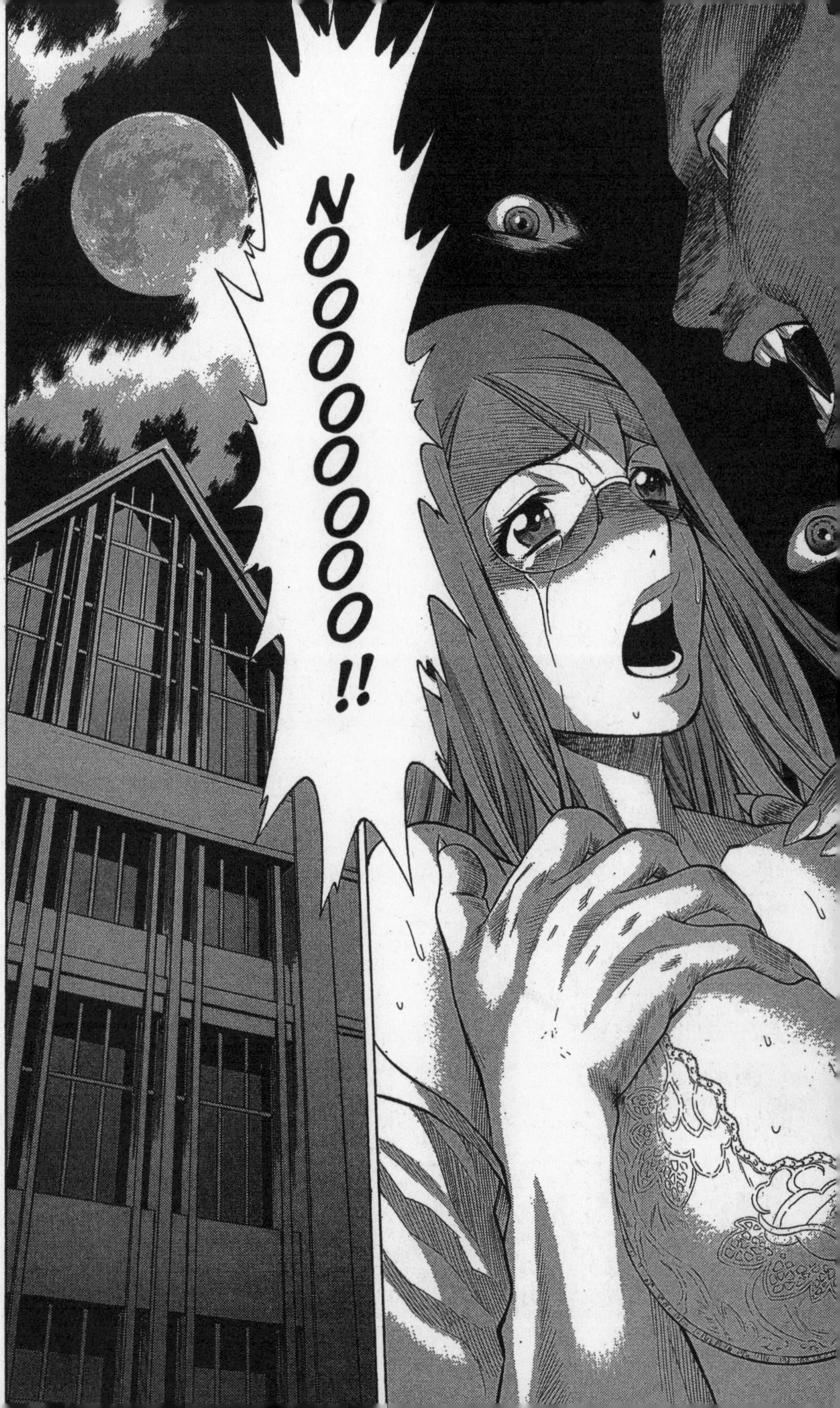
NOOOOOOOO!!

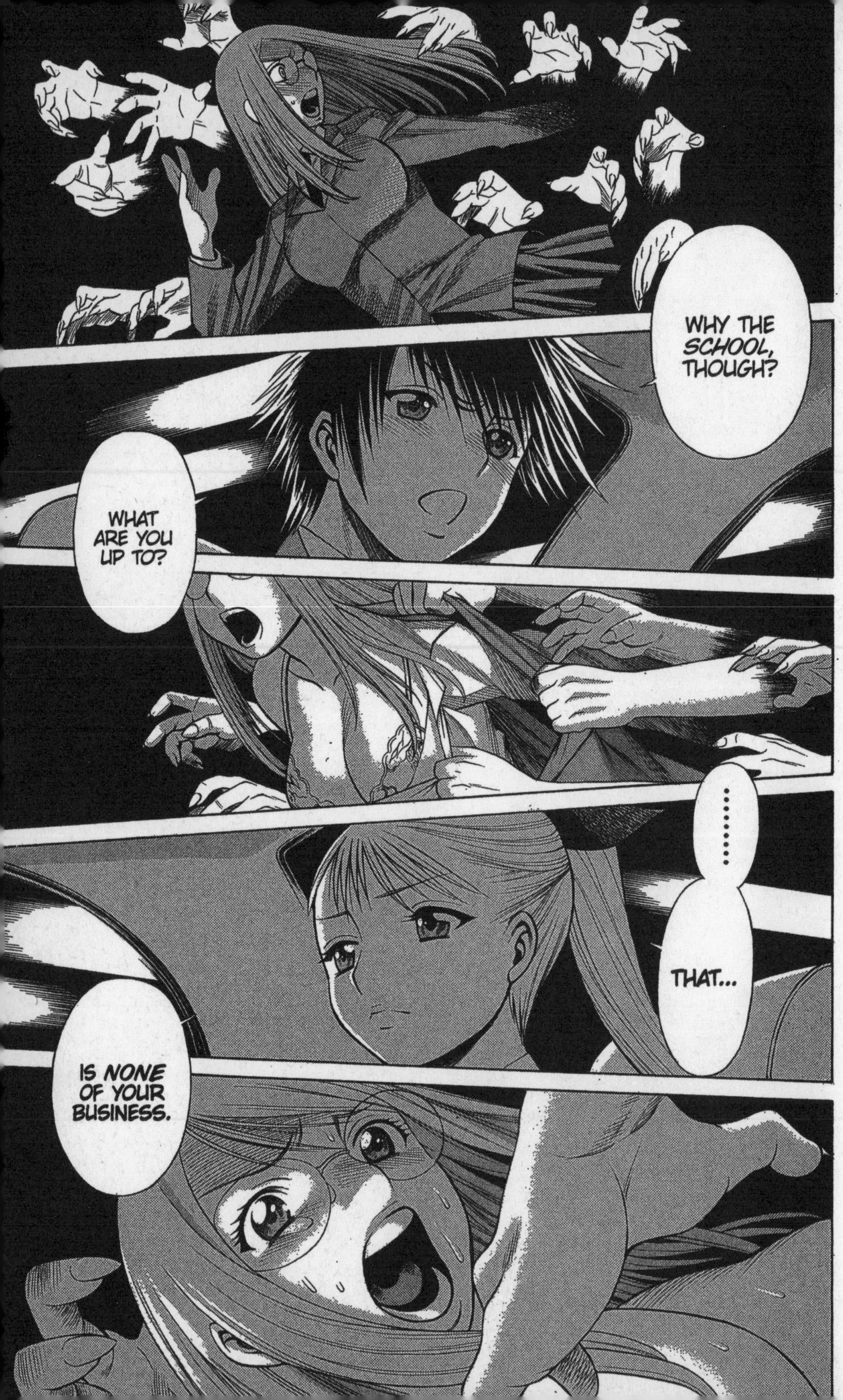
WHY THE *SCHOOL*, THOUGH?
WHAT ARE YOU UP TO?
....
THAT...
IS *NONE* OF YOUR BUSINESS.

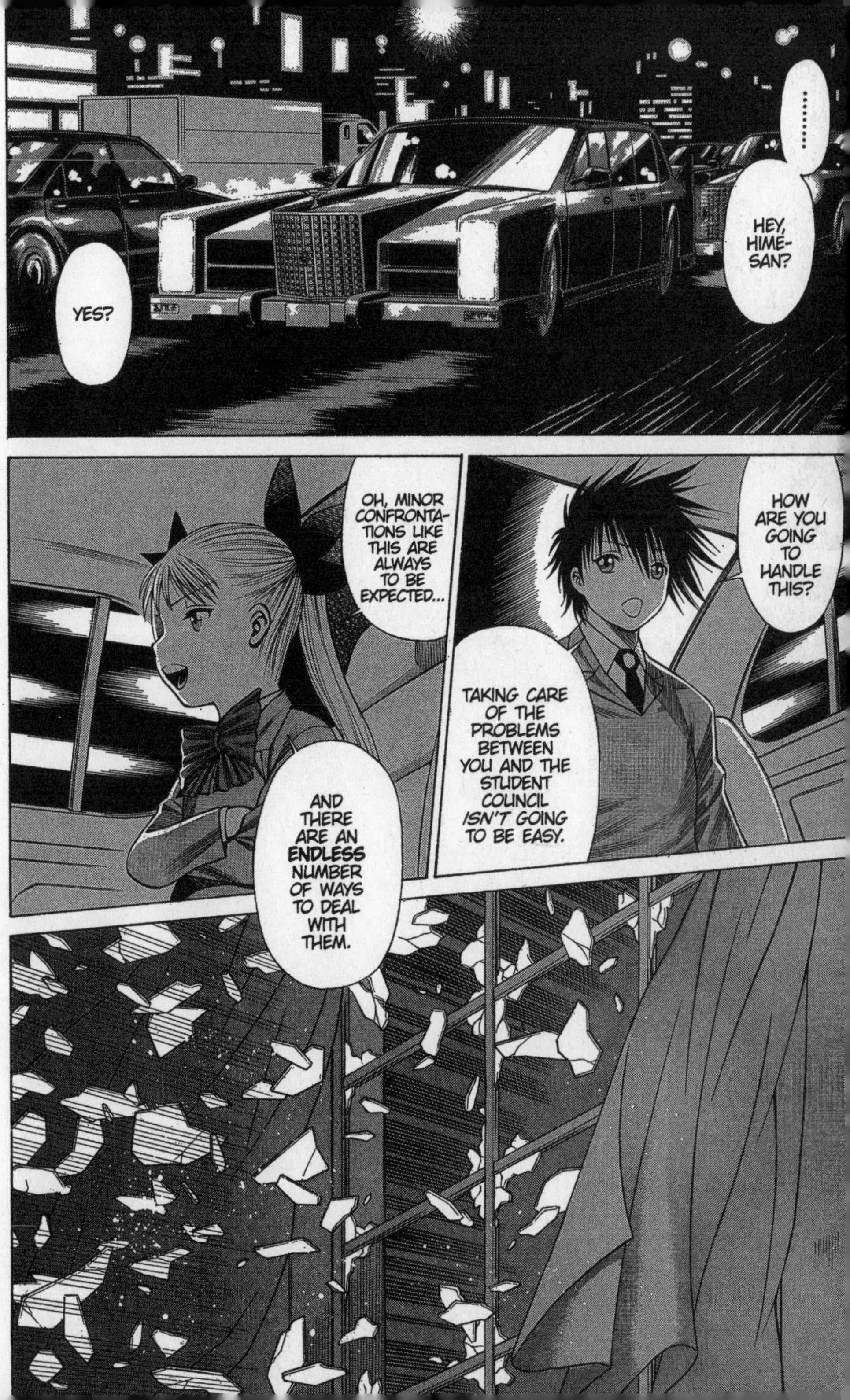
......
HEY, HIME-SAN?
YES?
HOW ARE YOU GOING TO HANDLE THIS?
TAKING CARE OF THE PROBLEMS BETWEEN YOU AND THE STUDENT COUNCIL *ISN'T* GOING TO BE EASY.
OH, MINOR CONFRONTATIONS LIKE THIS ARE ALWAYS TO BE EXPECTED...
AND THERE ARE AN **ENDLESS** NUMBER OF WAYS TO DEAL WITH THEM.

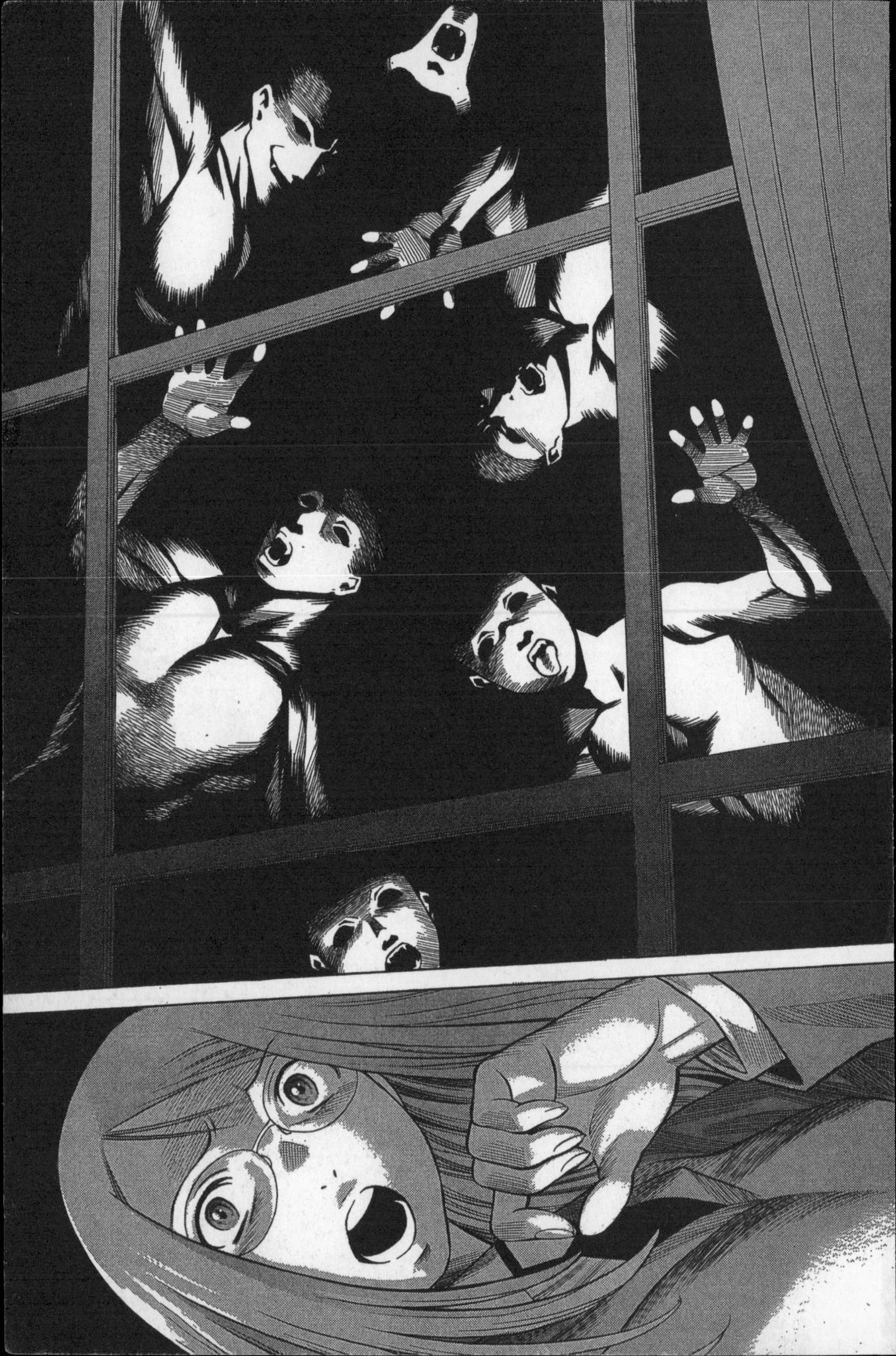

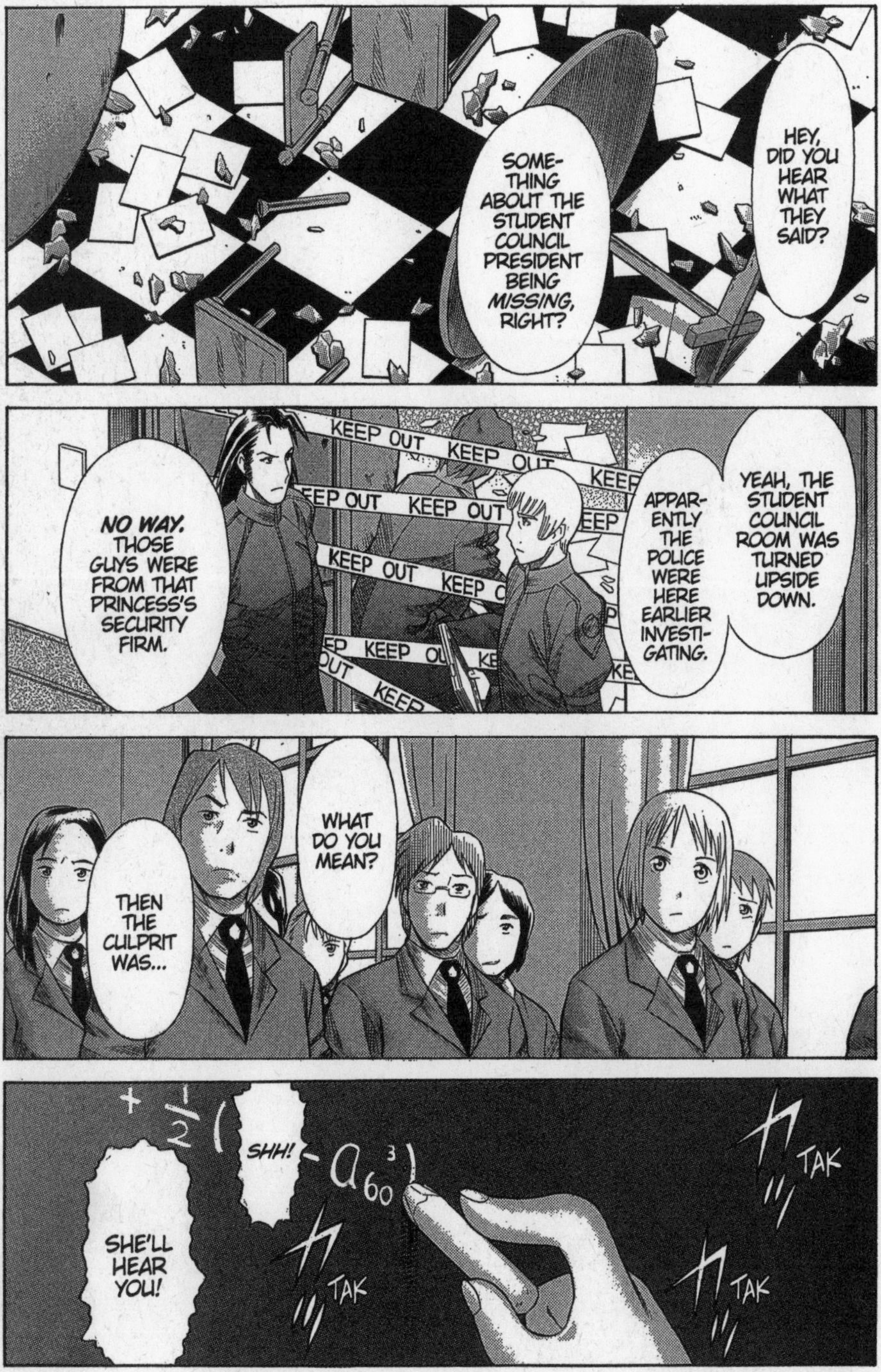
HEY, DID YOU HEAR WHAT THEY SAID?
SOME-THING ABOUT THE STUDENT COUNCIL PRESIDENT BEING *MISSING*, RIGHT?
YEAH, THE STUDENT COUNCIL ROOM WAS TURNED UPSIDE DOWN.
APPAR-ENTLY THE POLICE WERE HERE EARLIER INVESTI-GATING.
KEEP OUT
NO WAY. THOSE GUYS WERE FROM THAT PRINCESS'S SECURITY FIRM.
WHAT DO YOU MEAN?
THEN THE CULPRIT WAS...
TAK
TAK
SHH!
TAK
SHE'LL HEAR YOU!

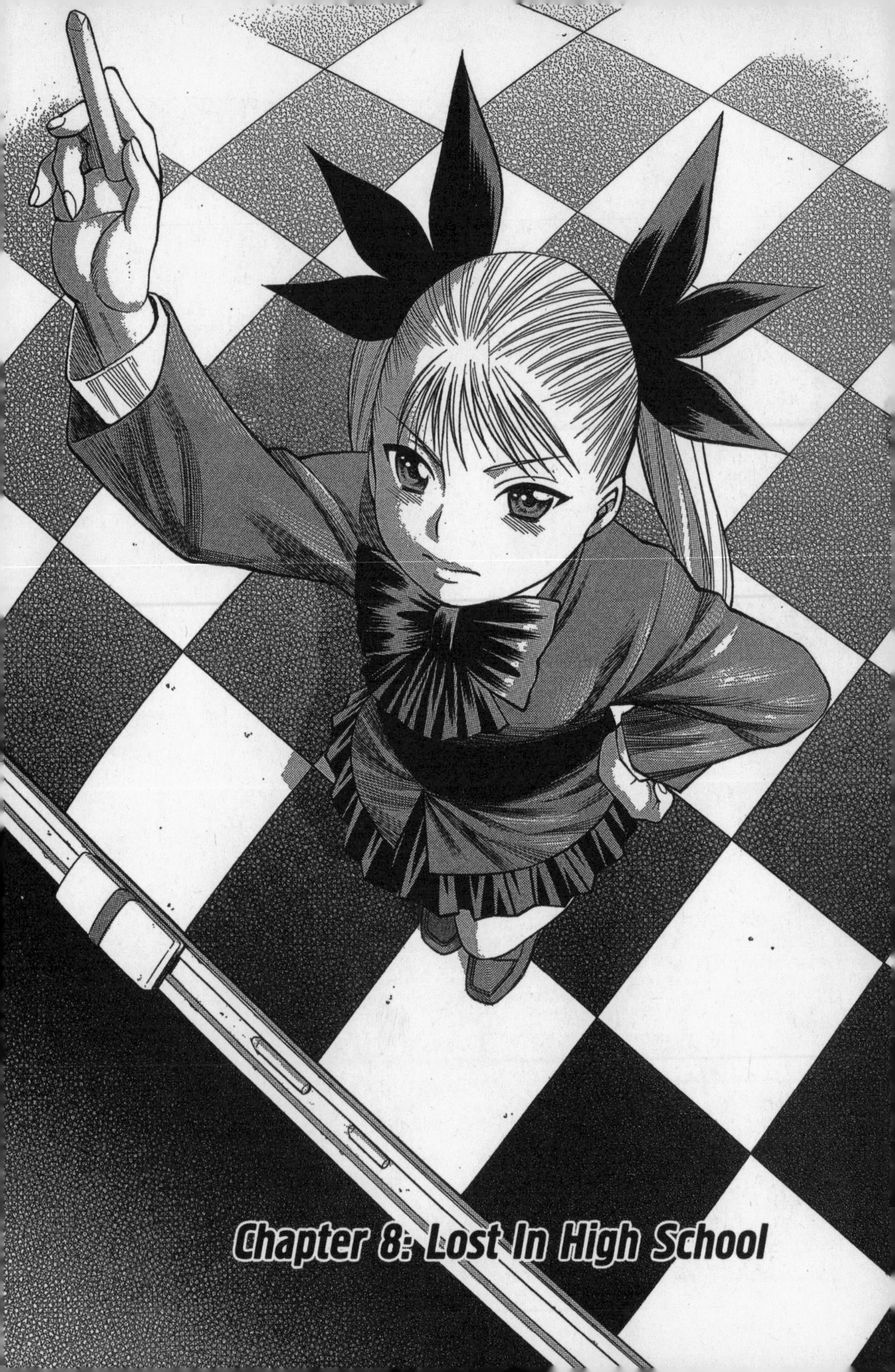

Chapter 8: Lost In High School

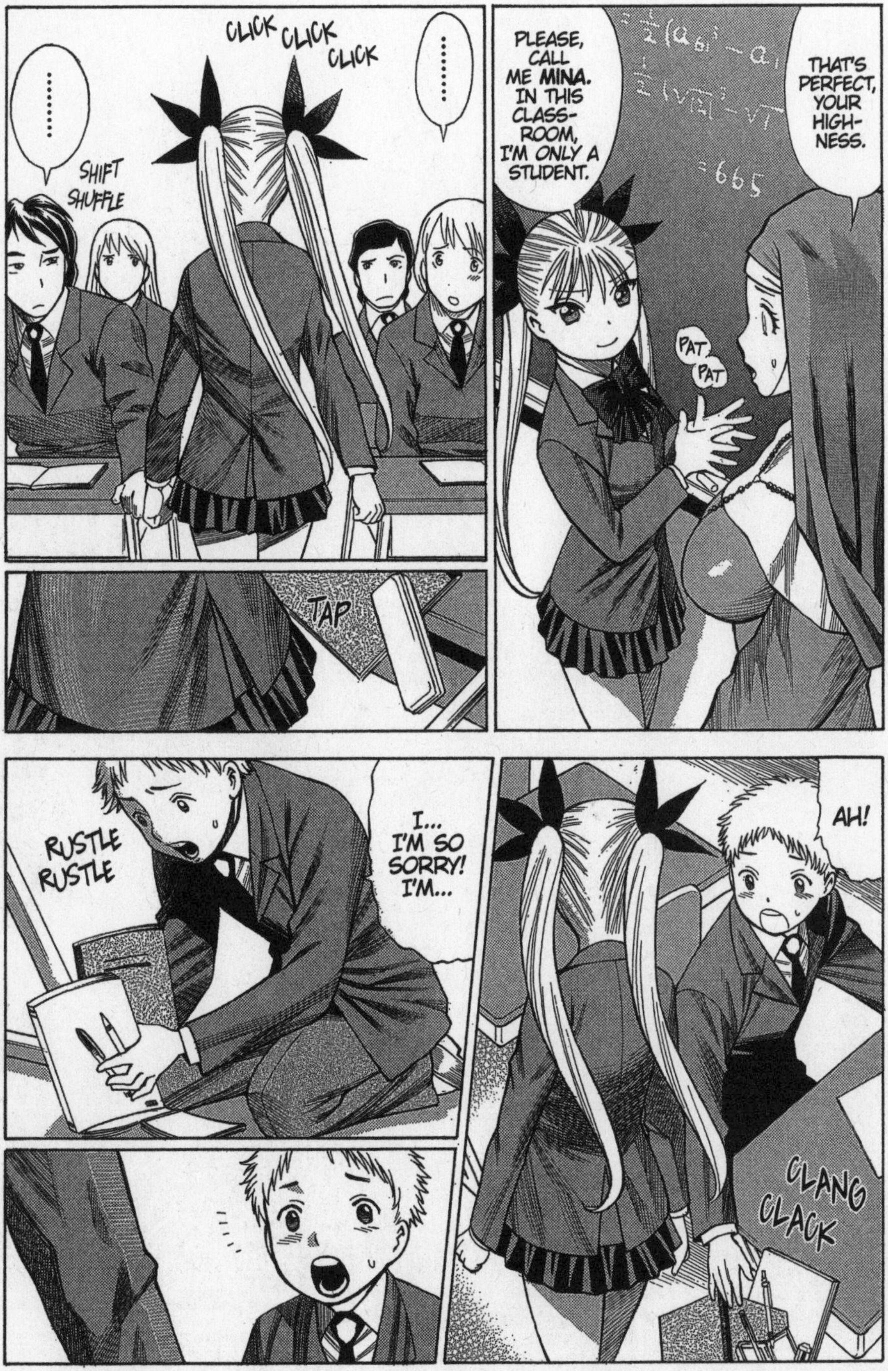

THAT'S PERFECT, YOUR HIGHNESS.
PLEASE, CALL ME MINA. IN THIS CLASSROOM, I'M ONLY A STUDENT.
PAT PAT
......
CLICK CLICK CLICK
......
SHIFT SHUFFLE
TAP
AH!
CLANG CLACK
I... I'M SO SORRY! I'M...
RUSTLE RUSTLE

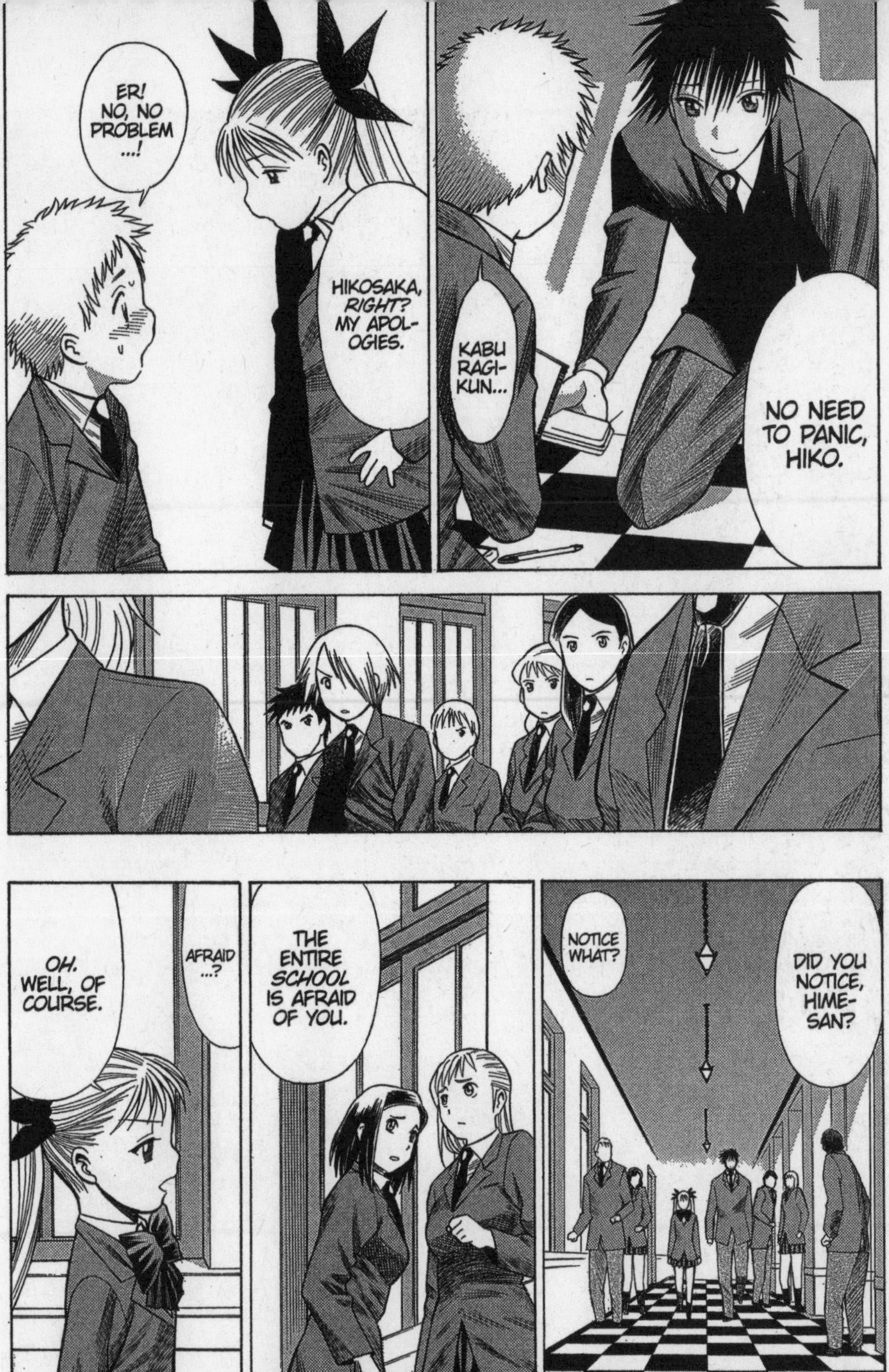
NO NEED TO PANIC, HIKO.
KABU RAGI-KUN...
HIKOSAKA, *RIGHT?* MY APOLOGIES.
ER! NO, NO PROBLEM ...!
DID YOU NOTICE, HIME-SAN?
NOTICE WHAT?
THE ENTIRE *SCHOOL* IS AFRAID OF YOU.
AFRAID ...?
OH. WELL, OF COURSE.

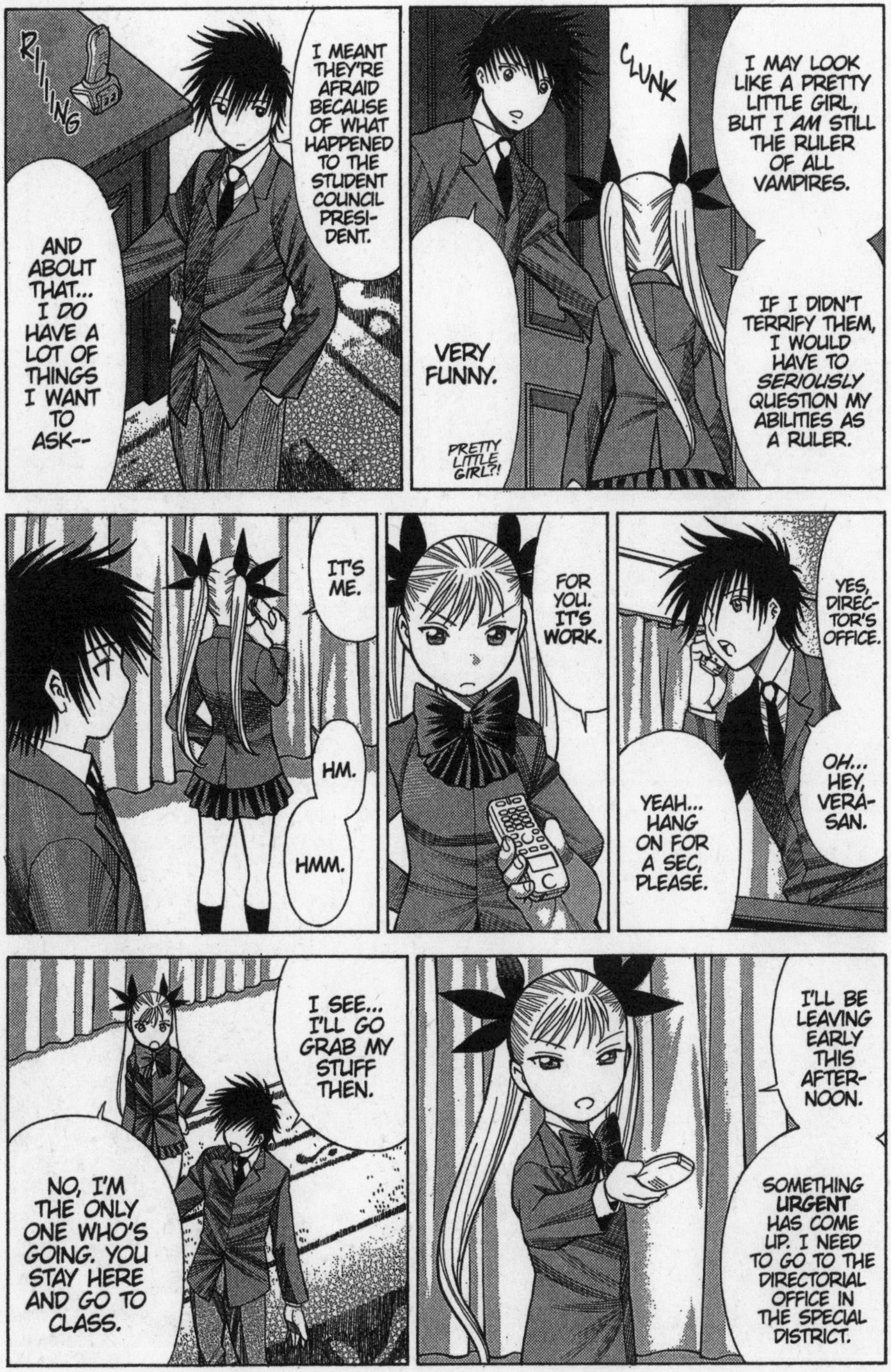
I MAY LOOK LIKE A PRETTY LITTLE GIRL, BUT I *AM* STILL THE RULER OF ALL VAMPIRES.
CLUNK
IF I DIDN'T TERRIFY THEM, I WOULD HAVE TO *SERIOUSLY* QUESTION MY ABILITIES AS A RULER.
VERY FUNNY.
PRETTY LITTLE GIRL?!
I MEANT THEY'RE AFRAID BECAUSE OF WHAT HAPPENED TO THE STUDENT COUNCIL PRESIDENT.
RIIIING
AND ABOUT THAT... I *DO* HAVE A LOT OF THINGS I WANT TO ASK--
YES, DIRECTOR'S OFFICE.
OH... HEY, VERA-SAN.
YEAH... HANG ON FOR A SEC, PLEASE.
FOR YOU. IT'S WORK.
IT'S ME.
HM.
HMM.
I'LL BE LEAVING EARLY THIS AFTERNOON.
SOMETHING **URGENT** HAS COME UP. I NEED TO GO TO THE DIRECTORIAL OFFICE IN THE SPECIAL DISTRICT.
I SEE... I'LL GO GRAB MY STUFF THEN.
NO, I'M THE ONLY ONE WHO'S GOING. YOU STAY HERE AND GO TO CLASS.

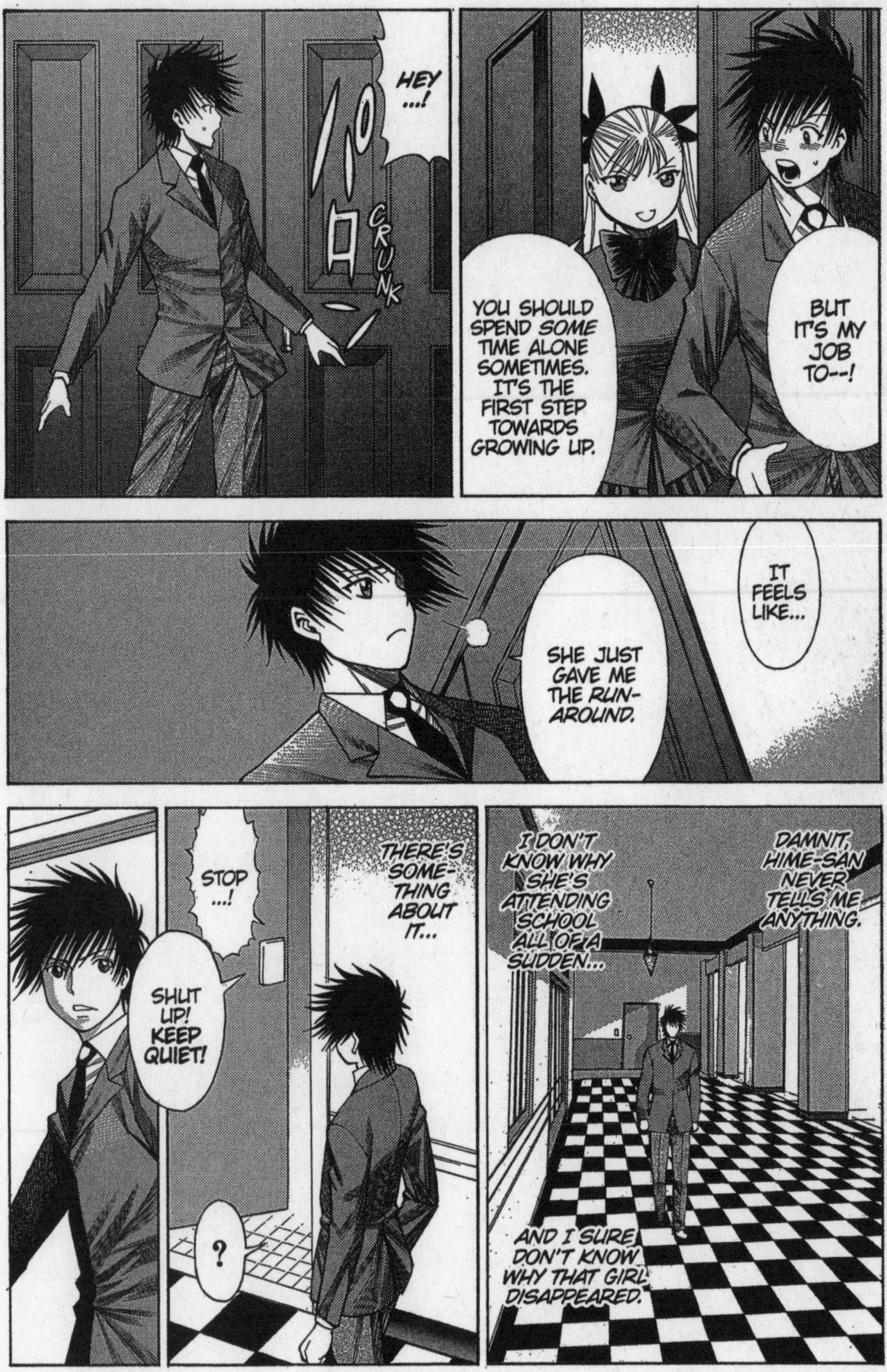
BUT IT'S MY JOB TO--!
YOU SHOULD SPEND SOME TIME ALONE SOMETIMES. IT'S THE FIRST STEP TOWARDS GROWING UP.
HEY ...!
CRUNK
IT FEELS LIKE...
SHE JUST GAVE ME THE RUN-AROUND.
DAMNIT, HIME-SAN NEVER TELLS ME ANYTHING.
I DON'T KNOW WHY SHE'S ATTENDING SCHOOL ALL OF A SUDDEN...
AND I SURE DON'T KNOW WHY THAT GIRL DISAPPEARED.
THERE'S SOME-THING ABOUT IT...
STOP ...!
?
SHUT UP! KEEP QUIET!

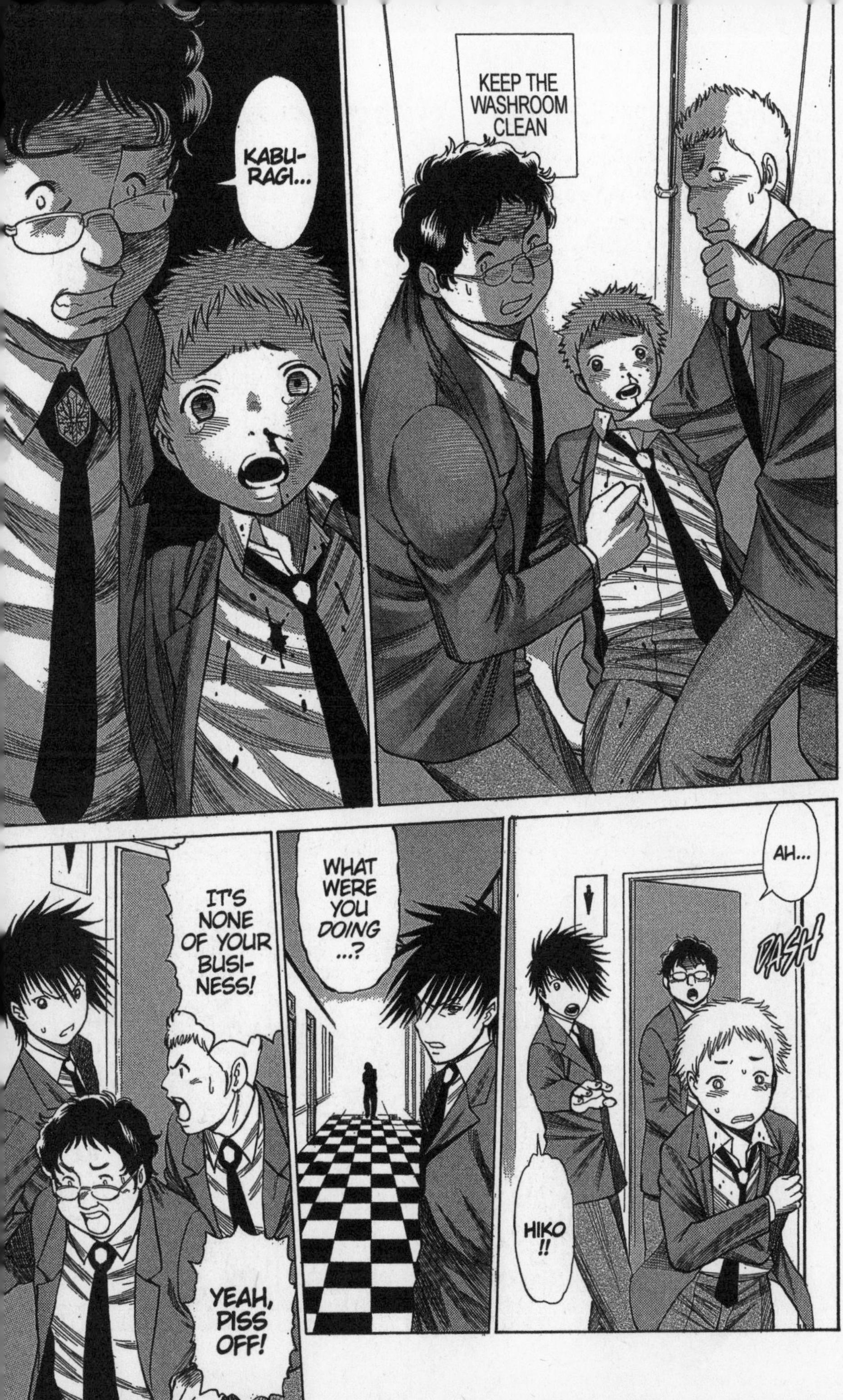
KEEP THE WASHROOM CLEAN
KABU-RAGI...
AH...
DASH
HIKO !!
WHAT WERE YOU DOING ...?
IT'S NONE OF YOUR BUSI-NESS!
YEAH, PISS OFF!

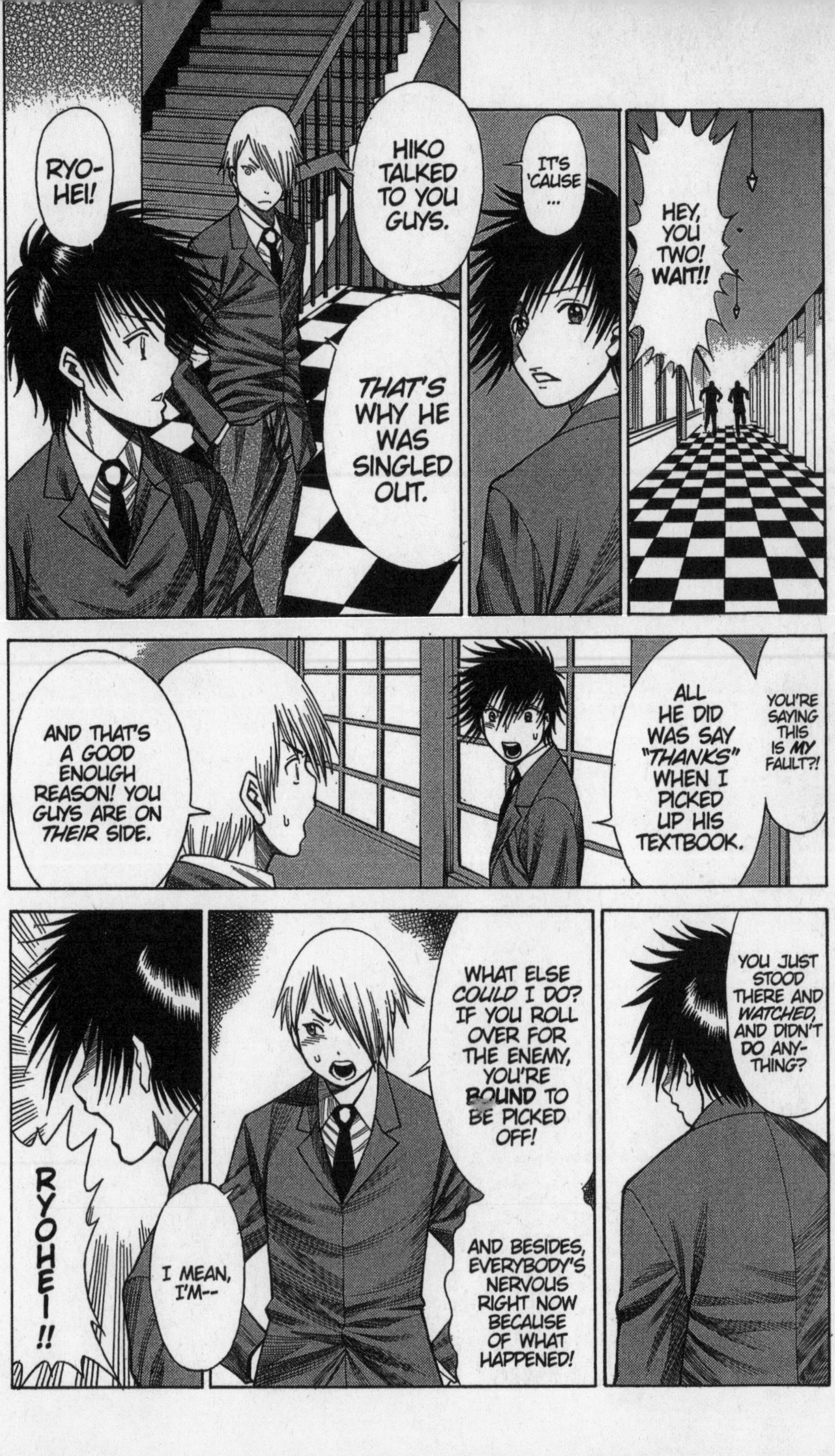

HEY, YOU TWO! WAIT!!
IT'S 'CAUSE ...
HIKO TALKED TO YOU GUYS.
THAT'S WHY HE WAS SINGLED OUT.
RYO-HEI!
ALL HE DID WAS SAY "THANKS" WHEN I PICKED UP HIS TEXTBOOK.
YOU'RE SAYING THIS IS MY FAULT?!
AND THAT'S A GOOD ENOUGH REASON! YOU GUYS ARE ON THEIR SIDE.
YOU JUST STOOD THERE AND WATCHED, AND DIDN'T DO ANY-THING?
WHAT ELSE COULD I DO? IF YOU ROLL OVER FOR THE ENEMY, YOU'RE BOUND TO BE PICKED OFF!
AND BESIDES, EVERYBODY'S NERVOUS RIGHT NOW BECAUSE OF WHAT HAPPENED!
I MEAN, I'M--
RYOHEI!!

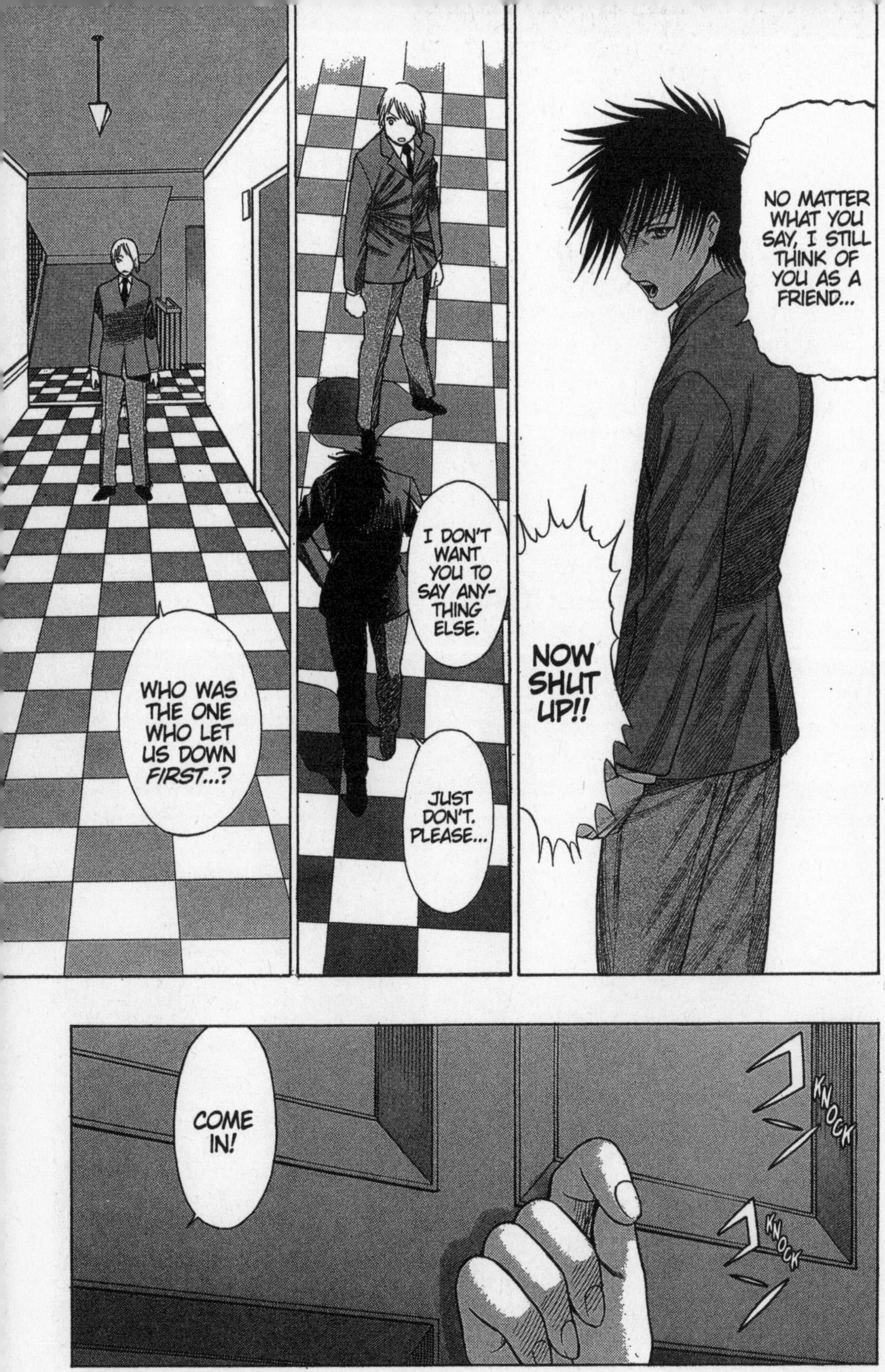
NO MATTER WHAT YOU SAY, I STILL THINK OF YOU AS A FRIEND...
NOW SHUT UP!!
I DON'T WANT YOU TO SAY ANY-THING ELSE.
JUST DON'T. PLEASE...
WHO WAS THE ONE WHO LET US DOWN *FIRST*...?
KNOCK
KNOCK
COME IN!

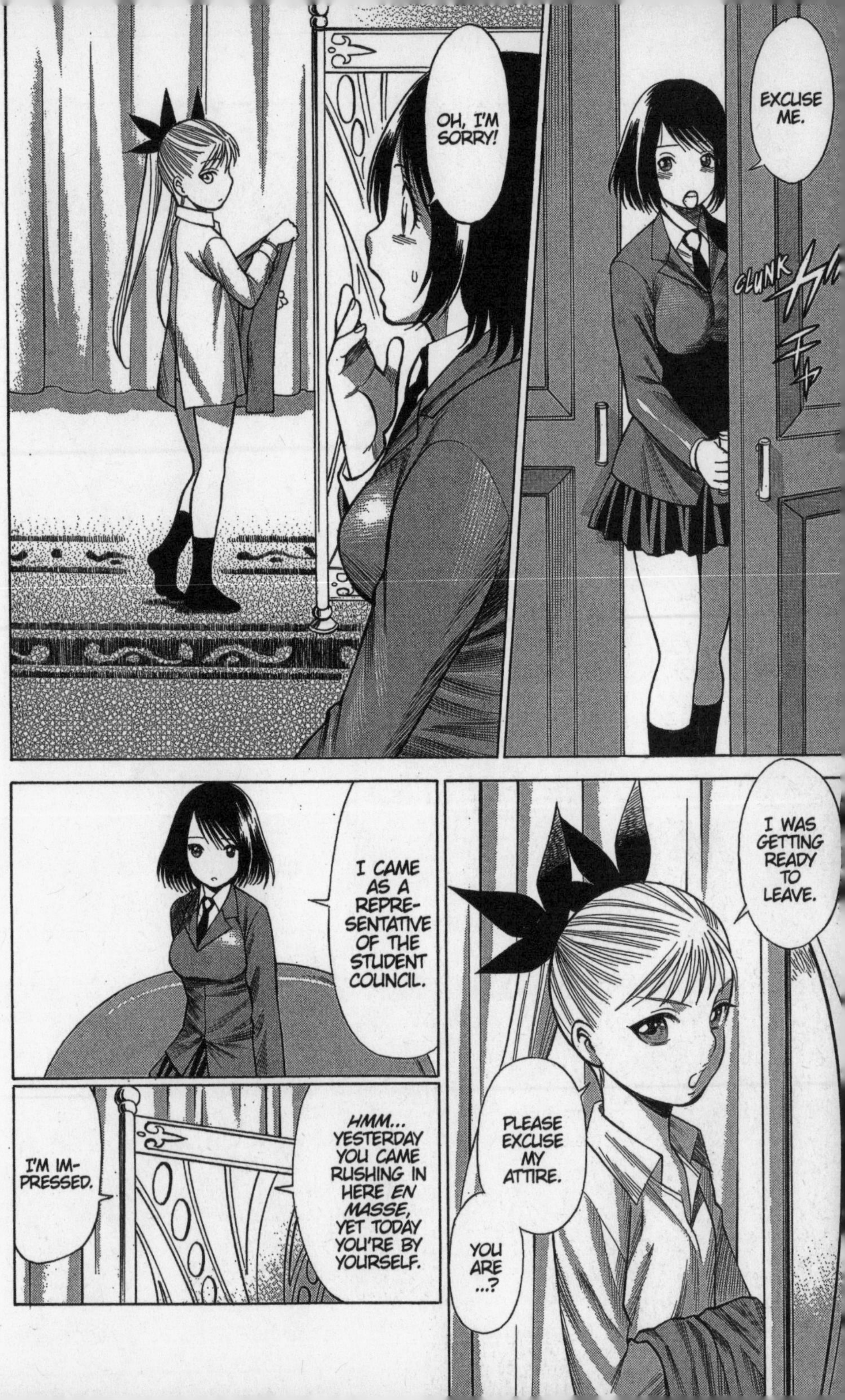
EXCUSE ME.
CLUNK
OH, I'M SORRY!
I WAS GETTING READY TO LEAVE.
PLEASE EXCUSE MY ATTIRE.
YOU ARE ...?
I CAME AS A REPRESENTATIVE OF THE STUDENT COUNCIL.
HMM... YESTERDAY YOU CAME RUSHING IN HERE *EN MASSE*, YET TODAY YOU'RE BY YOURSELF.
I'M IMPRESSED.

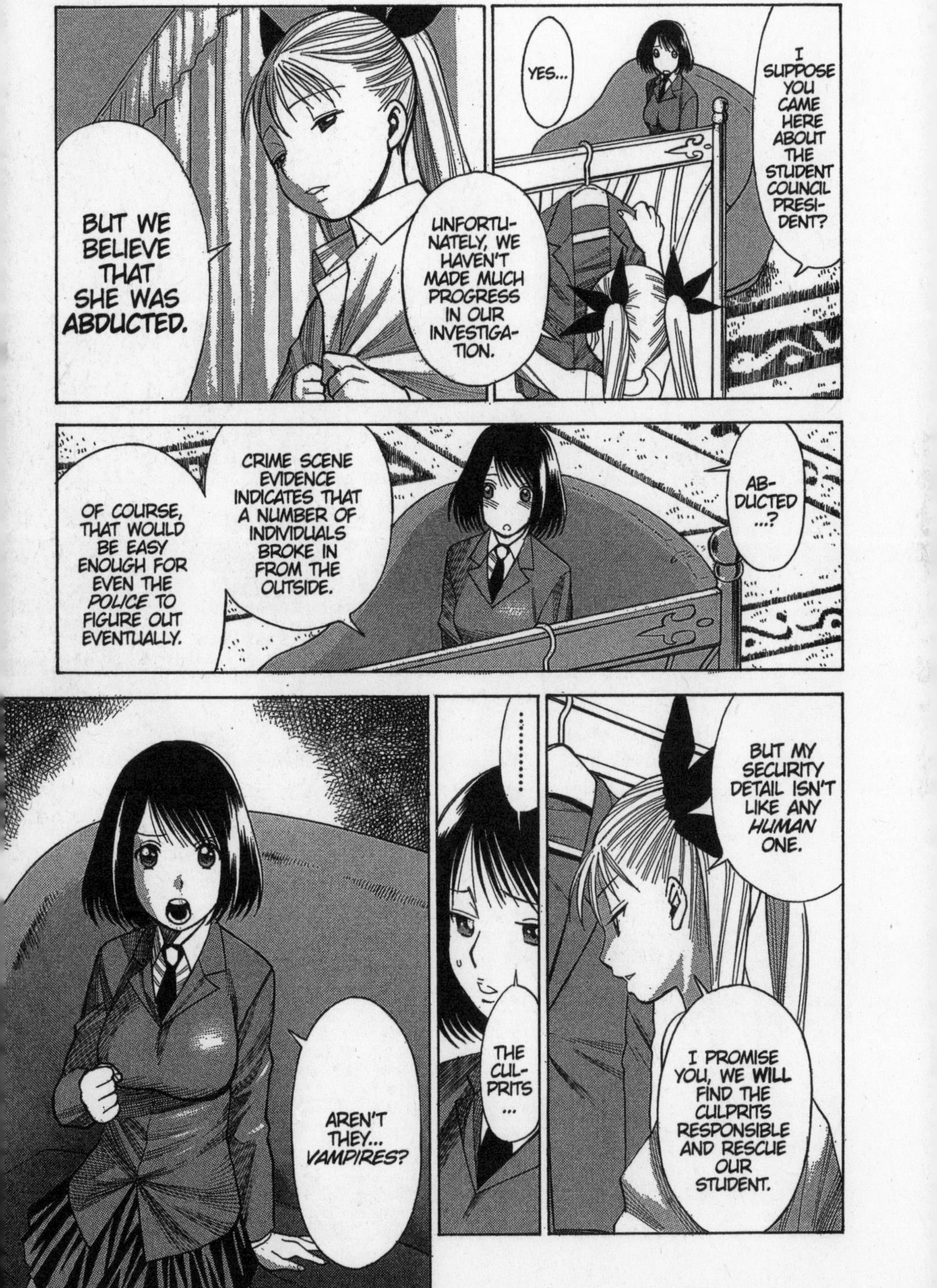
I SUPPOSE YOU CAME HERE ABOUT THE STUDENT COUNCIL PRESIDENT?
YES...
UNFORTUNATELY, WE HAVEN'T MADE MUCH PROGRESS IN OUR INVESTIGATION.
BUT WE BELIEVE THAT SHE WAS ABDUCTED.
ABDUCTED ...?
CRIME SCENE EVIDENCE INDICATES THAT A NUMBER OF INDIVIDUALS BROKE IN FROM THE OUTSIDE.
OF COURSE, THAT WOULD BE EASY ENOUGH FOR EVEN THE *POLICE* TO FIGURE OUT EVENTUALLY.
BUT MY SECURITY DETAIL ISN'T LIKE ANY *HUMAN* ONE.
I PROMISE YOU, WE **WILL** FIND THE CULPRITS RESPONSIBLE AND RESCUE OUR STUDENT.
......
THE CULPRITS ...
AREN'T THEY... *VAMPIRES?*

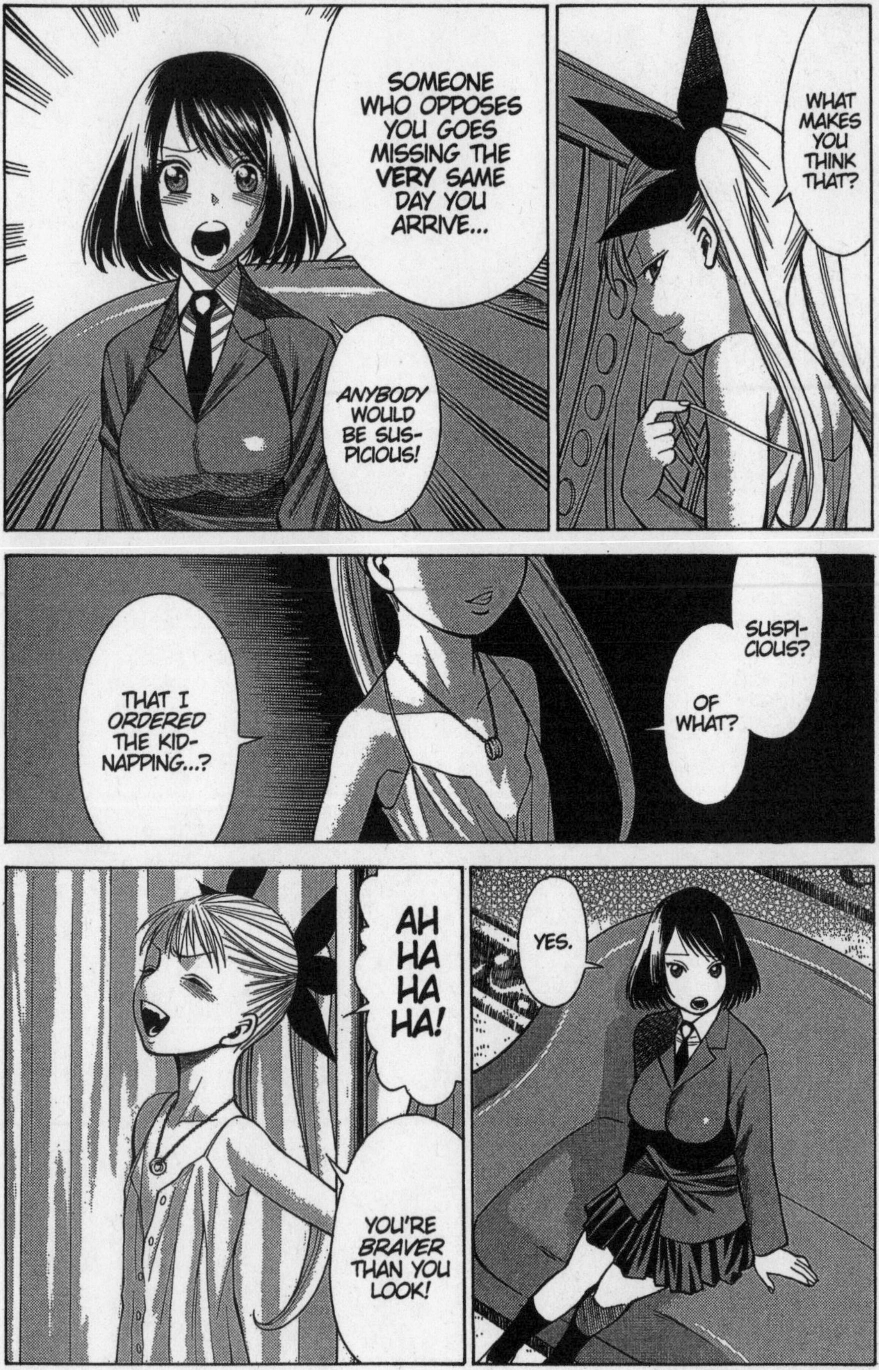
WHAT MAKES YOU THINK THAT?
SOMEONE WHO OPPOSES YOU GOES MISSING THE VERY SAME DAY YOU ARRIVE...
ANYBODY WOULD BE SUS-PICIOUS!
SUSPI-CIOUS?
OF WHAT?
THAT I ORDERED THE KID-NAPPING...?
YES.
AH HA HA HA!
YOU'RE BRAVER THAN YOU LOOK!

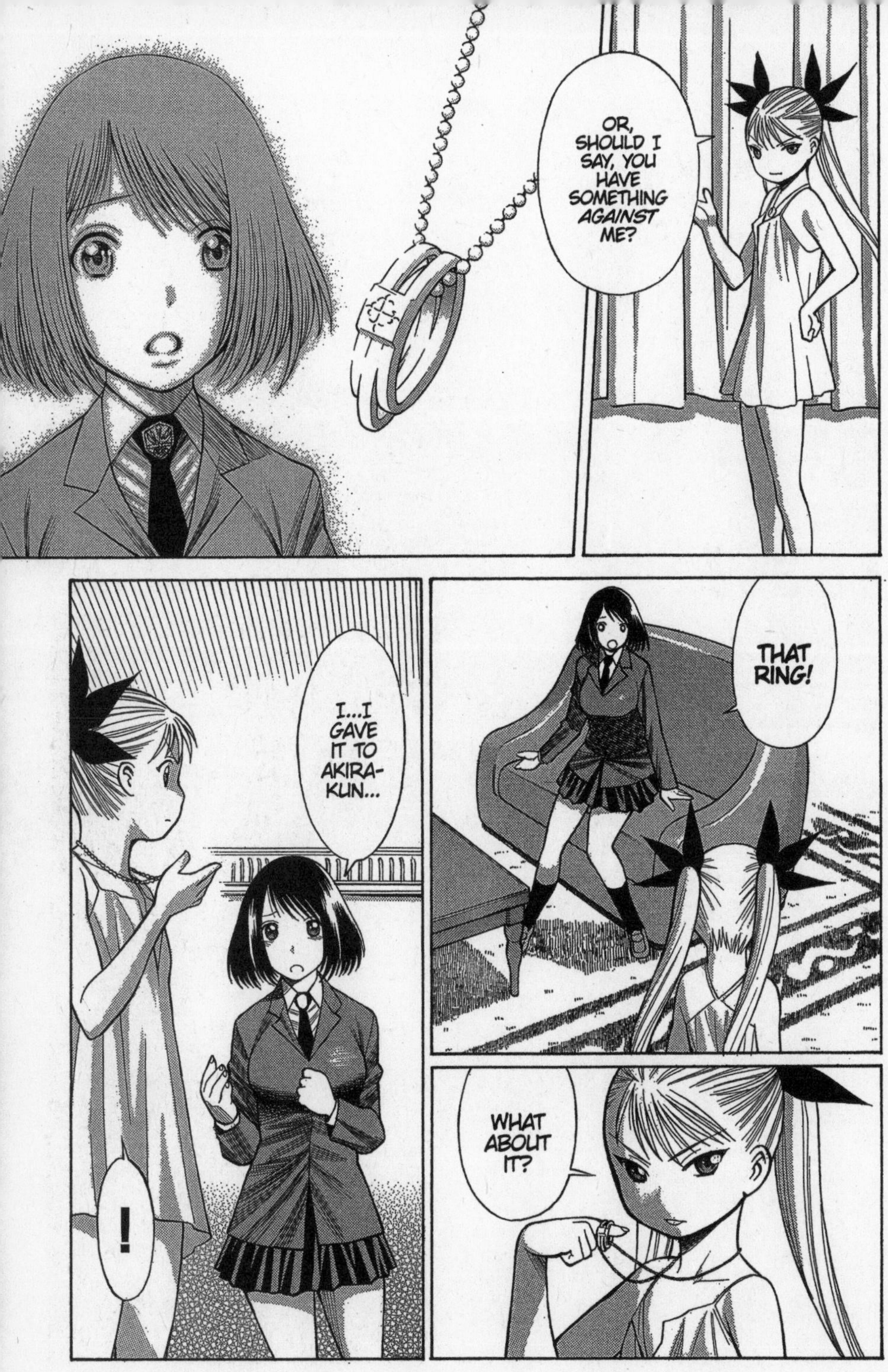
OR, SHOULD I SAY, YOU HAVE SOMETHING AGAINST ME?
THAT RING!
WHAT ABOUT IT?
I...I GAVE IT TO AKIRA-KUN...
!

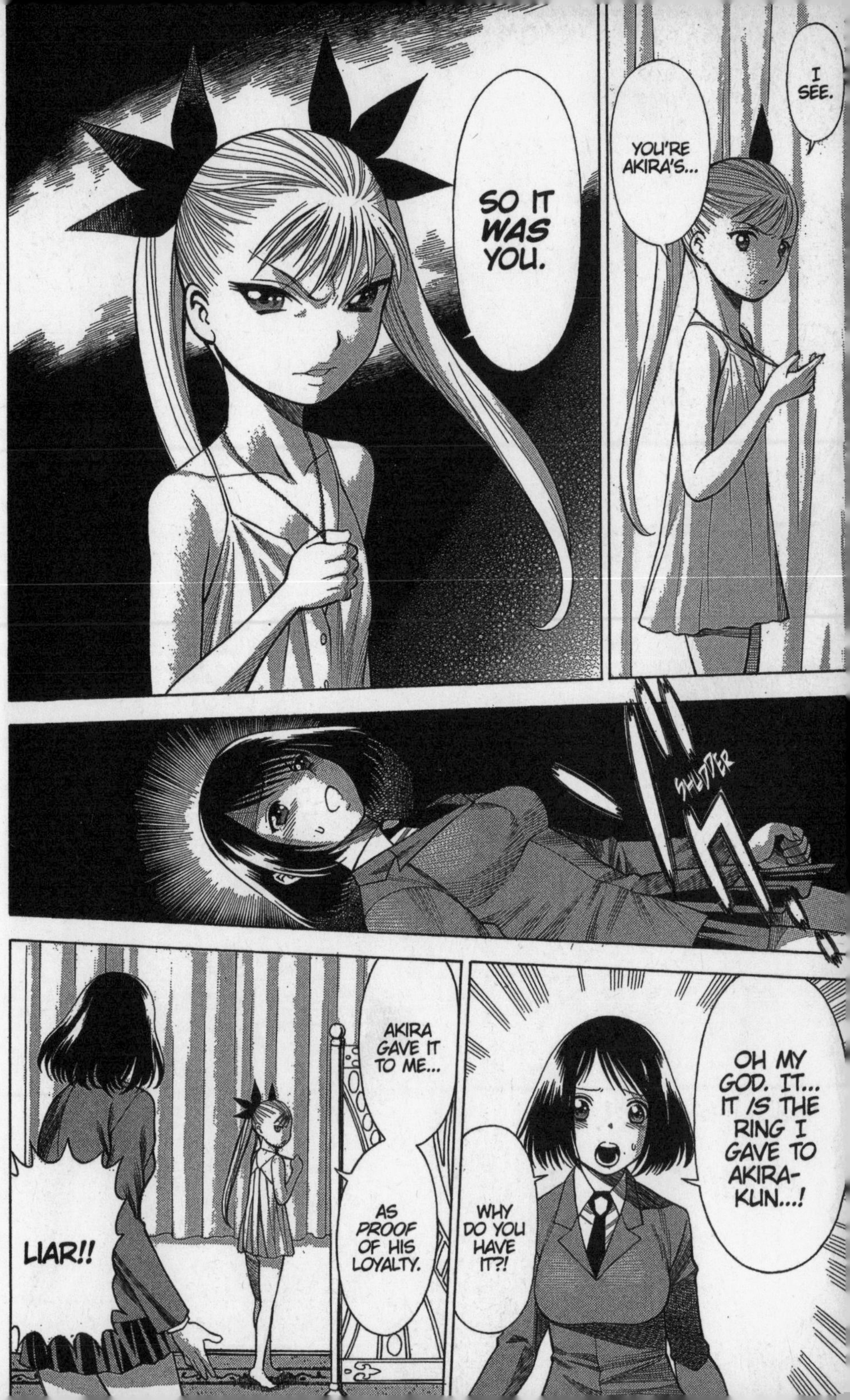
I SEE.
YOU'RE AKIRA'S...
SO IT *WAS* YOU.
SHUDDER
OH MY GOD. IT... IT *IS* THE RING I GAVE TO AKIRA-KUN...!
WHY DO YOU HAVE IT?!
AKIRA GAVE IT TO ME...
AS *PROOF* OF HIS LOYALTY.
LIAR!!

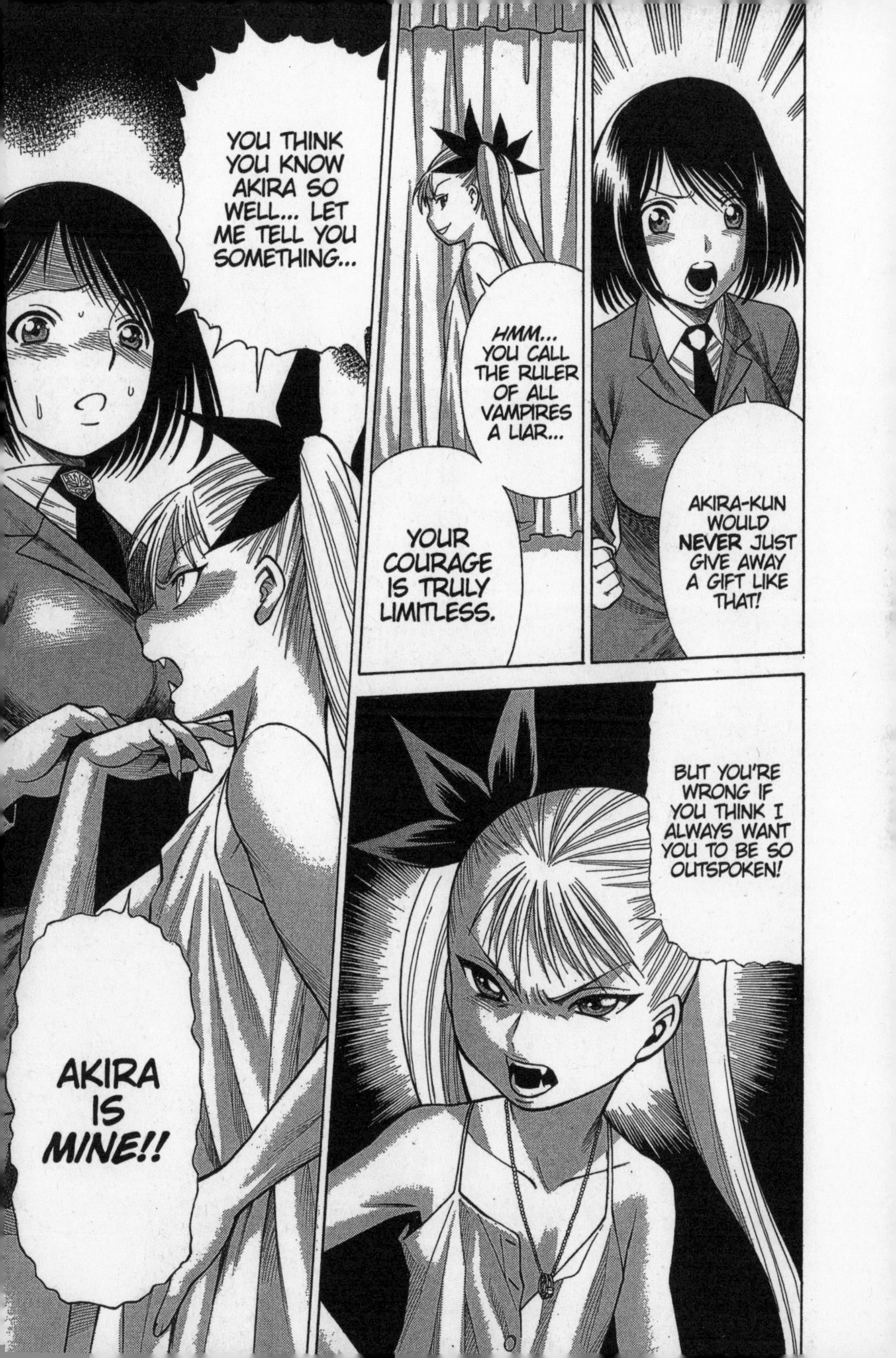
AKIRA-KUN WOULD NEVER JUST GIVE AWAY A GIFT LIKE THAT!
HMM... YOU CALL THE RULER OF ALL VAMPIRES A LIAR...
YOUR COURAGE IS TRULY LIMITLESS.
BUT YOU'RE WRONG IF YOU THINK I ALWAYS WANT YOU TO BE SO OUTSPOKEN!
YOU THINK YOU KNOW AKIRA SO WELL... LET ME TELL YOU SOMETHING...
AKIRA IS MINE!!

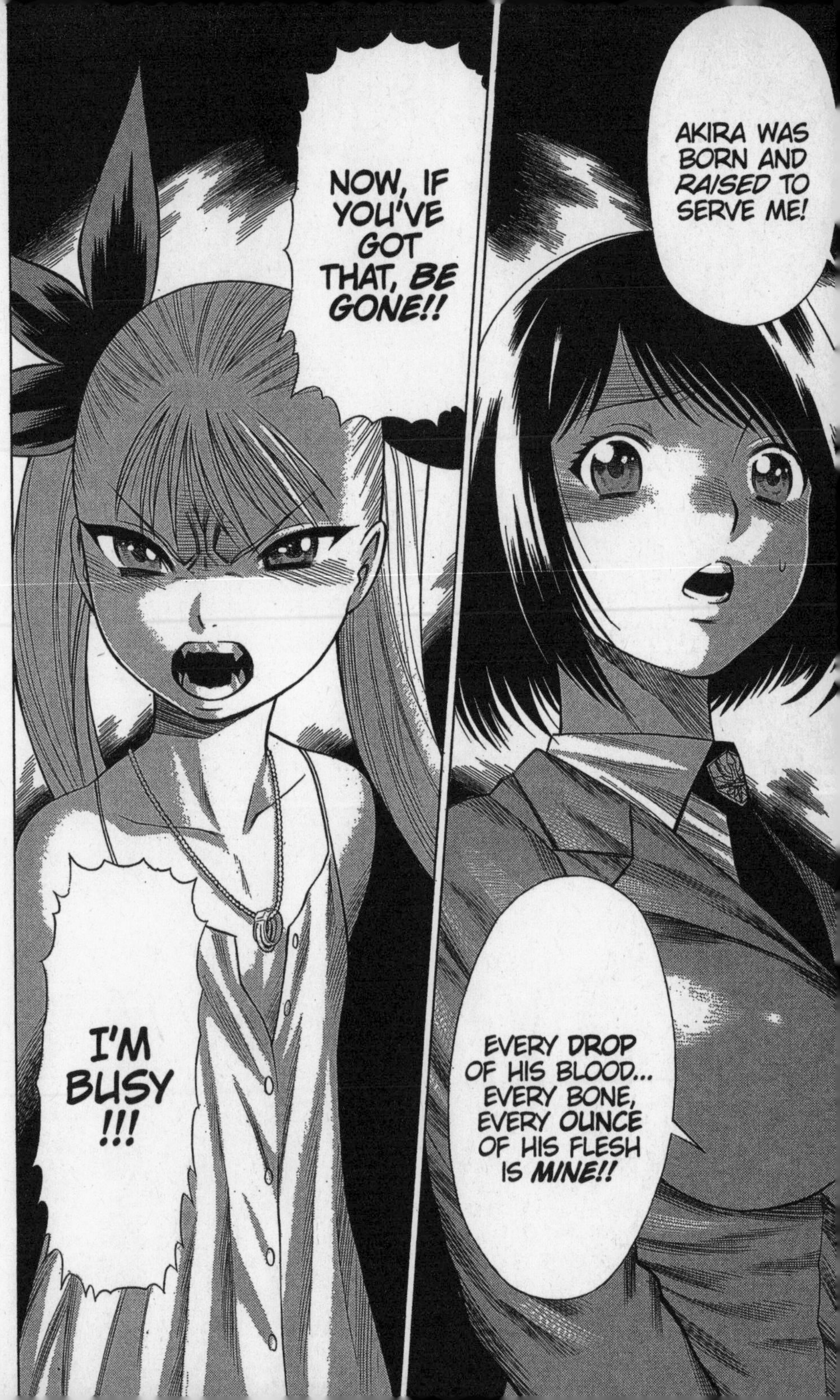
AKIRA WAS BORN AND *RAISED* TO SERVE ME!
EVERY DROP OF HIS BLOOD... EVERY BONE, EVERY OUNCE OF HIS FLESH IS ***MINE!!***
NOW, IF YOU'VE GOT THAT, ***BE GONE!!***
I'M BUSY !!!

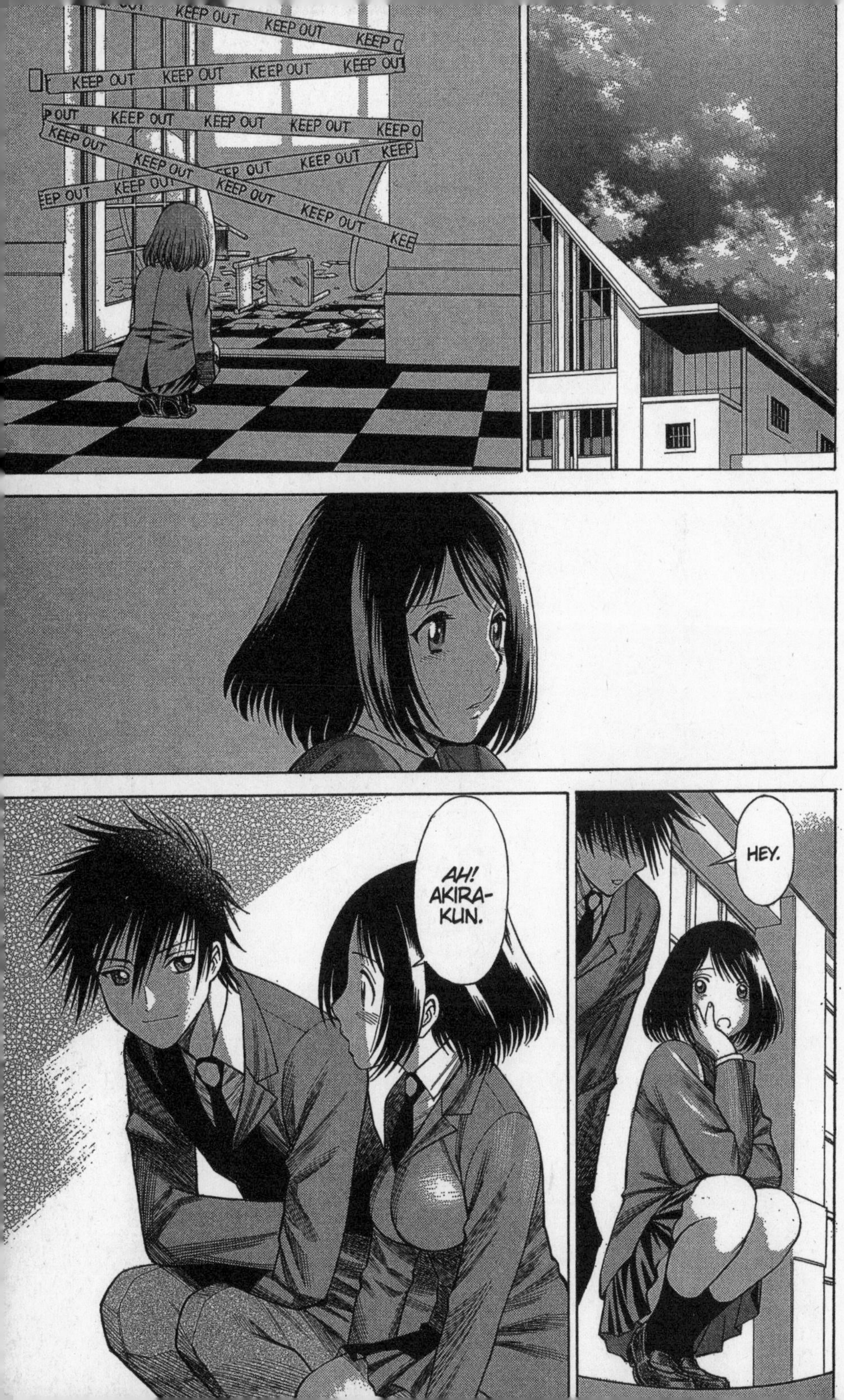
KEEP OUT
HEY.
AH! AKIRA-KUN.

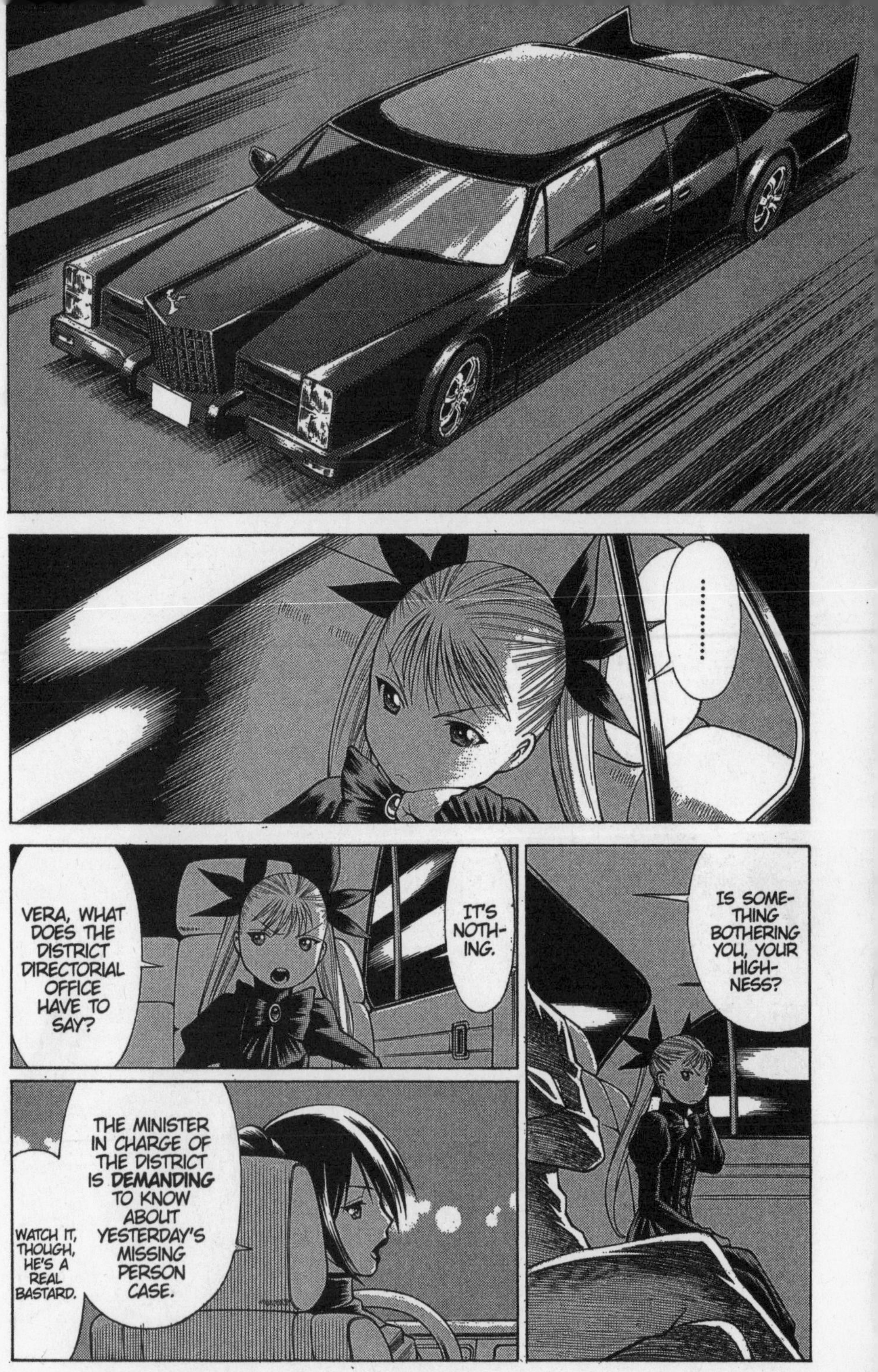
....
IS SOMETHING BOTHERING YOU, YOUR HIGHNESS?
IT'S NOTHING.
VERA, WHAT DOES THE DISTRICT DIRECTORIAL OFFICE HAVE TO SAY?
THE MINISTER IN CHARGE OF THE DISTRICT IS **DEMANDING** TO KNOW ABOUT YESTERDAY'S MISSING PERSON CASE.
WATCH IT, THOUGH, HE'S A REAL BASTARD.

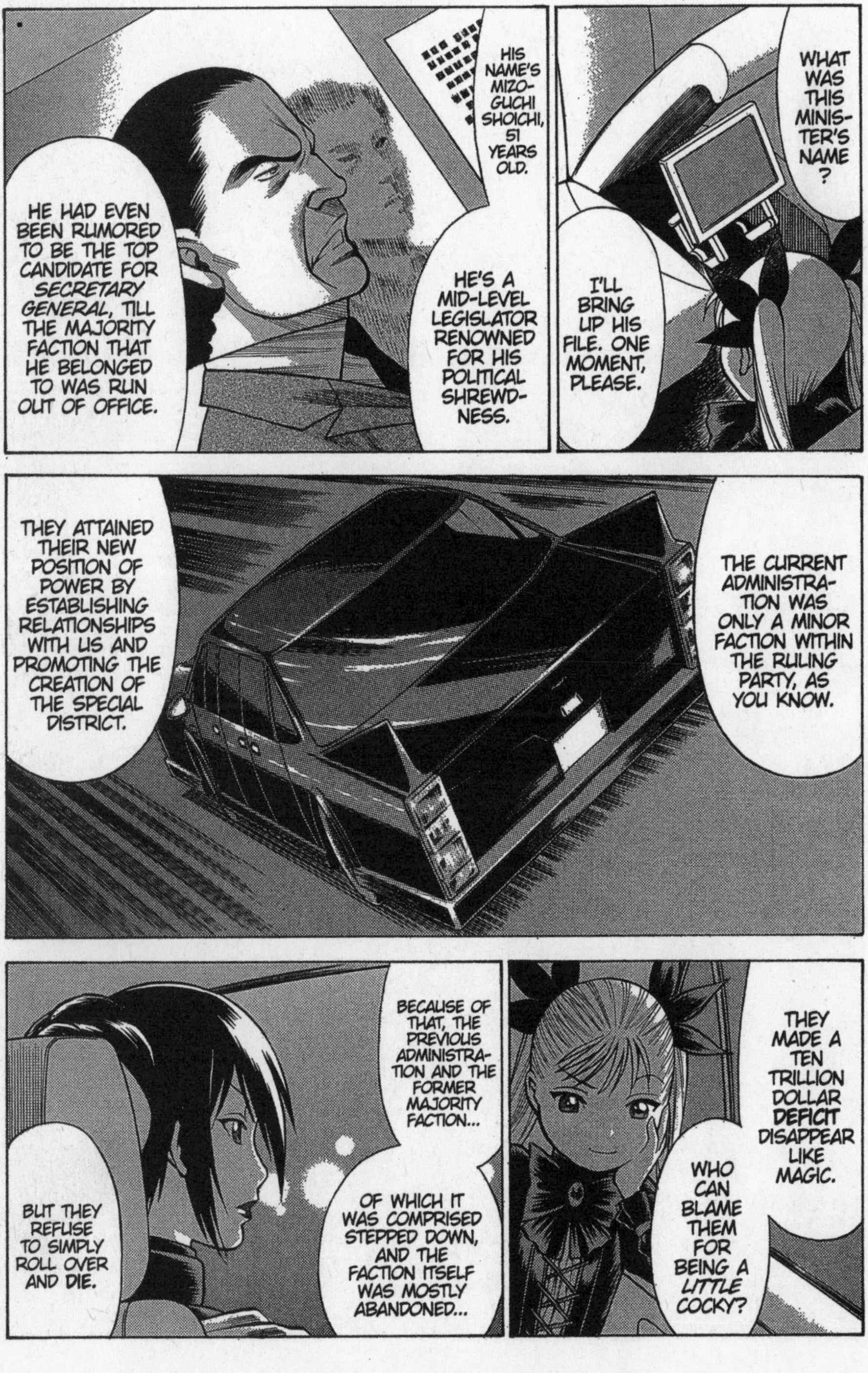

WHAT WAS THIS MINISTER'S NAME?
I'LL BRING UP HIS FILE. ONE MOMENT, PLEASE.
HIS NAME'S MIZOGUCHI SHOICHI, 51 YEARS OLD.
HE'S A MID-LEVEL LEGISLATOR RENOWNED FOR HIS POLITICAL SHREWDNESS.
HE HAD EVEN BEEN RUMORED TO BE THE TOP CANDIDATE FOR *SECRETARY GENERAL*, TILL THE MAJORITY FACTION THAT HE BELONGED TO WAS RUN OUT OF OFFICE.
THE CURRENT ADMINISTRATION WAS ONLY A MINOR FACTION WITHIN THE RULING PARTY, AS YOU KNOW.
THEY ATTAINED THEIR NEW POSITION OF POWER BY ESTABLISHING RELATIONSHIPS WITH US AND PROMOTING THE CREATION OF THE SPECIAL DISTRICT.
THEY MADE A TEN TRILLION DOLLAR **DEFICIT** DISAPPEAR LIKE MAGIC.
WHO CAN BLAME THEM FOR BEING A *LITTLE* COCKY?
BECAUSE OF THAT, THE PREVIOUS ADMINISTRATION AND THE FORMER MAJORITY FACTION...
OF WHICH IT WAS COMPRISED STEPPED DOWN, AND THE FACTION ITSELF WAS MOSTLY ABANDONED...
BUT THEY REFUSE TO SIMPLY ROLL OVER AND DIE.

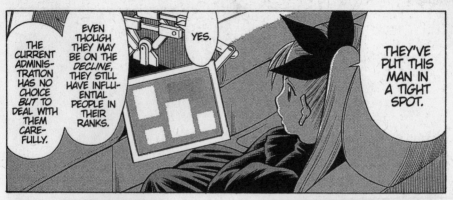

THEY'VE PUT THIS MAN IN A TIGHT SPOT.
YES.
EVEN THOUGH THEY MAY BE ON THE *DECLINE*, THEY STILL HAVE INFLUENTIAL PEOPLE IN THEIR RANKS.
THE CURRENT ADMINISTRATION HAS NO CHOICE *BUT* TO DEAL WITH THEM CAREFULLY.
AND SINCE HE DID NOT WIN A HIGH-PROFILE POSITION BECAUSE OF THE SPECIAL DISTRICT...
HE WOULD BE A PERFECT CHOICE FOR THEM TO STOP OUR ADVANCES.
SEVERAL ISSUES THAT WE HAD GOTTEN THE GOVERNMENT'S UNOFFICIAL CONSENT FOR HAVE ALREADY BEEN PUT ON *HOLD* THANKS TO THIS MAN.
HE'S TRYING TO MAKE A STATEMENT AND SOLIDIFY HIS STANDING WITH HIS FACTION.
HOW CONNIVING.
STUNTS LIKE THAT WON'T PLAY WELL WITH HIS ALLIES, THOUGH...
WHO'S THIS CHILD?
THE MINISTER'S GRANDSON, MIZOGUCHI SHINYA. HE'S FIVE.
HMM...
APPARENTLY, THE MINISTER IS A KIND-HEARTED GRANDFATHER WHO *DOTES* OVER HIS GRANDSON WHEN HE'S AT HOME.
....

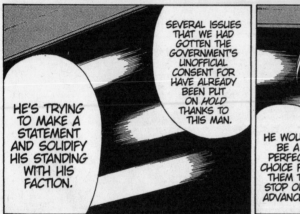

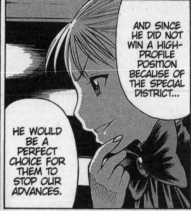

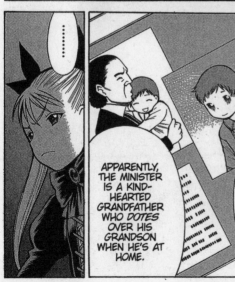

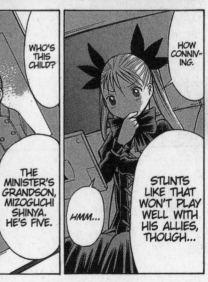

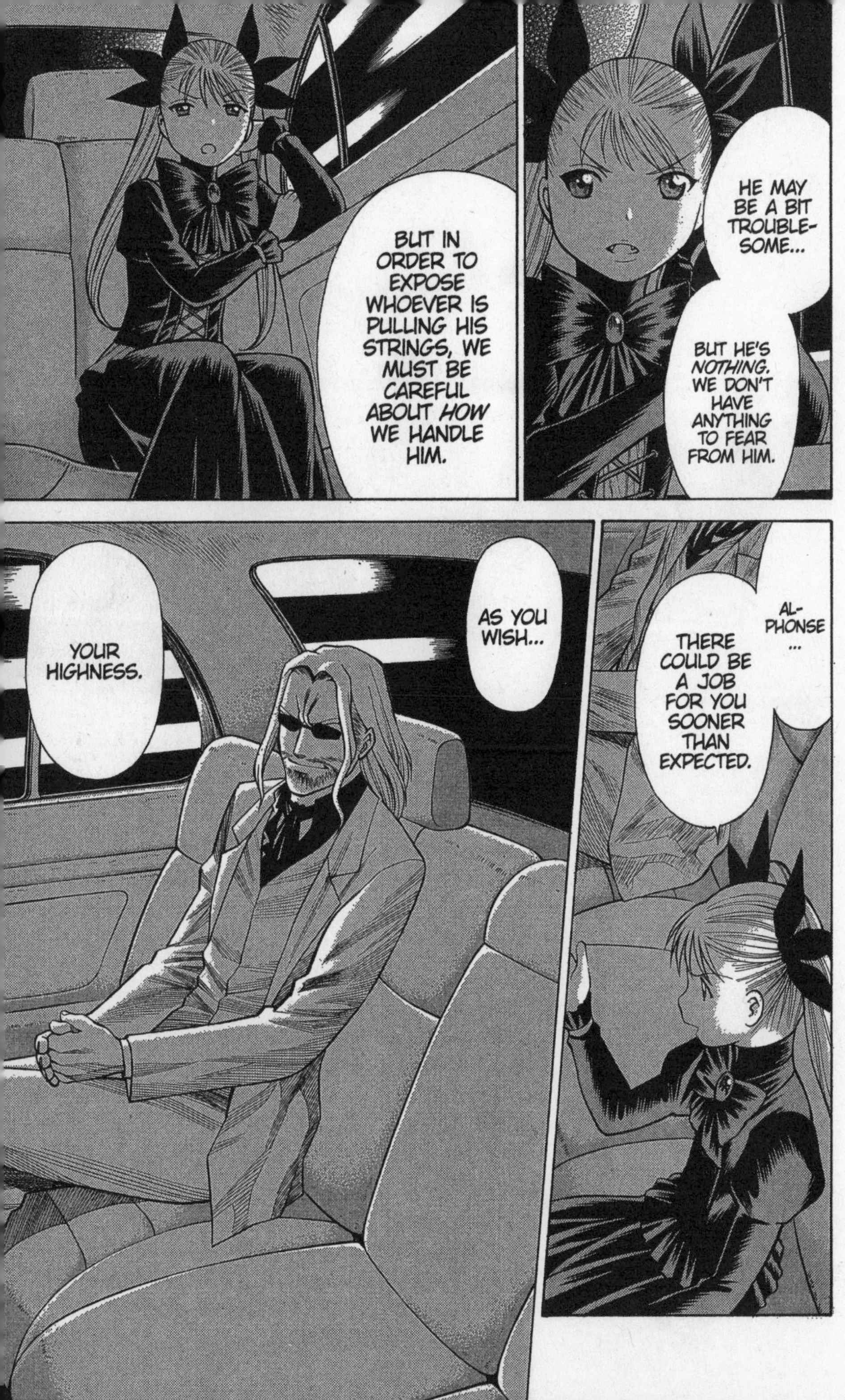
HE MAY BE A BIT TROUBLESOME...
BUT HE'S *NOTHING*. WE DON'T HAVE ANYTHING TO FEAR FROM HIM.
BUT IN ORDER TO EXPOSE WHOEVER IS PULLING HIS STRINGS, WE MUST BE CAREFUL ABOUT *HOW* WE HANDLE HIM.
ALPHONSE...
THERE COULD BE A JOB FOR YOU SOONER THAN EXPECTED.
AS YOU WISH...
YOUR HIGHNESS.

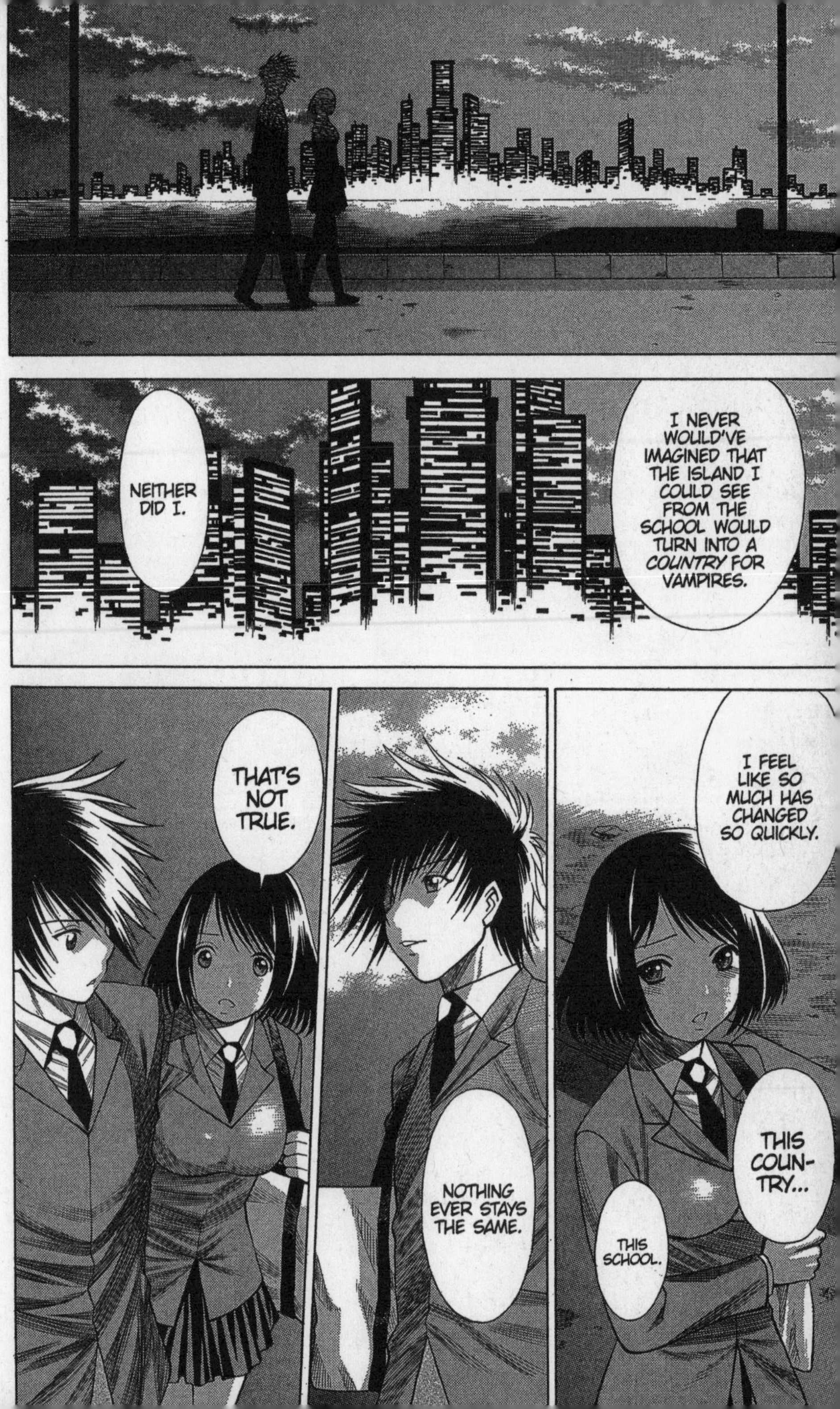
I NEVER WOULD'VE IMAGINED THAT THE ISLAND I COULD SEE FROM THE SCHOOL WOULD TURN INTO A *COUNTRY* FOR VAMPIRES.
NEITHER DID I.
I FEEL LIKE SO MUCH HAS CHANGED SO QUICKLY.
THIS COUN-TRY...
THIS SCHOOL.
NOTHING EVER STAYS THE SAME.
THAT'S NOT TRUE.

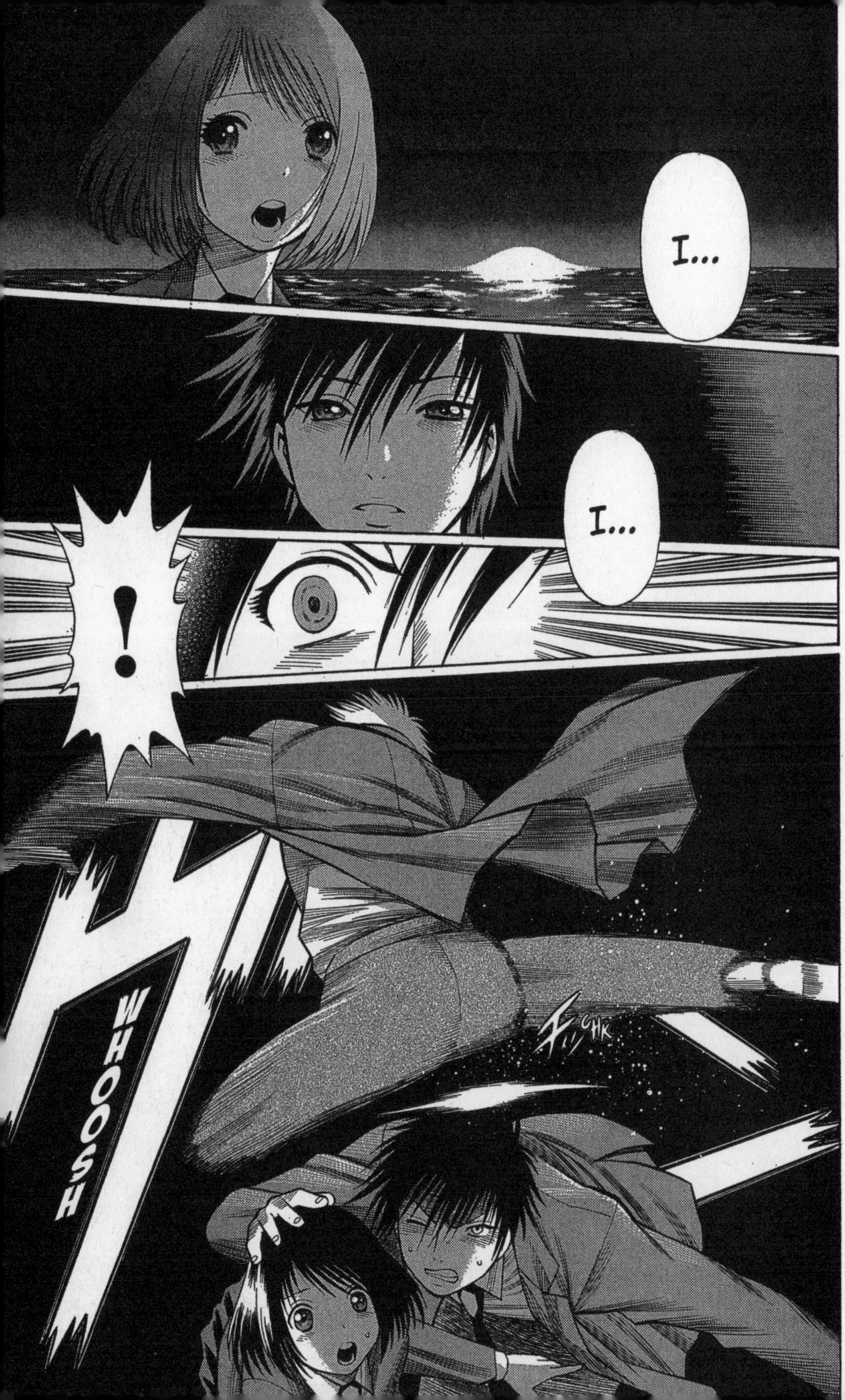
I...
I...
!
WHOOOSH
CHK

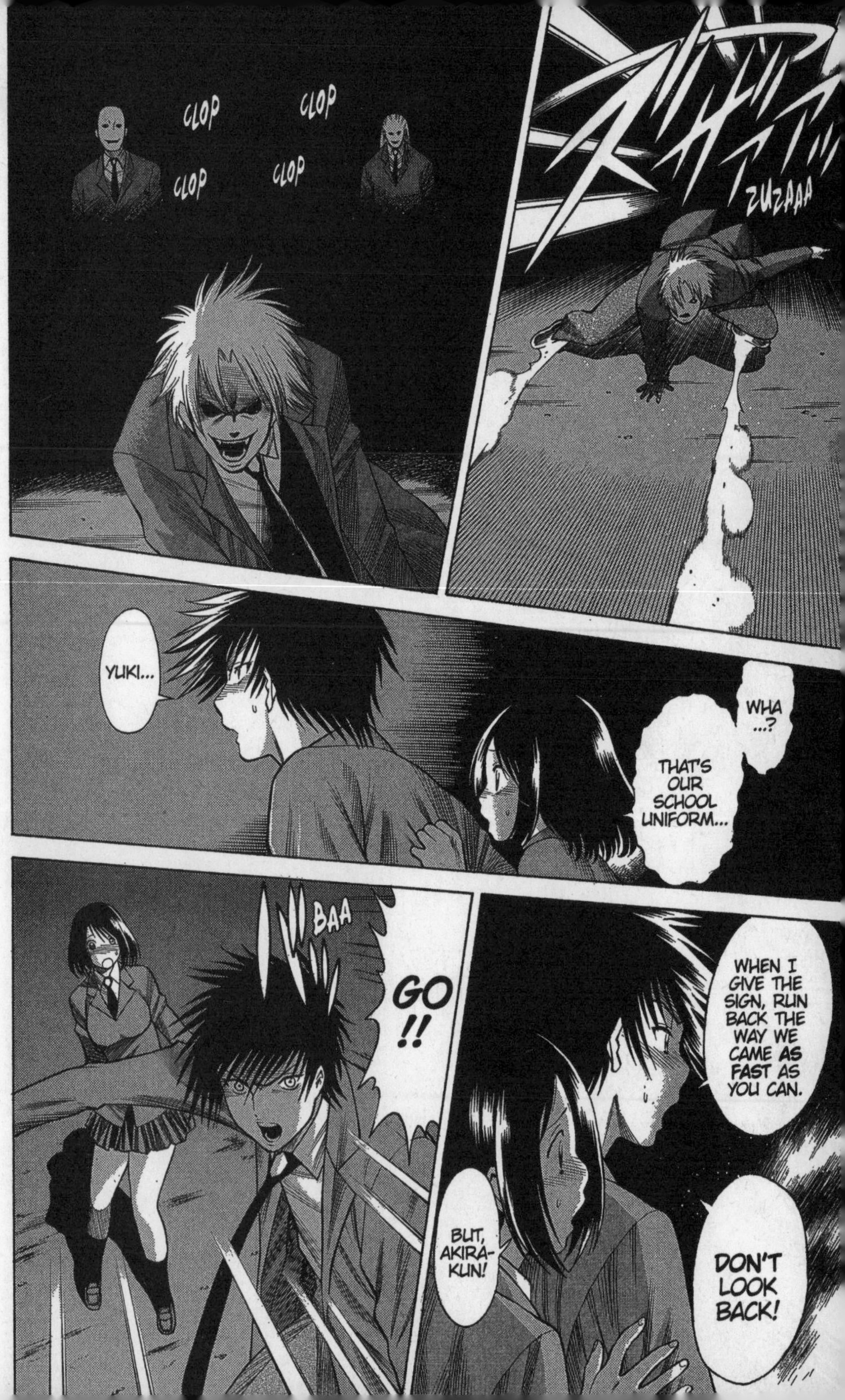
ZUZAAA
CLOP
CLOP
CLOP
CLOP
WHA ...?
THAT'S OUR SCHOOL UNIFORM...
YUKI...
WHEN I GIVE THE SIGN, RUN BACK THE WAY WE CAME AS FAST AS YOU CAN.
DON'T LOOK BACK!
BUT, AKIRA-KUN!
BAA
GO !!

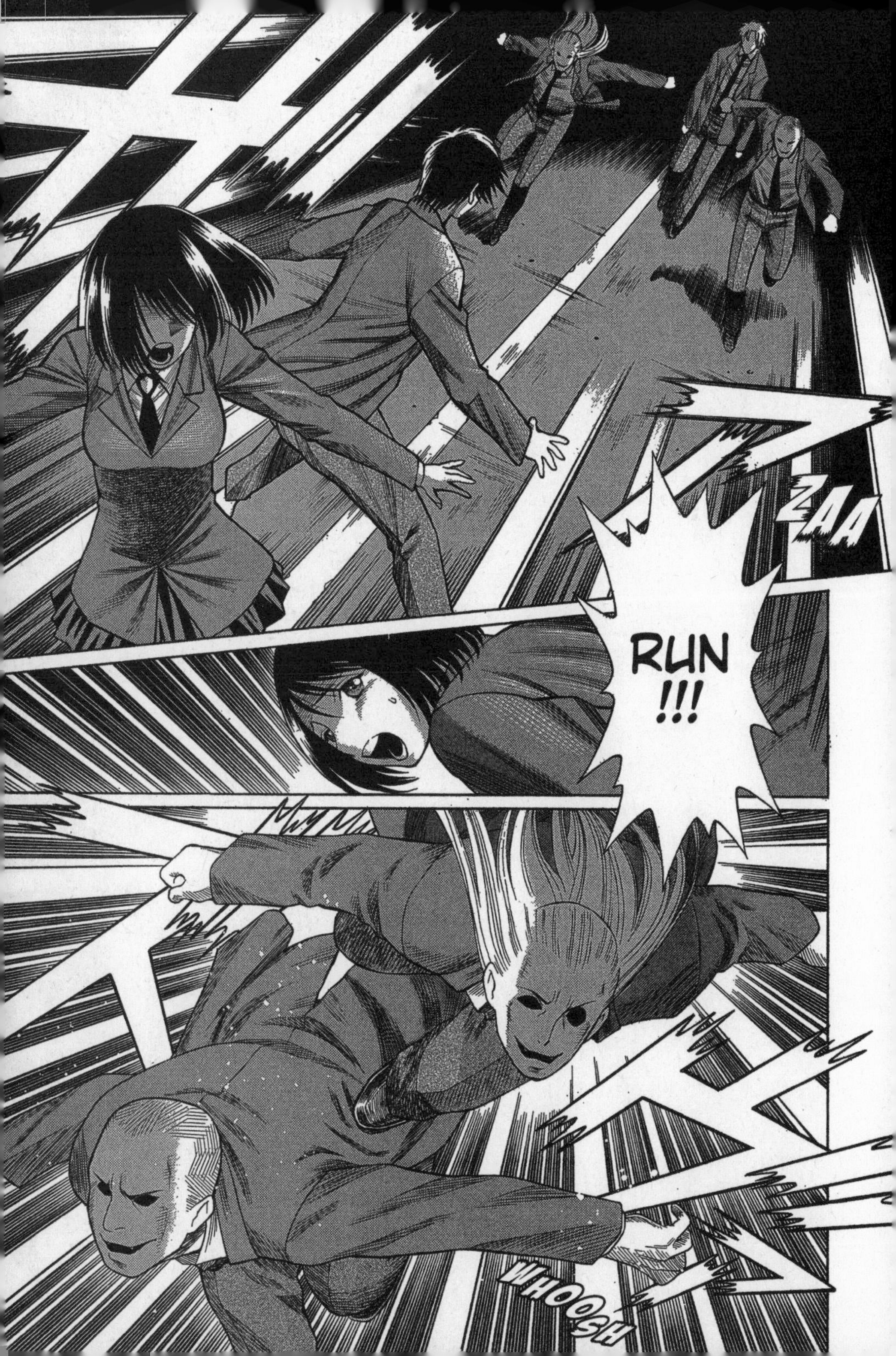
ZAA
RUN !!!
WHOOSH

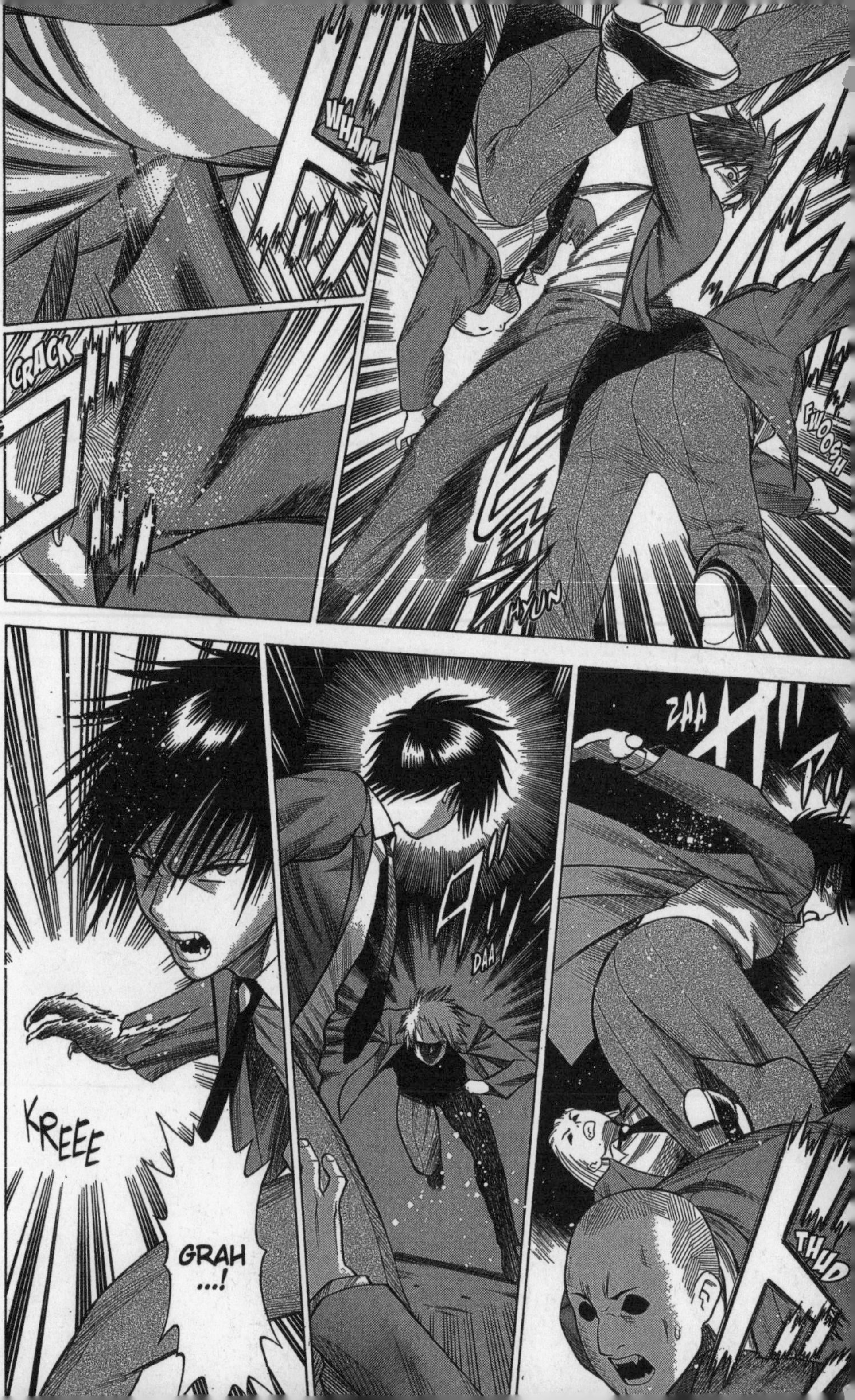
WHOOSH
HYUN
WHAM
CRACK
ZAA
THUD
DAA
KREEE
GRAH
...!

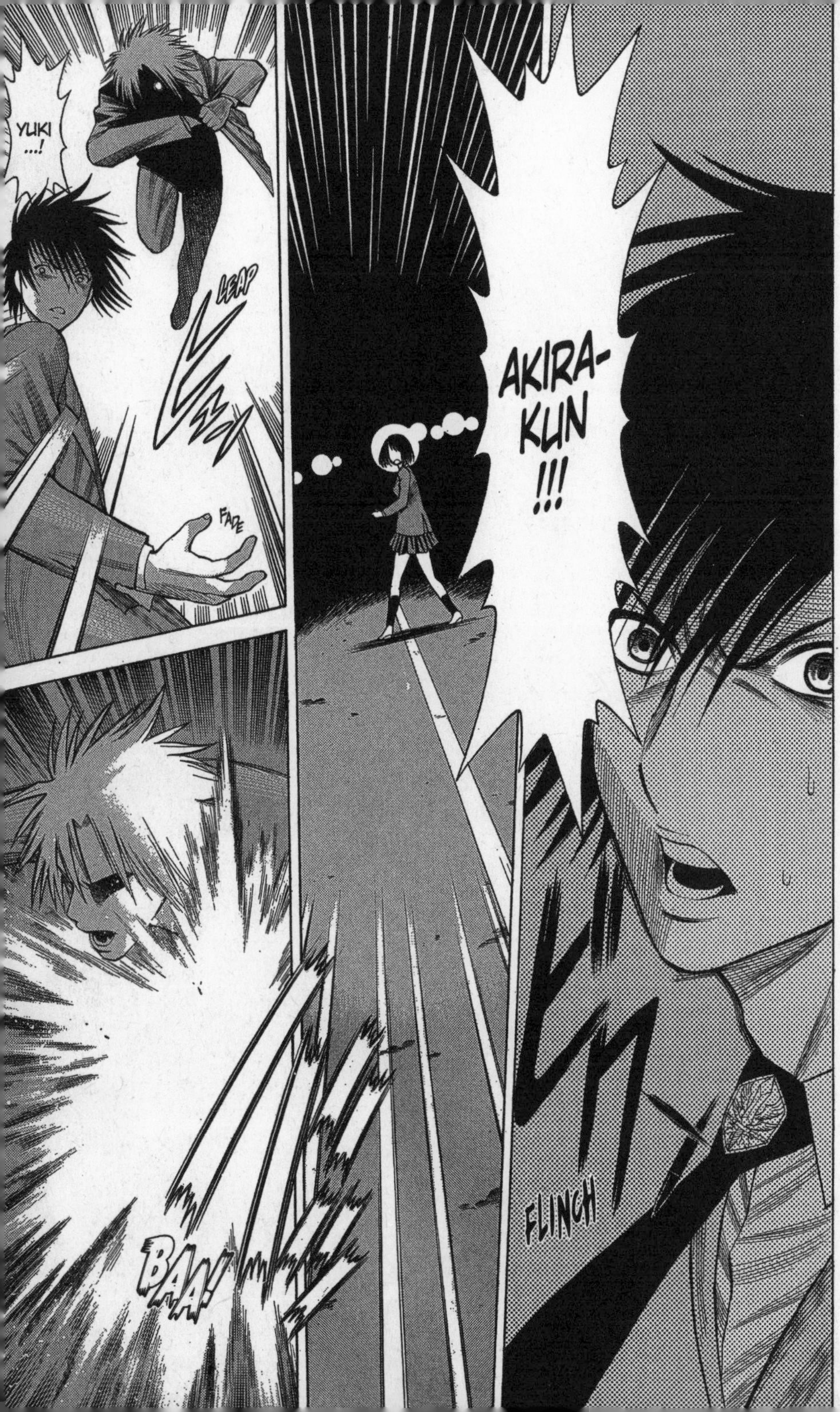
AKIRA-KUN!!!
FLINCH
YUKI...!
LEAP
FADE
BAA!

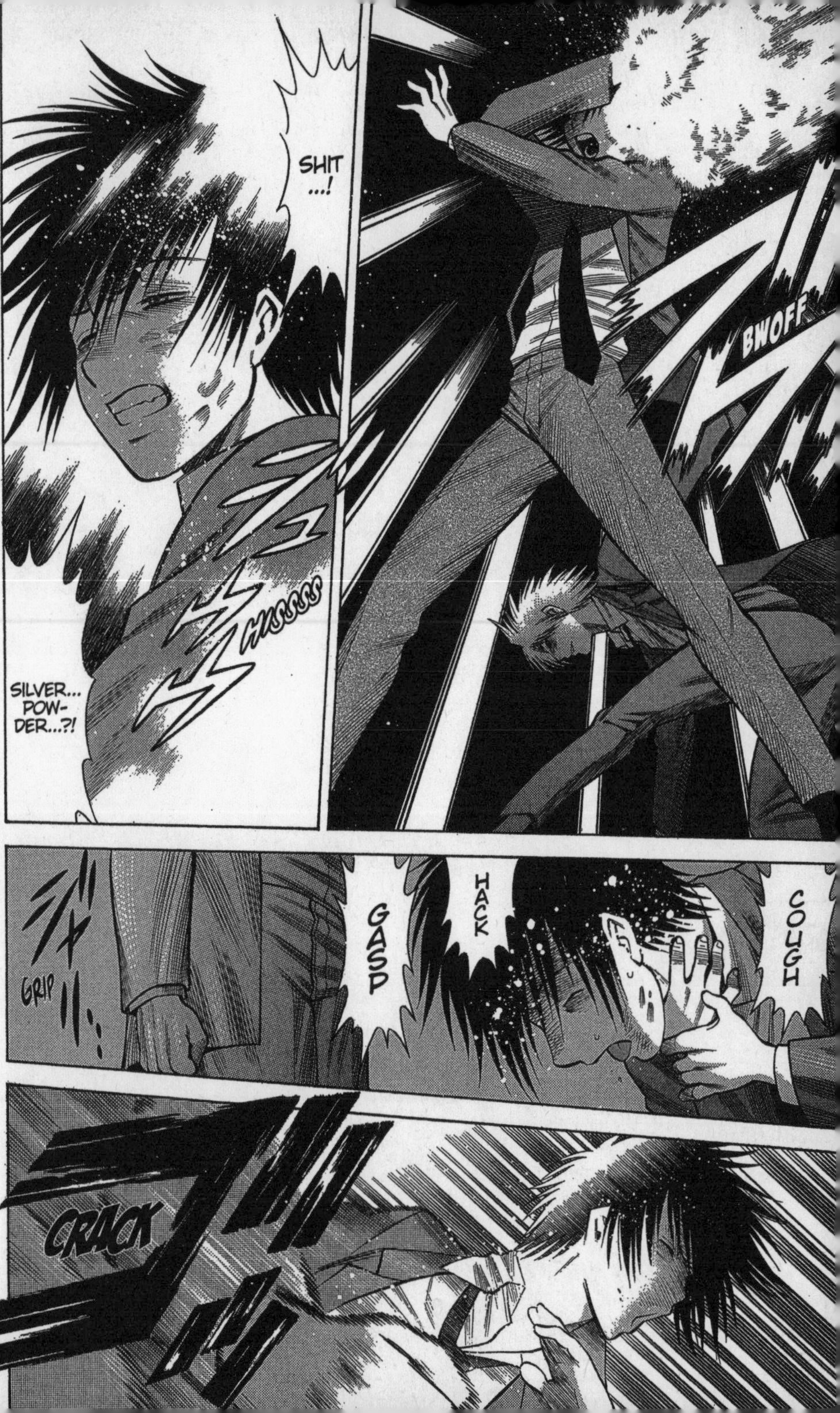
BWOFF
SHIT ...!
HISSSS
SILVER... POW-DER...?!
COUGH
HACK
GASP
GRIP
CRACK

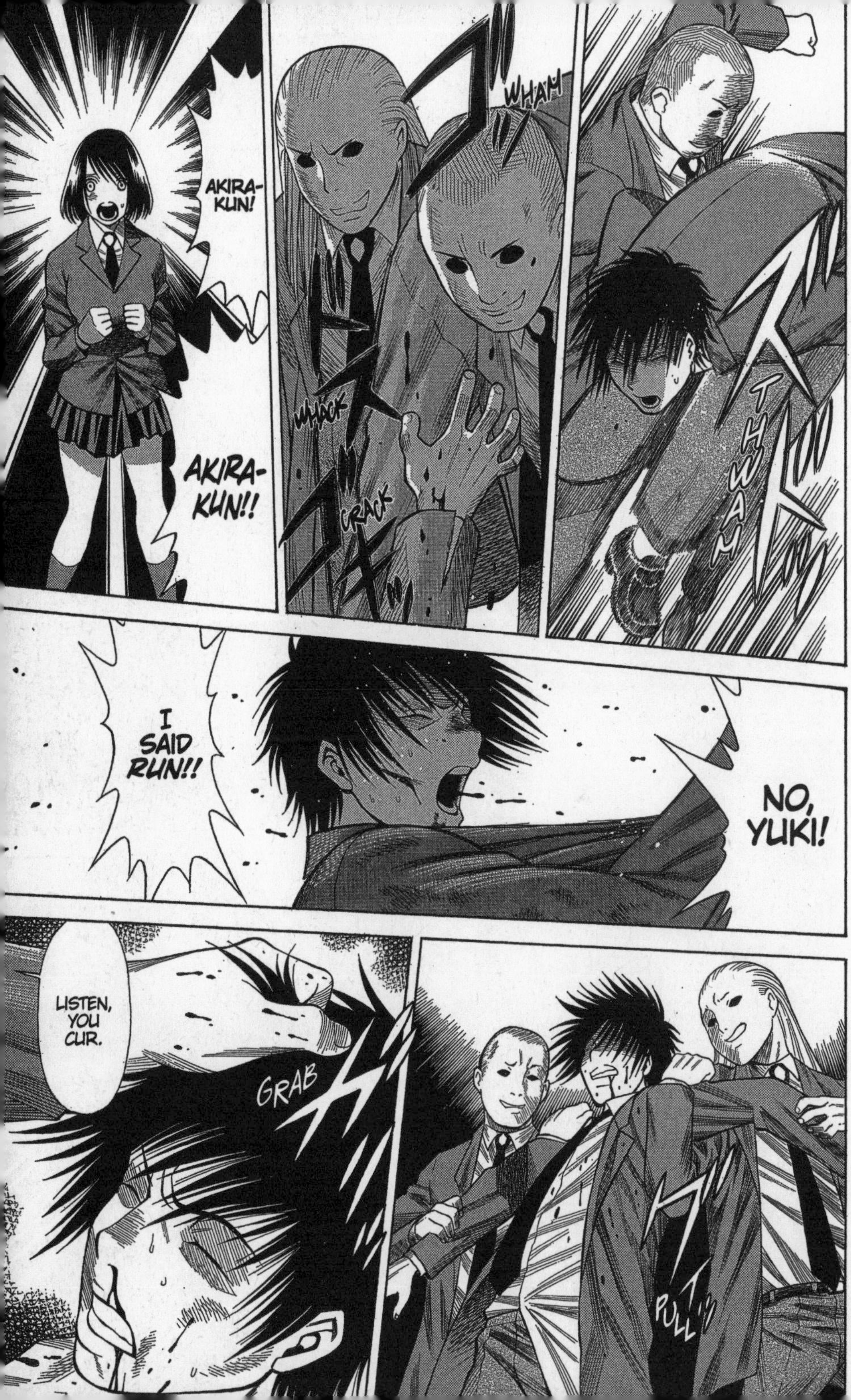
THWAM
WHAM
WHACK
CRACK
AKIRA-KUN!
AKIRA-KUN!!
NO, YUKI!
I SAID RUN!!
PULL
LISTEN, YOU CUR.
GRAB

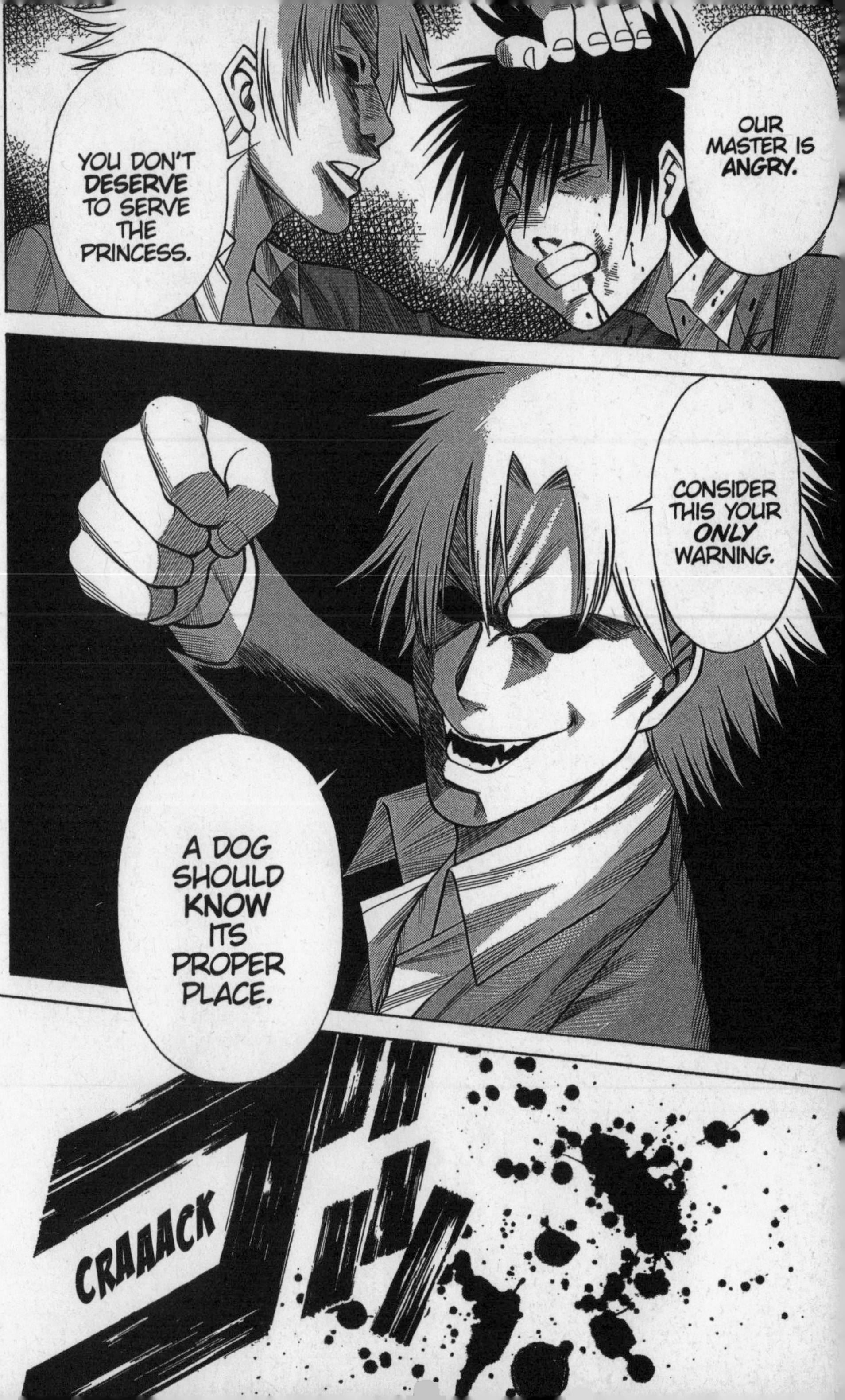
OUR MASTER IS ANGRY.
YOU DON'T DESERVE TO SERVE THE PRINCESS.
CONSIDER THIS YOUR ONLY WARNING.
A DOG SHOULD KNOW ITS PROPER PLACE.
CRAAACK

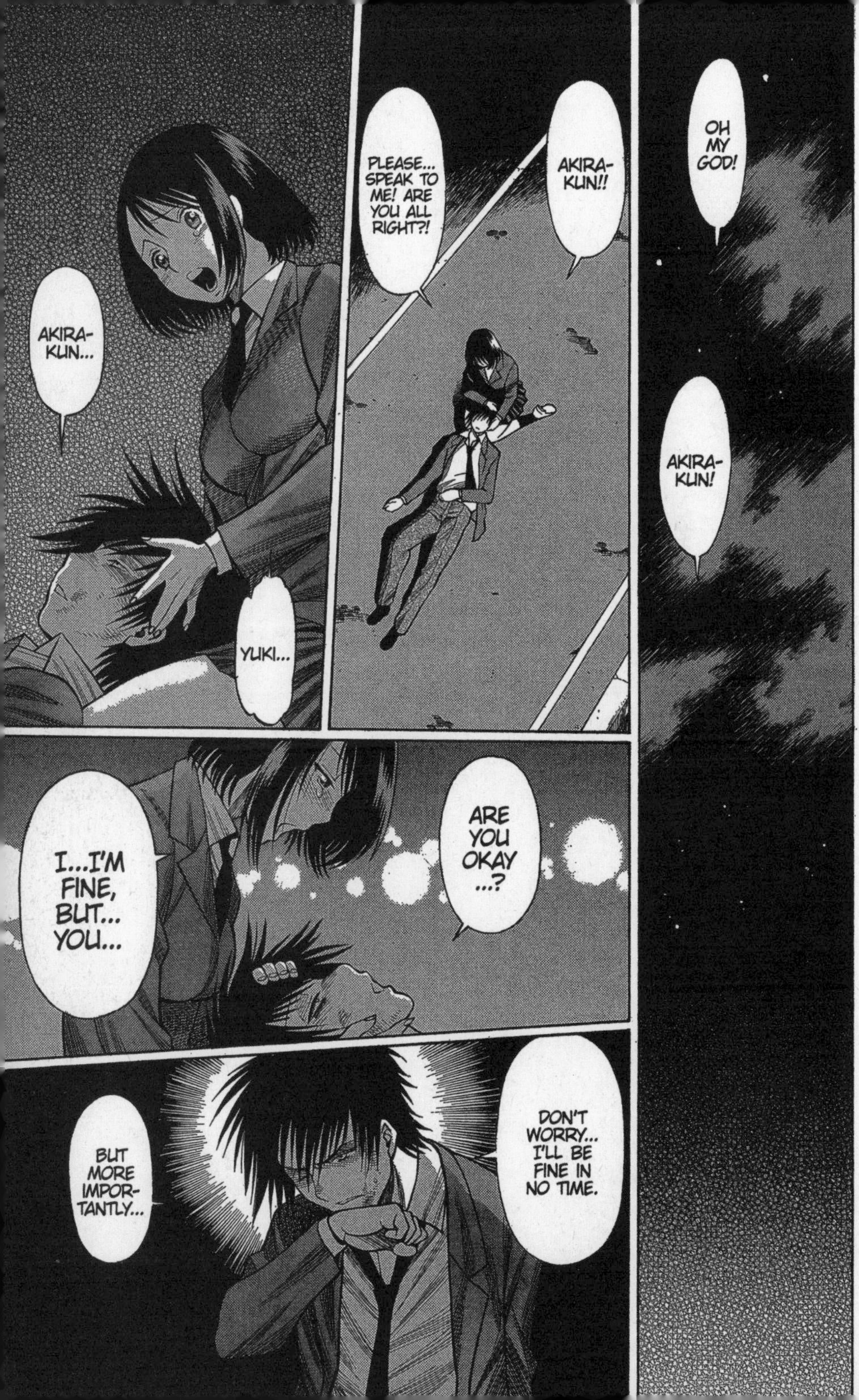
OH MY GOD!
AKIRA-KUN!
AKIRA-KUN!!
PLEASE... SPEAK TO ME! ARE YOU ALL RIGHT?!
AKIRA-KUN...
YUKI...
ARE YOU OKAY ...?
I...I'M FINE, BUT... YOU...
DON'T WORRY... I'LL BE FINE IN NO TIME.
BUT MORE IMPOR-TANTLY...

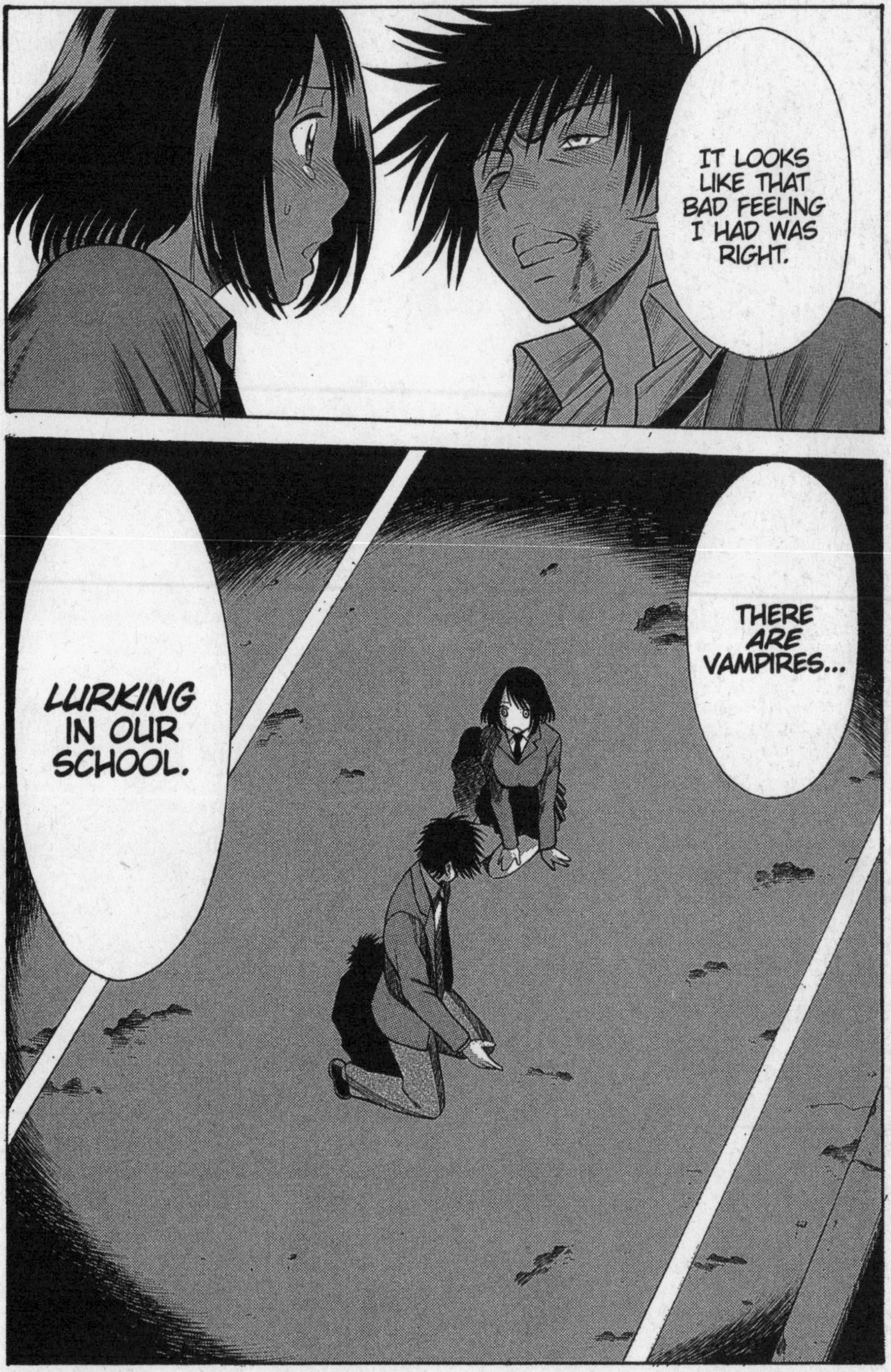
IT LOOKS LIKE THAT BAD FEELING I HAD WAS RIGHT.
THERE ARE VAMPIRES...
LURKING IN OUR SCHOOL.

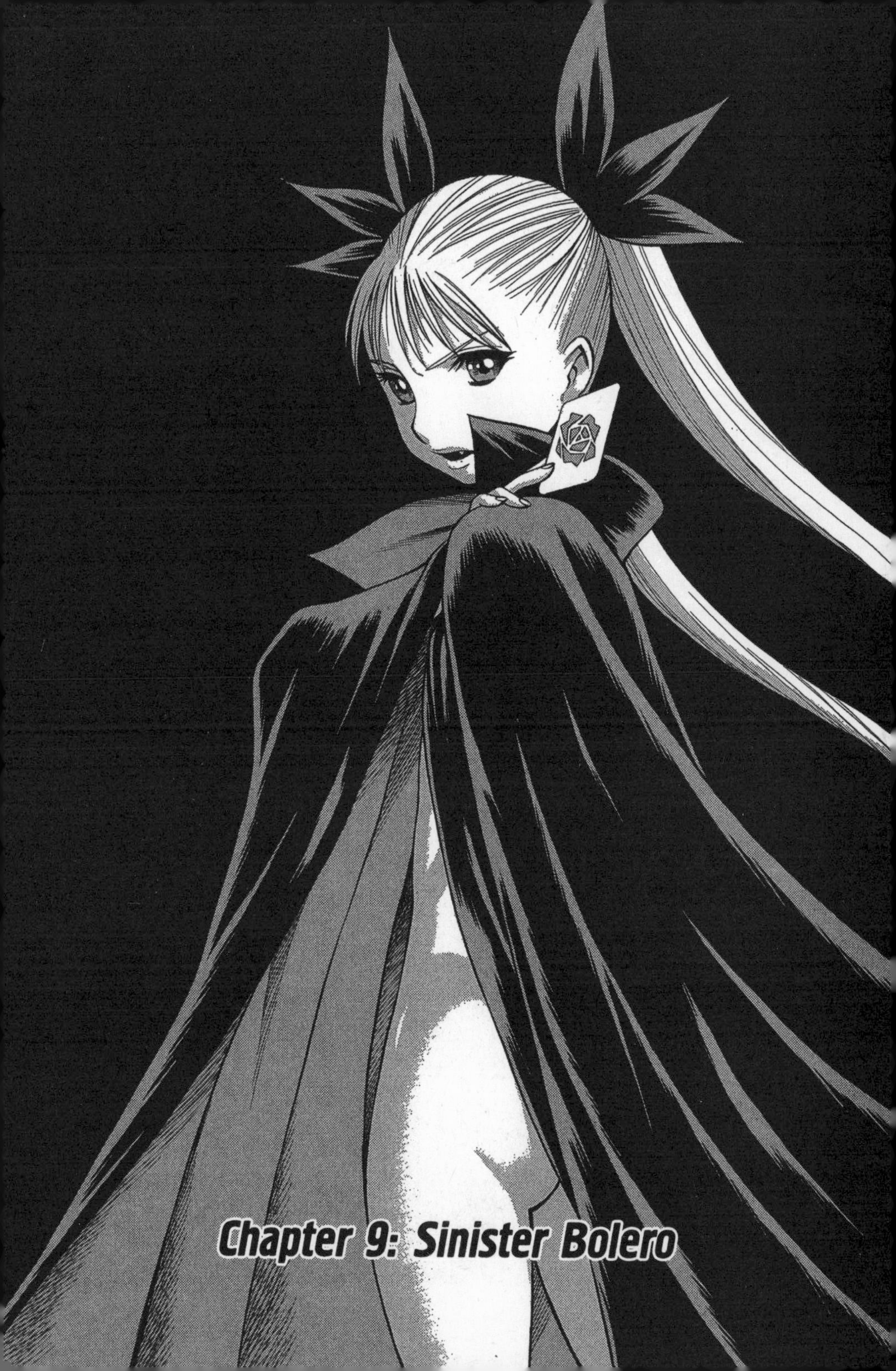
Chapter 9: Sinister Bolero

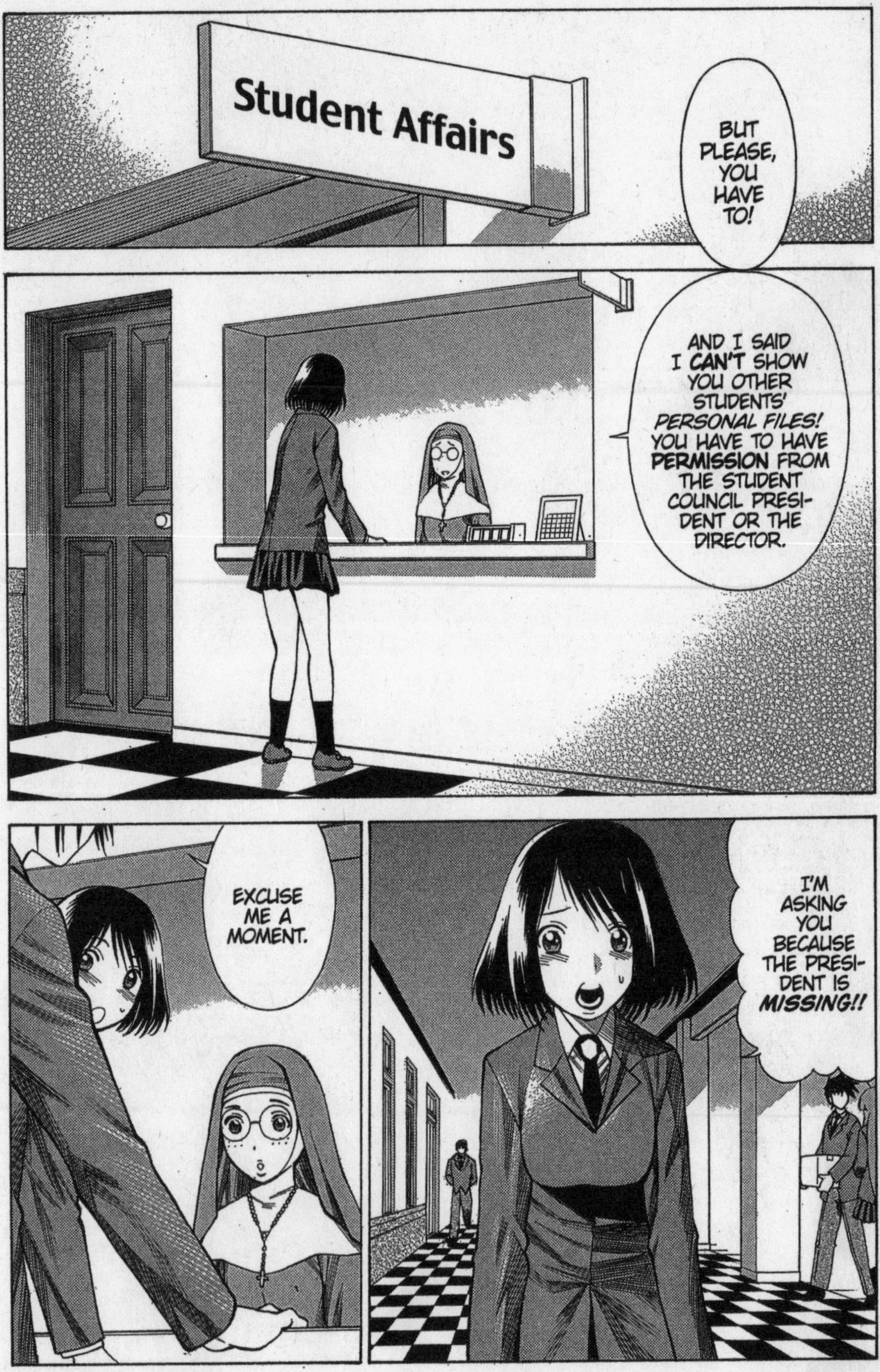
BUT PLEASE, YOU HAVE TO!
Student Affairs
AND I SAID I CAN'T SHOW YOU OTHER STUDENTS' PERSONAL FILES! YOU HAVE TO HAVE PERMISSION FROM THE STUDENT COUNCIL PRESI-DENT OR THE DIRECTOR.
I'M ASKING YOU BECAUSE THE PRESI-DENT IS MISSING!!
EXCUSE ME A MOMENT.

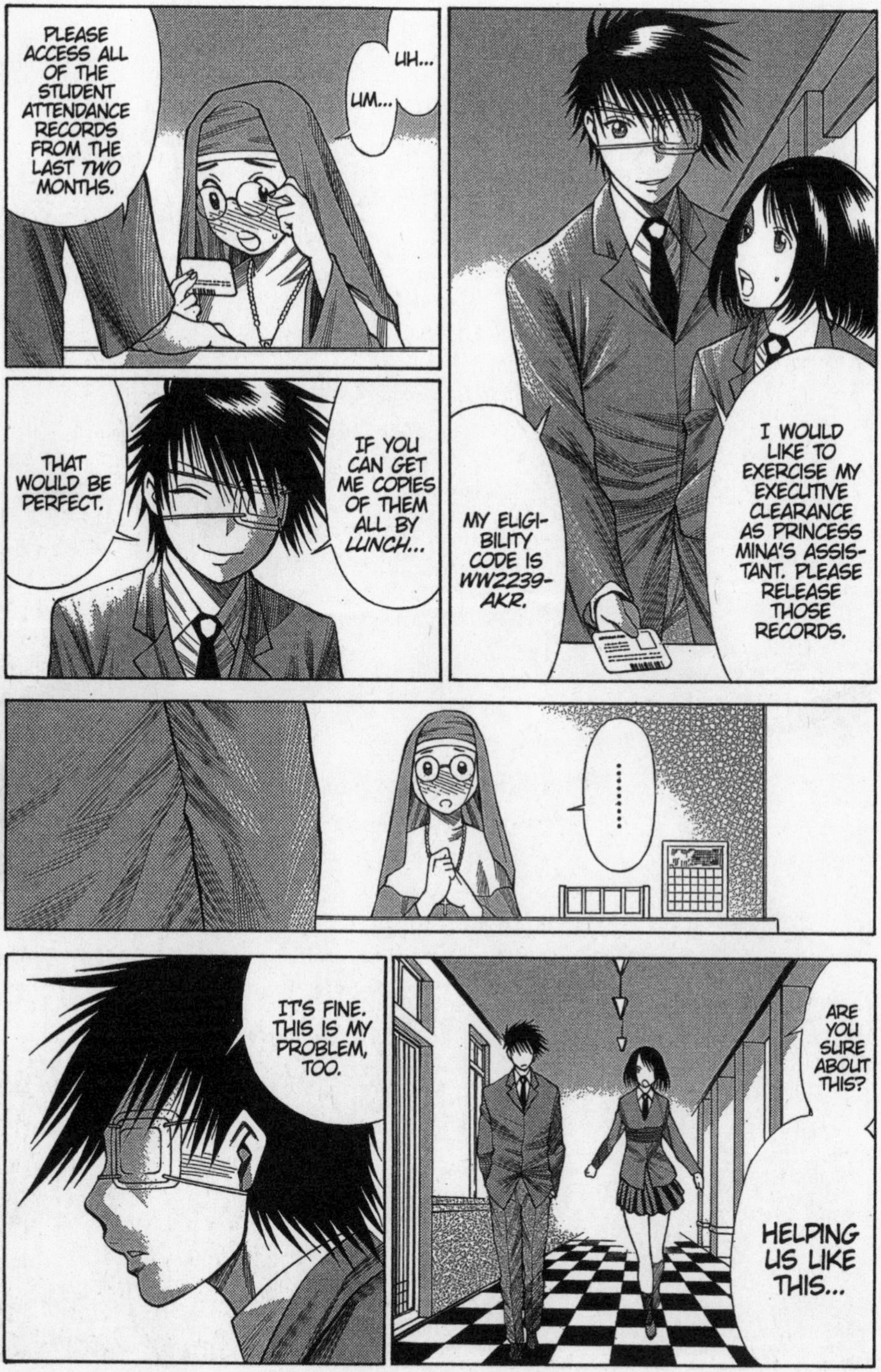
I WOULD LIKE TO EXERCISE MY EXECUTIVE CLEARANCE AS PRINCESS MINA'S ASSISTANT. PLEASE RELEASE THOSE RECORDS.
MY ELIGIBILITY CODE IS WW2239-AKR.
UH...
UM...
PLEASE ACCESS ALL OF THE STUDENT ATTENDANCE RECORDS FROM THE LAST TWO MONTHS.
IF YOU CAN GET ME COPIES OF THEM ALL BY LUNCH...
THAT WOULD BE PERFECT.
....
ARE YOU SURE ABOUT THIS?
HELPING US LIKE THIS...
IT'S FINE. THIS IS MY PROBLEM, TOO.

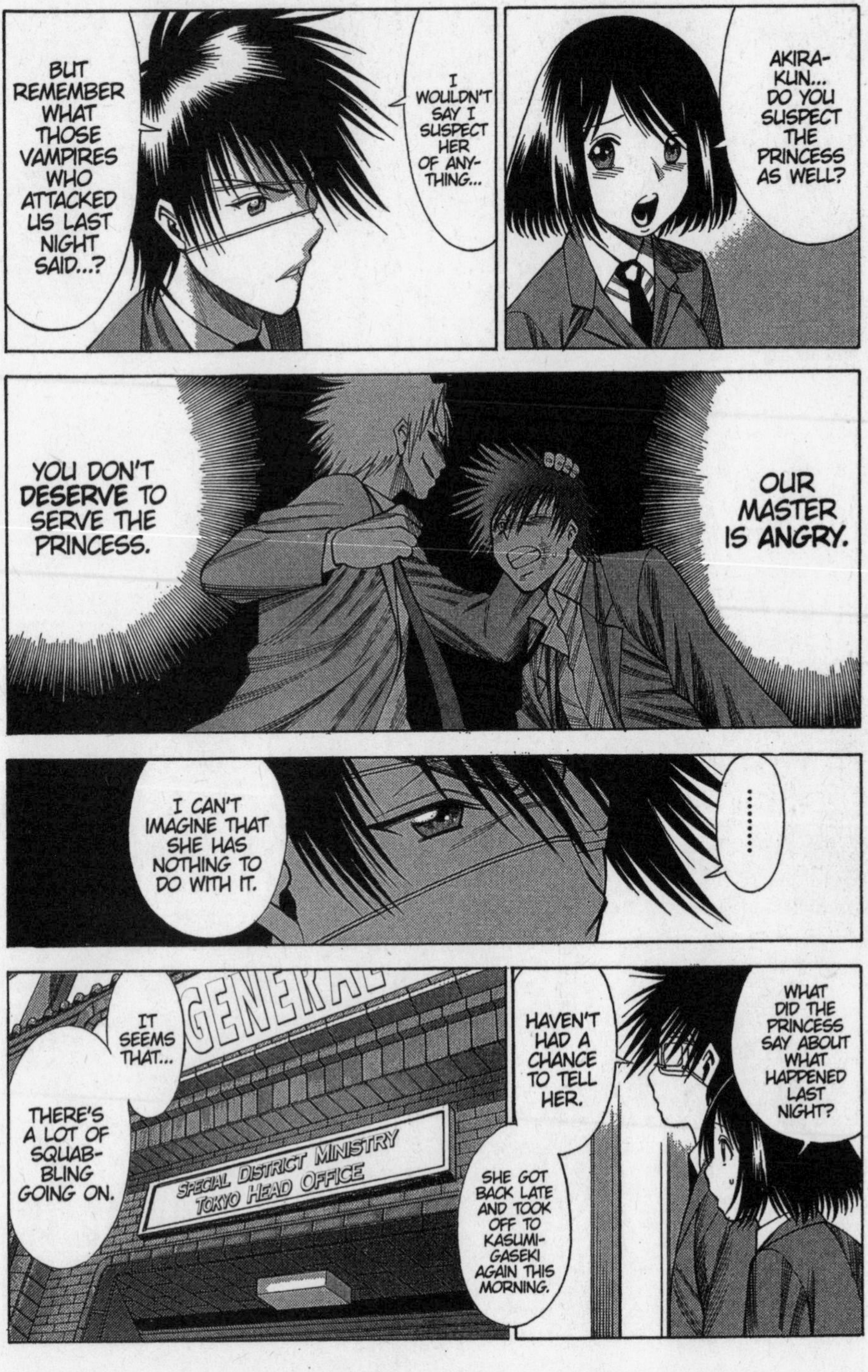
AKIRA-KUN... DO YOU SUSPECT THE PRINCESS AS WELL?
I WOULDN'T SAY I SUSPECT HER OF ANY-THING...
BUT REMEMBER WHAT THOSE VAMPIRES WHO ATTACKED US LAST NIGHT SAID...?
OUR MASTER IS ANGRY.
YOU DON'T DESERVE TO SERVE THE PRINCESS.
......
I CAN'T IMAGINE THAT SHE HAS NOTHING TO DO WITH IT.
WHAT DID THE PRINCESS SAY ABOUT WHAT HAPPENED LAST NIGHT?
HAVEN'T HAD A CHANCE TO TELL HER.
SHE GOT BACK LATE AND TOOK OFF TO KASUMI-GASEKI AGAIN THIS MORNING.
GENERAL
SPECIAL DISTRICT MINISTRY TOKYO HEAD OFFICE
IT SEEMS THAT...
THERE'S A LOT OF SQUAB-BLING GOING ON.

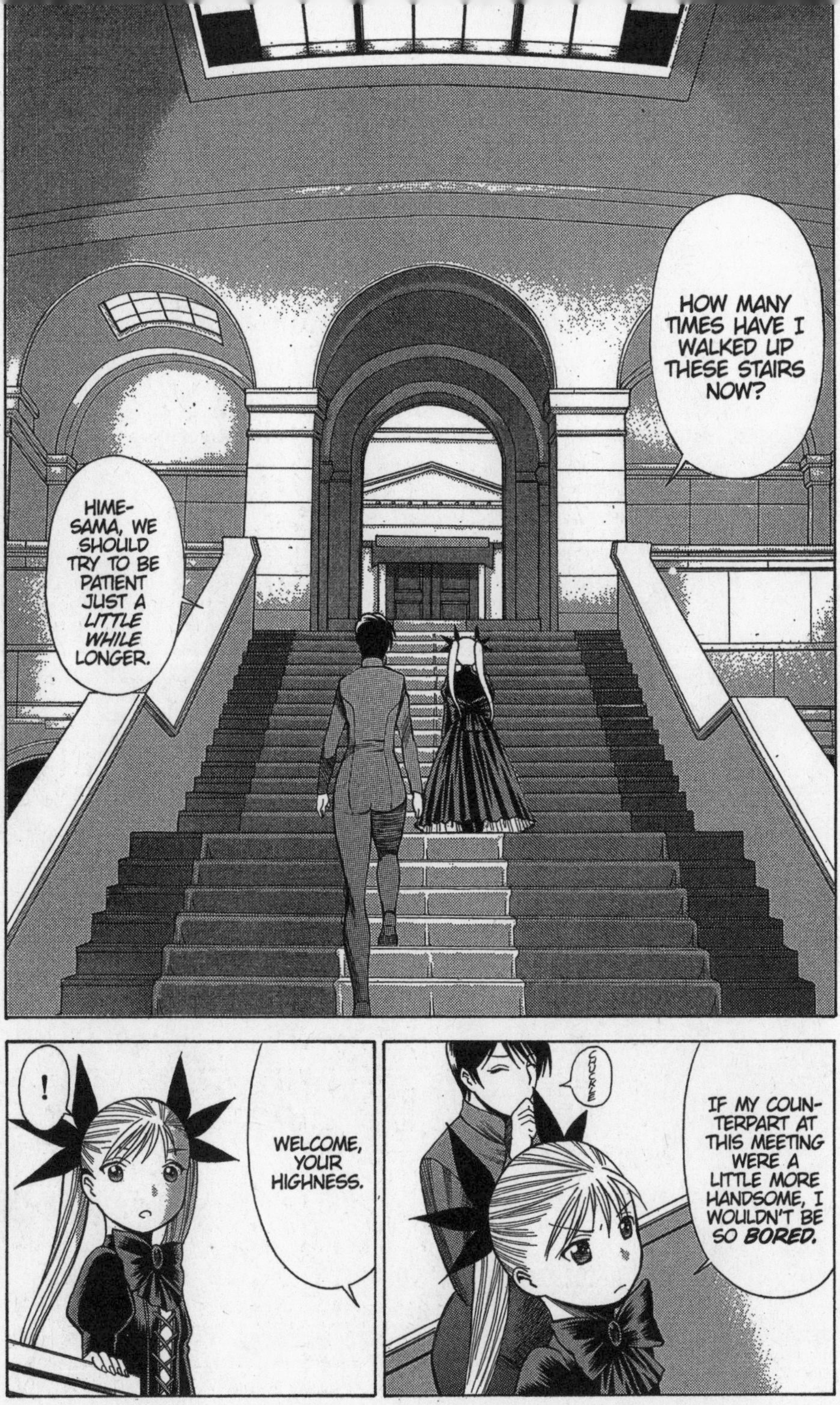
HOW MANY TIMES HAVE I WALKED UP THESE STAIRS NOW?
HIME-SAMA, WE SHOULD TRY TO BE PATIENT JUST A *LITTLE WHILE* LONGER.
IF MY COUNTERPART AT THIS MEETING WERE A LITTLE MORE HANDSOME, I WOULDN'T BE SO ***BORED.***
CHUCKLE
WELCOME, YOUR HIGHNESS.
!

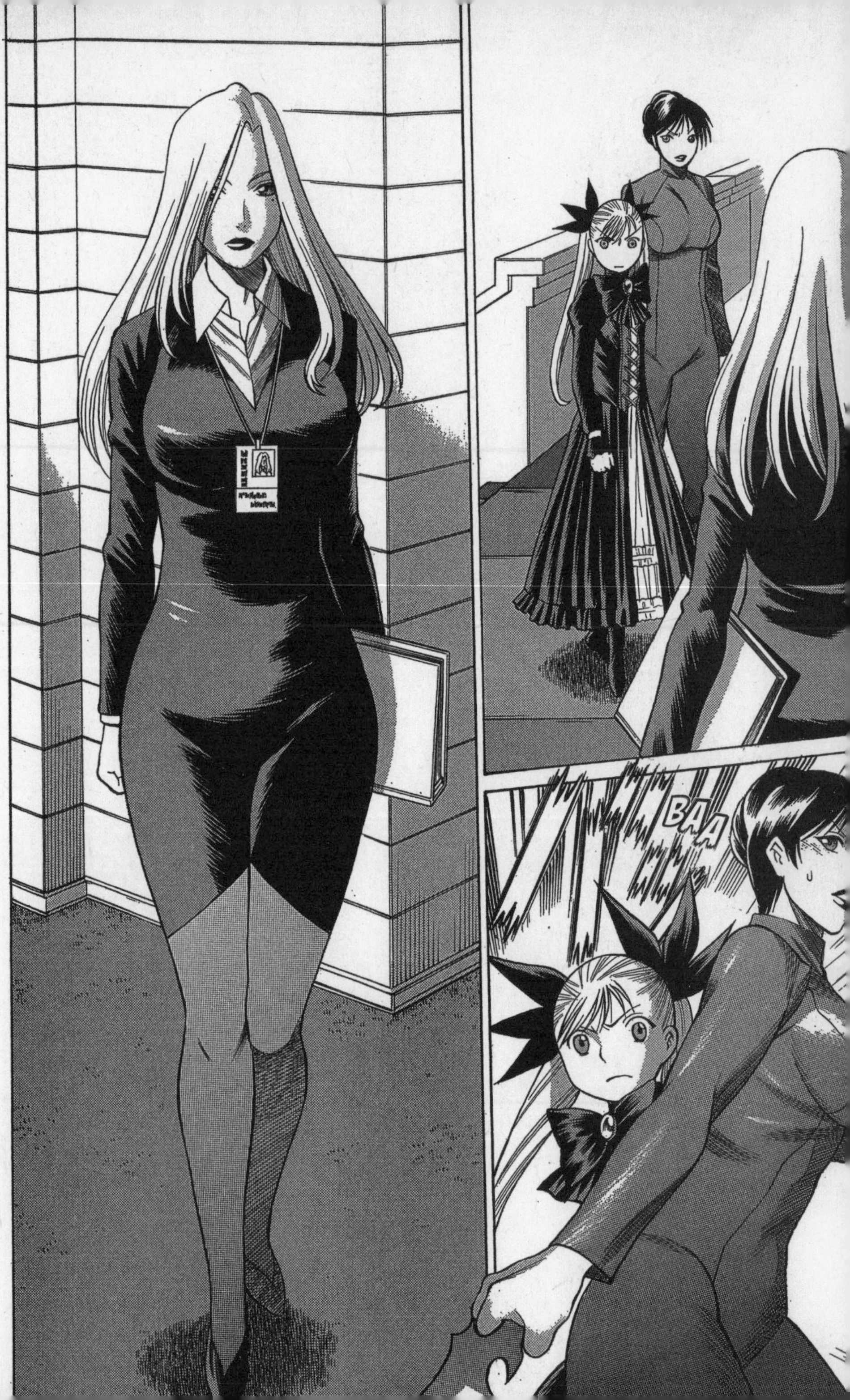
BAA

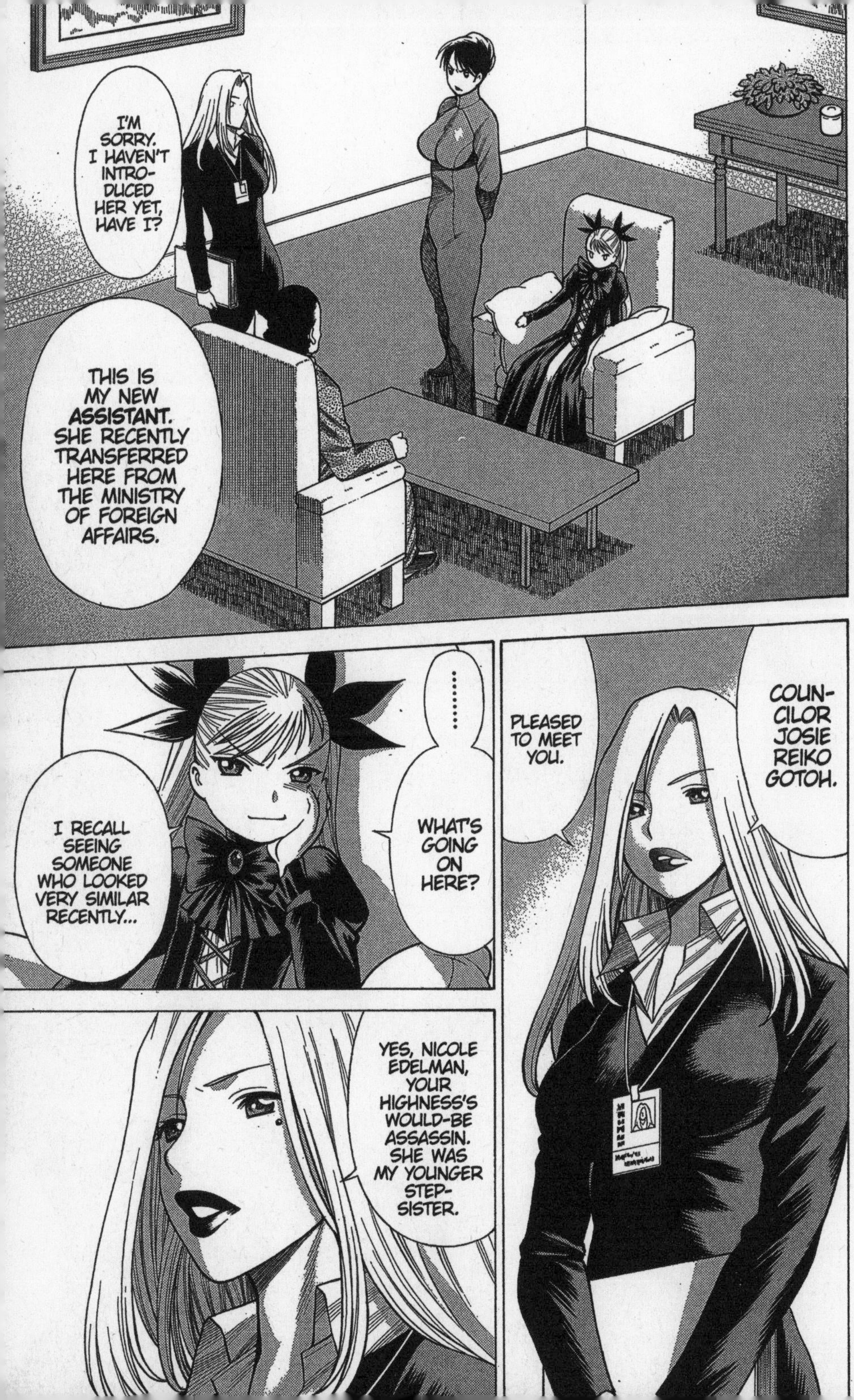
I'M SORRY. I HAVEN'T INTRO-DUCED HER YET, HAVE I?
THIS IS MY NEW **ASSISTANT.** SHE RECENTLY TRANSFERRED HERE FROM THE MINISTRY OF FOREIGN AFFAIRS.
COUN-CILOR JOSIE REIKO GOTOH.
PLEASED TO MEET YOU.
......
WHAT'S GOING ON HERE?
I RECALL SEEING SOMEONE WHO LOOKED VERY SIMILAR RECENTLY...
YES, NICOLE EDELMAN, YOUR HIGHNESS'S WOULD-BE ASSASSIN. SHE WAS MY YOUNGER STEP-SISTER.

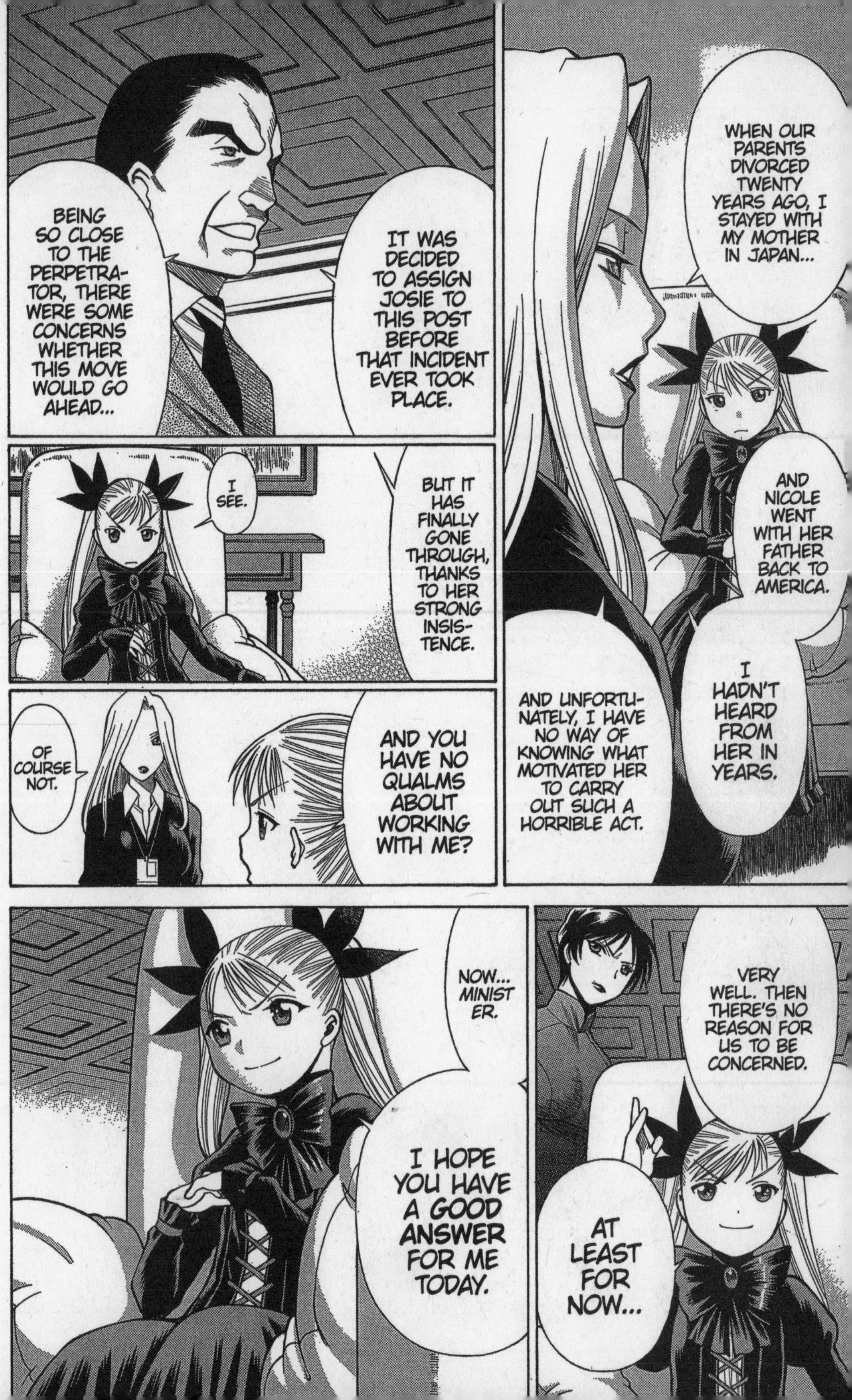
WHEN OUR PARENTS DIVORCED TWENTY YEARS AGO, I STAYED WITH MY MOTHER IN JAPAN...
AND NICOLE WENT WITH HER FATHER BACK TO AMERICA.
I HADN'T HEARD FROM HER IN YEARS.
AND UNFORTUNATELY, I HAVE NO WAY OF KNOWING WHAT MOTIVATED HER TO CARRY OUT SUCH A HORRIBLE ACT.
BEING SO CLOSE TO THE PERPETRATOR, THERE WERE SOME CONCERNS WHETHER THIS MOVE WOULD GO AHEAD...
IT WAS DECIDED TO ASSIGN JOSIE TO THIS POST BEFORE THAT INCIDENT EVER TOOK PLACE.
BUT IT HAS FINALLY GONE THROUGH, THANKS TO HER STRONG INSISTENCE.
I SEE.
AND YOU HAVE NO QUALMS ABOUT WORKING WITH ME?
OF COURSE NOT.
VERY WELL. THEN THERE'S NO REASON FOR US TO BE CONCERNED.
AT LEAST FOR NOW...
NOW... MINISTER.
I HOPE YOU HAVE A GOOD ANSWER FOR ME TODAY.

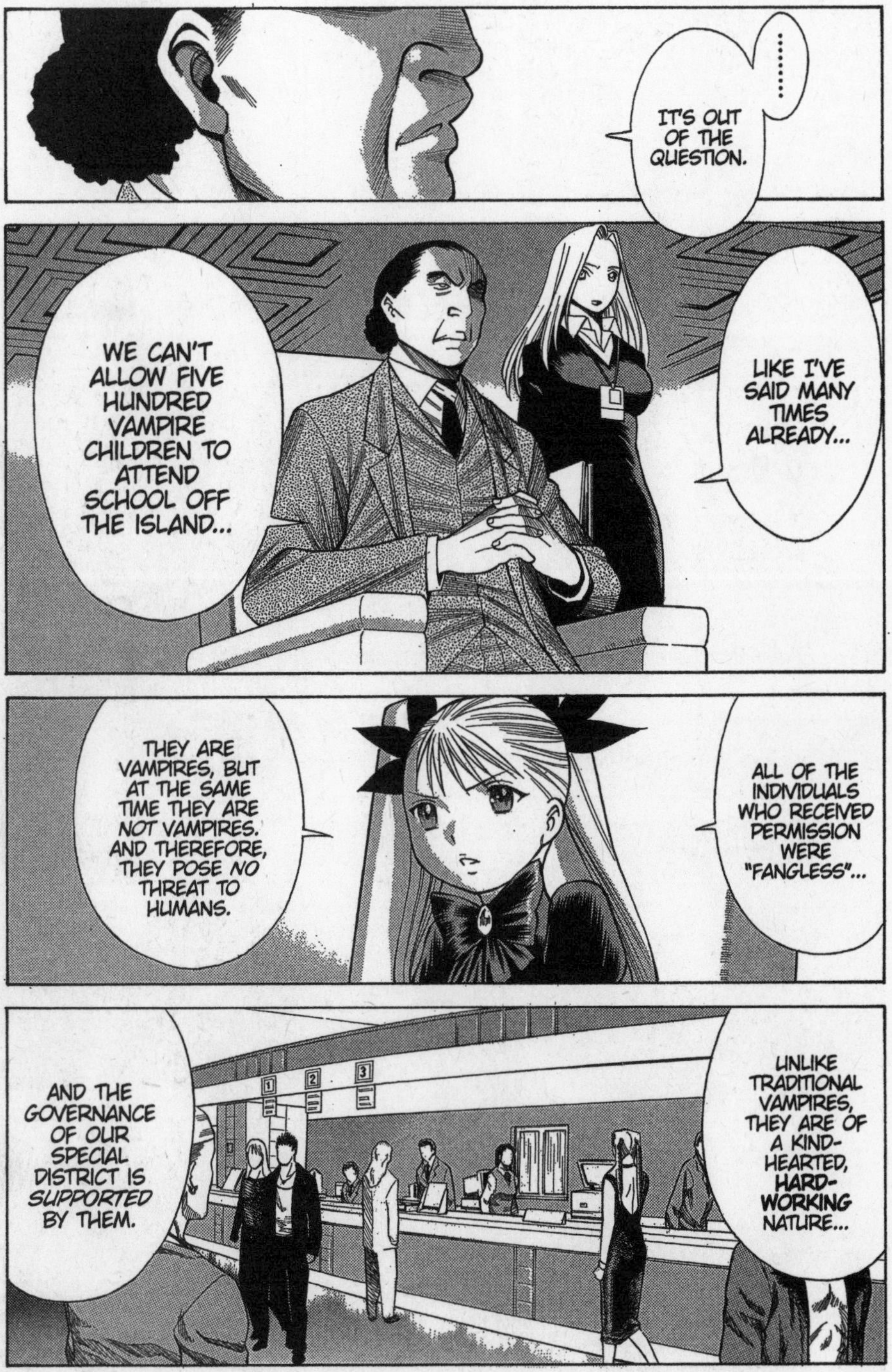
......
IT'S OUT OF THE QUESTION.
LIKE I'VE SAID MANY TIMES ALREADY...
WE CAN'T ALLOW FIVE HUNDRED VAMPIRE CHILDREN TO ATTEND SCHOOL OFF THE ISLAND...
ALL OF THE INDIVIDUALS WHO RECEIVED PERMISSION WERE "FANGLESS"...
THEY ARE VAMPIRES, BUT AT THE SAME TIME THEY ARE *NOT* VAMPIRES. AND THEREFORE, THEY POSE *NO* THREAT TO HUMANS.
UNLIKE TRADITIONAL VAMPIRES, THEY ARE OF A KIND-HEARTED, **HARD-WORKING** NATURE...
AND THE GOVERNANCE OF OUR SPECIAL DISTRICT IS *SUPPORTED* BY THEM.

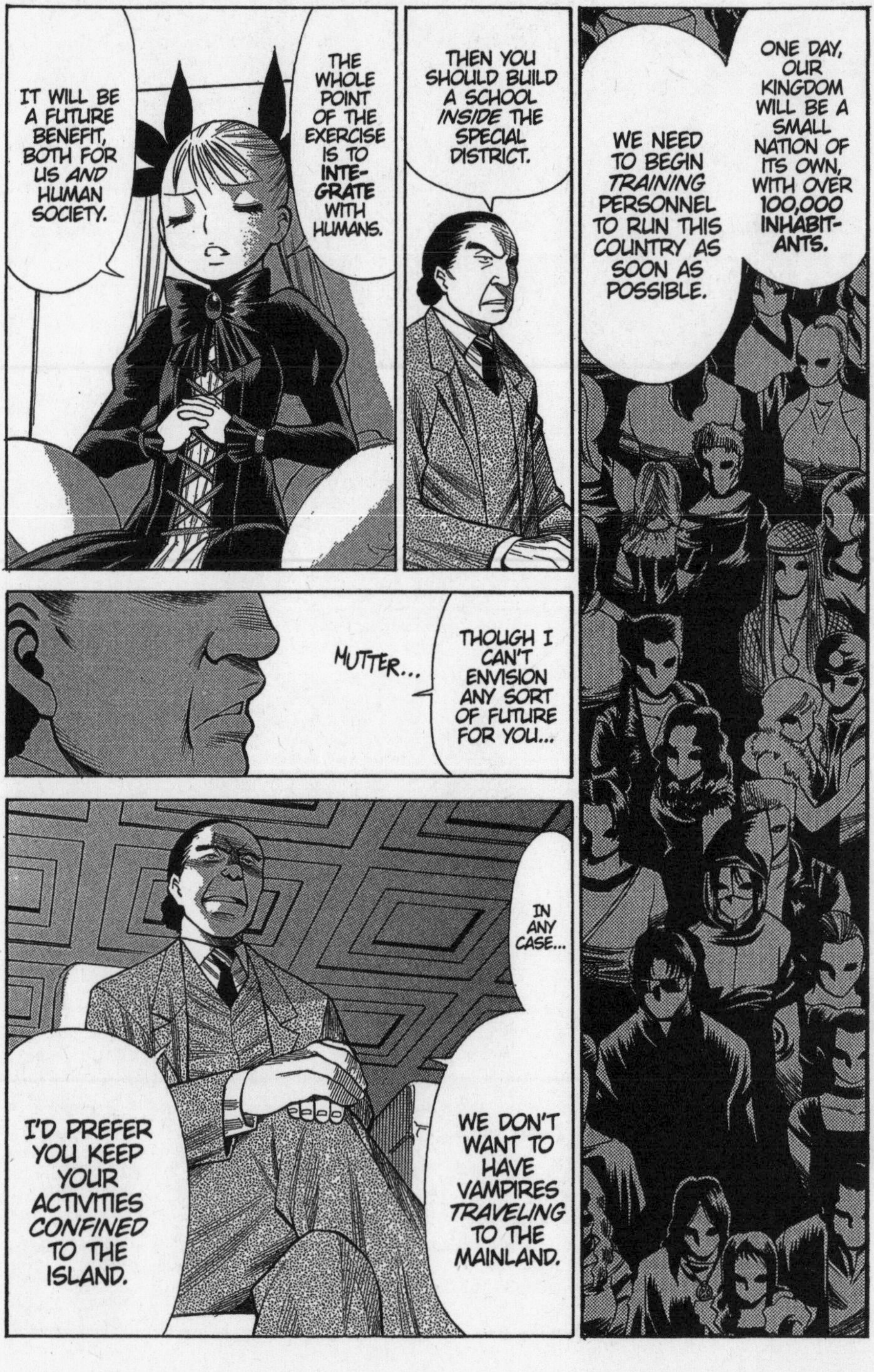
ONE DAY, OUR KINGDOM WILL BE A SMALL NATION OF ITS OWN, WITH OVER 100,000 INHABIT-ANTS.
WE NEED TO BEGIN *TRAINING* PERSONNEL TO RUN THIS COUNTRY AS SOON AS POSSIBLE.
THEN YOU SHOULD BUILD A SCHOOL *INSIDE* THE SPECIAL DISTRICT.
THE WHOLE POINT OF THE EXERCISE IS TO INTE-GRATE WITH HUMANS.
IT WILL BE A FUTURE BENEFIT, BOTH FOR US *AND* HUMAN SOCIETY.
THOUGH I CAN'T ENVISION ANY SORT OF FUTURE FOR YOU...
MUTTER...
IN ANY CASE...
WE DON'T WANT TO HAVE VAMPIRES *TRAVELING* TO THE MAINLAND.
I'D PREFER YOU KEEP YOUR ACTIVITIES *CONFINED* TO THE ISLAND.

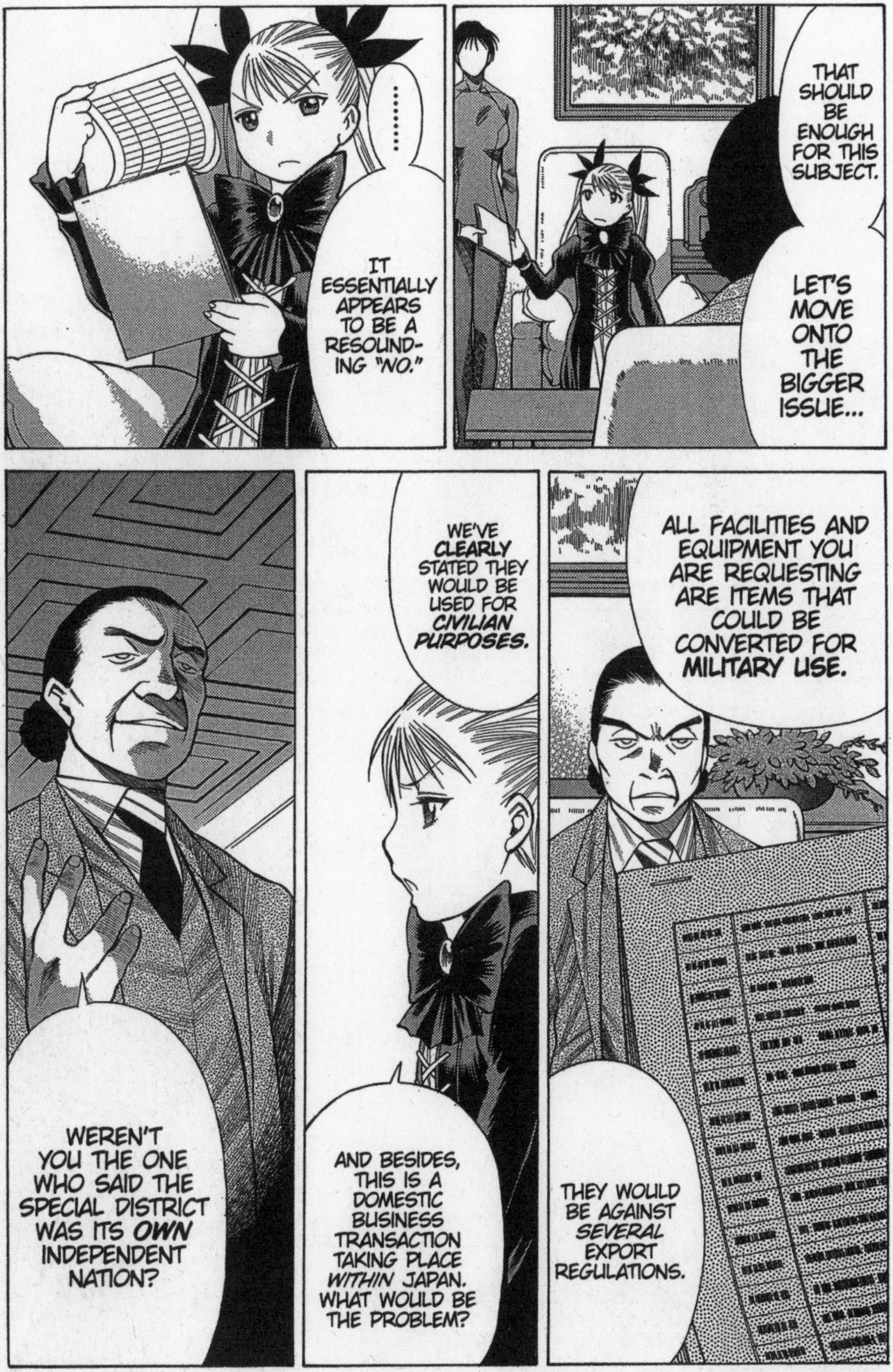
THAT SHOULD BE ENOUGH FOR THIS SUBJECT.
LET'S MOVE ONTO THE BIGGER ISSUE...
......
IT ESSENTIALLY APPEARS TO BE A RESOUNDING- ING "NO."
ALL FACILITIES AND EQUIPMENT YOU ARE REQUESTING ARE ITEMS THAT COULD BE CONVERTED FOR MILITARY USE.
THEY WOULD BE AGAINST SEVERAL EXPORT REGULATIONS.
WE'VE CLEARLY STATED THEY WOULD BE USED FOR CIVILIAN PURPOSES.
AND BESIDES, THIS IS A DOMESTIC BUSINESS TRANSACTION TAKING PLACE WITHIN JAPAN. WHAT WOULD BE THE PROBLEM?
WEREN'T YOU THE ONE WHO SAID THE SPECIAL DISTRICT WAS ITS OWN INDEPENDENT NATION?

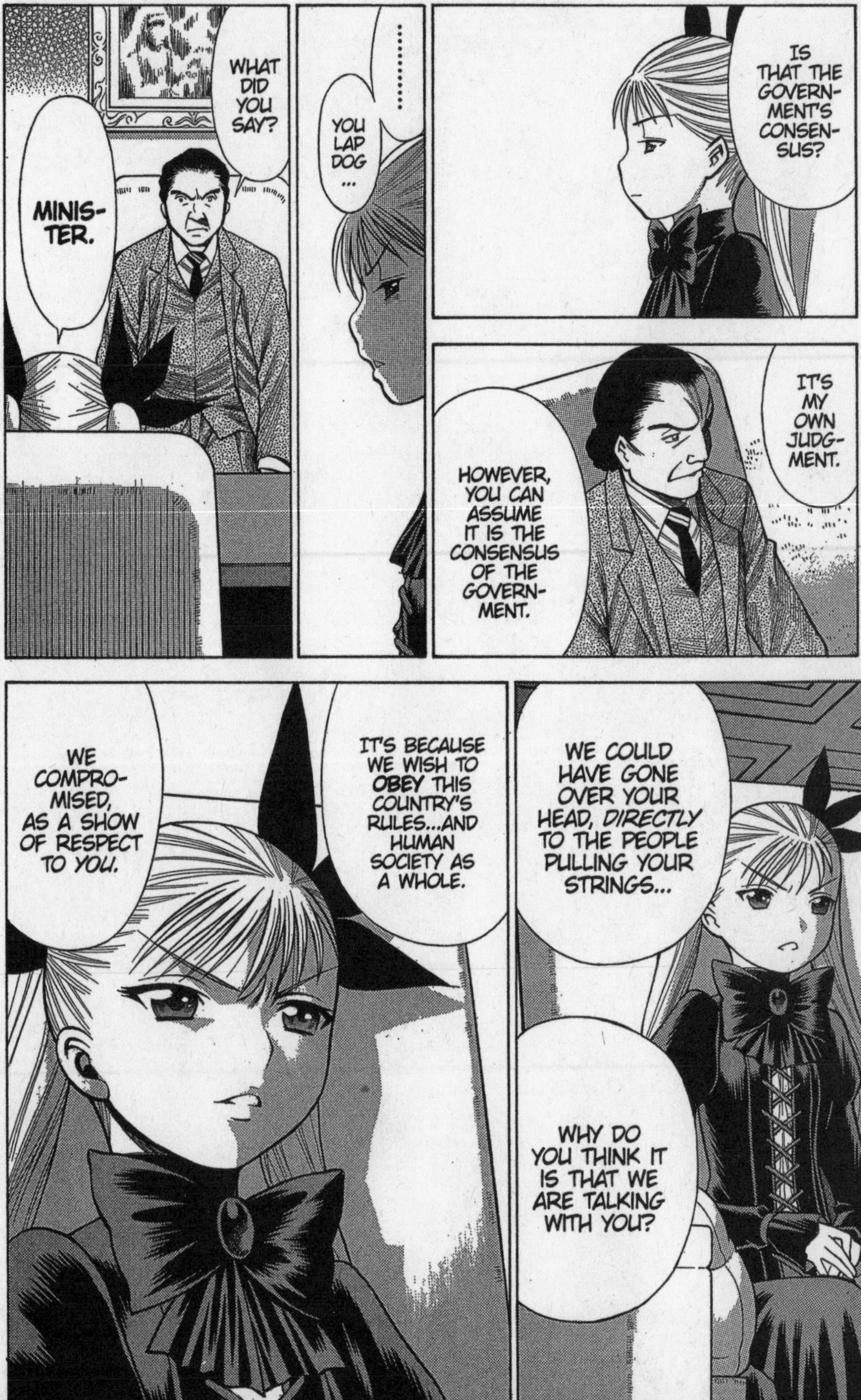
IS THAT THE GOVERNMENT'S CONSENSUS?
IT'S MY OWN JUDGMENT.
HOWEVER, YOU CAN ASSUME IT IS THE CONSENSUS OF THE GOVERNMENT.
......
YOU LAP DOG...
WHAT DID YOU SAY?
MINISTER.
WE COULD HAVE GONE OVER YOUR HEAD, *DIRECTLY* TO THE PEOPLE PULLING YOUR STRINGS...
WHY DO YOU THINK IT IS THAT WE ARE TALKING WITH YOU?
IT'S BECAUSE WE WISH TO **OBEY** THIS COUNTRY'S RULES...AND HUMAN SOCIETY AS A WHOLE.
WE COMPROMISED, AS A SHOW OF RESPECT TO *YOU*.

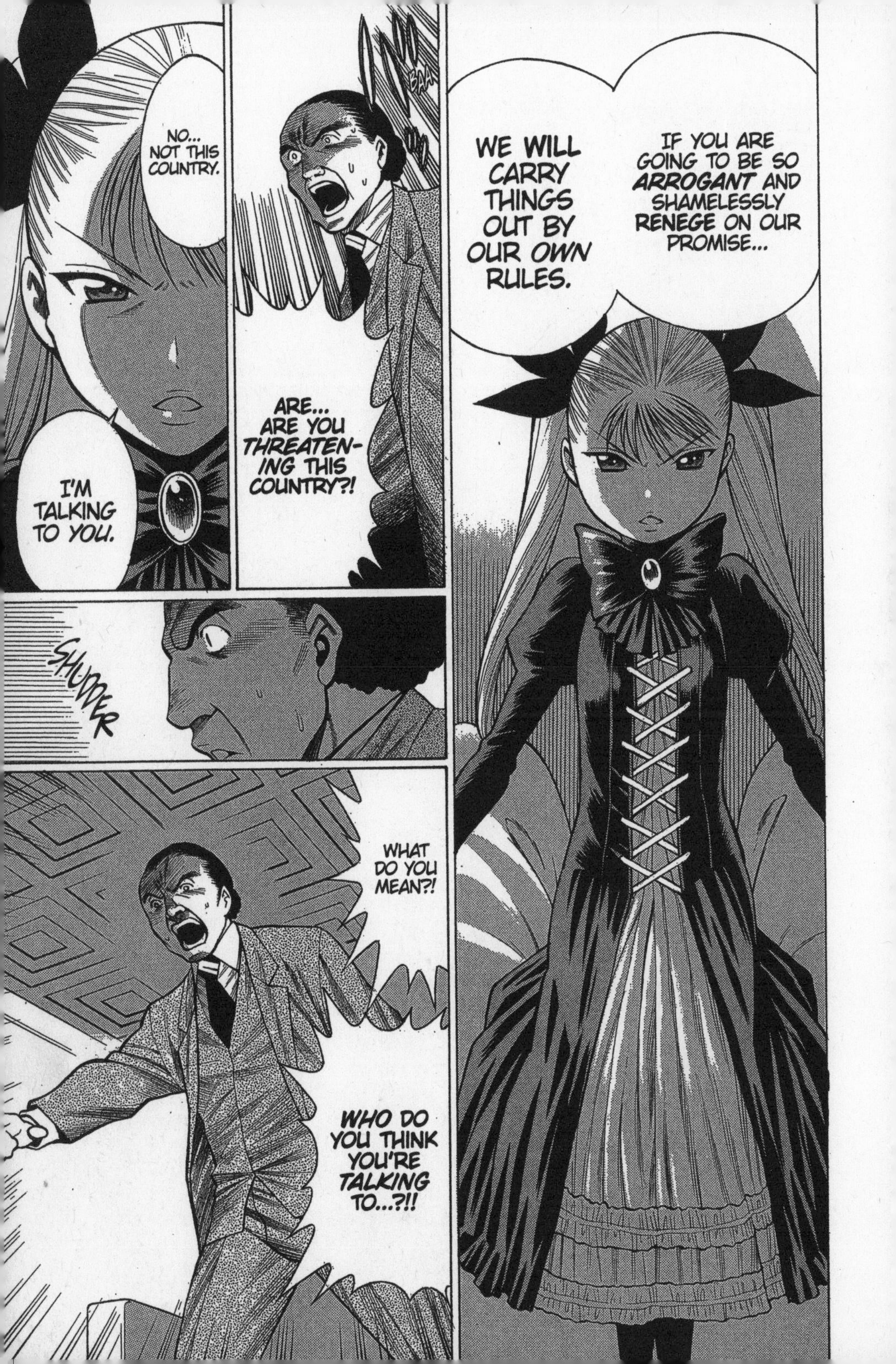
IF YOU ARE GOING TO BE SO ARROGANT AND SHAMELESSLY RENEGE ON OUR PROMISE...
WE WILL CARRY THINGS OUT BY OUR OWN RULES.
ARE... ARE YOU THREATENING THIS COUNTRY?!
NO... NOT THIS COUNTRY.
I'M TALKING TO YOU.
SHUDDER
WHAT DO YOU MEAN?!
WHO DO YOU THINK YOU'RE TALKING TO...?!!

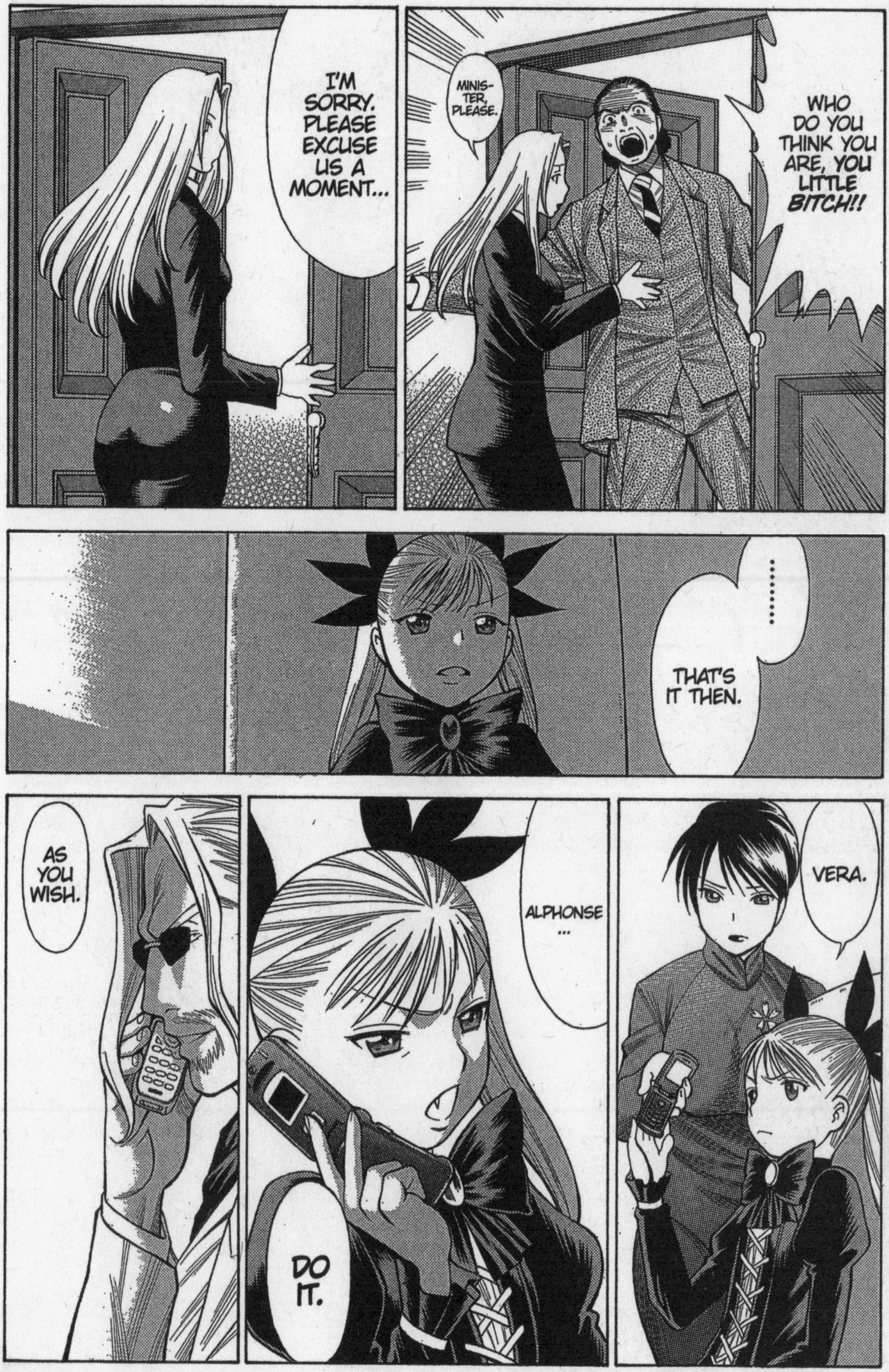
WHO DO YOU THINK YOU ARE, YOU LITTLE *BITCH!!*
MINISTER, PLEASE.
I'M SORRY. PLEASE EXCUSE US A MOMENT...
......
THAT'S IT THEN.
VERA.
ALPHONSE ...
DO IT.
AS YOU WISH.

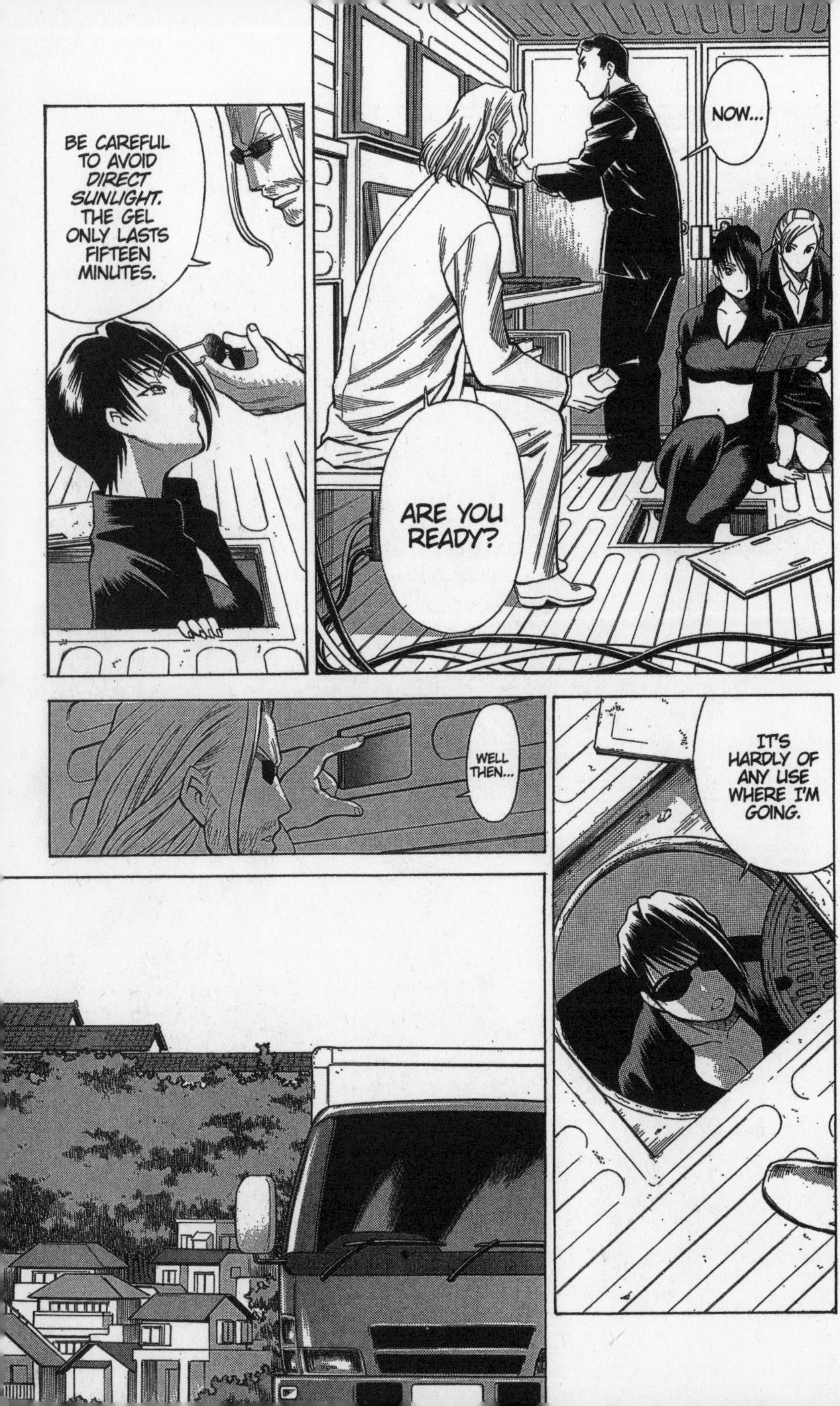

NOW...
ARE YOU READY?
BE CAREFUL TO AVOID DIRECT SUNLIGHT. THE GEL ONLY LASTS FIFTEEN MINUTES.
IT'S HARDLY OF ANY USE WHERE I'M GOING.
WELL THEN...

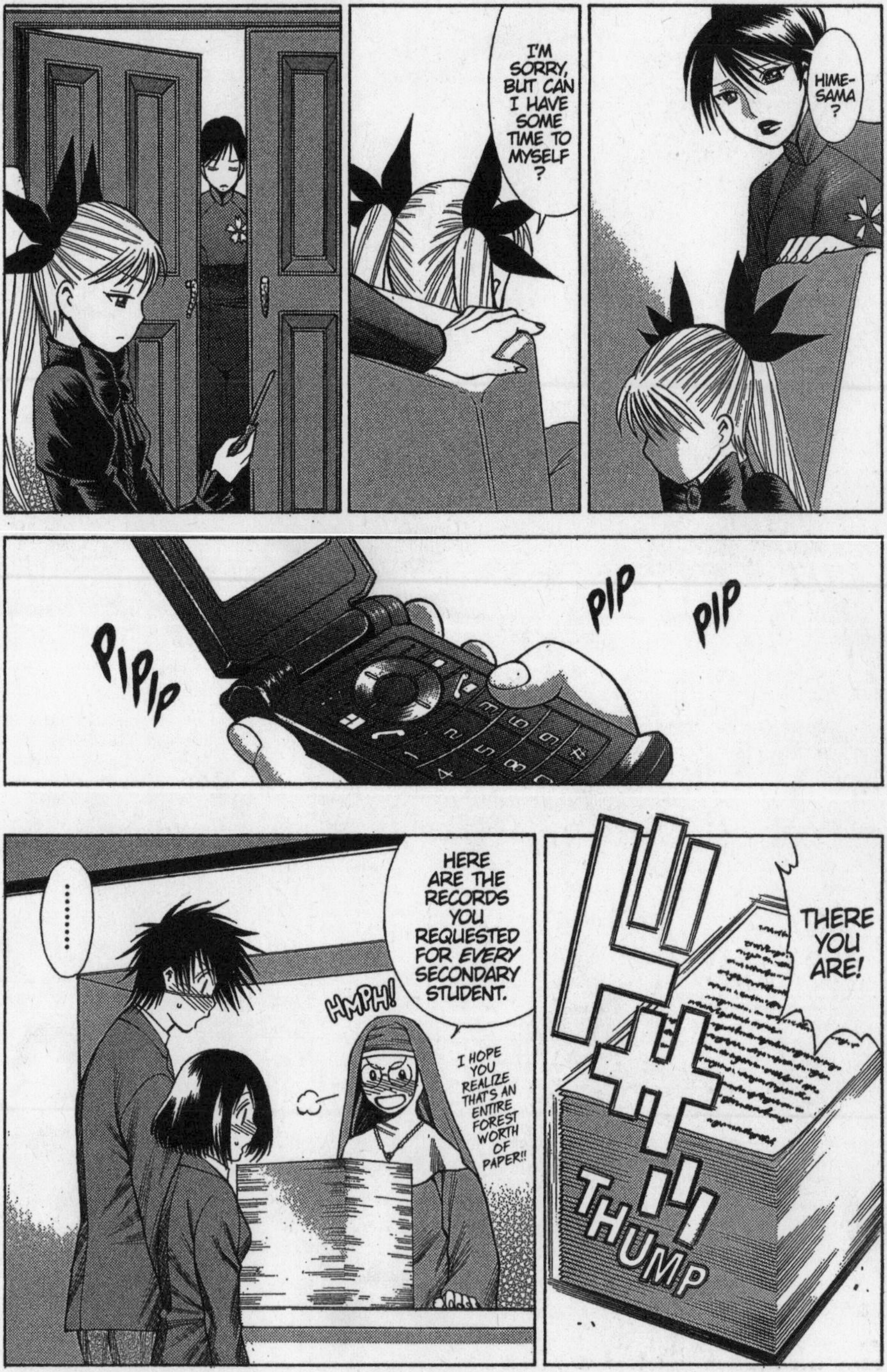
HIME-SAMA?
I'M SORRY, BUT CAN I HAVE SOME TIME TO MYSELF?
PIP
PIP
PIPIP
THERE YOU ARE!
THUMP
HERE ARE THE RECORDS YOU REQUESTED FOR *EVERY* SECONDARY STUDENT.
HMPH!
I HOPE YOU REALIZE THAT'S AN ENTIRE FOREST WORTH OF PAPER!!
....

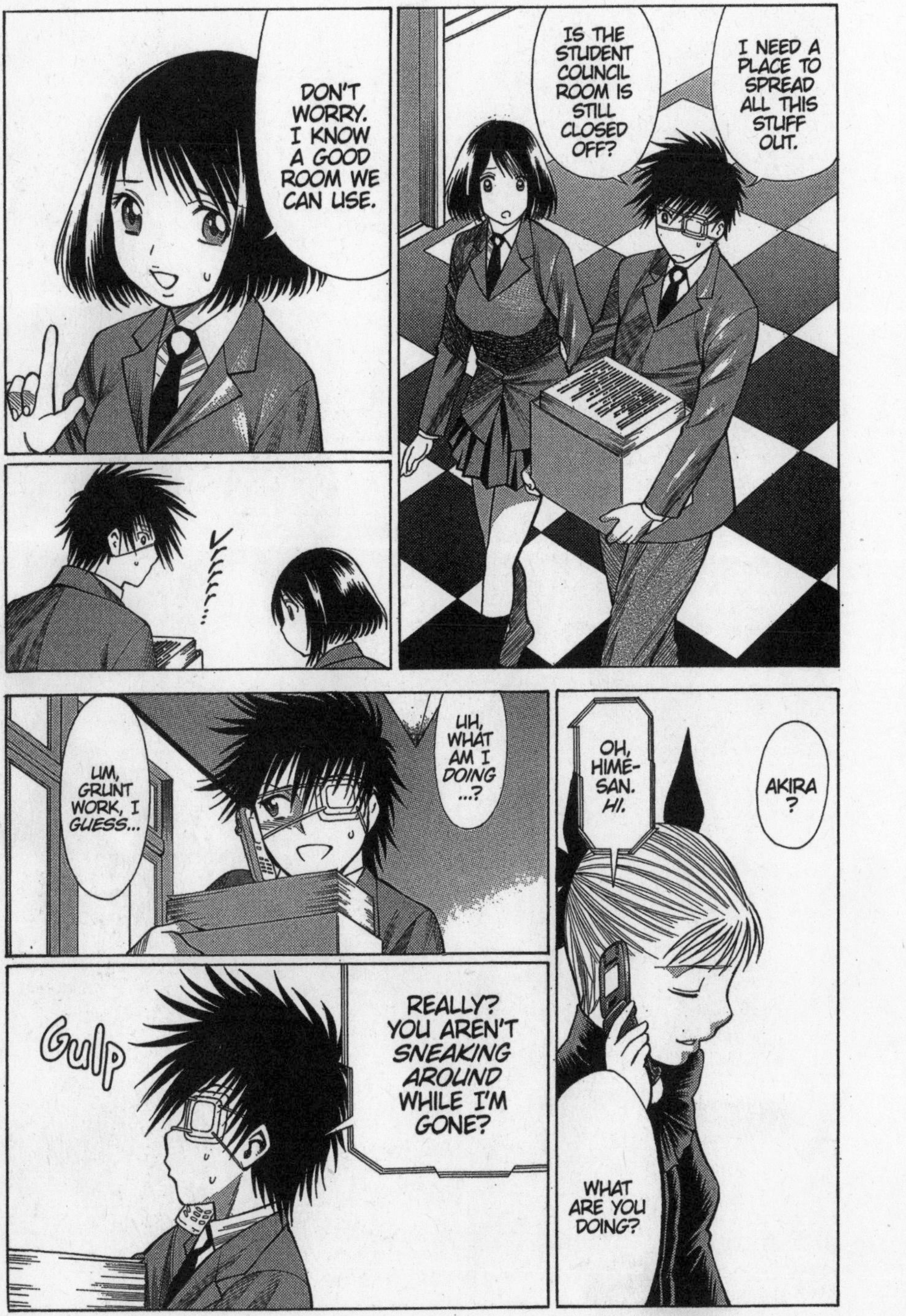
I NEED A PLACE TO SPREAD ALL THIS STUFF OUT.
IS THE STUDENT COUNCIL ROOM IS STILL CLOSED OFF?
DON'T WORRY. I KNOW A GOOD ROOM WE CAN USE.
AKIRA?
OH, HIME-SAN. HI.
WHAT ARE YOU DOING?
UH, WHAT AM I DOING ...?
UM, GRUNT WORK, I GUESS...
REALLY? YOU AREN'T SNEAKING AROUND WHILE I'M GONE?
Gulp

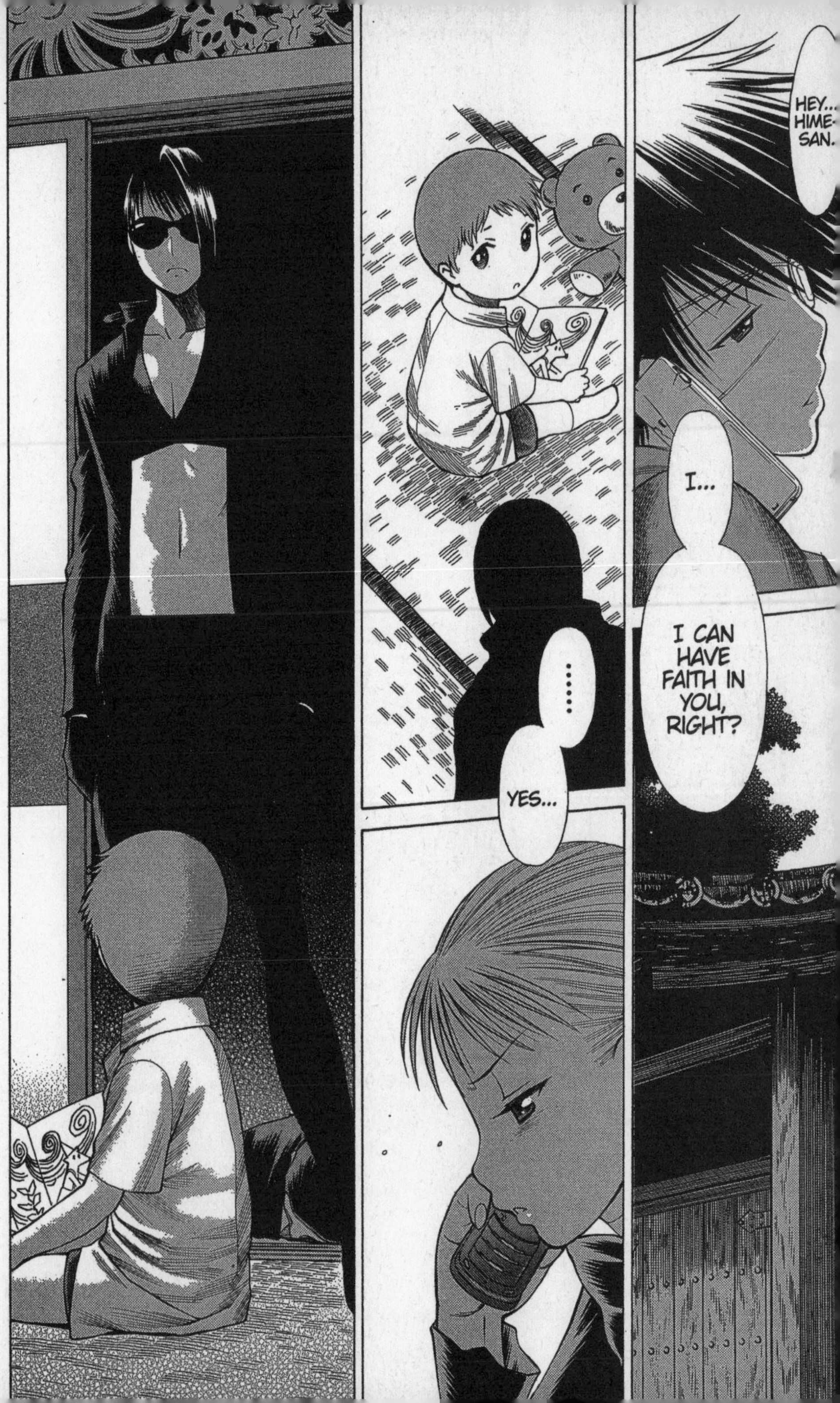
HEY... HIME-SAN.
I...
I CAN HAVE FAITH IN YOU, RIGHT?
......
YES...

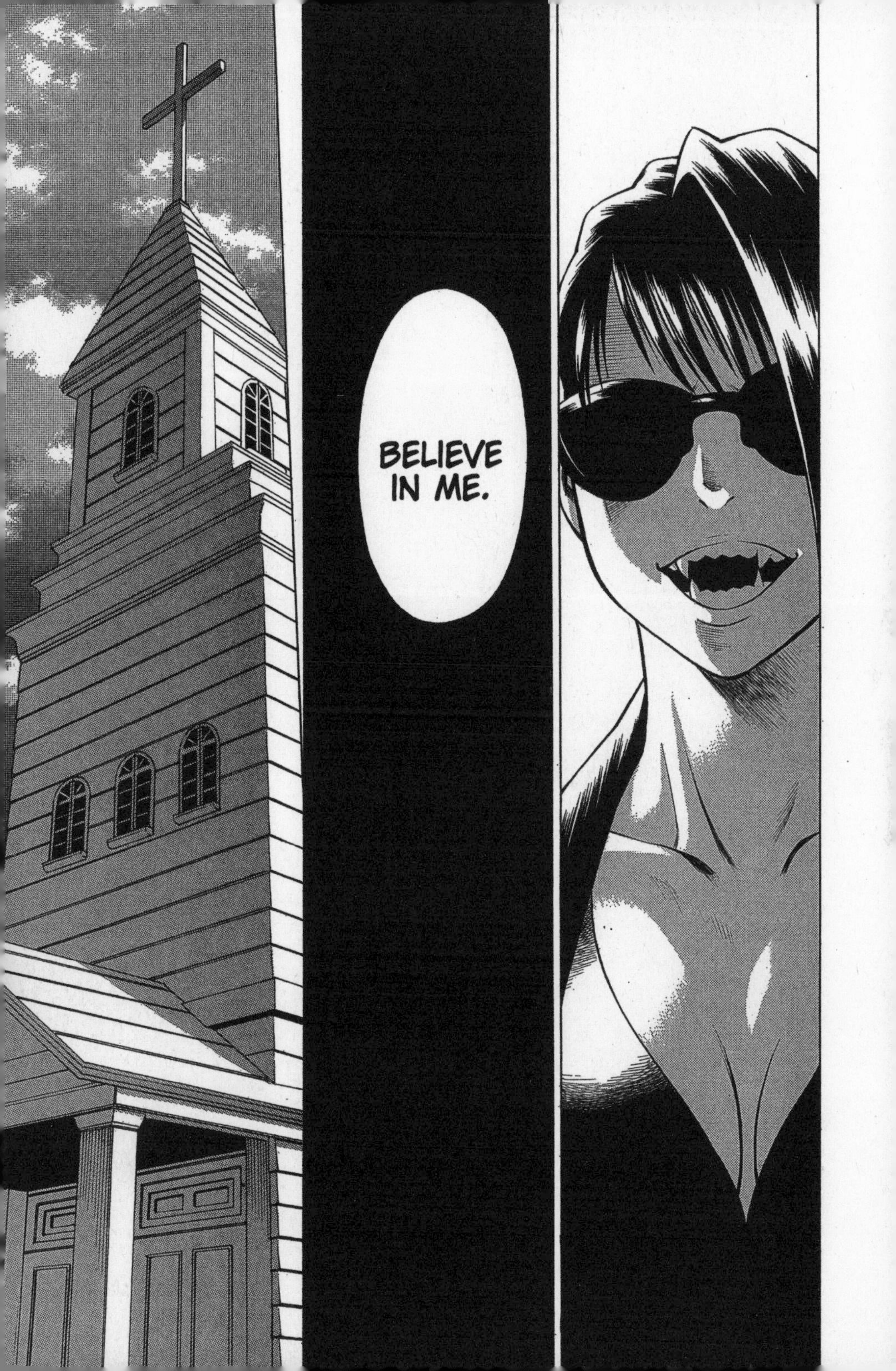
BELIEVE IN ME.

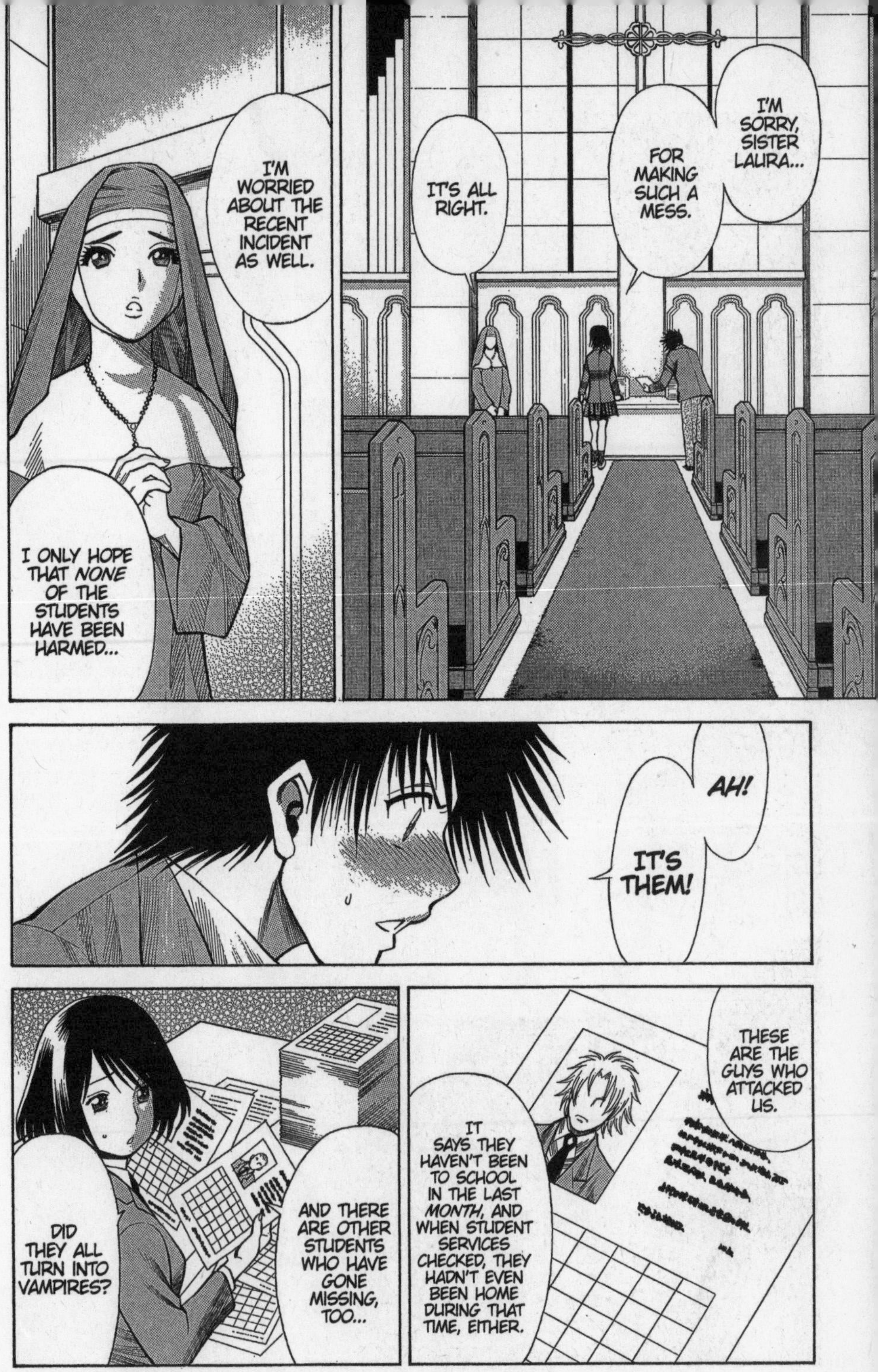
I'M SORRY, SISTER LAURA...
FOR MAKING SUCH A MESS.
IT'S ALL RIGHT.
I'M WORRIED ABOUT THE RECENT INCIDENT AS WELL.
I ONLY HOPE THAT *NONE* OF THE STUDENTS HAVE BEEN HARMED...
AH!
IT'S THEM!
THESE ARE THE GUYS WHO ATTACKED US.
IT SAYS THEY HAVEN'T BEEN TO SCHOOL IN THE LAST *MONTH*, AND WHEN STUDENT SERVICES CHECKED, THEY HADN'T EVEN BEEN HOME DURING THAT TIME, EITHER.
AND THERE ARE OTHER STUDENTS WHO HAVE GONE MISSING, TOO...
DID THEY ALL TURN INTO VAMPIRES?

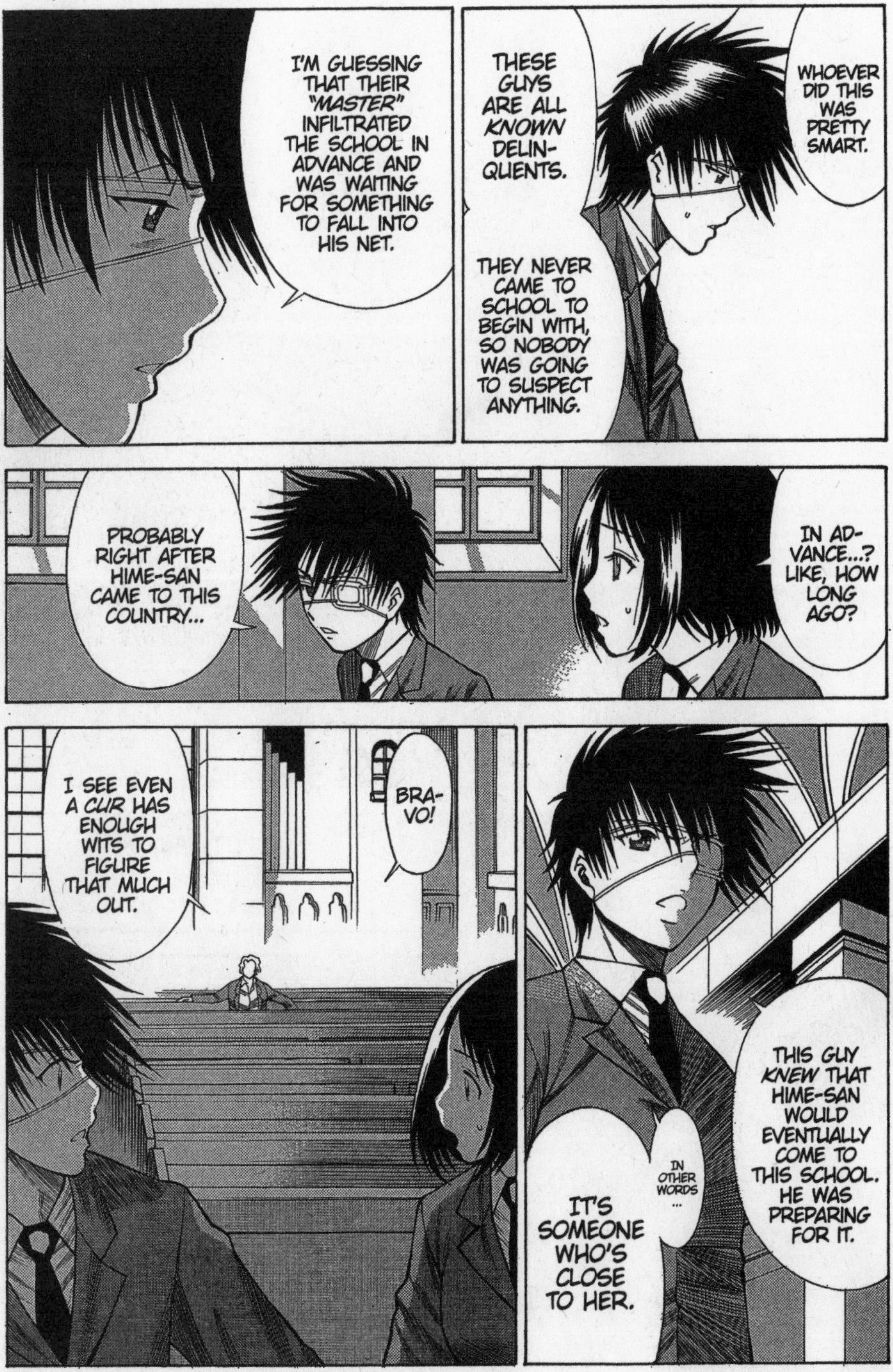
WHOEVER DID THIS WAS PRETTY SMART.
THESE GUYS ARE ALL *KNOWN* DELIN-QUENTS.
THEY NEVER CAME TO SCHOOL TO BEGIN WITH, SO NOBODY WAS GOING TO SUSPECT ANYTHING.
I'M GUESSING THAT THEIR *"MASTER"* INFILTRATED THE SCHOOL IN ADVANCE AND WAS WAITING FOR SOMETHING TO FALL INTO HIS NET.
IN AD-VANCE...? LIKE, HOW LONG AGO?
PROBABLY RIGHT AFTER HIME-SAN CAME TO THIS COUNTRY...
THIS GUY *KNEW* THAT HIME-SAN WOULD EVENTUALLY COME TO THIS SCHOOL. HE WAS PREPARING FOR IT.
IN OTHER WORDS ...
IT'S SOMEONE WHO'S CLOSE TO HER.
BRA-VO!
I SEE EVEN A *CUR* HAS ENOUGH WITS TO FIGURE THAT MUCH OUT.

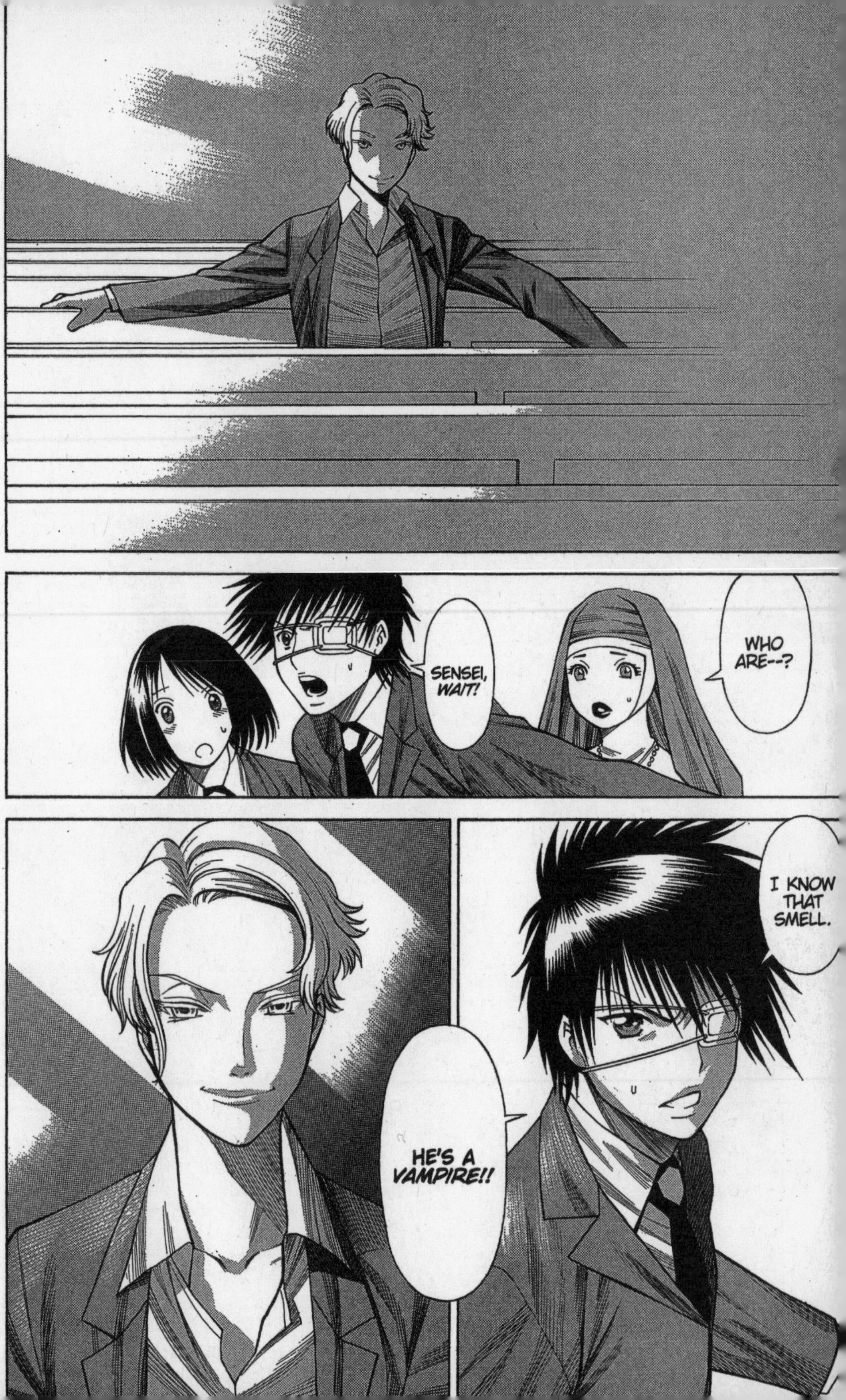
WHO ARE--?
SENSEI, WAIT!
I KNOW THAT SMELL.
HE'S A VAMPIRE!!

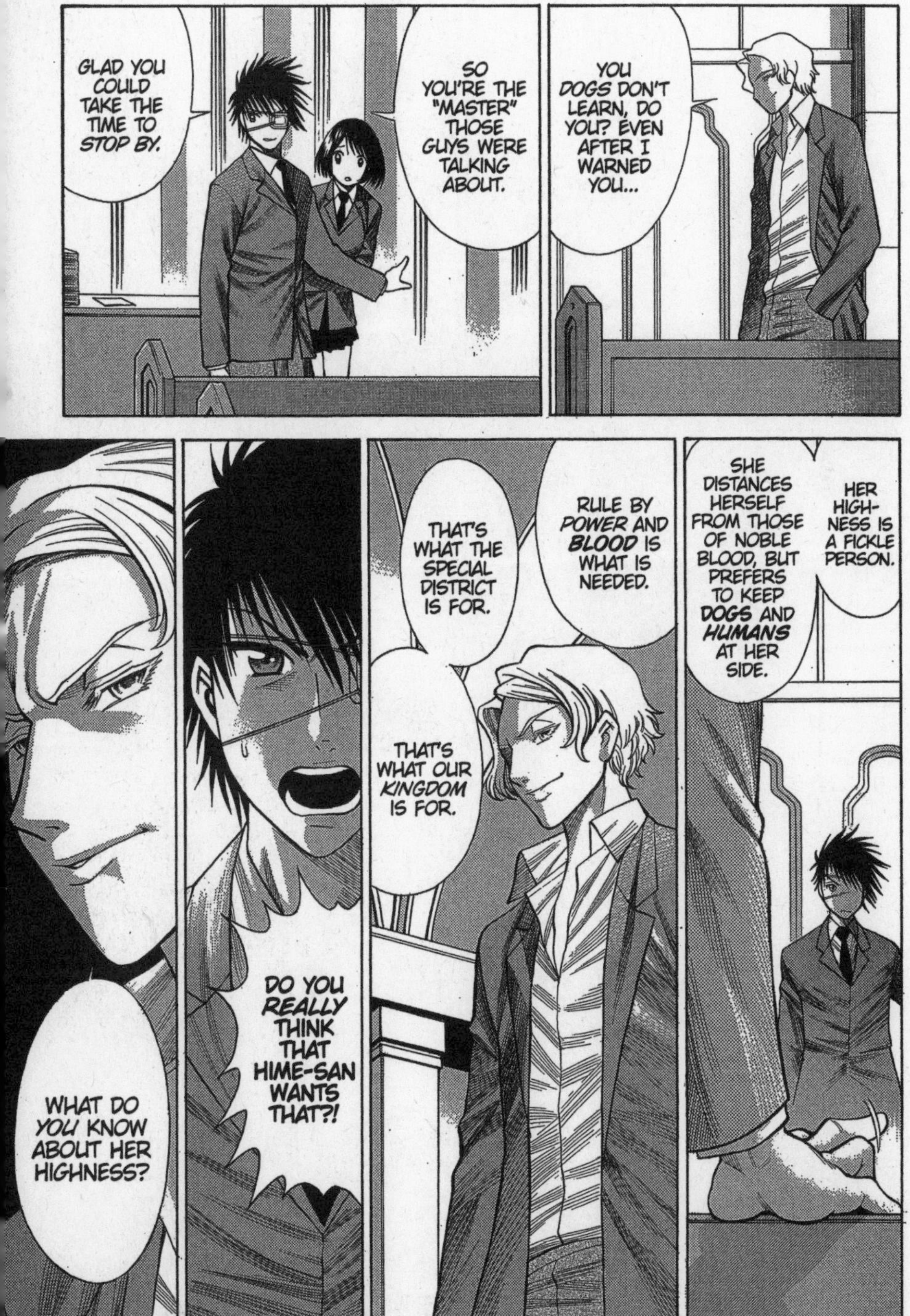
YOU DOGS DON'T LEARN, DO YOU? EVEN AFTER I WARNED YOU...
SO YOU'RE THE "MASTER" THOSE GUYS WERE TALKING ABOUT.
GLAD YOU COULD TAKE THE TIME TO STOP BY.
HER HIGHNESS IS A FICKLE PERSON.
SHE DISTANCES HERSELF FROM THOSE OF NOBLE BLOOD, BUT PREFERS TO KEEP DOGS AND HUMANS AT HER SIDE.
RULE BY POWER AND BLOOD IS WHAT IS NEEDED.
THAT'S WHAT THE SPECIAL DISTRICT IS FOR.
THAT'S WHAT OUR KINGDOM IS FOR.
DO YOU REALLY THINK THAT HIME-SAN WANTS THAT?!
WHAT DO YOU KNOW ABOUT HER HIGHNESS?

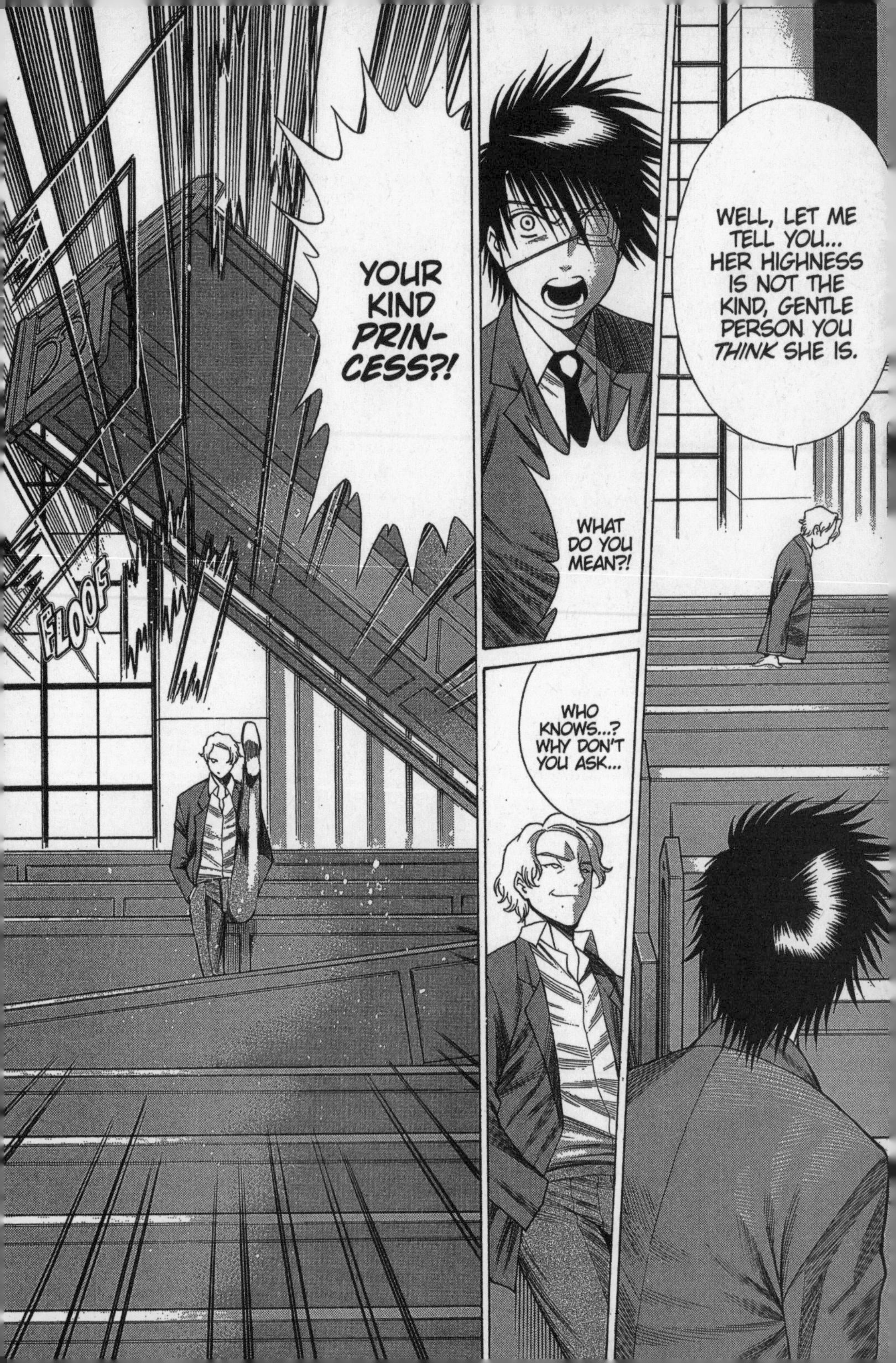
YOUR KIND PRIN- CESS?!
FLOOF
WELL, LET ME TELL YOU... HER HIGHNESS IS NOT THE KIND, GENTLE PERSON YOU *THINK* SHE IS.
WHAT DO YOU MEAN?!
WHO KNOWS...? WHY DON'T YOU ASK...

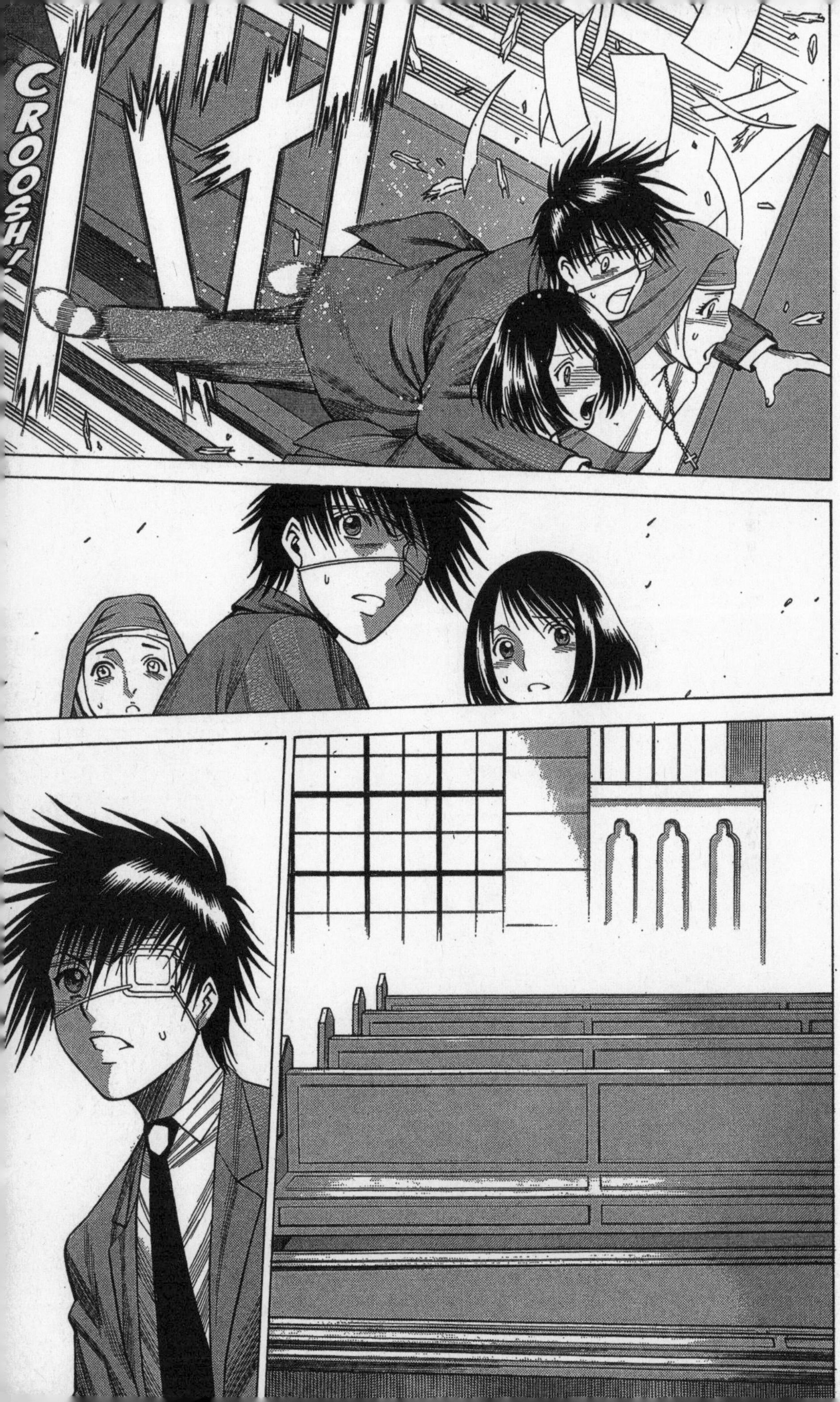
CROOOSH!

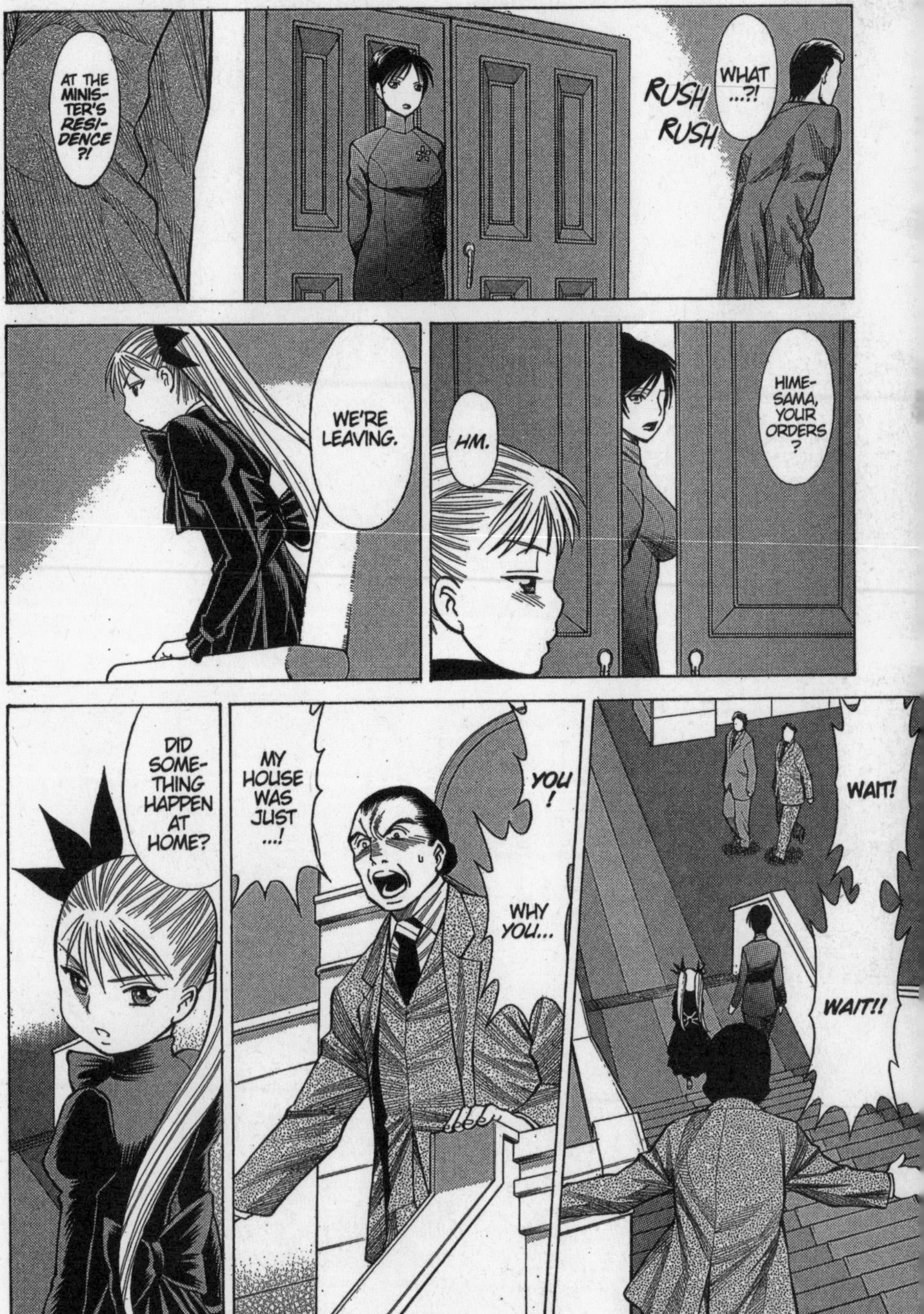
WHAT ...?!
RUSH RUSH
AT THE MINIS-TER'S RESI-DENCE ?!
HIME-SAMA, YOUR ORDERS ?
HM.
WE'RE LEAVING.
WAIT!
WAIT!!
YOU !
WHY YOU...
MY HOUSE WAS JUST ...!
DID SOME-THING HAPPEN AT HOME?

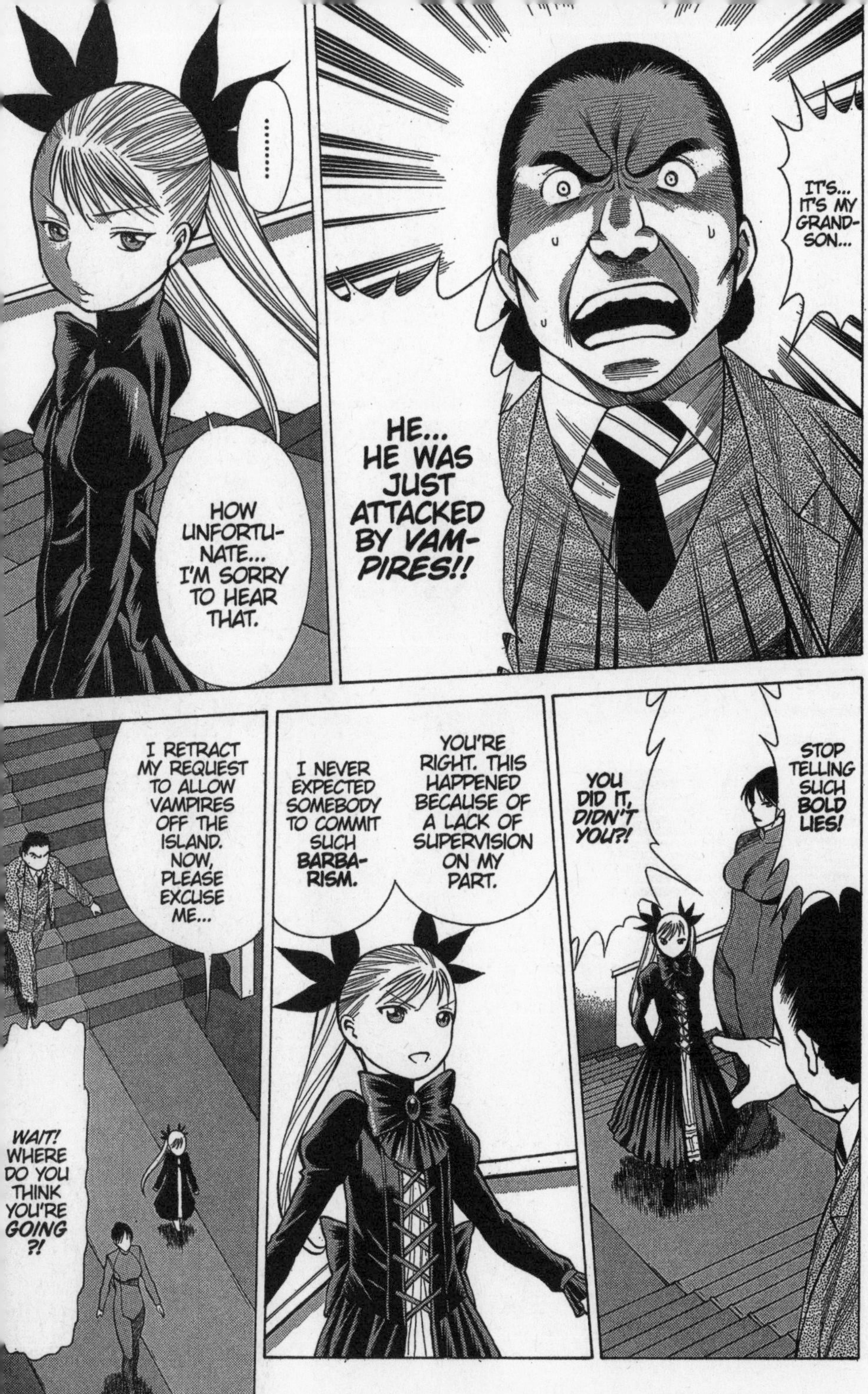

IT'S... IT'S MY GRANDSON...
HE... HE WAS JUST ATTACKED BY VAMPIRES!!
......
HOW UNFORTUNATE... I'M SORRY TO HEAR THAT.
STOP TELLING SUCH BOLD LIES!
YOU DID IT, DIDN'T YOU?!
YOU'RE RIGHT. THIS HAPPENED BECAUSE OF A LACK OF SUPERVISION ON MY PART.
I NEVER EXPECTED SOMEBODY TO COMMIT SUCH BARBARISM.
I RETRACT MY REQUEST TO ALLOW VAMPIRES OFF THE ISLAND. NOW, PLEASE EXCUSE ME...
WAIT! WHERE DO YOU THINK YOU'RE GOING?!

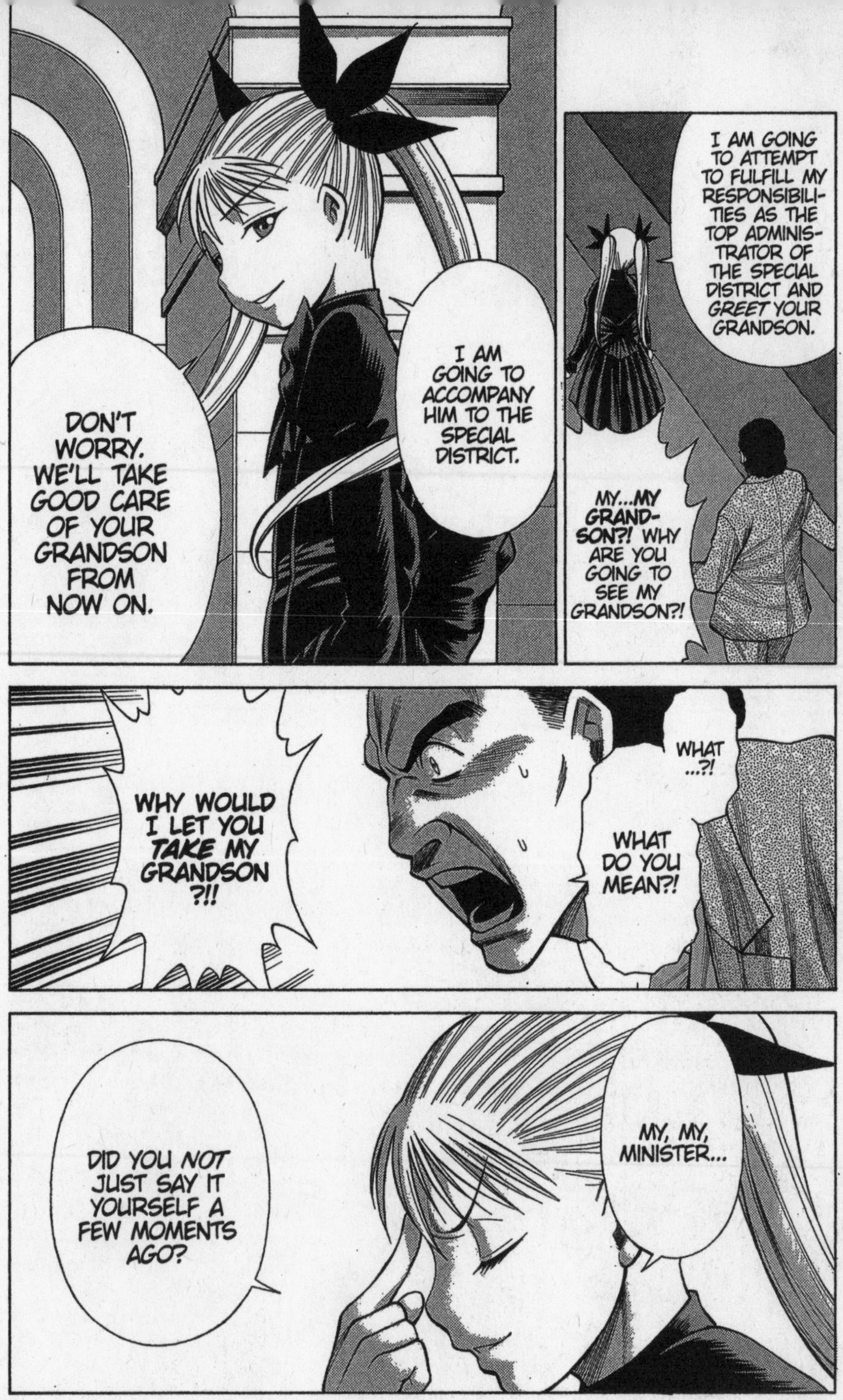
I AM GOING TO ATTEMPT TO FULFILL MY RESPONSIBILI-TIES AS THE TOP ADMINIS-TRATOR OF THE SPECIAL DISTRICT AND *GREET* YOUR GRANDSON.
MY...MY GRAND-SON?! WHY ARE YOU GOING TO SEE MY GRANDSON?!
I AM GOING TO ACCOMPANY HIM TO THE SPECIAL DISTRICT.
DON'T WORRY. WE'LL TAKE GOOD CARE OF YOUR GRANDSON FROM NOW ON.
WHAT ...?!
WHAT DO YOU MEAN?!
WHY WOULD I LET YOU *TAKE* MY GRANDSON ?!!
MY, MY, MINISTER...
DID YOU *NOT* JUST SAY IT YOURSELF A FEW MOMENTS AGO?

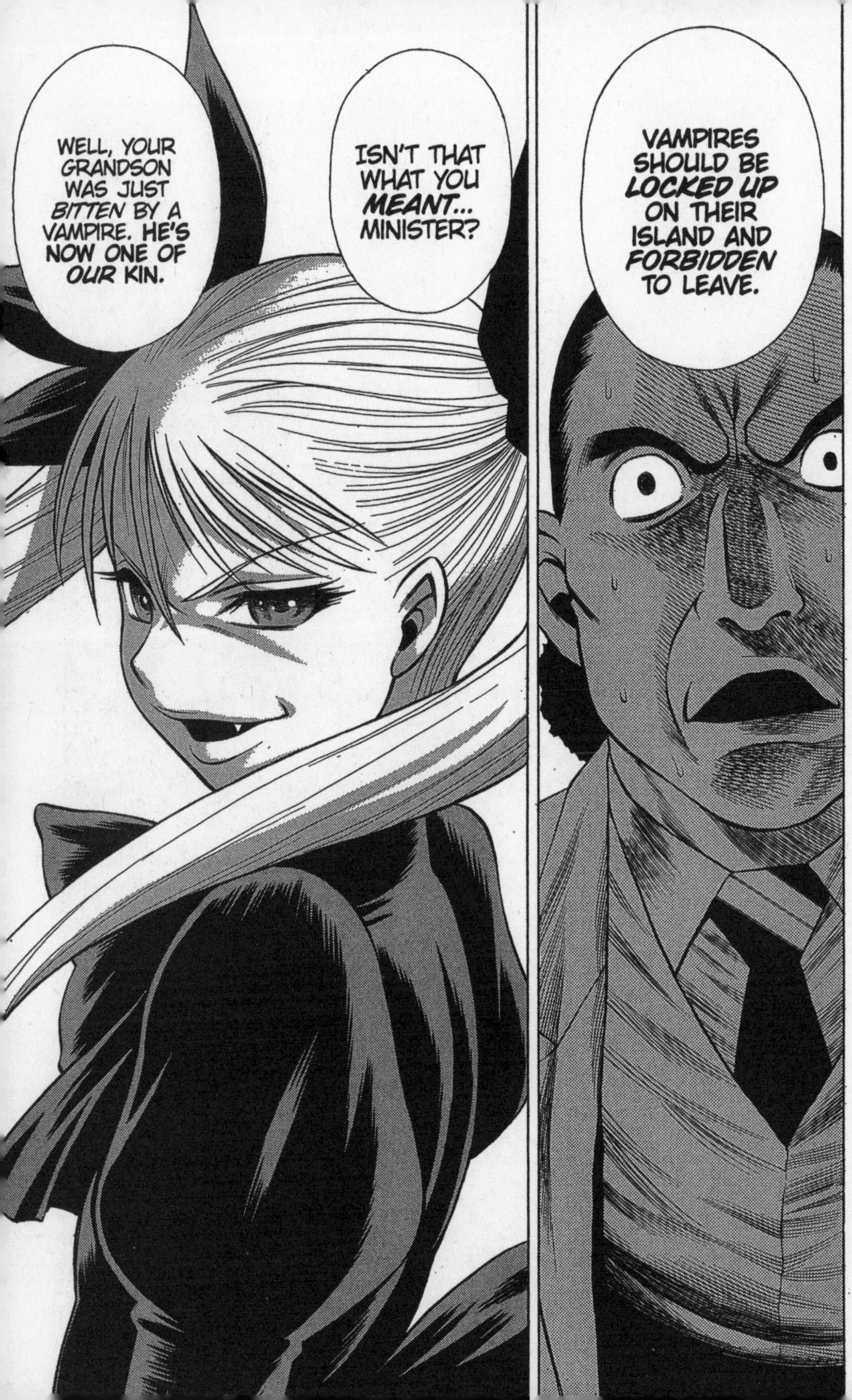
VAMPIRES SHOULD BE *LOCKED UP* ON THEIR ISLAND AND *FORBIDDEN* TO LEAVE.
WELL, YOUR GRANDSON WAS JUST *BITTEN* BY A VAMPIRE. HE'S NOW ONE OF *OUR* KIN.
ISN'T THAT WHAT YOU *MEANT*... MINISTER?

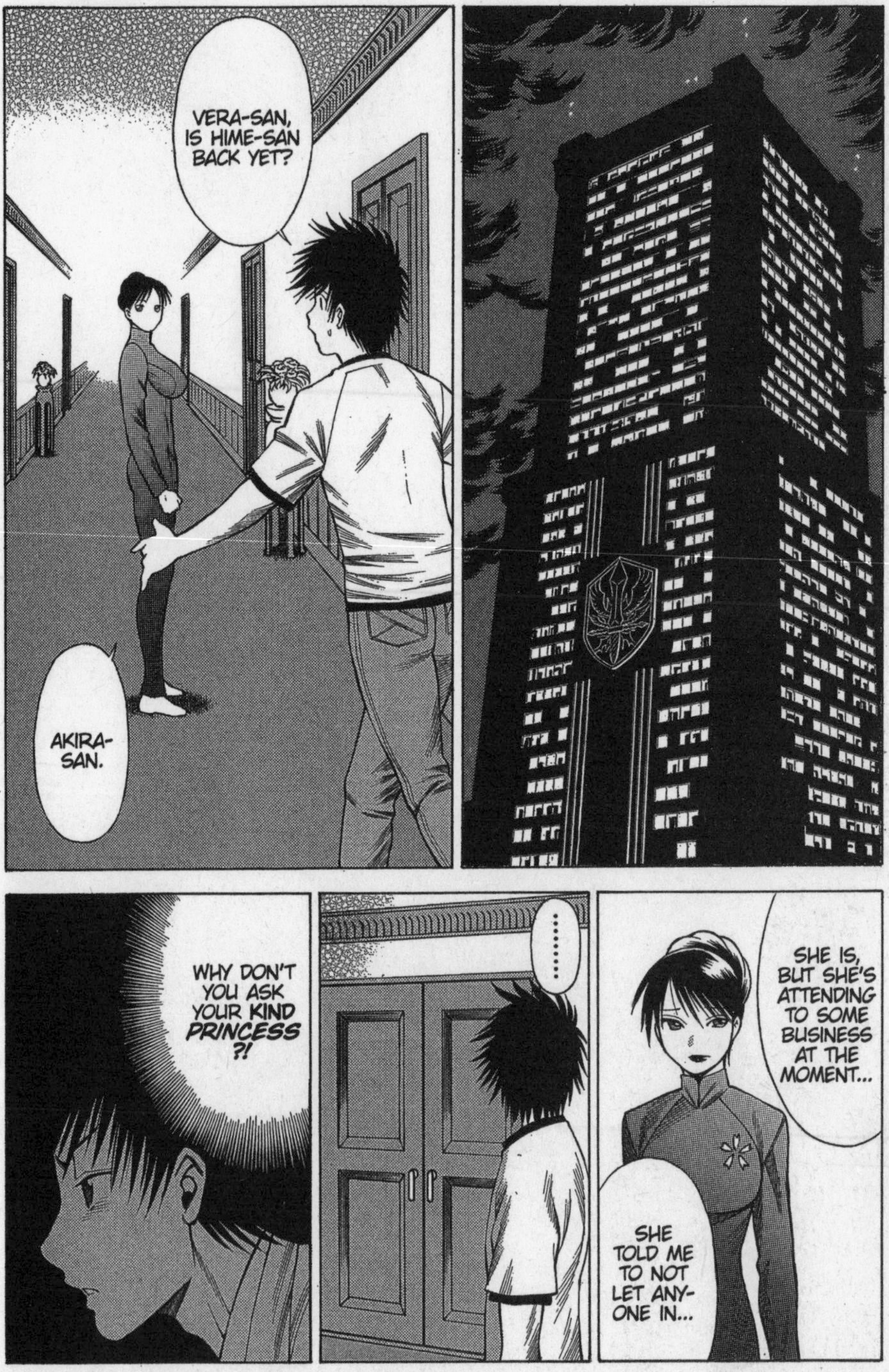
VERA-SAN, IS HIME-SAN BACK YET?
AKIRA-SAN.
SHE IS, BUT SHE'S ATTENDING TO SOME BUSINESS AT THE MOMENT...
SHE TOLD ME TO NOT LET ANY-ONE IN...
....
WHY DON'T YOU ASK YOUR KIND PRINCESS?!

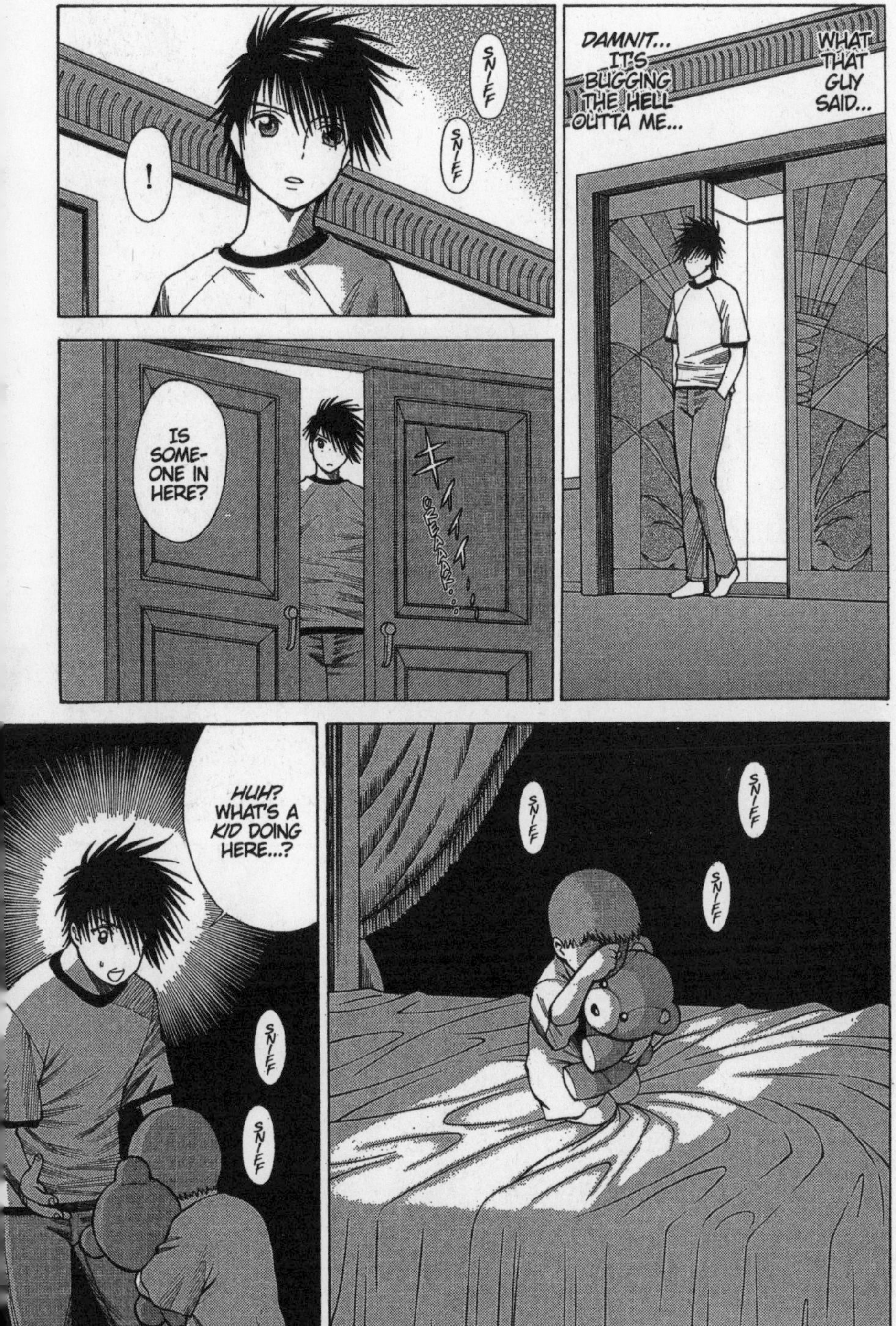
WHAT THAT GUY SAID...
DAMNIT... IT'S BUGGING THE HELL OUTTA ME...
SNIFF
SNIFF
!
CREAAAK...
IS SOMEONE IN HERE?
SNIFF
SNIFF
SNIFF
HUH? WHAT'S A KID DOING HERE...?
SNIFF
SNIFF

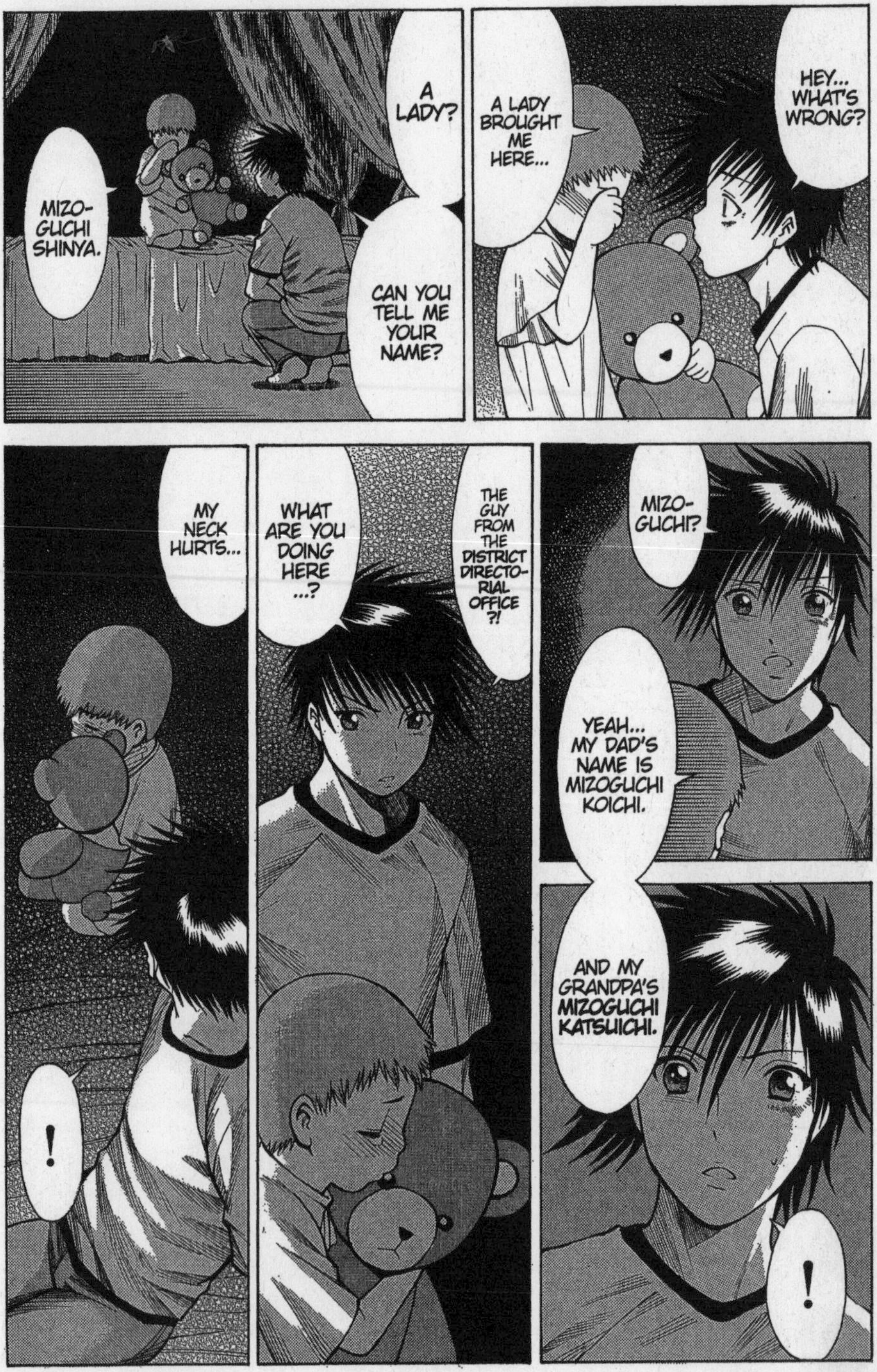
HEY... WHAT'S WRONG?
A LADY BROUGHT ME HERE...
A LADY?
CAN YOU TELL ME YOUR NAME?
MIZOGUCHI SHINYA.
MIZOGUCHI?
YEAH... MY DAD'S NAME IS MIZOGUCHI KOICHI.
AND MY GRANDPA'S MIZOGUCHI KATSUICHI.
!
THE GUY FROM THE DISTRICT DIRECTORIAL OFFICE?!
WHAT ARE YOU DOING HERE...?
MY NECK HURTS...
!

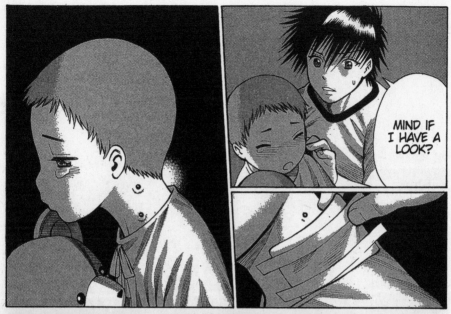

MIND IF I HAVE A LOOK?

......

I WANT TO GO HOME...

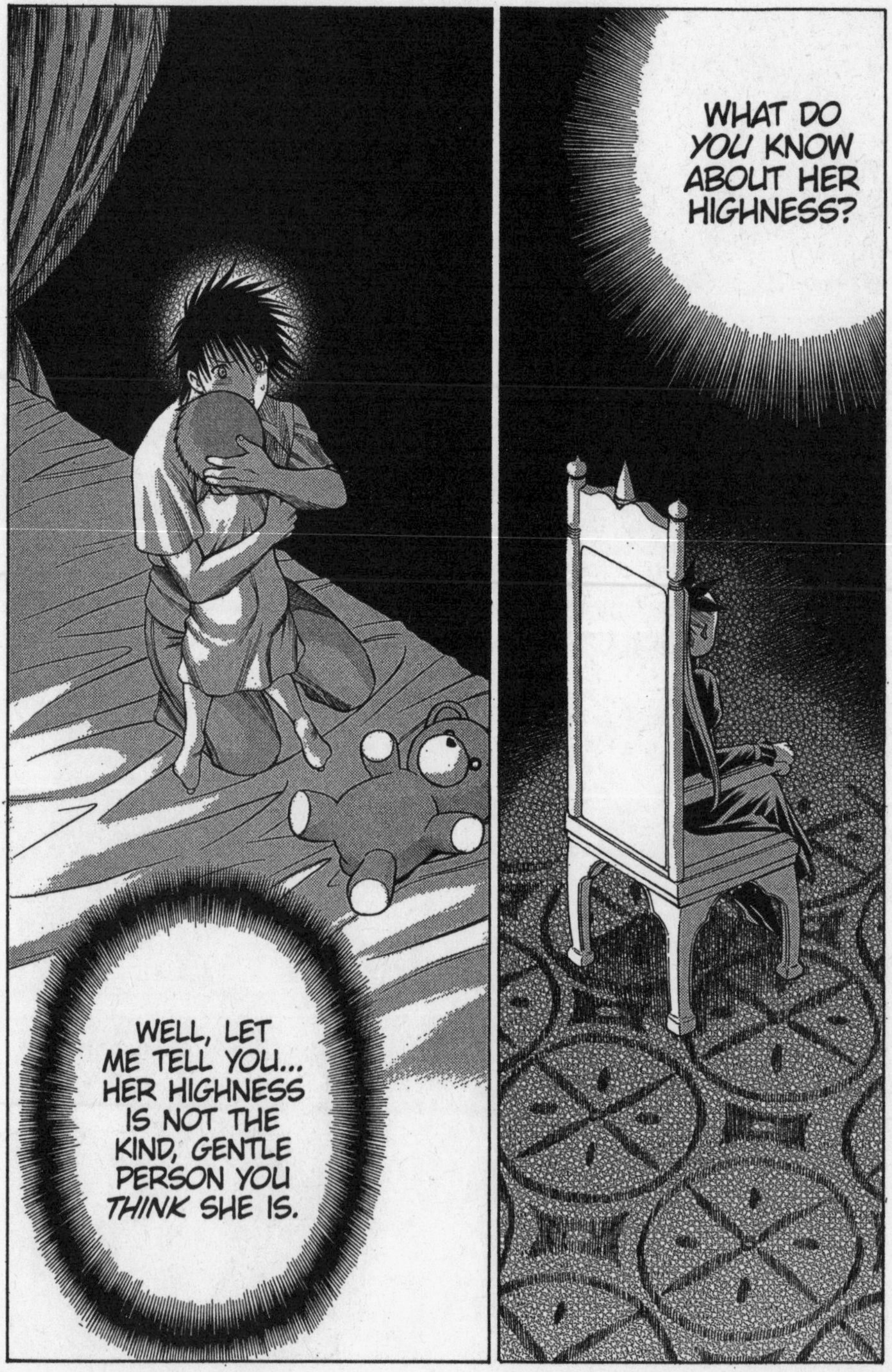
WHAT DO *YOU* KNOW ABOUT HER HIGHNESS?
WELL, LET ME TELL YOU... HER HIGHNESS IS NOT THE KIND, GENTLE PERSON YOU *THINK* SHE IS.

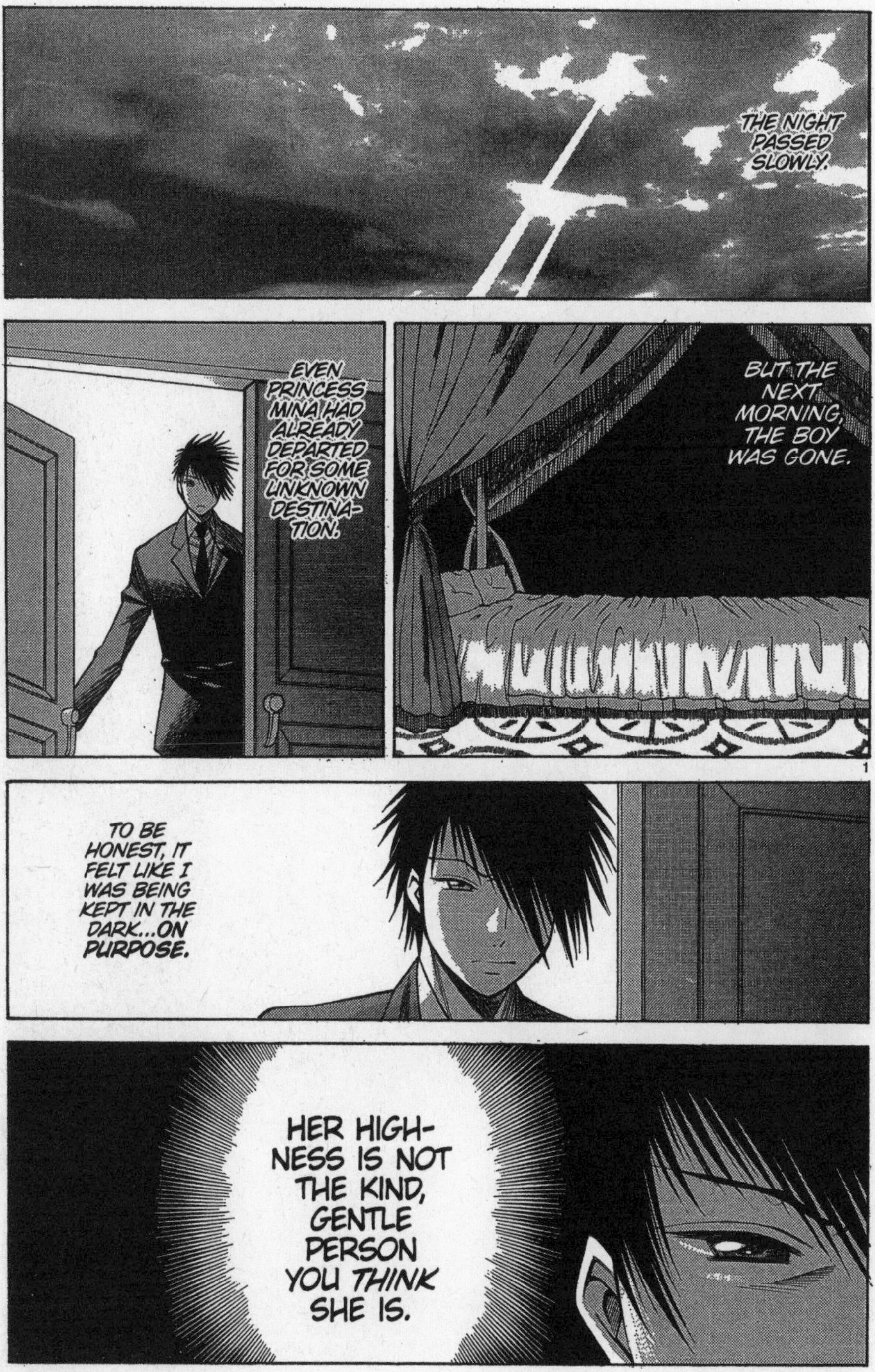
THE NIGHT PASSED SLOWLY.
BUT THE NEXT MORNING, THE BOY WAS GONE.
EVEN PRINCESS MINA HAD ALREADY DEPARTED FOR SOME UNKNOWN DESTINA-TION.
TO BE HONEST, IT FELT LIKE I WAS BEING KEPT IN THE DARK...ON PURPOSE.
HER HIGH-NESS IS NOT THE KIND, GENTLE PERSON YOU THINK SHE IS.

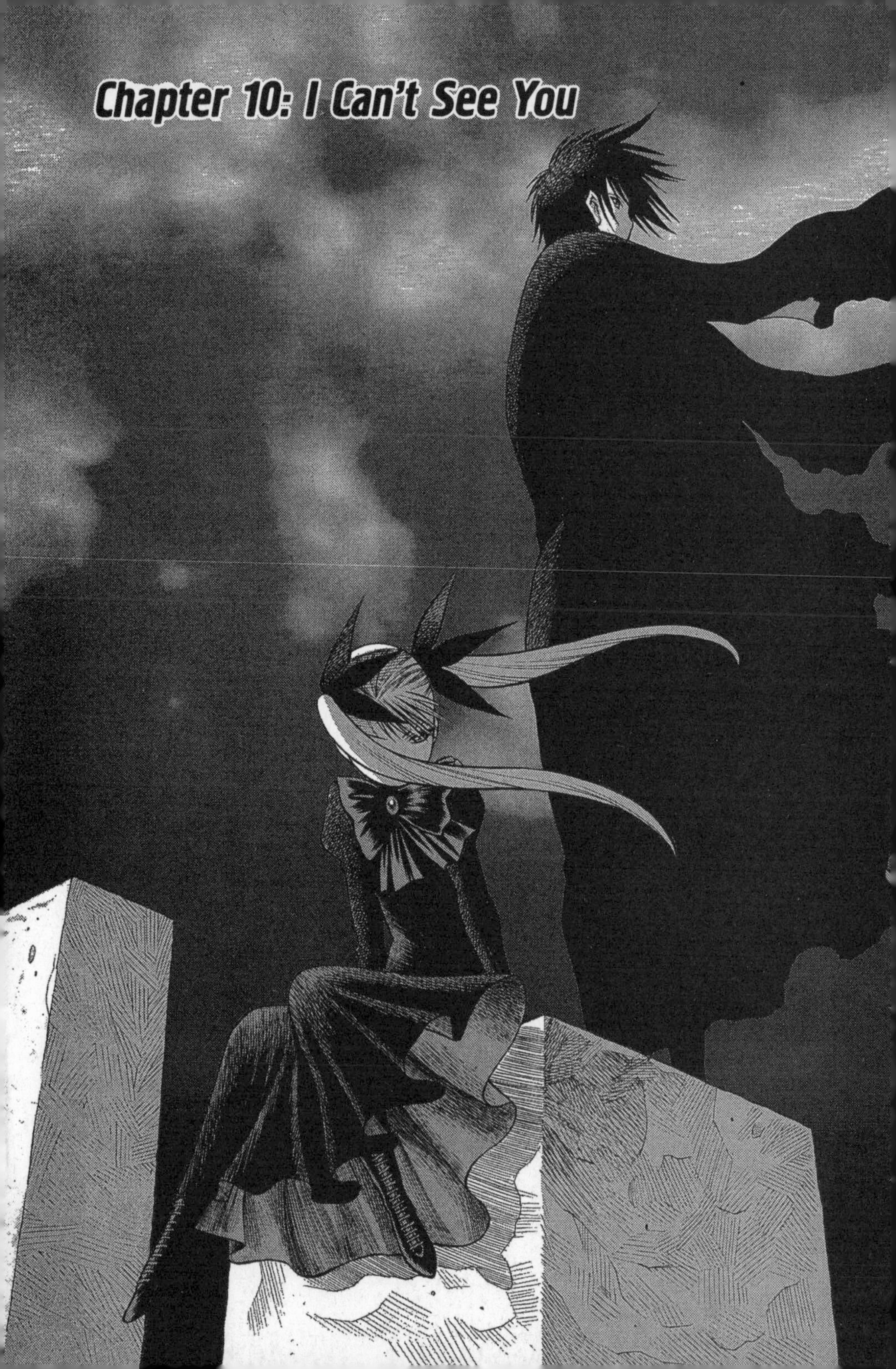
Chapter 10: I Can't See You

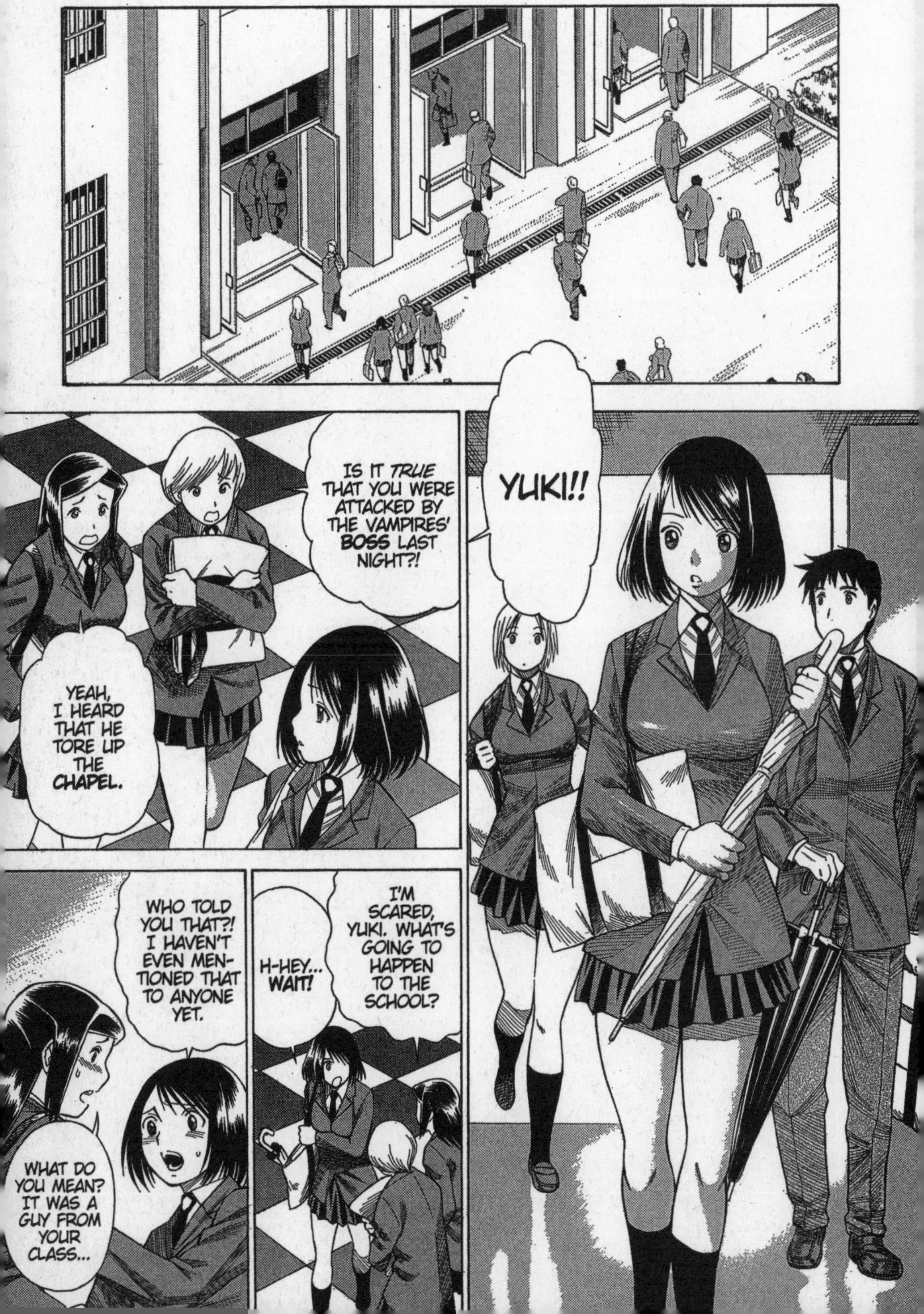
YUKI!!
IS IT *TRUE* THAT YOU WERE ATTACKED BY THE VAMPIRES' **BOSS** LAST NIGHT?!
YEAH, I HEARD THAT HE TORE UP THE **CHAPEL.**
I'M SCARED, YUKI. WHAT'S GOING TO HAPPEN TO THE SCHOOL?
H-HEY... **WAIT!**
WHO TOLD YOU THAT?! I HAVEN'T EVEN MEN-TIONED THAT TO ANYONE YET.
WHAT DO YOU MEAN? IT WAS A GUY FROM YOUR CLASS...

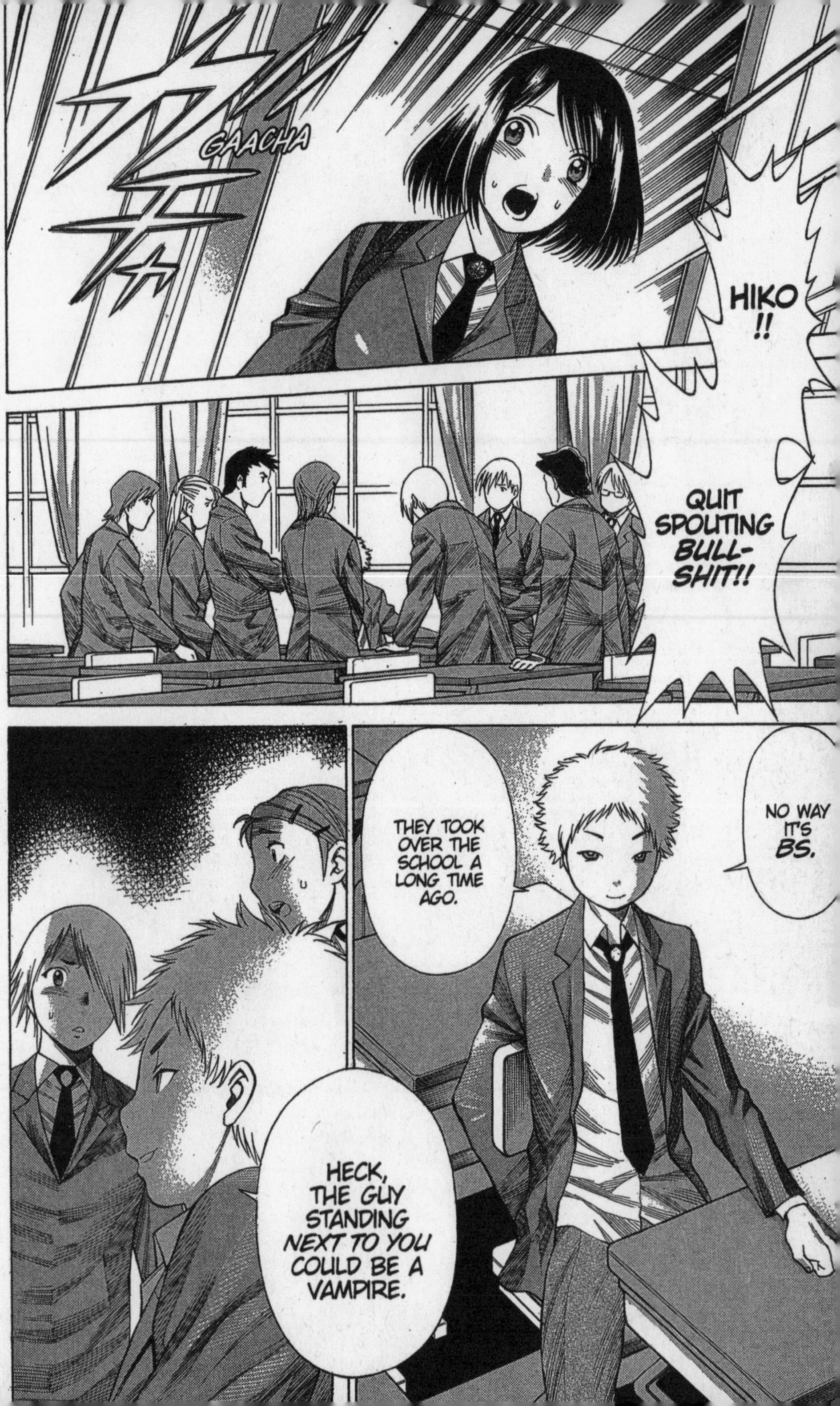
GAACHA
HIKO!!
QUIT SPOUTING *BULL-SHIT!!*
NO WAY IT'S *BS.*
THEY TOOK OVER THE SCHOOL A LONG TIME AGO.
HECK, THE GUY STANDING *NEXT TO YOU* COULD BE A VAMPIRE.

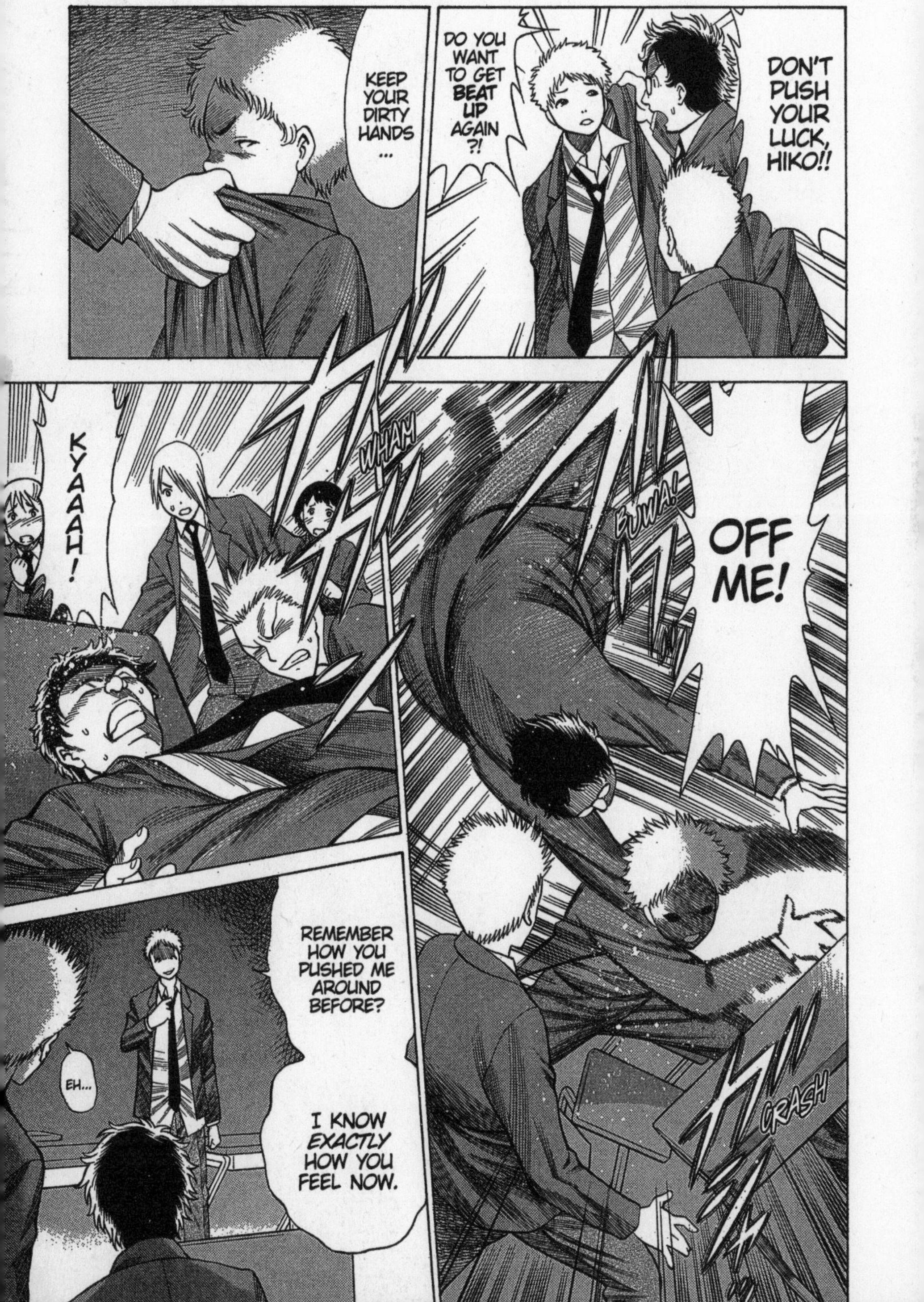
DON'T PUSH YOUR LUCK, HIKO!!
DO YOU WANT TO GET BEAT UP AGAIN ?!
KEEP YOUR DIRTY HANDS ...
OFF ME!
BUWA!
WHAM
CRASH
KYAAAH!
REMEMBER HOW YOU PUSHED ME AROUND BEFORE?
EH...
I KNOW *EXACTLY* HOW YOU FEEL NOW.

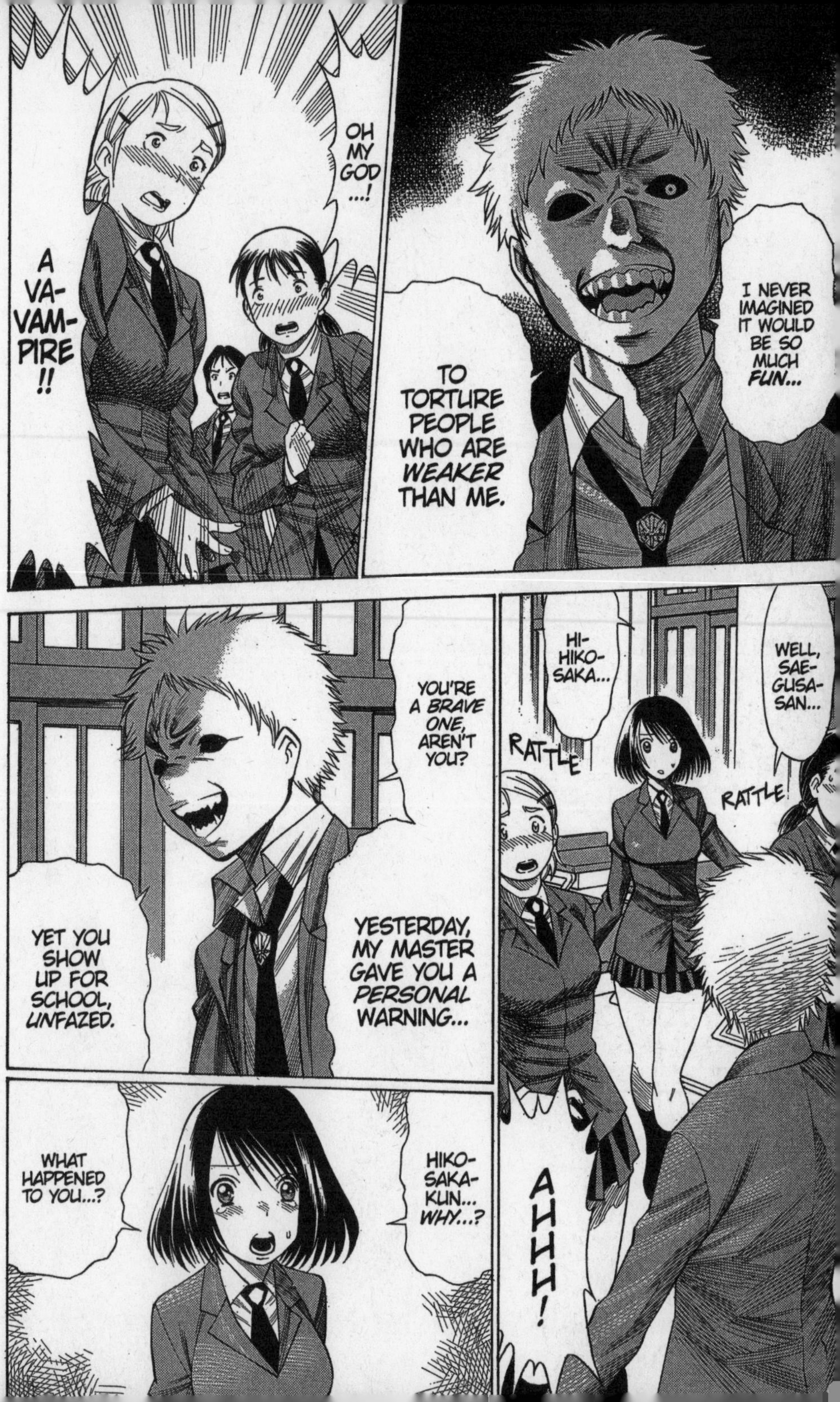
I NEVER IMAGINED IT WOULD BE SO MUCH FUN...
TO TORTURE PEOPLE WHO ARE WEAKER THAN ME.
OH MY GOD ...!
A VA-VAMPIRE!!
WELL, SAEGUSA-SAN...
HI-HIKOSAKA...
RATTLE
RATTLE
AHHH!
YOU'RE A BRAVE ONE, AREN'T YOU?
YESTERDAY, MY MASTER GAVE YOU A PERSONAL WARNING...
YET YOU SHOW UP FOR SCHOOL, UNFAZED.
HIKOSAKA-KUN... WHY...?
WHAT HAPPENED TO YOU...?

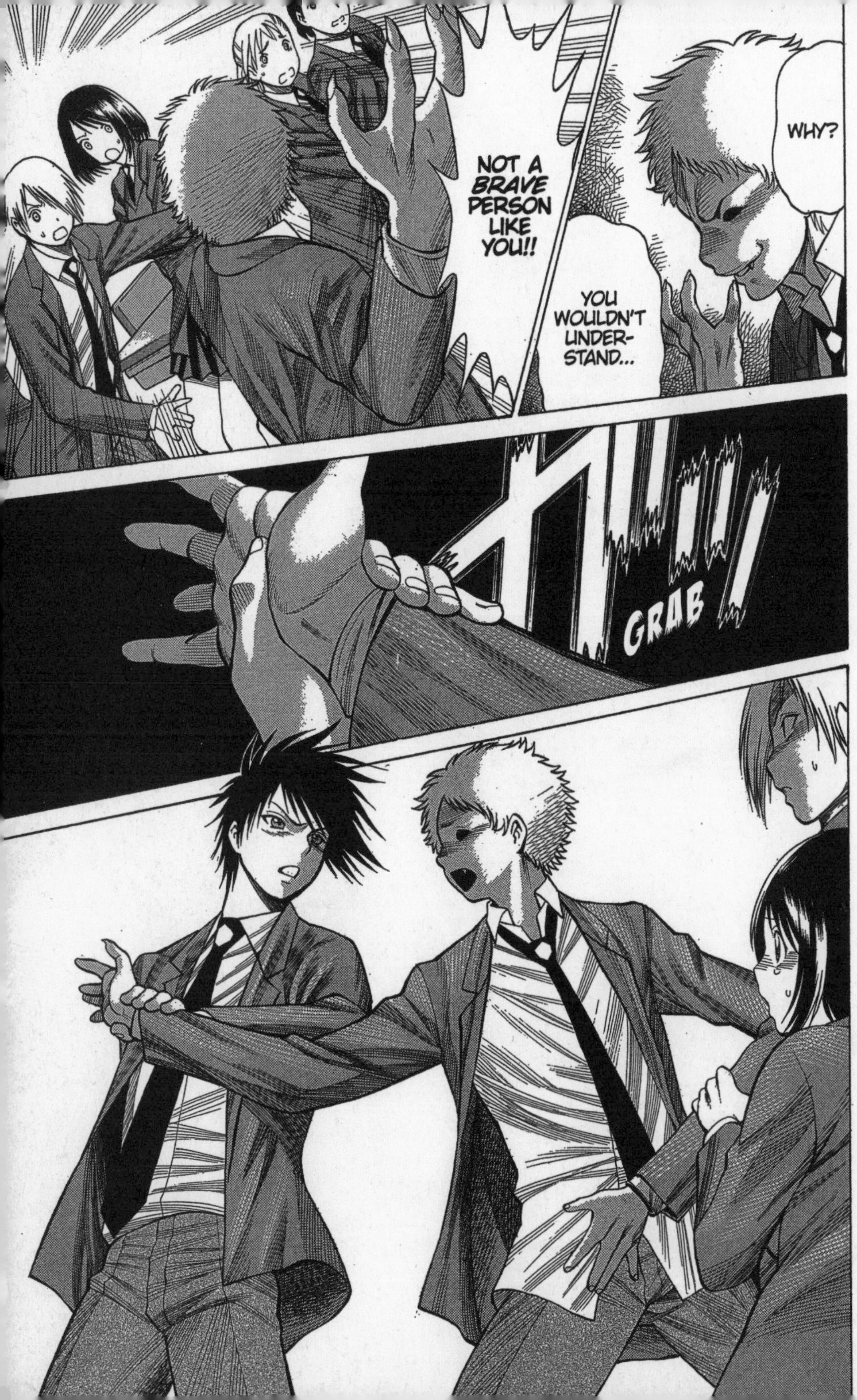
WHY?
YOU WOULDN'T UNDER-STAND...
NOT A BRAVE PERSON LIKE YOU!!
GRAB

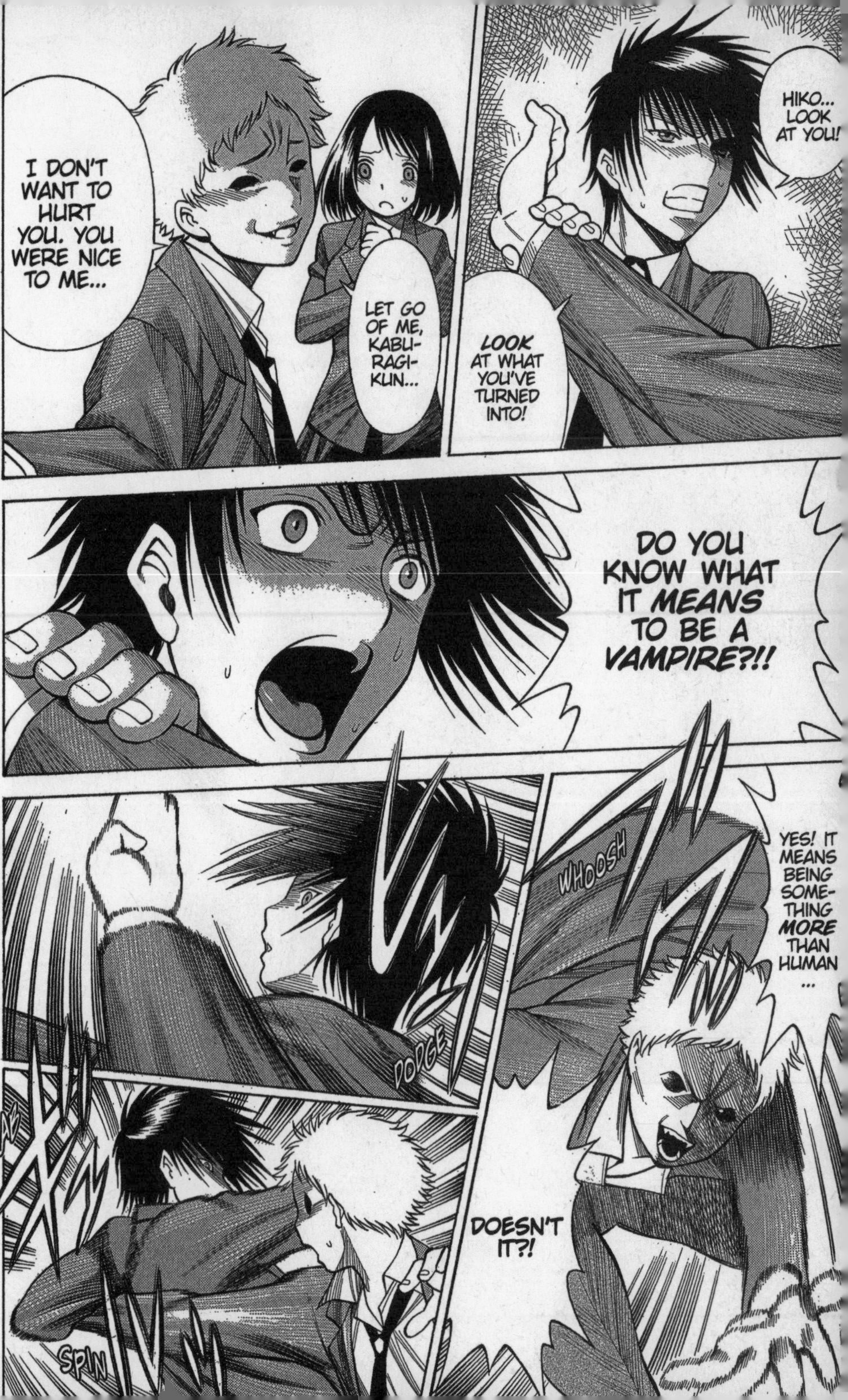
HIKO... LOOK AT YOU!
LOOK AT WHAT YOU'VE TURNED INTO!
LET GO OF ME, KABURAGI-KUN...
I DON'T WANT TO HURT YOU. YOU WERE NICE TO ME...
DO YOU KNOW WHAT IT MEANS TO BE A VAMPIRE?!!
YES! IT MEANS BEING SOMETHING MORE THAN HUMAN...
WHOOSH
DOESN'T IT?!
DODGE
GRAB
SPIN

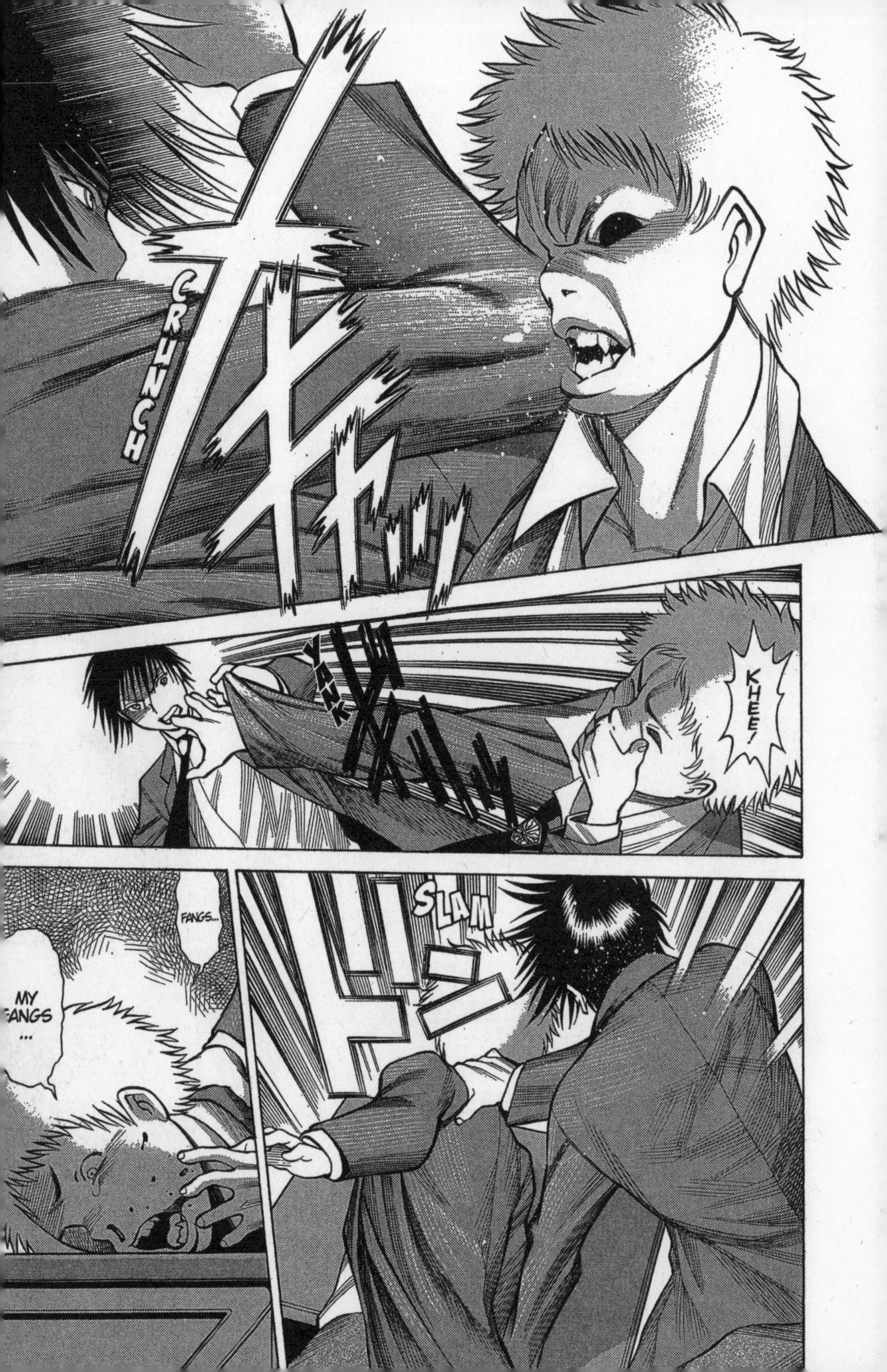
CRUNCH
KHEE!
YANK
SLAM
FANGS...
MY FANGS
...

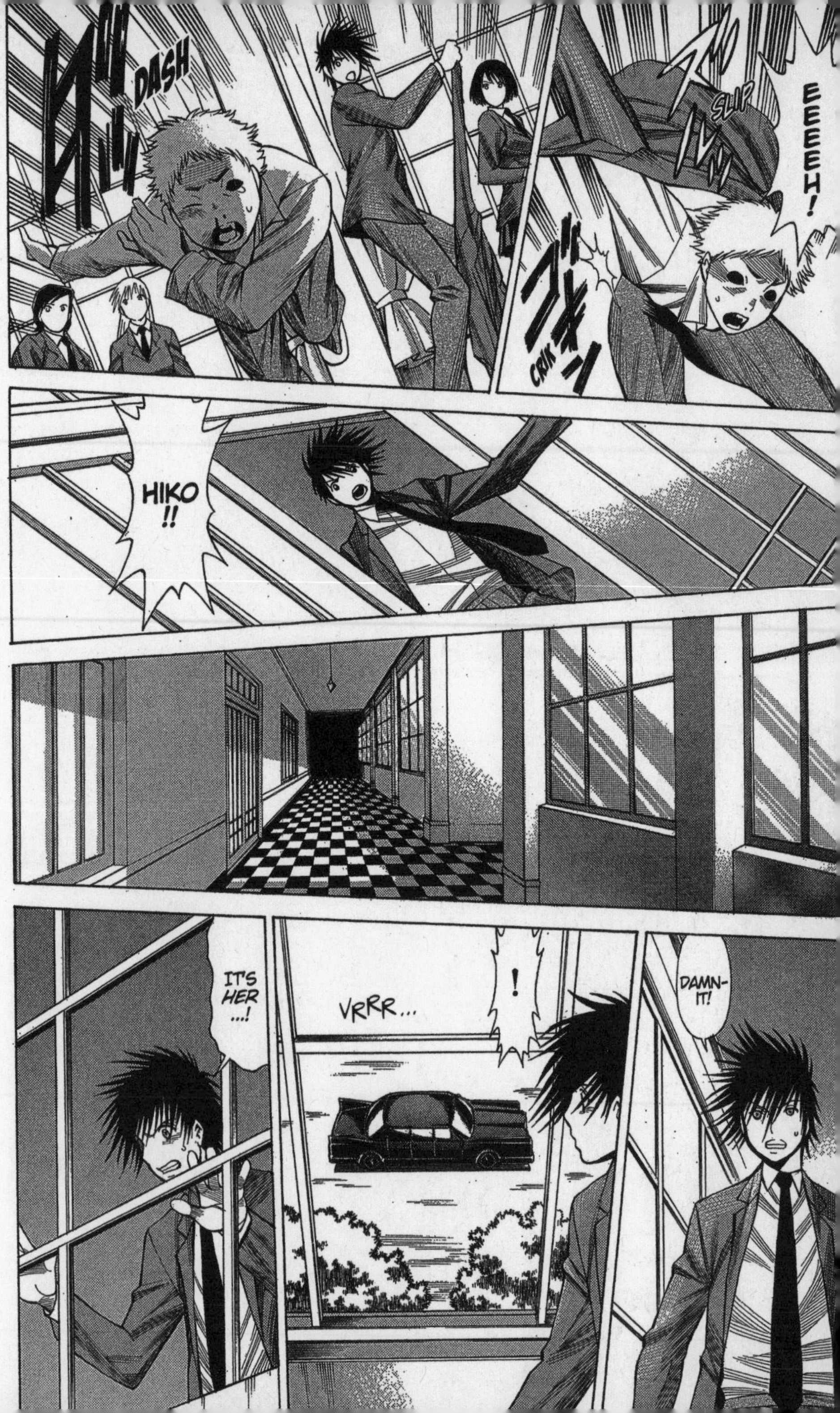

EEEEH!
SLIP
CRIK
DASH
HIKO !!
DAMN-IT!
!
VRRR...
IT'S HER ...!

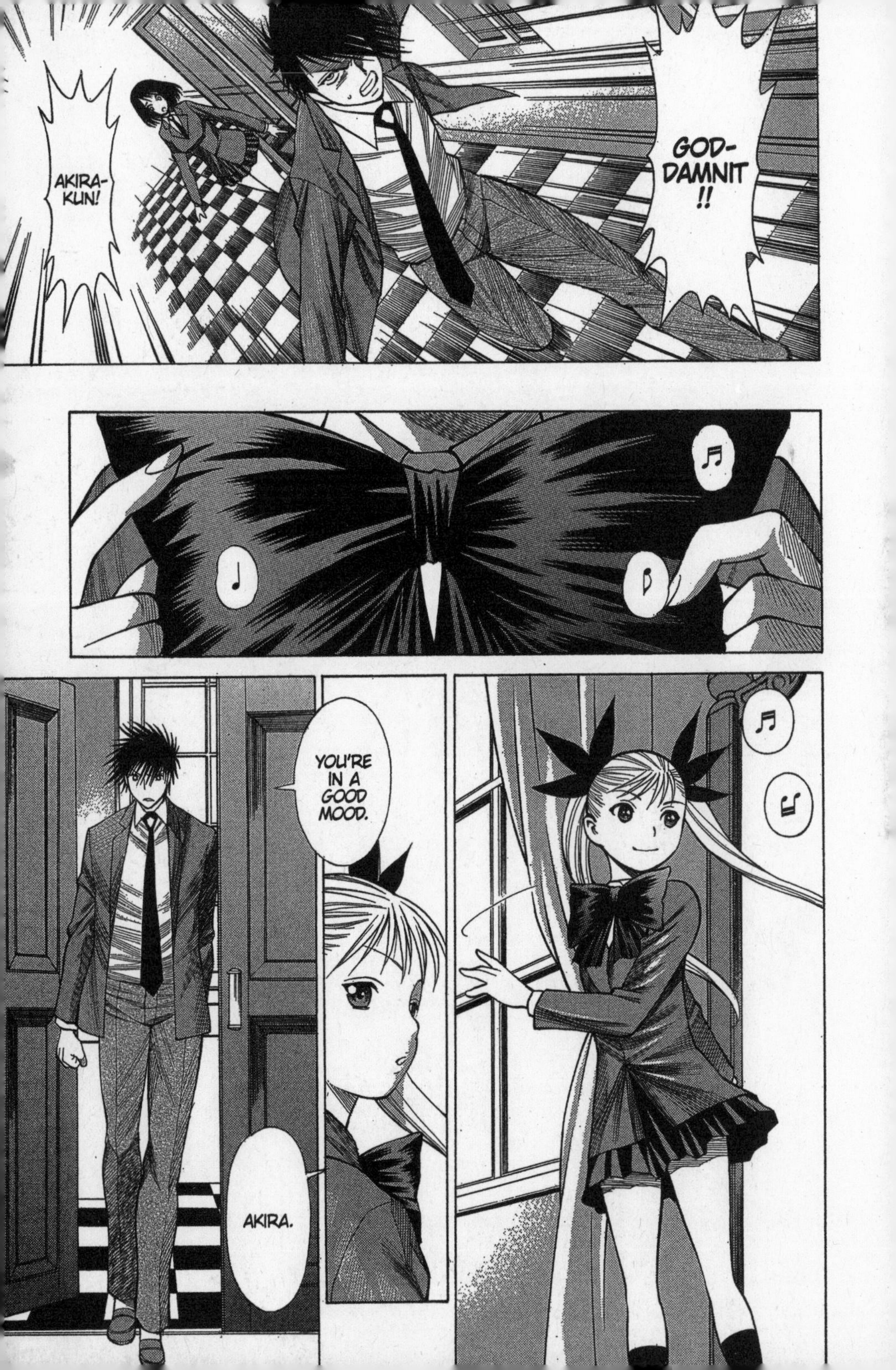
GOD-DAMNIT!!
AKIRA-KUN!
YOU'RE IN A GOOD MOOD.
AKIRA.

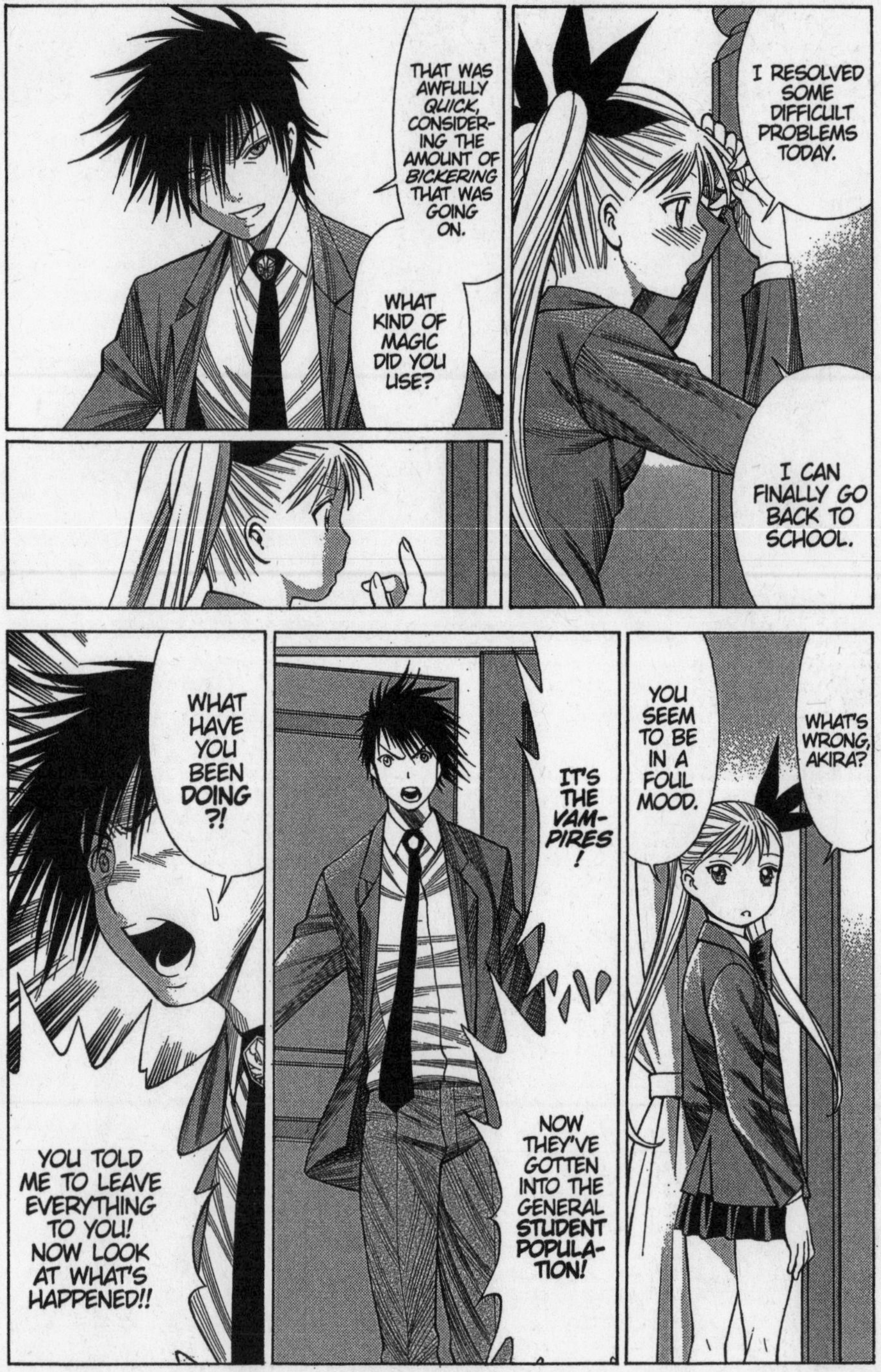
I RESOLVED SOME DIFFICULT PROBLEMS TODAY.
I CAN FINALLY GO BACK TO SCHOOL.
THAT WAS AWFULLY *QUICK*, CONSIDERING THE AMOUNT OF *BICKERING* THAT WAS GOING ON.
WHAT KIND OF MAGIC DID YOU USE?
WHAT'S WRONG, AKIRA?
YOU SEEM TO BE IN A FOUL MOOD.
IT'S THE *VAMPIRES*!
NOW THEY'VE GOTTEN INTO THE GENERAL STUDENT POPULATION!
WHAT HAVE YOU BEEN DOING?!
YOU TOLD ME TO LEAVE EVERYTHING TO YOU! NOW LOOK AT WHAT'S HAPPENED!!

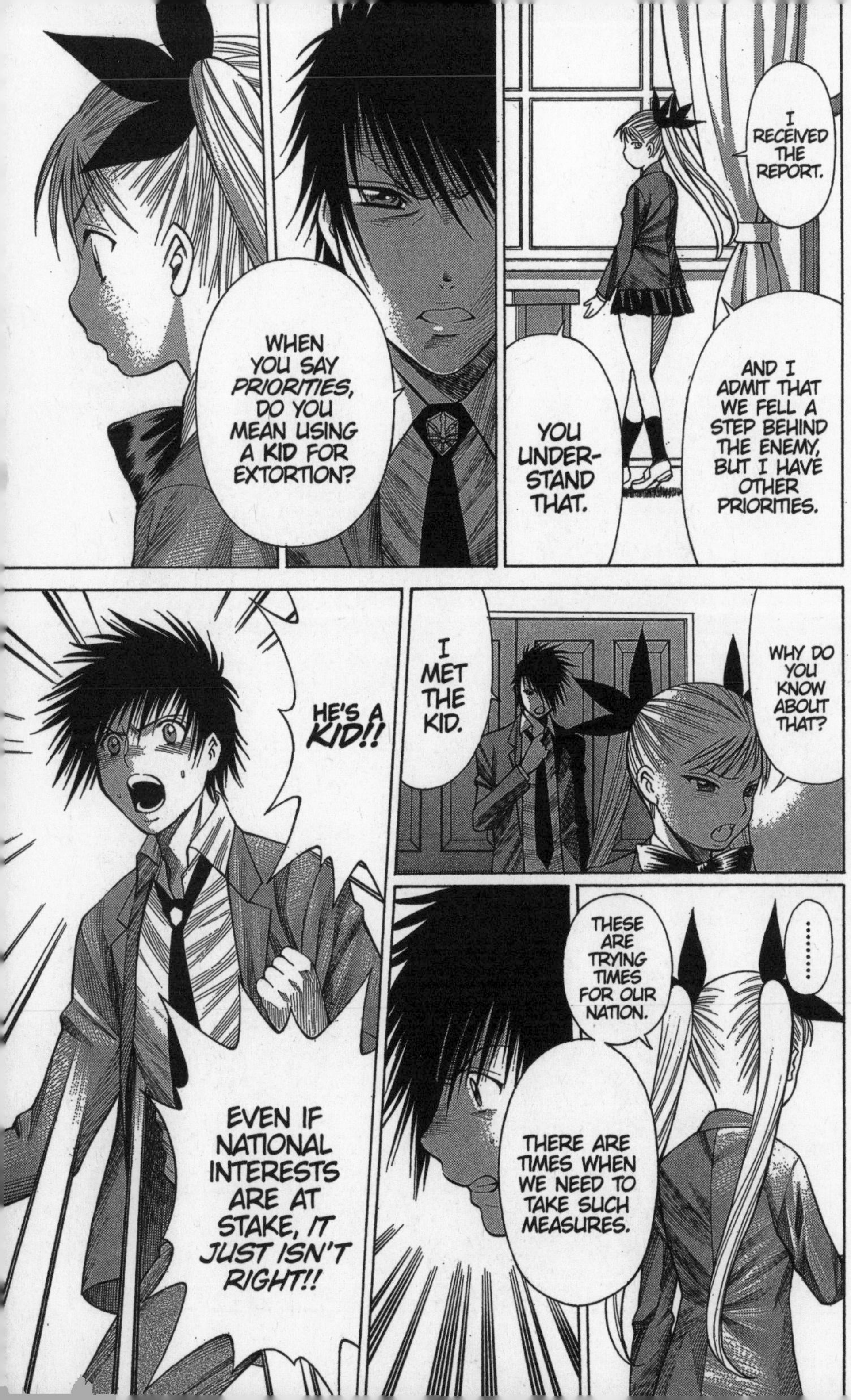
I RECEIVED THE REPORT.
AND I ADMIT THAT WE FELL A STEP BEHIND THE ENEMY, BUT I HAVE OTHER PRIORITIES.
YOU UNDER-STAND THAT.
WHEN YOU SAY *PRIORITIES*, DO YOU MEAN USING A KID FOR EXTORTION?
WHY DO YOU KNOW ABOUT THAT?
I MET THE KID.
......
THESE ARE TRYING TIMES FOR OUR NATION.
THERE ARE TIMES WHEN WE NEED TO TAKE SUCH MEASURES.
HE'S A ***KID!!***
EVEN IF NATIONAL INTERESTS ARE AT STAKE, *IT JUST ISN'T RIGHT!!*

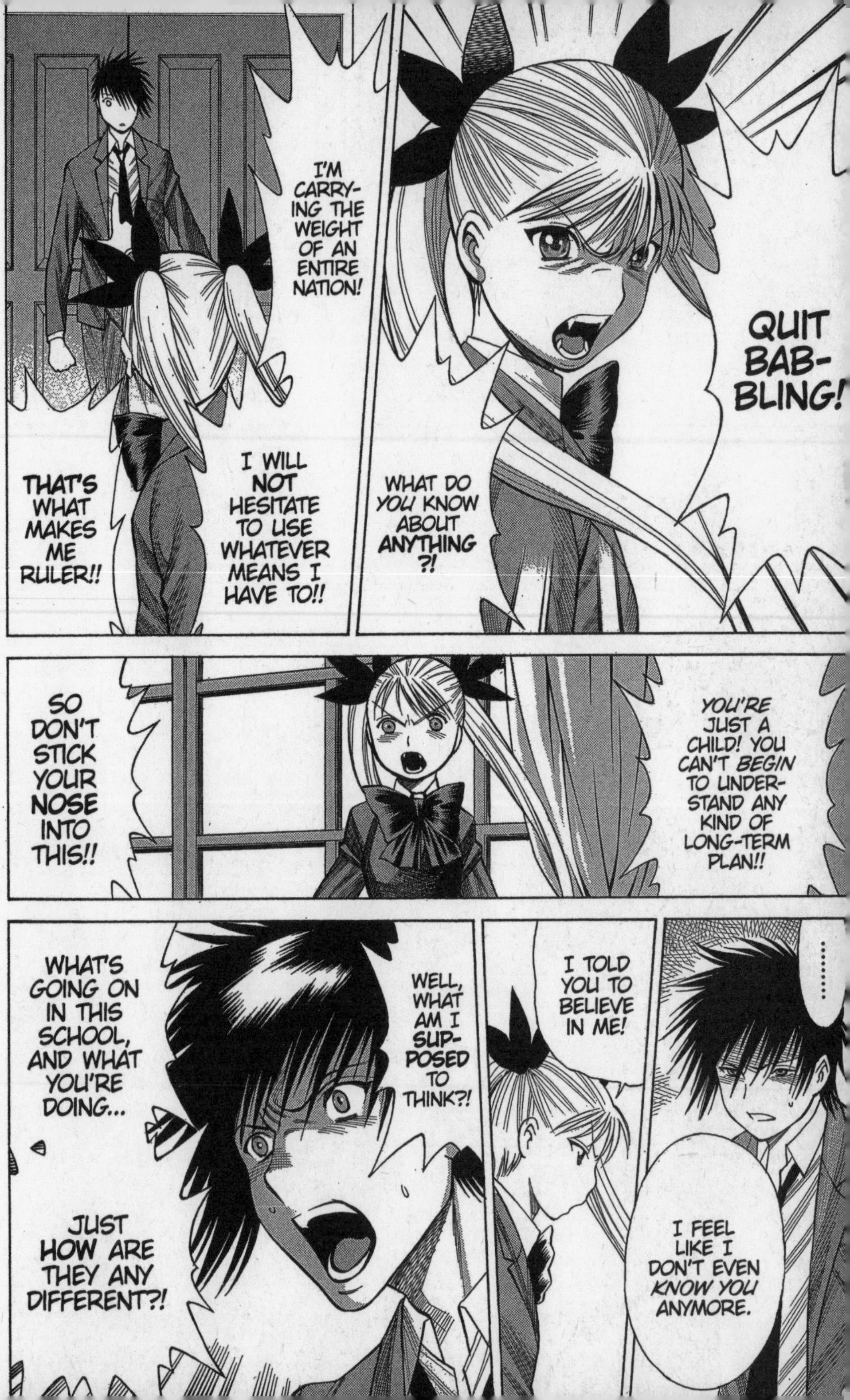
QUIT BAB-BLING!
WHAT DO YOU KNOW ABOUT ANYTHING?!
I'M CARRY-ING THE WEIGHT OF AN ENTIRE NATION!
I WILL NOT HESITATE TO USE WHATEVER MEANS I HAVE TO!!
THAT'S WHAT MAKES ME RULER!!
YOU'RE JUST A CHILD! YOU CAN'T BEGIN TO UNDER-STAND ANY KIND OF LONG-TERM PLAN!!
SO DON'T STICK YOUR NOSE INTO THIS!!
......
I FEEL LIKE I DON'T EVEN KNOW YOU ANYMORE.
I TOLD YOU TO BELIEVE IN ME!
WELL, WHAT AM I SUP-POSED TO THINK?!
WHAT'S GOING ON IN THIS SCHOOL, AND WHAT YOU'RE DOING...
JUST HOW ARE THEY ANY DIFFERENT?!

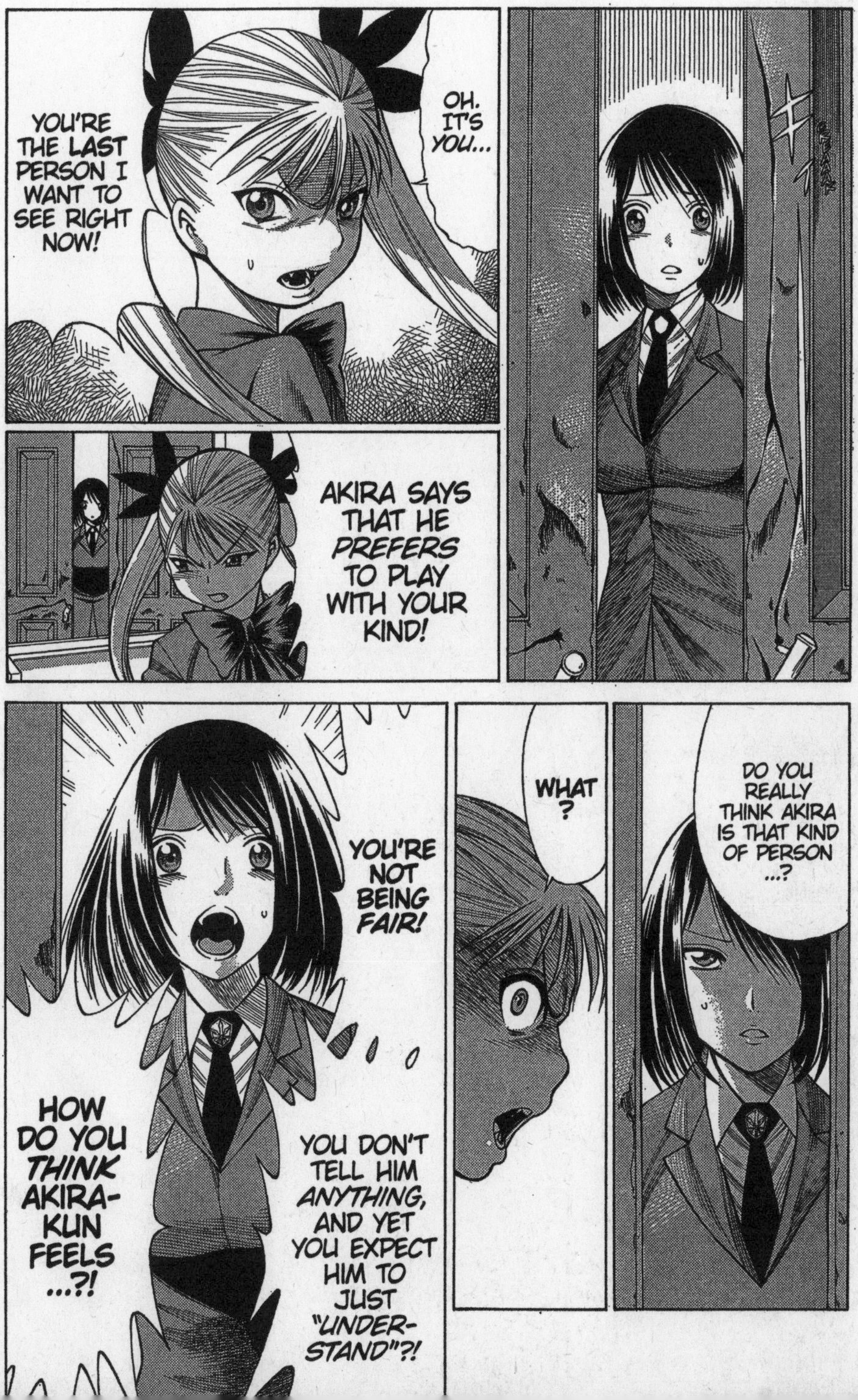
OH. IT'S YOU...
YOU'RE THE LAST PERSON I WANT TO SEE RIGHT NOW!
AKIRA SAYS THAT HE *PREFERS* TO PLAY WITH YOUR KIND!
DO YOU REALLY THINK AKIRA IS THAT KIND OF PERSON ...?
WHAT ?
YOU'RE NOT BEING *FAIR!*
YOU DON'T TELL HIM *ANYTHING,* AND YET YOU EXPECT HIM TO JUST *"UNDER-STAND"?!*
HOW DO YOU *THINK* AKIRA-KUN FEELS ...?!

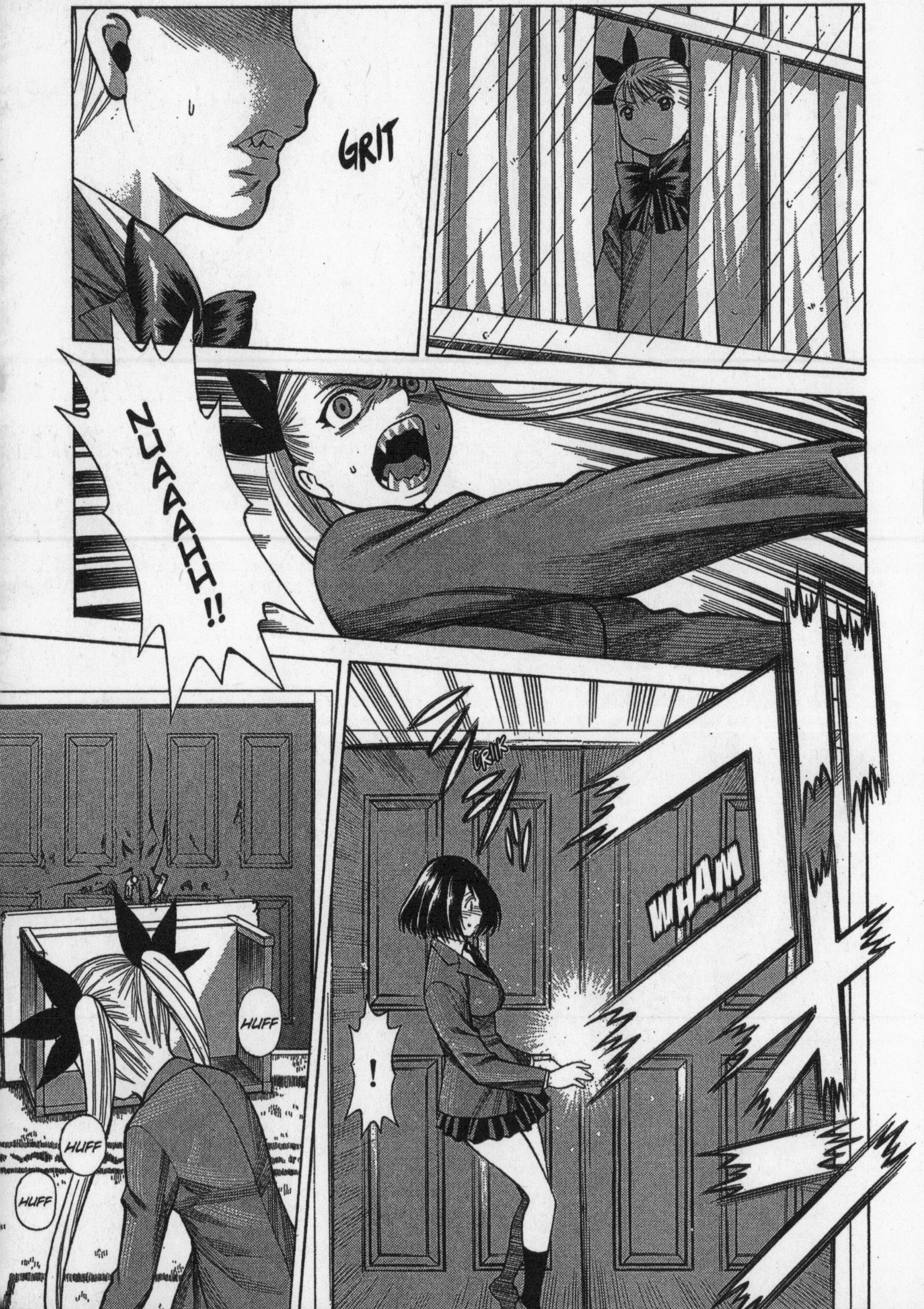
GRIT
NUAAAAHH!!
CRIIK
WHAM
!
HUFF
HUFF
HUFF

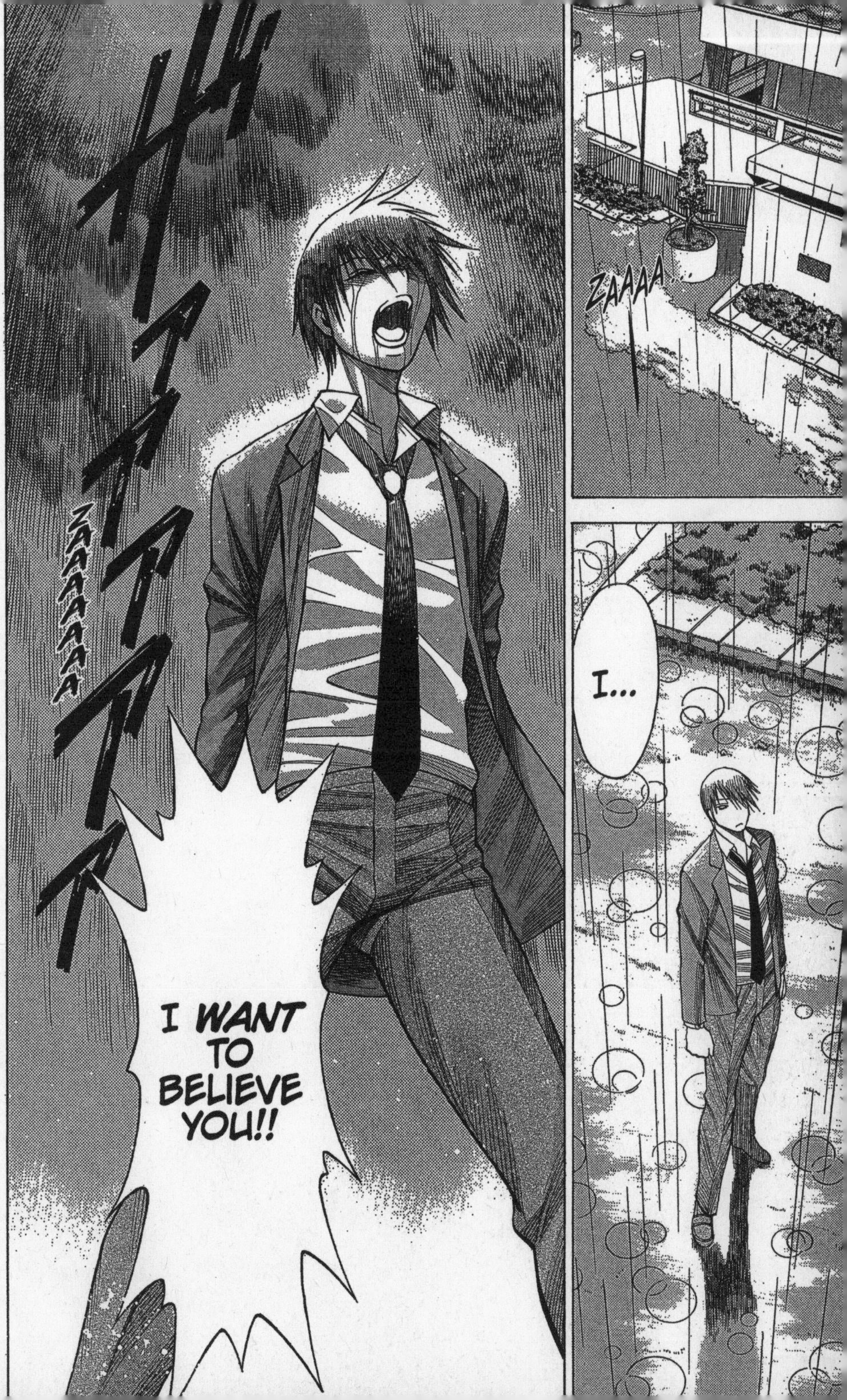
ZAAAA
I...
ZAAAAAAAA
I *WANT* TO BELIEVE YOU!!

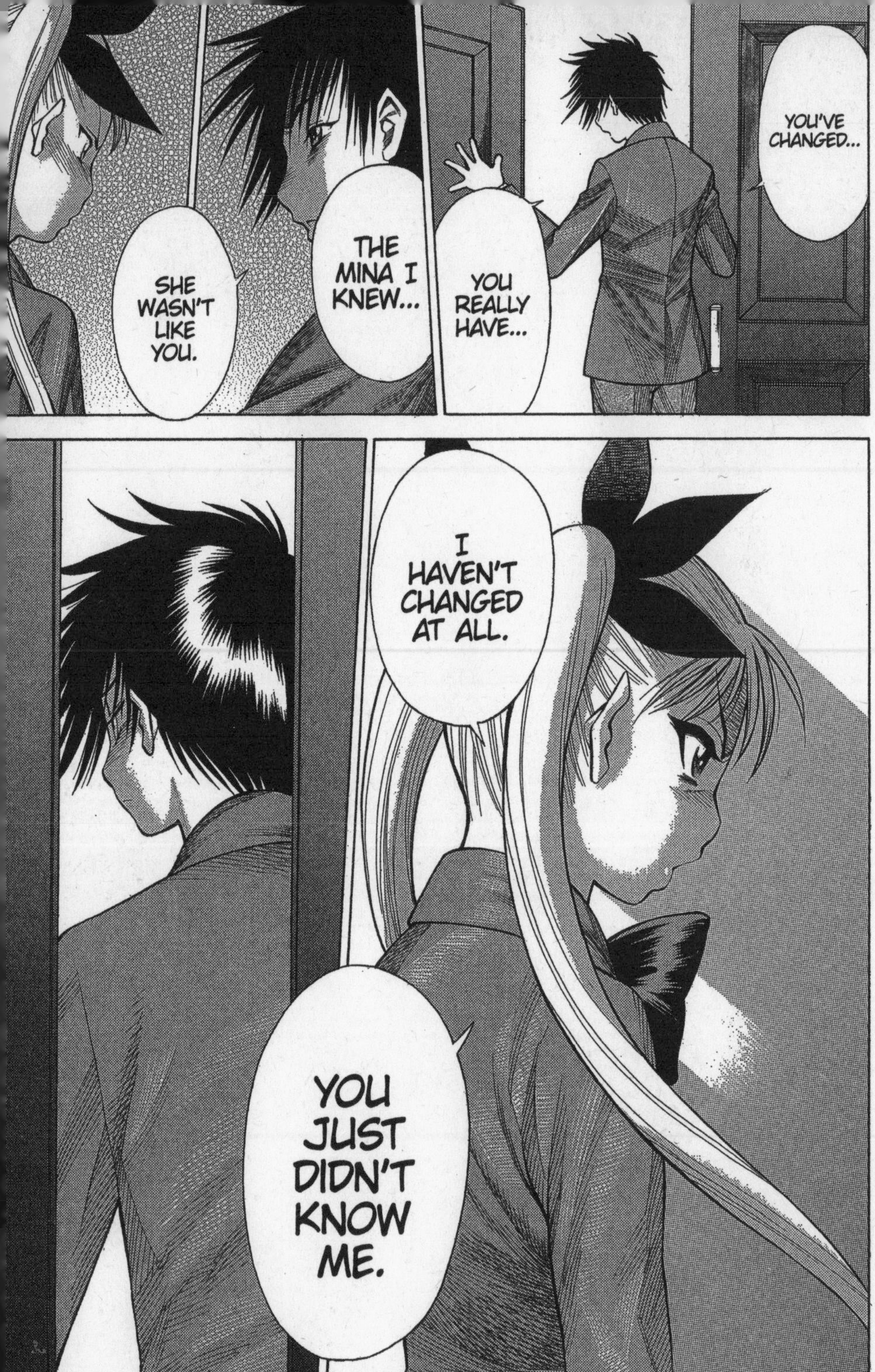
YOU'VE CHANGED...
YOU REALLY HAVE...
THE MINA I KNEW...
SHE WASN'T LIKE YOU.
I HAVEN'T CHANGED AT ALL.
YOU JUST DIDN'T KNOW ME.

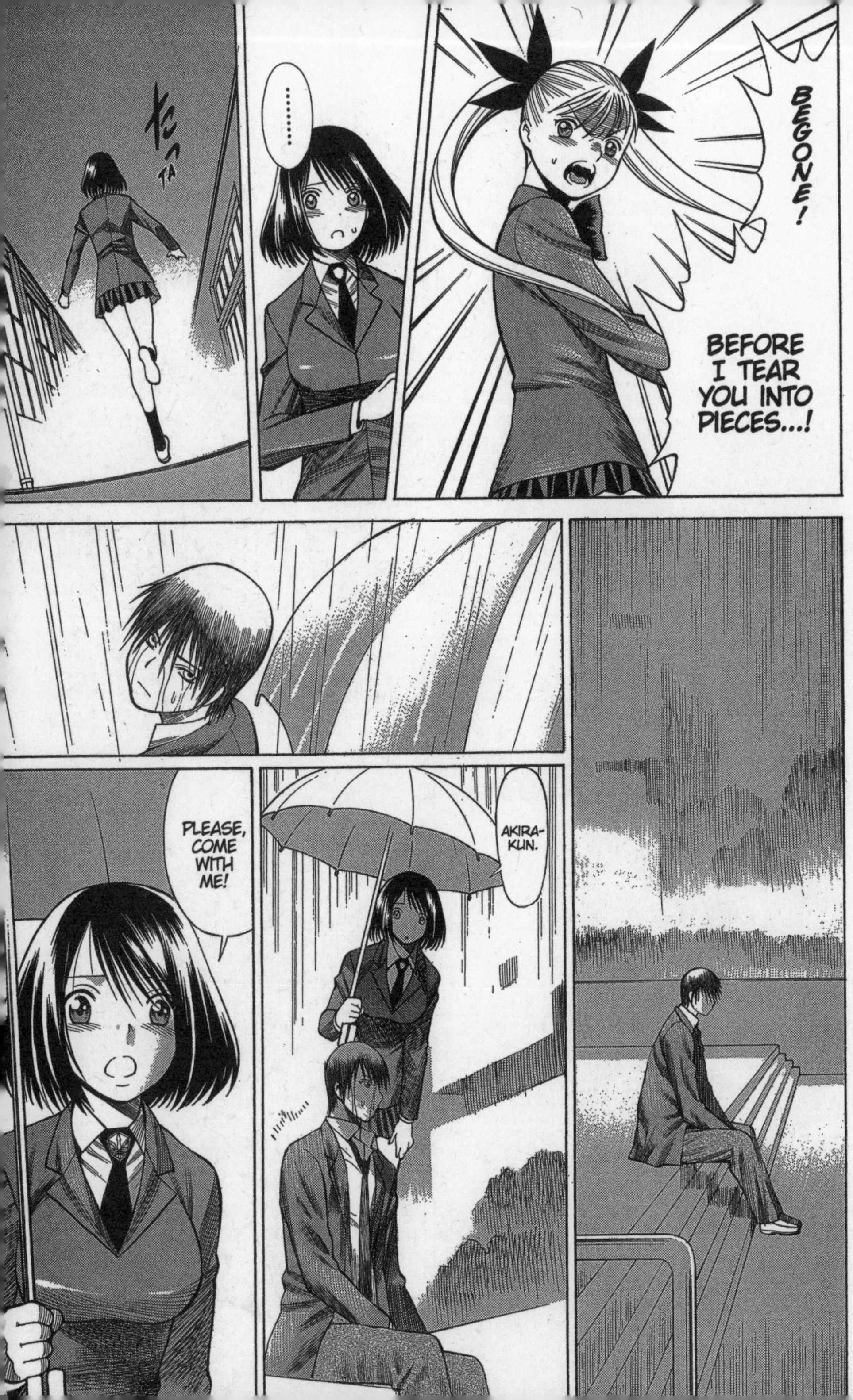
BEGONE!
BEFORE I TEAR YOU INTO PIECES...!
......
たっ TA
AKIRA-KUN.
PLEASE, COME WITH ME!

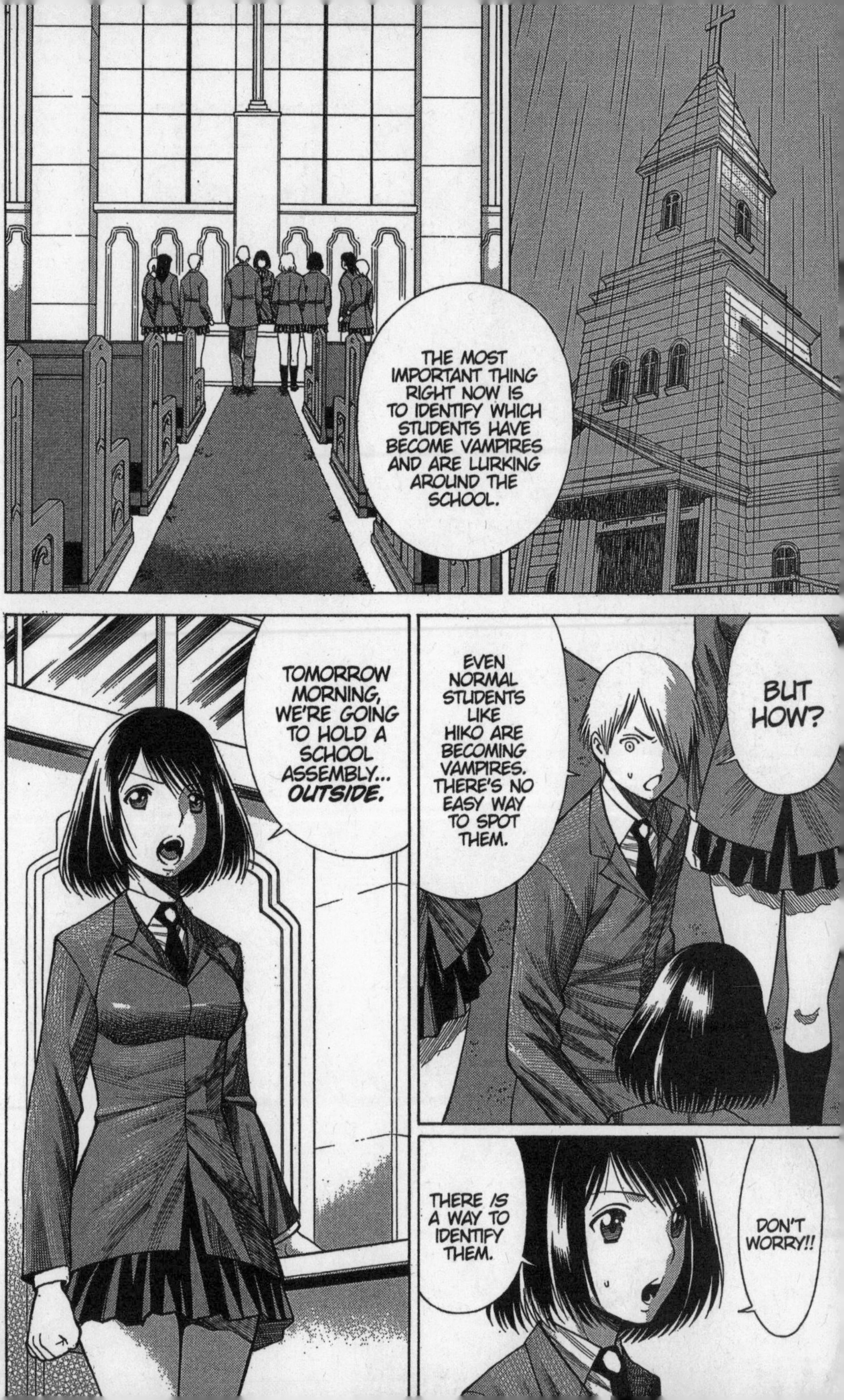
THE MOST IMPORTANT THING RIGHT NOW IS TO IDENTIFY WHICH STUDENTS HAVE BECOME VAMPIRES AND ARE LURKING AROUND THE SCHOOL.
BUT HOW?
EVEN NORMAL STUDENTS LIKE HIKO ARE BECOMING VAMPIRES. THERE'S NO EASY WAY TO SPOT THEM.
DON'T WORRY!!
THERE *IS* A WAY TO IDENTIFY THEM.
TOMORROW MORNING, WE'RE GOING TO HOLD A SCHOOL ASSEMBLY... ***OUTSIDE.***

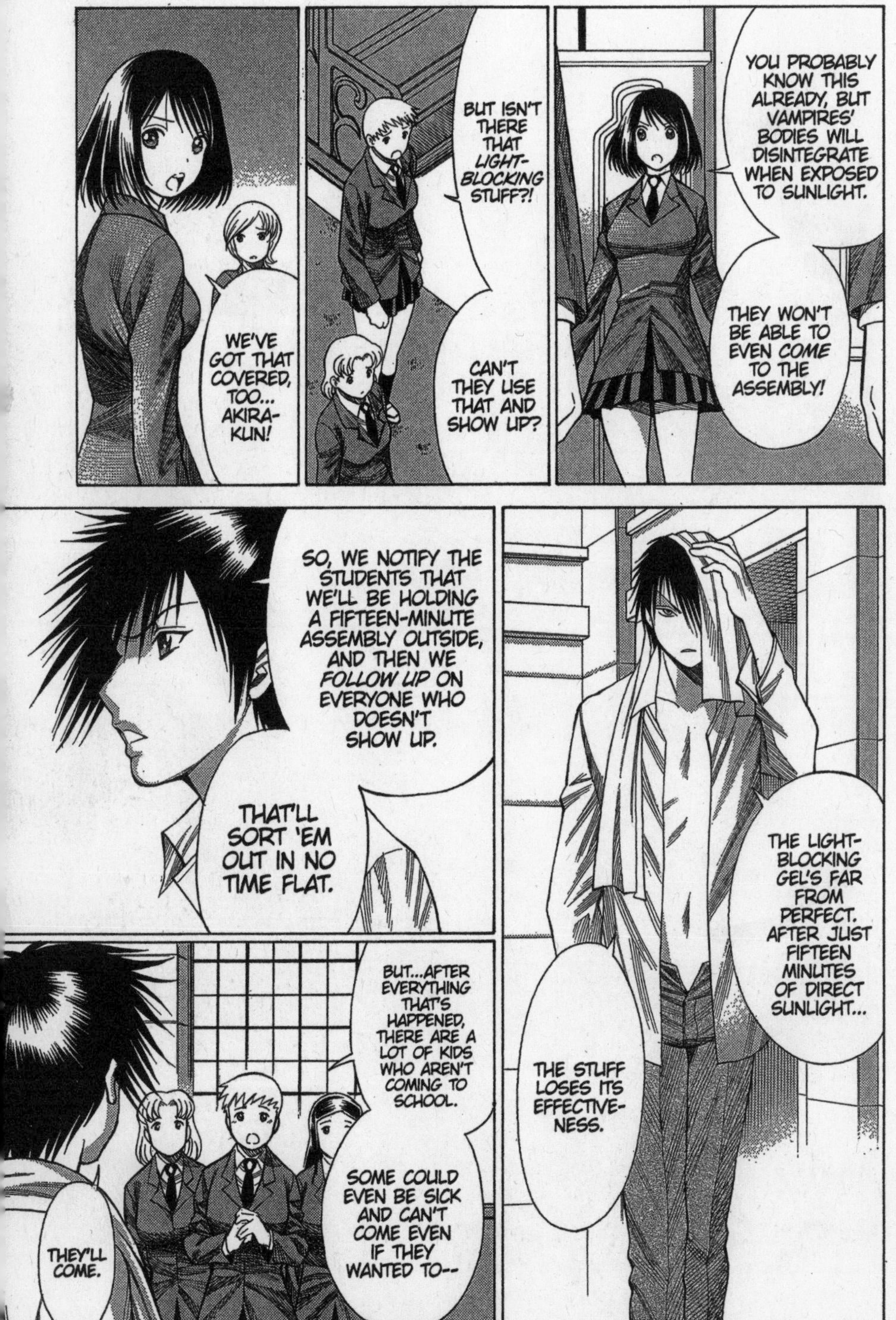
YOU PROBABLY KNOW THIS ALREADY, BUT VAMPIRES' BODIES WILL DISINTEGRATE WHEN EXPOSED TO SUNLIGHT.
THEY WON'T BE ABLE TO EVEN *COME* TO THE ASSEMBLY!
BUT ISN'T THERE THAT *LIGHT-BLOCKING* STUFF?!
CAN'T THEY USE THAT AND SHOW UP?
WE'VE GOT THAT COVERED, TOO... AKIRA-KUN!
THE LIGHT-BLOCKING GEL'S FAR FROM PERFECT. AFTER JUST FIFTEEN MINUTES OF DIRECT SUNLIGHT...
THE STUFF LOSES ITS EFFECTIVE-NESS.
SO, WE NOTIFY THE STUDENTS THAT WE'LL BE HOLDING A FIFTEEN-MINUTE ASSEMBLY OUTSIDE, AND THEN WE *FOLLOW UP* ON EVERYONE WHO DOESN'T SHOW UP.
THAT'LL SORT 'EM OUT IN NO TIME FLAT.
BUT...AFTER EVERYTHING THAT'S HAPPENED, THERE ARE A LOT OF KIDS WHO AREN'T COMING TO SCHOOL.
SOME COULD EVEN BE SICK AND CAN'T COME EVEN IF THEY WANTED TO--
THEY'LL COME.

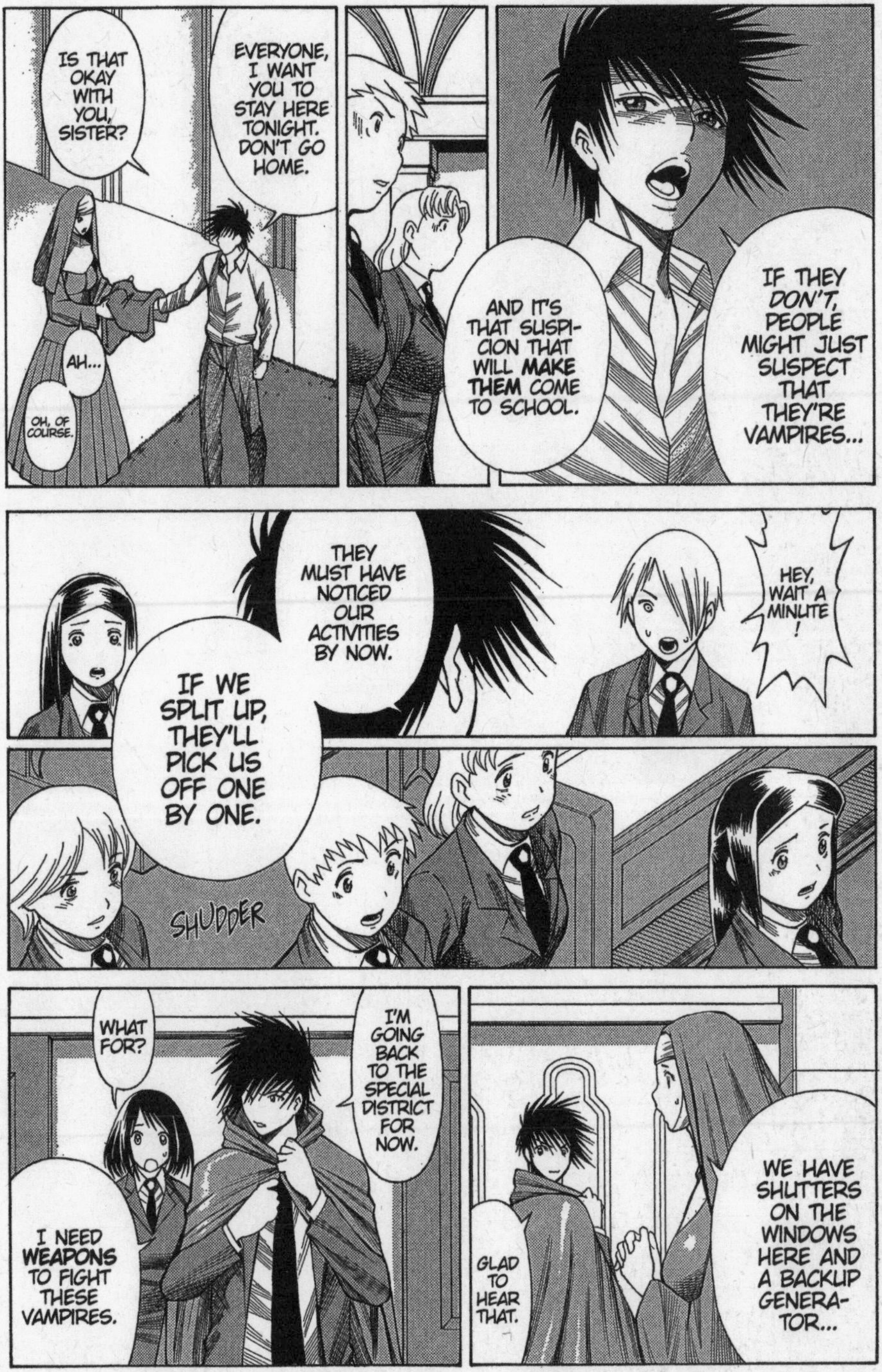
IF THEY DON'T, PEOPLE MIGHT JUST SUSPECT THAT THEY'RE VAMPIRES...
AND IT'S THAT SUSPICION THAT WILL MAKE THEM COME TO SCHOOL.
EVERYONE, I WANT YOU TO STAY HERE TONIGHT. DON'T GO HOME.
IS THAT OKAY WITH YOU, SISTER?
AH...
OH, OF COURSE.
HEY, WAIT A MINUTE!
THEY MUST HAVE NOTICED OUR ACTIVITIES BY NOW.
IF WE SPLIT UP, THEY'LL PICK US OFF ONE BY ONE.
SHUDDER
WE HAVE SHUTTERS ON THE WINDOWS HERE AND A BACKUP GENERATOR...
GLAD TO HEAR THAT.
I'M GOING BACK TO THE SPECIAL DISTRICT FOR NOW.
WHAT FOR?
I NEED WEAPONS TO FIGHT THESE VAMPIRES.

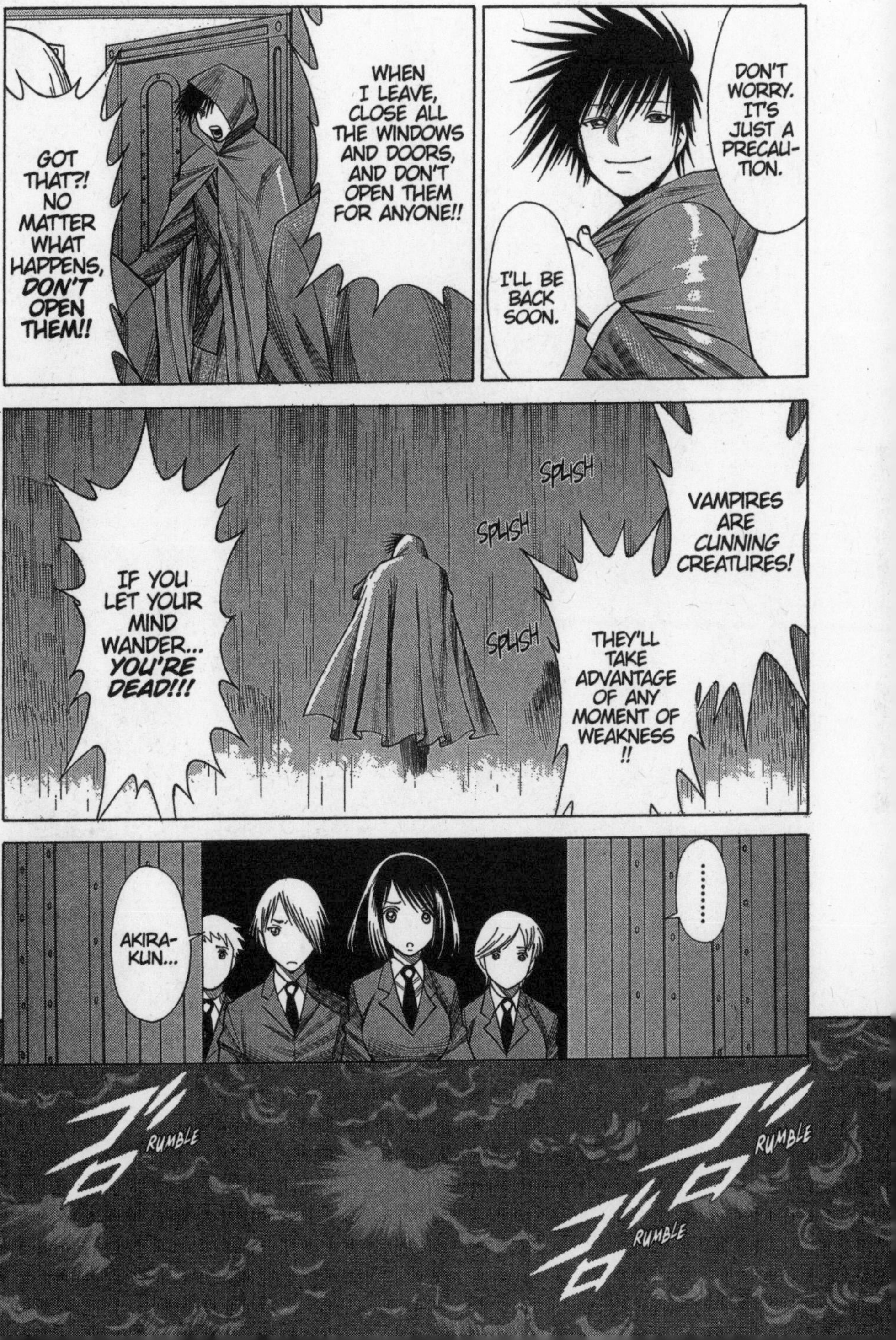
DON'T WORRY. IT'S JUST A PRECAU-TION.
I'LL BE BACK SOON.
WHEN I LEAVE, CLOSE ALL THE WINDOWS AND DOORS, AND DON'T OPEN THEM FOR ANYONE!!
GOT THAT?! NO MATTER WHAT HAPPENS, DON'T OPEN THEM!!
VAMPIRES ARE CUNNING CREATURES!
SPLISH
SPLISH
THEY'LL TAKE ADVANTAGE OF ANY MOMENT OF WEAKNESS !!
SPLISH
IF YOU LET YOUR MIND WANDER... YOU'RE DEAD!!!
....
AKIRA-KUN...
RUMBLE
RUMBLE
RUMBLE

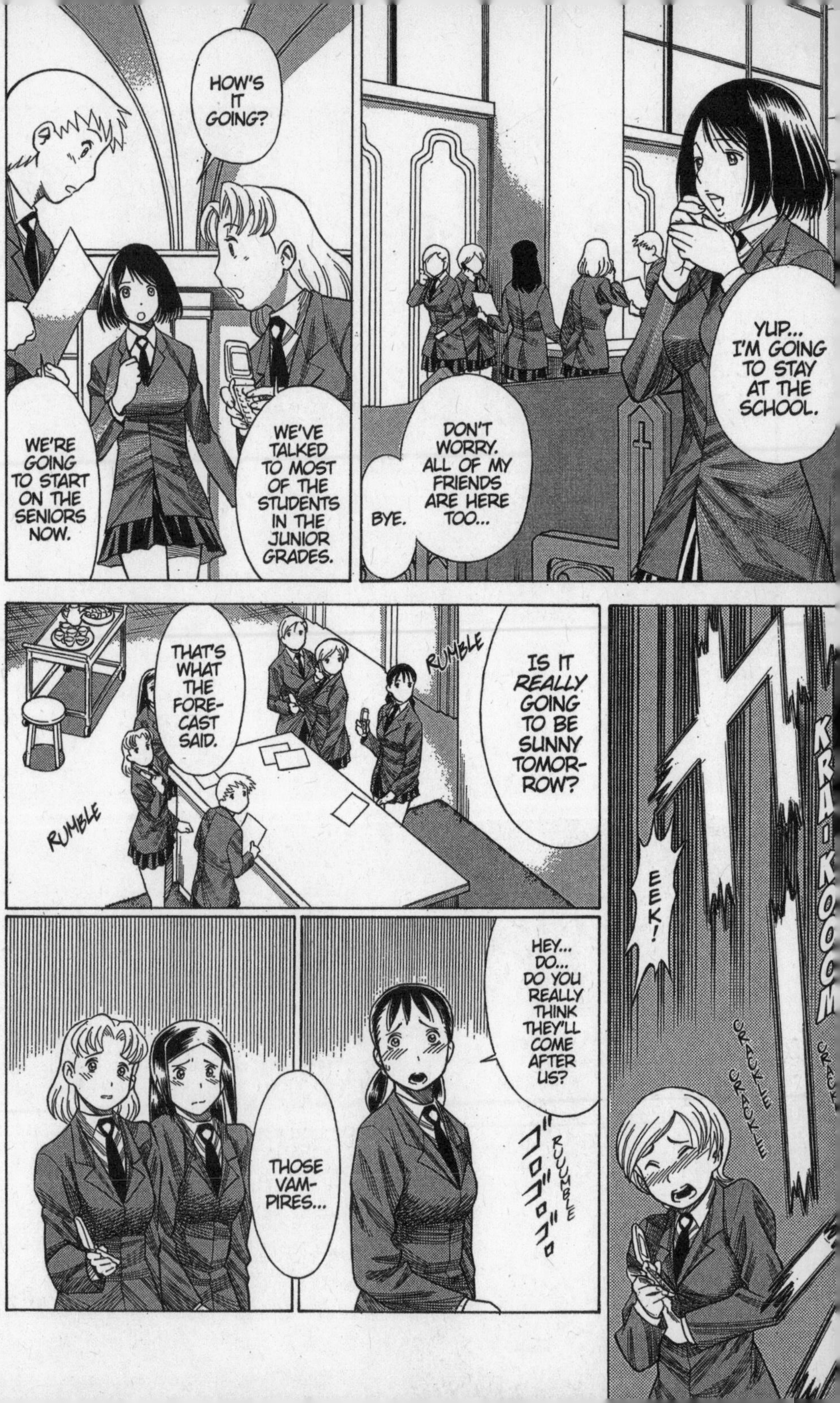
YUP... I'M GOING TO STAY AT THE SCHOOL.
DON'T WORRY. ALL OF MY FRIENDS ARE HERE TOO...
BYE.
HOW'S IT GOING?
WE'VE TALKED TO MOST OF THE STUDENTS IN THE JUNIOR GRADES.
WE'RE GOING TO START ON THE SENIORS NOW.
KRA-KOOOM
EEK!
CRACKLE
CRACKLE
CRACKLE
IS IT REALLY GOING TO BE SUNNY TOMORROW?
RUMBLE
THAT'S WHAT THE FORECAST SAID.
RUMBLE
HEY... DO... DO YOU REALLY THINK THEY'LL COME AFTER US?
RUUUMBLE
THOSE VAMPIRES...

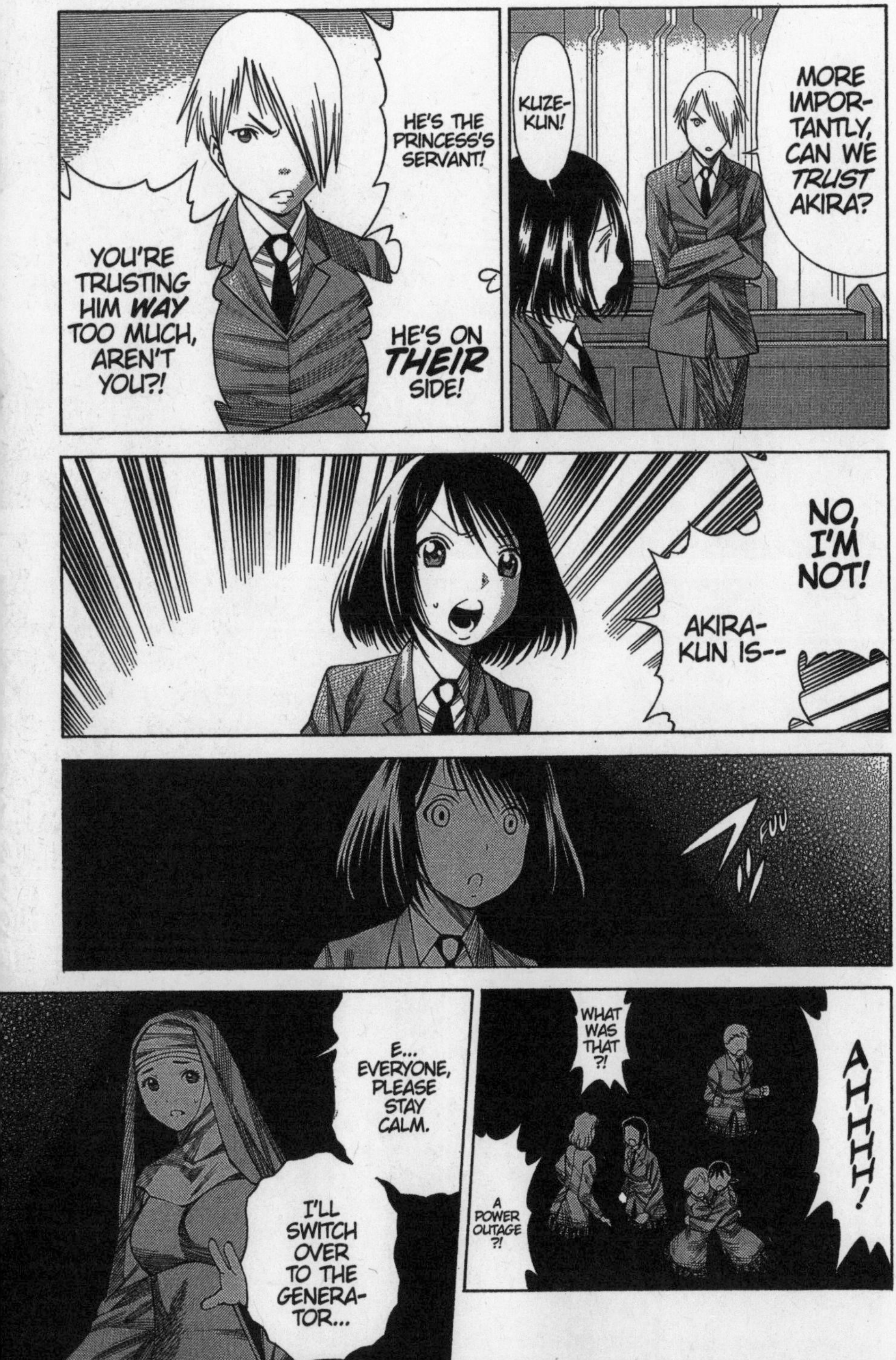
MORE IMPORTANTLY, CAN WE TRUST AKIRA?
KUZE-KUN!
HE'S THE PRINCESS'S SERVANT!
HE'S ON THEIR SIDE!
YOU'RE TRUSTING HIM WAY TOO MUCH, AREN'T YOU?!
NO, I'M NOT!
AKIRA-KUN IS--
FUU
AHHHH!
WHAT WAS THAT?!
A POWER OUTAGE?!
E... EVERYONE, PLEASE STAY CALM.
I'LL SWITCH OVER TO THE GENERATOR...

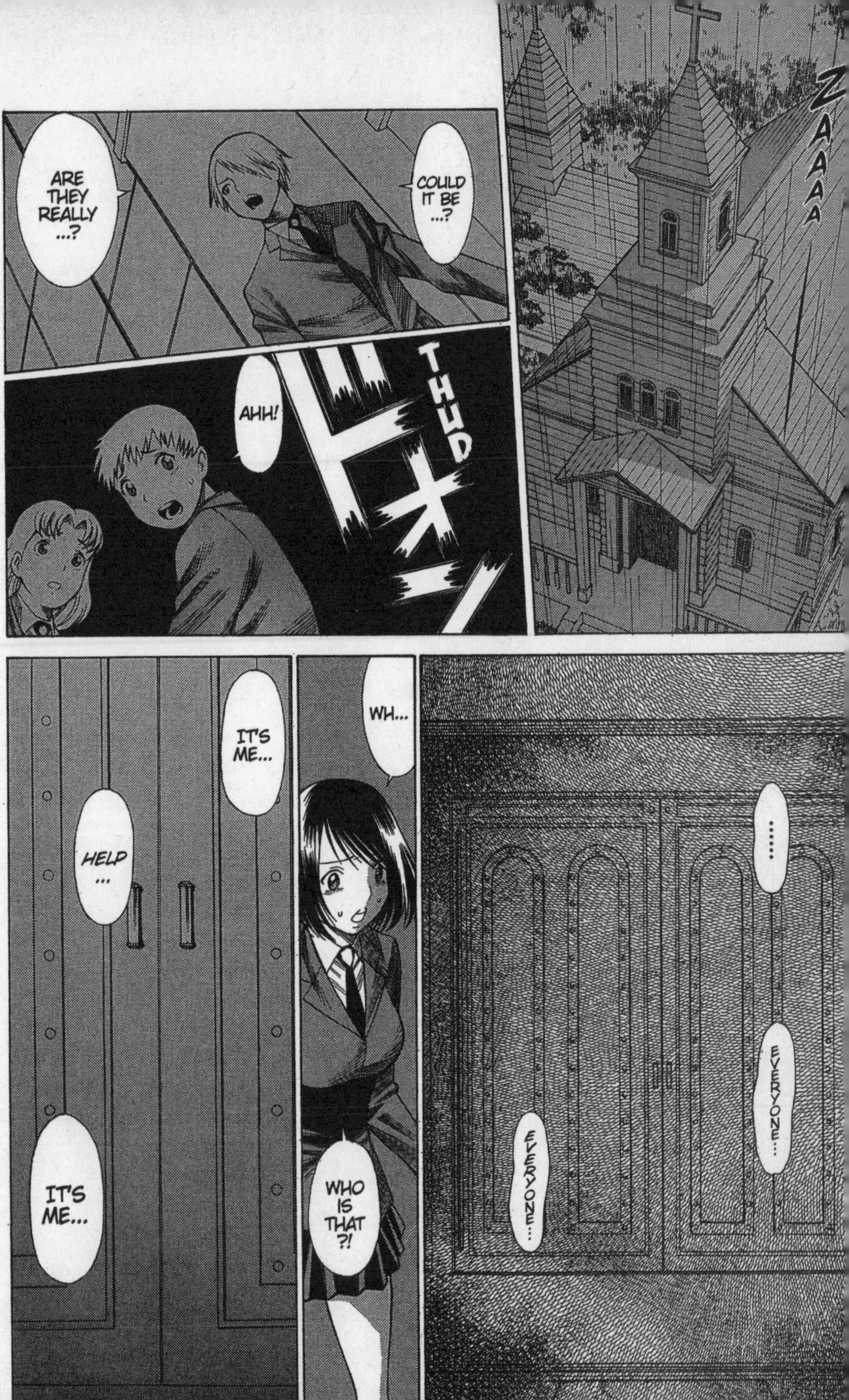
ZAAAA
COULD IT BE ...?
ARE THEY REALLY ...?
THUD
ドォン
AHH!
......
EVERYONE...
EVERYONE...
WH...
WHO IS THAT?!
IT'S ME...
HELP ...
IT'S ME...

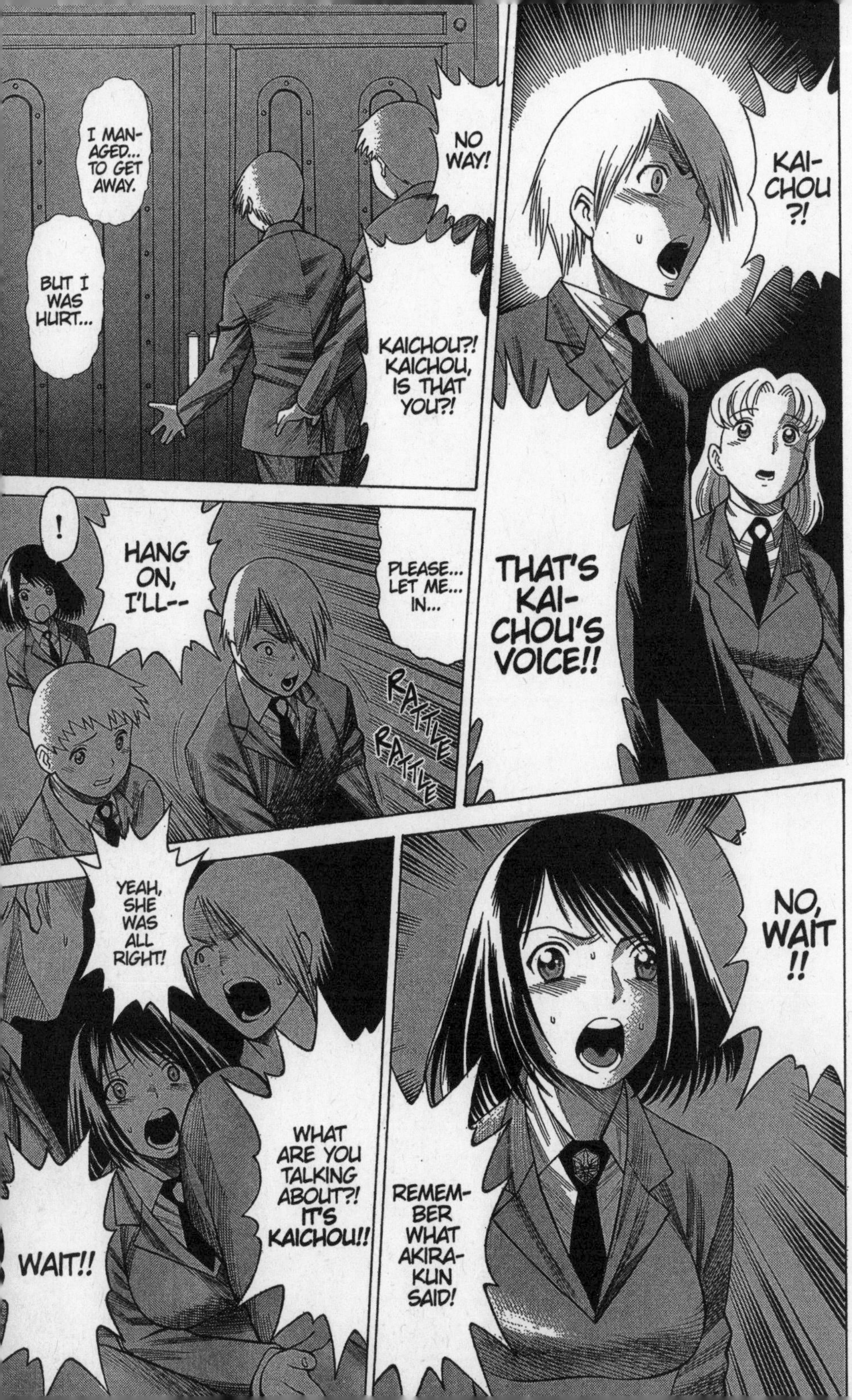
KAI-CHOU?!
THAT'S KAI-CHOU'S VOICE!!
NO WAY!
KAICHOU?! KAICHOU, IS THAT YOU?!
I MAN-AGED... TO GET AWAY.
BUT I WAS HURT...
PLEASE... LET ME... IN...
RATTLE RATTLE
HANG ON, I'LL--
!
NO, WAIT!!
REMEM-BER WHAT AKIRA-KUN SAID!
YEAH, SHE WAS ALL RIGHT!
WHAT ARE YOU TALKING ABOUT?! IT'S KAICHOU!!
WAIT!!

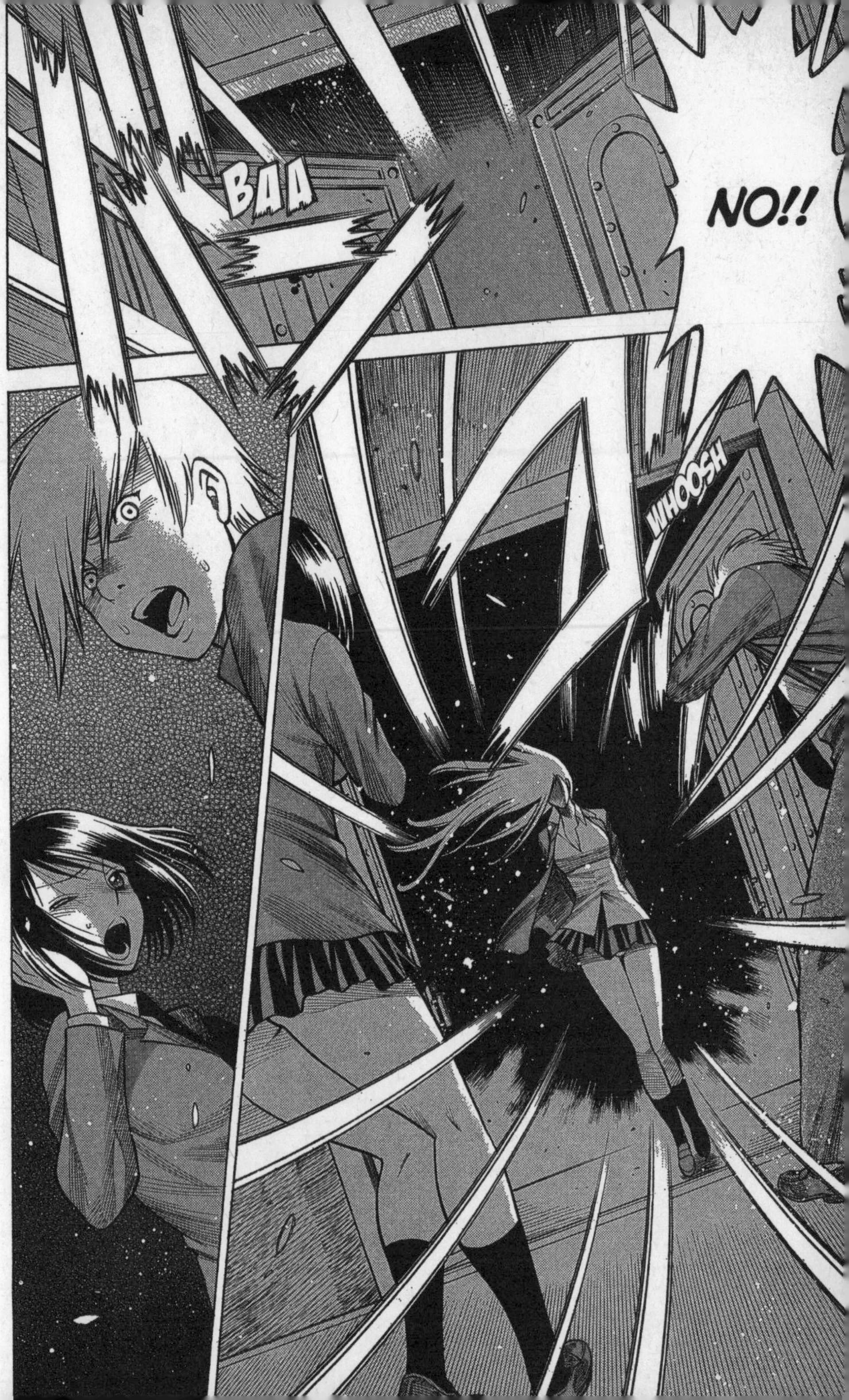
NO!!
BAA
WHOOSH

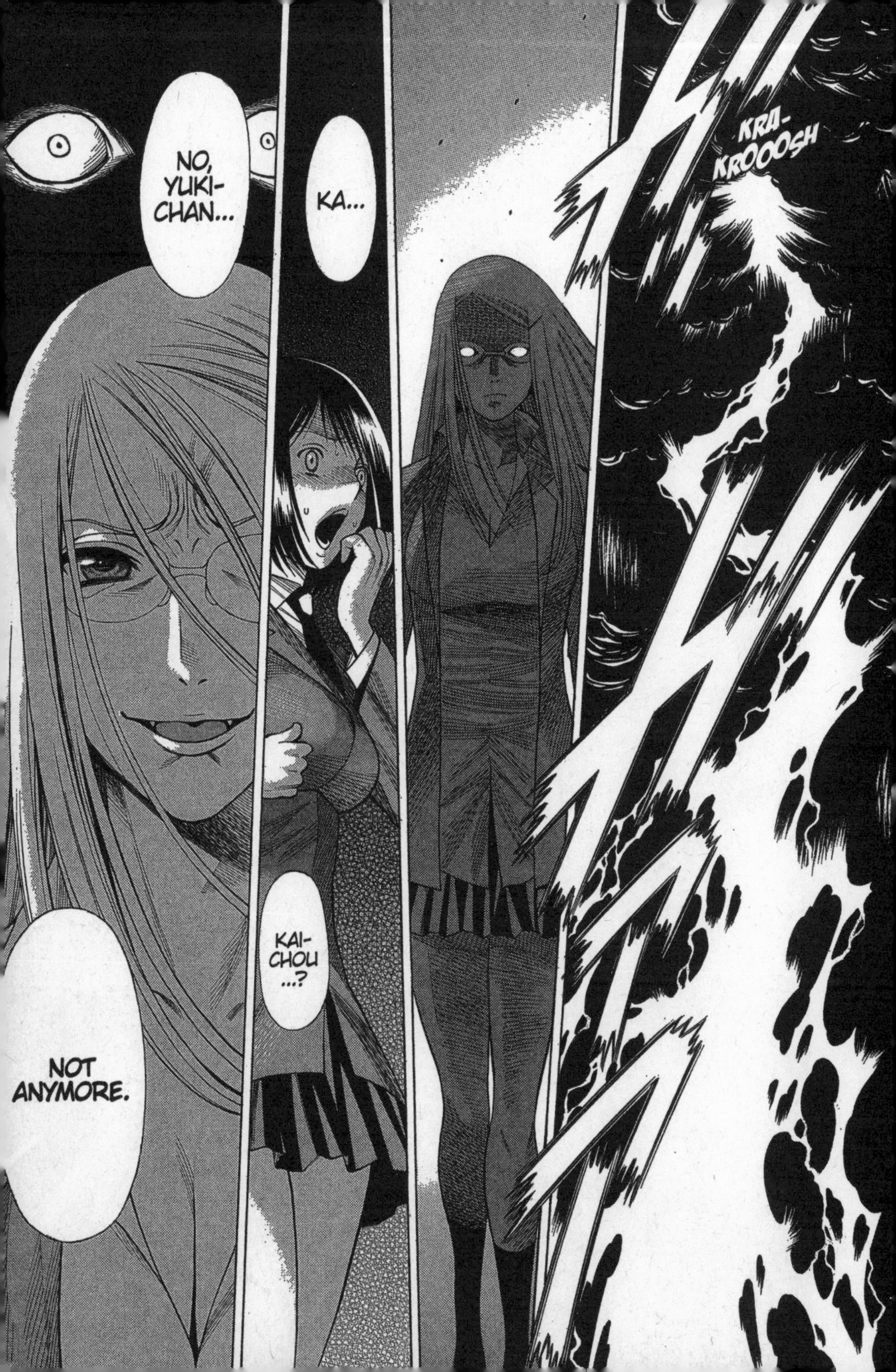
KRA-KROOOSH
KA...
KAI-CHOU...?
NO, YUKI-CHAN...
NOT ANYMORE.

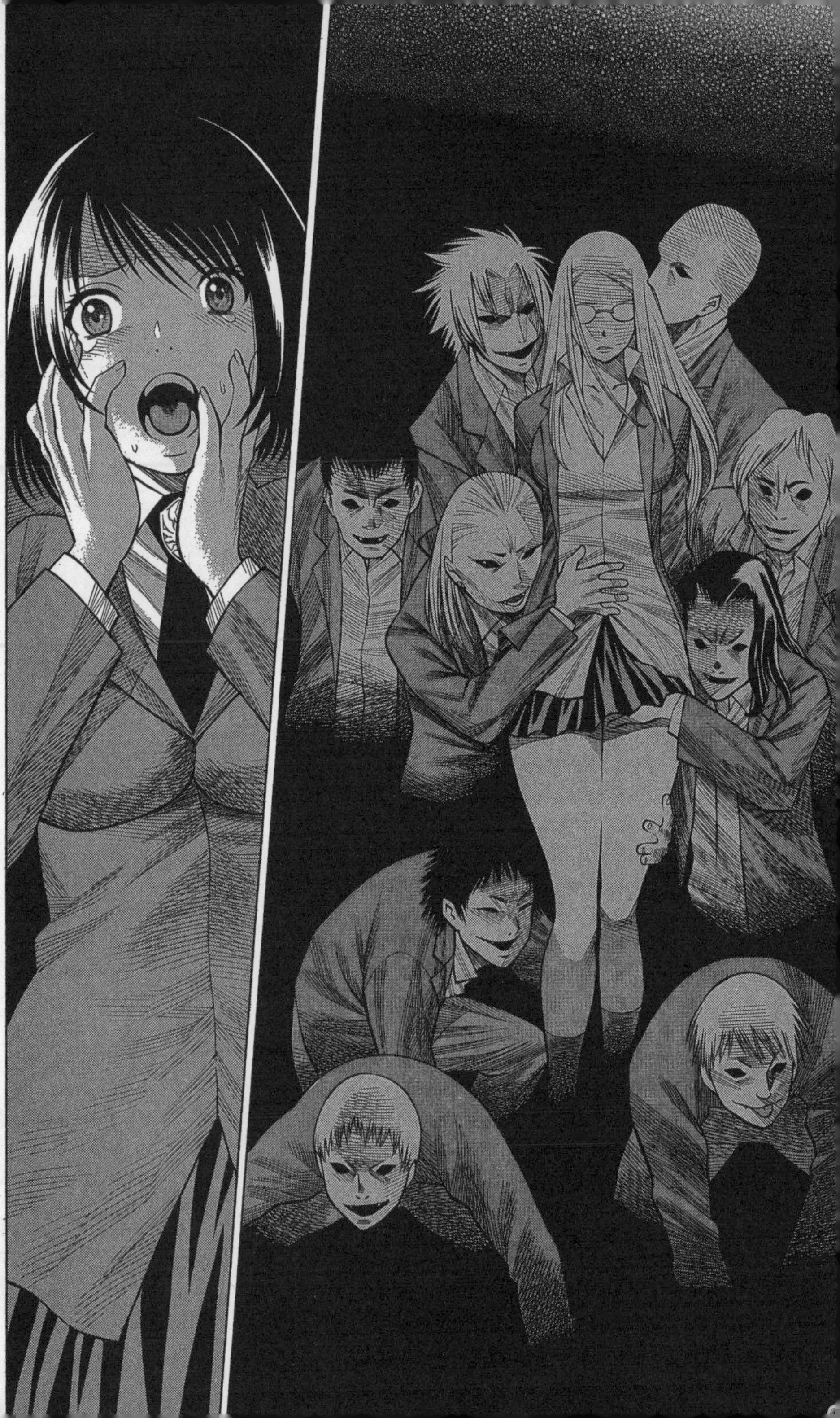

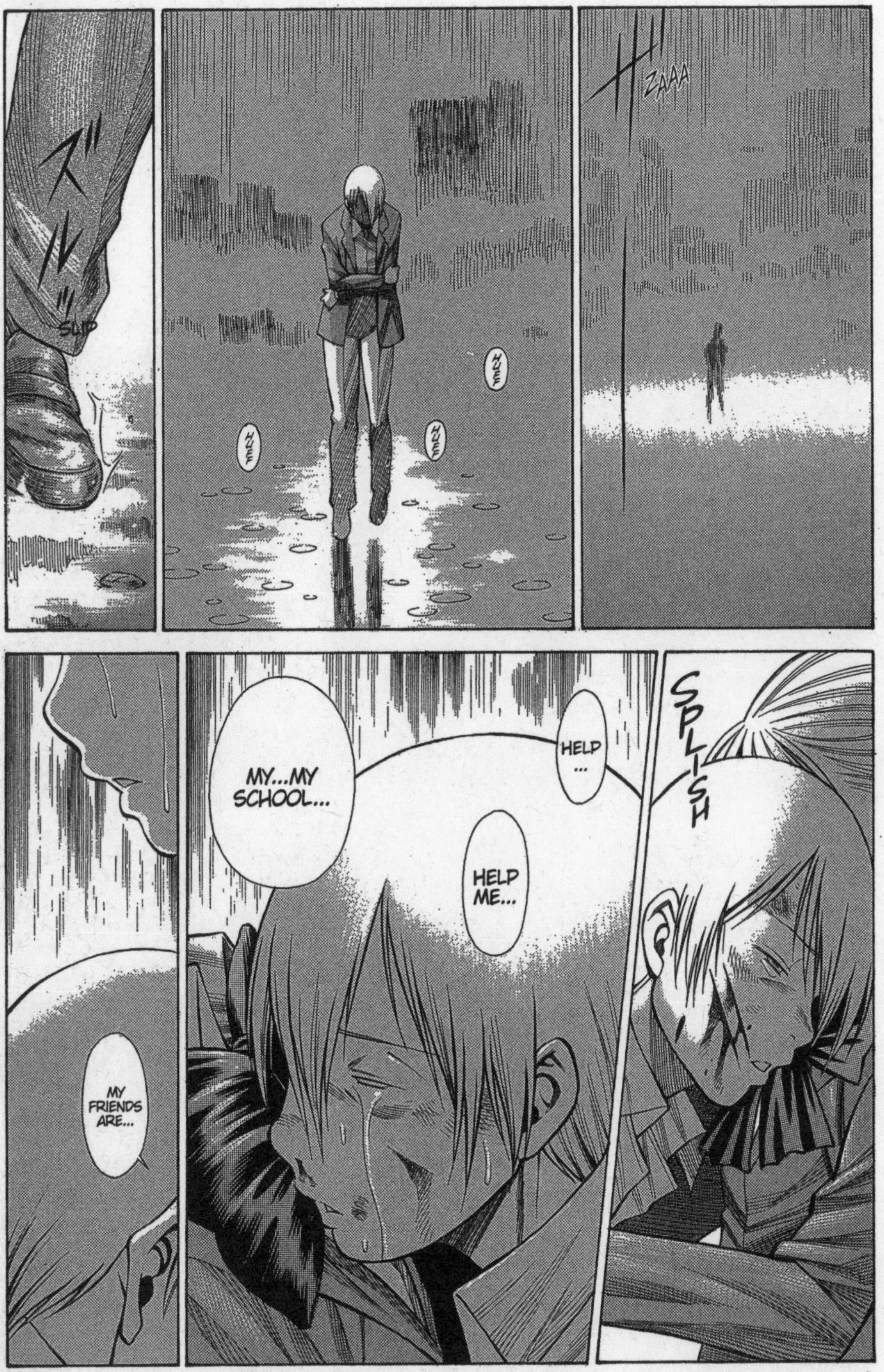
ZAAA
HUFF
HUFF
HUFF
ズル
SLIP
SPLISH
HELP ...
MY...MY SCHOOL...
HELP ME...
MY FRIENDS ARE...

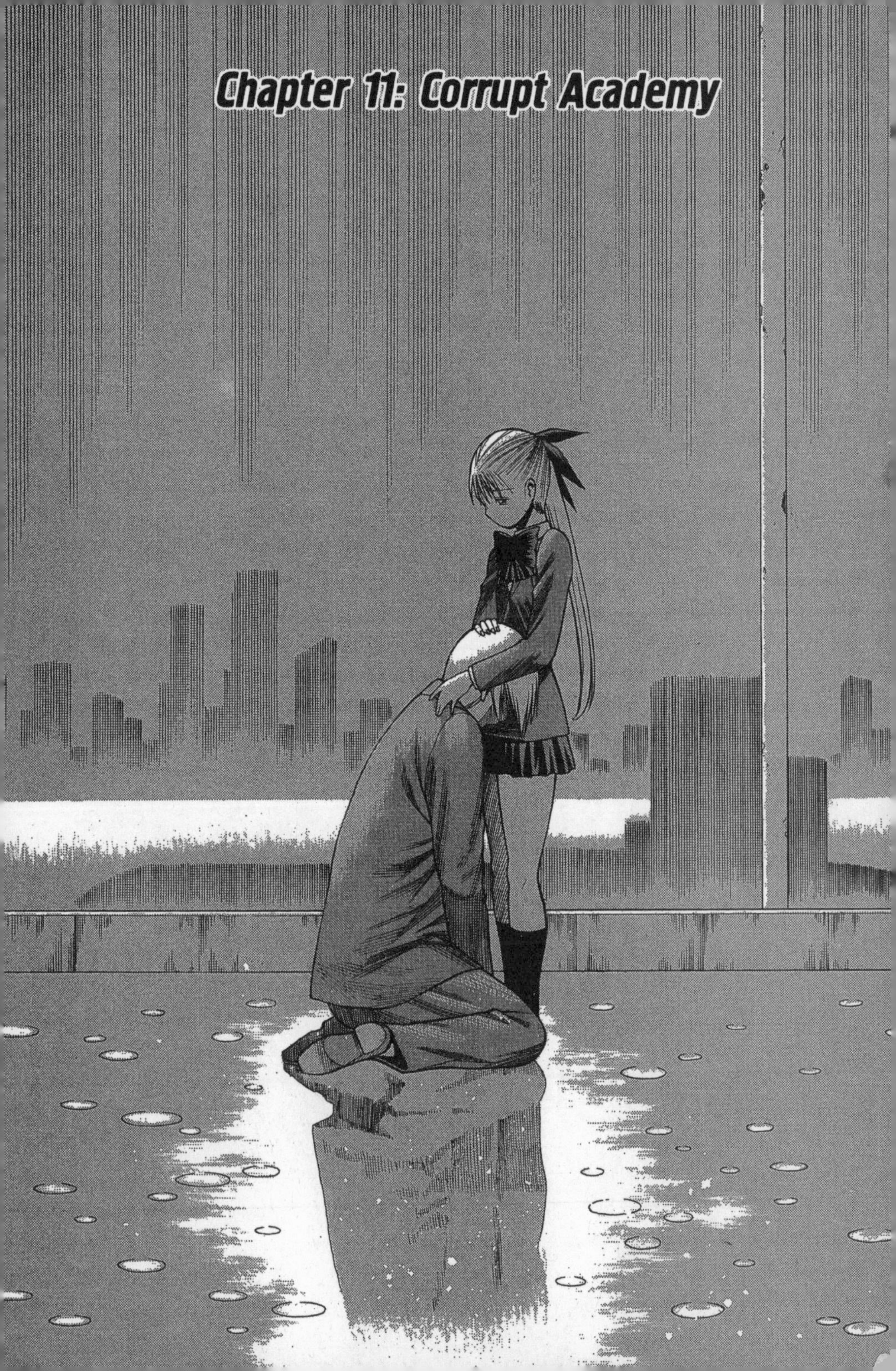
Chapter 11: Corrupt Academy

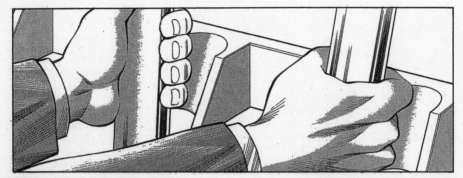

CLANG

CLANK

ARE YOU
SURE YOU
HAVE *TIME* TO
BE HANGING
AROUND
HERE, YOUNG
MAN?

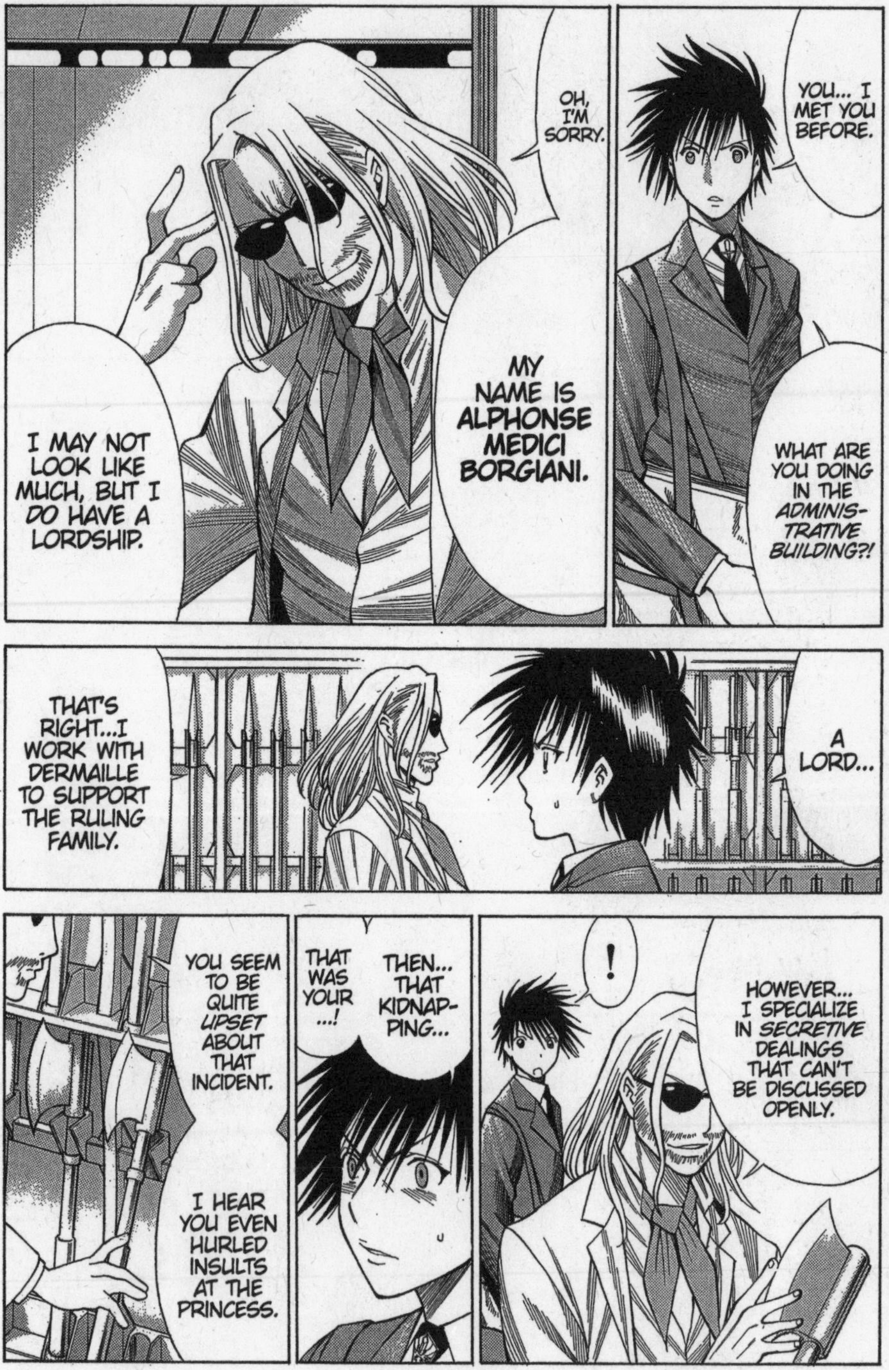
YOU... I MET YOU BEFORE.
WHAT ARE YOU DOING IN THE *ADMINISTRATIVE BUILDING?!*
OH, I'M SORRY.
MY NAME IS ALPHONSE MEDICI BORGIANI.
I MAY NOT LOOK LIKE MUCH, BUT I *DO* HAVE A LORDSHIP.
A LORD...
THAT'S RIGHT...I WORK WITH DERMAILLE TO SUPPORT THE RULING FAMILY.
!
HOWEVER... I SPECIALIZE IN *SECRETIVE* DEALINGS THAT CAN'T BE DISCUSSED OPENLY.
THEN... THAT KIDNAPPING...
THAT WAS YOUR ...!
YOU SEEM TO BE QUITE *UPSET* ABOUT THAT INCIDENT.
I HEAR YOU EVEN HURLED INSULTS AT THE PRINCESS.

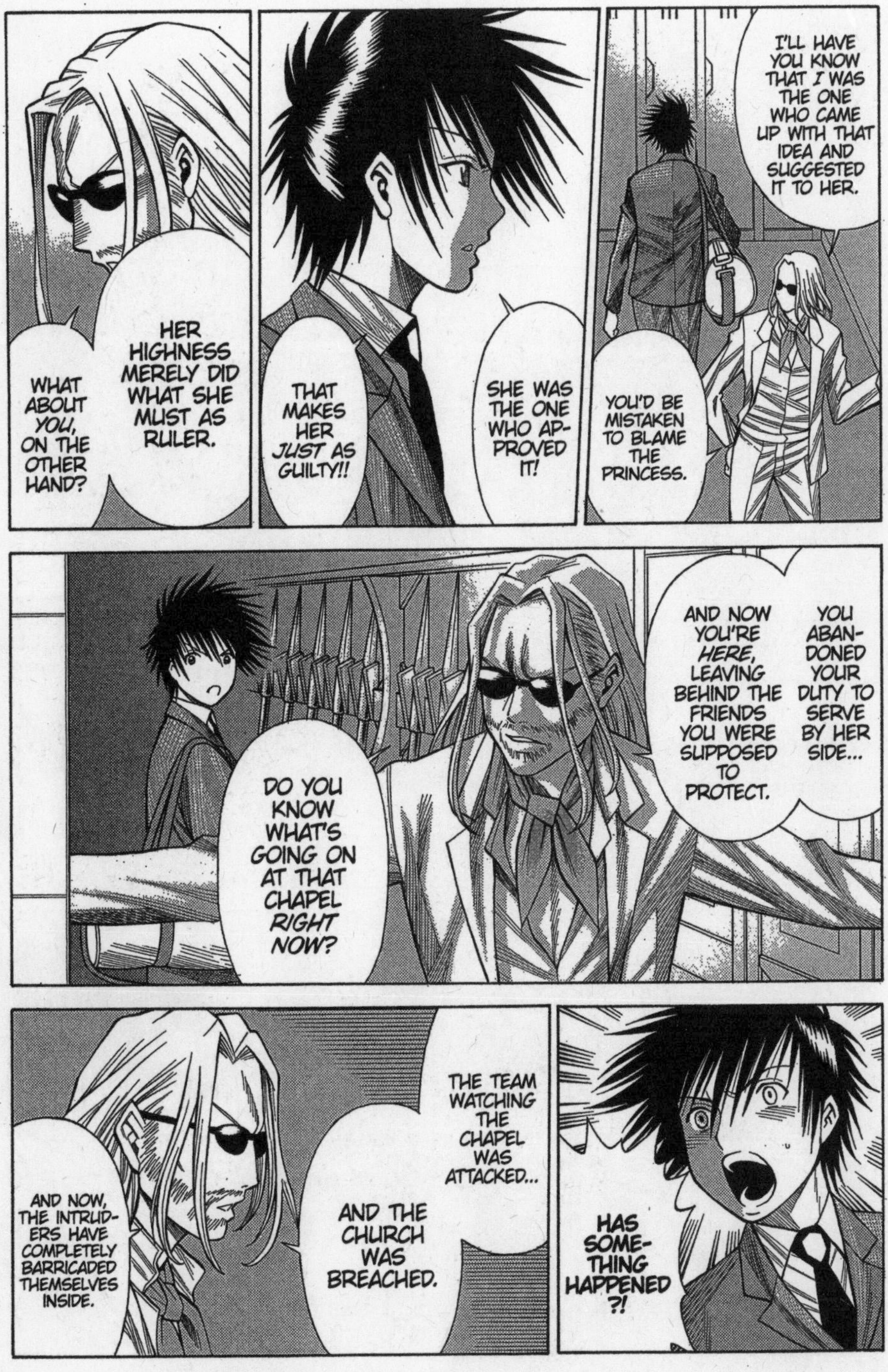
I'LL HAVE YOU KNOW THAT I WAS THE ONE WHO CAME UP WITH THAT IDEA AND SUGGESTED IT TO HER.
YOU'D BE MISTAKEN TO BLAME THE PRINCESS.
SHE WAS THE ONE WHO APPROVED IT!
THAT MAKES HER JUST AS GUILTY!!
HER HIGHNESS MERELY DID WHAT SHE MUST AS RULER.
WHAT ABOUT YOU, ON THE OTHER HAND?
YOU ABANDONED YOUR DUTY TO SERVE BY HER SIDE...
AND NOW YOU'RE HERE, LEAVING BEHIND THE FRIENDS YOU WERE SUPPOSED TO PROTECT.
DO YOU KNOW WHAT'S GOING ON AT THAT CHAPEL RIGHT NOW?
HAS SOMETHING HAPPENED?!
THE TEAM WATCHING THE CHAPEL WAS ATTACKED...
AND THE CHURCH WAS BREACHED.
AND NOW, THE INTRUDERS HAVE COMPLETELY BARRICADED THEMSELVES INSIDE.

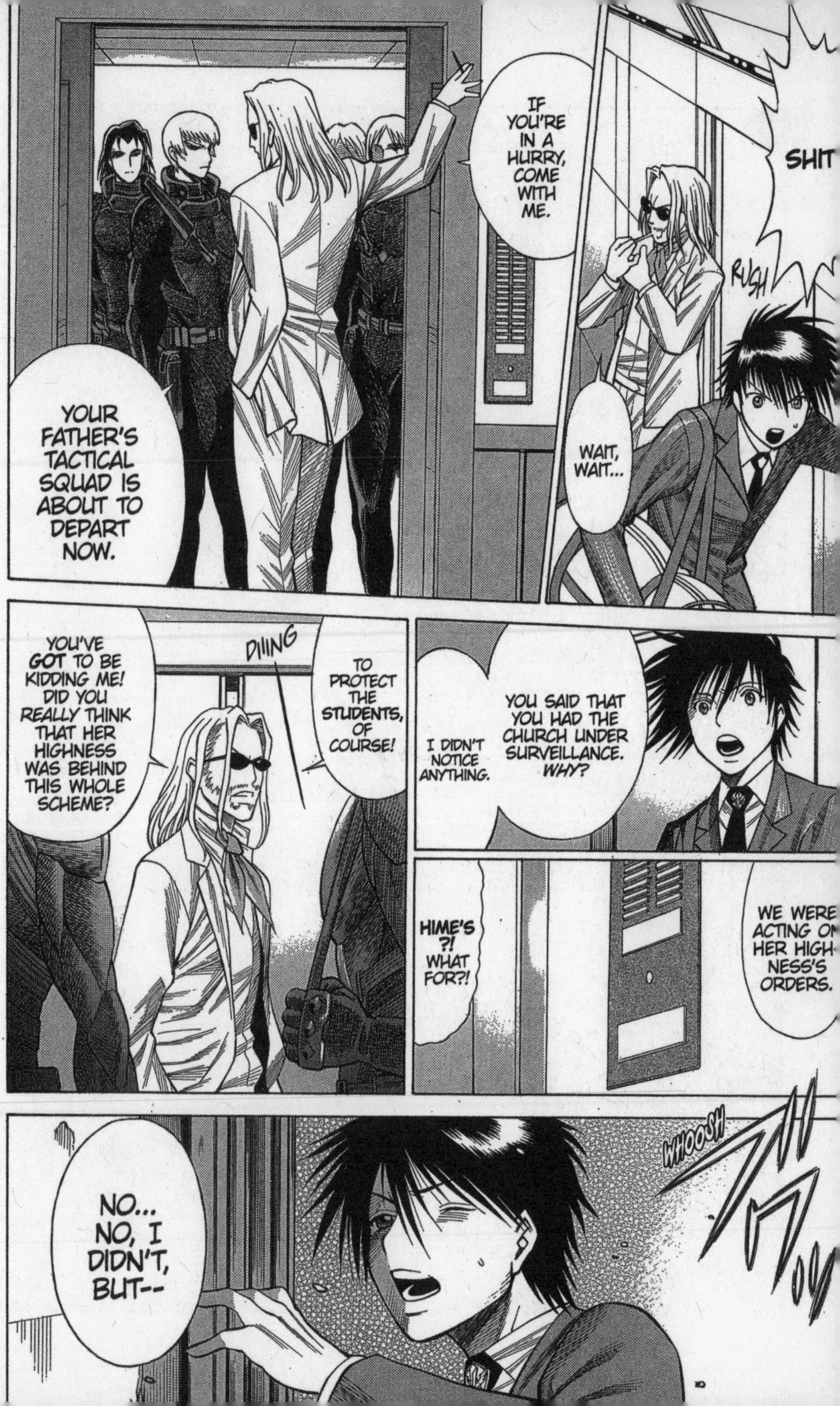
SHIT
IF YOU'RE IN A HURRY, COME WITH ME.
RUSH
WAIT, WAIT...
YOUR FATHER'S TACTICAL SQUAD IS ABOUT TO DEPART NOW.
YOU SAID THAT YOU HAD THE CHURCH UNDER SURVEILLANCE. WHY?
I DIDN'T NOTICE ANYTHING.
WE WERE ACTING ON HER HIGHNESS'S ORDERS.
HIME'S?! WHAT FOR?!
TO PROTECT THE STUDENTS, OF COURSE!
DIIING
YOU'VE GOT TO BE KIDDING ME! DID YOU REALLY THINK THAT HER HIGHNESS WAS BEHIND THIS WHOLE SCHEME?
WHOOSH
NO... NO, I DIDN'T, BUT--

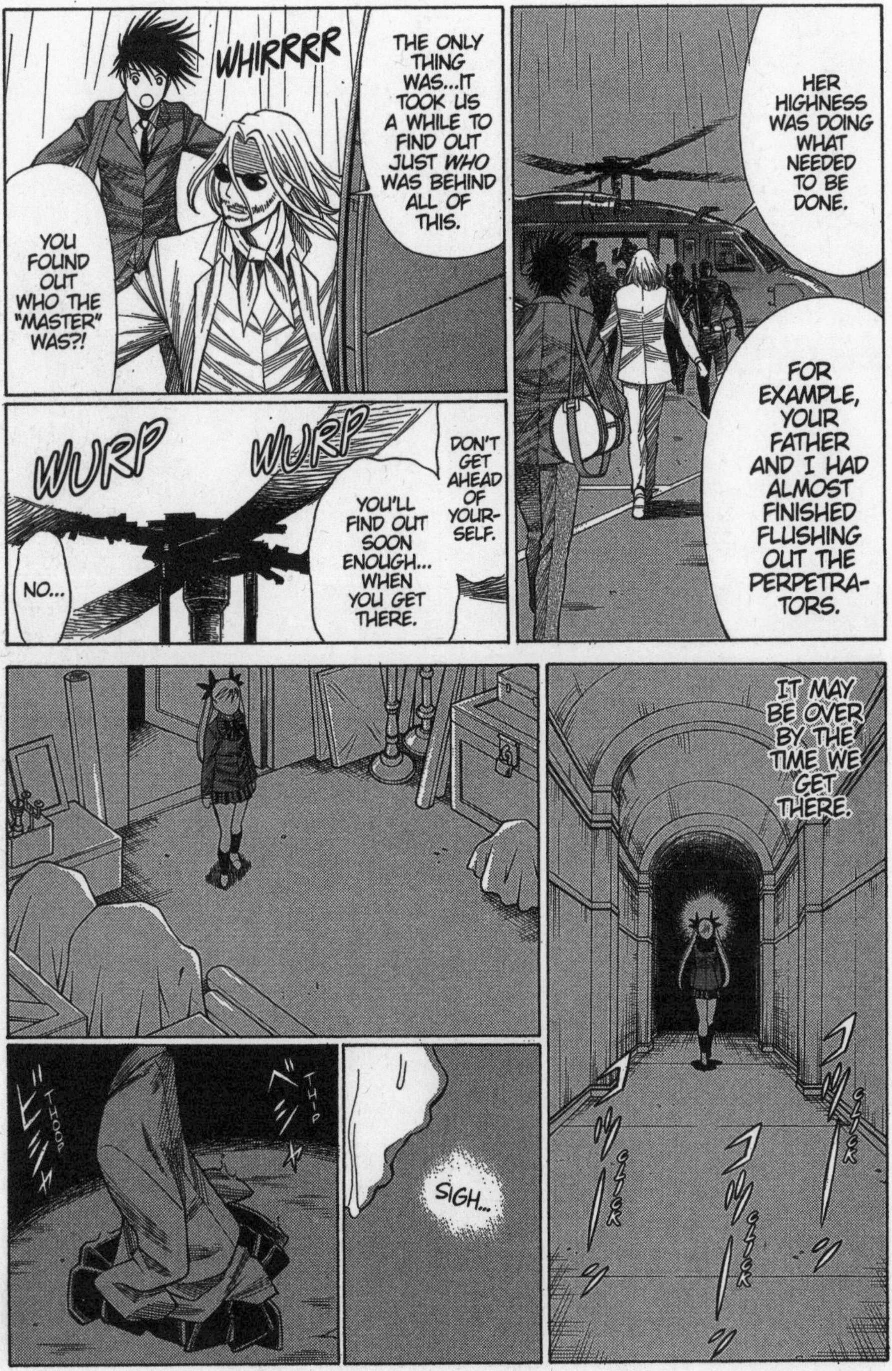
HER HIGHNESS WAS DOING WHAT NEEDED TO BE DONE.
FOR EXAMPLE, YOUR FATHER AND I HAD ALMOST FINISHED FLUSHING OUT THE PERPETRATORS.
THE ONLY THING WAS...IT TOOK US A WHILE TO FIND OUT JUST WHO WAS BEHIND ALL OF THIS.
WHIRRRR
YOU FOUND OUT WHO THE "MASTER" WAS?!
DON'T GET AHEAD OF YOUR-SELF.
YOU'LL FIND OUT SOON ENOUGH... WHEN YOU GET THERE.
WURP
WURP
NO...
IT MAY BE OVER BY THE TIME WE GET THERE.
CLICK
CLICK
CLICK
SIGH...
THIP
THOOP

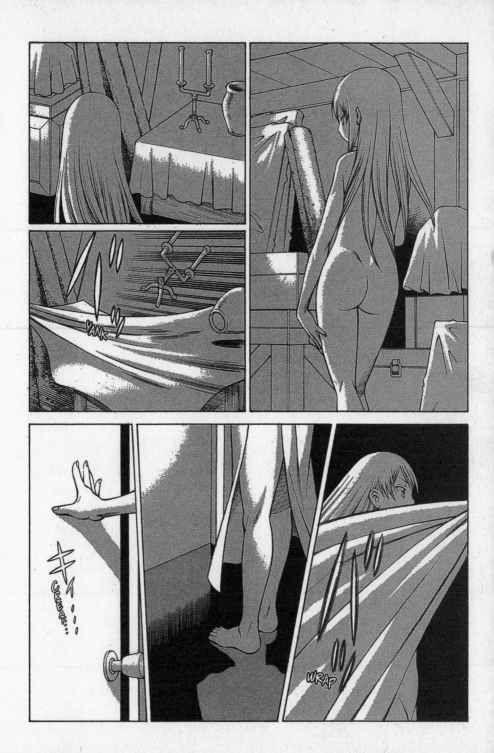

YANK

CREAK...

WRAP

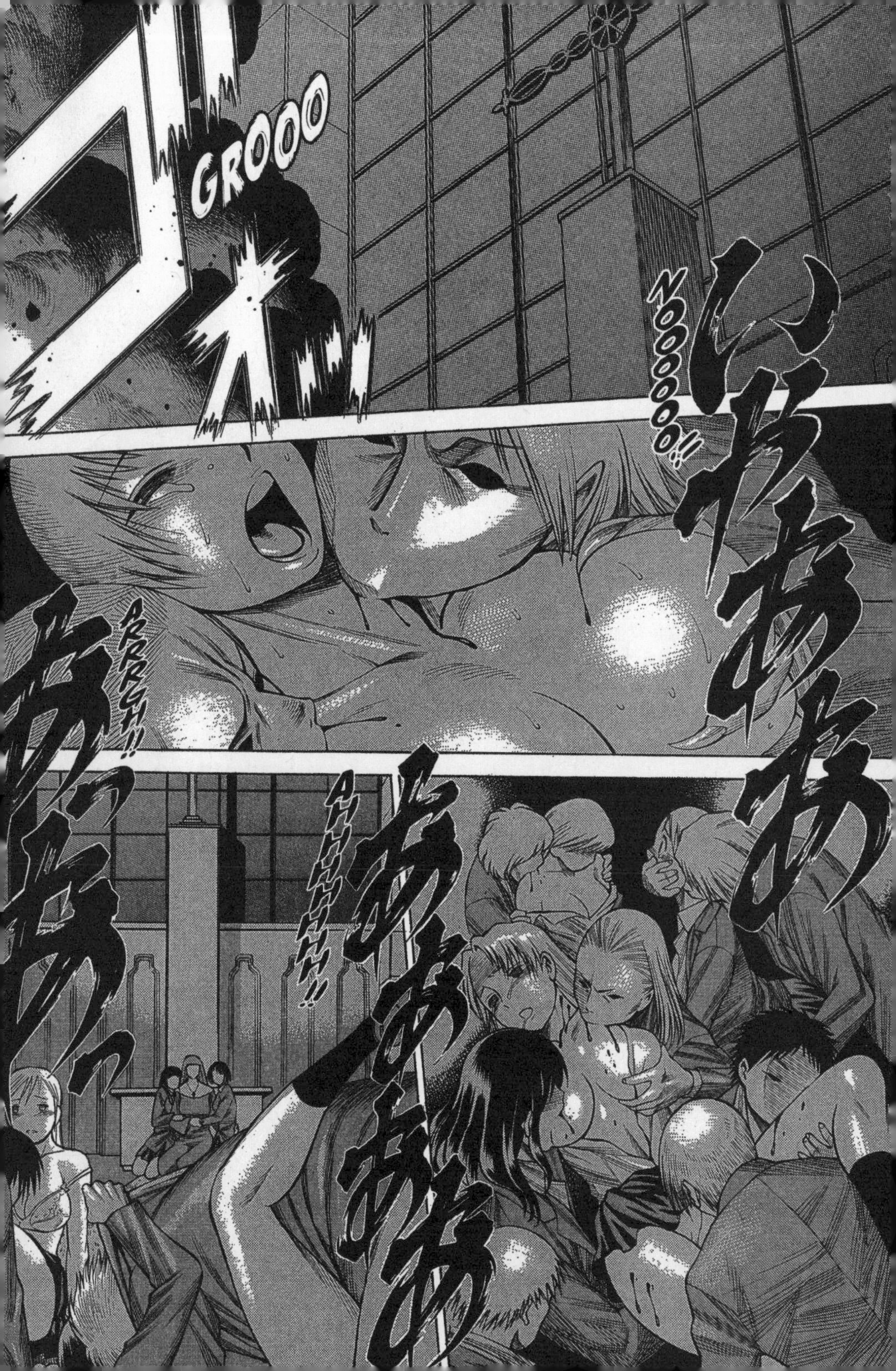
GROOO
NOOOOOOOO!!
ARRRGH!!
AHHHHHHHH!!

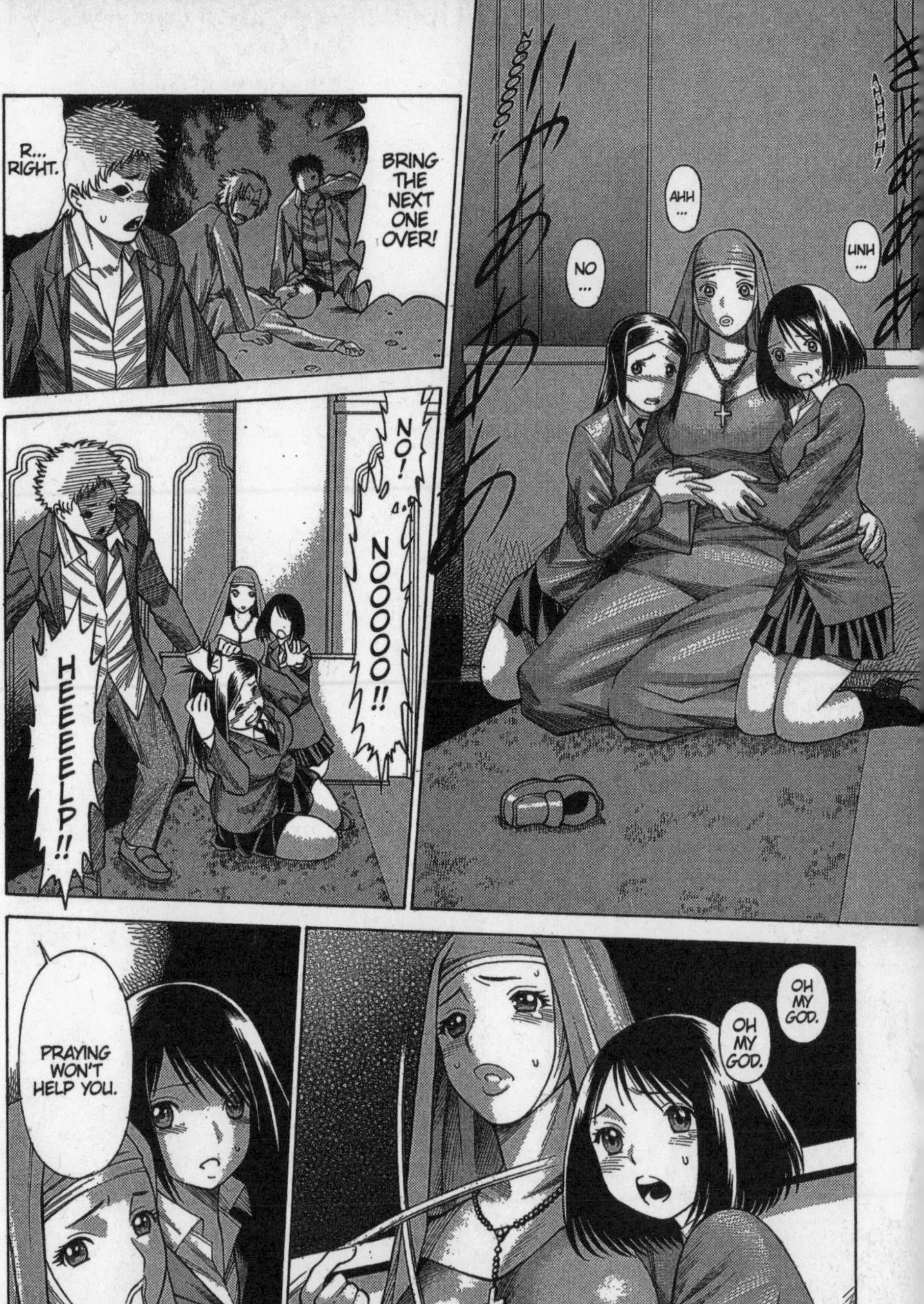
AAHHHH!
UNH ...
AHH ...
NO ...
NOOOOOO!!
BRING THE NEXT ONE OVER!
R... RIGHT.
NO! NOOOOOO!!
HEEEEELP!!
OH MY GOD.
OH MY GOD.
PRAYING WON'T HELP YOU.

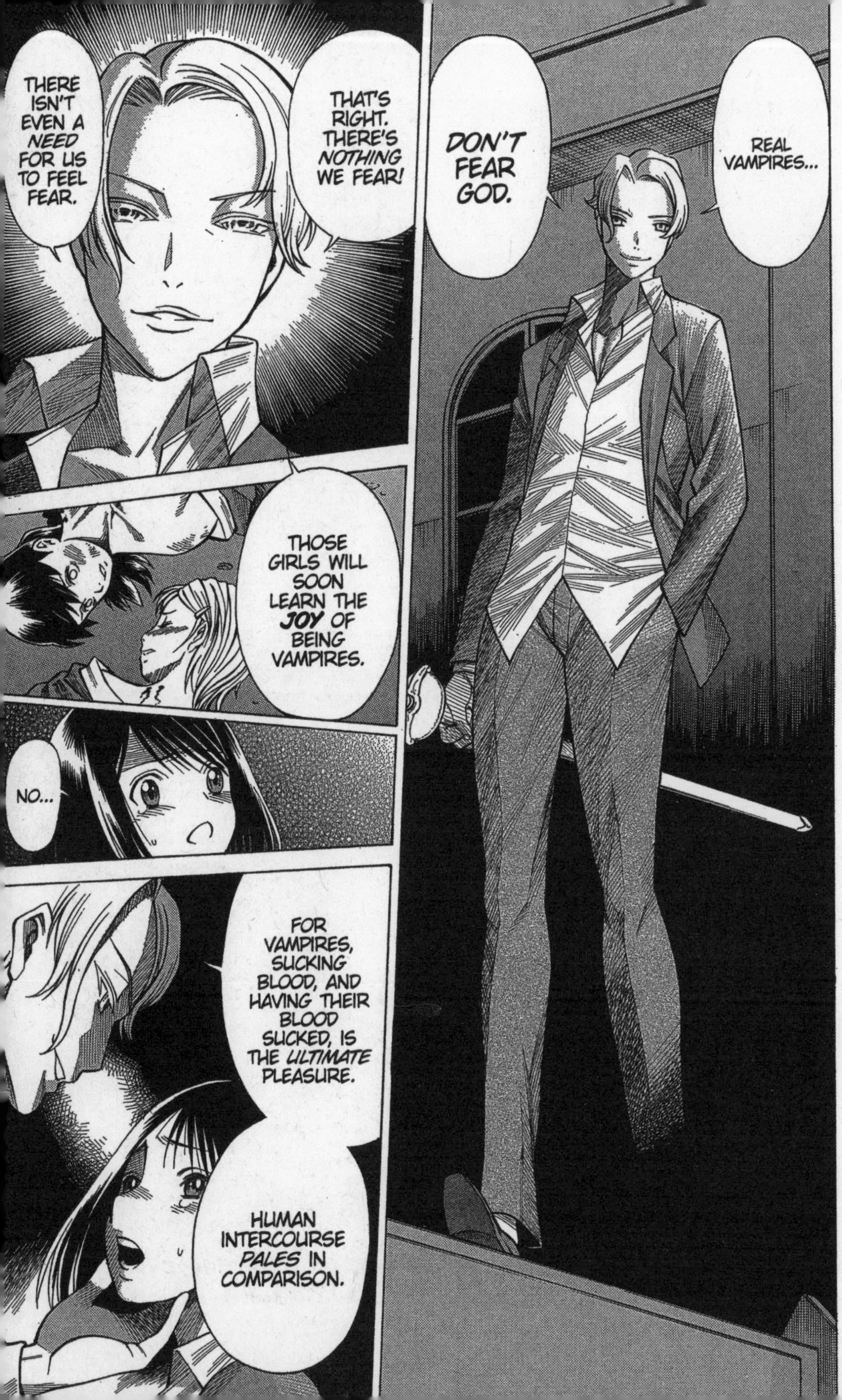
REAL VAMPIRES...
DON'T FEAR GOD.
THAT'S RIGHT. THERE'S *NOTHING* WE FEAR!
THERE ISN'T EVEN A *NEED* FOR US TO FEEL FEAR.
THOSE GIRLS WILL SOON LEARN THE **JOY** OF BEING VAMPIRES.
NO...
FOR VAMPIRES, SUCKING BLOOD, AND HAVING THEIR BLOOD SUCKED, IS THE *ULTIMATE* PLEASURE.
HUMAN INTERCOURSE *PALES* IN COMPARISON.

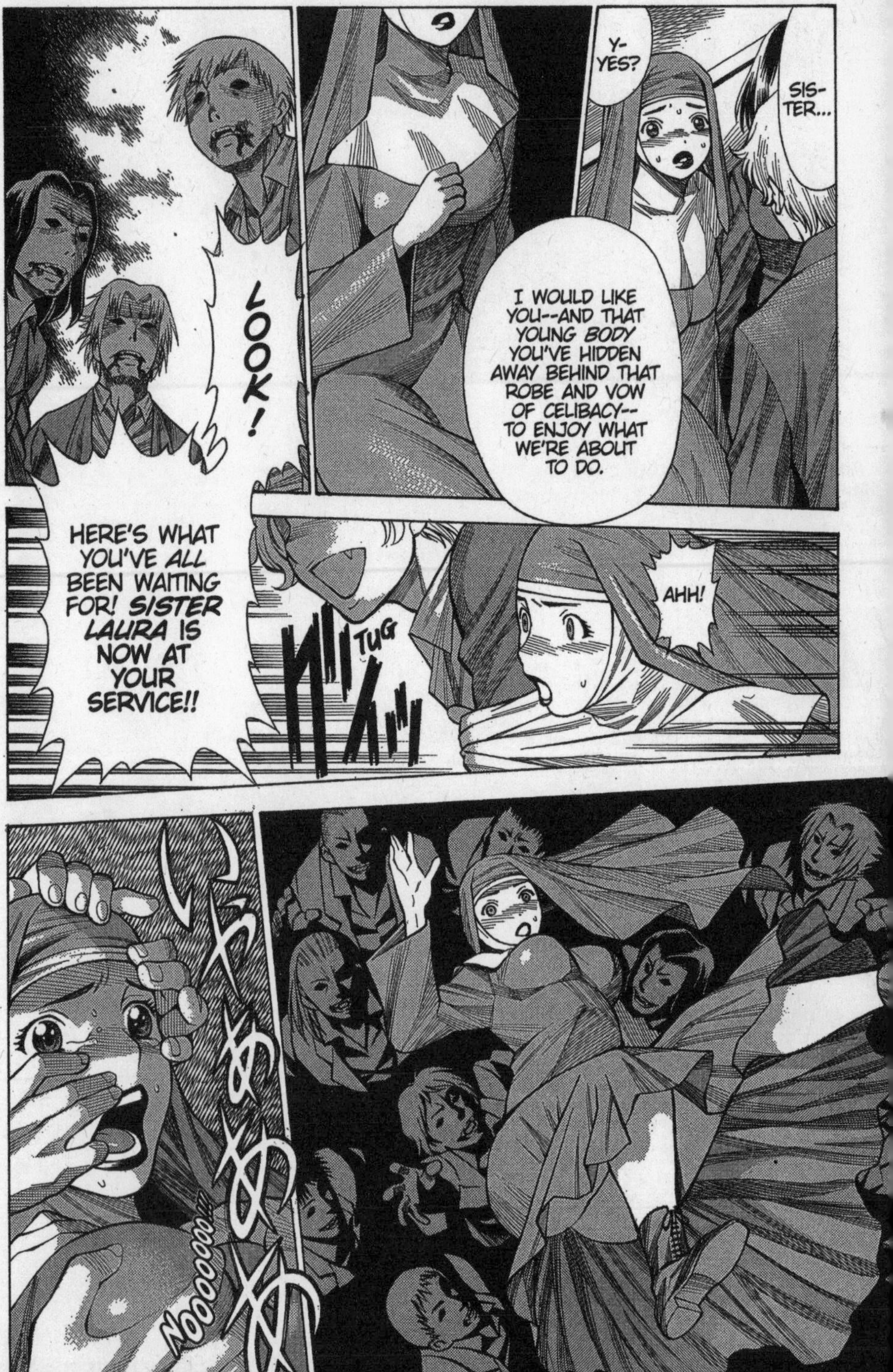
SIS-
TER...
Y-
YES?
I WOULD LIKE YOU--AND THAT YOUNG BODY YOU'VE HIDDEN AWAY BEHIND THAT ROBE AND VOW OF CELIBACY--TO ENJOY WHAT WE'RE ABOUT TO DO.
LOOK!
AHH!
TUG
HERE'S WHAT YOU'VE ALL BEEN WAITING FOR! SISTER LAURA IS NOW AT YOUR SERVICE!!
NOOOOOOO!!

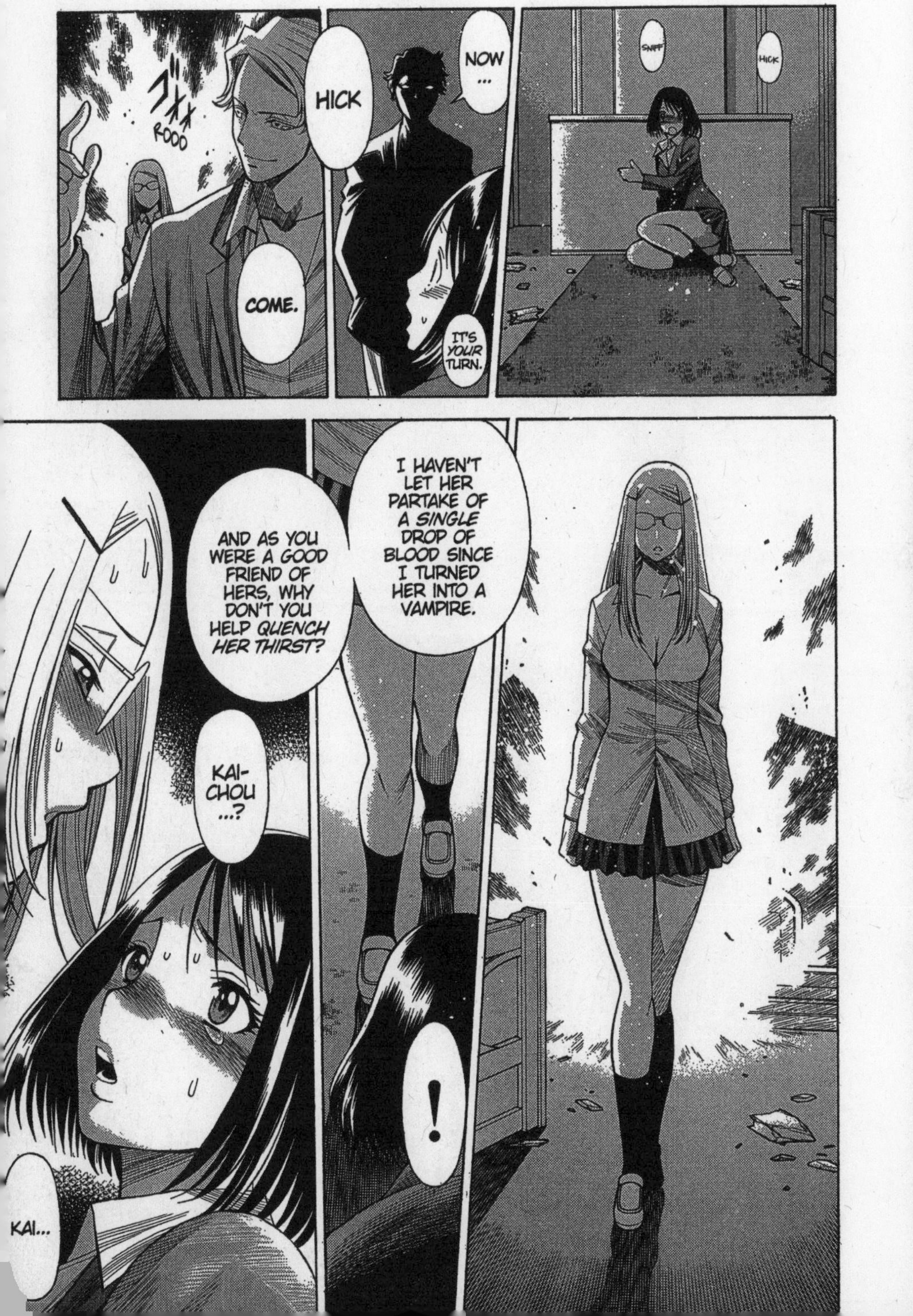
SNIFF
HICK
NOW...
HICK
IT'S YOUR TURN.
ゴオオ
ROOD
COME.
I HAVEN'T LET HER PARTAKE OF A SINGLE DROP OF BLOOD SINCE I TURNED HER INTO A VAMPIRE.
AND AS YOU WERE A GOOD FRIEND OF HERS, WHY DON'T YOU HELP QUENCH HER THIRST?
!
KAI-CHOU ...?
KAI...

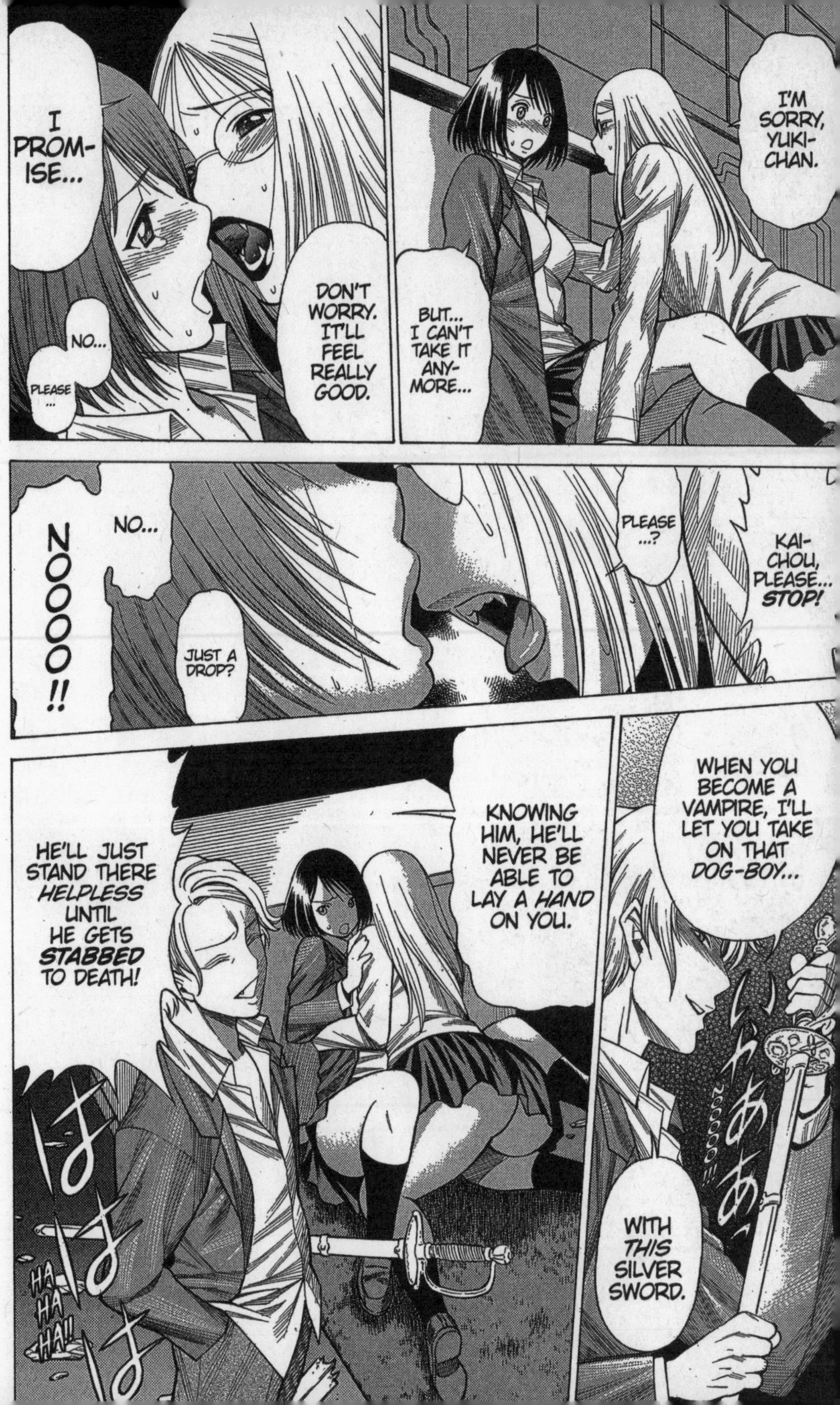
I'M SORRY, YUKI-CHAN.
BUT... I CAN'T TAKE IT ANYMORE...
DON'T WORRY. IT'LL FEEL REALLY GOOD.
I PROMISE...
NO...
PLEASE ...
KAI-CHOU, PLEASE... *STOP!*
PLEASE ...?
JUST A DROP?
NO...
NOOOOO!!
WHEN YOU BECOME A VAMPIRE, I'LL LET YOU TAKE ON THAT *DOG-BOY*...
WITH *THIS* SILVER SWORD.
KNOWING HIM, HE'LL NEVER BE ABLE TO LAY A *HAND* ON YOU.
HE'LL JUST STAND THERE *HELPLESS* UNTIL HE GETS *STABBED* TO DEATH!
HA HA HA HA!!

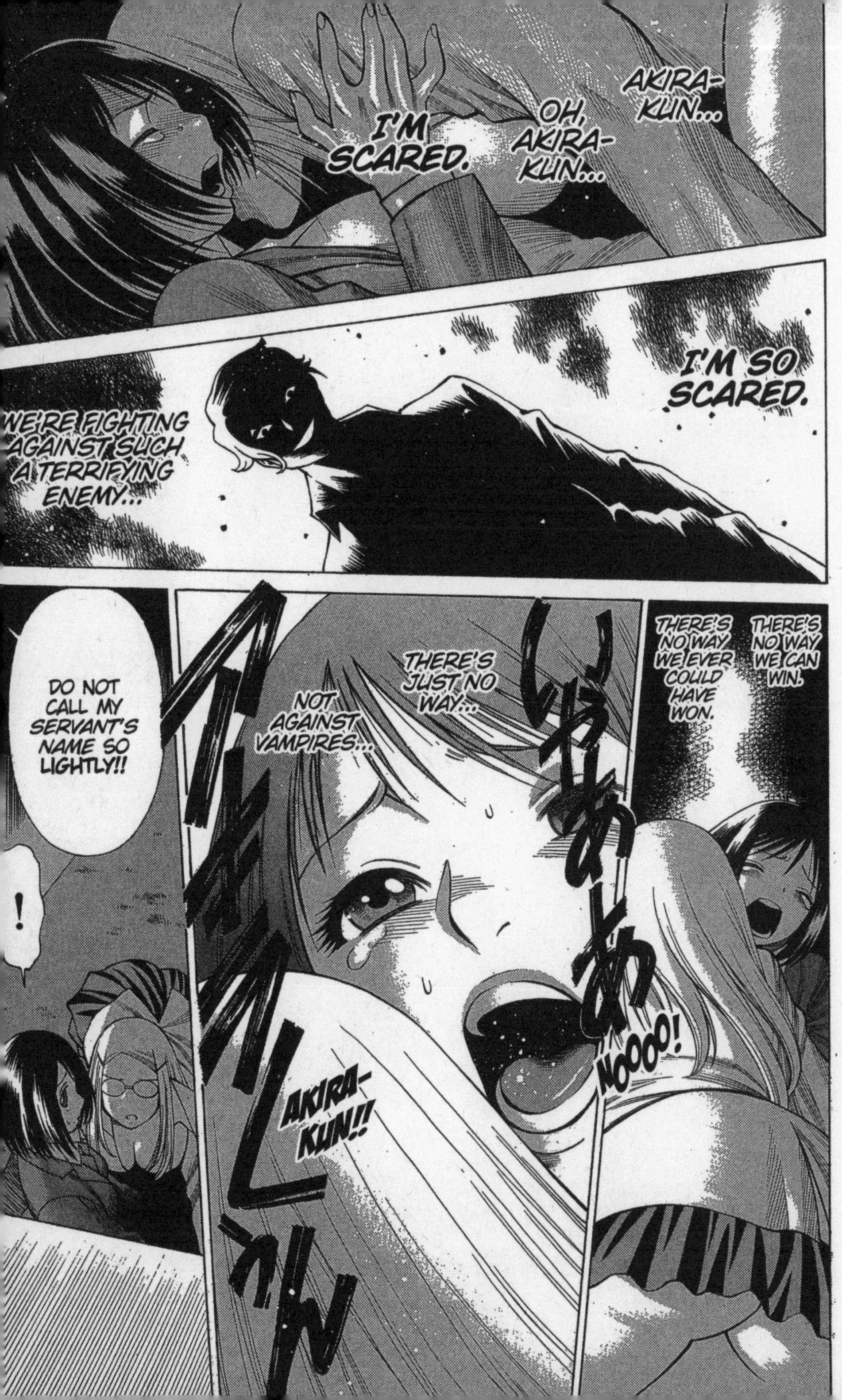

AKIRA-KUN...
OH, AKIRA-KUN...
I'M SCARED.
I'M SO SCARED.
WE'RE FIGHTING AGAINST SUCH A TERRIFYING ENEMY...
THERE'S NO WAY WE CAN WIN.
THERE'S NO WAY WE EVER COULD HAVE WON.
THERE'S JUST NO WAY...
NOT AGAINST VAMPIRES...
NOOOO!
AKIRA-KUN!!
DO NOT CALL MY SERVANT'S NAME SO LIGHTLY!!
!

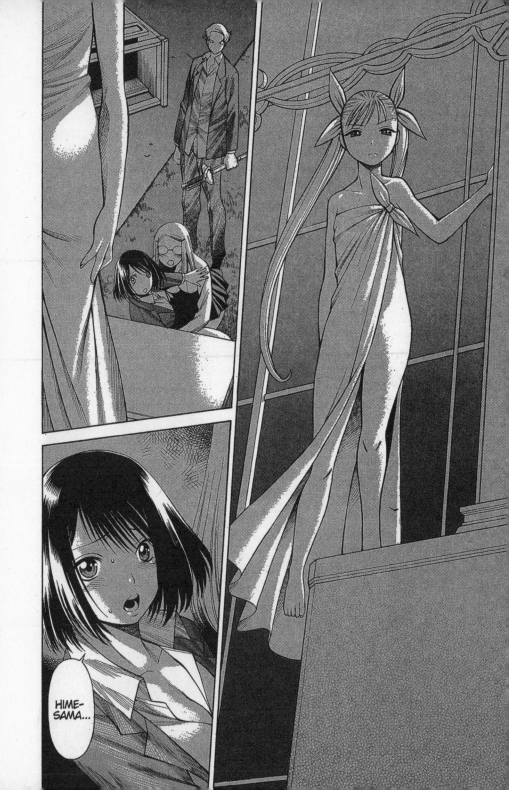

HIME-
SAMA...

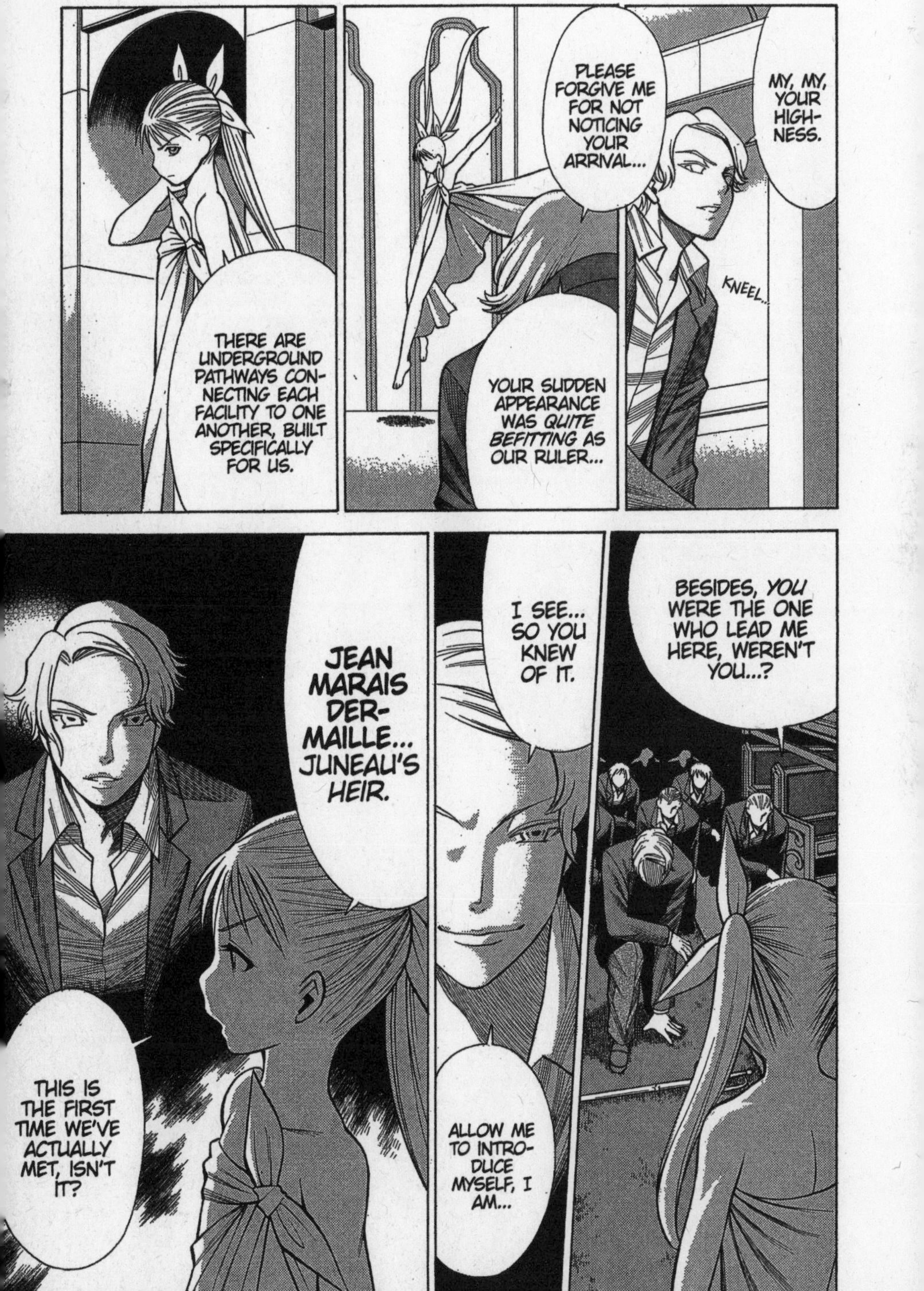
MY, MY, YOUR HIGHNESS.
KNEEL...
PLEASE FORGIVE ME FOR NOT NOTICING YOUR ARRIVAL...
YOUR SUDDEN APPEARANCE WAS *QUITE* BEFITTING AS OUR RULER...
THERE ARE UNDERGROUND PATHWAYS CONNECTING EACH FACILITY TO ONE ANOTHER, BUILT SPECIFICALLY FOR US.
BESIDES, *YOU* WERE THE ONE WHO LEAD ME HERE, WEREN'T YOU...?
I SEE... SO YOU KNEW OF IT.
ALLOW ME TO INTRODUCE MYSELF, I AM...
JEAN MARAIS DERMAILLE... JUNEAU'S HEIR.
THIS IS THE FIRST TIME WE'VE ACTUALLY MET, ISN'T IT?

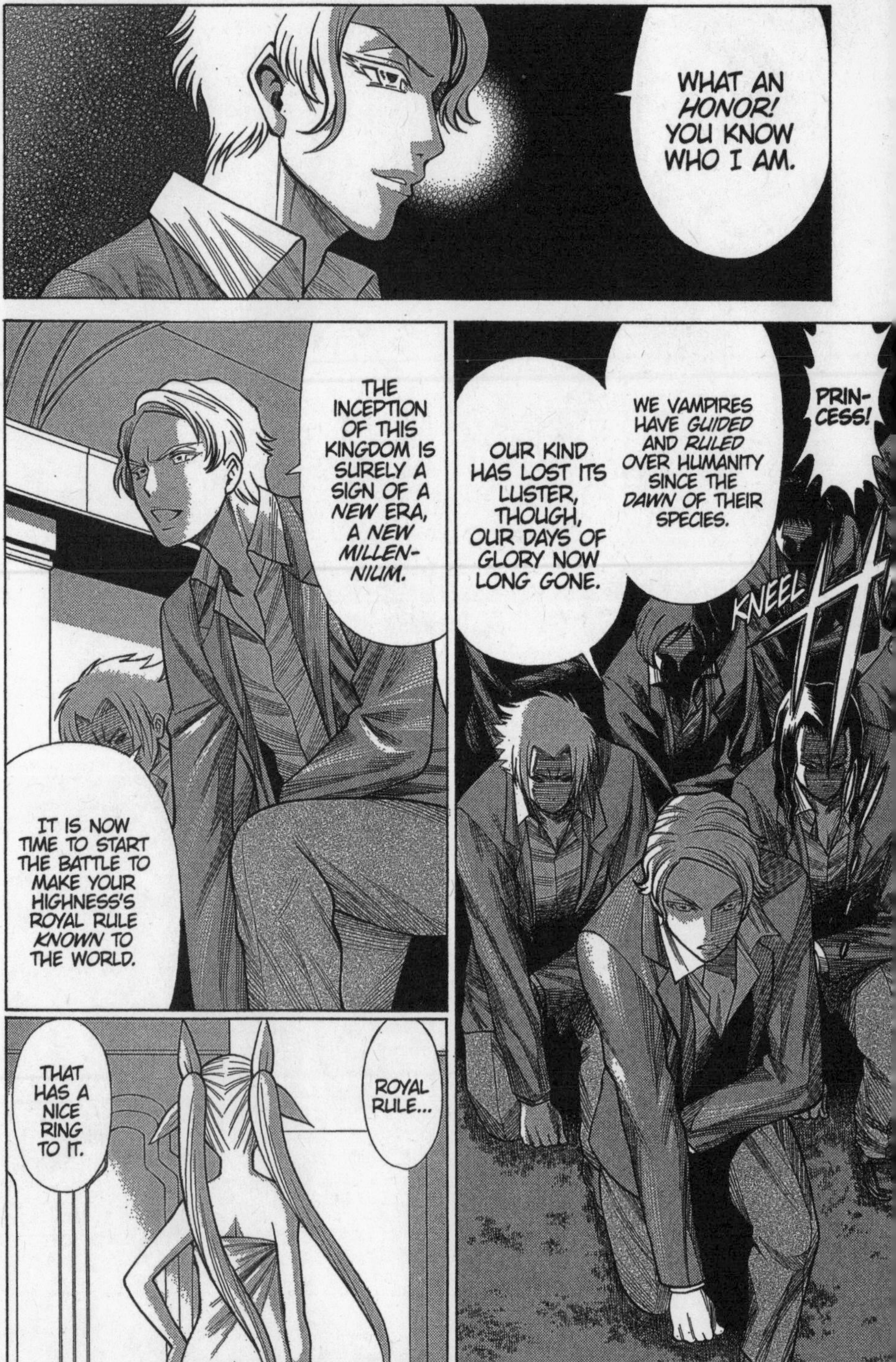
WHAT AN HONOR! YOU KNOW WHO I AM.
PRIN-CESS!
KNEEL
WE VAMPIRES HAVE GUIDED AND RULED OVER HUMANITY SINCE THE DAWN OF THEIR SPECIES.
OUR KIND HAS LOST ITS LUSTER, THOUGH, OUR DAYS OF GLORY NOW LONG GONE.
THE INCEPTION OF THIS KINGDOM IS SURELY A SIGN OF A NEW ERA, A NEW MILLEN-NIUM.
IT IS NOW TIME TO START THE BATTLE TO MAKE YOUR HIGHNESS'S ROYAL RULE KNOWN TO THE WORLD.
ROYAL RULE...
THAT HAS A NICE RING TO IT.

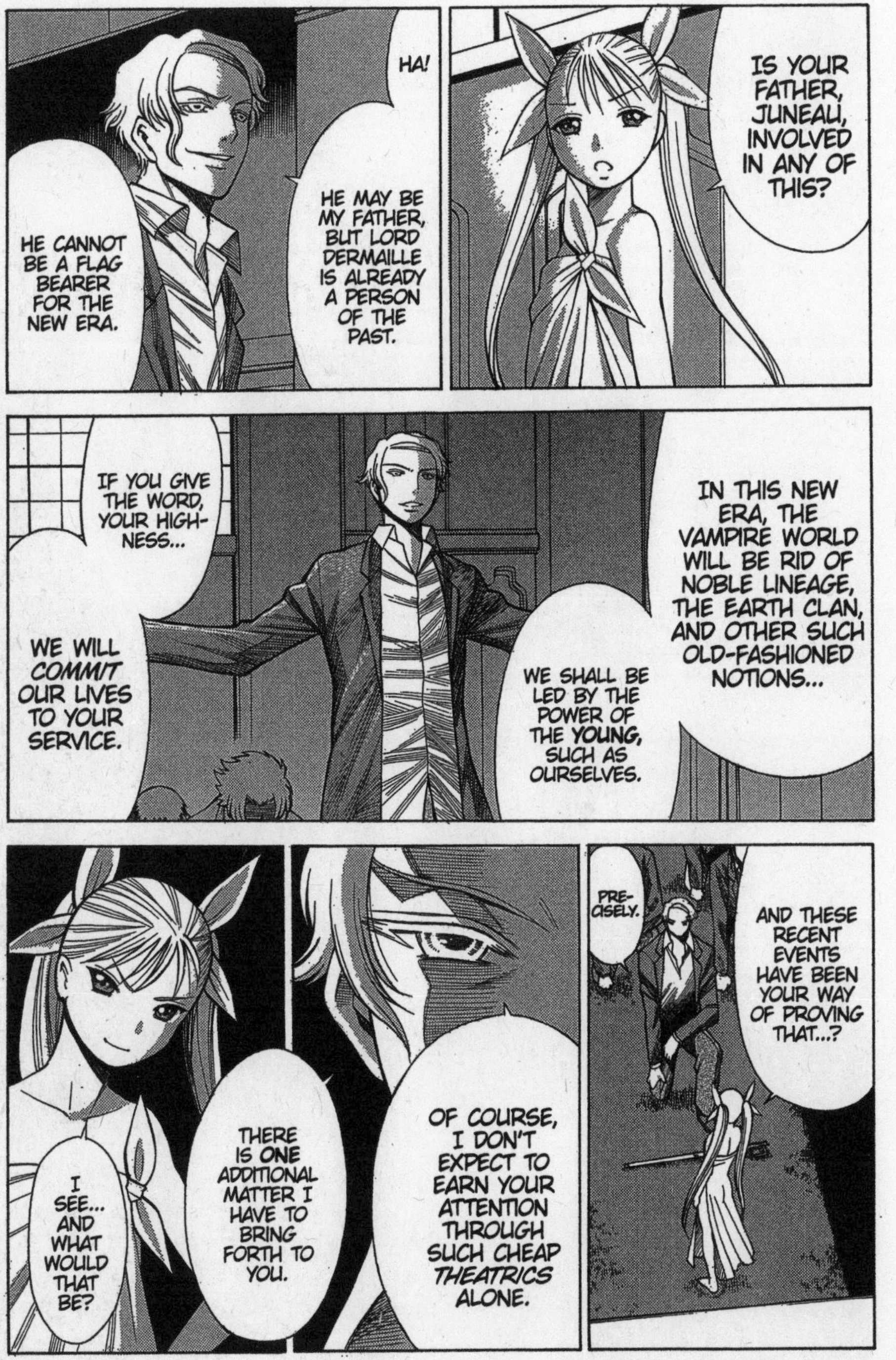
IS YOUR FATHER, JUNEAU, INVOLVED IN ANY OF THIS?
HA!
HE MAY BE MY FATHER, BUT LORD DERMAILLE IS ALREADY A PERSON OF THE PAST.
HE CANNOT BE A FLAG BEARER FOR THE NEW ERA.
IN THIS NEW ERA, THE VAMPIRE WORLD WILL BE RID OF NOBLE LINEAGE, THE EARTH CLAN, AND OTHER SUCH OLD-FASHIONED NOTIONS...
WE SHALL BE LED BY THE POWER OF THE **YOUNG**, SUCH AS OURSELVES.
IF YOU GIVE THE WORD, YOUR HIGH-NESS...
WE WILL *COMMIT* OUR LIVES TO YOUR SERVICE.
AND THESE RECENT EVENTS HAVE BEEN YOUR WAY OF PROVING THAT...?
PRE-CISELY.
OF COURSE, I DON'T EXPECT TO EARN YOUR ATTENTION THROUGH SUCH CHEAP *THEATRICS* ALONE.
THERE IS **ONE** ADDITIONAL MATTER I HAVE TO BRING FORTH TO YOU.
I SEE... AND WHAT WOULD THAT BE?

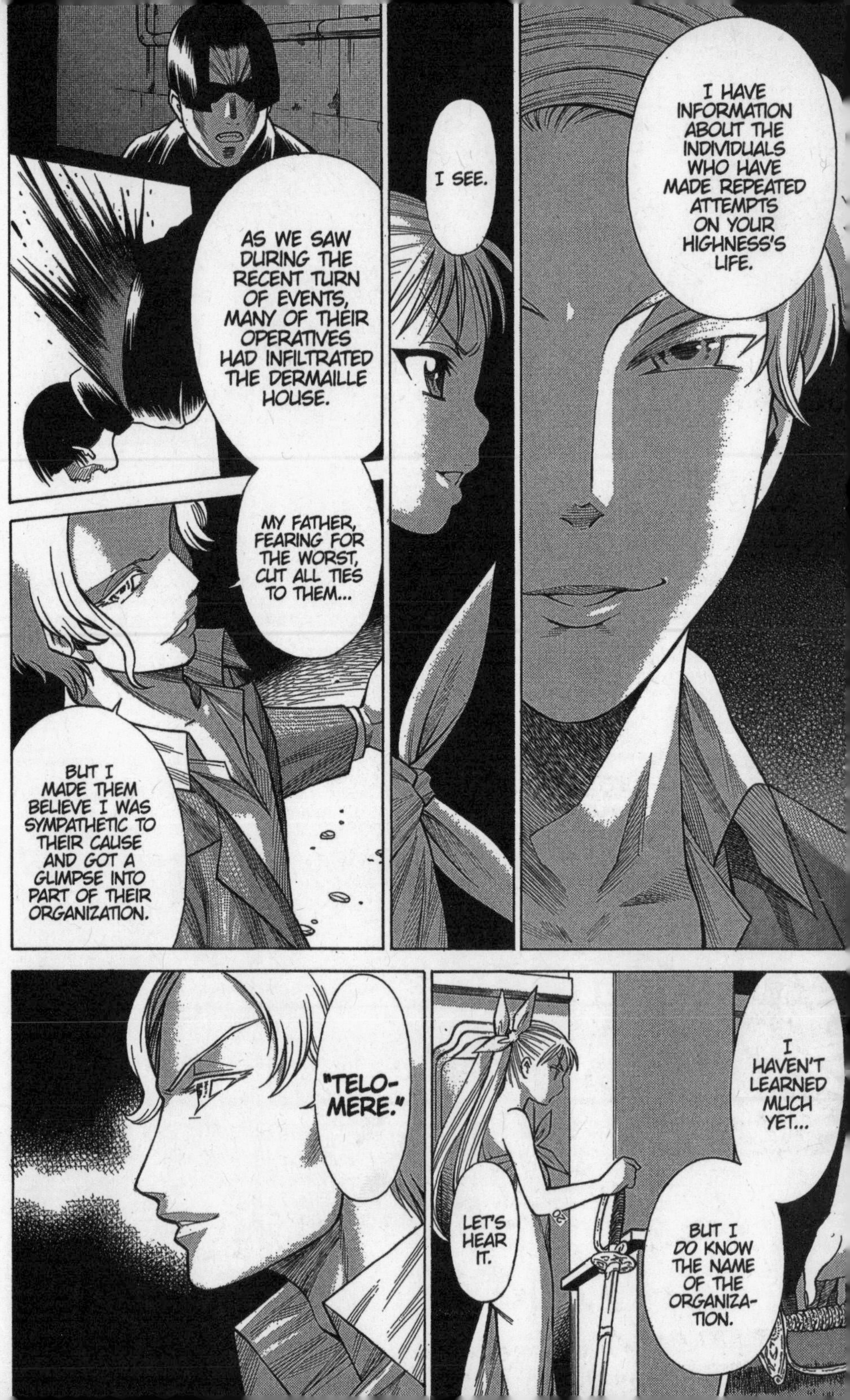
I HAVE INFORMATION ABOUT THE INDIVIDUALS WHO HAVE MADE REPEATED ATTEMPTS ON YOUR HIGHNESS'S LIFE.
I SEE.
AS WE SAW DURING THE RECENT TURN OF EVENTS, MANY OF THEIR OPERATIVES HAD INFILTRATED THE DERMAILLE HOUSE.
MY FATHER, FEARING FOR THE WORST, CUT ALL TIES TO THEM...
BUT I MADE THEM BELIEVE I WAS SYMPATHETIC TO THEIR CAUSE AND GOT A GLIMPSE INTO PART OF THEIR ORGANIZATION.
I HAVEN'T LEARNED MUCH YET...
BUT I DO KNOW THE NAME OF THE ORGANIZATION.
LET'S HEAR IT.
"TELOMERE."

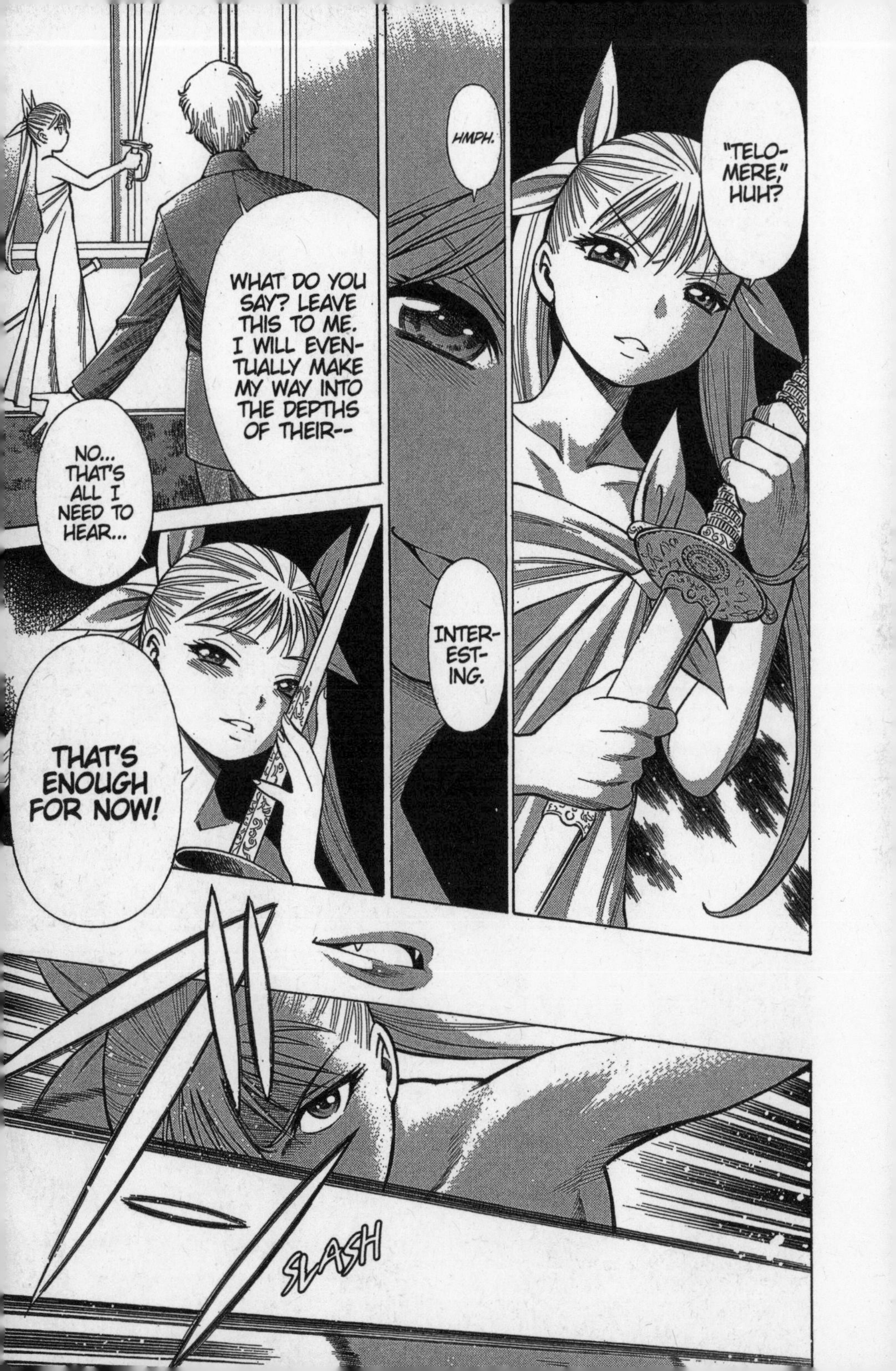
"TELOMERE," HUH?
HMPH.
INTERESTING.
WHAT DO YOU SAY? LEAVE THIS TO ME. I WILL EVENTUALLY MAKE MY WAY INTO THE DEPTHS OF THEIR--
NO... THAT'S ALL I NEED TO HEAR...
THAT'S ENOUGH FOR NOW!
SLASH

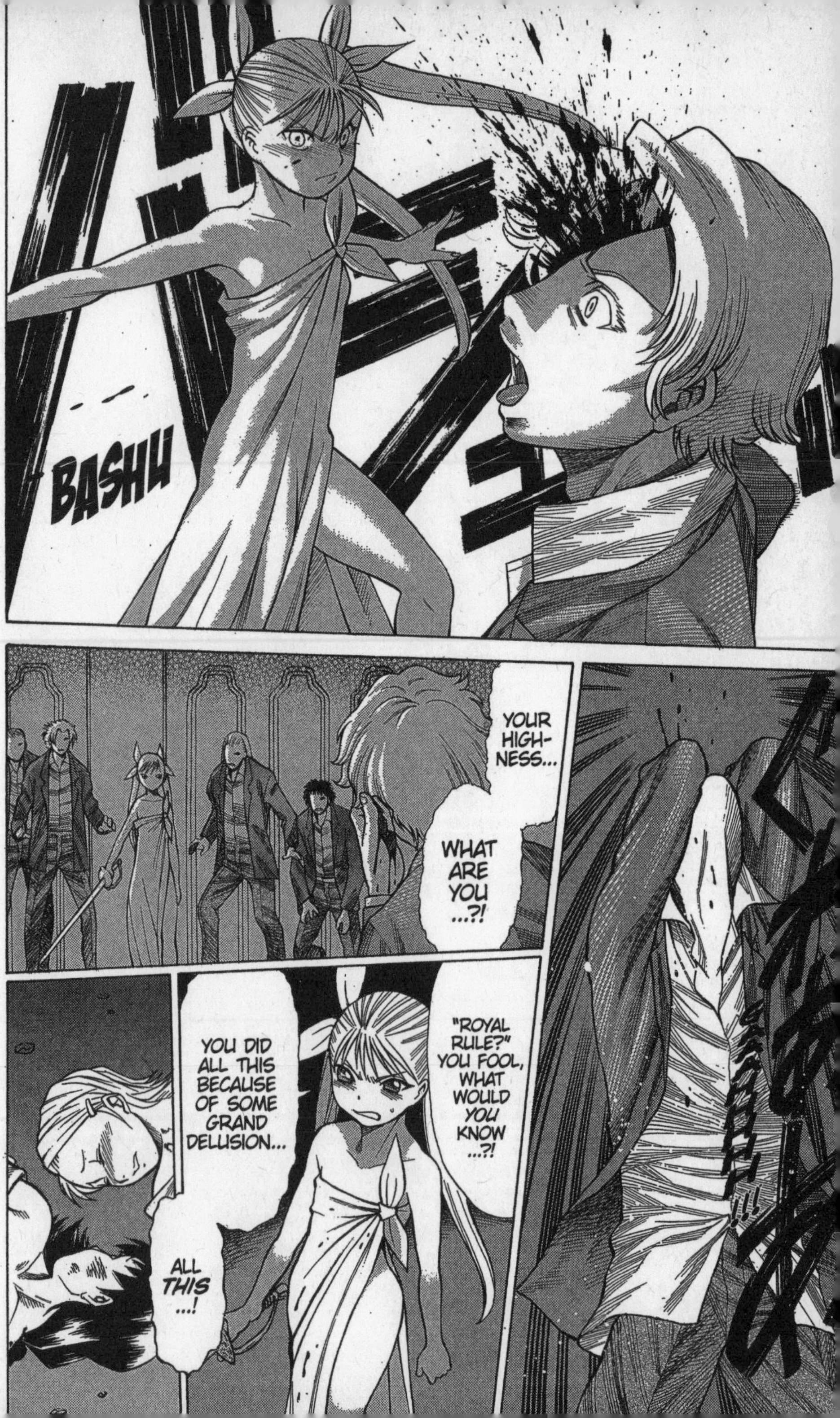
BASHU
YOUR HIGH-NESS...
WHAT ARE YOU ...?!
"ROYAL RULE?" YOU FOOL, WHAT WOULD YOU KNOW ...?!
YOU DID ALL THIS BECAUSE OF SOME GRAND DELUSION...
ALL THIS ...!

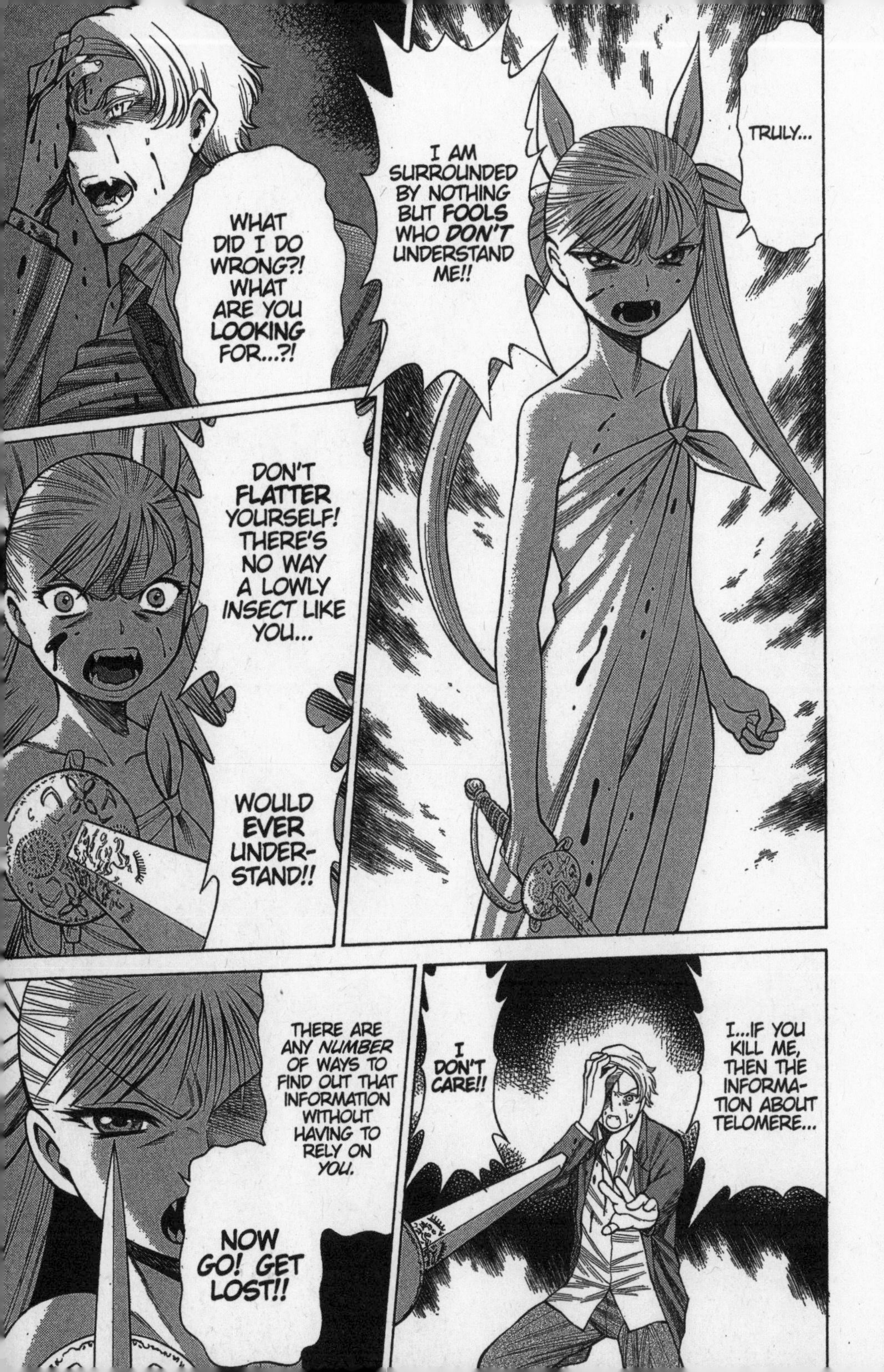
TRULY...
I AM SURROUNDED BY NOTHING BUT FOOLS WHO *DON'T* UNDERSTAND ME!!
WHAT DID I DO WRONG?! WHAT ARE YOU LOOKING FOR...?!
DON'T FLATTER YOURSELF! THERE'S NO WAY A LOWLY INSECT LIKE YOU...
WOULD EVER UNDER-STAND!!
I...IF YOU KILL ME, THEN THE INFORMATION ABOUT TELOMERE...
I DON'T CARE!!
THERE ARE ANY *NUMBER* OF WAYS TO FIND OUT THAT INFORMATION WITHOUT HAVING TO RELY ON *YOU*.
NOW GO! GET LOST!!

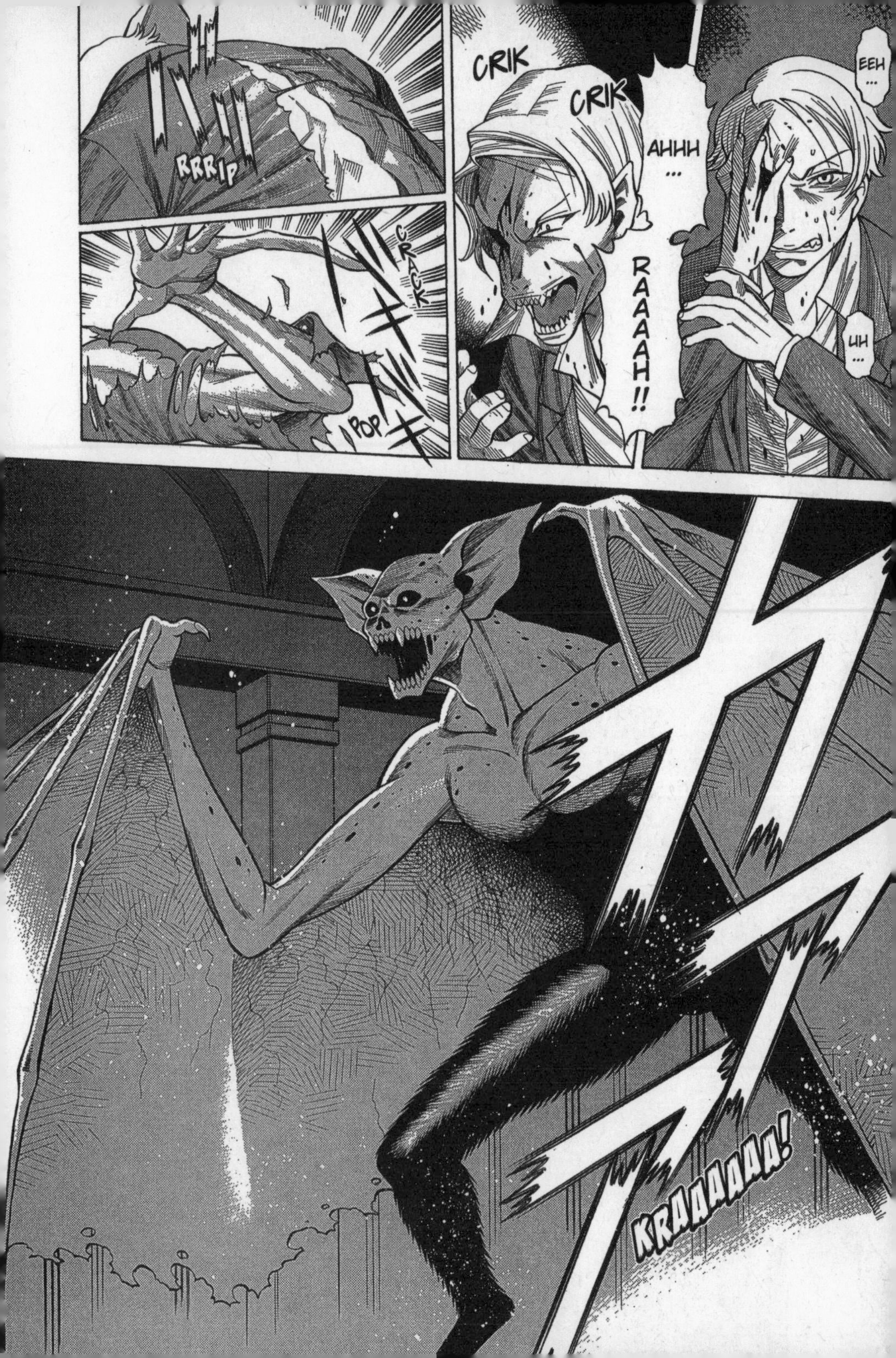

EEH ...
UH ...
CRIK
CRIK
AHHH ...
RAAAAAH!!
RRRIP
CRACK
POP
KRAAAAAAA!

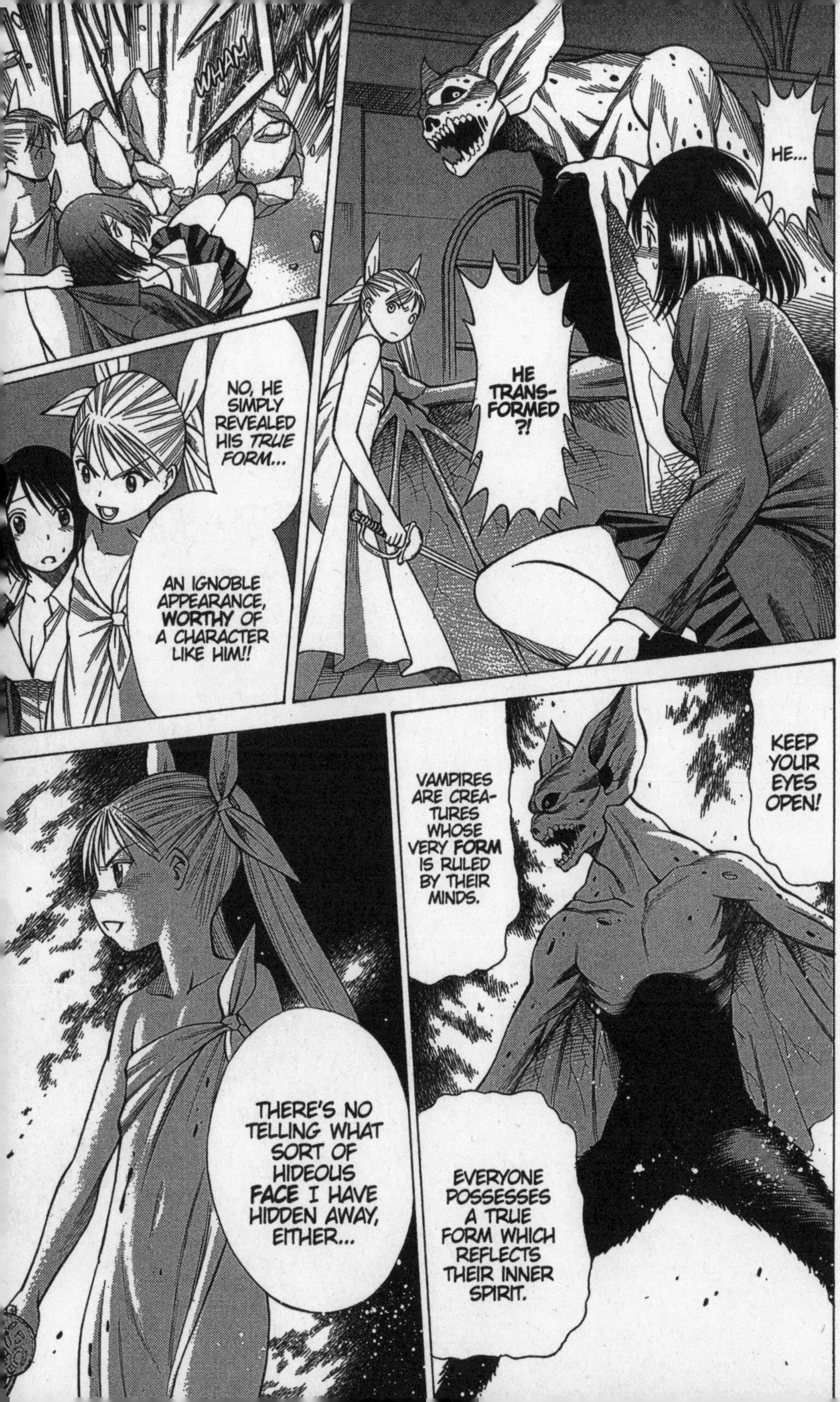
HE...
HE TRANSFORMED?!
WHAM
NO, HE SIMPLY REVEALED HIS *TRUE FORM*...
AN IGNOBLE APPEARANCE, **WORTHY** OF A CHARACTER LIKE HIM!!
KEEP YOUR EYES OPEN!
VAMPIRES ARE CREATURES WHOSE VERY **FORM** IS RULED BY THEIR MINDS.
EVERYONE POSSESSES A TRUE FORM WHICH REFLECTS THEIR INNER SPIRIT.
THERE'S NO TELLING WHAT SORT OF HIDEOUS **FACE** I HAVE HIDDEN AWAY, EITHER...

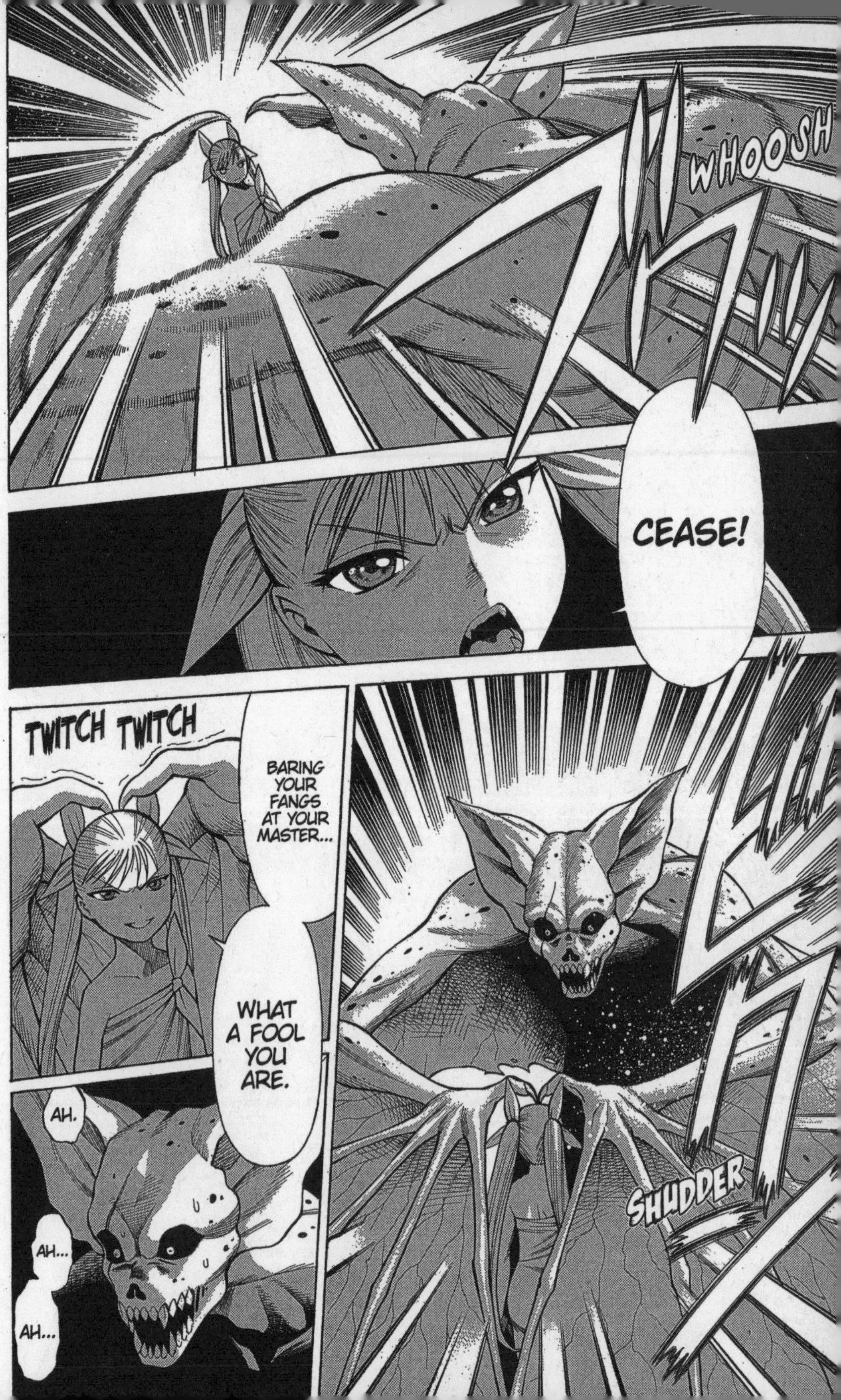
WHOOSH
CEASE!
SHUDDER
TWITCH TWITCH
BARING YOUR FANGS AT YOUR MASTER...
WHAT A FOOL YOU ARE.
AH.
AH...
AH...

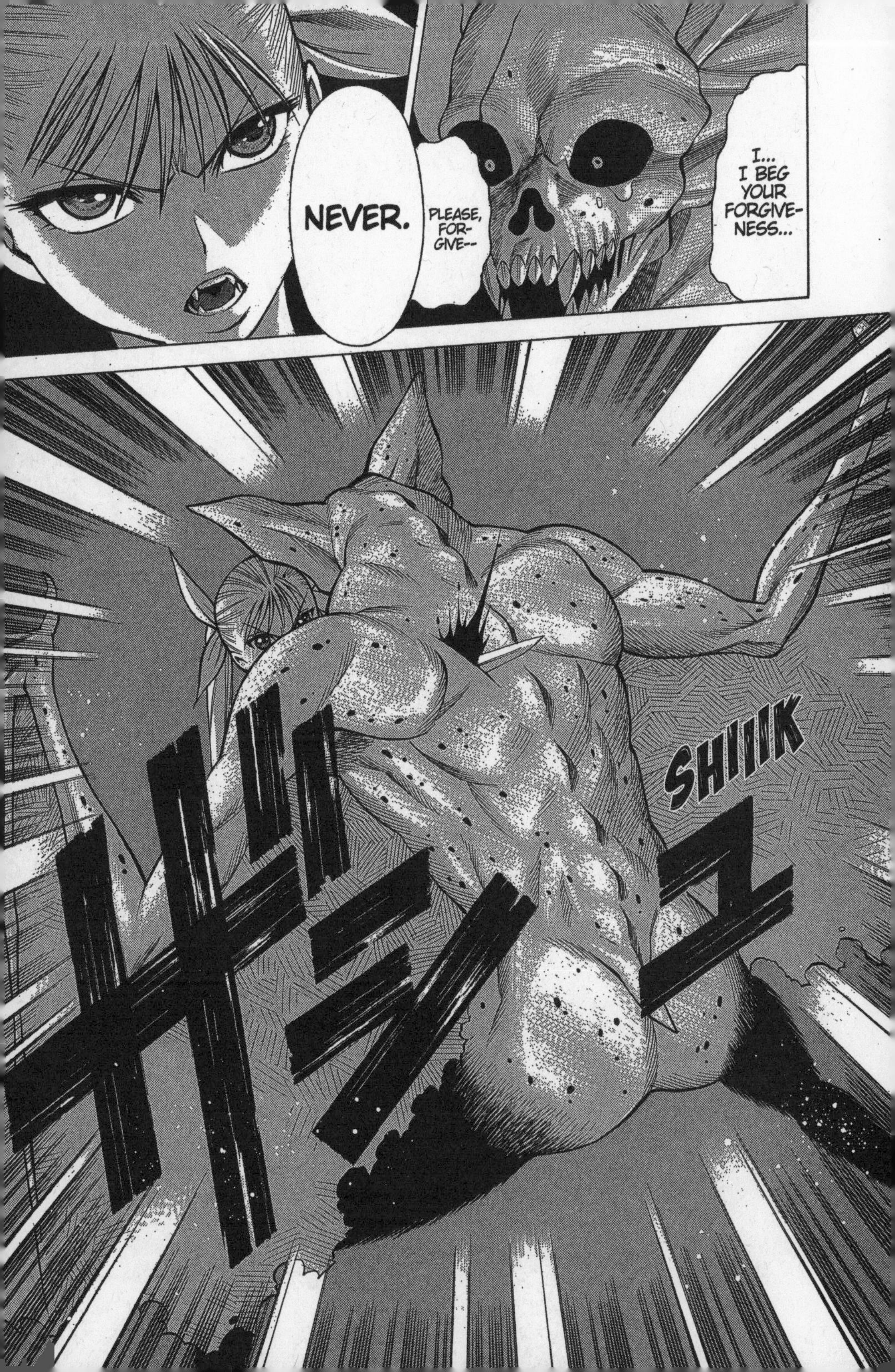
I... I BEG YOUR FORGIVE-NESS...
PLEASE, FOR-GIVE--
NEVER.
SHIIIK

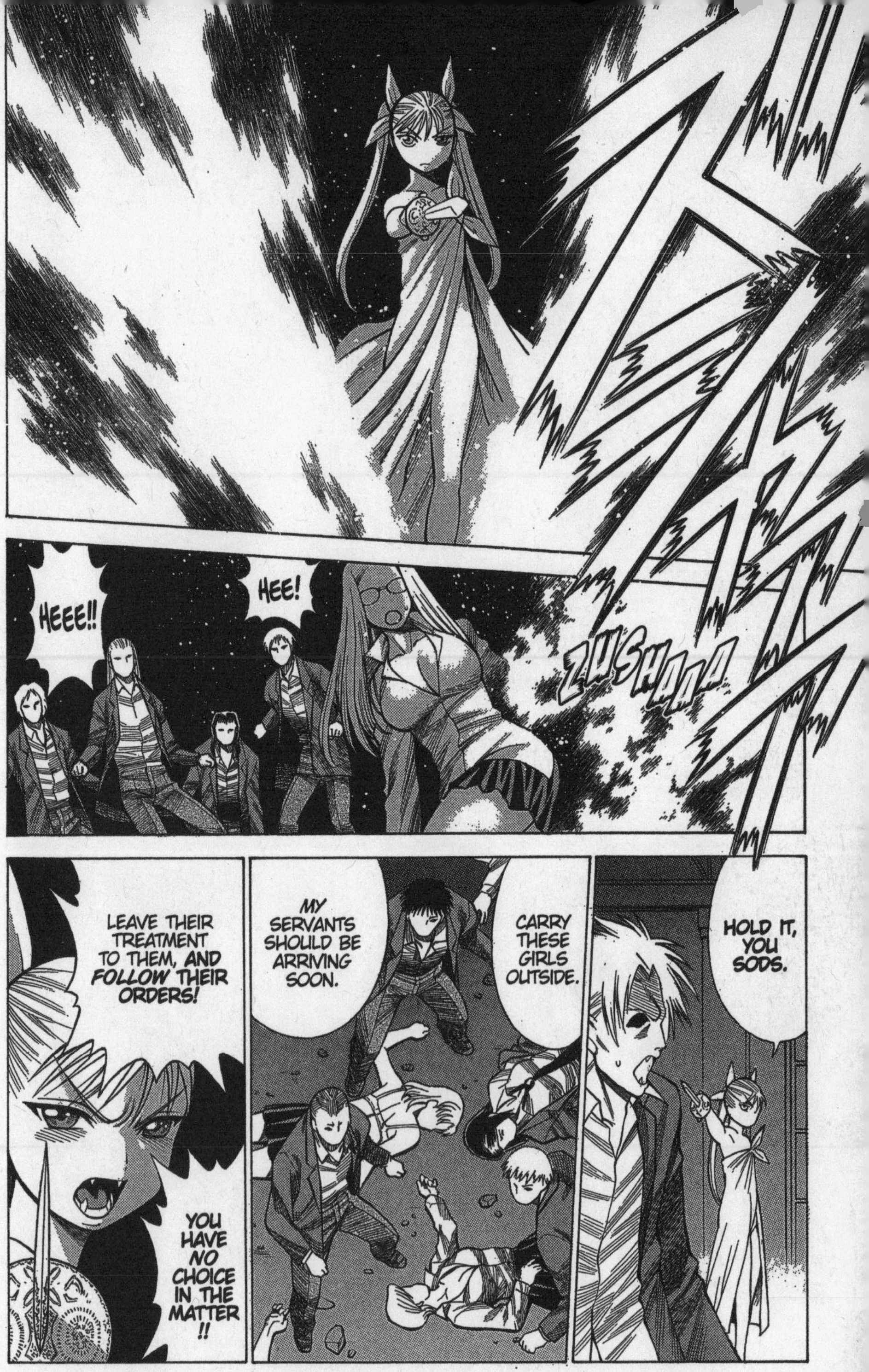
ZUSHAAA
HEE!
HEEE!!
HOLD IT, YOU SODS.
CARRY THESE GIRLS OUTSIDE.
MY SERVANTS SHOULD BE ARRIVING SOON.
LEAVE THEIR TREATMENT TO THEM, AND *FOLLOW* THEIR ORDERS!
YOU HAVE *NO* CHOICE IN THE MATTER!!

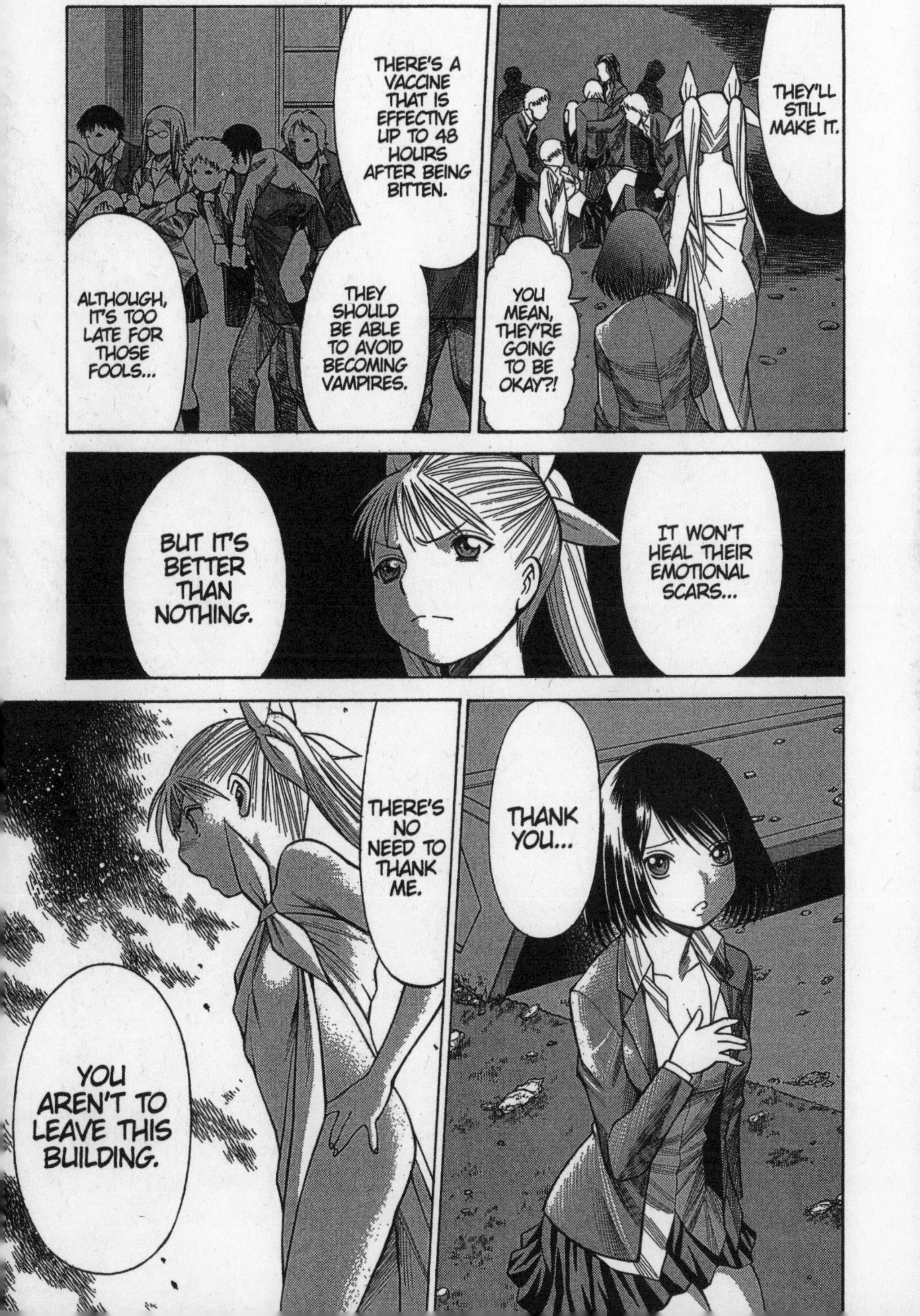
THEY'LL STILL MAKE IT.
YOU MEAN, THEY'RE GOING TO BE OKAY?!
THERE'S A VACCINE THAT IS EFFECTIVE UP TO 48 HOURS AFTER BEING BITTEN.
THEY SHOULD BE ABLE TO AVOID BECOMING VAMPIRES.
ALTHOUGH, IT'S TOO LATE FOR THOSE FOOLS...
IT WON'T HEAL THEIR EMOTIONAL SCARS...
BUT IT'S BETTER THAN NOTHING.
THANK YOU...
THERE'S NO NEED TO THANK ME.
YOU AREN'T TO LEAVE THIS BUILDING.

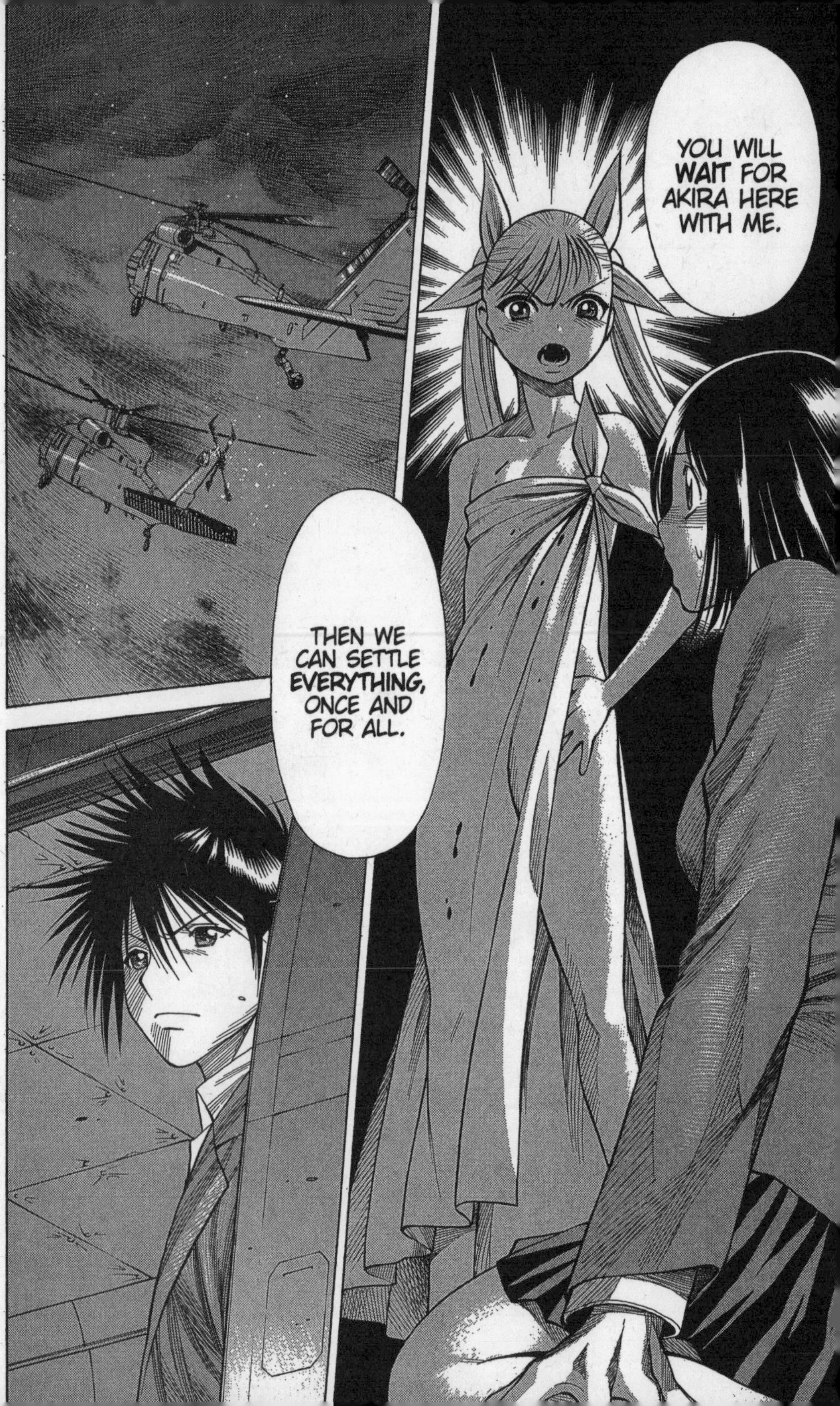
YOU WILL WAIT FOR AKIRA HERE WITH ME.
THEN WE CAN SETTLE EVERYTHING, ONCE AND FOR ALL.

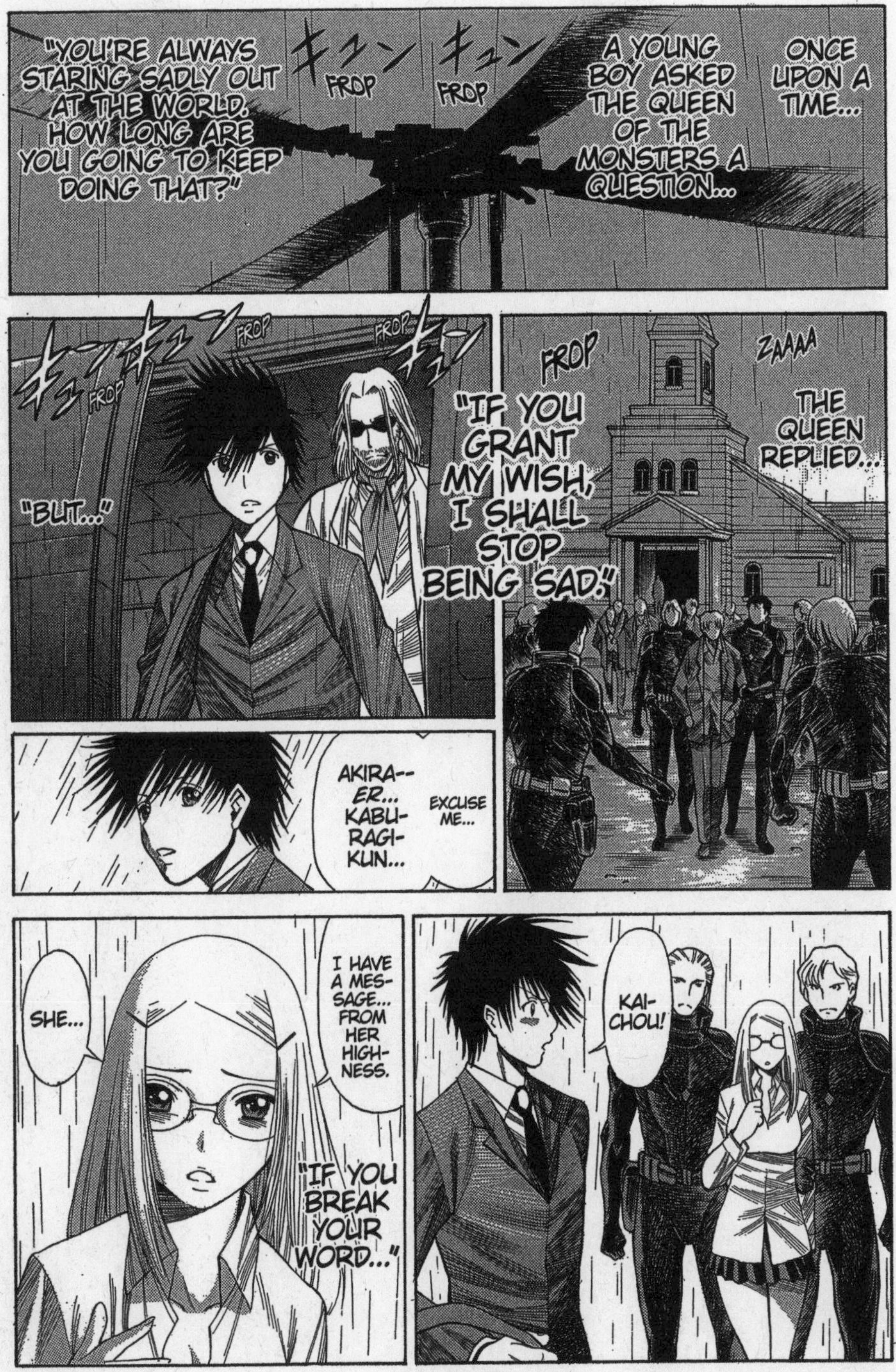
ONCE UPON A TIME...
A YOUNG BOY ASKED THE QUEEN OF THE MONSTERS A QUESTION...
キュン
FROP
キュン
FROP
"YOU'RE ALWAYS STARING SADLY OUT AT THE WORLD. HOW LONG ARE YOU GOING TO KEEP DOING THAT?"
ZAAAA
THE QUEEN REPLIED...
FROP
"IF YOU GRANT MY WISH, I SHALL STOP BEING SAD."
FROP
FROP
FROP
"BUT..."
EXCUSE ME...
AKIRA-- ER... KABU-RAGI-KUN...
KAI-CHOU!
I HAVE A MES-SAGE... FROM HER HIGH-NESS.
SHE...
"IF YOU BREAK YOUR WORD..."

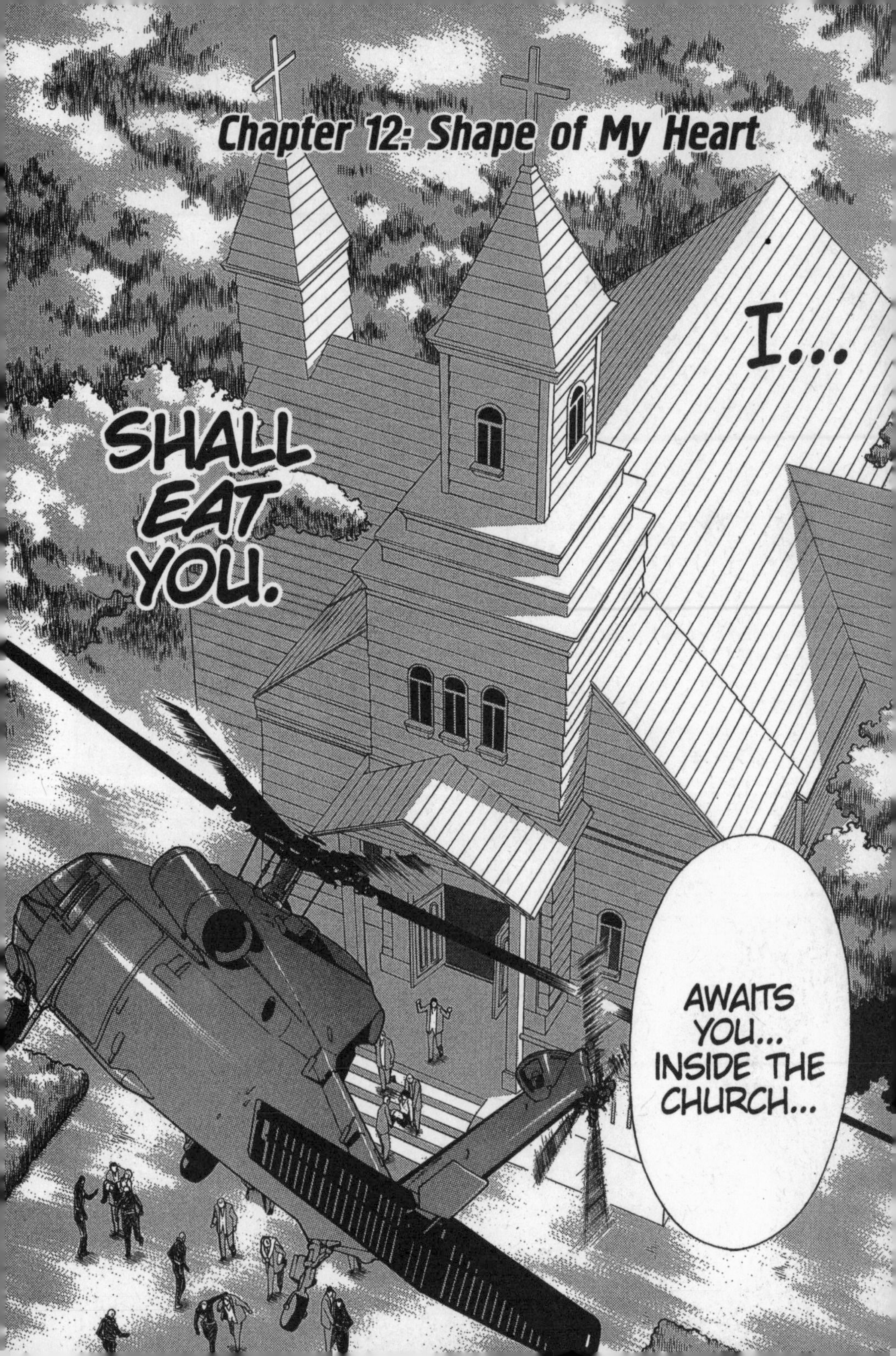
Chapter 12: Shape of My Heart
I...
SHALL EAT YOU.
AWAITS YOU... INSIDE THE CHURCH...

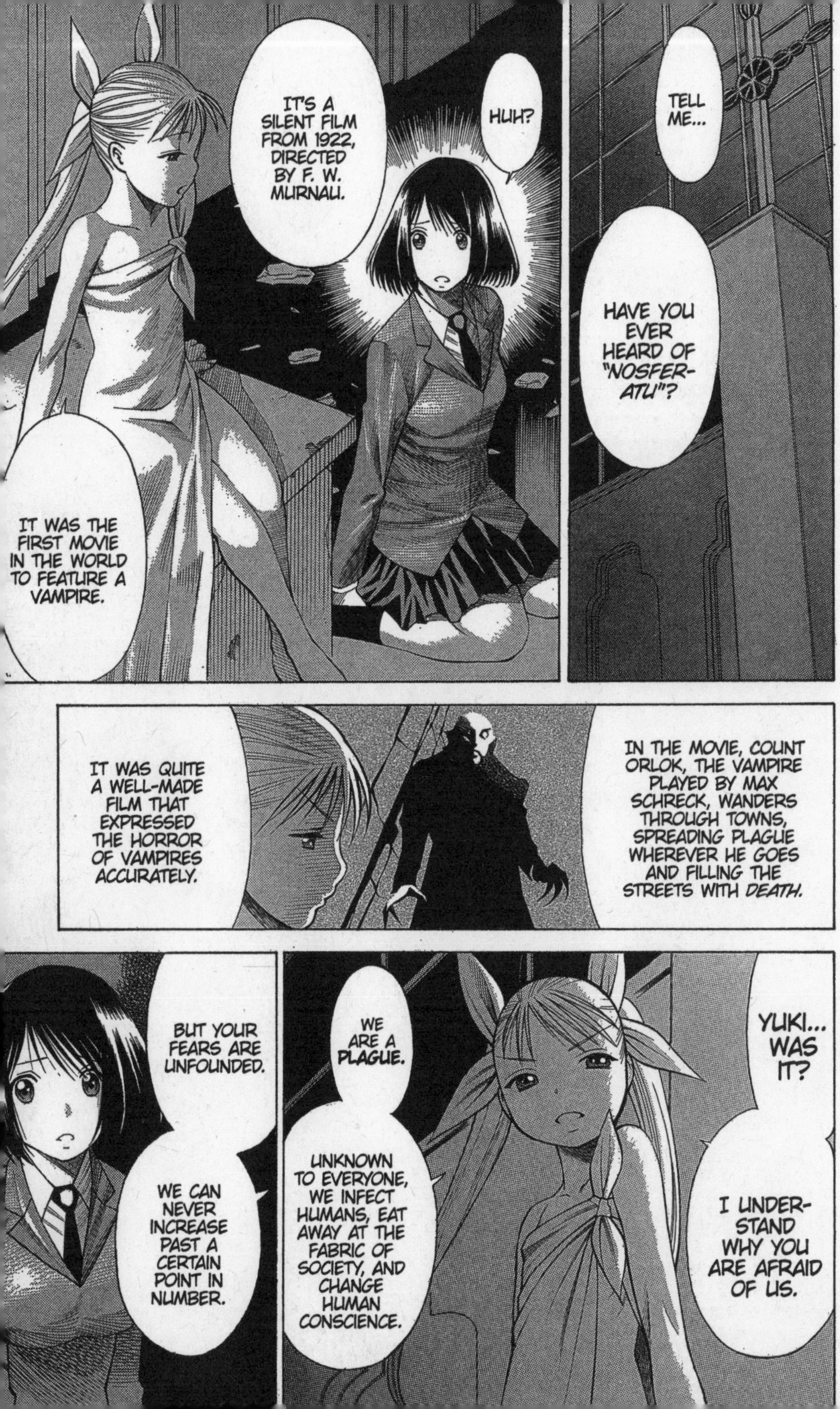
TELL ME...
HAVE YOU EVER HEARD OF "NOSFERATU"?
HUH?
IT'S A SILENT FILM FROM 1922, DIRECTED BY F. W. MURNAU.
IT WAS THE FIRST MOVIE IN THE WORLD TO FEATURE A VAMPIRE.
IN THE MOVIE, COUNT ORLOK, THE VAMPIRE PLAYED BY MAX SCHRECK, WANDERS THROUGH TOWNS, SPREADING PLAGUE WHEREVER HE GOES AND FILLING THE STREETS WITH *DEATH*.
IT WAS QUITE A WELL-MADE FILM THAT EXPRESSED THE HORROR OF VAMPIRES ACCURATELY.
YUKI... WAS IT?
I UNDER-STAND WHY YOU ARE AFRAID OF US.
WE ARE A PLAGUE.
UNKNOWN TO EVERYONE, WE INFECT HUMANS, EAT AWAY AT THE FABRIC OF SOCIETY, AND CHANGE HUMAN CONSCIENCE.
BUT YOUR FEARS ARE UNFOUNDED.
WE CAN NEVER INCREASE PAST A CERTAIN POINT IN NUMBER.

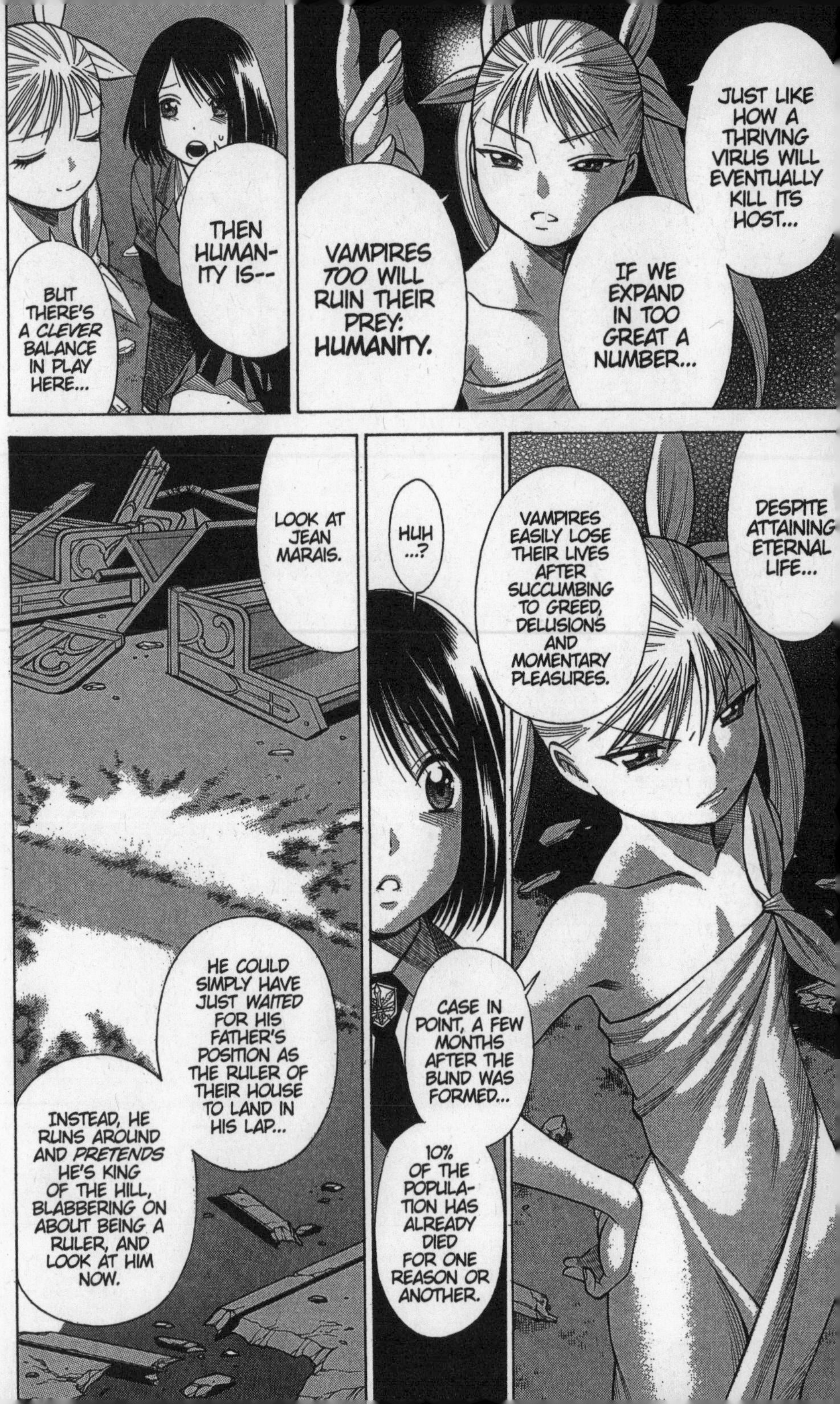
JUST LIKE HOW A THRIVING VIRUS WILL EVENTUALLY KILL ITS HOST...
IF WE EXPAND IN TOO GREAT A NUMBER...
VAMPIRES *TOO* WILL RUIN THEIR PREY: HUMANITY.
THEN HUMANITY IS--
BUT THERE'S A *CLEVER* BALANCE IN PLAY HERE...
DESPITE ATTAINING ETERNAL LIFE...
VAMPIRES EASILY LOSE THEIR LIVES AFTER SUCCUMBING TO GREED, DELUSIONS AND MOMENTARY PLEASURES.
HUH ...?
CASE IN POINT, A FEW MONTHS AFTER THE BUND WAS FORMED...
10% OF THE POPULATION HAS ALREADY DIED FOR ONE REASON OR ANOTHER.
LOOK AT JEAN MARAIS.
HE COULD SIMPLY HAVE JUST *WAITED* FOR HIS FATHER'S POSITION AS THE RULER OF THEIR HOUSE TO LAND IN HIS LAP...
INSTEAD, HE RUNS AROUND AND *PRETENDS* HE'S KING OF THE HILL, BLABBERING ON ABOUT BEING A RULER, AND LOOK AT HIM NOW.

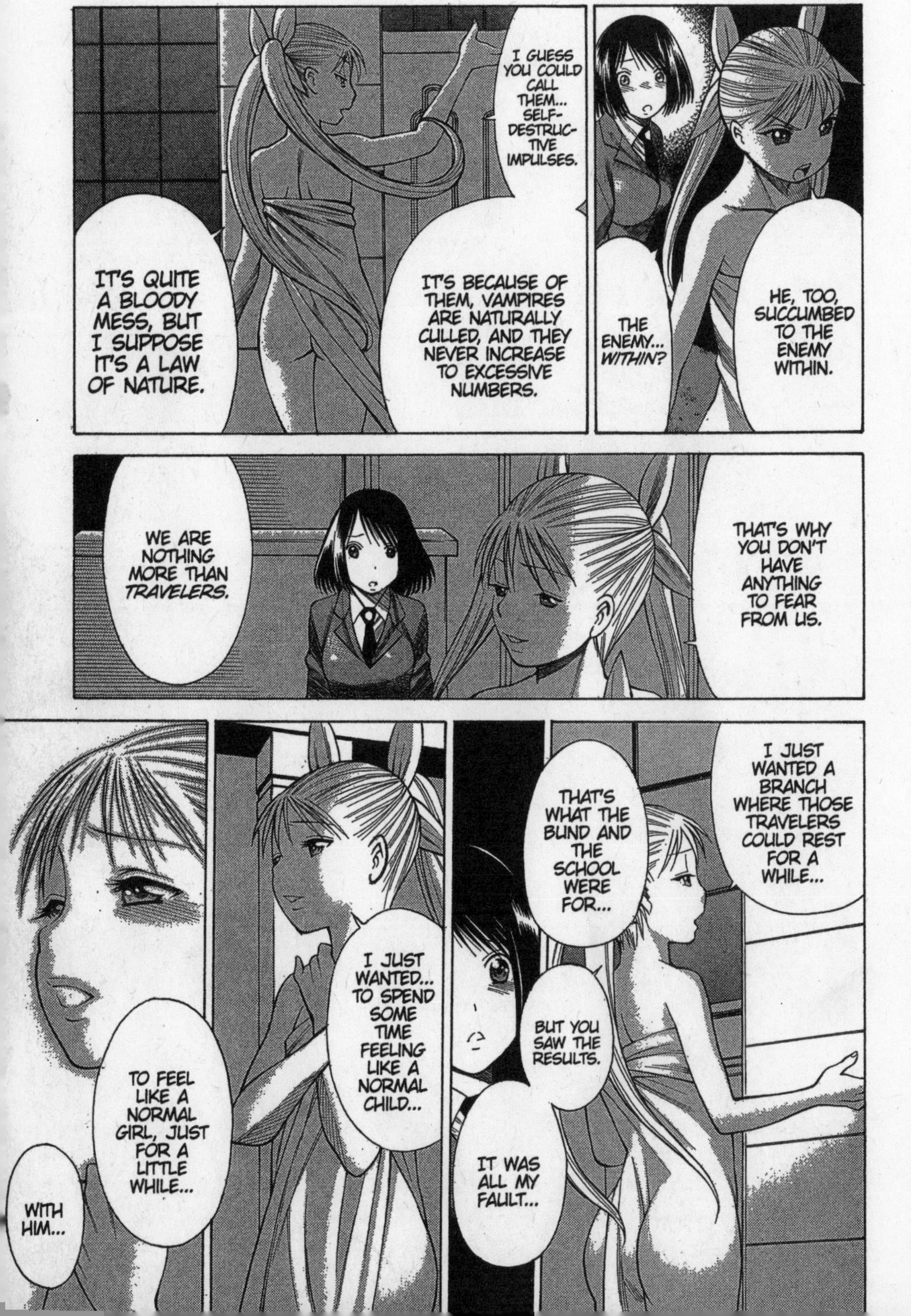
HE, TOO, SUCCUMBED TO THE ENEMY WITHIN.
THE ENEMY... *WITHIN?*
I GUESS YOU COULD CALL THEM... SELF-DESTRUCTIVE IMPULSES.
IT'S BECAUSE OF THEM, VAMPIRES ARE NATURALLY CULLED, AND THEY NEVER INCREASE TO EXCESSIVE NUMBERS.
IT'S QUITE A BLOODY MESS, BUT I SUPPOSE IT'S A LAW OF NATURE.
THAT'S WHY YOU DON'T HAVE ANYTHING TO FEAR FROM US.
WE ARE NOTHING MORE THAN *TRAVELERS.*
I JUST WANTED A BRANCH WHERE THOSE TRAVELERS COULD REST FOR A WHILE...
THAT'S WHAT THE BUND AND THE SCHOOL WERE FOR...
BUT YOU SAW THE RESULTS.
IT WAS ALL MY FAULT...
I JUST WANTED... TO SPEND SOME TIME FEELING LIKE A NORMAL CHILD...
TO FEEL LIKE A NORMAL GIRL, JUST FOR A LITTLE WHILE...
WITH HIM...

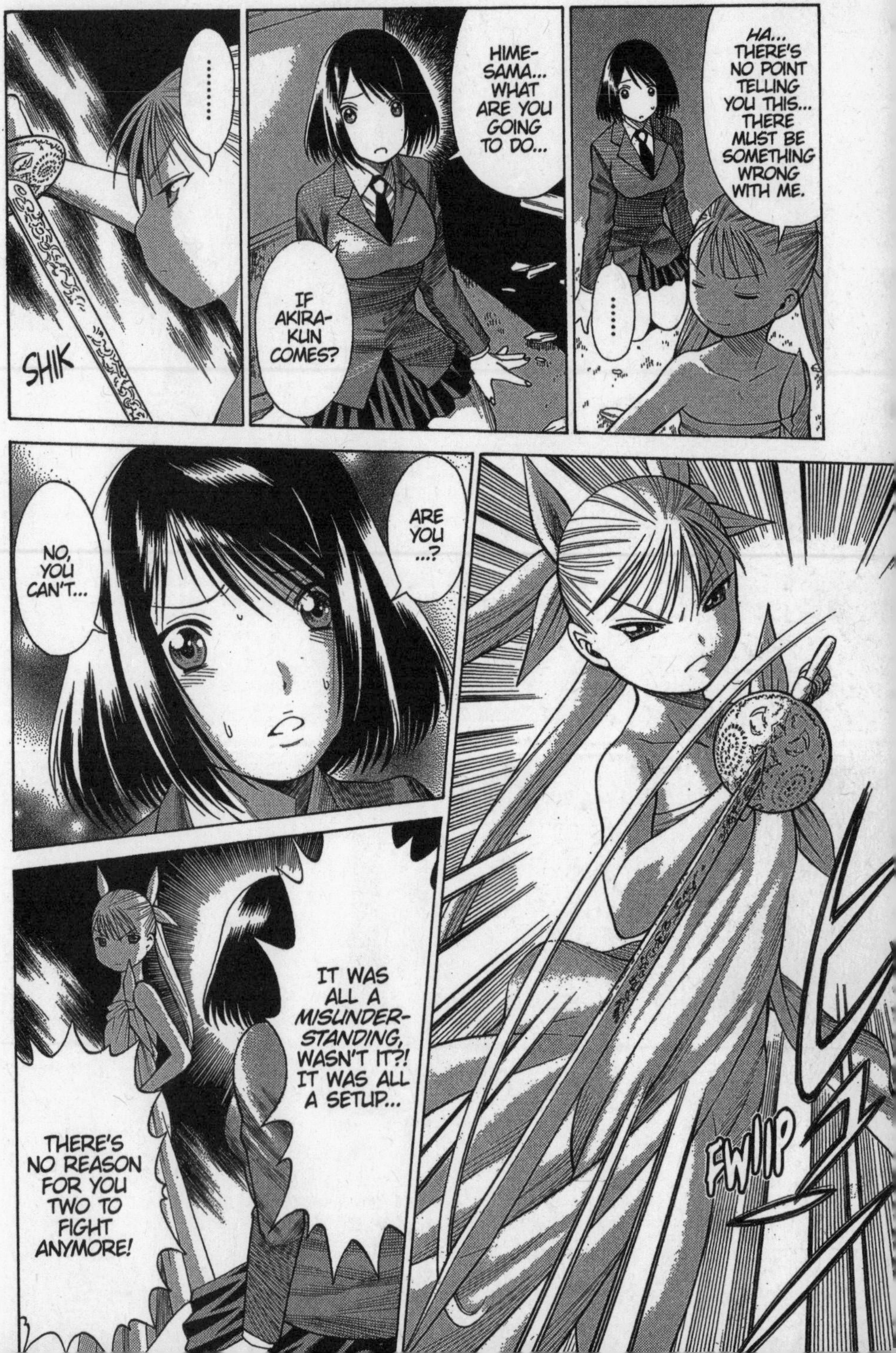
HA... THERE'S NO POINT TELLING YOU THIS... THERE MUST BE SOMETHING WRONG WITH ME.
......
HIME-SAMA... WHAT ARE YOU GOING TO DO...
IF AKIRA-KUN COMES?
....
SHIK
FWIP
ARE YOU ...?
NO, YOU CAN'T...
IT WAS ALL A MISUNDERSTANDING, WASN'T IT?! IT WAS ALL A SETUP...
THERE'S NO REASON FOR YOU TWO TO FIGHT ANYMORE!

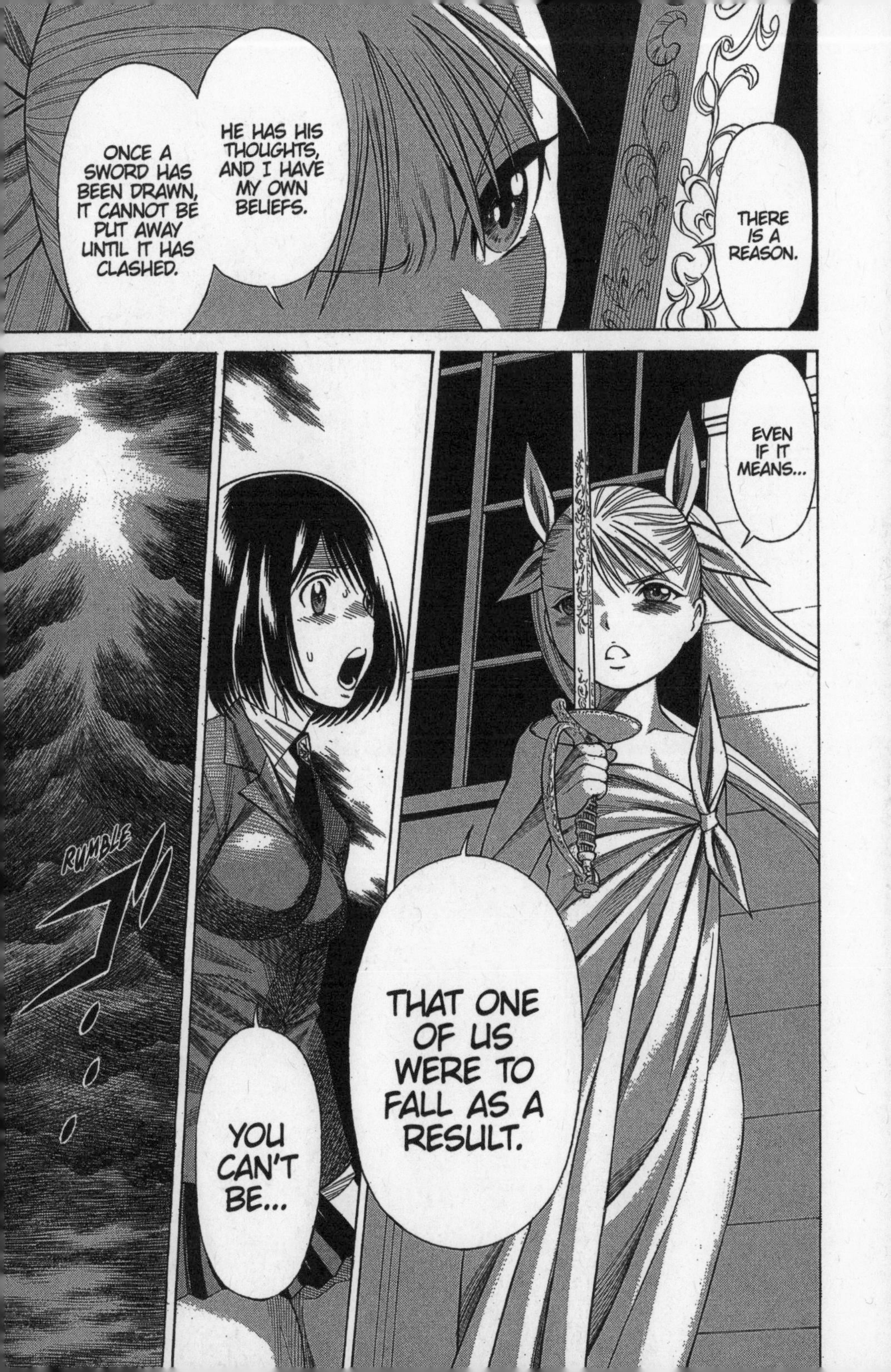
THERE IS A REASON.
HE HAS HIS THOUGHTS, AND I HAVE MY OWN BELIEFS.
ONCE A SWORD HAS BEEN DRAWN, IT CANNOT BE PUT AWAY UNTIL IT HAS CLASHED.
EVEN IF IT MEANS...
THAT ONE OF US WERE TO FALL AS A RESULT.
YOU CAN'T BE...
RUMBLE

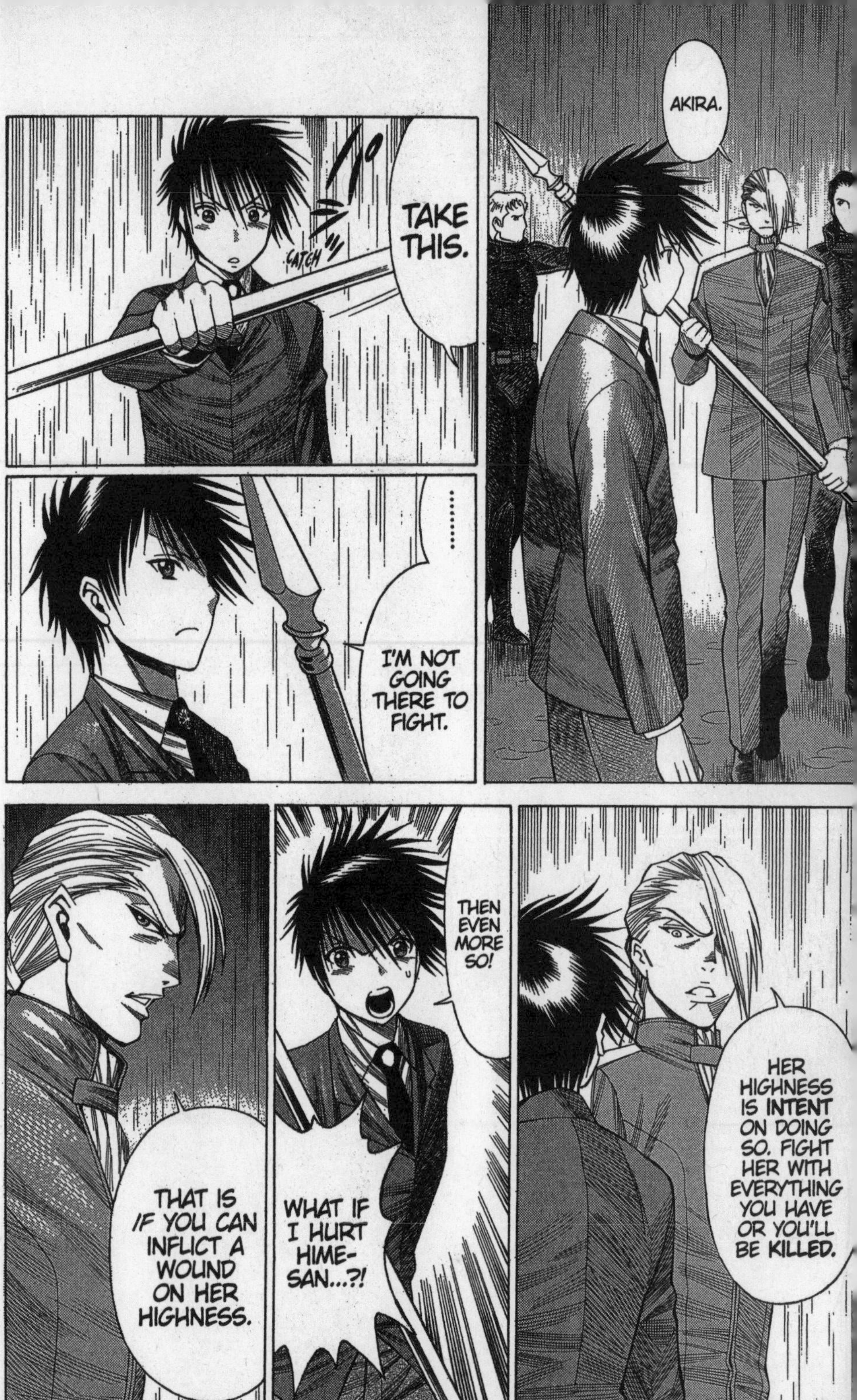
AKIRA.
TAKE THIS.
CATCH
......
I'M NOT GOING THERE TO FIGHT.
HER HIGHNESS IS INTENT ON DOING SO. FIGHT HER WITH EVERYTHING YOU HAVE OR YOU'LL BE KILLED.
THEN EVEN MORE SO!
WHAT IF I HURT HIME-SAN...?!
THAT IS IF YOU CAN INFLICT A WOUND ON HER HIGHNESS.

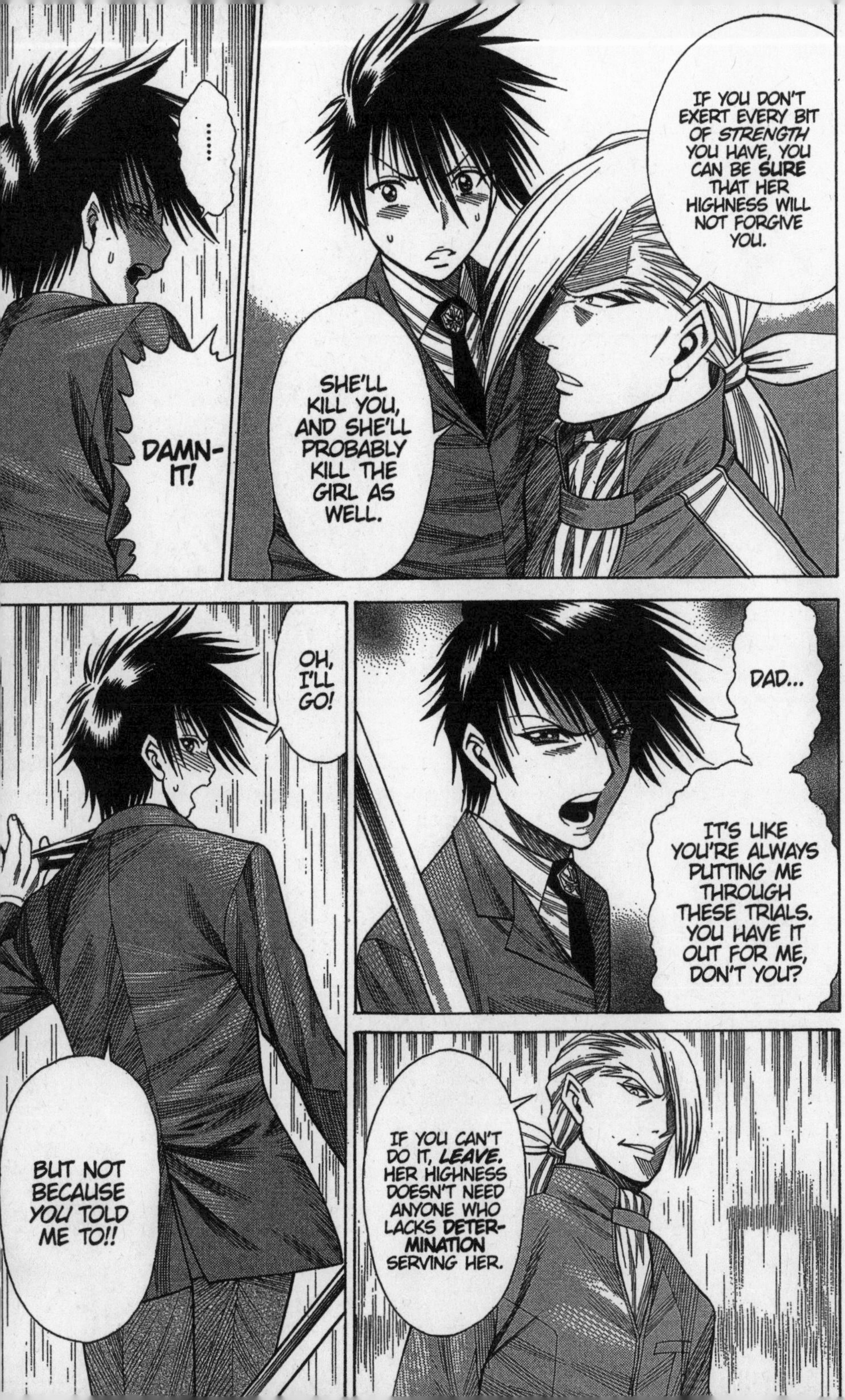
IF YOU DON'T EXERT EVERY BIT OF STRENGTH YOU HAVE, YOU CAN BE SURE THAT HER HIGHNESS WILL NOT FORGIVE YOU.
SHE'LL KILL YOU, AND SHE'LL PROBABLY KILL THE GIRL AS WELL.
......
DAMN-IT!
DAD...
IT'S LIKE YOU'RE ALWAYS PUTTING ME THROUGH THESE TRIALS. YOU HAVE IT OUT FOR ME, DON'T YOU?
IF YOU CAN'T DO IT, LEAVE. HER HIGHNESS DOESN'T NEED ANYONE WHO LACKS DETERMINATION SERVING HER.
OH, I'LL GO!
BUT NOT BECAUSE YOU! TOLD ME TO!!

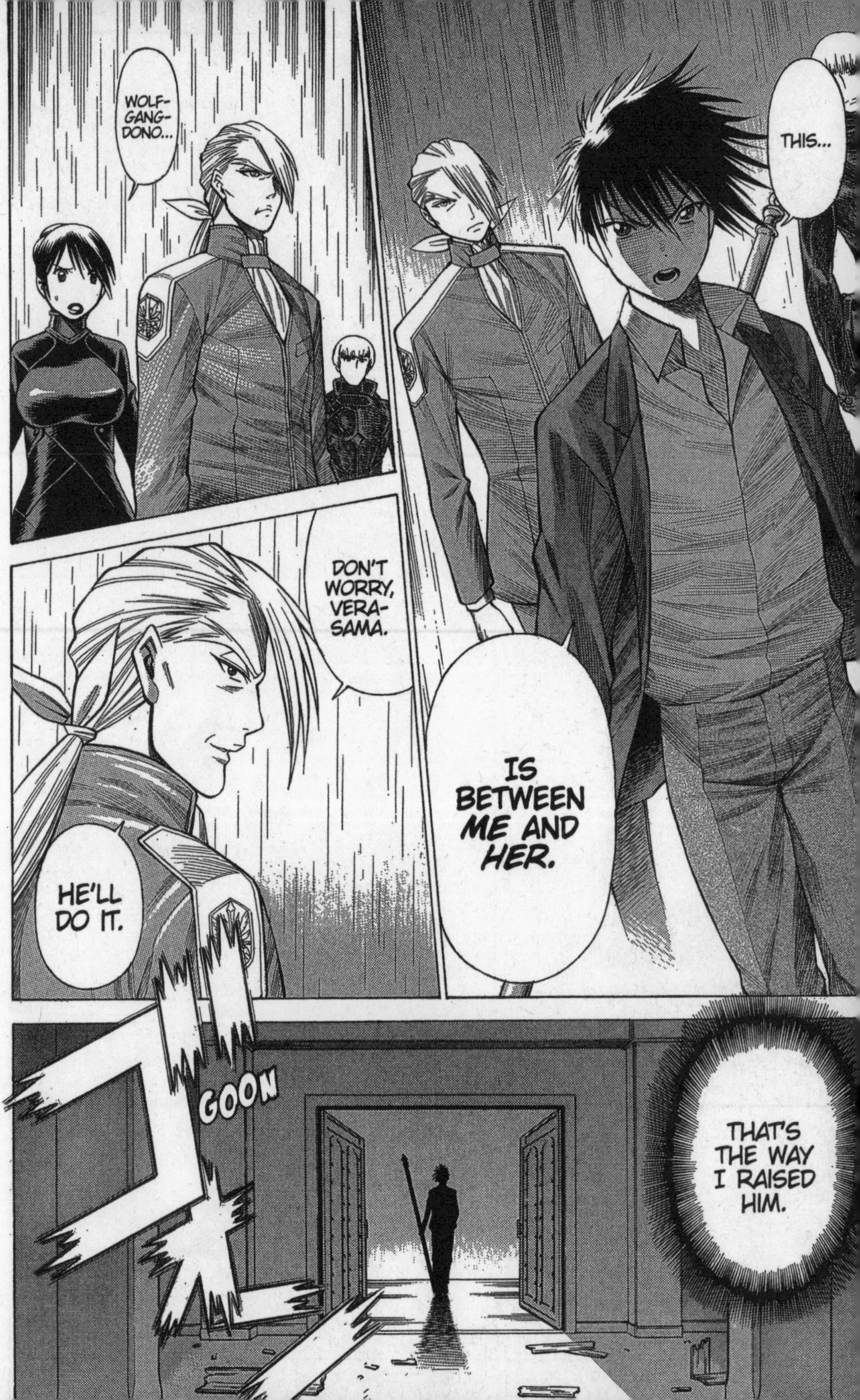
THIS...
IS BETWEEN ME AND HER.
WOLF-GANG-DONO...
DON'T WORRY, VERA-SAMA.
HE'LL DO IT.
THAT'S THE WAY I RAISED HIM.
GOON

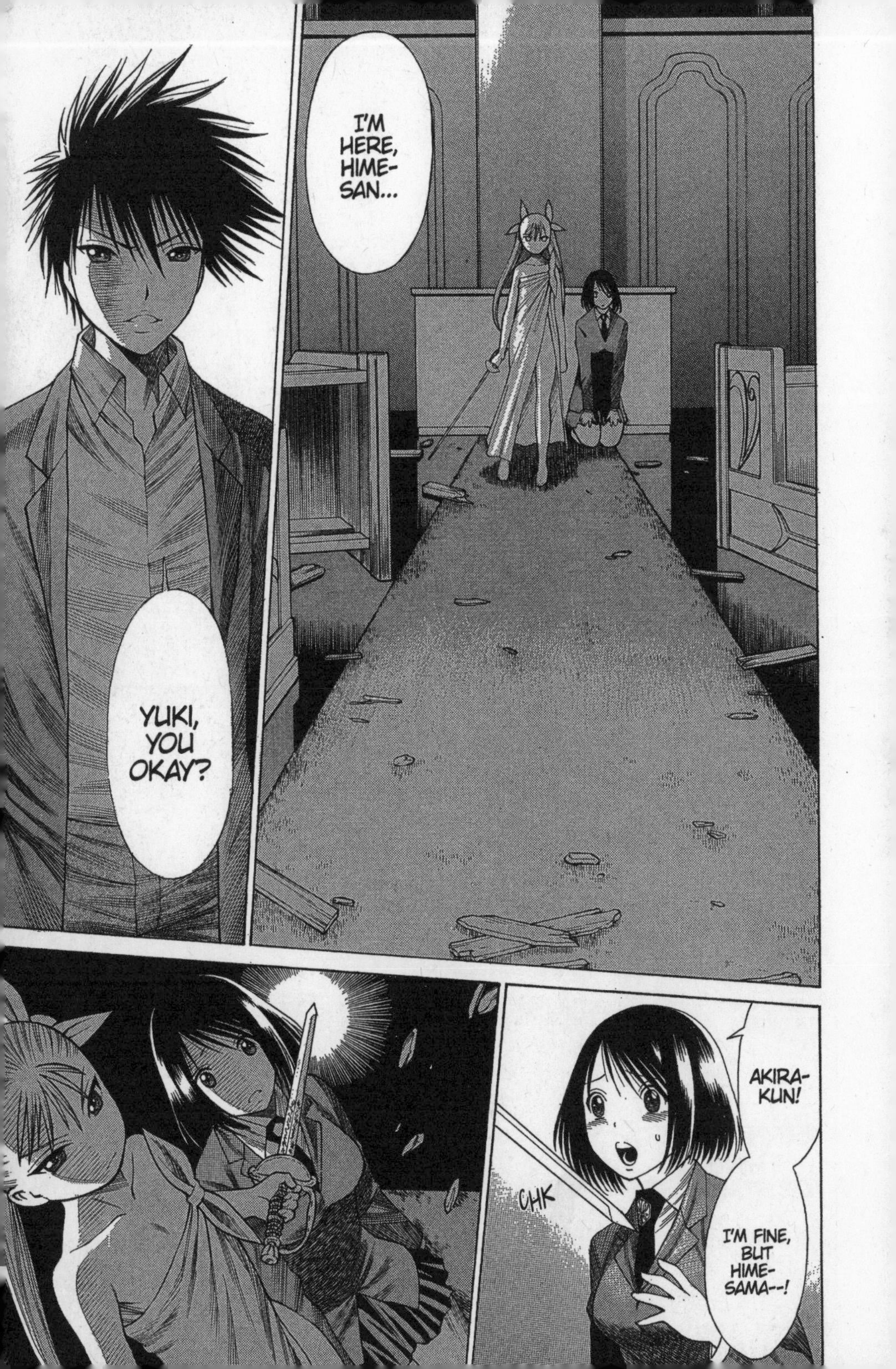
I'M HERE, HIME-SAN...
YUKI, YOU OKAY?
AKIRA-KUN!
CHK
I'M FINE, BUT HIME-SAMA--!

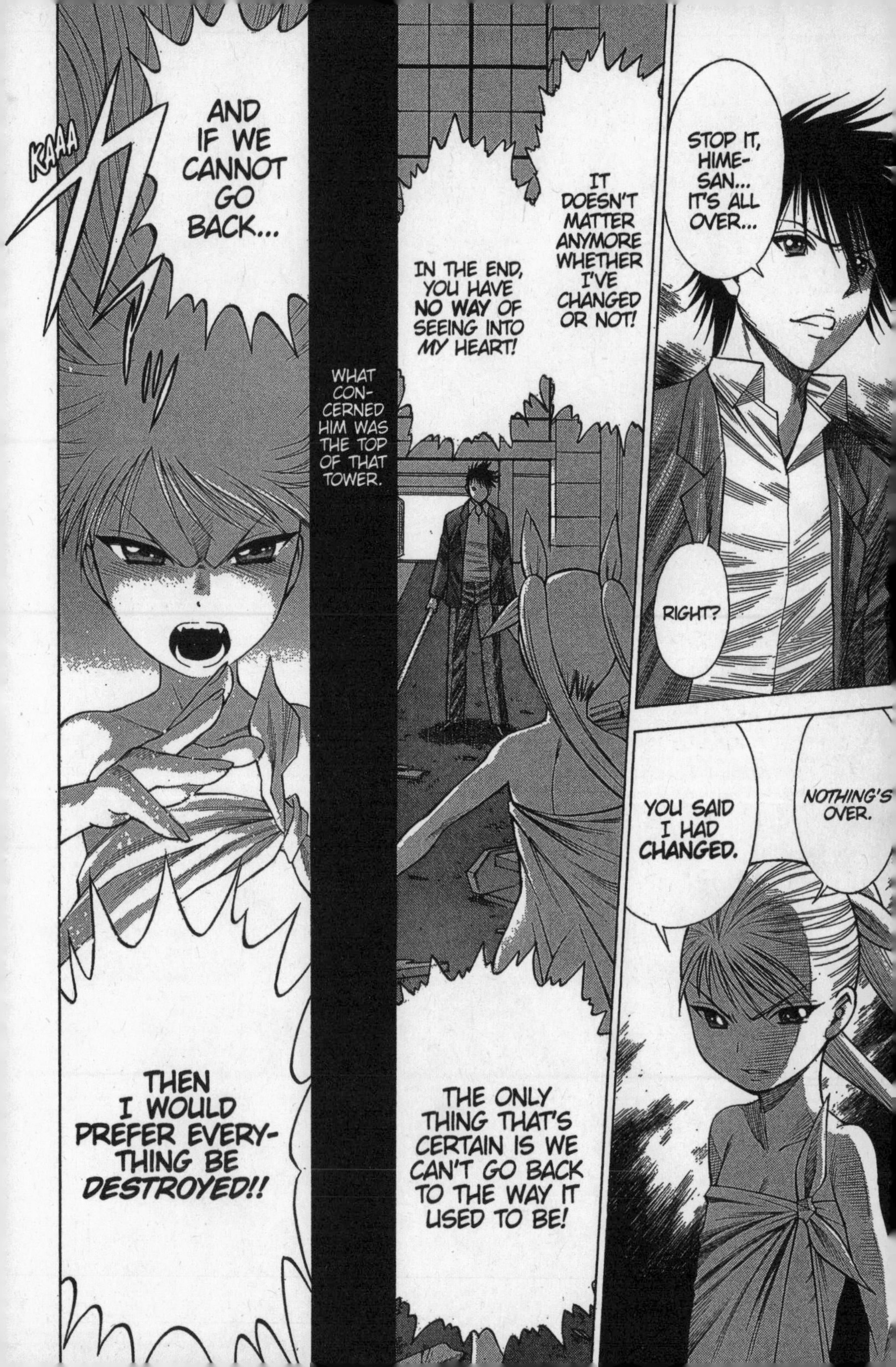
STOP IT, HIME-SAN... IT'S ALL OVER...
RIGHT?
NOTHING'S OVER.
YOU SAID I HAD CHANGED.
IT DOESN'T MATTER ANYMORE WHETHER I'VE CHANGED OR NOT!
IN THE END, YOU HAVE NO WAY OF SEEING INTO MY HEART!
WHAT CON-CERNED HIM WAS THE TOP OF THAT TOWER.
THE ONLY THING THAT'S CERTAIN IS WE CAN'T GO BACK TO THE WAY IT USED TO BE!
KAAA
AND IF WE CANNOT GO BACK...
THEN I WOULD PREFER EVERY-THING BE DESTROYED!!

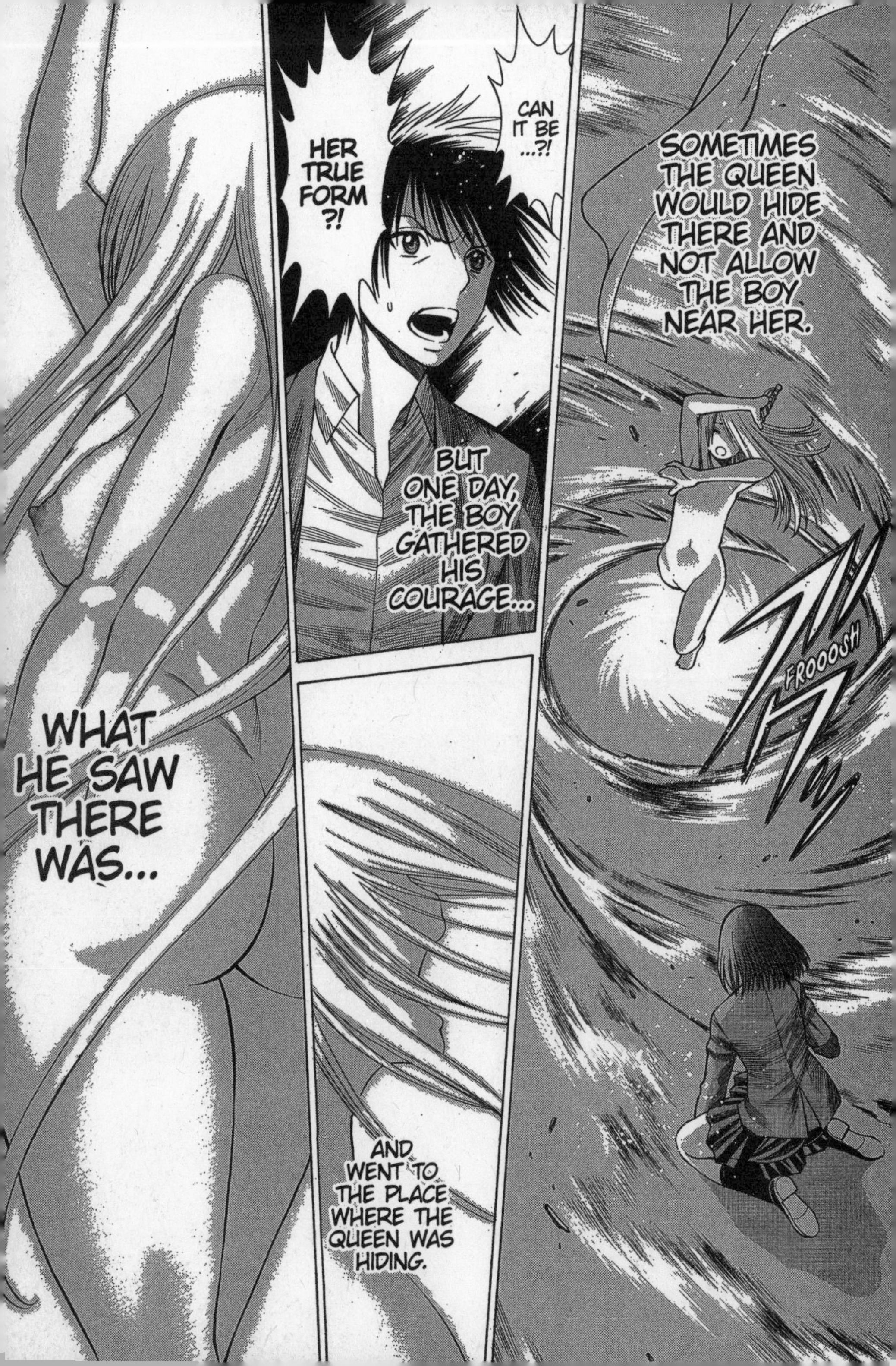
SOMETIMES THE QUEEN WOULD HIDE THERE AND NOT ALLOW THE BOY NEAR HER.
FROOOSH
CAN IT BE ...?!
HER TRUE FORM ?!
BUT ONE DAY, THE BOY GATHERED HIS COURAGE...
AND WENT TO THE PLACE WHERE THE QUEEN WAS HIDING.
WHAT HE SAW THERE WAS...

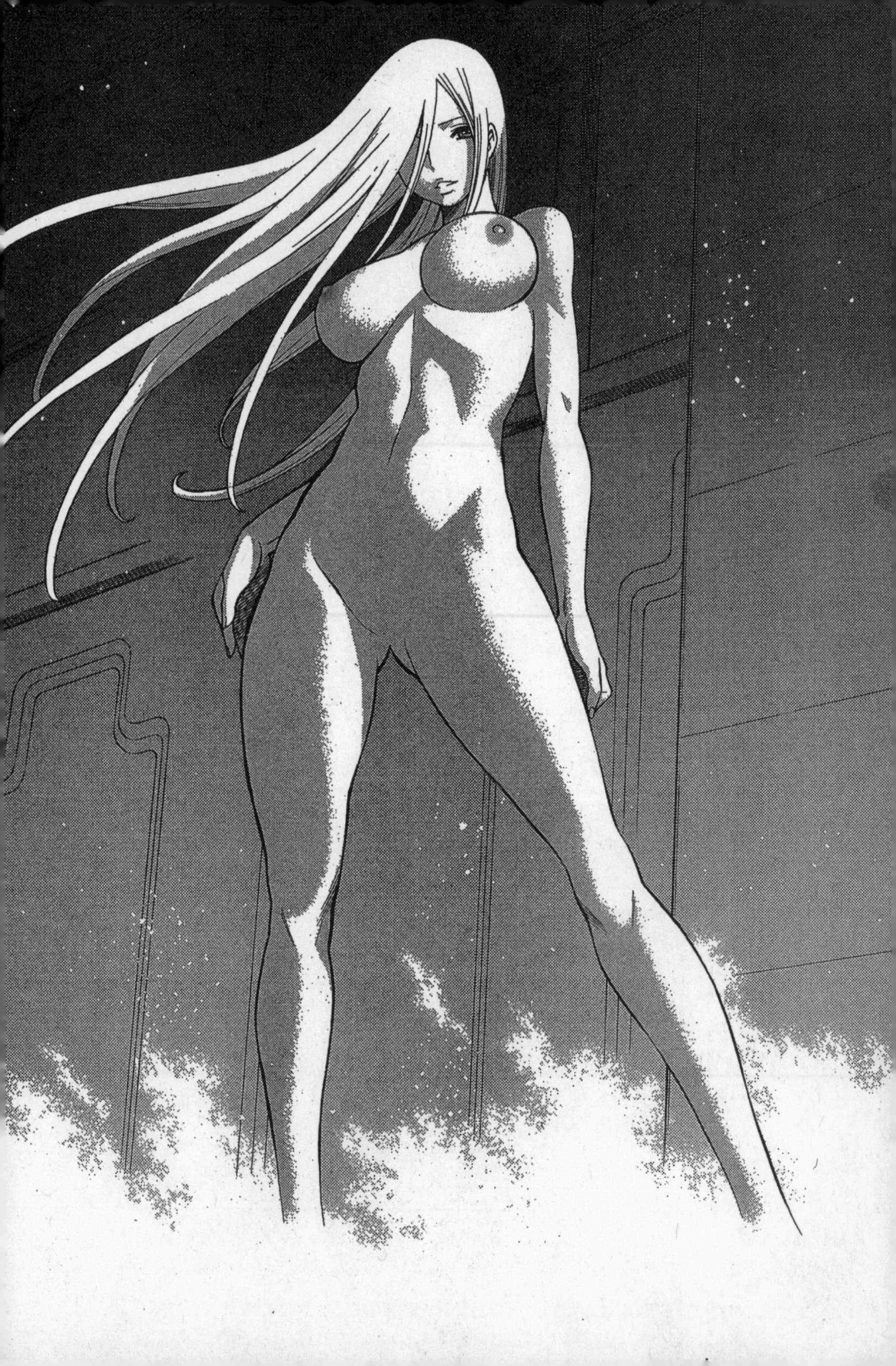

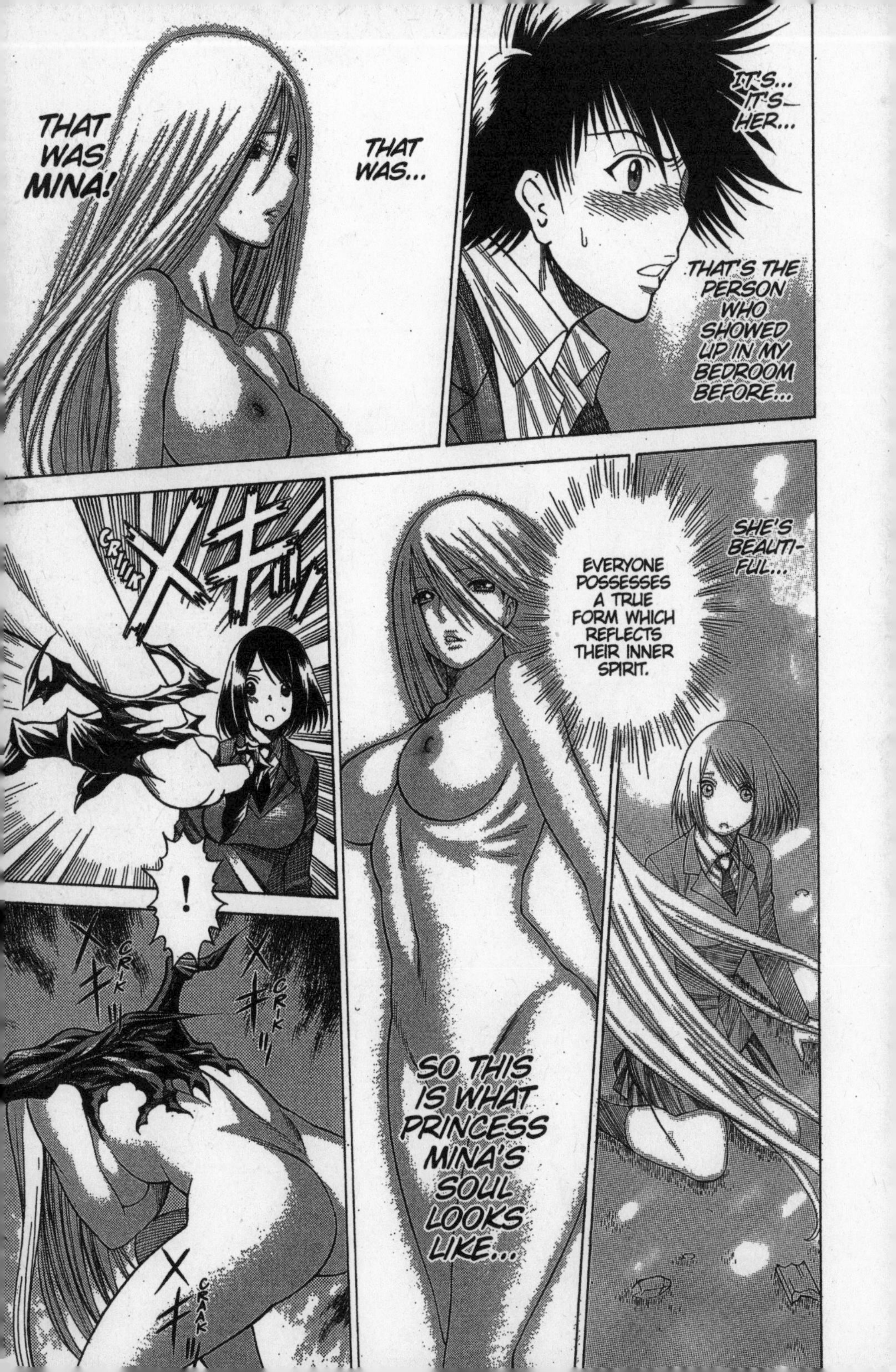
IT'S... IT'S HER...
THAT'S THE PERSON WHO SHOWED UP IN MY BEDROOM BEFORE...
THAT WAS...
THAT WAS MINA!
SHE'S BEAUTI-FUL...
EVERYONE POSSESSES A TRUE FORM WHICH REFLECTS THEIR INNER SPIRIT.
SO THIS IS WHAT PRINCESS MINA'S SOUL LOOKS LIKE...
CRUUK
!
CRIK
CRIK
CRAAK

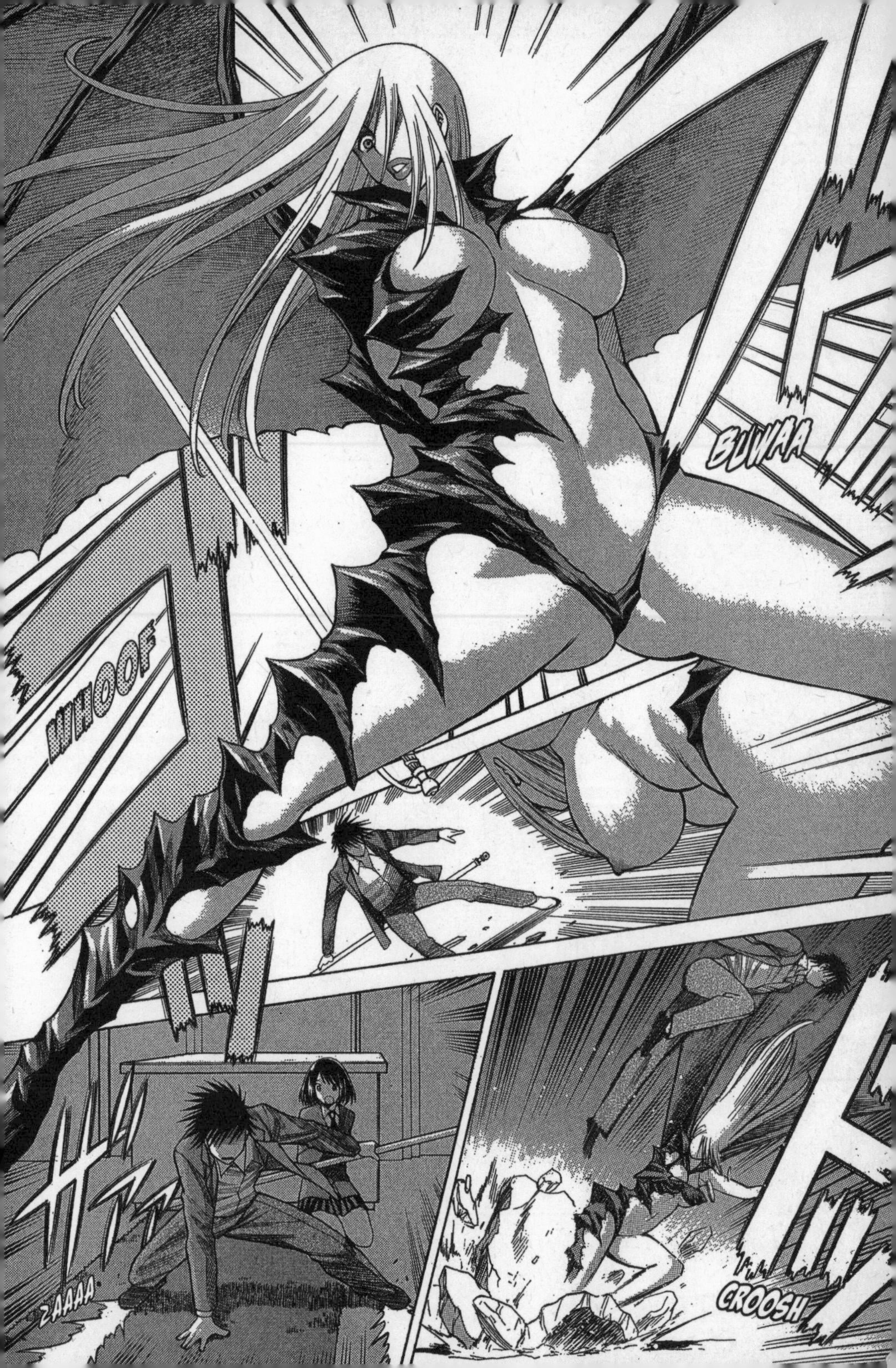
BUWAA
WHOOF
CROOSH
ZAAAA

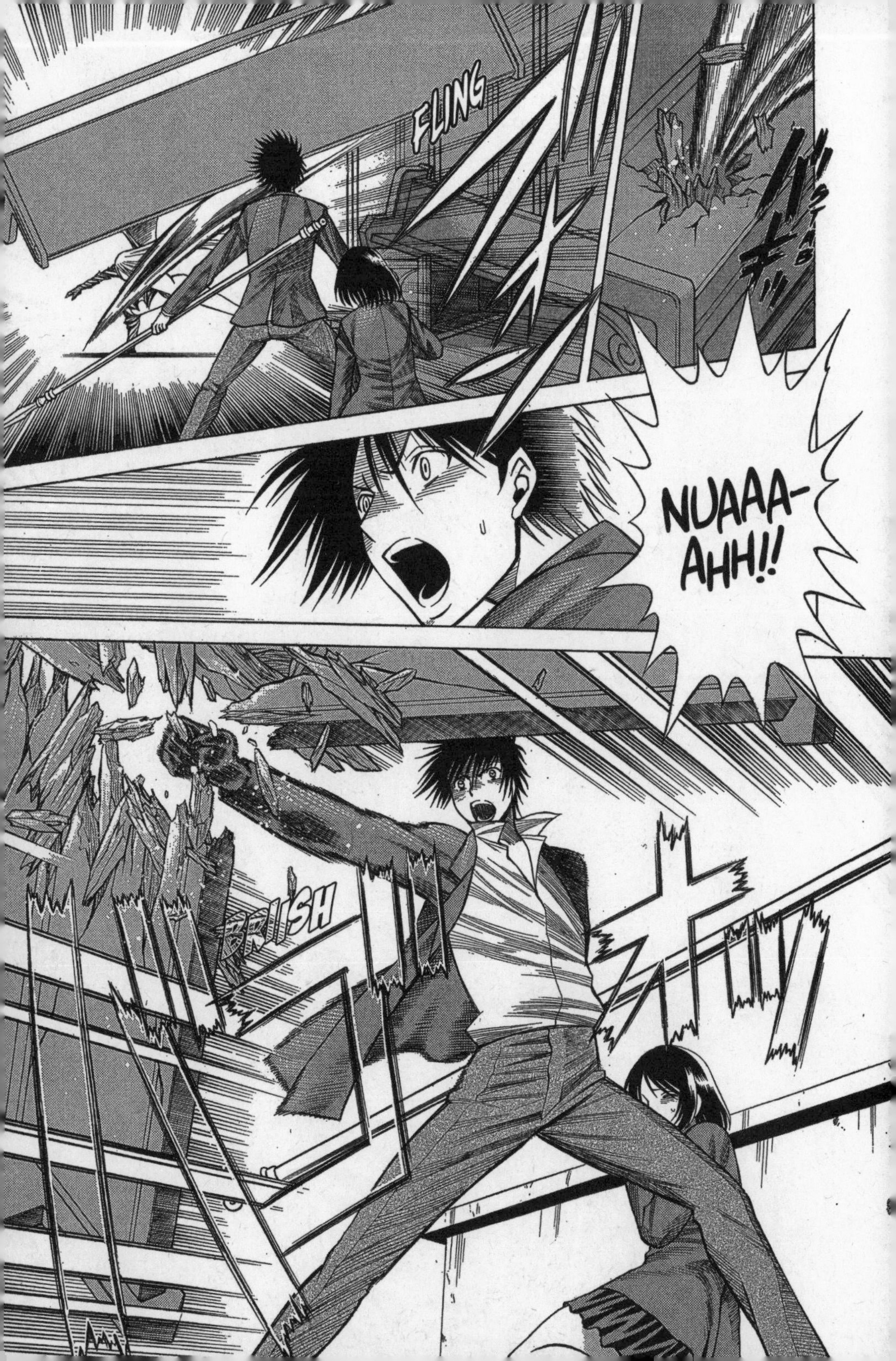
STAB
FLING
NUAAA-AHH!!
BRUSH

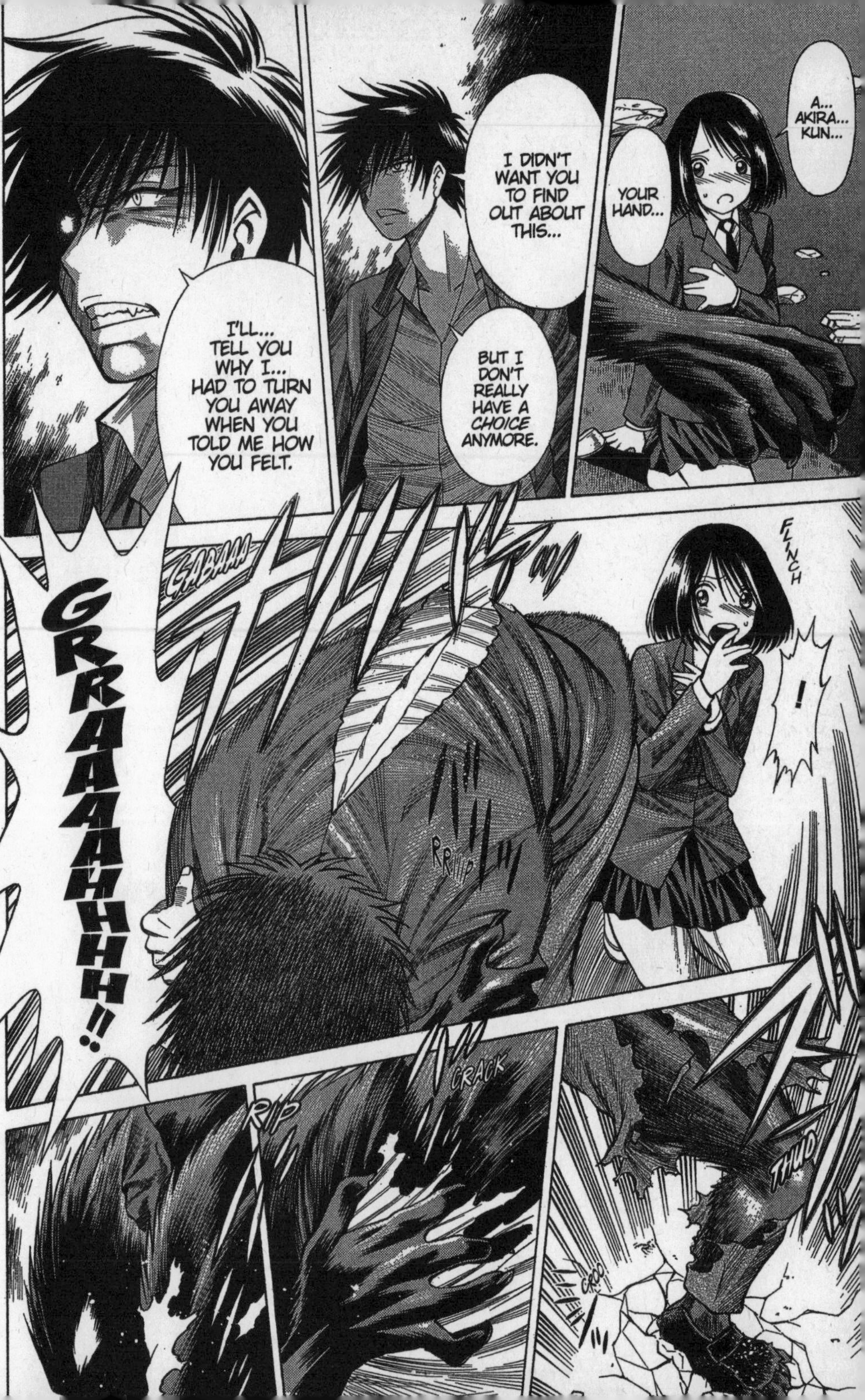
A... AKIRA... KUN...
YOUR HAND...
I DIDN'T WANT YOU TO FIND OUT ABOUT THIS...
BUT I DON'T REALLY HAVE A *CHOICE* ANYMORE.
I'LL... TELL YOU WHY I... HAD TO TURN YOU AWAY WHEN YOU TOLD ME HOW YOU FELT.
FLINCH
!
GABAAA
RRIIP
GRRAAAAHHHH!!
THUD
CRACK
RIP

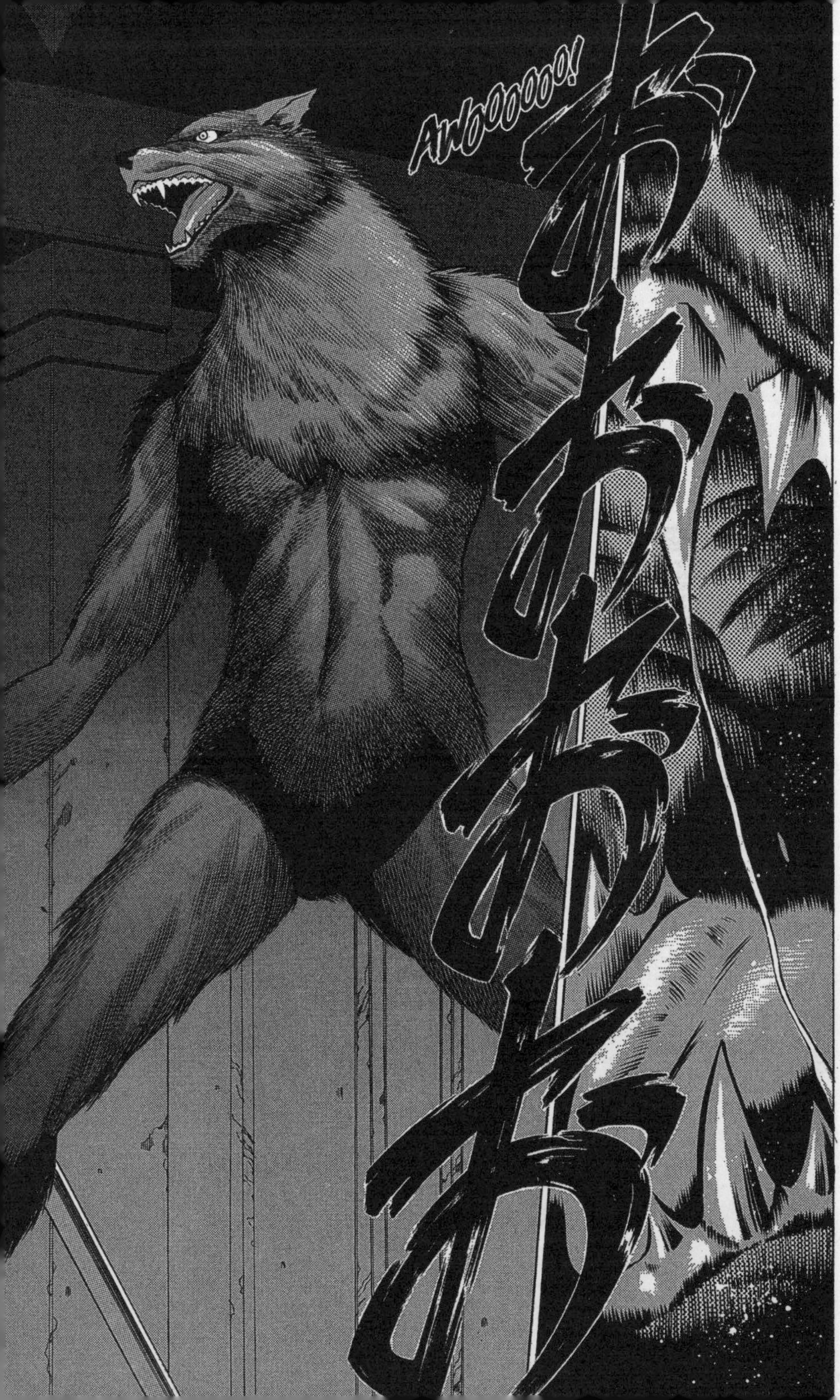
Awooooooo!

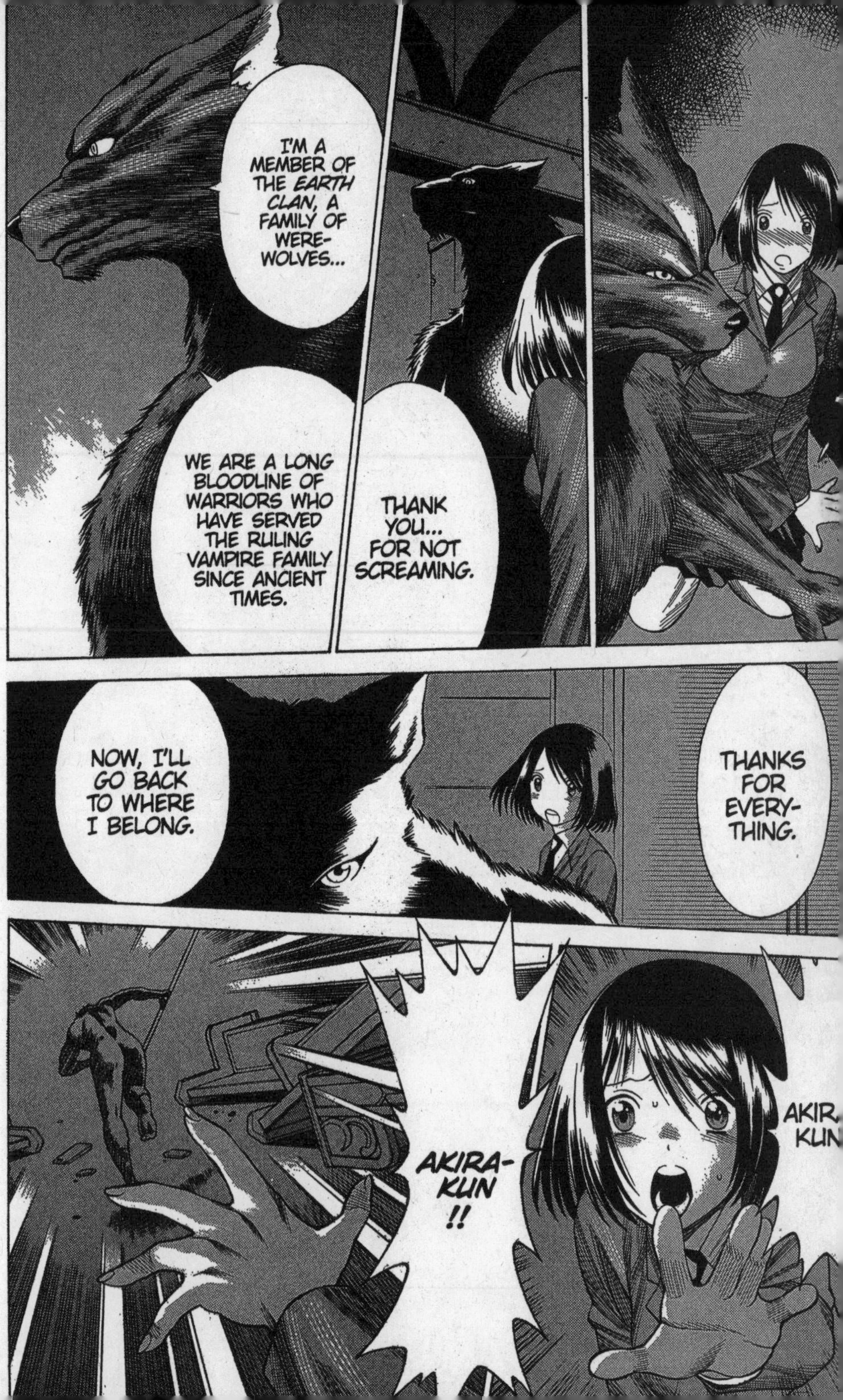
THANK YOU... FOR NOT SCREAMING.
I'M A MEMBER OF THE *EARTH CLAN*, A FAMILY OF WERE-WOLVES...
WE ARE A LONG BLOODLINE OF WARRIORS WHO HAVE SERVED THE RULING VAMPIRE FAMILY SINCE ANCIENT TIMES.
THANKS FOR EVERY-THING.
NOW, I'LL GO BACK TO WHERE I BELONG.
AKIR KUN
AKIRA-KUN !!

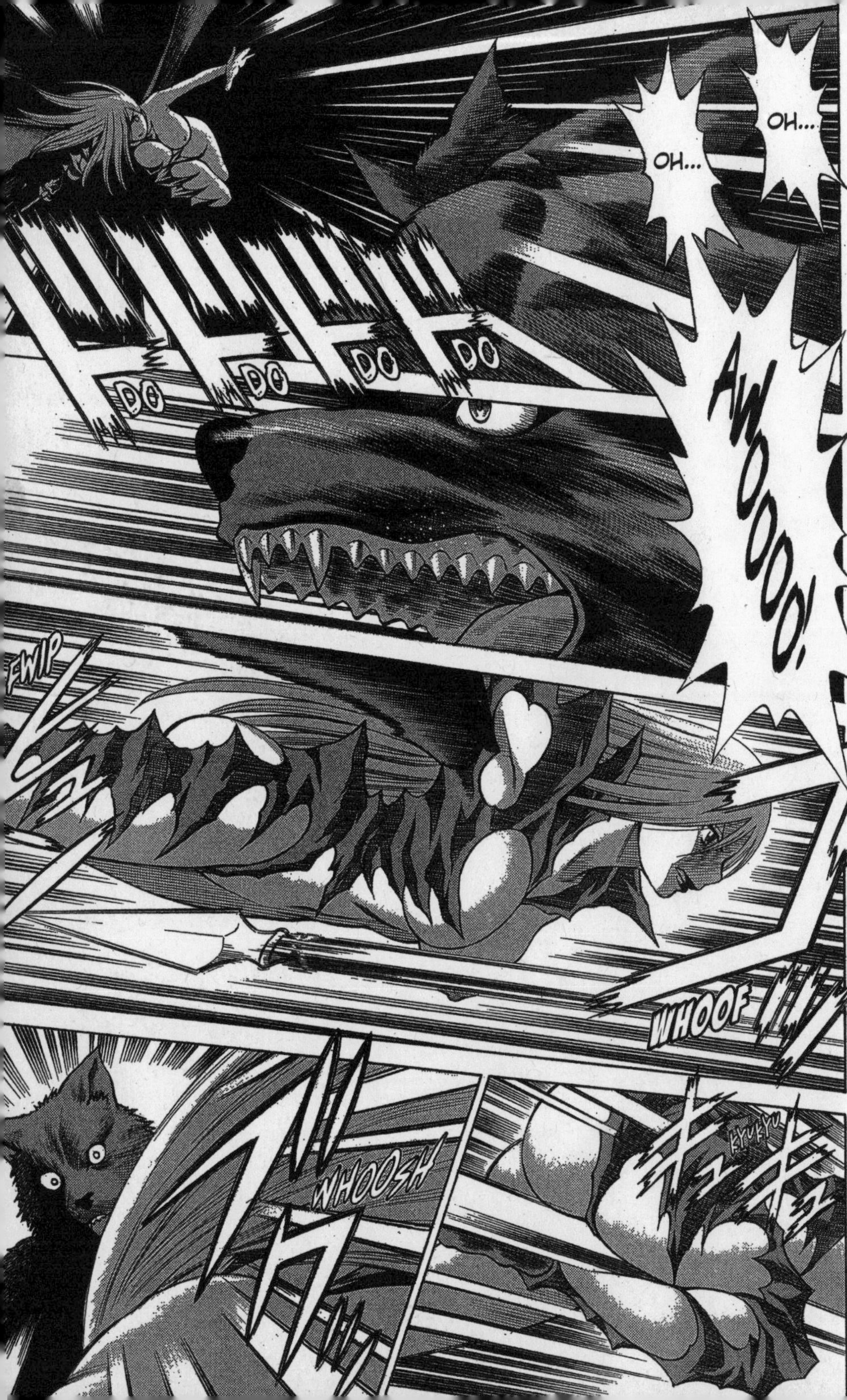
OH...
OH...
AWOOOOO!
DO DO DO DO
FWIP
WHOOF
KYUKYU
WHOOSH

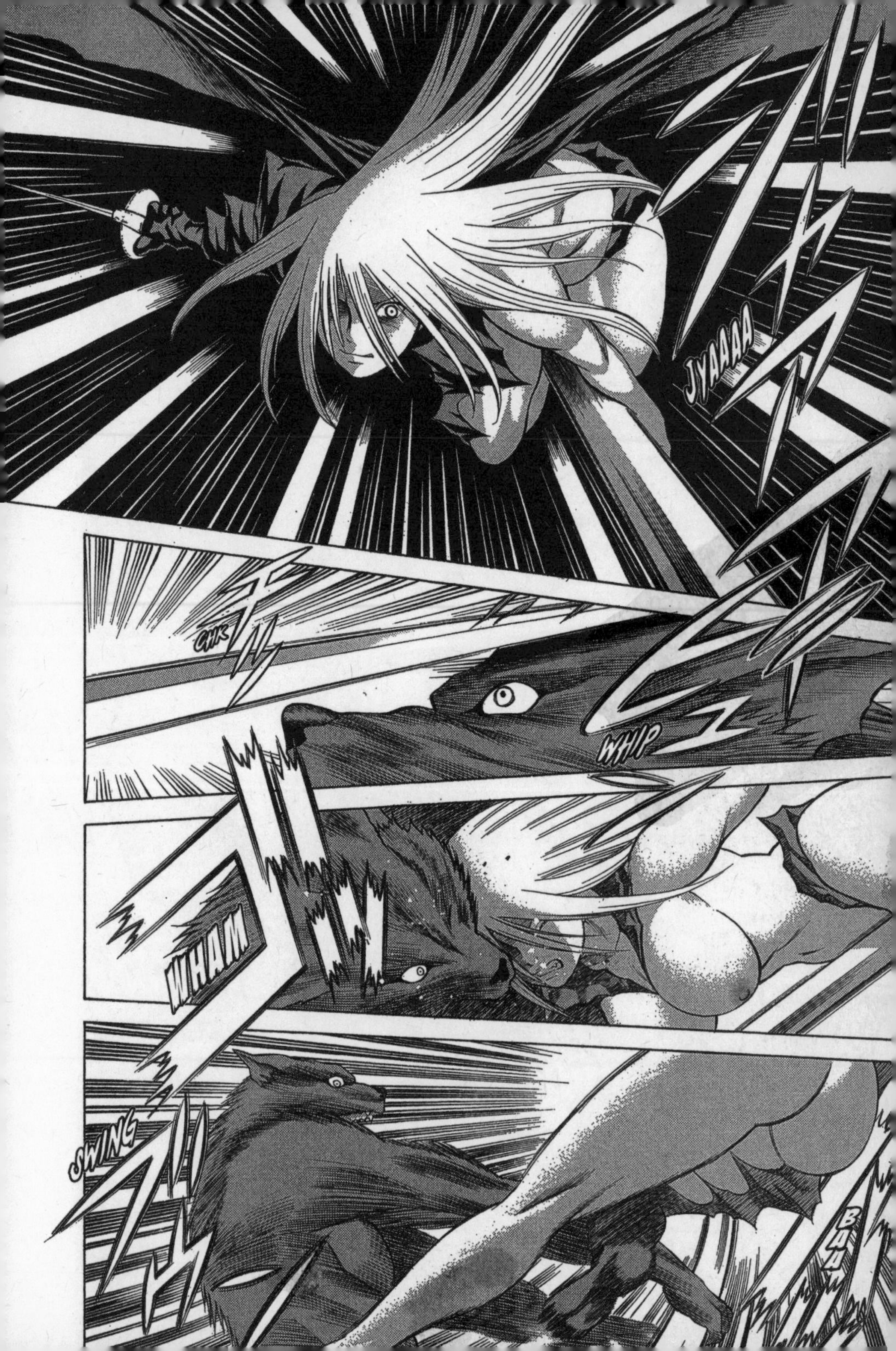
JYAAAA
WHIP
CHK
WHAM
BAA
SWING

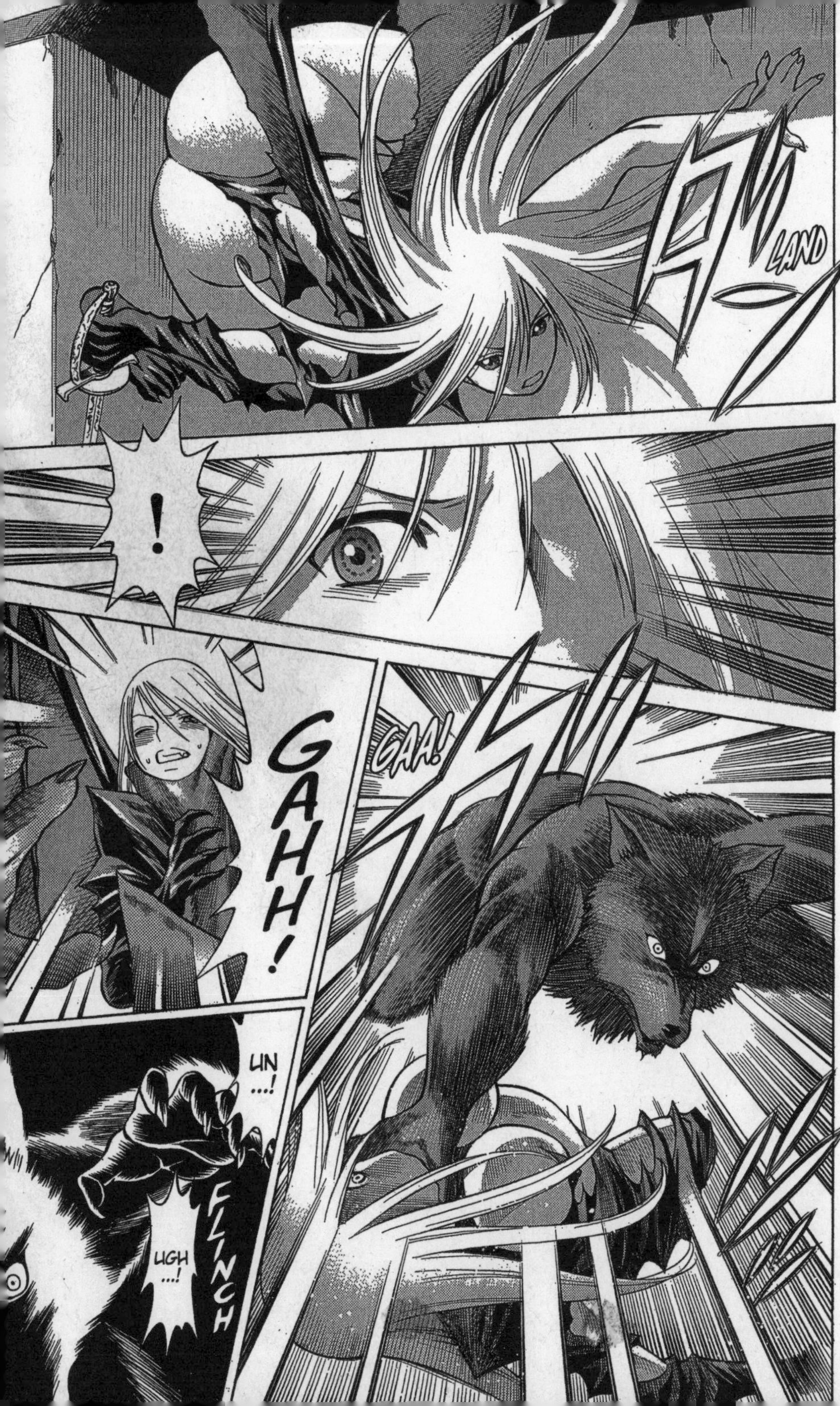
LAND
!
GAA!
GAHH!
UN ...!
FLINCH
UGH ...!

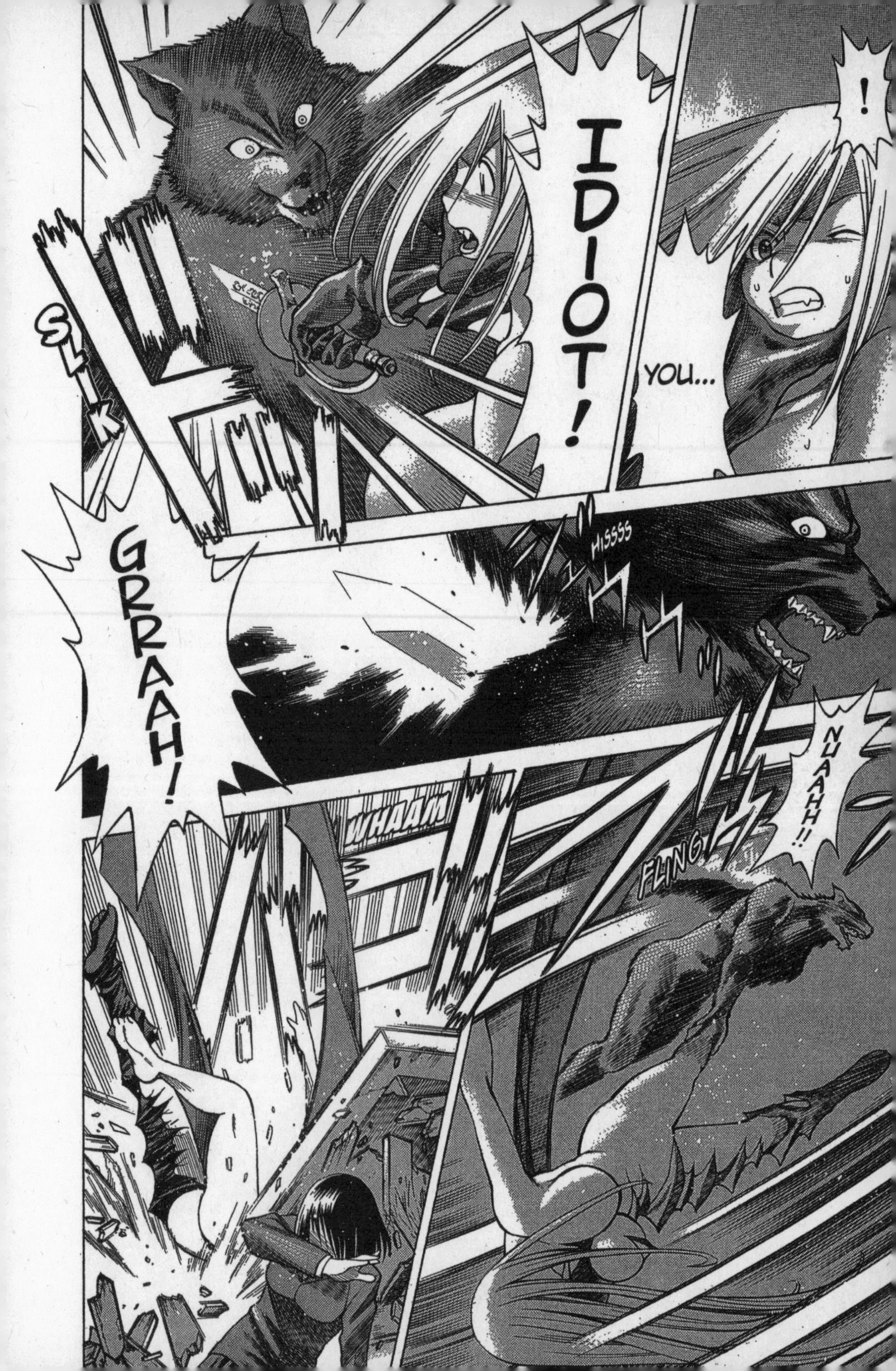
!
YOU...
IDIOT!
SLIK
HISSSS
GRRAAH!
NUAAHH!!
FLING
WHAAM

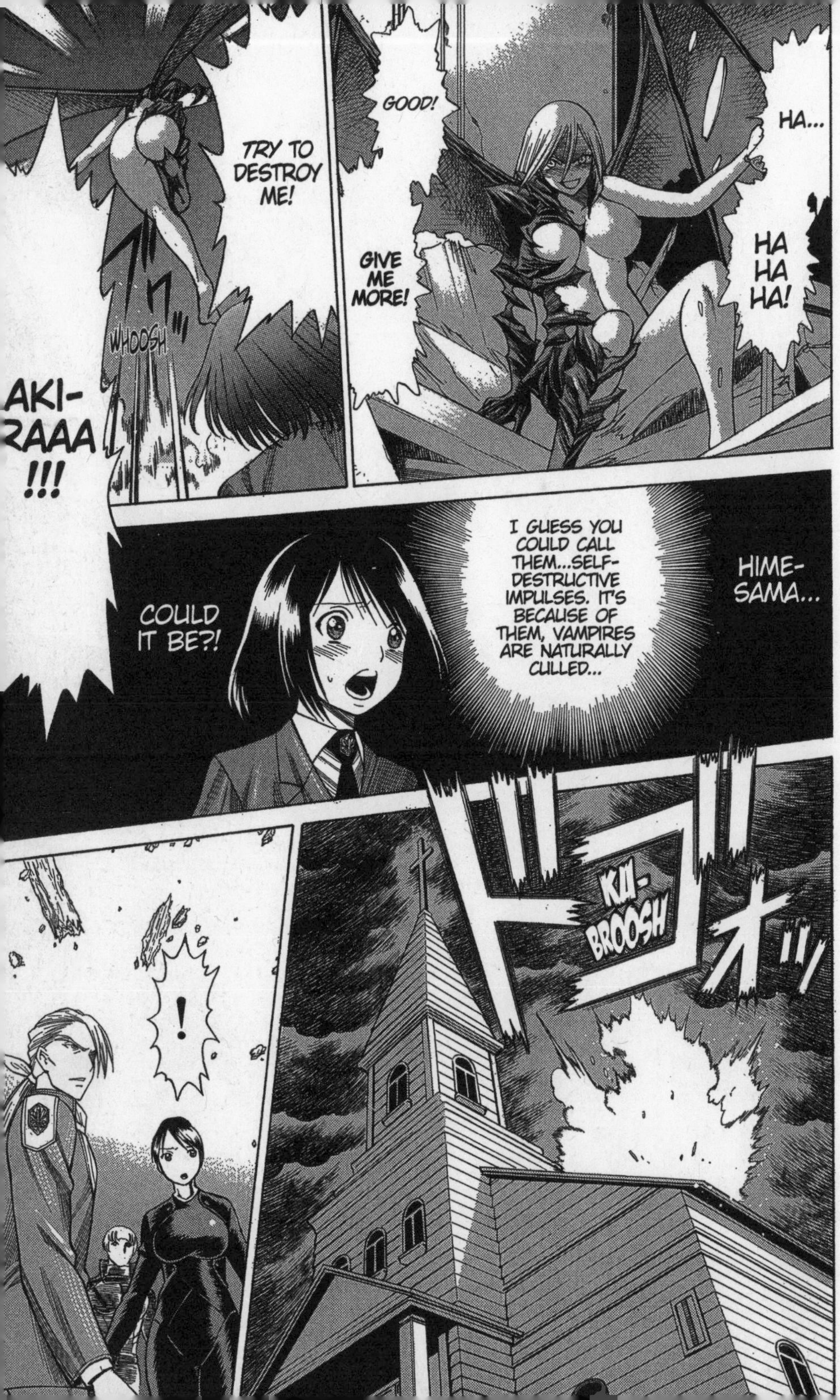
HA...
HA HA HA!
GOOD!
GIVE ME MORE!
TRY TO DESTROY ME!
WHOOSH
AKI-RAAA!!!
HIME-SAMA...
I GUESS YOU COULD CALL THEM...SELF-DESTRUCTIVE IMPULSES. IT'S BECAUSE OF THEM, VAMPIRES ARE NATURALLY CULLED...
COULD IT BE?!
KU-BROOSH
!

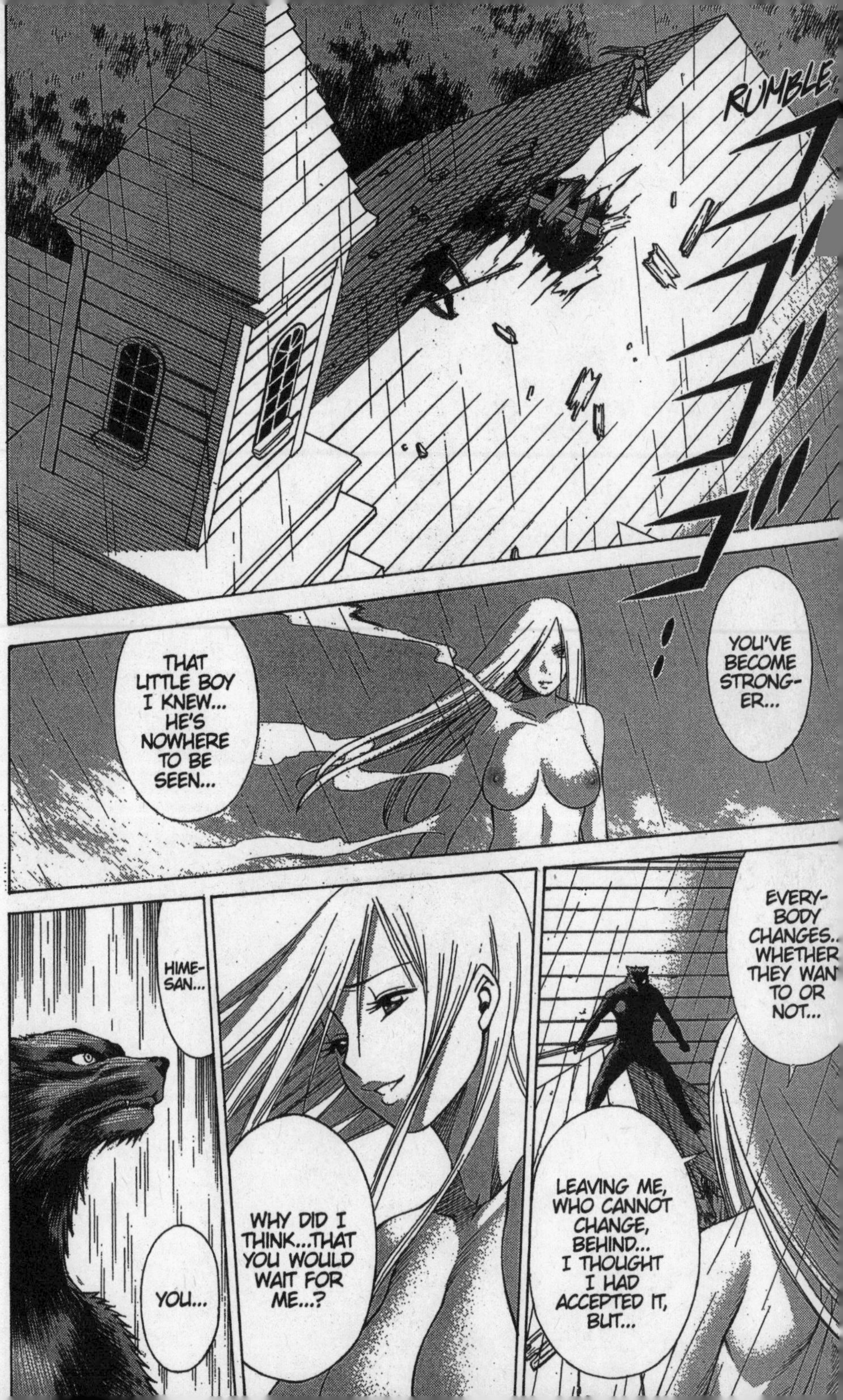
RUMBLE
YOU'VE BECOME STRONG-ER...
THAT LITTLE BOY I KNEW... HE'S NOWHERE TO BE SEEN...
EVERY-BODY CHANGES.. WHETHER THEY WAN TO OR NOT...
LEAVING ME, WHO CANNOT CHANGE, BEHIND... I THOUGHT I HAD ACCEPTED IT, BUT...
WHY DID I THINK...THAT YOU WOULD WAIT FOR ME...?
HIME-SAN...
YOU...

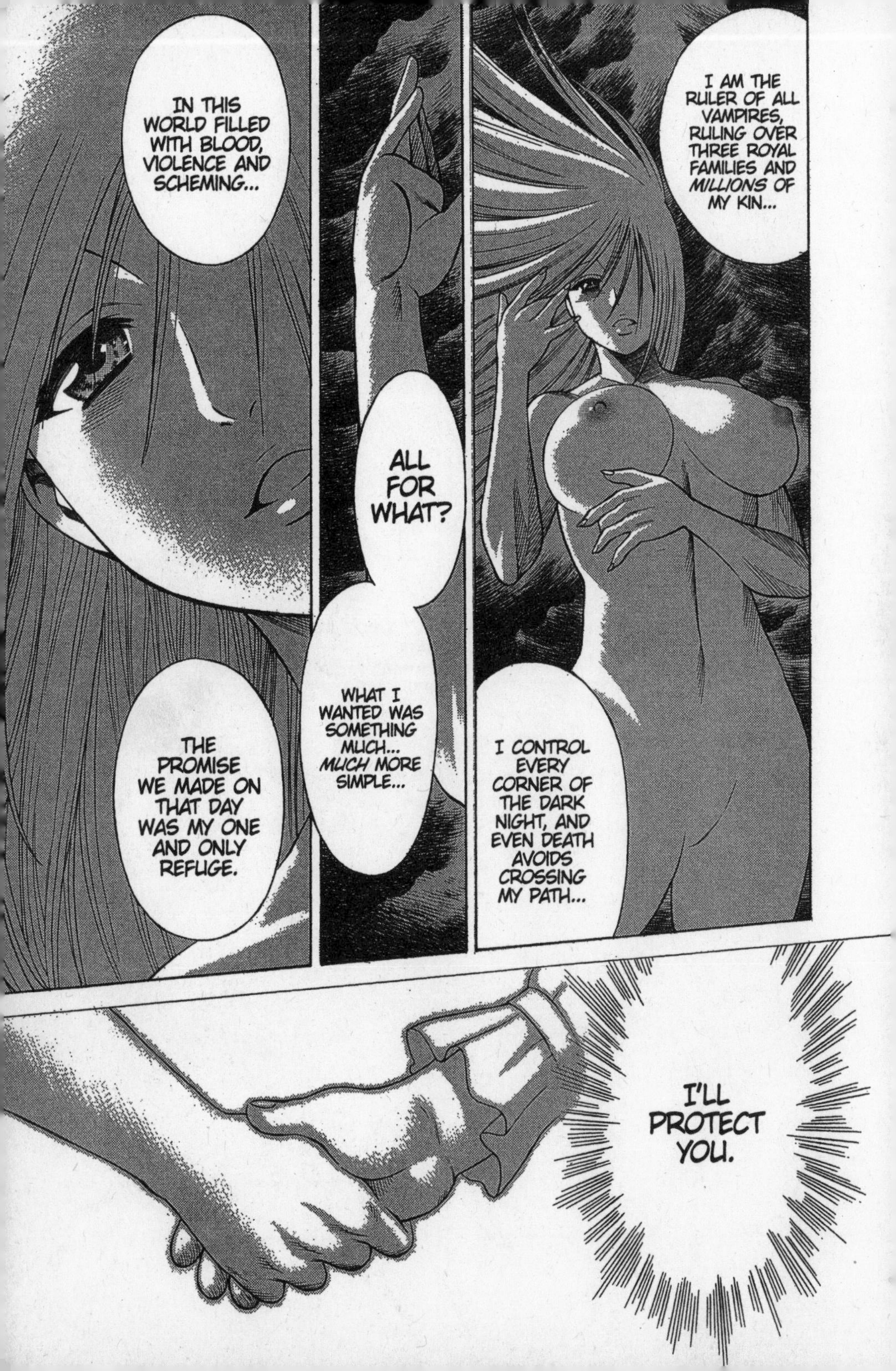
I AM THE RULER OF ALL VAMPIRES, RULING OVER THREE ROYAL FAMILIES AND *MILLIONS* OF MY KIN...
I CONTROL EVERY CORNER OF THE DARK NIGHT, AND EVEN DEATH AVOIDS CROSSING MY PATH...
ALL FOR WHAT?
WHAT I WANTED WAS SOMETHING MUCH... *MUCH* MORE SIMPLE...
IN THIS WORLD FILLED WITH BLOOD, VIOLENCE AND SCHEMING...
THE PROMISE WE MADE ON THAT DAY WAS MY ONE AND ONLY REFUGE.
I'LL PROTECT YOU.

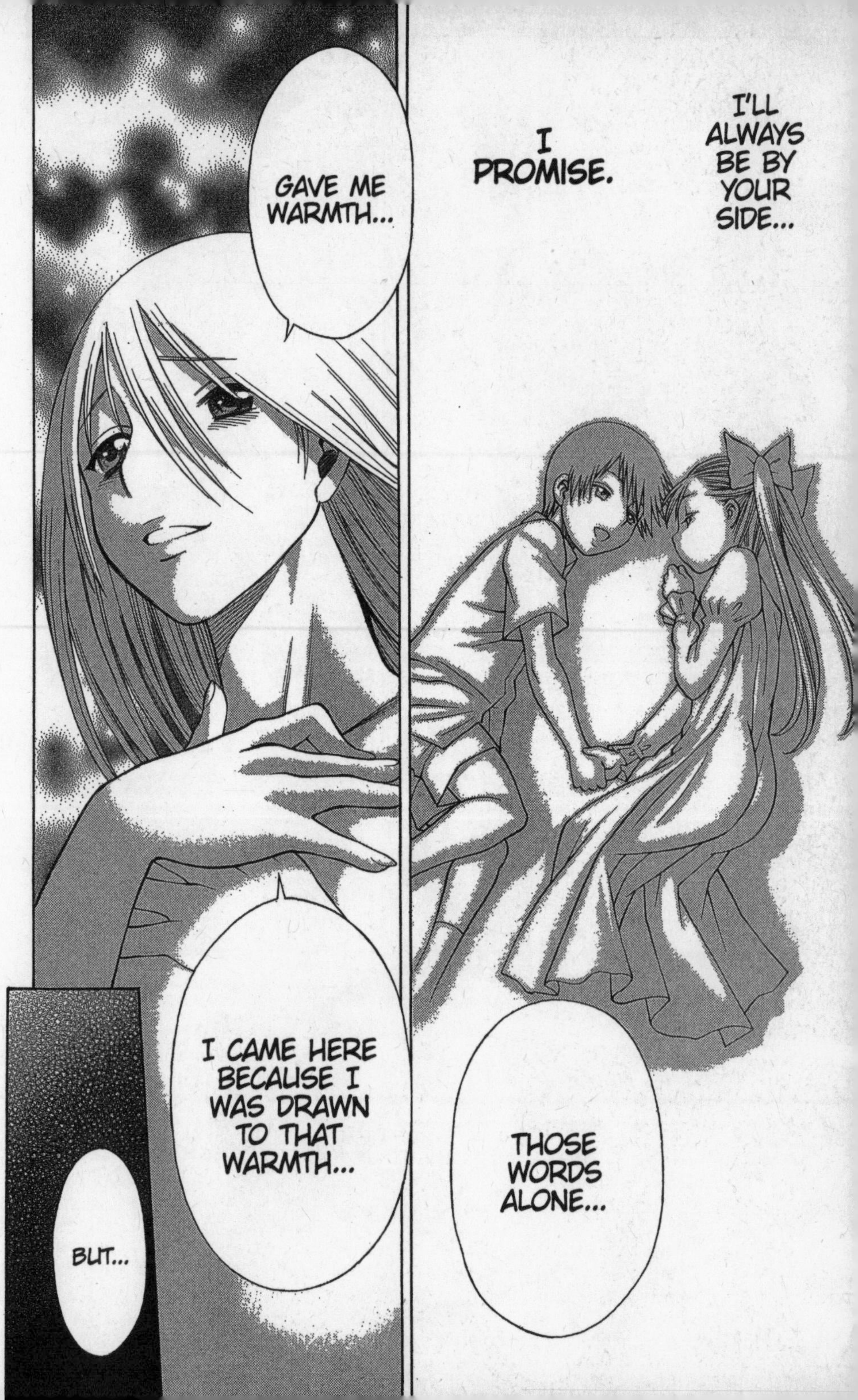
I'LL ALWAYS BE BY YOUR SIDE...
I PROMISE.
THOSE WORDS ALONE...
GAVE ME WARMTH...
I CAME HERE BECAUSE I WAS DRAWN TO THAT WARMTH...
BUT...

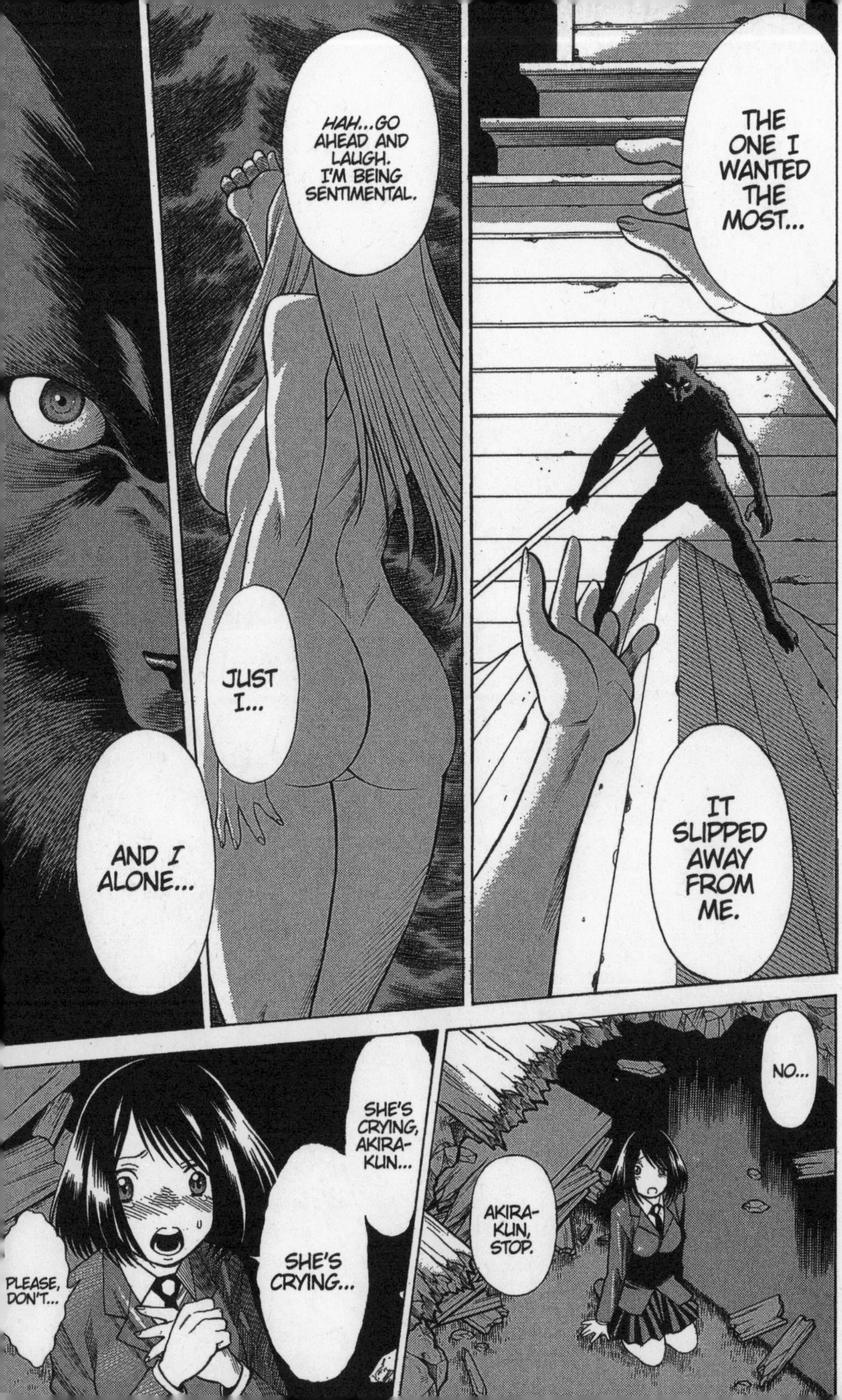
THE ONE I WANTED THE MOST...
IT SLIPPED AWAY FROM ME.
HAH...GO AHEAD AND LAUGH. I'M BEING SENTIMENTAL.
JUST I...
AND I ALONE...
NO...
AKIRA-KUN, STOP.
SHE'S CRYING, AKIRA-KUN...
SHE'S CRYING...
PLEASE, DON'T...

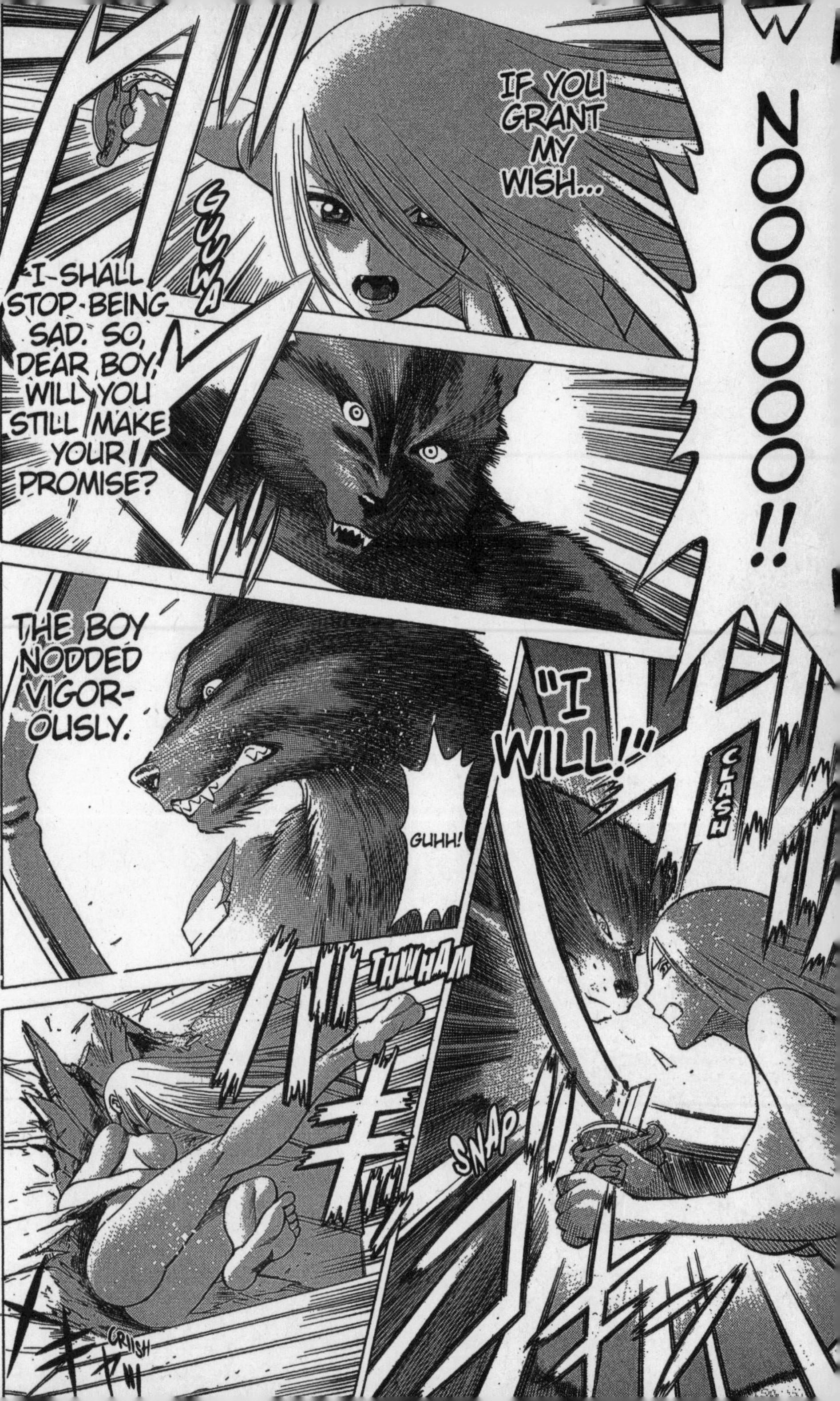
NOOOOOOO!!
IF YOU GRANT MY WISH...
GUUWA
I-SHALL STOP-BEING SAD. SO, DEAR BOY, WILL YOU STILL MAKE YOUR PROMISE?
"I WILL!"
CLASH
THE BOY NODDED VIGOR-OUSLY.
GUHH!
THWHAM
SNAP
CRUSH

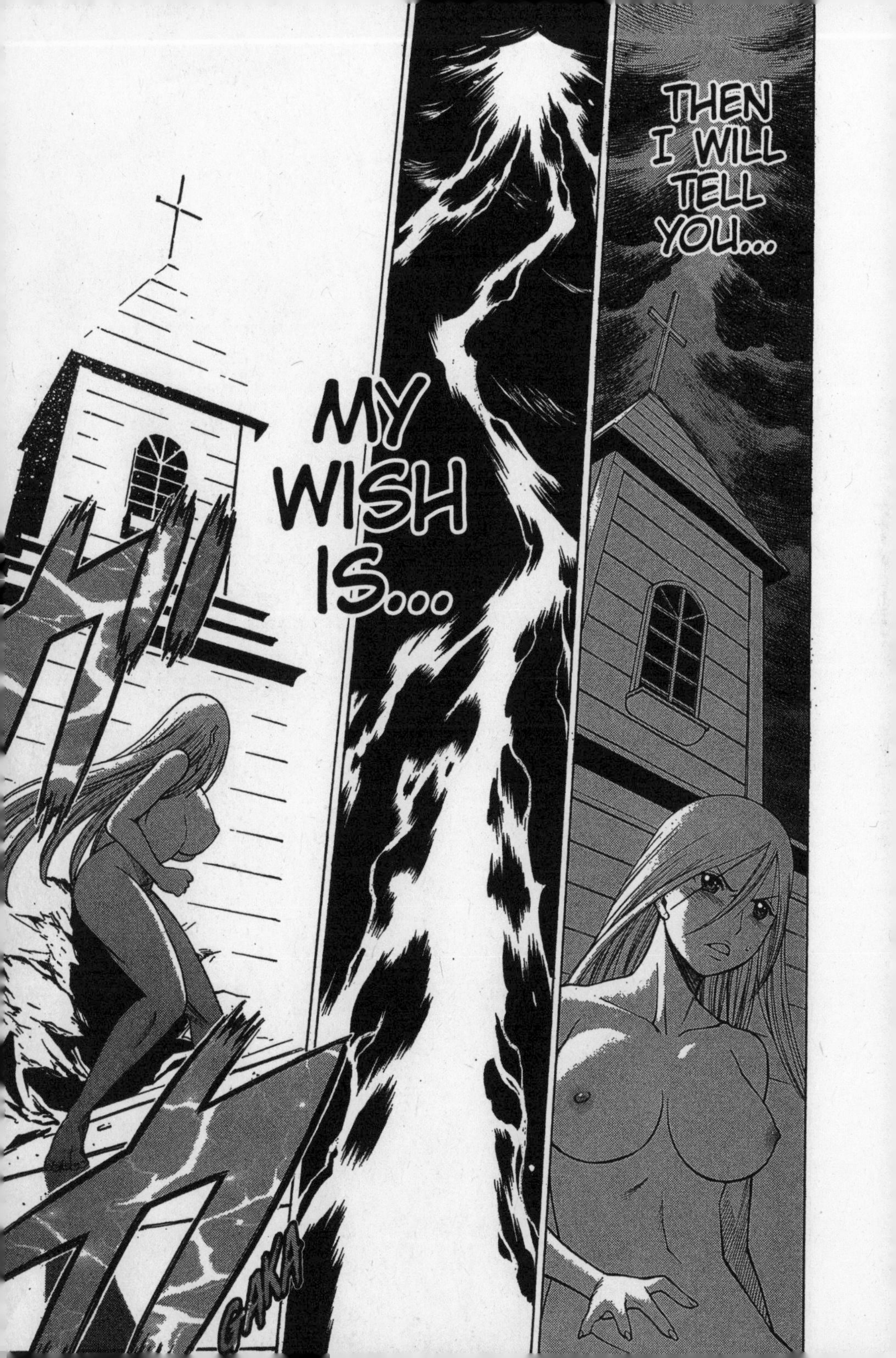
THEN I WILL TELL YOU...
MY WISH IS...
GAKA

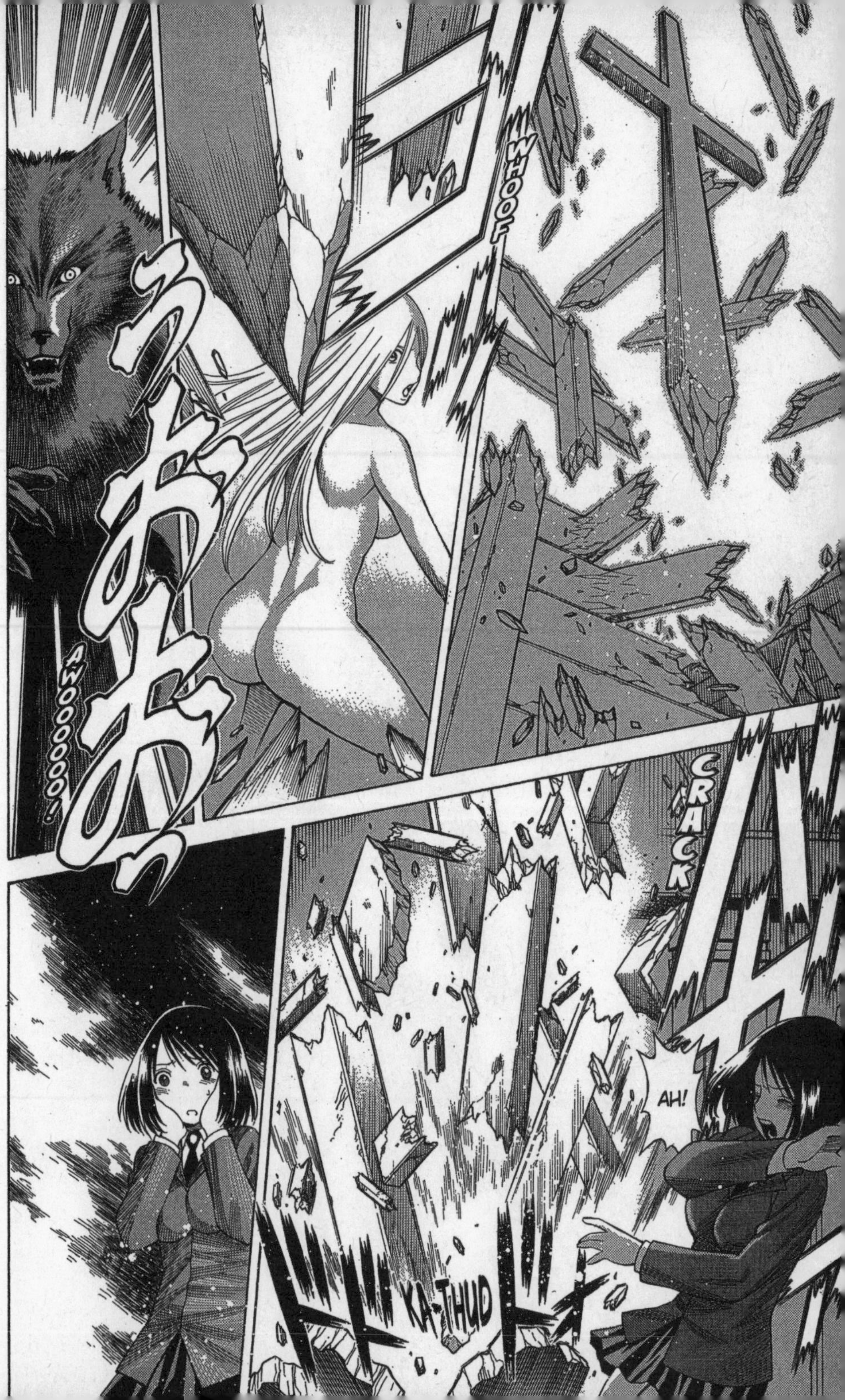
WHOOF
AWOOOOOOO!
CRACK
AH!
KA-THUD

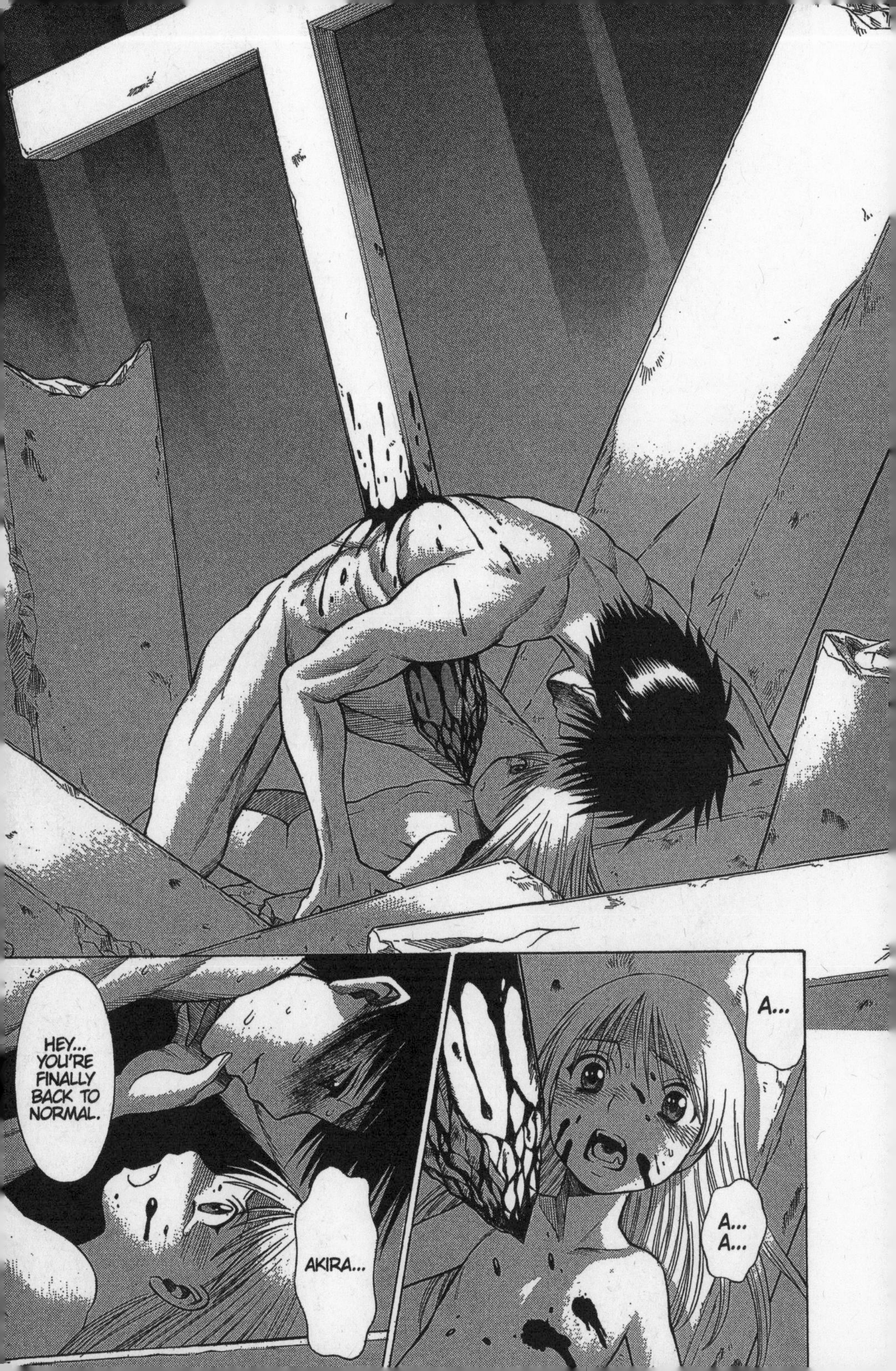
A...
A... A...
HEY... YOU'RE FINALLY BACK TO NORMAL.
AKIRA...

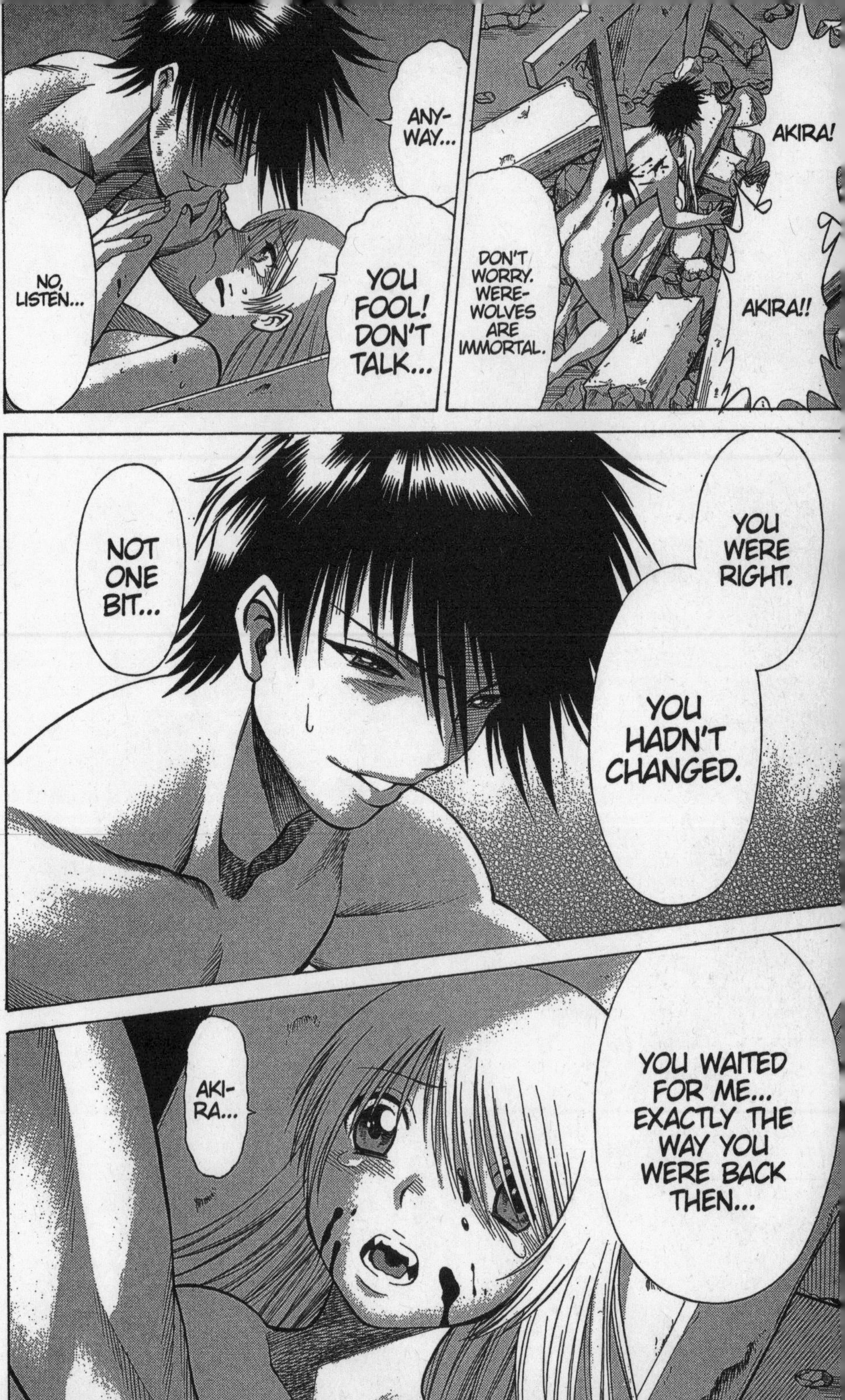
AKIRA!
AKIRA!!
DON'T WORRY. WERE-WOLVES ARE IMMORTAL.
YOU FOOL! DON'T TALK...
ANY-WAY...
NO, LISTEN...
YOU WERE RIGHT.
YOU HADN'T CHANGED.
NOT ONE BIT...
YOU WAITED FOR ME... EXACTLY THE WAY YOU WERE BACK THEN...
AKI-RA...

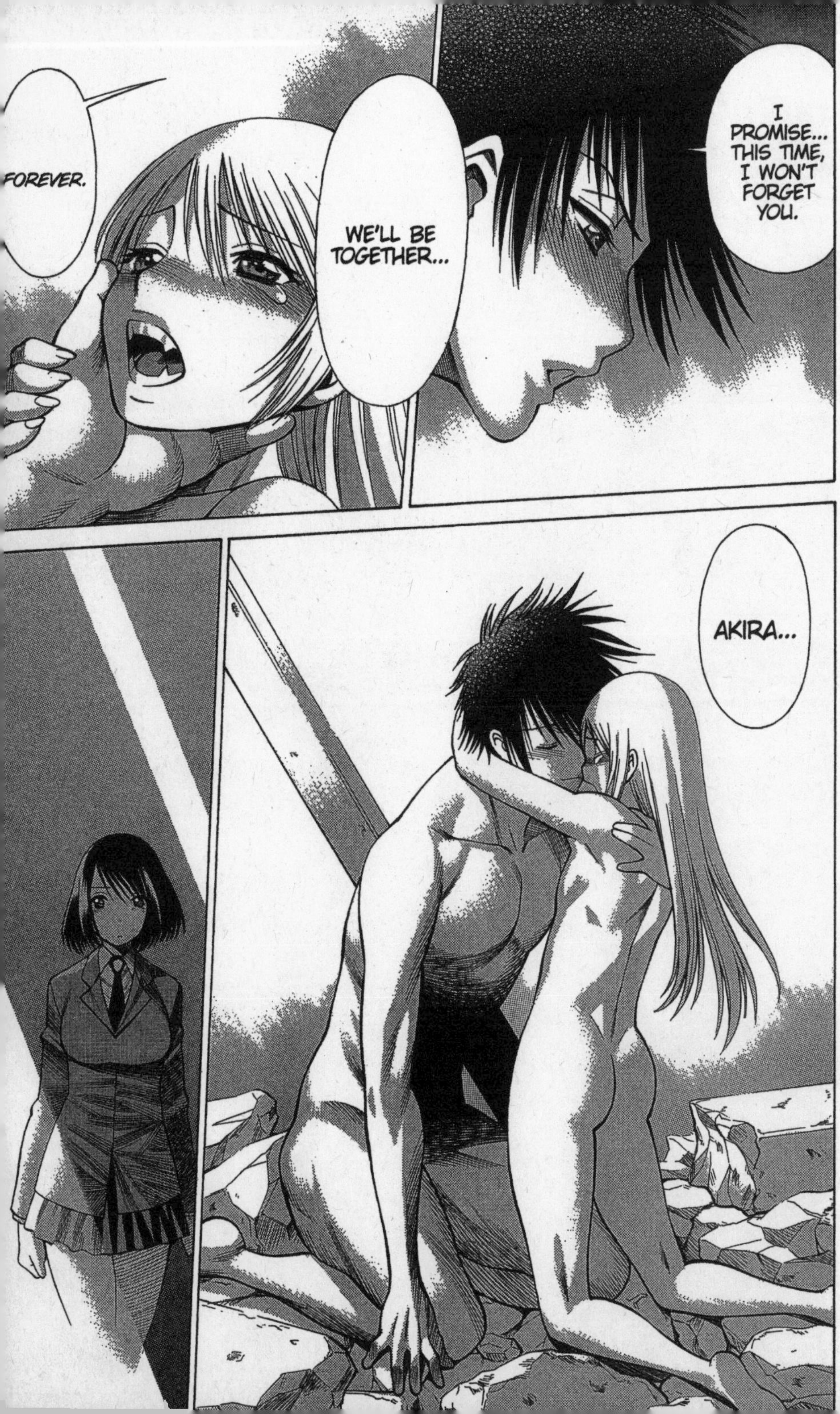
I PROMISE... THIS TIME, I WON'T FORGET YOU.
WE'LL BE TOGETHER...
FOREVER.
AKIRA...

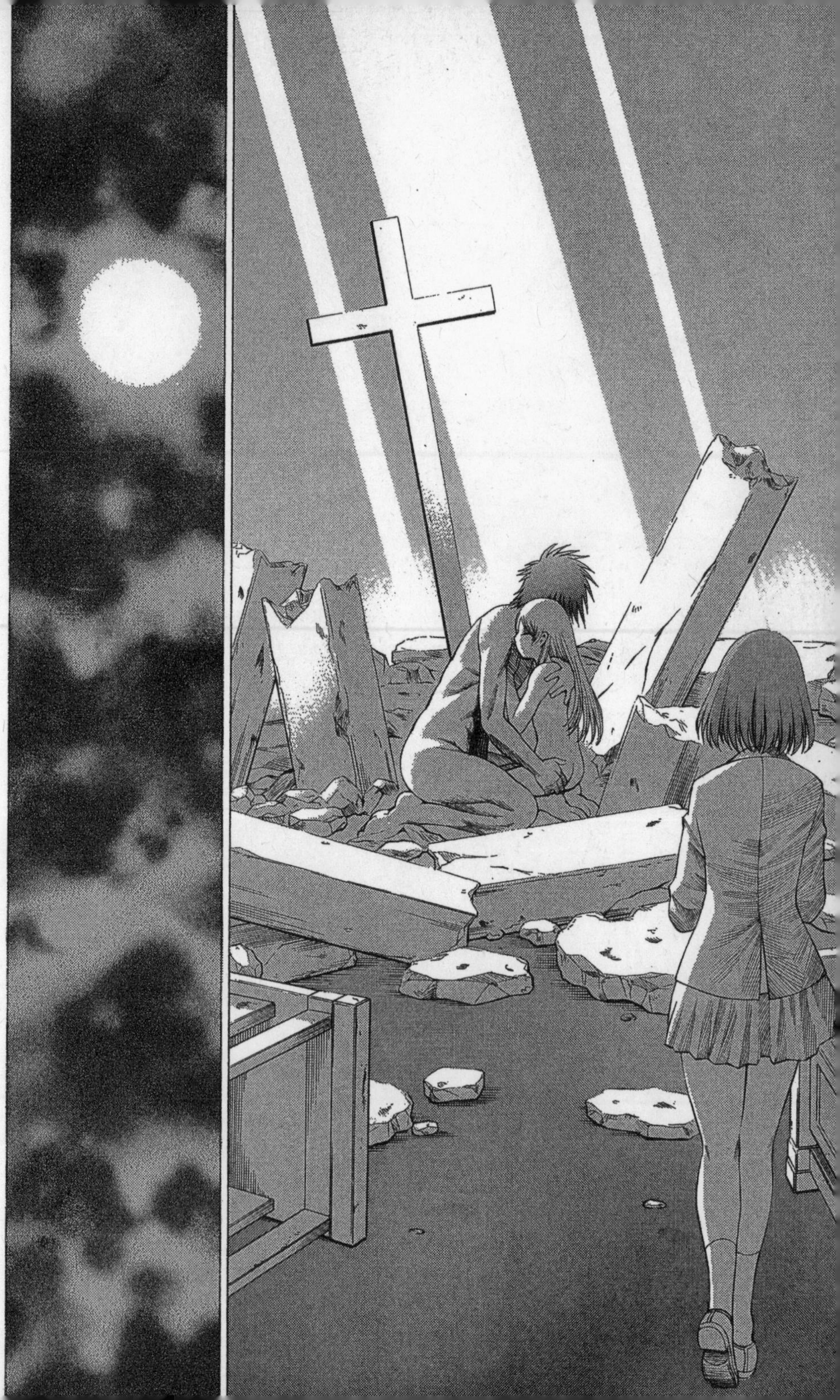

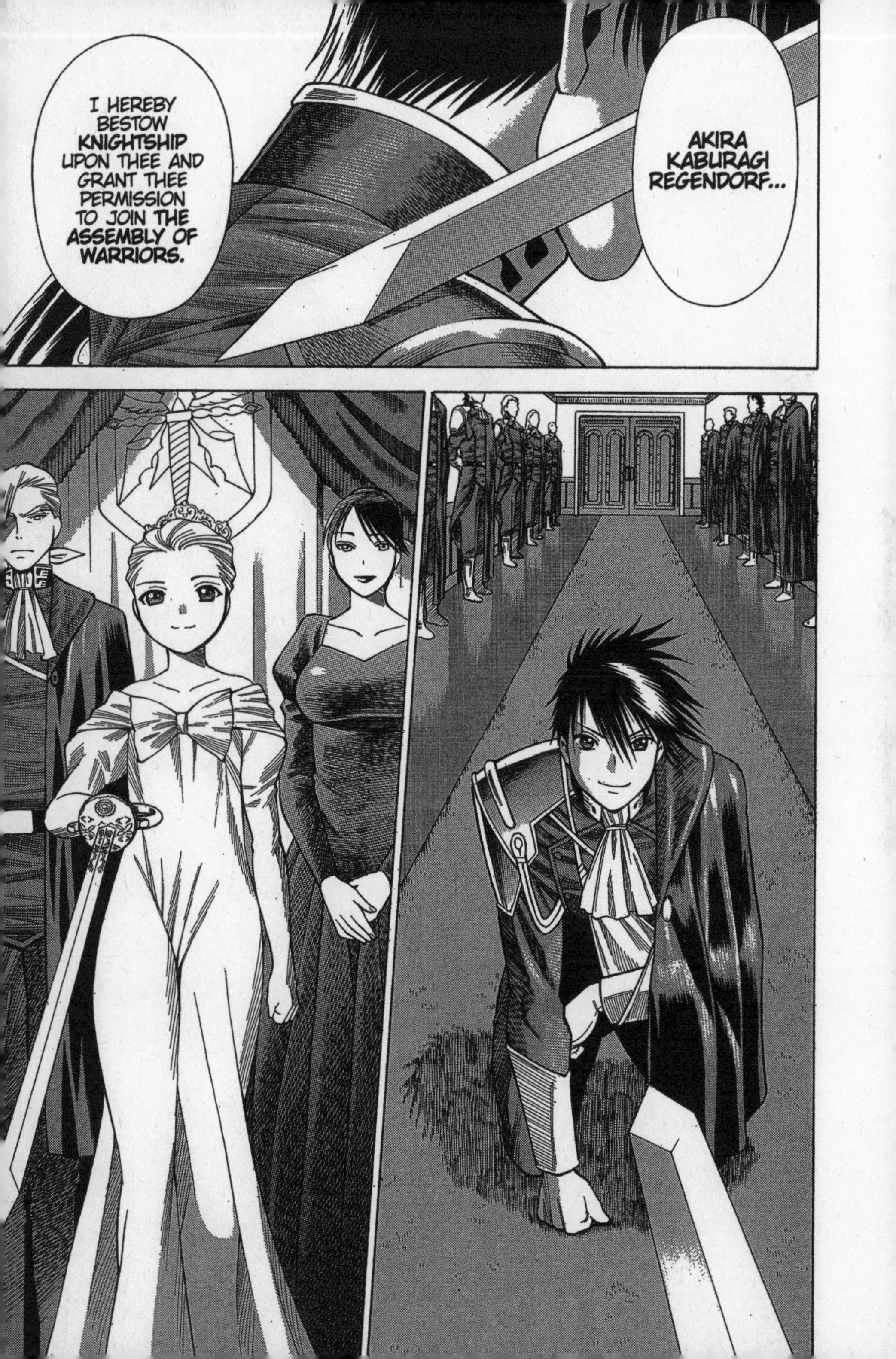
AKIRA KABURAGI REGENDORF...
I HEREBY BESTOW KNIGHTSHIP UPON THEE AND GRANT THEE PERMISSION TO JOIN THE ASSEMBLY OF WARRIORS.

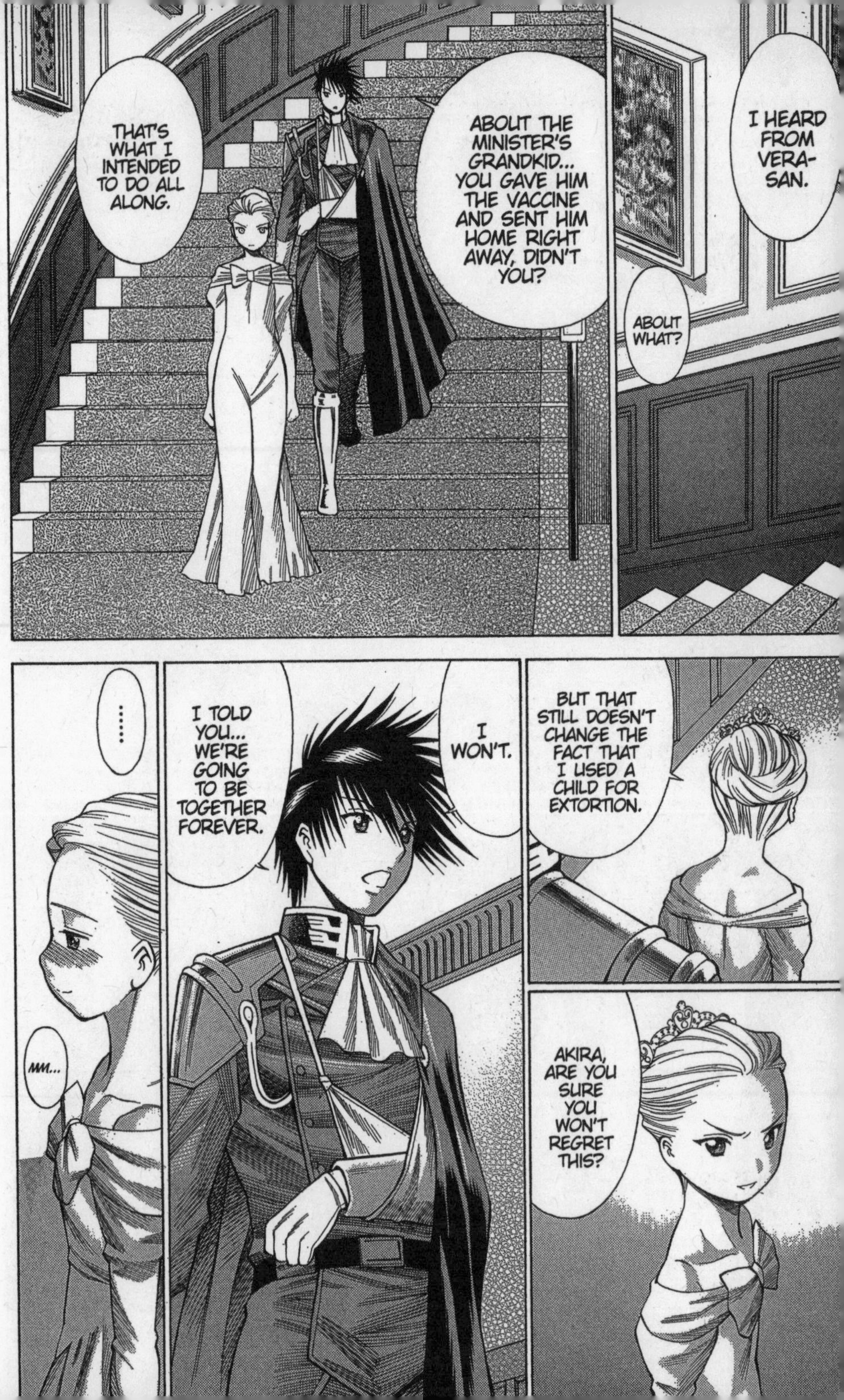

I HEARD FROM VERA-SAN.
ABOUT WHAT?
ABOUT THE MINISTER'S GRANDKID... YOU GAVE HIM THE VACCINE AND SENT HIM HOME RIGHT AWAY, DIDN'T YOU?
THAT'S WHAT I INTENDED TO DO ALL ALONG.
BUT THAT STILL DOESN'T CHANGE THE FACT THAT I USED A CHILD FOR EXTORTION.
AKIRA, ARE YOU SURE YOU WON'T REGRET THIS?
I WON'T.
I TOLD YOU... WE'RE GOING TO BE TOGETHER FOREVER.
......
MM...

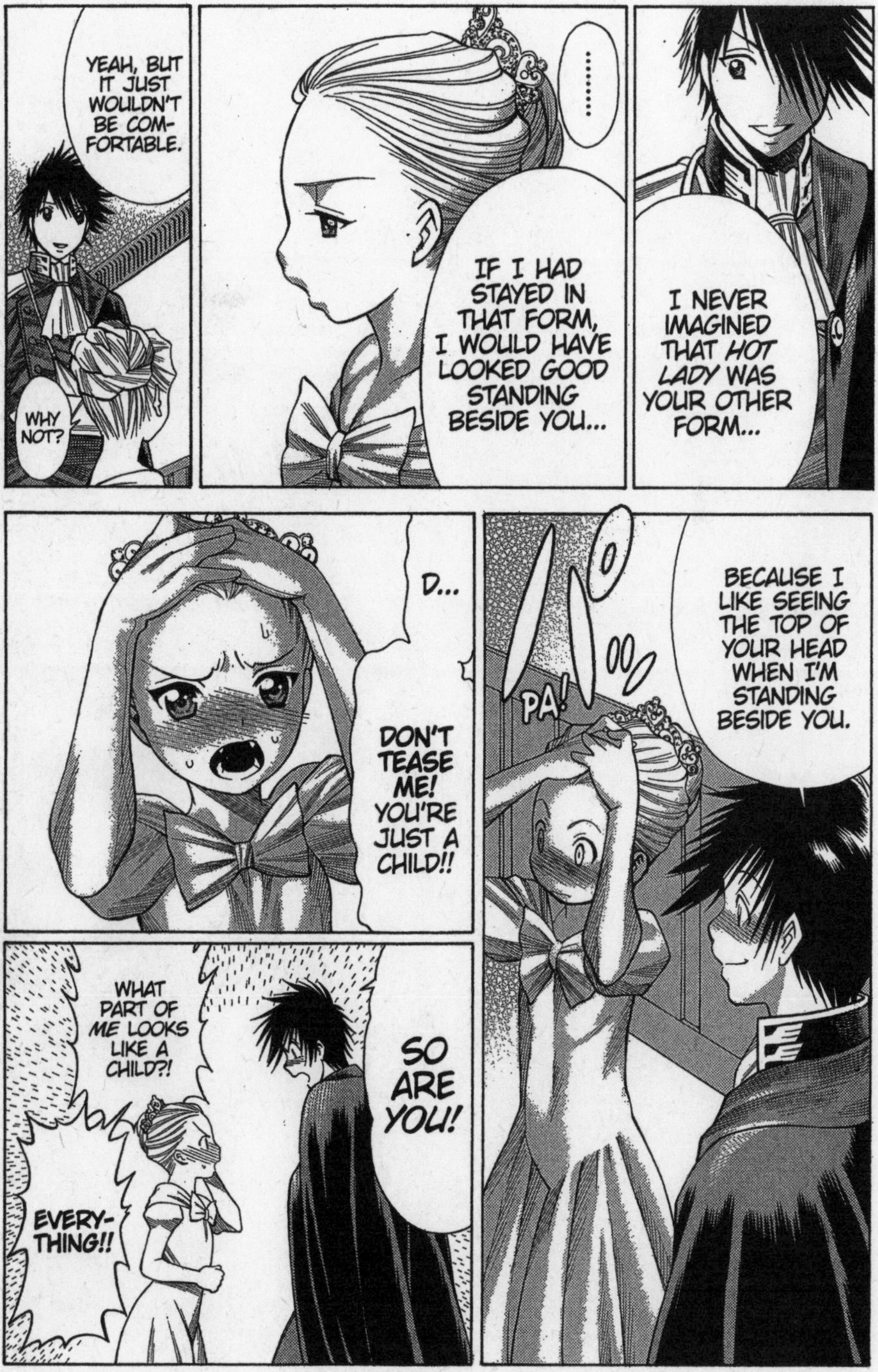
I NEVER IMAGINED THAT *HOT LADY* WAS YOUR OTHER FORM...
......
IF I HAD STAYED IN THAT FORM, I WOULD HAVE LOOKED GOOD STANDING BESIDE YOU...
YEAH, BUT IT JUST WOULDN'T BE COM-FORTABLE.
WHY NOT?
BECAUSE I LIKE SEEING THE TOP OF YOUR HEAD WHEN I'M STANDING BESIDE YOU.
PA!
D...
DON'T TEASE ME! YOU'RE JUST A CHILD!!
SO ARE YOU!
WHAT PART OF *ME* LOOKS LIKE A CHILD?!
EVERY-THING!!

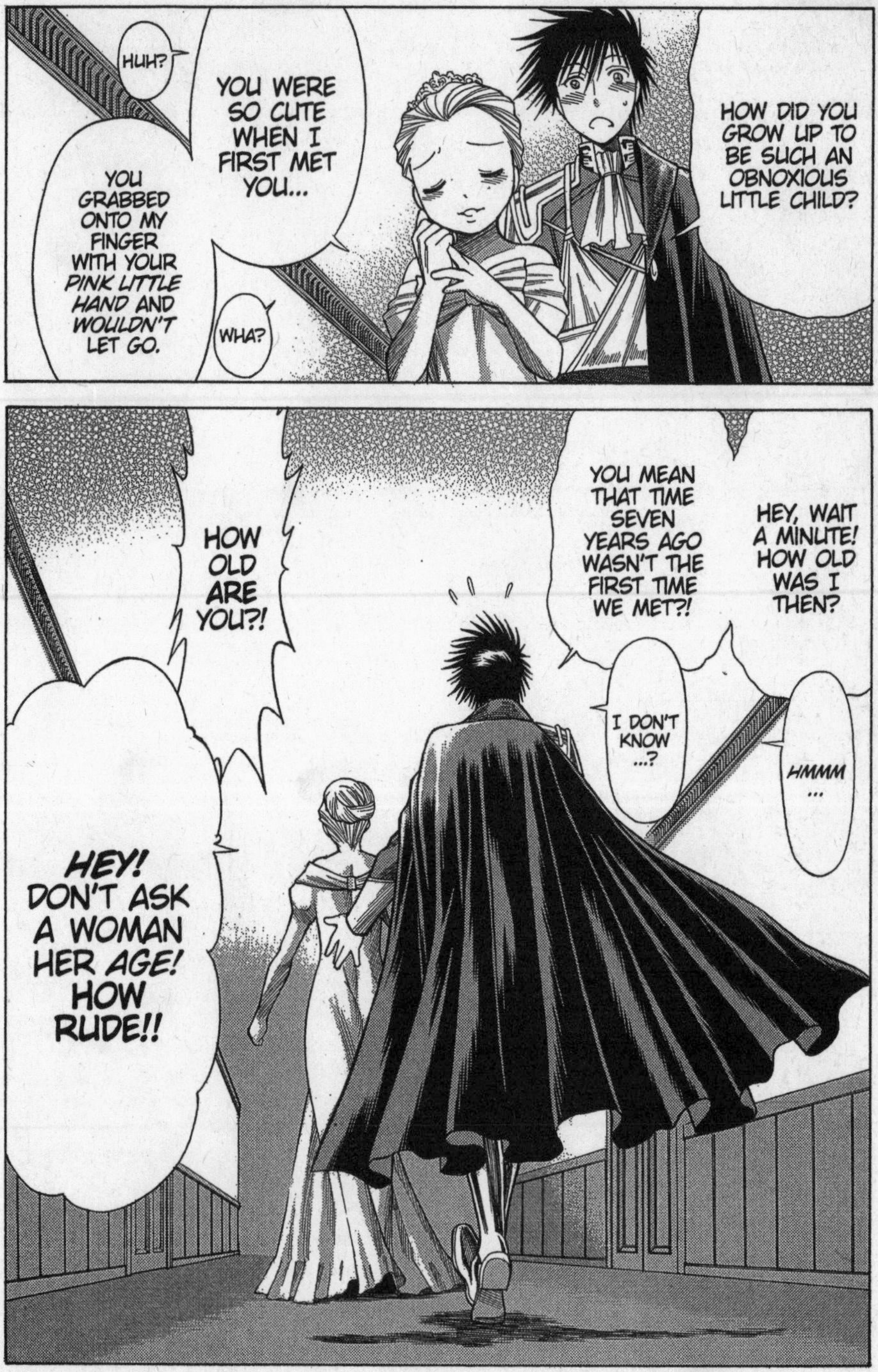

HOW DID YOU GROW UP TO BE SUCH AN OBNOXIOUS LITTLE CHILD?
YOU WERE SO CUTE WHEN I FIRST MET YOU...
HUH?
YOU GRABBED ONTO MY FINGER WITH YOUR *PINK LITTLE HAND* AND *WOULDN'T* LET GO.
WHA?
HEY, WAIT A MINUTE! HOW OLD WAS I THEN?
YOU MEAN THAT TIME SEVEN YEARS AGO WASN'T THE FIRST TIME WE MET?!
HMMM ...
I DON'T KNOW ...?
HOW OLD ARE YOU?!
HEY! DON'T ASK A WOMAN HER *AGE!* HOW RUDE!!

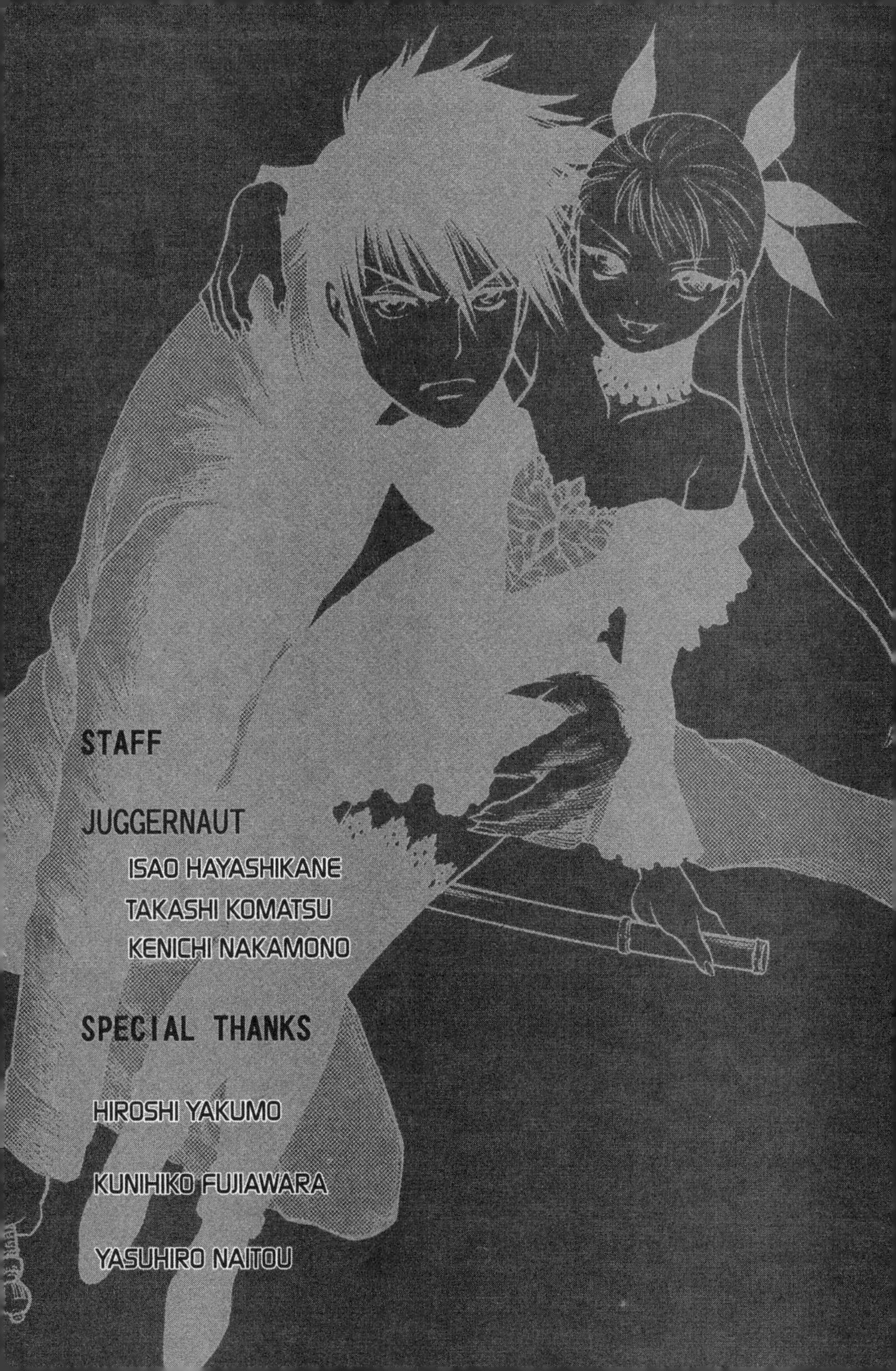
STAFF
JUGGERNAUT
ISAO HAYASHIKANE
TAKASHI KOMATSU
KENICHI NAKAMONO
SPECIAL THANKS
HIROSHI YAKUMO
KUNIHIKO FUJIAWARA
YASUHIRO NAITOU

DANCE with the VAMPIRE MAID

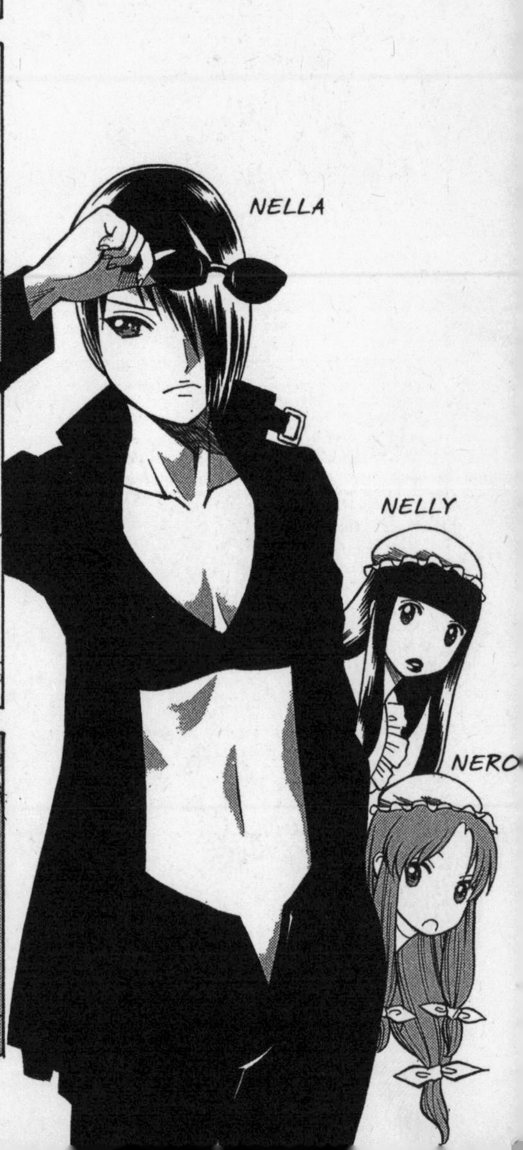
NELLA
NELLY
NERO

Other Side

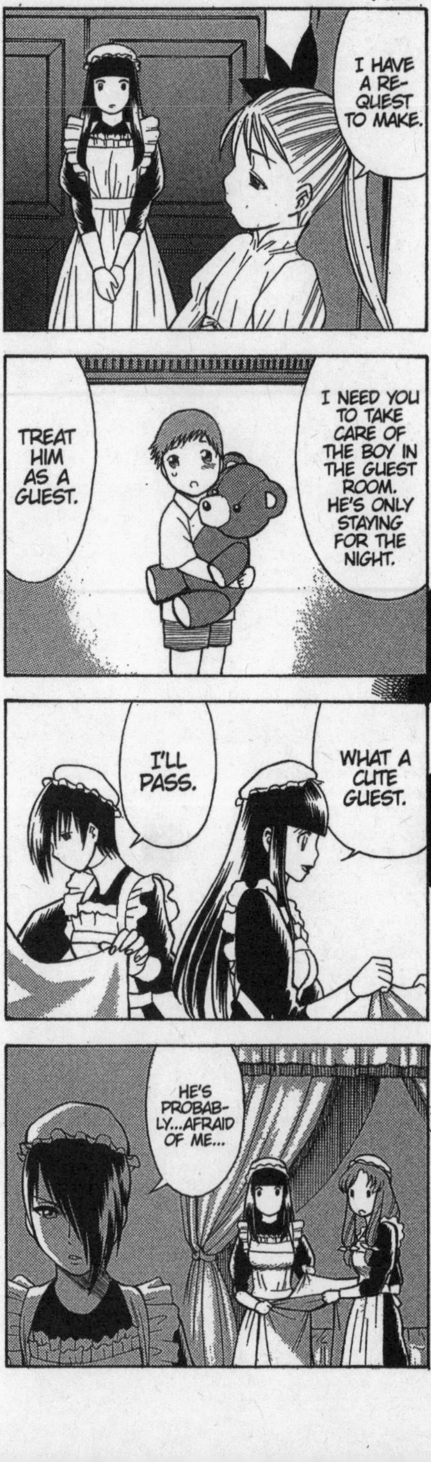
I HAVE A REQUEST TO MAKE.
I NEED YOU TO TAKE CARE OF THE BOY IN THE GUEST ROOM. HE'S ONLY STAYING FOR THE NIGHT.
TREAT HIM AS A GUEST.
WHAT A CUTE GUEST.
I'LL PASS.
HE'S PROBABLY...AFRAID OF ME...

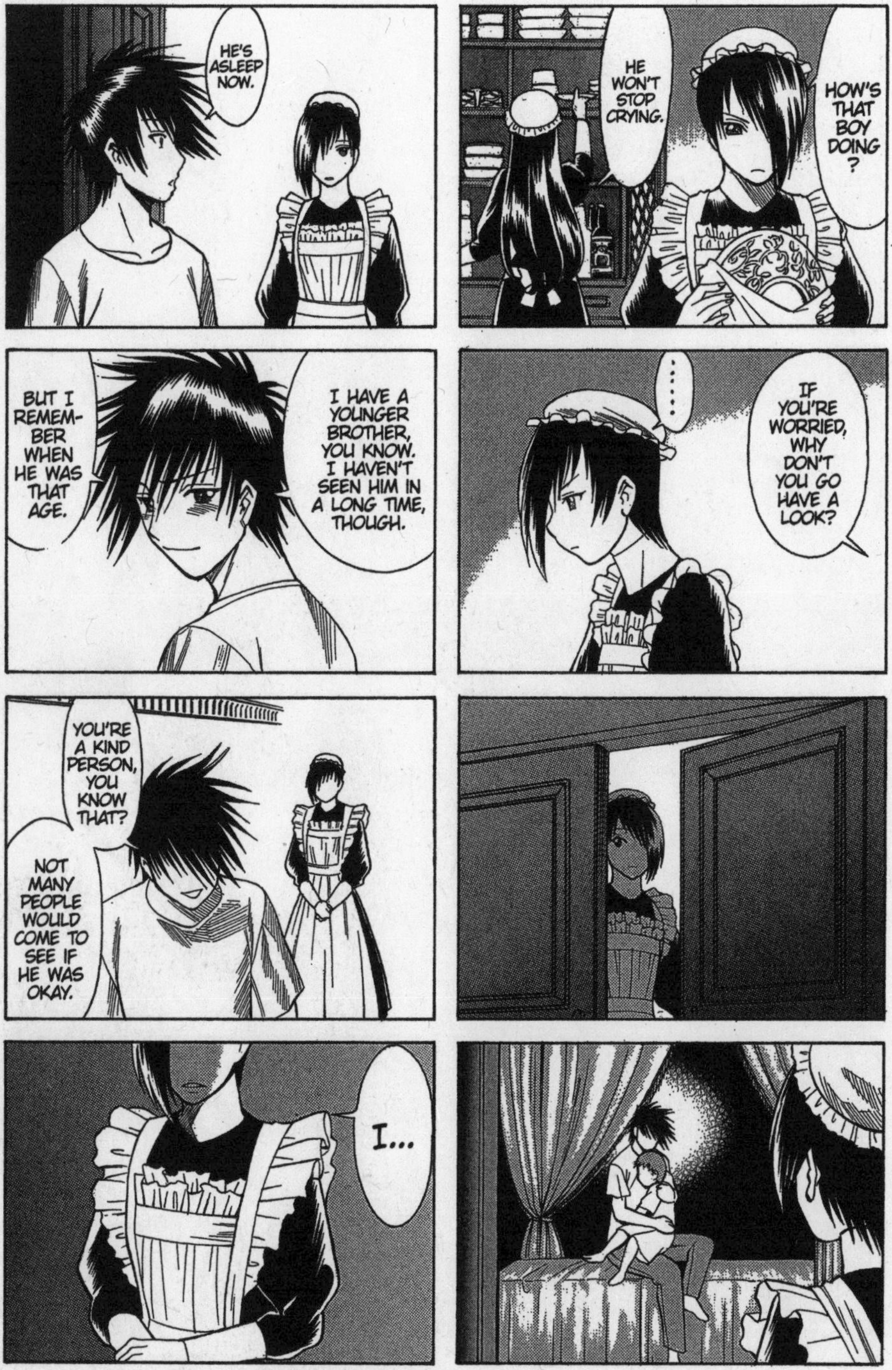
HOW'S THAT BOY DOING?
HE WON'T STOP CRYING.
HE'S ASLEEP NOW.
IF YOU'RE WORRIED, WHY DON'T YOU GO HAVE A LOOK?
......
I HAVE A YOUNGER BROTHER, YOU KNOW. I HAVEN'T SEEN HIM IN A LONG TIME, THOUGH.
BUT I REMEMBER WHEN HE WAS THAT AGE.
YOU'RE A KIND PERSON, YOU KNOW THAT?
NOT MANY PEOPLE WOULD COME TO SEE IF HE WAS OKAY.
I...

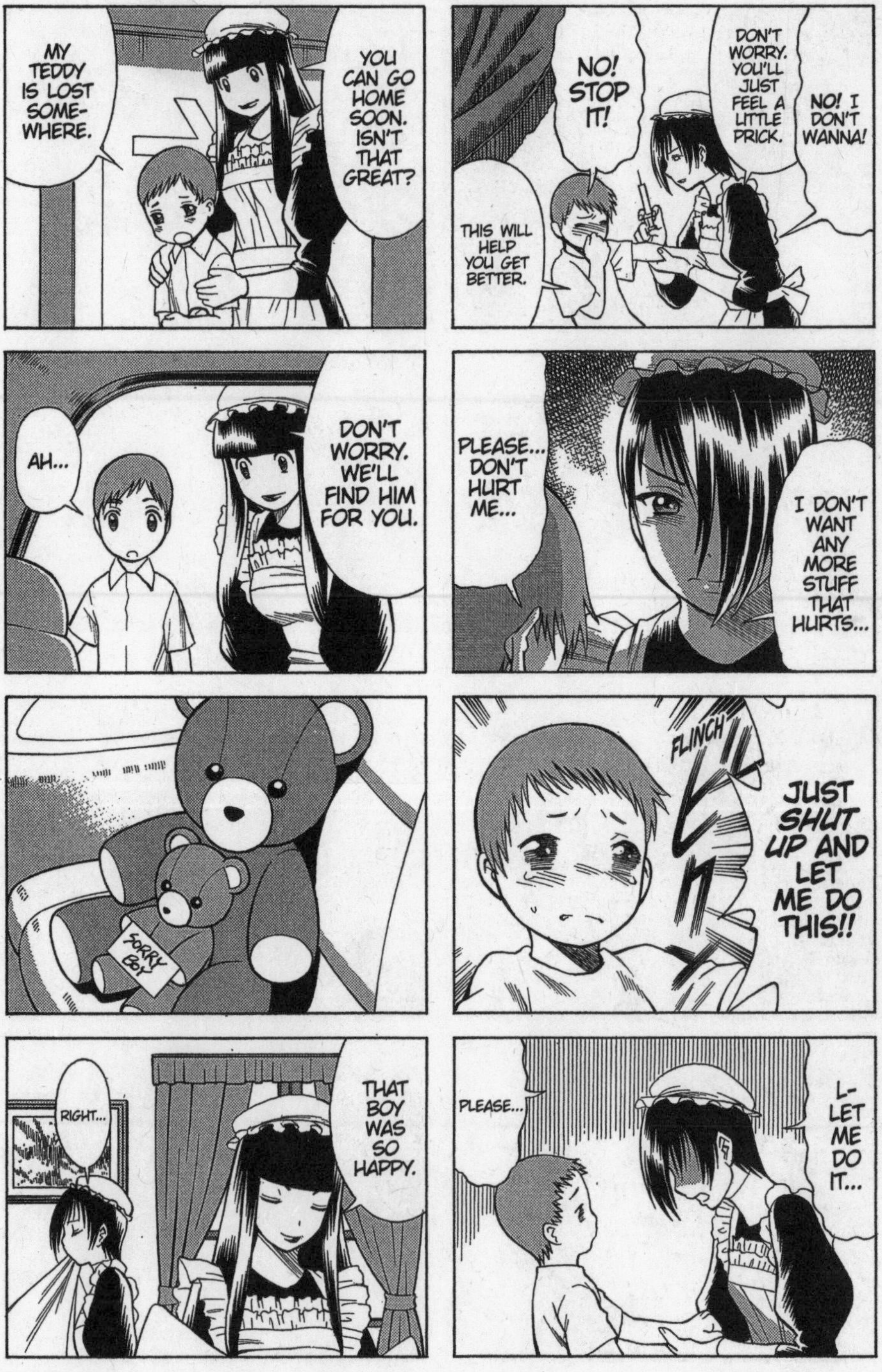
NO! I DON'T WANNA!
DON'T WORRY. YOU'LL JUST FEEL A LITTLE PRICK.
NO! STOP IT!
THIS WILL HELP YOU GET BETTER.
YOU CAN GO HOME SOON. ISN'T THAT GREAT?
MY TEDDY IS LOST SOME-WHERE.
I DON'T WANT ANY MORE STUFF THAT HURTS...
PLEASE... DON'T HURT ME...
DON'T WORRY. WE'LL FIND HIM FOR YOU.
AH...
FLINCH
JUST SHUT UP AND LET ME DO THIS!!
SORRY BOY
L-LET ME DO IT...
PLEASE...
THAT BOY WAS SO HAPPY.
RIGHT...

After Side

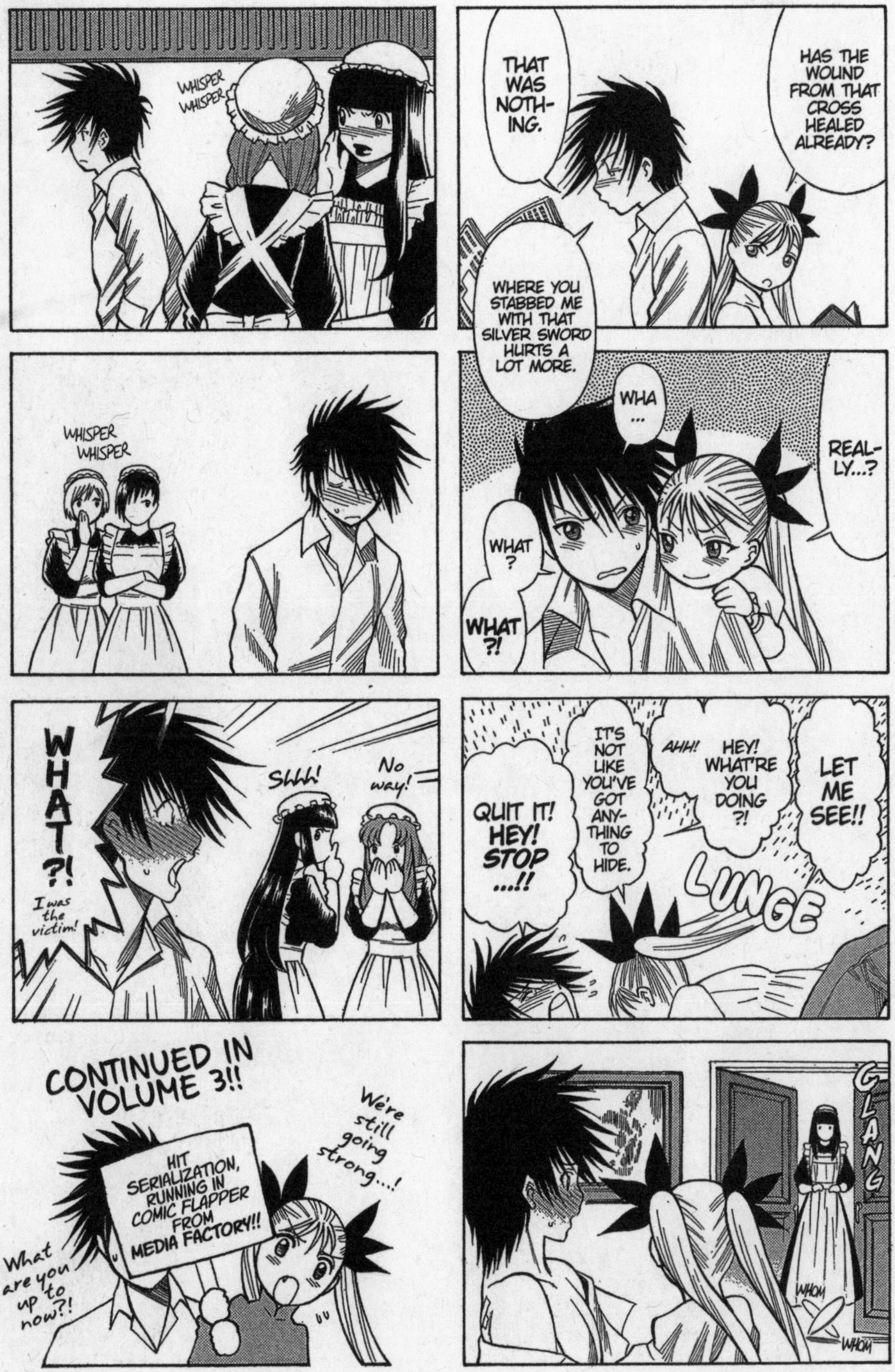
HAS THE WOUND FROM THAT CROSS HEALED ALREADY?
THAT WAS NOTHING.
WHERE YOU STABBED ME WITH THAT SILVER SWORD HURTS A LOT MORE.
WHISPER WHISPER
REAL-LY...?
WHA...
WHAT?
WHAT?!
WHISPER WHISPER
LET ME SEE!!
HEY! WHAT'RE YOU DOING?!
AHH!
IT'S NOT LIKE YOU'VE GOT ANYTHING TO HIDE.
QUIT IT! HEY! STOP...!!
LUNGE
No way!
Shhh!
WHAT?!
I was the victim!
CLANG
WHOM
WHOM
CONTINUED IN VOLUME 3!!
We're still going strong...!
HIT SERIALIZATION, RUNNING IN COMIC FLAPPER FROM MEDIA FACTORY!!
What are you up to now?!

Tamaki Nozomu Presents Dance In The Vampire Bund 3

DANCE IN THE VAMPIRE BUND
3
NOZOMU TAMAKI

On nous réconcilia:

Nous nous embrassâmes.

et depuis ce temps-là nous sommes ennemis mortels.

We reconciled

and we embraced.

And since then,

we have been mortal enemies――

Alain René Lesage, Le Diable boiteux

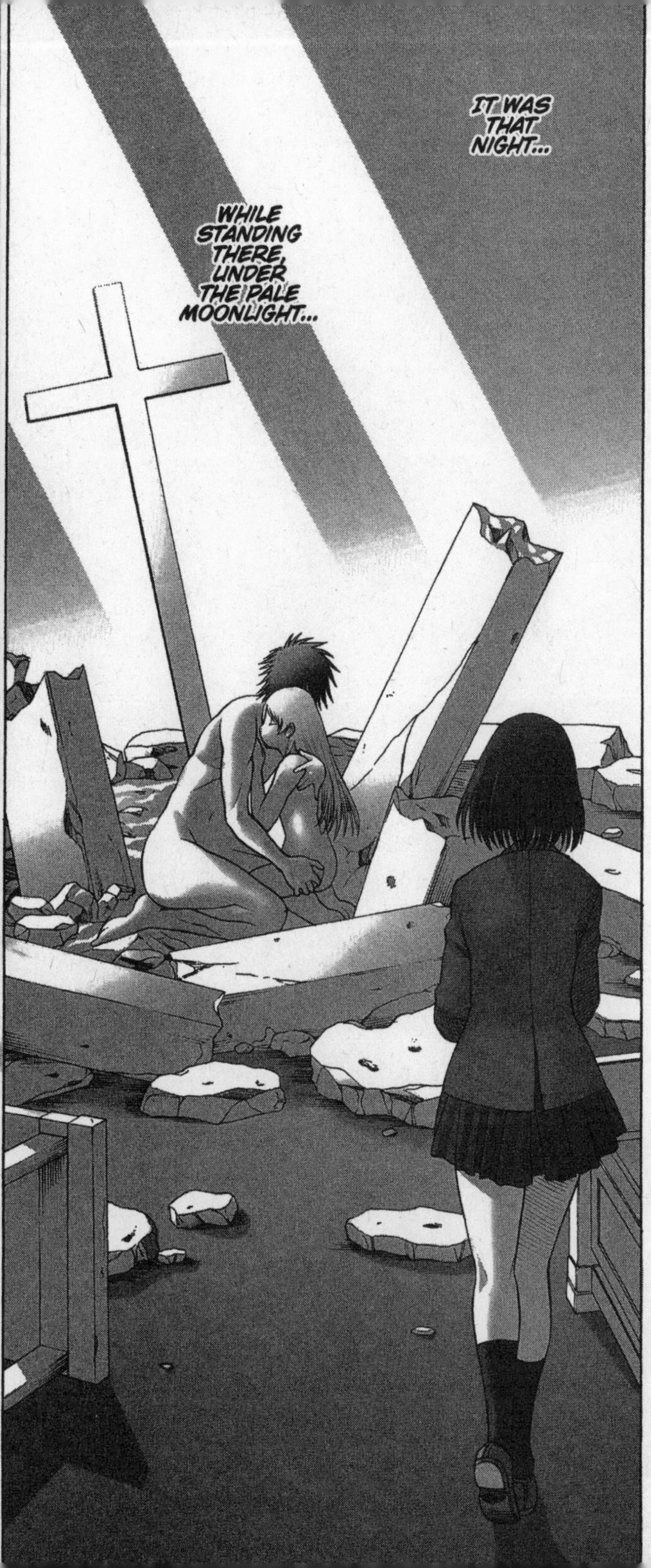
IT WAS THAT NIGHT...
WHILE STANDING THERE, UNDER THE PALE MOONLIGHT...
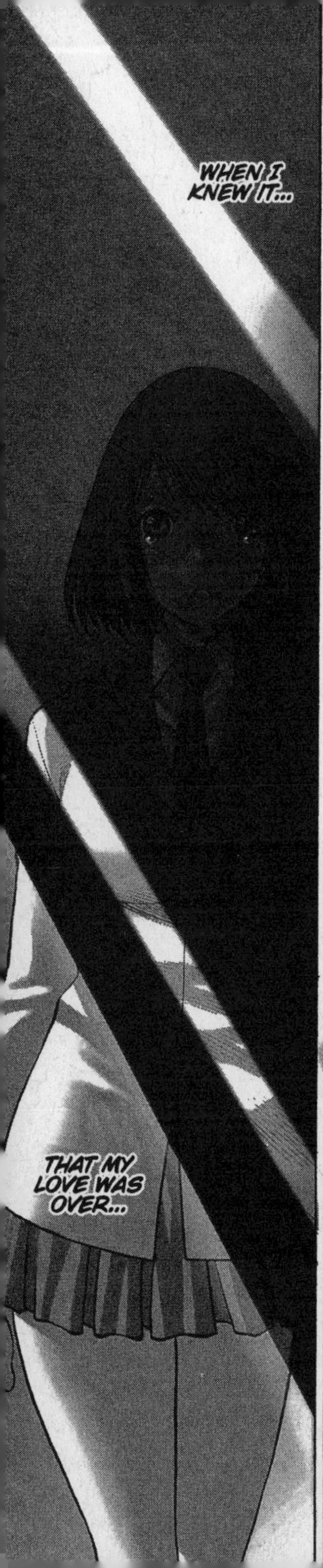
WHEN I KNEW IT...
THAT MY LOVE WAS OVER...

Chapter 13: A Solemn Promise

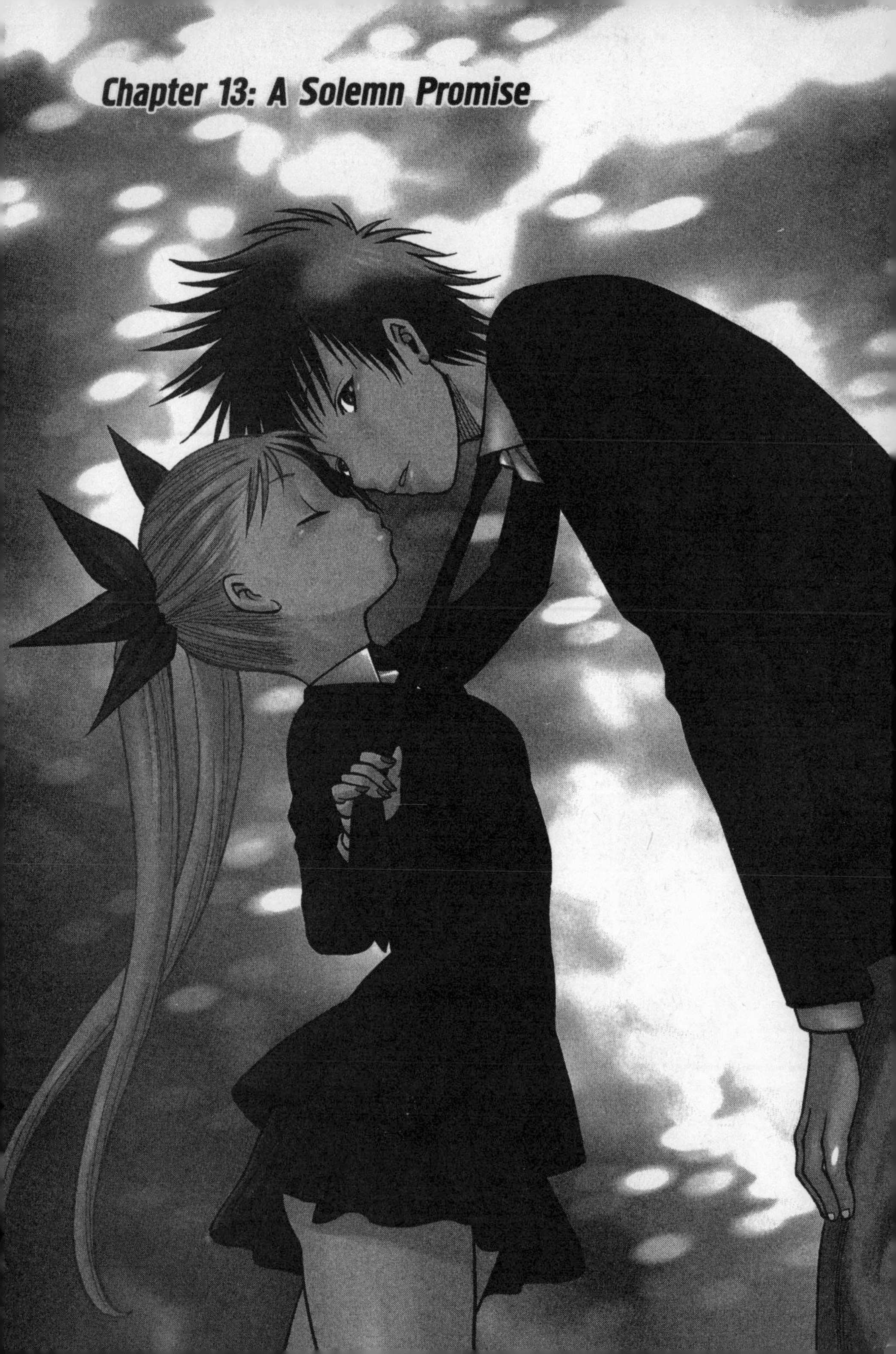

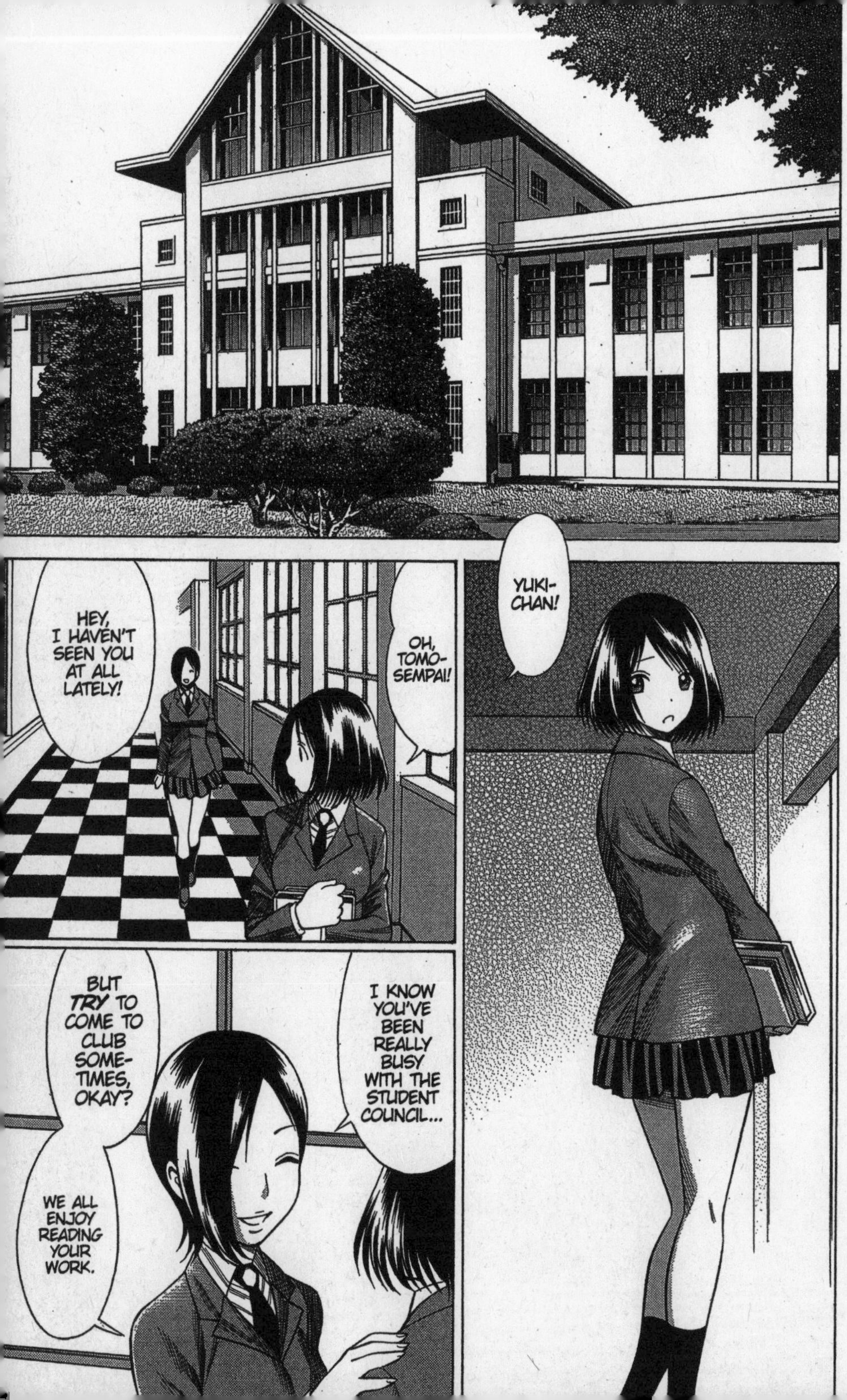
YUKI-CHAN!
OH, TOMO-SEMPAI!
HEY, I HAVEN'T SEEN YOU AT ALL LATELY!
I KNOW YOU'VE BEEN REALLY BUSY WITH THE STUDENT COUNCIL...
BUT *TRY* TO COME TO CLUB SOMETIMES, OKAY?
WE ALL ENJOY READING YOUR WORK.

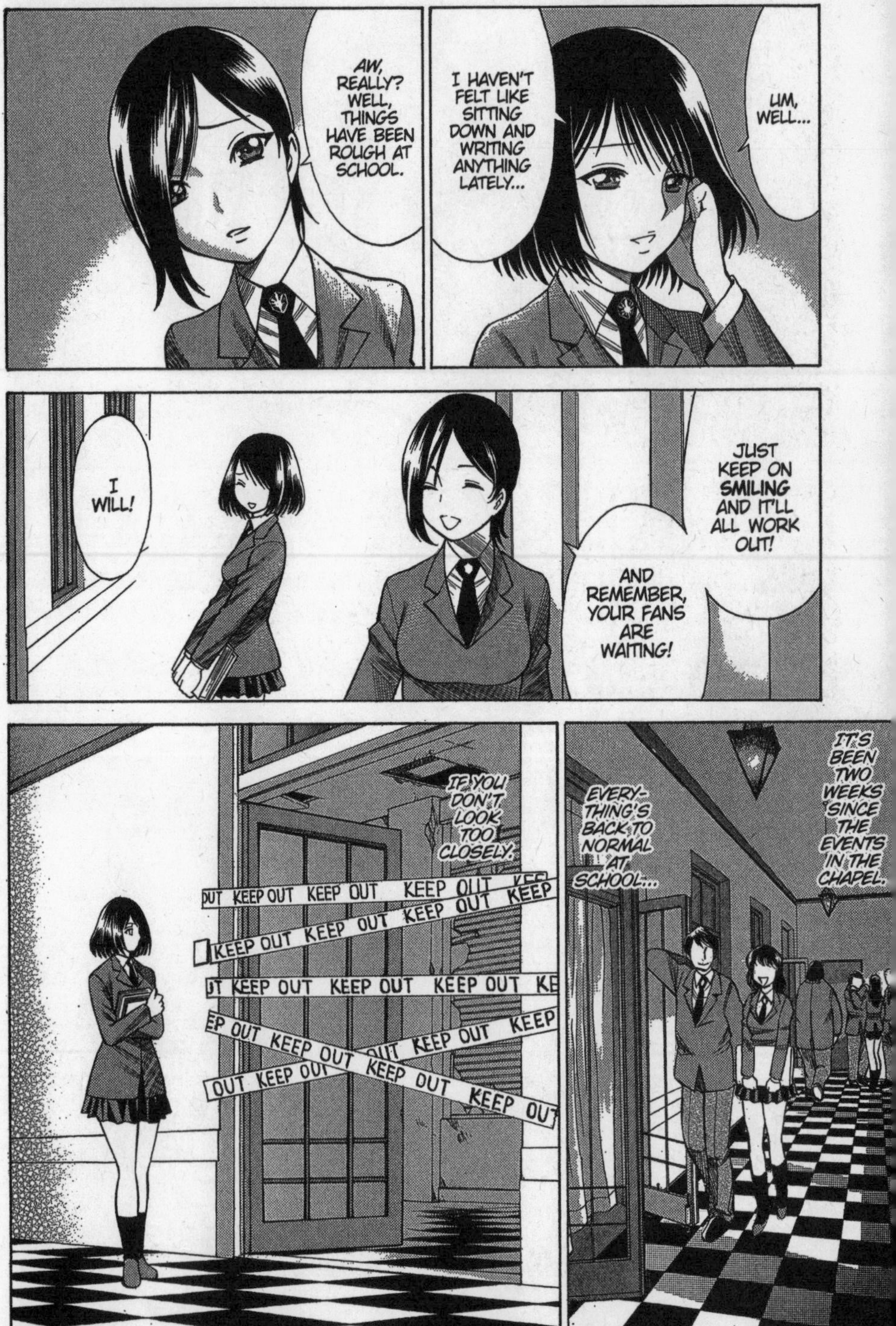
UM, WELL...
I HAVEN'T FELT LIKE SITTING DOWN AND WRITING ANYTHING LATELY...
AW, REALLY? WELL, THINGS HAVE BEEN ROUGH AT SCHOOL.
JUST KEEP ON SMILING AND IT'LL ALL WORK OUT!
AND REMEMBER, YOUR FANS ARE WAITING!
I WILL!
IT'S BEEN TWO WEEKS SINCE THE EVENTS IN THE CHAPEL.
EVERY-THING'S BACK TO NORMAL AT SCHOOL...
IF YOU DON'T LOOK TOO CLOSELY.
KEEP OUT

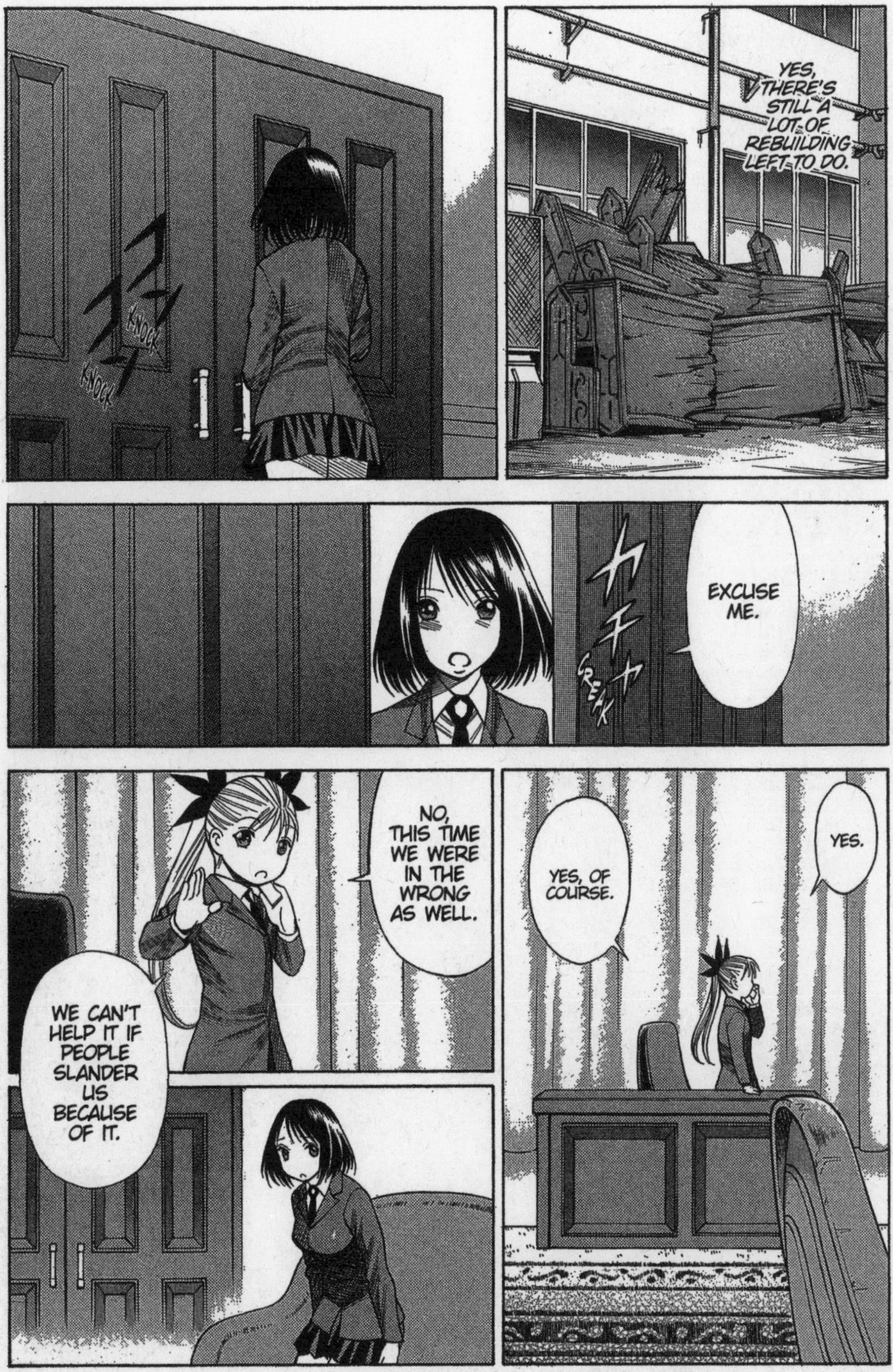
YES, THERE'S STILL A LOT OF REBUILDING LEFT TO DO.
KNOCK
KNOCK
EXCUSE ME.
CREAK
YES.
YES, OF COURSE.
NO, THIS TIME WE WERE IN THE WRONG AS WELL.
WE CAN'T HELP IT IF PEOPLE SLANDER US BECAUSE OF IT.

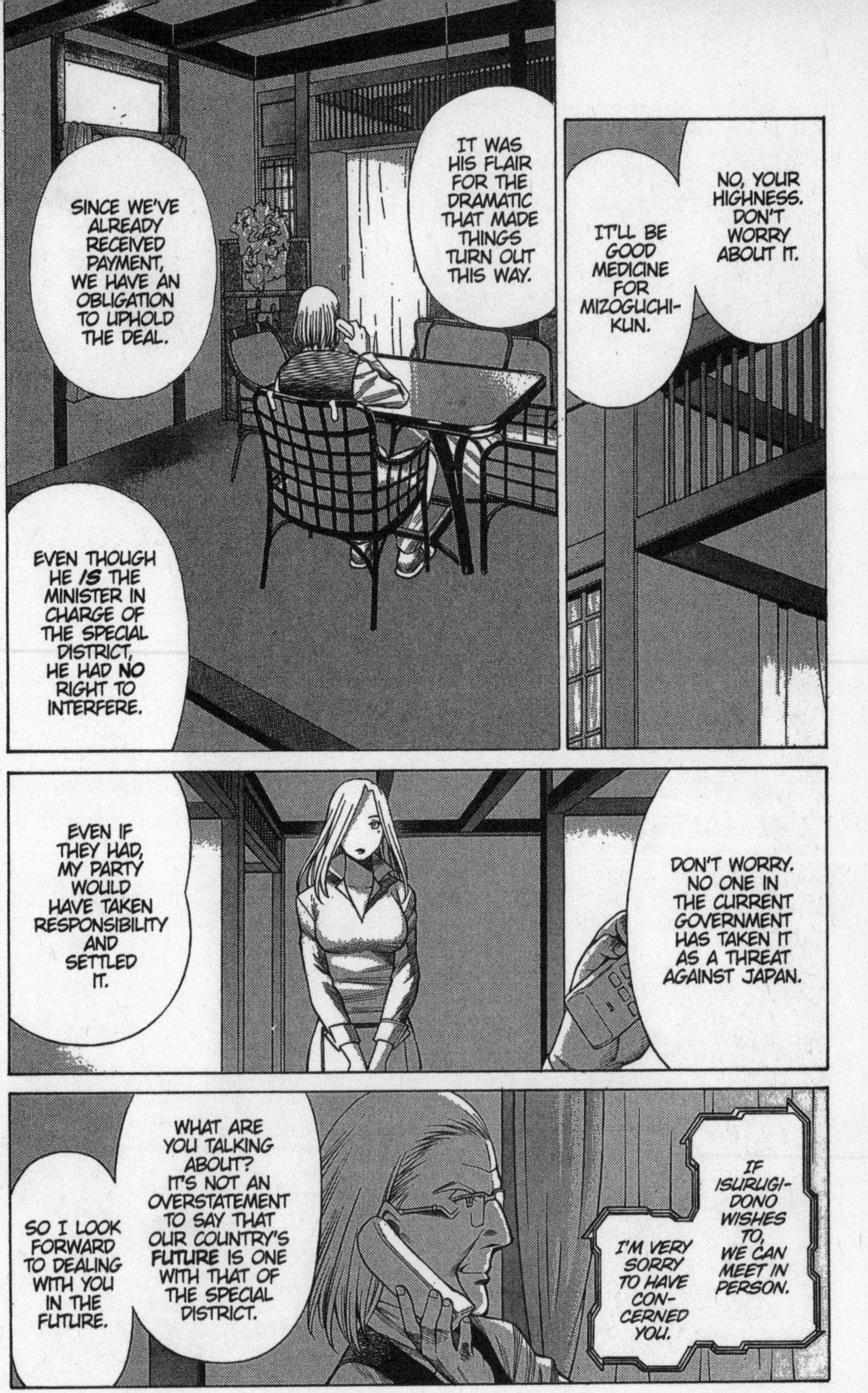
NO, YOUR HIGHNESS. DON'T WORRY ABOUT IT.
IT'LL BE GOOD MEDICINE FOR MIZOGUCHI-KUN.
IT WAS HIS FLAIR FOR THE DRAMATIC THAT MADE THINGS TURN OUT THIS WAY.
SINCE WE'VE ALREADY RECEIVED PAYMENT, WE HAVE AN OBLIGATION TO UPHOLD THE DEAL.
EVEN THOUGH HE *IS* THE MINISTER IN CHARGE OF THE SPECIAL DISTRICT, HE HAD **NO** RIGHT TO INTERFERE.
DON'T WORRY. NO ONE IN THE CURRENT GOVERNMENT HAS TAKEN IT AS A THREAT AGAINST JAPAN.
EVEN IF THEY HAD, MY PARTY WOULD HAVE TAKEN RESPONSIBILITY AND SETTLED IT.
IF ISURUGI-DONO WISHES TO, WE CAN MEET IN PERSON.
I'M VERY SORRY TO HAVE CONCERNED YOU.
WHAT ARE YOU TALKING ABOUT? IT'S NOT AN OVERSTATEMENT TO SAY THAT OUR COUNTRY'S **FUTURE** IS ONE WITH THAT OF THE SPECIAL DISTRICT.
SO I LOOK FORWARD TO DEALING WITH YOU IN THE FUTURE.

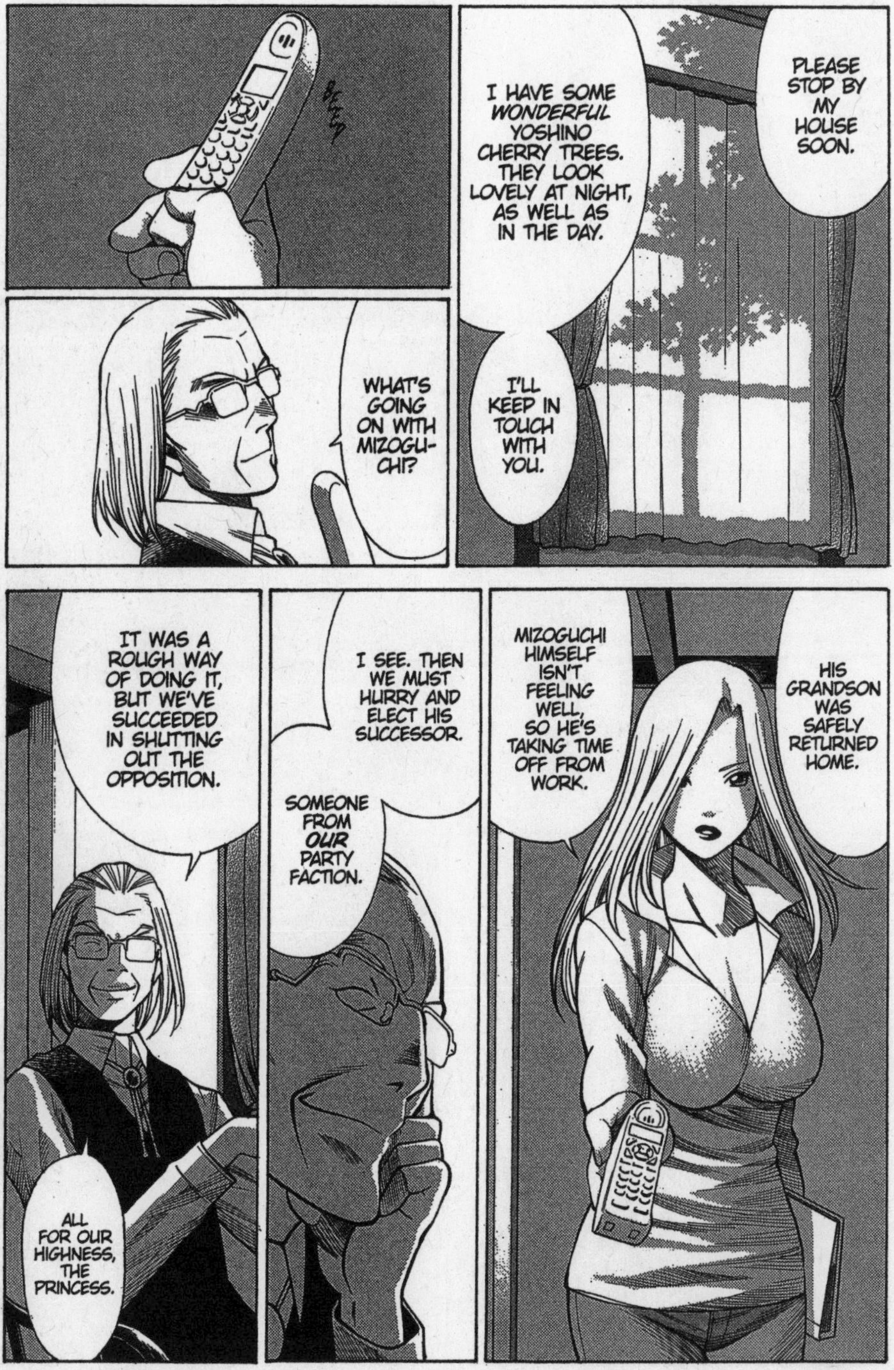
PLEASE STOP BY MY HOUSE SOON.
I HAVE SOME *WONDERFUL* YOSHINO CHERRY TREES. THEY LOOK LOVELY AT NIGHT, AS WELL AS IN THE DAY.
I'LL KEEP IN TOUCH WITH YOU.
WHAT'S GOING ON WITH MIZOGU-CHI?
HIS GRANDSON WAS SAFELY RETURNED HOME.
MIZOGUCHI HIMSELF ISN'T FEELING WELL, SO HE'S TAKING TIME OFF FROM WORK.
I SEE. THEN WE MUST HURRY AND ELECT HIS SUCCESSOR.
SOMEONE FROM ***OUR*** PARTY FACTION.
IT WAS A ROUGH WAY OF DOING IT, BUT WE'VE SUCCEEDED IN SHUTTING OUT THE OPPOSITION.
ALL FOR OUR HIGHNESS, THE PRINCESS.

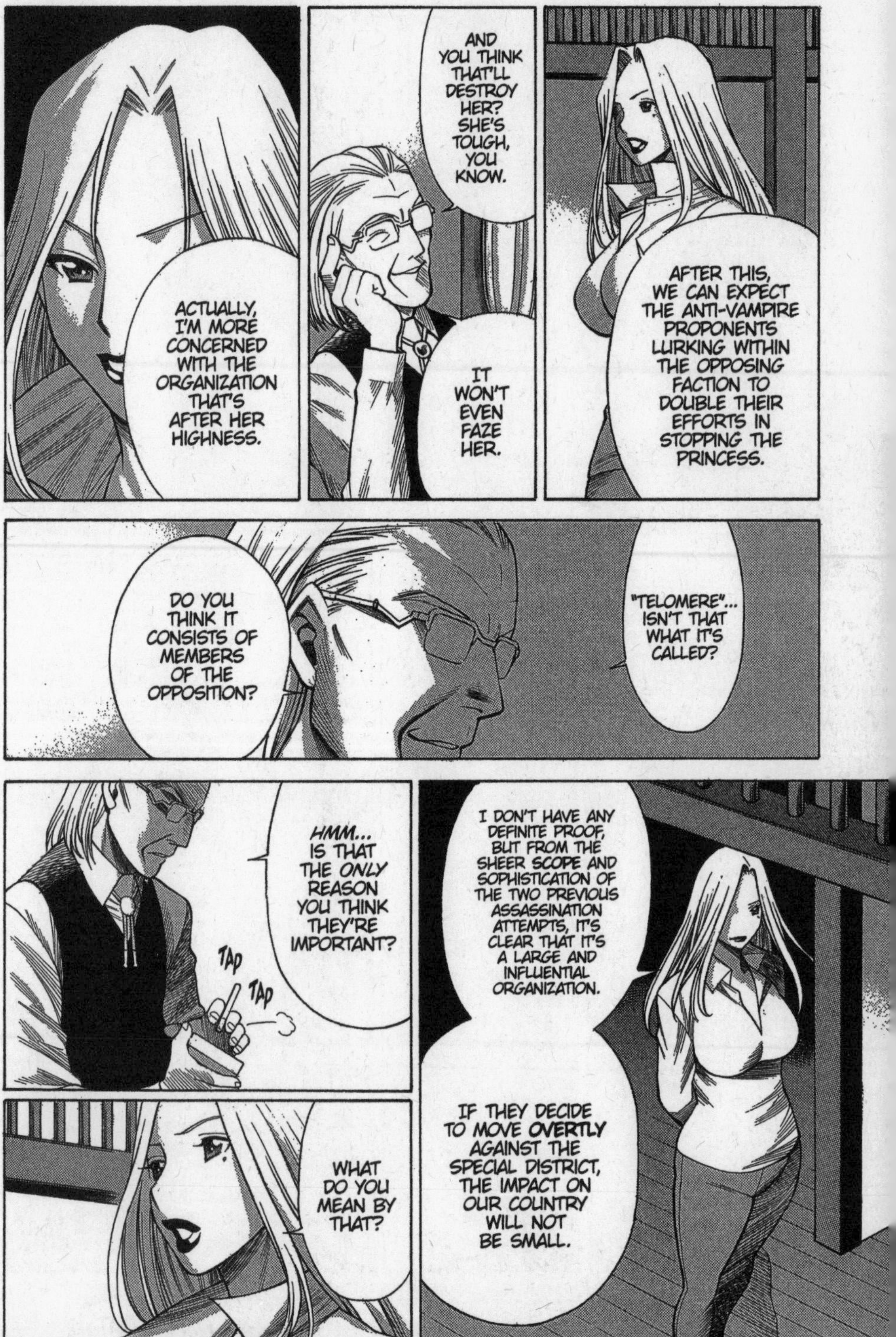
AFTER THIS, WE CAN EXPECT THE ANTI-VAMPIRE PROPONENTS LURKING WITHIN THE OPPOSING FACTION TO DOUBLE THEIR EFFORTS IN STOPPING THE PRINCESS.
AND YOU THINK THAT'LL DESTROY HER? SHE'S TOUGH, YOU KNOW.
IT WON'T EVEN FAZE HER.
ACTUALLY, I'M MORE CONCERNED WITH THE ORGANIZATION THAT'S AFTER HER HIGHNESS.
"TELOMERE"... ISN'T THAT WHAT IT'S CALLED?
DO YOU THINK IT CONSISTS OF MEMBERS OF THE OPPOSITION?
I DON'T HAVE ANY DEFINITE PROOF, BUT FROM THE SHEER SCOPE AND SOPHISTICATION OF THE TWO PREVIOUS ASSASSINATION ATTEMPTS, IT'S CLEAR THAT IT'S A LARGE AND INFLUENTIAL ORGANIZATION.
IF THEY DECIDE TO MOVE **OVERTLY** AGAINST THE SPECIAL DISTRICT, THE IMPACT ON OUR COUNTRY WILL NOT BE SMALL.
HMM... IS THAT THE *ONLY* REASON YOU THINK THEY'RE IMPORTANT?
TAP
TAP
WHAT DO YOU MEAN BY THAT?

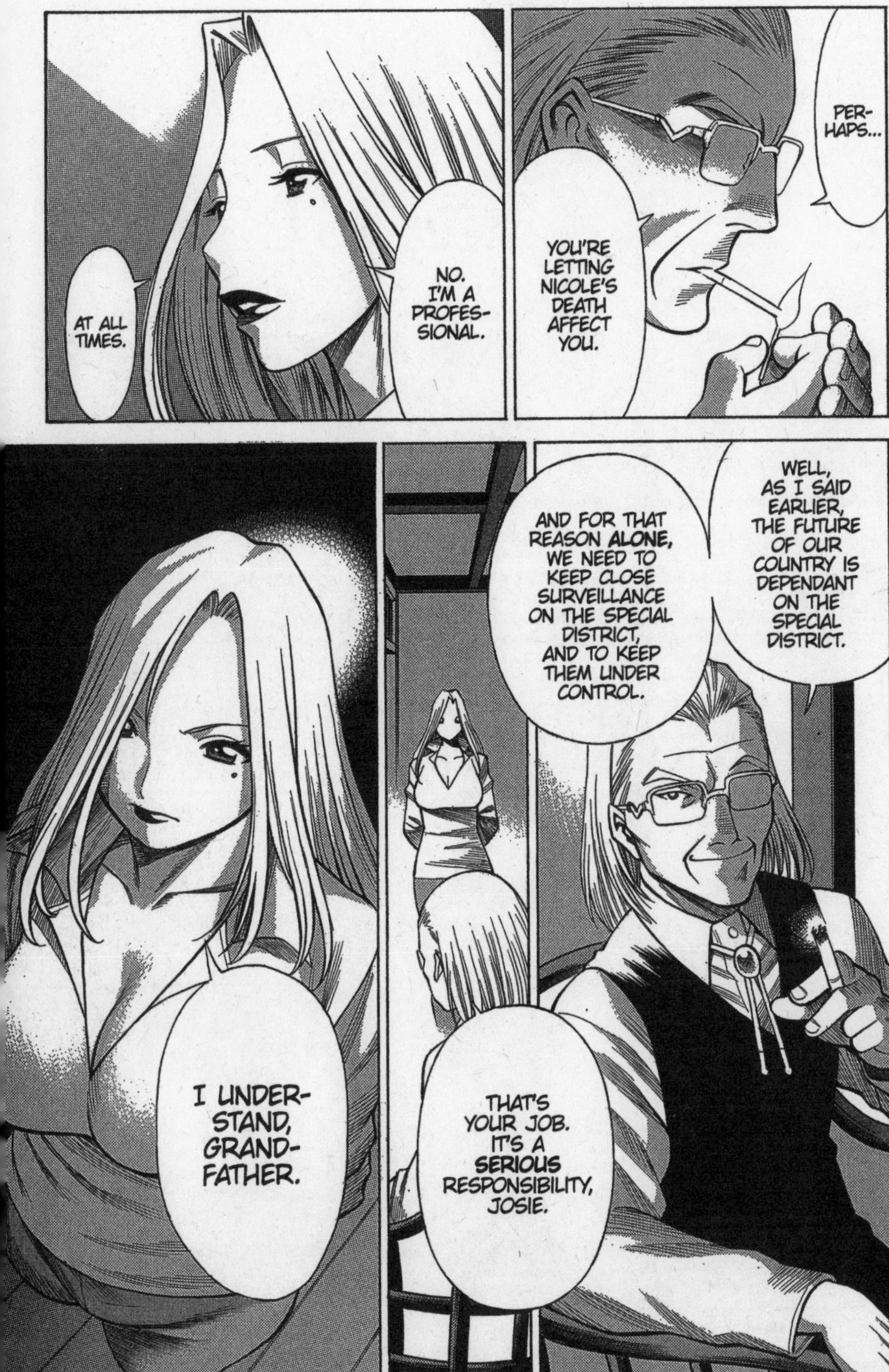
PER-HAPS...
YOU'RE LETTING NICOLE'S DEATH AFFECT YOU.
NO. I'M A PROFES-SIONAL.
AT ALL TIMES.
WELL, AS I SAID EARLIER, THE FUTURE OF OUR COUNTRY IS DEPENDANT ON THE SPECIAL DISTRICT.
AND FOR THAT REASON ALONE, WE NEED TO KEEP CLOSE SURVEILLANCE ON THE SPECIAL DISTRICT, AND TO KEEP THEM UNDER CONTROL.
THAT'S YOUR JOB. IT'S A SERIOUS RESPONSIBILITY, JOSIE.
I UNDER-STAND, GRAND-FATHER.

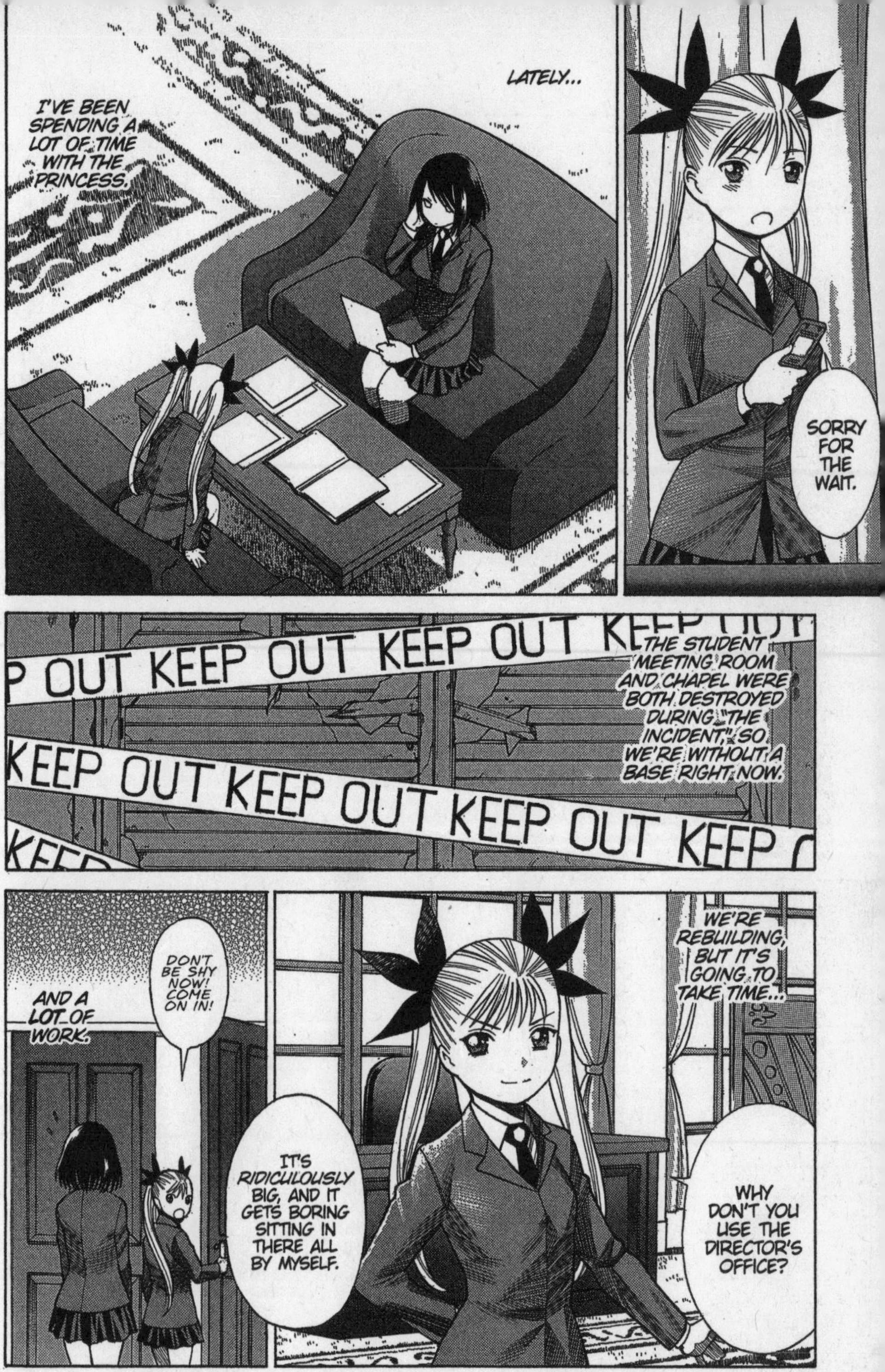
SORRY FOR THE WAIT.
LATELY...
I'VE BEEN SPENDING A LOT OF TIME WITH THE PRINCESS.
P OUT KEEP OUT KEEP OUT KE
THE STUDENT MEETING ROOM AND CHAPEL WERE BOTH DESTROYED DURING "THE INCIDENT," SO WE'RE WITHOUT A BASE RIGHT NOW.
KEEP OUT KEEP OUT KEEP OUT KEEP
WE'RE REBUILDING, BUT IT'S GOING TO TAKE TIME...
WHY DON'T YOU USE THE DIRECTOR'S OFFICE?
IT'S *RIDICULOUSLY* BIG, AND IT GETS BORING SITTING IN THERE ALL BY MYSELF.
DON'T BE SHY NOW! COME ON IN!
AND A LOT OF WORK.

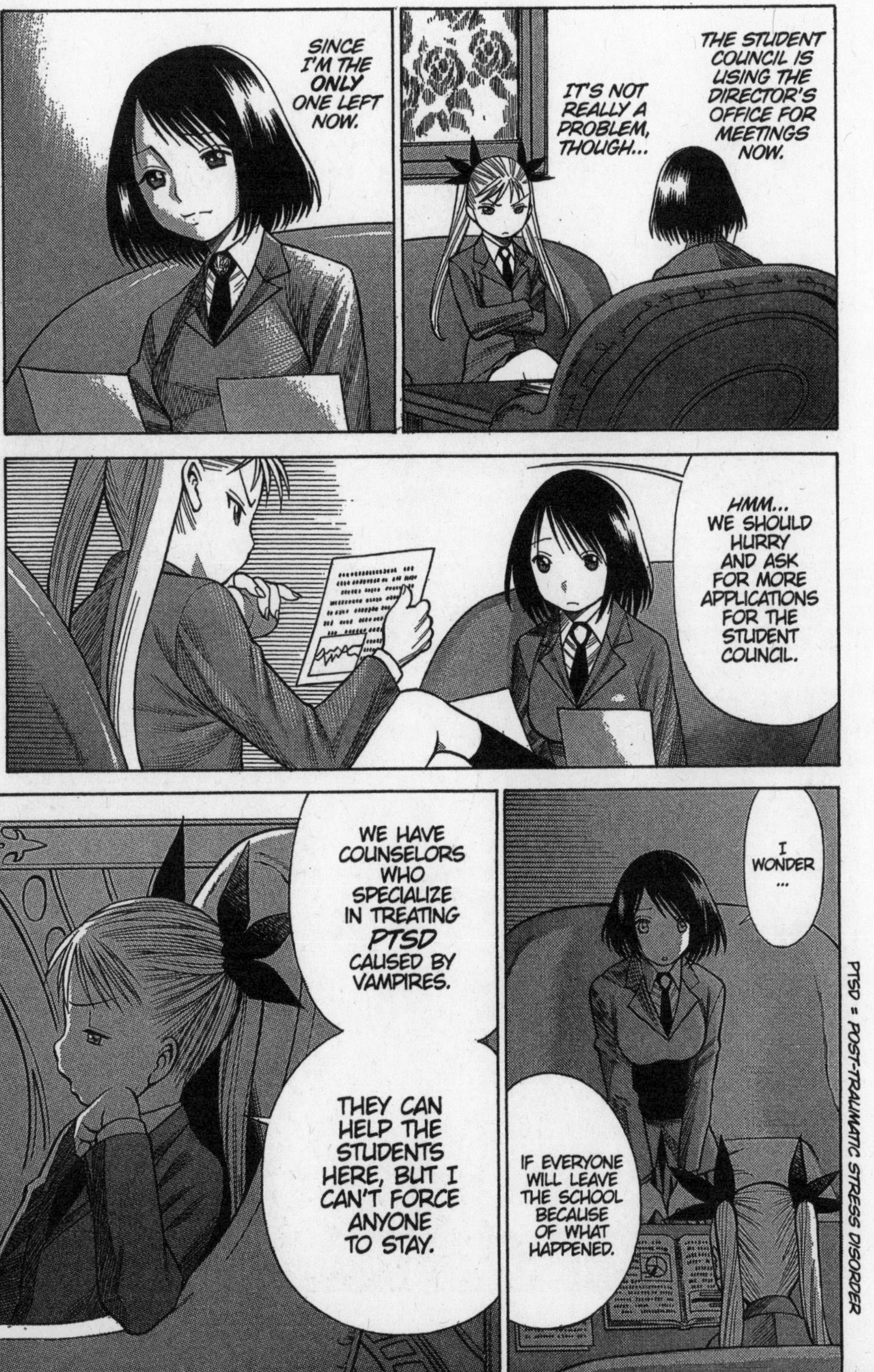
THE STUDENT COUNCIL IS USING THE DIRECTOR'S OFFICE FOR MEETINGS NOW.
IT'S NOT REALLY A PROBLEM, THOUGH...
SINCE I'M THE **ONLY** ONE LEFT NOW.
HMM... WE SHOULD HURRY AND ASK FOR MORE APPLICATIONS FOR THE STUDENT COUNCIL.
I WONDER ...
IF EVERYONE WILL LEAVE THE SCHOOL BECAUSE OF WHAT HAPPENED.
WE HAVE COUNSELORS WHO SPECIALIZE IN TREATING *PTSD* CAUSED BY VAMPIRES.
THEY CAN HELP THE STUDENTS HERE, BUT I CAN'T FORCE ANYONE TO STAY.

PTSD = POST-TRAUMATIC STRESS DISORDER

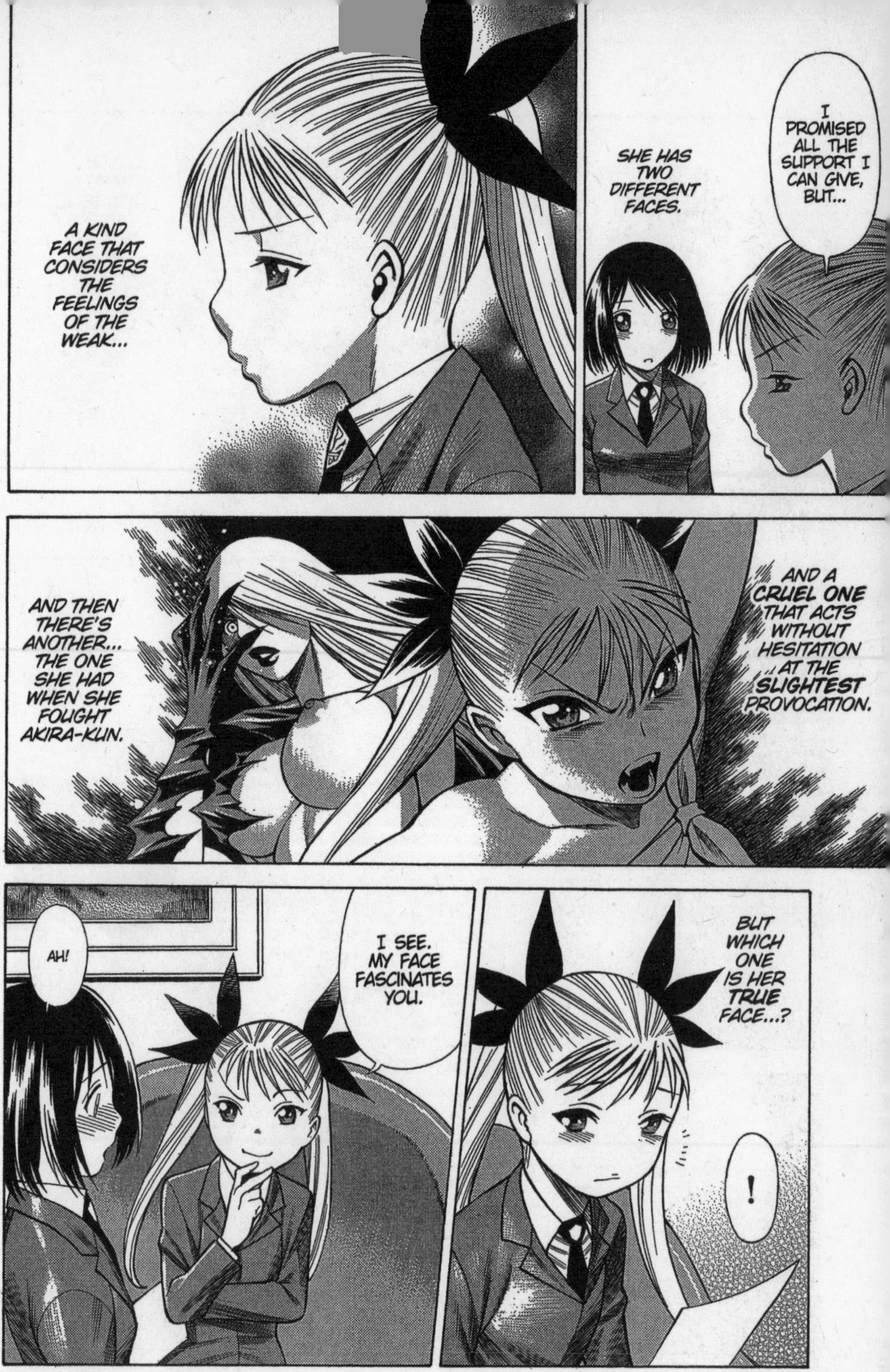
I PROMISED ALL THE SUPPORT I CAN GIVE, BUT...
SHE HAS TWO DIFFERENT FACES.
A KIND FACE THAT CONSIDERS THE FEELINGS OF THE WEAK...
AND A CRUEL ONE THAT ACTS WITHOUT HESITATION ...AT THE SLIGHTEST PROVOCATION.
AND THEN THERE'S ANOTHER... THE ONE SHE HAD WHEN SHE FOUGHT AKIRA-KUN.
BUT WHICH ONE IS HER TRUE FACE...?
!
I SEE. MY FACE FASCINATES YOU.
AH!

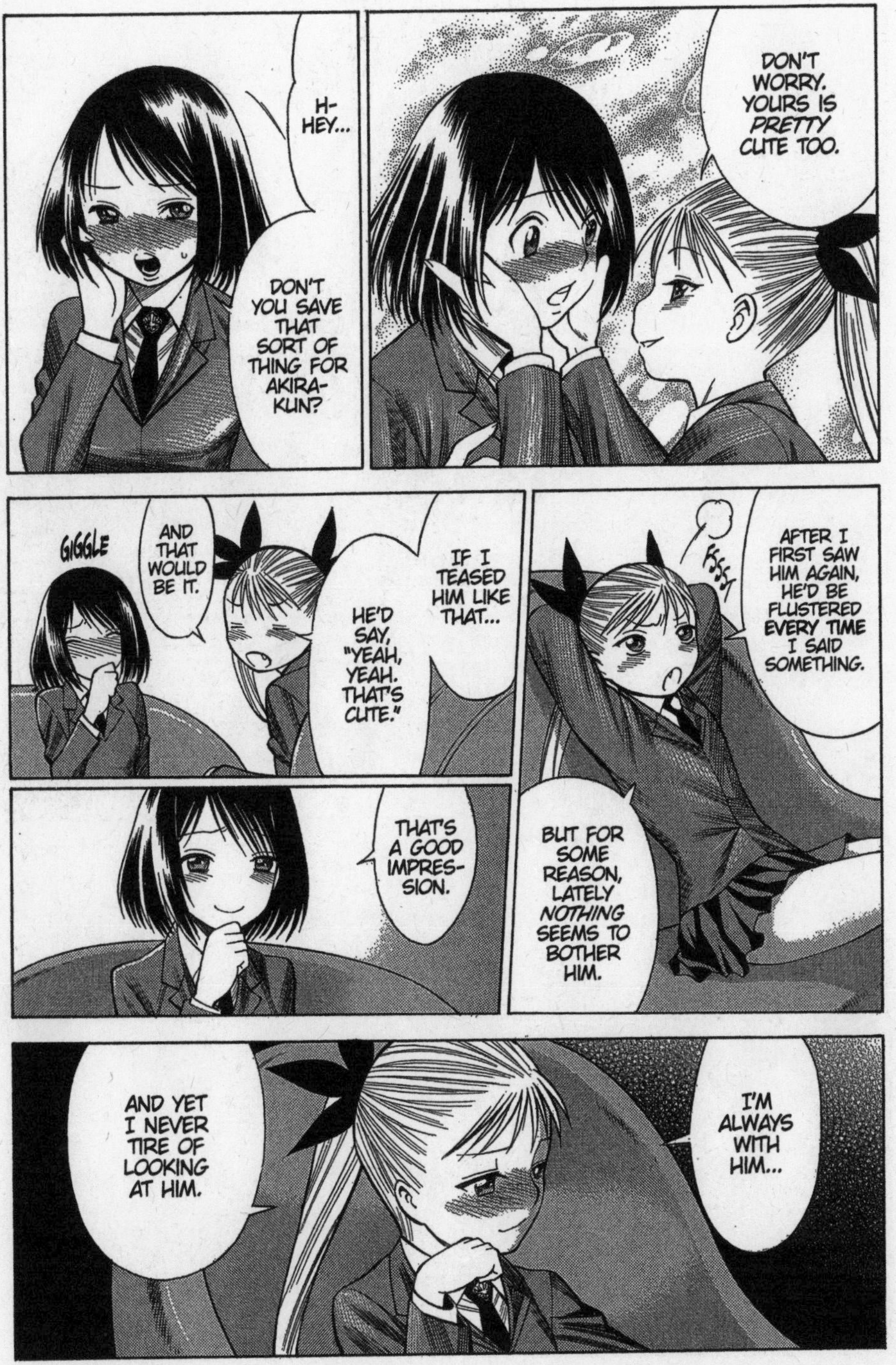
DON'T WORRY. YOURS IS PRETTY CUTE TOO.
H-HEY...
DON'T YOU SAVE THAT SORT OF THING FOR AKIRA-KUN?
AFTER I FIRST SAW HIM AGAIN, HE'D BE FLUSTERED EVERY TIME I SAID SOMETHING.
BUT FOR SOME REASON, LATELY NOTHING SEEMS TO BOTHER HIM.
IF I TEASED HIM LIKE THAT...
HE'D SAY, "YEAH, YEAH. THAT'S CUTE."
AND THAT WOULD BE IT.
GIGGLE
THAT'S A GOOD IMPRESSION.
I'M ALWAYS WITH HIM...
AND YET I NEVER TIRE OF LOOKING AT HIM.

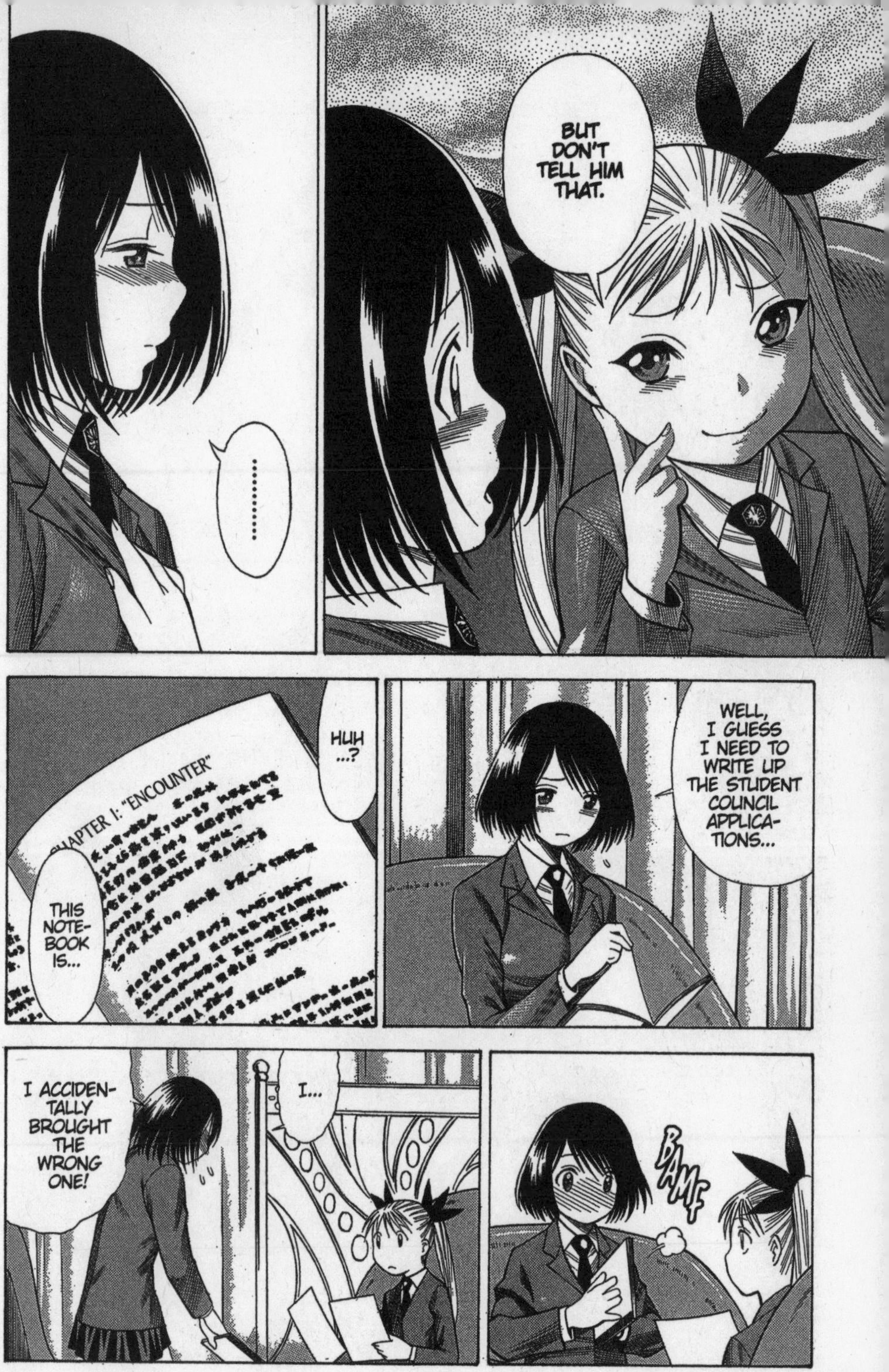
BUT DON'T TELL HIM THAT.
......
WELL, I GUESS I NEED TO WRITE UP THE STUDENT COUNCIL APPLICATIONS...
HUH ...?
CHAPTER 1: "ENCOUNTER"
THIS NOTE-BOOK IS...
BAMF
I...
I ACCIDEN-TALLY BROUGHT THE WRONG ONE!

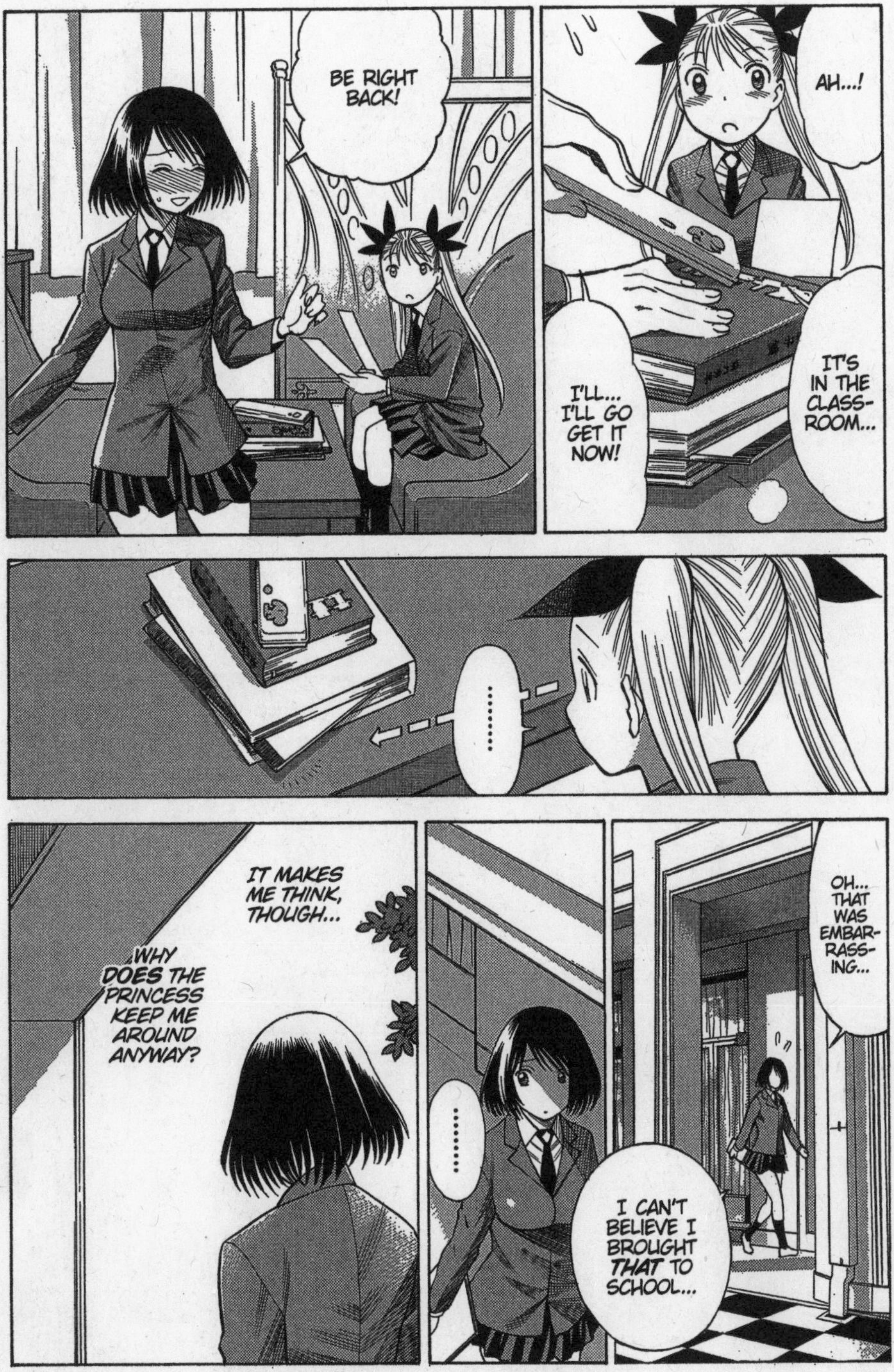
AH...!
IT'S IN THE CLASSROOM...
I'LL... I'LL GO GET IT NOW!
BE RIGHT BACK!
....
OH... THAT WAS EMBARRASSING...
I CAN'T BELIEVE I BROUGHT *THAT* TO SCHOOL...
....
IT MAKES ME THINK, THOUGH...
WHY **DOES** THE PRINCESS KEEP ME AROUND ANYWAY?

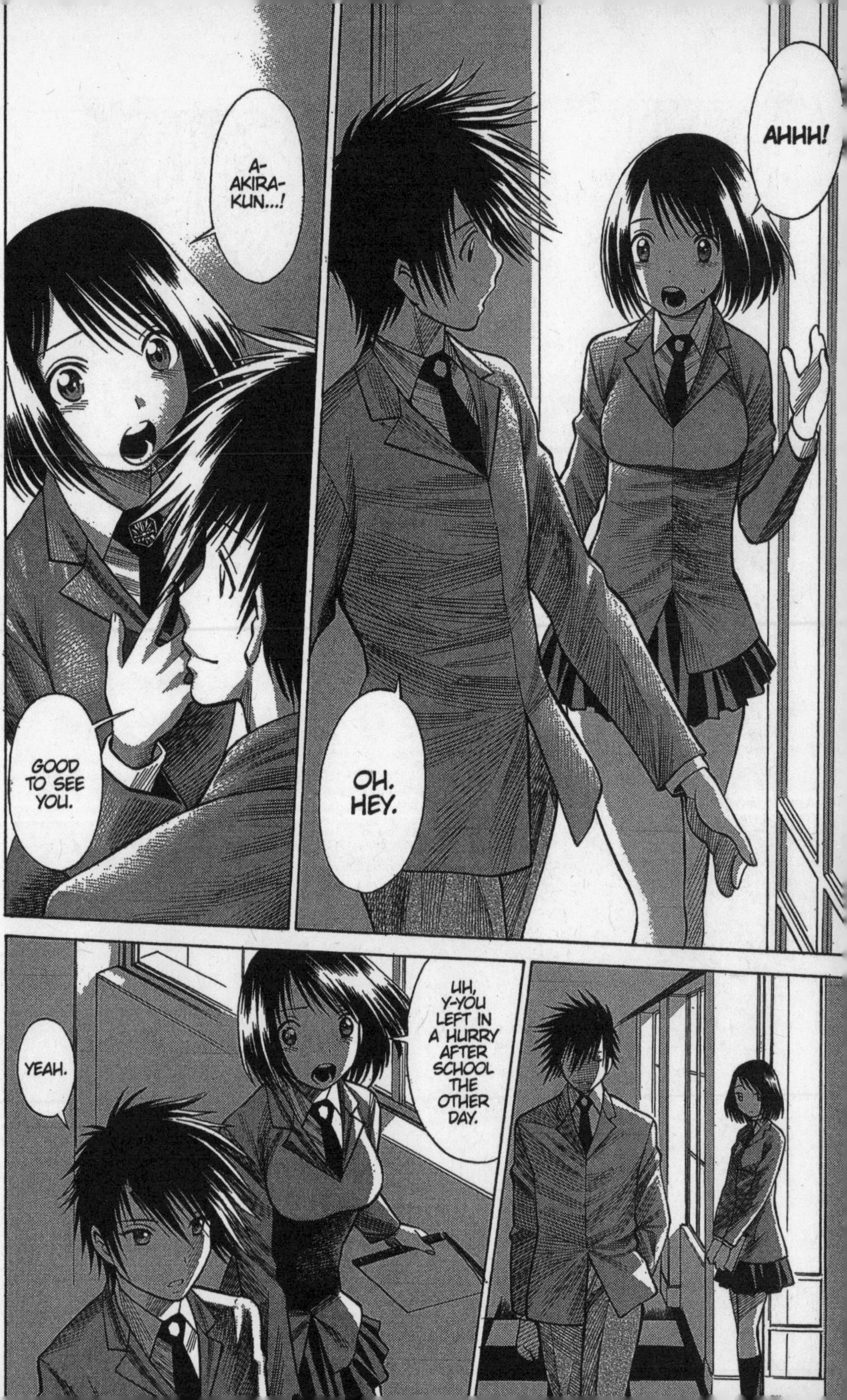
AHHH!
OH. HEY.
A-AKIRA-KUN...!
GOOD TO SEE YOU.
UH, Y-YOU LEFT IN A HURRY AFTER SCHOOL THE OTHER DAY.
YEAH.

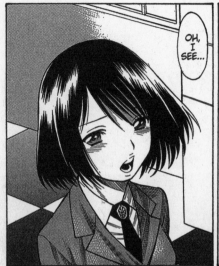

I WENT TO VISIT RYOHEI IN THE HOSPITAL.
THEY WOULDN'T LET ME SEE HIM THOUGH.
OH, I SEE...
......
EVER SINCE THAT NIGHT...
IT'S LIKE AKIRA-KUN HAS BEEN TRYING TO AVOID ME.

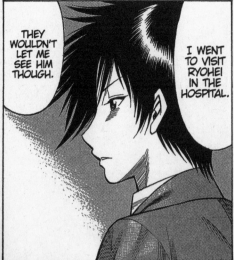

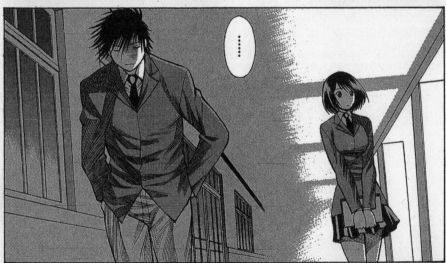

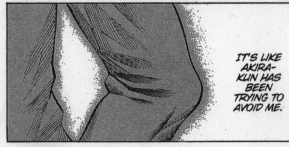

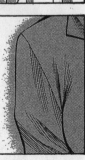

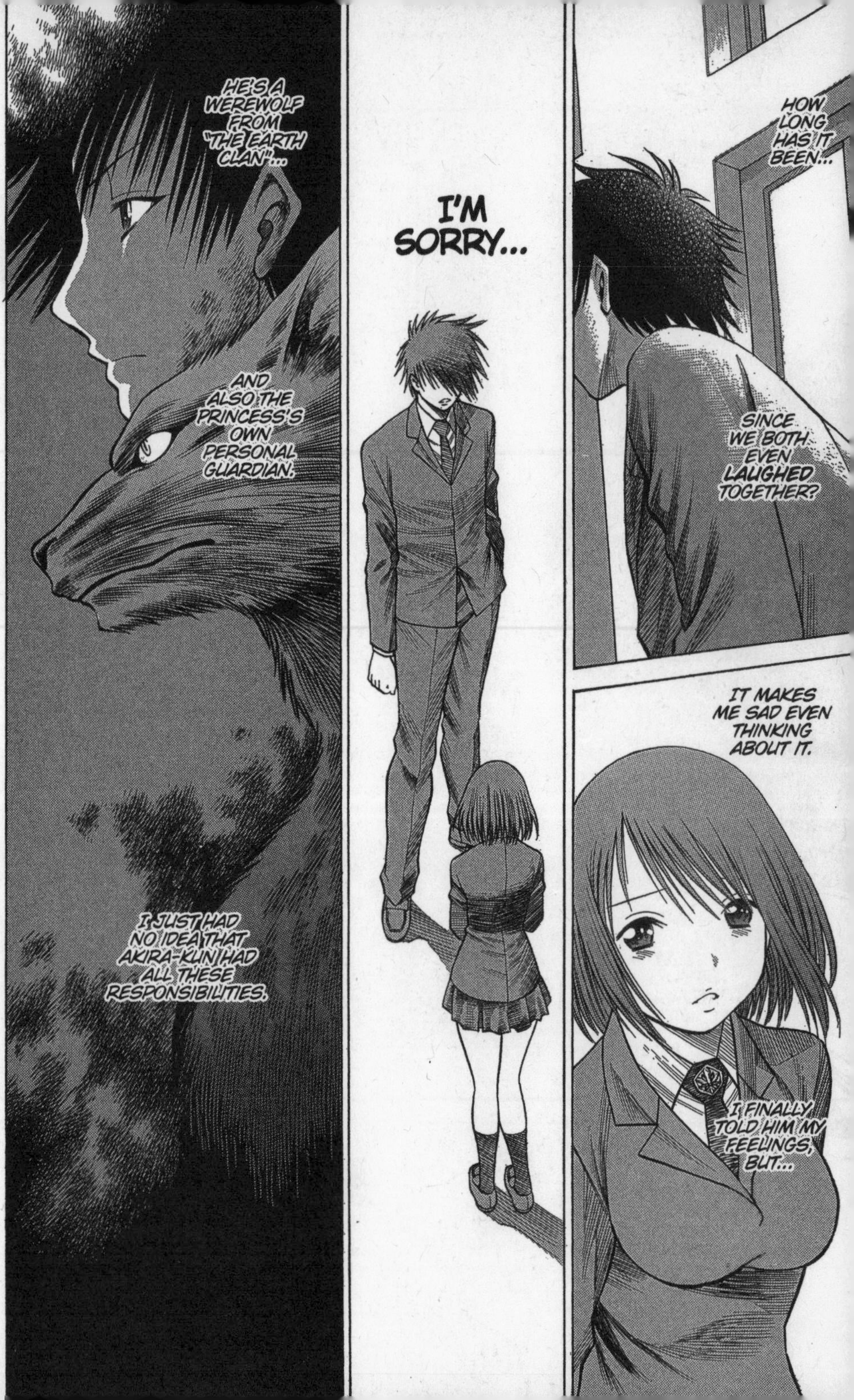
HOW LONG HAS IT BEEN...
SINCE WE BOTH EVEN LAUGHED TOGETHER?
IT MAKES ME SAD EVEN THINKING ABOUT IT.
I FINALLY TOLD HIM MY FEELINGS, BUT...
I'M SORRY...
HE'S A WEREWOLF FROM "THE EARTH CLAN"...
AND ALSO THE PRINCESS'S OWN PERSONAL GUARDIAN.
I JUST HAD NO IDEA THAT AKIRA-KUN HAD ALL THESE RESPONSIBILITIES.

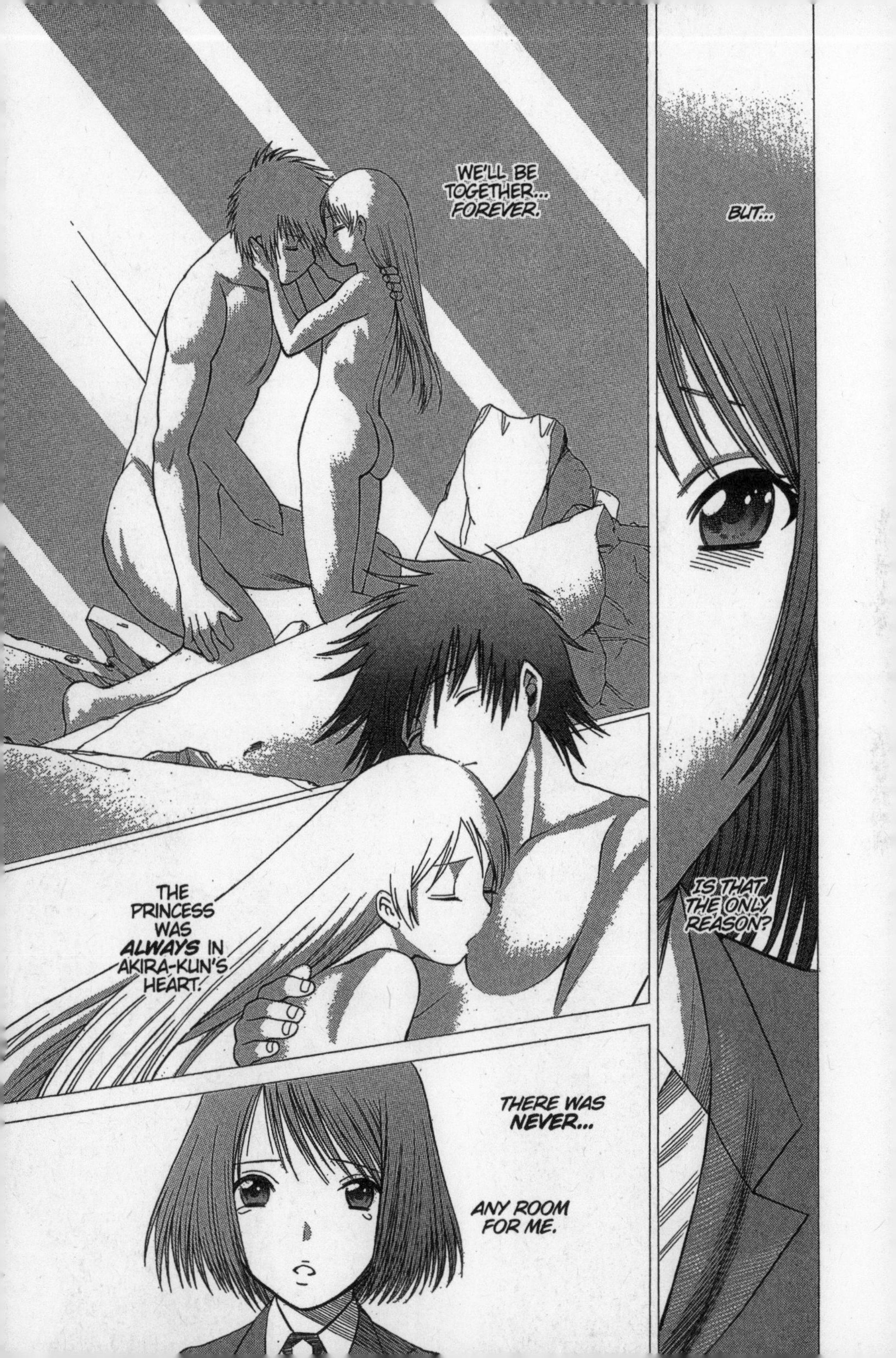
BUT...
IS THAT THE ONLY REASON?
WE'LL BE TOGETHER... FOREVER.
THE PRINCESS WAS ALWAYS IN AKIRA-KUN'S HEART.
THERE WAS NEVER...
ANY ROOM FOR ME.

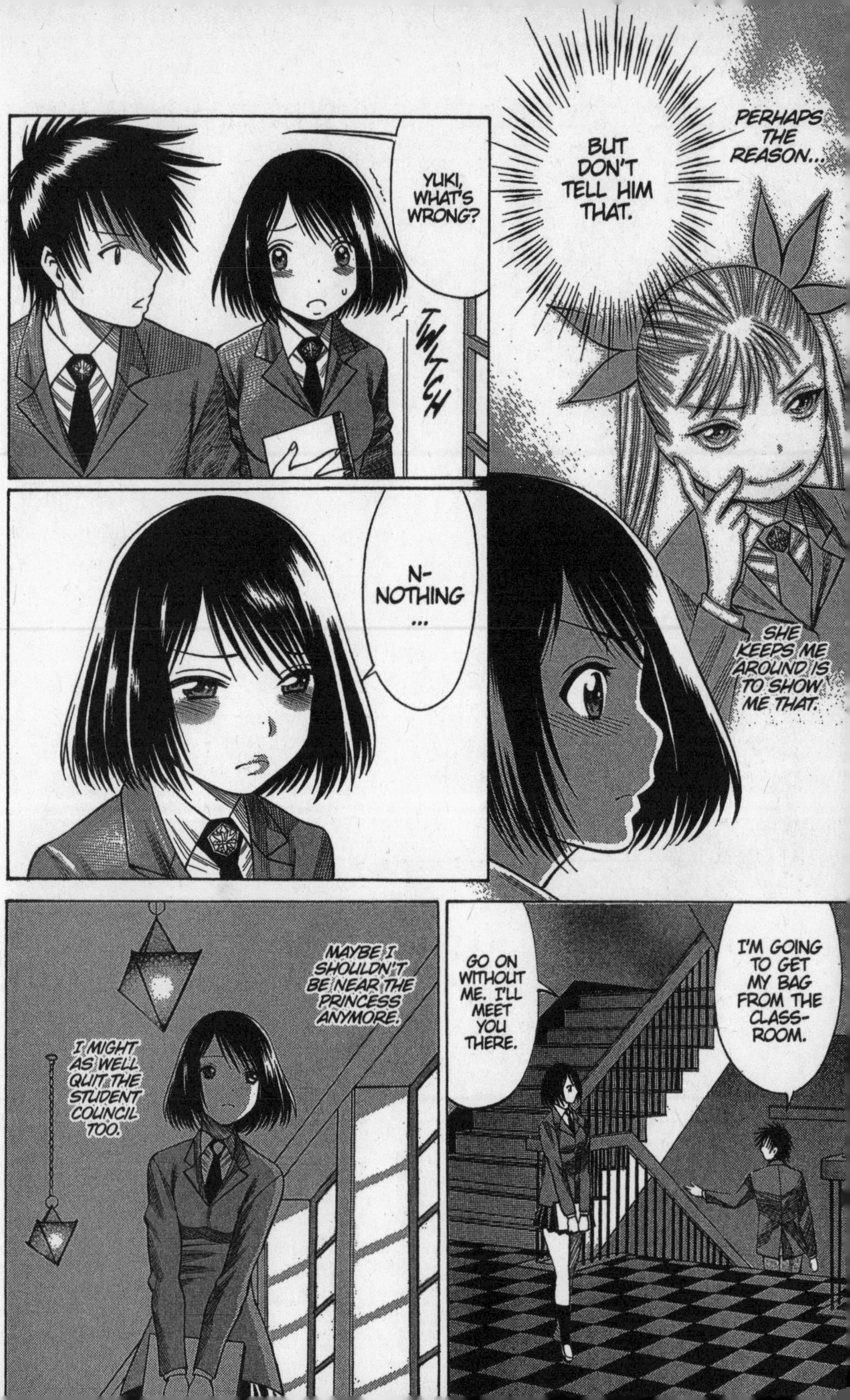
PERHAPS THE REASON...
BUT DON'T TELL HIM THAT.
SHE KEEPS ME AROUND IS TO SHOW ME THAT.
YUKI, WHAT'S WRONG?
TWITCH
N-NOTHING ...
I'M GOING TO GET MY BAG FROM THE CLASS-ROOM.
GO ON WITHOUT ME. I'LL MEET YOU THERE.
MAYBE I SHOULDN'T BE NEAR THE PRINCESS ANYMORE.
I MIGHT AS WELL QUIT THE STUDENT COUNCIL TOO.

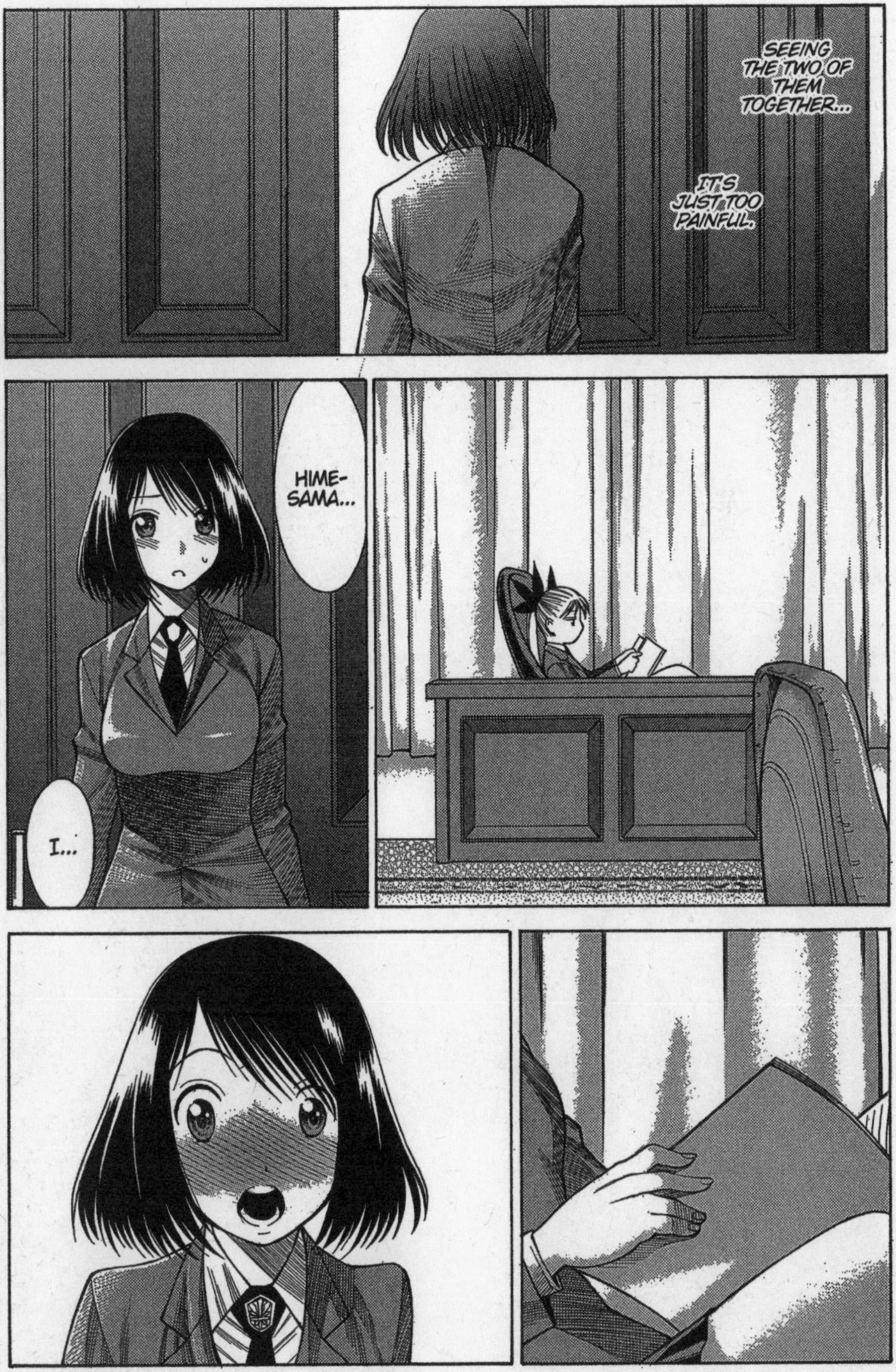
SEEING THE TWO OF THEM TOGETHER...
IT'S JUST TOO PAINFUL.
HIME-SAMA...
I...

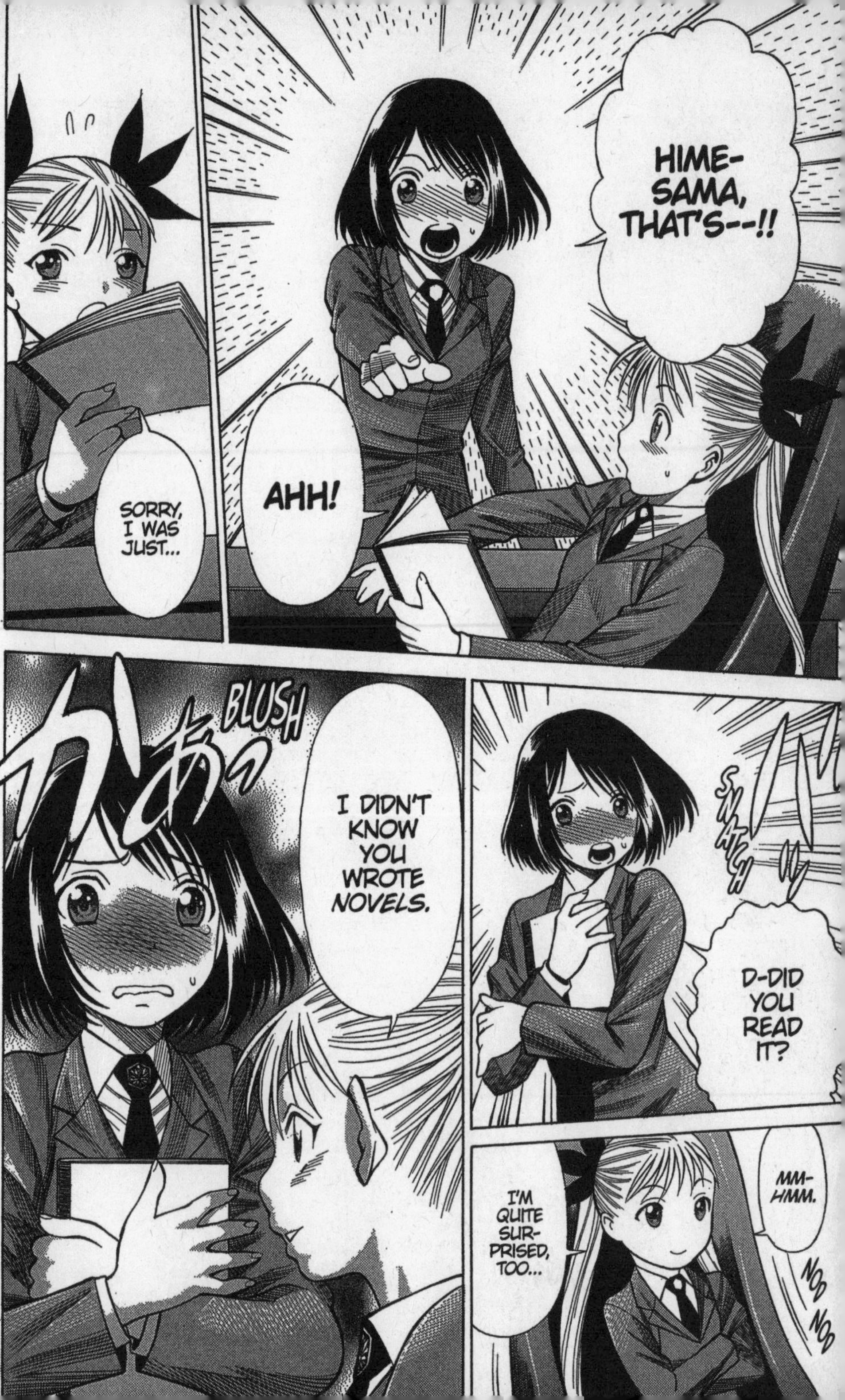
HIME-SAMA, THAT'S--!!
AHH!
SORRY, I WAS JUST...
SNATCH
D-DID YOU READ IT?
MM-HMM.
NOD NOD
I'M QUITE SUR-PRISED, TOO...
BLUSH
I DIDN'T KNOW YOU WROTE *NOVELS.*

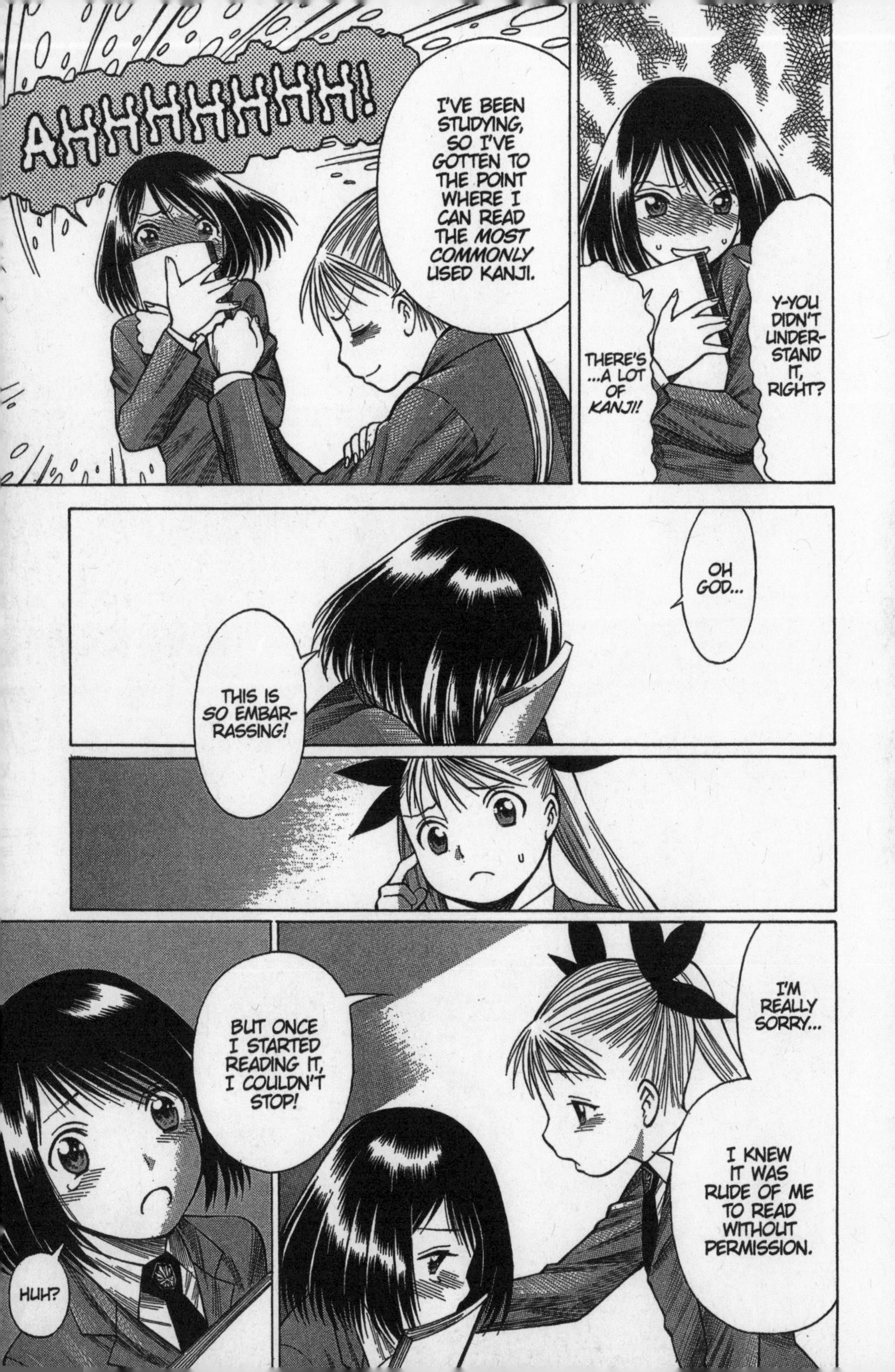
Y-YOU DIDN'T UNDER-STAND IT, RIGHT?
THERE'S ...A LOT OF *KANJI!*
AHHHHHHHH!
I'VE BEEN STUDYING, SO I'VE GOTTEN TO THE POINT WHERE I CAN READ THE *MOST COMMONLY* USED KANJI.
OH GOD...
THIS IS SO EMBAR-RASSING!
I'M REALLY SORRY...
I KNEW IT WAS RUDE OF ME TO READ WITHOUT PERMISSION.
BUT ONCE I STARTED READING IT, I COULDN'T STOP!
HUH?

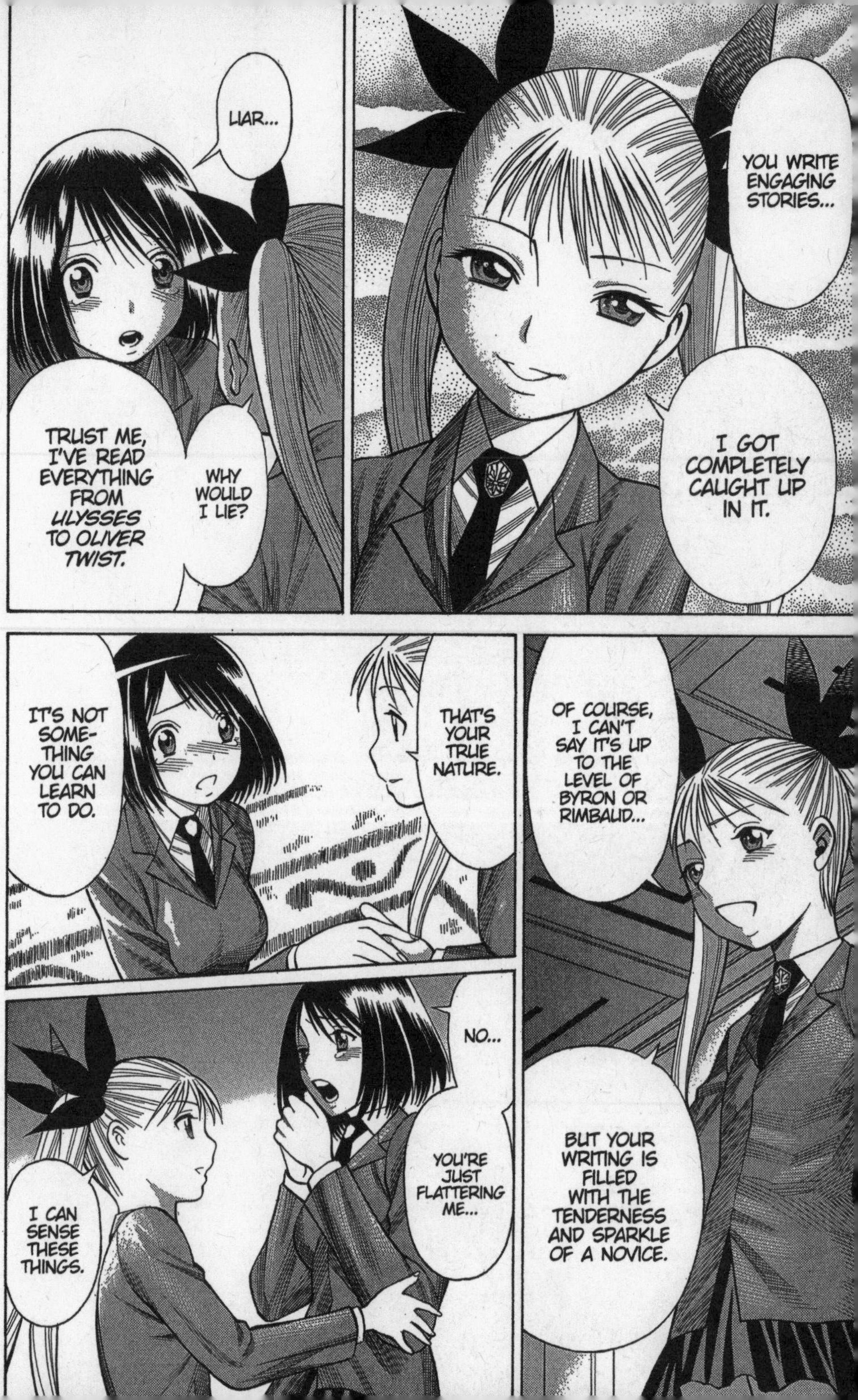
YOU WRITE ENGAGING STORIES...
I GOT COMPLETELY CAUGHT UP IN IT.
LIAR...
WHY WOULD I LIE?
TRUST ME, I'VE READ EVERYTHING FROM *ULYSSES* TO *OLIVER TWIST*.
OF COURSE, I CAN'T SAY IT'S UP TO THE LEVEL OF BYRON OR RIMBAUD...
BUT YOUR WRITING IS FILLED WITH THE TENDERNESS AND SPARKLE OF A NOVICE.
THAT'S YOUR TRUE NATURE.
IT'S NOT SOME-THING YOU CAN LEARN TO DO.
NO...
YOU'RE JUST FLATTERING ME...
I CAN SENSE THESE THINGS.

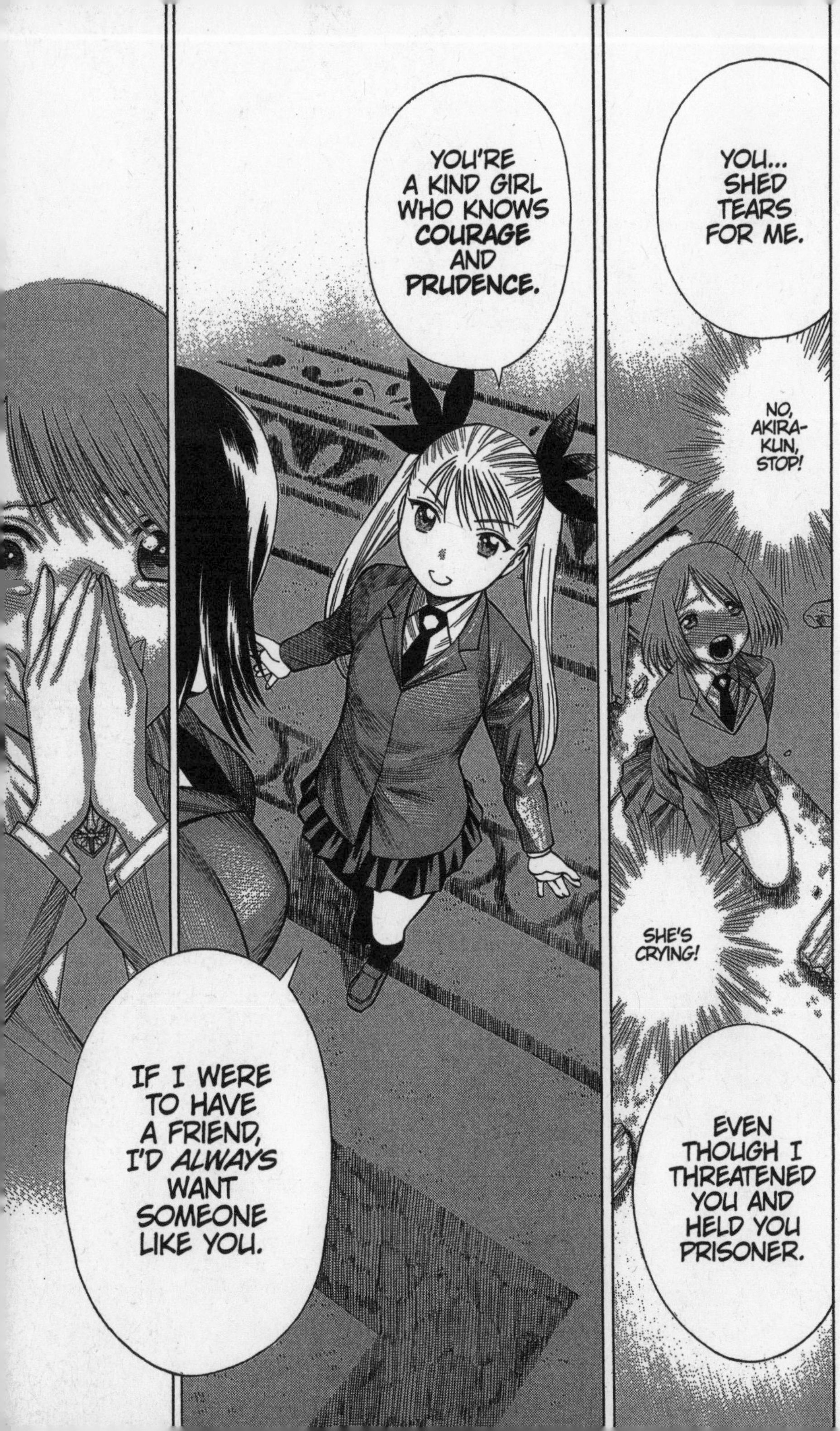
YOU... SHED TEARS FOR ME.
NO, AKIRA-KUN, STOP!
SHE'S CRYING!
EVEN THOUGH I THREATENED YOU AND HELD YOU PRISONER.
YOU'RE A KIND GIRL WHO KNOWS COURAGE AND PRUDENCE.
IF I WERE TO HAVE A FRIEND, I'D *ALWAYS* WANT SOMEONE LIKE YOU.

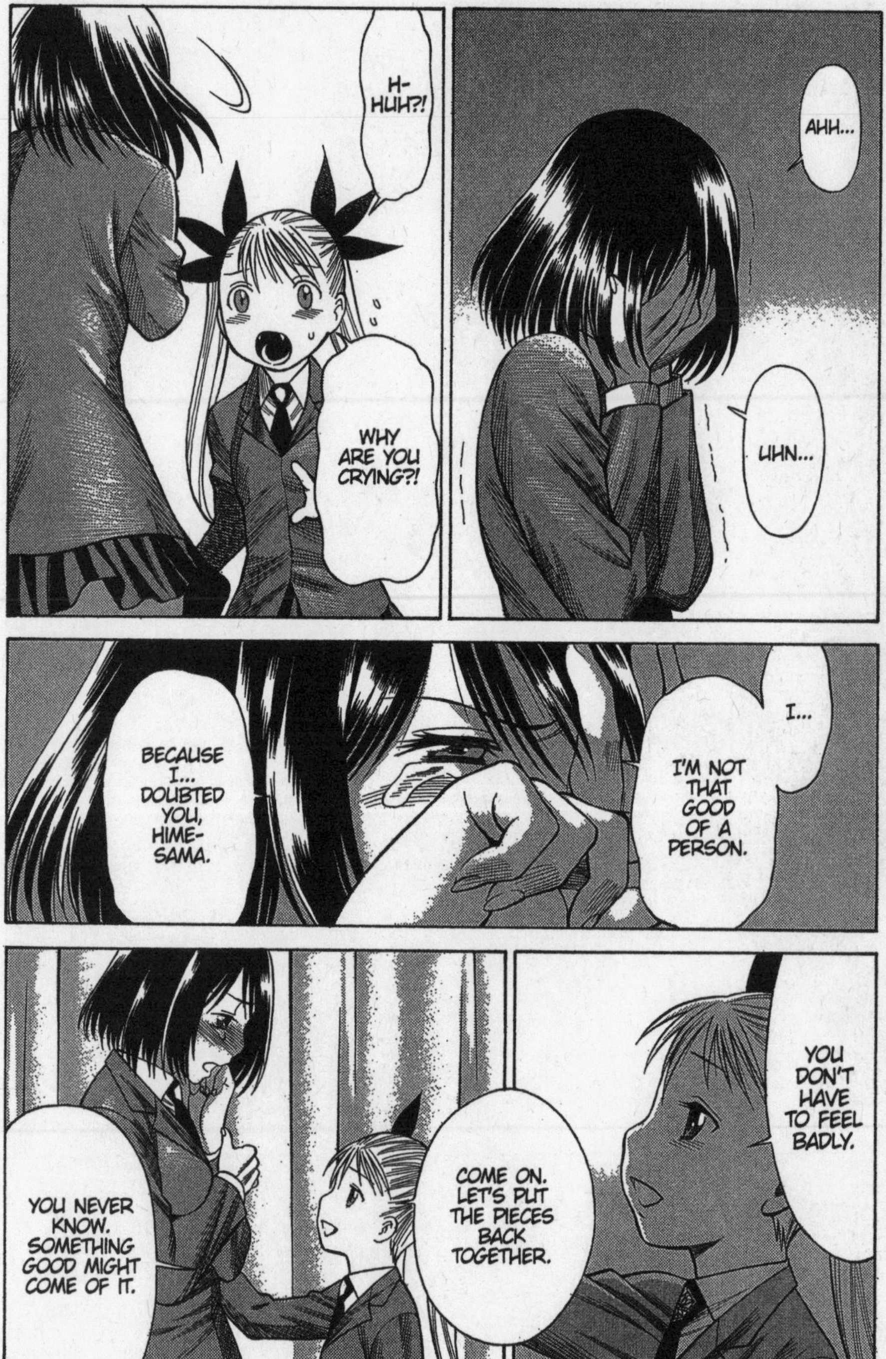
AHH...
UHN...
H-HUH?!
WHY ARE YOU CRYING?!
I...
I'M NOT THAT GOOD OF A PERSON.
BECAUSE I... DOUBTED YOU, HIME-SAMA.
YOU DON'T HAVE TO FEEL BADLY.
COME ON. LET'S PUT THE PIECES BACK TOGETHER.
YOU NEVER KNOW. SOMETHING GOOD MIGHT COME OF IT.

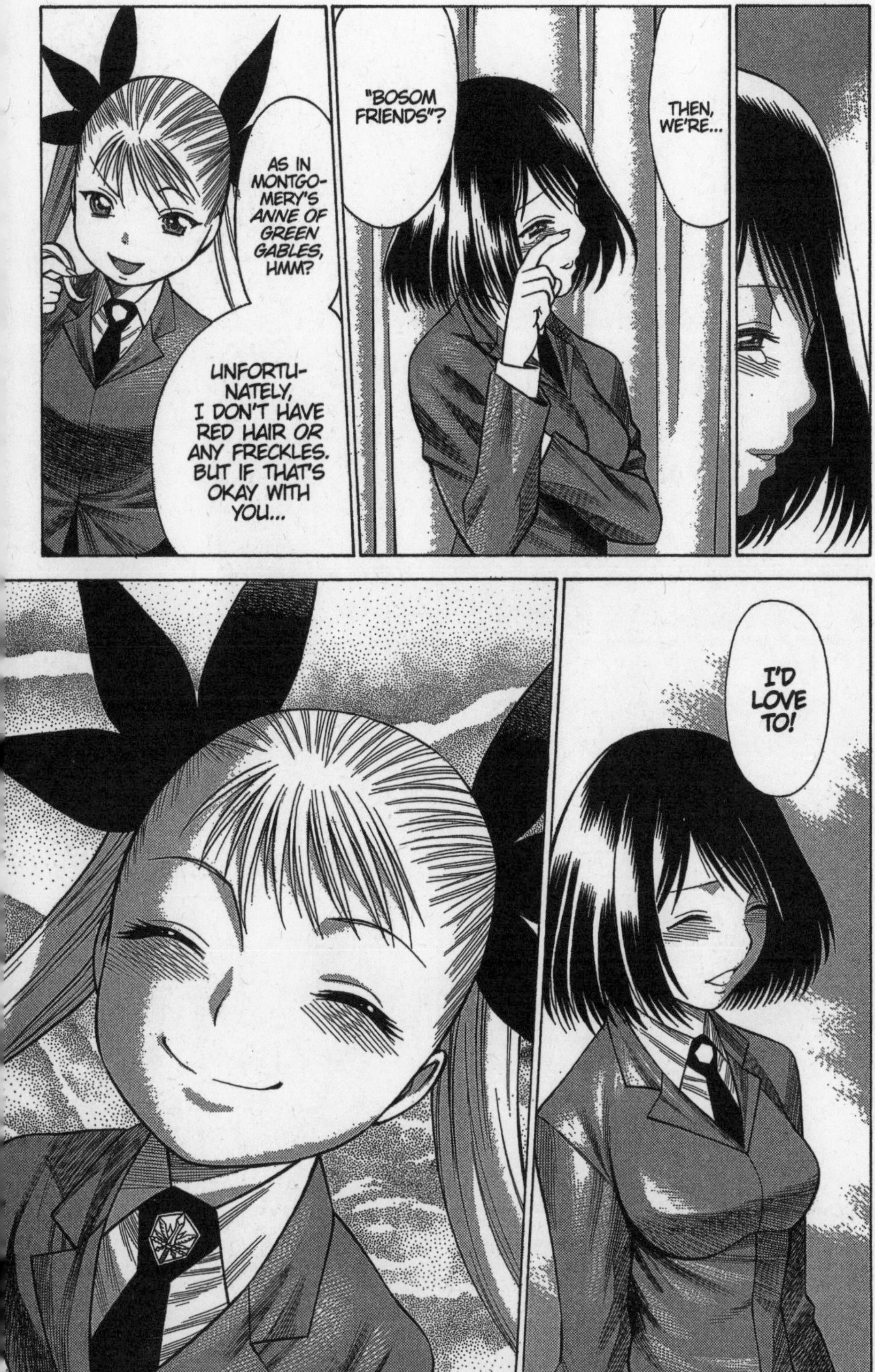
THEN, WE'RE...
"BOSOM FRIENDS"?
AS IN MONTGO-MERY'S *ANNE OF GREEN GABLES*, HMM?
UNFORTU-NATELY, I DON'T HAVE RED HAIR OR ANY FRECKLES. BUT IF THAT'S OKAY WITH YOU...
I'D LOVE TO!

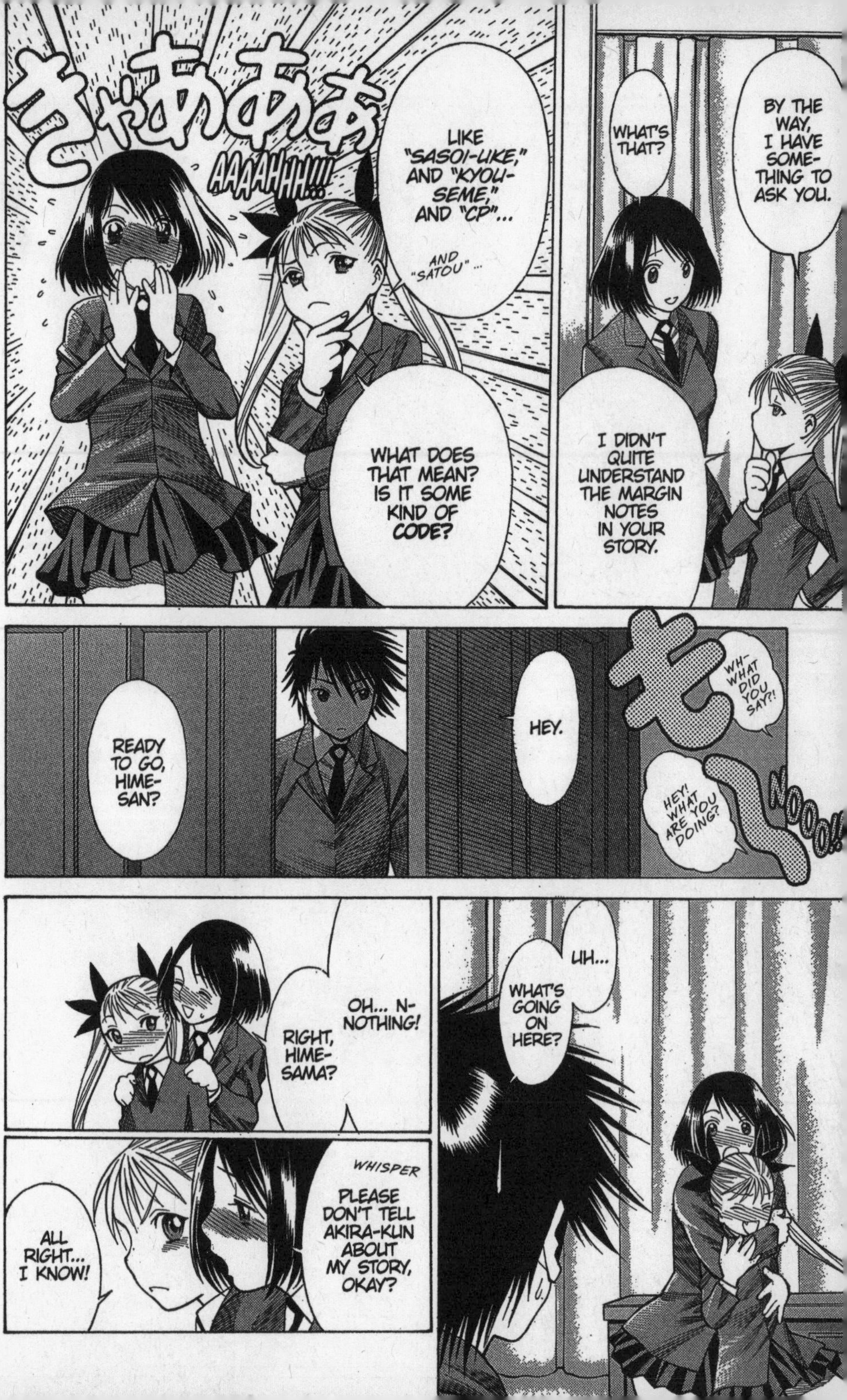
BY THE WAY, I HAVE SOMETHING TO ASK YOU.
WHAT'S THAT?
I DIDN'T QUITE UNDERSTAND THE MARGIN NOTES IN YOUR STORY.
LIKE "SASOI-UKE," AND "KYOU-SEME," AND "CP"...
AND "SATOU"...
WHAT DOES THAT MEAN? IS IT SOME KIND OF CODE?
きゃあああ
AAAAHHH!!!...
WH-WHAT DID YOU SAY?!
HEY! WHAT ARE YOU DOING?
NOOO!!
HEY.
READY TO GO, HIME-SAN?
UH...
WHAT'S GOING ON HERE?
OH... N-NOTHING!
RIGHT, HIME-SAMA?
WHISPER
PLEASE DON'T TELL AKIRA-KUN ABOUT MY STORY, OKAY?
ALL RIGHT... I KNOW!

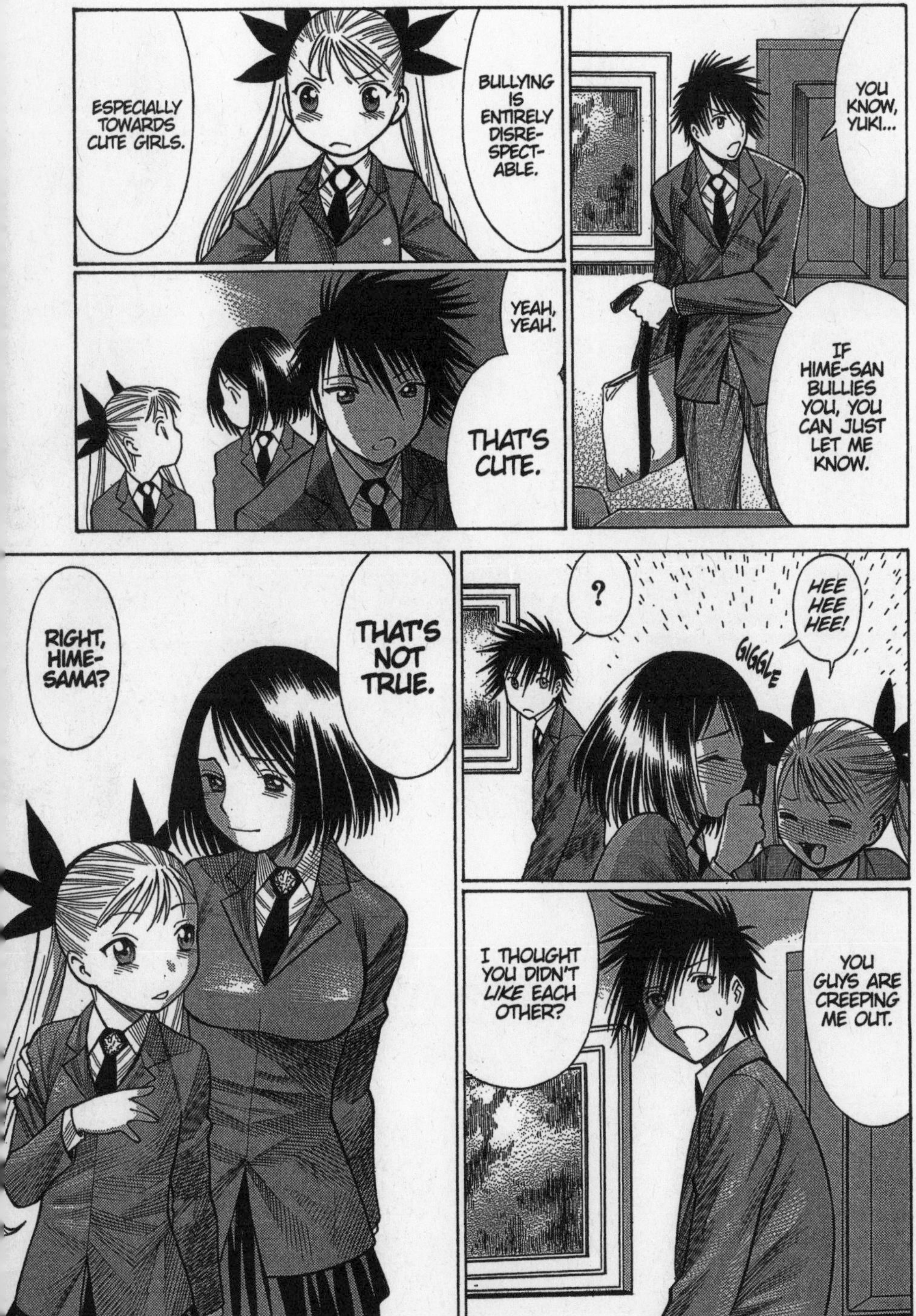
YOU KNOW, YUKI...
IF HIME-SAN BULLIES YOU, YOU CAN JUST LET ME KNOW.
BULLYING IS ENTIRELY DISRE-SPECT-ABLE.
ESPECIALLY TOWARDS CUTE GIRLS.
YEAH, YEAH.
THAT'S CUTE.
HEE HEE HEE!
GIGGLE
?
YOU GUYS ARE CREEPING ME OUT.
I THOUGHT YOU DIDN'T *LIKE* EACH OTHER?
THAT'S NOT TRUE.
RIGHT, HIME-SAMA?

SINCE WHEN...?

EXACTLY.

WE'RE BOSOM FRIENDS!

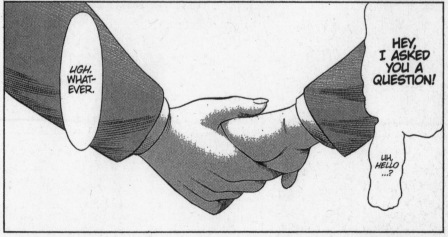

UGH. WHATEVER.

HEY, I ASKED YOU A QUESTION!

UH, HELLO...?

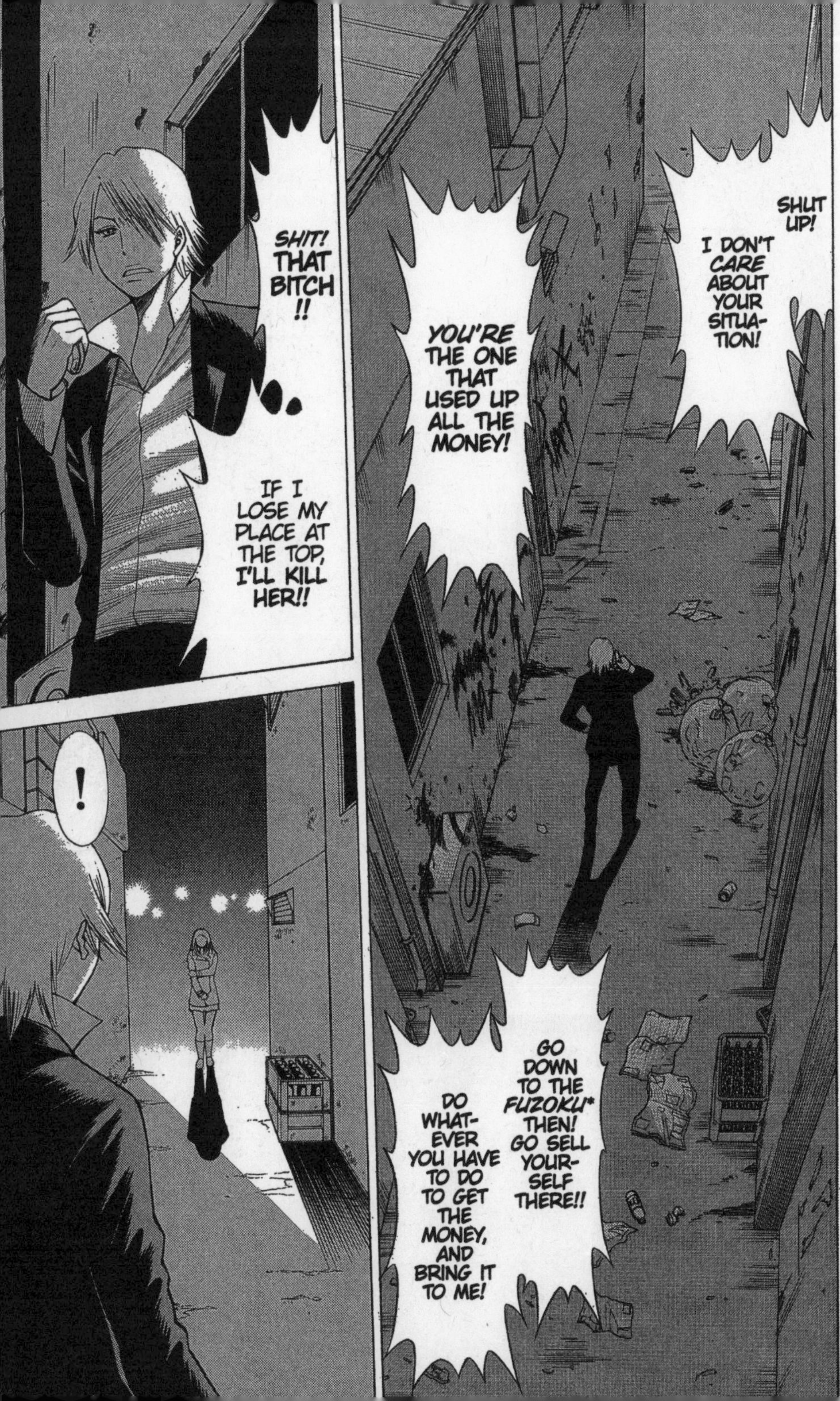
SHUT UP!
I DON'T CARE ABOUT YOUR SITUATION!
YOU'RE THE ONE THAT USED UP ALL THE MONEY!
GO DOWN TO THE *FUZOKU** THEN! GO SELL YOURSELF THERE!!
DO WHATEVER YOU HAVE TO DO TO GET THE MONEY, AND BRING IT TO ME!
SHIT! THAT BITCH!!
IF I LOSE MY PLACE AT THE TOP, I'LL KILL HER!!
!

A prostitution establishment, many of which cater to a specific sexual fetish.

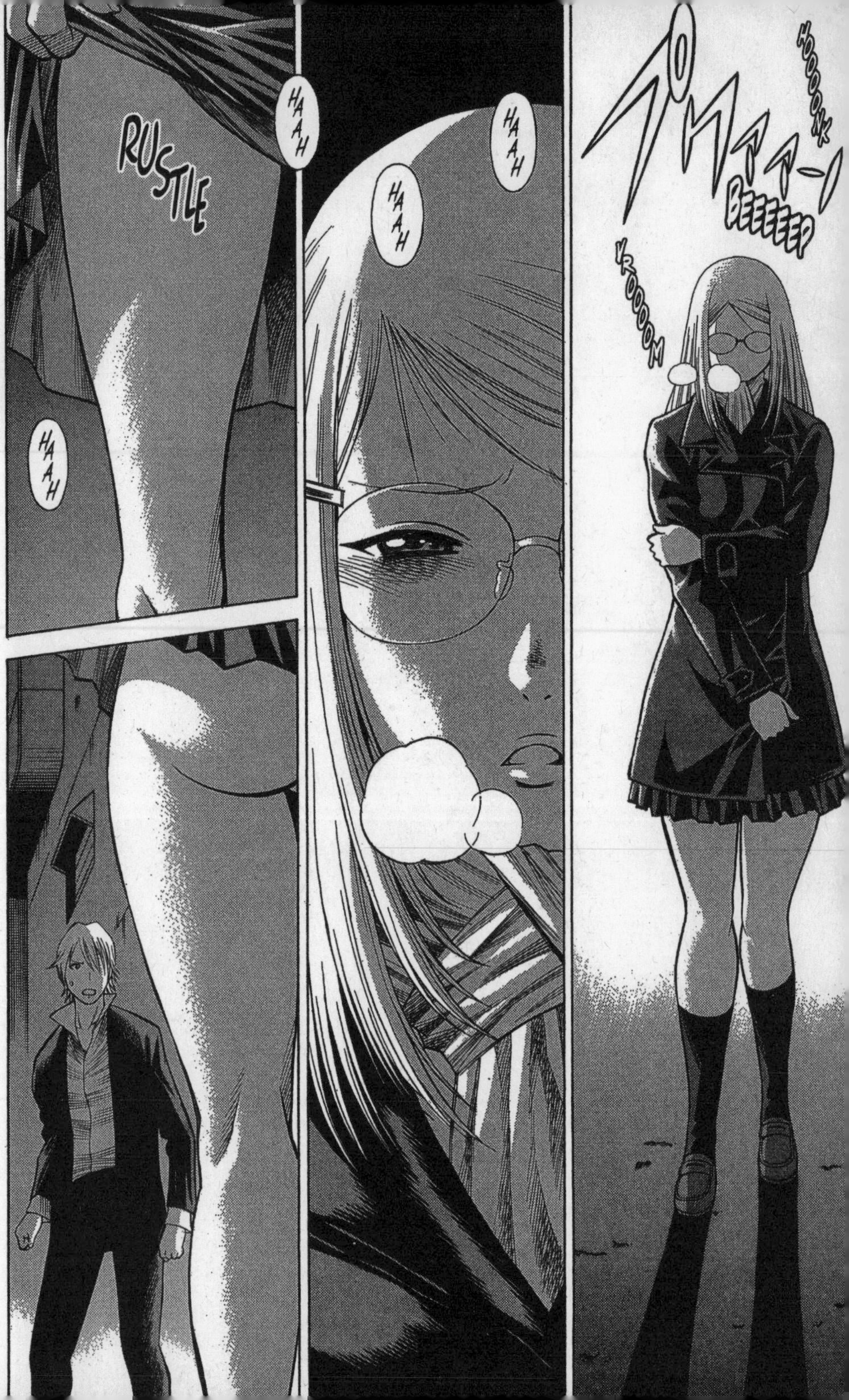
HOOOONK
BEEEEEP
VROOOOM
HAAAH
HAAAH
HAAAH
RUSTLE
HAAAH

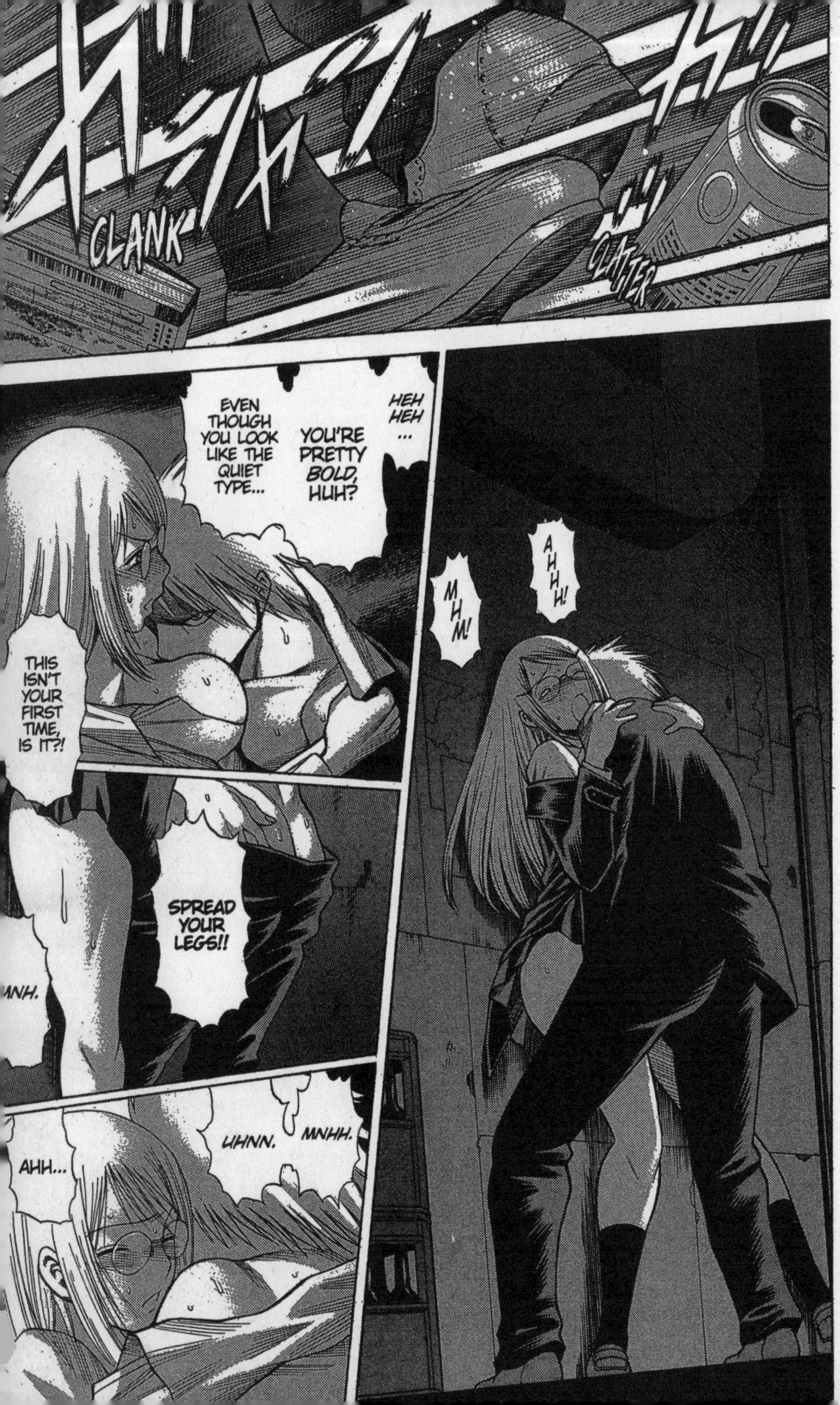
CLATTER
CLANK
AHHH!
MHM!
HEH HEH...
YOU'RE PRETTY BOLD, HUH?
EVEN THOUGH YOU LOOK LIKE THE QUIET TYPE...
THIS ISN'T YOUR FIRST TIME, IS IT?!
SPREAD YOUR LEGS!!
MNH.
MNHH.
UHNN.
AHH...

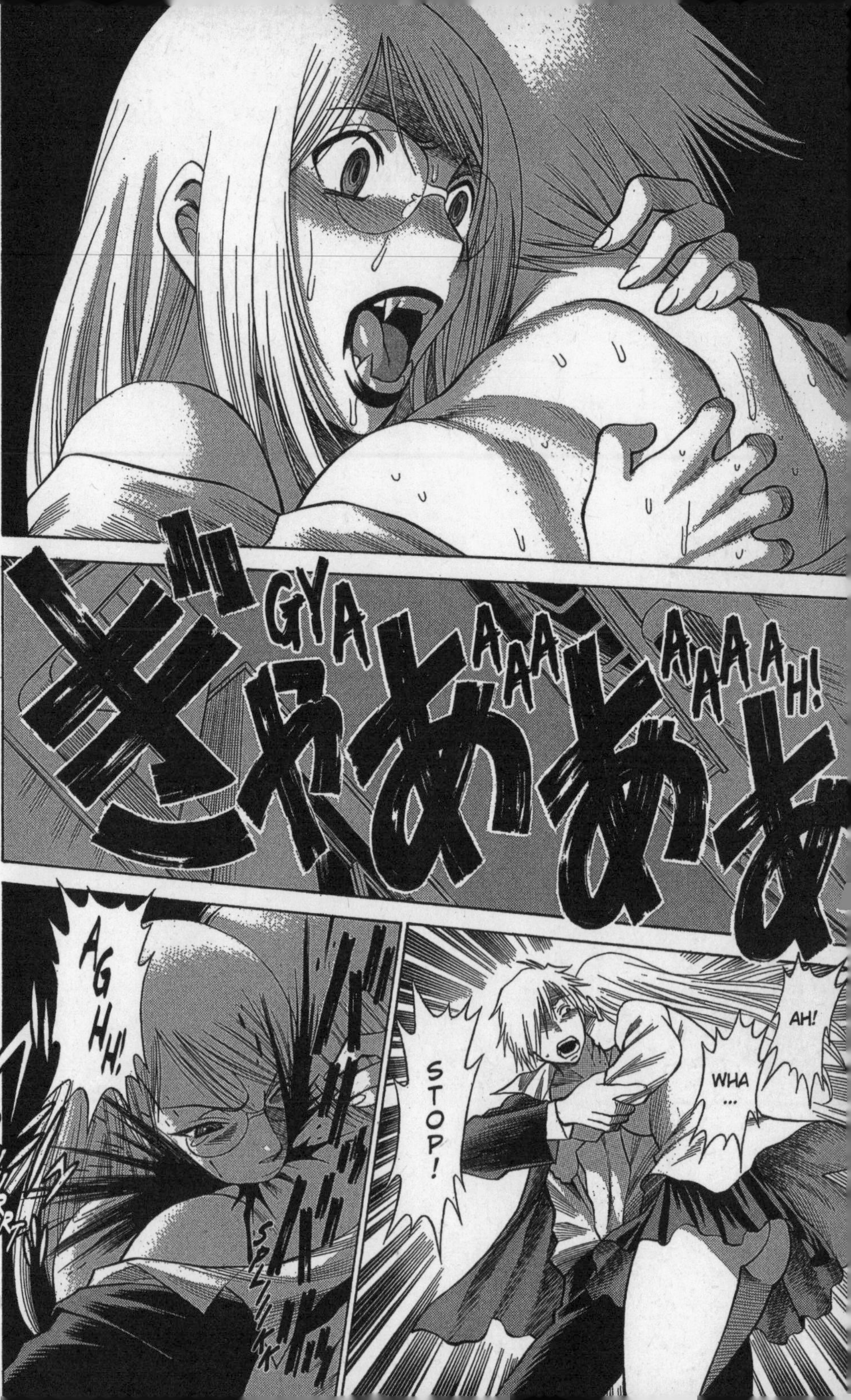
ぎゃあああ
GYAAAAAAAH!
AH!
WHA ...
STOP!
AGHH!
SPLIIIKK
SPLUURRT

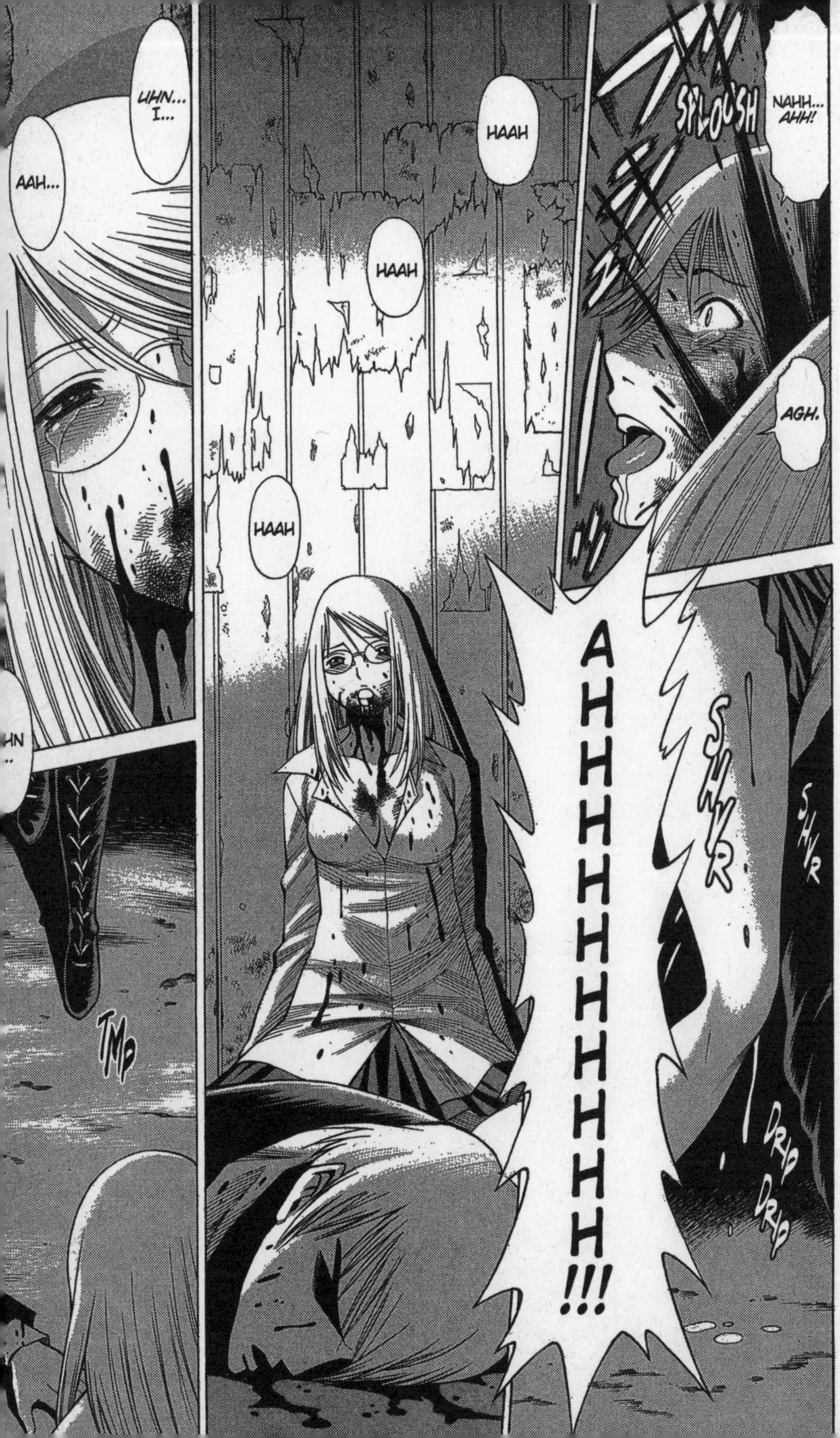
SPLOOSH
NAHH... AHH!
AGH.
AHHHHHHHHHHHHH!!!
SHVR
SHVR
DRIP
DRIP
DRIP
HAAH
HAAH
HAAH
UHN... I...
AAH...
TMP

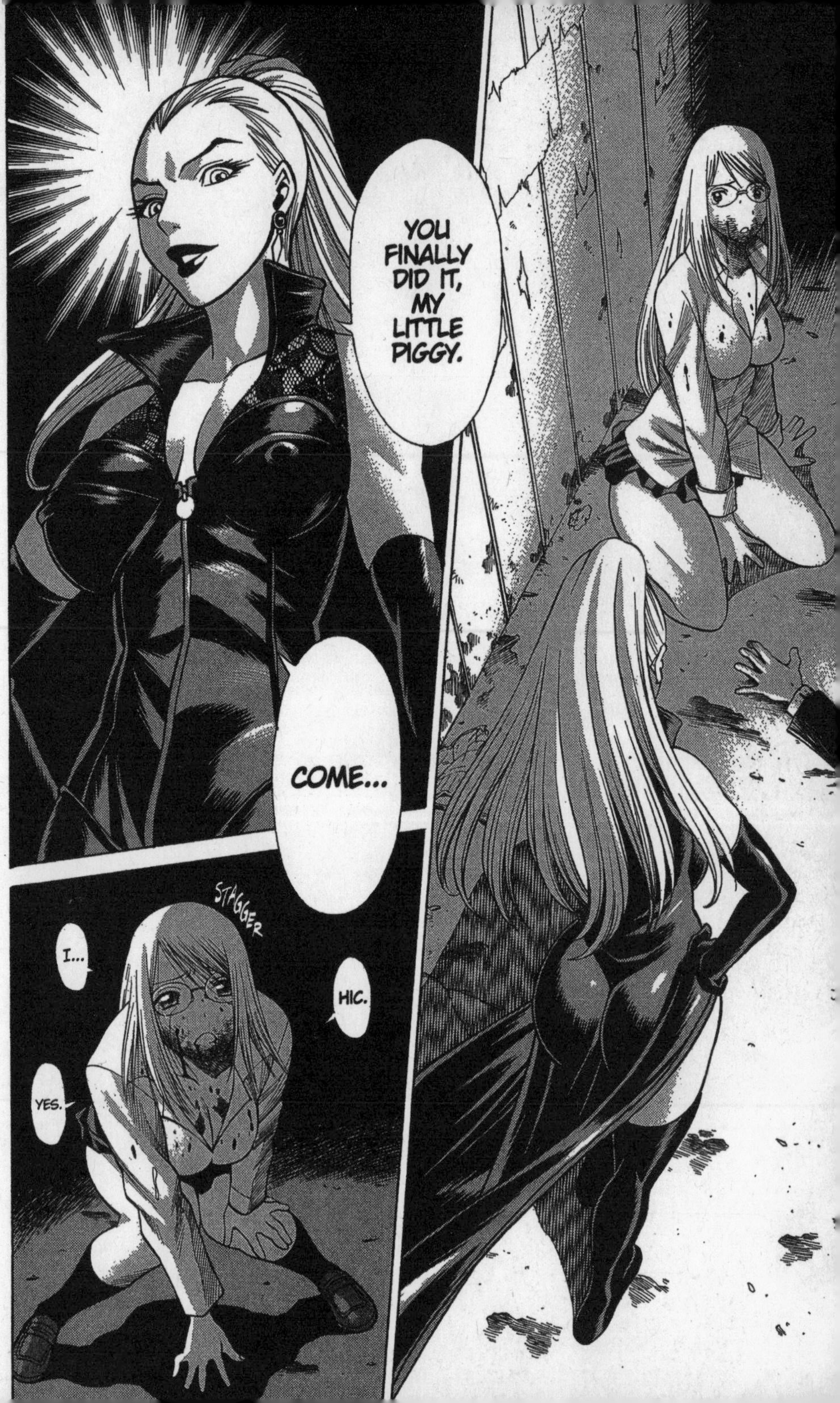
YOU FINALLY DID IT, MY LITTLE PIGGY.
COME...
STAGGER
I...
HIC.
YES.

Chapter 14: Moving Shadows

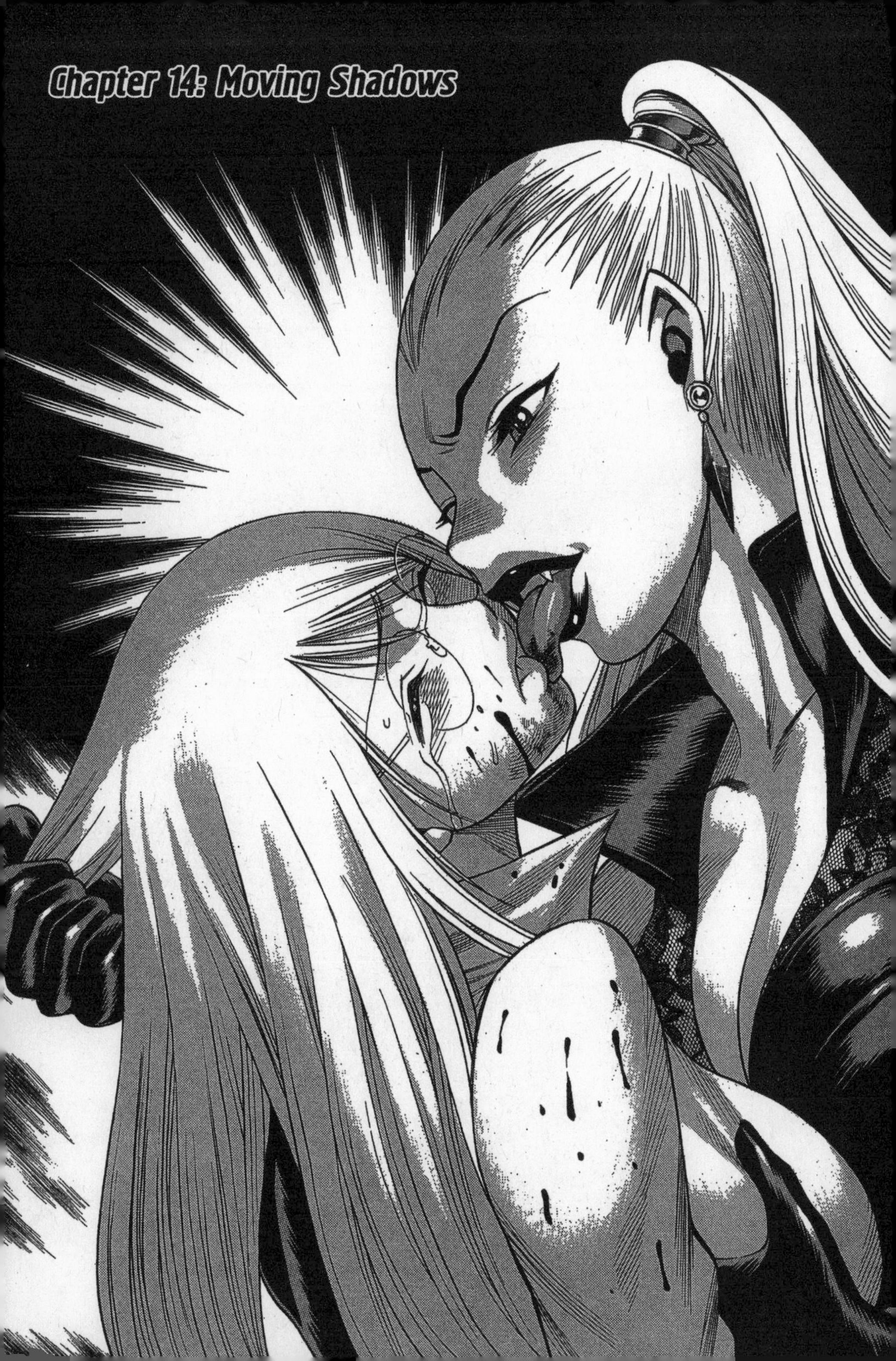

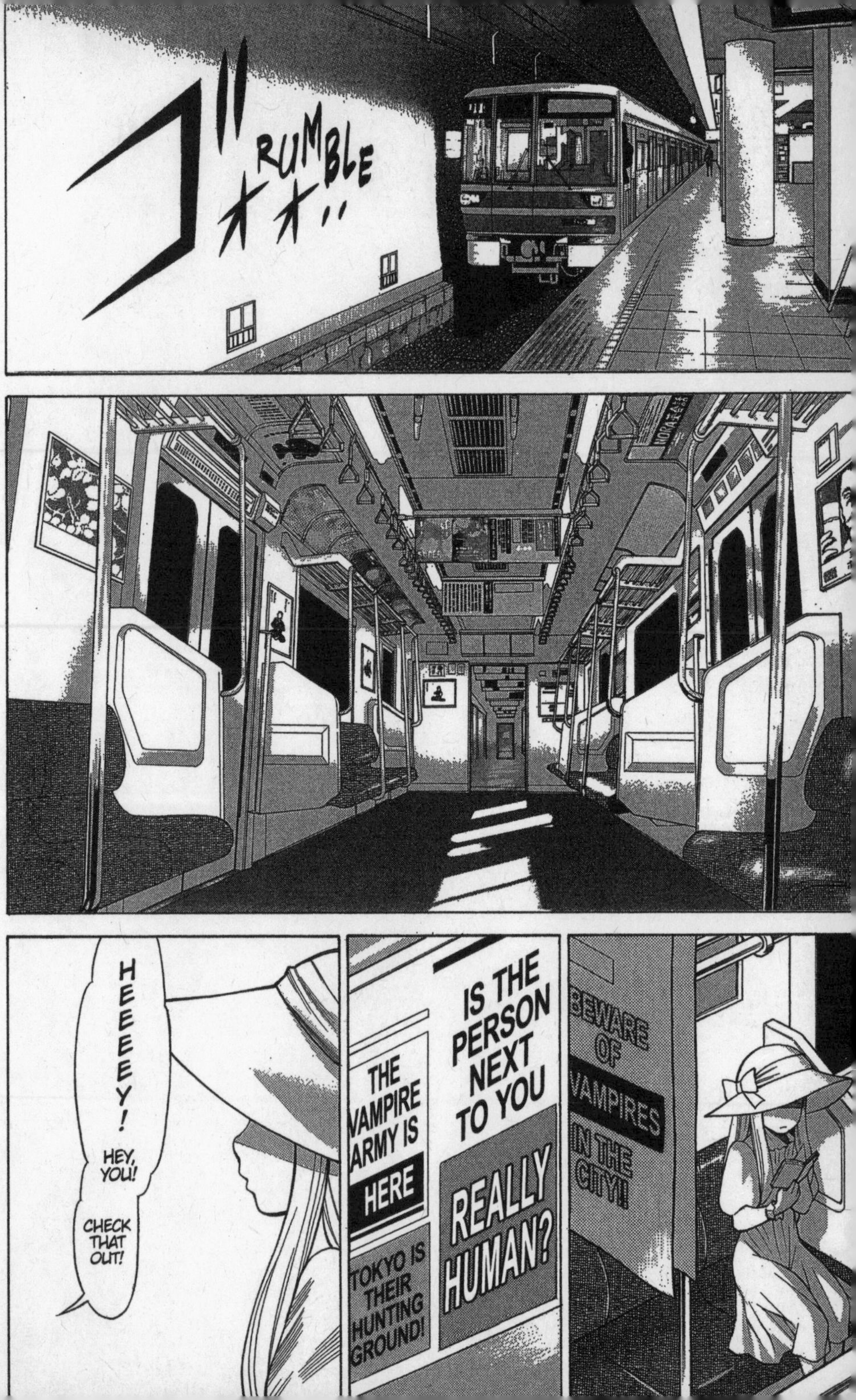
RUMBLE
BEWARE OF VAMPIRES IN THE CITY!
IS THE PERSON NEXT TO YOU REALLY HUMAN?
THE VAMPIRE ARMY IS HERE
TOKYO IS THEIR HUNTING GROUND!
HEEEEEY! HEY, YOU! CHECK THAT OUT!

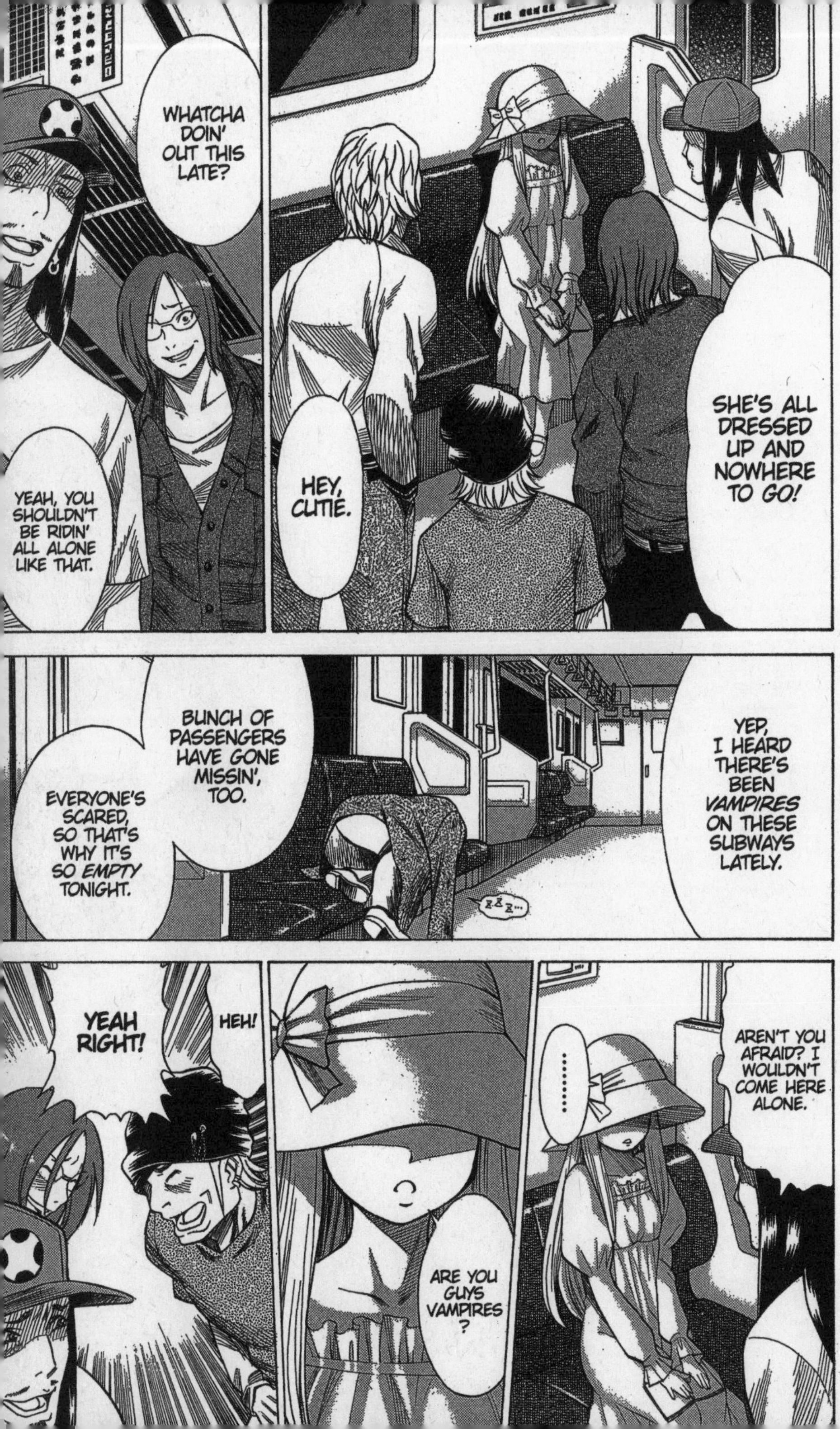
SHE'S ALL DRESSED UP AND NOWHERE TO GO!
HEY, CUTIE.
WHATCHA DOIN' OUT THIS LATE?
YEAH, YOU SHOULDN'T BE RIDIN' ALL ALONE LIKE THAT.
YEP, I HEARD THERE'S BEEN VAMPIRES ON THESE SUBWAYS LATELY.
BUNCH OF PASSENGERS HAVE GONE MISSIN', TOO.
EVERYONE'S SCARED, SO THAT'S WHY IT'S SO EMPTY TONIGHT.
AREN'T YOU AFRAID? I WOULDN'T COME HERE ALONE.
......
ARE YOU GUYS VAMPIRES?
HEH!
YEAH RIGHT!

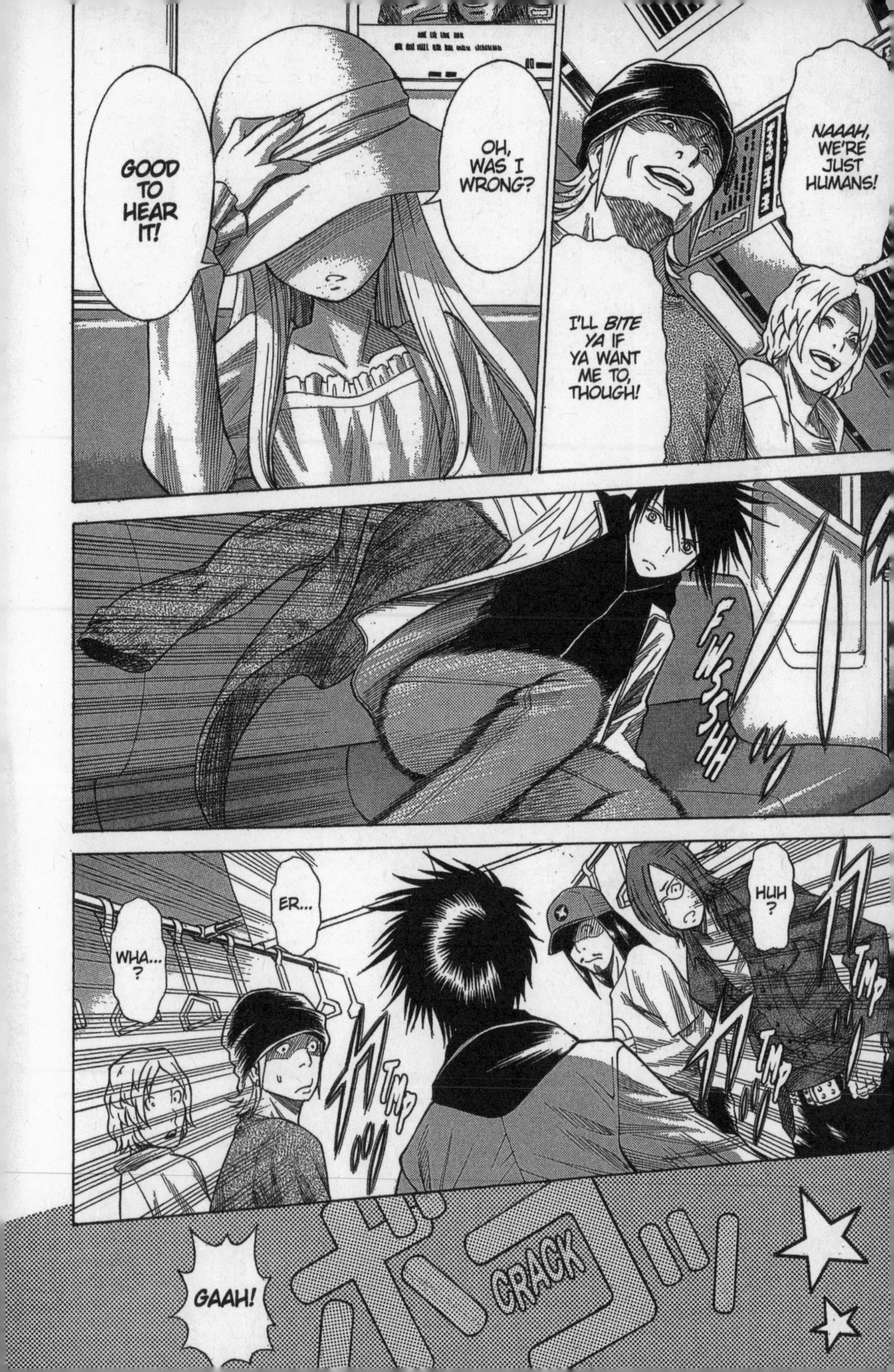
NAAAH, WE'RE JUST HUMANS!
I'LL *BITE* YA IF YA WANT ME TO, THOUGH!
OH, WAS I WRONG?
GOOD TO HEAR IT!
FWSSHH
HUH?
TMP
TMP
ER...
WHA...?
TMP
CRACK
GAAH!

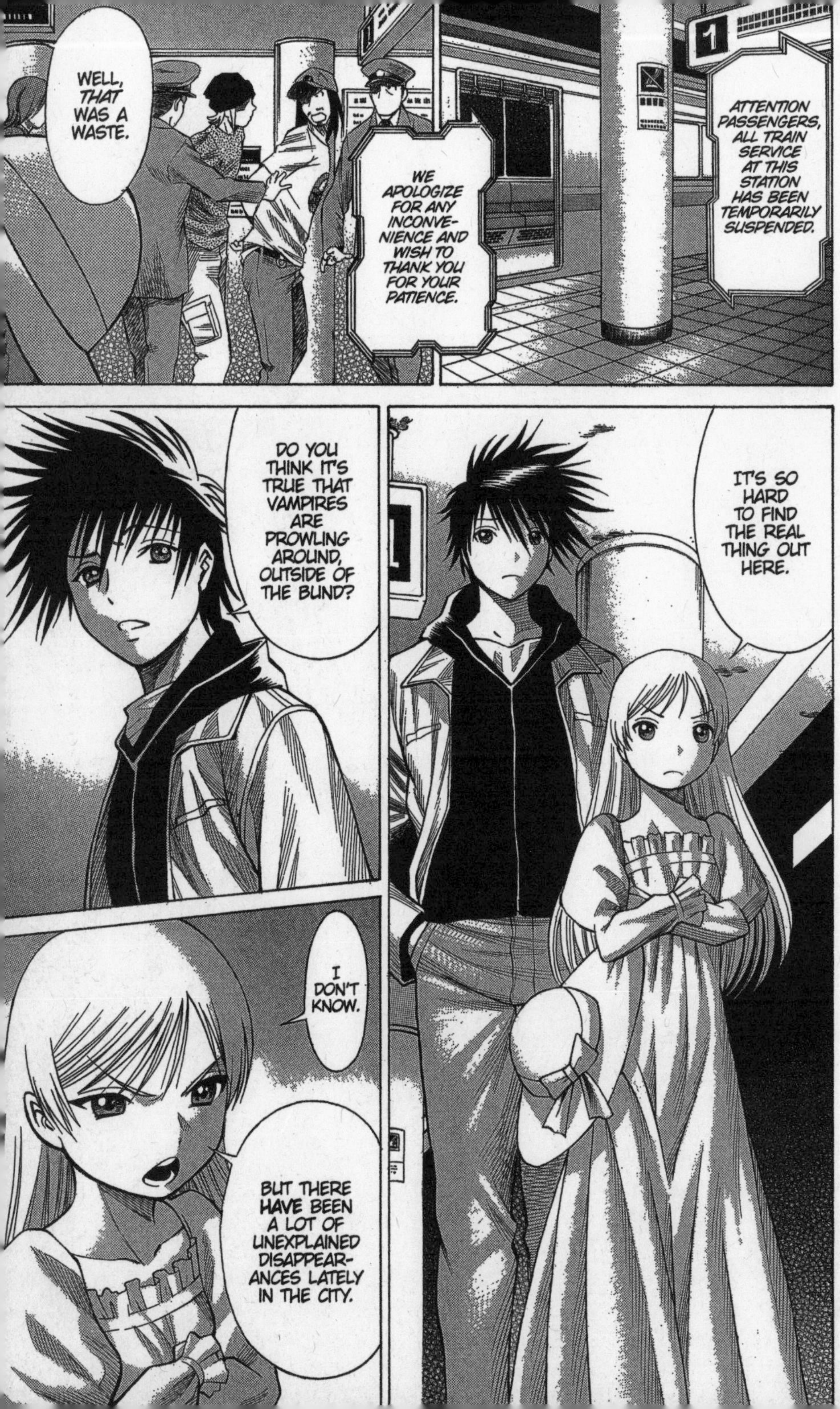
ATTENTION PASSENGERS, ALL TRAIN SERVICE AT THIS STATION HAS BEEN TEMPORARILY SUSPENDED.
WE APOLOGIZE FOR ANY INCONVE-NIENCE AND WISH TO THANK YOU FOR YOUR PATIENCE.
WELL, THAT WAS A WASTE.
IT'S SO HARD TO FIND THE REAL THING OUT HERE.
DO YOU THINK IT'S TRUE THAT VAMPIRES ARE PROWLING AROUND, OUTSIDE OF THE BUND?
I DON'T KNOW.
BUT THERE HAVE BEEN A LOT OF UNEXPLAINED DISAPPEAR-ANCES LATELY IN THE CITY.

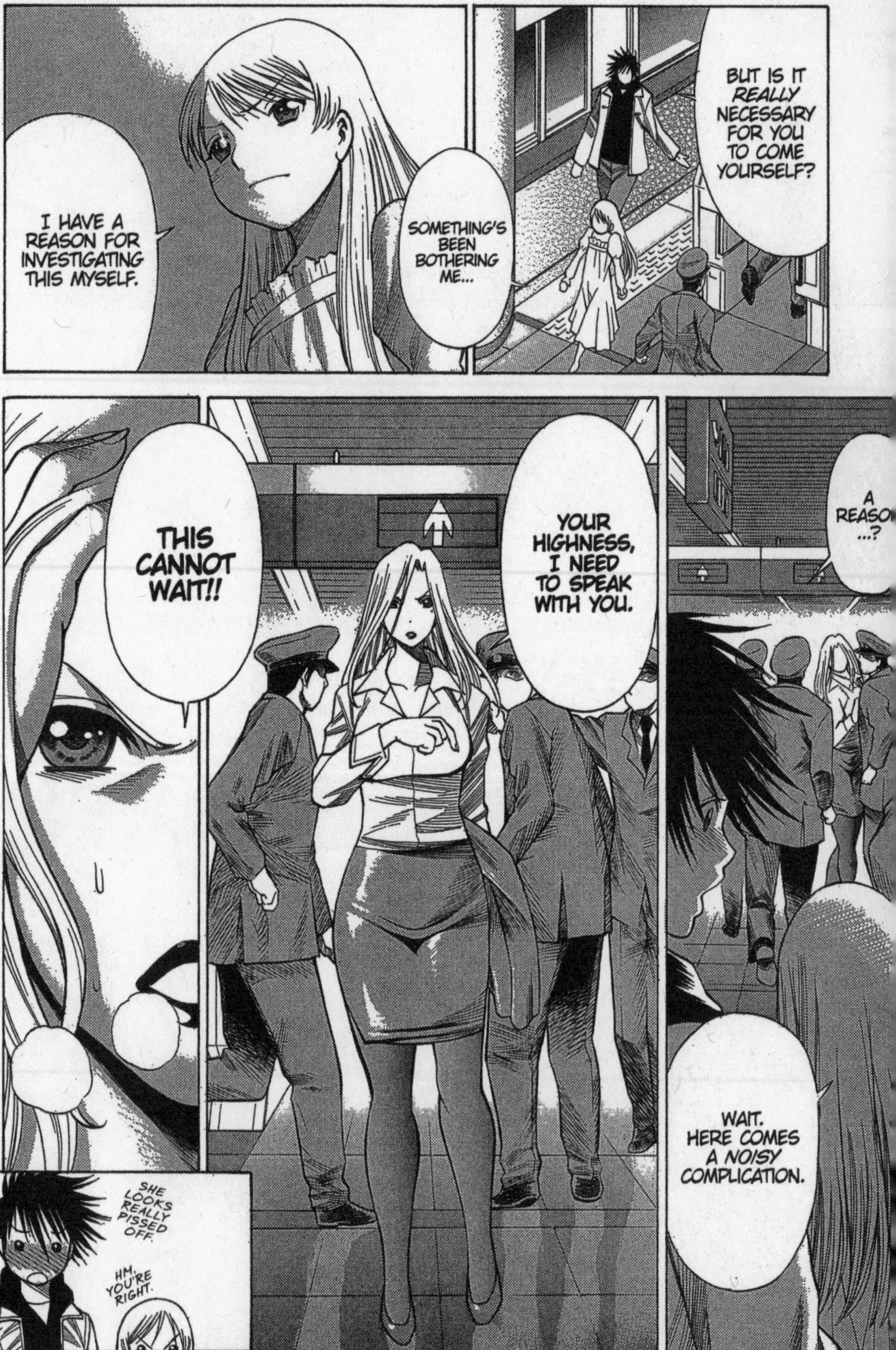
BUT IS IT *REALLY* NECESSARY FOR YOU TO COME YOURSELF?
SOMETHING'S BEEN BOTHERING ME...
I HAVE A REASON FOR INVESTIGATING THIS MYSELF.
A REASO ...?
WAIT. HERE COMES A *NOISY* COMPLICATION.
YOUR HIGHNESS, I NEED TO SPEAK WITH YOU.
THIS CANNOT WAIT!!
SHE LOOKS REALLY PISSED OFF.
HM. YOU'RE RIGHT.

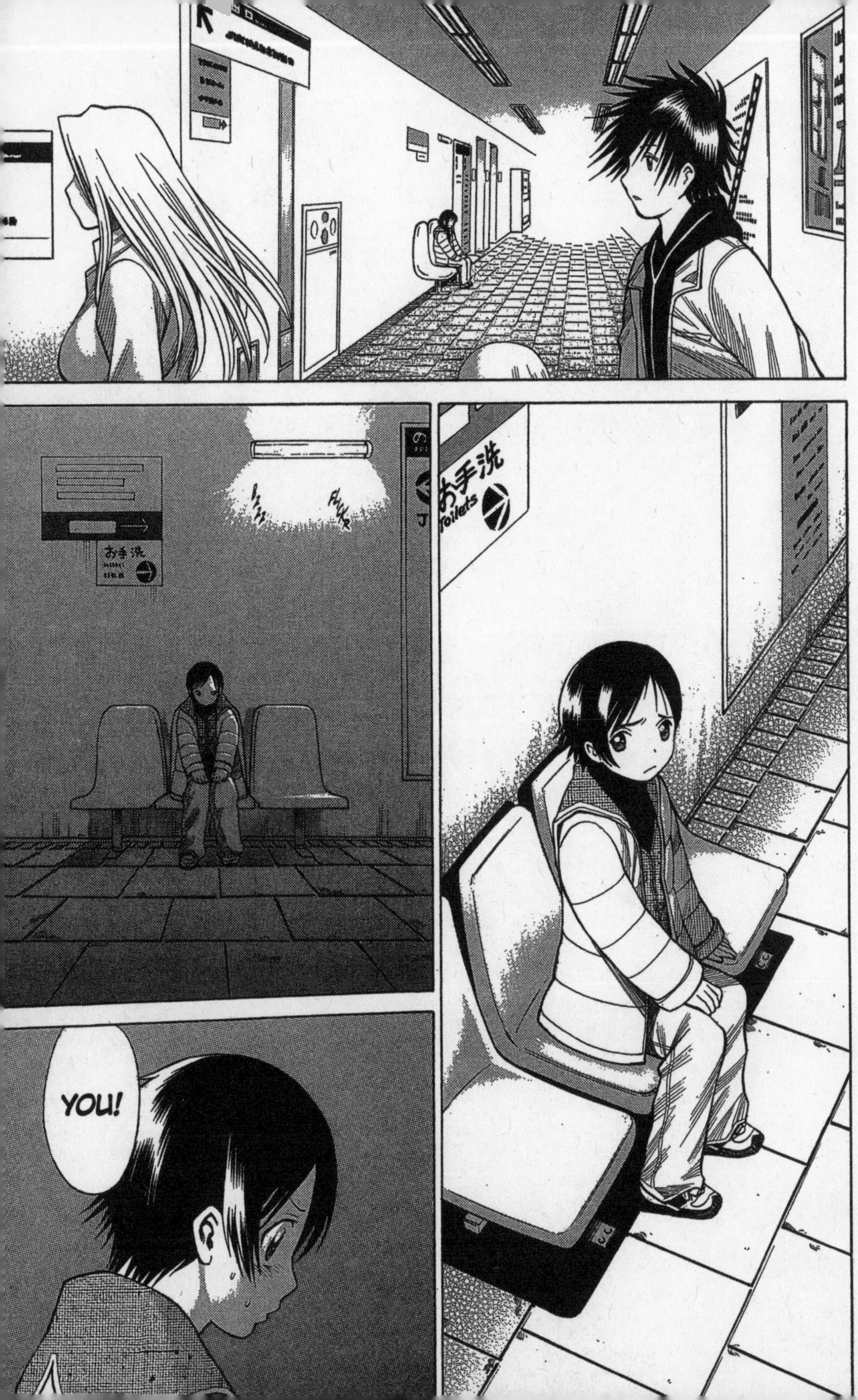
お手洗
Toilets
FLICKR
BZZZ
お手洗
YOU!

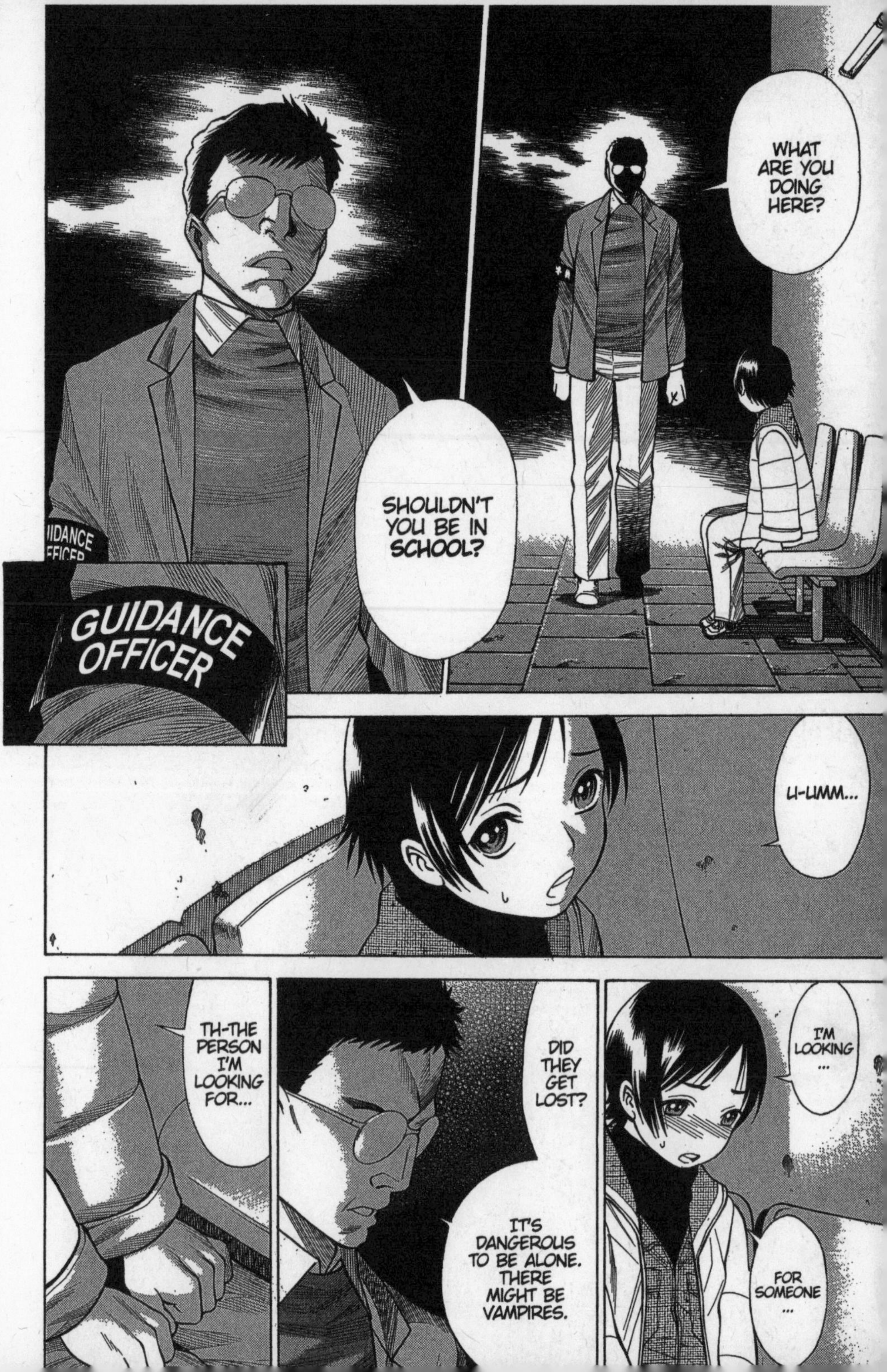
WHAT ARE YOU DOING HERE?
SHOULDN'T YOU BE IN SCHOOL?
GUIDANCE OFFICER
U-UMM...
I'M LOOKING ...
FOR SOMEONE ...
DID THEY GET LOST?
IT'S DANGEROUS TO BE ALONE. THERE MIGHT BE VAMPIRES.
TH-THE PERSON I'M LOOKING FOR...

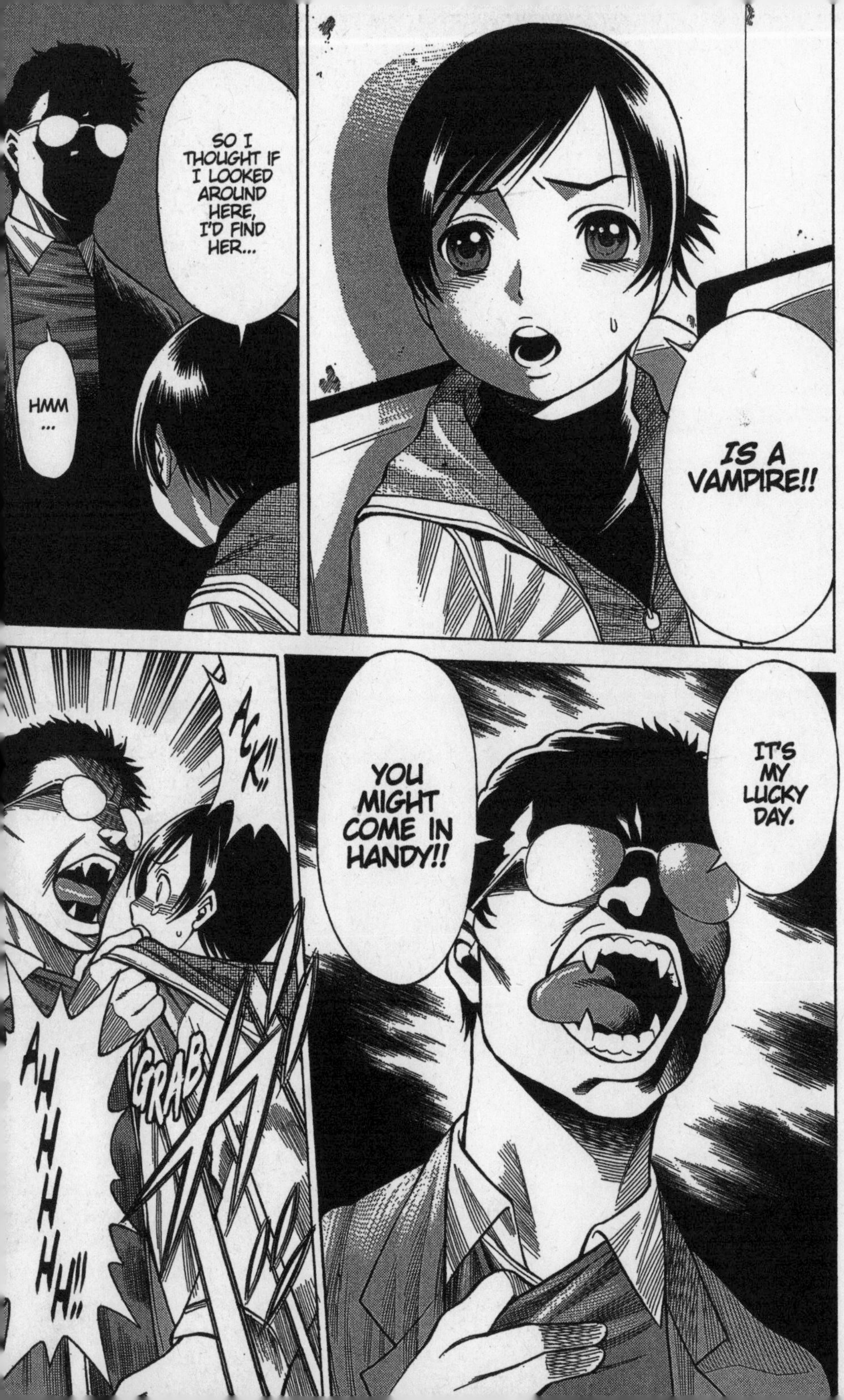
IS A VAMPIRE!!
SO I THOUGHT IF I LOOKED AROUND HERE, I'D FIND HER...
HMM...
IT'S MY LUCKY DAY.
YOU MIGHT COME IN HANDY!!
ACK!!
GRAB
AHHHHHH!!

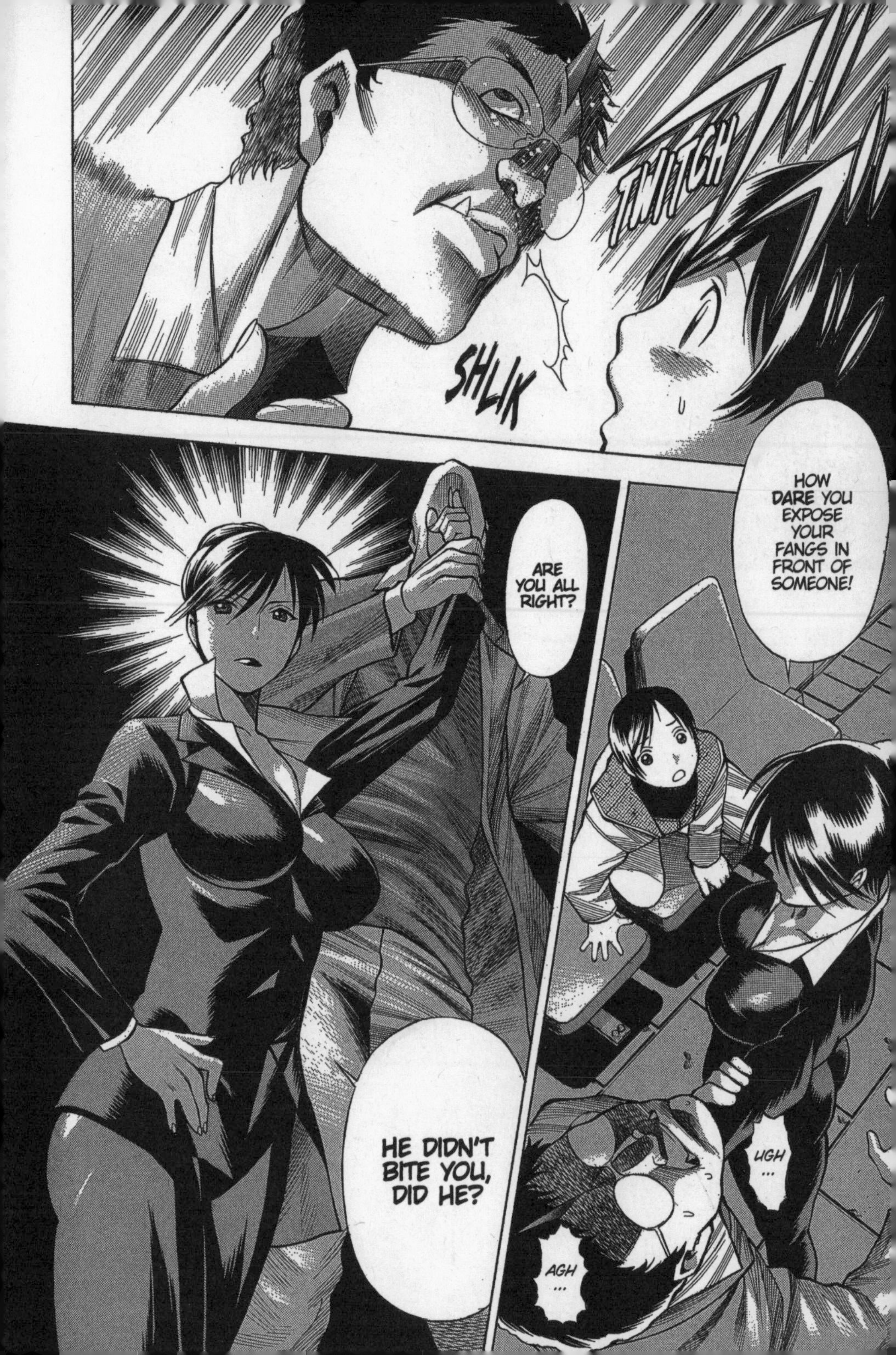
TWITCH
SHLIK
HOW DARE YOU EXPOSE YOUR FANGS IN FRONT OF SOMEONE!
UGH ...
AGH ...
ARE YOU ALL RIGHT?
HE DIDN'T BITE YOU, DID HE?

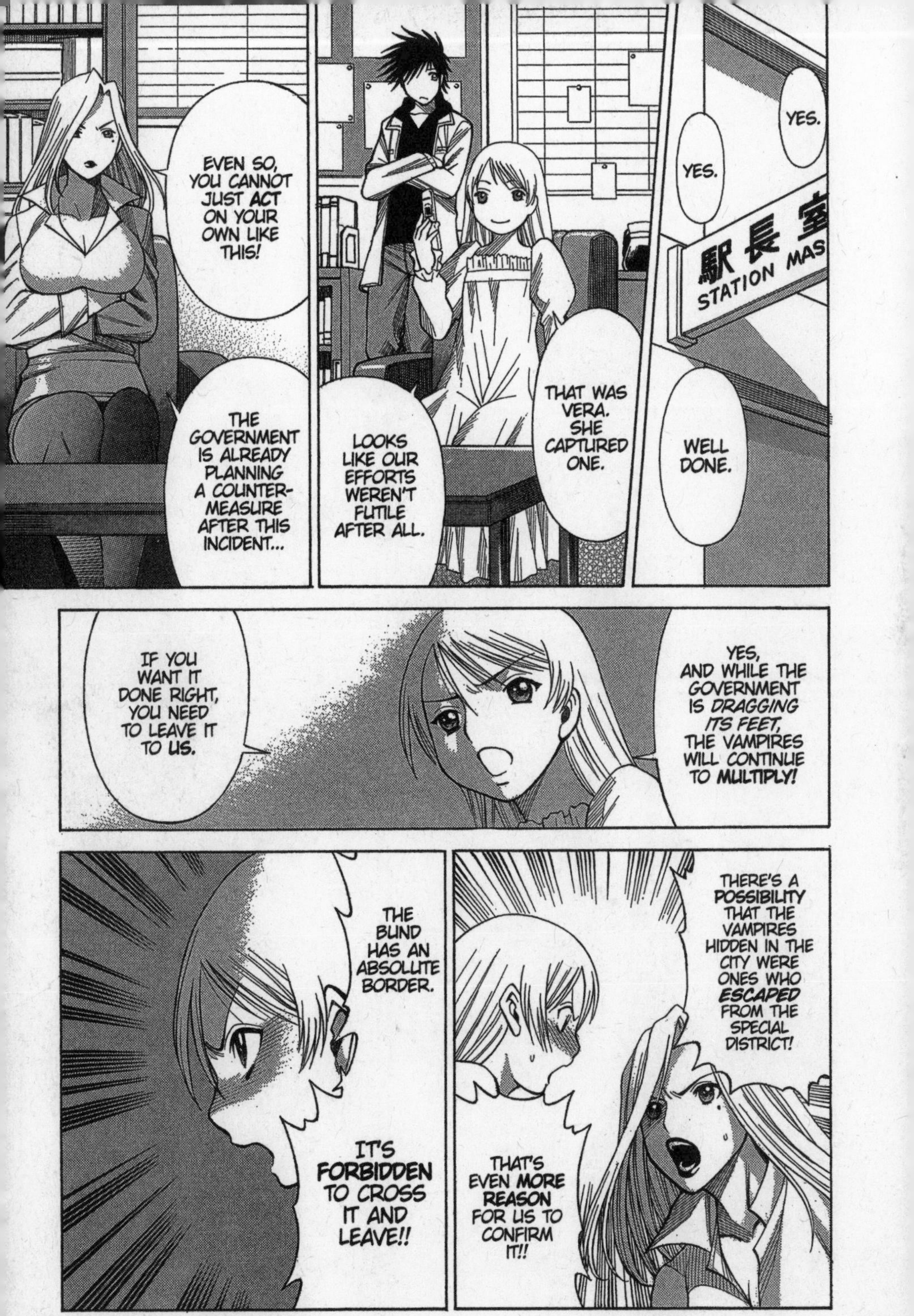
YES.
YES.
駅長室
STATION MAS
WELL DONE.
THAT WAS VERA. SHE CAPTURED ONE.
LOOKS LIKE OUR EFFORTS WEREN'T FUTILE AFTER ALL.
EVEN SO, YOU CANNOT JUST **ACT** ON YOUR OWN LIKE THIS!
THE GOVERNMENT IS ALREADY PLANNING A COUNTER-MEASURE AFTER THIS INCIDENT...
YES, AND WHILE THE GOVERNMENT IS *DRAGGING ITS FEET*, THE VAMPIRES WILL CONTINUE TO **MULTIPLY!**
IF YOU WANT IT DONE RIGHT, YOU NEED TO LEAVE IT TO **US.**
THERE'S A **POSSIBILITY** THAT THE VAMPIRES HIDDEN IN THE CITY WERE ONES WHO **ESCAPED** FROM THE SPECIAL DISTRICT!
THAT'S EVEN **MORE REASON** FOR US TO CONFIRM IT!!
THE BUND HAS AN ABSOLUTE BORDER.
IT'S **FORBIDDEN** TO CROSS IT AND LEAVE!!

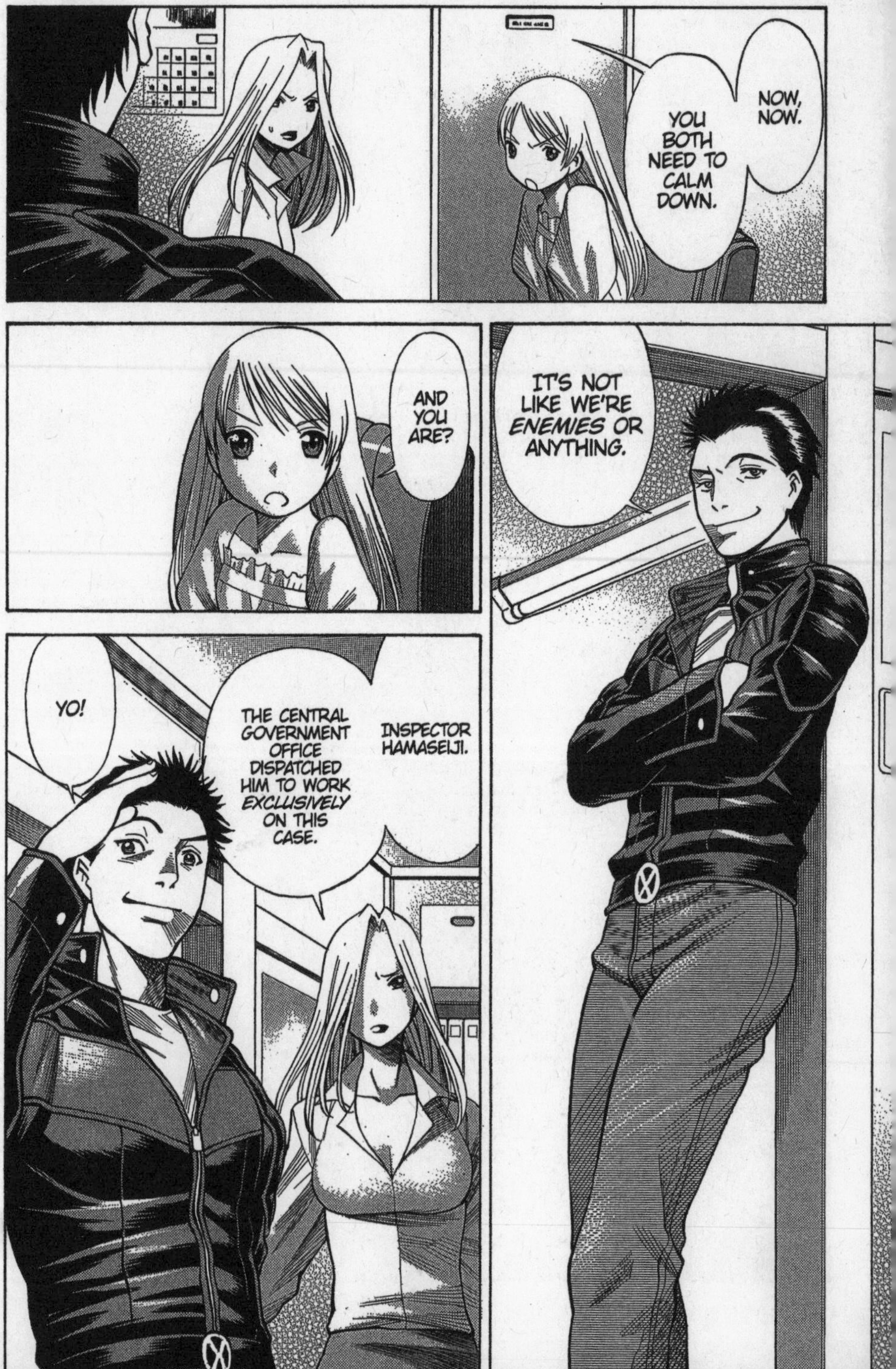
NOW, NOW.
YOU BOTH NEED TO CALM DOWN.
IT'S NOT LIKE WE'RE *ENEMIES* OR ANYTHING.
AND YOU ARE?
INSPECTOR HAMASEIJI.
THE CENTRAL GOVERNMENT OFFICE DISPATCHED HIM TO WORK *EXCLUSIVELY* ON THIS CASE.
YO!

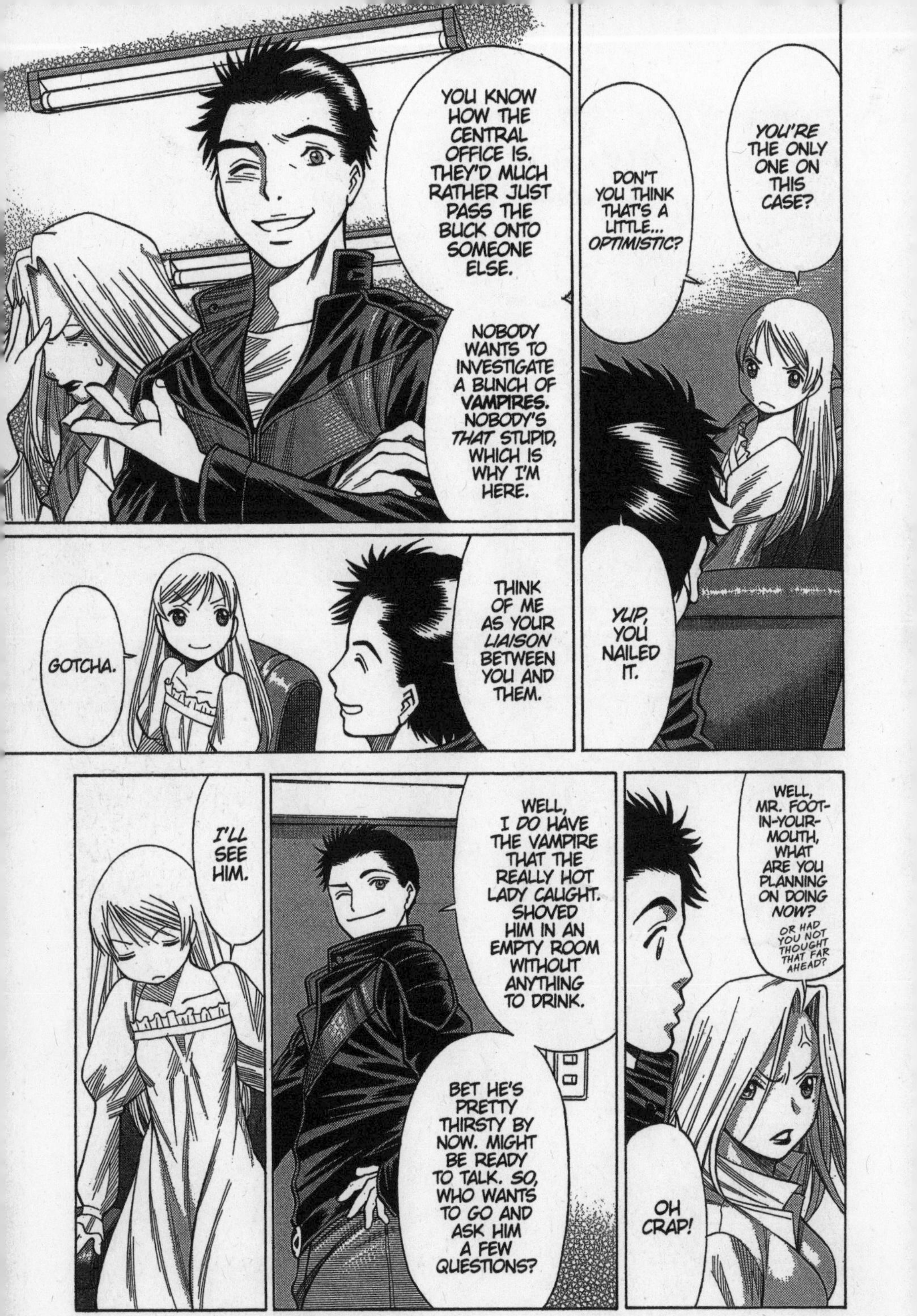
YOU'RE THE ONLY ONE ON THIS CASE?
DON'T YOU THINK THAT'S A LITTLE... OPTIMISTIC?
YUP, YOU NAILED IT.
YOU KNOW HOW THE CENTRAL OFFICE IS. THEY'D MUCH RATHER JUST PASS THE BUCK ONTO SOMEONE ELSE.
NOBODY WANTS TO INVESTIGATE A BUNCH OF VAMPIRES. NOBODY'S THAT STUPID, WHICH IS WHY I'M HERE.
THINK OF ME AS YOUR LIAISON BETWEEN YOU AND THEM.
GOTCHA.
WELL, MR. FOOT-IN-YOUR-MOUTH, WHAT ARE YOU PLANNING ON DOING NOW?
OR HAD YOU NOT THOUGHT THAT FAR AHEAD?
OH CRAP!
WELL, I DO HAVE THE VAMPIRE THAT THE REALLY HOT LADY CAUGHT. SHOVED HIM IN AN EMPTY ROOM WITHOUT ANYTHING TO DRINK.
BET HE'S PRETTY THIRSTY BY NOW. MIGHT BE READY TO TALK. SO, WHO WANTS TO GO AND ASK HIM A FEW QUESTIONS?
I'LL SEE HIM.

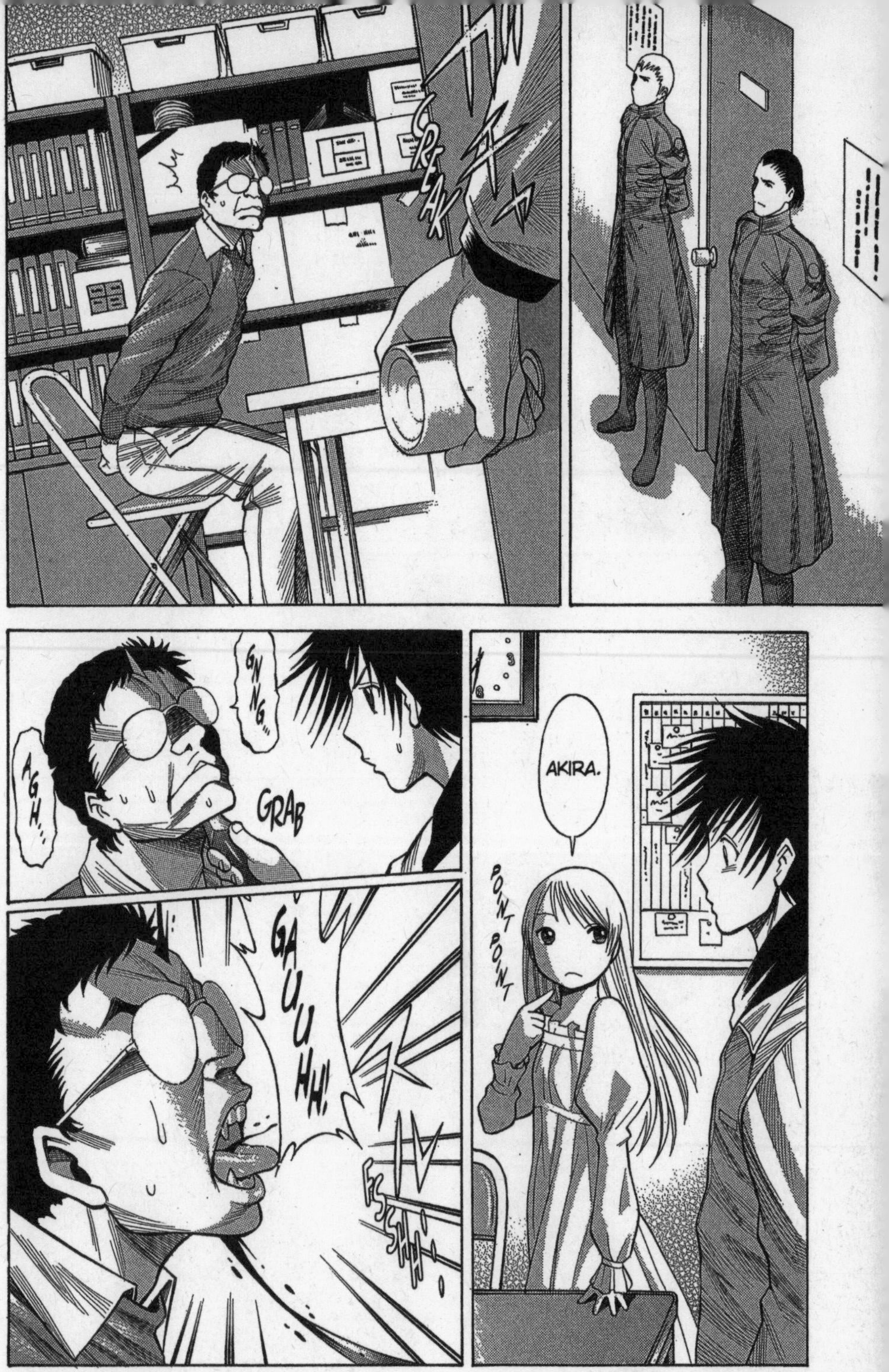
CREAK
AKIRA.
POINT POINT
GNNG...
GRAB
AGH...
GAUUUHH!
FSSHH!

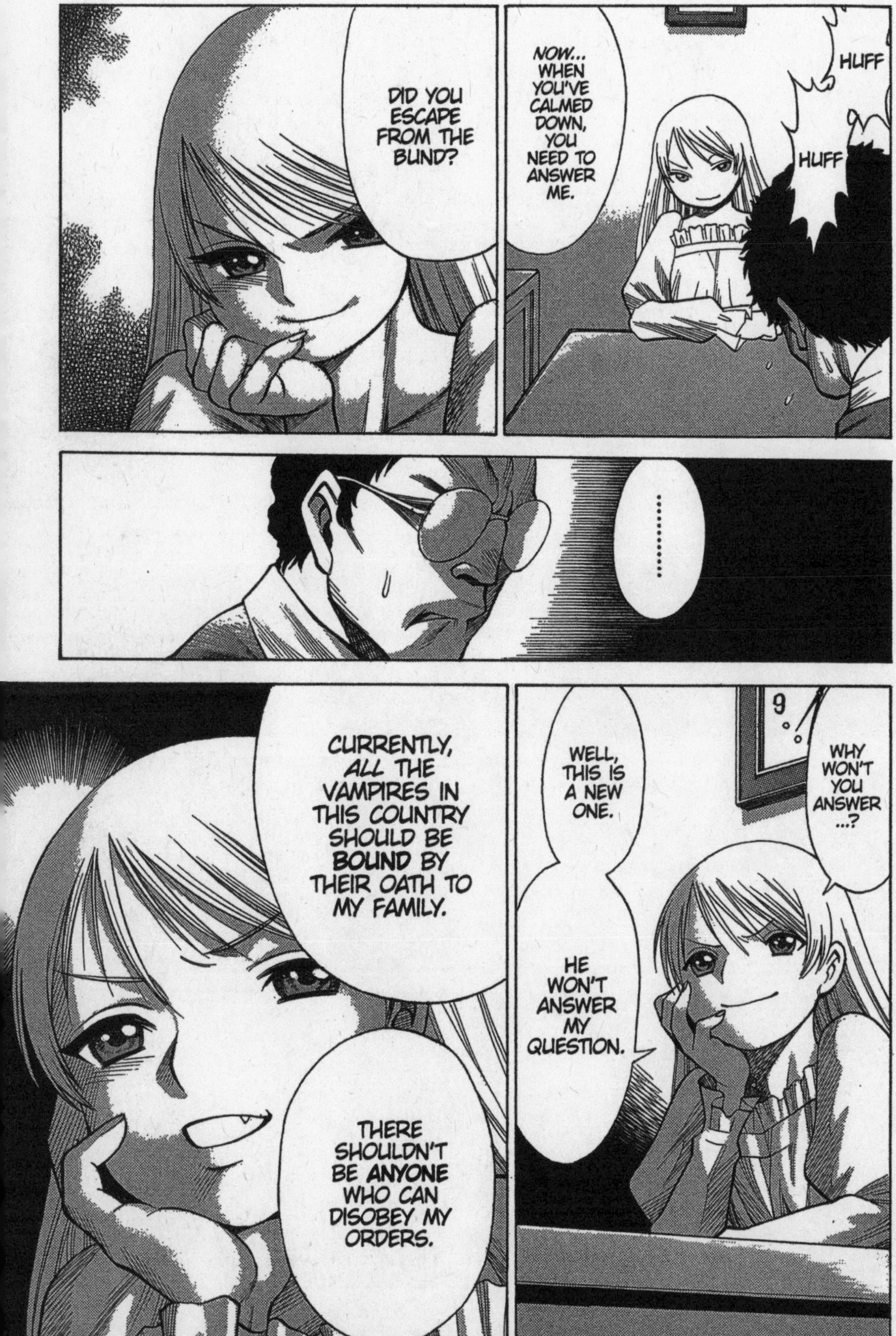
HUFF
HUFF
NOW... WHEN YOU'VE CALMED DOWN, YOU NEED TO ANSWER ME.
DID YOU ESCAPE FROM THE BUND?
....
WHY WON'T YOU ANSWER ...?
WELL, THIS IS A NEW ONE.
HE WON'T ANSWER MY QUESTION.
CURRENTLY, ALL THE VAMPIRES IN THIS COUNTRY SHOULD BE BOUND BY THEIR OATH TO MY FAMILY.
THERE SHOULDN'T BE ANYONE WHO CAN DISOBEY MY ORDERS.

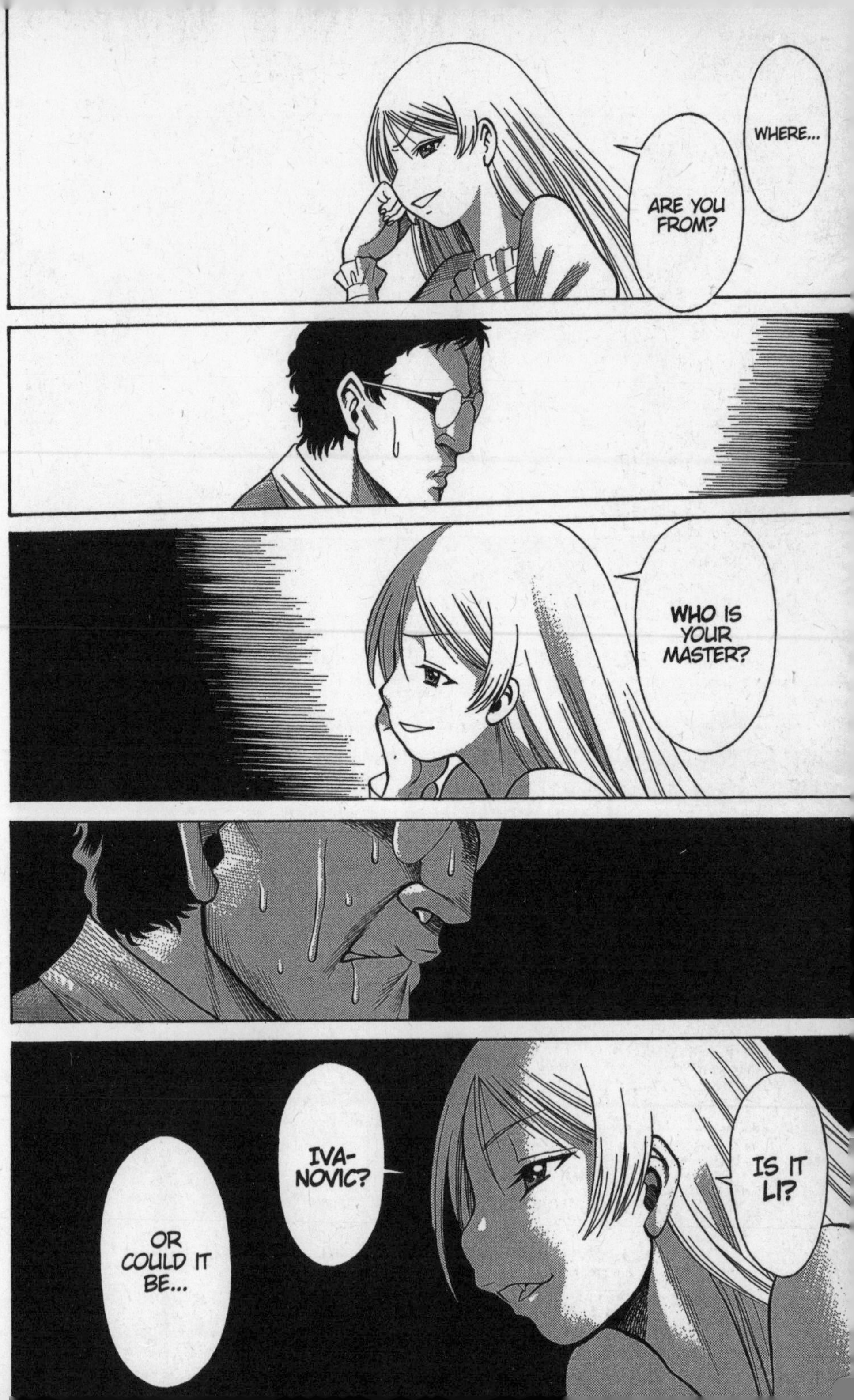
WHERE...
ARE YOU FROM?
WHO IS YOUR MASTER?
IS IT LI?
IVA-NOVIC?
OR COULD IT BE...

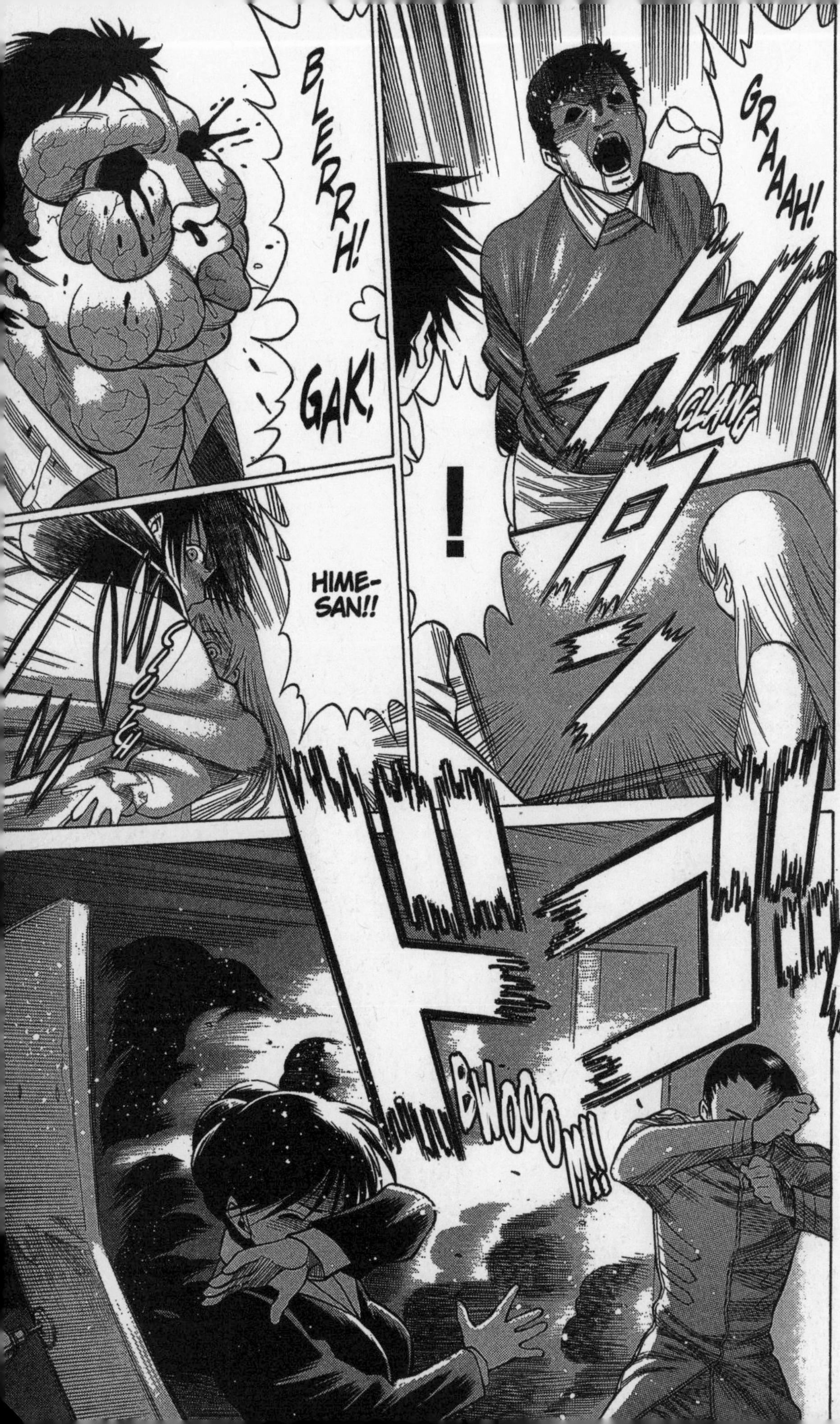
GRAAAH!
CLANG
!
BLERRH!
GAK!
HIME-SAN!!
BWOOOOM!!

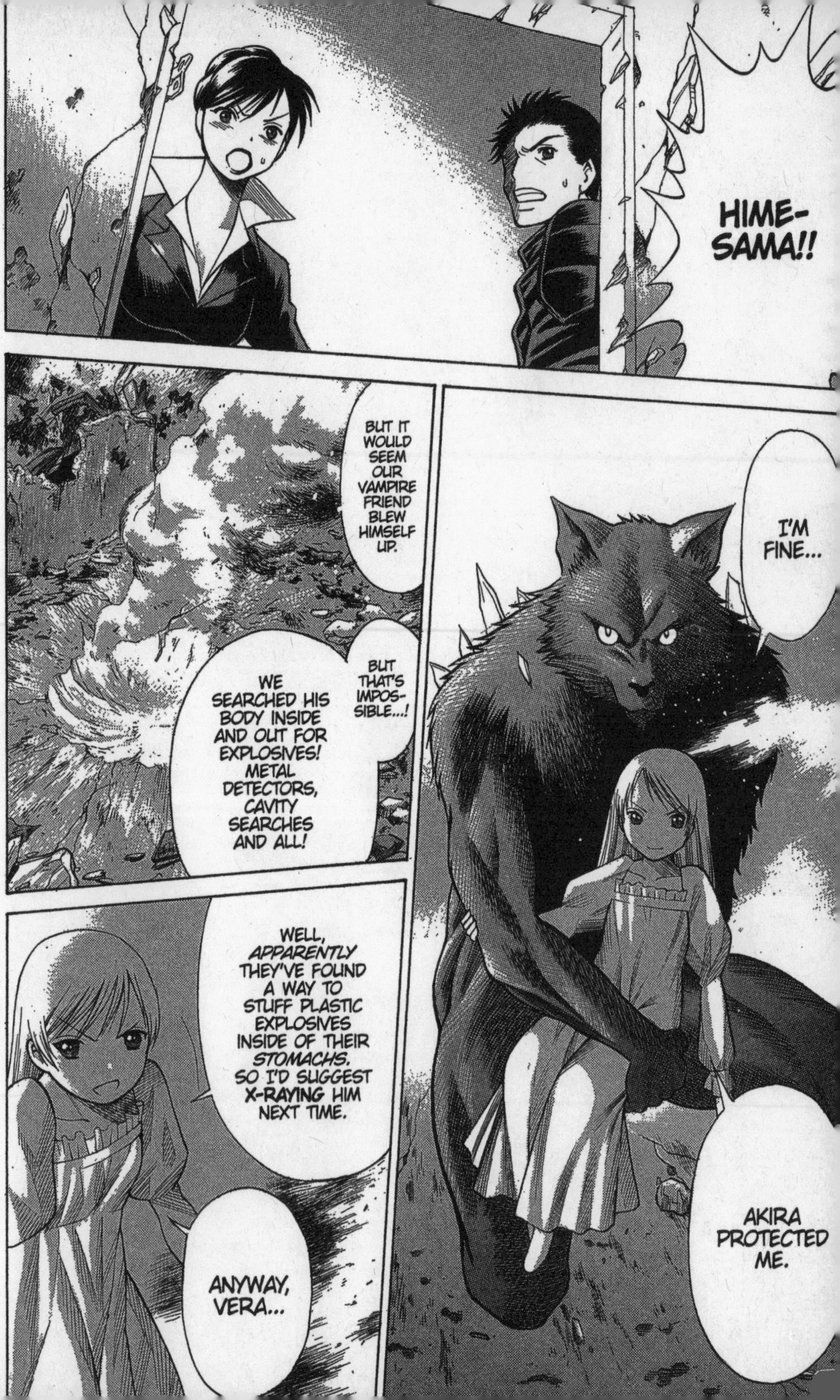
HIME-SAMA!!
I'M FINE...
AKIRA PROTECTED ME.
BUT IT WOULD SEEM OUR VAMPIRE FRIEND BLEW HIMSELF UP.
BUT THAT'S IMPOS-SIBLE...!
WE SEARCHED HIS BODY INSIDE AND OUT FOR EXPLOSIVES! METAL DETECTORS, CAVITY SEARCHES AND ALL!
WELL, APPARENTLY THEY'VE FOUND A WAY TO STUFF PLASTIC EXPLOSIVES INSIDE OF THEIR STOMACHS. SO I'D SUGGEST X-RAYING HIM NEXT TIME.
ANYWAY, VERA...

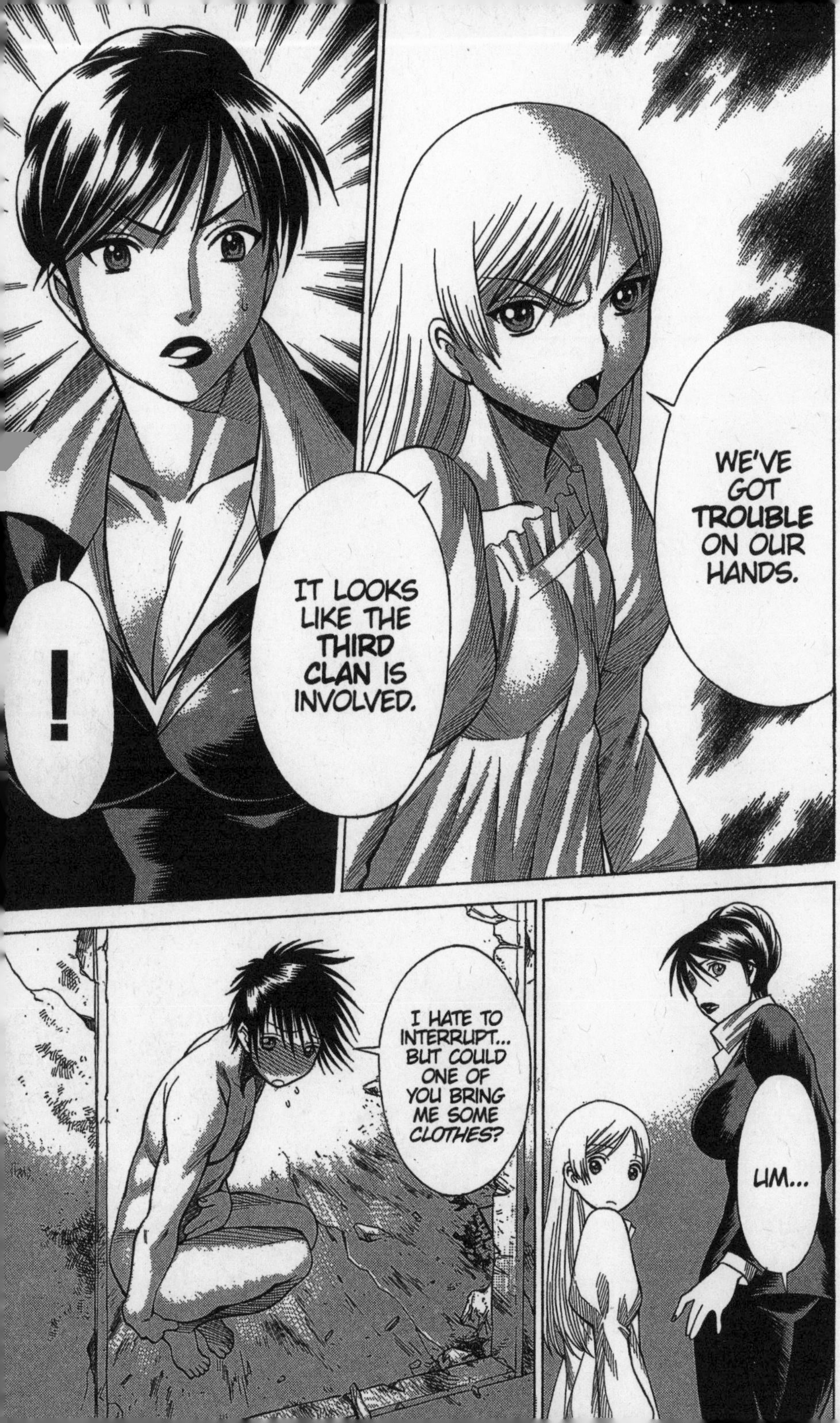
WE'VE GOT TROUBLE ON OUR HANDS.
IT LOOKS LIKE THE THIRD CLAN IS INVOLVED.
!
UM...
I HATE TO INTERRUPT... BUT COULD ONE OF YOU BRING ME SOME CLOTHES?

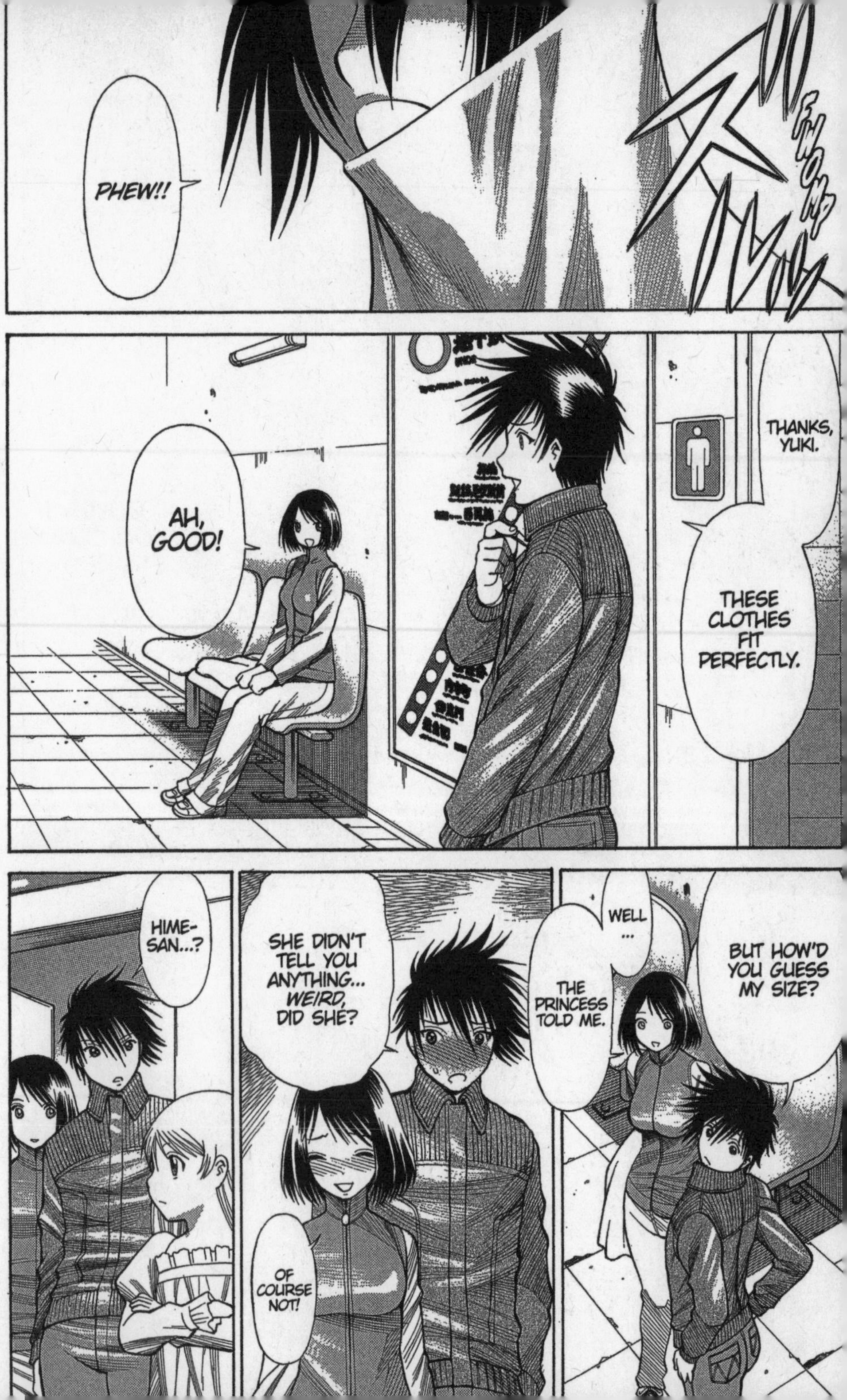
FWOMP
PHEW!!
THANKS, YUKI.
THESE CLOTHES FIT PERFECTLY.
AH, GOOD!
BUT HOW'D YOU GUESS MY SIZE?
WELL ...
THE PRINCESS TOLD ME.
SHE DIDN'T TELL YOU ANYTHING... *WEIRD*, DID SHE?
OF COURSE NOT!
HIME-SAN...?

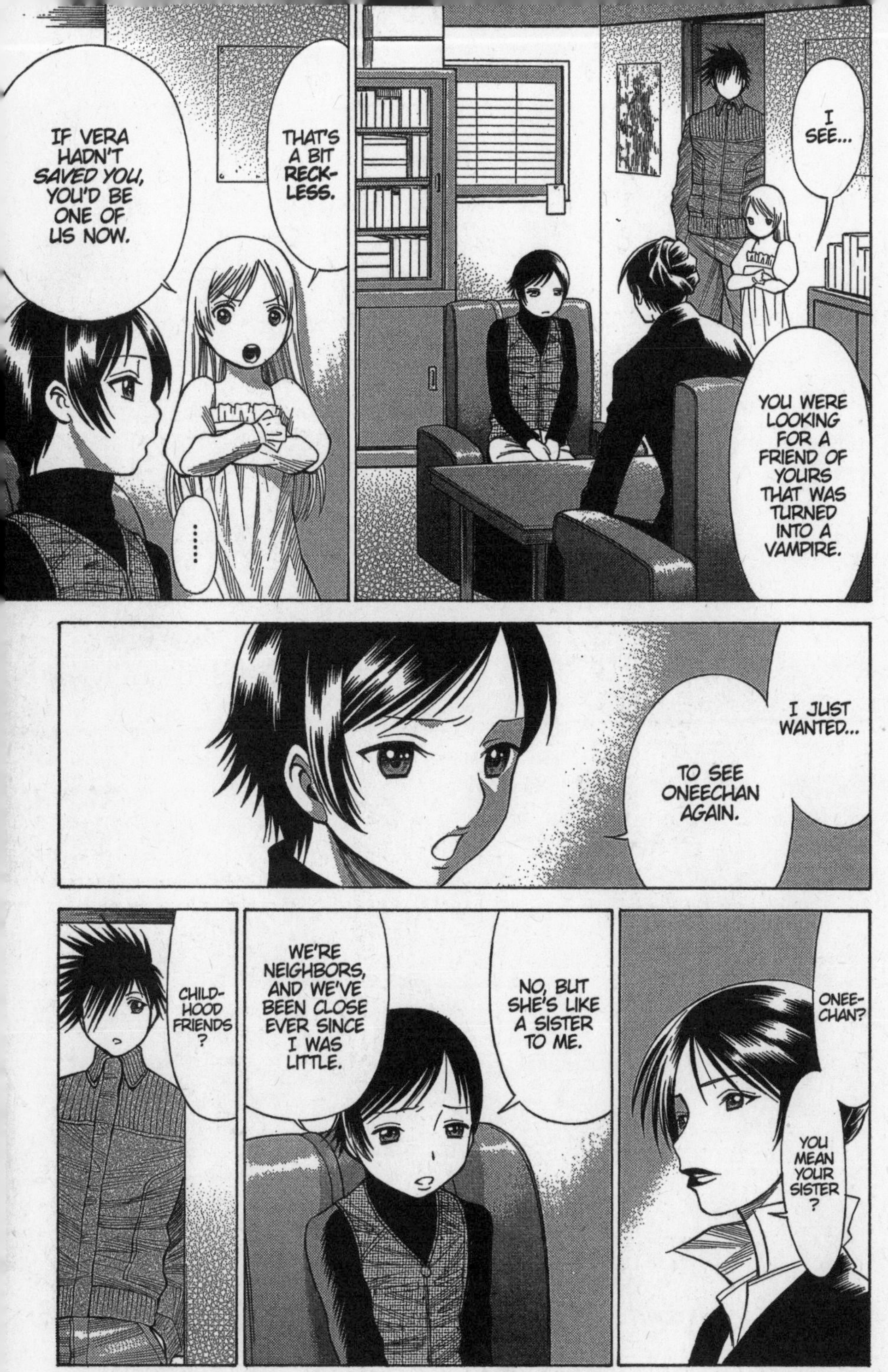
I SEE...
YOU WERE LOOKING FOR A FRIEND OF YOURS THAT WAS TURNED INTO A VAMPIRE.
THAT'S A BIT RECK-LESS.
IF VERA HADN'T SAVED YOU, YOU'D BE ONE OF US NOW.
......
I JUST WANTED...
TO SEE ONEECHAN AGAIN.
ONEE-CHAN?
YOU MEAN YOUR SISTER?
NO, BUT SHE'S LIKE A SISTER TO ME.
WE'RE NEIGHBORS, AND WE'VE BEEN CLOSE EVER SINCE I WAS LITTLE.
CHILD-HOOD FRIENDS?

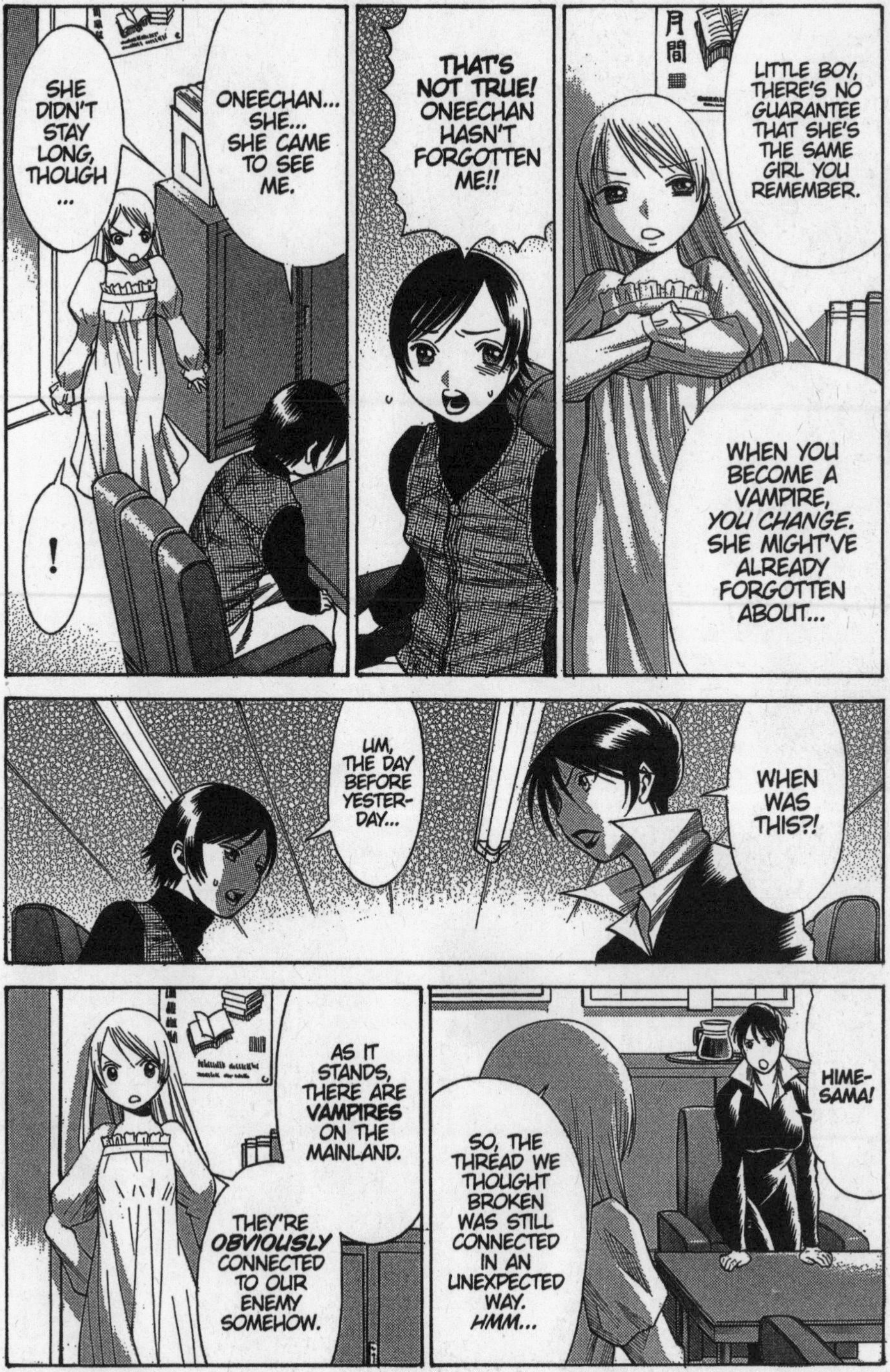
LITTLE BOY, THERE'S NO GUARANTEE THAT SHE'S THE SAME GIRL YOU REMEMBER.
WHEN YOU BECOME A VAMPIRE, YOU CHANGE. SHE MIGHT'VE ALREADY FORGOTTEN ABOUT...
THAT'S NOT TRUE! ONEECHAN HASN'T FORGOTTEN ME!!
ONEECHAN... SHE... SHE CAME TO SEE ME.
SHE DIDN'T STAY LONG, THOUGH...
!
WHEN WAS THIS?!
UM, THE DAY BEFORE YESTERDAY...
HIME-SAMA!
SO, THE THREAD WE THOUGHT BROKEN WAS STILL CONNECTED IN AN UNEXPECTED WAY. HMM...
AS IT STANDS, THERE ARE VAMPIRES ON THE MAINLAND.
THEY'RE OBVIOUSLY CONNECTED TO OUR ENEMY SOMEHOW.

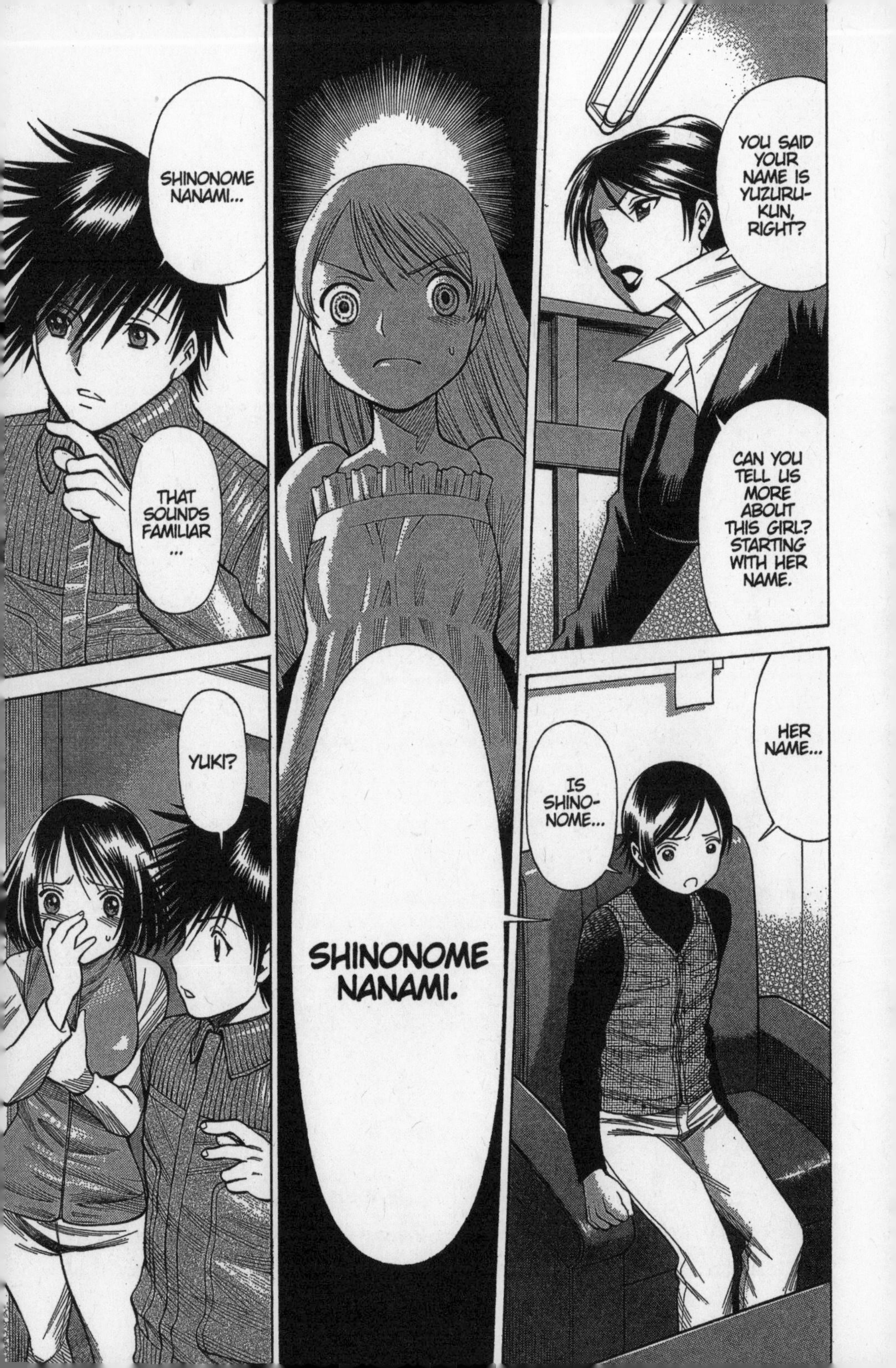
YOU SAID YOUR NAME IS YUZURU-KUN, RIGHT?
CAN YOU TELL US MORE ABOUT THIS GIRL? STARTING WITH HER NAME.
HER NAME...
IS SHINO-NOME...
SHINONOME NANAMI.
SHINONOME NANAMI...
THAT SOUNDS FAMILIAR ...
YUKI?

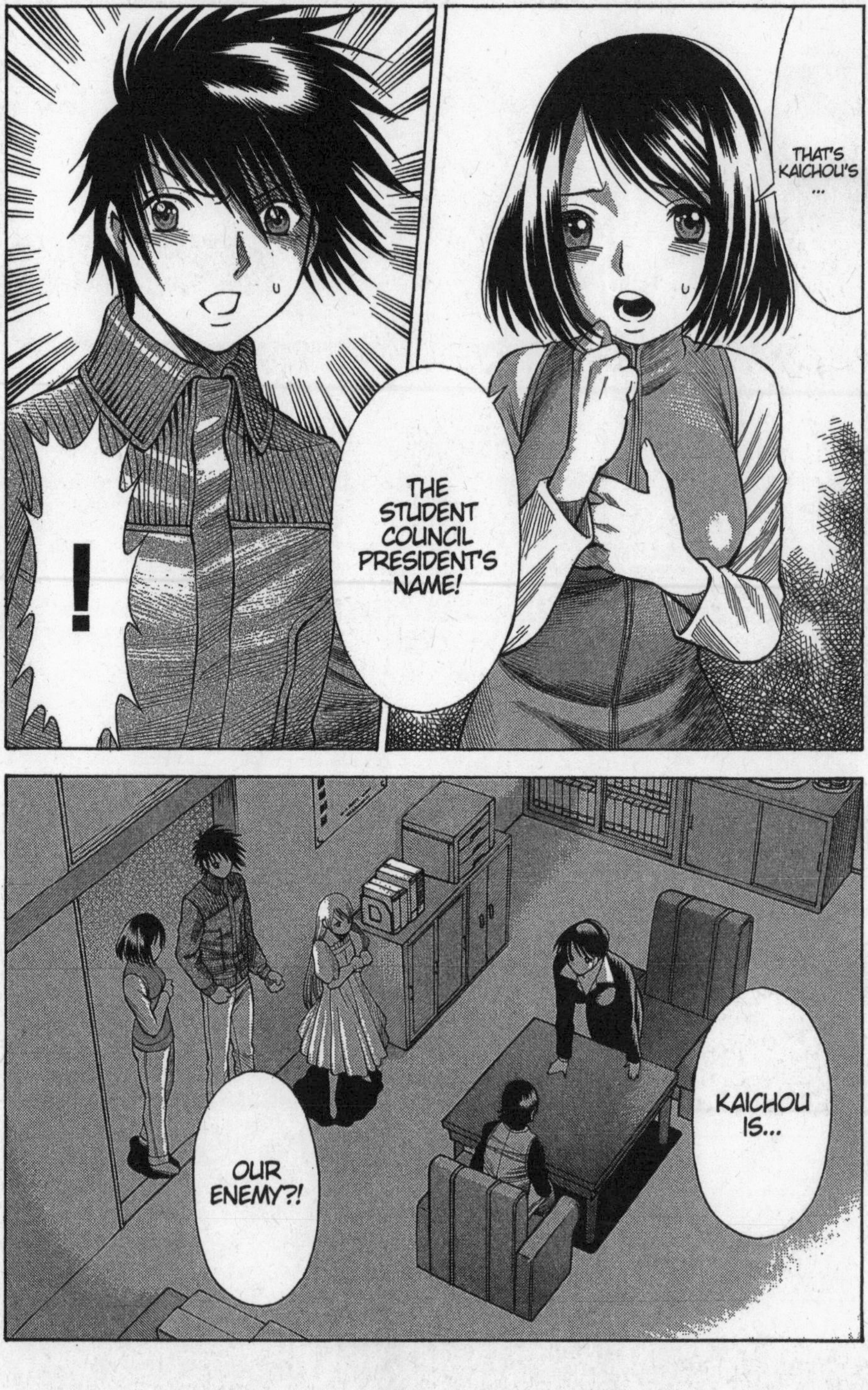
THAT'S KAICHOU'S ...
THE STUDENT COUNCIL PRESIDENT'S NAME!
!
KAICHOU IS...
OUR ENEMY?!

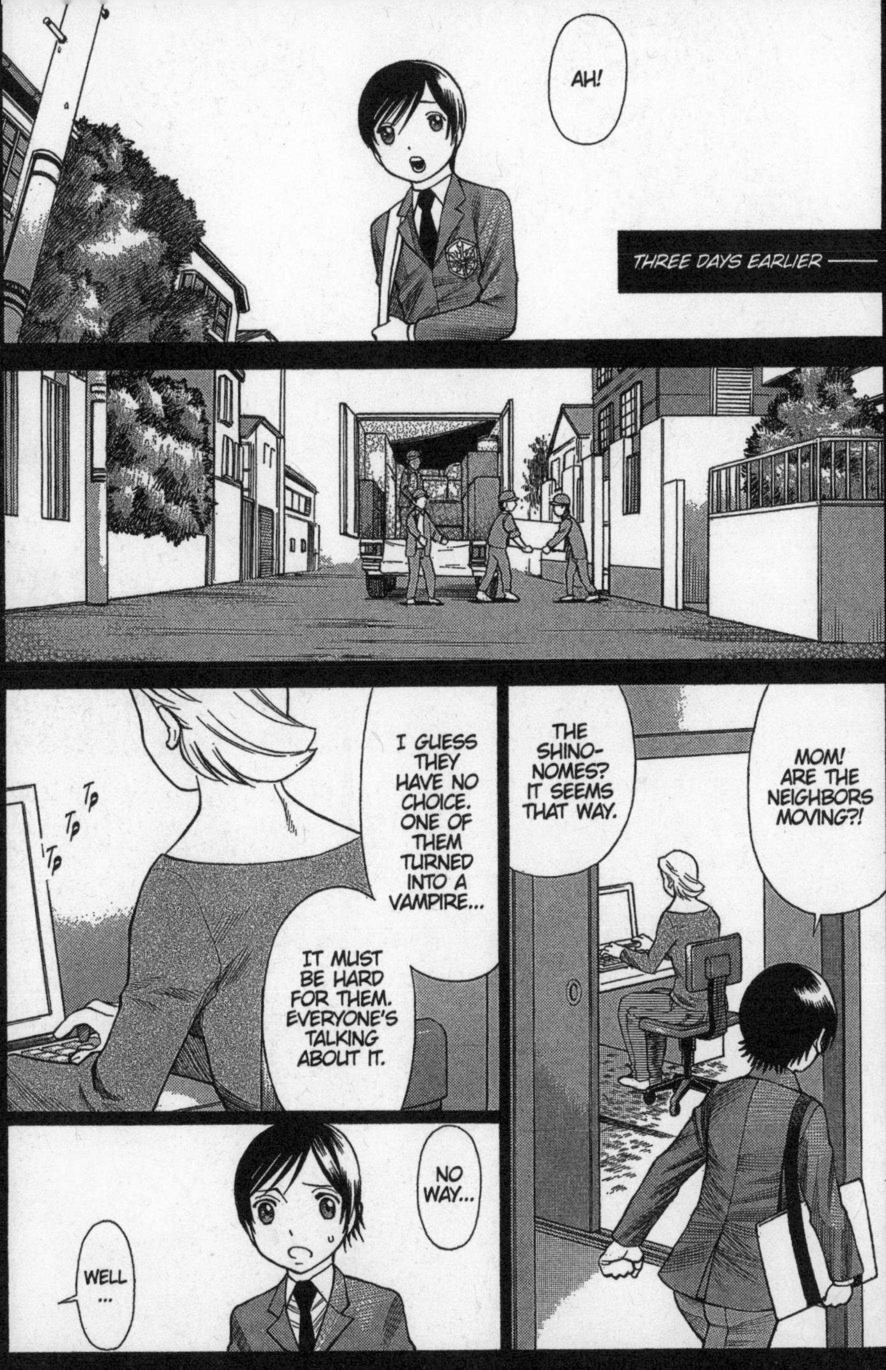
AH!
THREE DAYS EARLIER ——
MOM! ARE THE NEIGHBORS MOVING?!
THE SHINO-NOMES? IT SEEMS THAT WAY.
I GUESS THEY HAVE NO CHOICE. ONE OF THEM TURNED INTO A VAMPIRE...
IT MUST BE HARD FOR THEM. EVERYONE'S TALKING ABOUT IT.
Tp Tp Tp
NO WAY...
WELL ...

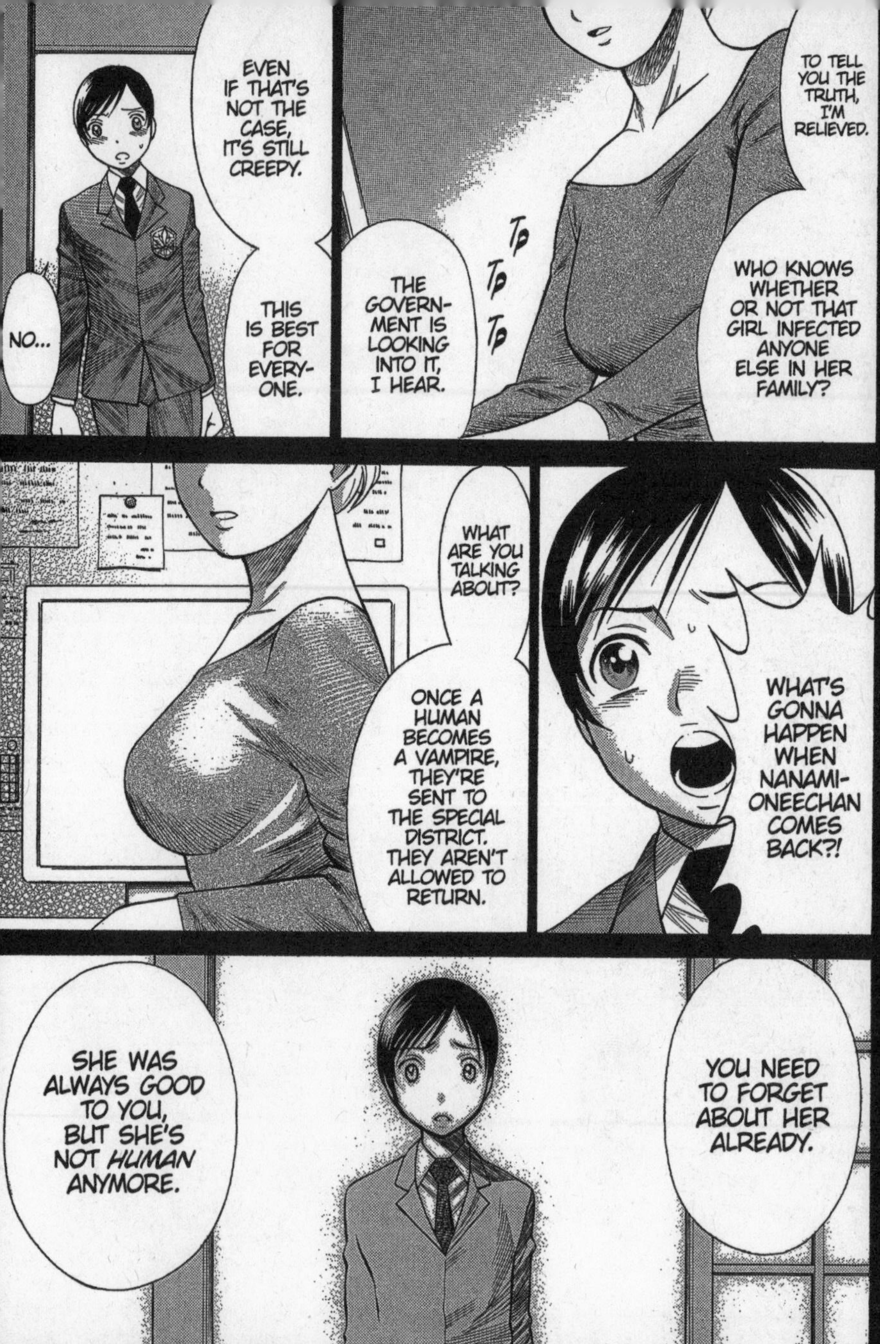
TO TELL YOU THE TRUTH, I'M RELIEVED.
WHO KNOWS WHETHER OR NOT THAT GIRL INFECTED ANYONE ELSE IN HER FAMILY?
Tp Tp Tp
THE GOVERNMENT IS LOOKING INTO IT, I HEAR.
EVEN IF THAT'S NOT THE CASE, IT'S STILL CREEPY.
THIS IS BEST FOR EVERYONE.
NO...
WHAT'S GONNA HAPPEN WHEN NANAMI-ONEECHAN COMES BACK?!
WHAT ARE YOU TALKING ABOUT?
ONCE A HUMAN BECOMES A VAMPIRE, THEY'RE SENT TO THE SPECIAL DISTRICT. THEY AREN'T ALLOWED TO RETURN.
YOU NEED TO FORGET ABOUT HER ALREADY.
SHE WAS ALWAYS GOOD TO YOU, BUT SHE'S NOT *HUMAN* ANYMORE.

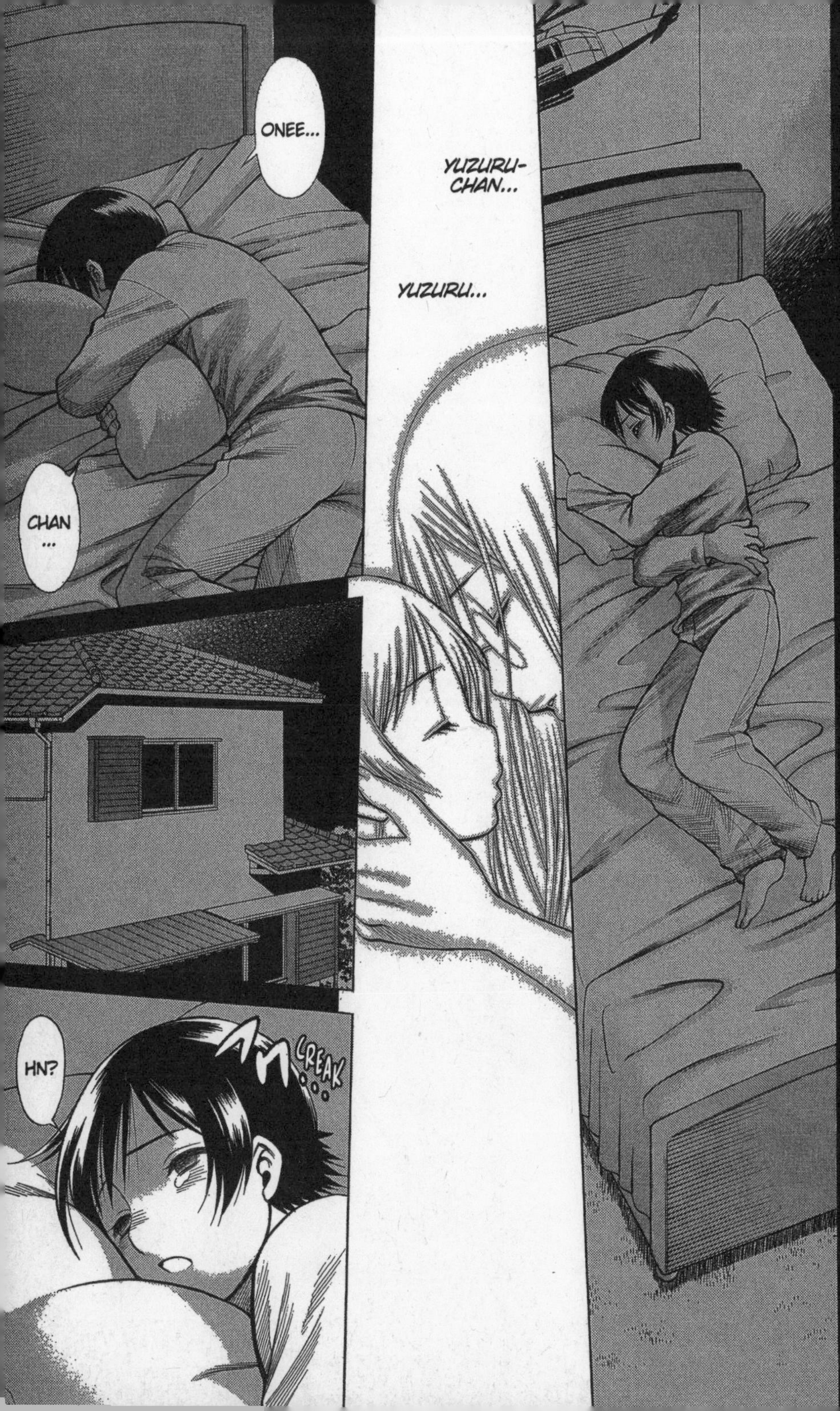
YUZURU-CHAN...
YUZURU...
ONEE...
CHAN...
HN?
CREAK...

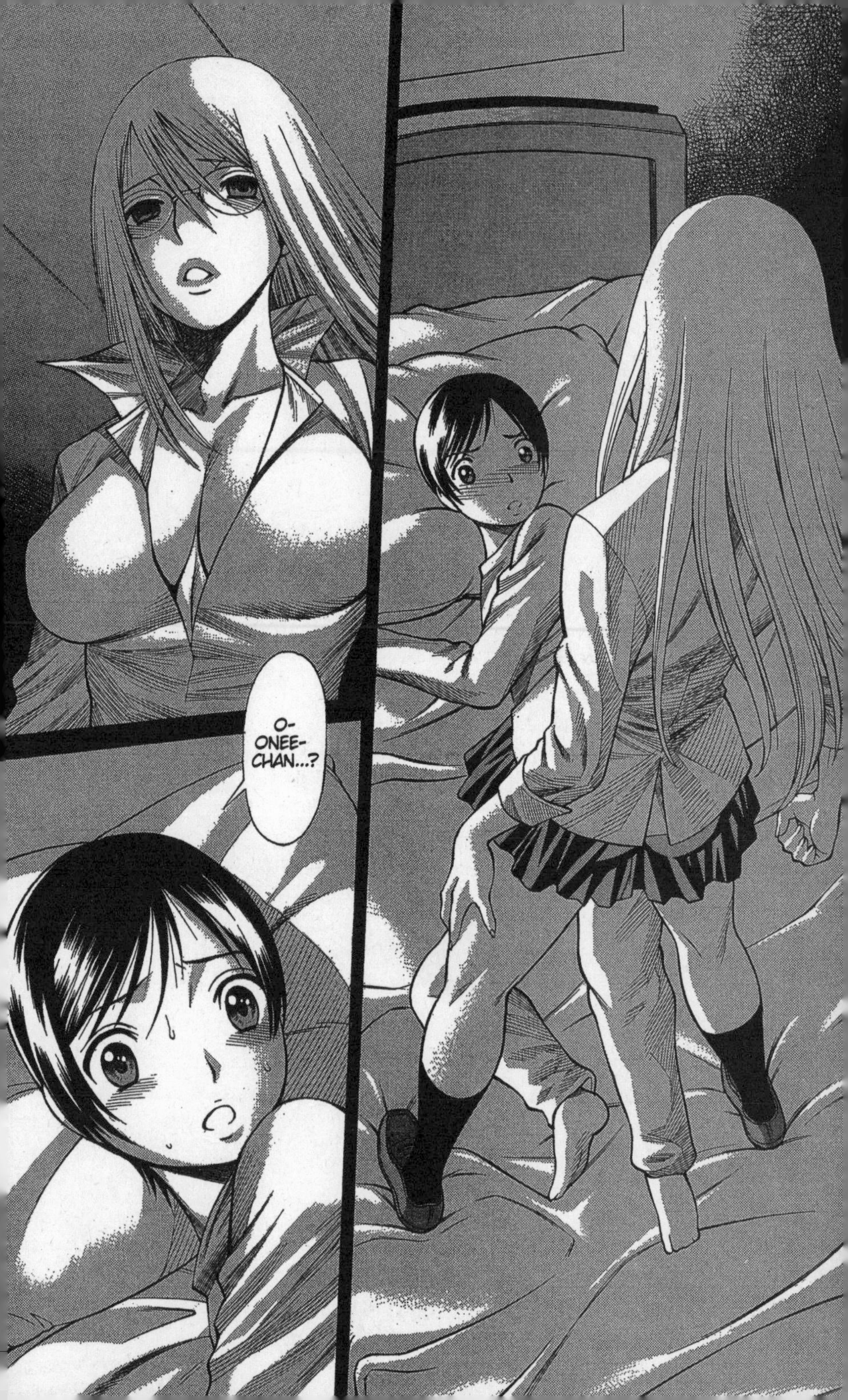
O-ONEE-CHAN...?

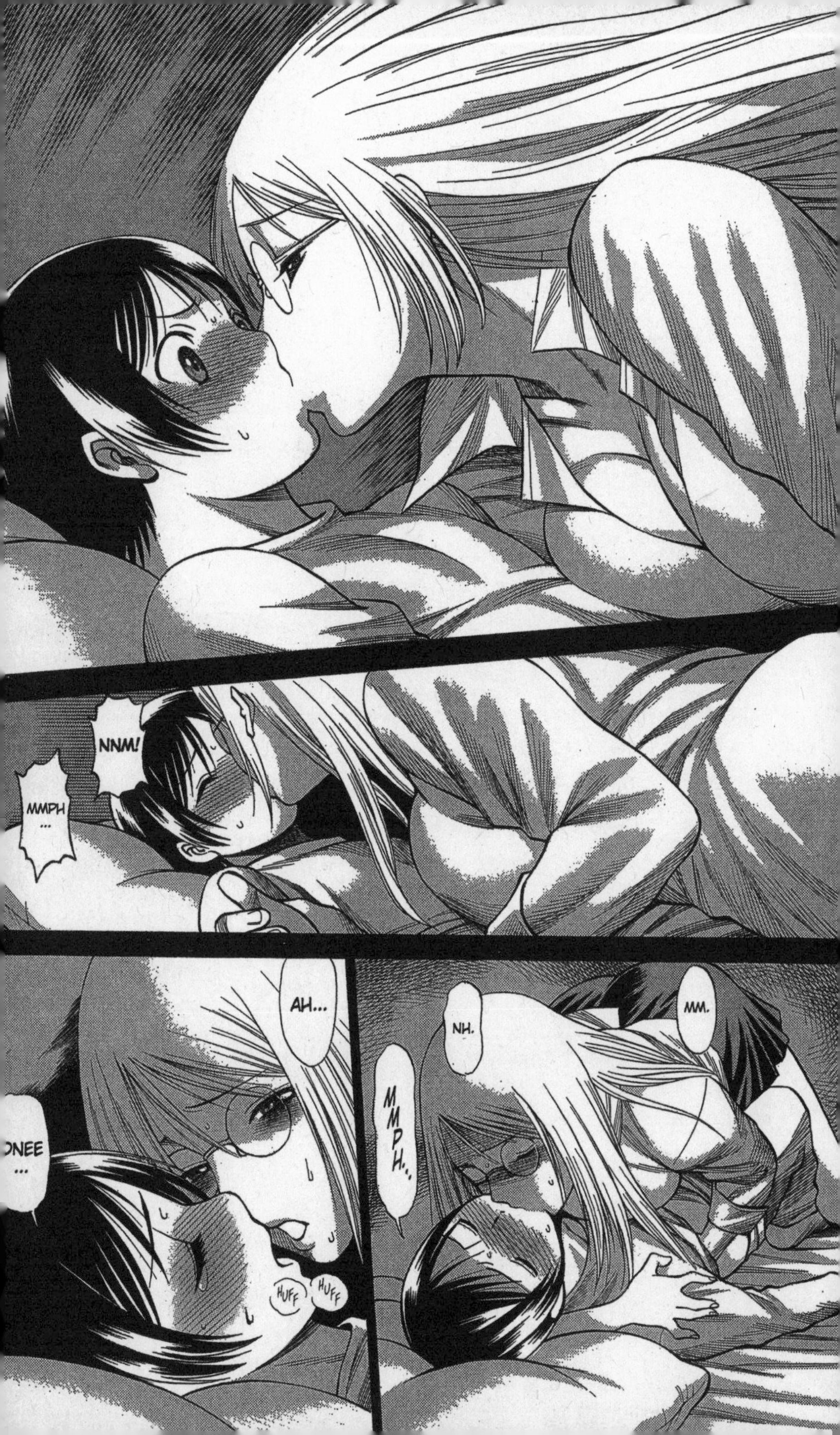
NNM!
MMPH...
MM.
NH.
MMPH...
AH...
ONEE...
HUFF
HUFF

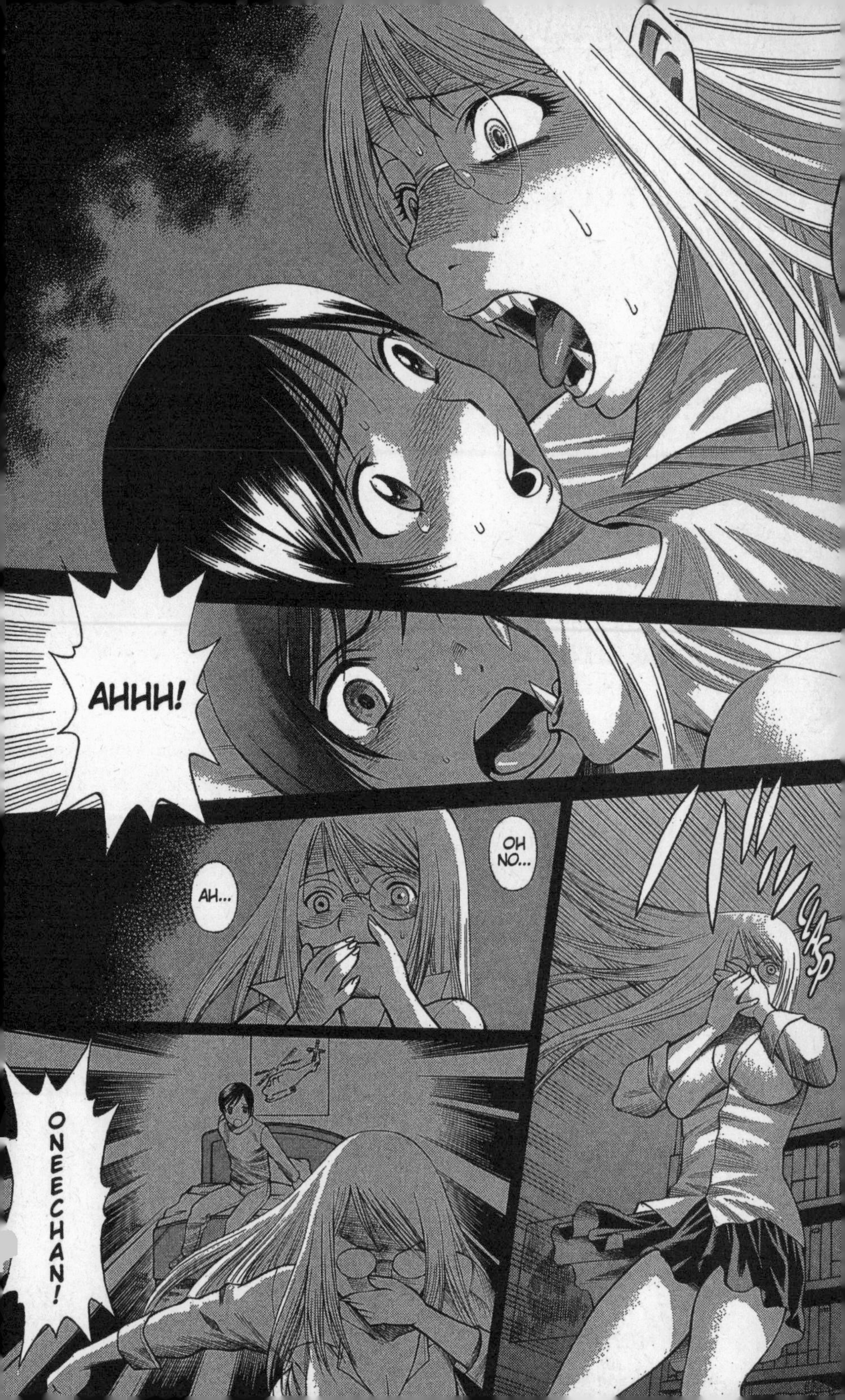
AHHH!
GASP
OH NO...
AH...
ONEECHAN!

Chapter 15: Children of the Night

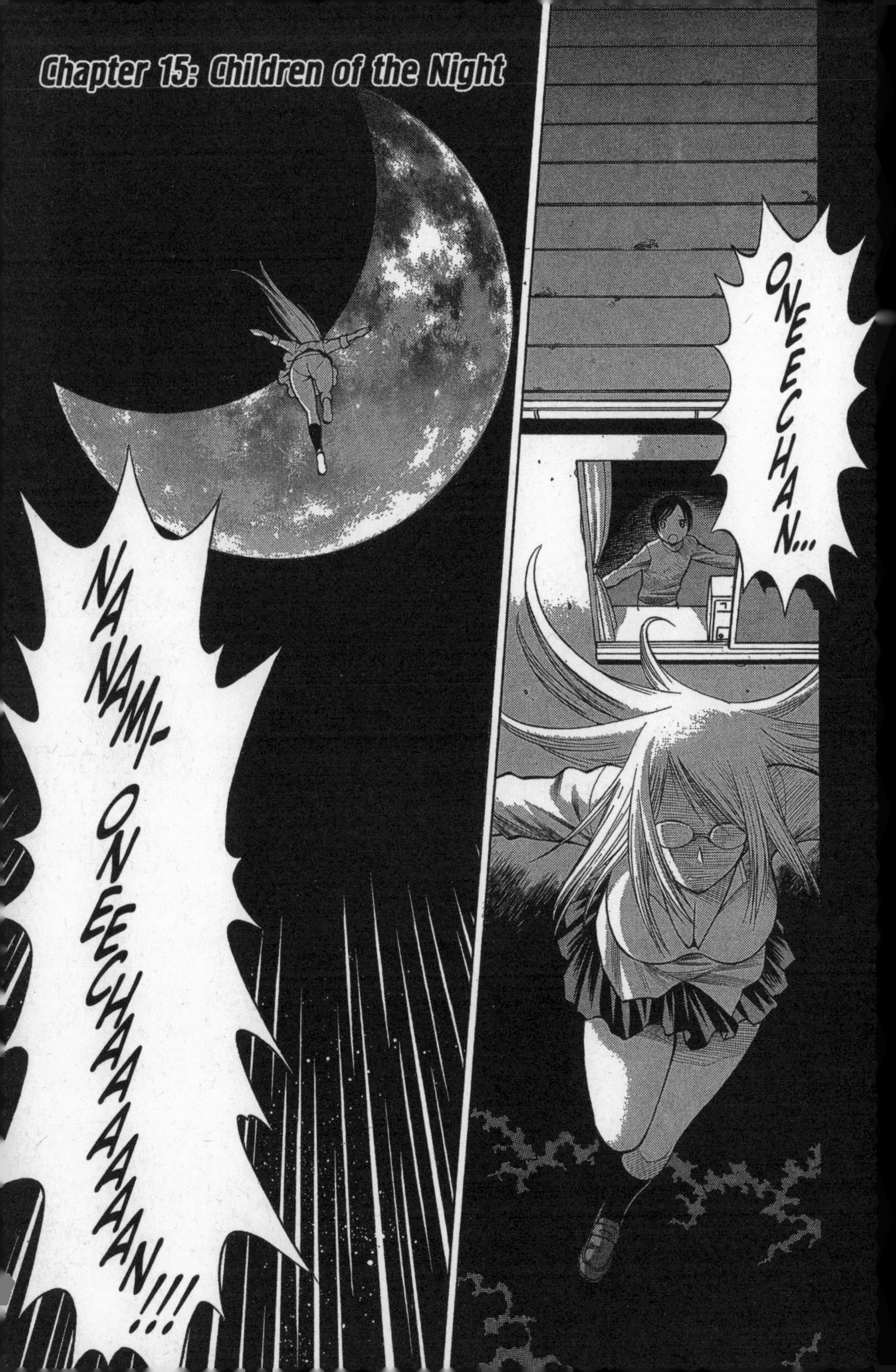

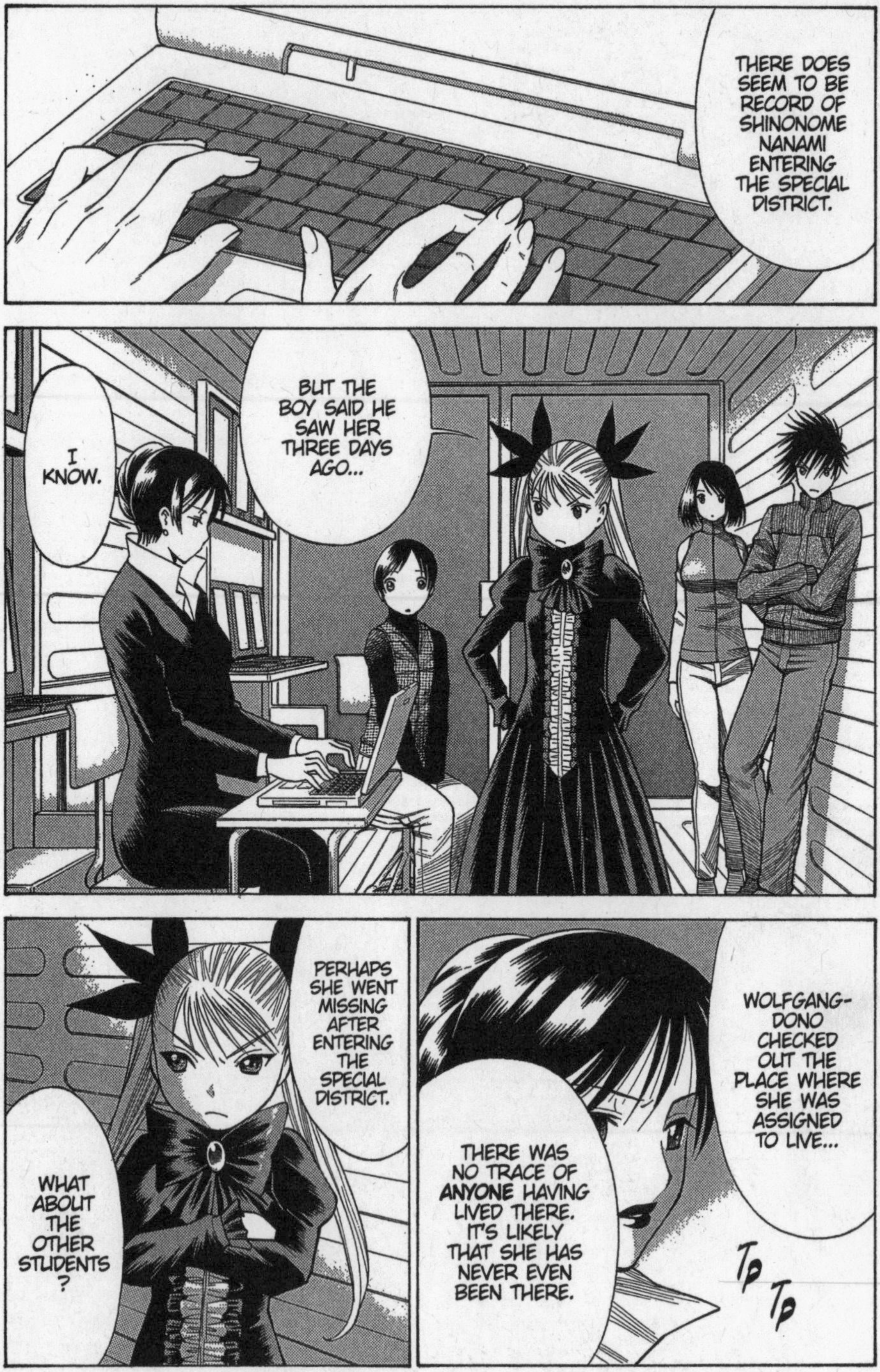
THERE DOES SEEM TO BE RECORD OF SHINONOME NANAMI ENTERING THE SPECIAL DISTRICT.
BUT THE BOY SAID HE SAW HER THREE DAYS AGO...
I KNOW.
WOLFGANG-DONO CHECKED OUT THE PLACE WHERE SHE WAS ASSIGNED TO LIVE...
THERE WAS NO TRACE OF ANYONE HAVING LIVED THERE. IT'S LIKELY THAT SHE HAS NEVER EVEN BEEN THERE.
Tp Tp
PERHAPS SHE WENT MISSING AFTER ENTERING THE SPECIAL DISTRICT.
WHAT ABOUT THE OTHER STUDENTS?

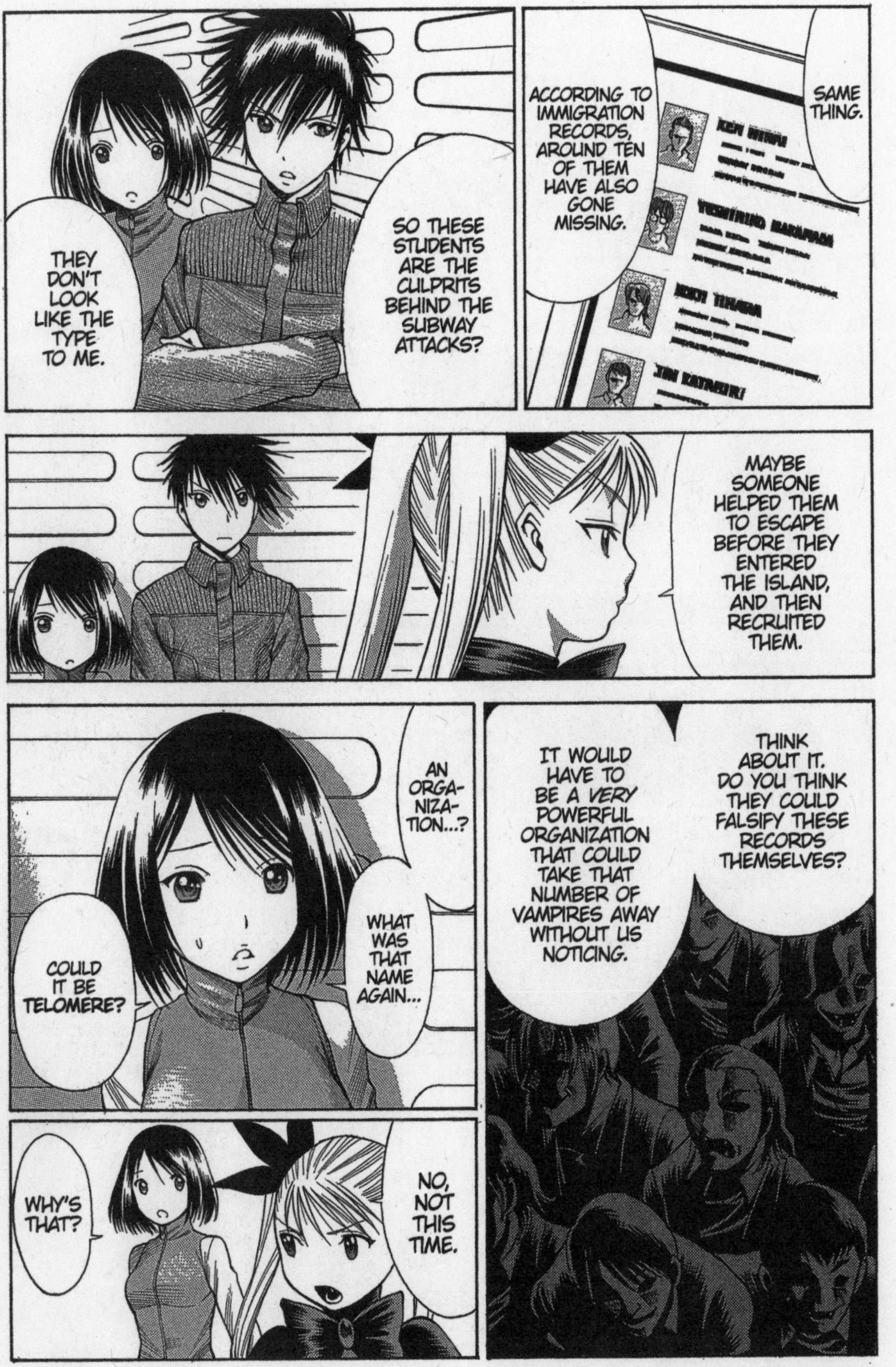
SAME THING.
ACCORDING TO IMMIGRATION RECORDS, AROUND TEN OF THEM HAVE ALSO GONE MISSING.
SO THESE STUDENTS ARE THE CULPRITS BEHIND THE SUBWAY ATTACKS?
THEY DON'T LOOK LIKE THE TYPE TO ME.
MAYBE SOMEONE HELPED THEM TO ESCAPE BEFORE THEY ENTERED THE ISLAND, AND THEN RECRUITED THEM.
THINK ABOUT IT. DO YOU THINK THEY COULD FALSIFY THESE RECORDS THEMSELVES?
IT WOULD HAVE TO BE A *VERY* POWERFUL ORGANIZATION THAT COULD TAKE THAT NUMBER OF VAMPIRES AWAY WITHOUT US NOTICING.
AN ORGA-NIZA-TION...?
WHAT WAS THAT NAME AGAIN...
COULD IT BE TELOMERE?
NO, NOT THIS TIME.
WHY'S THAT?

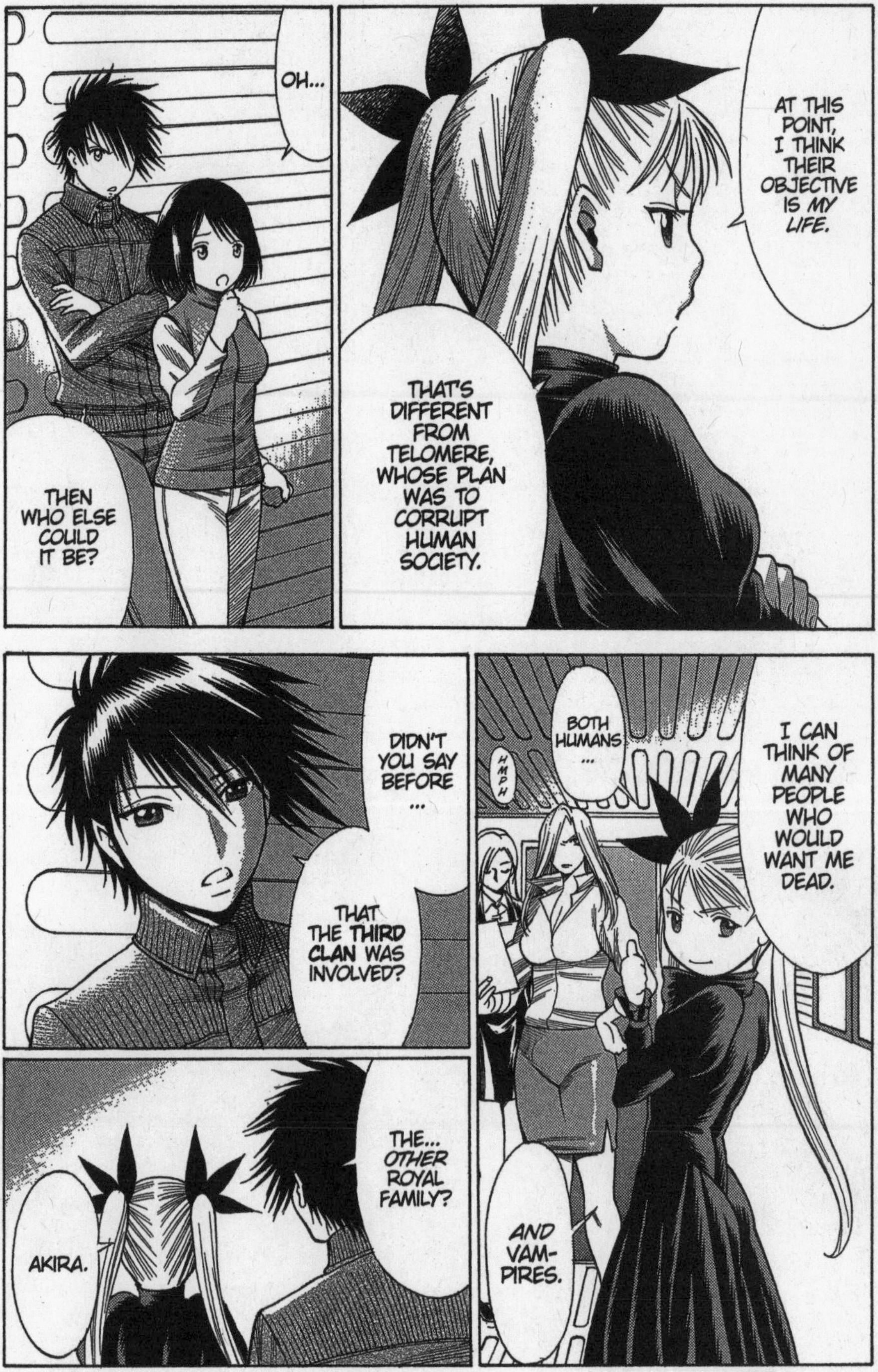
AT THIS POINT, I THINK THEIR OBJECTIVE IS *MY* LIFE.
THAT'S DIFFERENT FROM TELOMERE, WHOSE PLAN WAS TO CORRUPT HUMAN SOCIETY.
OH...
THEN WHO ELSE COULD IT BE?
I CAN THINK OF MANY PEOPLE WHO WOULD WANT ME DEAD.
BOTH HUMANS ...
HMPH
AND VAMPIRES.
DIDN'T YOU SAY BEFORE ...
THAT THE **THIRD CLAN** WAS INVOLVED?
THE... *OTHER* ROYAL FAMILY?
AKIRA.

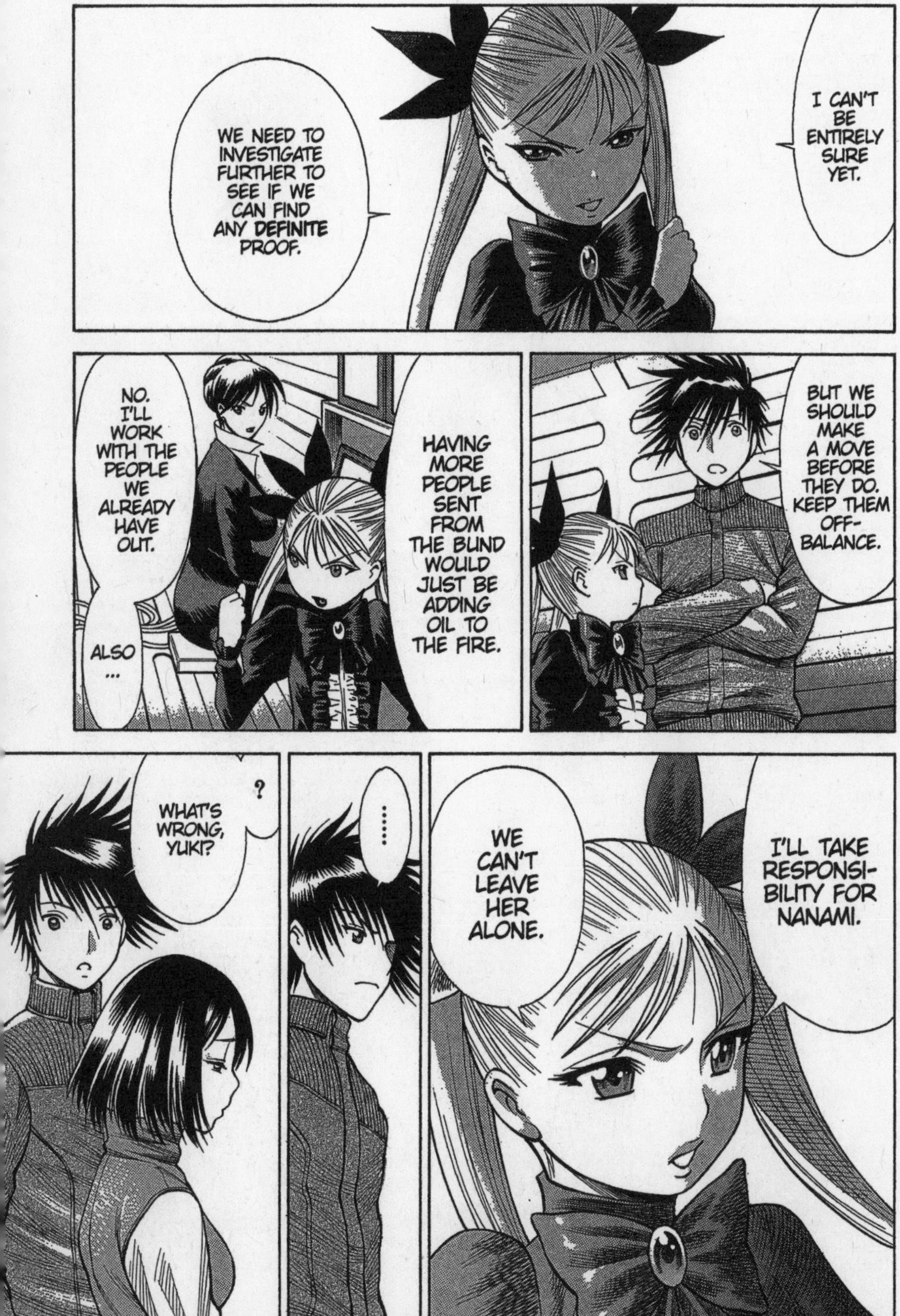
I CAN'T BE ENTIRELY SURE YET.
WE NEED TO INVESTIGATE FURTHER TO SEE IF WE CAN FIND ANY DEFINITE PROOF.
BUT WE SHOULD MAKE A MOVE BEFORE THEY DO. KEEP THEM OFF-BALANCE.
HAVING MORE PEOPLE SENT FROM THE BUND WOULD JUST BE ADDING OIL TO THE FIRE.
NO. I'LL WORK WITH THE PEOPLE WE ALREADY HAVE OUT.
ALSO ...
I'LL TAKE RESPONSI-BILITY FOR NANAMI.
WE CAN'T LEAVE HER ALONE.
......
?
WHAT'S WRONG, YUKI?

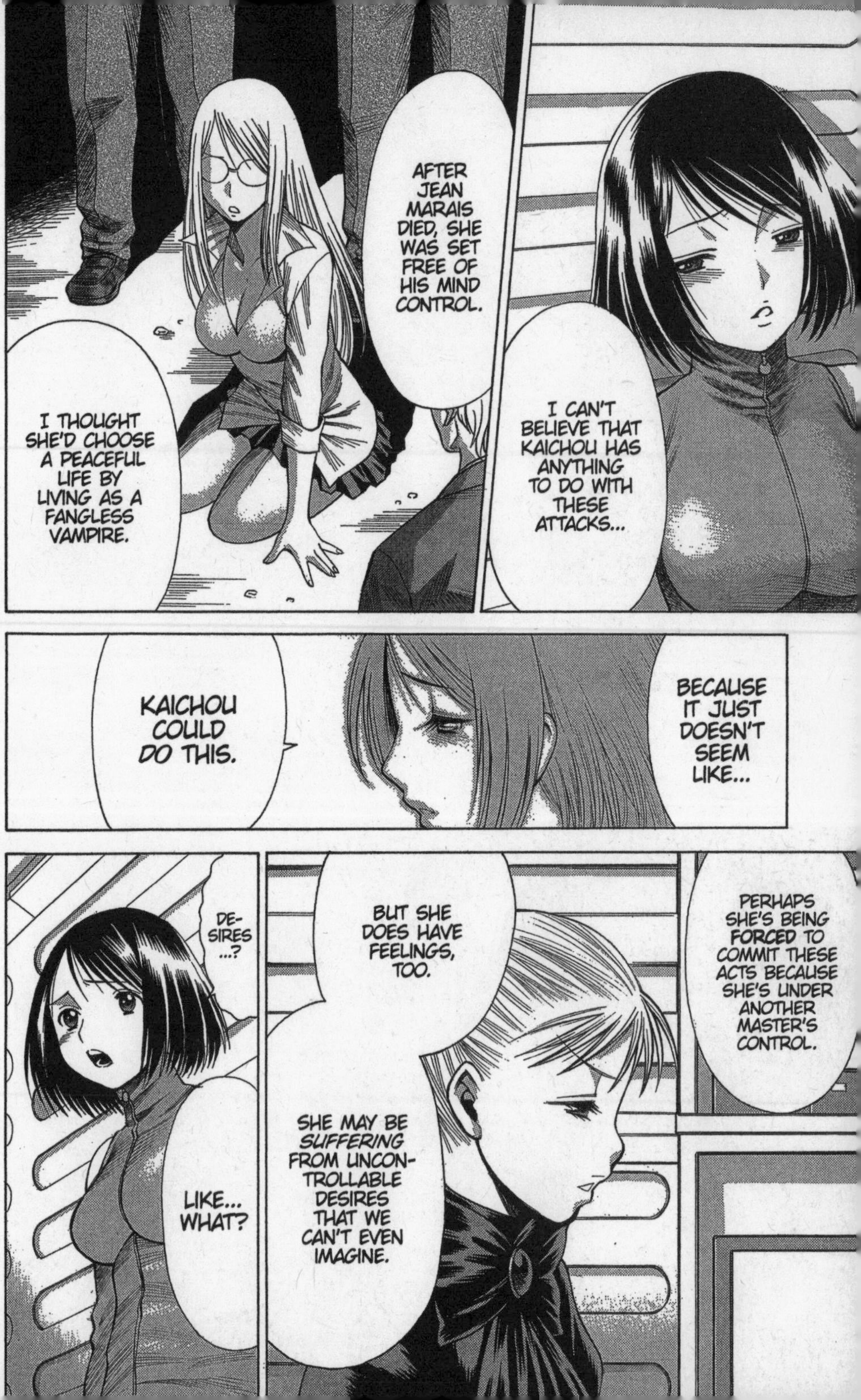
I CAN'T BELIEVE THAT KAICHOU HAS ANYTHING TO DO WITH THESE ATTACKS...
AFTER JEAN MARAIS DIED, SHE WAS SET FREE OF HIS MIND CONTROL.
I THOUGHT SHE'D CHOOSE A PEACEFUL LIFE BY LIVING AS A FANGLESS VAMPIRE.
BECAUSE IT JUST DOESN'T SEEM LIKE...
KAICHOU COULD *DO* THIS.
PERHAPS SHE'S BEING FORCED TO COMMIT THESE ACTS BECAUSE SHE'S UNDER ANOTHER MASTER'S CONTROL.
BUT SHE DOES HAVE FEELINGS, TOO.
SHE MAY BE *SUFFERING* FROM UNCON-TROLLABLE DESIRES THAT WE CAN'T EVEN IMAGINE.
DE-SIRES ...?
LIKE... WHAT?

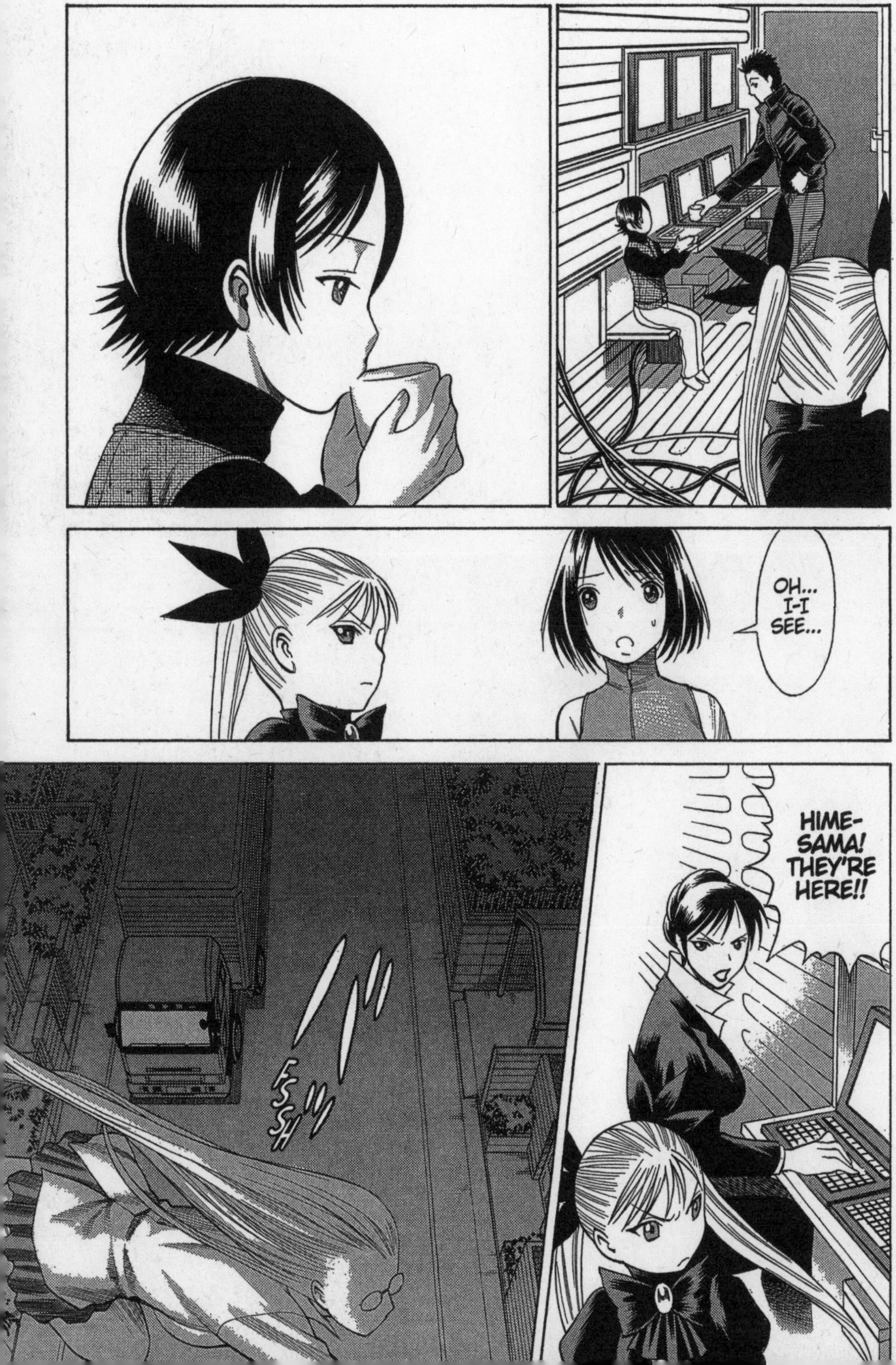
OH... I-I SEE...
HIME-SAMA! THEY'RE HERE!!
FSSH

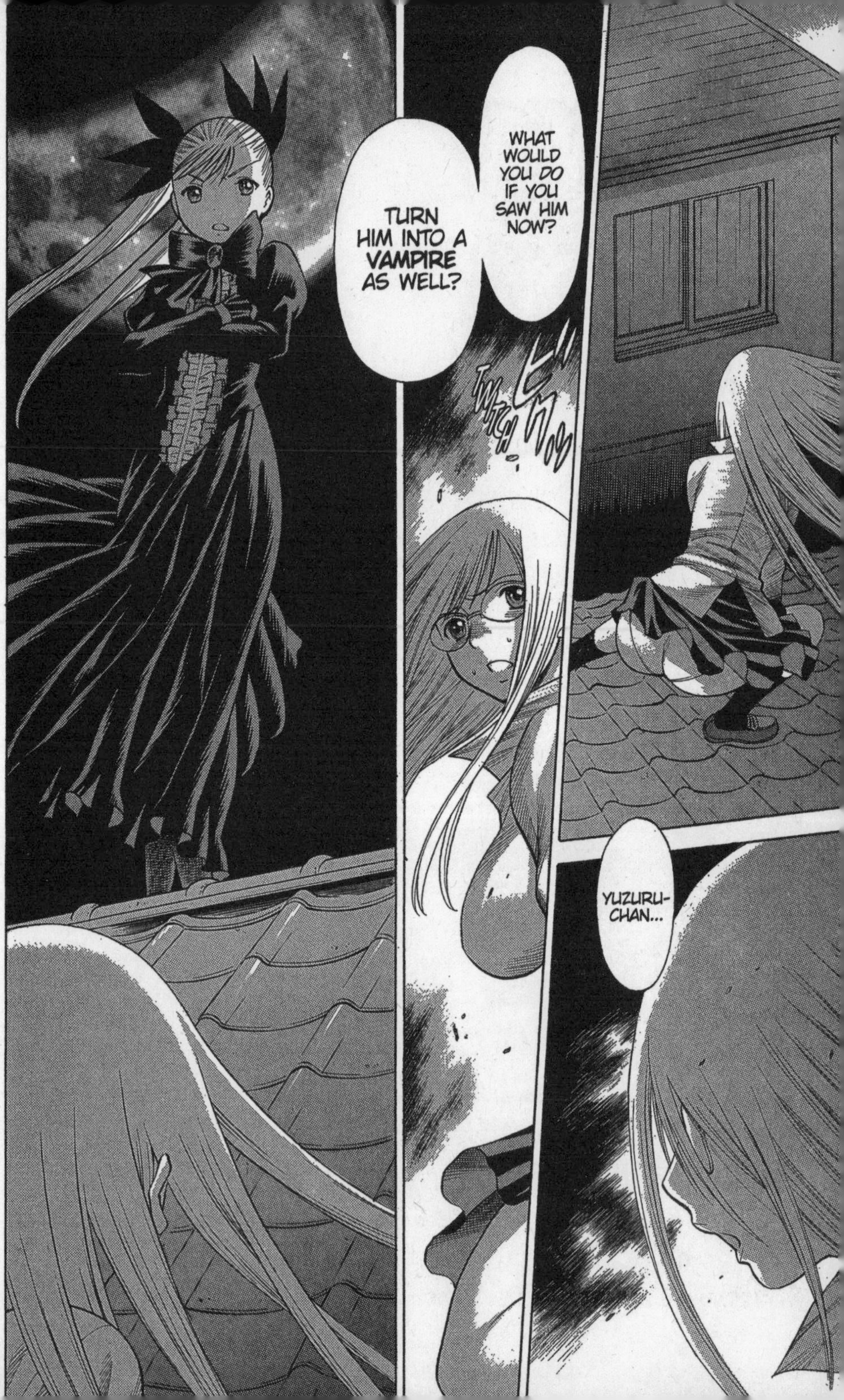
WHAT WOULD YOU DO IF YOU SAW HIM NOW?
TURN HIM INTO A VAMPIRE AS WELL?
YUZURU-CHAN...

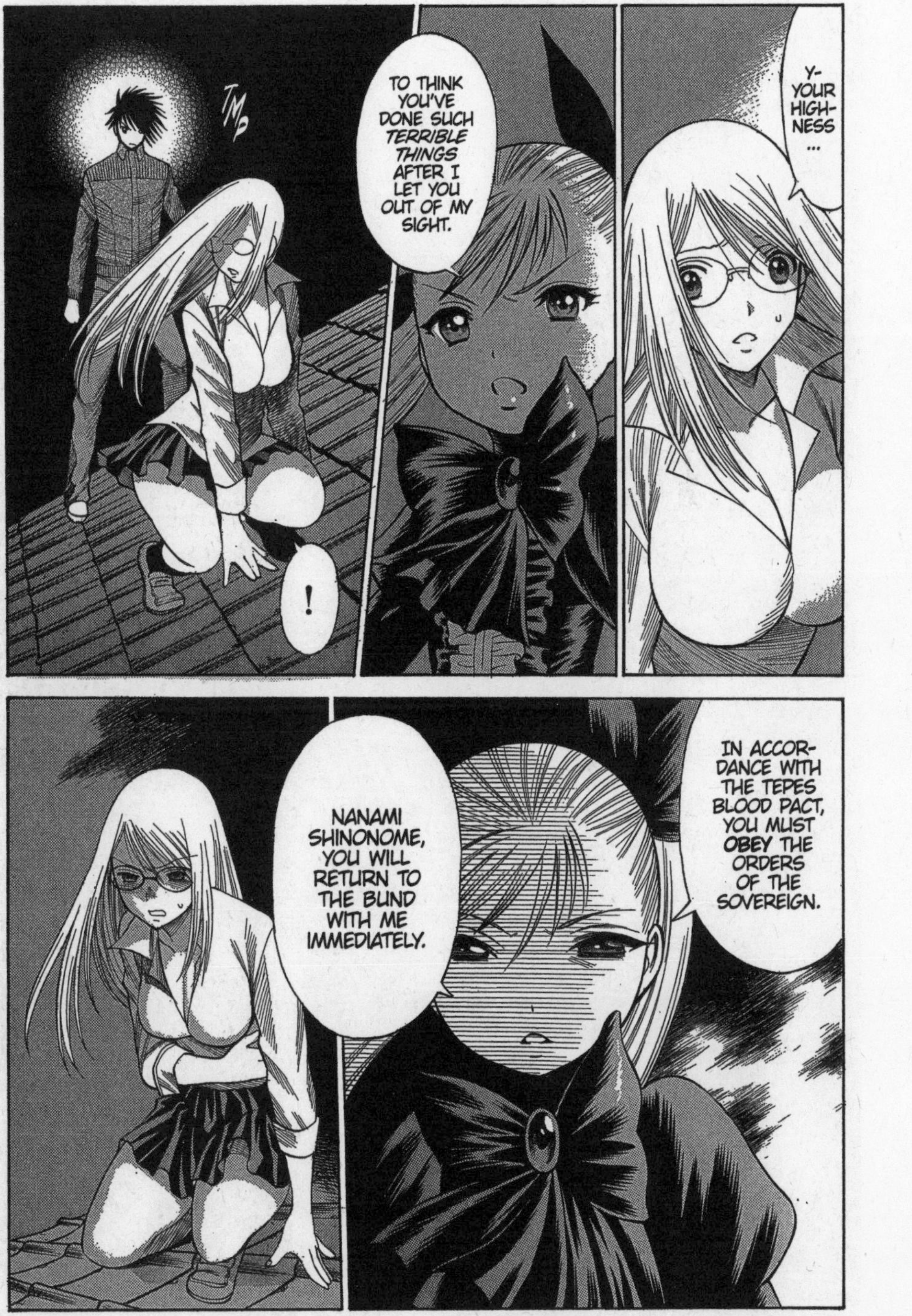
Y-YOUR HIGHNESS...
TO THINK YOU'VE DONE SUCH *TERRIBLE THINGS* AFTER I LET YOU OUT OF MY SIGHT.
TMP
!
IN ACCORDANCE WITH THE TEPES BLOOD PACT, YOU MUST **OBEY** THE ORDERS OF THE SOVEREIGN.
NANAMI SHINONOME, YOU WILL RETURN TO THE BUND WITH ME IMMEDIATELY.

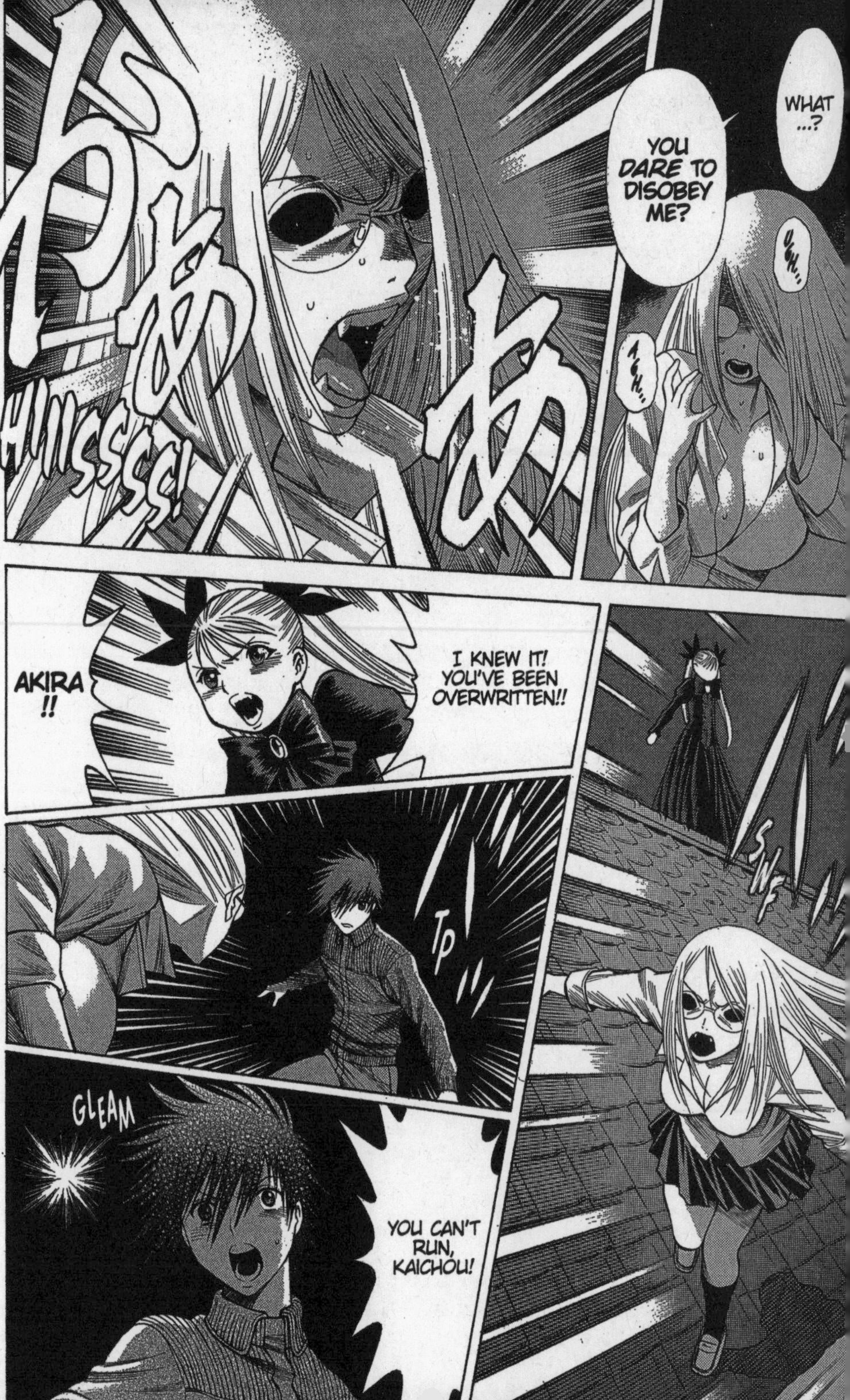
WHAT ...?
YOU DARE TO DISOBEY ME?
UGH...
AGH...
HIIISSSS!
SWF
I KNEW IT! YOU'VE BEEN OVERWRITTEN!!
AKIRA !!
TP
YOU CAN'T RUN, KAICHOU!
GLEAM

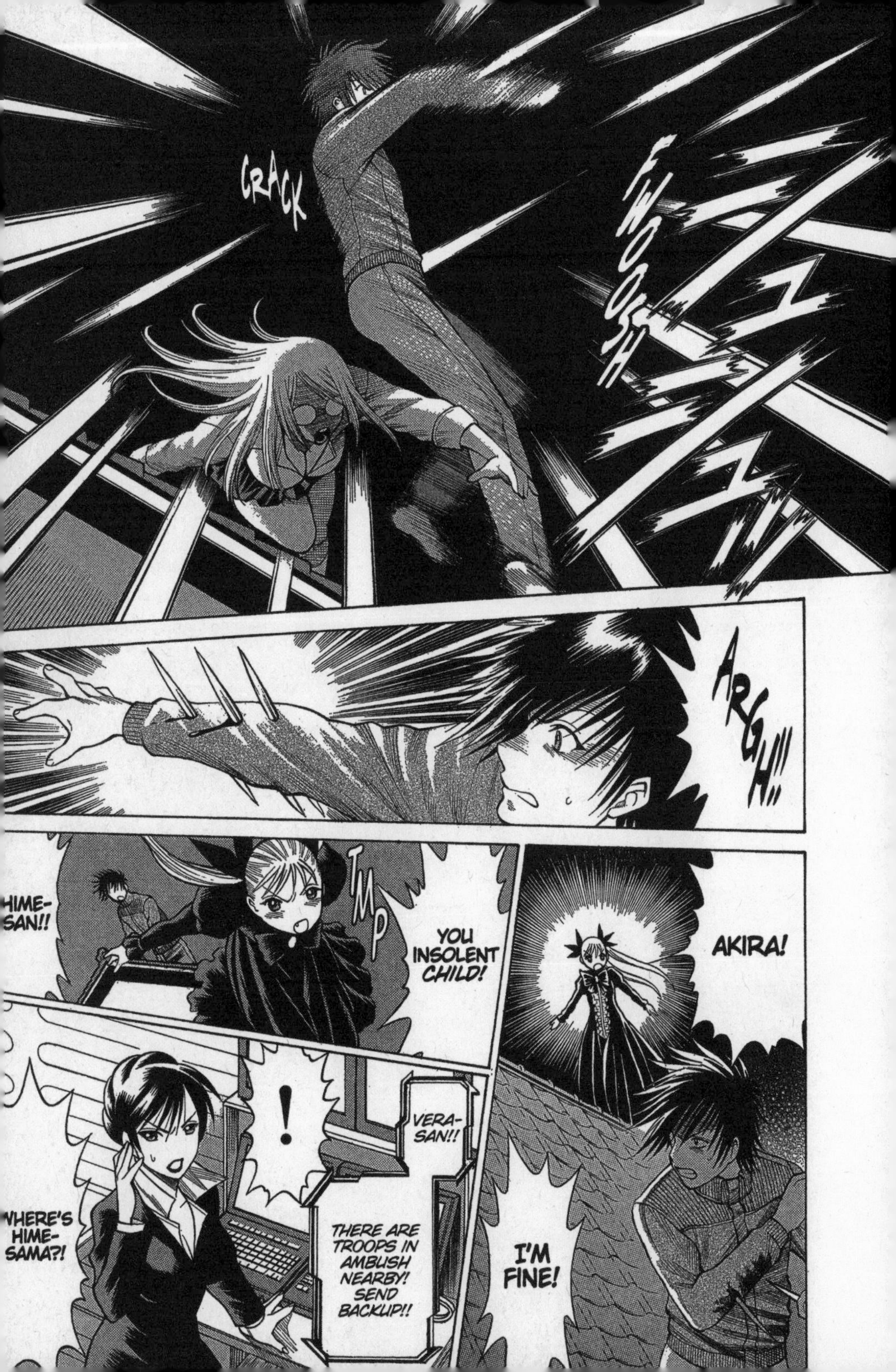
FWOOSH
CRACK
ARGH!!
AKIRA!
I'M FINE!
TMP
YOU INSOLENT CHILD!
HIME-SAN!!
VERA-SAN!!
!
THERE ARE TROOPS IN AMBUSH NEARBY! SEND BACKUP!!
WHERE'S HIME-SAMA?!

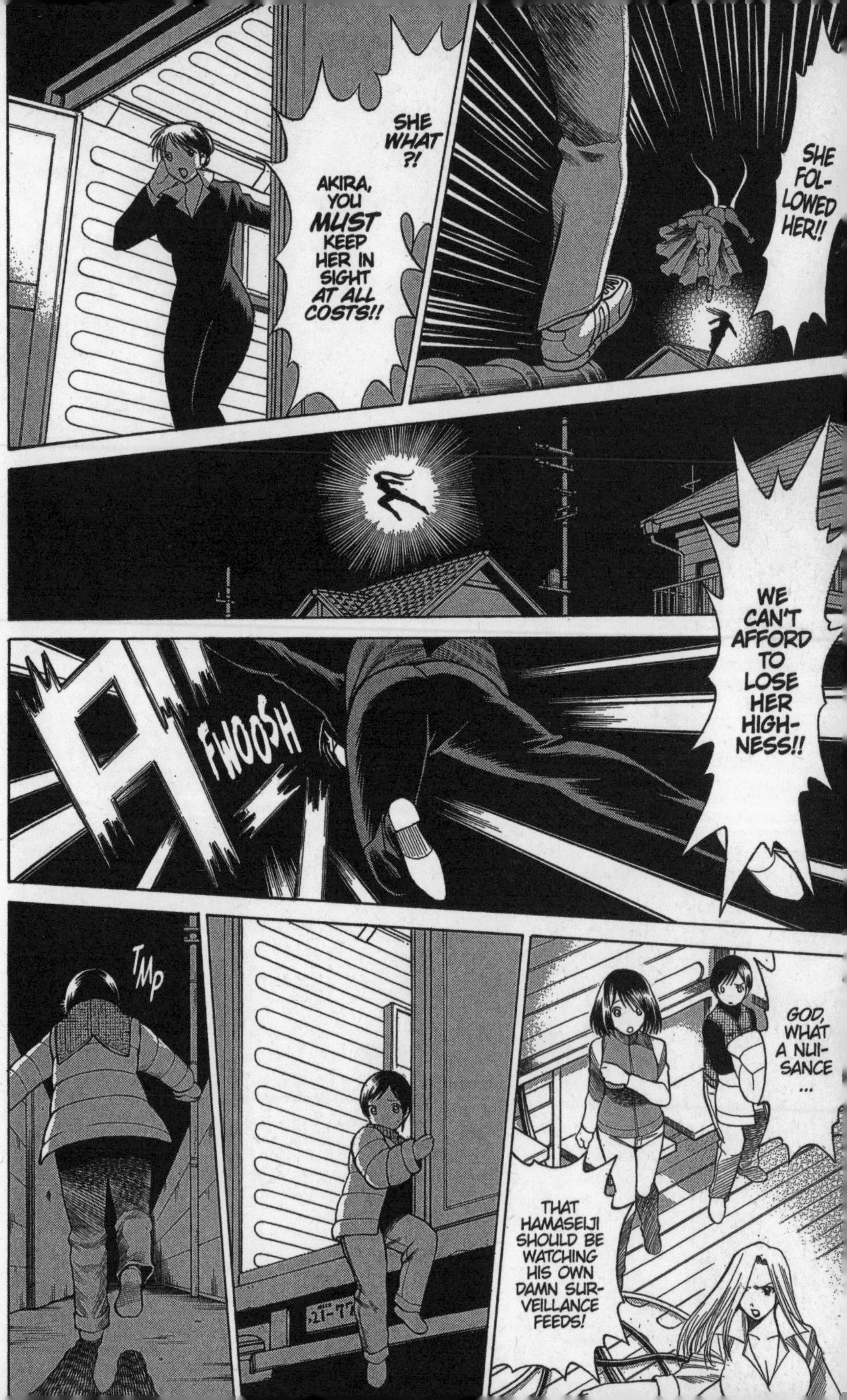
SHE FOL-LOWED HER!!
SHE WHAT?!
AKIRA, YOU MUST KEEP HER IN SIGHT AT ALL COSTS!!
WE CAN'T AFFORD TO LOSE HER HIGH-NESS!!
FWOOSH
GOD, WHAT A NUI-SANCE...
THAT HAMASEIJI SHOULD BE WATCHING HIS OWN DAMN SUR-VEILLANCE FEEDS!
TMP

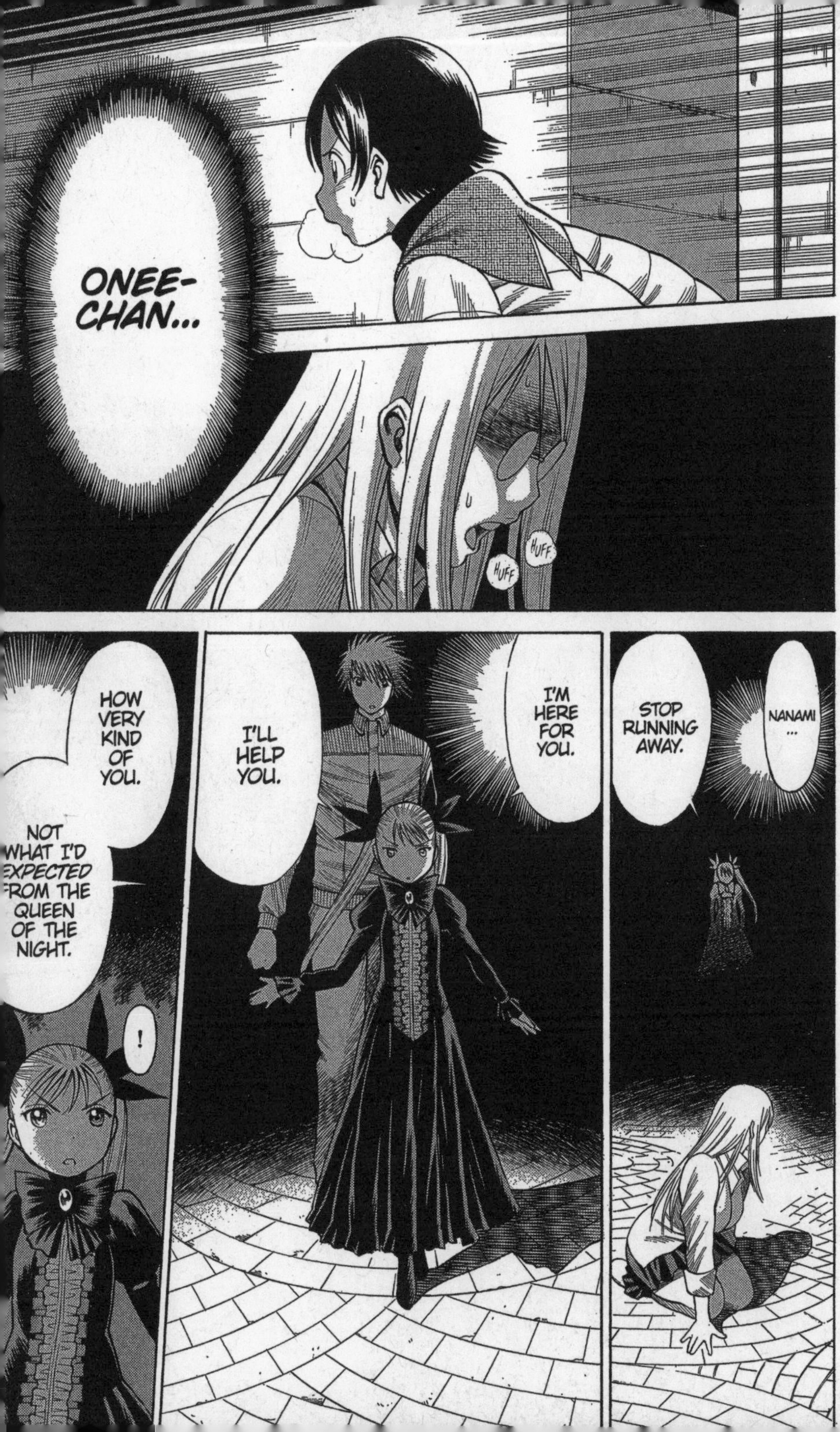
ONEE-CHAN...
HUFF
HUFF
NANAMI ...
STOP RUNNING AWAY.
I'M HERE FOR YOU.
I'LL HELP YOU.
HOW VERY KIND OF YOU.
NOT WHAT I'D EXPECTED FROM THE QUEEN OF THE NIGHT.
!

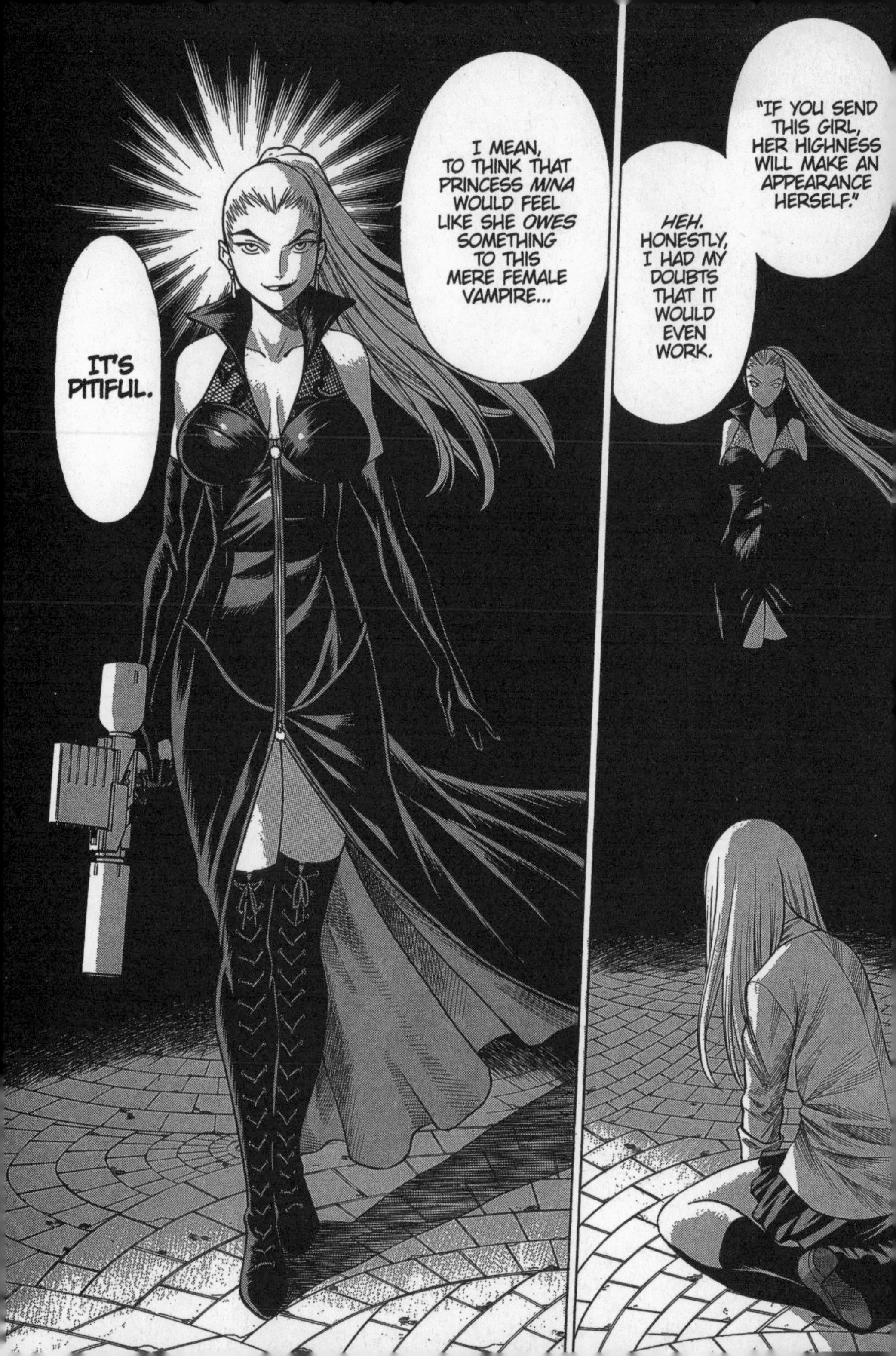
"IF YOU SEND THIS GIRL, HER HIGHNESS WILL MAKE AN APPEARANCE HERSELF."
HEH. HONESTLY, I HAD MY DOUBTS THAT IT WOULD EVEN WORK.
I MEAN, TO THINK THAT PRINCESS *MINA* WOULD FEEL LIKE SHE *OWES* SOMETHING TO THIS MERE FEMALE VAMPIRE...
IT'S PITIFUL.

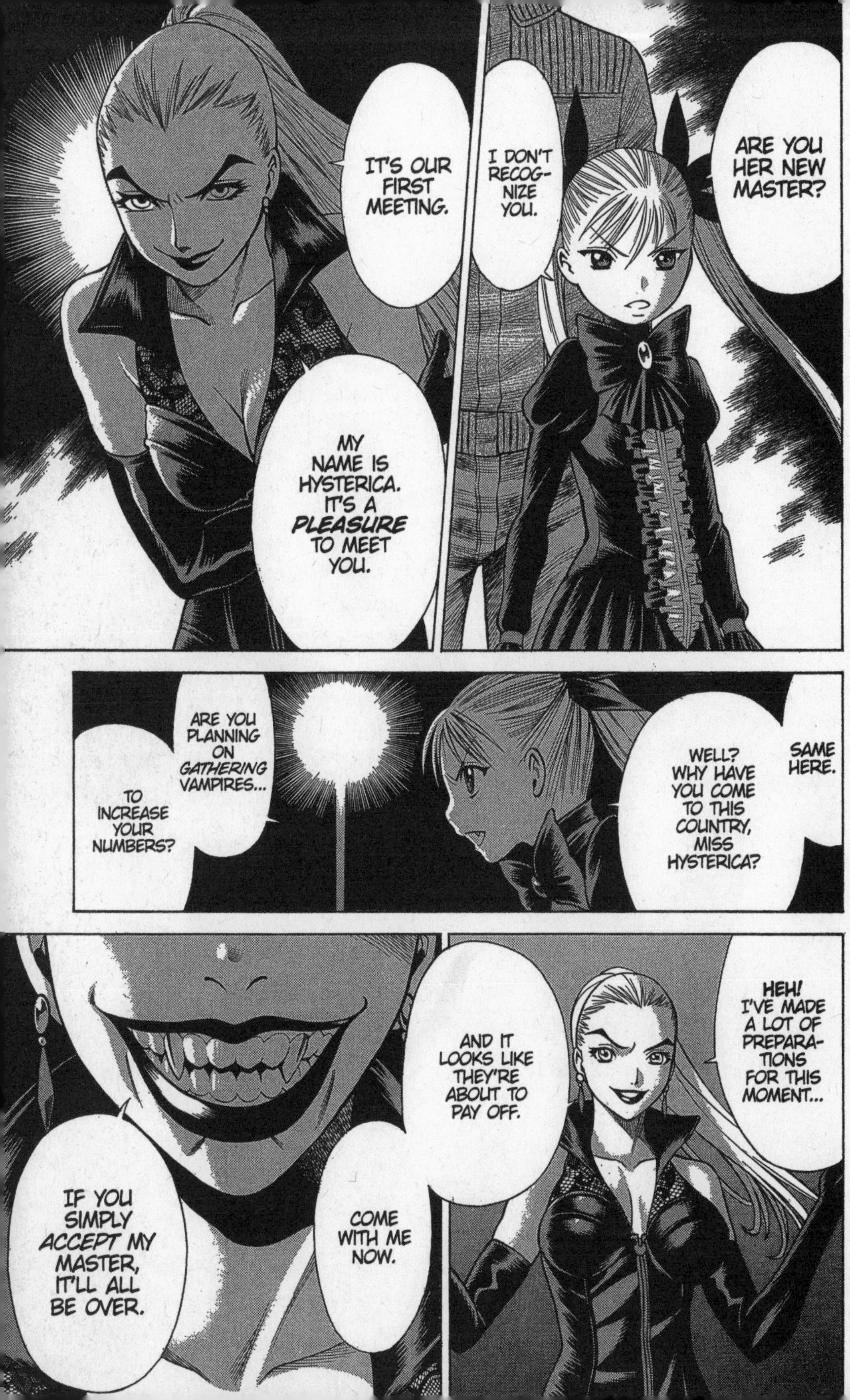
ARE YOU HER NEW MASTER?
I DON'T RECOG-NIZE YOU.
IT'S OUR FIRST MEETING.
MY NAME IS HYSTERICA. IT'S A *PLEASURE* TO MEET YOU.
SAME HERE.
WELL? WHY HAVE YOU COME TO THIS COUNTRY, MISS HYSTERICA?
ARE YOU PLANNING ON *GATHERING* VAMPIRES...
TO INCREASE YOUR NUMBERS?
HEH! I'VE MADE A LOT OF PREPARA-TIONS FOR THIS MOMENT...
AND IT LOOKS LIKE THEY'RE ABOUT TO PAY OFF.
COME WITH ME NOW.
IF YOU SIMPLY *ACCEPT* MY MASTER, IT'LL ALL BE OVER.

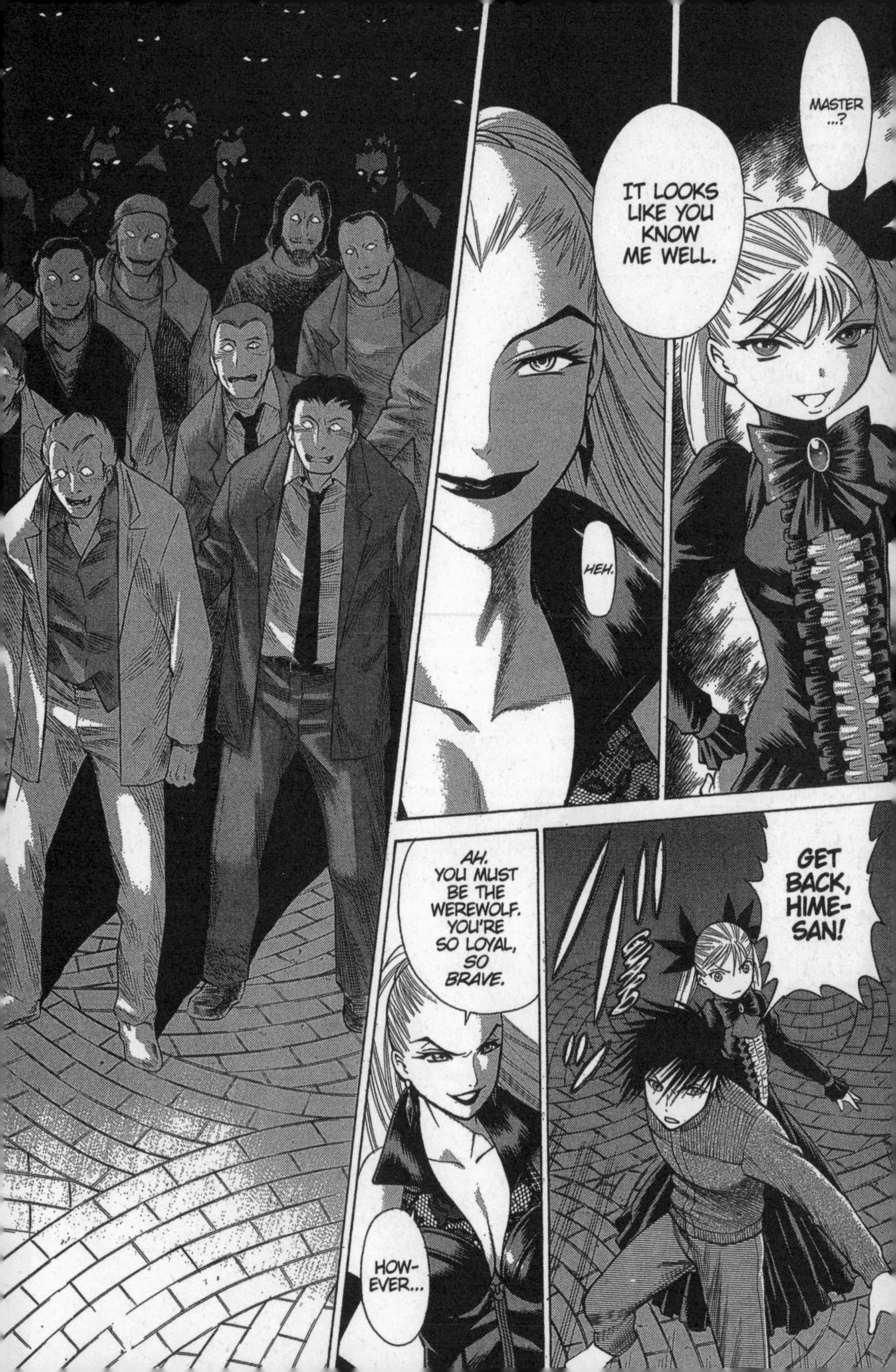
MASTER ...?
IT LOOKS LIKE YOU KNOW ME WELL.
HEH.
GET BACK, HIME-SAN!
AH. YOU MUST BE THE WEREWOLF. YOU'RE SO LOYAL, SO BRAVE.
HOW-EVER...

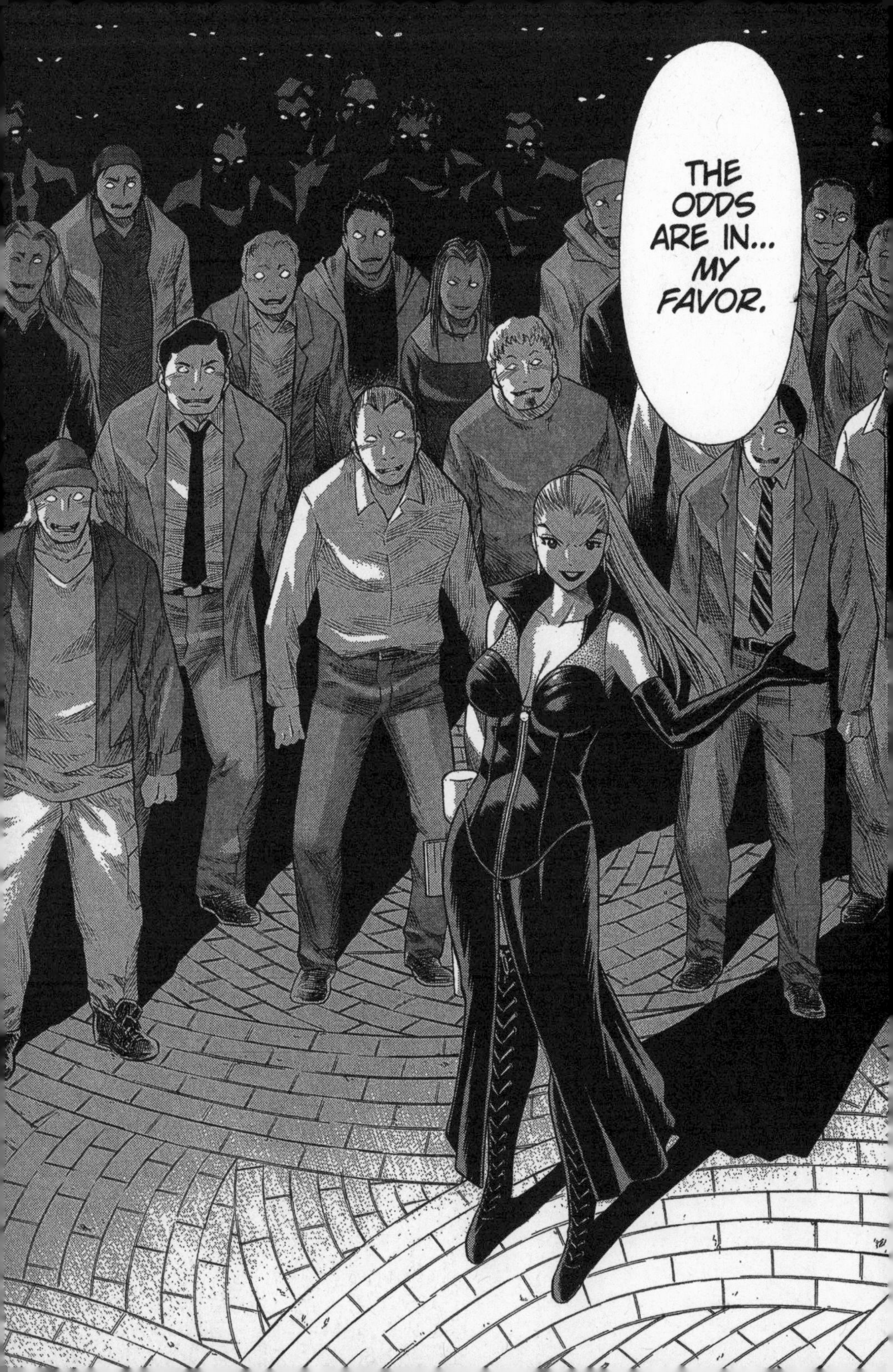
THE ODDS ARE IN... MY FAVOR.

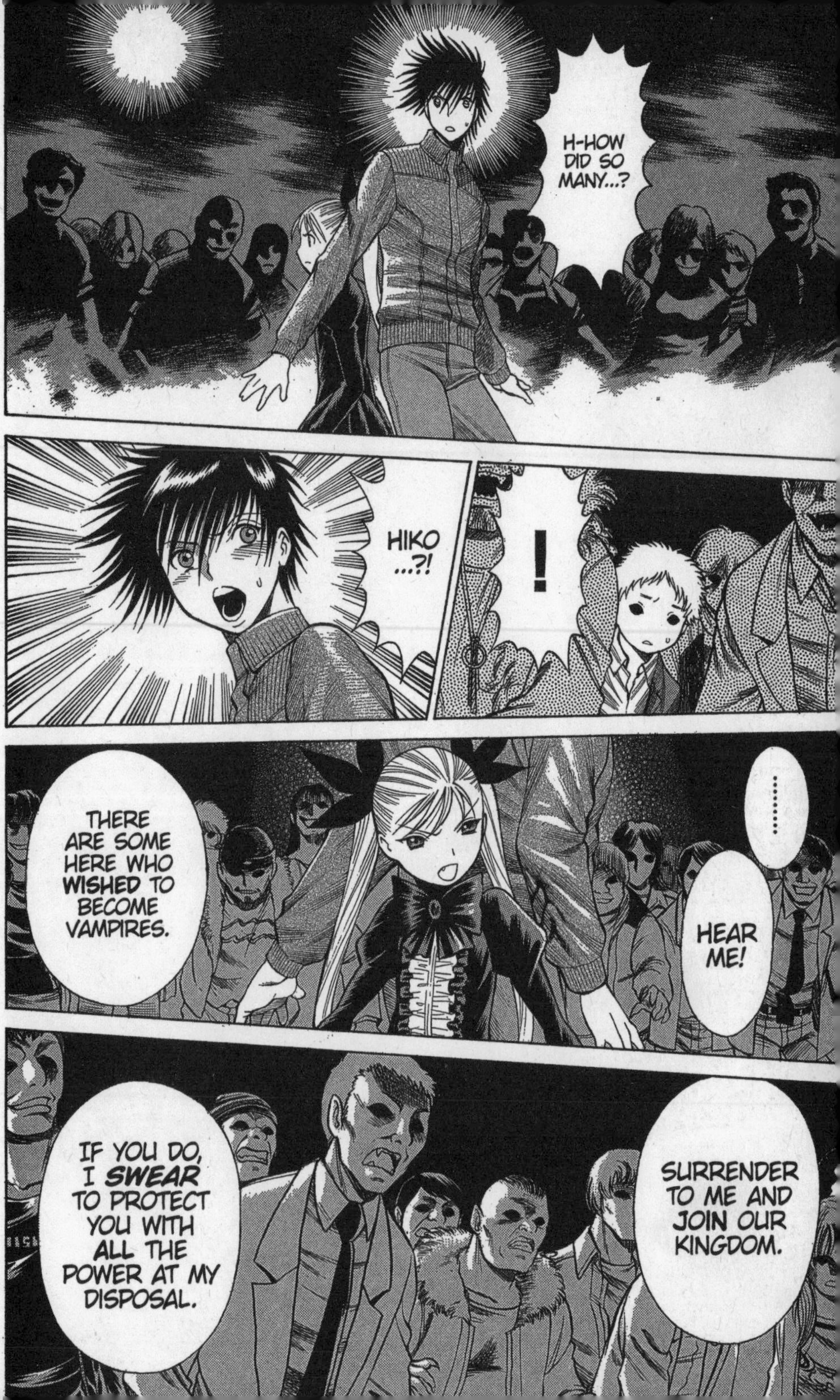
H-HOW DID SO MANY...?
!
HIKO ...?!
......
HEAR ME!
THERE ARE SOME HERE WHO WISHED TO BECOME VAMPIRES.
SURRENDER TO ME AND JOIN OUR KINGDOM.
IF YOU DO, I SWEAR TO PROTECT YOU WITH ALL THE POWER AT MY DISPOSAL.

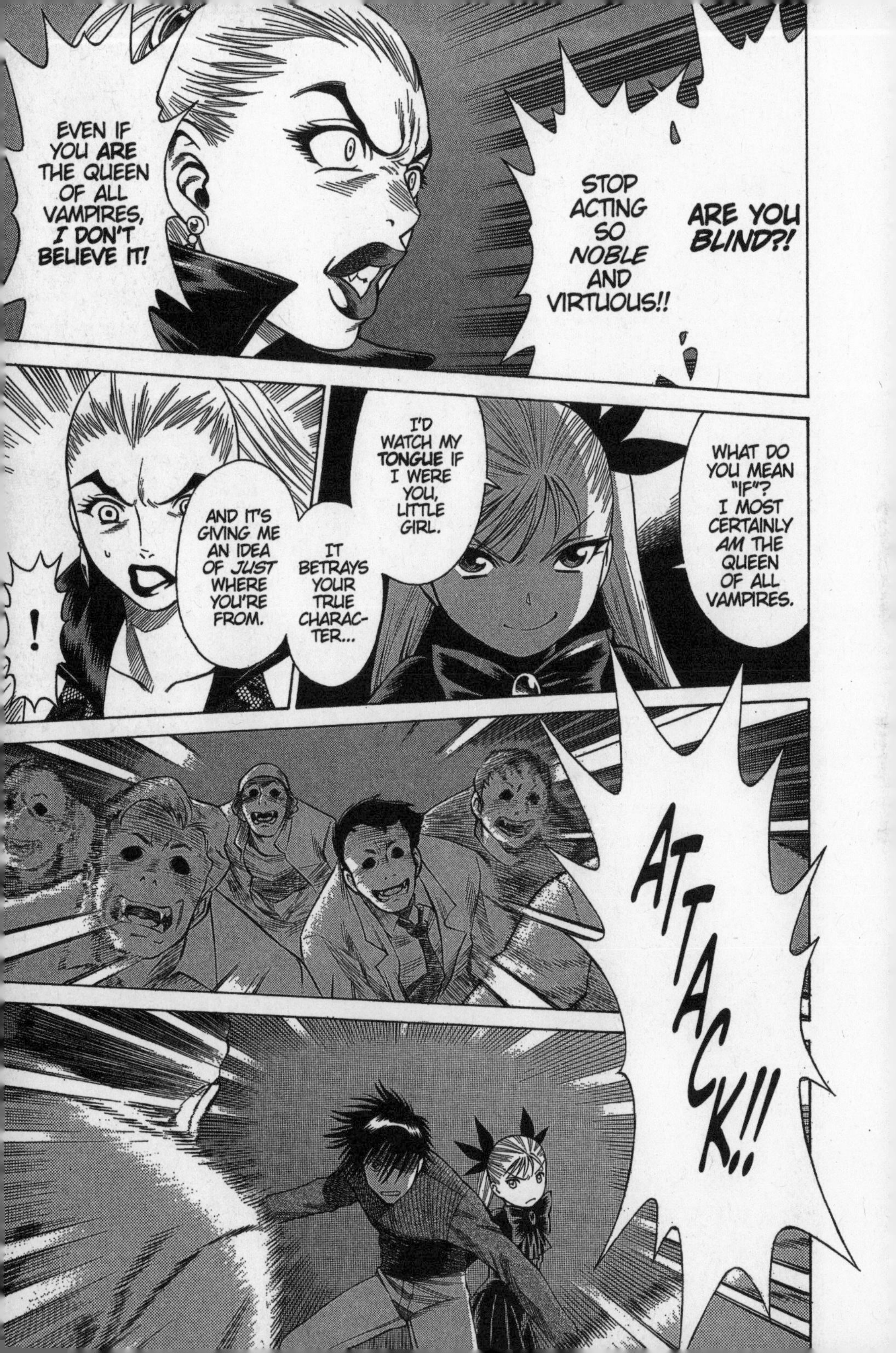
ARE YOU BLIND?!
STOP ACTING SO NOBLE AND VIRTUOUS!!
EVEN IF YOU ARE THE QUEEN OF ALL VAMPIRES, I DON'T BELIEVE IT!
WHAT DO YOU MEAN "IF"? I MOST CERTAINLY AM THE QUEEN OF ALL VAMPIRES.
I'D WATCH MY TONGUE IF I WERE YOU, LITTLE GIRL.
IT BETRAYS YOUR TRUE CHARACTER...
AND IT'S GIVING ME AN IDEA OF JUST WHERE YOU'RE FROM.
!
ATTACK!!

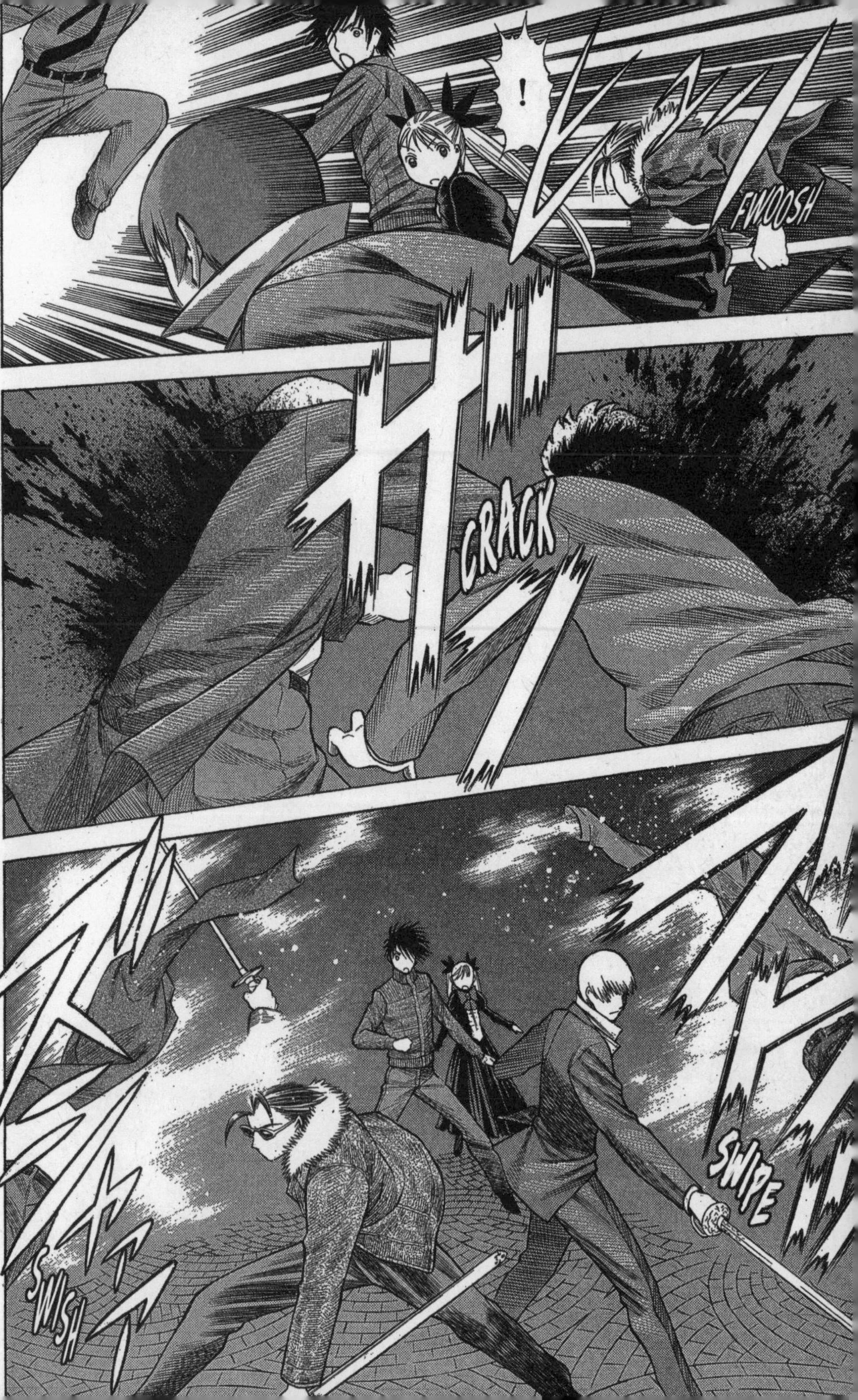
!
FWOOSH
CRACK
SWIPE
SWISH

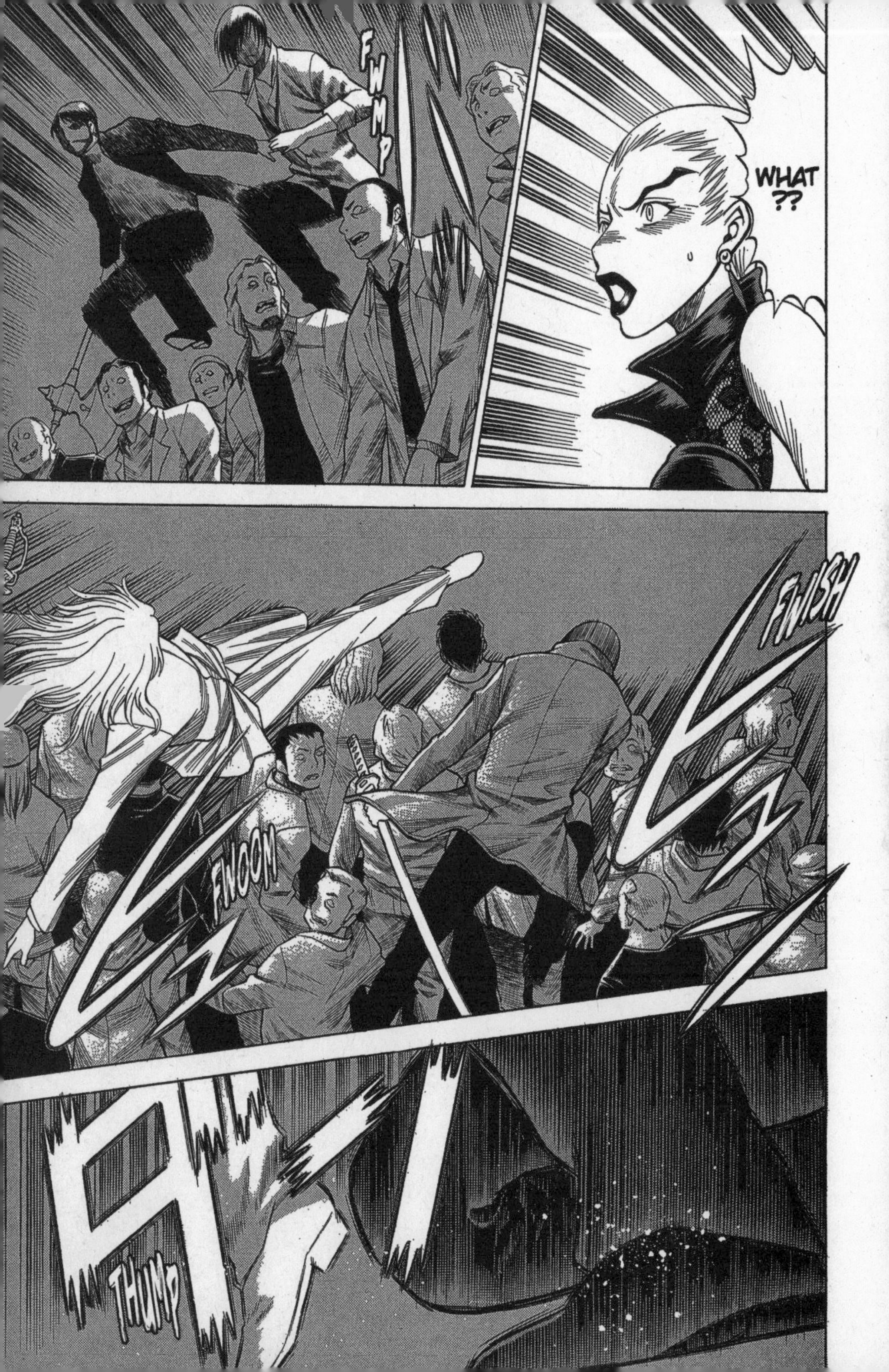
WHAT ??
FWMP
FWISH
FWOOM
THUMP

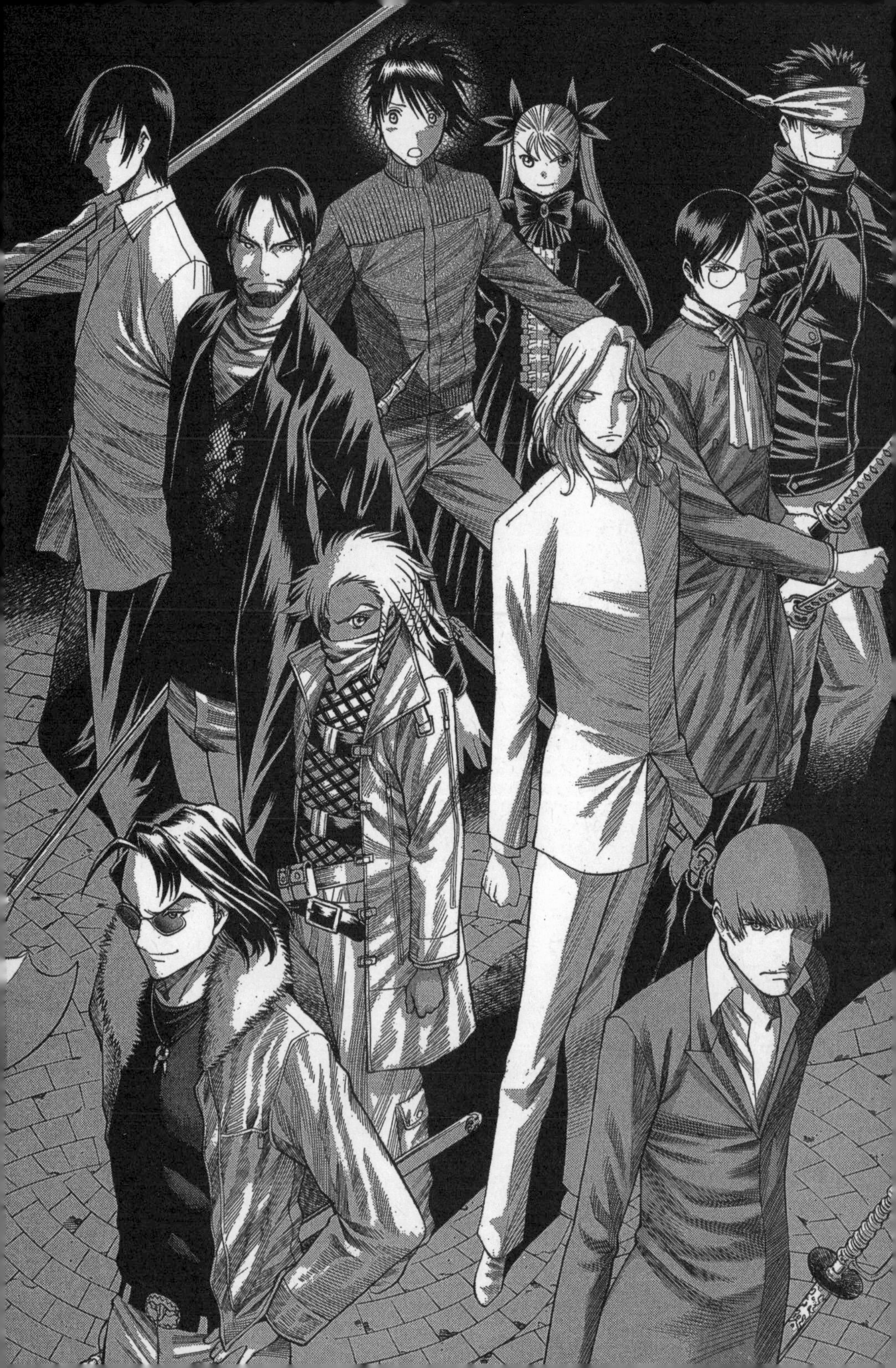

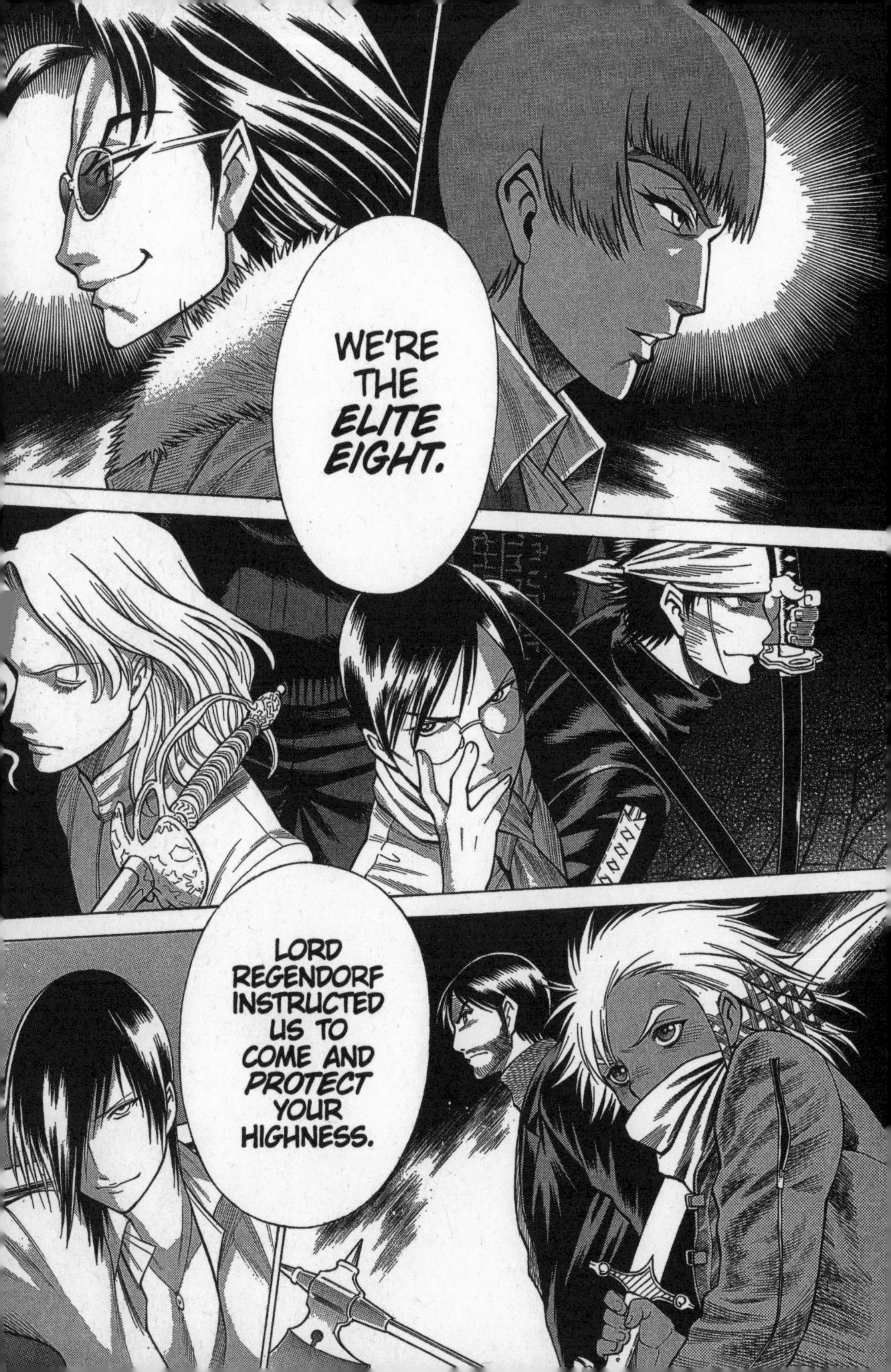
WE'RE THE ELITE EIGHT.
LORD REGENDORF INSTRUCTED US TO COME AND PROTECT YOUR HIGHNESS.

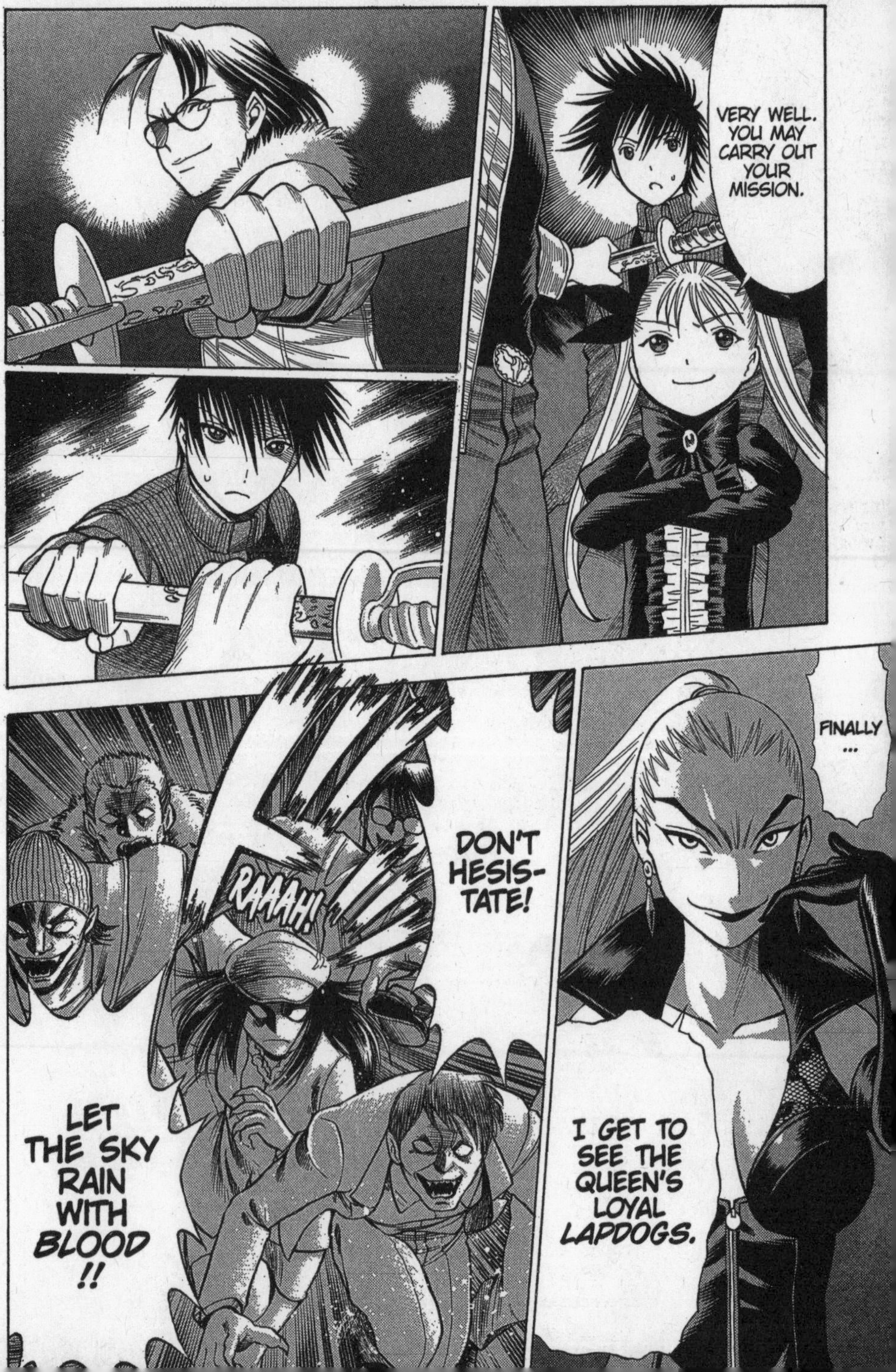
VERY WELL. YOU MAY CARRY OUT YOUR MISSION.
FINALLY ...
I GET TO SEE THE QUEEN'S LOYAL LAPDOGS.
DON'T HESIS-TATE!
RAAAH!
LET THE SKY RAIN WITH BLOOD !!

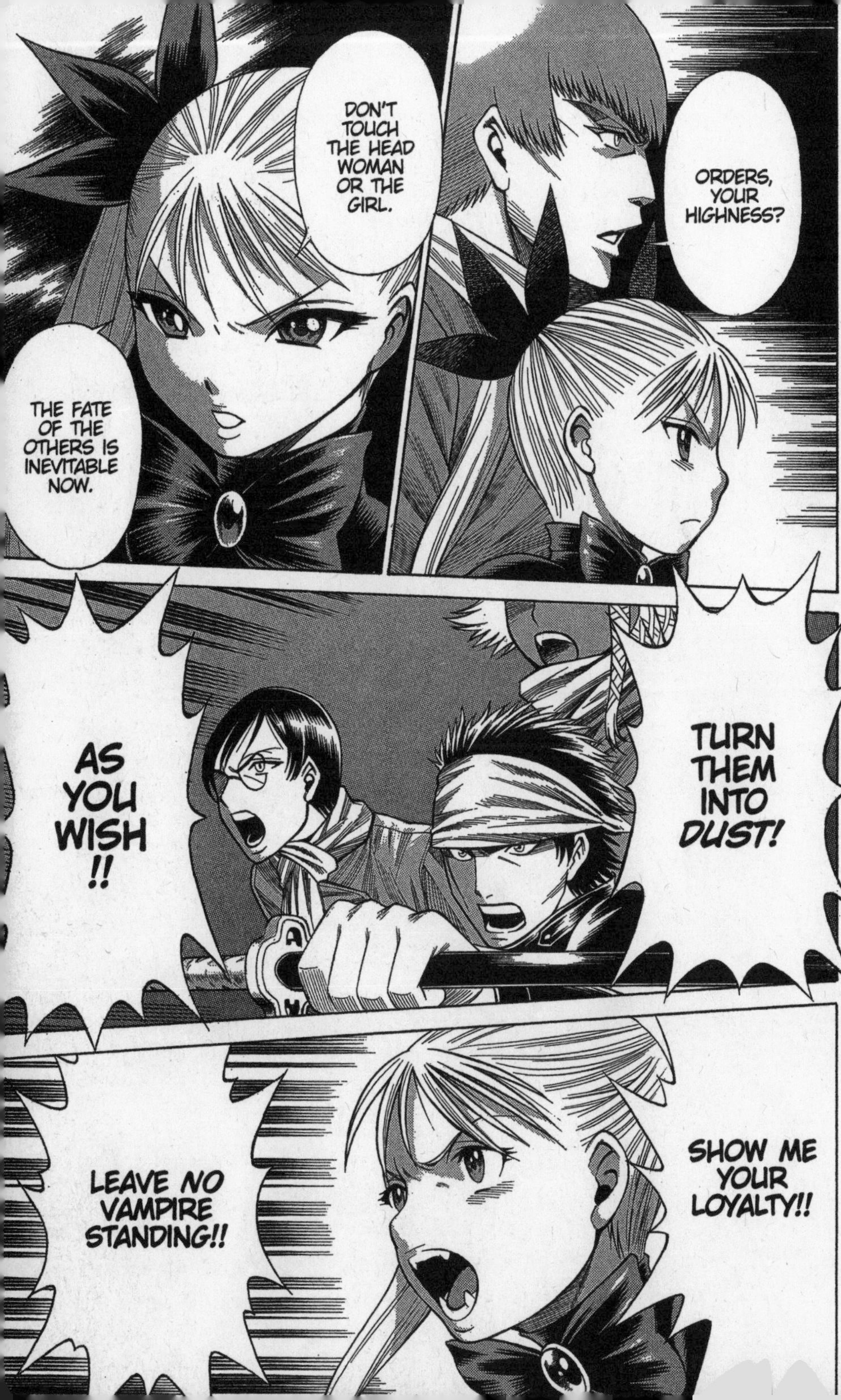
ORDERS, YOUR HIGHNESS?
DON'T TOUCH THE HEAD WOMAN OR THE GIRL.
THE FATE OF THE OTHERS IS INEVITABLE NOW.
TURN THEM INTO DUST!
AS YOU WISH !!
SHOW ME YOUR LOYALTY!!
LEAVE NO VAMPIRE STANDING!!

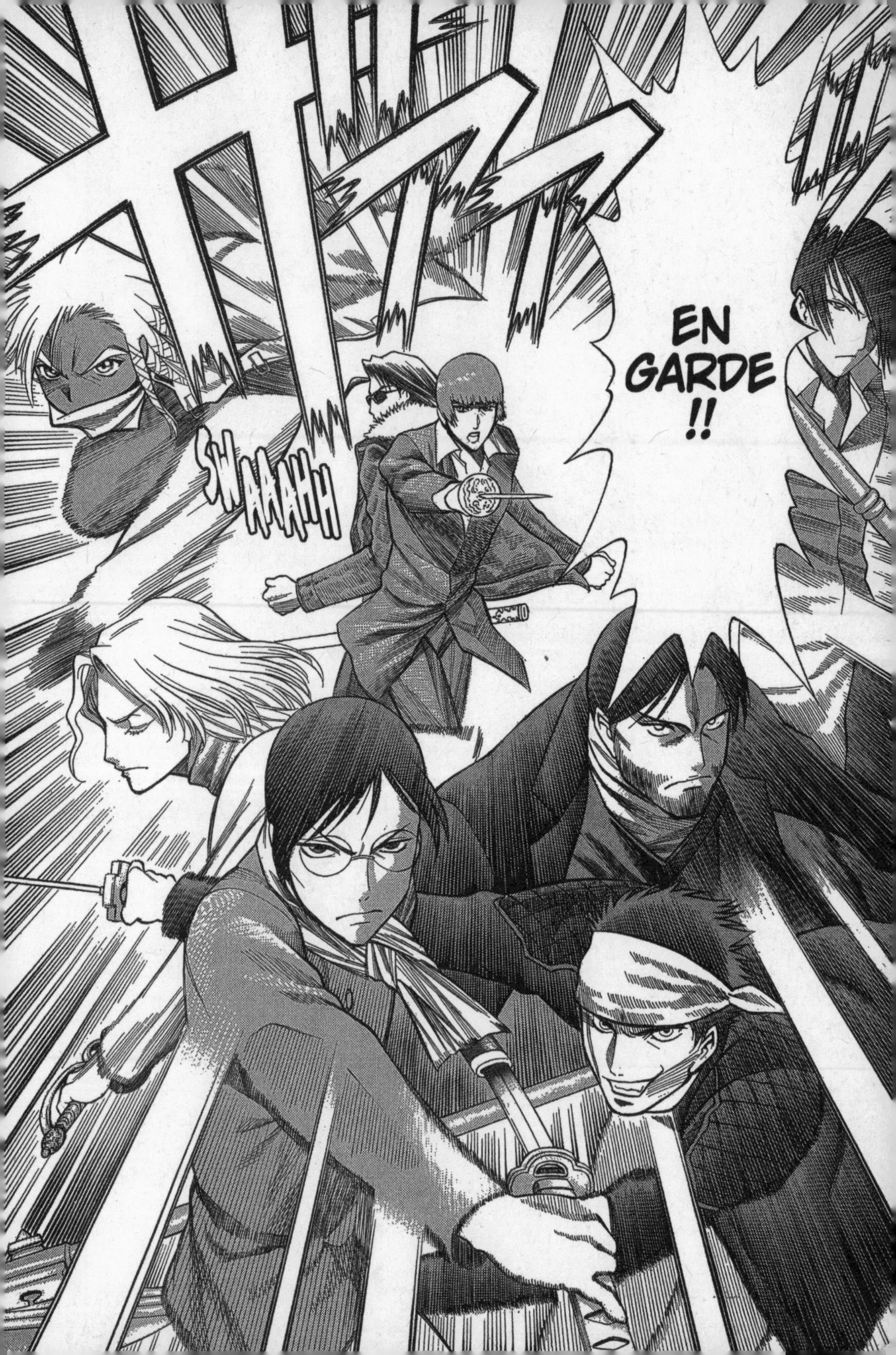
EN GARDE !!
SWAAAHH

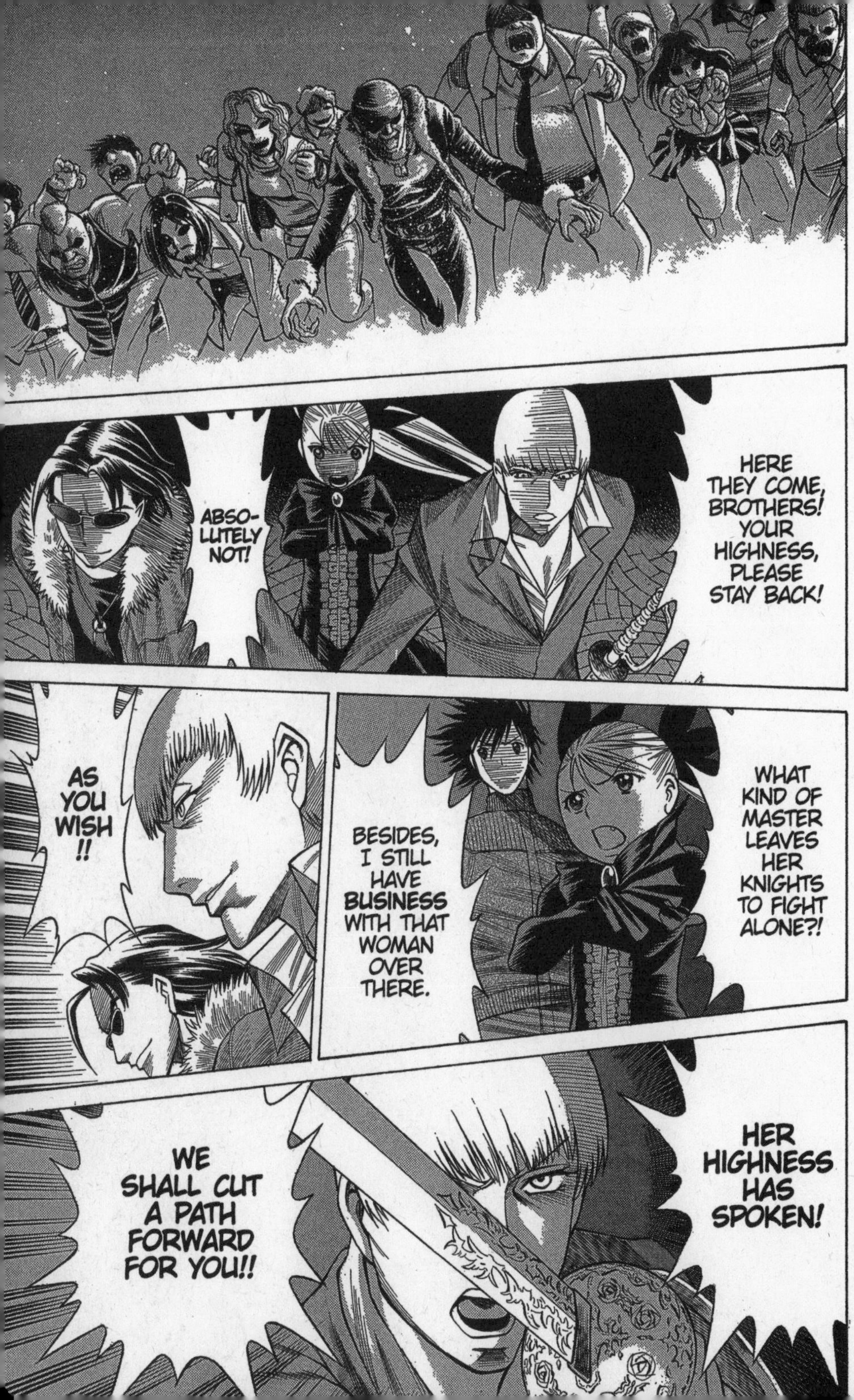
HERE THEY COME, BROTHERS! YOUR HIGHNESS, PLEASE STAY BACK!
ABSO-LUTELY NOT!
WHAT KIND OF MASTER LEAVES HER KNIGHTS TO FIGHT ALONE?!
BESIDES, I STILL HAVE BUSINESS WITH THAT WOMAN OVER THERE.
AS YOU WISH!!
HER HIGHNESS HAS SPOKEN!
WE SHALL CUT A PATH FORWARD FOR YOU!!

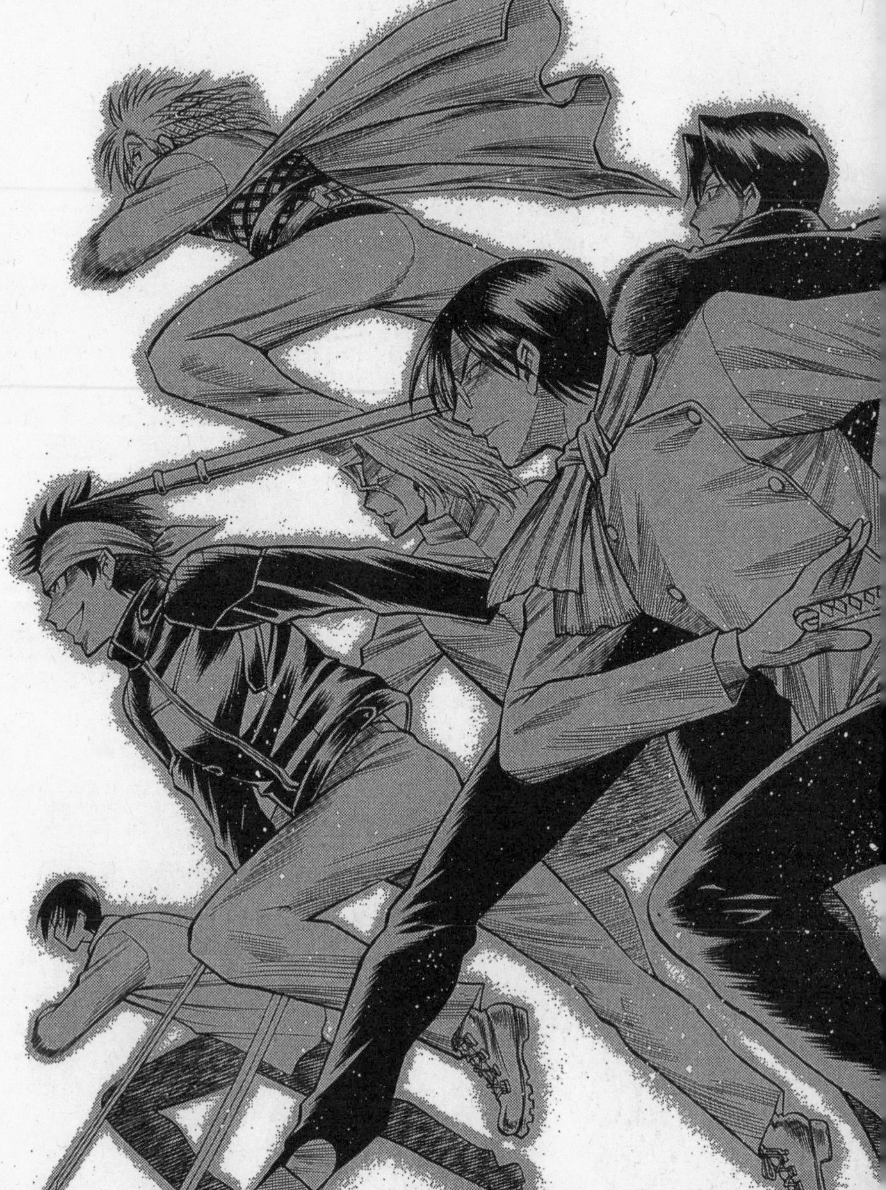

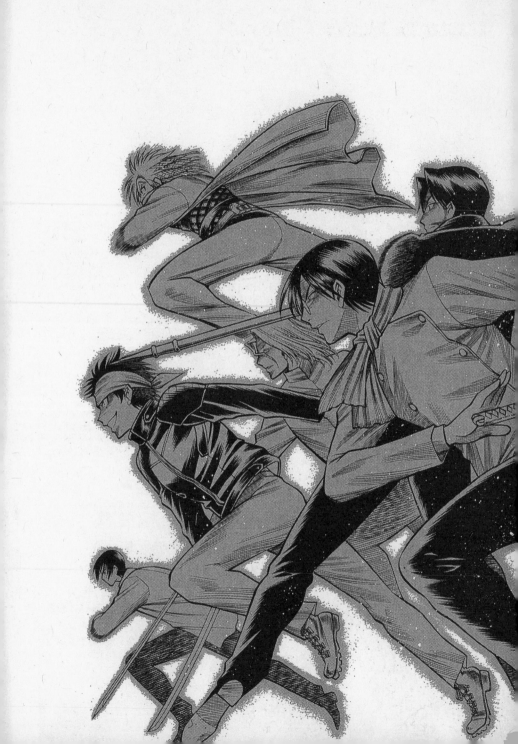

Chapter 16: Werewolf ~Beowulf~

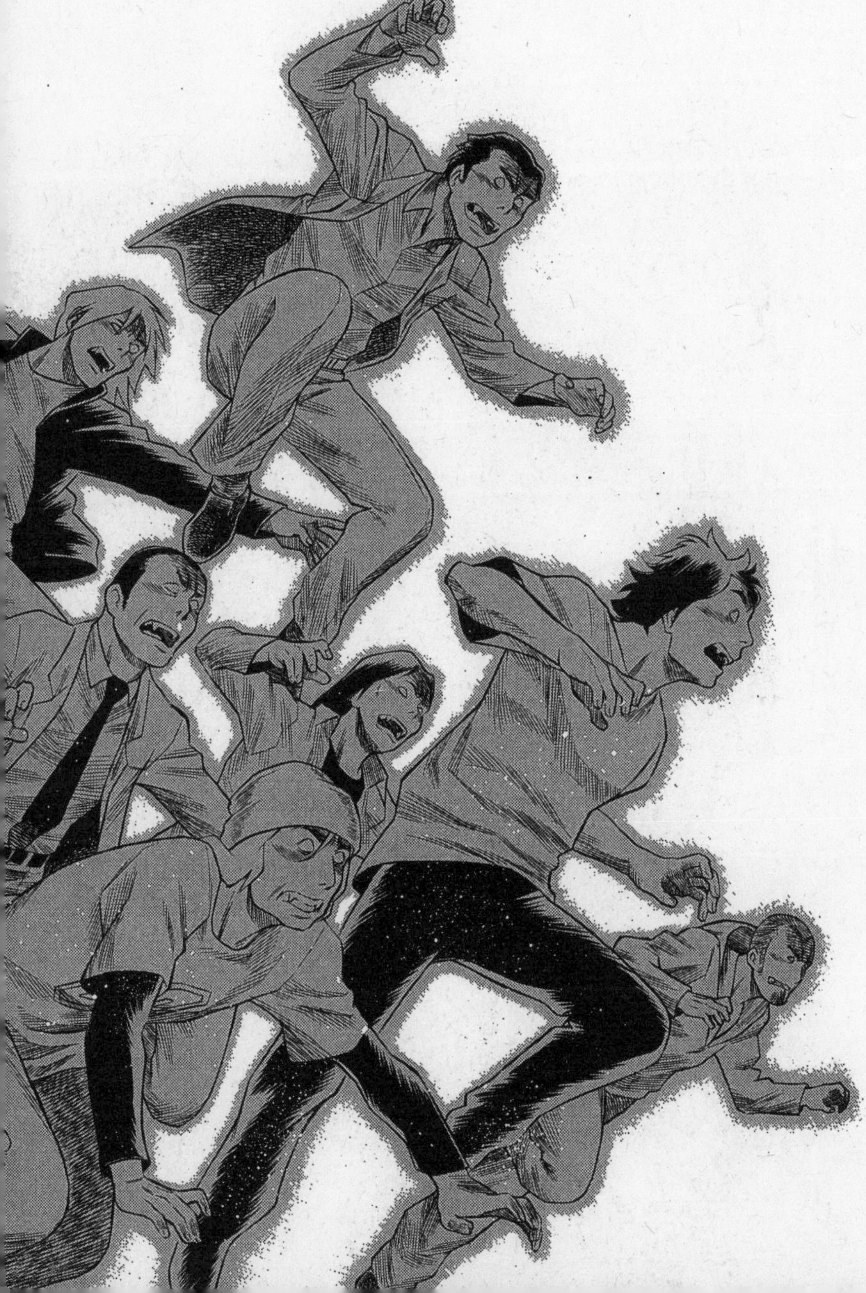

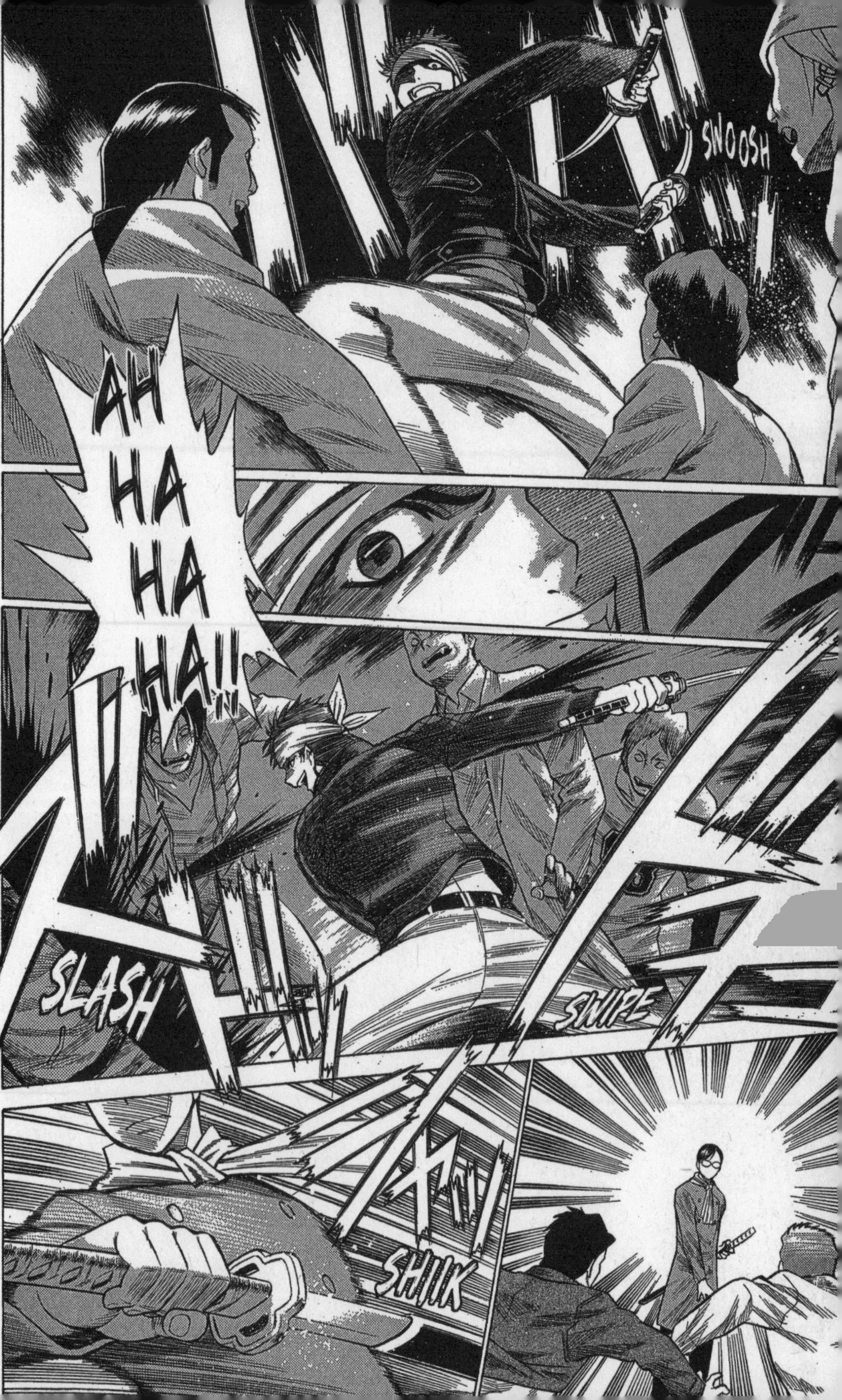
SWOOSH
AH HA HA HA HA!!
SWIPE
SLASH
SHIIK

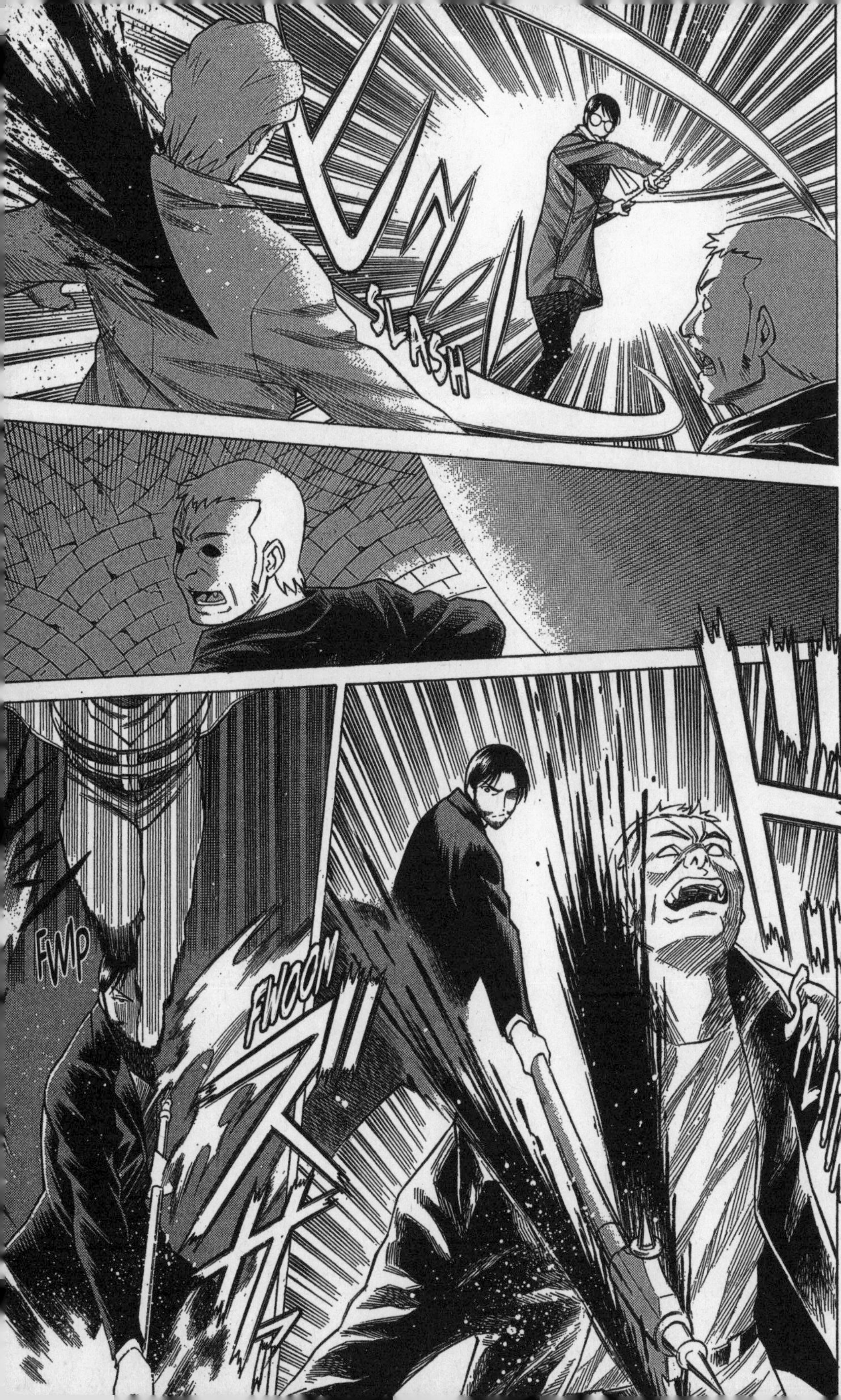
SLASH
FWOOM
FWP

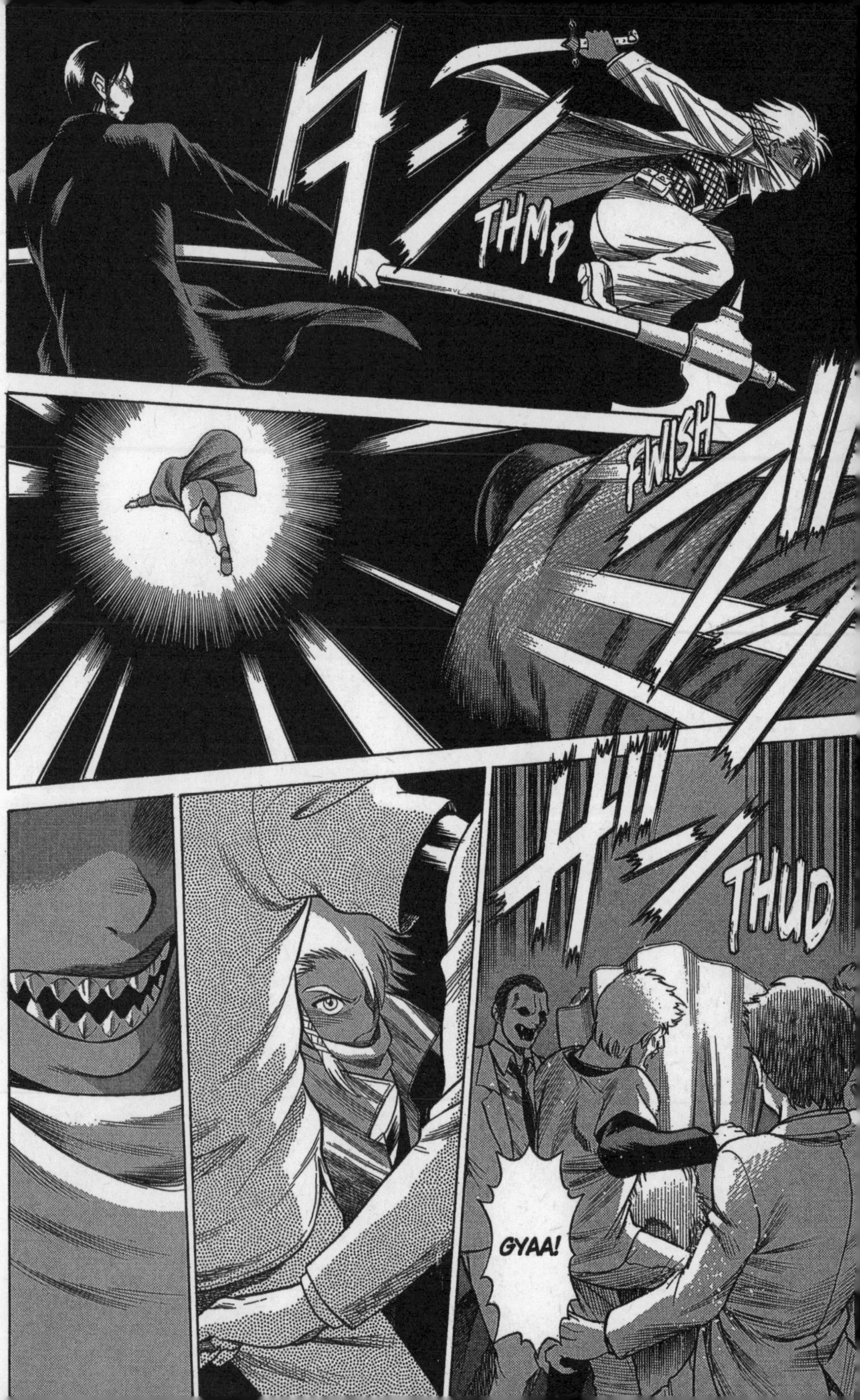
THMP
FWISH
THUD
GYAA!

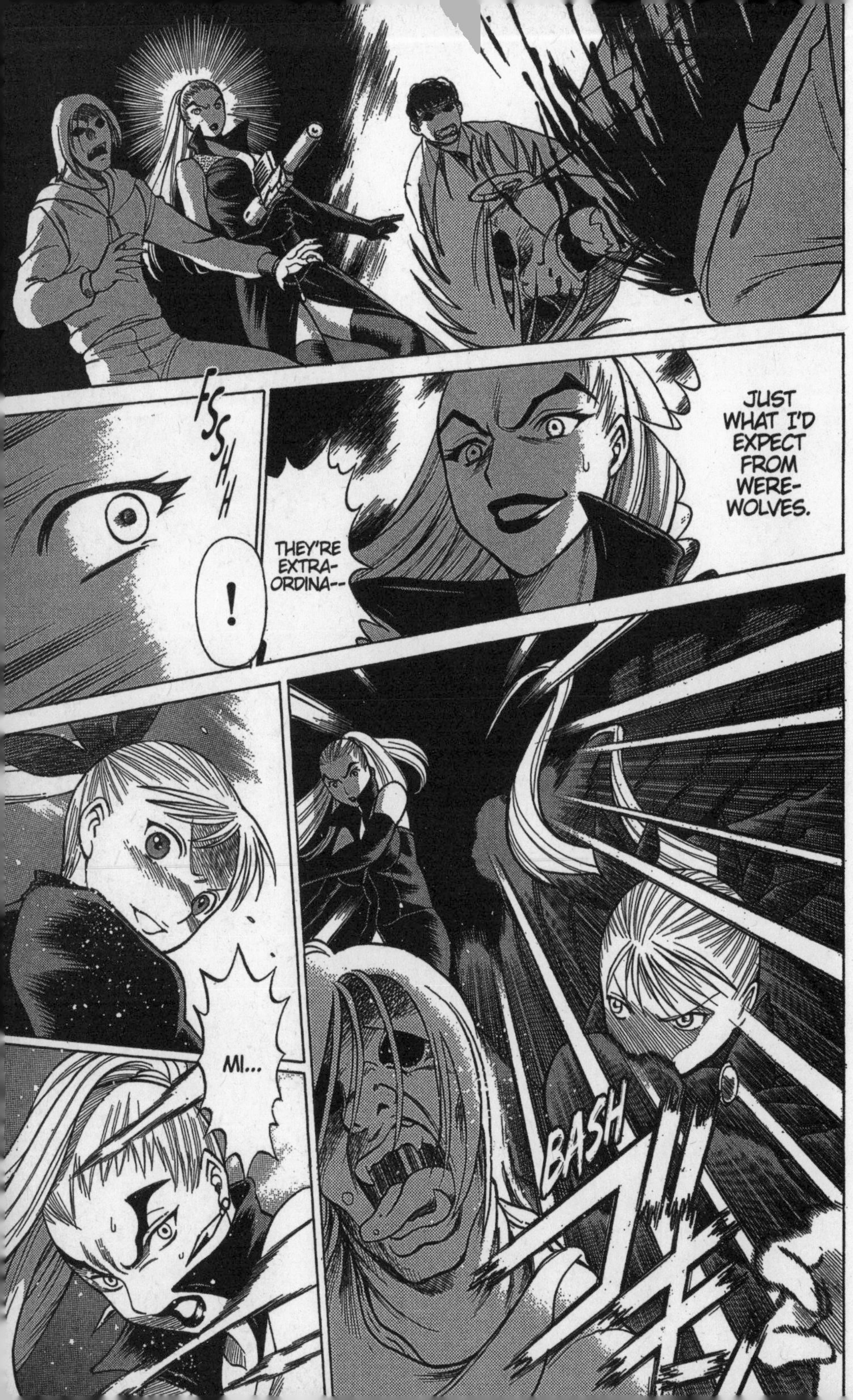
JUST WHAT I'D EXPECT FROM WERE-WOLVES.
THEY'RE EXTRA-ORDINA--
FSSHH
!
BASH
MI...

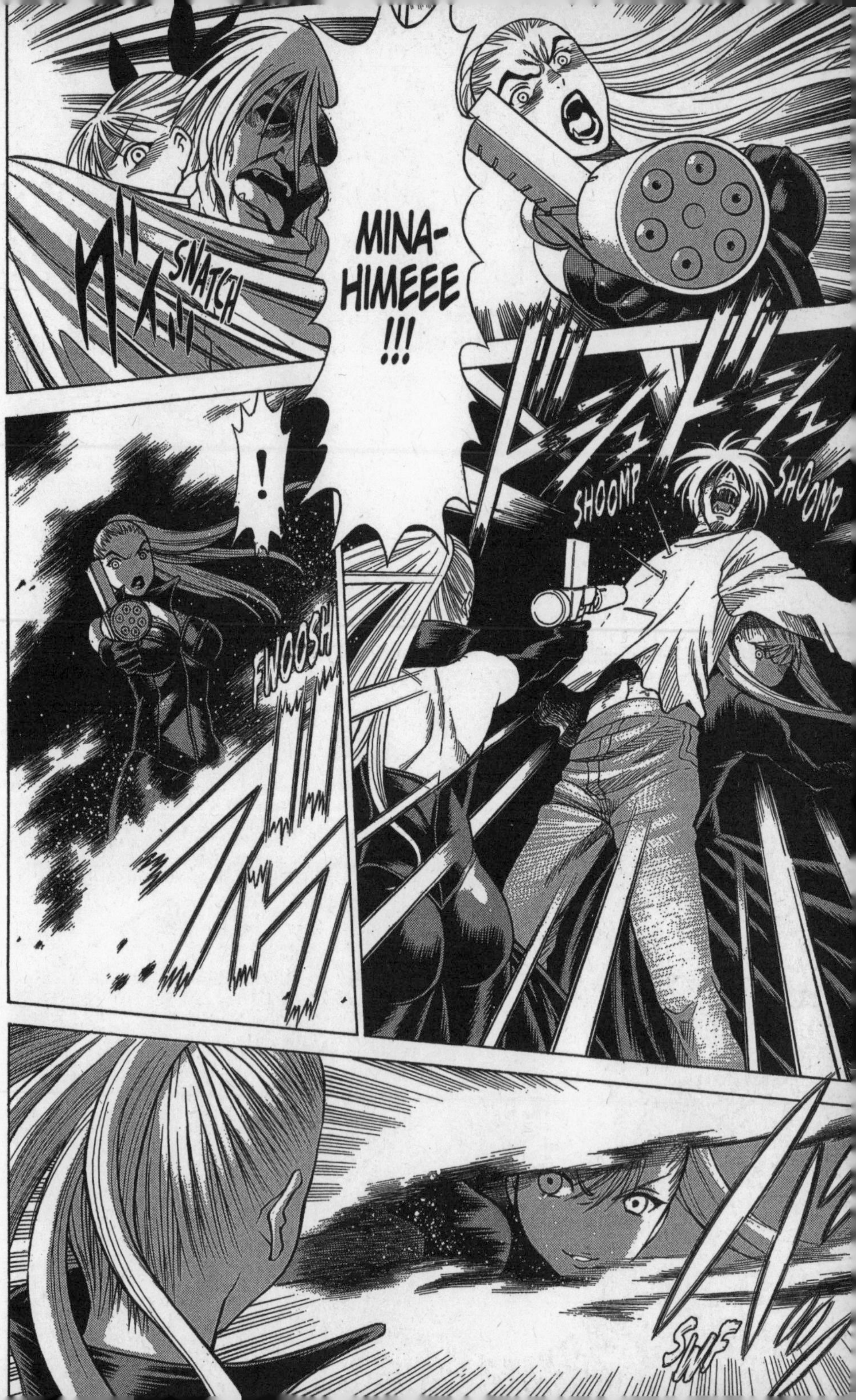
MINA-
HIMEEE
!!!
SNATCH
SHOOMP
SHOOMP
!
FWOOSH
SWF

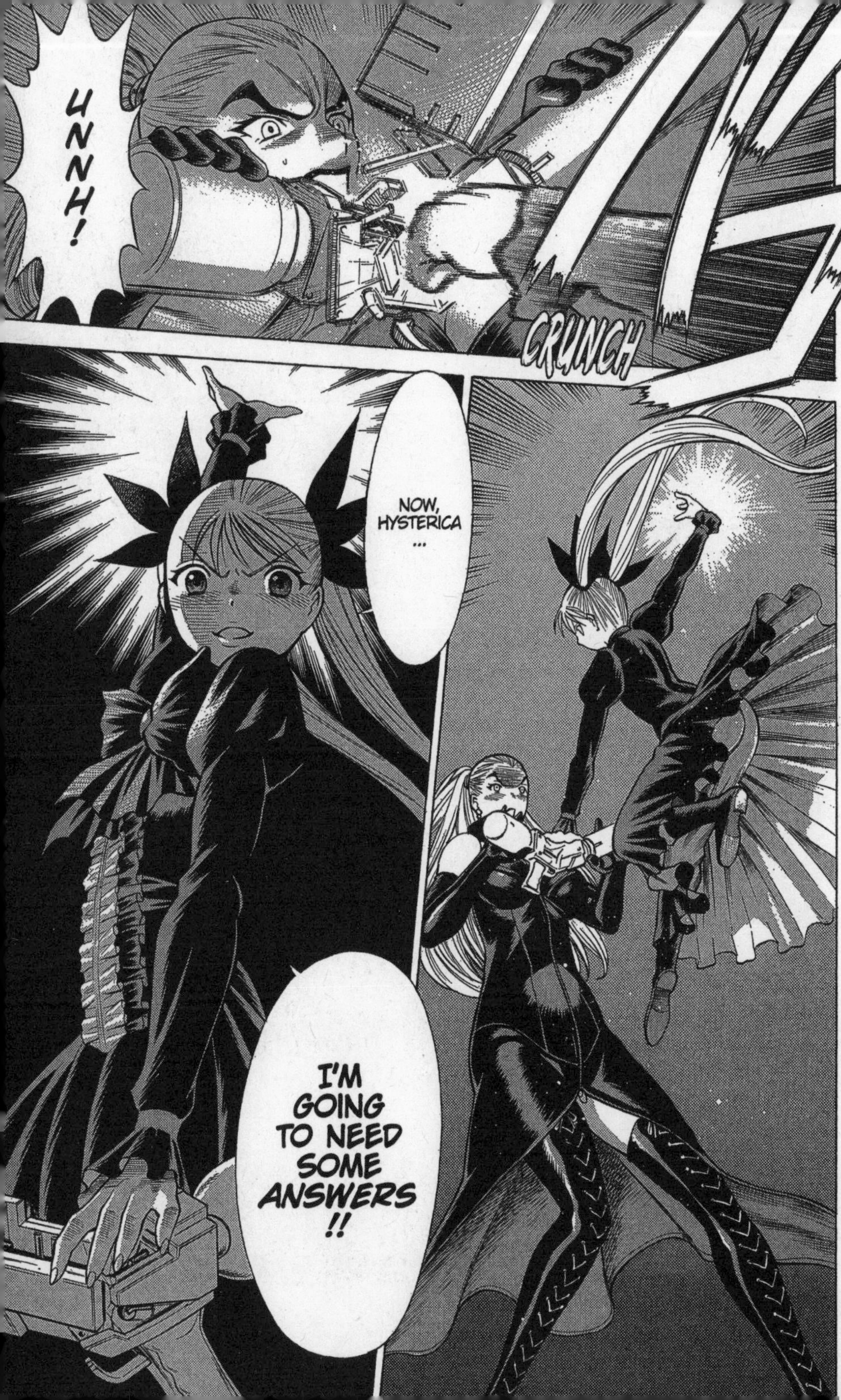
UNNH!
CRUNCH
NOW, HYSTERICA ...
I'M GOING TO NEED SOME ANSWERS!!

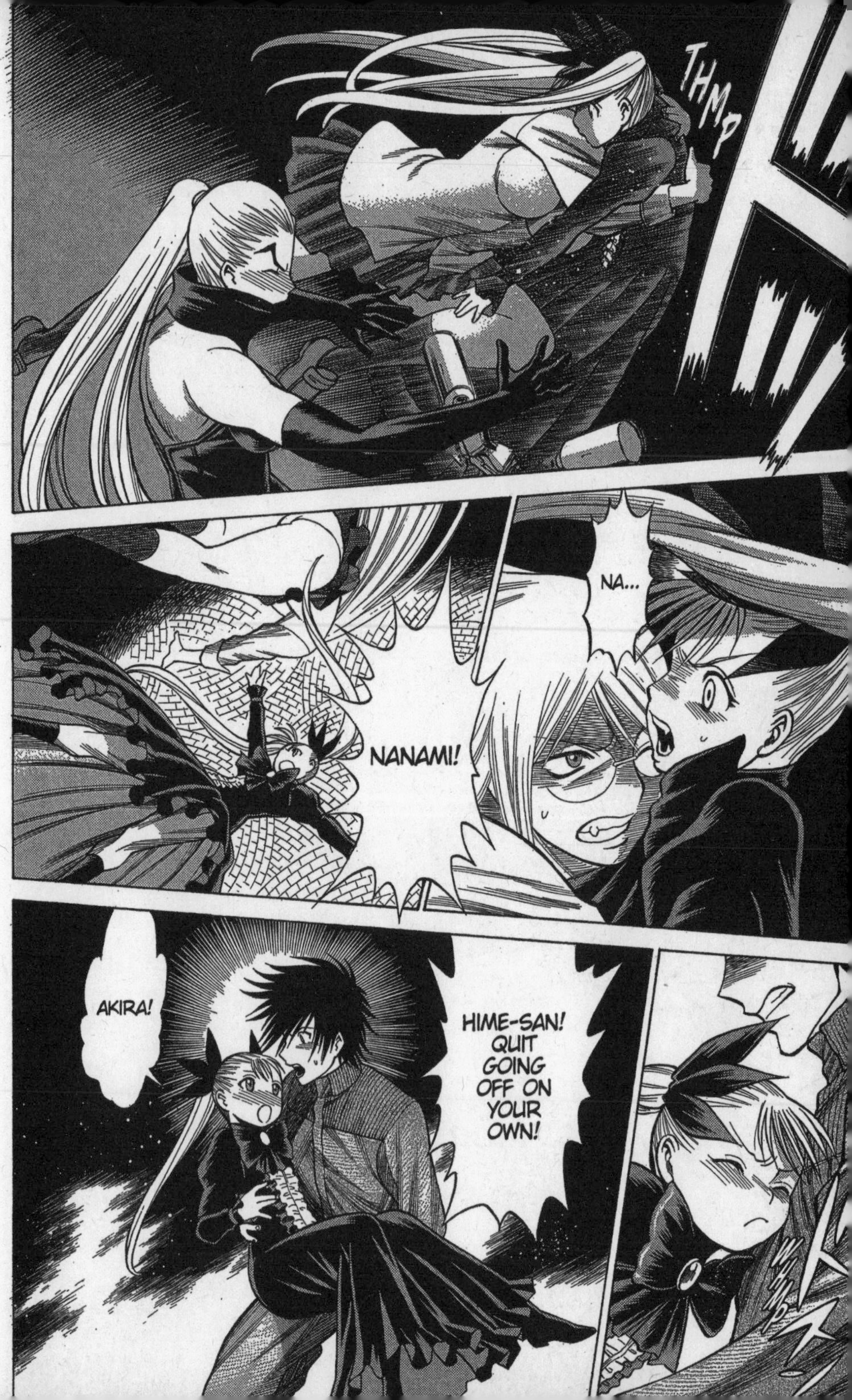
THMP
NA...
NANAMI!
HIME-SAN! QUIT GOING OFF ON YOUR OWN!
AKIRA!

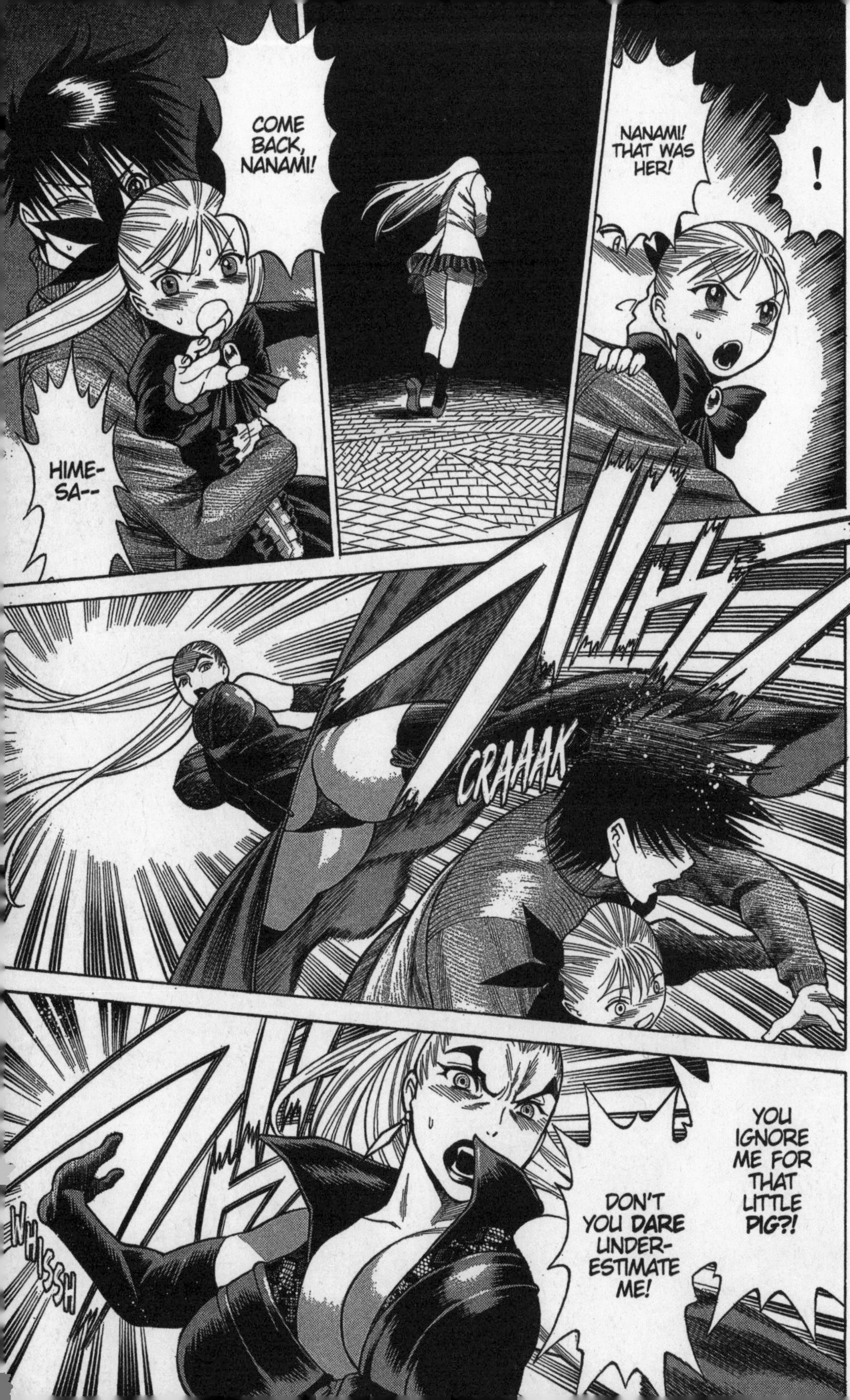
!
NANAMI! THAT WAS HER!
COME BACK, NANAMI!
HIME-SA--
CRAAAK
YOU IGNORE ME FOR THAT LITTLE PIG?!
DON'T YOU DARE UNDER-ESTIMATE ME!
WHISSH

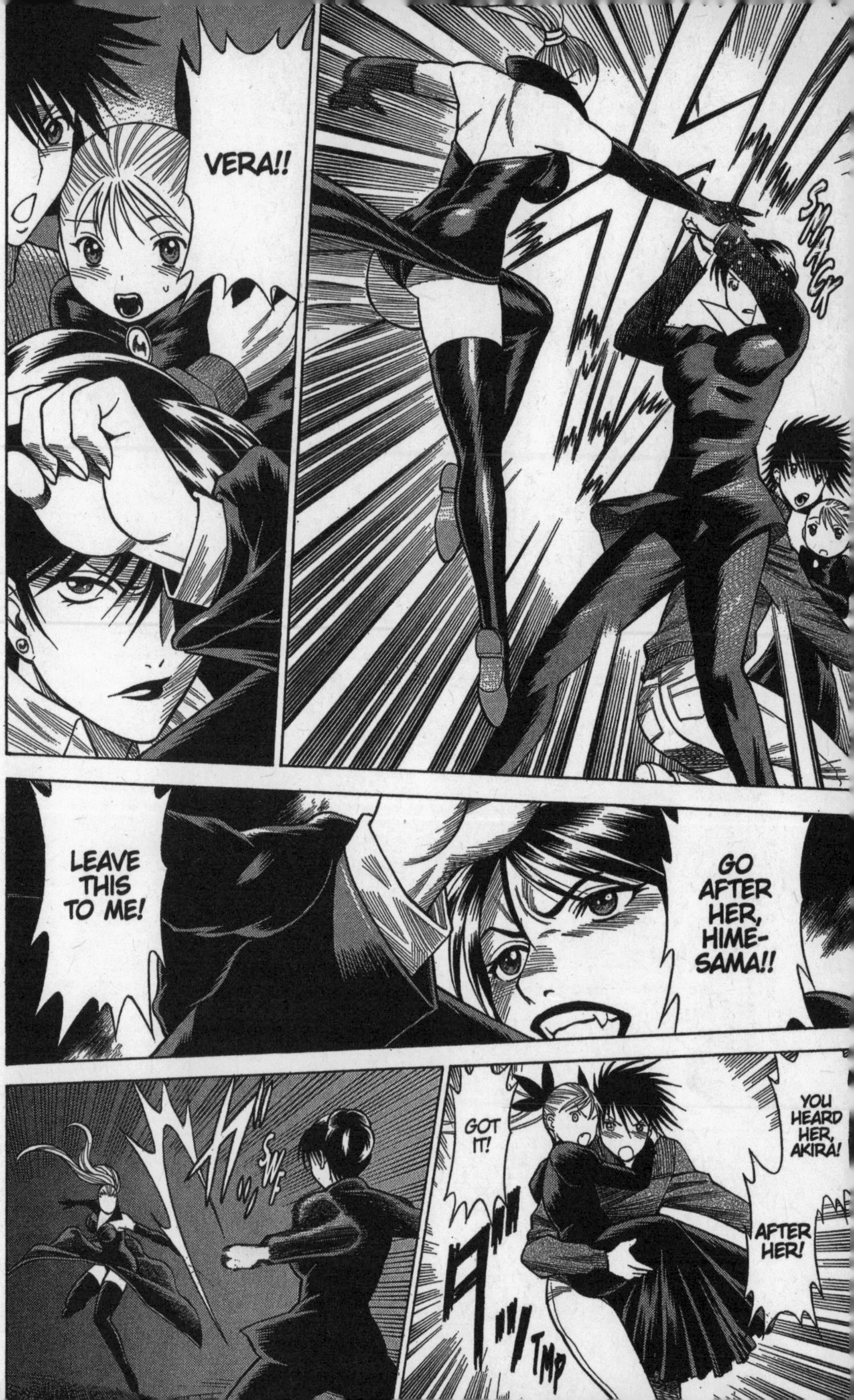
SMACK
VERA!!
GO AFTER HER, HIME-SAMA!!
LEAVE THIS TO ME!
YOU HEARD HER, AKIRA!
GOT IT!
AFTER HER!
TMP
SWF

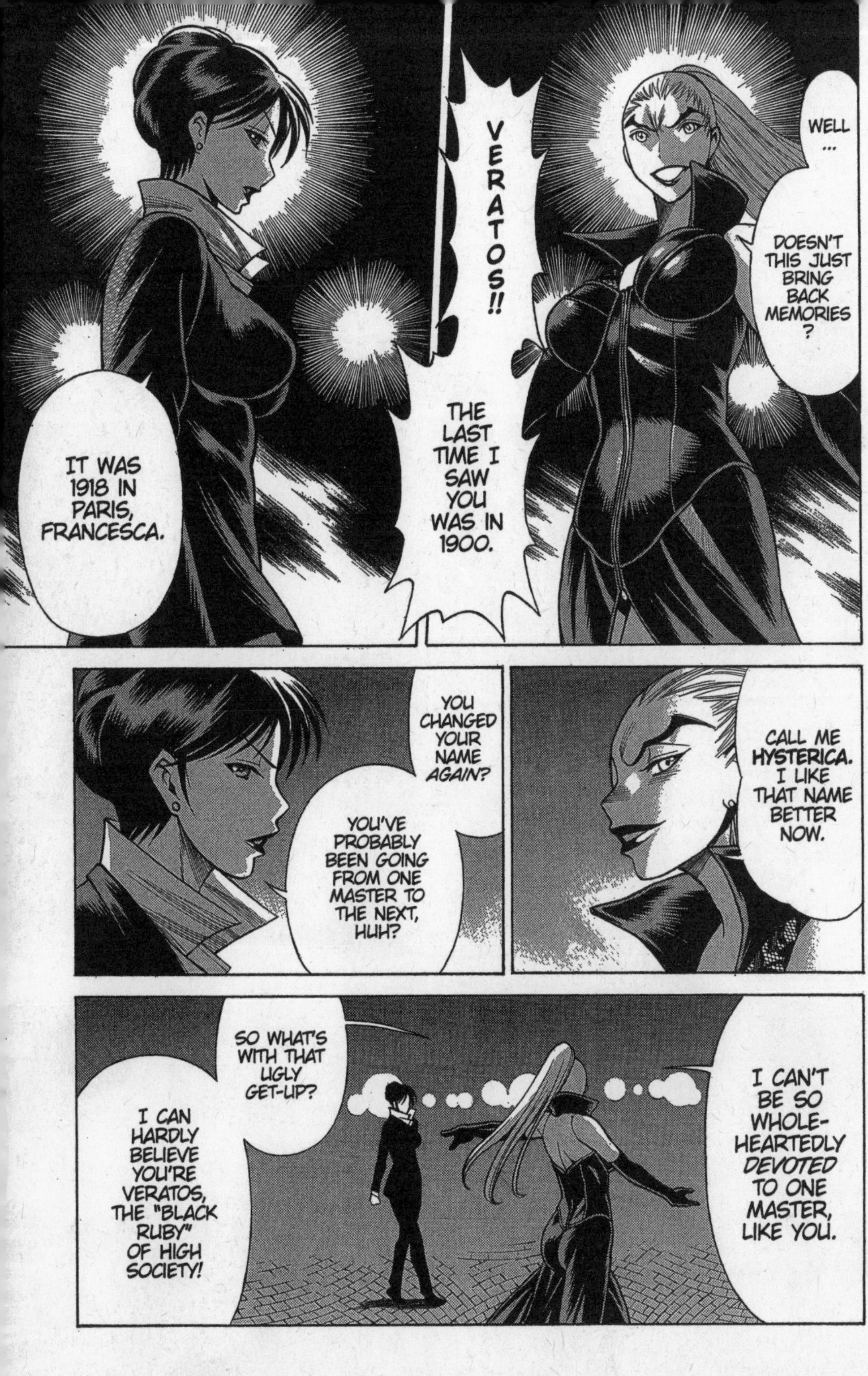
WELL ...
DOESN'T THIS JUST BRING BACK MEMORIES?
VERATOS!!
THE LAST TIME I SAW YOU WAS IN 1900.
IT WAS 1918 IN PARIS, FRANCESCA.
CALL ME **HYSTERICA.** I LIKE THAT NAME BETTER NOW.
YOU CHANGED YOUR NAME *AGAIN?*
YOU'VE PROBABLY BEEN GOING FROM ONE MASTER TO THE NEXT, HUH?
I CAN'T BE SO WHOLE-HEARTEDLY *DEVOTED* TO ONE MASTER, LIKE YOU.
SO WHAT'S WITH THAT UGLY GET-UP?
I CAN HARDLY BELIEVE YOU'RE VERATOS, THE "BLACK RUBY" OF HIGH SOCIETY!

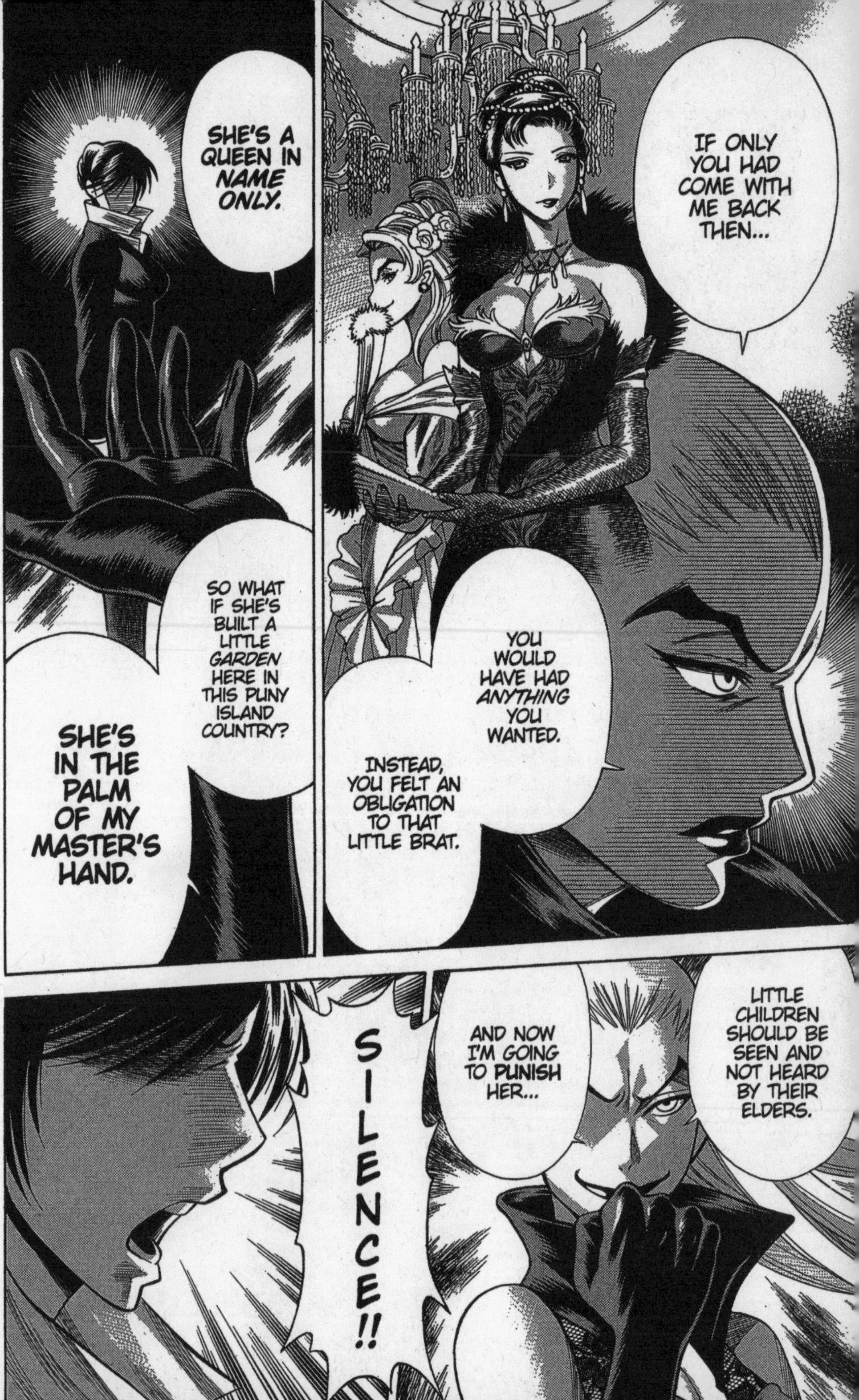
IF ONLY YOU HAD COME WITH ME BACK THEN...
YOU WOULD HAVE HAD *ANYTHING* YOU WANTED.
INSTEAD, YOU FELT AN OBLIGATION TO THAT LITTLE BRAT.
SHE'S A QUEEN IN *NAME ONLY.*
SO WHAT IF SHE'S BUILT A LITTLE *GARDEN* HERE IN THIS PUNY ISLAND COUNTRY?
SHE'S IN THE PALM OF MY MASTER'S HAND.
LITTLE CHILDREN SHOULD BE SEEN AND NOT HEARD BY THEIR ELDERS.
AND NOW I'M GOING TO **PUNISH** HER...
SILENCE!!

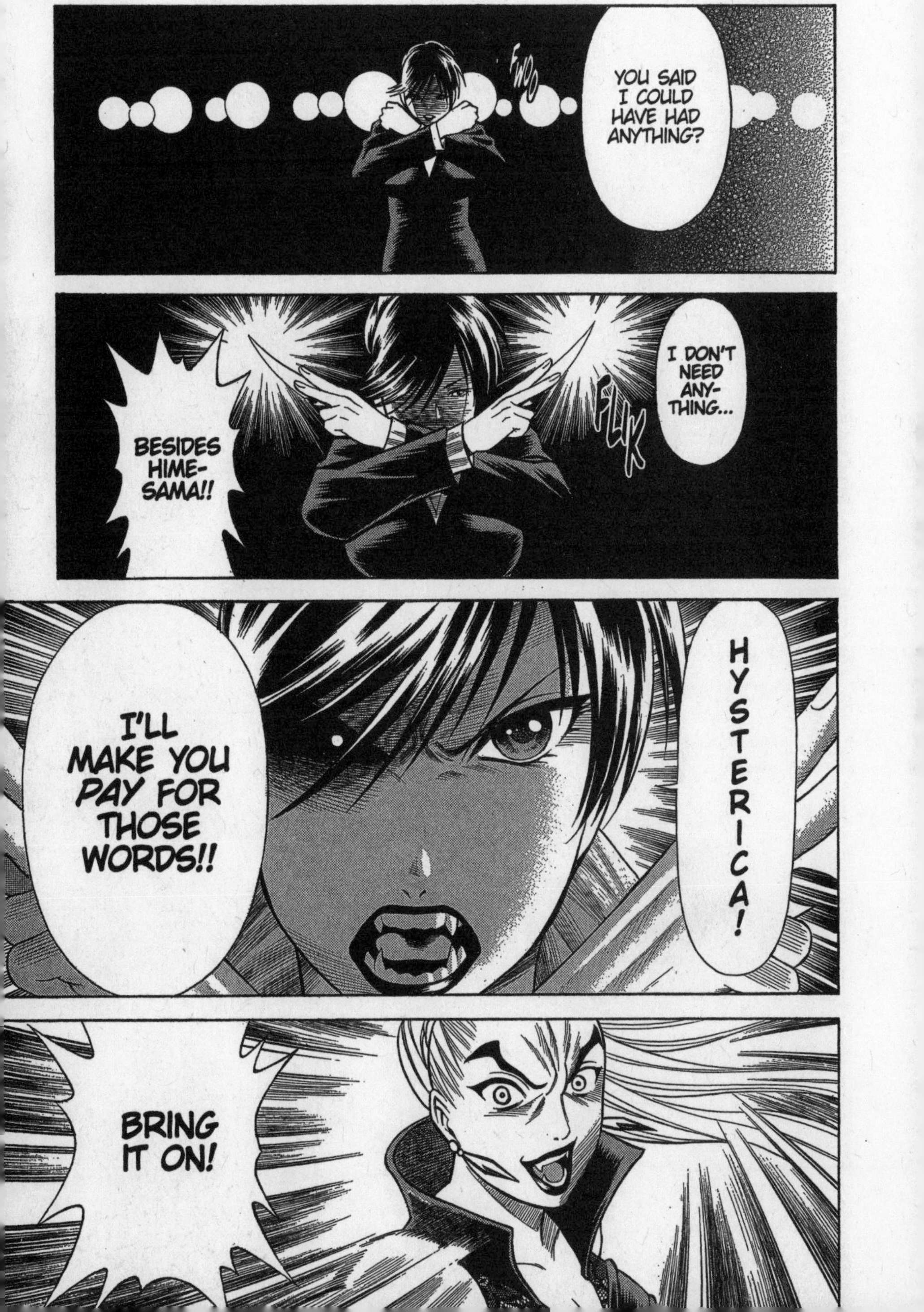
YOU SAID I COULD HAVE HAD ANYTHING?
FWOO
I DON'T NEED ANYTHING...
FLIK
BESIDES HIME-SAMA!!
HYSTERICA!
I'LL MAKE YOU *PAY* FOR THOSE WORDS!!
BRING IT ON!

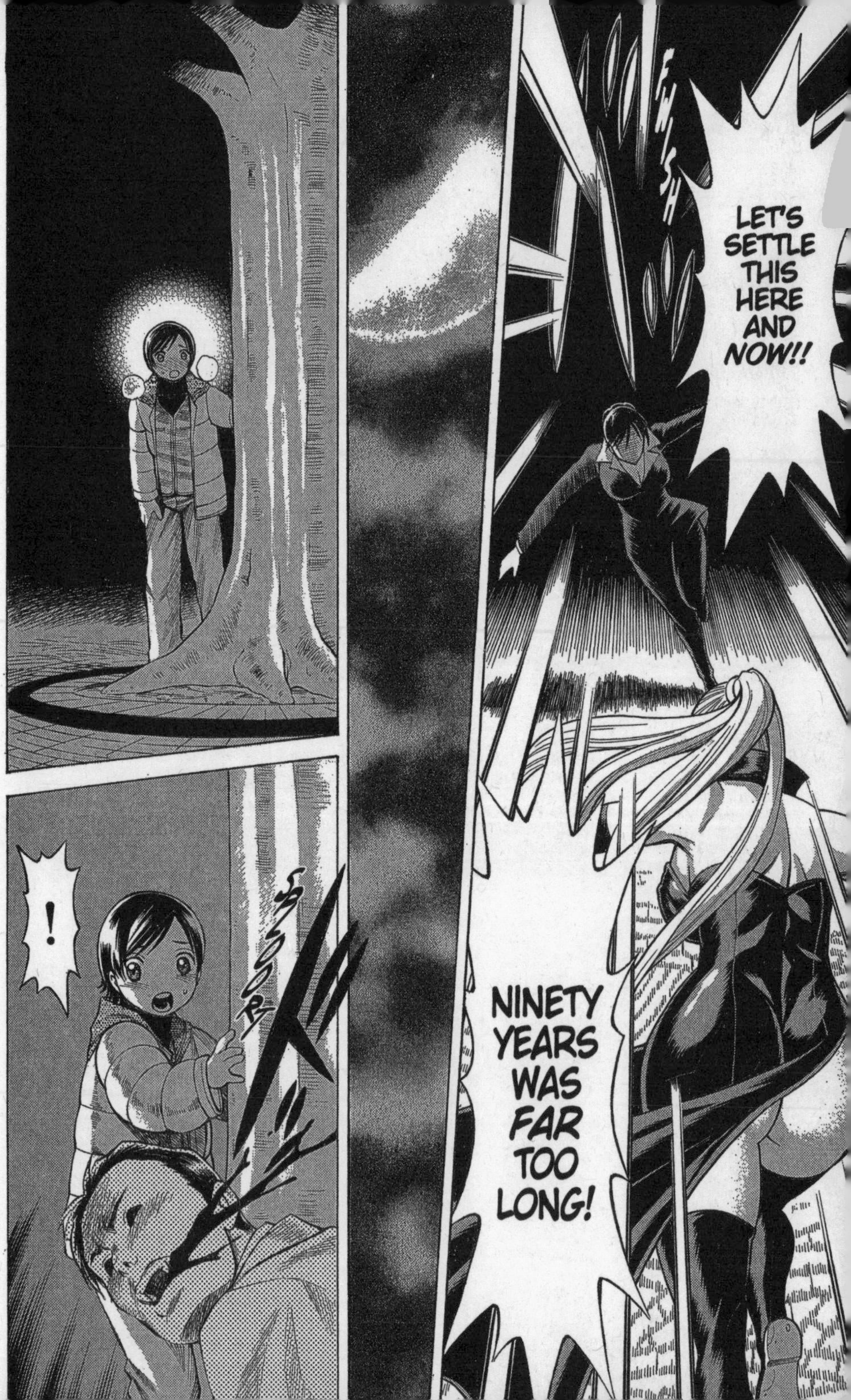
FWISH
LET'S SETTLE THIS HERE AND NOW!!
NINETY YEARS WAS FAR TOO LONG!
!

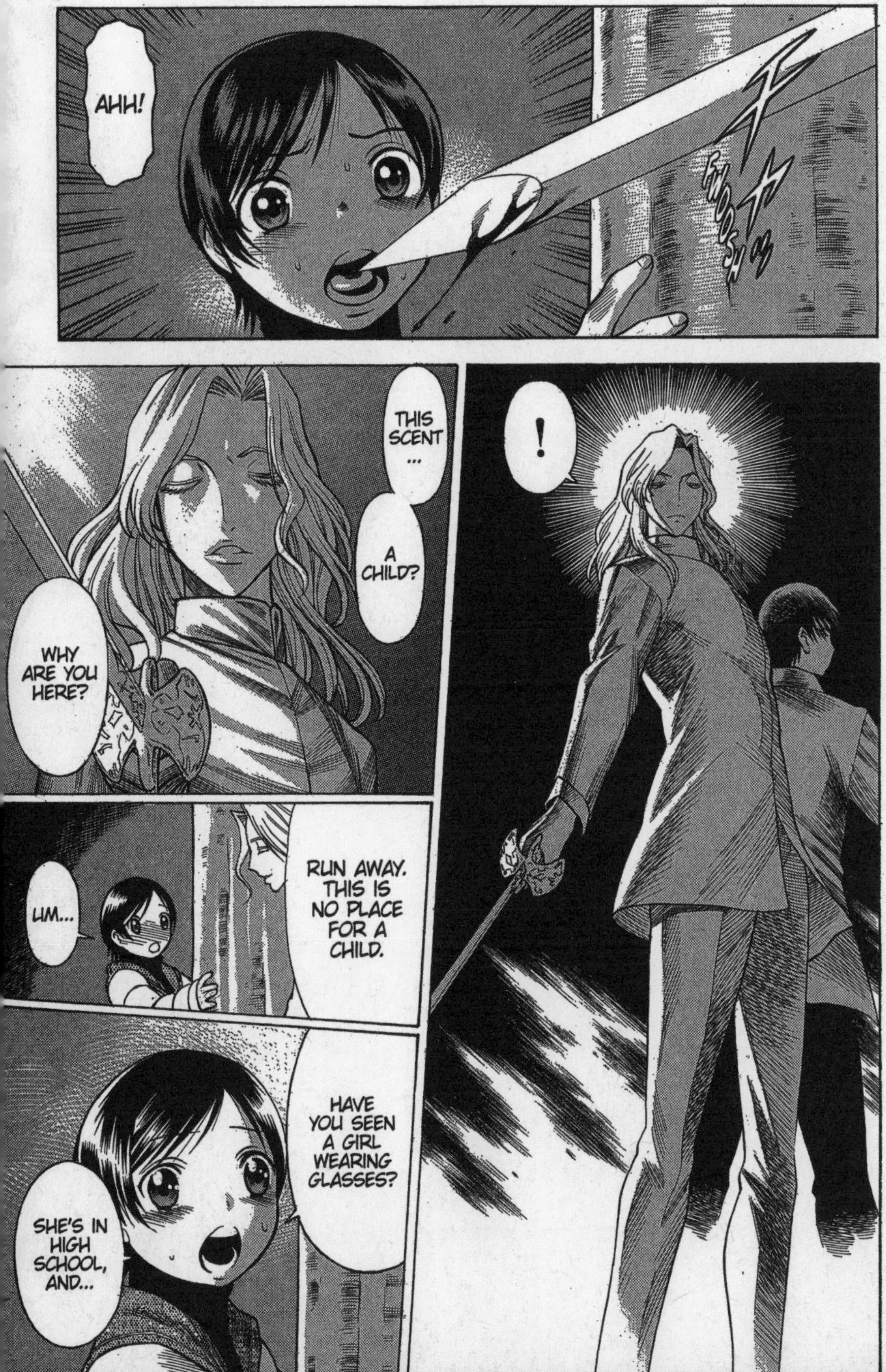
FWOOSH
AHH!
!
THIS SCENT ...
A CHILD?
WHY ARE YOU HERE?
RUN AWAY. THIS IS NO PLACE FOR A CHILD.
UM...
HAVE YOU SEEN A GIRL WEARING GLASSES?
SHE'S IN HIGH SCHOOL, AND...

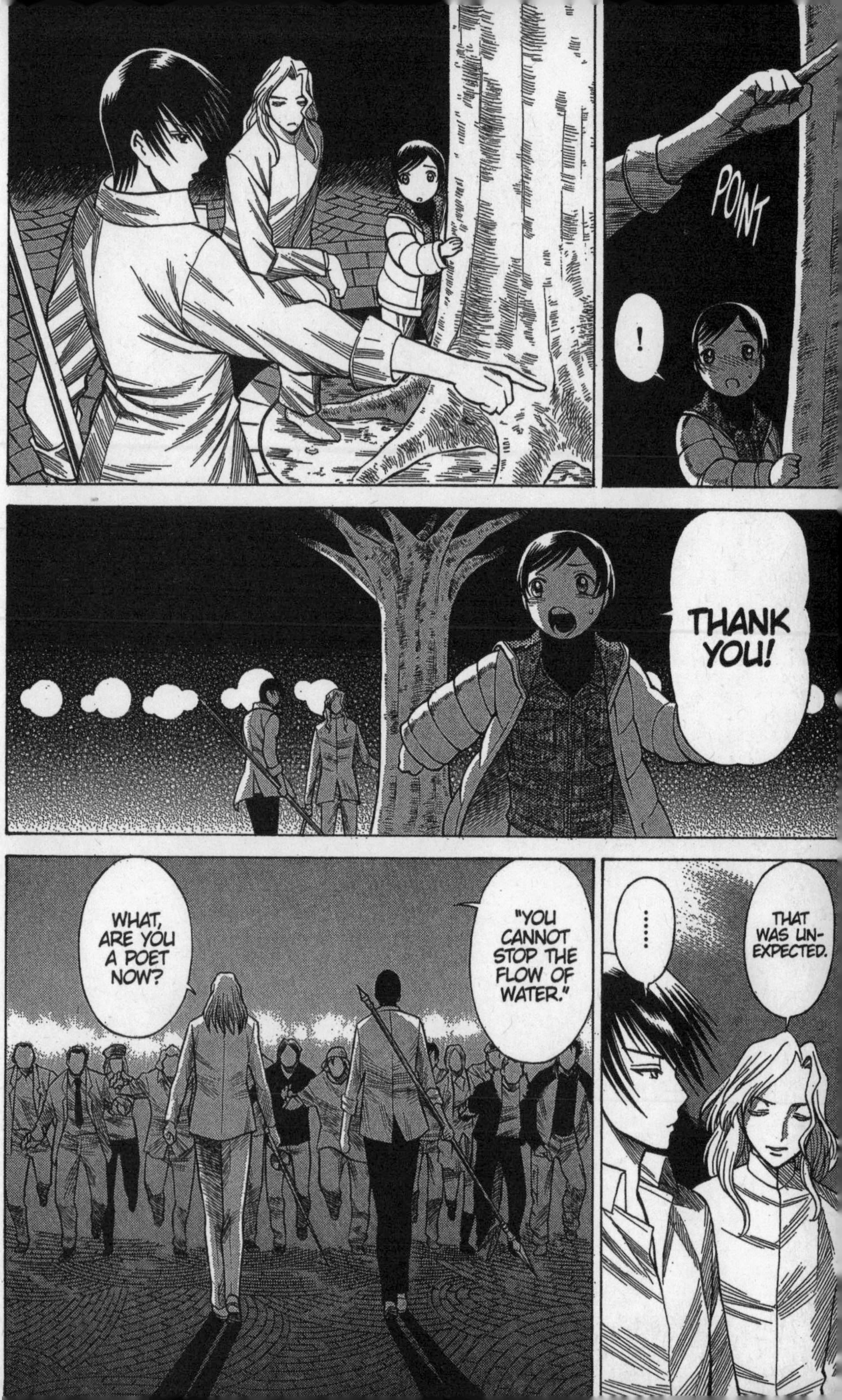
POINT
!
THANK YOU!
THAT WAS UN-EXPECTED.
……
"YOU CANNOT STOP THE FLOW OF WATER."
WHAT, ARE YOU A POET NOW?

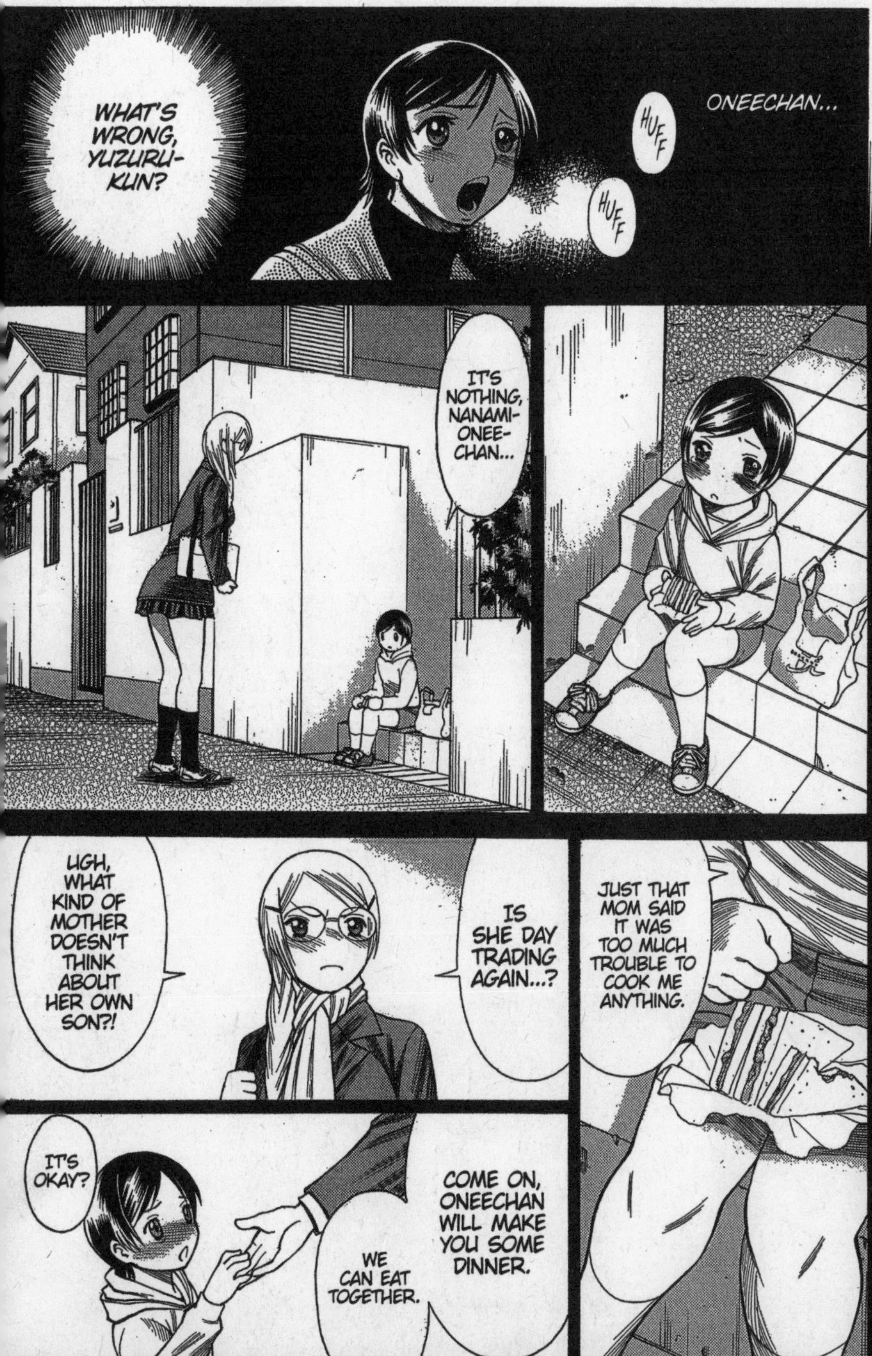
ONEECHAN...
HUFF
HUFF
WHAT'S WRONG, YUZURU-KUN?
IT'S NOTHING, NANAMI-ONEE-CHAN...
JUST THAT MOM SAID IT WAS TOO MUCH TROUBLE TO COOK ME ANYTHING.
IS SHE DAY TRADING AGAIN...?
UGH, WHAT KIND OF MOTHER DOESN'T THINK ABOUT HER OWN SON?!
COME ON, ONEECHAN WILL MAKE YOU SOME DINNER.
WE CAN EAT TOGETHER.
IT'S OKAY?

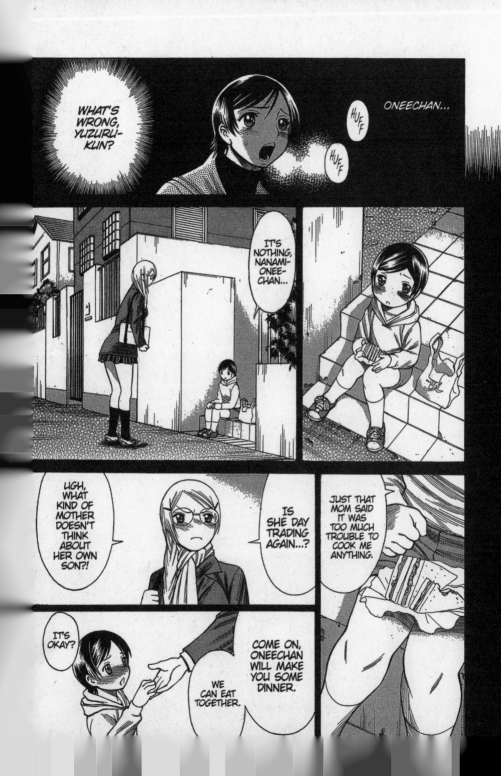

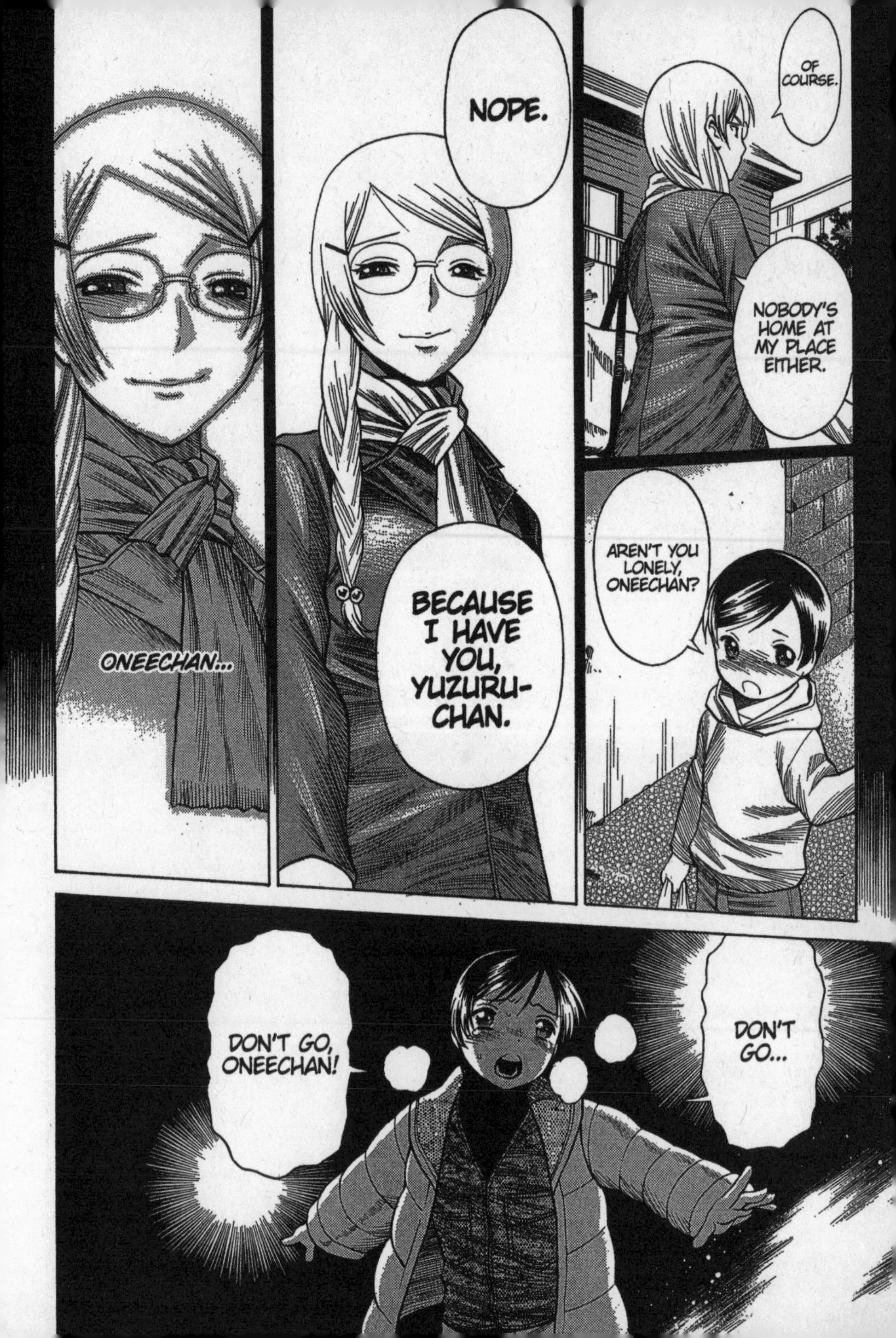
OF COURSE.
NOBODY'S HOME AT MY PLACE EITHER.
AREN'T YOU LONELY, ONEECHAN?
NOPE.
BECAUSE I HAVE YOU, YUZURU-CHAN.
ONEECHAN...
DON'T GO...
DON'T GO, ONEECHAN!

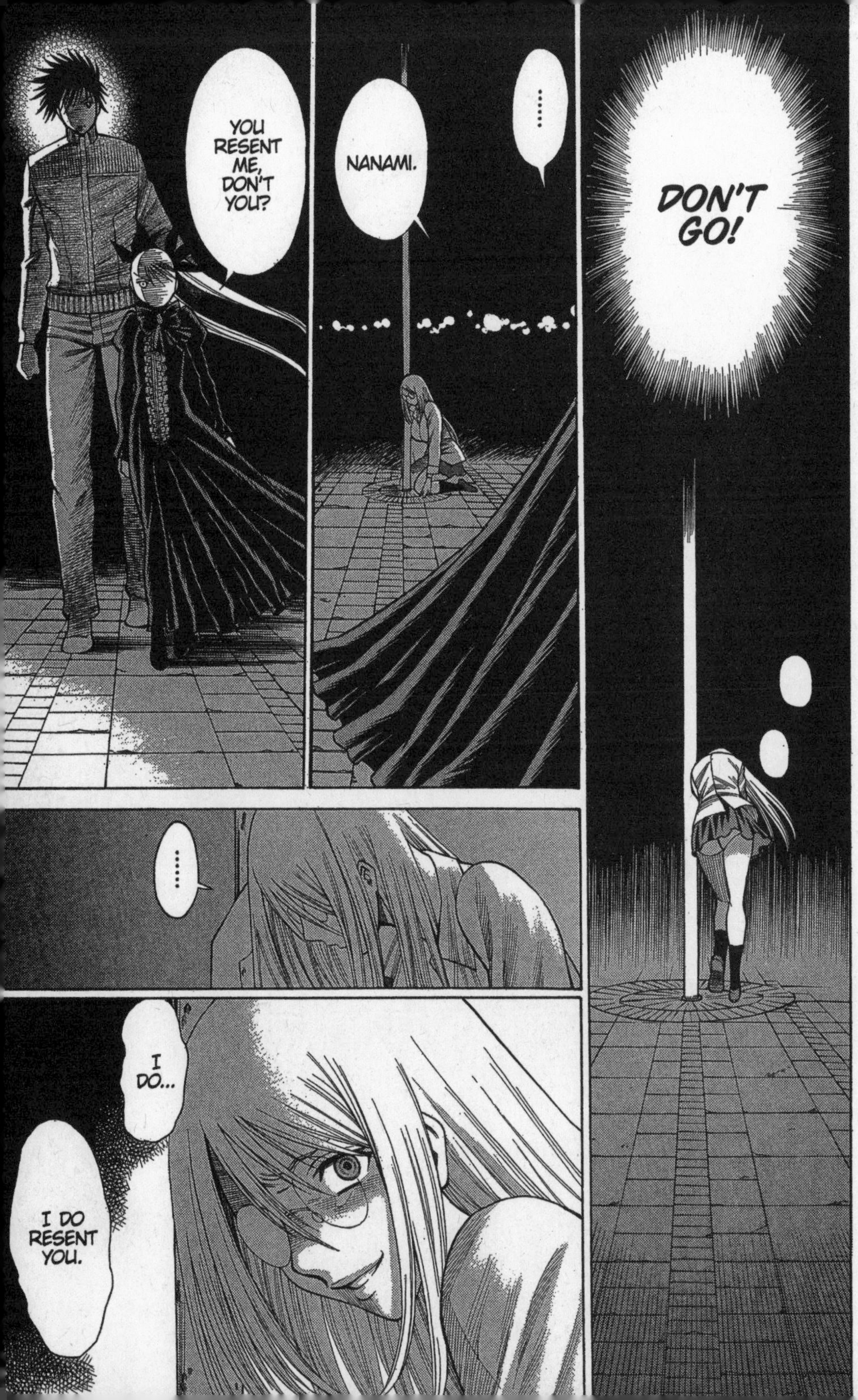
DON'T GO!
......
NANAMI.
YOU RESENT ME, DON'T YOU?
......
I DO...
I DO RESENT YOU.

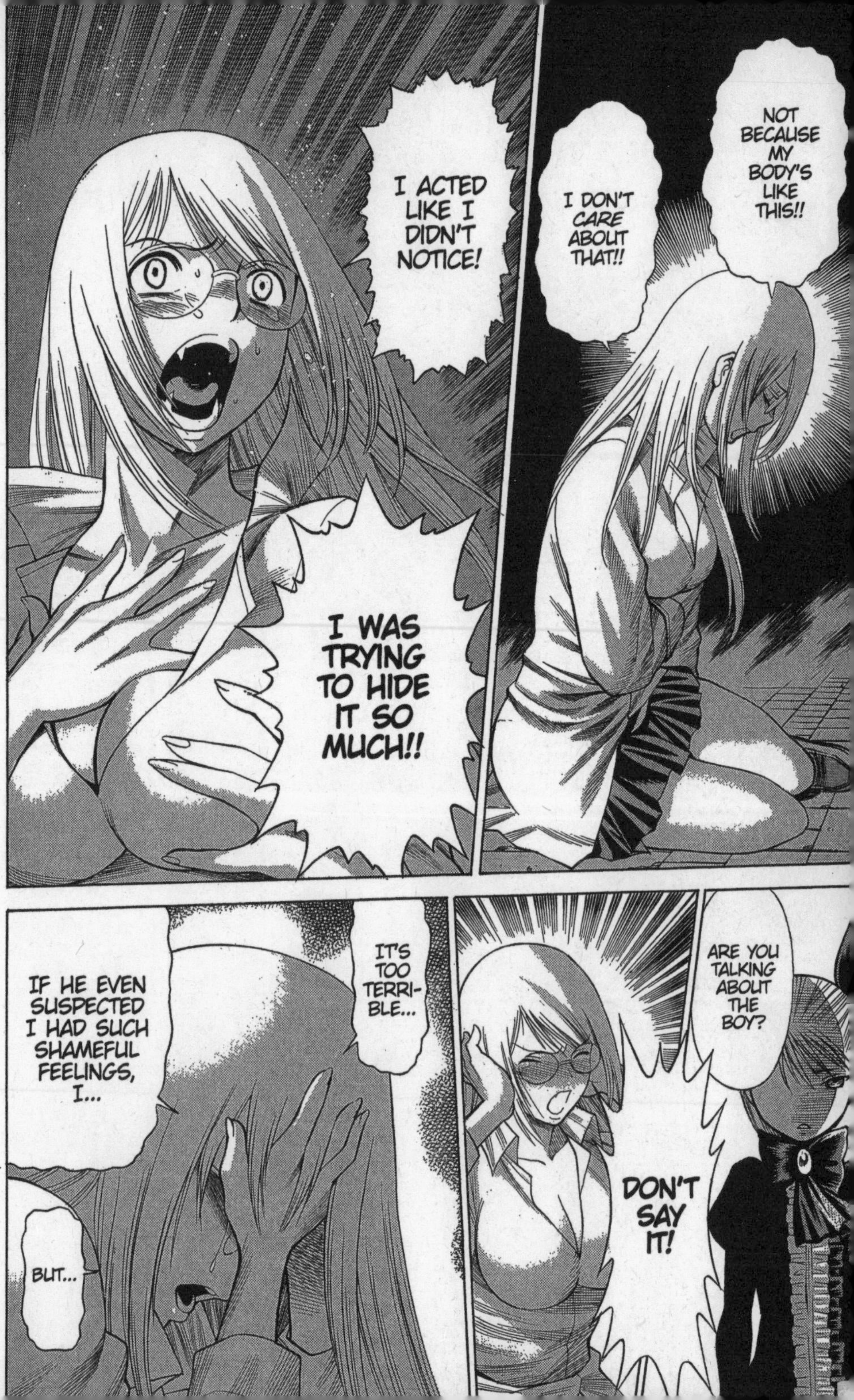
NOT BECAUSE MY BODY'S LIKE THIS!!
I DON'T *CARE* ABOUT THAT!!
I ACTED LIKE I DIDN'T NOTICE!
I WAS TRYING TO HIDE IT SO MUCH!!
ARE YOU TALKING ABOUT THE BOY?
DON'T SAY IT!
IT'S TOO TERRI-BLE...
IF HE EVEN SUSPECTED I HAD SUCH SHAMEFUL FEELINGS, I...
BUT...

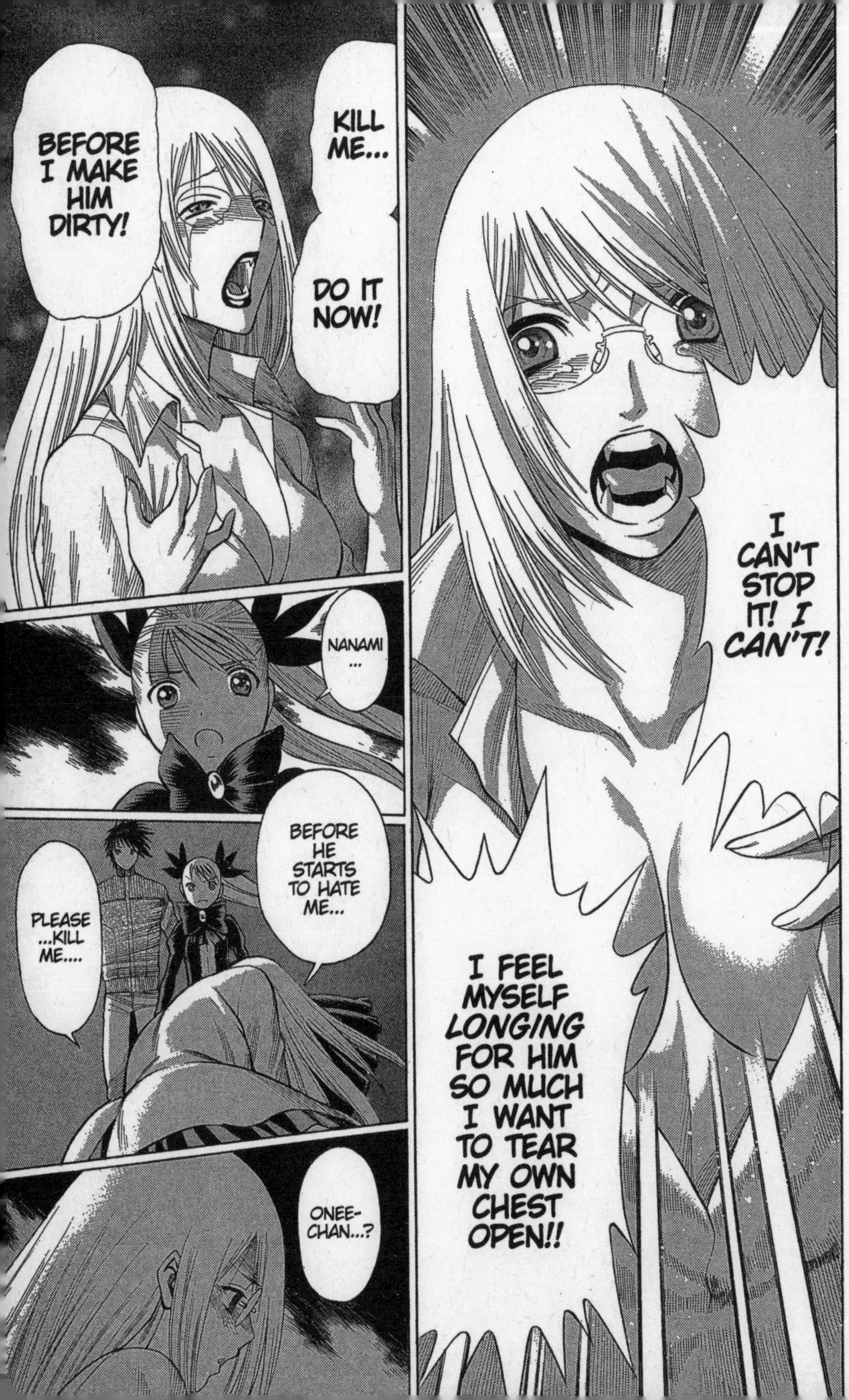

I CAN'T STOP IT! I CAN'T!
I FEEL MYSELF LONGING FOR HIM SO MUCH I WANT TO TEAR MY OWN CHEST OPEN!!
KILL ME...
DO IT NOW!
BEFORE I MAKE HIM DIRTY!
NANAMI ...
BEFORE HE STARTS TO HATE ME...
PLEASE ...KILL ME....
ONEE-CHAN...?

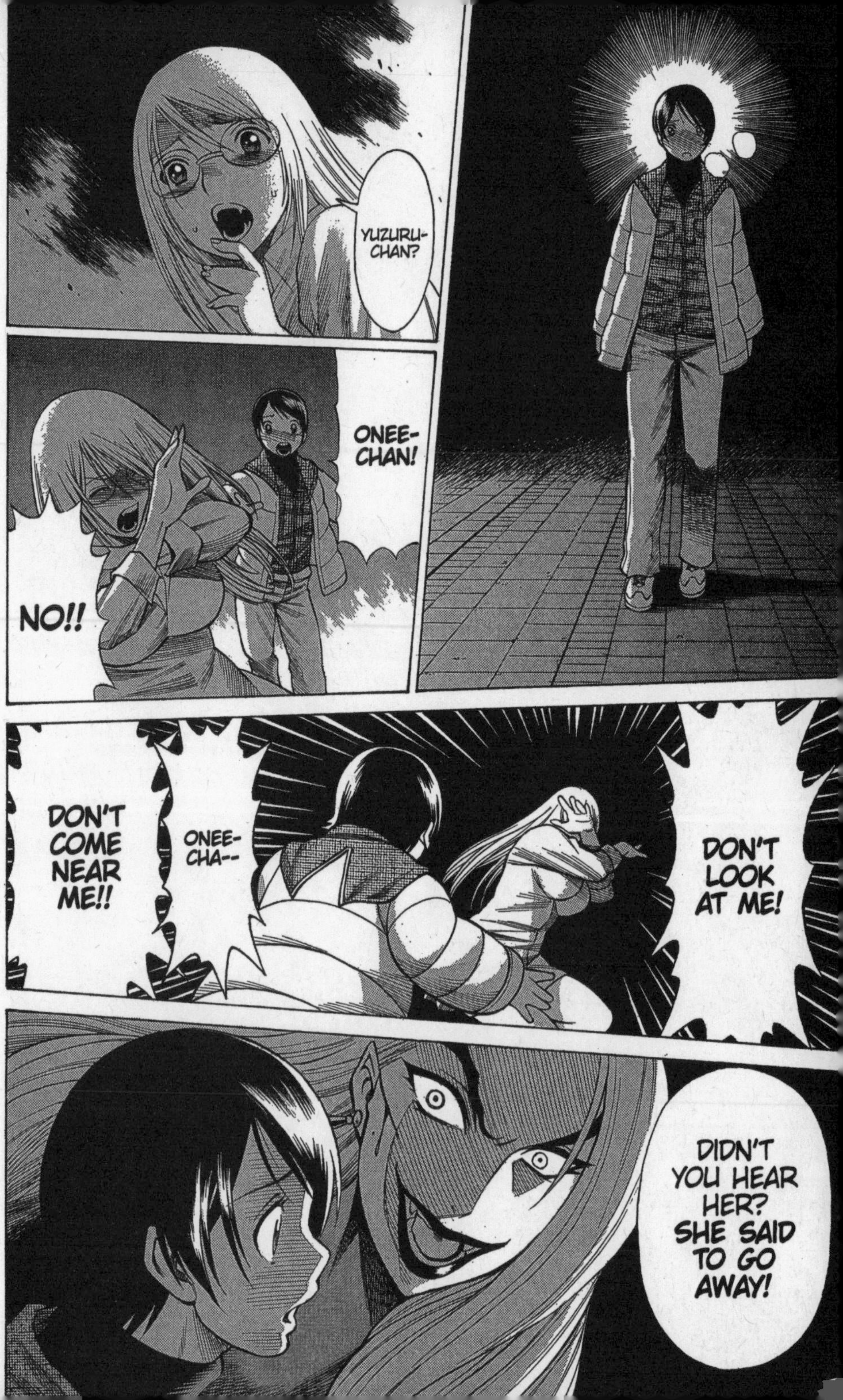
YUZURU-CHAN?
ONEE-CHAN!
NO!!
DON'T LOOK AT ME!
ONEE-CHA--
DON'T COME NEAR ME!!
DIDN'T YOU HEAR HER? SHE SAID TO GO AWAY!

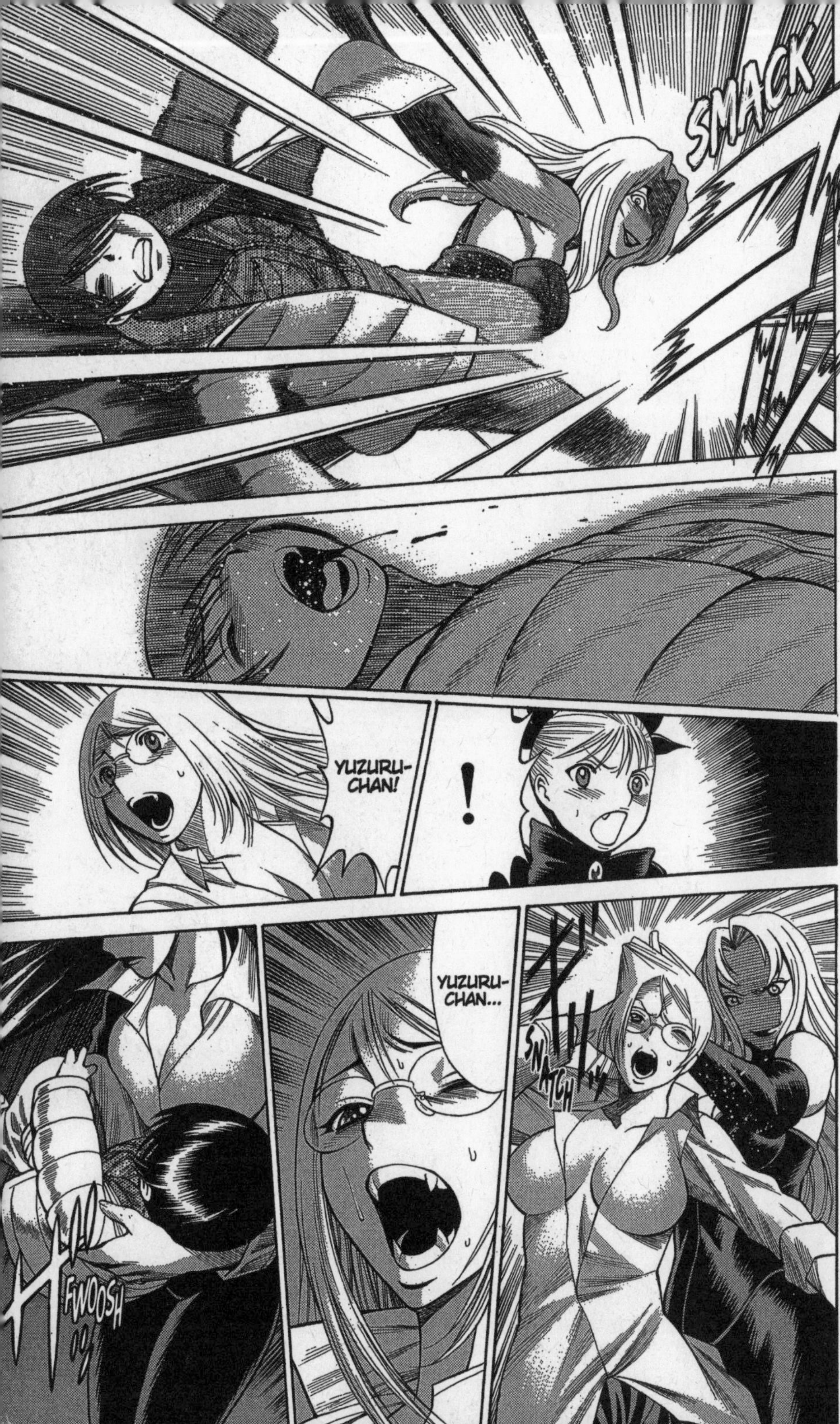
SMACK
!
YUZURU-CHAN!
SNATCH
YUZURU-CHAN...
FWOOSH

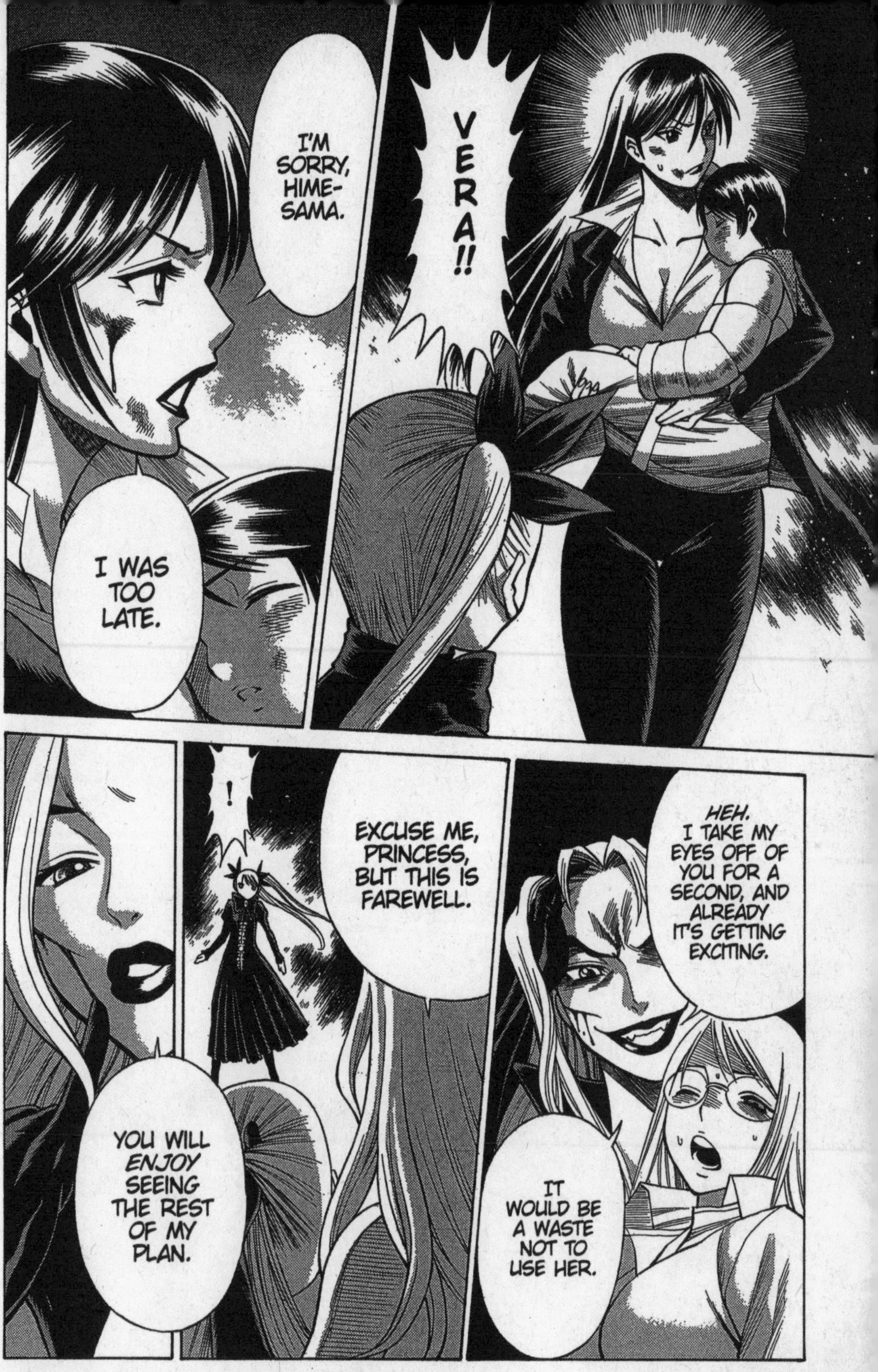
VERA!!
I'M SORRY, HIME-SAMA.
I WAS TOO LATE.
HEH. I TAKE MY EYES OFF OF YOU FOR A SECOND, AND ALREADY IT'S GETTING EXCITING.
IT WOULD BE A WASTE NOT TO USE HER.
EXCUSE ME, PRINCESS, BUT THIS IS FAREWELL.
!
YOU WILL *ENJOY* SEEING THE REST OF MY PLAN.

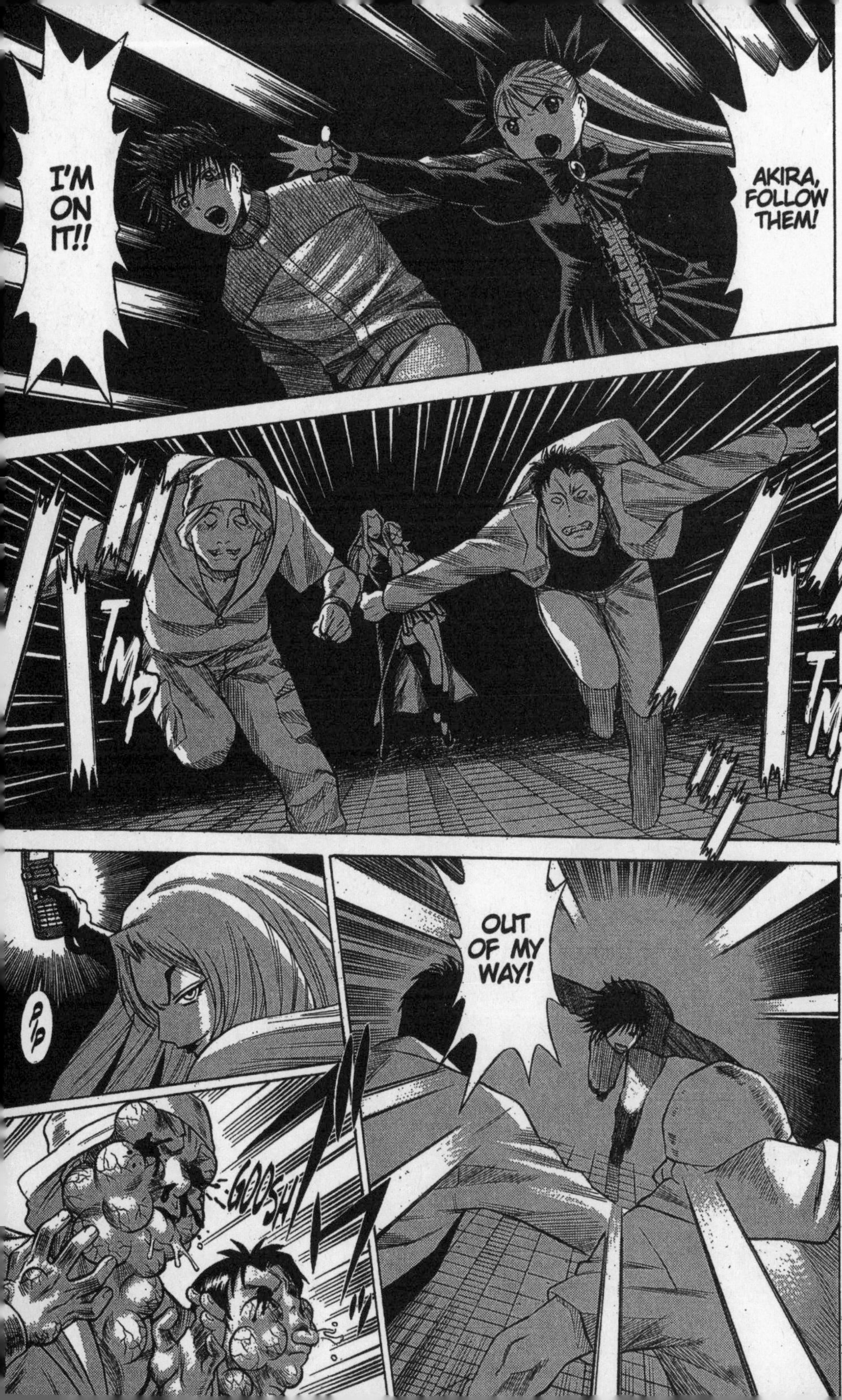
AKIRA, FOLLOW THEM!
I'M ON IT!!
TMP
TMP
OUT OF MY WAY!
GOOSH
PIP

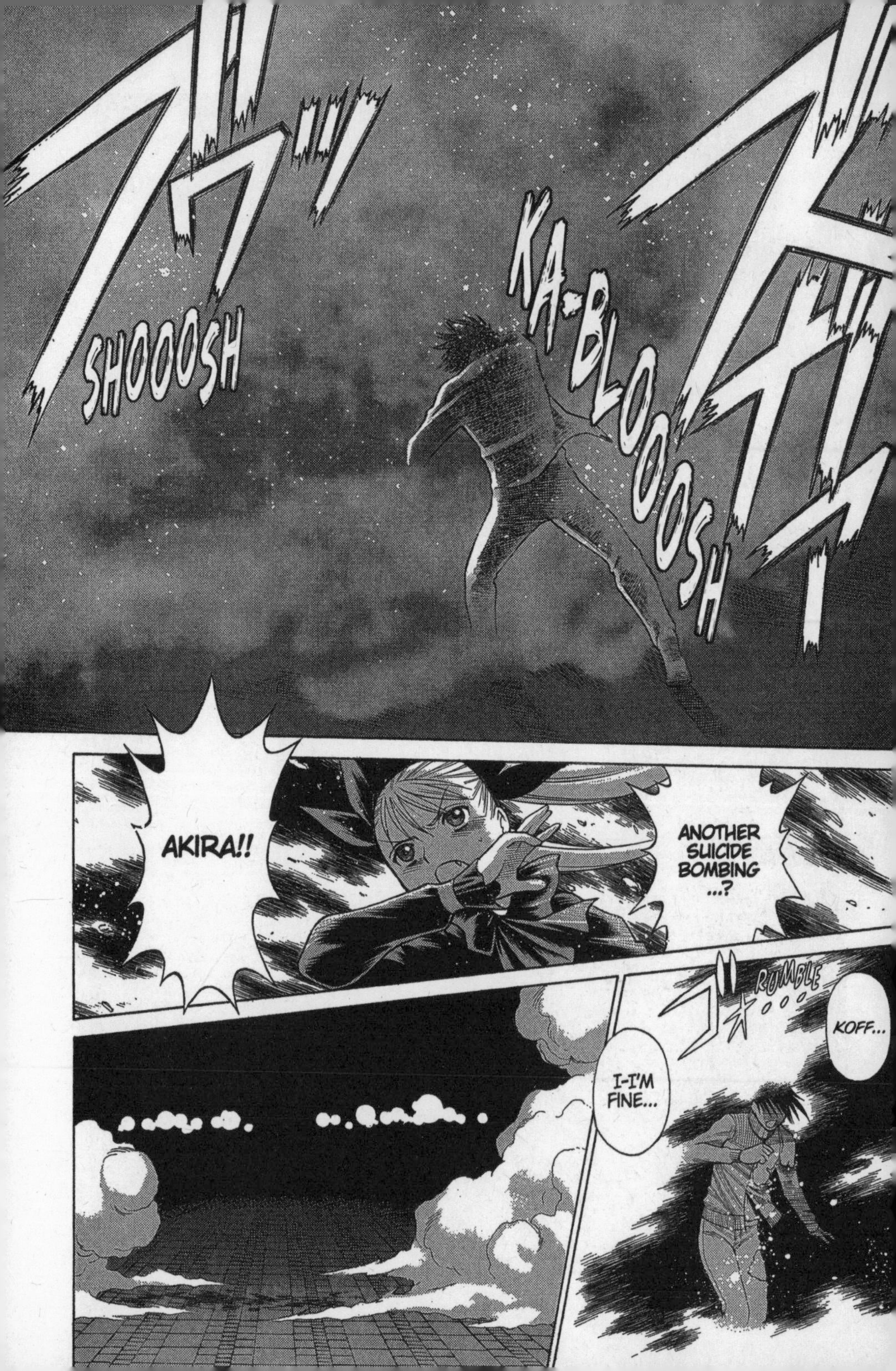
KA-BLOOOSH
SHOOSH
ANOTHER SUICIDE BOMBING ...?
AKIRA!!
RUMBLE
KOFF...
I-I'M FINE...

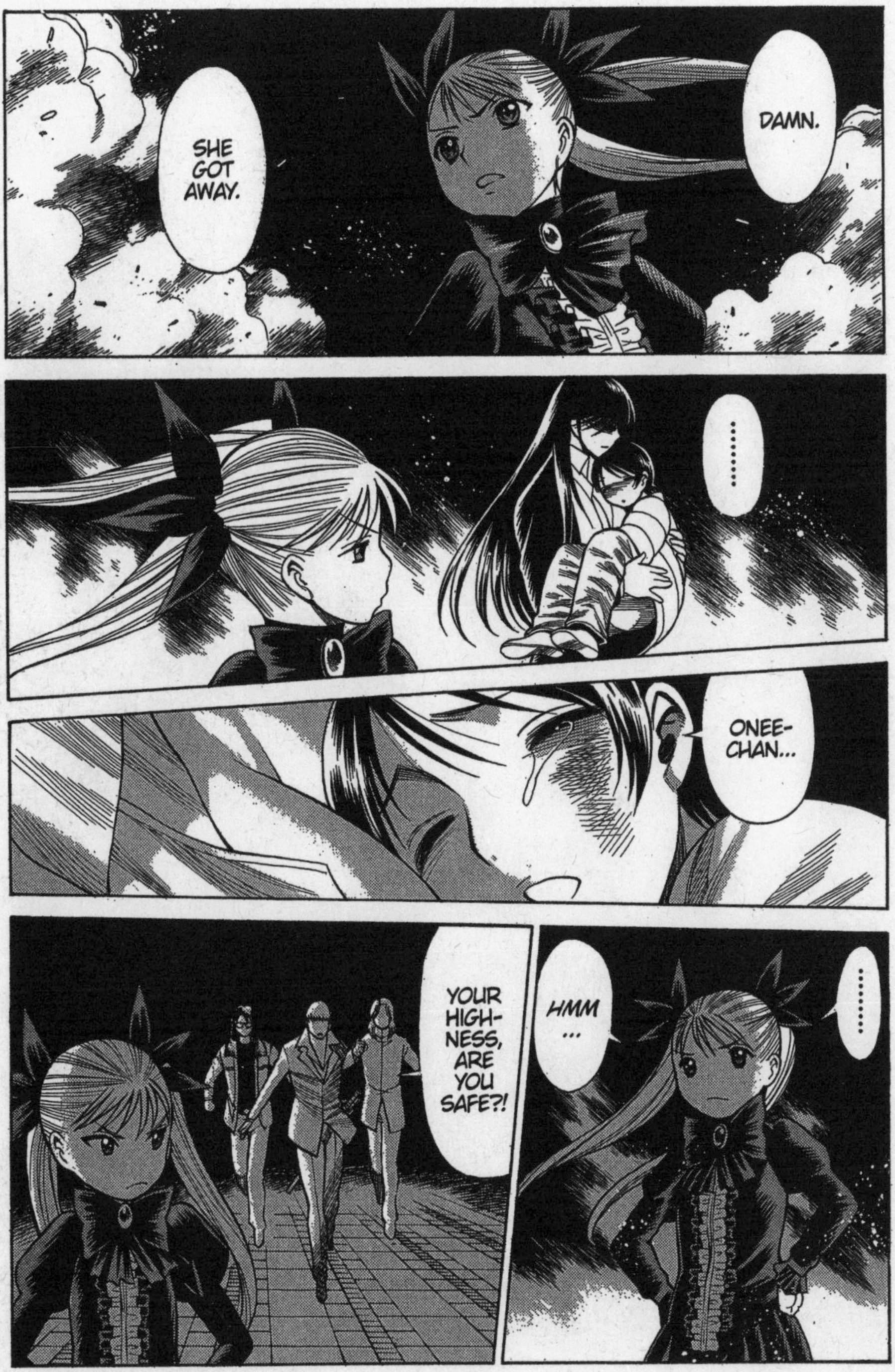
DAMN.
SHE GOT AWAY.
......
ONEE-CHAN...
......
HMM ...
YOUR HIGHNESS, ARE YOU SAFE?!

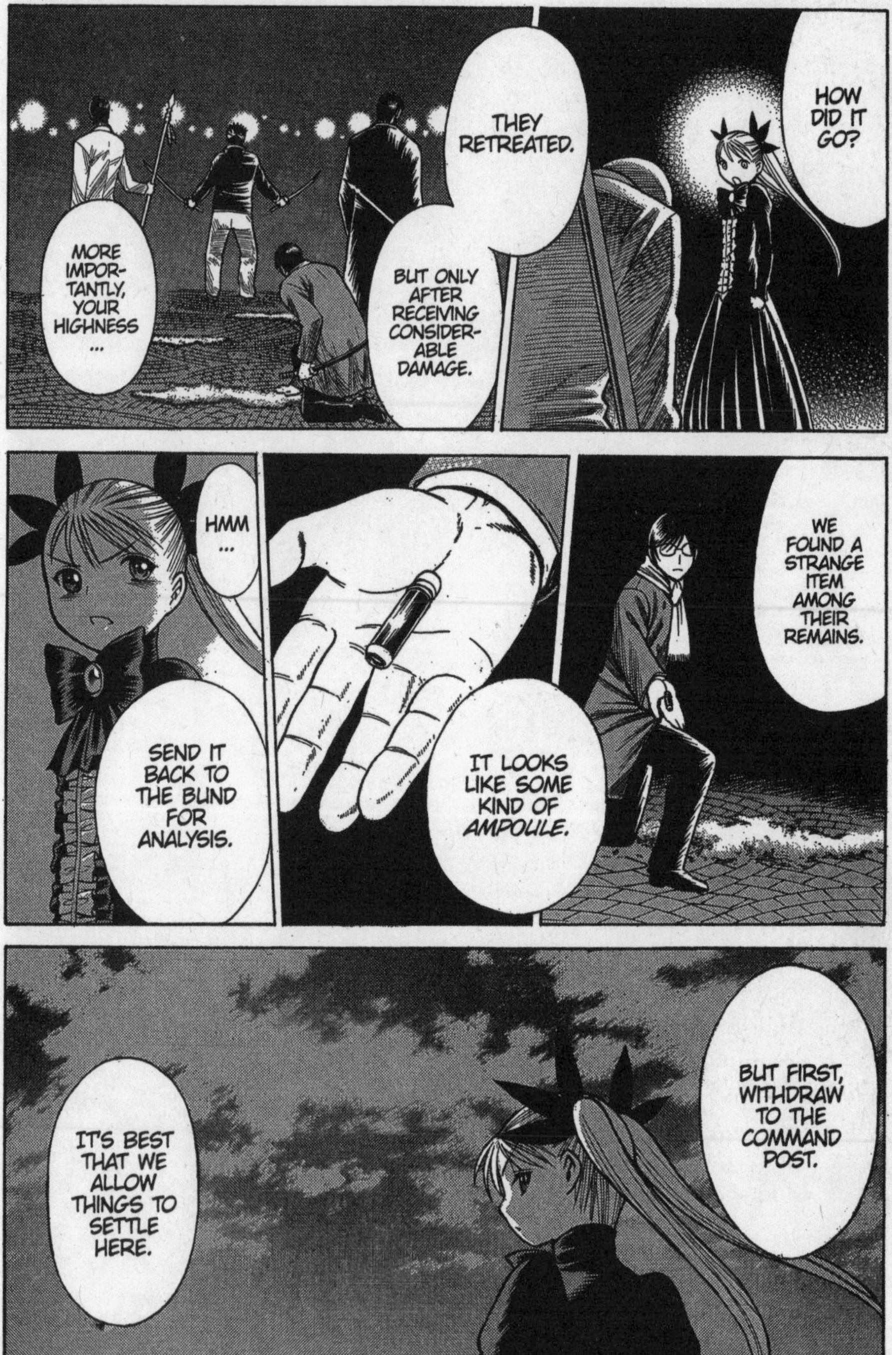
HOW DID IT GO?
THEY RETREATED.
BUT ONLY AFTER RECEIVING CONSIDERABLE DAMAGE.
MORE IMPORTANTLY, YOUR HIGHNESS ...
WE FOUND A STRANGE ITEM AMONG THEIR REMAINS.
IT LOOKS LIKE SOME KIND OF *AMPOULE.*
HMM ...
SEND IT BACK TO THE BUND FOR ANALYSIS.
BUT FIRST, WITHDRAW TO THE COMMAND POST.
IT'S BEST THAT WE ALLOW THINGS TO SETTLE HERE.

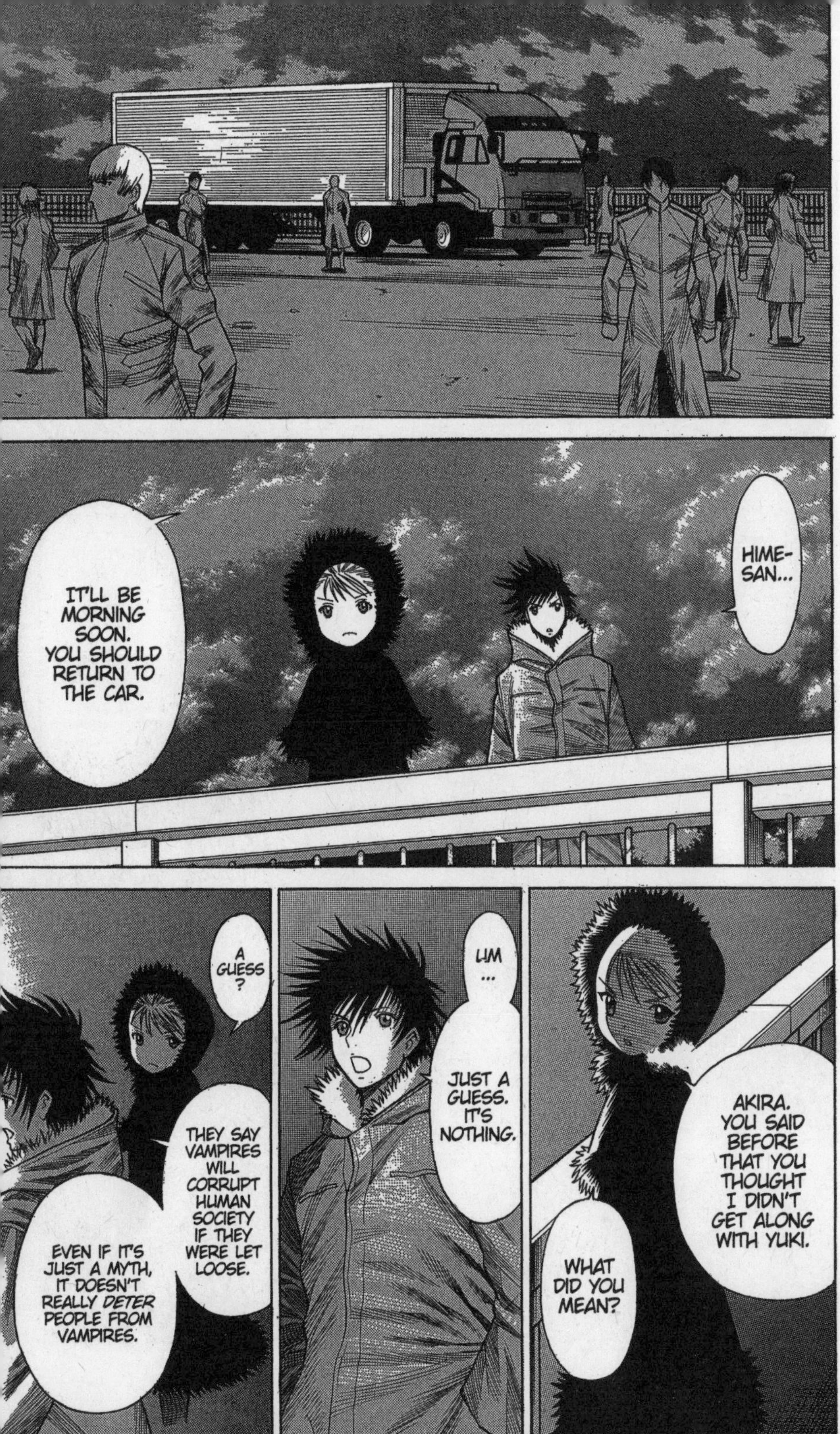
HIME-SAN...
IT'LL BE MORNING SOON. YOU SHOULD RETURN TO THE CAR.
AKIRA. YOU SAID BEFORE THAT YOU THOUGHT I DIDN'T GET ALONG WITH YUKI.
WHAT DID YOU MEAN?
UM ...
JUST A GUESS. IT'S NOTHING.
A GUESS?
THEY SAY VAMPIRES WILL CORRUPT HUMAN SOCIETY IF THEY WERE LET LOOSE.
EVEN IF IT'S JUST A MYTH, IT DOESN'T REALLY *DETER* PEOPLE FROM VAMPIRES.

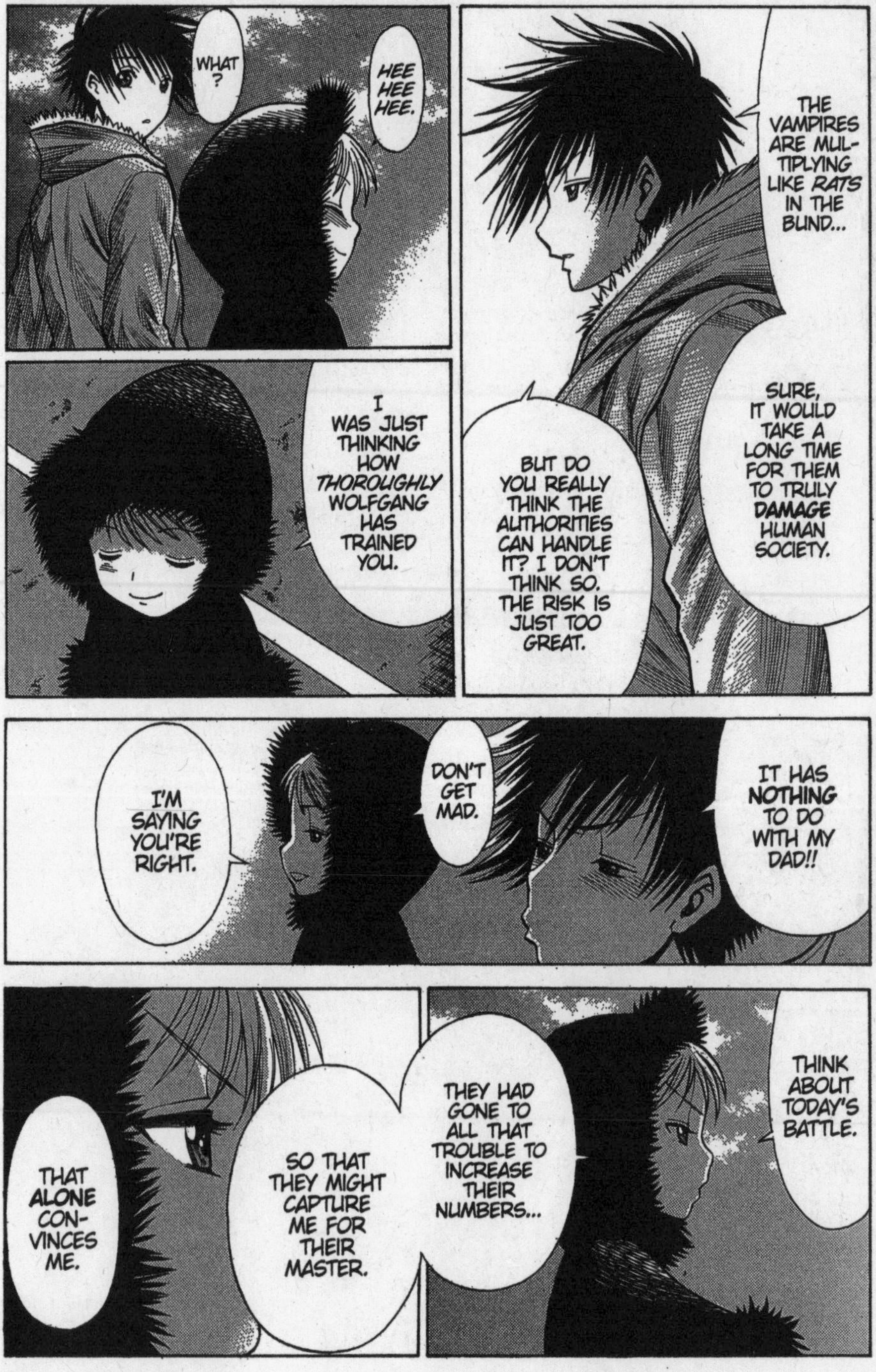
THE VAMPIRES ARE MULTIPLYING LIKE *RATS* IN THE BUND...
SURE, IT WOULD TAKE A LONG TIME FOR THEM TO TRULY **DAMAGE** HUMAN SOCIETY.
BUT DO YOU REALLY THINK THE AUTHORITIES CAN HANDLE IT? I DON'T THINK SO. THE RISK IS JUST TOO GREAT.
HEE HEE HEE.
WHAT?
I WAS JUST THINKING HOW *THOROUGHLY* WOLFGANG HAS TRAINED YOU.
IT HAS **NOTHING** TO DO WITH MY DAD!!
DON'T GET MAD.
I'M SAYING YOU'RE RIGHT.
THINK ABOUT TODAY'S BATTLE.
THEY HAD GONE TO ALL THAT TROUBLE TO INCREASE THEIR NUMBERS...
SO THAT THEY MIGHT CAPTURE ME FOR THEIR MASTER.
THAT **ALONE** CONVINCES ME.

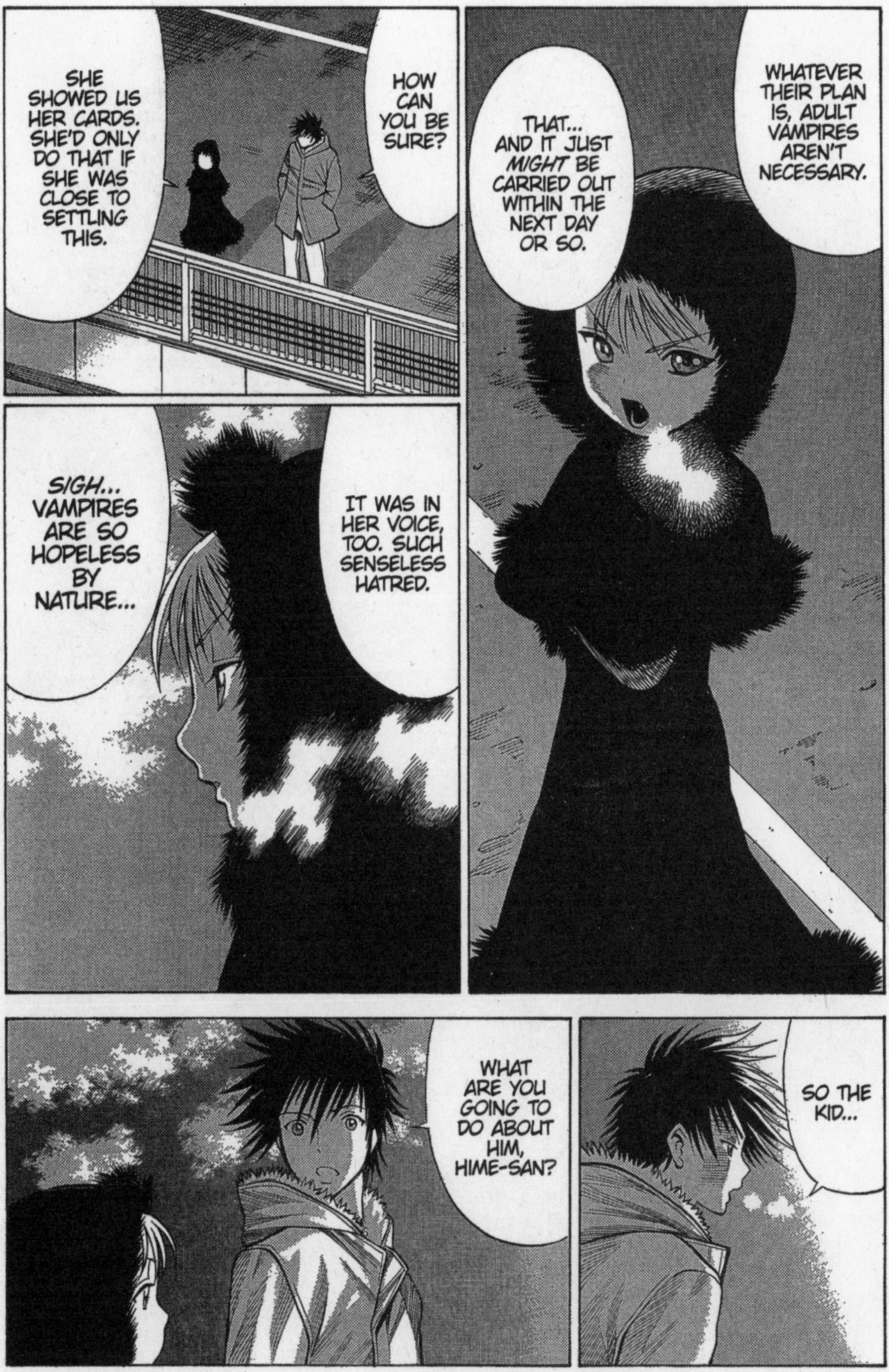
WHATEVER THEIR PLAN IS, ADULT VAMPIRES AREN'T NECESSARY.
THAT... AND IT JUST *MIGHT* BE CARRIED OUT WITHIN THE NEXT DAY OR SO.
HOW CAN YOU BE SURE?
SHE SHOWED US HER CARDS. SHE'D ONLY DO THAT IF SHE WAS CLOSE TO SETTLING THIS.
IT WAS IN HER VOICE, TOO. SUCH SENSELESS HATRED.
SIGH... VAMPIRES ARE SO HOPELESS BY NATURE...
SO THE KID...
WHAT ARE YOU GOING TO DO ABOUT HIM, HIME-SAN?

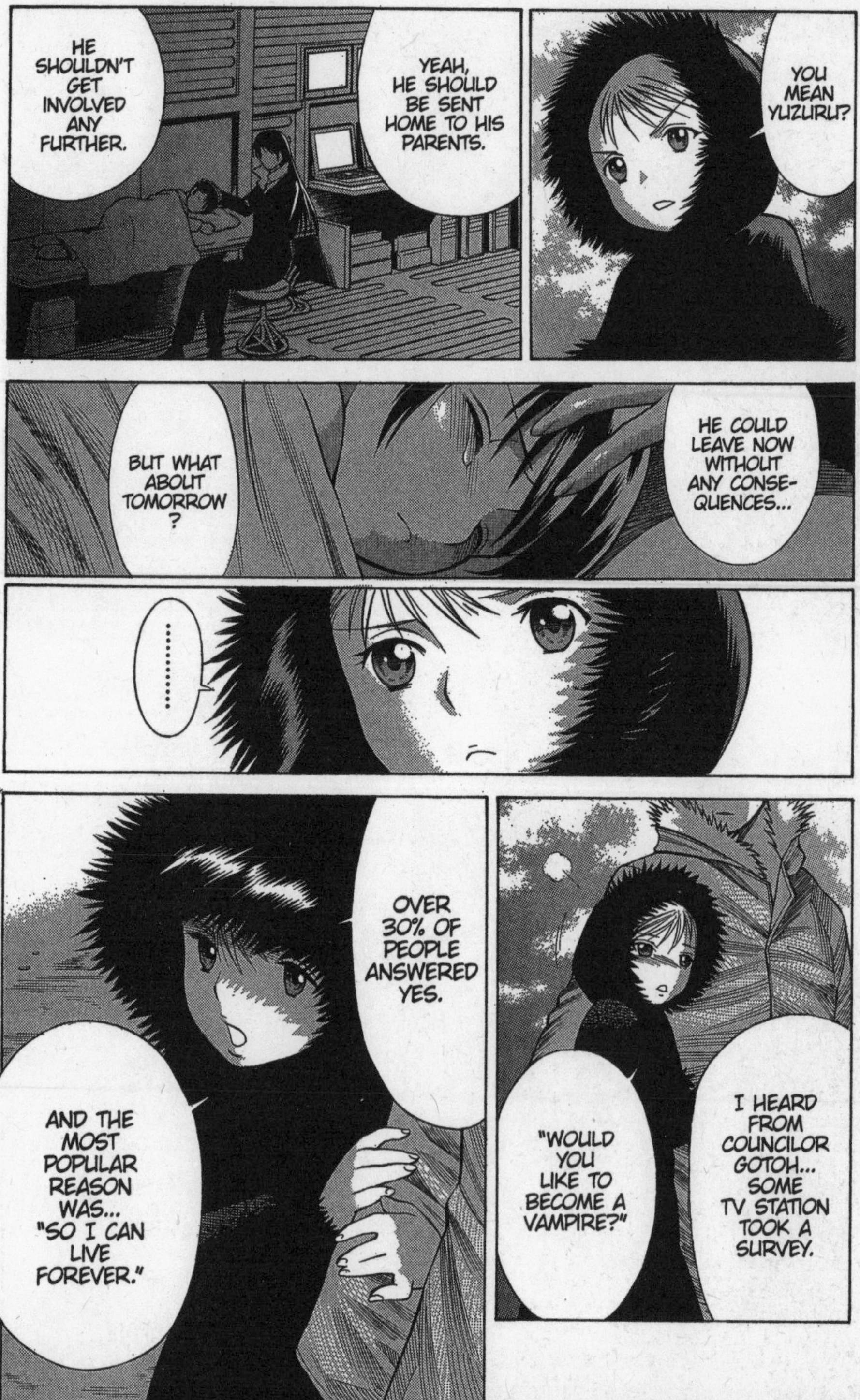
YOU MEAN YUZURU?
YEAH, HE SHOULD BE SENT HOME TO HIS PARENTS.
HE SHOULDN'T GET INVOLVED ANY FURTHER.
HE COULD LEAVE NOW WITHOUT ANY CONSE-QUENCES...
BUT WHAT ABOUT TOMORROW?
......
I HEARD FROM COUNCILOR GOTOH... SOME TV STATION TOOK A SURVEY.
"WOULD YOU LIKE TO BECOME A VAMPIRE?"
OVER 30% OF PEOPLE ANSWERED YES.
AND THE MOST POPULAR REASON WAS... "SO I CAN LIVE FOREVER."

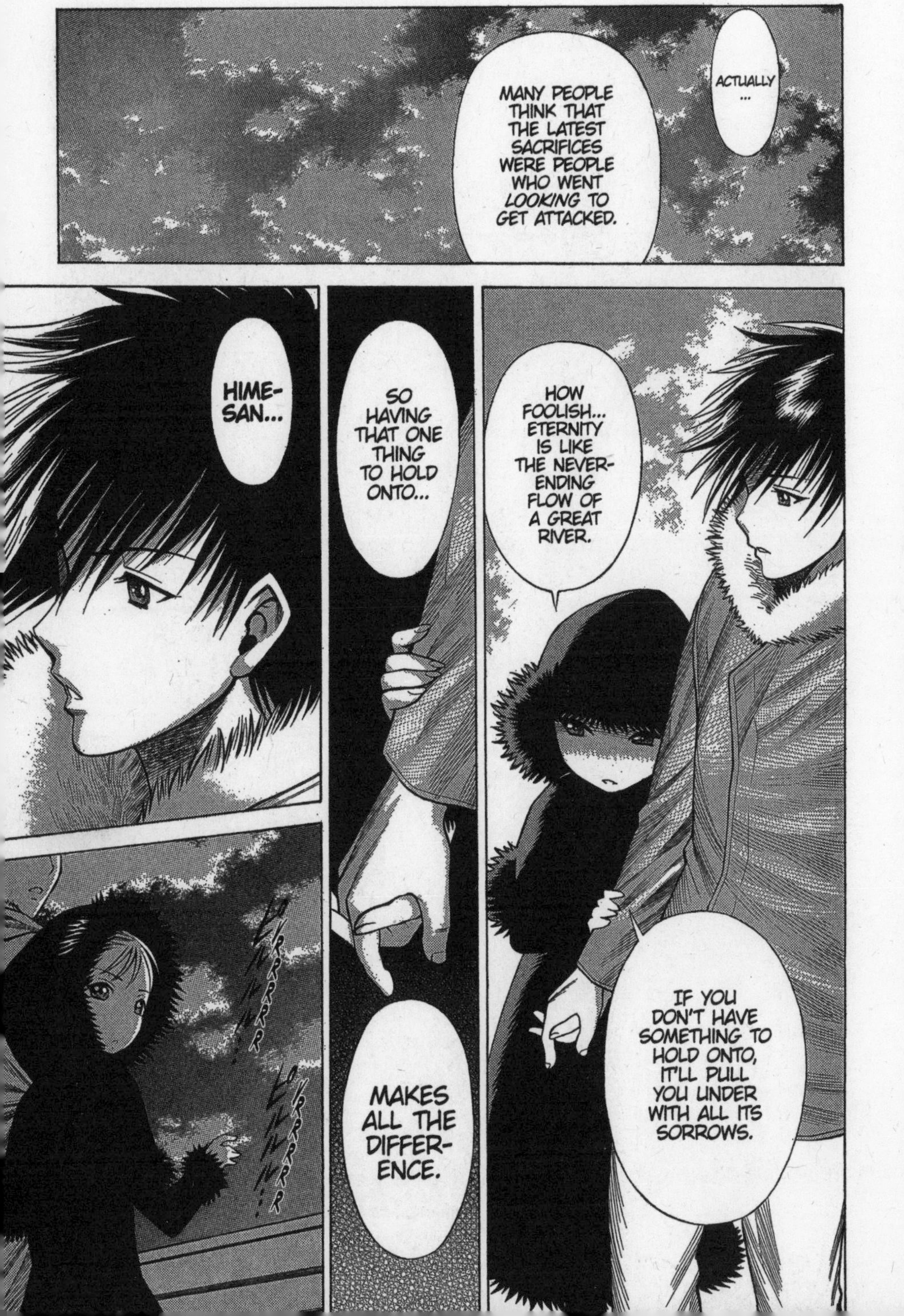
ACTUALLY...
MANY PEOPLE THINK THAT THE LATEST SACRIFICES WERE PEOPLE WHO WENT *LOOKING* TO GET ATTACKED.
HOW FOOLISH... ETERNITY IS LIKE THE NEVER-ENDING FLOW OF A GREAT RIVER.
IF YOU DON'T HAVE SOMETHING TO HOLD ONTO, IT'LL PULL YOU UNDER WITH ALL ITS SORROWS.
SO HAVING THAT ONE THING TO HOLD ONTO...
MAKES ALL THE DIFFER-ENCE.
HIME-SAN...

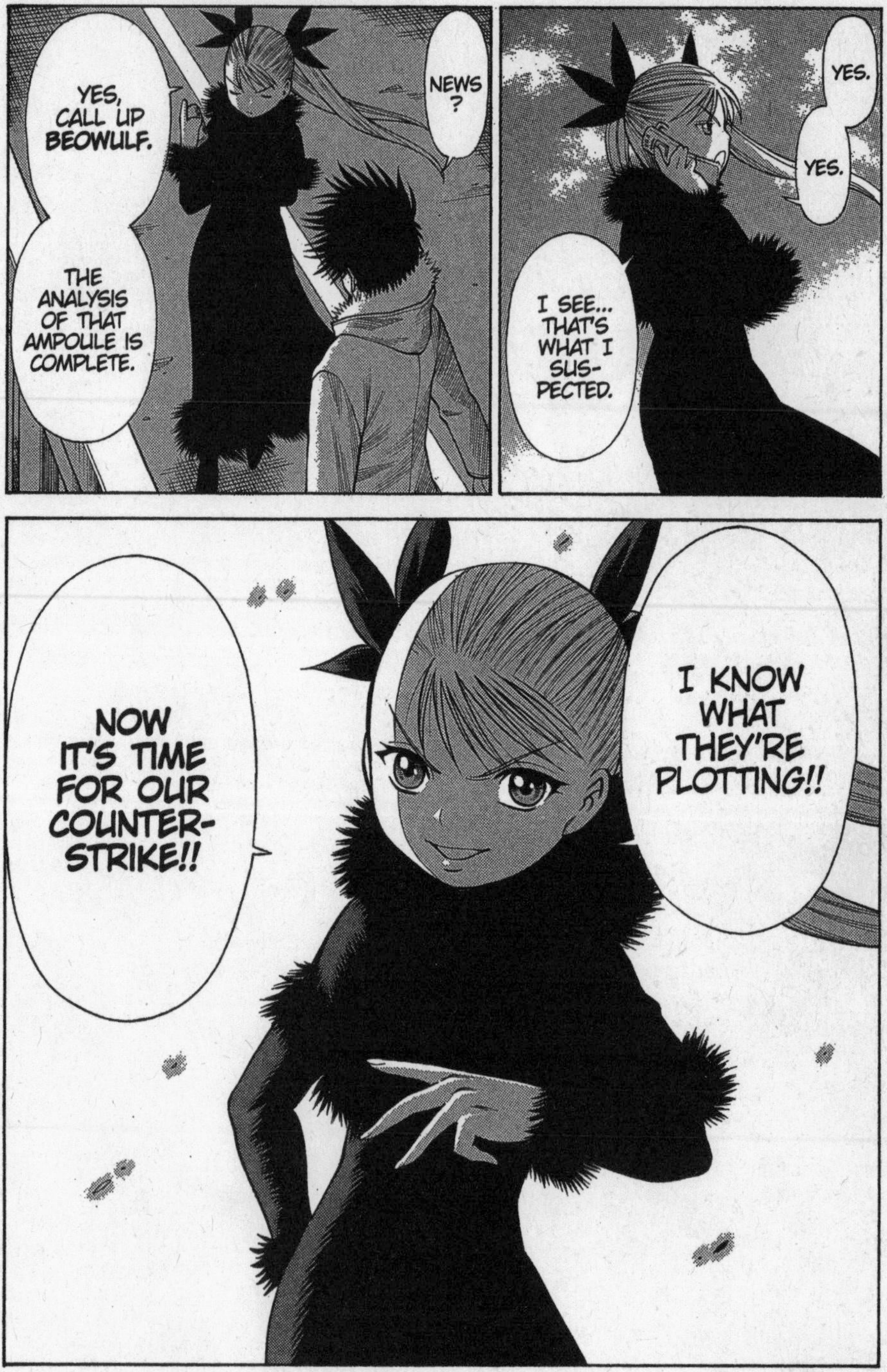
YES.
YES.
I SEE... THAT'S WHAT I SUS-PECTED.
NEWS?
YES, CALL UP BEOWULF.
THE ANALYSIS OF THAT AMPOULE IS COMPLETE.
I KNOW WHAT THEY'RE PLOTTING!!
NOW IT'S TIME FOR OUR COUNTER-STRIKE!!

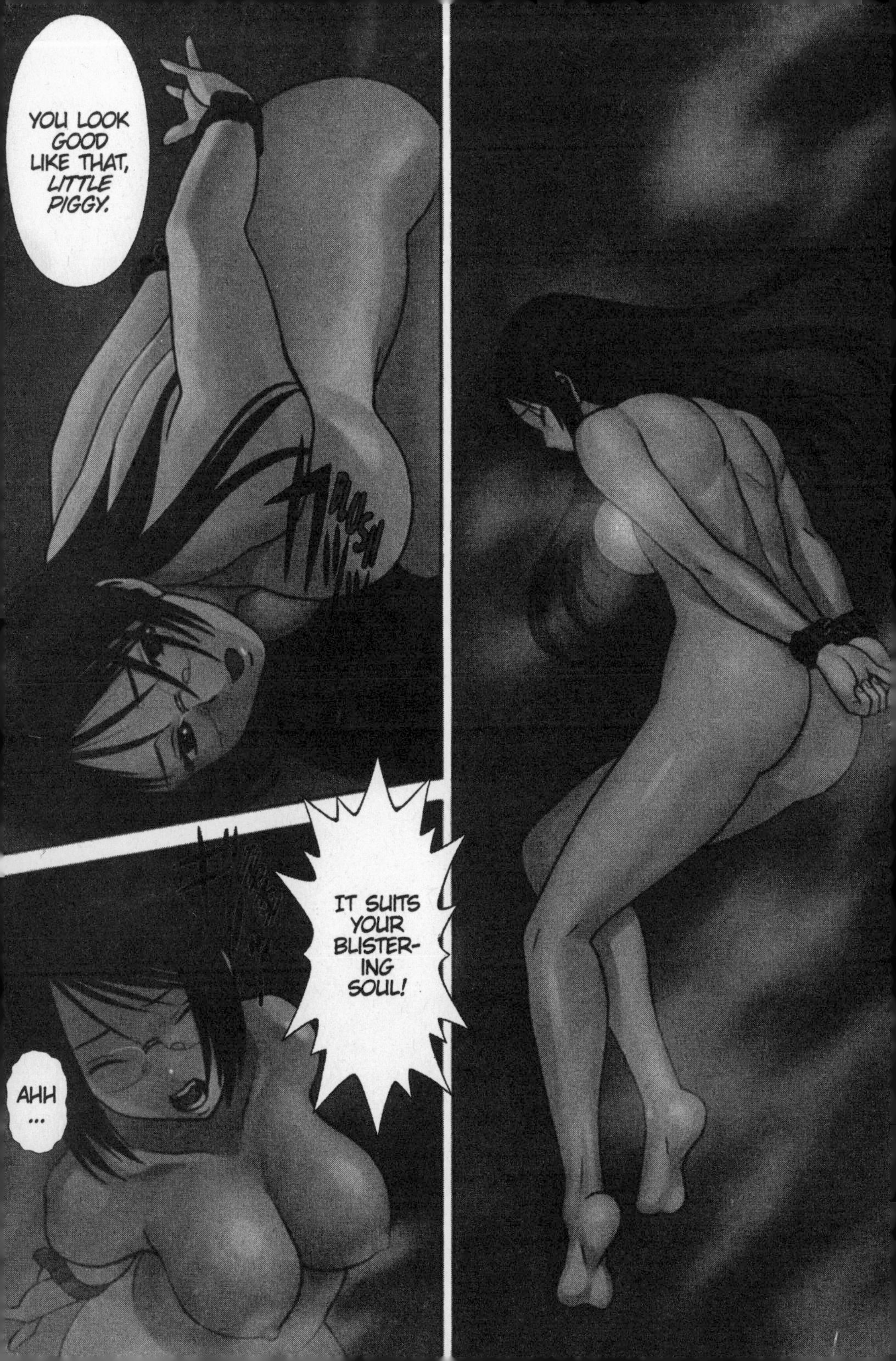
YOU LOOK GOOD LIKE THAT, LITTLE PIGGY.
IT SUITS YOUR BLISTER-ING SOUL!
AHH ...

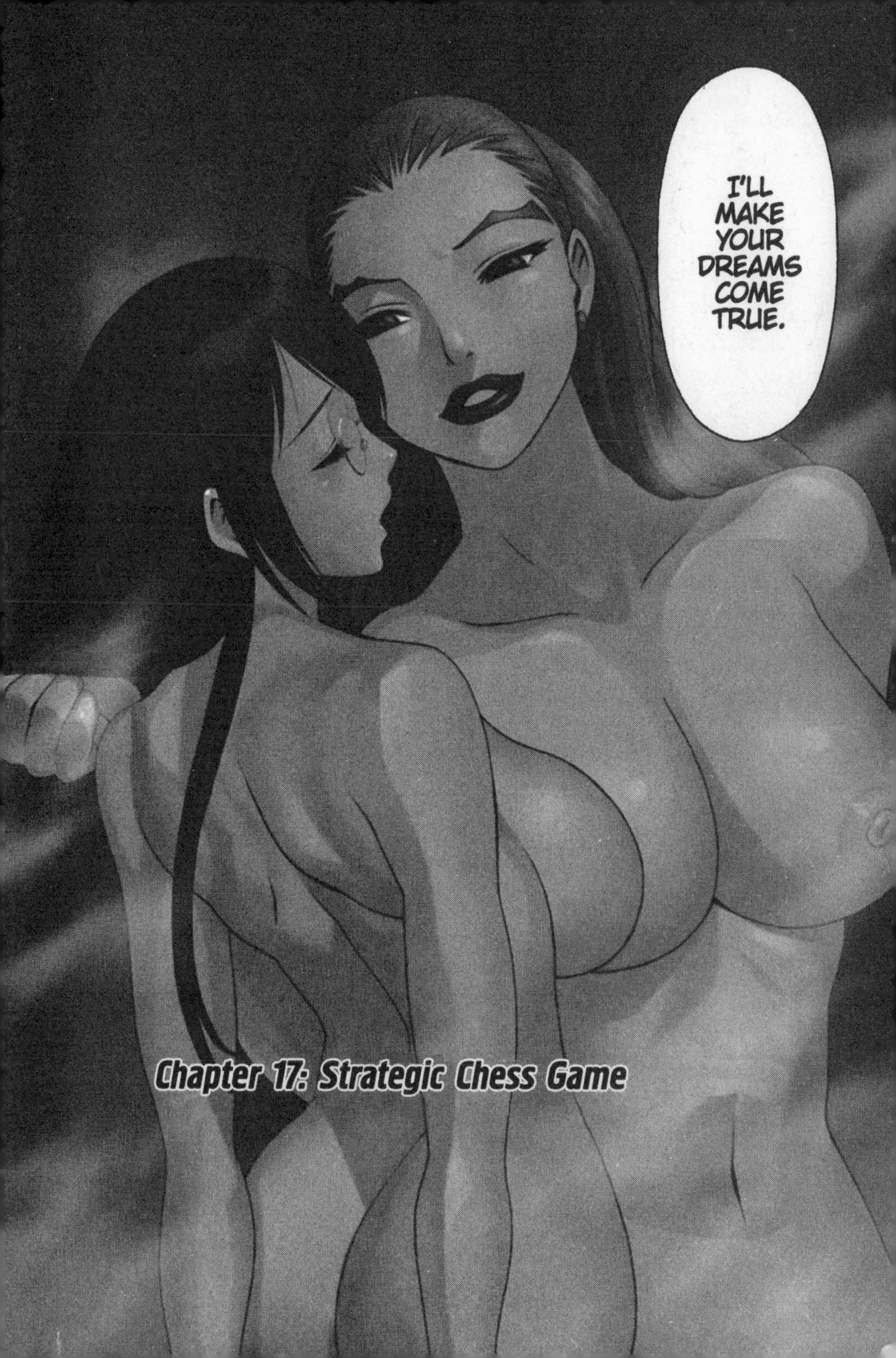
I'LL MAKE YOUR DREAMS COME TRUE.
Chapter 17: Strategic Chess Game

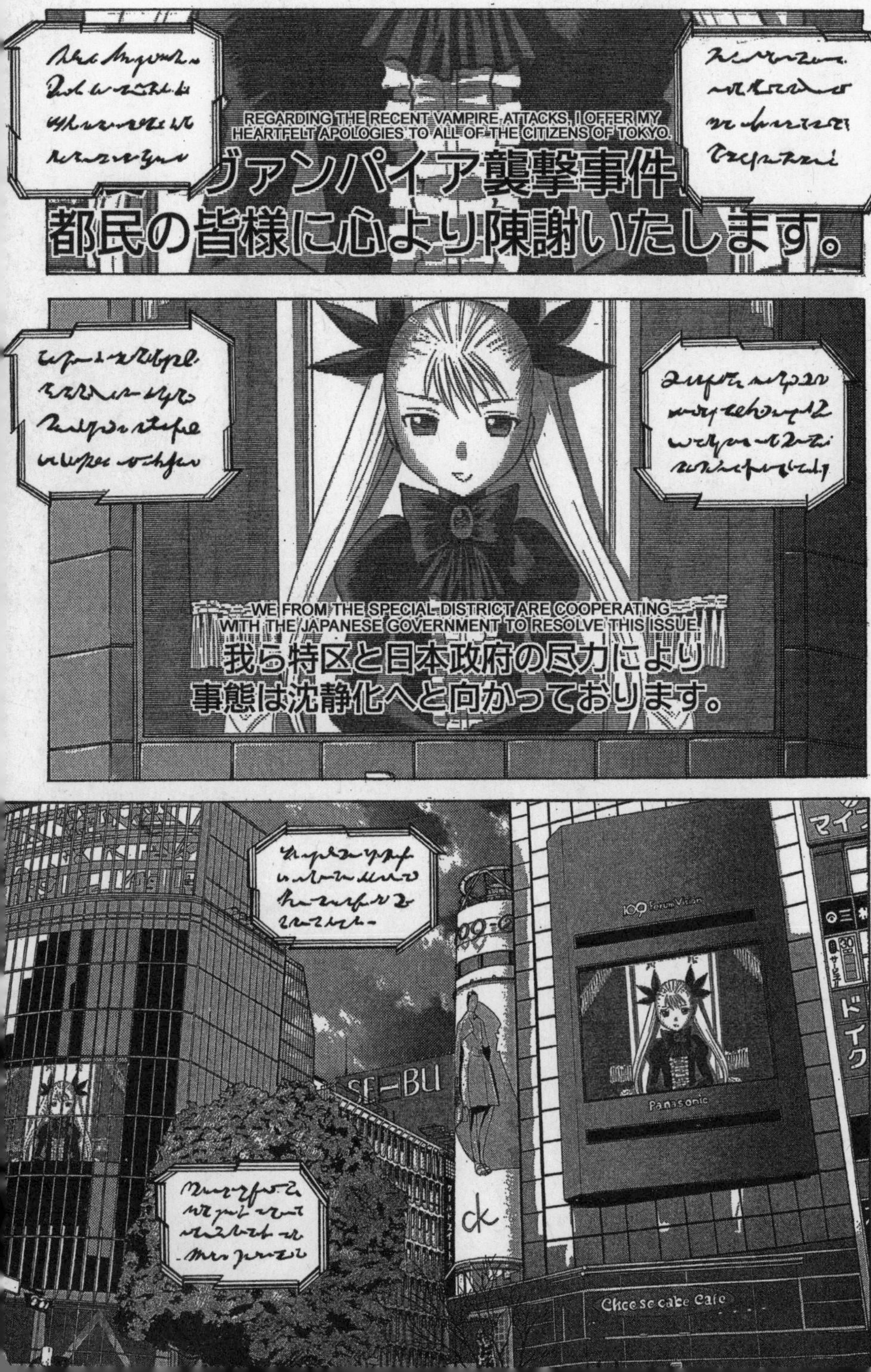
REGARDING THE RECENT VAMPIRE ATTACKS, I OFFER MY HEARTFELT APOLOGIES TO ALL OF THE CITIZENS OF TOKYO.
ヴァンパイア襲撃事件
都民の皆様に心より陳謝いたします。
WE FROM THE SPECIAL DISTRICT ARE COOPERATING WITH THE JAPANESE GOVERNMENT TO RESOLVE THIS ISSUE.
我ら特区と日本政府の尽力により
事態は沈静化へと向かっております。
109 Forum Vision
Panasonic
SE-BU
ck
ドイク
Cheesecake Cafe

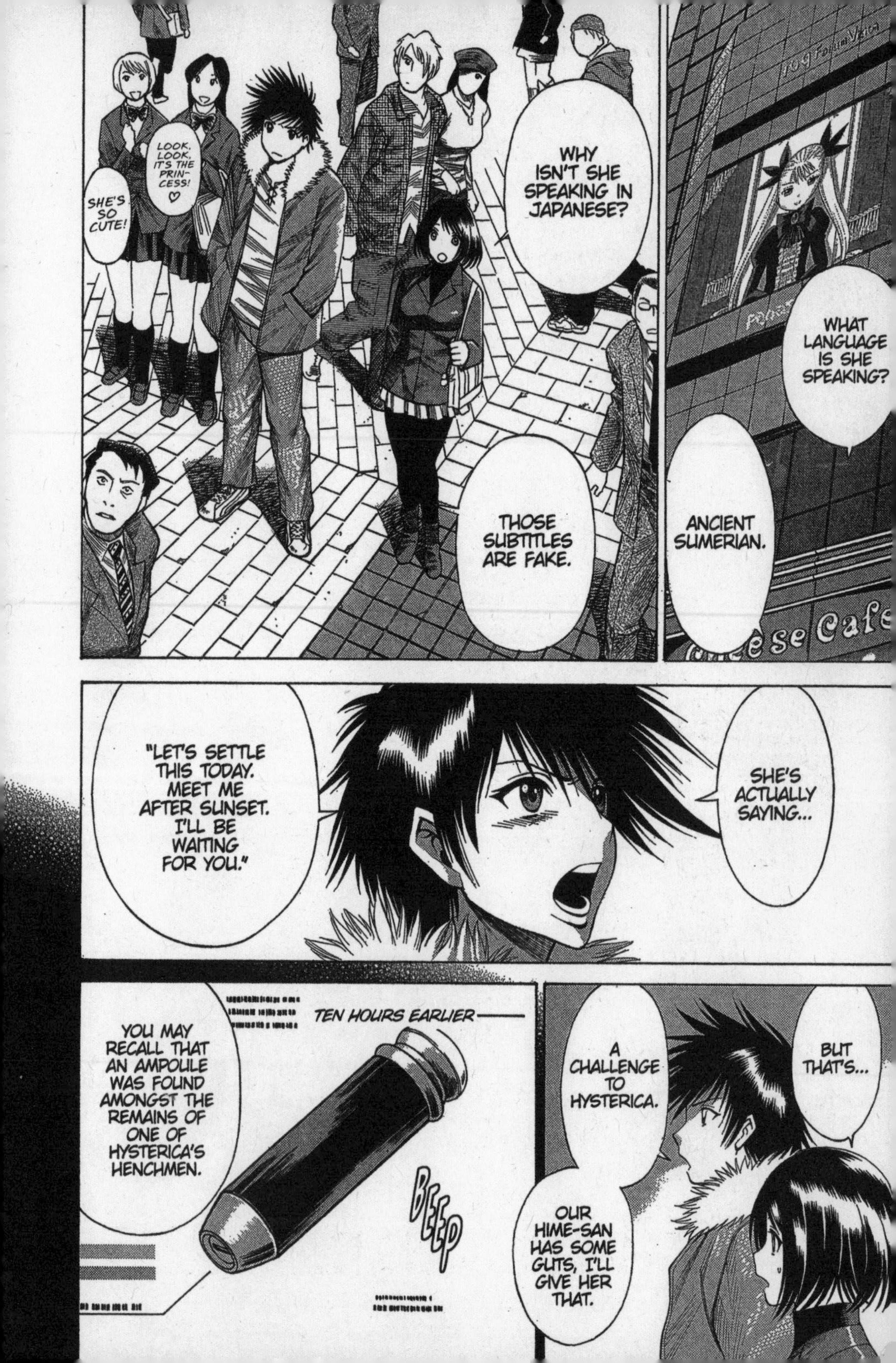
WHAT LANGUAGE IS SHE SPEAKING?
ANCIENT SUMERIAN.
Chinese Cafe
WHY ISN'T SHE SPEAKING IN JAPANESE?
THOSE SUBTITLES ARE FAKE.
LOOK, LOOK, IT'S THE PRINCESS! ♡
SHE'S SO CUTE!
SHE'S ACTUALLY SAYING...
"LET'S SETTLE THIS TODAY. MEET ME AFTER SUNSET. I'LL BE WAITING FOR YOU."
BUT THAT'S...
A CHALLENGE TO HYSTERICA.
OUR HIME-SAN HAS SOME GUTS, I'LL GIVE HER THAT.
TEN HOURS EARLIER—
YOU MAY RECALL THAT AN AMPOULE WAS FOUND AMONGST THE REMAINS OF ONE OF HYSTERICA'S HENCHMEN.
BEEP

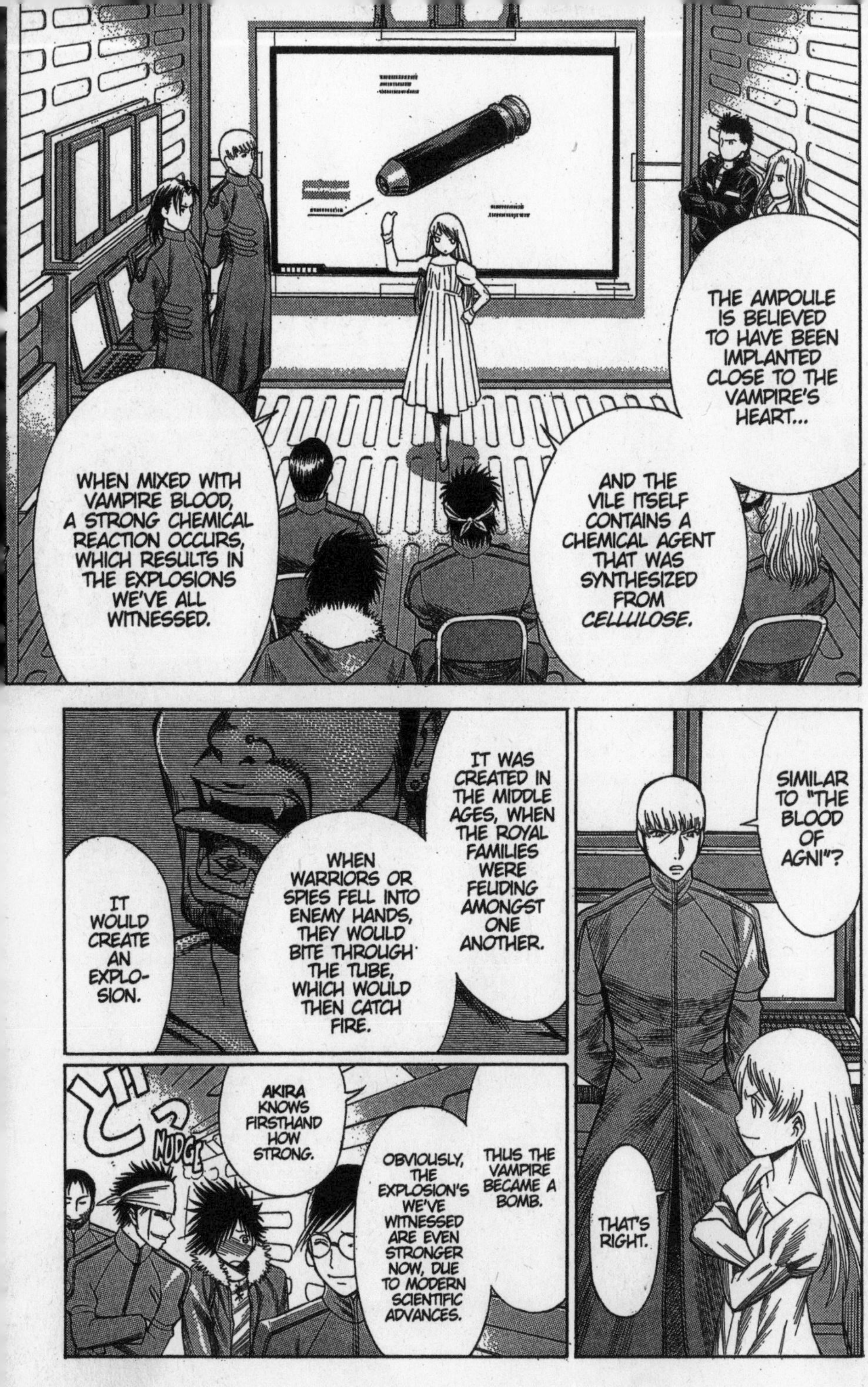
THE AMPOULE IS BELIEVED TO HAVE BEEN IMPLANTED CLOSE TO THE VAMPIRE'S HEART...
AND THE VILE ITSELF CONTAINS A CHEMICAL AGENT THAT WAS SYNTHESIZED FROM *CELLULOSE.*
WHEN MIXED WITH VAMPIRE BLOOD, A STRONG CHEMICAL REACTION OCCURS, WHICH RESULTS IN THE EXPLOSIONS WE'VE ALL WITNESSED.
SIMILAR TO "THE BLOOD OF AGNI"?
THAT'S RIGHT.
IT WAS CREATED IN THE MIDDLE AGES, WHEN THE ROYAL FAMILIES WERE FEUDING AMONGST ONE ANOTHER.
WHEN WARRIORS OR SPIES FELL INTO ENEMY HANDS, THEY WOULD BITE THROUGH THE TUBE, WHICH WOULD THEN CATCH FIRE.
IT WOULD CREATE AN EXPLO-SION.
THUS THE VAMPIRE BECAME A BOMB.
OBVIOUSLY, THE EXPLOSION'S WE'VE WITNESSED ARE EVEN STRONGER NOW, DUE TO MODERN SCIENTIFIC ADVANCES.
AKIRA KNOWS FIRSTHAND HOW STRONG.
NUDGE

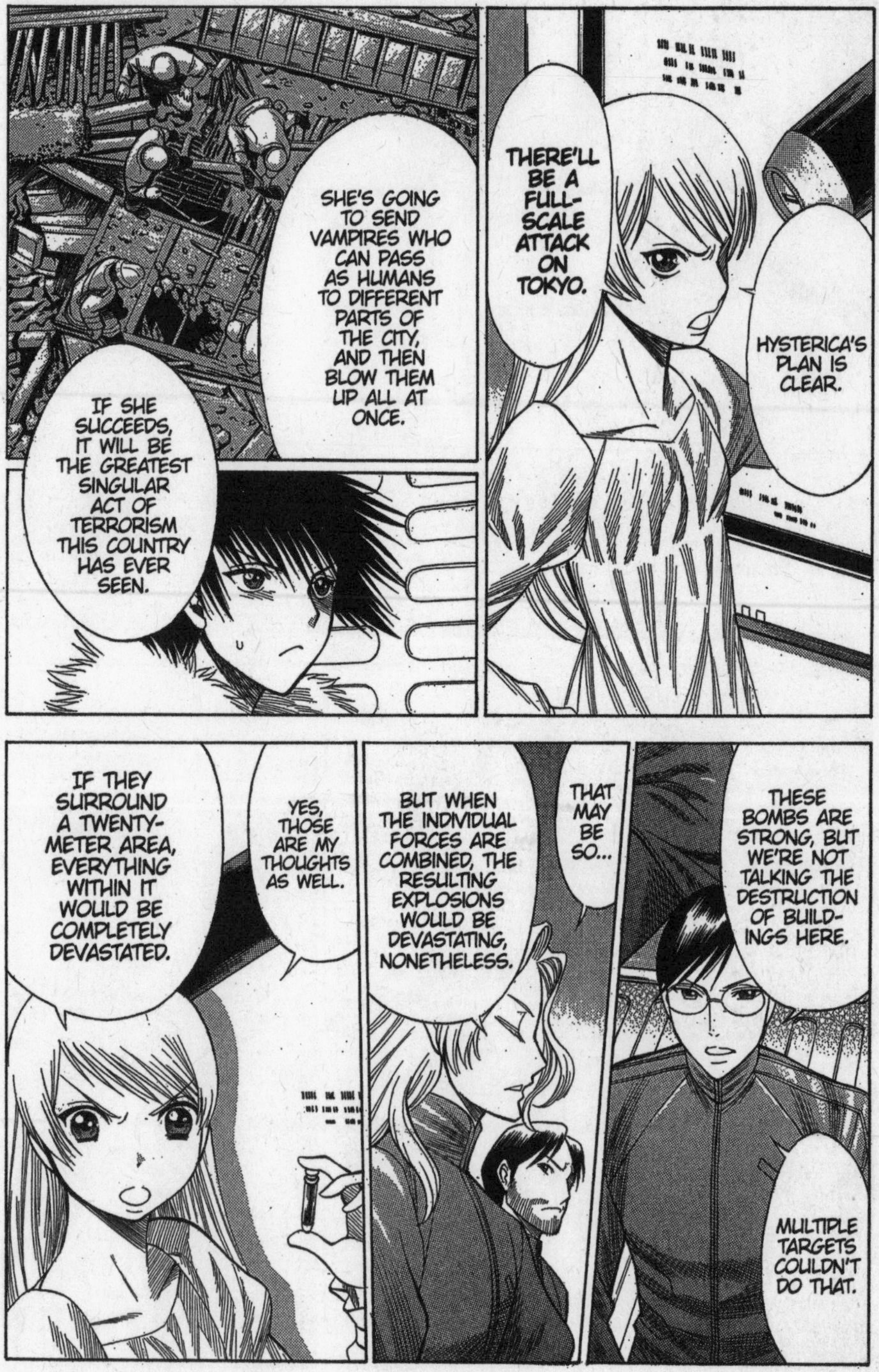
HYSTERICA'S PLAN IS CLEAR.
THERE'LL BE A FULL-SCALE ATTACK ON TOKYO.
SHE'S GOING TO SEND VAMPIRES WHO CAN PASS AS HUMANS TO DIFFERENT PARTS OF THE CITY, AND THEN BLOW THEM UP ALL AT ONCE.
IF SHE SUCCEEDS, IT WILL BE THE GREATEST SINGULAR ACT OF TERRORISM THIS COUNTRY HAS EVER SEEN.
THESE BOMBS ARE STRONG, BUT WE'RE NOT TALKING THE DESTRUCTION OF BUILDINGS HERE.
MULTIPLE TARGETS COULDN'T DO THAT.
THAT MAY BE SO...
BUT WHEN THE INDIVIDUAL FORCES ARE COMBINED, THE RESULTING EXPLOSIONS WOULD BE DEVASTATING, NONETHELESS.
YES, THOSE ARE MY THOUGHTS AS WELL.
IF THEY SURROUND A TWENTY-METER AREA, EVERYTHING WITHIN IT WOULD BE COMPLETELY DEVASTATED.

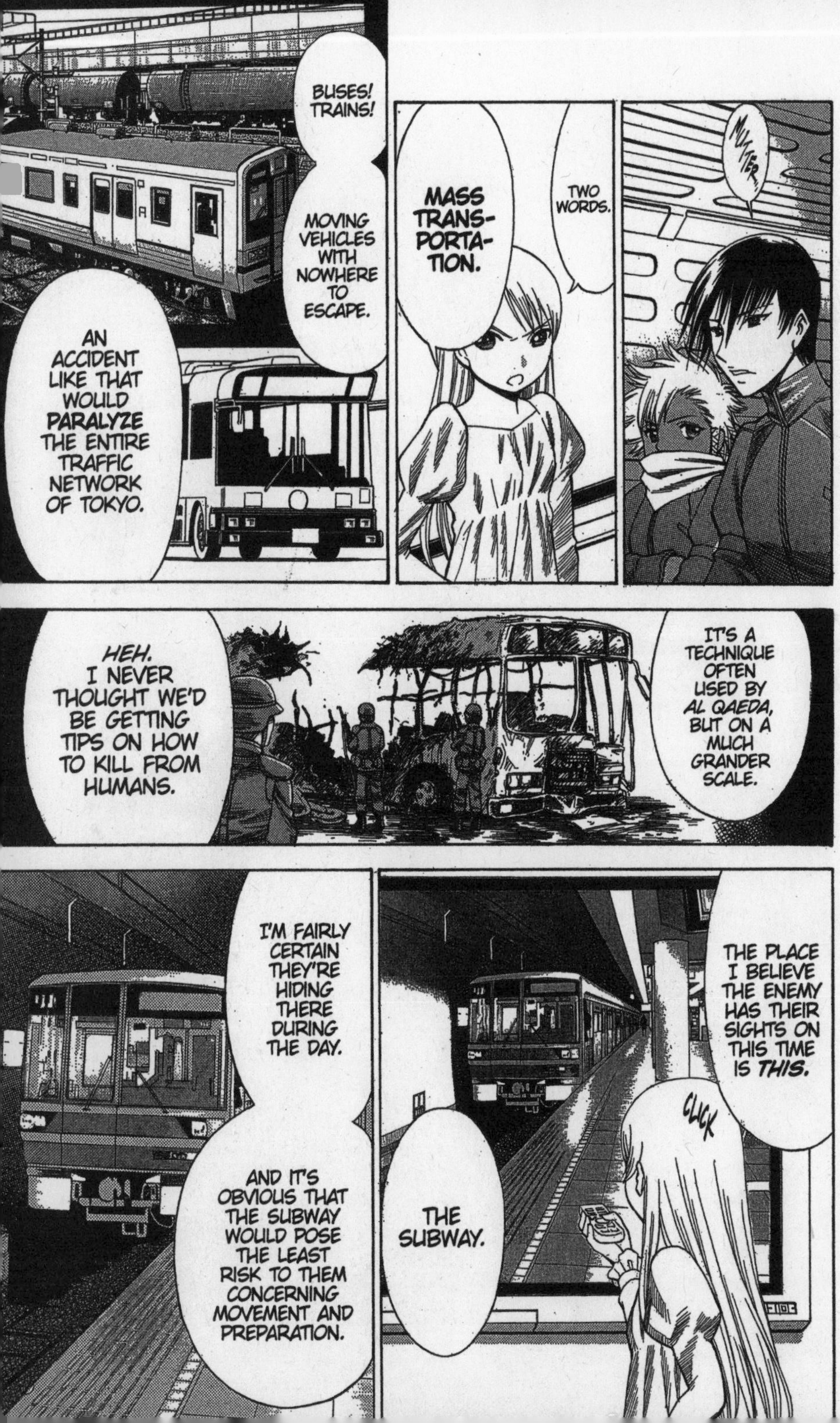
MUTTER
TWO WORDS.
MASS TRANSPORTATION.
BUSES! TRAINS!
MOVING VEHICLES WITH NOWHERE TO ESCAPE.
AN ACCIDENT LIKE THAT WOULD PARALYZE THE ENTIRE TRAFFIC NETWORK OF TOKYO.
IT'S A TECHNIQUE OFTEN USED BY AL QAEDA, BUT ON A MUCH GRANDER SCALE.
HEH. I NEVER THOUGHT WE'D BE GETTING TIPS ON HOW TO KILL FROM HUMANS.
THE PLACE I BELIEVE THE ENEMY HAS THEIR SIGHTS ON THIS TIME IS THIS.
CLICK
THE SUBWAY.
I'M FAIRLY CERTAIN THEY'RE HIDING THERE DURING THE DAY.
AND IT'S OBVIOUS THAT THE SUBWAY WOULD POSE THE LEAST RISK TO THEM CONCERNING MOVEMENT AND PREPARATION.

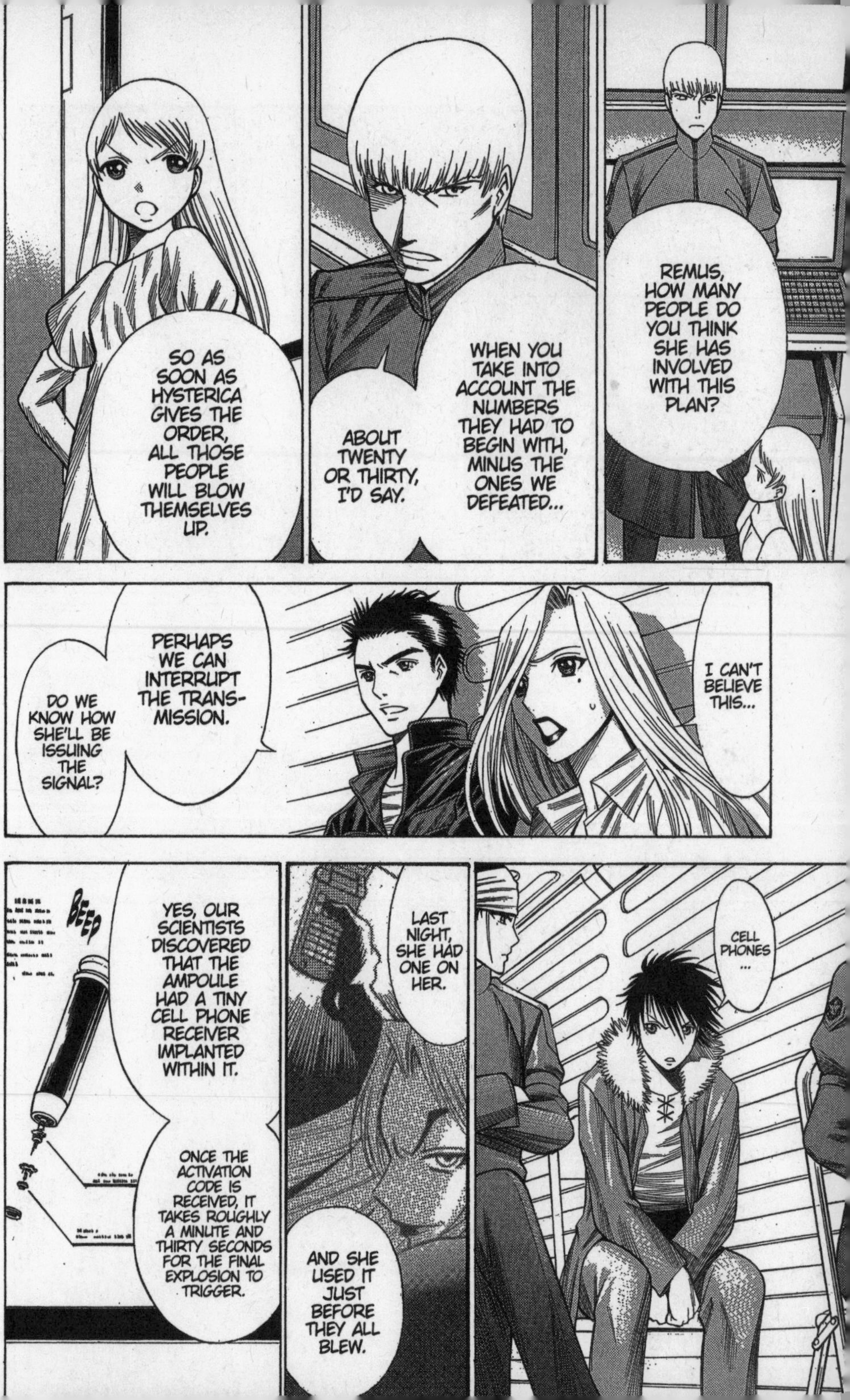
REMUS, HOW MANY PEOPLE DO YOU THINK SHE HAS INVOLVED WITH THIS PLAN?
WHEN YOU TAKE INTO ACCOUNT THE NUMBERS THEY HAD TO BEGIN WITH, MINUS THE ONES WE DEFEATED...
ABOUT TWENTY OR THIRTY, I'D SAY.
SO AS SOON AS HYSTERICA GIVES THE ORDER, ALL THOSE PEOPLE WILL BLOW THEMSELVES UP.
I CAN'T BELIEVE THIS...
PERHAPS WE CAN INTERRUPT THE TRANS-MISSION.
DO WE KNOW HOW SHE'LL BE ISSUING THE SIGNAL?
CELL PHONES ...
LAST NIGHT, SHE HAD ONE ON HER.
AND SHE USED IT JUST BEFORE THEY ALL BLEW.
BEEP
YES, OUR SCIENTISTS DISCOVERED THAT THE AMPOULE HAD A TINY CELL PHONE RECEIVER IMPLANTED WITHIN IT.
ONCE THE ACTIVATION CODE IS RECEIVED, IT TAKES ROUGHLY A MINUTE AND THIRTY SECONDS FOR THE FINAL EXPLOSION TO TRIGGER.

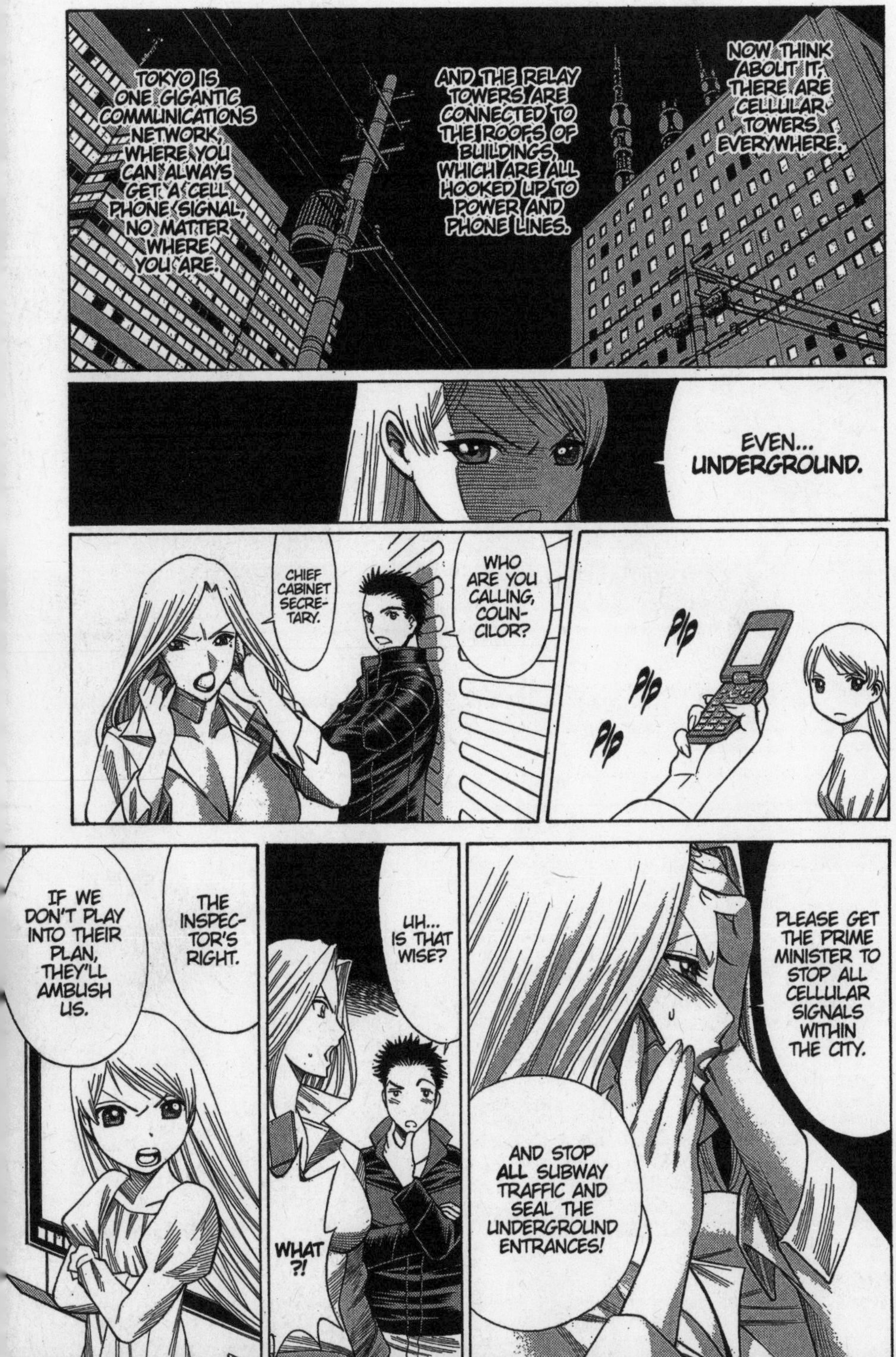
NOW THINK ABOUT IT, THERE ARE CELLULAR TOWERS EVERYWHERE.
AND THE RELAY TOWERS ARE CONNECTED TO THE ROOFS OF BUILDINGS, WHICH ARE ALL HOOKED UP TO POWER AND PHONE LINES.
TOKYO IS ONE GIGANTIC COMMUNICATIONS NETWORK, WHERE YOU CAN ALWAYS GET A CELL PHONE SIGNAL, NO MATTER WHERE YOU ARE.
EVEN... UNDERGROUND.
PIP
PIP
PIP
WHO ARE YOU CALLING, COUN-CILOR?
CHIEF CABINET SECRE-TARY.
PLEASE GET THE PRIME MINISTER TO STOP ALL CELLULAR SIGNALS WITHIN THE CITY.
AND STOP ALL SUBWAY TRAFFIC AND SEAL THE UNDERGROUND ENTRANCES!
UH... IS THAT WISE?
WHAT ?!
THE INSPEC-TOR'S RIGHT.
IF WE DON'T PLAY INTO THEIR PLAN, THEY'LL AMBUSH US.

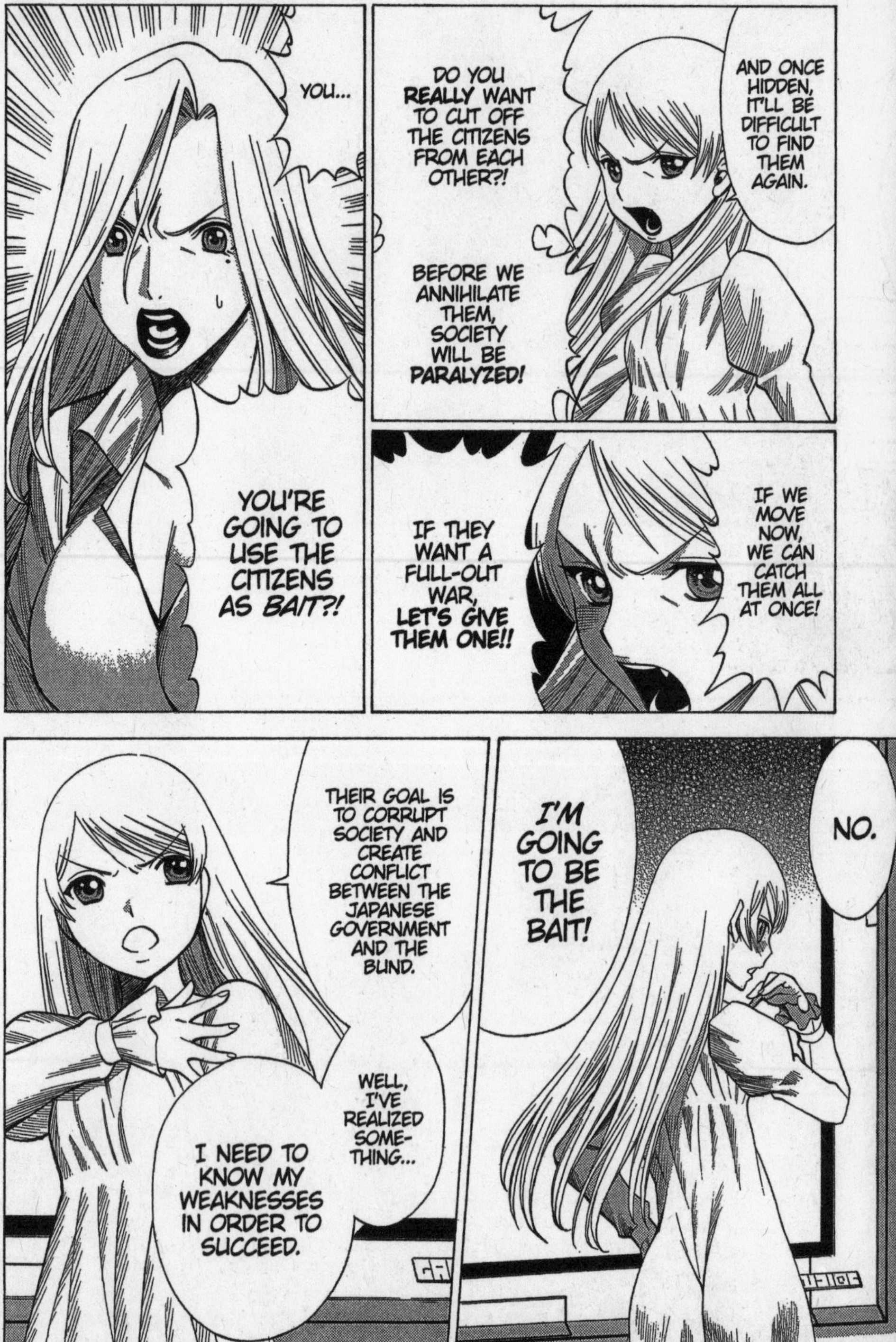
AND ONCE HIDDEN, IT'LL BE DIFFICULT TO FIND THEM AGAIN.
DO YOU REALLY WANT TO CUT OFF THE CITIZENS FROM EACH OTHER?!
BEFORE WE ANNIHILATE THEM, SOCIETY WILL BE PARALYZED!
IF WE MOVE NOW, WE CAN CATCH THEM ALL AT ONCE!
IF THEY WANT A FULL-OUT WAR, LET'S GIVE THEM ONE!!
YOU...
YOU'RE GOING TO USE THE CITIZENS AS *BAIT*?!
NO.
I'M GOING TO BE THE BAIT!
THEIR GOAL IS TO CORRUPT SOCIETY AND CREATE CONFLICT BETWEEN THE JAPANESE GOVERNMENT AND THE BUND.
WELL, I'VE REALIZED SOME-THING...
I NEED TO KNOW MY WEAKNESSES IN ORDER TO SUCCEED.

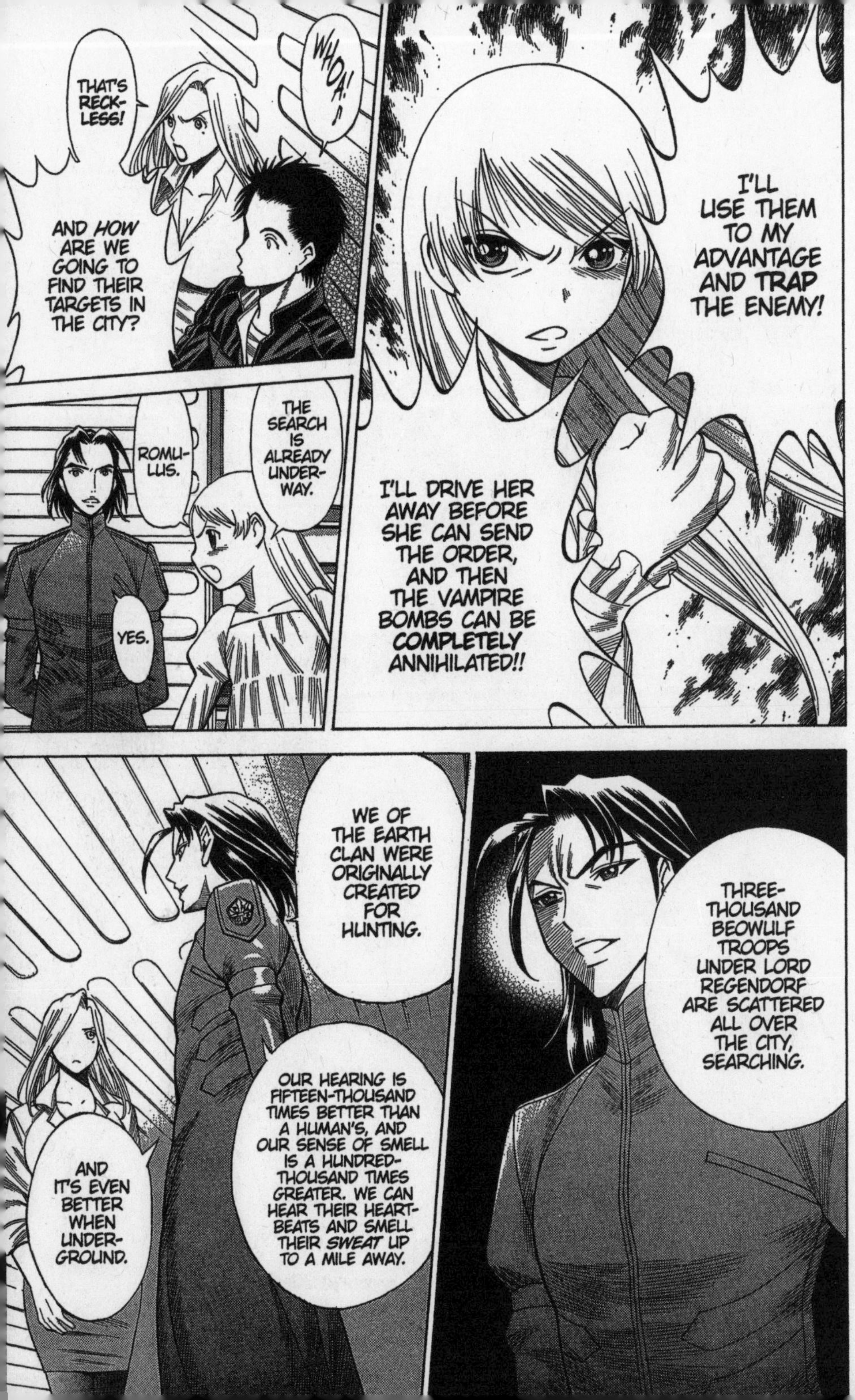
I'LL USE THEM TO MY ADVANTAGE AND TRAP THE ENEMY!
I'LL DRIVE HER AWAY BEFORE SHE CAN SEND THE ORDER, AND THEN THE VAMPIRE BOMBS CAN BE COMPLETELY ANNIHILATED!!
WHOA!
THAT'S RECKLESS!
AND *HOW* ARE WE GOING TO FIND THEIR TARGETS IN THE CITY?
THE SEARCH IS ALREADY UNDERWAY.
ROMULUS.
YES.
THREE-THOUSAND BEOWULF TROOPS UNDER LORD REGENDORF ARE SCATTERED ALL OVER THE CITY, SEARCHING.
WE OF THE EARTH CLAN WERE ORIGINALLY CREATED FOR HUNTING.
OUR HEARING IS FIFTEEN-THOUSAND TIMES BETTER THAN A HUMAN'S, AND OUR SENSE OF SMELL IS A HUNDRED-THOUSAND TIMES GREATER. WE CAN HEAR THEIR HEARTBEATS AND SMELL THEIR *SWEAT* UP TO A MILE AWAY.
AND IT'S EVEN BETTER WHEN UNDERGROUND.

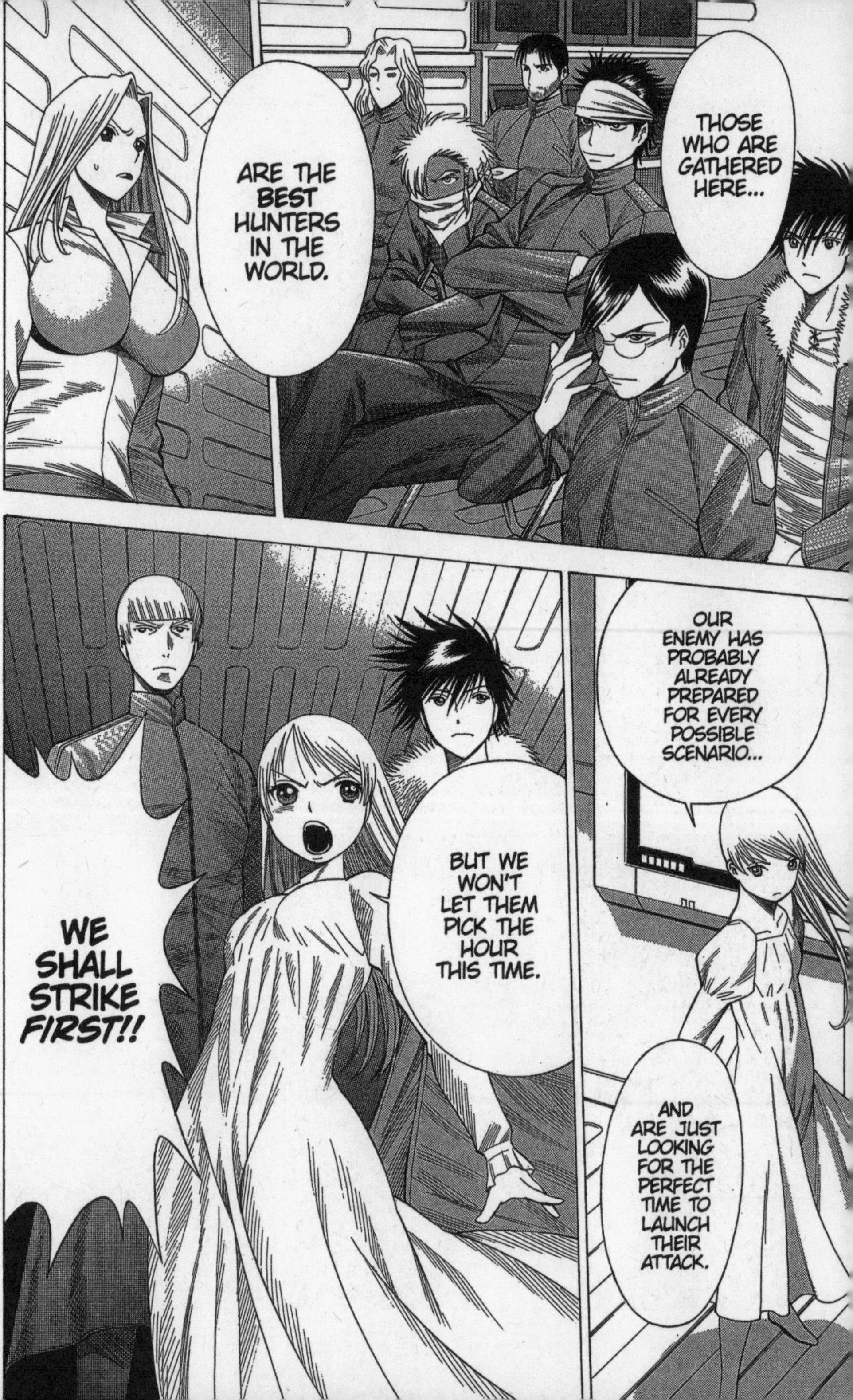

THOSE WHO ARE GATHERED HERE...
ARE THE BEST HUNTERS IN THE WORLD.
OUR ENEMY HAS PROBABLY ALREADY PREPARED FOR EVERY POSSIBLE SCENARIO...
AND ARE JUST LOOKING FOR THE PERFECT TIME TO LAUNCH THEIR ATTACK.
BUT WE WON'T LET THEM PICK THE HOUR THIS TIME.
WE SHALL STRIKE FIRST!!

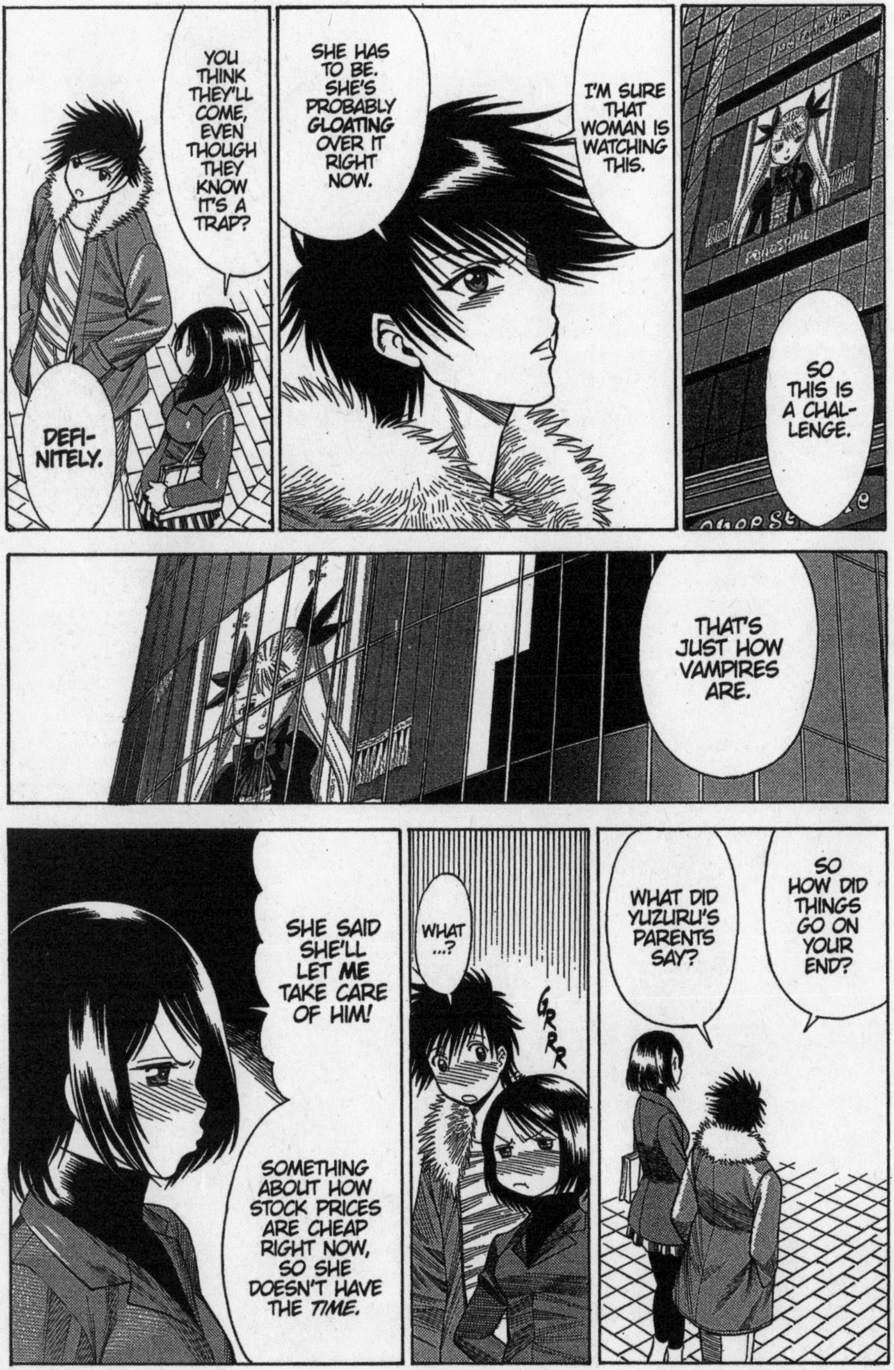

SO THIS IS A CHAL-LENGE.
I'M SURE THAT WOMAN IS WATCHING THIS.
SHE HAS TO BE. SHE'S PROBABLY GLOATING OVER IT RIGHT NOW.
YOU THINK THEY'LL COME, EVEN THOUGH THEY KNOW IT'S A TRAP?
DEFI-NITELY.
THAT'S JUST HOW VAMPIRES ARE.
SO HOW DID THINGS GO ON YOUR END?
WHAT DID YUZURU'S PARENTS SAY?
WHAT ...?
GRRR
SHE SAID SHE'LL LET ME TAKE CARE OF HIM!
SOMETHING ABOUT HOW STOCK PRICES ARE CHEAP RIGHT NOW, SO SHE DOESN'T HAVE THE *TIME*.

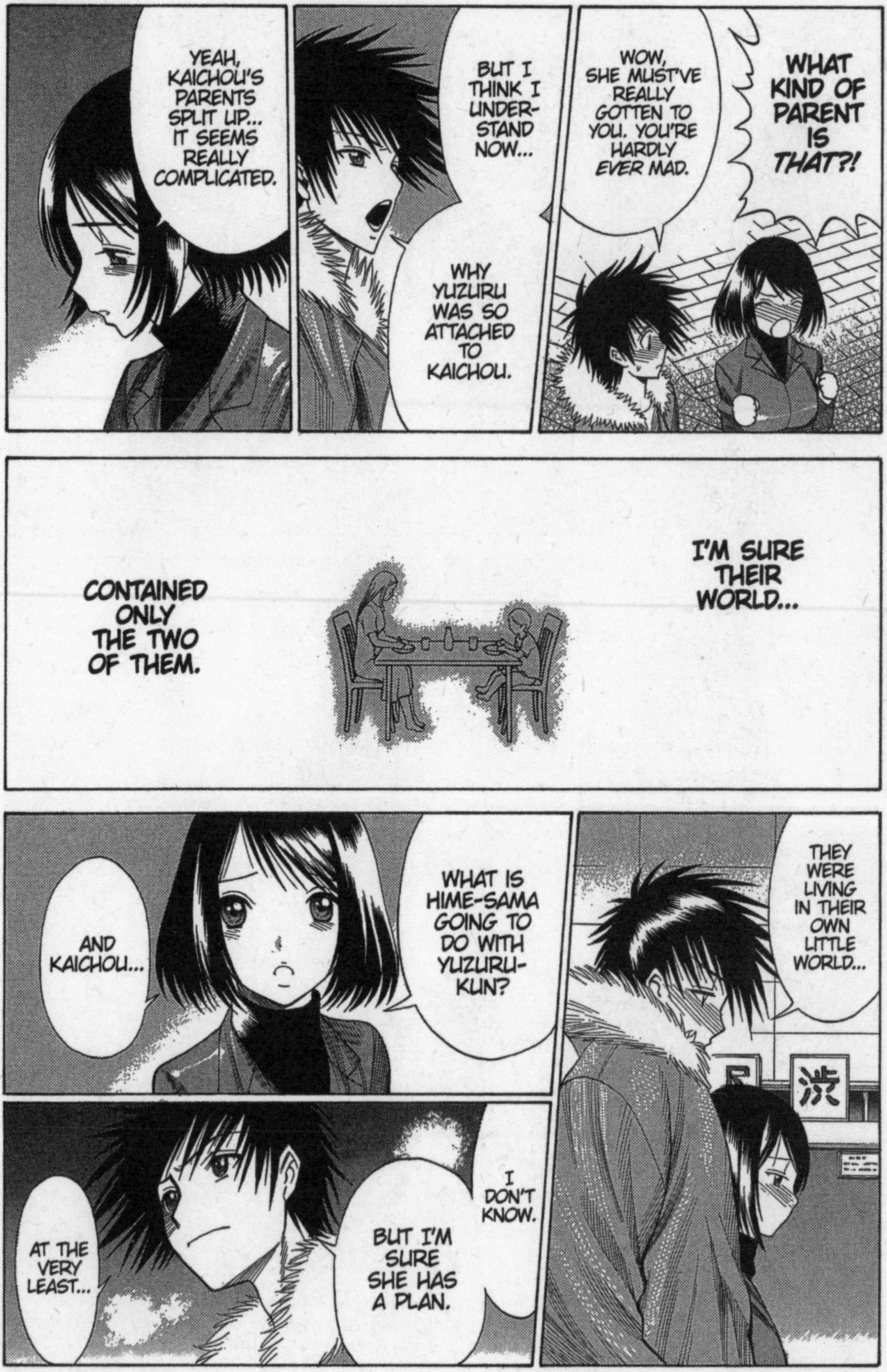
WHAT KIND OF PARENT IS *THAT?!*
WOW, SHE MUST'VE REALLY GOTTEN TO YOU. YOU'RE HARDLY *EVER* MAD.
BUT I THINK I UNDER-STAND NOW...
WHY YUZURU WAS SO ATTACHED TO KAICHOU.
YEAH, KAICHOU'S PARENTS SPLIT UP... IT SEEMS REALLY COMPLICATED.
I'M SURE THEIR WORLD...
CONTAINED ONLY THE TWO OF THEM.
THEY WERE LIVING IN THEIR OWN LITTLE WORLD...
WHAT IS HIME-SAMA GOING TO DO WITH YUZURU-KUN?
AND KAICHOU...
I DON'T KNOW.
BUT I'M SURE SHE HAS A PLAN.
AT THE VERY LEAST...

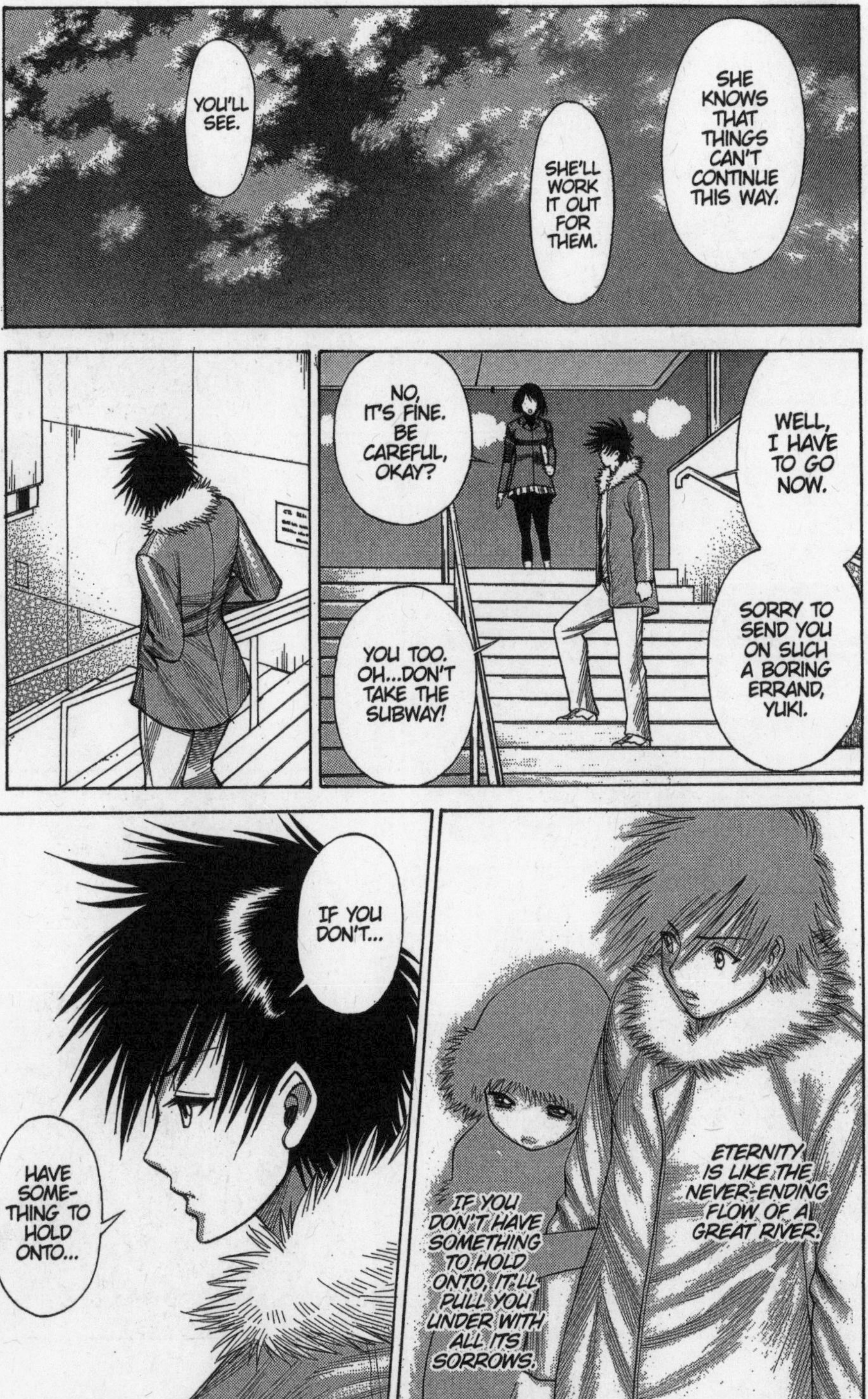
SHE KNOWS THAT THINGS CAN'T CONTINUE THIS WAY.
SHE'LL WORK IT OUT FOR THEM.
YOU'LL SEE.
WELL, I HAVE TO GO NOW.
SORRY TO SEND YOU ON SUCH A BORING ERRAND, YUKI.
NO, IT'S FINE. BE CAREFUL, OKAY?
YOU TOO. OH...DON'T TAKE THE SUBWAY!
ETERNITY IS LIKE THE NEVER-ENDING FLOW OF A GREAT RIVER.
IF YOU DON'T HAVE SOMETHING TO HOLD ONTO, IT'LL PULL YOU UNDER WITH ALL ITS SORROWS.
IF YOU DON'T...
HAVE SOME-THING TO HOLD ONTO...

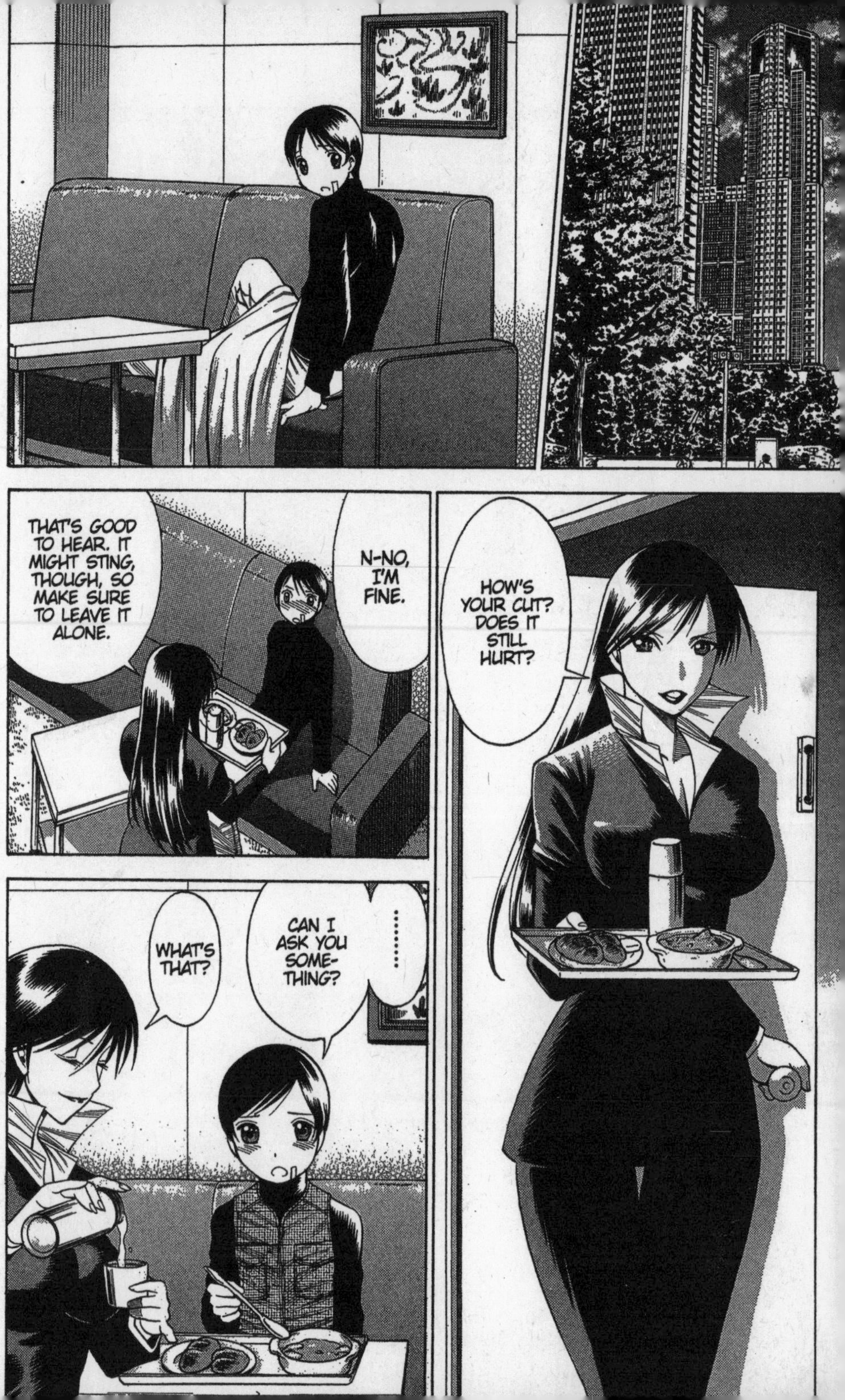
HOW'S YOUR CUT? DOES IT STILL HURT?
N-NO, I'M FINE.
THAT'S GOOD TO HEAR. IT MIGHT STING, THOUGH, SO MAKE SURE TO LEAVE IT ALONE.
......
CAN I ASK YOU SOME-THING?
WHAT'S THAT?

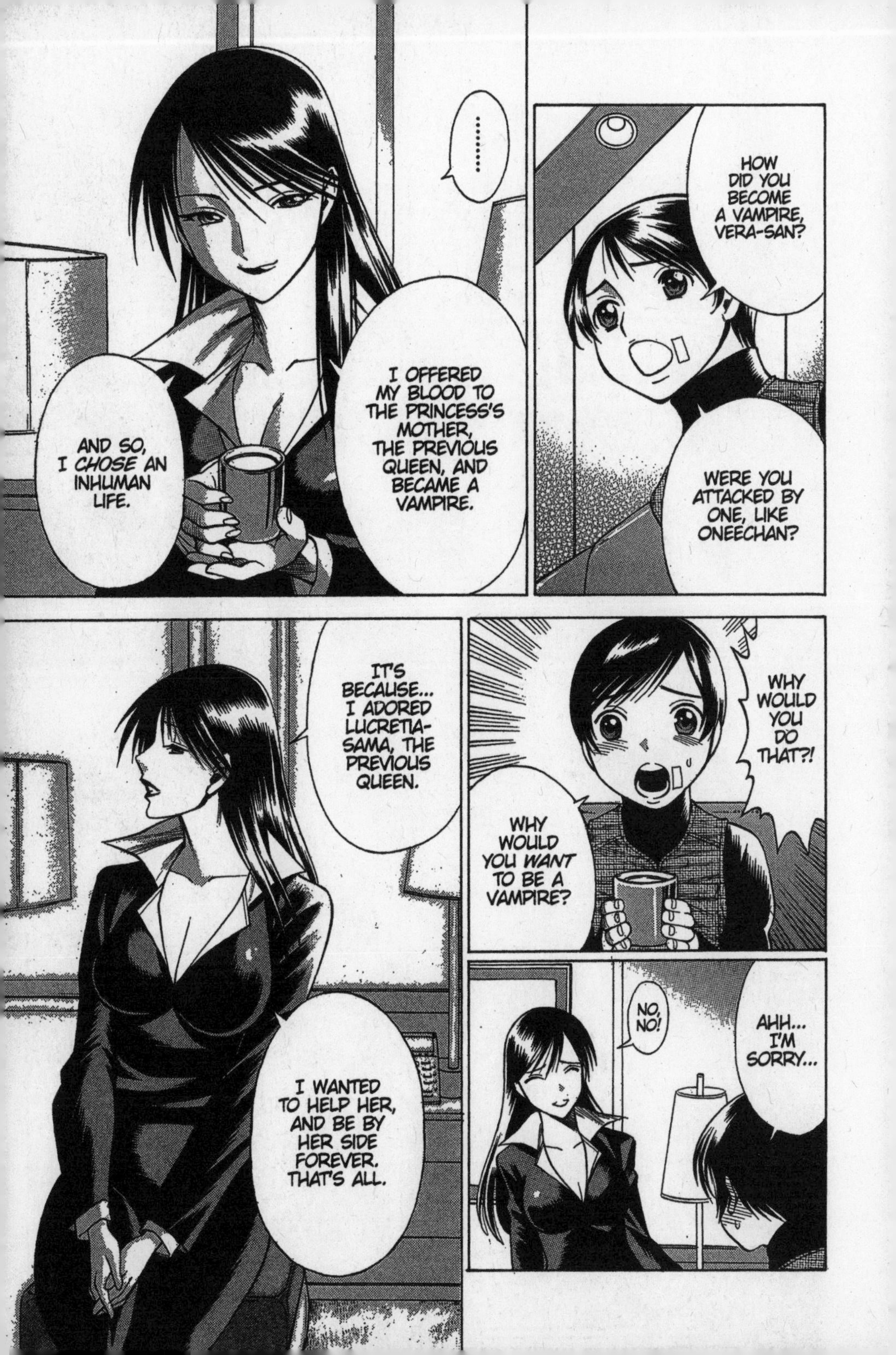
HOW DID YOU BECOME A VAMPIRE, VERA-SAN?
WERE YOU ATTACKED BY ONE, LIKE ONEECHAN?
......
I OFFERED MY BLOOD TO THE PRINCESS'S MOTHER, THE PREVIOUS QUEEN, AND BECAME A VAMPIRE.
AND SO, I *CHOSE* AN INHUMAN LIFE.
WHY WOULD YOU DO THAT?!
WHY WOULD YOU *WANT* TO BE A VAMPIRE?
AHH... I'M SORRY...
NO, NO!
IT'S BECAUSE... I ADORED LUCRETIA-SAMA, THE PREVIOUS QUEEN.
I WANTED TO HELP HER, AND BE BY HER SIDE FOREVER. THAT'S ALL.

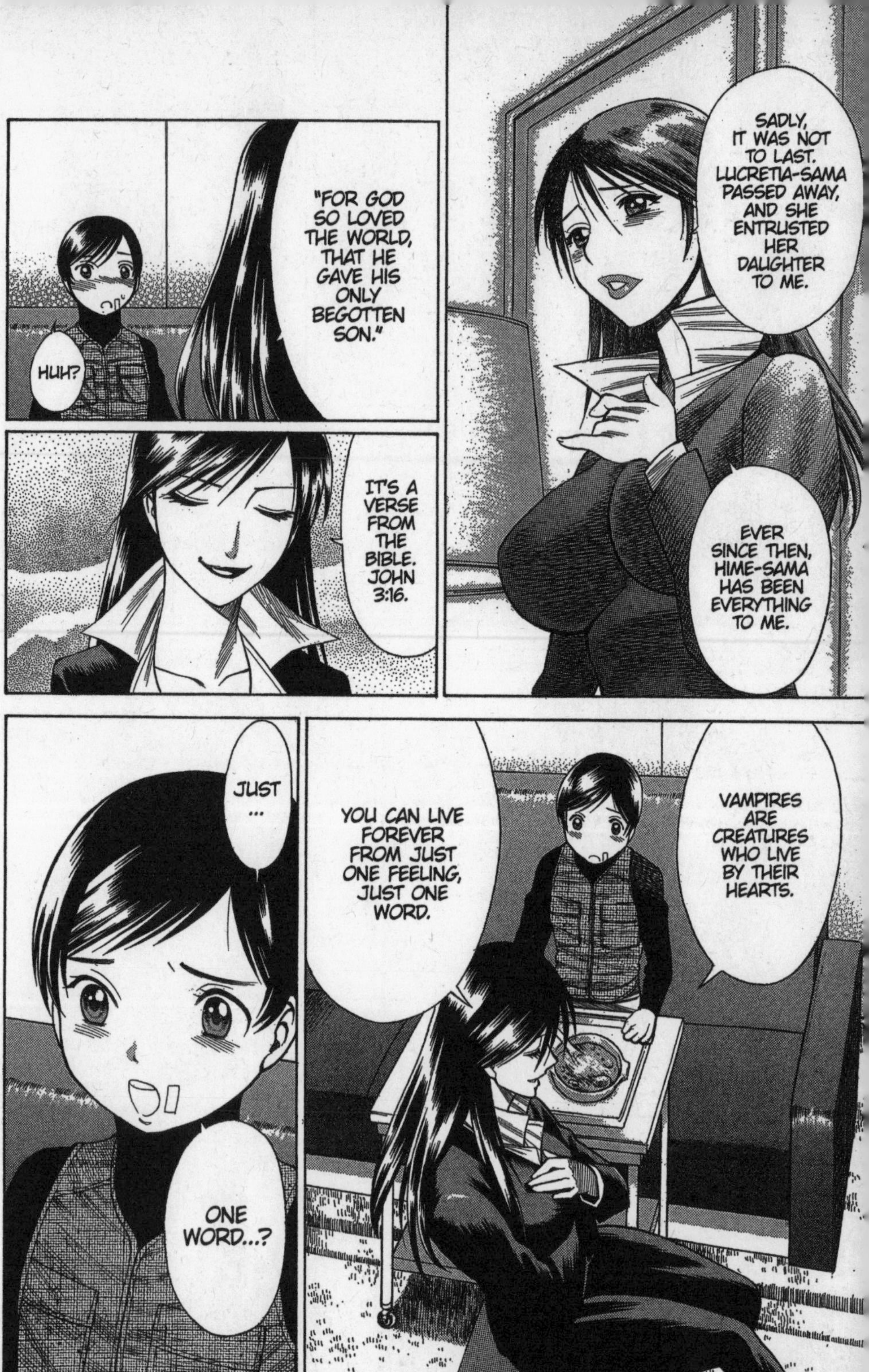
SADLY, IT WAS NOT TO LAST. LUCRETIA-SAMA PASSED AWAY, AND SHE ENTRUSTED HER DAUGHTER TO ME.
EVER SINCE THEN, HIME-SAMA HAS BEEN EVERYTHING TO ME.
"FOR GOD SO LOVED THE WORLD, THAT HE GAVE HIS ONLY BEGOTTEN SON."
HUH?
IT'S A VERSE FROM THE BIBLE. JOHN 3:16.
VAMPIRES ARE CREATURES WHO LIVE BY THEIR HEARTS.
YOU CAN LIVE FOREVER FROM JUST ONE FEELING, JUST ONE WORD.
JUST ...
ONE WORD...?

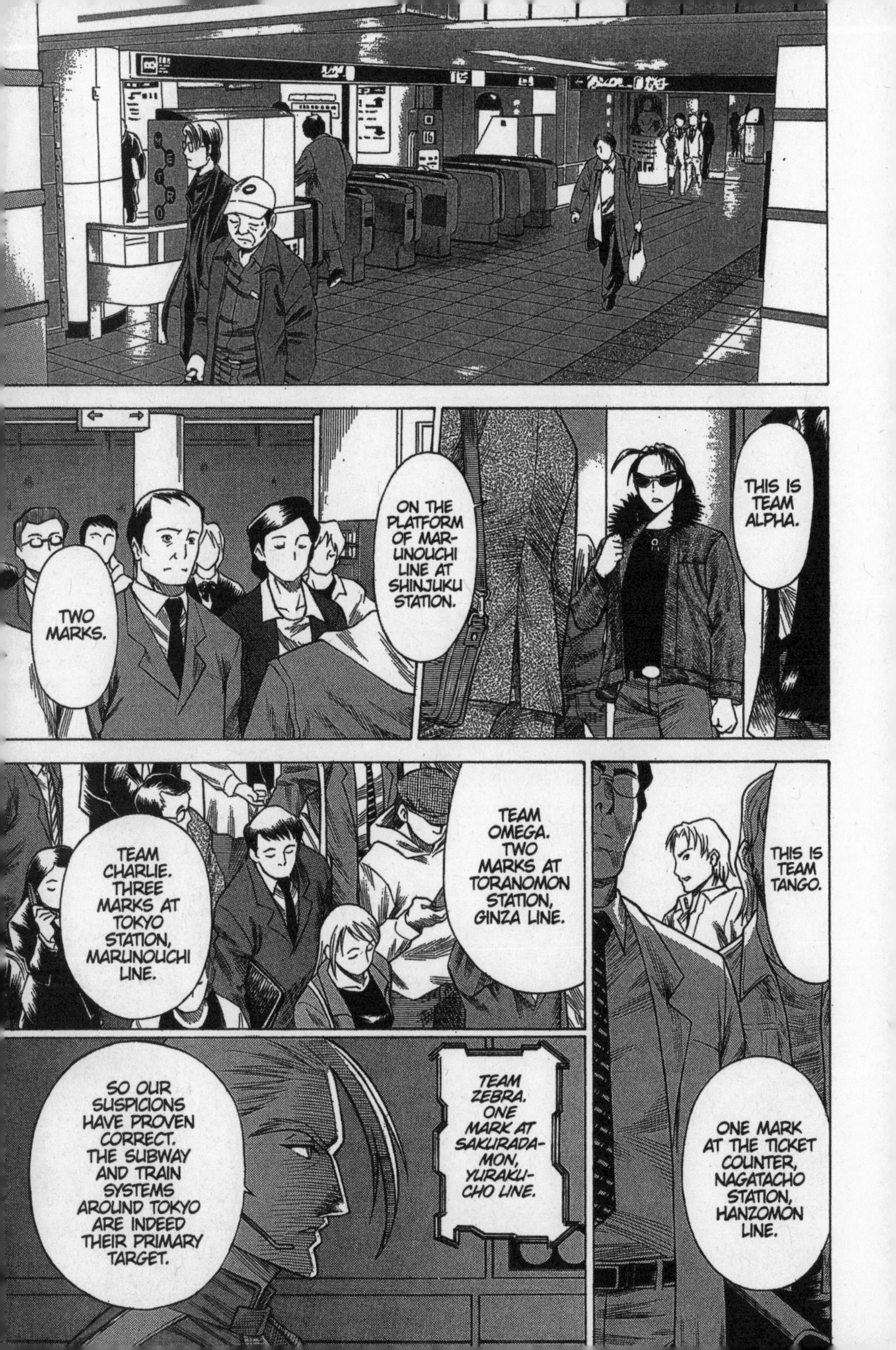
THIS IS TEAM ALPHA.
ON THE PLATFORM OF MARUNOUCHI LINE AT SHINJUKU STATION.
TWO MARKS.
THIS IS TEAM TANGO.
ONE MARK AT THE TICKET COUNTER, NAGATACHO STATION, HANZOMON LINE.
TEAM OMEGA. TWO MARKS AT TORANOMON STATION, GINZA LINE.
TEAM CHARLIE. THREE MARKS AT TOKYO STATION, MARUNOUCHI LINE.
TEAM ZEBRA. ONE MARK AT SAKURADAMON, YURAKUCHO LINE.
SO OUR SUSPICIONS HAVE PROVEN CORRECT. THE SUBWAY AND TRAIN SYSTEMS AROUND TOKYO ARE INDEED THEIR PRIMARY TARGET.

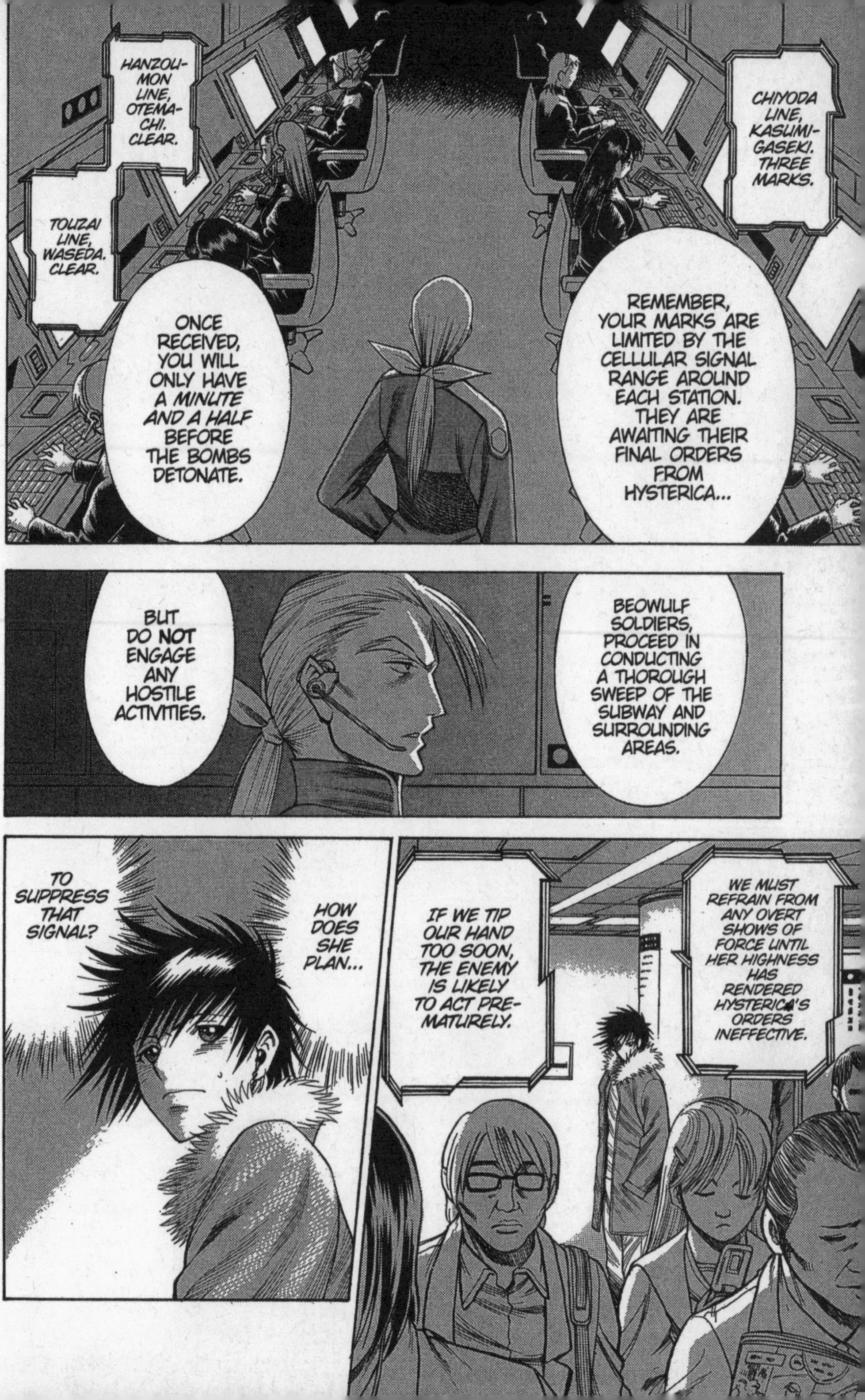
CHIYODA LINE, KASUMI-GASEKI. THREE MARKS.
HANZOU-MON LINE, OTEMA-CHI. CLEAR.
TOUZAI LINE, WASEDA. CLEAR.
REMEMBER, YOUR MARKS ARE LIMITED BY THE CELLULAR SIGNAL RANGE AROUND EACH STATION. THEY ARE AWAITING THEIR FINAL ORDERS FROM HYSTERICA...
ONCE RECEIVED, YOU WILL ONLY HAVE A *MINUTE AND A HALF* BEFORE THE BOMBS DETONATE.
BEOWULF SOLDIERS, PROCEED IN CONDUCTING A THOROUGH SWEEP OF THE SUBWAY AND SURROUNDING AREAS.
BUT DO **NOT** ENGAGE ANY HOSTILE ACTIVITIES.
WE MUST REFRAIN FROM ANY OVERT SHOWS OF FORCE UNTIL HER HIGHNESS HAS RENDERED HYSTERICA'S ORDERS INEFFECTIVE.
IF WE TIP OUR HAND TOO SOON, THE ENEMY IS LIKELY TO ACT PRE-MATURELY.
HOW DOES SHE PLAN...
TO SUPPRESS THAT SIGNAL?

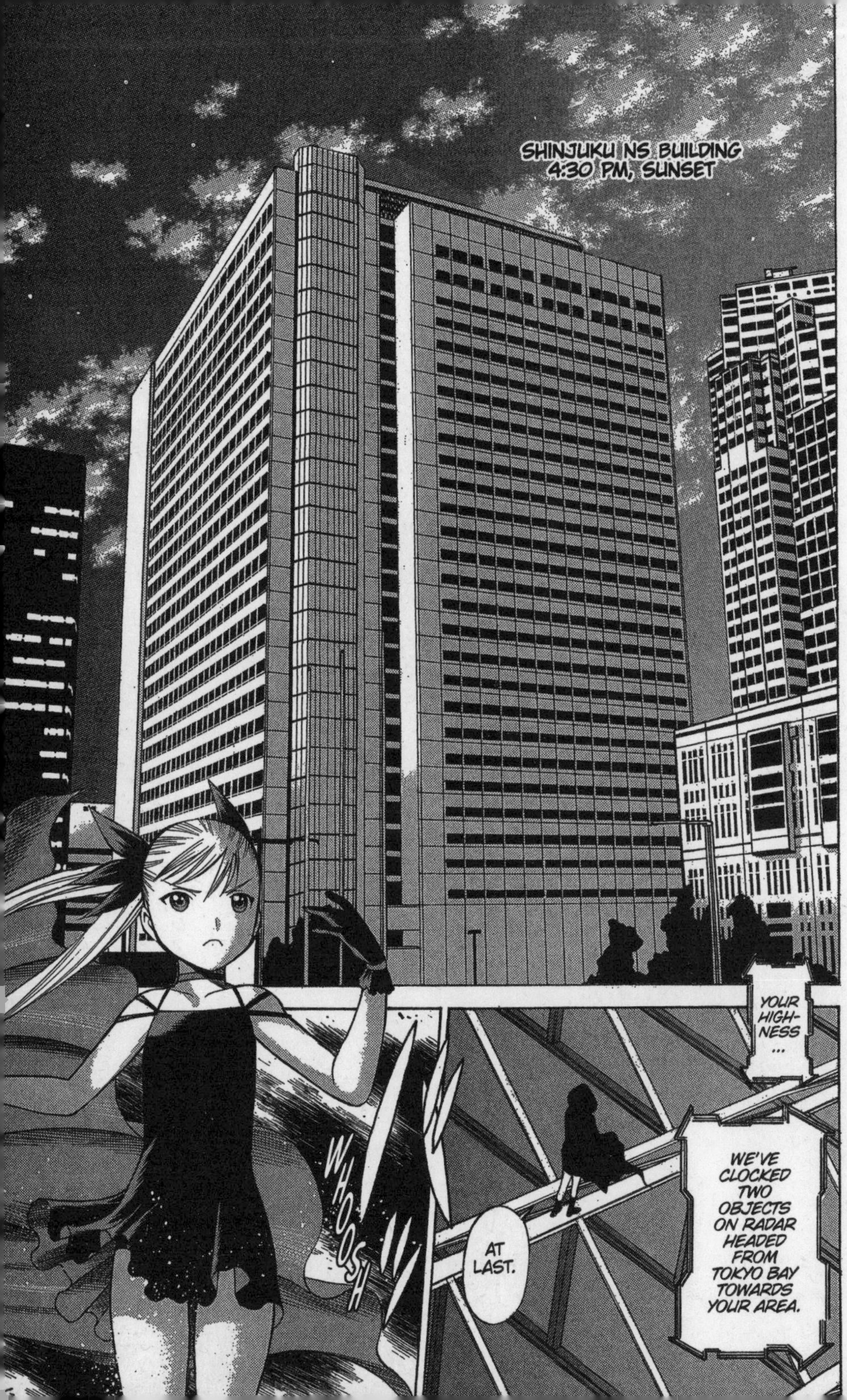
SHINJUKU NS BUILDING
4:30 PM, SUNSET
YOUR HIGH-NESS ...
WE'VE CLOCKED TWO OBJECTS ON RADAR HEADED FROM TOKYO BAY TOWARDS YOUR AREA.
AT LAST.
WHOOSH

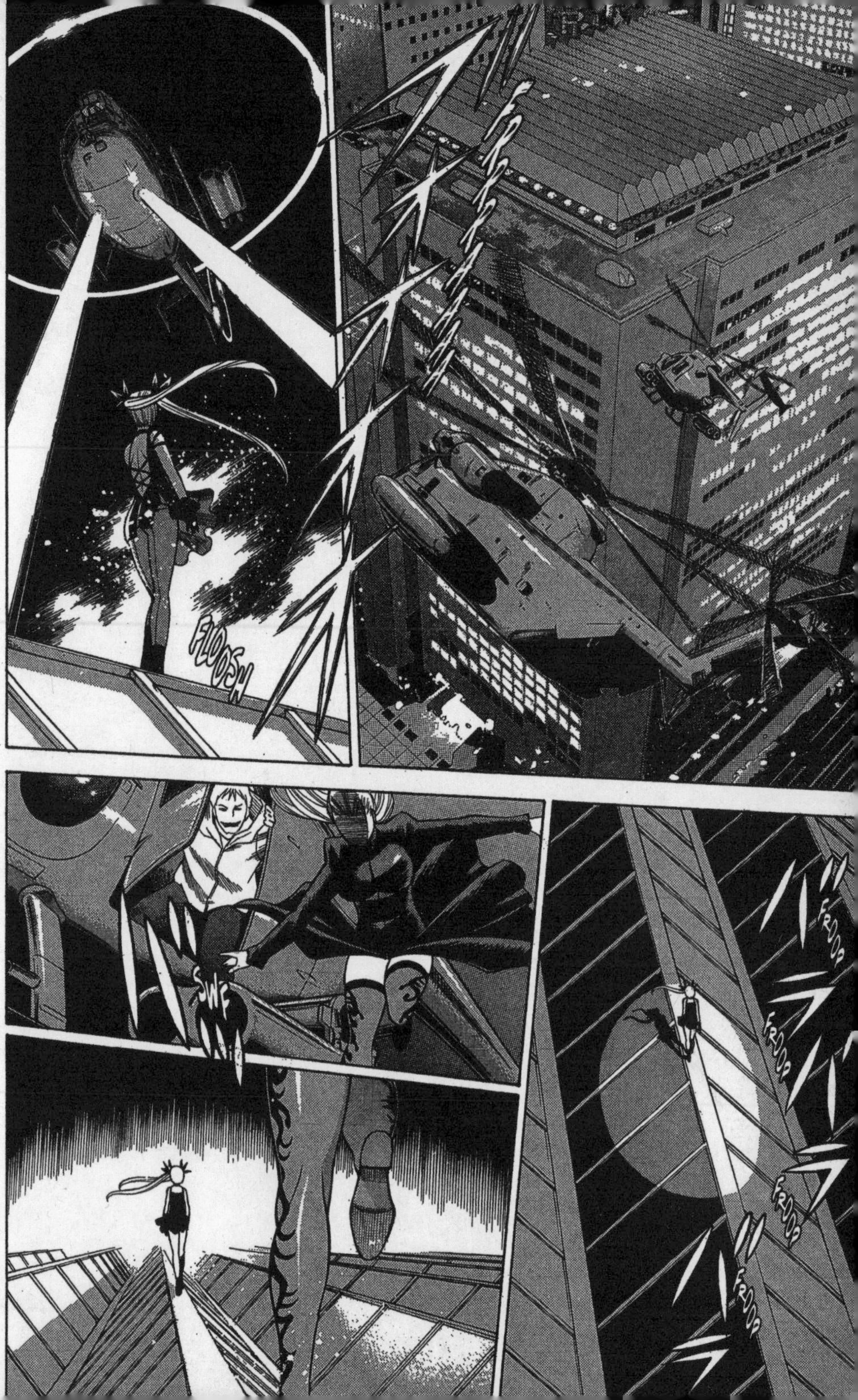
FLOOSH
FROOP
FROOP
FROOP
FROOP
SWF

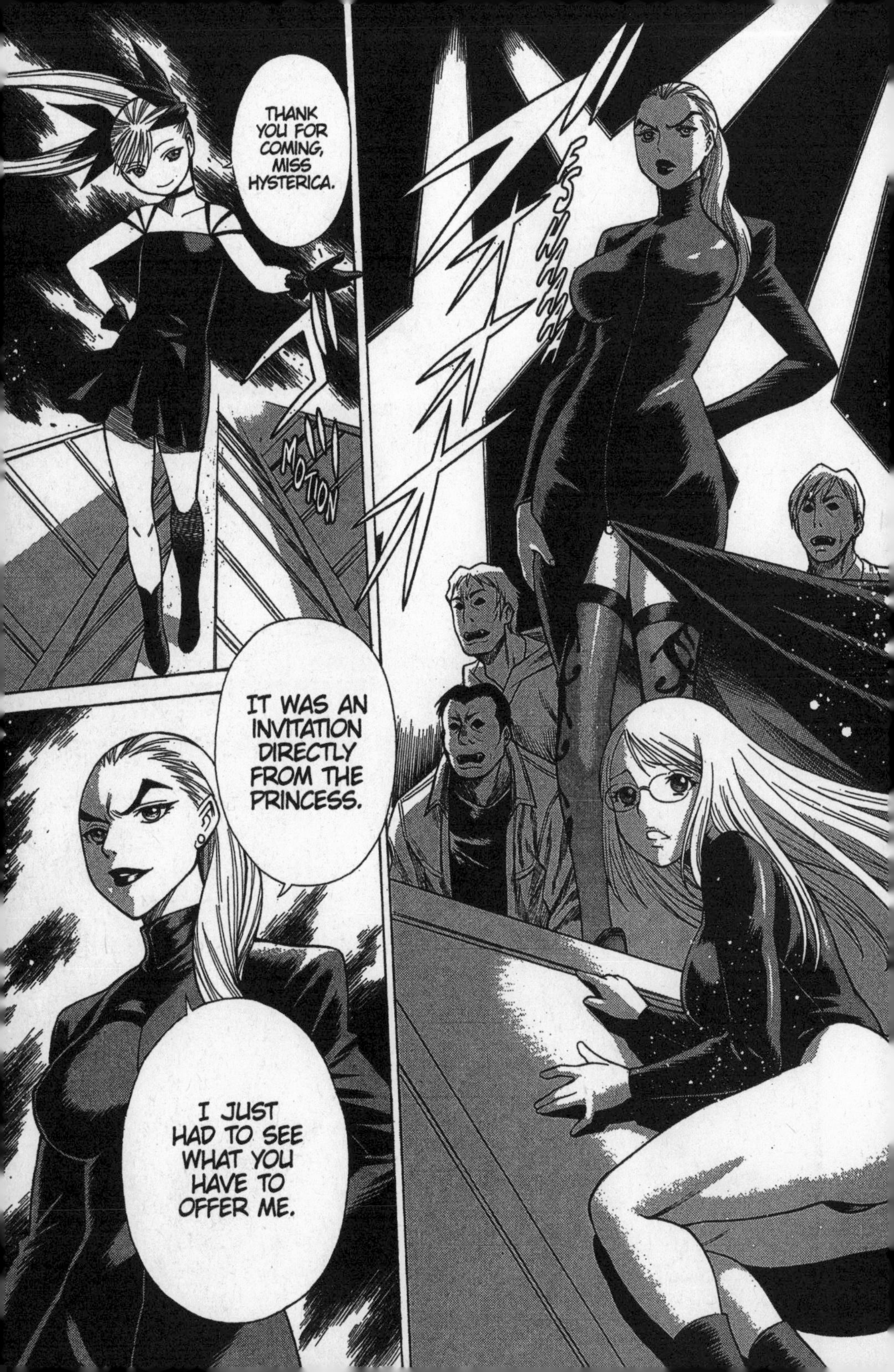
FESHHHHH
THANK YOU FOR COMING, MISS HYSTERICA.
MOTION
IT WAS AN INVITATION DIRECTLY FROM THE PRINCESS.
I JUST HAD TO SEE WHAT YOU HAVE TO OFFER ME.

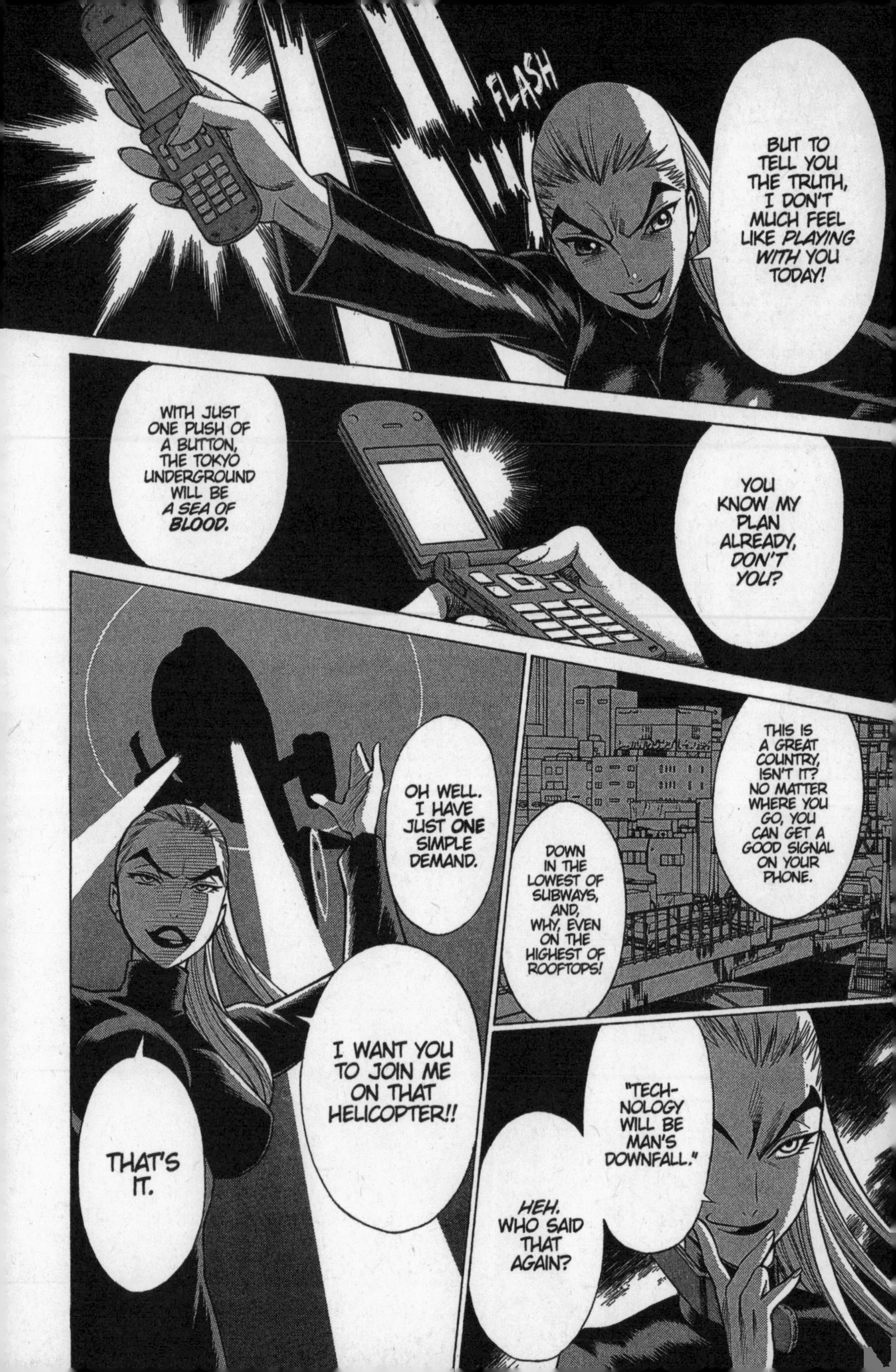
FLASH
BUT TO TELL YOU THE TRUTH, I DON'T MUCH FEEL LIKE *PLAYING WITH* YOU TODAY!
YOU KNOW MY PLAN ALREADY, *DON'T YOU?*
WITH JUST ONE PUSH OF A BUTTON, THE TOKYO UNDERGROUND WILL BE *A SEA OF BLOOD.*
THIS IS A GREAT COUNTRY, ISN'T IT? NO MATTER WHERE YOU GO, YOU CAN GET A GOOD SIGNAL ON YOUR PHONE.
DOWN IN THE LOWEST OF SUBWAYS, AND, WHY, EVEN ON THE HIGHEST OF ROOFTOPS!
"TECH-NOLOGY WILL BE MAN'S DOWNFALL."
HEH. WHO SAID THAT AGAIN?
OH WELL. I HAVE JUST ONE SIMPLE DEMAND.
I WANT YOU TO JOIN ME ON THAT HELICOPTER!!
THAT'S IT.

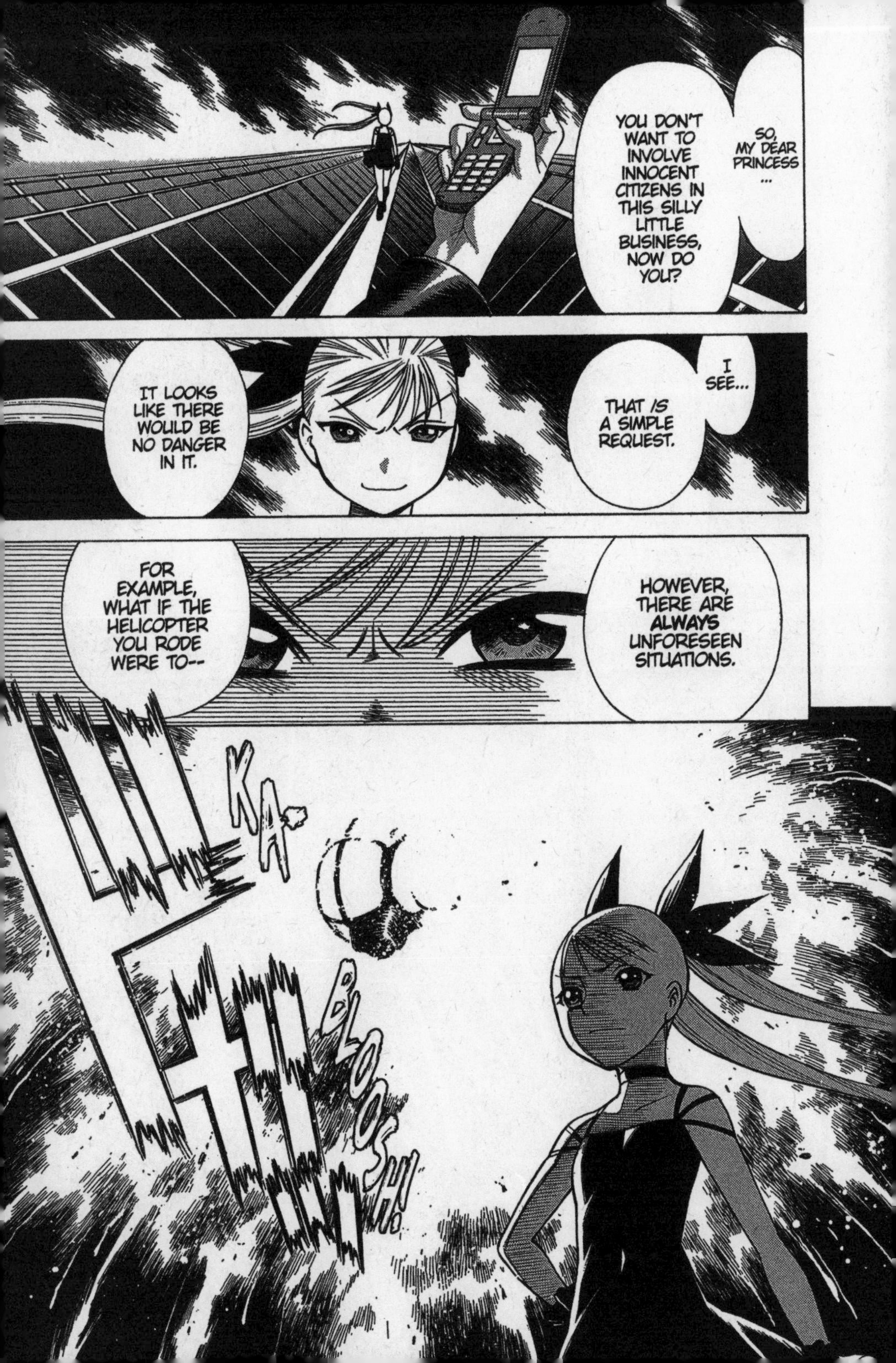
SO, MY DEAR PRINCESS ...
YOU DON'T WANT TO INVOLVE INNOCENT CITIZENS IN THIS SILLY LITTLE BUSINESS, NOW DO YOU?
I SEE...
THAT IS A SIMPLE REQUEST.
IT LOOKS LIKE THERE WOULD BE NO DANGER IN IT.
HOWEVER, THERE ARE ALWAYS UNFORESEEN SITUATIONS.
FOR EXAMPLE, WHAT IF THE HELICOPTER YOU RODE WERE TO--
KA
BLOOSH!!

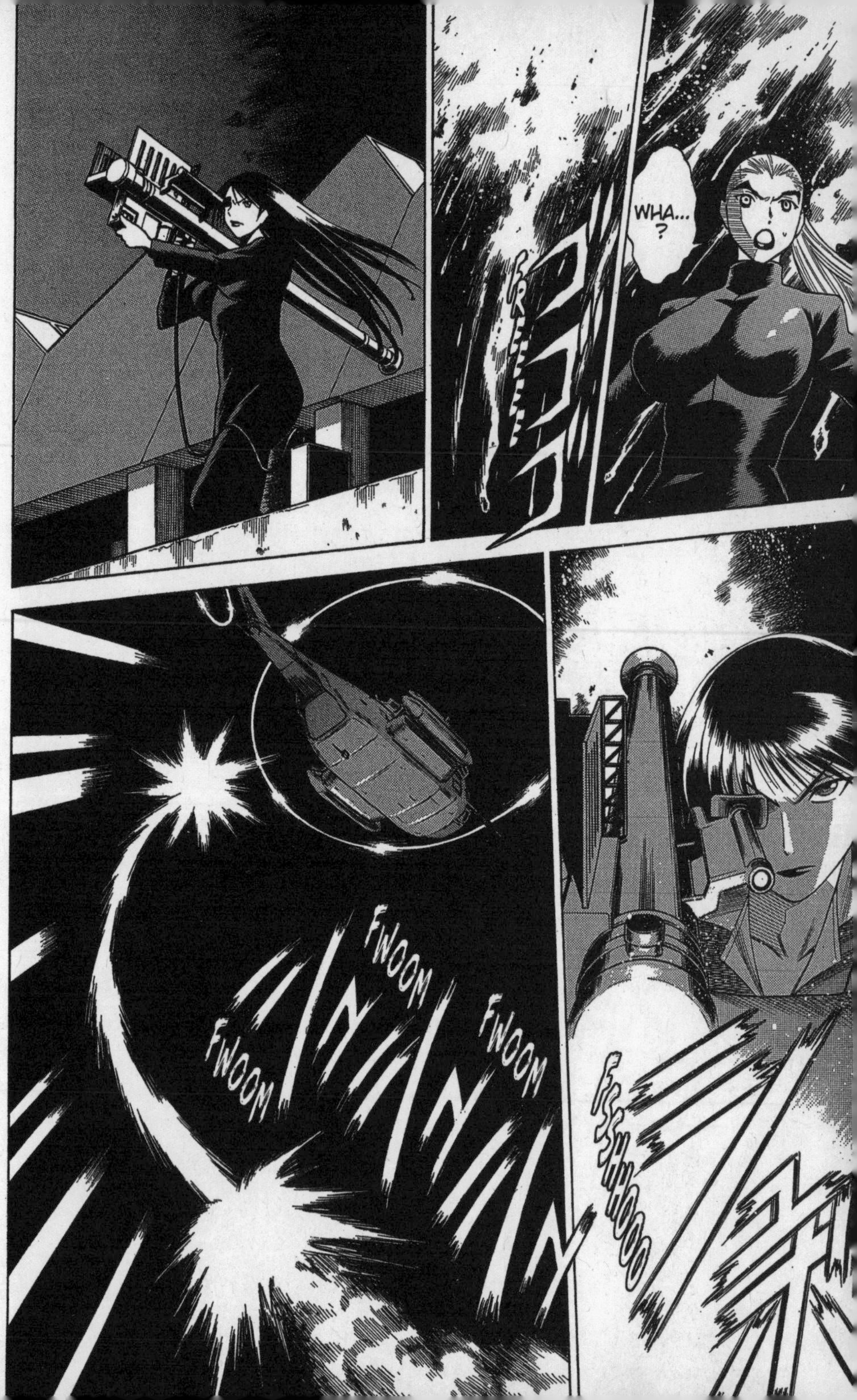
WHA... ?
FR
FSHHOOO
FWOOM
FWOOM
FWOOM

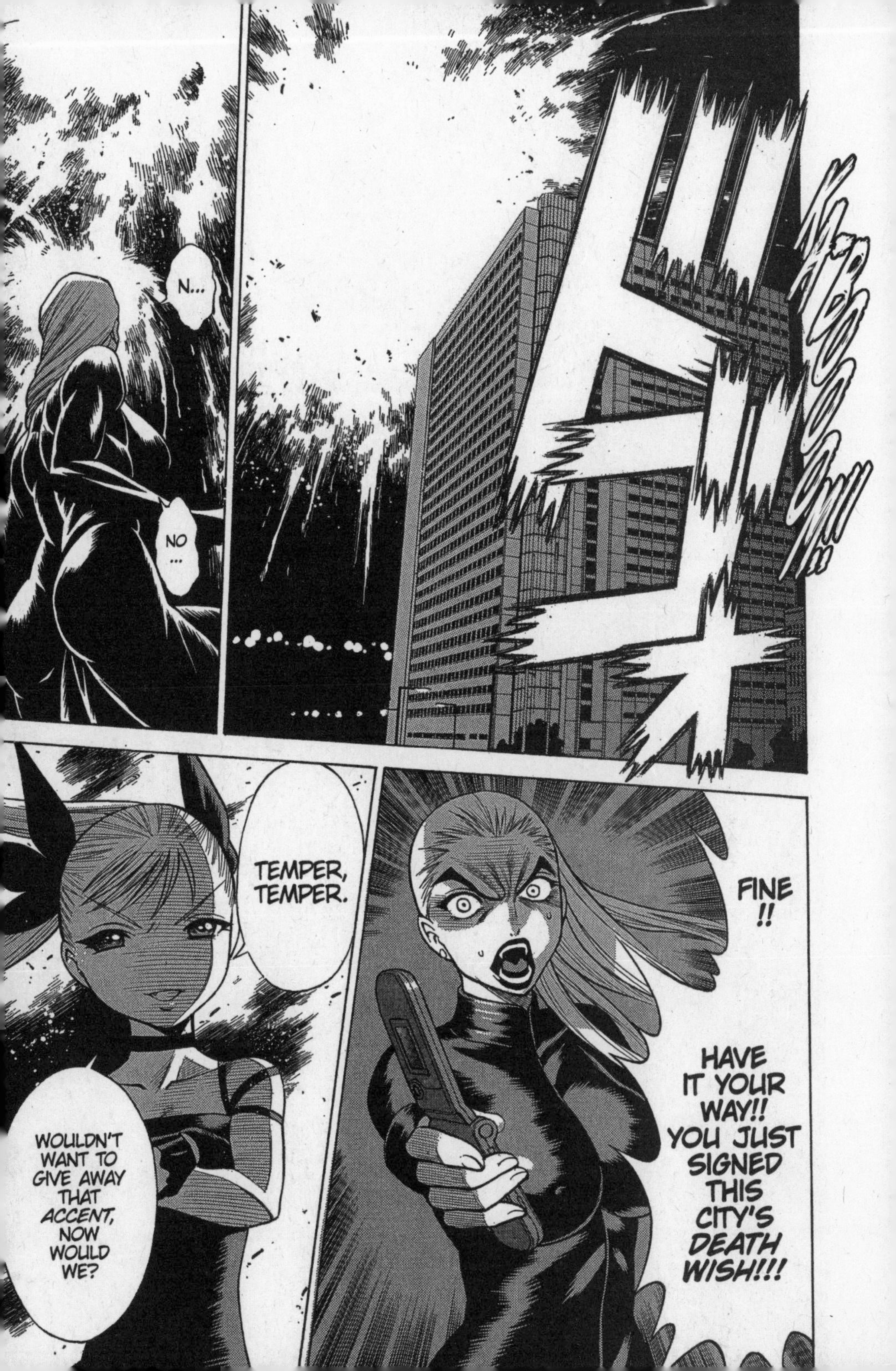
N...
NO ...
FINE !!
HAVE IT YOUR WAY!! YOU JUST SIGNED THIS CITY'S DEATH WISH!!!
TEMPER, TEMPER.
WOULDN'T WANT TO GIVE AWAY THAT ACCENT, NOW WOULD WE?

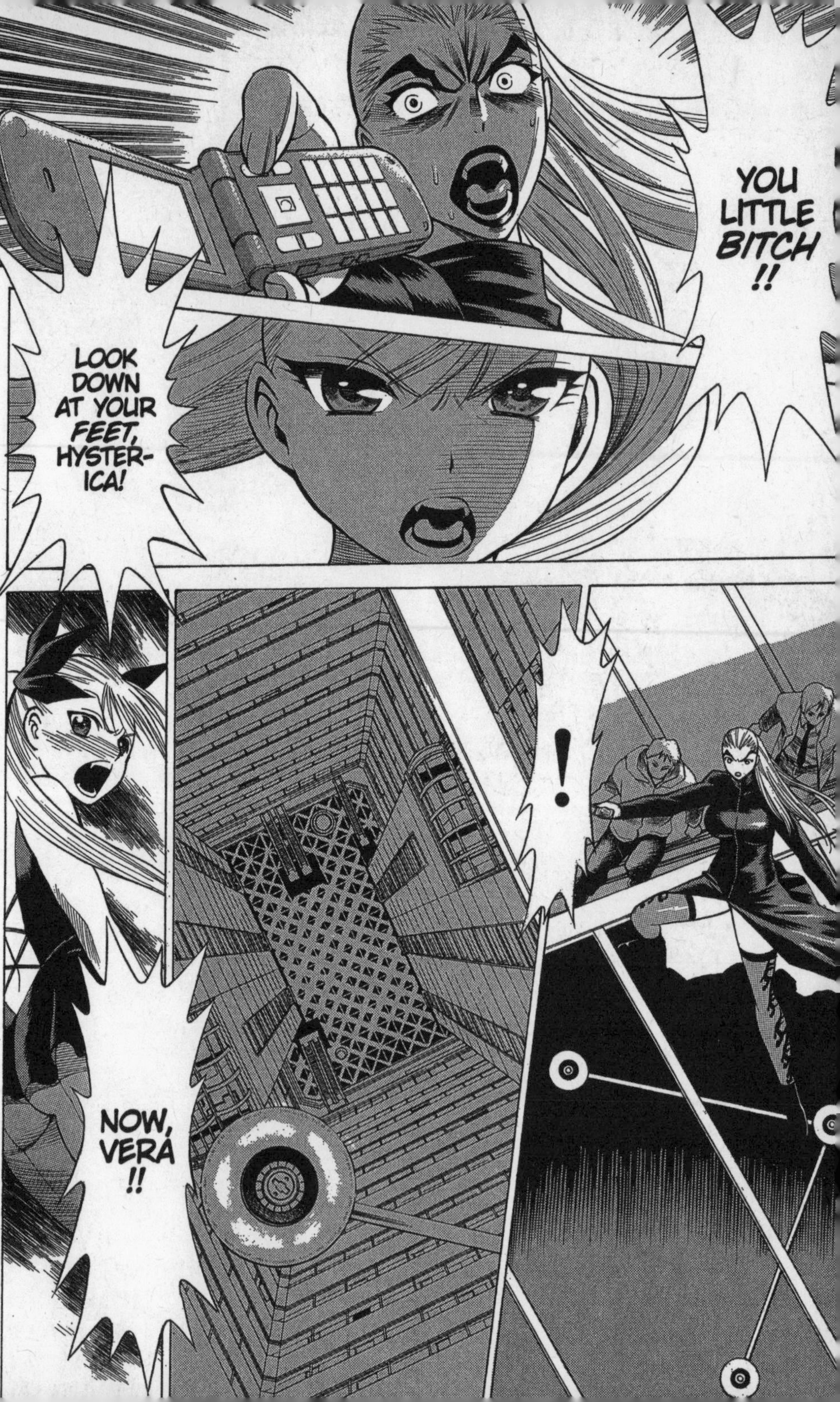
YOU LITTLE BITCH!!
LOOK DOWN AT YOUR FEET, HYSTER-ICA!
!
NOW, VERA!!

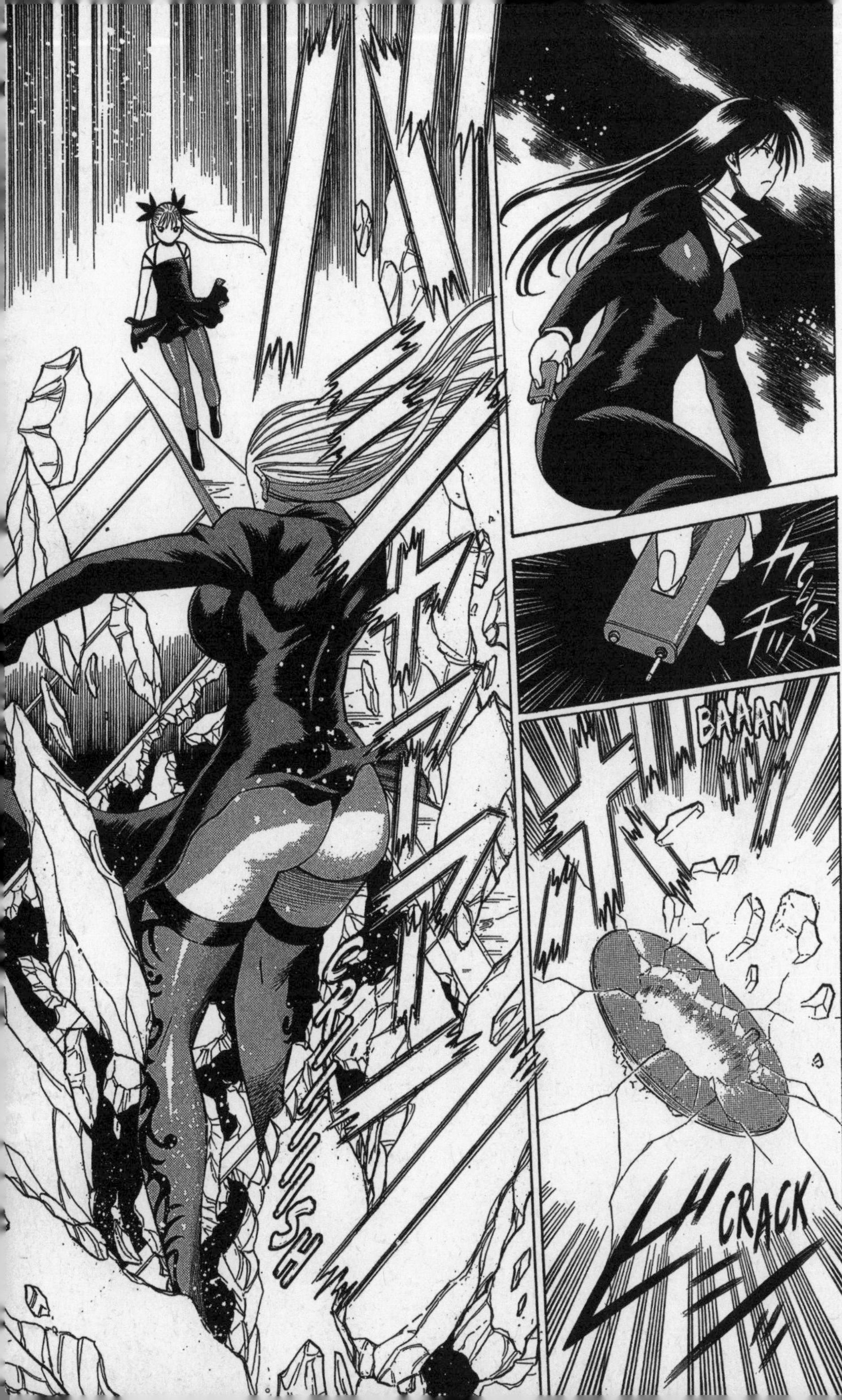
CLICK
BAAAM
CRACK
SPLIIIISH

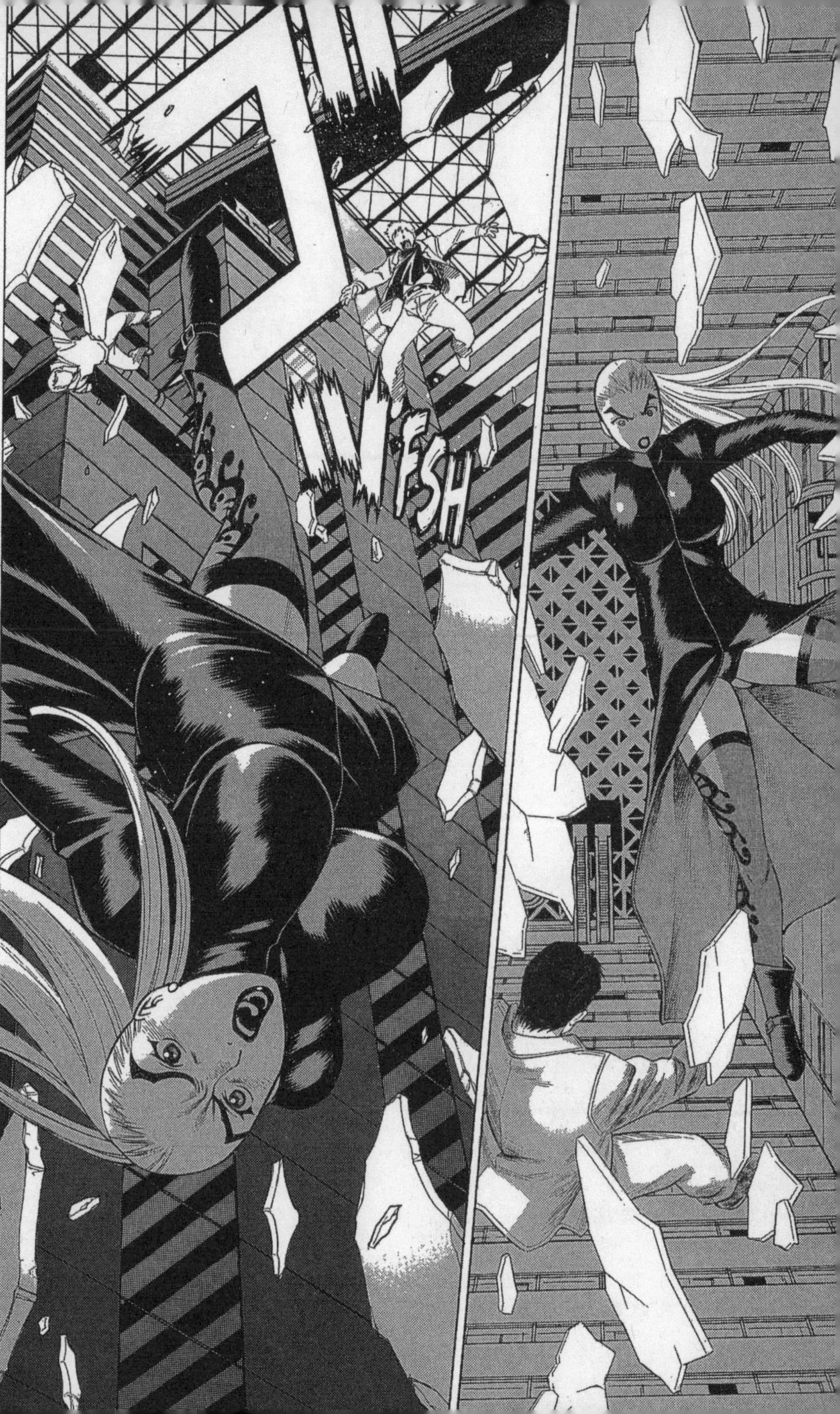
FSH

Dance In The Vampire Bund

We reconciled
and then we embraced.

And ever since then, we've been mortal enemies ———

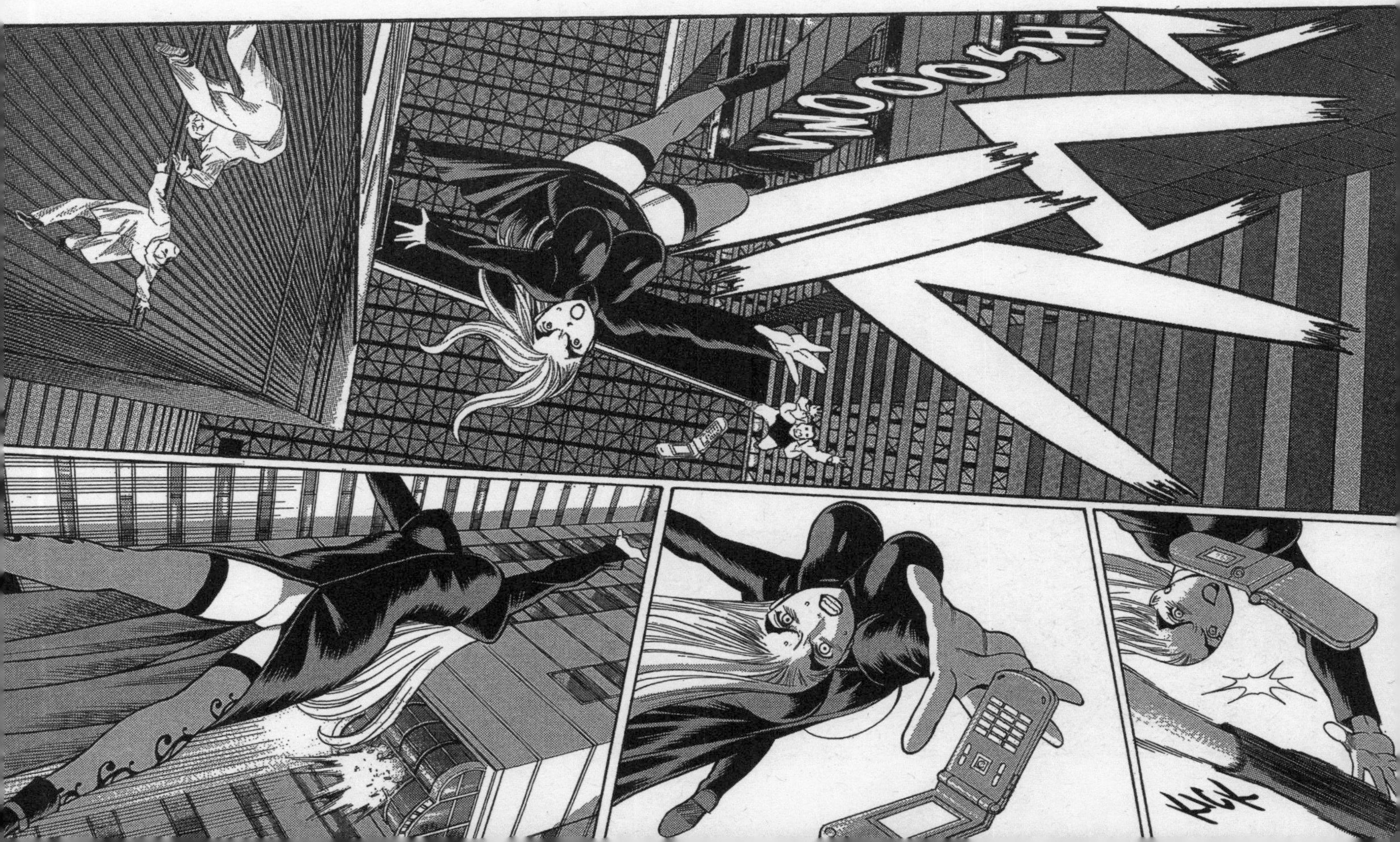
VWOOOSH
KICK

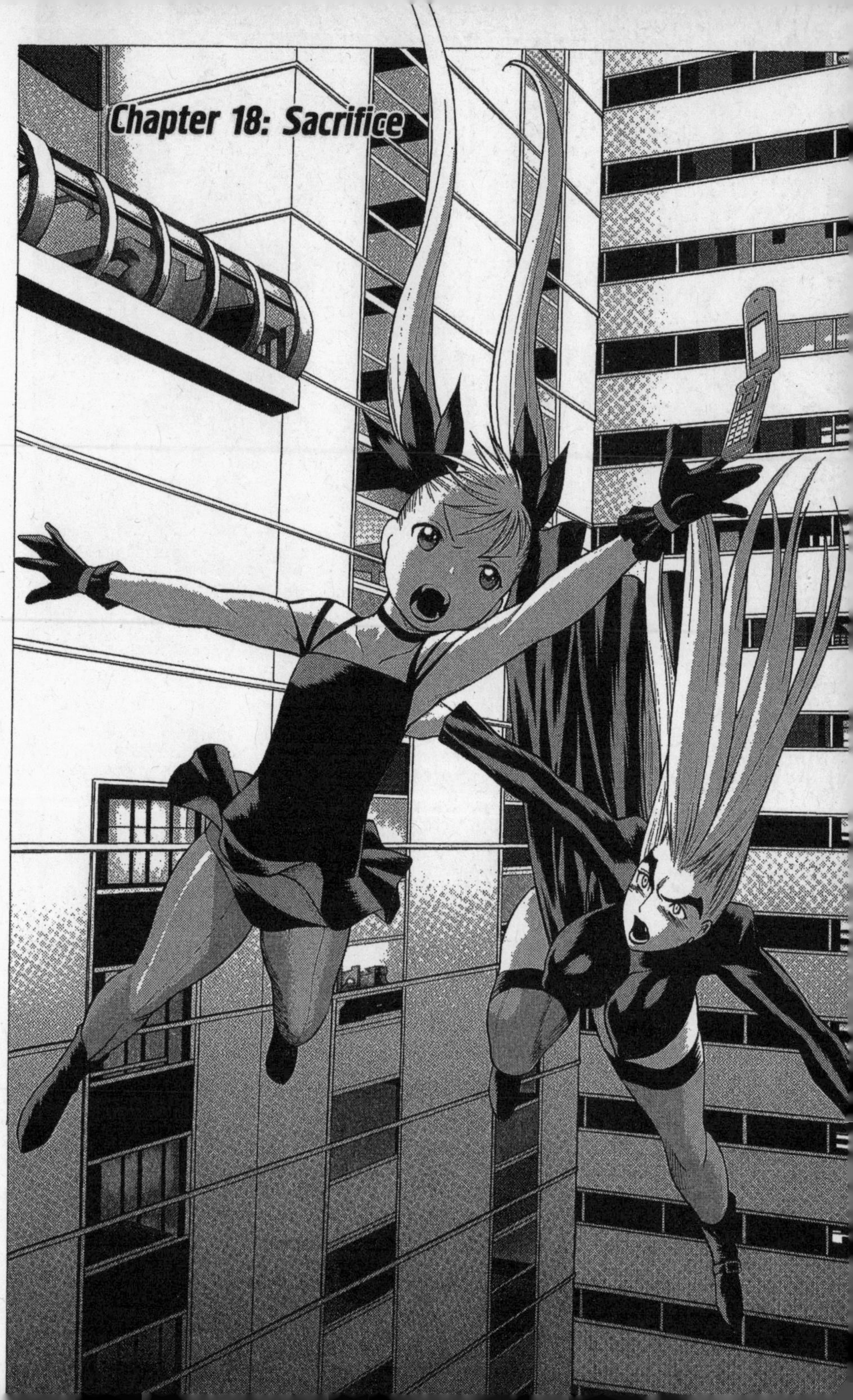
Chapter 18: Sacrifice

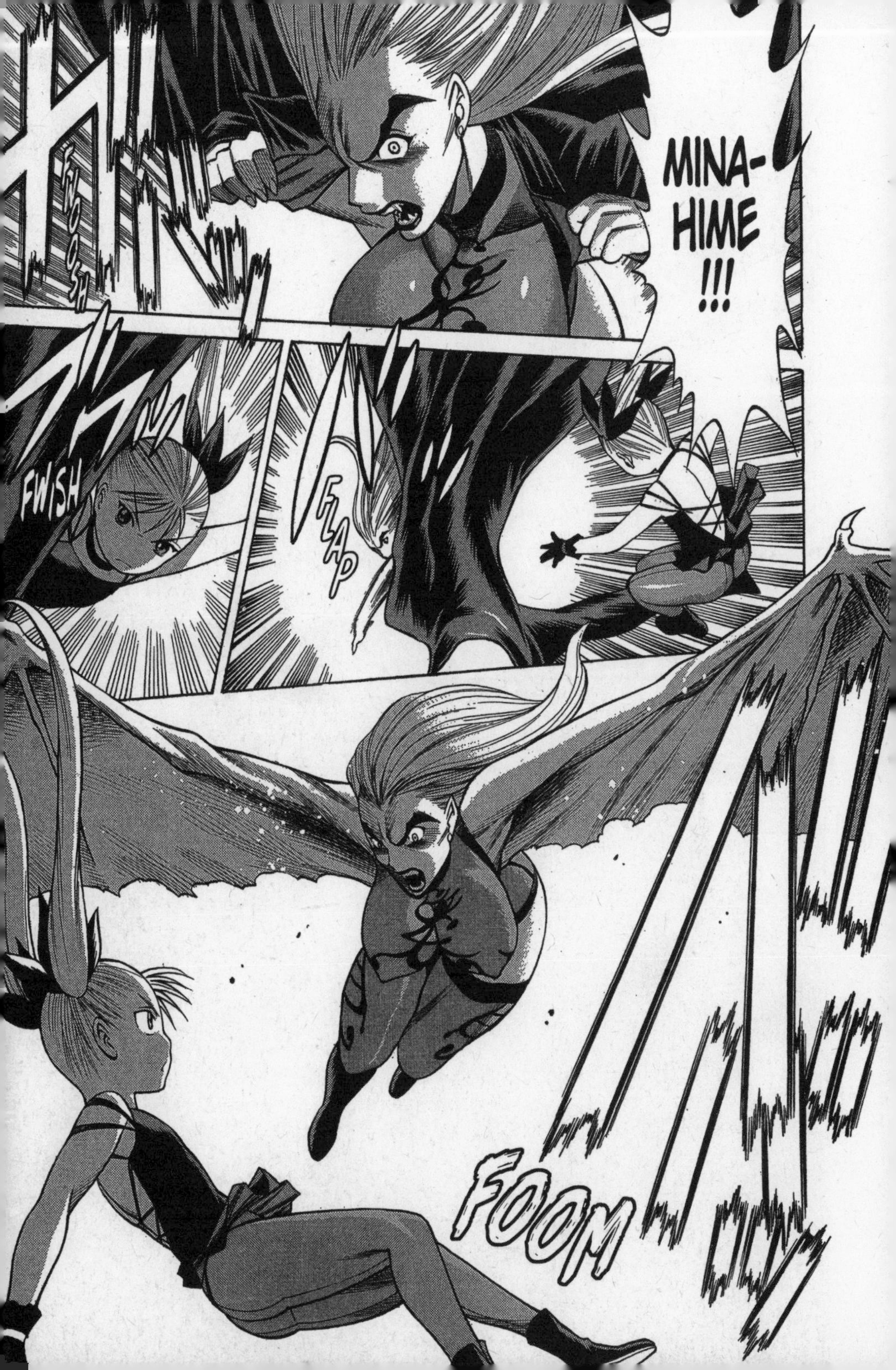
MINA-HIME!!!
FWOOSH
FLAP
FWISH
FOOM

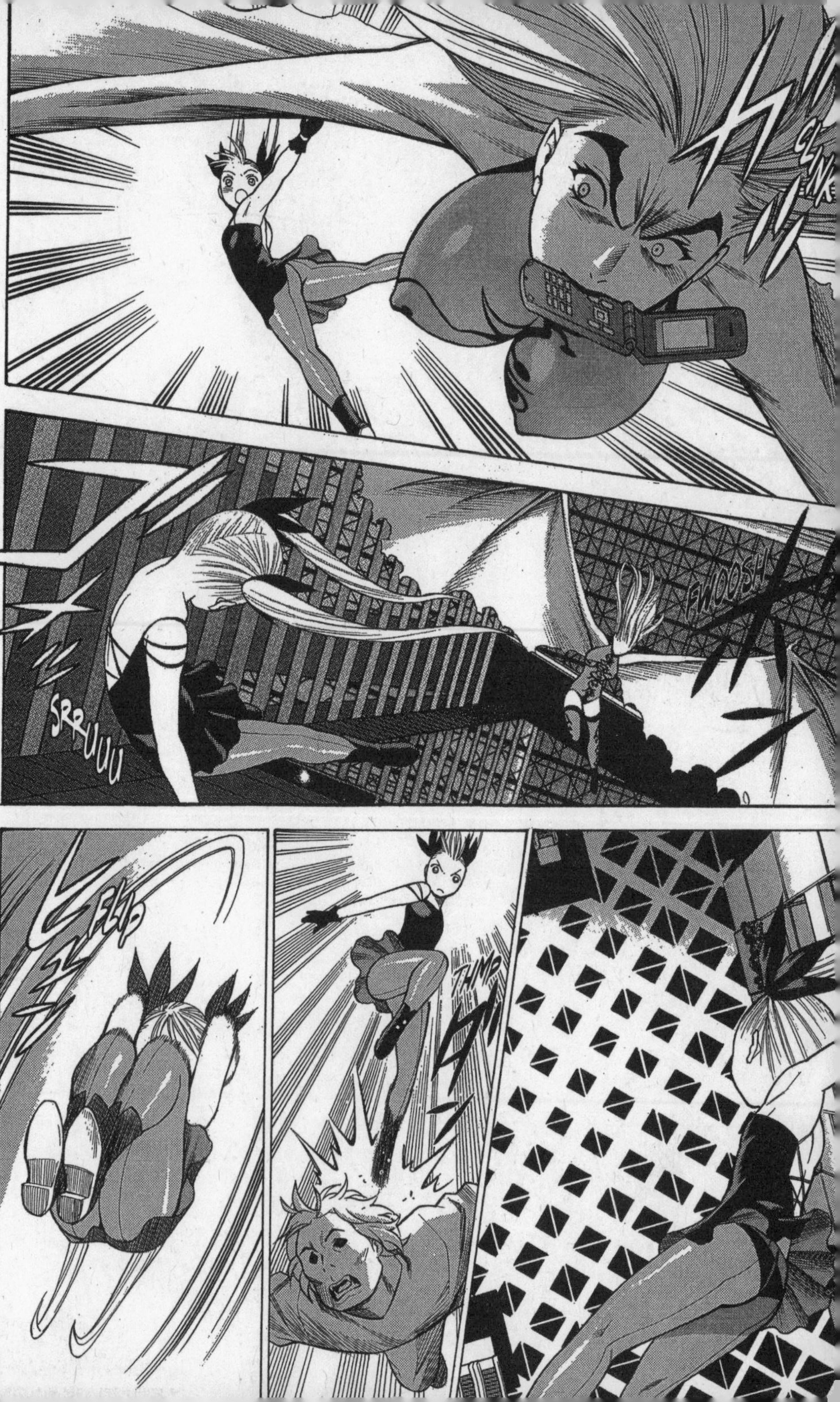
CLINK
FWOOSH
SRRUUU
THMP
FLIP

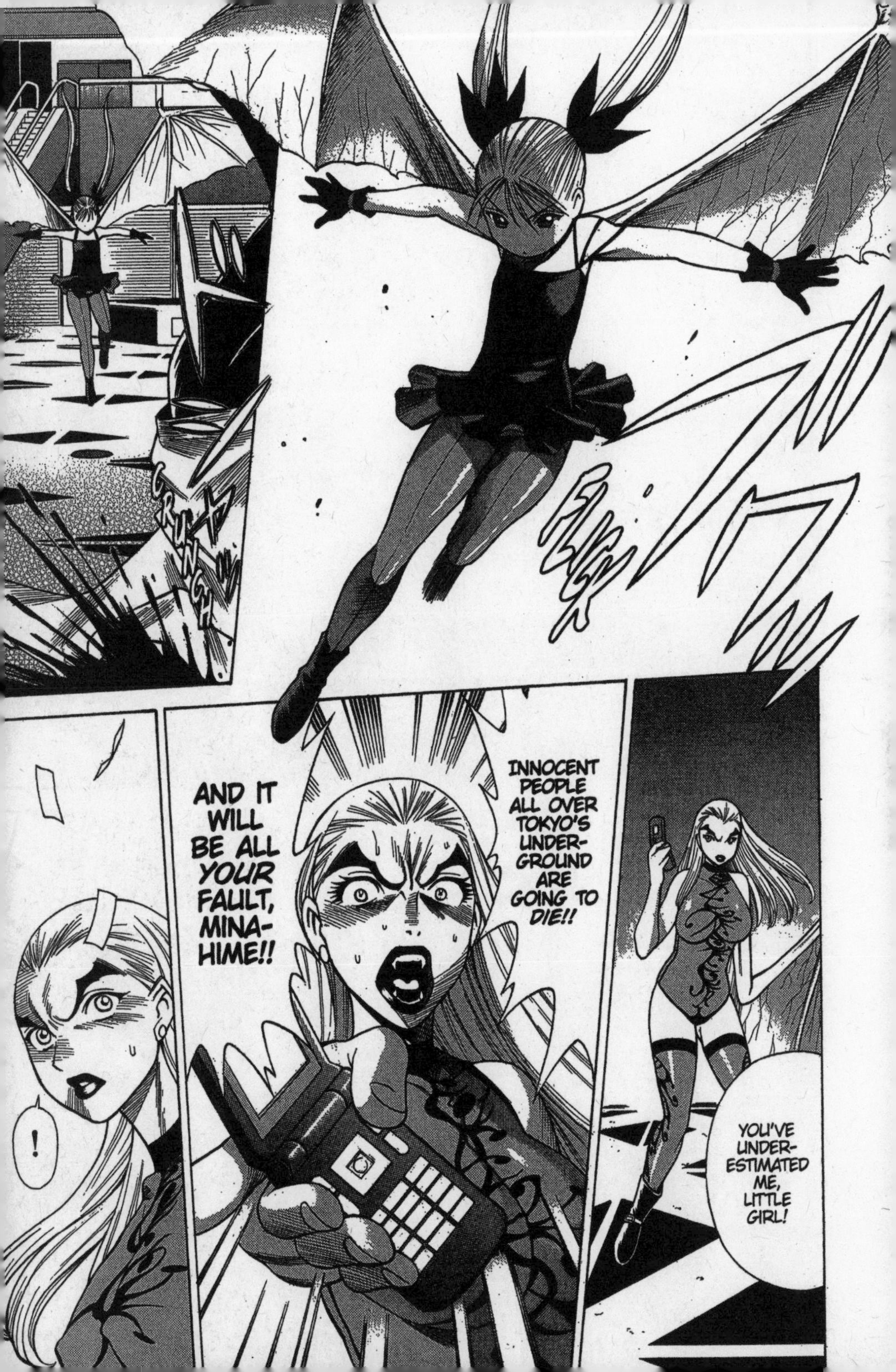
FLICK
CRUNCH
YOU'VE UNDER-ESTIMATED ME, LITTLE GIRL!
INNOCENT PEOPLE ALL OVER TOKYO'S UNDER-GROUND ARE GOING TO DIE!!
AND IT WILL BE ALL YOUR FAULT, MINA-HIME!!
!

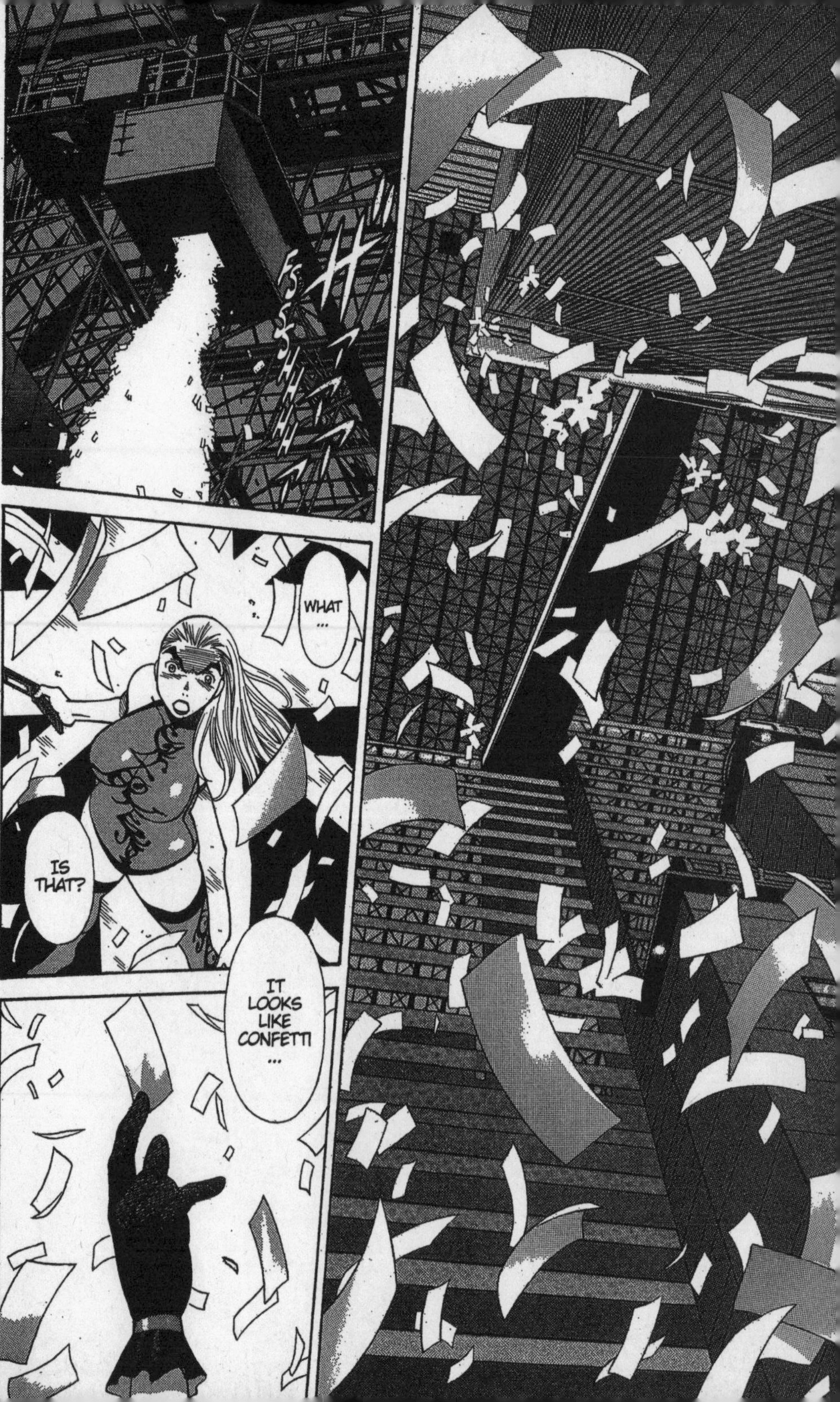
FSSHHHH
WHAT ...
IS THAT?
IT LOOKS LIKE CONFETTI ...

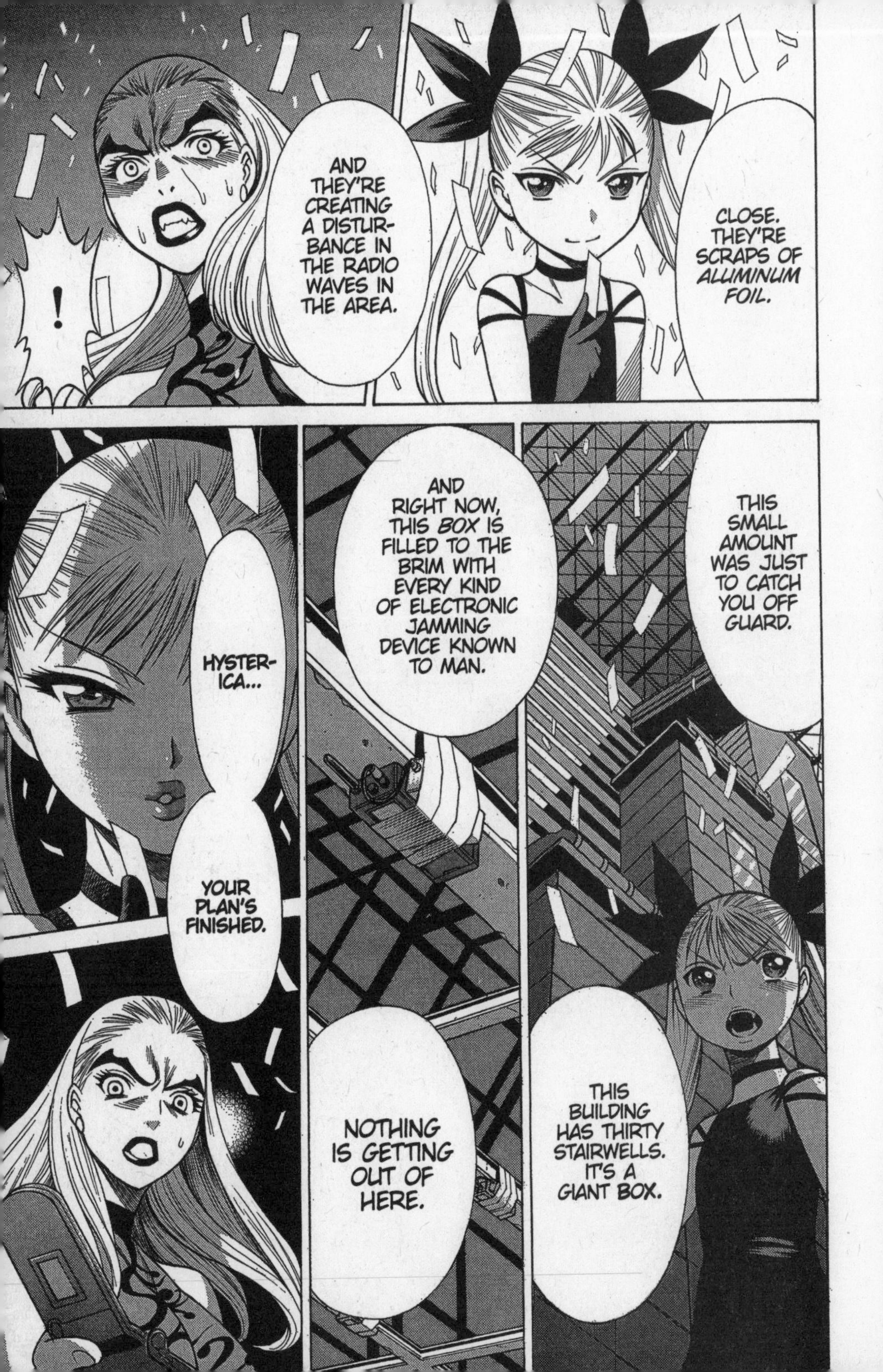
CLOSE. THEY'RE SCRAPS OF *ALUMINUM FOIL.*
AND THEY'RE CREATING A DISTURBANCE IN THE RADIO WAVES IN THE AREA.
!
THIS SMALL AMOUNT WAS JUST TO CATCH YOU OFF GUARD.
THIS BUILDING HAS THIRTY STAIRWELLS. IT'S A GIANT BOX.
AND RIGHT NOW, THIS *BOX* IS FILLED TO THE BRIM WITH EVERY KIND OF ELECTRONIC JAMMING DEVICE KNOWN TO MAN.
NOTHING IS GETTING OUT OF HERE.
HYSTERICA...
YOUR PLAN'S FINISHED.

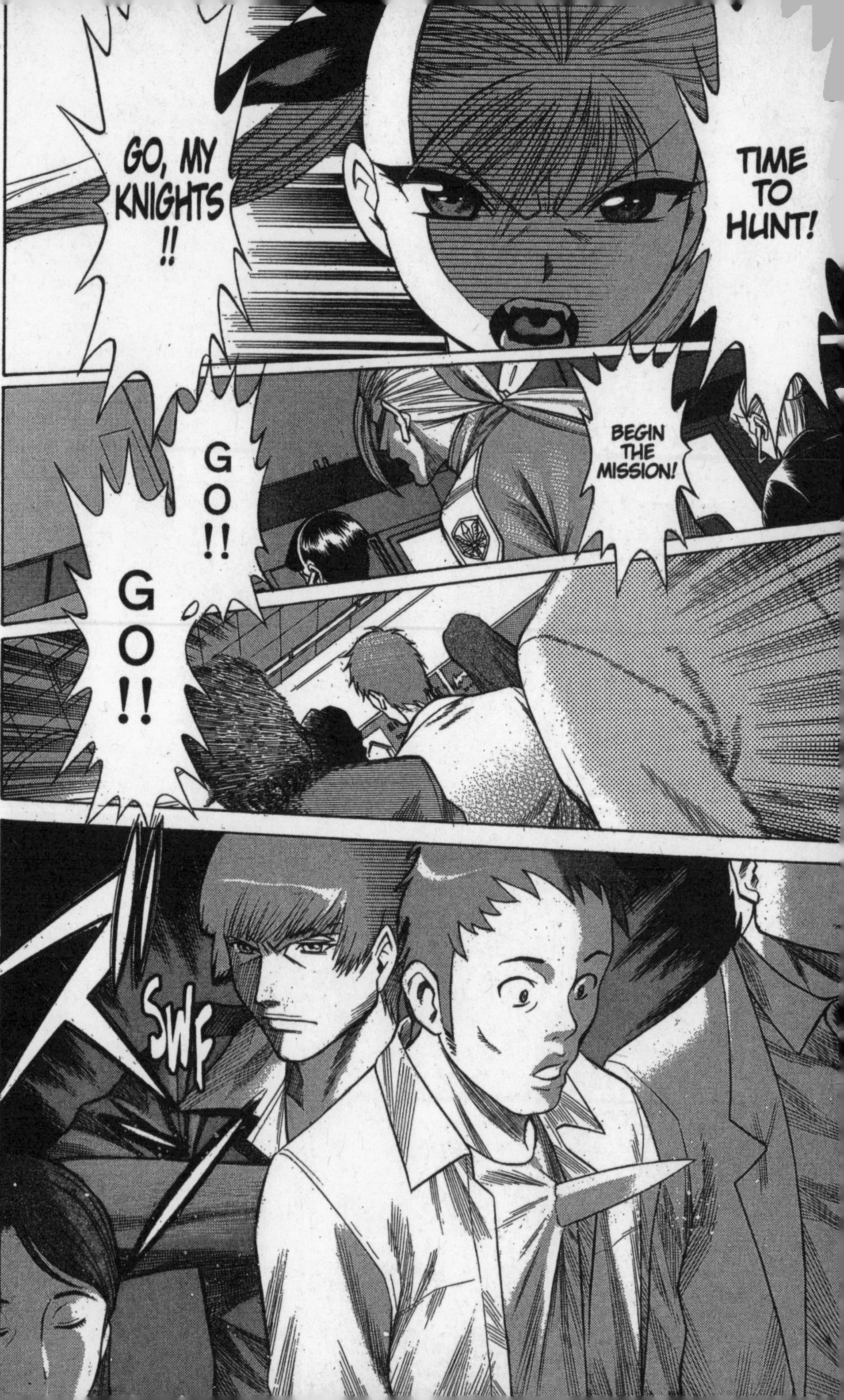
TIME TO HUNT!
GO, MY KNIGHTS!!
BEGIN THE MISSION!
GO!!
GO!!
SWF

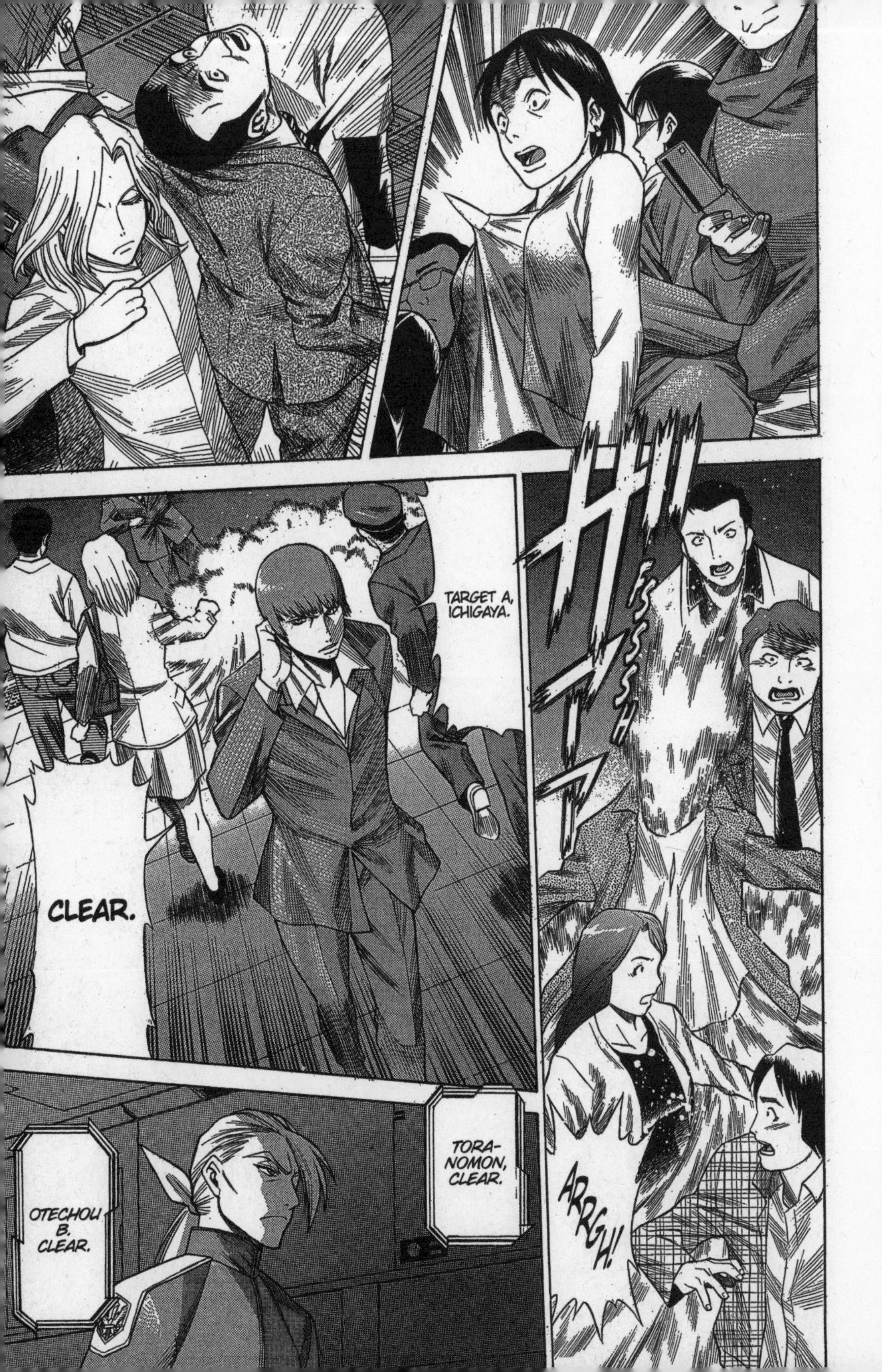

FSSSH
ARRGH!
TARGET A, ICHIGAYA.
CLEAR.
TORA-NOMON, CLEAR.
OTECHOU B. CLEAR.

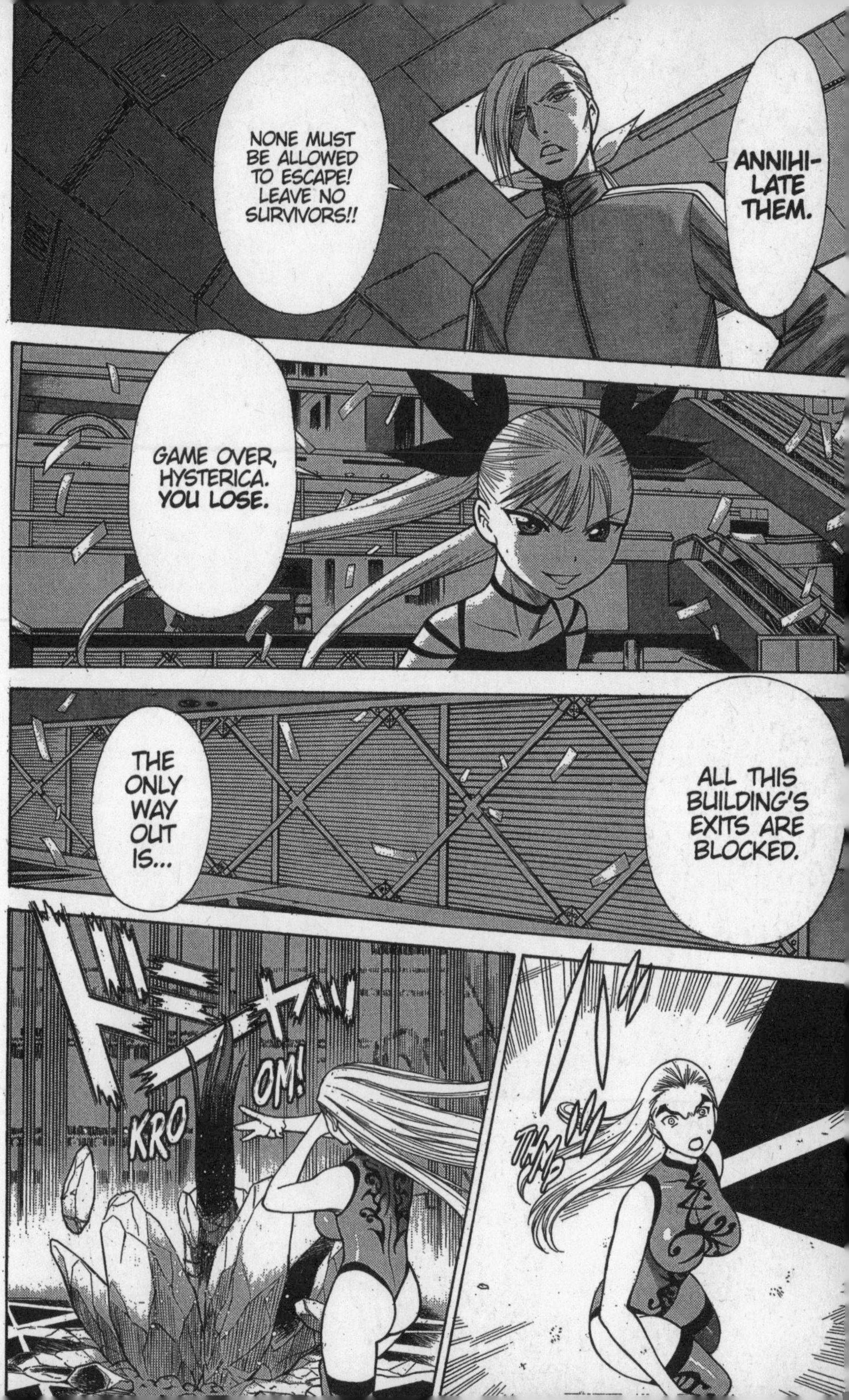
ANNIHI-LATE THEM.
NONE MUST BE ALLOWED TO ESCAPE! LEAVE NO SURVIVORS!!
GAME OVER, HYSTERICA. YOU LOSE.
ALL THIS BUILDING'S EXITS ARE BLOCKED.
THE ONLY WAY OUT IS...
THMP
KRO OM!

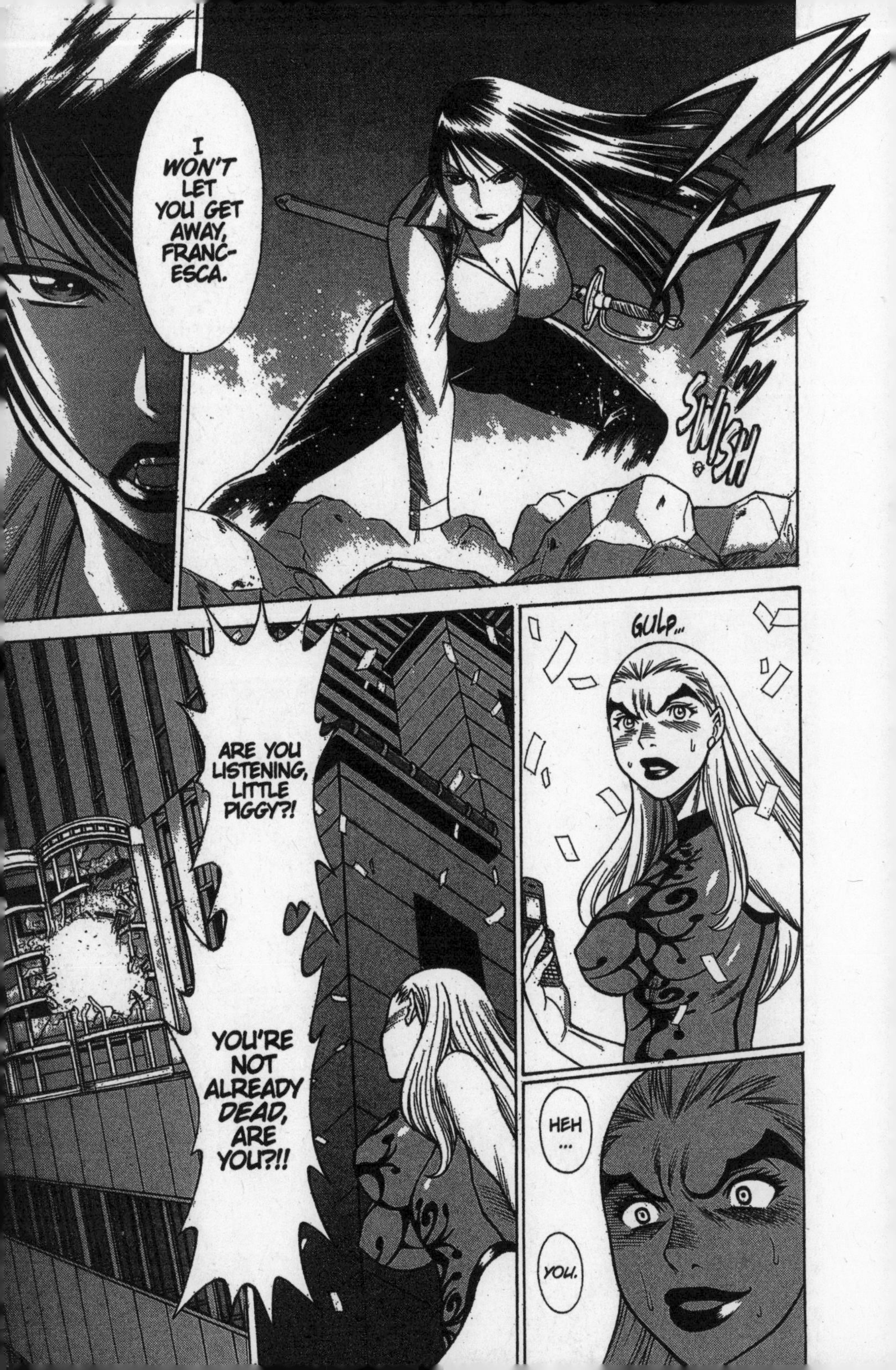
SWISH
I WON'T LET YOU GET AWAY, FRANC-ESCA.
GULP...
HEH...
YOU.
ARE YOU LISTENING, LITTLE PIGGY?!
YOU'RE NOT ALREADY DEAD, ARE YOU?!!

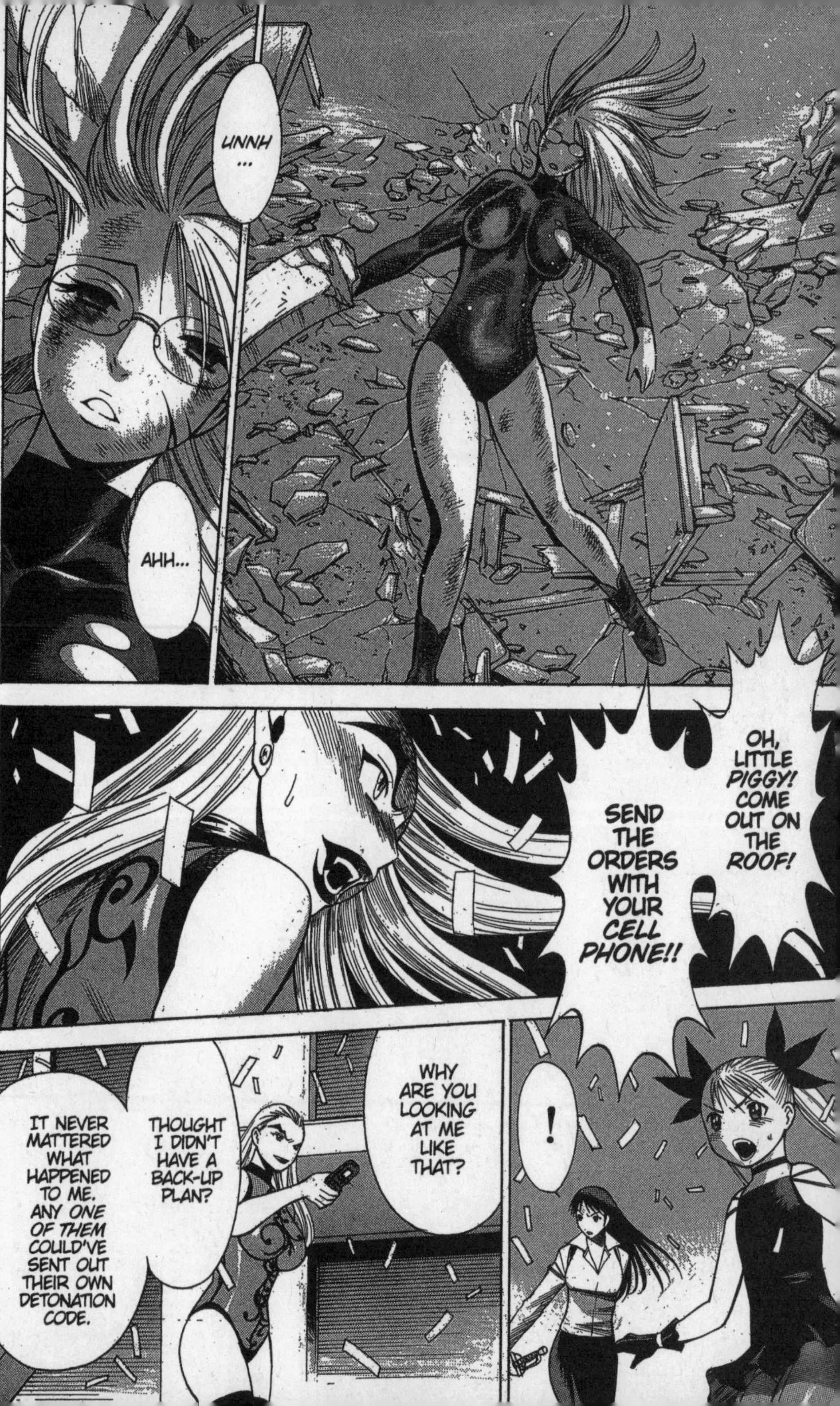
UNNH ...
AHH...
OH, LITTLE PIGGY! COME OUT ON THE ROOF!
SEND THE ORDERS WITH YOUR CELL PHONE!!
!
WHY ARE YOU LOOKING AT ME LIKE THAT?
THOUGHT I DIDN'T HAVE A BACK-UP PLAN?
IT NEVER MATTERED WHAT HAPPENED TO ME. ANY ONE OF THEM COULD'VE SENT OUT THEIR OWN DETONATION CODE.

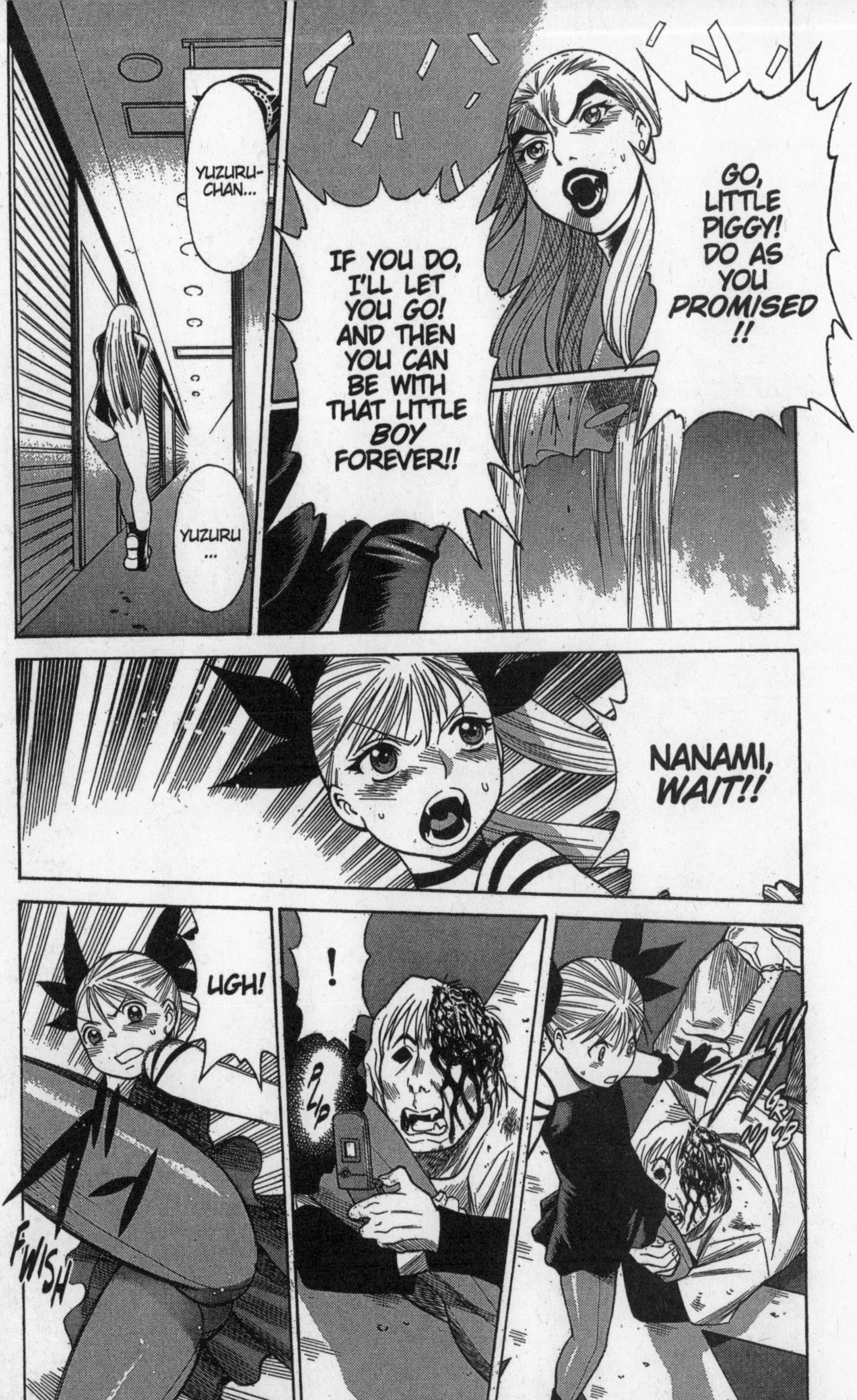
GO, LITTLE PIGGY! DO AS YOU PROMISED!!
IF YOU DO, I'LL LET YOU GO! AND THEN YOU CAN BE WITH THAT LITTLE BOY FOREVER!!
YUZURU-CHAN...
YUZURU...
NANAMI, WAIT!!
GRAB
!
UGH!
FWISH

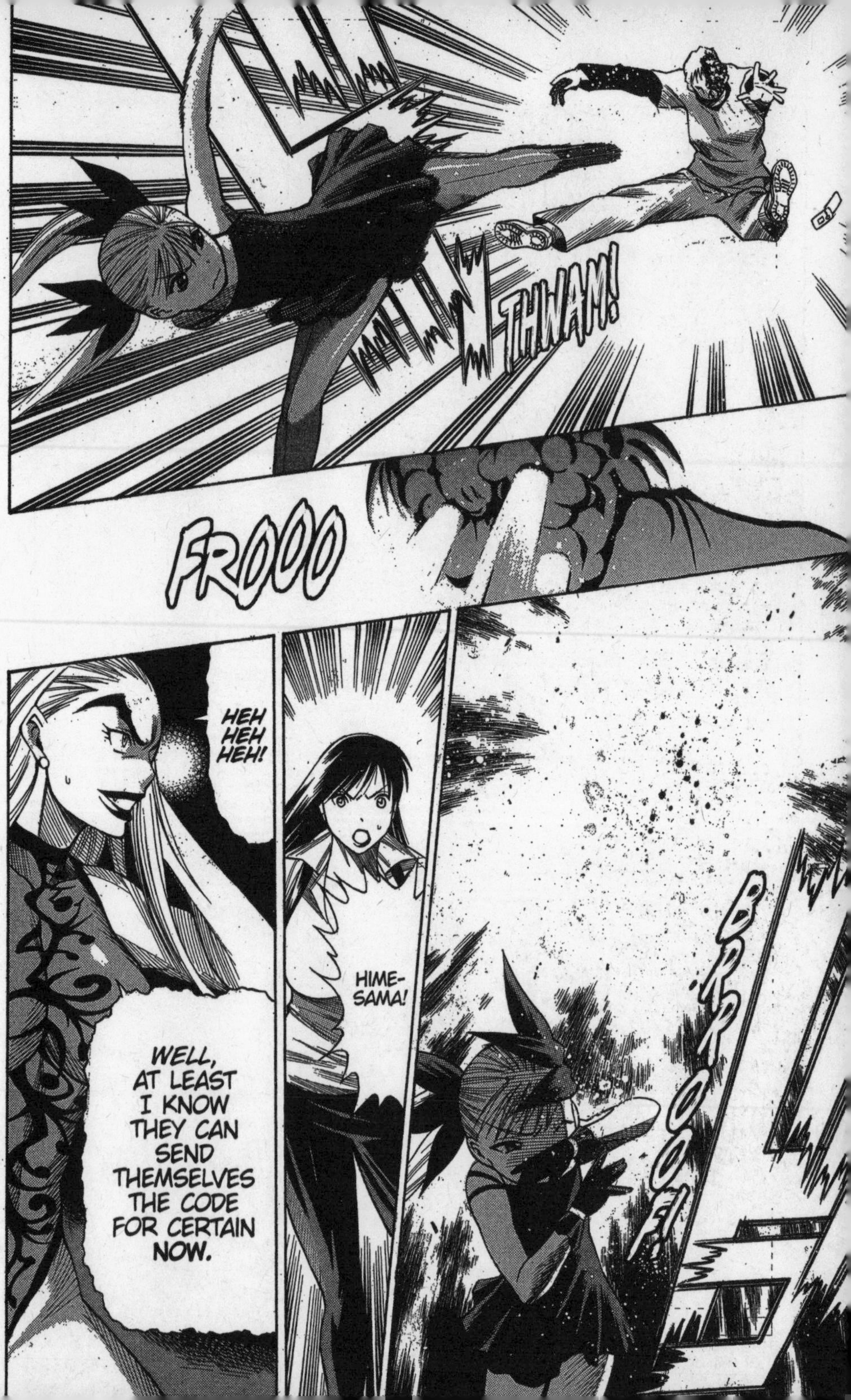
THWAM!
FROOO
HIME-SAMA!
HEH HEH HEH!
WELL, AT LEAST I KNOW THEY CAN SEND THEMSELVES THE CODE FOR CERTAIN NOW.

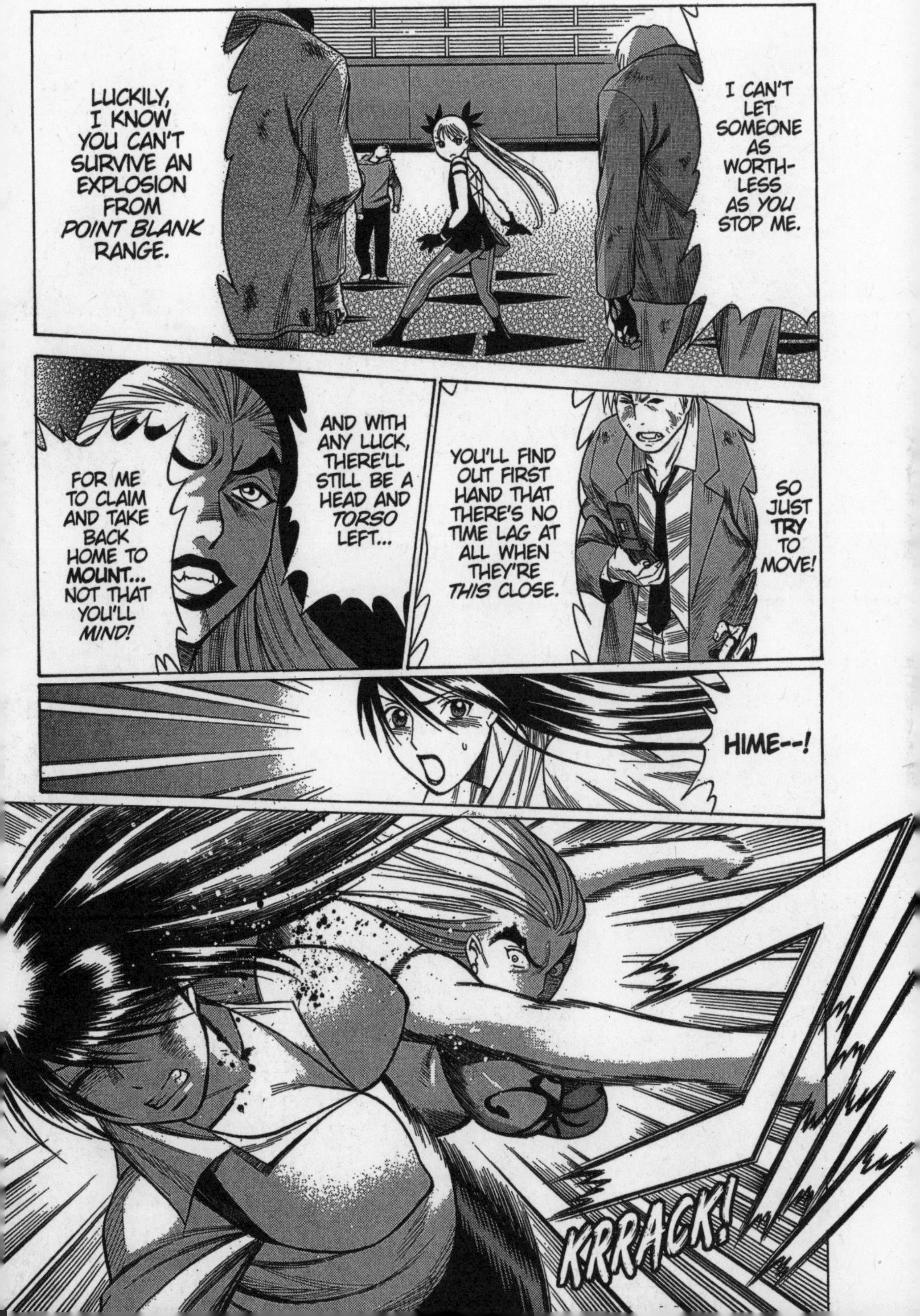
I CAN'T LET SOMEONE AS WORTHLESS AS *YOU* STOP ME.
LUCKILY, I KNOW YOU CAN'T SURVIVE AN EXPLOSION FROM *POINT BLANK* RANGE.
SO JUST **TRY** TO MOVE!
YOU'LL FIND OUT FIRST HAND THAT THERE'S NO TIME LAG AT ALL WHEN THEY'RE *THIS* CLOSE.
AND WITH ANY LUCK, THERE'LL STILL BE A HEAD AND *TORSO* LEFT...
FOR ME TO CLAIM AND TAKE BACK HOME TO **MOUNT**... NOT THAT YOU'LL *MIND!*
HIME--!
KRRACK!

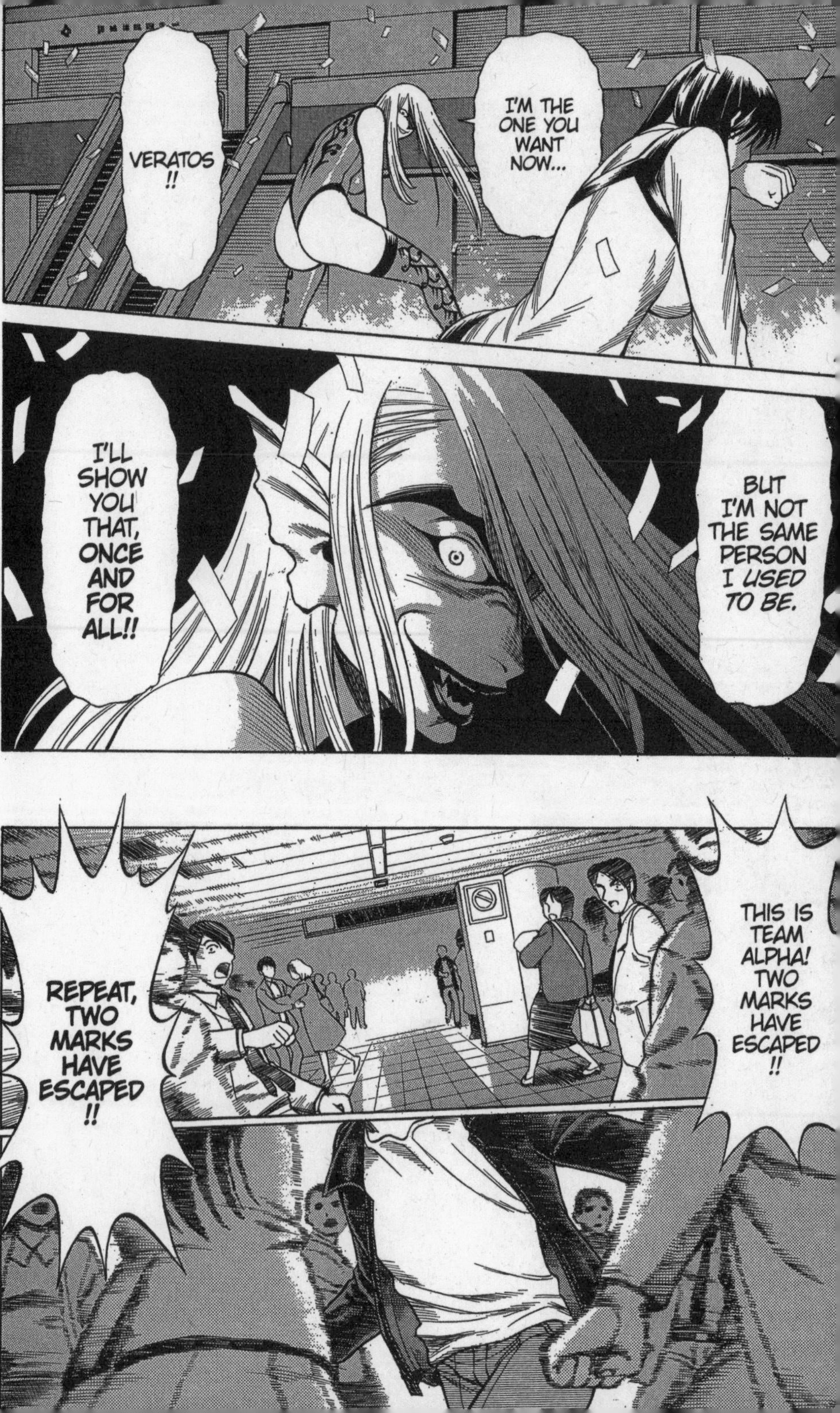
I'M THE ONE YOU WANT NOW...
VERATOS !!
BUT I'M NOT THE SAME PERSON I *USED TO BE.*
I'LL SHOW YOU THAT, ONCE AND FOR ALL!!
THIS IS TEAM ALPHA! TWO MARKS HAVE ESCAPED !!
REPEAT, TWO MARKS HAVE ESCAPED !!

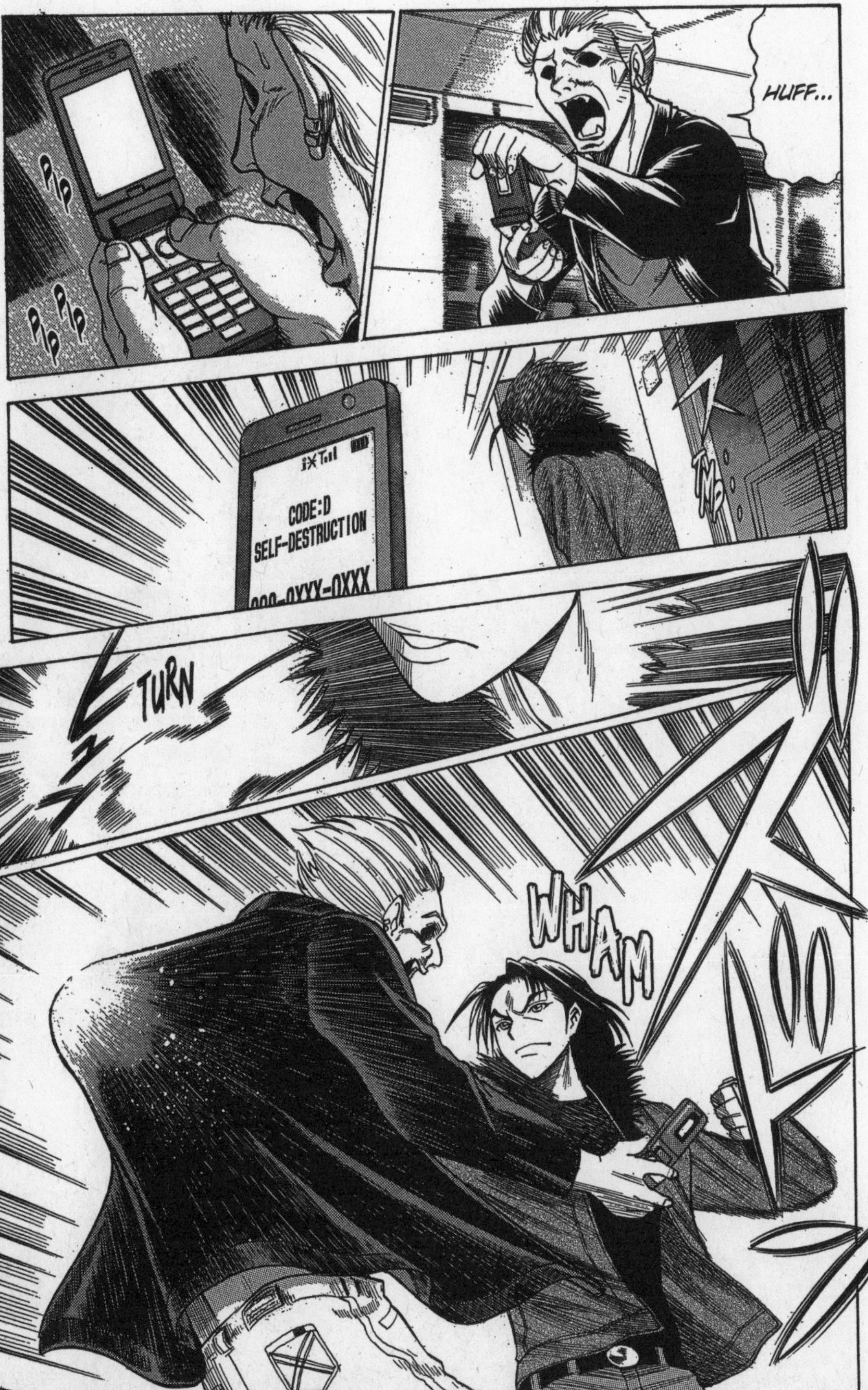

HUFF...
PIP PIP
PIP PIP PIP
CODE:D
SELF-DESTRUCTION
TURN
WHAM

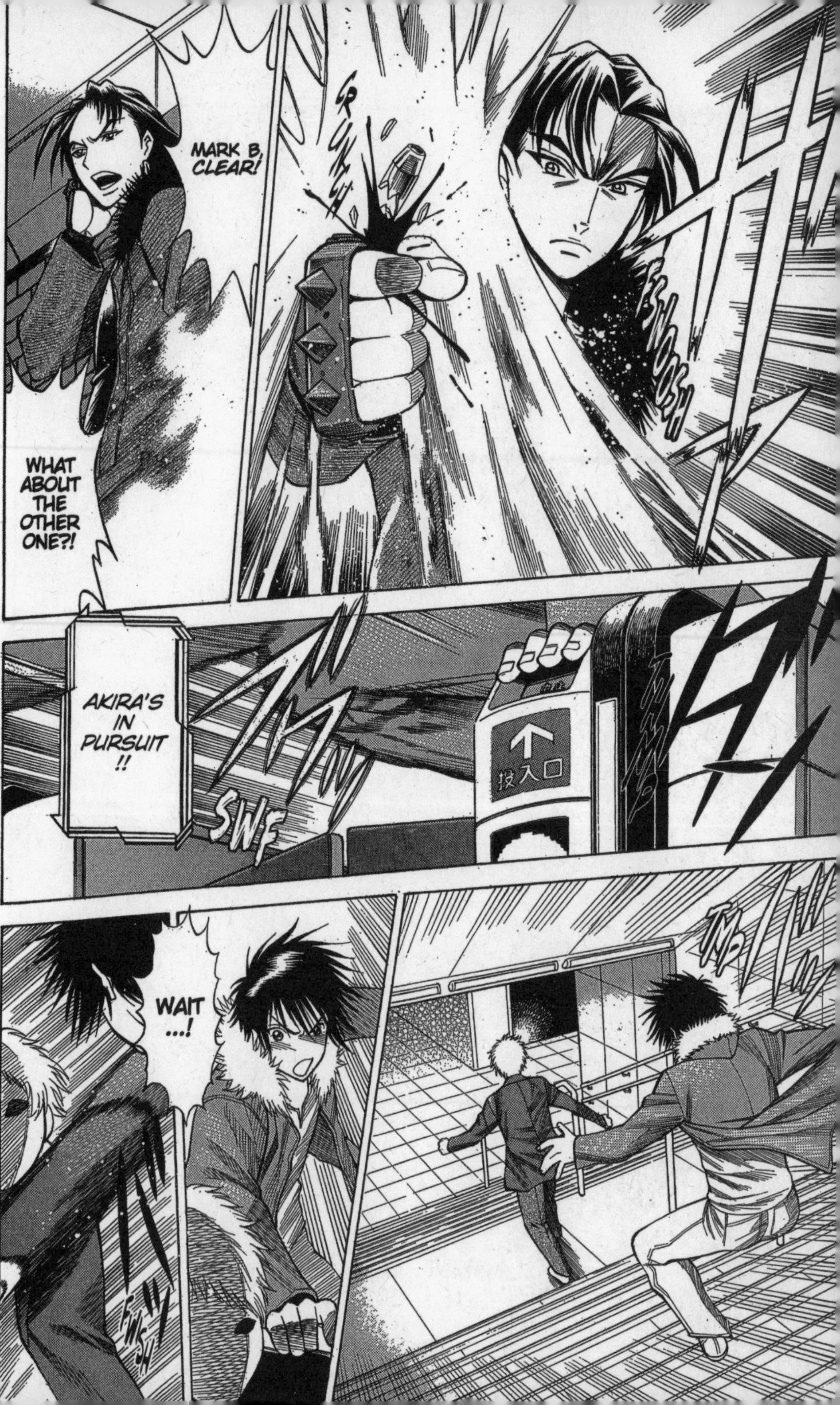
MARK B, CLEAR!
WHAT ABOUT THE OTHER ONE?!
AKIRA'S IN PURSUIT !!
SWF
投入口
WAIT ...!

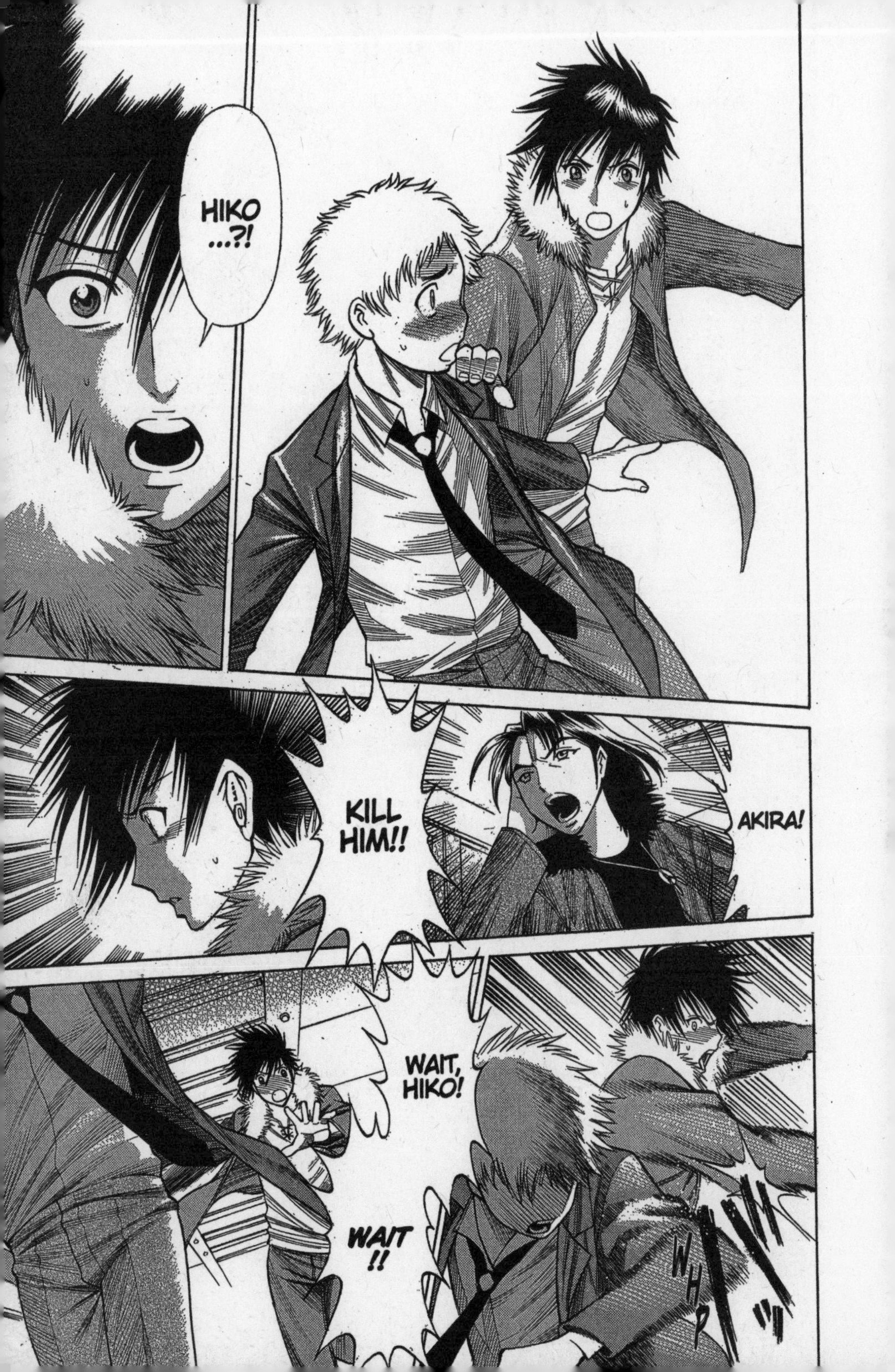
HIKO ...?!
AKIRA!
KILL HIM!!
WAIT, HIKO!
WAIT !!
WHP

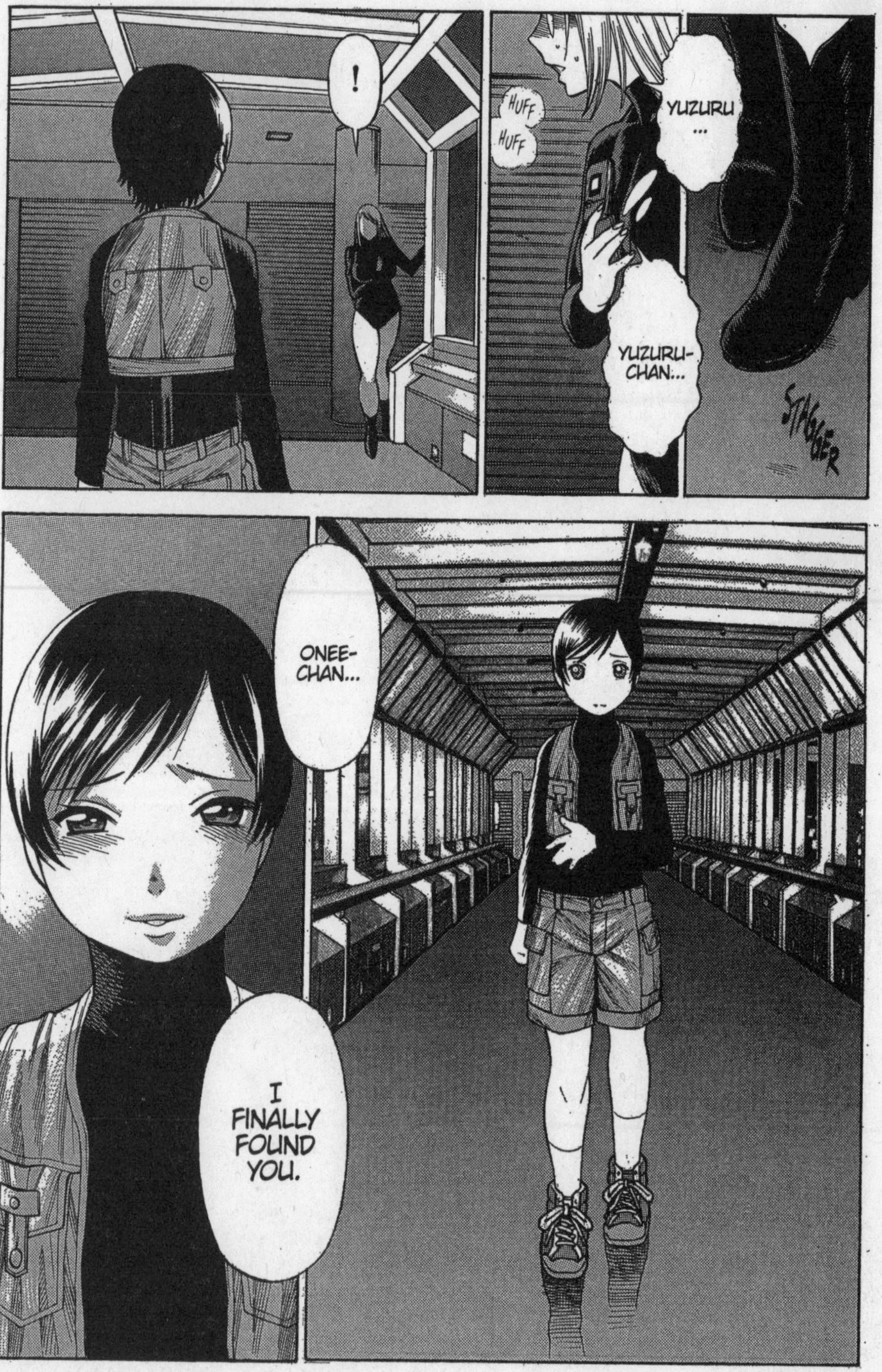
STAGGER
YUZURU ...
HUFF
HUFF
YUZURU-CHAN...
!
ONEE-CHAN...
I FINALLY FOUND YOU.

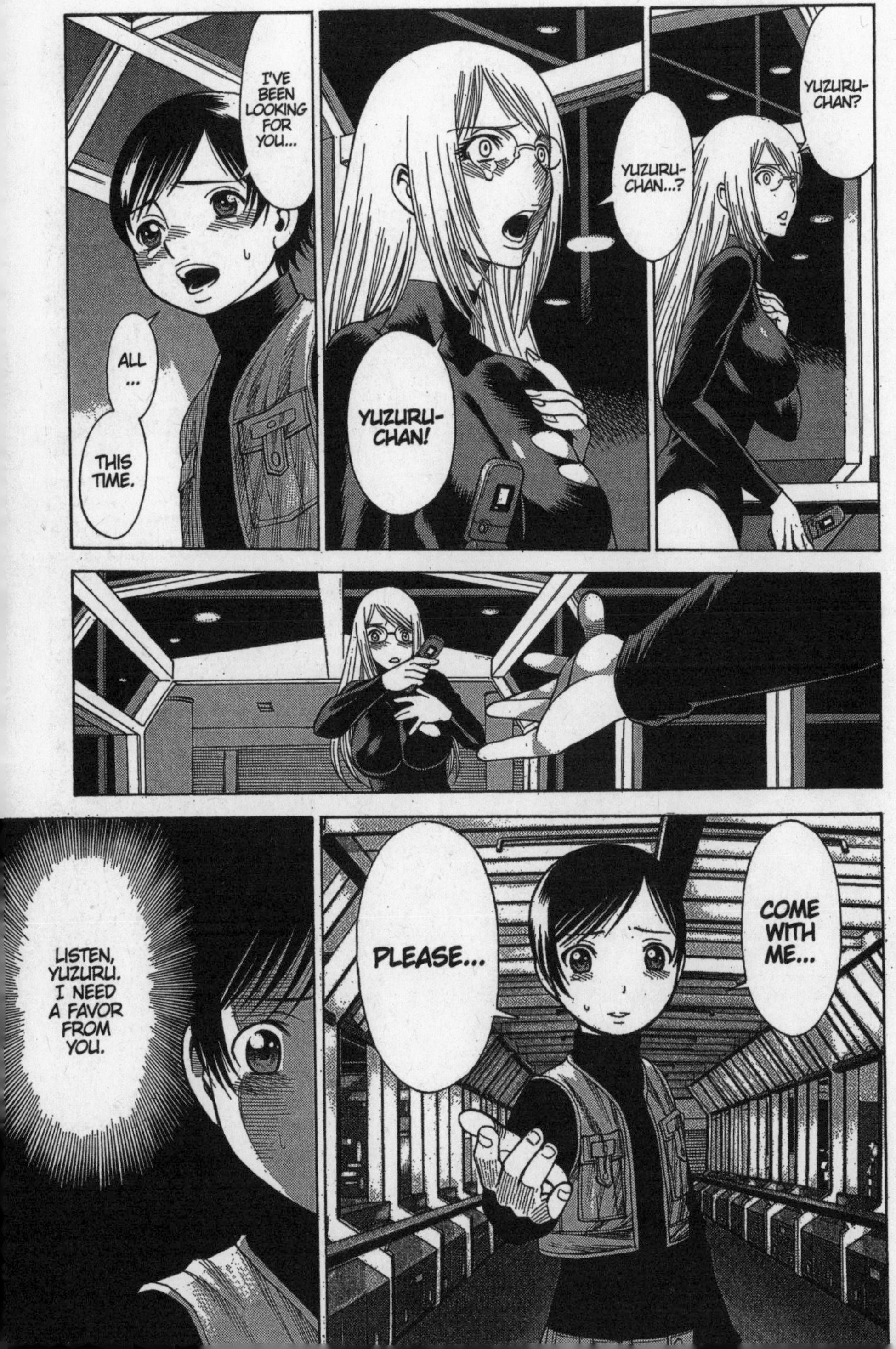
YUZURU-CHAN?
YUZURU-CHAN...?
YUZURU-CHAN!
I'VE BEEN LOOKING FOR YOU...
ALL...
THIS TIME.
COME WITH ME...
PLEASE...
LISTEN, YUZURU. I NEED A FAVOR FROM YOU.

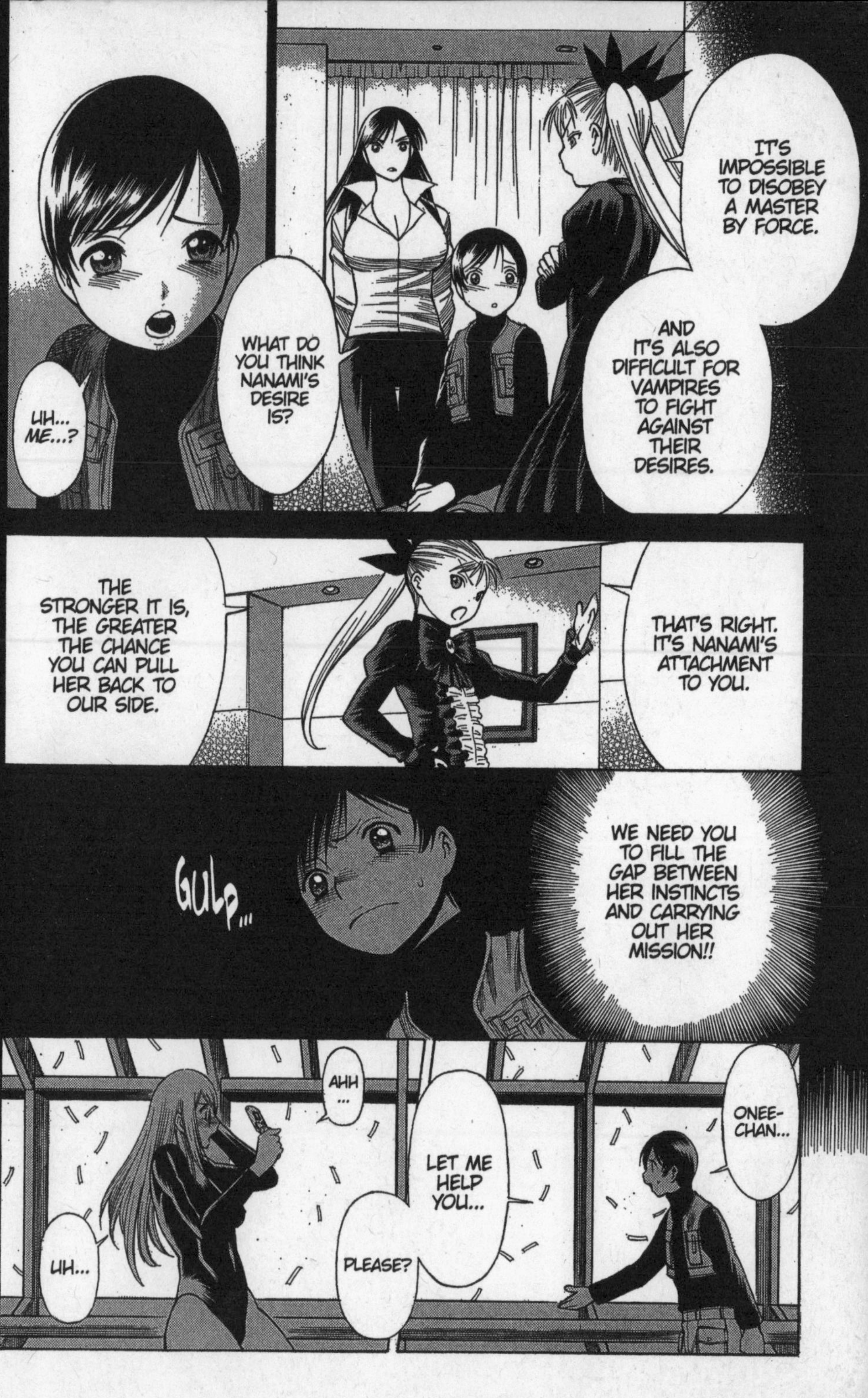
IT'S IMPOSSIBLE TO DISOBEY A MASTER BY FORCE.
AND IT'S ALSO DIFFICULT FOR VAMPIRES TO FIGHT AGAINST THEIR DESIRES.
WHAT DO YOU THINK NANAMI'S DESIRE IS?
UH... ME...?
THAT'S RIGHT. IT'S NANAMI'S ATTACHMENT TO YOU.
THE STRONGER IT IS, THE GREATER THE CHANCE YOU CAN PULL HER BACK TO OUR SIDE.
WE NEED YOU TO FILL THE GAP BETWEEN HER INSTINCTS AND CARRYING OUT HER MISSION!!
GULP...
ONEE-CHAN...
LET ME HELP YOU...
PLEASE?
AHH...
UH...

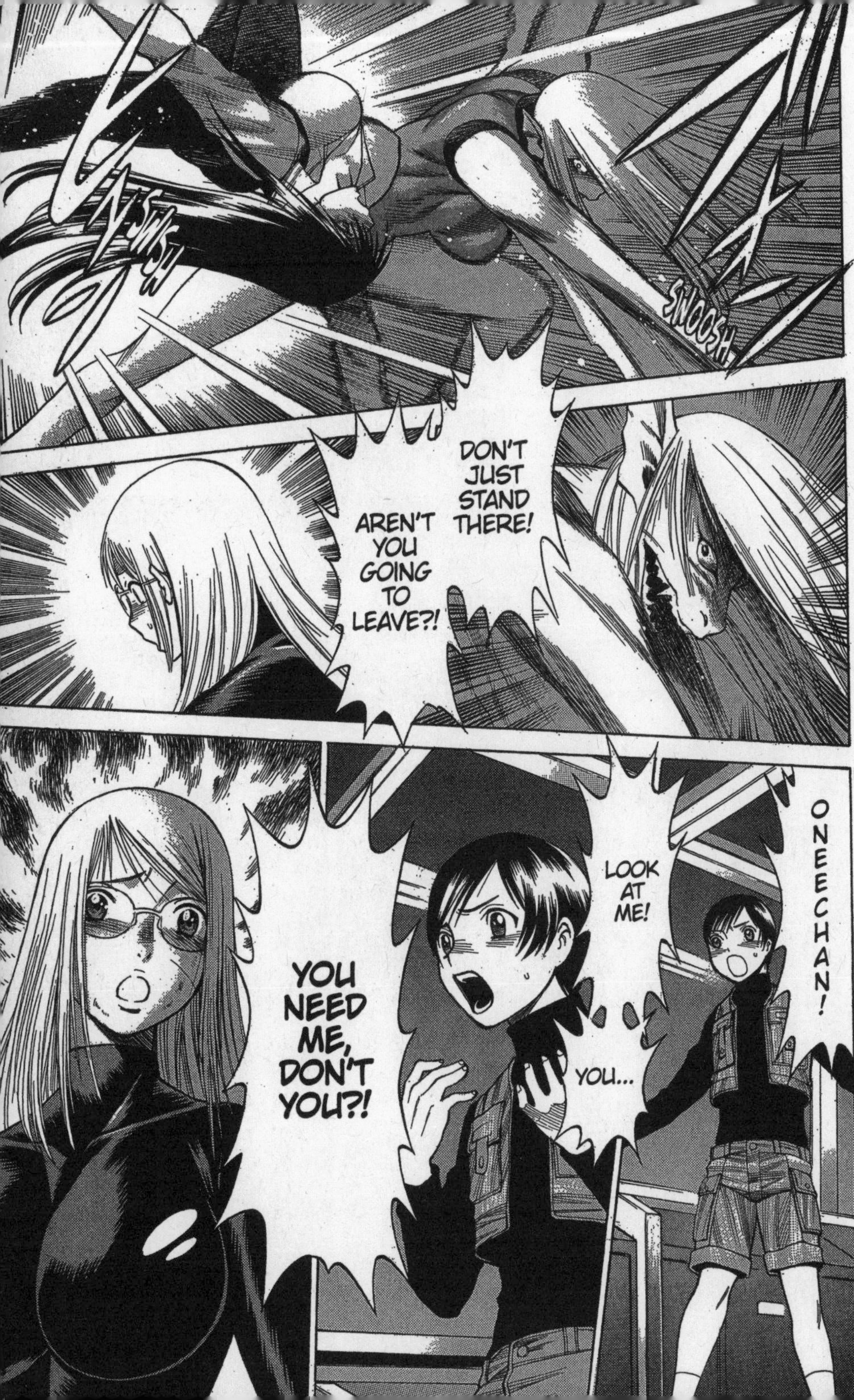
SWOOSH
SWISH
DON'T JUST STAND THERE!
AREN'T YOU GOING TO LEAVE?!
ONEECHAN!
LOOK AT ME!
YOU...
YOU NEED ME, DON'T YOU?!

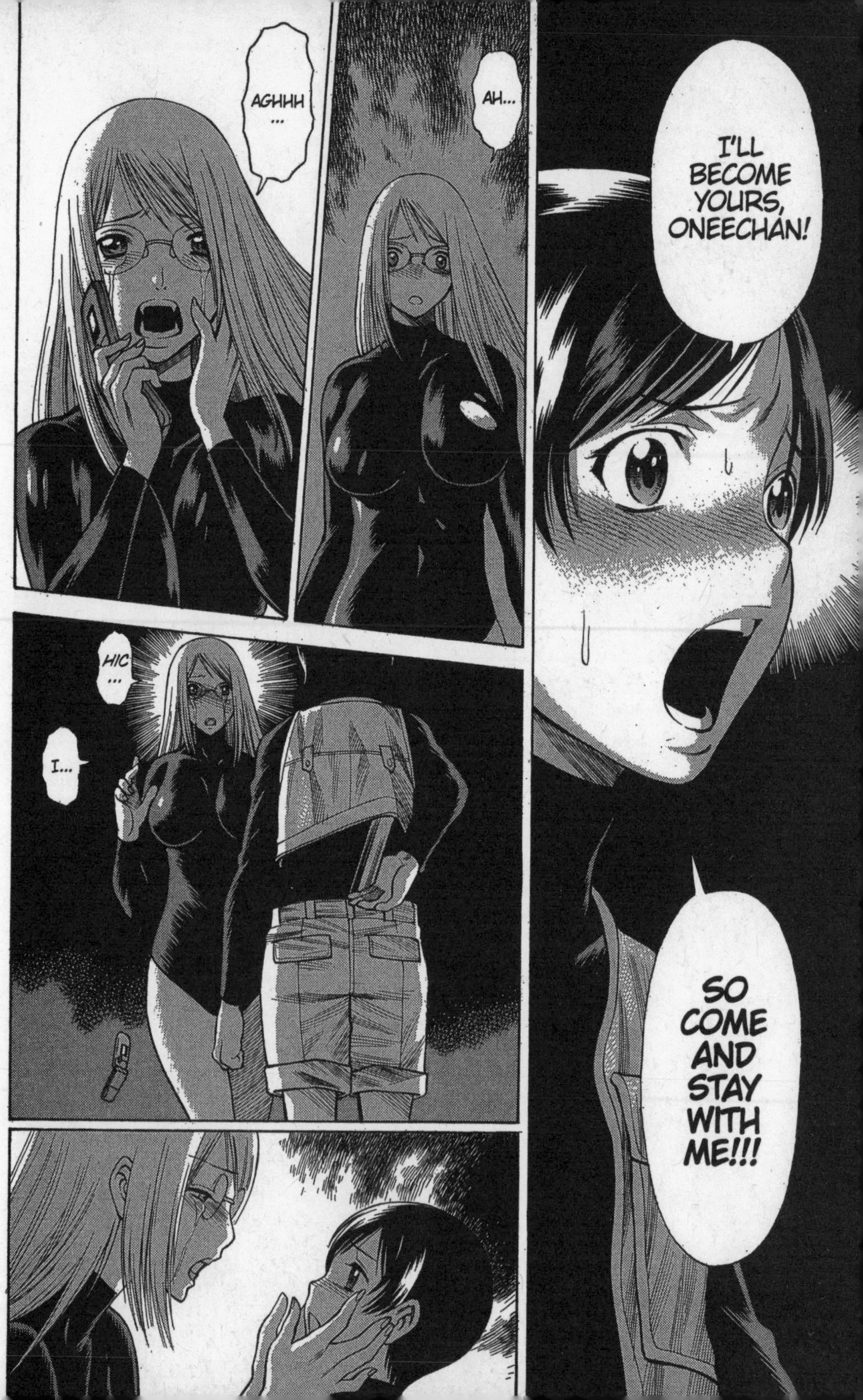
I'LL BECOME YOURS, ONEECHAN!
SO COME AND STAY WITH ME!!!
AH...
AGHHH ...
HIC ...
I...

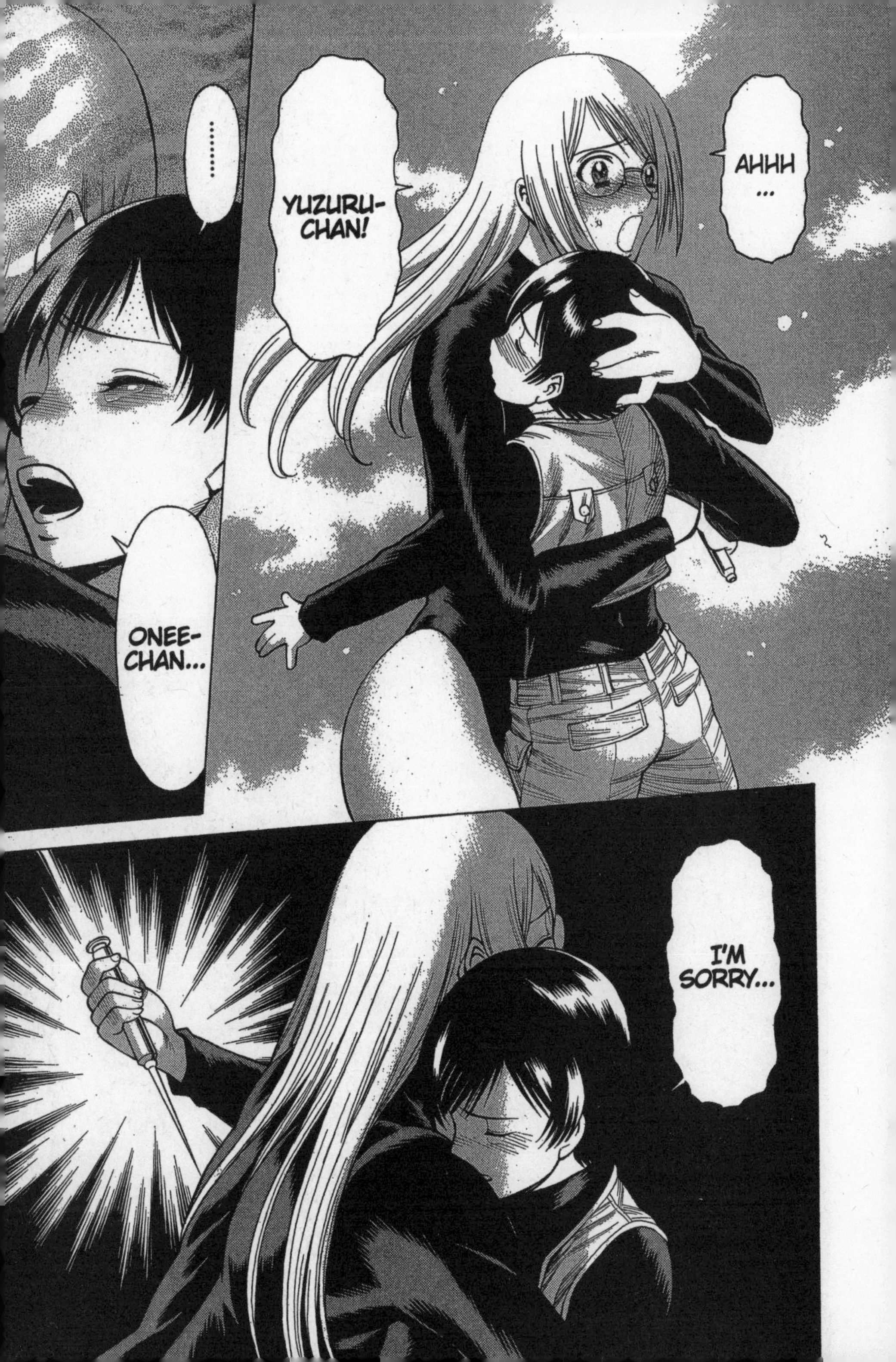
AHHH ...
YUZURU-CHAN!
......
ONEE-CHAN...
I'M SORRY...

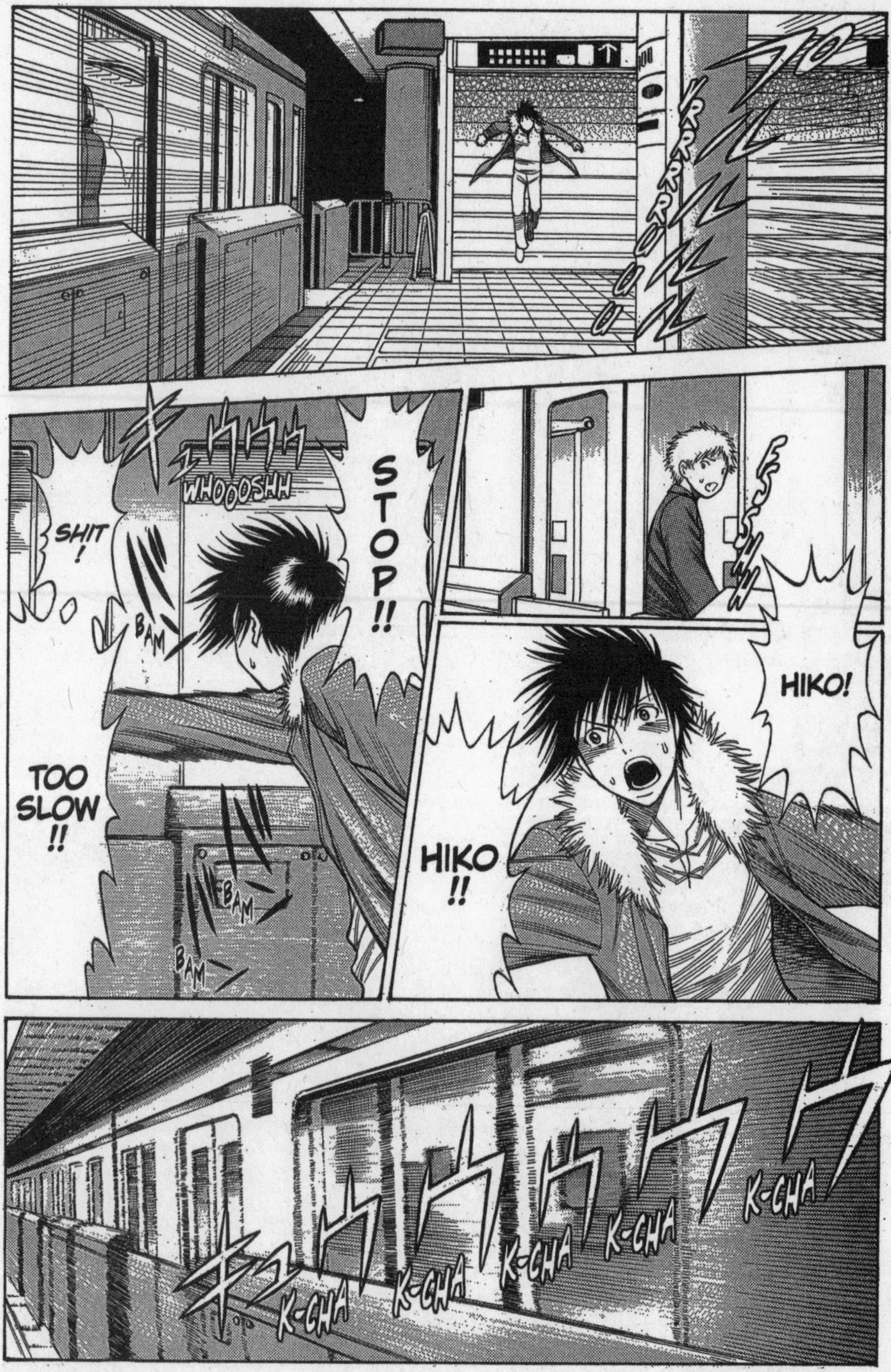
VRRRRUUU
FSSHH
HIKO!
HIKO!!
STOP!!
WHOOOSHH
SHIT!
BAM
TOO SLOW!!
BAM
BAM
K-CHA
K-CHA
K-CHA
K-CHA
K-CHA
K-CHA

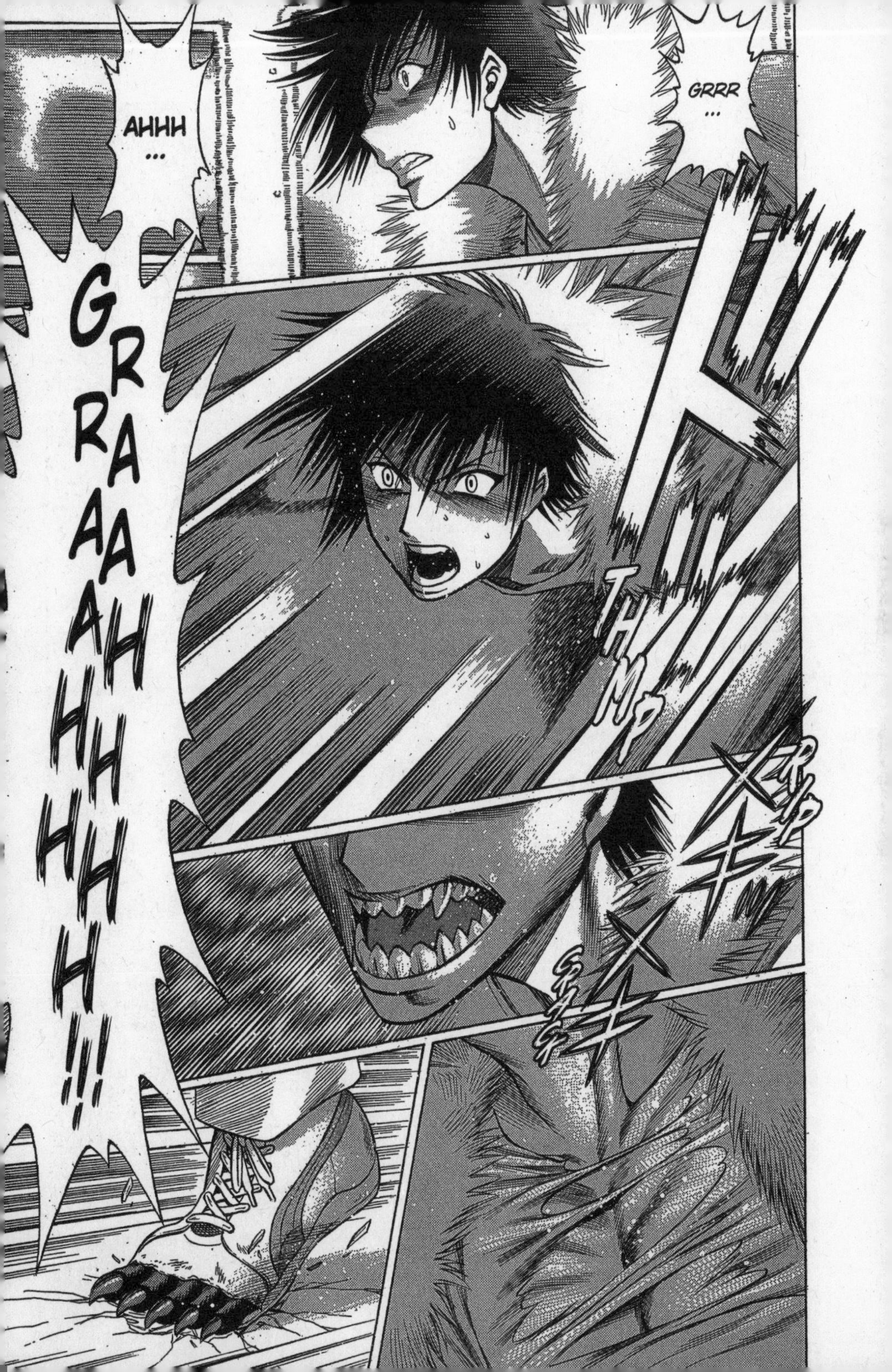
GRRR ...
AHHH ...
THUMP
RRIP
CRACK
GRRAAAAHHHHHHH!!!

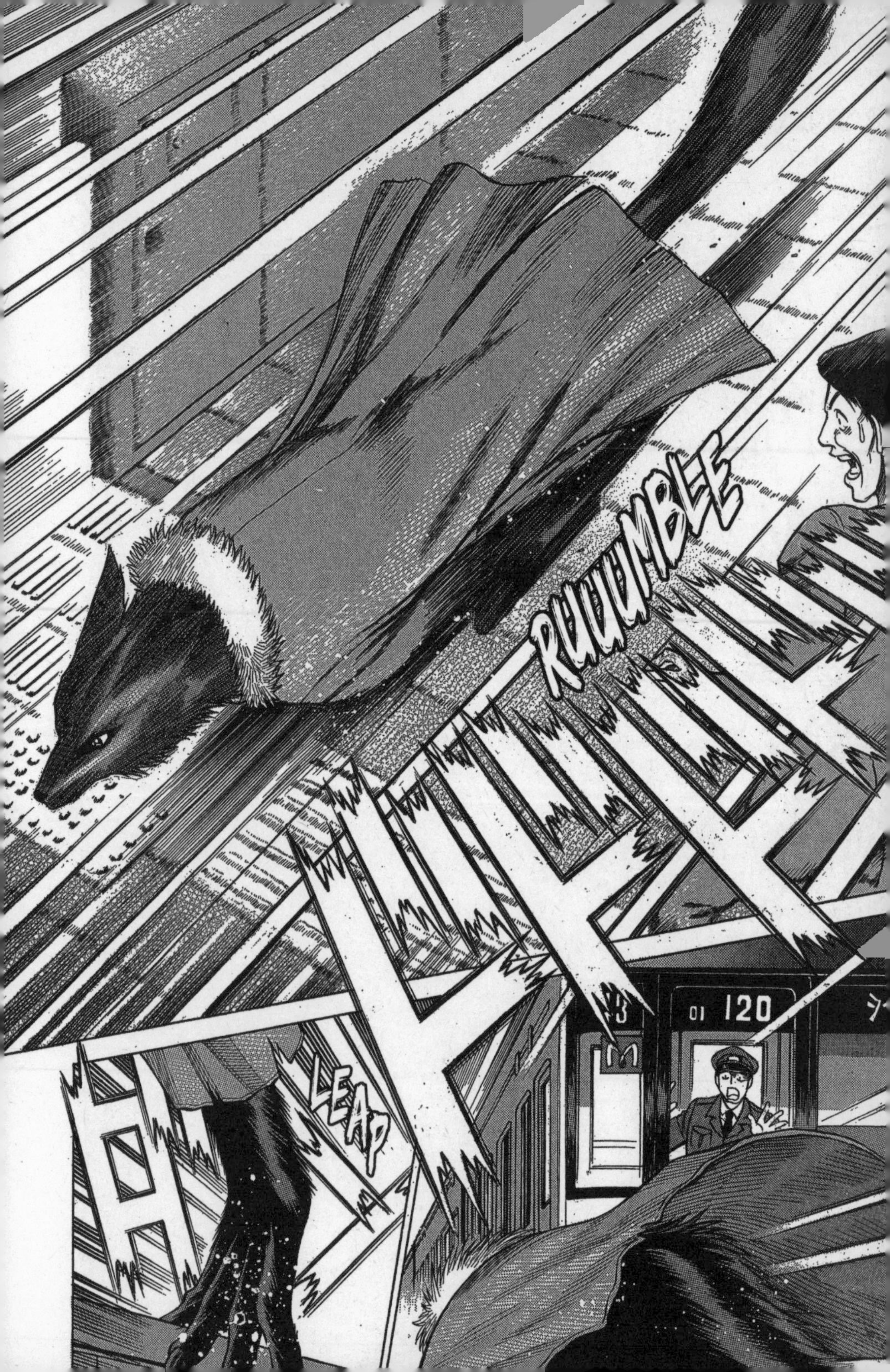
RUUUMBLEE
01 120
LEAP

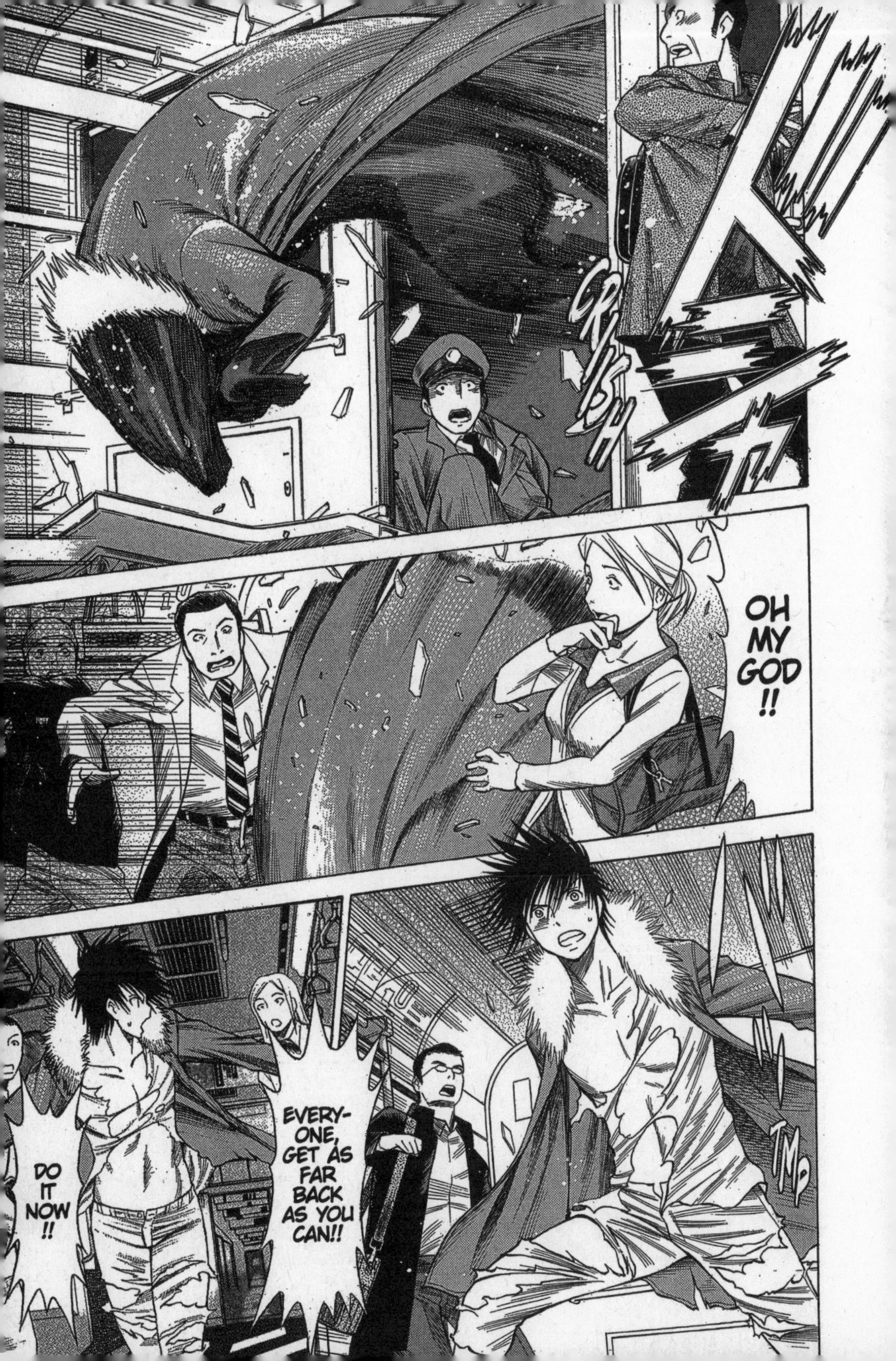
CRASH
OH MY GOD!!
TMP
EVERY-ONE, GET AS FAR BACK AS YOU CAN!!
DO IT NOW!!

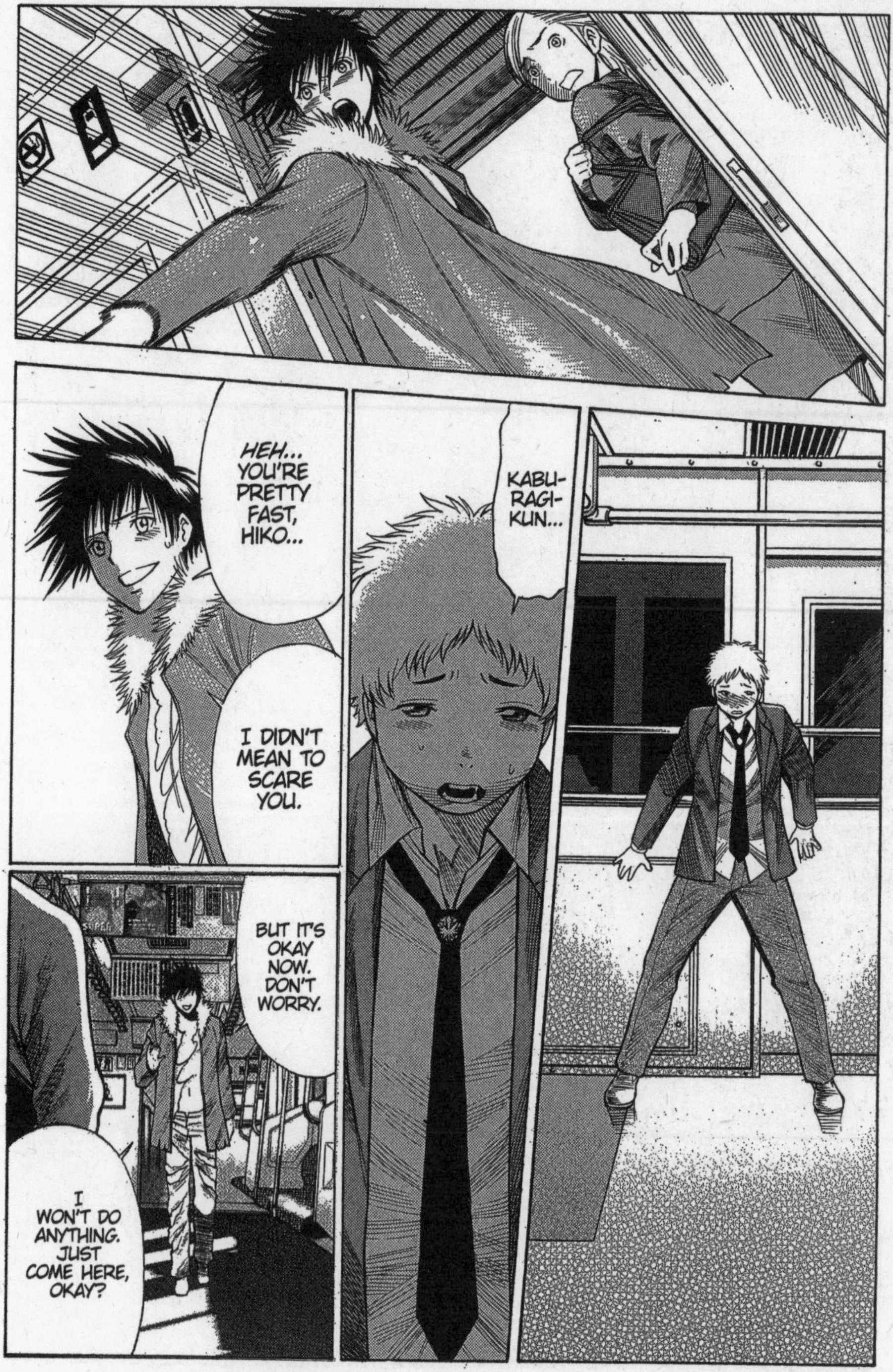
KABU-RAGI-KUN...
HEH... YOU'RE PRETTY FAST, HIKO...
I DIDN'T MEAN TO SCARE YOU.
BUT IT'S OKAY NOW. DON'T WORRY.
I WON'T DO ANYTHING. JUST COME HERE, OKAY?

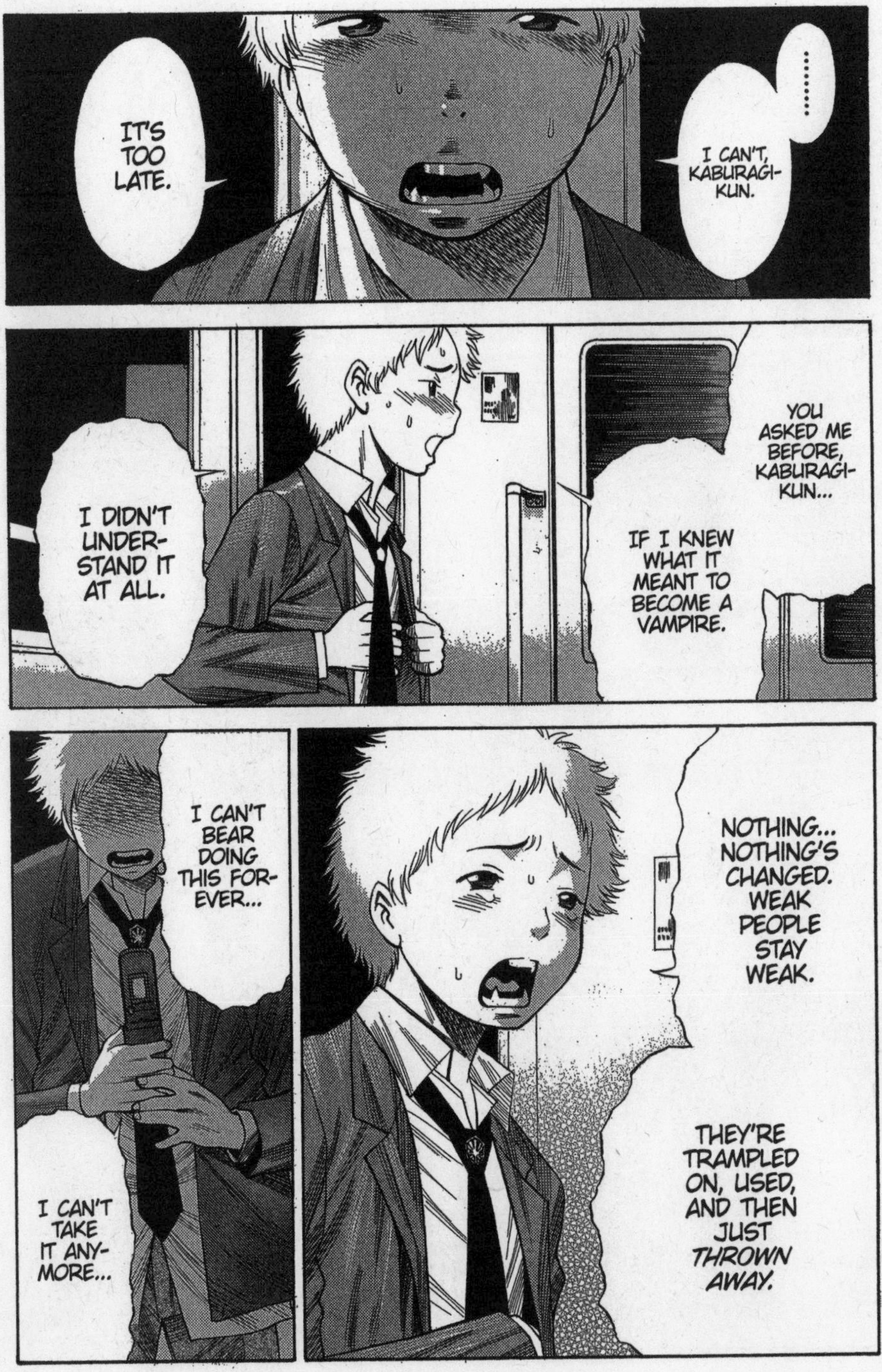
......
I CAN'T, KABURAGI-KUN.
IT'S TOO LATE.
YOU ASKED ME BEFORE, KABURAGI-KUN...
IF I KNEW WHAT IT MEANT TO BECOME A VAMPIRE.
I DIDN'T UNDERSTAND IT AT ALL.
NOTHING... NOTHING'S CHANGED. WEAK PEOPLE STAY WEAK.
THEY'RE TRAMPLED ON, USED, AND THEN JUST *THROWN AWAY.*
I CAN'T BEAR DOING THIS FOREVER...
I CAN'T TAKE IT ANYMORE...

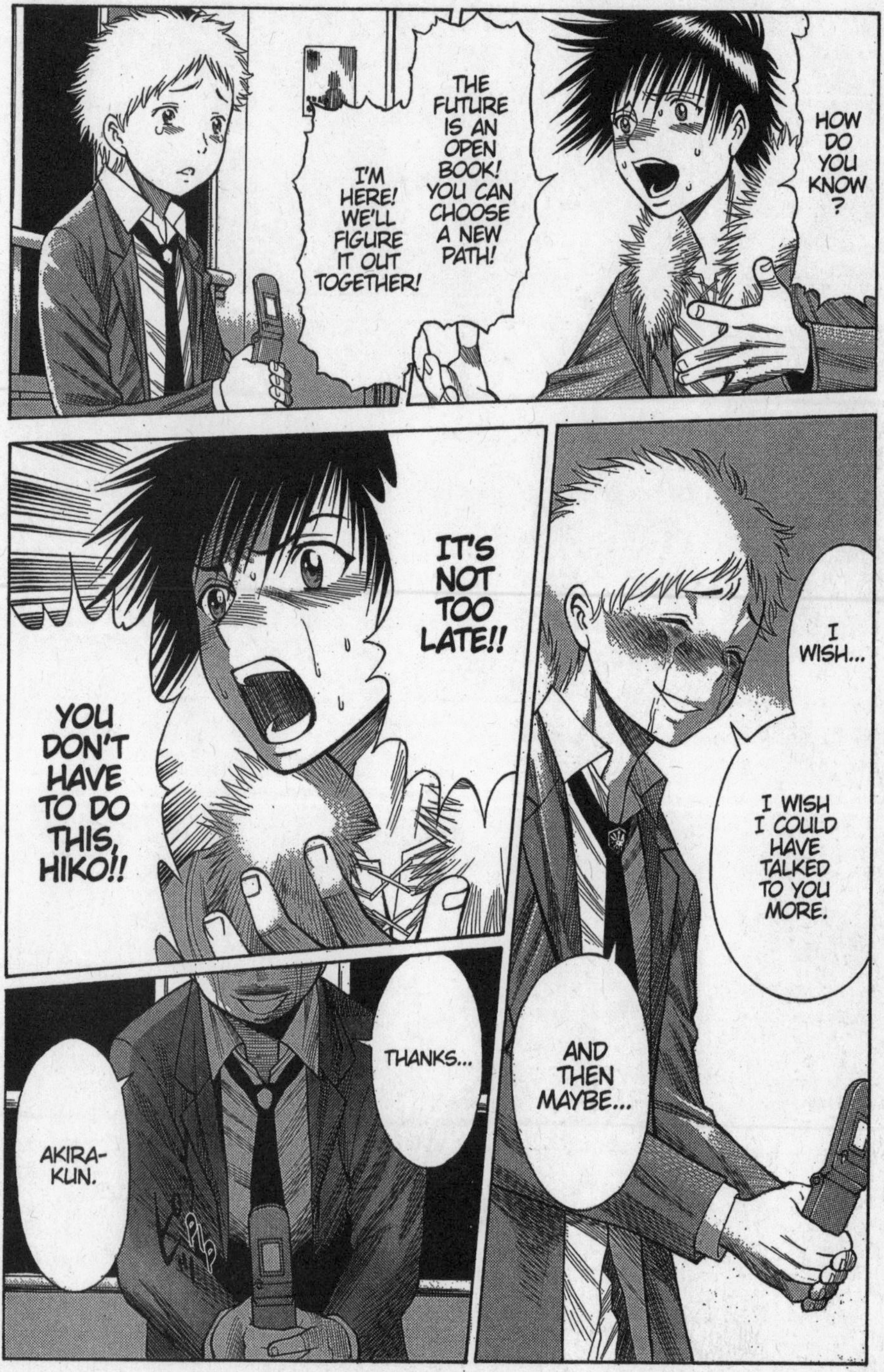
HOW DO YOU KNOW?
THE FUTURE IS AN OPEN BOOK! YOU CAN CHOOSE A NEW PATH!
I'M HERE! WE'LL FIGURE IT OUT TOGETHER!
I WISH...
I WISH I COULD HAVE TALKED TO YOU MORE.
AND THEN MAYBE...
IT'S NOT TOO LATE!!
YOU DON'T HAVE TO DO THIS, HIKO!!
THANKS...
AKIRA-KUN.

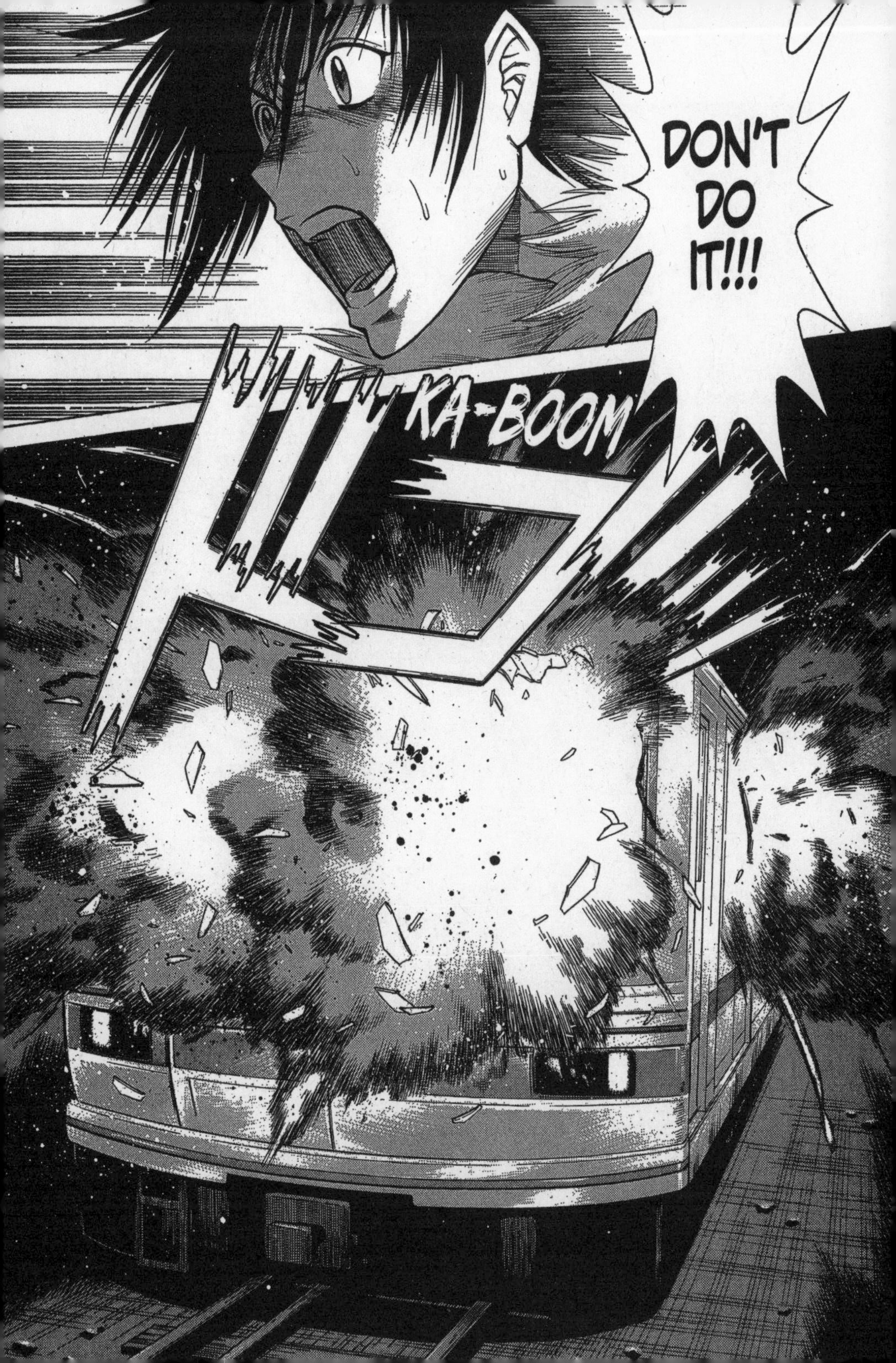
DON'T DO IT!!!
KA-BOOM

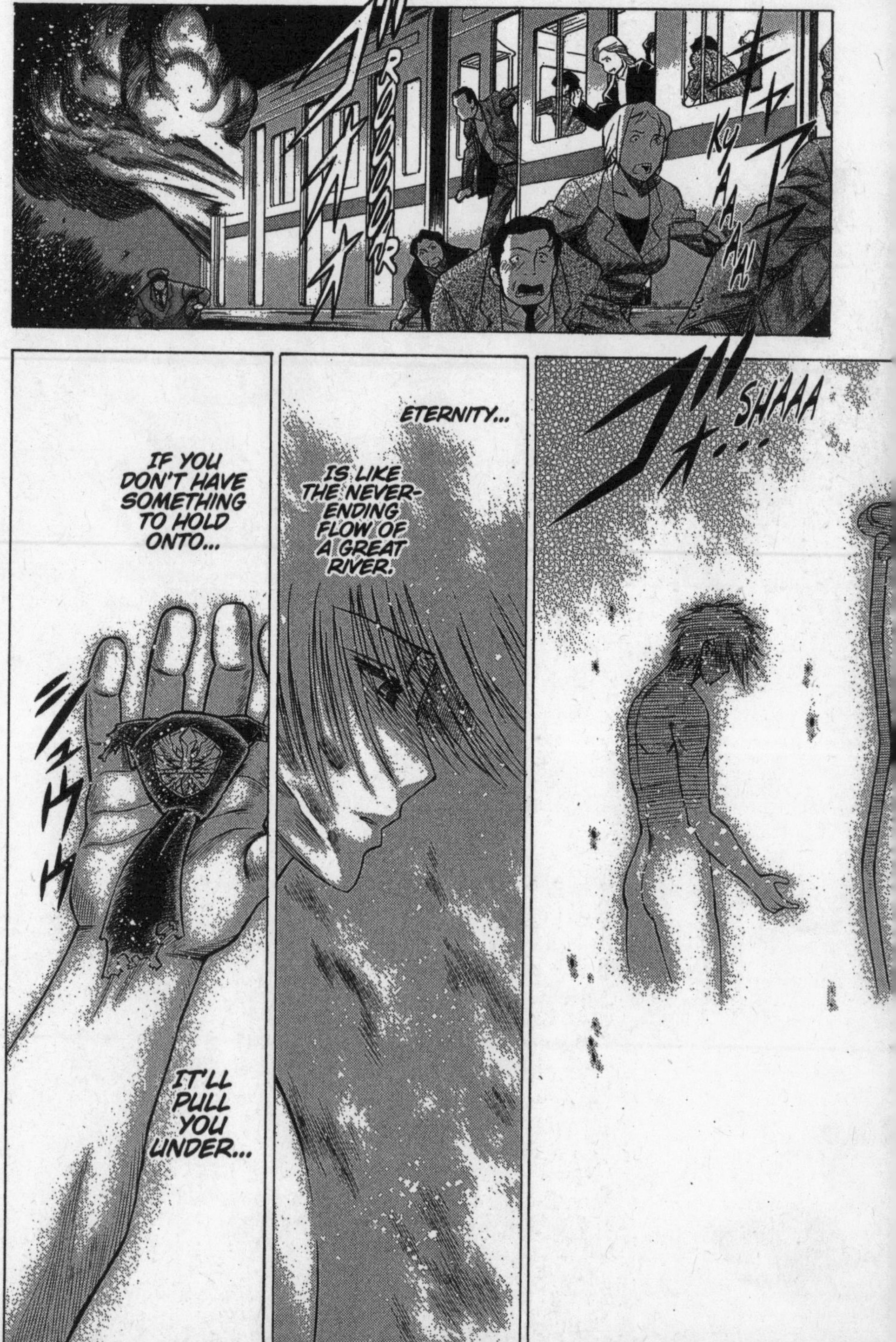
KYAAAAAH!
ROOOOOOR
SHAAA
ETERNITY...
IS LIKE THE NEVER-ENDING FLOW OF A GREAT RIVER.
IF YOU DON'T HAVE SOMETHING TO HOLD ONTO...
IT'LL PULL YOU UNDER...

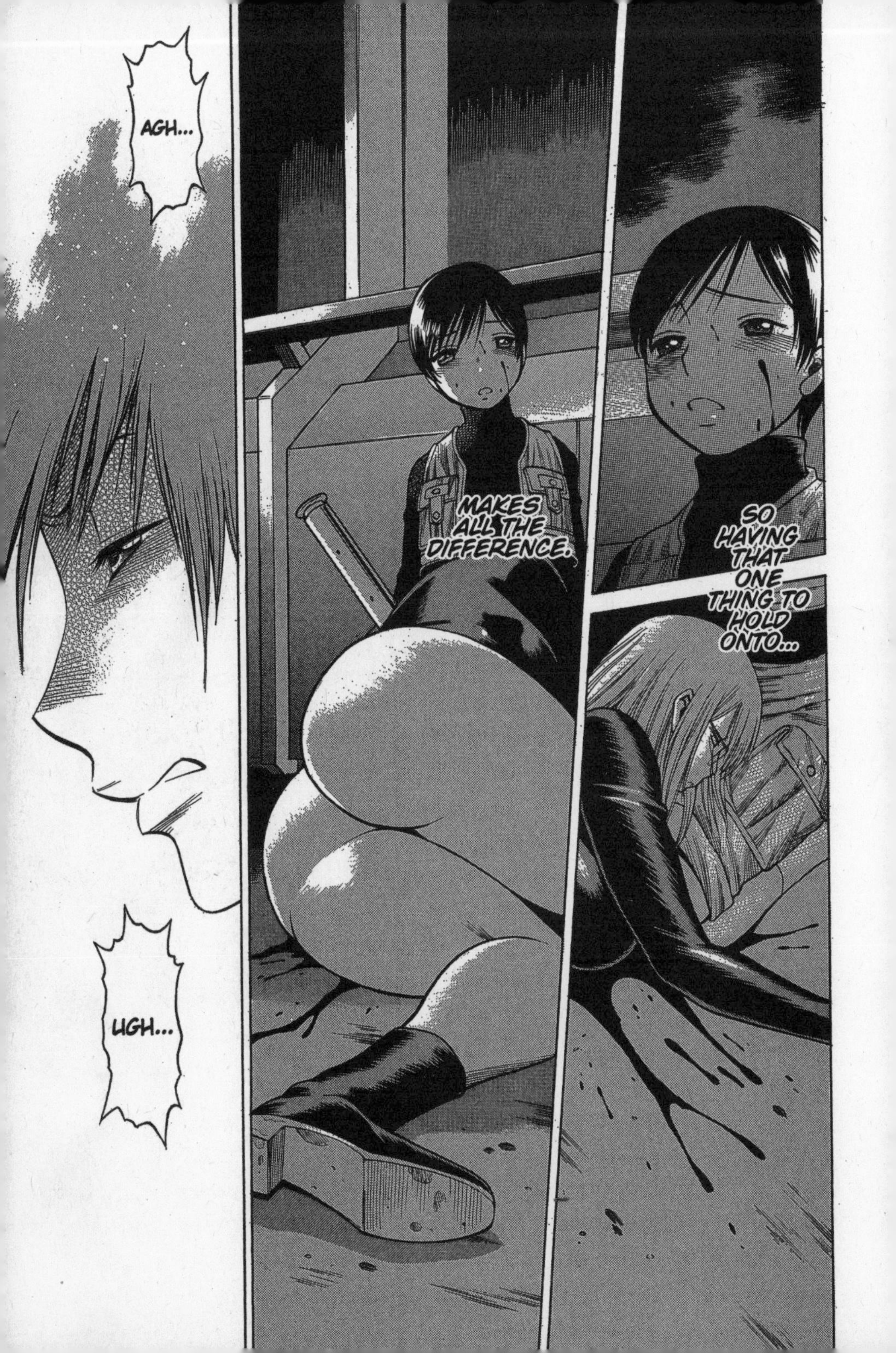
SO HAVING THAT ONE THING TO HOLD ONTO...
MAKES ALL THE DIFFERENCE.
AGH...
UGH...

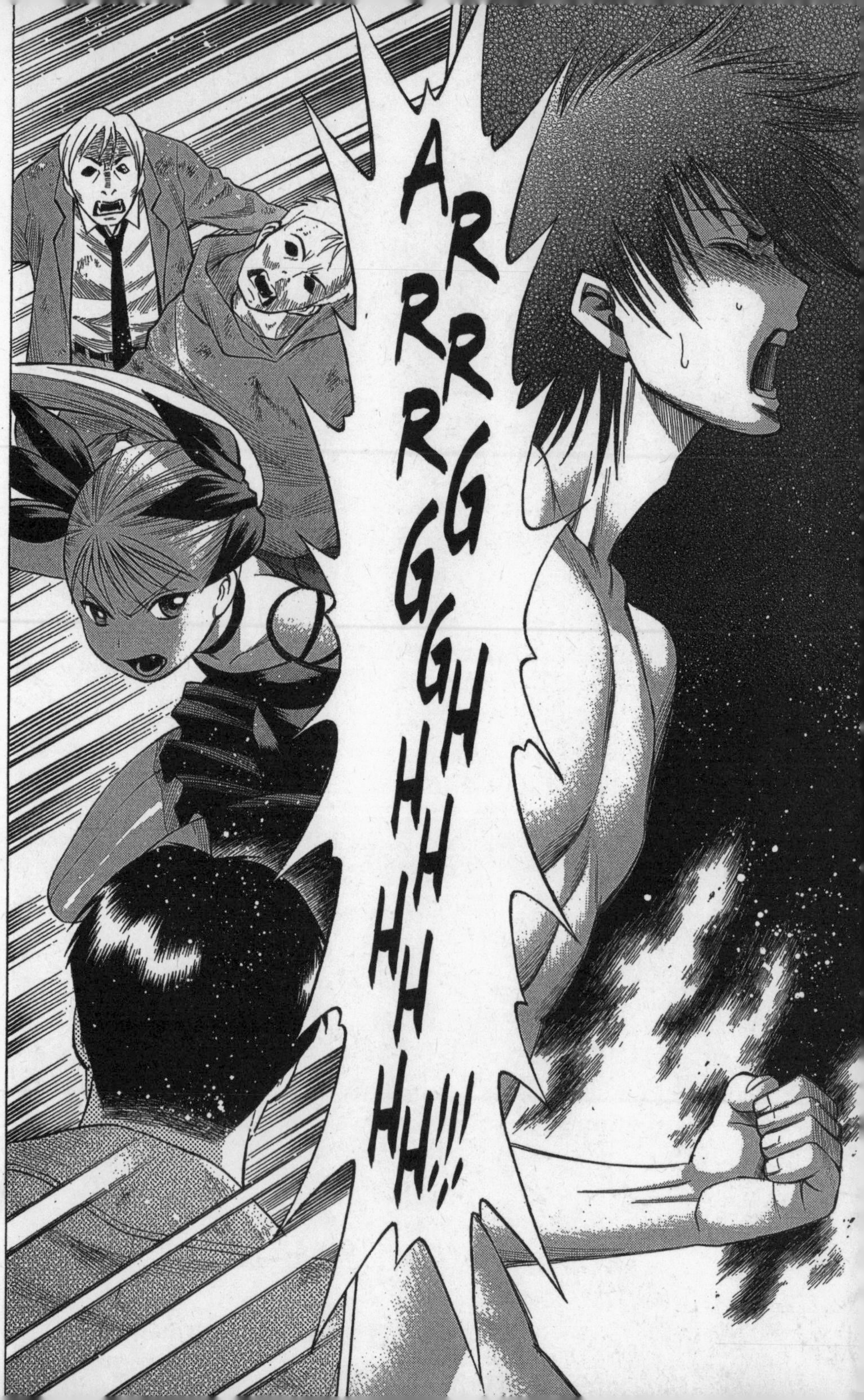
ARRRRGGGHHHHHHHHH!!!

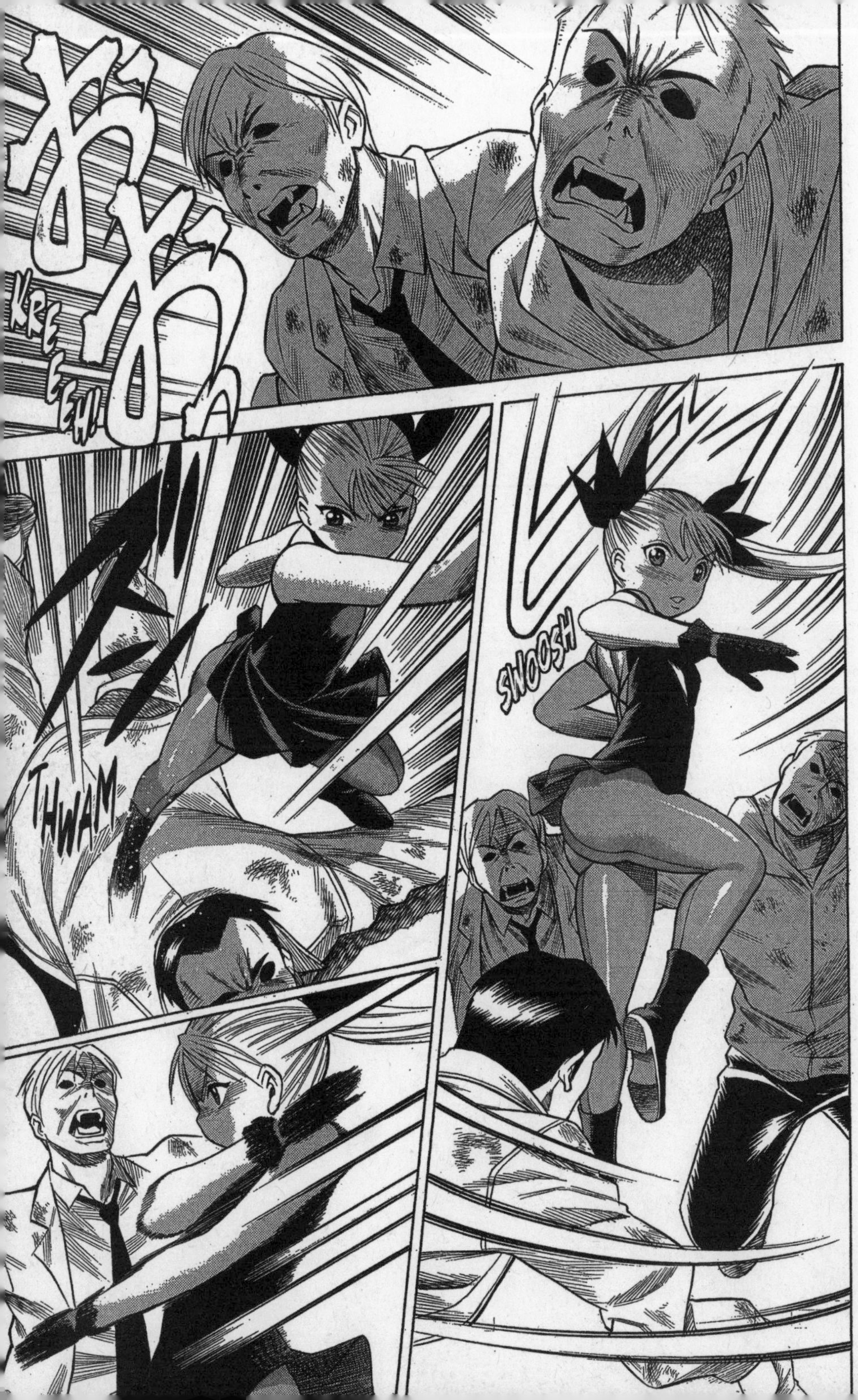
KREEEH
SWOOSH
THWAM

Chapter 19: Body and Mind

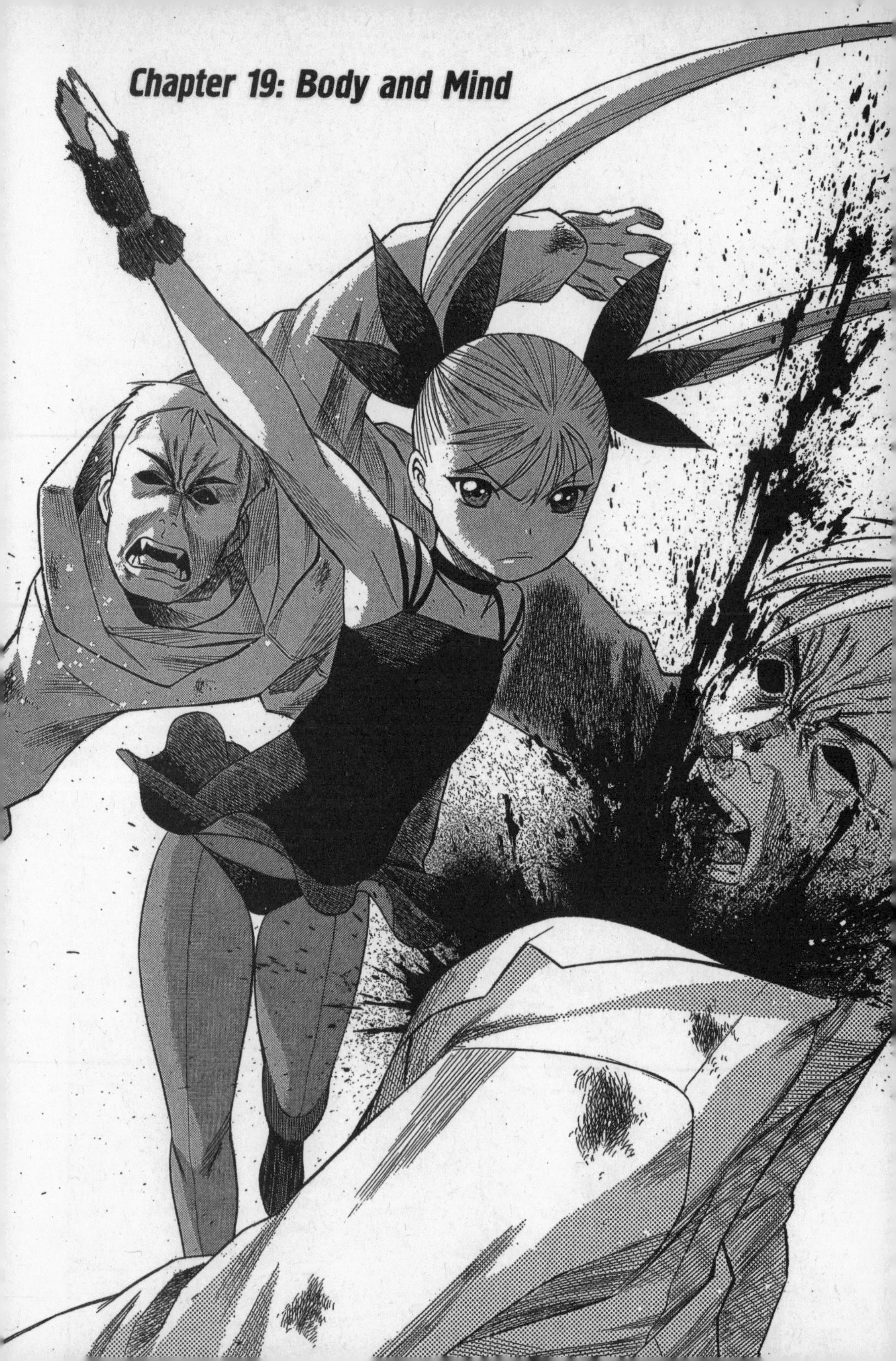

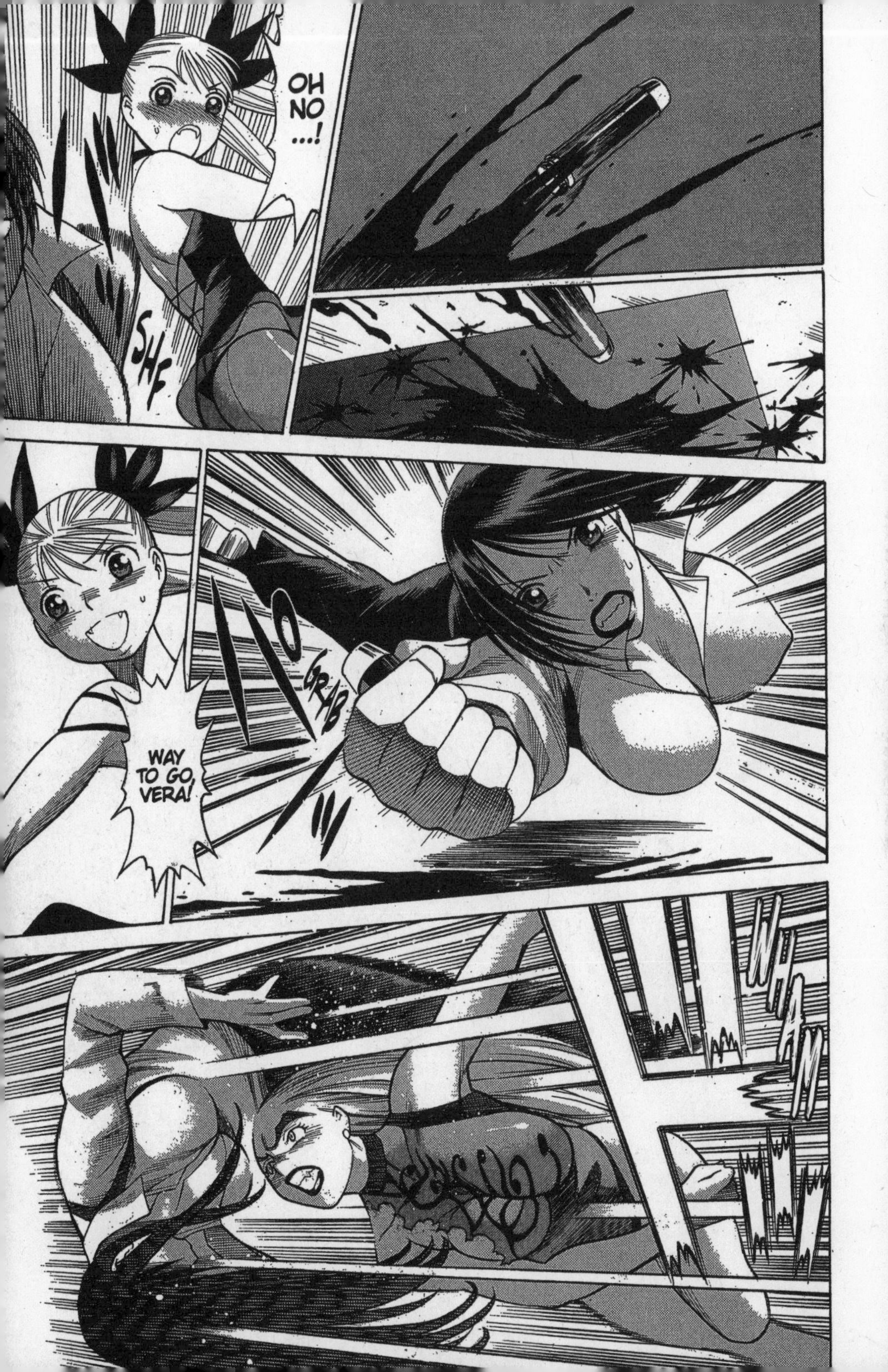
OH NO ...!
SHF
GRAB
WAY TO GO, VERA!
WHAM

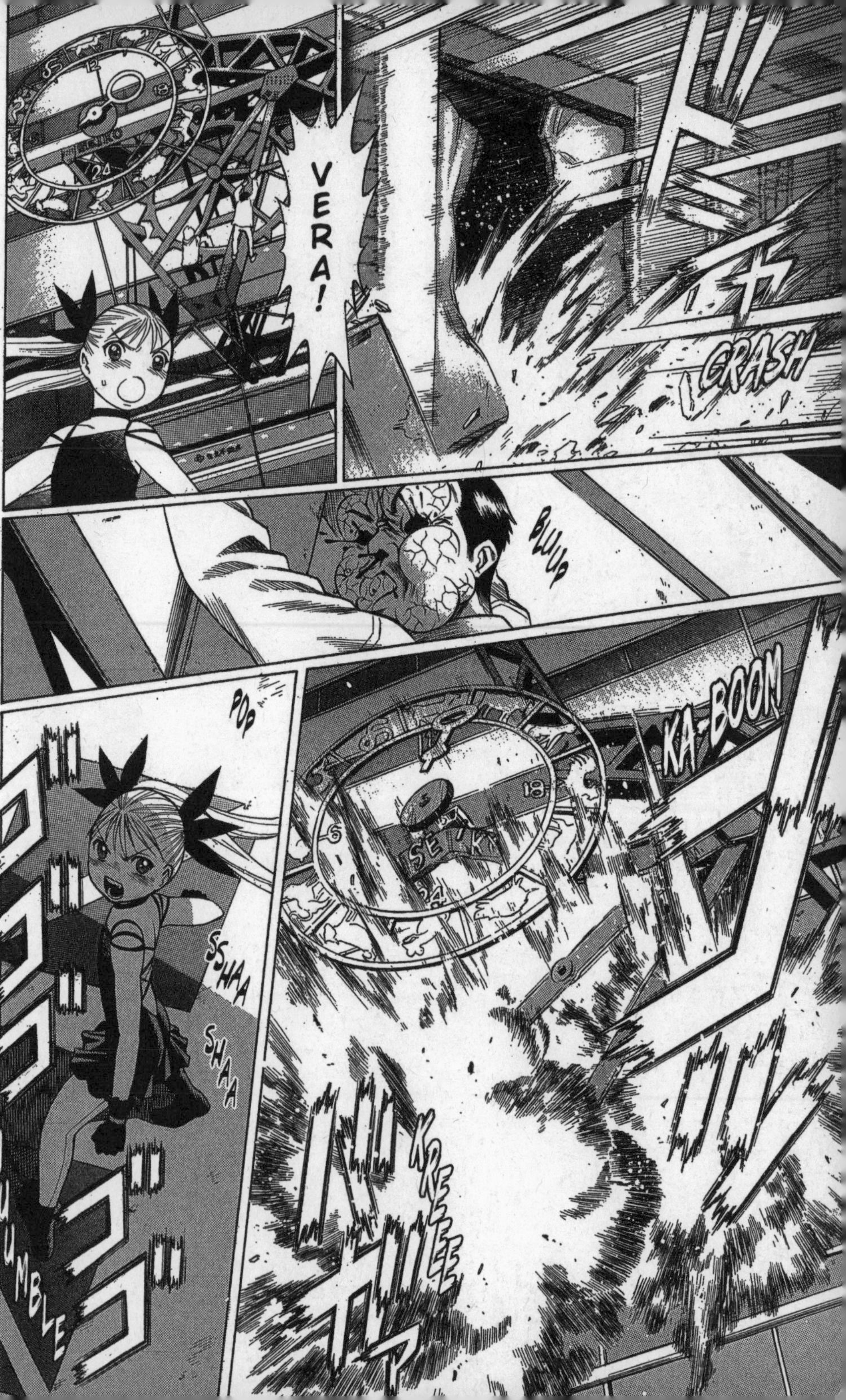

CRASH
VERA!
BLUUP
KA-BOOM
KREEEE
POP
SSHAA
SHAA
RUUUMBLE

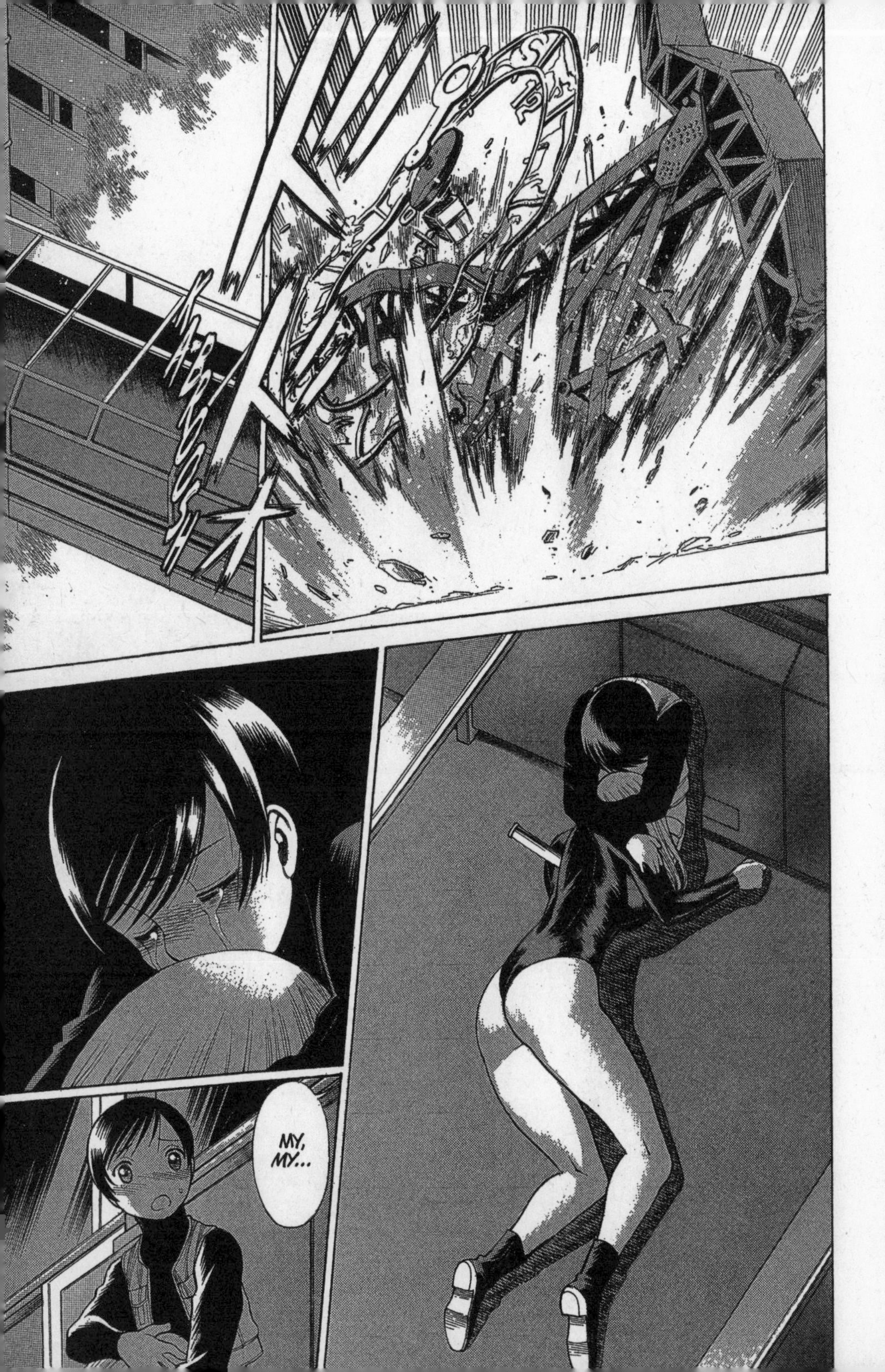
MY, MY...

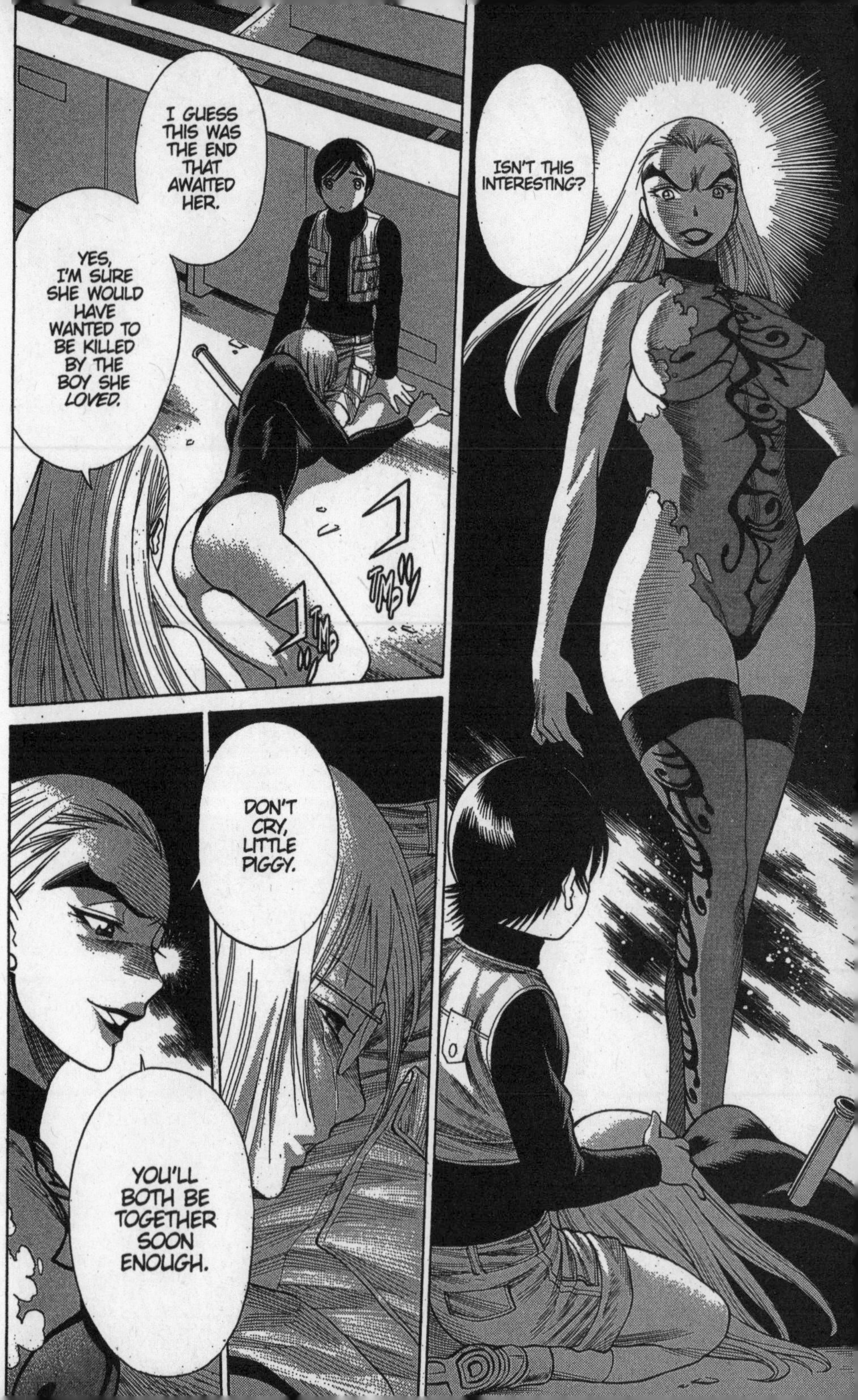
ISN'T THIS INTERESTING?
I GUESS THIS WAS THE END THAT AWAITED HER.
YES, I'M SURE SHE WOULD HAVE WANTED TO BE KILLED BY THE BOY SHE LOVED.
TMP
TMP
DON'T CRY, LITTLE PIGGY.
YOU'LL BOTH BE TOGETHER SOON ENOUGH.

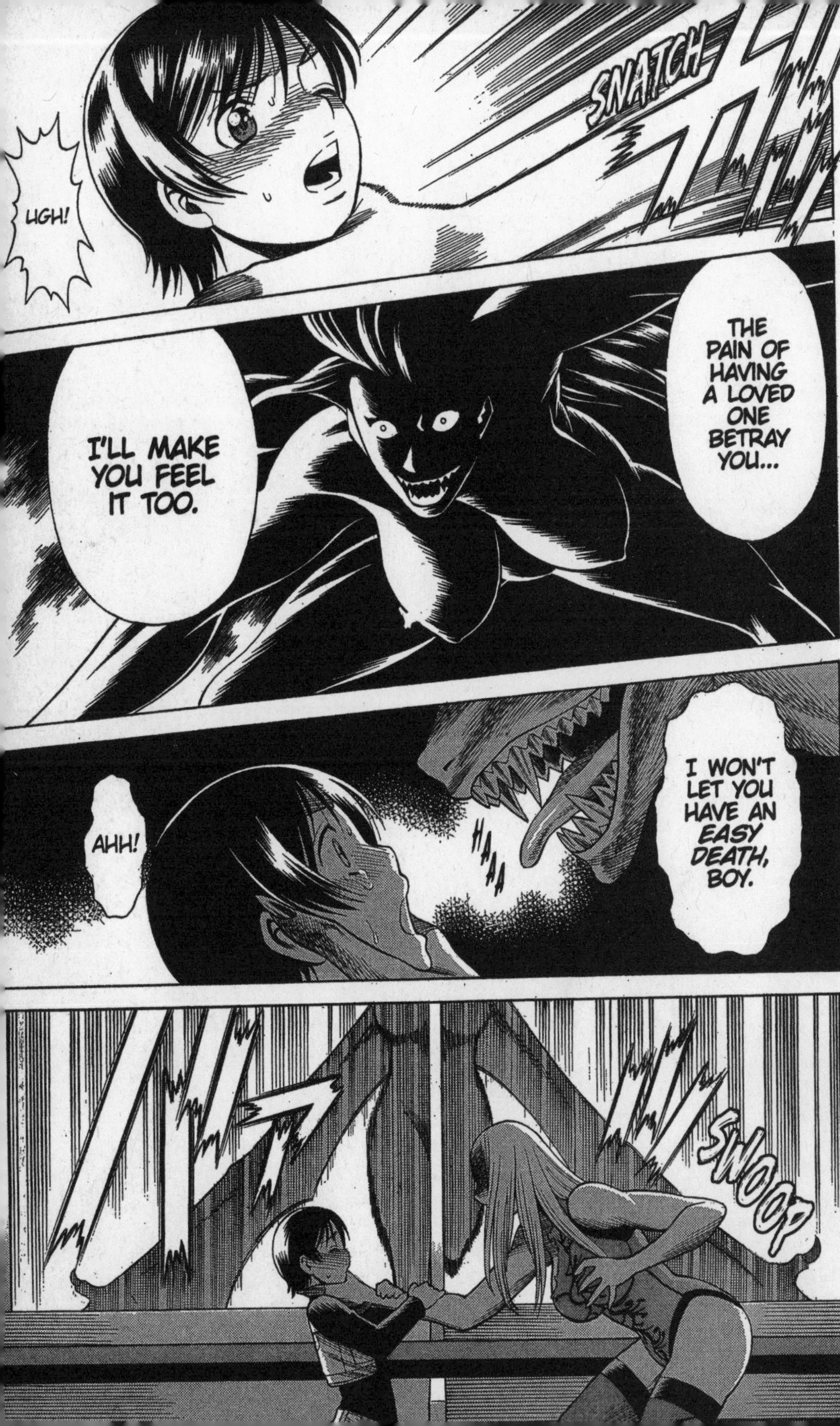
SNATCH
UGH!
THE PAIN OF HAVING A LOVED ONE BETRAY YOU...
I'LL MAKE YOU FEEL IT TOO.
I WON'T LET YOU HAVE AN EASY DEATH, BOY.
HAAA
AHH!
SWOOP

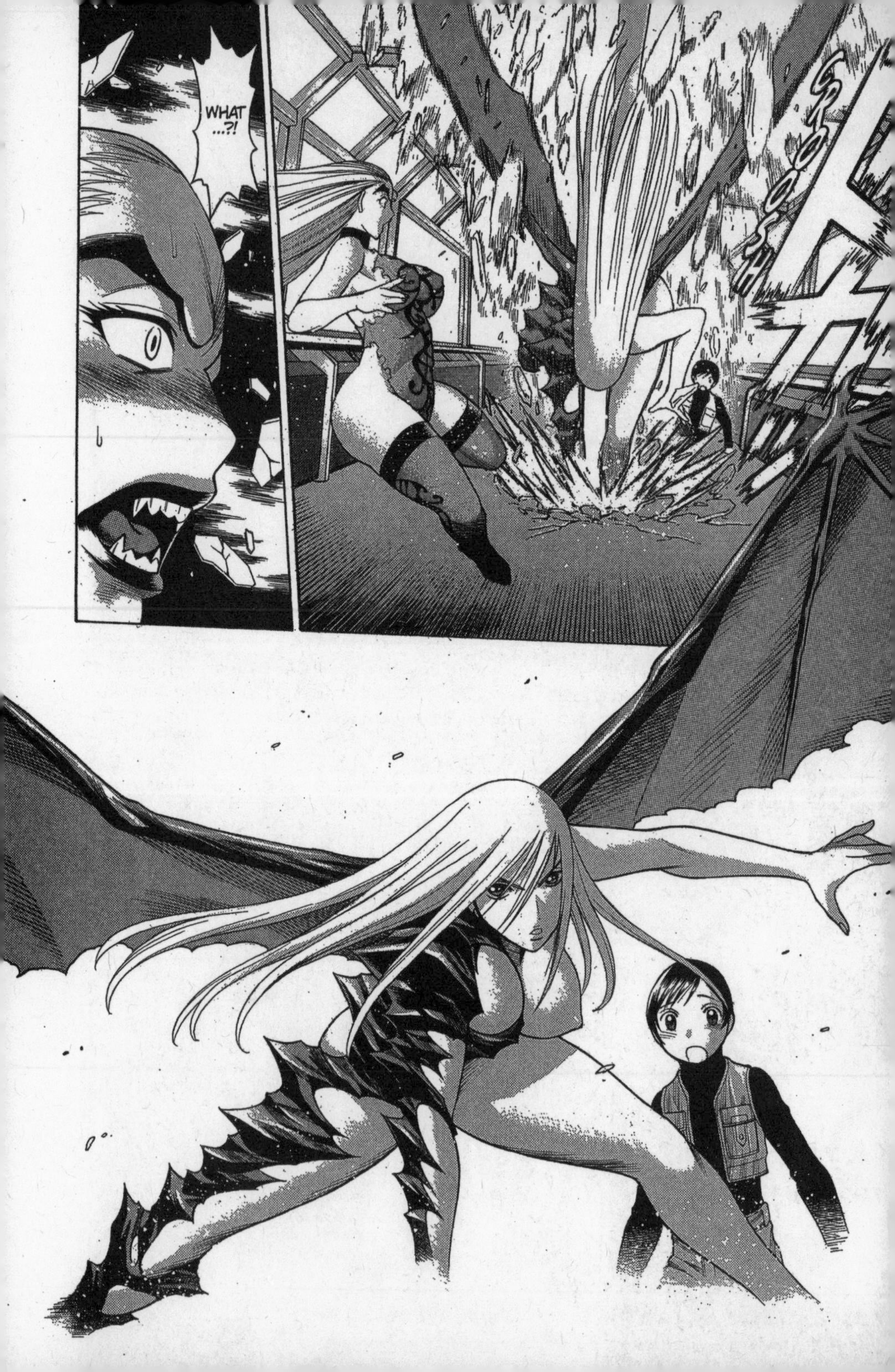
GROOOSH
WHAT ...?!

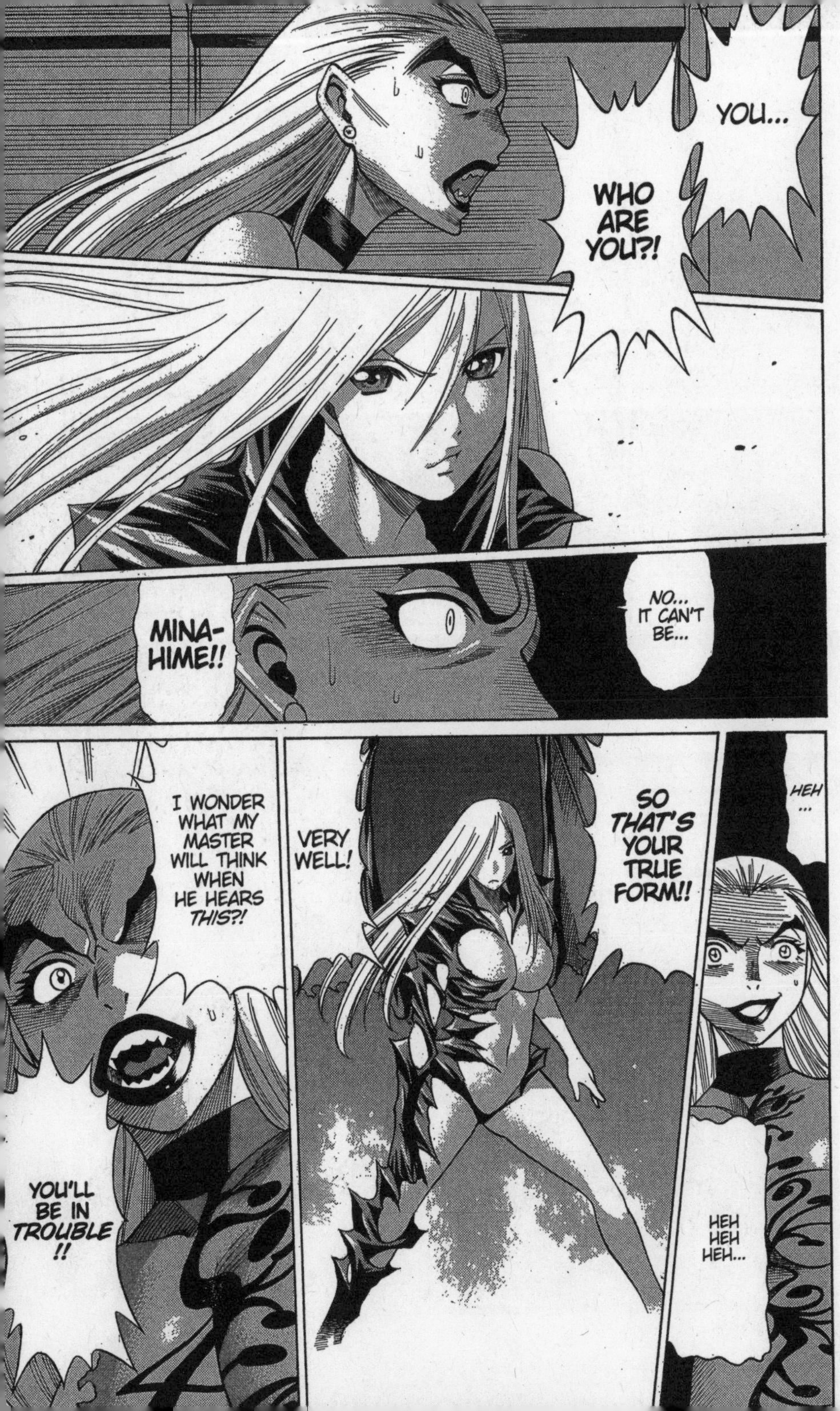
YOU...
WHO ARE YOU?!
NO... IT CAN'T BE...
MINA-HIME!!
HEH ...
SO THAT'S YOUR TRUE FORM!!
HEH HEH HEH...
VERY WELL!
I WONDER WHAT MY MASTER WILL THINK WHEN HE HEARS THIS?!
YOU'LL BE IN TROUBLE !!

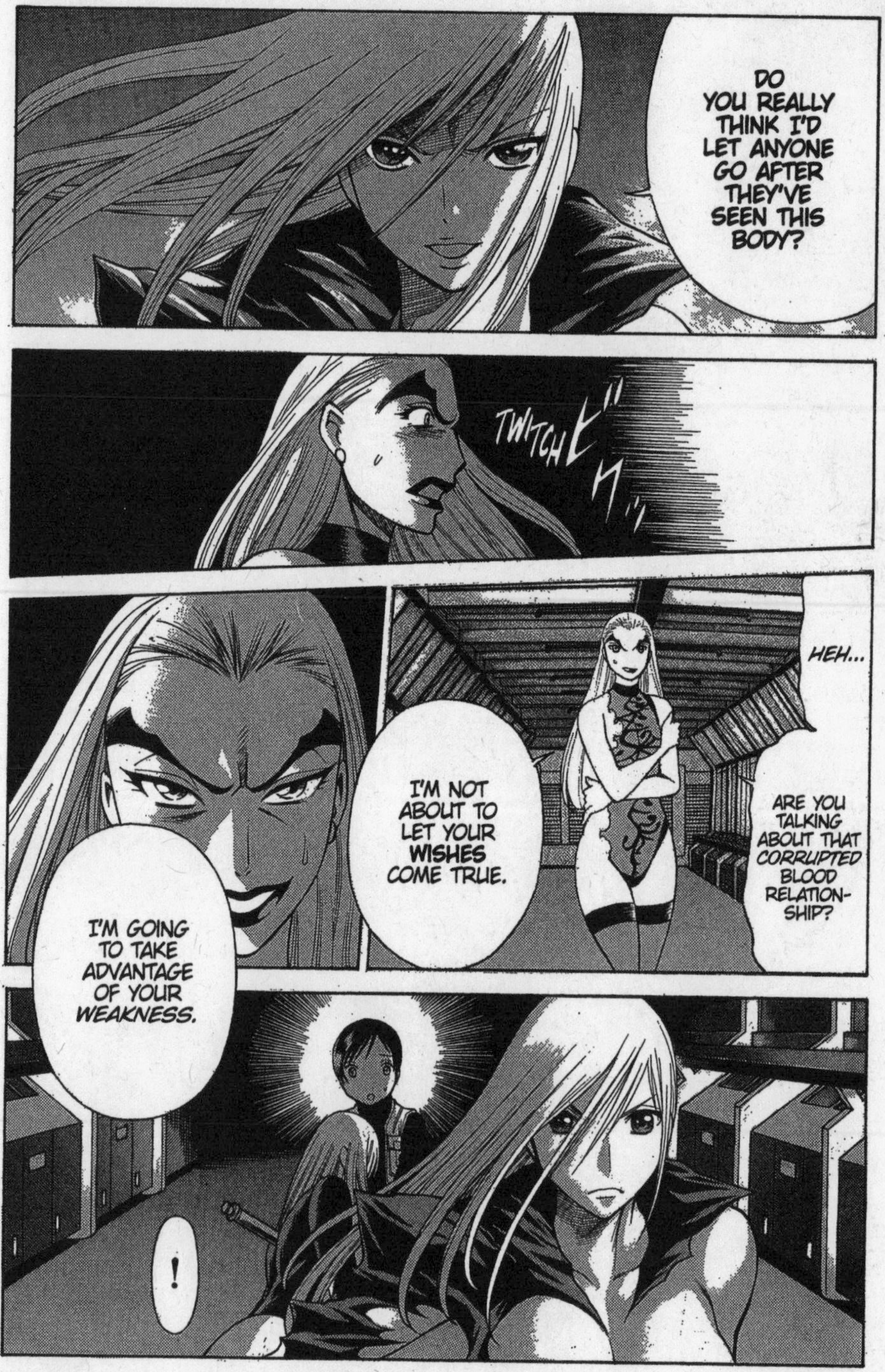
DO YOU REALLY THINK I'D LET ANYONE GO AFTER THEY'VE SEEN THIS BODY?
TWITCH
HEH...
ARE YOU TALKING ABOUT THAT CORRUPTED BLOOD RELATIONSHIP?
I'M NOT ABOUT TO LET YOUR WISHES COME TRUE.
I'M GOING TO TAKE ADVANTAGE OF YOUR WEAKNESS.
!

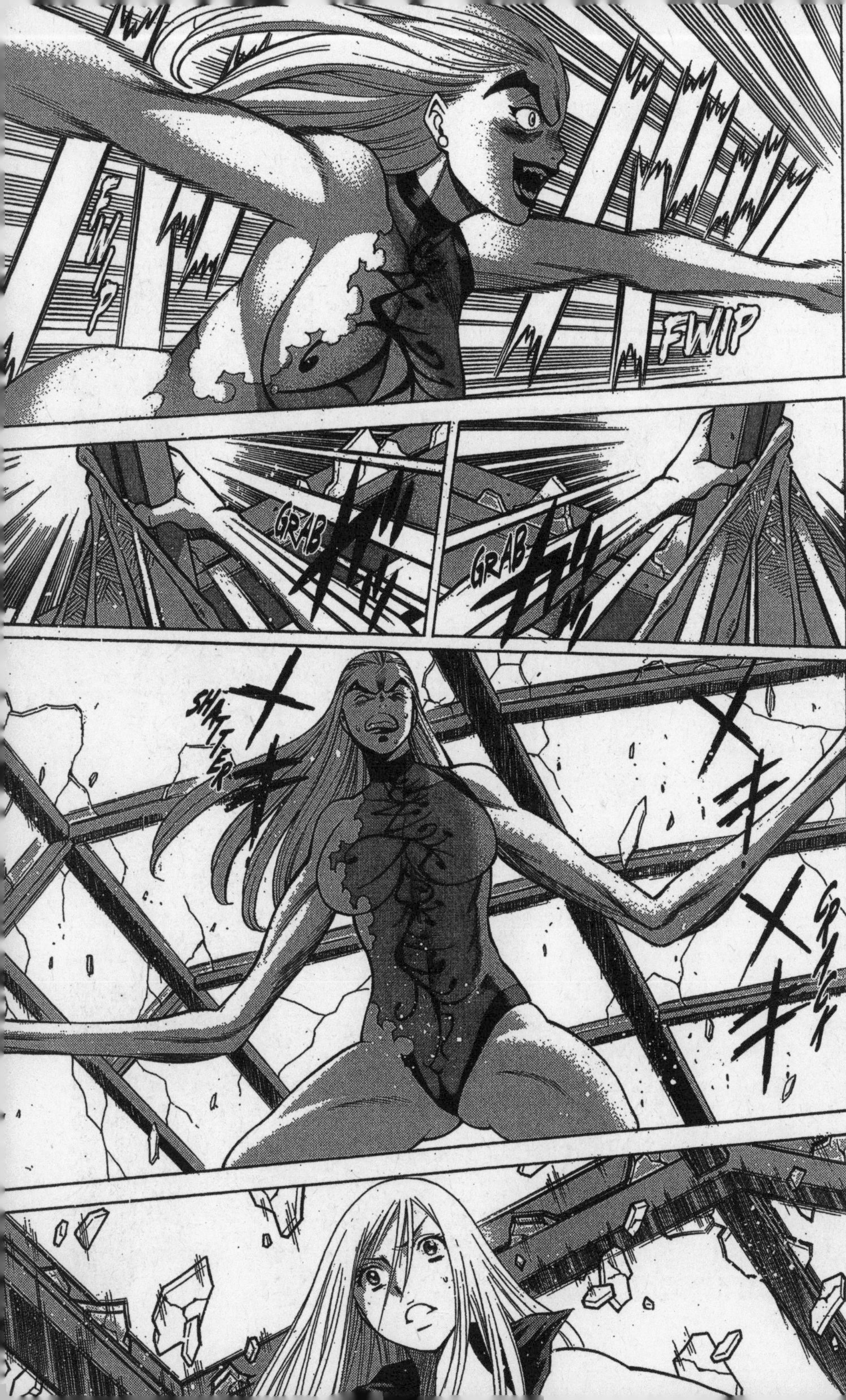
FWIP
FWIP
GRAB
GRAB
CRACK
SHATTER

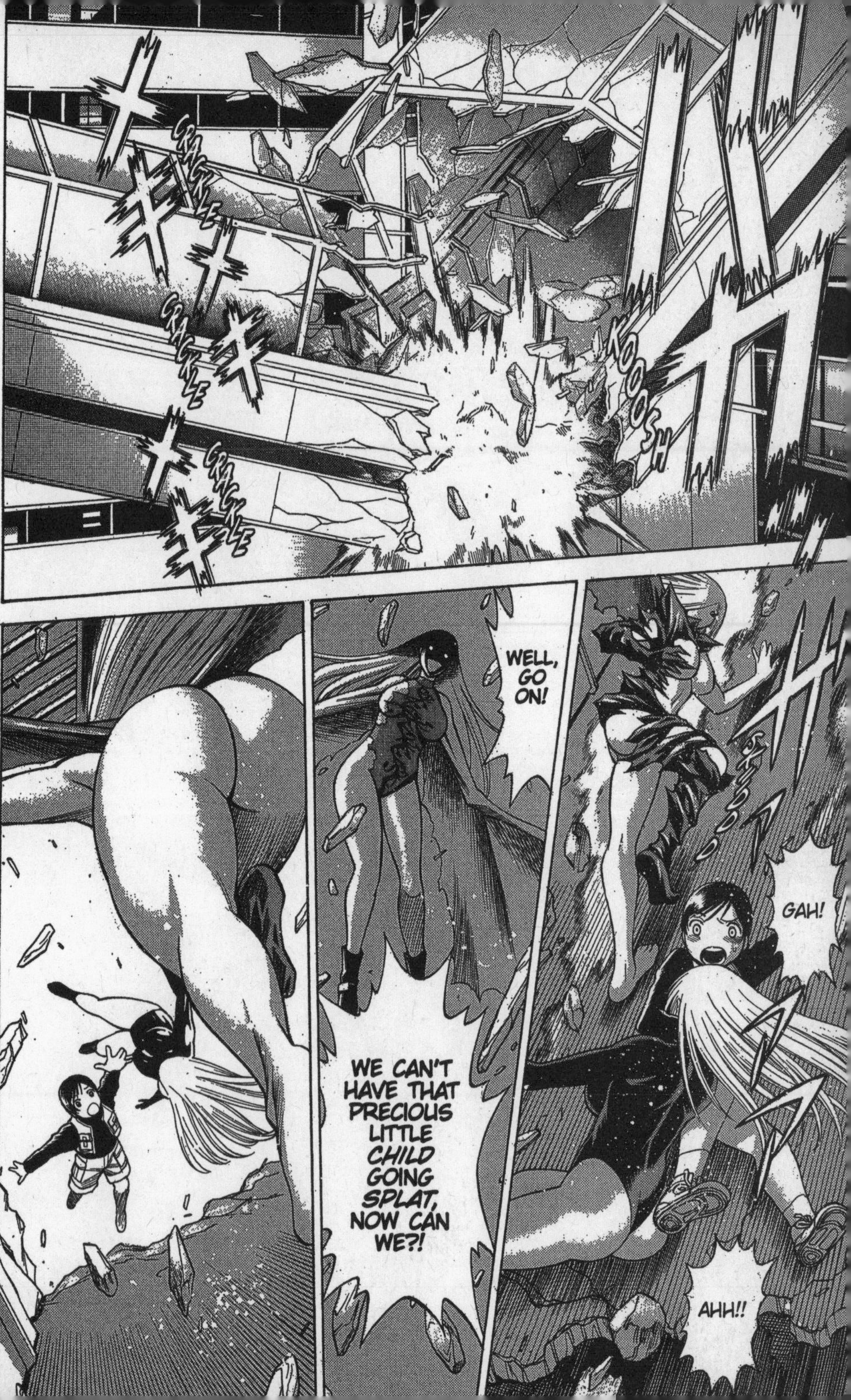
CRACKLE
CRACKLE
CRACKLE
KOOOSH
WELL, GO ON!
GAH!
WE CAN'T HAVE THAT PRECIOUS LITTLE *CHILD* GOING *SPLAT*, NOW CAN WE?!
AHH!!

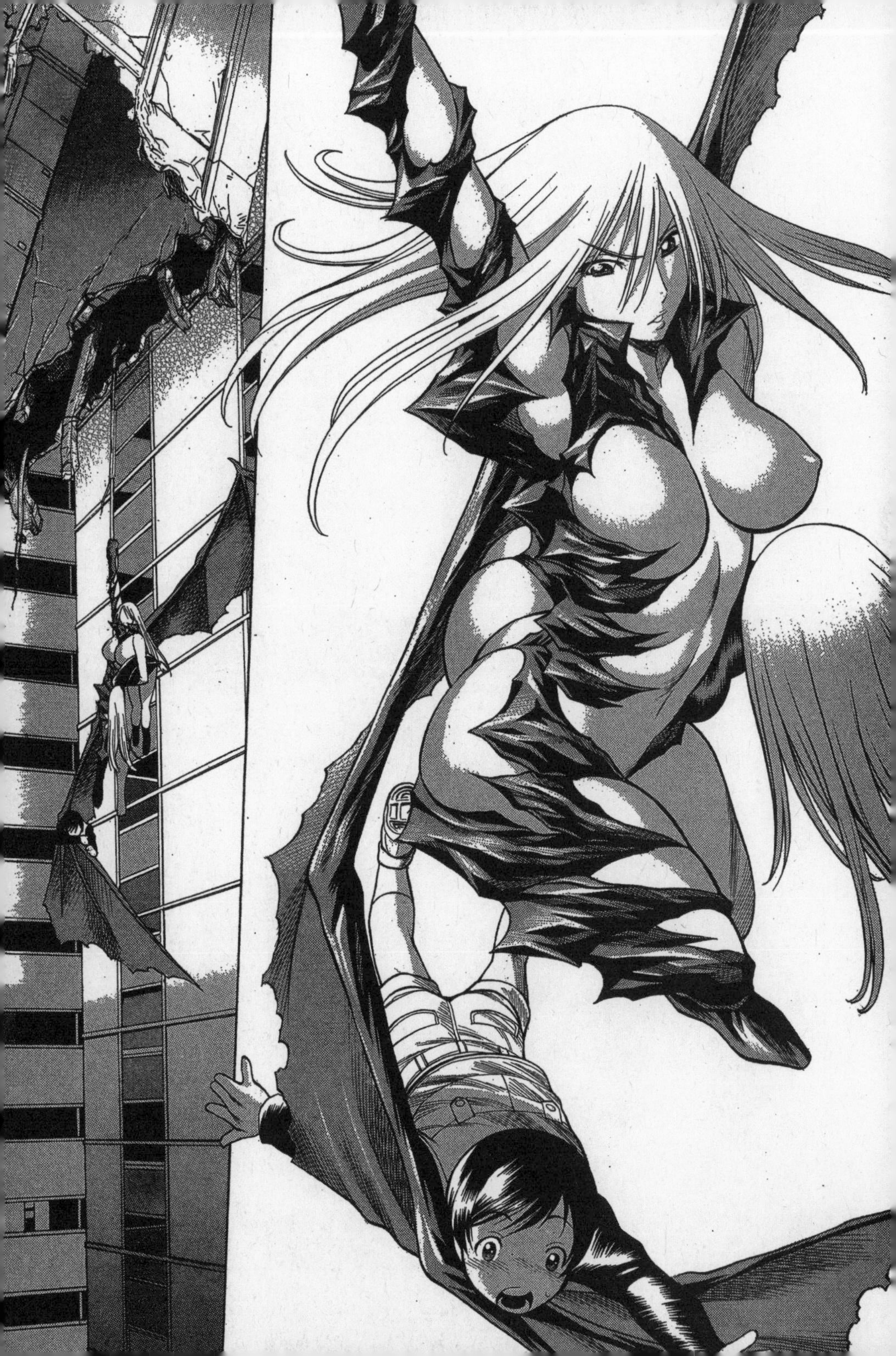

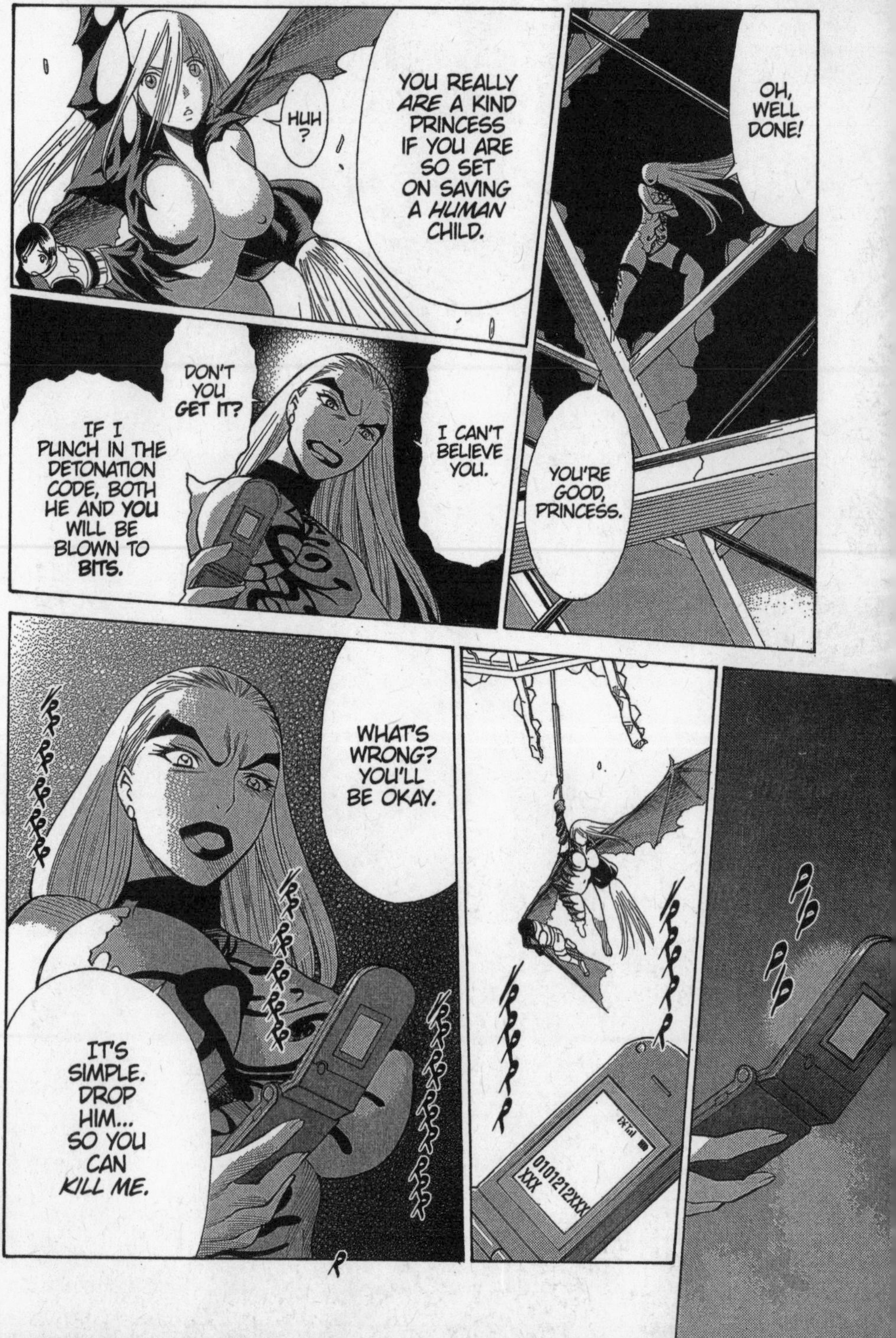
OH, WELL DONE!
YOU'RE GOOD, PRINCESS.
YOU REALLY ARE A KIND PRINCESS IF YOU ARE SO SET ON SAVING A HUMAN CHILD.
HUH?
I CAN'T BELIEVE YOU.
DON'T YOU GET IT?
IF I PUNCH IN THE DETONATION CODE, BOTH HE AND YOU WILL BE BLOWN TO BITS.
0101212XXX
XXX
WHAT'S WRONG? YOU'LL BE OKAY.
IT'S SIMPLE. DROP HIM... SO YOU CAN KILL ME.

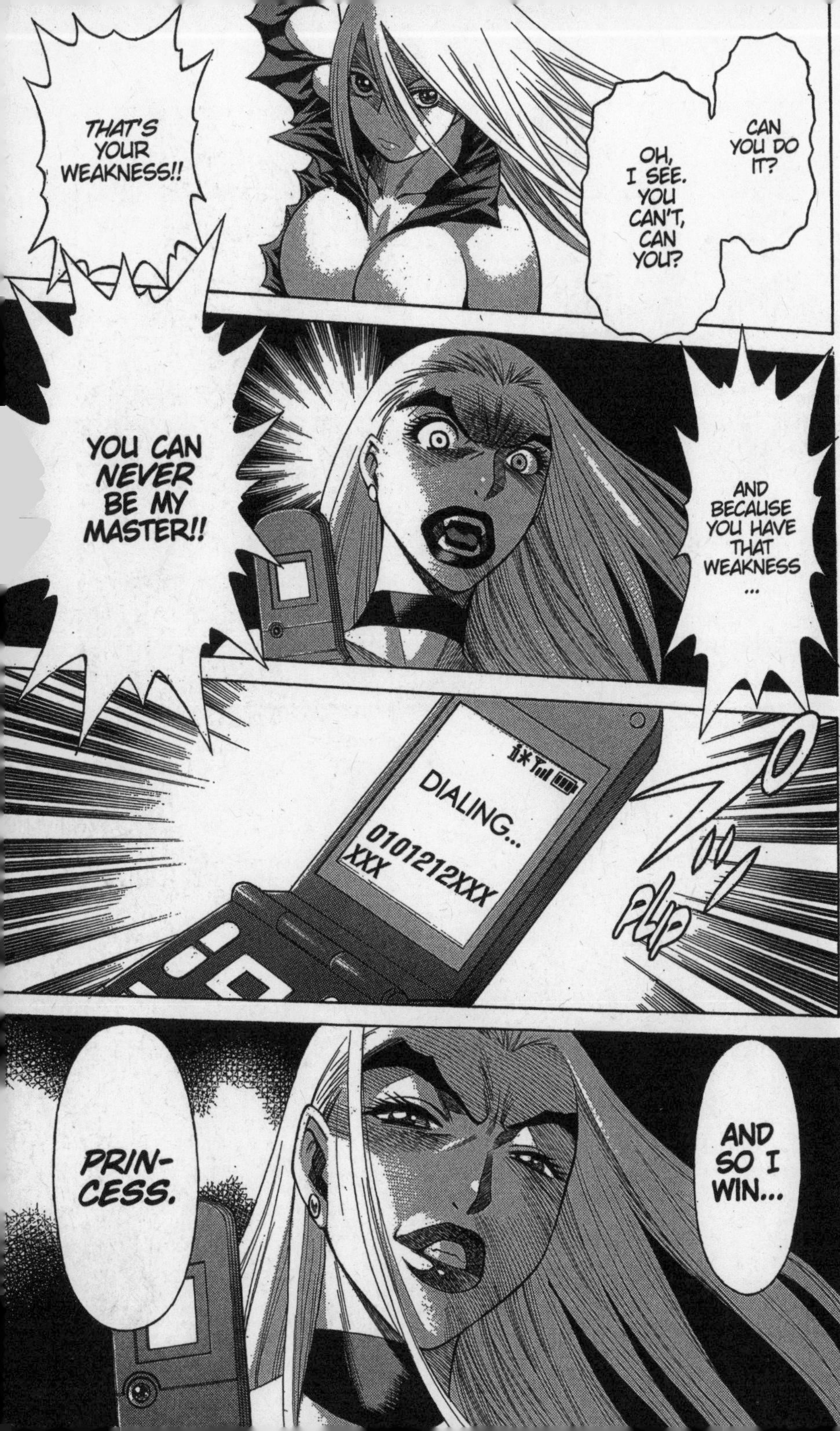
CAN YOU DO IT?
OH, I SEE. YOU CAN'T, CAN YOU?
THAT'S YOUR WEAKNESS!!
AND BECAUSE YOU HAVE THAT WEAKNESS ...
YOU CAN NEVER BE MY MASTER!!
PLIP
DIALING...
0101212XXX XXX
AND SO I WIN...
PRIN-CESS.

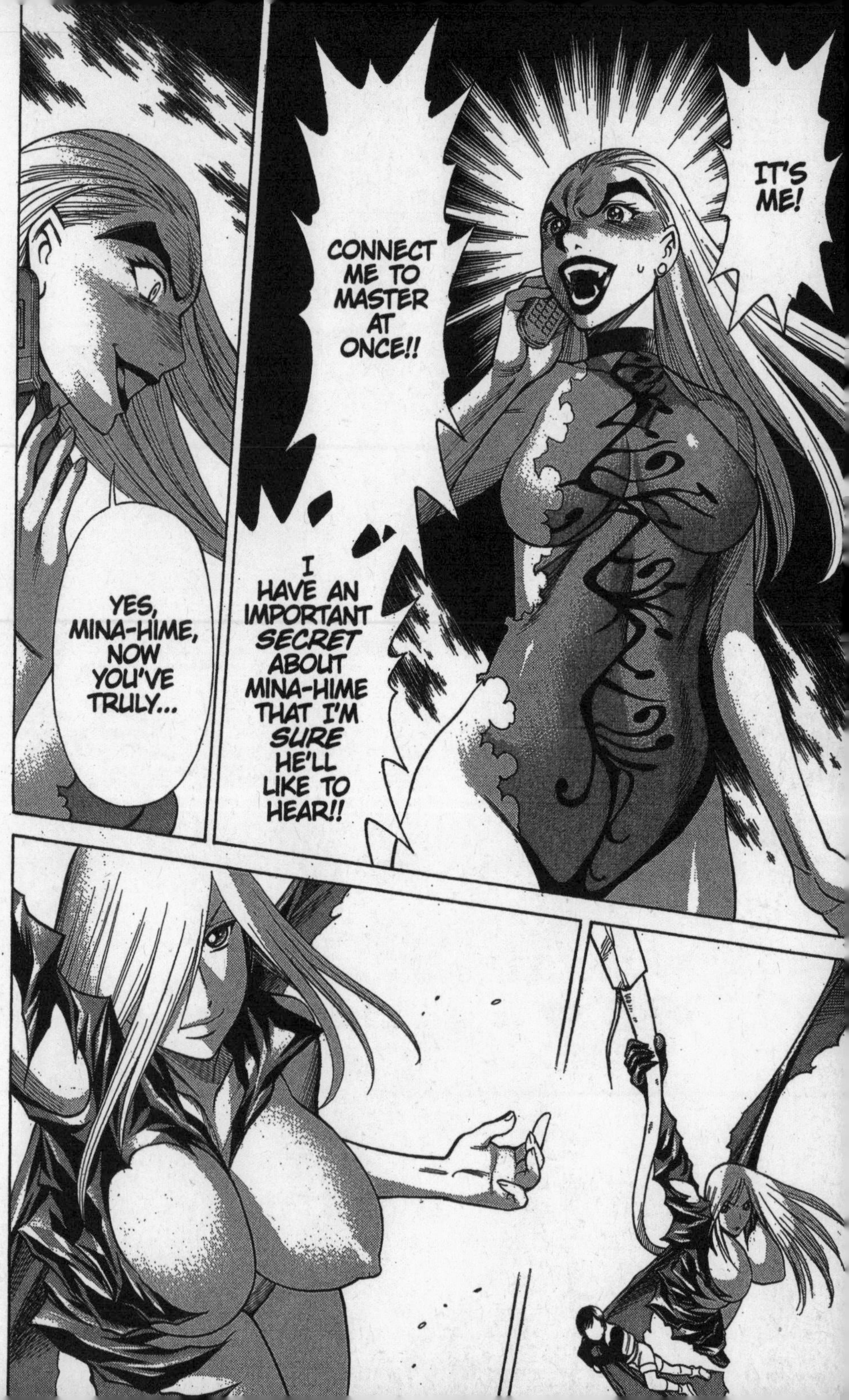
IT'S ME!
CONNECT ME TO MASTER AT ONCE!!
I HAVE AN IMPORTANT SECRET ABOUT MINA-HIME THAT I'M SURE HE'LL LIKE TO HEAR!!
YES, MINA-HIME, NOW YOU'VE TRULY...

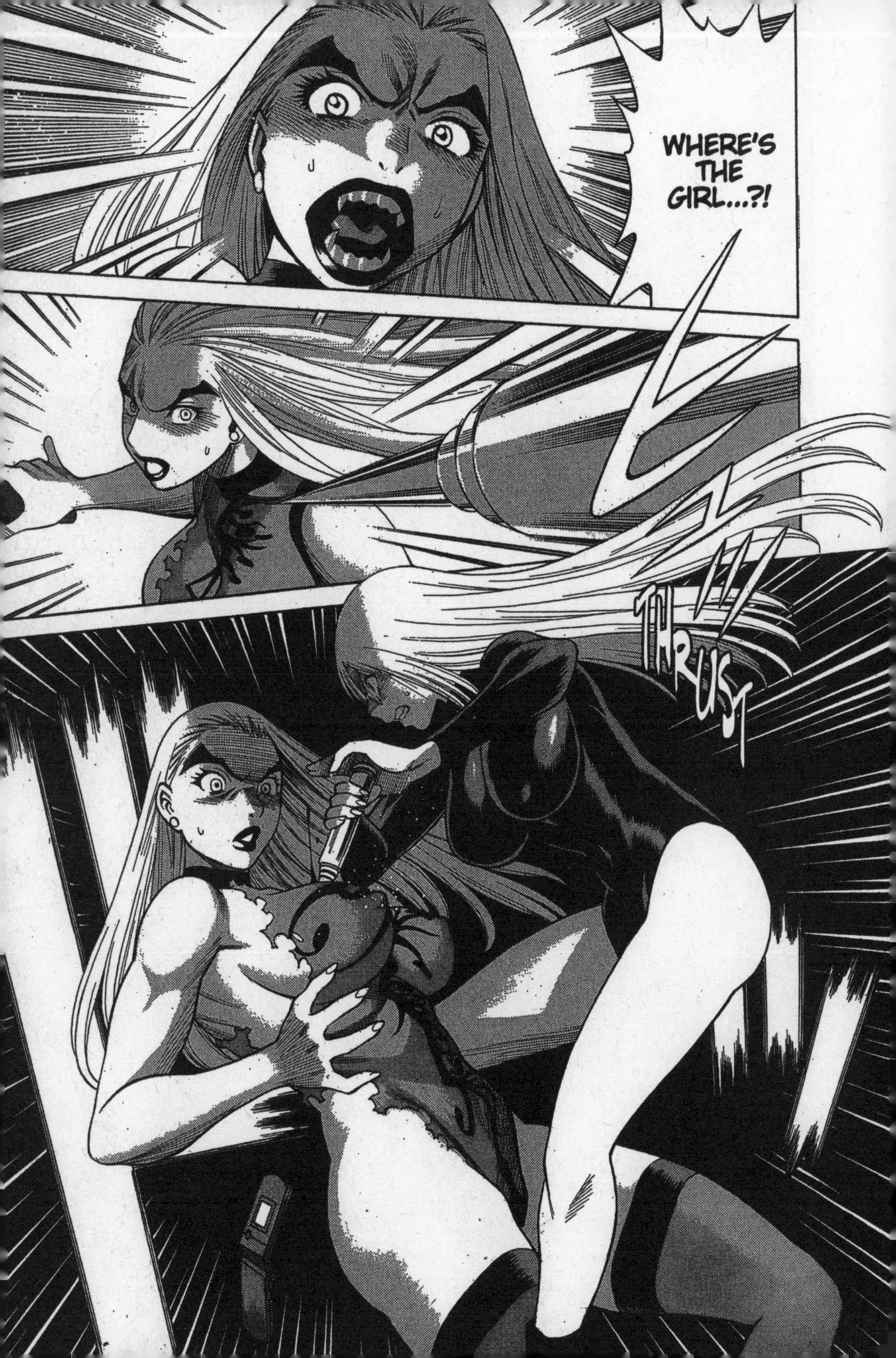
WHERE'S THE GIRL...?!
THRUST

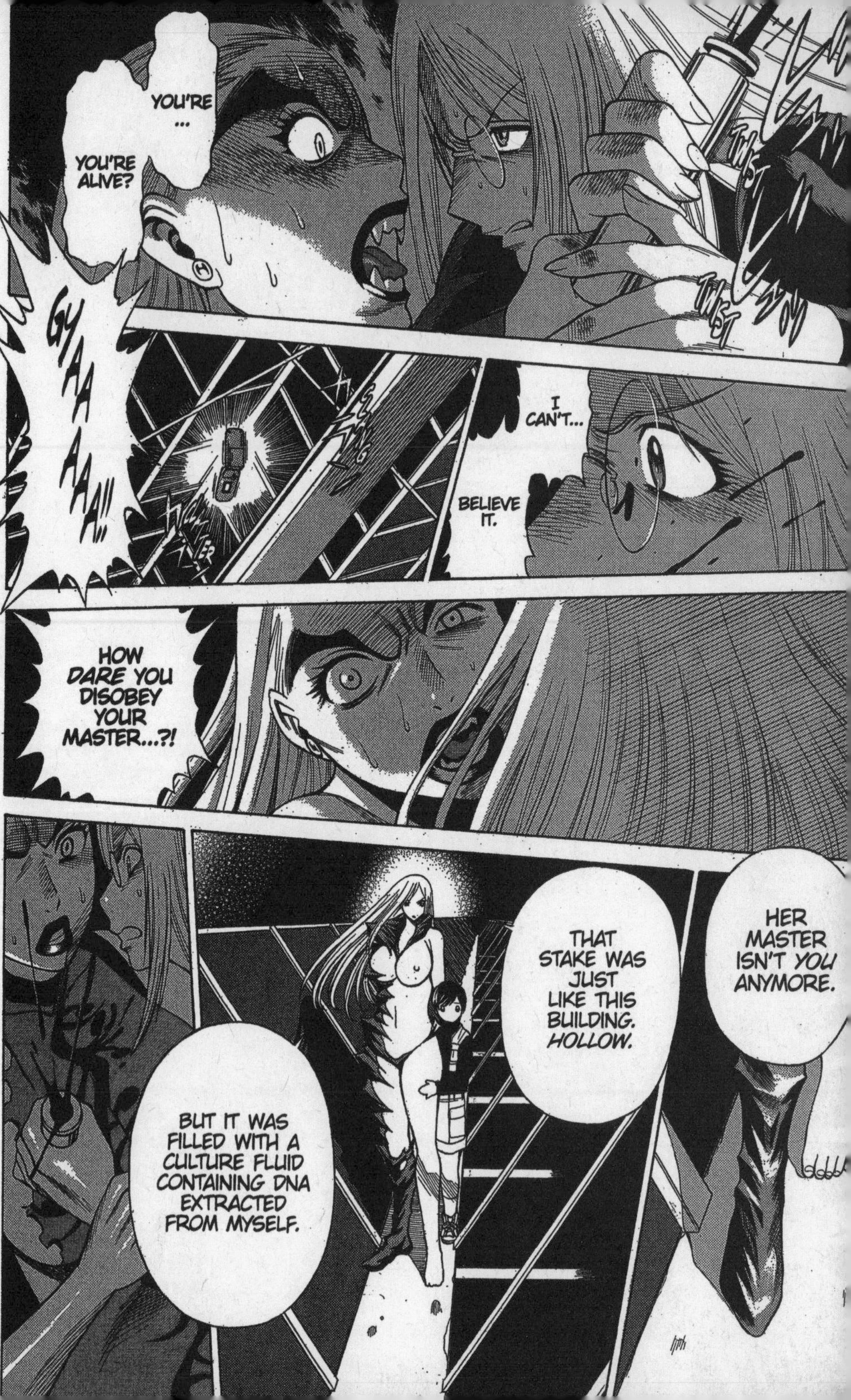
YOU'RE ...
YOU'RE ALIVE?
I CAN'T...
BELIEVE IT.
GYAAAAAA!!
HOW DARE YOU DISOBEY YOUR MASTER...?!
HER MASTER ISN'T YOU ANYMORE.
THAT STAKE WAS JUST LIKE THIS BUILDING. HOLLOW.
BUT IT WAS FILLED WITH A CULTURE FLUID CONTAINING DNA EXTRACTED FROM MYSELF.

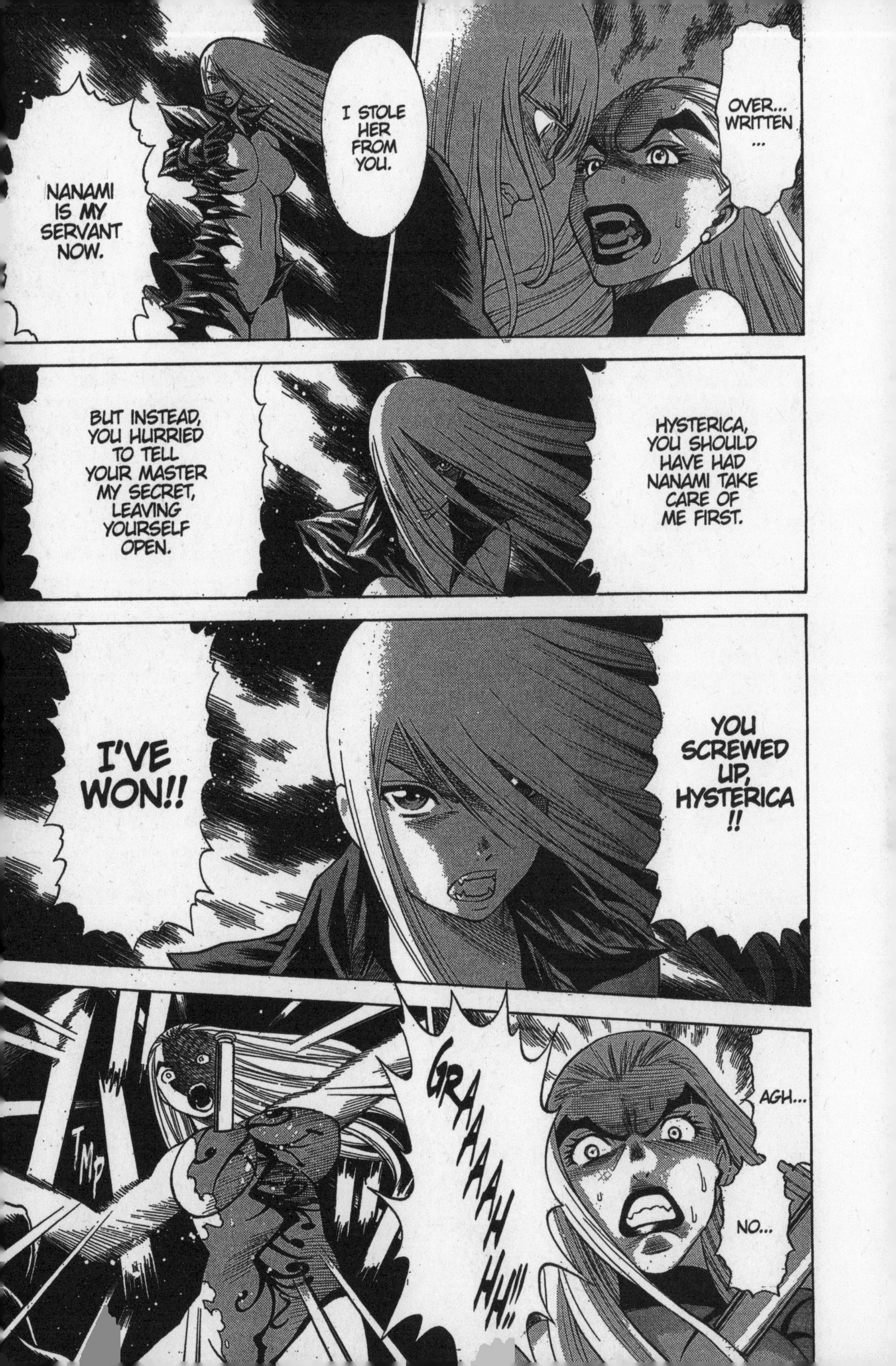
OVER... WRITTEN ...
I STOLE HER FROM YOU.
NANAMI IS MY SERVANT NOW.
HYSTERICA, YOU SHOULD HAVE HAD NANAMI TAKE CARE OF ME FIRST.
BUT INSTEAD, YOU HURRIED TO TELL YOUR MASTER MY SECRET, LEAVING YOURSELF OPEN.
YOU SCREWED UP, HYSTERICA !!
I'VE WON!!
AGH...
NO...
GRAAAAAHHH!!
TMP

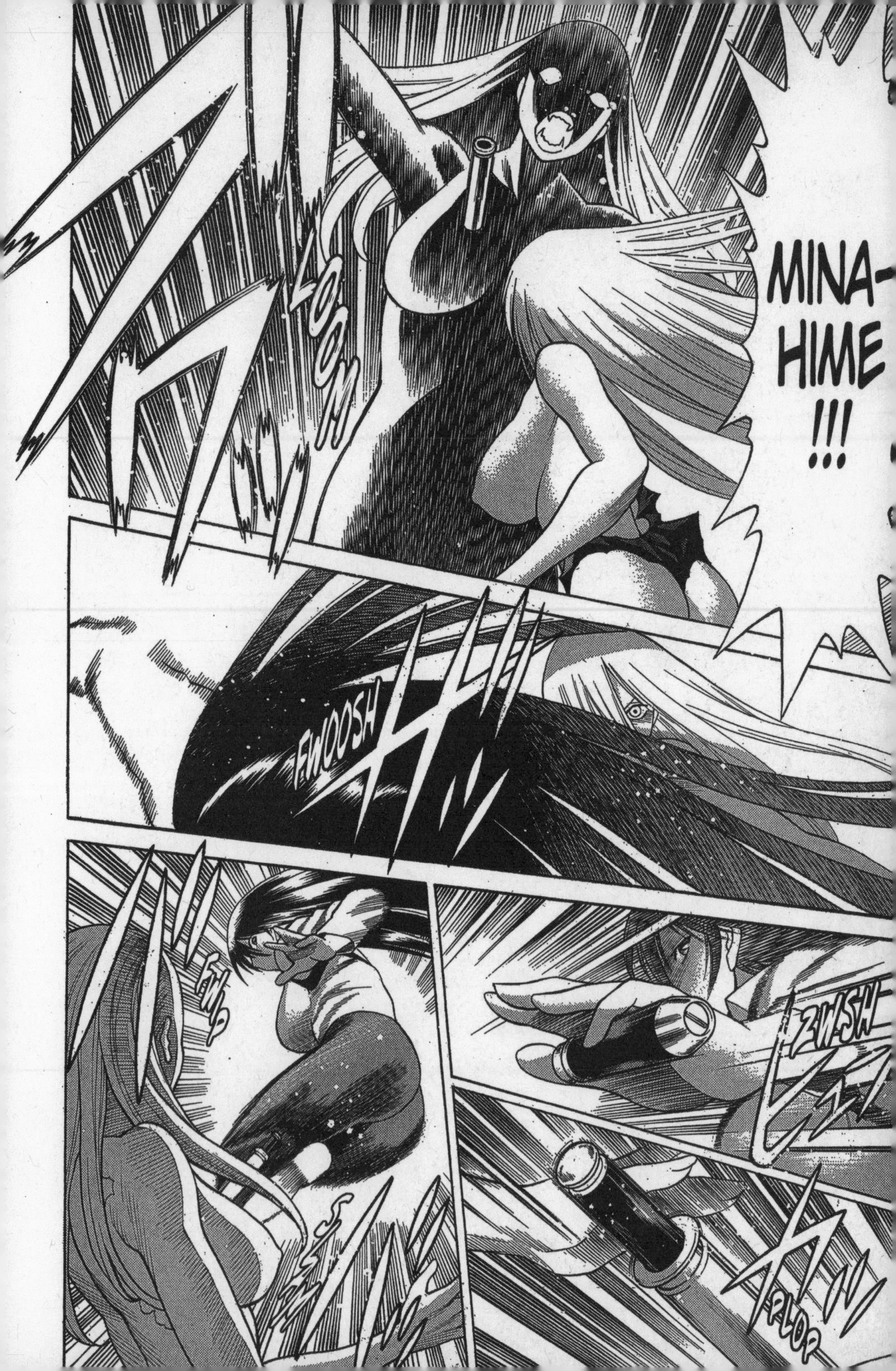
MINA-HIME !!!
LOOOM
FWOOSH
ZWSH
PLOP
FWIP

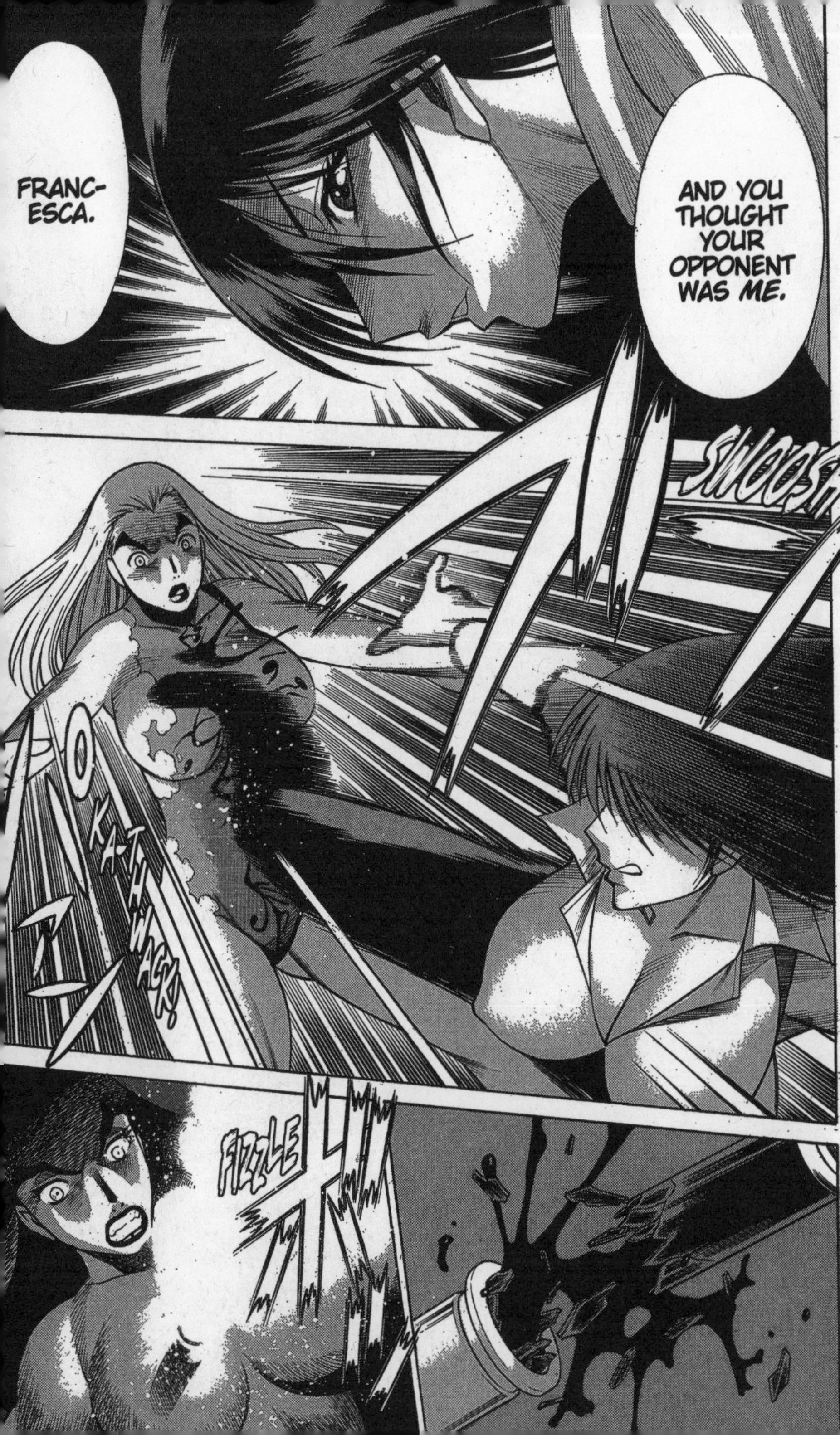
AND YOU THOUGHT YOUR OPPONENT WAS ME.
FRANC-ESCA.
SWOOSH
KA-THWACK!
FIZZLE

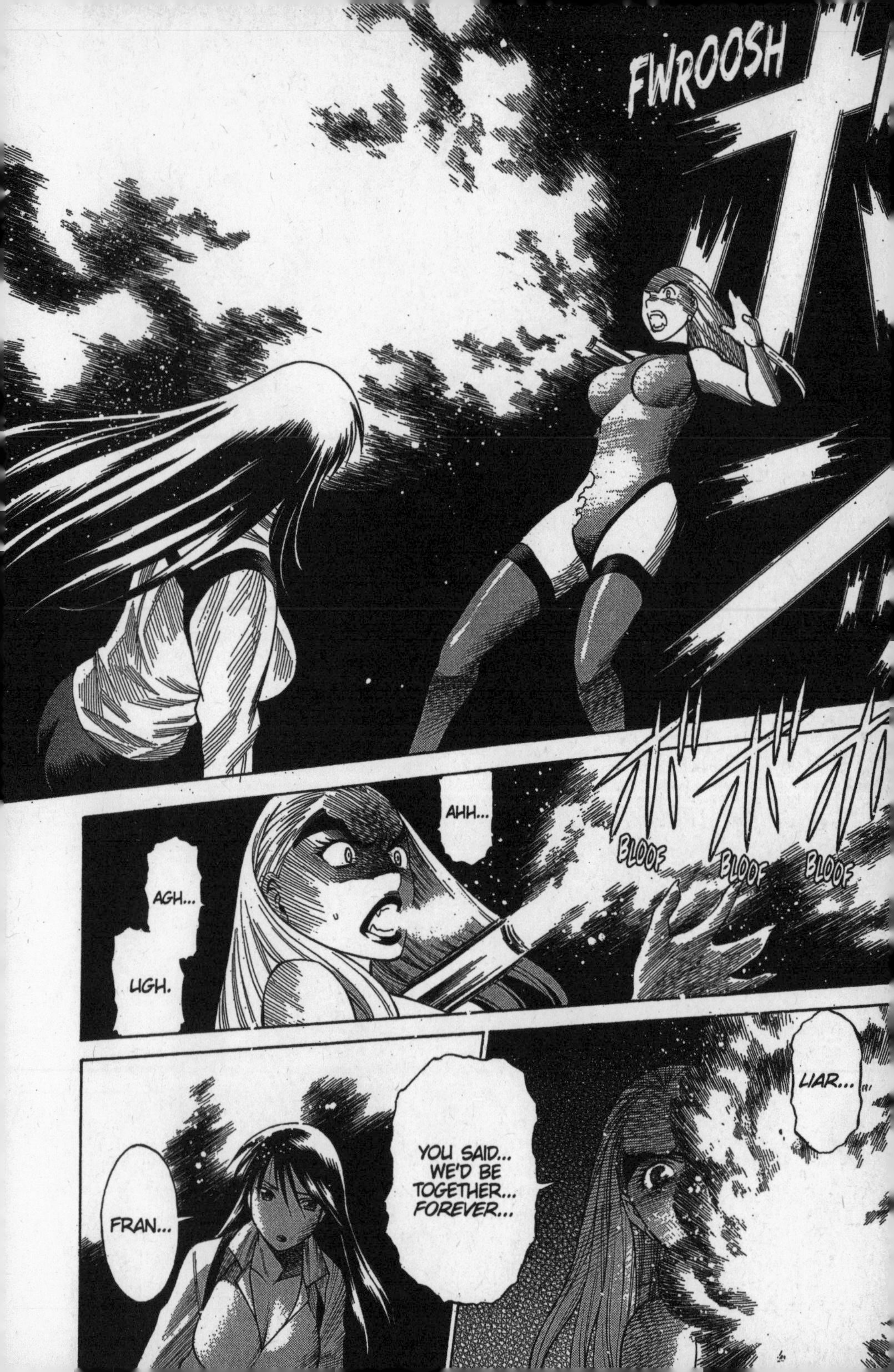
FWROOSH
BLOOF
BLOOF
BLOOF
AHH...
AGH...
UGH.
LIAR...
YOU SAID... WE'D BE TOGETHER... FOREVER...
FRAN...

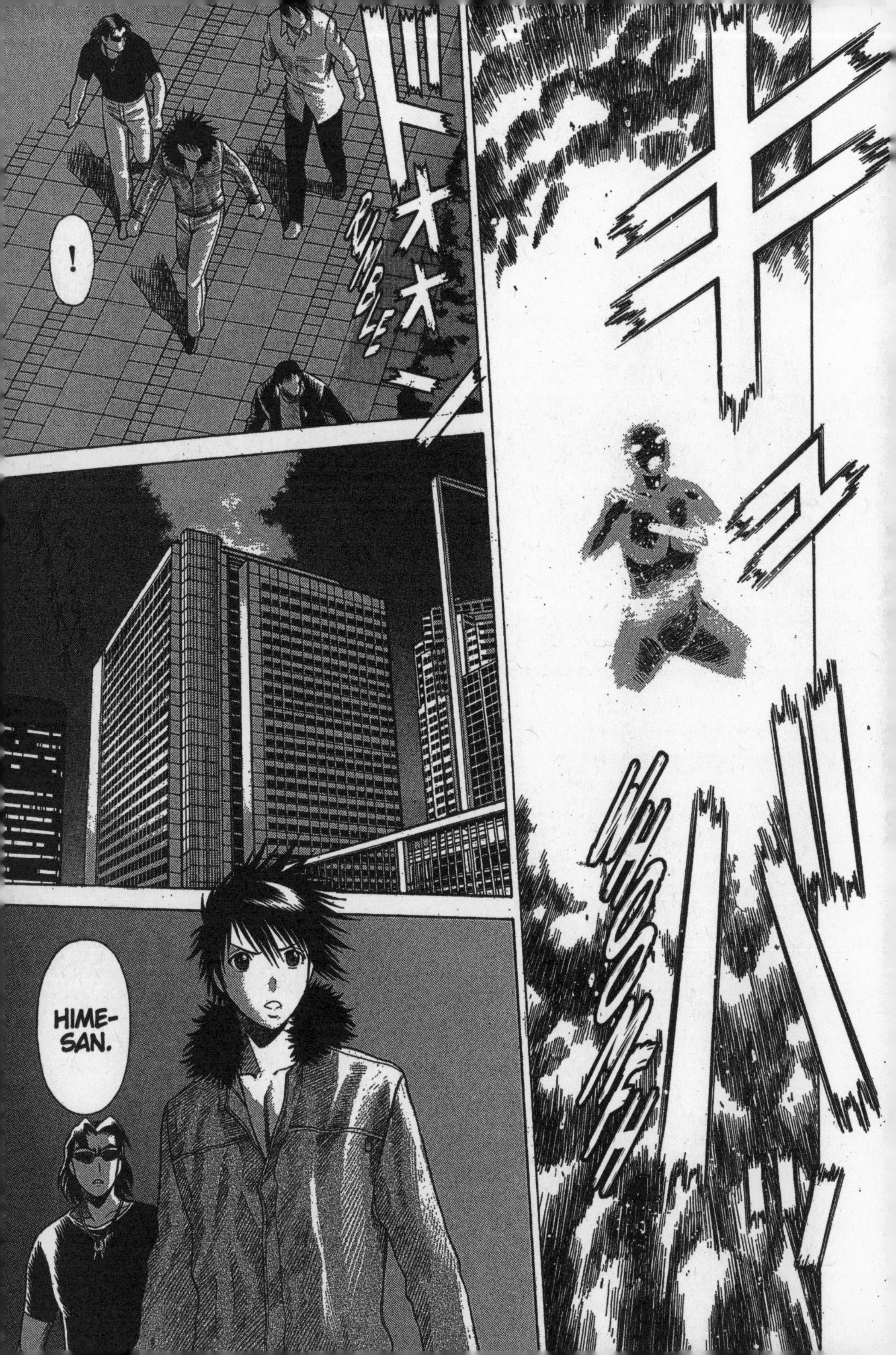

WHOOOOSHHH
!
RUMBLE
HIME-SAN.

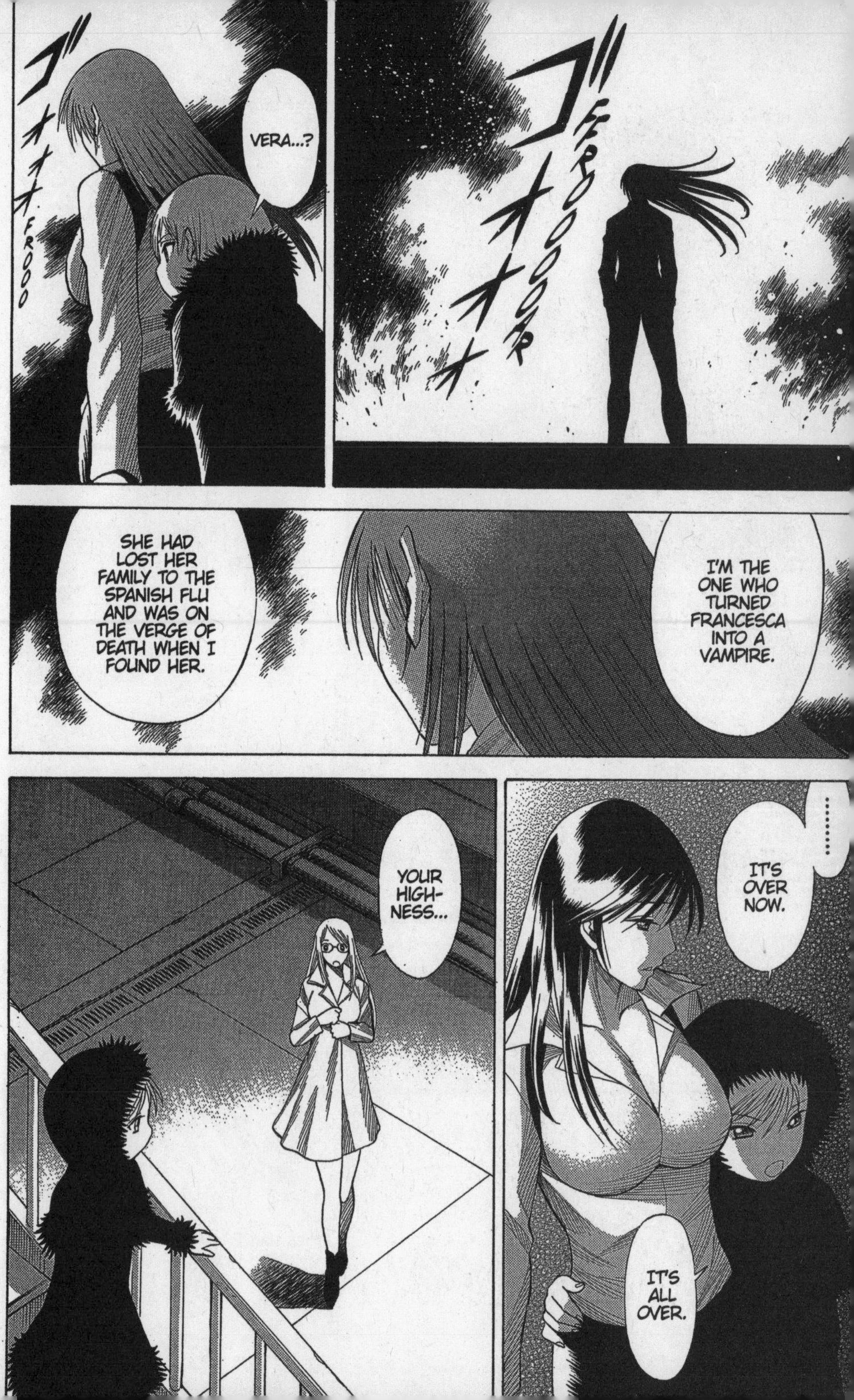
FROOOOOOR
VERA...?
FROOO
I'M THE ONE WHO TURNED FRANCESCA INTO A VAMPIRE.
SHE HAD LOST HER FAMILY TO THE SPANISH FLU AND WAS ON THE VERGE OF DEATH WHEN I FOUND HER.
......
IT'S OVER NOW.
IT'S ALL OVER.
YOUR HIGH-NESS...

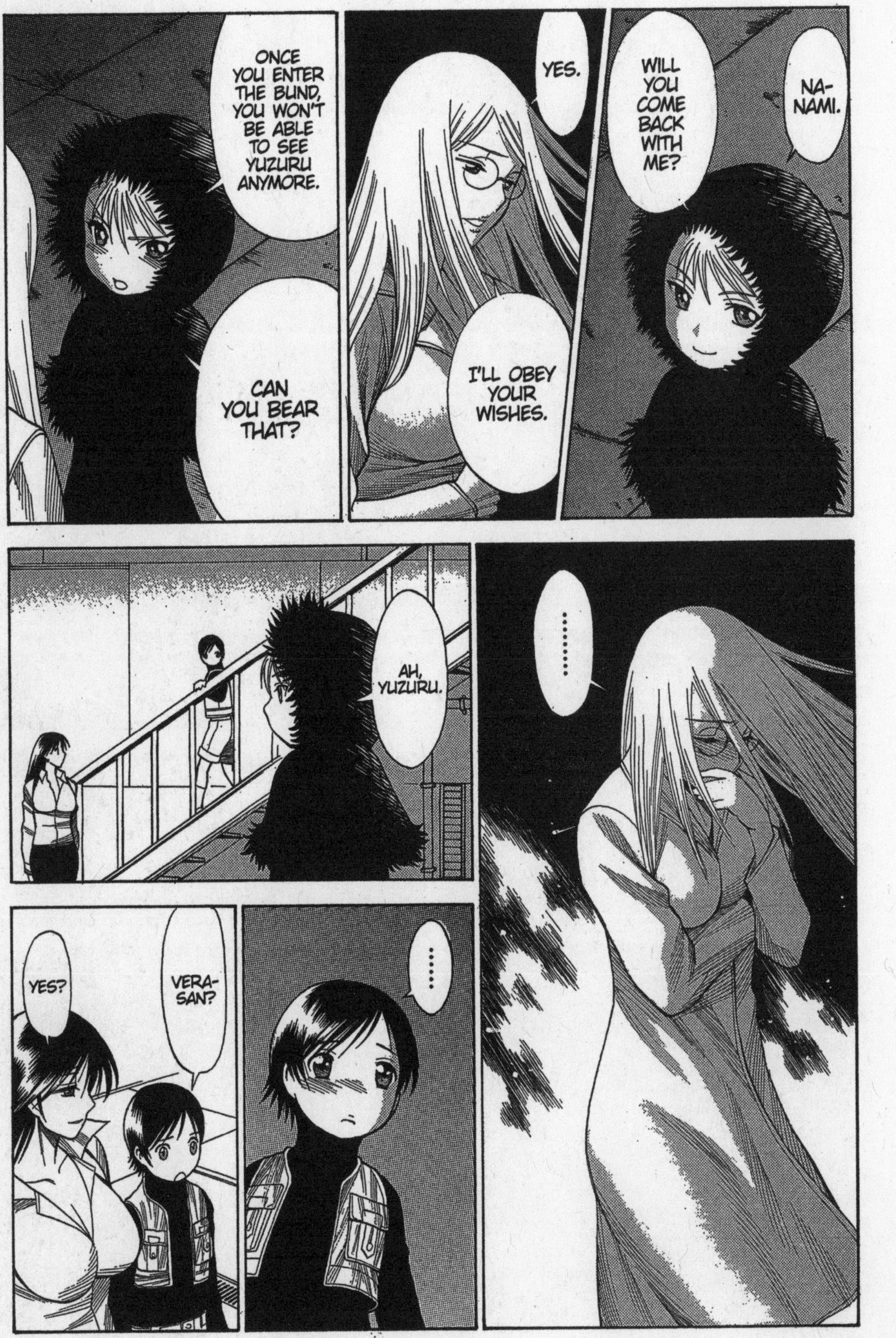
NA-NAMI.
WILL YOU COME BACK WITH ME?
YES.
I'LL OBEY YOUR WISHES.
ONCE YOU ENTER THE BUND, YOU WON'T BE ABLE TO SEE YUZURU ANYMORE.
CAN YOU BEAR THAT?
....
AH, YUZURU.
......
VERA-SAN?
YES?

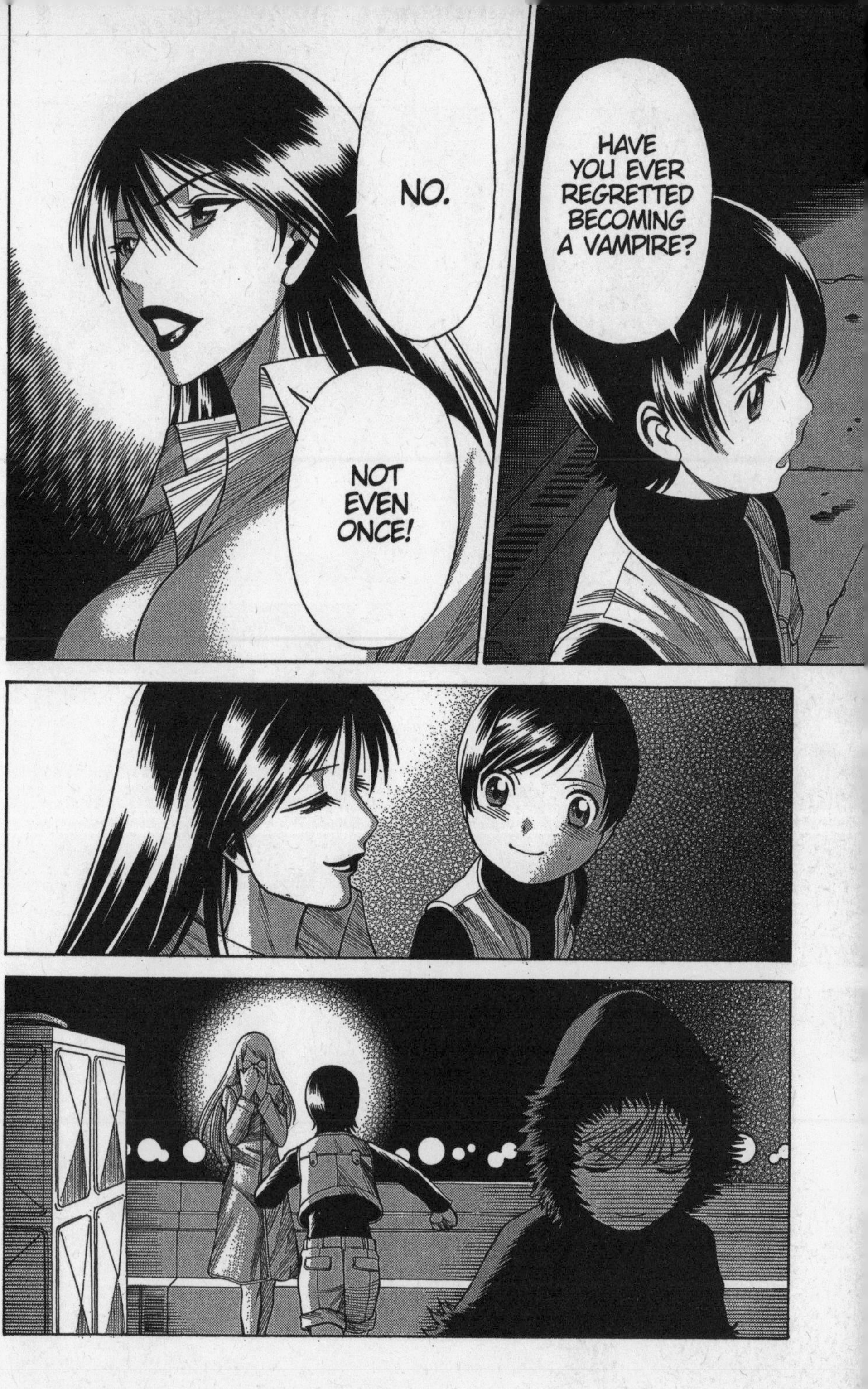
HAVE YOU EVER REGRETTED BECOMING A VAMPIRE?
NO.
NOT EVEN ONCE!

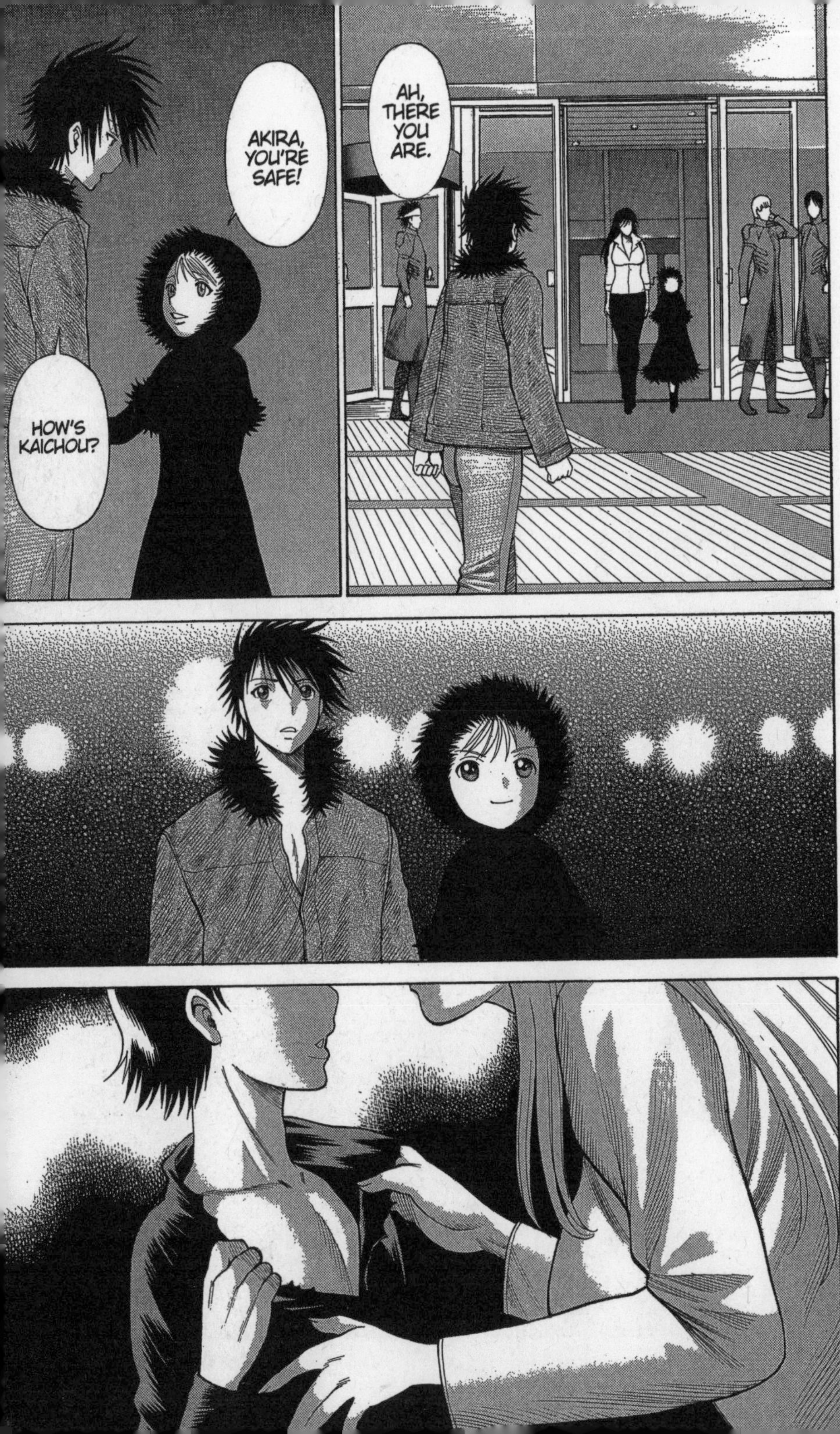
AH, THERE YOU ARE.
AKIRA, YOU'RE SAFE!
HOW'S KAICHOU?

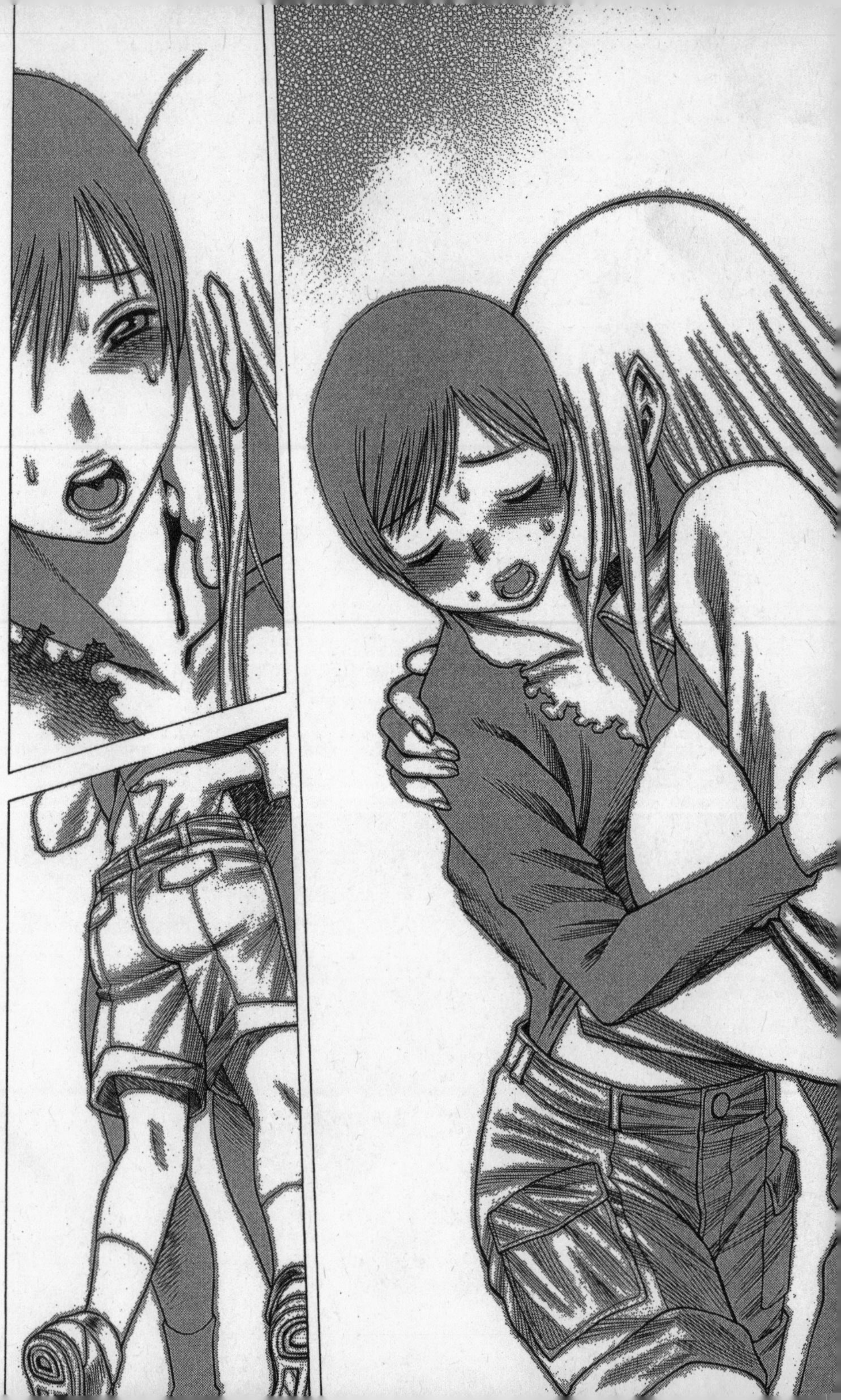

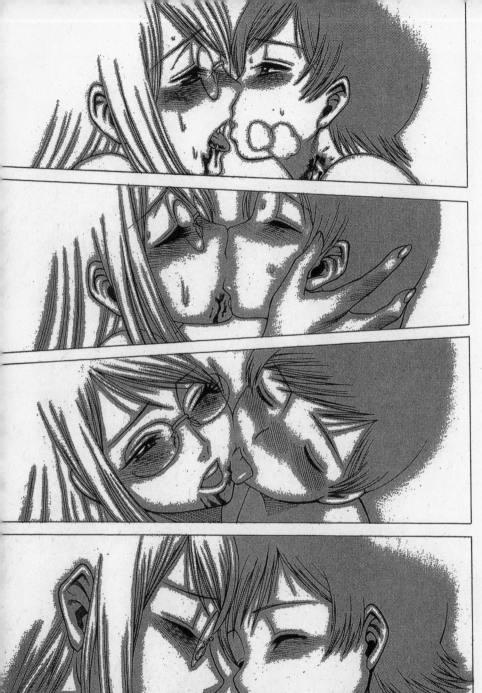

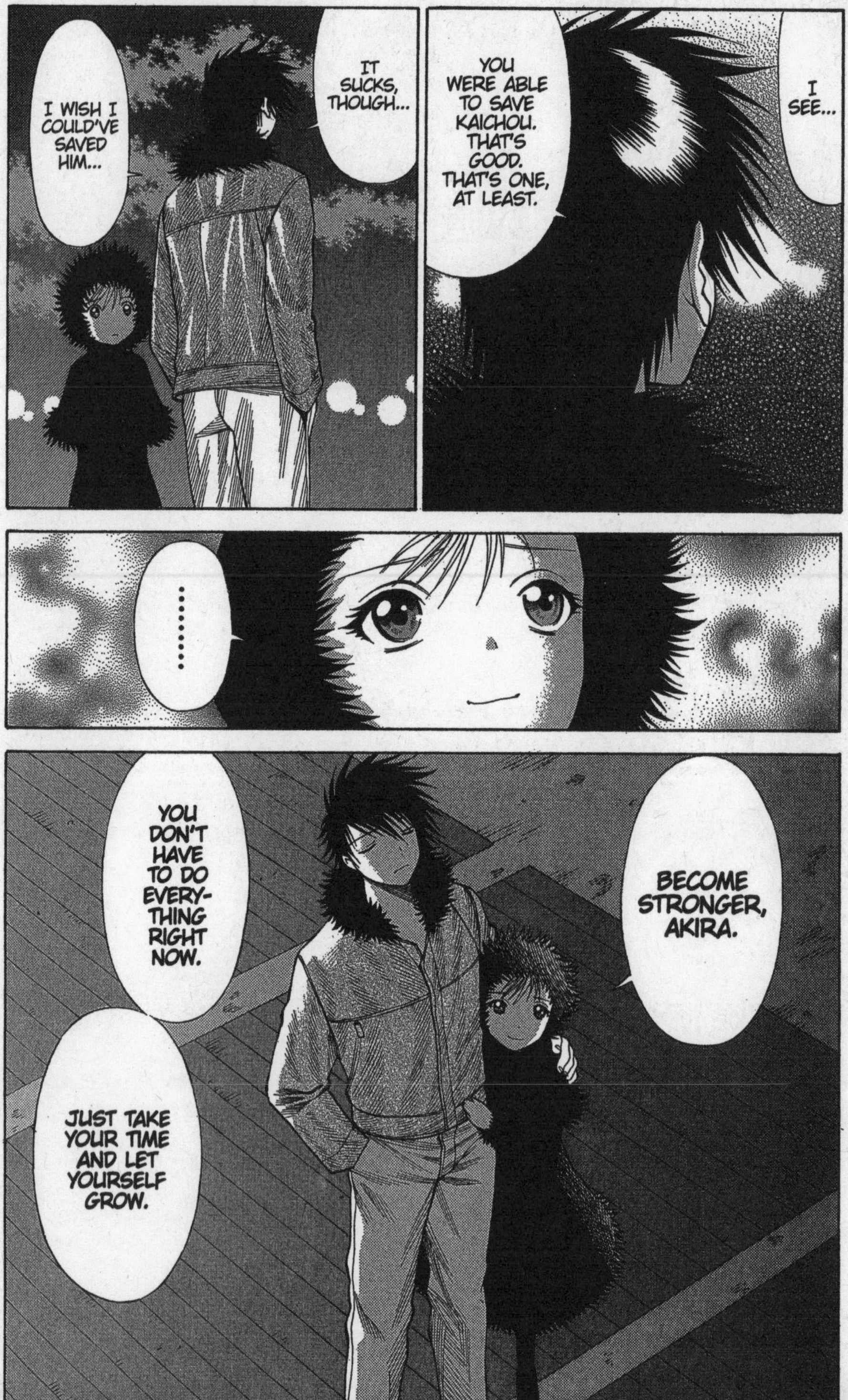
I SEE...
YOU WERE ABLE TO SAVE KAICHOU. THAT'S GOOD. THAT'S ONE, AT LEAST.
IT SUCKS, THOUGH...
I WISH I COULD'VE SAVED HIM...
....
BECOME STRONGER, AKIRA.
YOU DON'T HAVE TO DO EVERY-THING RIGHT NOW.
JUST TAKE YOUR TIME AND LET YOURSELF GROW.

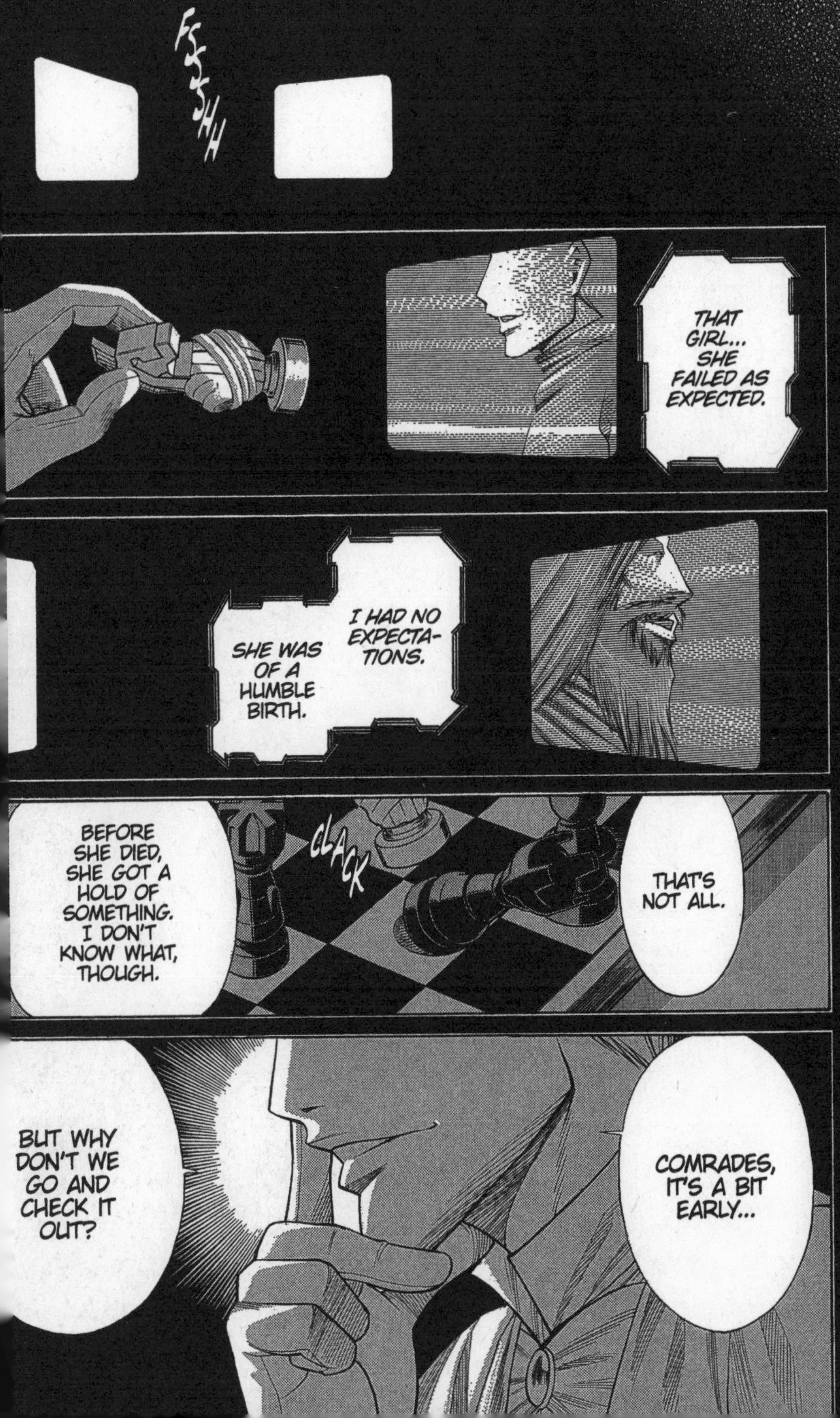
FSSSHH
THAT GIRL... SHE FAILED AS EXPECTED.
I HAD NO EXPECTATIONS.
SHE WAS OF A HUMBLE BIRTH.
THAT'S NOT ALL.
CLACK
BEFORE SHE DIED, SHE GOT A HOLD OF SOMETHING. I DON'T KNOW WHAT, THOUGH.
COMRADES, IT'S A BIT EARLY...
BUT WHY DON'T WE GO AND CHECK IT OUT?

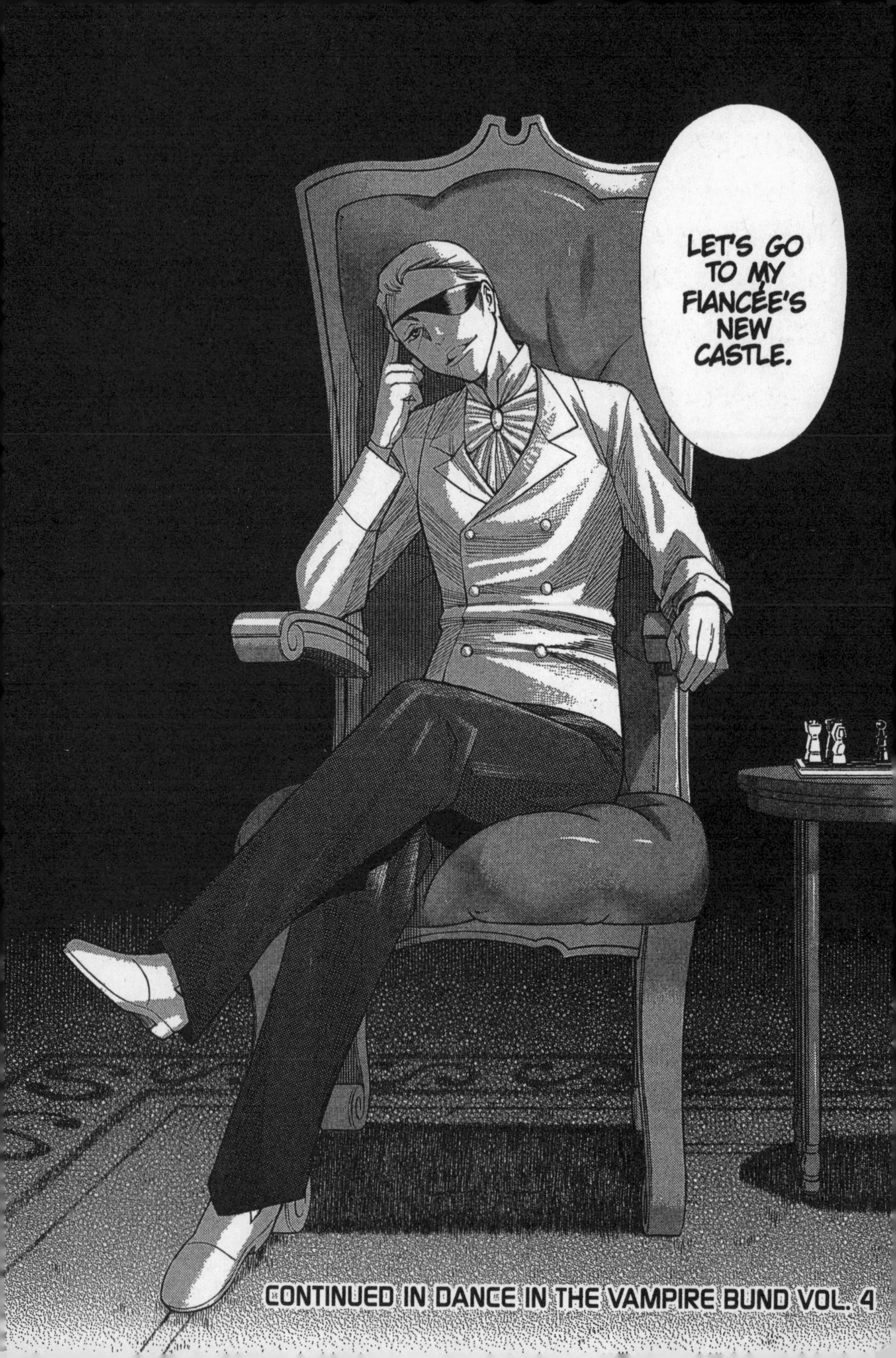
LET'S GO TO MY FIANCÉE'S NEW CASTLE.
CONTINUED IN DANCE IN THE VAMPIRE BUND VOL. 4

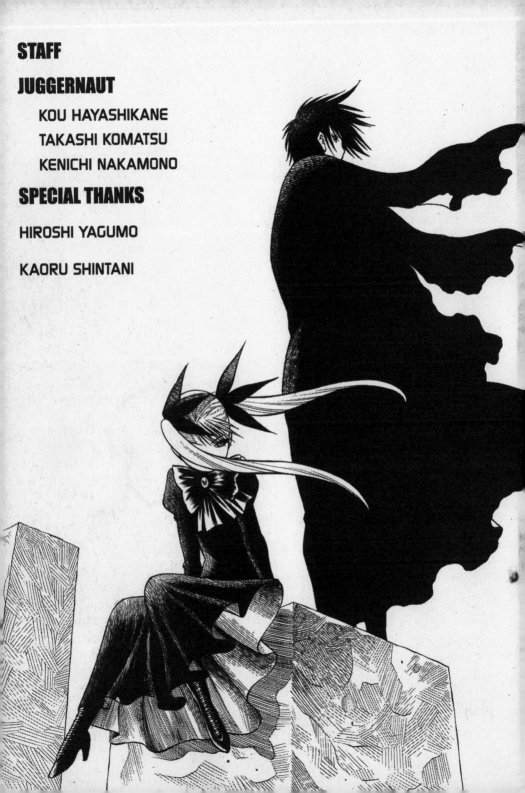

STAFF

JUGGERNAUT

KOU HAYASHIKANE

TAKASHI KOMATSU

KENICHI NAKAMONO

SPECIAL THANKS

HIROSHI YAGUMO

KAORU SHINTANI

DANCE with the VAMPIRE MAID

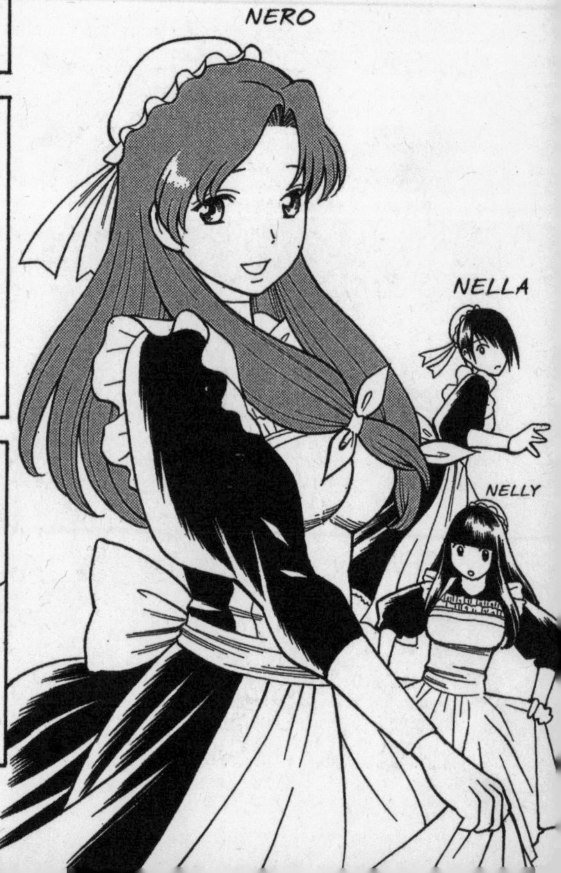
NERO
NELLA
NELLY

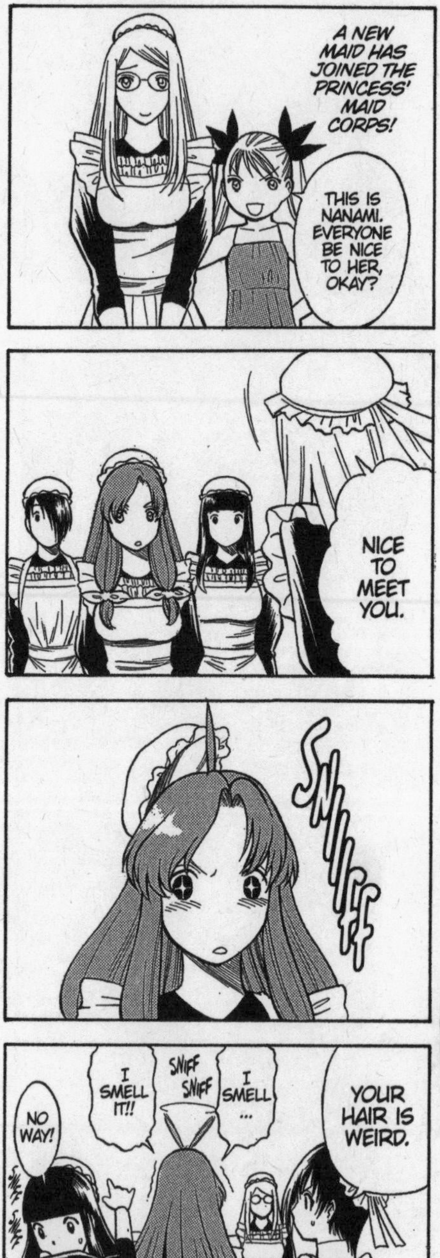
A NEW MAID HAS JOINED THE PRINCESS' MAID CORPS!
THIS IS NANAMI. EVERYONE BE NICE TO HER, OKAY?
NICE TO MEET YOU.
SNIIIFF
YOUR HAIR IS WEIRD.
I SMELL ...
SNIFF SNIFF
I SMELL IT!!
NO WAY!

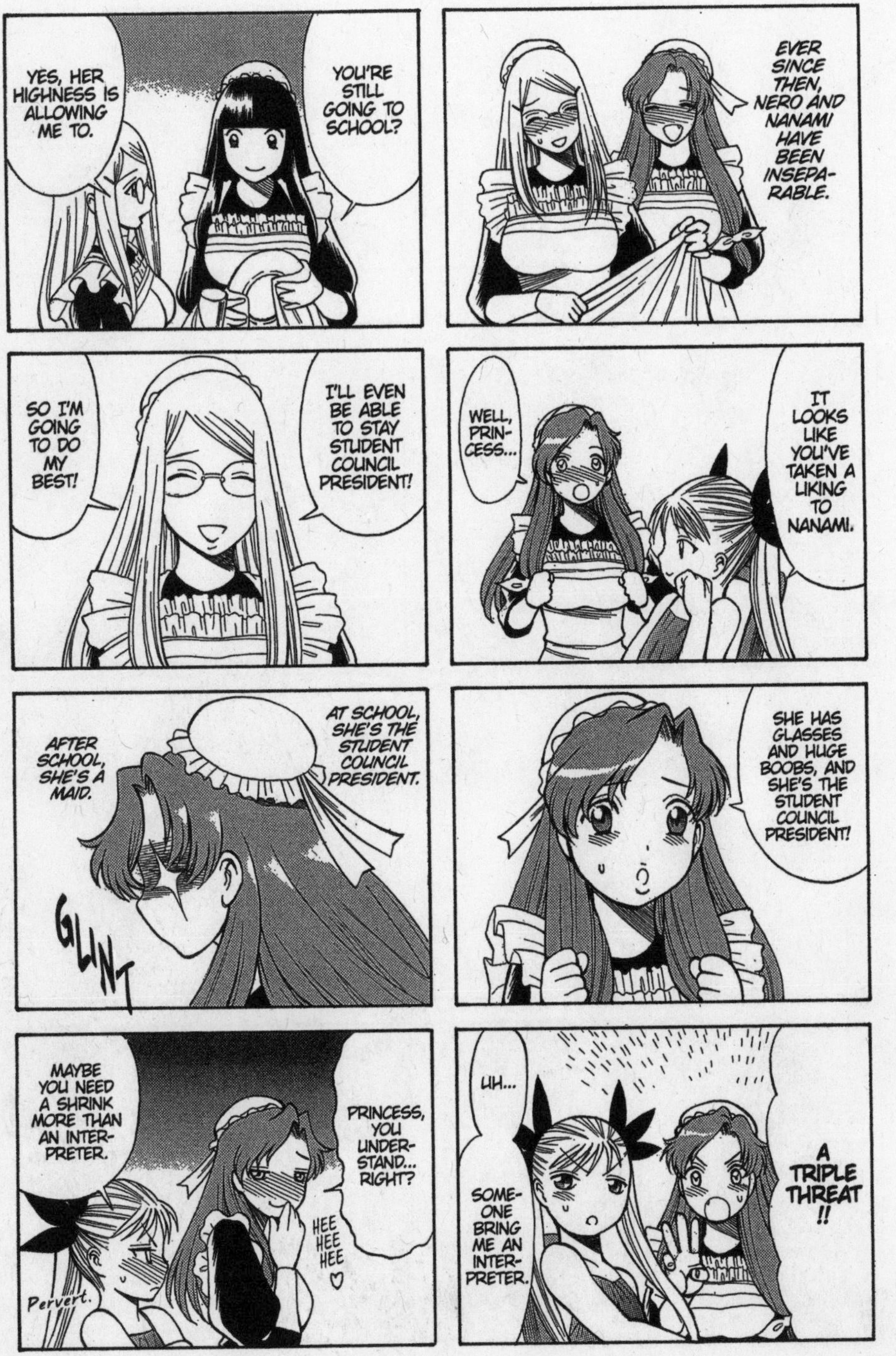
EVER SINCE THEN, NERO AND NANAMI HAVE BEEN INSEPARABLE.
YOU'RE STILL GOING TO SCHOOL?
YES, HER HIGHNESS IS ALLOWING ME TO.
IT LOOKS LIKE YOU'VE TAKEN A LIKING TO NANAMI.
WELL, PRINCESS...
I'LL EVEN BE ABLE TO STAY STUDENT COUNCIL PRESIDENT!
SO I'M GOING TO DO MY BEST!
SHE HAS GLASSES AND HUGE BOOBS, AND SHE'S THE STUDENT COUNCIL PRESIDENT!
AT SCHOOL, SHE'S THE STUDENT COUNCIL PRESIDENT.
AFTER SCHOOL, SHE'S A MAID.
GLINT
A TRIPLE THREAT!!
UH...
SOMEONE BRING ME AN INTERPRETER.
PRINCESS, YOU UNDERSTAND... RIGHT?
HEE HEE HEE ♡
MAYBE YOU NEED A SHRINK MORE THAN AN INTERPRETER.
Pervert.

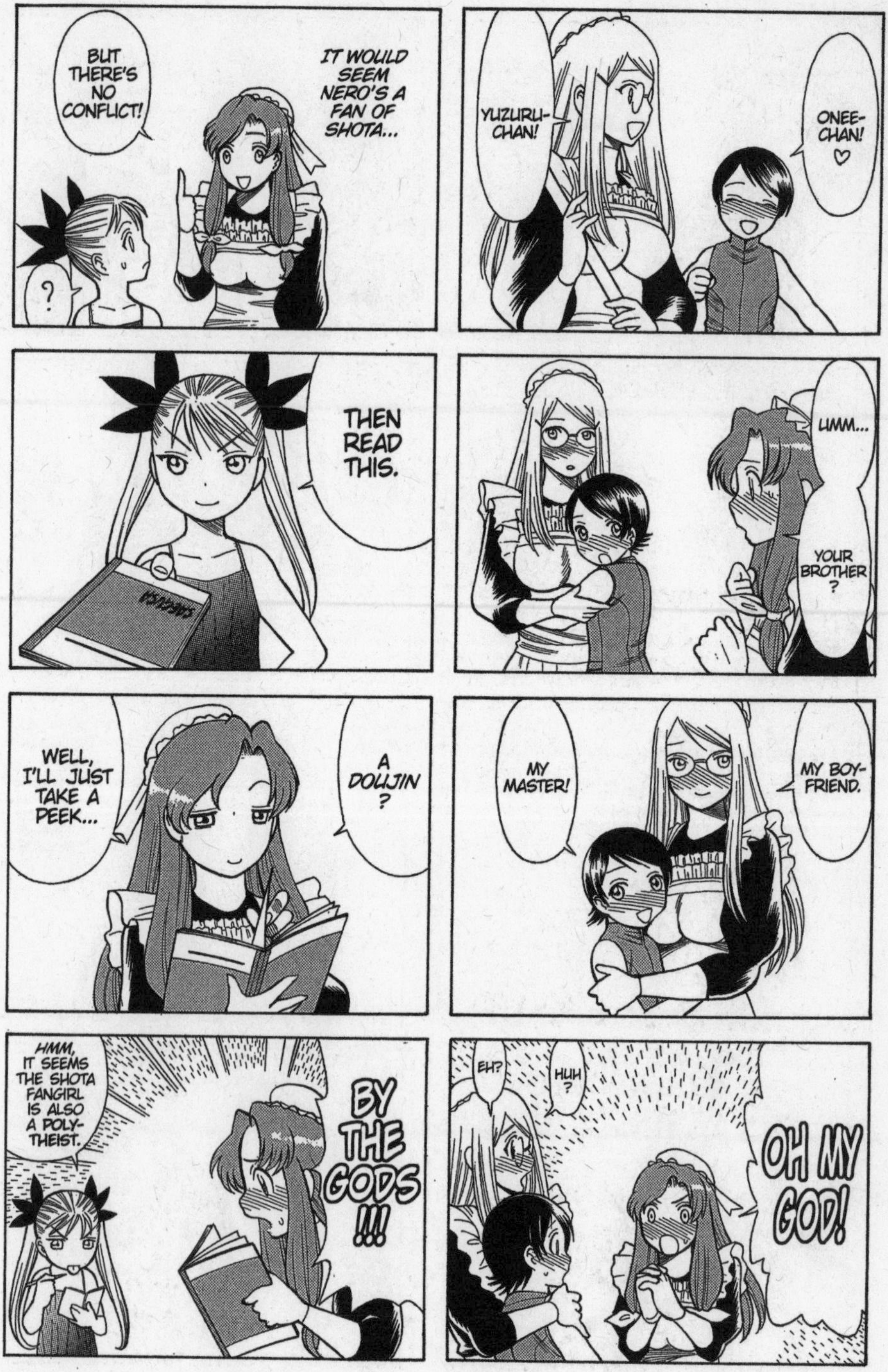
ONEE-CHAN! ♡
YUZURU-CHAN!
IT WOULD SEEM NERO'S A FAN OF SHOTA...
BUT THERE'S NO CONFLICT!
?
UMM...
YOUR BROTHER?
THEN READ THIS.
MY BOY-FRIEND.
MY MASTER!
A DOUJIN?
WELL, I'LL JUST TAKE A PEEK...
OH MY GOD!
HUH?
EH?
BY THE GODS!!!
HMM, IT SEEMS THE SHOTA FANGIRL IS ALSO A POLY-THEIST.

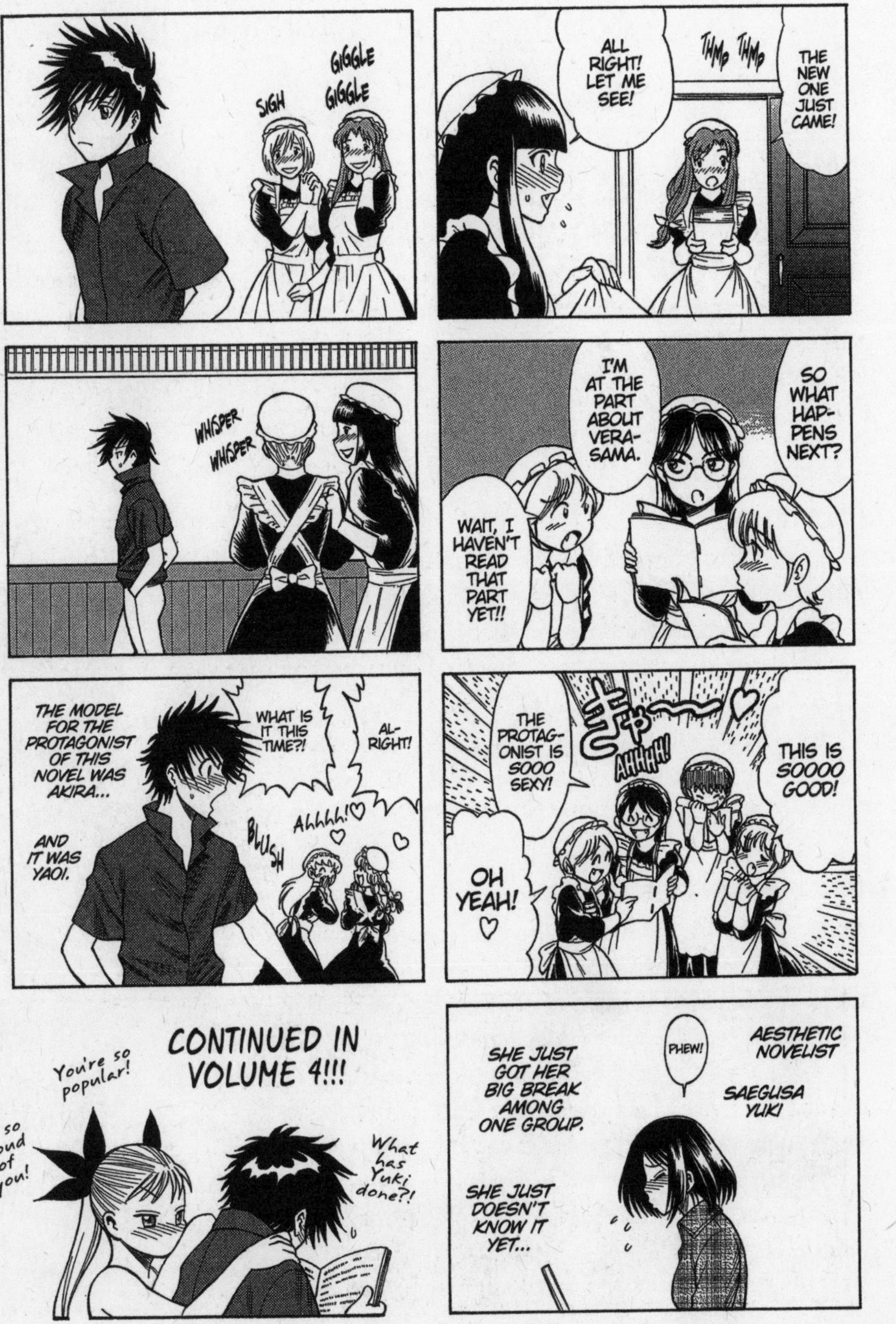
THE NEW ONE JUST CAME!
THMP THMP
ALL RIGHT! LET ME SEE!
SIGH
GIGGLE GIGGLE
SO WHAT HAP-PENS NEXT?
I'M AT THE PART ABOUT VERA-SAMA.
WAIT, I HAVEN'T READ THAT PART YET!!
WHISPER WHISPER
THIS IS SOOOO GOOD!
きゃ～～♡
AHHHH!
THE PROTAG-ONIST IS SOOO SEXY!
OH YEAH! ♡
AL-RIGHT!
WHAT IS IT THIS TIME?!
THE MODEL FOR THE PROTAGONIST OF THIS NOVEL WAS AKIRA...
BLUSH
Ahhhh! ♡
AND IT WAS YAOI.
AESTHETIC NOVELIST
SAEGUSA YUKI
PHEW!
SHE JUST GOT HER BIG BREAK AMONG ONE GROUP.
SHE JUST DOESN'T KNOW IT YET...
CONTINUED IN VOLUME 4!!!
You're so popular!
What has Yuki done?!
I'm so proud of you!

TRANSLATION NOTES

VAMPIRE BUND

Bund refers to an embankment or embanked quay, and comes from the Urdu word *band*, which in turn is related to the German word bund ("federation" or "union") and the English words *bind* and *band*. A famous waterfront area in Shanghai, China is also named "The Bund."
In all cases, *bund* is a term used to describe some sort of colony or collective, and as such a Vampire Bund would be an area (in this case a man-made island) set aside for vampires to live on.

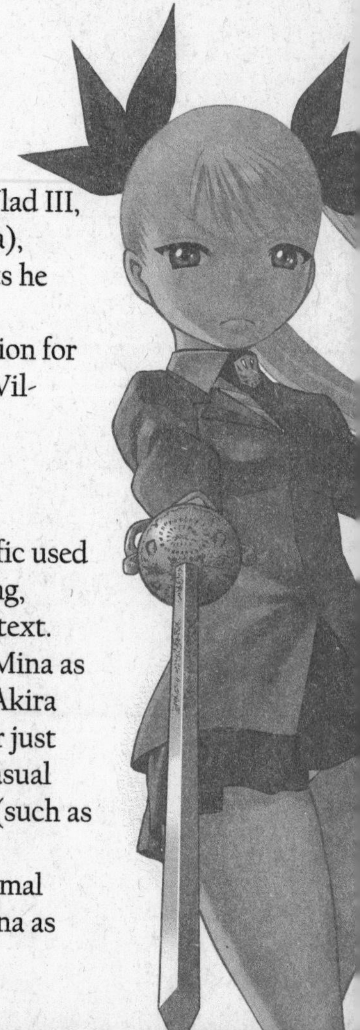

MINA TEPEŞ

The name Ţepeş comes from the common Russian nickname, *Vlad Ţepeş* (Vlad The Impaler) given to Vlad III, Prince of Wallachia (a state in what is now Romania), which he earned for the extremely cruel punishments he inflicted on his people. In the Western world he is probably better known as Vlad Dracula, the inspiration for Bram Stoker's famous novel. Mina is a reference to Wilhelmina Murray, also of Bram Stoker's novel.

HIME-SAMA

"Hime" is literally "princess" and "sama" is an honorific used to indicate respect towards a person of higher ranking, although it can also be used in a joking/sarcastic context. Several characters (such as Akira and Vera) refer to Mina as "Hime-sama" as a sign of respect and/or friendship (Akira also calls her by the less-respectful "san" honorific, or just plain "Hime" on occasion, to indicate his relatively casual relationship and attitude towards her) while others (such as Wolfgang and Juneau) refer to her more formally as "Princess" or "Her Highness." Similarly, in certain formal contexts even the characters who usually refer to Mina as "Hime-sama" will refer to her as "Princess" instead.

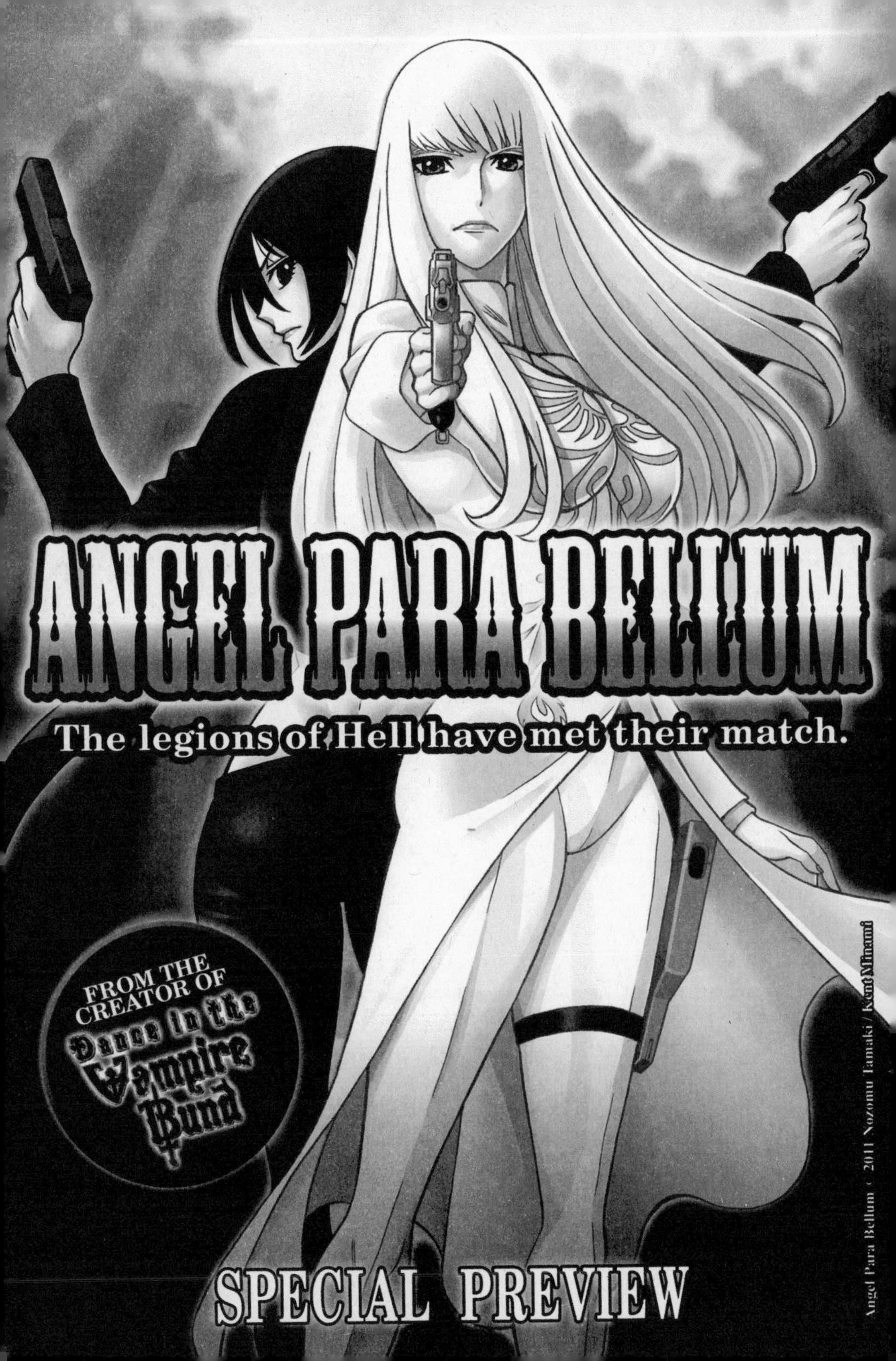
ANGEL PARA BELLUM
The legions of Hell have met their match.
FROM THE CREATOR OF
Dance in the Vampire Bund
SPECIAL PREVIEW
Angel Para Bellum © 2011 Nozomu Tamaki / Kent Minami

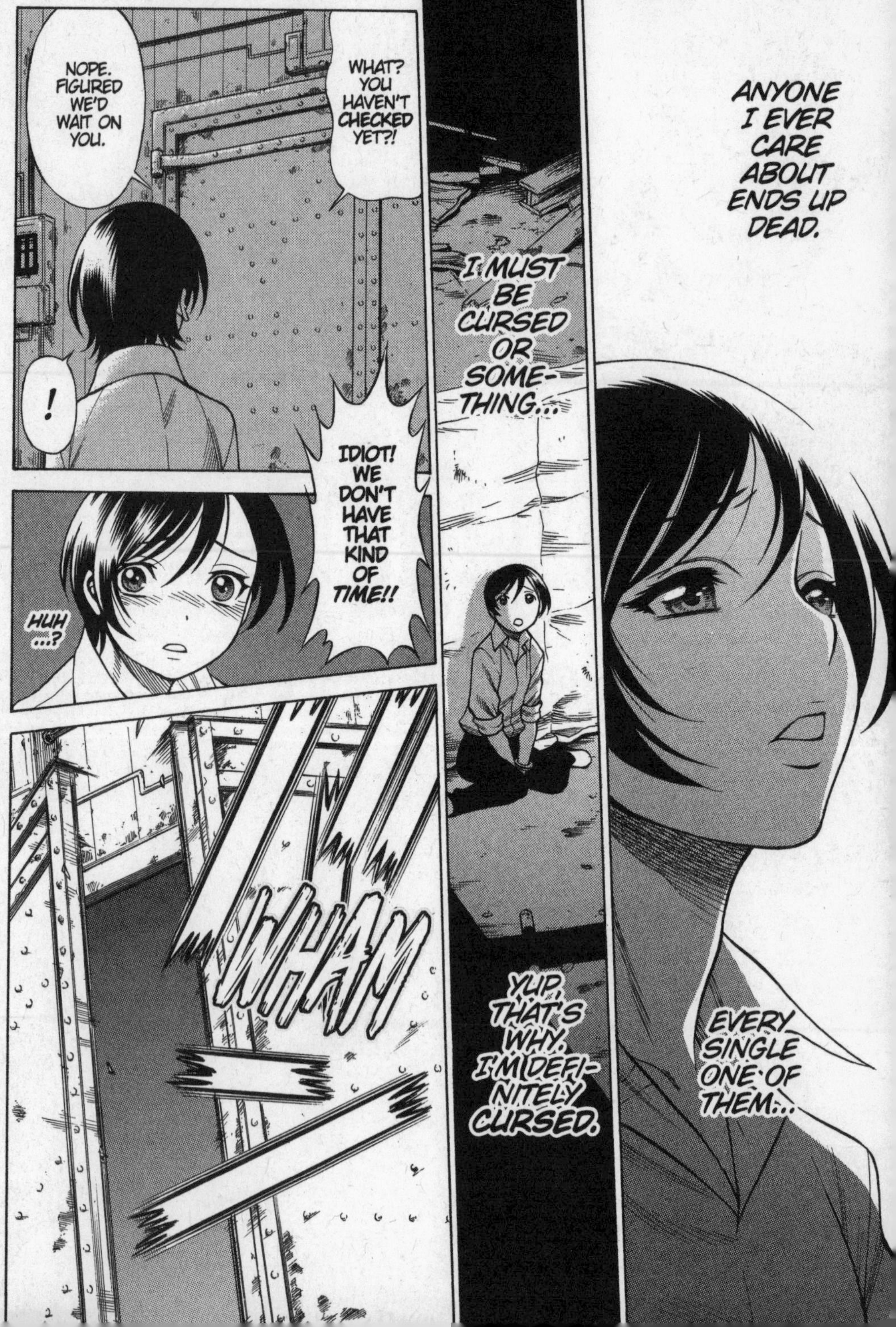
ANYONE I EVER CARE ABOUT ENDS UP DEAD.
EVERY SINGLE ONE OF THEM...
I MUST BE CURSED OR SOMETHING...
YUP, THAT'S WHY. I'M DEFINITELY CURSED.
WHAT? YOU HAVEN'T CHECKED YET?!
NOPE. FIGURED WE'D WAIT ON YOU.
!
IDIOT! WE DON'T HAVE THAT KIND OF TIME!!
HUH ...?
WHAM

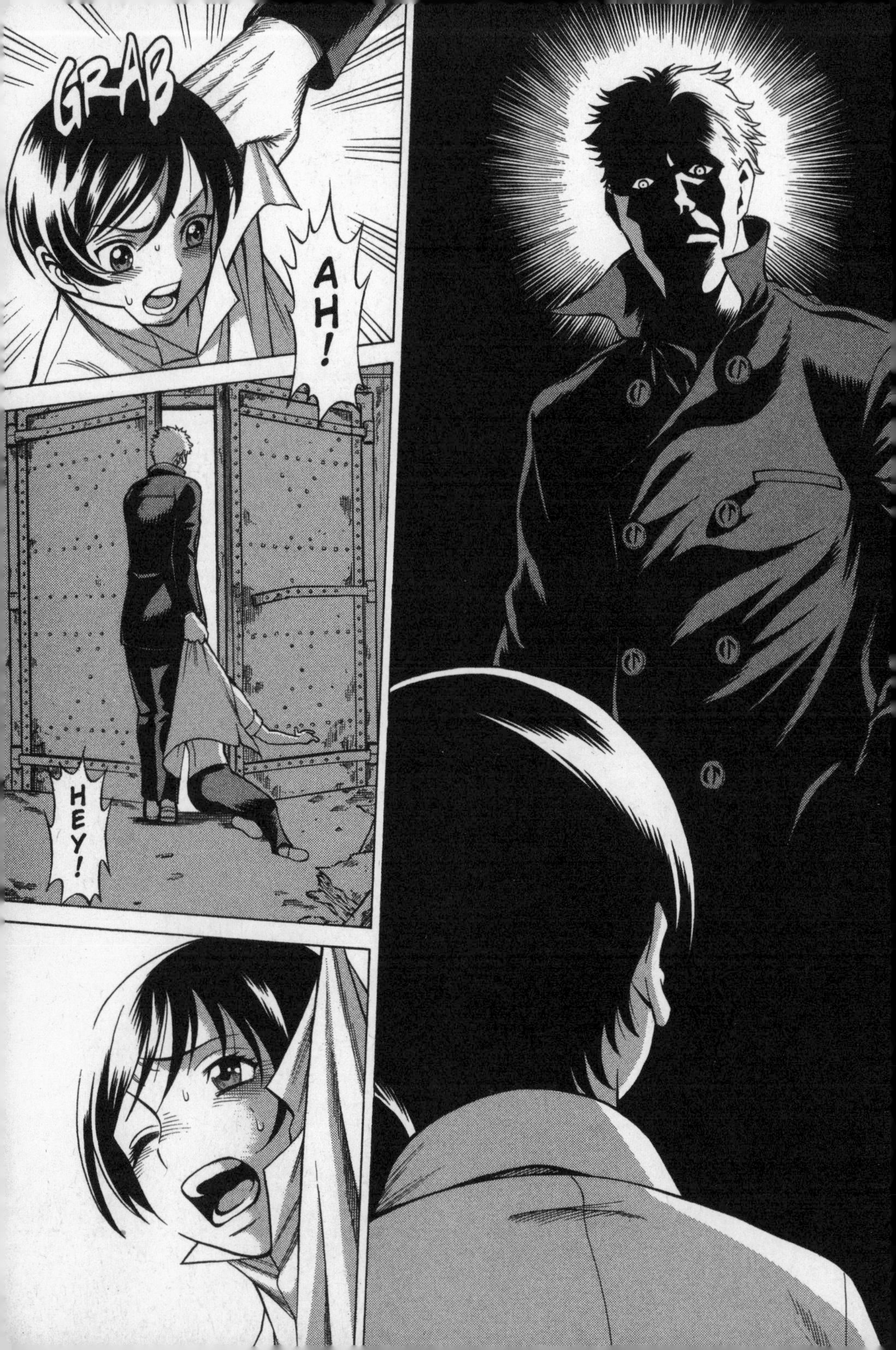
GRAB
AH!
HEY!

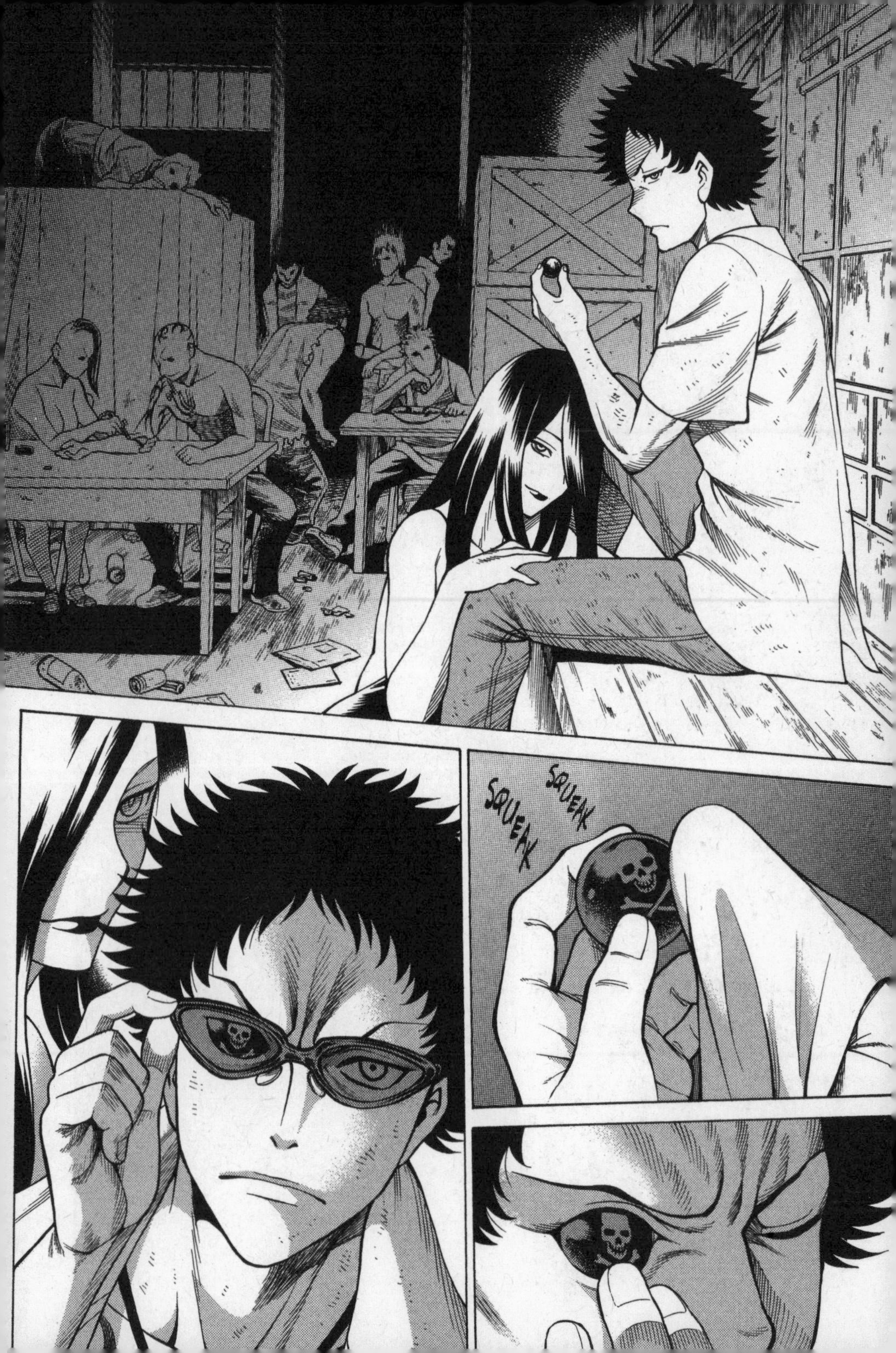
SQUEAK
SQUEAK

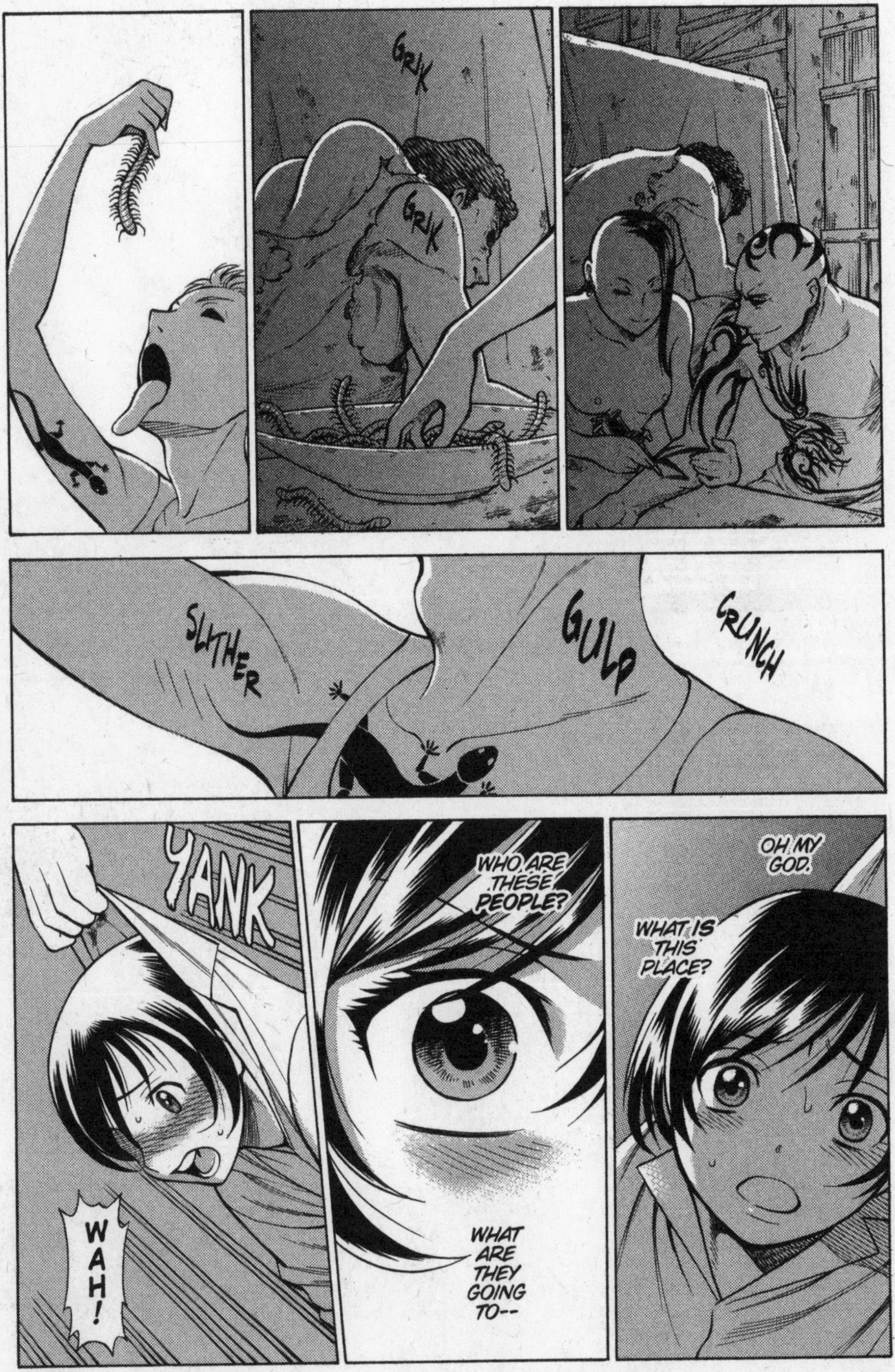
GRIK
GRIK
CRUNCH
GULP
SLITHER
OH MY GOD.
WHAT IS THIS PLACE?
WHO ARE THESE PEOPLE?
WHAT ARE THEY GOING TO--
YANK
WAH!

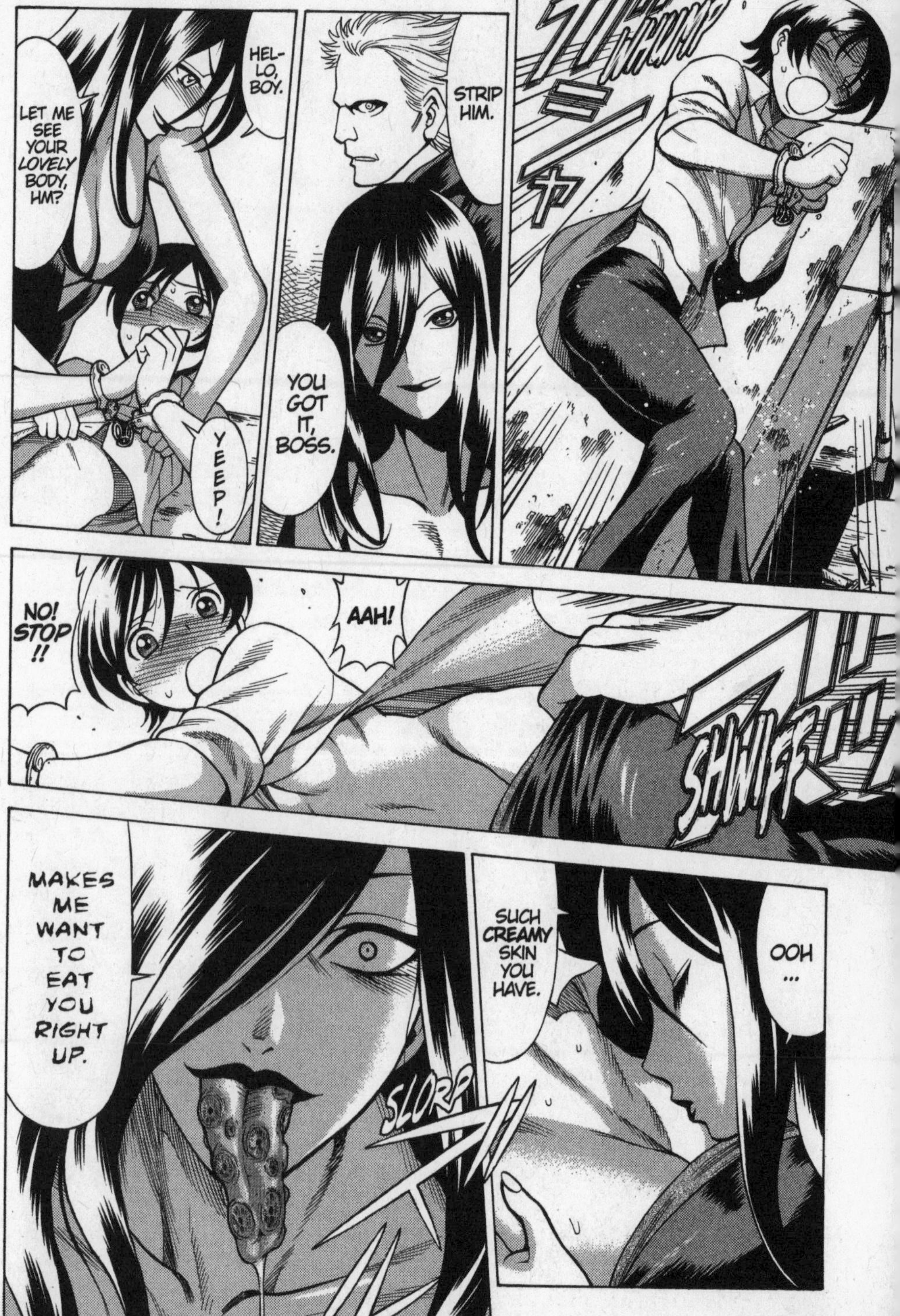

STRIP HIM.
YOU GOT IT, BOSS.
HEL-LO, BOY.
LET ME SEE YOUR LOVELY BODY, HM?
YEEP!
SHWIFF
AAH!
NO! STOP!!
OOH ...
SUCH CREAMY SKIN YOU HAVE.
MAKES ME WANT TO EAT YOU RIGHT UP.
SLORP

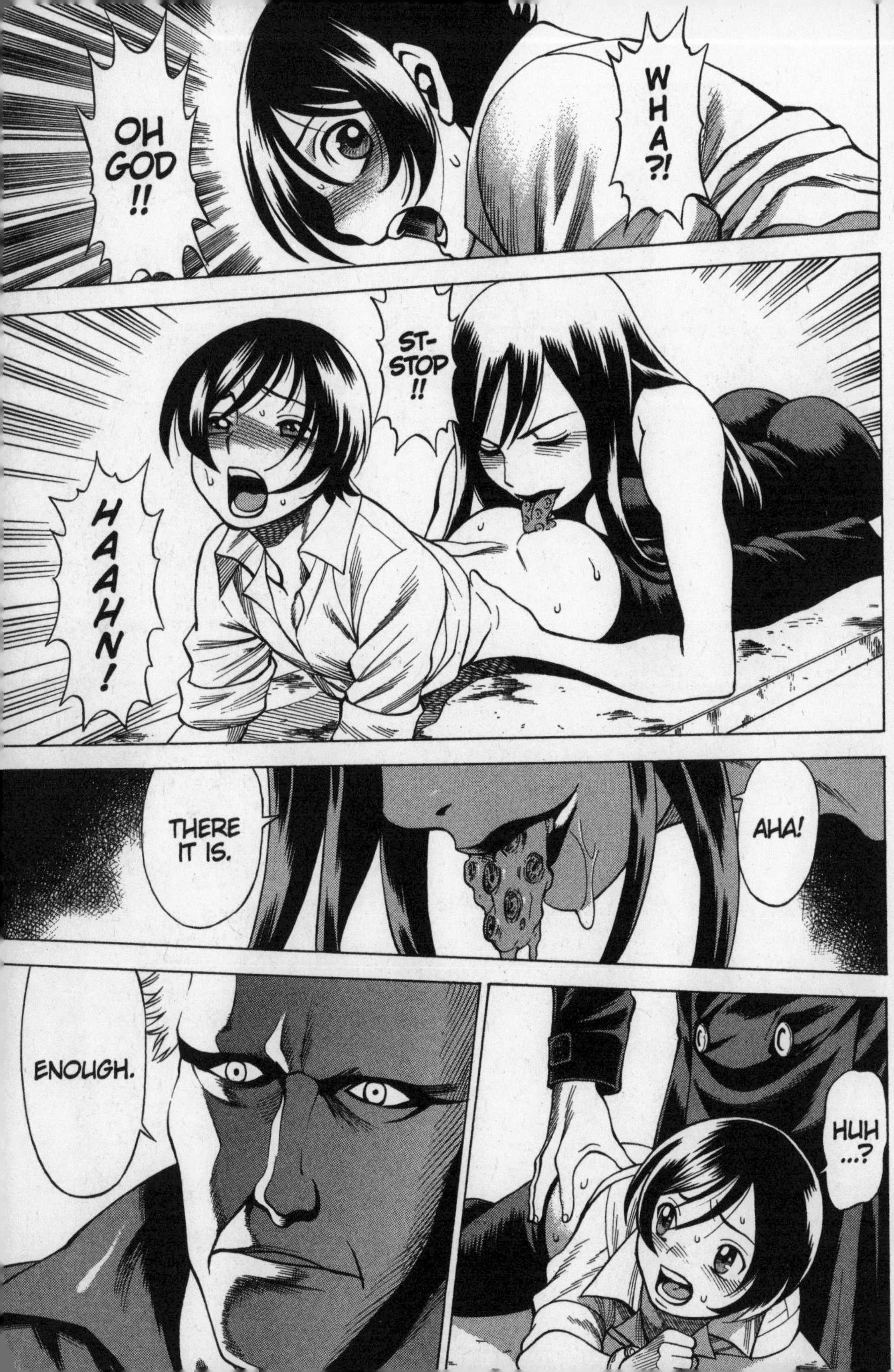
WHA?!
OH GOD!!
ST-STOP!!
HAAAHN!
AHA!
THERE IT IS.
HUH...?
ENOUGH.

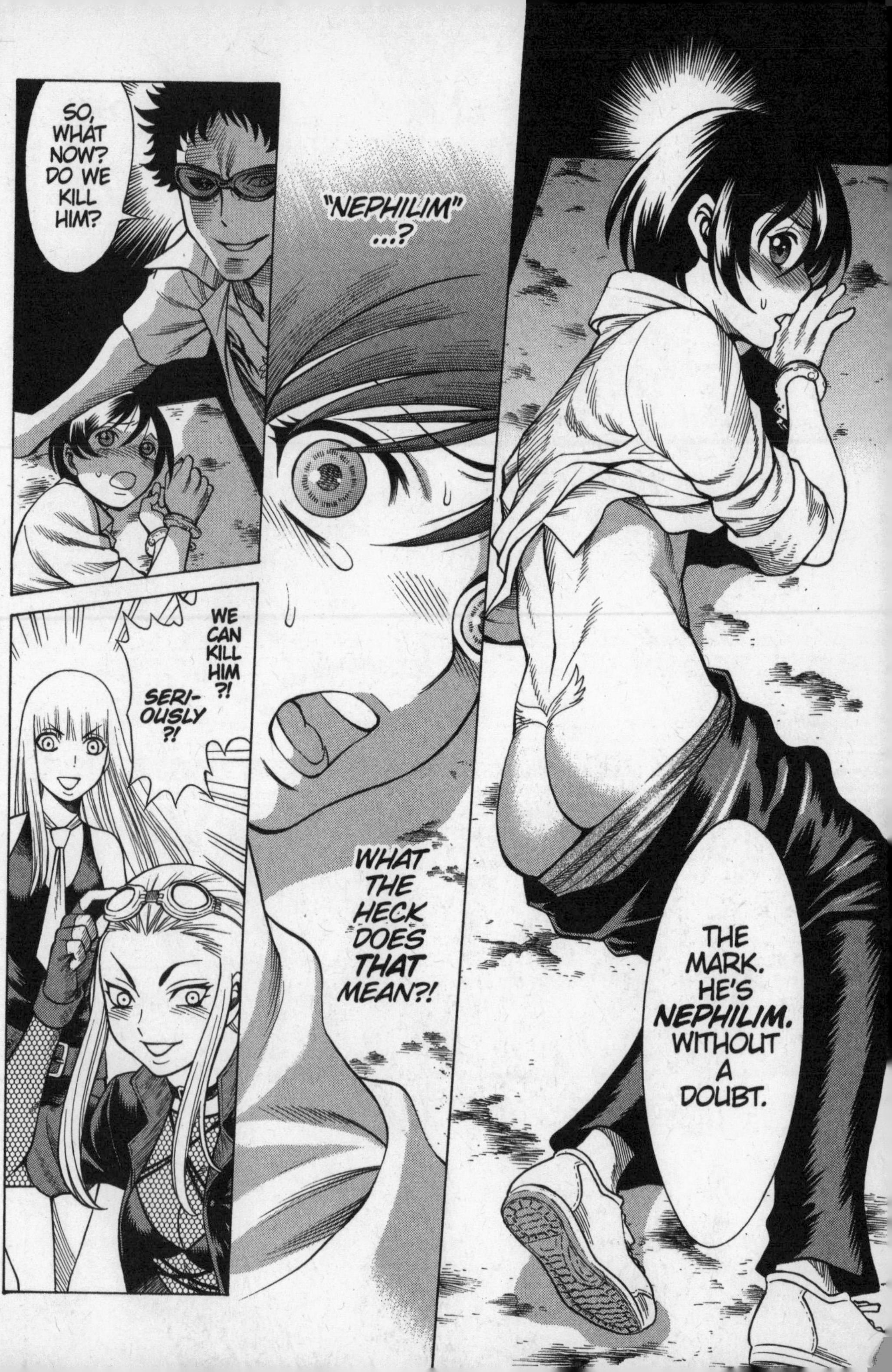
THE MARK. HE'S NEPHILIM. WITHOUT A DOUBT.
"NEPHILIM" ...?
WHAT THE HECK DOES THAT MEAN?!
SO, WHAT NOW? DO WE KILL HIM?
WE CAN KILL HIM?!
SERI-OUSLY?!

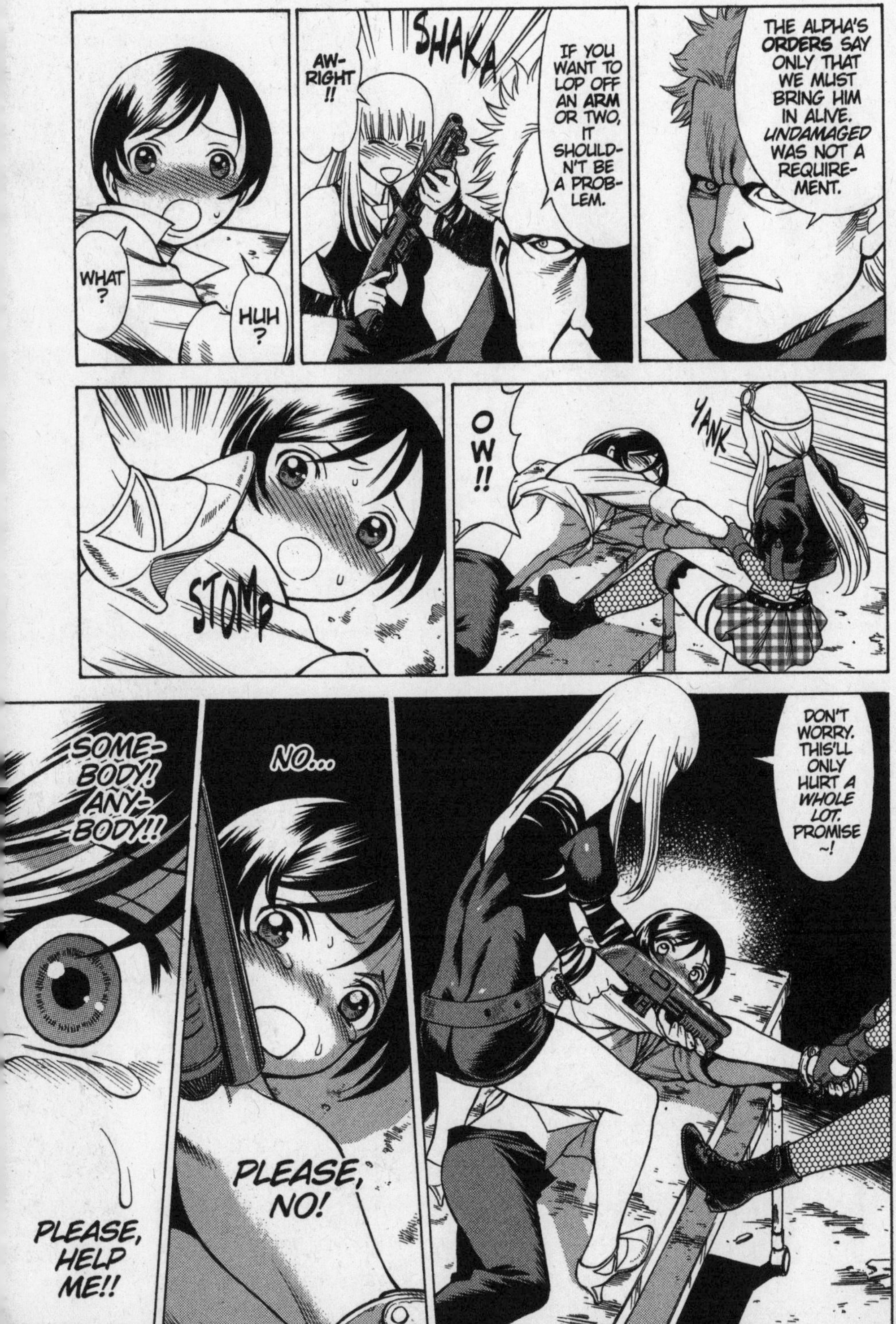
THE ALPHA'S ORDERS SAY ONLY THAT WE MUST BRING HIM IN ALIVE. UNDAMAGED WAS NOT A REQUIREMENT.
IF YOU WANT TO LOP OFF AN ARM OR TWO, IT SHOULDN'T BE A PROBLEM.
SHAKA
AW-RIGHT!!
HUH?
WHAT?
YANK
OW!!
STOMP
DON'T WORRY. THIS'LL ONLY HURT A WHOLE LOT. PROMISE~!
NO...
PLEASE, NO!
SOMEBODY! ANYBODY!!
PLEASE, HELP ME!!

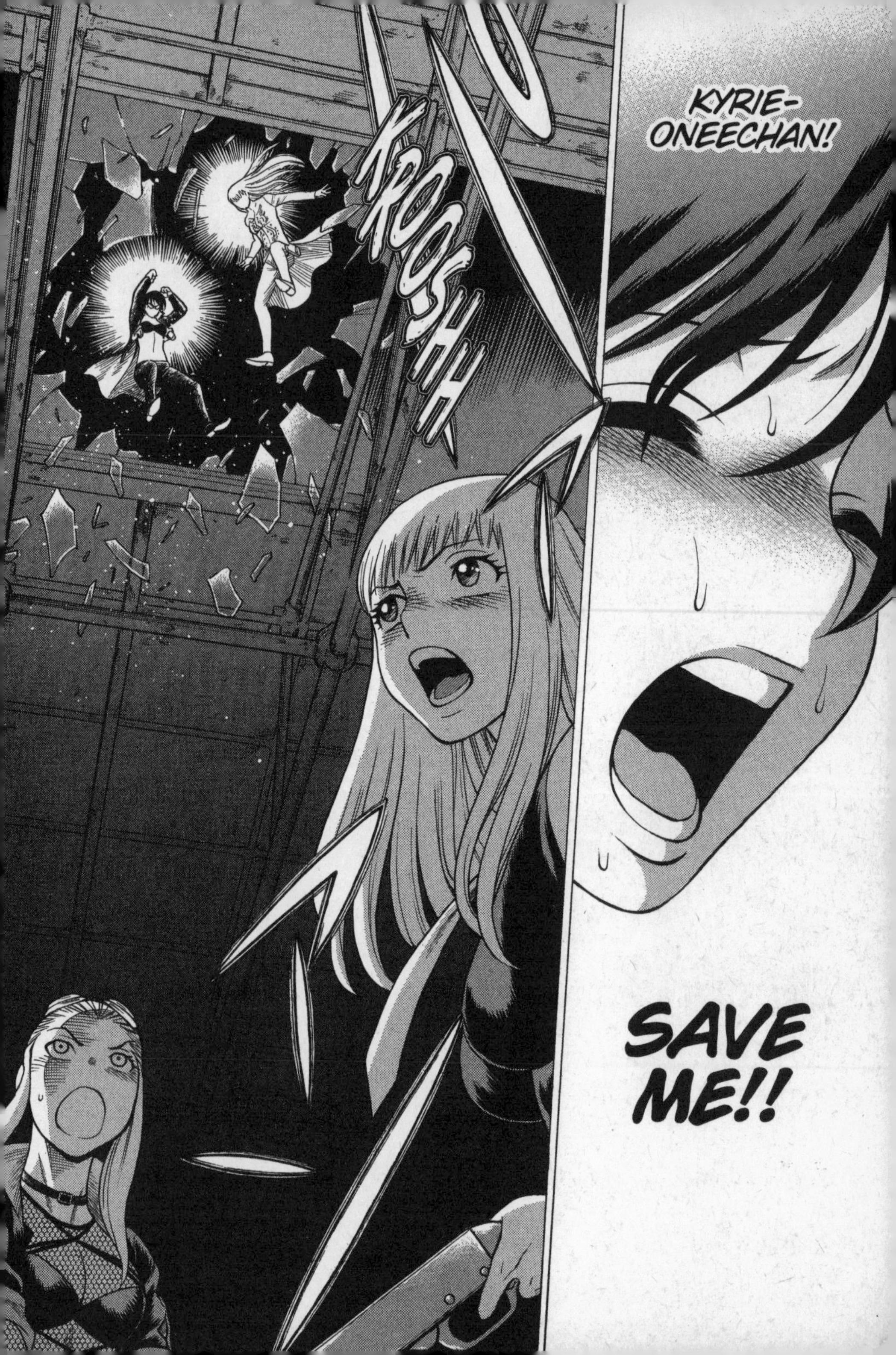
KYRIE-ONEECHAN!
SAVE ME!!
KROOSHHH

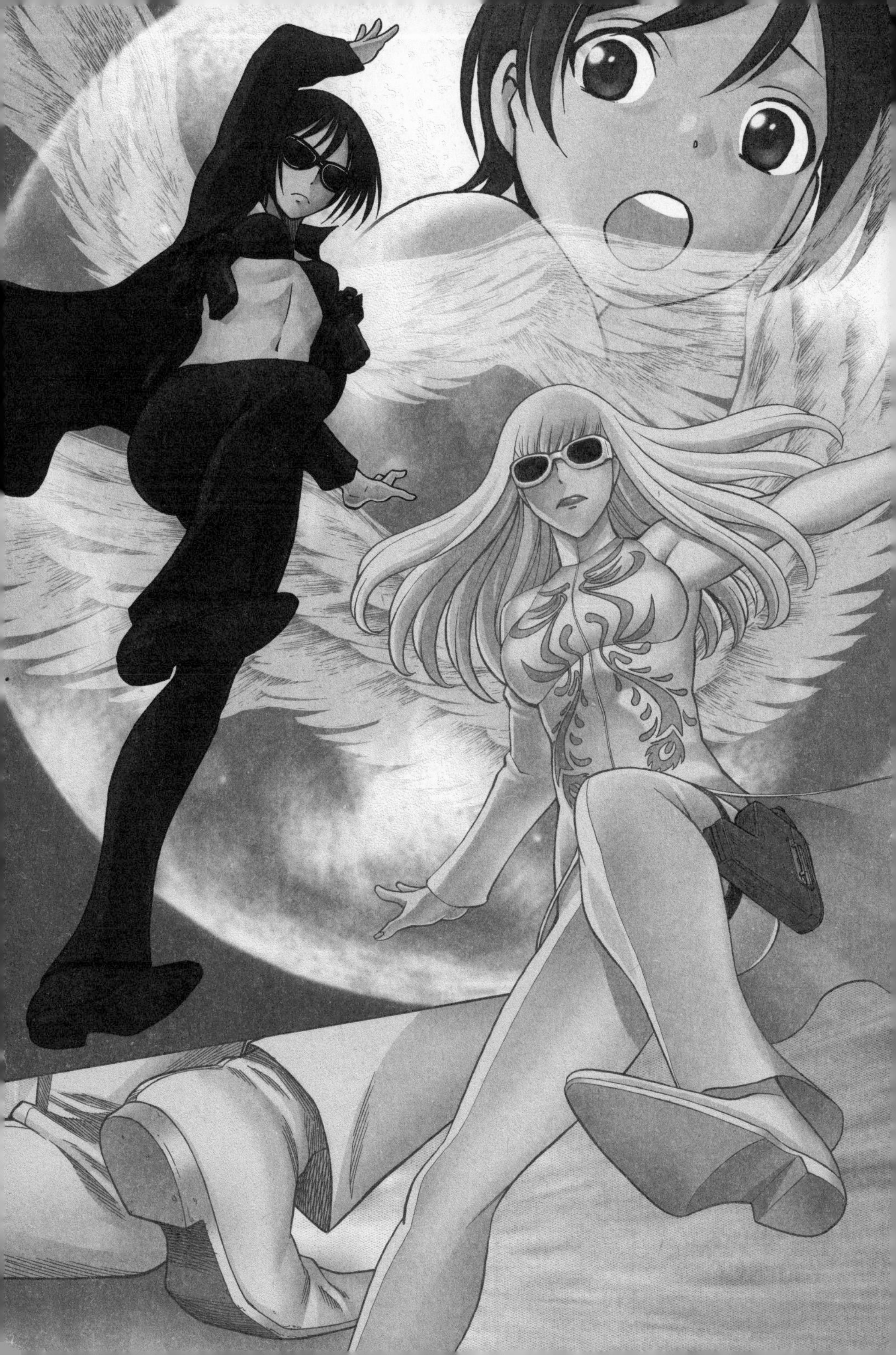

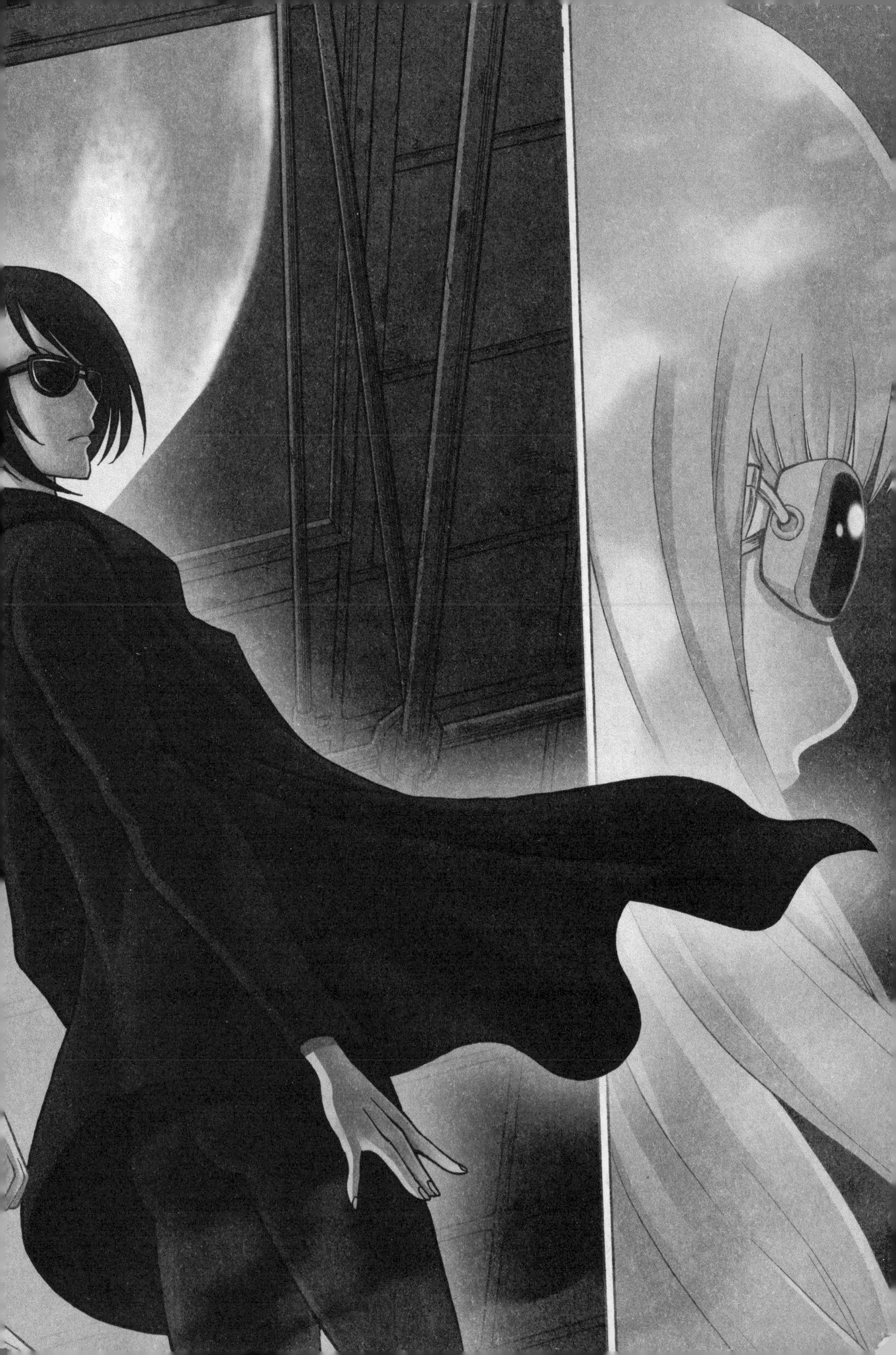